GREEK AND LATIN AUTHORS

800 B.C. – A.D. 1000

Biographical Dictionaries in

THE WILSON AUTHORS SERIES

Greek and Latin Authors 800 B.C.– A.D. 1000
European Authors 1000 – 1900
British Authors Before 1800
British Authors of the Nineteenth Century
American Authors 1600 – 1900

Twentieth Century Authors
Twentieth Century Authors: First Supplement
World Authors 1950 – 1970
World Authors 1970 – 1975

The Junior Book of Authors
More Junior Authors
Third Book of Junior Authors
Fourth Book of Junior Authors and Illustrators

GREEK AND LATIN AUTHORS
800 B.C. – A.D. 1000

A Volume in the Wilson Authors Series

---

by

MICHAEL GRANT

THE H. W. WILSON COMPANY

NEW YORK

1980

93—414

Library of Congress Cataloging in Publication Data

Grant, Michael, 1914 —
  Greek and Latin authors, 800 B.C.-A.D. 1000.

  (The Wilson authors series)
  Includes bibliographies.
  SUMMARY: Biographical sketches of 376 Greek and Latin authors covering the years 800 B.C. to 1000 A.D. Includes a list of works of doubtful attribution and a chronological list of authors by century.
    1.   Classical literature — Dictionaries.   [1.   Authors, Greek — Dictionaries.   2.   Authors, Latin — Dictionaries.   3.   Classical literature — Dictionaries]   I.   Title.
  II.   Series: Wilson authors series.
  PA31.G7   880'.9 [920]   79-27446
  ISBN 0-8242-0640-1

PRINTED IN THE UNITED STATES OF AMERICA

CONTENTS

viii

LIST OF ILLUSTRATIONS, WITH CREDITS

PREFACE

THE LITERATURE of the Greeks and Romans is a storehouse of immense richness and variety. In pursuance of the policy of The Wilson Authors Series, GREEK AND LATIN AUTHORS: 800 B.C.– A.D. 1000 is an endeavor to grasp within the compass of a single volume the essential features of the writers of the classical period and its aftermath who created this literature. I am conscious of the inevitable inadequacy of any such attempt, but all the same I hope the book will be useful — if only for the grandeur of the subject.

The authors included extend from the beginnings of ancient Greece to A.D. 1000, linking the volume up with *European Authors: 1000–1900*. It has not, of course, been possible to find room for every known writer throughout this long period, since otherwise the volume would have been far too long or the entries too short. It is hoped, however, that among the more than three hundred and seventy figures who appear no one of real importance has been omitted. An Appendix lists a few works of unknown or disputed authorship; another gives a chronological list of authors by century.

Each sketch consists of an account of the writer's life, a description of the titles and contents of his or her works, and critical commentary on the nature and quality of those works. Where relevant, there is a brief discussion on the influence of an author's works on later literature. Each sketch is followed by a bibliography covering the most useful editions, translations (which have lately proliferated), and books devoted to the writer in question (especially those so recently published that most current bibliographical works have not so far included them). In the all too few instances where a more or less realistic representation of an author was available in photographic form, it has been included with the sketch.

I owe warm thanks to all publishers and librarians and other scholars who have taken trouble to keep me informed. I also very much appreciate the helpful and imaginative editorial assistance that I have invariably received from various members of the General Publications Department of The H.W. Wilson Company. My wife has played an indispensable part in the whole enterprise.

MICHAEL GRANT
Lucca, 1979

KEY TO PRONUNCIATION

As in other volumes in The Wilson Authors Series, indications of the pronunciation of authors' names have been included. In the case of these ancient Greek and Latin names, it should be noted that very little is known about how they were actually pronounced in antiquity. In consequence, the pronunciations in current American and British usage are given instead; the few instances in which these differ appreciably from one another have been indicated.

SYMBOLS USED

ā as in lāte

a as in cap

ȧ as in ȧsk

ä as in cärt

â as in câre

ē as in scēne

e as in get

ẽ as in hẽr

ī as in fīne

i as in tip

ō as in tōne

o as in mop

ô as in ôrb

ū as in rūle

u as in up

ou as in out

o͞o as in so͞on

o͝o as in fo͝ot

g as in good

ng as in song

s as in sat

sh as in shall

th as in thin

t̶h̶ as in t̶hat

v as in even

w as in we

y as in yet

z as in haze

ə the schwa, an unaccented, neutral vowel such as the *e* in mittən

' as in battle (bat' t'l)

' = main accent

ACCIUS, LUCIUS, Latin poet and playwright, was born in 170 B.C., perhaps at Pisaurum (Pesaro) in Umbria, of parents who were former slaves (freedmen); he may have died in about 86 B.C. Only about seven hundred lines of his writings survive.

He lived mainly at Rome, where he formed many influential connections. His patron was the nobleman Decimus Junius Brutus Callaicus. Among his friends was the tragic poet Pacuvius. When Pacuvius was eighty and Accius was thirty, they both presented plays at the same games. After both had died, Accius' reputation surpassed that of Pacuvius. Accius' tragedies were credited by the literary critic Quintilian with "extraordinary cleverness in making apt replies." But owing to our fragmentary knowledge of his work and of the development of Roman tragic poetry as a whole, it is difficult to discern today in what respect he differed from his predecessors. His *Atreus* has left us one of the most famous of Latin tags, *oderint dum metuant,* "let them hate provided that they fear."

We know the names of more than forty of Accius' tragedies dealing with Greek mythological themes. Their plots seem to have been taken mainly from Euripides, though to some extent also from Sophocles and occasionally from Aeschylus and post-Euripidean dramatists. Accius also wrote two *fabulae praetextae* (plays on Roman historical subjects): the *Aeneadae,* or *Decius,* on the self-immolation of the Roman commander Publius Decius Mus the Younger at the battle of Sentinum in 295 B.C.; and *Brutus,* on the expulsion of the Tarquins in c. 507 B.C. by the legendary ancestor of Accius' patron. From these two plays between forty and fifty lines have been preserved. Accius was the last of the tragic poets of Republican Rome and was considered in imperial times the greatest of all Rome's tragedians.

Accius also wrote a number of compositions outside the field of tragedy. Among them was the *Didascalica,* a work of nine books dealing with the history of literature, especially drama. From the twenty-two lines that survive it appears that various poetic meters may have been used, and perhaps prose as well. The *Sotadica,* with its erotic

ak' ki us

verse, has sometimes been identified with the *Didascalica* but was probably a separate work. The *Pragmatica* seems to have been concerned with stage directions. The *Annals,* written in hexameters, dealt with the calendar and with festivals, and the *Praxidica* with astronomy or agriculture. The subject of the *Parerga* is unknown. In one of his works Accius advocated reforms in spelling. On several occasions he engaged in vigorous controversies on literary matters with the satirist Lucilius.

WORKS (lost except for fragments)—*Tragedies on Greek models:* Achilles, Aegisthus, Agamemnonidae, Alcestis, Alcmaeon, Alphesiboea, Amphitruo, Andromeda, Antenoridae, Antigona, Armorum Judicium, Astyanax, Athamas, Atreus, Bacchae, Chrysippus, Clutaemestra, Deiphobus, Diomedes, Epigoni, Epinausimache, Erigona, Eriphyla (possibly the same as the Epigoni), Eurysaces, Hecuba, Hellenes, Io (perhaps, or this may be an alternative title for the Prometheus), Medea, Melanippus, Meleager, Minos (or Minotaurus), Myrmidones (possibly the same play as the Achilles), Neoptolemus, Nuctegresia, Oenomaus, Pelopidae, Persidae (perhaps the same as the Amphitruo), Philocteta, Phinidae, Phoenissae, Prometheus, Thebais (perhaps the same as the Phoenissae), Stasiastae (or Tropaeum Liberi, Trophy of Dionysus), Telephus, Tereus. *Tragedies on Roman historical themes:* Aeneadae vel Decius, Brutus. *Works outside the field of tragedy:* Didascalica, Sotadica, Pragmatica, Annals, Praxidica, Parerga.
EDITIONS—A. Klotz, Scaenicorum Romanorum Fragmenta, 3rd ed., v 1, 1953.
ABOUT—H. J. Mette, Die römische Tragödie (Lustrum, v 9), 1964; M. Coffey *in* Fifty Years (and Twelve) of Classical Scholarship, 1968; W. Beare, The Roman Stage, 3rd ed. revised, 1969; G. Williams *in* D. Daiches and A. Thorlby, eds., Literature and Western Civilisation, v 1: The Classical World, 1972.

ACHILLES TATIUS, Greek novelist from Alexandria, lived and wrote, as recent papyrus discoveries show, in the second century A.D. and not several hundred years later as had hitherto been believed. About his life nothing is known.

His chief extant work, *Leucippe and Clitophon,* in eight books, is a romance of love and adventure told in the first person by Clitophon himself. A storm at sea delivers the young lovers into the hands of Egyptian pirates; this is the first of a whole series of melodramatic happenings, described in

a kil' les   ta' ti us or a kil' lēz   tā shi us

1

breathless succession. Achilles Tatius' fiction, though he adds a spicy twist of his own, follows traditional lines. There are the customary disasters and frustrations of true love. Time after time it is hard for Clitophon to believe that his beloved is still alive, for on no less than three occasions she is apparently killed. This sort of exaggeration, which occurs fairly frequently, suggests that Achilles Tatius is making fun of well-worn themes.

A new touch was the willingness of Clitophon, in the absence of Leucippe, to go to bed with another woman. Although this happened, admittedly, under coercion, the scene shows a new ironical tolerance of human weakness, implying criticism of the impossibly high standards of sexual restraint maintained by other writers of romances. Achilles Tatius took a keen, and occasionally prurient, interest in sex and love and unlike other novelists was not content with simple love at first sight but dwelt on the gradual stages of courtship and on the arts which caused it to progress. He was also well aware of the irresistible erotic urge and the agitations and disturbances it causes. Towards the sufferings of love, as with other sufferings, he was unusually sympathetic. For the most part, blind Fortune is more prominent in his fiction than religious intervention. Yet, like contemporary Platonists, Achilles Tatius compared the amorous passion with religious Mysteries; one of the gods of his native country, Serapis, plays an important part in his work.

He is a writer who loves marvels; and he devotes all the inquisitive, encyclopedic credulity of his age to building up digressions on a great variety of curious subjects. But he is not entirely serious, and when, for example, he writes at length about the healing fragrance of the elephant's breath, after the animal has been feeding on the leaf of the black rose, he is mocking the current taste for imaginative anthropology. Furthermore, although his main story, for all its exuberance, is told lucidly enough, with characters more human than in previous Greek novels, the language, when not pseudonaive, is sometimes artificial to a laughable degree. However, men and women of Byzantine times, and the people of Elizabethan Eng-

land as well, loved reading Achilles Tatius; and translations of *Leucippe and Clitophon* influenced the development of the European novel.

WORKS—Besides the Leucippe and Clitophon, other writings that are now lost have been ascribed to Achilles Tatius, including a Miscellaneous History of Great and Famous Men, an etymology, and a partially preserved book, On the Sphere, which, however, may not be his work.
EDITIONS—E. Vilborg, 1955. *With translation:* S. Gaselee, Achilles Tatius (Loeb ed.), revised ed., 1969.
ABOUT—E. H. Haight, Essays on the Greek Romances, 1943; Q. Cataudella, Il romanzo classico, 1958; P. Grimal, Romans grecs et latins, 1958; B. E. Perry, The Ancient Romance, 1967.

AELIAN (Claudius Aelianus), Greek writer of popular science and philosophy, was born in about A.D. 170 at Praeneste (Palestrina in Italy), lived in Rome, and died in 235. His writings enjoyed a great vogue.

On the Characteristics of Animals, or more properly *The Peculiarities of Animals,* in seventeen books, illustrates the wonders of the natural world by describing such themes as the musical gifts of dolphins, the loyalty of dogs, the teachability of elephants, and the mechanical skills of bees. Aelian also uses these qualities of the various animals in the manner of the Stoic philosophers, to censure the corruption of mankind, although a series of stories on the love-lives of animals is interspersed, in order to introduce an erotic element. Aelian seems to be drawing on some collection of marvels from natural history produced in second century Alexandria. A large part of his *Various History,* or *Miscellaneous Stories,* has also survived. Apart from the initial portion, which deals with inanimate nature, this is a human counterpart of *The Characteristics of Animals.* It is filled with chatty, often inane, and uncritical anecdotes, mostly about famous political or literary characters. Aelian has also left us a collection of twenty *Rustic Epistles*—brief stylistic exercises—as well as fragments of two works containing material derived from orators and comic poets and designed to demonstrate the workings of providence and divine justice. His lost writ-

ē′ li ən

ings include an invective against Elagabalus, which was no doubt not published until after that emperor's death in A.D. 222.

Foolish but readable, Aelian practiced, or affected, an artless simplicity of style and lack of arrangement. His comparatively pure form of Attic Greek won him praise and so, above all, did the moralizing tone of his writings, which earned him great popularity among early Christian authors. He also influenced the bestiaries and medical treatises of the Middle Ages. He is probably to be distinguished from the Aelian who wrote a book (the *Tactica*) on the obsolete Macedonian phalanx, probably in the earlier part of the second century A.D.

WORKS—On the Characteristics (Peculiarities) of Animals (De Proprietatibus Animalium); Various History or Miscellaneous Stories (Varia Storia); Rustic Epistles or Peasants' Letters (Epistulae Rusticae). *Fragments:* On Providence, On Special Providences.

EDITIONS—A. M. Leone, Epistulae Rusticae, 1974. *With translation:* A. R. Benner and F. H. Fobes, The Rustic Epistles, *in* The Letters of Alciphron, Aelian and Philostratus (Loeb ed.), 1949; A. F. Schofield, On the Characteristics of Animals (Loeb ed.), 1958–59.

ABOUT—R. R. Bolgar, The Classical Heritage, 1954 (on manuscripts used in the fifteenth century, and French and Italian translations of the sixteenth century); U. Treu and K. Treu, Claudius Aelianus, Die tanzenden Pferde von Sybaris: Tiergeschichten, 1978.

AENEAS of Stymphalus. See Aeneas Tacticus

AENEAS TACTICUS, Greek military writer of the fourth or early third century B.C., is possibly identifiable with Aeneas of Stymphalus, who was general of the Arcadian League in the Peloponnese in 367 B.C.

He was the author of a collection of military treatises, one of which, *On the Defense of Fortified Positions,* has survived. Consisting of a series of short chapters mainly relating to various aspects of the technique of resisting sieges—"how to hold out when besieged"—it is a manual of a somewhat elementary nature, written for the guidance of the garrison commander who faces attack by a well-organized professional army but

e nē′ ás tak′ ti kus

has little else but a citizen-militia at his disposal. The fluid nature of ancient sieges is made apparent, and the factor of morale is not neglected, since it is pointed out that the citizen, when faced with external danger, is inclined to think more of his own property than of the common interest. Moreover, light is thrown upon contemporary conditions by the author's assumption that the principal danger is not the enemy outside the walls but a disaffected faction within, ready to betray the city to its attackers.

There is a certain fresh vividness in Aeneas' selection of examples that suggests he was a man of action rather than a literary figure. His somewhat uncouth style (foreshadowing in some respects the uniform Greek *Koine* [common speech] of the future) conveys the same message. It shows few signs of the influence of the Attic literary tradition, due perhaps partly to the author's ignorance of it but also to a purely practical approach to questions of style, which gave his writing the clarity he was looking for— though his unskillful arrangement sometimes operates in the opposite direction. Aeneas is curiously isolated in classical literature, from the standpoints of his style and dialect and subject matter.

EDITIONS with translation—Illinois Greek Club, Aeneas Tacticus, Asclepiodotus, Onasander (Loeb ed.), 1923; A. Dain and A. M. Bon, Énée le Tacticien: Poliorcétique (Budé ed.), 1967.

ABOUT—L. W. Hunter (revised by S. A. Handford), Aineiou Poliorketika, 1927.

AESCHINES, Greek orator, c. 397 or 389 – c. 322 B.C., lacked the aristocratic background of his fellow Athenian and rival Demosthenes, his father being a schoolteacher and his mother an employee of mystery cults. He served in the army with some distinction as a young man and then for a time attempted a professional career on the stage, for which his fine voice and impressive appearance suited him; he also occupied a minor government office. Then he embarked on a political career as a supporter first of Aristophon and then of the latter's opponent Eubulus, during whose financial con-

es′ ki nēz (Brit. ēs′ ki nēz)

3

AESCHINES

AESCHINES

trollership of Athens Aeschines' brother held an important post. In 347/6 both Aeschines and Demosthenes were members of the Council *(Boule)*. Aeschines supported Eubulus in seeking to check the expansion of the Macedonian king Philip II by organizing a common peace among the Greek city-states. However, the attempt failed. Aeschines and Demosthenes then served on a deputation to Philip that resulted in an alliance (the Peace of Philocrates) between Macedonia and the Athenian League. But the alliance came to nothing, because of Philip's continued aggressive activity. Aeschines sought to reconcile Athenian public opinion to the gains that the Peace of Philocrates had brought to Macedonia, but Demosthenes, in his speech *On the Peace,* insinuated that Aeschines had been bribed by Philip to take this view, and in 346/5 initiated his prosecution. Aeschines countered by his speech *Against Timarchus* (a supporter of Demosthenes), maintaining that the man's notorious immorality debarred him from speaking in public and retaining the rights of a citizen; and Timarchus was found guilty. Three years later, however, Demosthenes returned to the attack in his speech *On the Fraudulent Embassy,* to which Aeschines replied in an oration with the same title that narrowly gained him acquittal.

After Philip's decisive victory over the city-states at Chaeronea (338), Aeschines retired from public life; he subsequently emerged from retirement on only two occasions—when he saw favorable opportunities to strike at Demosthenes. In 336, when it was proposed in the Council by a certain Ctesiphon that Demosthenes should be awarded a crown for his services to the city, Aeschines assailed the measure, and six years later he proceeded with the prosecution of its proposer. This speech, *Against Ctesiphon,* however, was successfully rebutted by Demosthenes in his oration *On the Crown.* Aeschines, since he failed to obtain the necessary minimum of one-fifth of the votes cast and was unable or unwilling to pay the fine that such a failure incurred, was deprived of his civic rights. He left Athens for Asia Minor; and it was recorded, on doubtful authority, that he inaugurated the teaching of rhetoric at Rhodes.

Aeschines' general policy had been to find an understanding with Macedonia that would leave Athens independent and avoid war. Though a self-made man, without professional training in rhetoric, and lacking also Demosthenes' special capacity to make apt use of historical argument, he possessed considerable learning, of which he was proud, and his presence and delivery produced a strong effect upon his audiences. Favoring a dignified style and a statuesque pose, without extravagant gestures, he spoke with convincing and persuasive force, sometimes rising to torrential vigor. He was a master of diversionary tactics and legalistic arguments, in which he preferred, however, to employ vivid description rather than close logical reasoning. But his main strength lay in his wit. He was much funnier than Demosthenes, and in the course of the unrestrained abuse which they exchanged with one another, Aeschines made fun of his opponent's peculiarities with uproarious success, while Demosthenes remained grimly serious. Their violent attacks and counterattacks supply an important part of our evidence for the relations between Athens and Macedonia in the 340s and 330s B.C.

WORKS—*Speeches:* Against Timarchus; On the Fraudulent Embassy (De Falsa Legatione); Against

Ctesiphon. Twelve letters ascribed to Aeschines are spurious.
EDITIONS with translation—C. D. Adams, Aeschines: Speeches, 1919; G. de Budé and V. Martin, Eschine: Discours (Budé ed.), 1927–28.
ABOUT—G. Kennedy, The Art of Persuasion in Greece, 1963; A. Anastassiou and D. Irmer, Kleine attische Redner, 1977.

AESCHYLUS, Greek poet and tragic dramatist, was born in 525 or 524 B.C. and died in 456. His birthplace was Eleusis near Athens, and he was the son of Euphorion, a landowner of noble family. His brother Cynegirus was killed fighting against the Persians at Marathon (490), and he himself likewise fought in the battle, as was recorded in his epitaph—probably written by himself —which makes no mention of his achievements as a dramatist. He seems to have taken part also in the battle of Salamis (480), though reports that he was a participant in the further engagements at Artemisium (in the same year) and Plataea (479) are less certain. Aeschylus was not only strongly patriotic but also deeply religious, and it has been conjectured from a passage of the comic dramatist Aristophanes that he was initiated into the Eleusinian Mysteries, honoring the goddess Demeter. It was believed that he was prosecuted for violating their secrecy but acquitted on the plea that he had done so unknowingly. Between c. 478 and c. 472 Aeschylus visited the court of King Hiero I of Syracuse; he returned to Sicily in 458, or later, and died on the island, at Gela. An anecdote relates that he was killed by a tortoise dropped on his bald head by an eagle. His son Euphorion was also a tragic poet.

A manuscript catalogue of his plays includes 72 titles, but there are at least ten more attributed to him, for the most part convincingly, by other sources. The first of his thirteen victories in dramatic competitions was in 484. The custom was for each playwright to produce four plays (a tetralogy) at each contest, comprising a trilogy of tragedies and a satyric drama. (For further information, see below under WORKS and also under Sophocles and Euripides.)

es′ ki lus (Brit. ē′ ski lus)

In Aeschylus' play the *Persians* (472), Xerxes, the young and bold king of Persia, has gone forth in 480 at the head of an enormous army collected from the nations of his empire to conquer the whole of Greece, with the particular intention of taking vengeance upon the Athenians, who had heavily defeated his father, Darius, ten years earlier at Marathon. Meanwhile, at home in Persia, the Elders (the chorus of the play), whom the king had appointed as regents during his absence, are worried by the lack of all news from him and his army; they gather in solemn session to deliberate on what may have happened. To the session comes Queen Mother Atossa, seeking the Elders' interpretation of a dream she has had that seems to portend disaster for her son; the Elders direct her to pray to the gods and to propitiate the Earth and the spirits of the dead with offerings, in the hope of warding off the evil outcome forecast by the dream. Before departing, she enquires what strength Athens could oppose to the might of Persia, and they tell her of the city's prowess. Then comes a messenger, in urgent haste, reporting the destruction of the Persian fleet at Salamis and the hardships of the army on its homeward march. On hearing this news, Atossa sacrifices at the tomb of her husband Darius; and the spirit of the dead king, conjured up by the incantations of the chorus, dissuades the Persians from any further schemes for invading Greece, foretells that their sacrilege and arrogance will cause them to be defeated at Plataea, and attributes Xerxes' failure to his presumptuous infatuation with revenge. At the end of the play Xerxes himself appears in distress to illustrate the downfall of his mad pride.

Seven Against Thebes (467) tells the story of the Theban Polyneices and six champions from Argos he has enlisted against his brother Eteocles, with whom he is disputing the throne of Thebes left vacant by the abdication and exile of their blinded father Oedipus. Warned by the seer Tiresias that the Argives are determined upon a supreme assault, Eteocles heartens his fellow Thebans and quells the lamentations of their terrified women, the chorus of the tragedy. A scout informs him that the enemy is at hand and describes their leaders, one standing at each of the seven gates of the city. Eteocles dispatches a Theban hero to face each of them. One of the seven is Polyneices himself, and Eteocles goes out to confront him. He ignores the chorus's plea that he should not shed his brother's blood; and they review the curse that has weighed upon the royal house of Thebes ever since Laius, father of Oedipus, disobeyed Apollo's order not to beget a child. The chorus recall Oedipus' own curse on his two sons and his pronouncement that they will perish at one another's hands. Presently the scout returns to report that, whereas the enemy has been repulsed at six of the gates, at the seventh both Eteocles and Polyneices lie dead, struck down by one another. Their sisters, Antigone and Ismene, lament them; but a herald comes to announce the official decision that, whereas Eteocles is to be buried with full honors, Polyneices, the attacker of his own city, must lie unburied to be eaten by the dogs. Antigone declares that she will defy the order, whatever the consequences; and half the chorus join her, while the rest depart with Eteocles' funeral procession.

Suppliant Women (463) is about the fifty daughters of Danaus, whom the fifty sons of Aegyptus, Danaus' brother, have tried to compel to become their wives. But the Danaids, detesting the violence of their cousins, flee with their father to Argos, the home of their ancestress Io, who had been the mistress of Zeus. There they seek sanctuary from King Pelasgus. This he is reluctant to grant them but is overborne by the vote of the Argive people. The thwarted bridegrooms arrive in pursuit, preceded by their herald, who demands the surrender of the young women: but, despite his threats of war, the demand is rejected.

Aeschylus continued this story in two other plays, which have only survived in fragmentary condition: *The Egyptians* and the *Danaids.* Danaus, forced to give way to his nephews' insistence on taking his daughters, orders them to kill their husbands on the wedding night. All obey except one, Hypermnestra, who spares her bridegroom because she loves him. She is brought to trial, but the goddess Aphrodite defends her on the grounds that the love of man and woman is hallowed by the love of Heaven for Earth.

The *Oresteia* (458), consisting of the *Agamemnon, The Libation Bearers (Choephoroi),* and *The Eumenides (Furies* —literally, *Kindly Ones),* is the only complete trilogy extant. Its plot is taken from the legend of the Argive royal house of Atreus, in which crime bred crime through many generations. The action of the first play takes place at the palace of Agamemnon in an atmosphere of mingled hope and foreboding. The end of the Trojan War is near. However, it is revealed that before sailing for Troy Agamemnon had sacrificed his own daughter Iphigenia in order to obtain a fair wind. During the ten years of his absence, his wife Clytemnestra has brooded over this deed, sending their son Orestes away, ruling over Argos with her lover Aegisthus, and awaiting the moment of revenge. Now comes the news, flashed by a chain of beacons, that Troy has fallen. Clytemnestra is jubilant, but the chorus of Argive elders think of the crime that started the war and the price that has been paid for victory.

Presently the victorious king appears, with a captive Trojan girl, Cassandra, in his train. It is a strained reunion. Clytemnestra is fulsome, Agamemnon cold and wary, but eventually she entices him into the palace and kills him; whereupon Cassandra, after seeing horrifying visions of the crimes of the house of Atreus, past and present, despairingly follows him, and dies in her turn. Soon the interior of the palace is revealed, and the chorus is horrified to see the bodies of Agamemnon and Cassandra and to recognize Clytemnestra standing over them. She answers the elders' protests by recalling the sacrifice of Iphigenia, and when Aegisthus appears he tries to overawe them by a show of force. The elders can only hope that one day Agamemnon's son will avenge him.

In the *Libation Bearers* Orestes, after years of exile, returns to Argos under orders from Apollo to avenge his father's death. He sees his sister Electra, accompanied by a group of slave women (the chorus), taking libations to pour at Agamemnon's tomb. After a hesitant recognition Electra joins Orestes in an awe-inspiring invocation of their dead father's spirit; and they are filled with a passion for revenge.

Orestes contrives to kill Aegisthus and

then, sword in hand, faces his mother. For a moment he falters, but his friend Pylades sternly reminds him of Apollo's command, and they lead her into the palace. Again the interior is thrown open. Orestes in his turn is seen standing over the bodies of Clytemnestra and Aegisthus. While he is justifying his vengeance, he sees avenging Furies appearing to haunt him, and he flees to seek purification at Apollo's shrine at Delphi.

The opening scene of the *Eumenides* is set in Delphi. The suppliant Orestes, surrounded by a chorus of sleeping Furies, is reassured by Apollo and sent away to Athens for judgment. The ghost of Clytemnestra angrily arouses the Furies, and they set off on his trail. The scene now changes to Athens, before Athena's temple on the Acropolis. The Furies and Orestes submit their rival claims and justifications to Athena, who founds the homicide court of the Areopagus to hear the case. The Furies prosecute, and Apollo defends; the judges are evenly divided, but Athena gives her casting vote to Orestes. She then calms the enraged Furies, persuading them to take on a new function and settle in Attica as revered and beneficent powers, the Eumenides, or Kindly Ones. And so they are conducted in a procession to their new underground sanctuary on the Areopagus.

The plot of the later *Prometheus Bound,* and the two lost plays that were produced as its sequels, is concerned with Prometheus' endeavor to oppose Zeus, and the outcome of that effort. Zeus, when he had overthrown his father Kronos and established himself in supreme power, decided to destroy all human beings, since they had become contemptuous of the gods. Zeus's cousin Prometheus, on the other hand, had helped men and women in many ways. In particular, he had granted them Hope, which prevented them from brooding on their mortality, and he had stolen fire from heaven and given it to them, to become the source of all technical inventions.

And now he opposes Zeus's intention to destroy mankind. In consequence, the god punishes him, ordering that he should be chained forever to a crag in the Caucasus, and it is at this point that the play begins. Zeus's henchmen Might and Violence bring Prometheus to the place as a prisoner, and Hephaestus, god of fire, nails him to the rock. He is first visited by the Daughters of Oceanus, the chorus of the play, who weep for him; then by their father Oceanus, who urges him to submit to Zeus's will; and finally by Io, a mortal girl, who, because Zeus has seduced her, has been transformed into a heifer by Zeus's wife Hera and driven mad by a gadfly that pursues her all over the world.

Prometheus foretells to Io that after many generations a descendant of hers is destined to set him free. He also reveals that Zeus will beget a son fated to overthrow him. The identity of the boy's mother (Thetis) is a secret known only to Prometheus, so that, as long as he does not disclose it, his enemy's downfall is assured. At the end of the play Hermes, messenger of Zeus, orders him to reveal what he knows, but Prometheus refuses. The rock is then struck by lightning, and the Daughters of Oceanus, refusing to leave him, are swallowed up in an earthquake.

Prometheus Bound was part of a trilogy, but the other two plays, *Prometheus Unbound* and *Prometheus the Firebearer,* have only survived in fragments. It appears, however, that after a passage of thirty thousand years Zeus and Prometheus become reconciled: Zeus changes his attitude and becomes eager to promote the welfare of mankind, and in consequence Prometheus saves him from destruction by revealing his secret.

Although there had been shadowy predecessors, Aeschylus is generally regarded as the real founder of Greek tragedy. His most important technical innovation was the introduction of a second actor, who created the possibility of tragic dialogue; and it seems to have been he, once again, who organized its stage presentation on the lines that subsequently became traditional. Aeschylus was also responsible for a new and exalted seriousness, a lofty intellectual tone conveyed through a densely charged poetry of massive grandeur and stiffly gorgeous, exuberant complexity, reinforced by spectacular and often barbaric stage effects. In veiled, oracular utterance, loaded with a multiplicity of inventive words and images, he was able, by virtue of his enormous imaginative power, to infuse into the traditional mythology almost incommunicable truth about the universe and the human soul.

Most of his characters are devised as the embodiments of some mighty passion or principle that determines all their words and actions. The fates of human beings are seen to depend on the interaction of two factors, their own will and the often inscrutable rulings of the divine powers controlling the world. The human characters in Aeschylus' dramas, among whom the remorseless, dominant Clytemnestra stands out supreme, possess powerful personalities that by no means fall short of the terrible challenges they have to meet. The choruses are often designed as foils to set off a leading personage, though they, too, are characterized in distinct terms, varying strongly from one play to another.

The plots move unrelentingly forward as the divine plan works itself out. The grouping of plays into trilogies was a practice especially well fitted to depict this slow but certain operation. Aeschylus wanted above all to impress on his audience the lesson of the eventual fulfillment of providential Law, by which the clashing aims of human beings and gods alike are ultimately brought to reconciliation. He is deeply preoccupied with the traditional ideas of inherited evil, curses that ruin a house, and the hazards of great wealth. Yet a curse, he often seems to feel, will not strike its victim down unless he has encouraged it to do so by his own arrogance *(hubris)*. Even wealth, although already perilous in itself, musc be accompanied by *hubris* before it can bring disaster. Justice, however long postponed, will be done in the end; and it may somehow be possible, at long last, to escape from the disastrous chain of evil and even to recognize the cruelest tortures of suffering as elements in the pattern of a vast and beneficent heavenly design.

Much attention has been devoted in recent years to the reflection of current political events and developments in Aeschylus' plays. His was an age when the antithesis of tyranny and liberty was in everyone's mind. The defeat of Persia in its wars against the Greeks was manifestly an example of down-

fall through *hubris,* and the salvation of the new, brash, increasingly powerful city-state of Athens depended on a firm reconstruction, under divine auspices, of its rival and conflicting elements. Scholars have also detected reflections of Aeschylus' Sicilian experiences.

After his death, the Athenian people decreed that anyone desiring to produce one of Aeschylus' tragedies should be granted a chorus by the authorities, and the statement in his anonymously written biography that his plays gained many posthumous victories may well be true. His dramatic successors Sophocles and Euripides followed, in their different ways, along the lines he had laid down; and so did all the subsequent tragic theater of Europe and America.

WORKS—*Lost plays:* The Laius, Oedipus, and satyr play the Sphinx formed a tetralogy with the Seven Against Thebes. The Egyptians, Danaids, and satyric Amymone formed a tetralogy with the Suppliant Women. The Proteus was the satyr play of the Oresteia. A tetralogy the Lykourgeia comprised the Edonians, Bassarids, Youths (Neaniskoi), and the satyric Lycurgus. No subject connection can be traced at present between the Persians and other productions of the same year: the Phineus, Glaucus the Sea God, and the satyric Prometheus. *Other plays by Aeschylus:* Alcmene, Argives, Argo, Atalanta, Athamas, Award of Armor, Bacchae, Bone-Gatherers, Builders of the Bridal Chamber, Cabiri, Callisto, Carians (or Europa), Cercyon, Children of Heracles, Circe (satyric), Conjurers of the Dead, Cretan Women, Cycnus, Eleusinians, Epigoni, Etnaeans, Eurytion, Glaucus the Sea God, Heliades, Heralds, Huntresses, Hypsipyle, Iphigenia, Isthmiasts (satyric), Ixion, Lemnians, Lion, Memnon, Myrmidons, Mysians, Necromancers, Nemea, Nereids, Net-Drawers (about the infant Perseus), Niobe, Nurses, Orithyia, Palamedes, Penelope, Pentheus, Perrhaebians, Philoctetes, Phineus, Phercides, Polydectes, Priestesses, Processional, Ransom of Hector, Semele, Sisyphus (perhaps two plays), Telephus, Tenes, Toxotides (on the death of Actaeon), Weighing of Souls, Women of Salamis, Xantriai.

EDITIONS—P. Groeneboom (except the Suppliants), 1928–52; H. J. Rose, 1957–58; Persians: H. D. Broadhead, 1960; Suppliants: H. F. Johansen and O. Smith, v 1, 1970; Agamemnon: J. D. Denniston and D. Page, 1957; Eumenides: G. Pompella, 1973; Fragments: H. J. Mette, Die Fragmente der Tragödien des Aischylos, 1959. *With translation:* Prometheus Bound and Oresteia: G. Thomson, 1932, 1938; Agamemnon: E. Fraenkel, 1950; Fragments: H. J. Mette, Der verlorene Aischylos 1963. *Translations*—H. W. Smyth (Loeb ed.), 1922, 1957 (also supplement to latter by H. Lloyd-Jones); D. Greene and R. Lattimore, The Complete Greek Tragedies, 1954, 1956; P. Vellacott (Penguin ed.), 1956, 1961; F. L. Lucas, Greek Drama for the

Common Reader, 1967. For translations of individual plays *see* A. M. W. Green, Classics in Translation: A Selective Bibliography (1930–76), 1976; F. Raphael and K. McLeish, The Oresteia, 1978.

ABOUT—W. B. Stanford, Aeschylus in His Style, 1942; K. Reinhardt, Aischylos als Regisseur und Theologe, 1949; F. Solmsen, Hesiod and Aeschylus, 1949; J. H. Finley, Pindar and Aeschylus, 1955; J. de Romilly, La crainte et l'angoisse dans le théâtre d'Éschyle, 1958; M. Werre de Haas, Aeschylus, 1961; G. A. Murray, Aeschylus: The Creator of Tragedy, 1962; A. Lesky, Greek Tragedy, 1966; A. J. Podlecki, Political Background of Aeschylean Tragedy, 1966; A. H. Ahrens, The Plays of Aeschylus, 1966; H. W. Smyth, Aeschylean Tragedy, 1969; J. Herington, The Author of the Prometheus Bound, 1970; H. Lloyd-Jones, The Justice of Zeus, 1971; T. B. L. Webster, Greek Tragedy (Greece & Rome: New Surveys in the Classics, no 5), 1971; H. Hemmel, Wege zu Aischylos, 1974; E. Petrounias, Funktion und Thematik der Bilder bei Aischylos, 1976; R. Böhme, Bühnenbearbeitung äschyleischer Tragödien, 1977; M. Gagarin, Aeschylean Drama, 1977; M. Griffith, The Authenticity of Prometheus Bound, 1977; O. Taplin, The Stagecraft of Aeschylus, 1978; W. G. Thalmann, Dramatic Art in Aeschylus' Seven Against Thebes, 1978.

AESOP, Greek writer of fables, lived in the early sixth century B.C. and came from Thrace (not Phrygia in Asia Minor, as was asserted later); he was taken to the island of Samos, where he worked as a slave.

The kind of fable he told was of Eastern, and probably Babylonian, origin. The Assyrian *Book of Ahikar,* which shows how fables of various kinds can attach themselves to the person of a famous sage, was known in a Greek translation in the fourth century B.C., but the interest in such tales probably went back to the sixth century and may have been spread by Aesop himself. It is unlikely, however, that he ever wrote or published anything himself. He was apparently a famous teller of tales, living in an age when written prose was reserved for the serious works of history and philosophy that were just beginning to appear.

Aesop's fables were mentioned by Herodotus and Aristophanes, so that there must have been a collection of them by their time, and possibly a life of Aesop himself. However, the oldest collection of which we have any knowledge was made by Demetrius of Phaleron in the fourth century B.C., and the earliest collection of which any por-

ē′ sop

tion is extant today is the *Collectio Augustana.* A fragment of this work on a papyrus of the first century A.D., preserved formerly at Augsburg (after which it is named), is now at Munich. In the same period Phaedrus, a freedman of Augustus, wrote five books of so-called Aesop's fables in Latin verse, and some two centuries later Babrius used an Aesopic collection for his Greek metrical version. These collections, and the *Lives* or *Romances* of Aesop in the forms in which they have come down to us, bear the marks of such repeated alteration that their connection with him is tenuous or nonexistent; yet his name continued to be associated with such productions, and in the fourth century A.D. the emperor Julian the Apostate described him as "the Homer or Thucydides or Plato of fables." Later, the Byzantines produced several new collections of Aesopic fables, and they have penetrated European literature very deeply.

EDITIONS with translation—S. A. Handford (Penguin ed.), 1954; D. B. Hull, 1960; L. W. Daly, Aesop Without Morals: The Famous Fables, and a Life of Aesop, 1961; G. Poethke (German), 1974.

ABOUT—R. C. D. Kovacs, The Aesopic Fable in Ancient Rhetorical Theory and Practice, 1950; B. E. Perry, Aesopica, 1952, *and* Babrius and Phaedrus (Loeb ed.), 1965; M. Pugliarello, Le origini della favolistica classica, 1973.

AFRANIUS, LUCIUS, Latin comic poet and playwright, was born in (probably) about 150 B.C.; his death date is uncertain. A reference by Cicero suggests that he was an orator and, therefore, a Roman citizen.

Afranius was one of three known practitioners of the *fabula togata,* comic drama with subject matter based on Italian life. The three or four hundred scattered lines and about forty titles of his plays that survive indicate that he concentrated on domestic drama. The title of *Women of Brundusium* names the Italian town (Brindisi) that formed its background. *The Divorce* dealt with, among other things, the interference of a father with the marriage of his daughter. *Saved from the Sea* (if that is the meaning of *Exceptus*) seems to have been about a young man who was rejected by a Neapolitan

a frä′ ni us

9

woman and escaped drowning when a fisherman pulled him out of the sea. *The Fire* showed a conflagration on the stage—and was revived by the emperor Nero (who was himself accused of arson). *The Impostor,* brought back to the theater in 57 B.C., presented a husband who led a life of dissipation, out of which his father-in-law sought to frighten him by threatening to fetch the wife back to her parental home. The play contained a scene in which a child intervened in a quarrel between its parents. *Bucco Adopted,* if an authentic title of Afranius, shows the influence of native Italian productions, in which Bucco was a stock character, the fat fool. (These productions were known as Atellan farces *[fabulae Atellanae]* after the town of Atella in Campania, though they may have originated in some other part of Italy.)

The literary critic Quintilian, while singling out Afranius as the best writer of *comoediae togatae,* complained of Afranius' liking for pederastic themes, though no trace of this has survived in extant fragments. Afranius borrowed from Terence and, like him, discussed literary questions through the speakers of his prologues. In the prologue to his *Compitalia* (the name of a festival in honor of the household gods or Lares) he also acknowledged a debt to the Greek comic poet Menander, whose method of introducing a play through the mouth of a deity or personification Afranius seems to have adopted. His avowed admiration for Menander (and for Terence, who, although he wrote in Latin, employed Greek themes) prompts the suspicion that the Italianness of Afranius' own plays may only have been superficial.

WORKS—His plays (lost except for fragments) included Brundusinae (Women of Brundusium), Bucco Adoptatus (Bucco Adopted), Compitalia, Divortium (The Divorce), Emancipatus (son freed from father's power), Epistula (The Letter), Exceptus (Saved from the Sea?), Fratriae (Sisters-in-Law), Incendium (The Fire), Privignus (The Stepson), Simulans (The Impostor), Thais, Vopiscus (one of a pair of twins born alive after the other did not survive).
EDITIONS—O. Ribbeck, Comicorum Romanorum Fragmenta, 2nd ed., 1897.
ABOUT—W. Beare, The Roman Stage, 3rd ed. revised, 1969; A. P. Bagniolini, Note sulla lingua di Afranio, 1977.

AGATHIAS, Greek (Byzantine) poet and historian, was born at Myrina in Aeolis (western Asia Minor) in about A.D. 531 and died in about 580.

After receiving from the rhetoricians of Alexandria an education of the traditional high quality, he studied law at Constantinople and practiced there as an advocate *(scholasticus)* and this became his nickname or surname. He was also a member of a circle of writers of occasional poetry who were close to the court of Justinian I. Agathias himself published a seven- or eight-book *Circle* of little poems written by himself and his contemporaries. The poems were arranged according to subject, and many of them, including a hundred of his own composition, were subsequently incorporated in the enlarged Greek Anthology compiled by Cephalas in the tenth century. They are predominantly epigrams, but a number of them are elegies: epitaphs, dedications, and pieces on obscene subjects. As an epigrammatist Agathias was too prolix to be entirely successful, but his best (and shortest) poems are those relating to love and are warm, intimate, and honest. The 123-line prologue which he later added to his collection throws light on the literary ideas of the time.

After completing the *Circle,* Agathias started work on his prose *Histories,* which were designed to continue and bring up to date Procopius' *History of the Wars of Justinian.* Agathias' *Histories,* of which probably only the surviving five books were completed, have as their main themes the campaign of the imperial general Narses in Italy from 552 to 555 and the holding operation against the Sassanian Persians on the eastern frontier (in Lazica) from 554 to the truce of 557. This military narrative occupies the first four books. The fifth provides a firsthand account of an earthquake at Constantinople in 557, a plague in 558, and the Huns' attempted raid on that city in 559. Around this narrative core are woven numerous digressions concerned chiefly with personalities, antiquities, and ethnology. They tell us a good deal about the intellectual interests of the writer and his contempo-

à ga' thi às

raries. Particularly significant are discussions about the Franks and about Persian history and customs.

Although he lacks Procopius' insight and experience, Agathias provides a detailed, contemporary, and valuable account of the penultimate decade of the reign of Justinian, to whose policy of expansion he is on the whole favorable. He is also a source useful to orientalists and students of the origins and early history of France, Germany, and Russia. But his florid and sometimes bizarre style tends to result in obscurity. He is a self-conscious archaizer, who not only shuns modernisms but deliberately searches out obsolete and recondite words and forms. Though he himself was a Christian, his desire to recapture the spirit of pagan antiquity causes him to omit all references to Christianity from his writings. Nevertheless, he avoids Procopius' emphasis on the role of chance in history and has no theory of historical causation apart from the Divine Will.

EDITIONS (of the Histories)—R. Keydell, Agathiae Myrinaei Historiarum Libri Quinque, 1967; S. Costanza, Historiarum Libri Quinque, 1971. *With translation:* M. V. Levchenko, Agafij: O Tsarstvovanii Iustiniana, 1953; J. D. C. Frendo, Agathias: The Histories, 1975. ABOUT—A. Cameron, Agathias, 1970.

AGATHON, Greek tragic poet, c. 447 – c. 401 B.C., the son of Tisamenus, was born into a rich and aristocratic Athenian family. He was handsome, elegant, and sociable. The fictional setting of Plato's *Symposium* is the house of Agathon, whose first victory as a tragic dramatist (416 B.C.) is being celebrated by a party at which Aristophanes, Alcibiades, and Socrates are present.

In 411 Agathon heard and admired the speech made in his own defense by Antiphon, leader of the oligarchic extremists, which may suggest that Agathon's own political sympathies were not dissimilar. In the same year he was caricatured by Aristophanes in the *Thesmophoriazusae* as an idle and effeminate esthete who appears at his dressing table in female attire, assuring his fellow tragedian Euripides and his father-in-law that his purpose is to get the feel

ag′ à thon

of the woman's part he is writing. Aristophanes' lost comedy *Gerytades* apparently accorded Agathon more caustic treatment still. In 407 Agathon moved (like Euripides) to the court of King Archelaus in Macedonia, where he remained. Two years later Aristophanes, relenting in his judgment of Agathon, makes the god Dionysus, in the *Frogs,* describe him punningly as "a good *[agathos]* poet, much missed by his friends."

Next to Aeschylus, Sophocles, and Euripides, Agathon was the most distinguished of Athenian tragic dramatists; but only forty lines of his work survive. His style was noted for its elaboration, reflected also in florid musical effects. The eulogy of love that Plato ascribes to him in the *Symposium* is so heavily loaded with rhetorical figures of paradox and antithesis that Plato must have intended a parody, an impression that is confirmed by the fragments of Agathon's plays. Moreover, in early life, he had been a pupil of the sophist Prodicus, who would have fostered such tendencies. This desire to fascinate the listener by mere sound led to a new independence in the lyrical sections of Agathon's plays, which he treated, according to Aristotle, as interludes or entr'actes; and choral innovations of this type formed the most striking feature of his tragedies. They also abounded in epigrammatic phrases, well adapted to quotation, but their plots, we learn from the same source, were often much too involved: for example, he tried to cram the whole of a lengthy story such as the Sack of Troy into a single play. However, Aristotle refers very favorably to another work, the *Antheus,* in which Agathon moved away from customary mythology and invented the entire plot himself, devising a romantic tale that ended in the death of the hero by a woman's contrivance. He was evidently a talented modernizer whose breaks with tradition pleased some and shocked others.

WORKS—His plays included the Aërope, Antheus (rather than Anthos), Alcmaeon, The Mysians, Telephus, Thyestes.
EDITIONS—A. Nauck, Tragicorum Graecorum Fragmenta (Teubner ed.), revised ed., 1964.
ABOUT—P. Lévèque, Agathon, 1955.

ALCAEUS, Greek poet, was born about 620 B.C. in the city of Mytilene on the island of Lesbos. We learn much about his life from the surviving fragments of his poems. When the hereditary monarchy of the city came to an end in the middle of the seventh century B.C., various groups of nobles competed for power, and Alcaeus belonged to one of these groups. While he was still a boy, his brothers, with the help of Pittacus (later considered one of the Seven Sages of Greece), overthrew the autocrat Melanchrus. Later, when Mytilene was at war with Athens over the control of the Propontis (Gallipoli), Alcaeus fought at Pittacus' side —although on one occasion, according to his own rueful admission (which may already have been something of a literary convention), he threw down his shield and ran away. At some stage Alcaeus and his friends had to retreat to Pyrrha, at the other end of the island, in order to get away from Melanchrus' successor Myrsilus. In due course, however, Myrsilus was killed (to Alcaeus' delight) and was succeeded by Pittacus, whom Alcaeus now violently abused for his acceptance of autocratic power (and much else). Retreating into exile in Egypt, Alcaeus may have visited Thrace and Boeotia and may have gone to Lydia as well. According to later and dubious literary evidence, Pittacus, before resigning his office in 580, pardoned Alcaeus; at all events Alcaeus seems to have returned home before his death, of which the date is uncertain. He was a friend and contemporary of Sappho.

Many of the surviving fragments of his poems are concerned with combative political themes, relating to the power struggle at Mytilene. They contain fierce personal attacks, particularly directed against Pittacus. Alcaeus was happy to sing of Pittacus' well-stocked armory, enumerating its brightly gleaming weapons. He also dealt with the mythology of the Trojan war and composed hymns in honor of various gods—Apollo, Hermes, Hephaestus, Athena Itonia, Eros, and perhaps Artemis—and sang of Bacchus and the Muses as well. We owe this information to Horace, who added that another of Alcaeus' themes was the boy Lycus, whose beauty he praised. Other Roman writers

al kī′ us

also speak of this erotic branch of Alcaeus' poetry. The subject of drinking and other themes intended for recitation at table played a substantial part in his work; sometimes these pieces contained a philosophical undercurrent.

Alcaeus was a fighter and a feaster, a man of action who personified the bellicose, power-hungry aristocracy that had bred him. His vigorous hatreds were not all that inspired him, however, for he also had a keen eye for beauty, a skillful capacity for evoking various (though mainly masculine) moods, and a power of lucid, straightforward communication, seen at its best in his charmingly direct accounts of unprofound emotions. Writing in the vernacular dialect of Aeolis (the region to which Lesbos belonged), he employed a remarkably wide range of meters (including one type of four-line stanza named after him), which later lyric poets, Greek and Roman alike, were eager to emulate. In other respects, too, his influence was considerable, and Horace in particular was proud to claim him as a model and once imitated a famous comparison of the state to a ship at sea, a comparison that Alcaeus had liked especially, though he was not its originator.

EDITIONS—E. Lobel and D. L. Page, Poetarum Lesbiorum Fragmenta, 2nd ed., 1963; E. M. Voight, Sappho et Alcaeus, Fragmenta, 1971. *With translation:* J. M. Edmonds, Lyra Graeca (Loeb ed.), v 1, revised ed., 1928.
ABOUT—M. Treu, Alkaios, 1952; C. A. Mastrelli, La lingua di Alceo, 1954; D. L. Page, Sappho and Alcaeus, 1955; C. M. Bowra, Greek Lyric Poetry, 2nd ed., 1962; D. A. Campbell, Greek Lyric Poetry, 1967; H. Martin, Alcaeus, 1972; G. M. Kirkwood, Early Greek Monody, 1974.

ALCMAN, Greek poet. The evidence for his life is elusive, but it has been suggested that he flourished in the middle or, more probably, the latter part of the seventh century B.C. However, it has also been argued that at least one of his poems might conceivably have been written as late as 570. He worked in Sparta, which later claimed to be his birthplace, and he wrote a language that is basically Laconian (Spartan) vernacular. An

alk′ man

earlier tradition had it that he had come to Sparta from abroad. Indeed, one of his poems claims that a certain man came from Sardis in Lydia (western Asia Minor); and since this man is thought to have been himself, it is possible that he was a Lydian or, more likely, an Asiatic (Ionian) Greek. In any event, he was said to have been a slave, granted his freedom because of his cleverness.

Alcman wrote lyric poems, which were later collected into six books, though only fragments of them have come down to us. The most substantial comprises a papyrus containing about one hundred verses from a *Song of Maidens* (Partheneion). We learn that the choir which sang it consisted of eleven girls, led by a certain Hagesichora (if this was her real name; the word means choir-leader). After recounting a heroic myth, the slaying of the sons of Hippocoön by Heracles—a story that illustrates the punishment of pride—the chorus converse and jest with one another and compare the looks of Hagesichora with another of their number, Agido; other chorus members, too, receive praise. While the song seems to have been sung at night in competition with another choir, its exact structure remains controversial, as does its purpose and character. It has been variously attributed to local Spartan festivals of Artemis Orthia, Castor and Pollux, Dionysus, and Helen. Alcman seems to be telling the old stories from a Laconian viewpoint, glorifying local heroes and heroines whenever the opportunity offered. The atmosphere is that of a happy party, and the loosely constructed verses seem to echo the conversation of the young women who were the singers. A further two leaves of papyrus, discovered twenty years ago, provide a portion of another song, which is once again designed for singing by a chorus of girls. Here, too, there is light-hearted bantering, expressed with a charming and colorful freshness.

Other fragments came from hymns to gods and goddesses—Apollo, Aphrodite, Athena, Hera, Castor and Pollux, and Dionysus, whose nocturnal festival the poem in his honor apparently describes. There is also a poem on the origins of the universe, giving prominence to Thetis, and other pieces that have been interpreted as preludes to recitations of Homer. Alcman wrote love poems as well and indeed acquired a reputation as the founder of erotic poetry. Other subjects to which he devoted attention were eating and drinking, especially the former, since he writes about mashed peas and complains that in the Spartan spring there are flowers enough but not much to eat. Yet Alcman is also profoundly observant of nature. He knows the ways of horses and birds, and he can imitate the song of a partridge. A fragment describing the stillness of night is particularly moving. It tells how mountain and valley are lapped in sleep, together with all the creatures of land and air and sea. A contrast is implied between nature, which is at rest, and the unrest of the human heart.

Alcman is also sensitive about the oncoming of age, expressing sadness because he can no longer take part in the dance and because he is not like a kingfisher, which is carried over the waves by its mate when it grows old.

EDITIONS—A. Garzya, ed., Alcmane: I frammenti, 1954; D. L. Page, Poetae Melici Graeci, 1962. *With translation:* J. M. Edmonds, Lyra Graeca (Loeb ed.), v 1, revised ed., 1928; G. Davenport, Partheneia and Fragments (Arion, v 8, no 4), 1969.
ABOUT—D. L. Page, Alcman: The Partheneion, 1951; C. M. Bowra, Greek Lyric Poetry, 2nd ed., 1962; D. A. Campbell, Greek Lyric Poetry, 1967.

ALCUIN. See *British Authors Before 1800* (H. W. Wilson, 1952)

ALEXANDER OF APHRODISIAS, Greek philosopher, came from the city of that name (now Kehre) in western Asia Minor. A pupil of the Aristotelian (Peripatetic) Aristocles of Messana (Messina) in Sicily, he subsequently became head of the Aristotelian school (Lyceum) at Athens, at the very end of the second century A.D. He dedicated his book *On Fate* to the Roman emperors Septimius Severus (193–211) and Caracalla (211–17).

Alexander was the most able of the Greek
af rō di′ si ås

commentators on Aristotle, whose teaching he set out to restore to its original purity by purging it of subsequent accretions. In antiquity these commentaries were the most influential branch of his writings, earning him the title of The Expositor from respectful later commentators. On the whole, he restricts himself to the exposition of Aristotle's doctrines, treating them as a coherent system and attempting little variation or criticism. However, he also puts forward a few independent theories of his own, including a denial of the immortality of the soul and an assertion of the unalterable unity of the mental faculties of human beings.

In the Middle Ages, however, Alexander was chiefly known for his other and more original writings, which attracted both Christian and Arabic philosophers. The most important of them are *On Fate,* in which he defends free will against the Stoic doctrine of Necessity, and *On the Soul,* in which he tries to embroider upon Aristotle's beliefs concerning the soul and the intellect. In the latter work, fraught with difficult obscurities, Alexander saw the divine intellect —the external, immaterial form or first cause—as the actualizer or paradigm for the human intellect and the performer of the abstractions it needs. He appears to have exercised an influence on Plotinus' mystical notion of the intellect *(nous),* and his doctrine of the divine intellect, revived by Averroes, was keenly debated in the thirteenth century.

WORKS—*Surviving commentaries:* on Aristotle, Prior Analytics I, Topics, Meteorologica, On Sensation and Metaphysics I–IV; fragments of lost commentaries are quoted by later commentators. The most serious loss is his commentary on the Physics. *Other works:* On the Soul, On Fate, On Mixture and Growth. Treatises of uncertain authenticity to which his name has been attached are named Doubts and Ethical Problems. There are other tractates also which have been attributed to him but are certainly spurious.
EDITIONS—R. B. Todd, On Stoic Physics (De Mixtione, On Mixture), 1976; also see other works listed *in* Oxford Classical Dictionary, 2nd ed., 1970, p 42. *Translations*—On Fate: A. Fitzgerald, 1931.
ABOUT—G. Théry, Alexandre d'Aphrodise, 1926; P. Moraux, Alexandre d'Aphrodise, 1942; P. Merlan, Monopsychism, Mysticism, Metaconsciousness, 1963; G. Movia, Alessandro di Afrodisia: Tra naturalismo e misticismo, 1970; P. L. Donini, Tre studi sull'Aristotelismo nel secondo secolo, 1974.

ALEXIS, Greek comic poet, was born in about 375 B.C. at Thurii (Sybaris) in southern Italy and lived for most of his life at Athens, dying in about 275.

Alexis wrote 245 plays, of which about 140 titles and 340 fragments (amounting to 1000 lines) survive. He was a leading figure, perhaps *the* leading figure, in the Athenian Middle Comedy, which came between the Old Comedy of Aristophanes and the New Comedy of Menander. Middle Comedy was experimental and by no means homogeneous. Hellenistic theory saw its typical features as the absence of political criticism and the presence of mythological burlesque. Such evidence as we possess about Alexis' plays shows at least a dozen travesties of the traditional mythology. Various attempts have also been made, without complete success, to deduce from this exiguous material Alexis' role in the transition between the Old and New Comedy. It appears that his treatment of the chorus mirrored first the former and then, subsequently, the latter, in which the song-and-dance had become merely a fill-in between acts indicated by the notice "chorus." He also seems to have been largely responsible for the substantial role played in Greek comedy from this time on by the character of the social "parasite." Indeed, the term as applied to humans probably originated with Alexis. A play of his, attributable to the 330s, provides an example of a type of plot particularly associated with New Comedy, combining a love story and a confidence trick. His work also provides instances of verbal cleverness and wit —for example, in a description of gate-crashers at parties—while at the same time he is capable of considerable beauty of language, accompanied by a certain reflective profundity.

The much better known Menander, pioneer of New Comedy, was reported to be a nephew or pupil of Alexis—since Menander was a native Athenian, the latter is more probable. In later years Alexis' plays were well known to the Romans: Caecilius Statius, Turpilius, and perhaps Plautus as well were among those who adapted them.

WORKS—The Carthaginian; The Changeling; The De-
à lek' sis

ceiver; Demetrius; Drummed Out of the Service; The Exile; The Girl from . . . [names of various cities]; The Heiress; The Letter; Linus; The Lyre-Player; The Matriarchy; The Nurse; Odysseus the Weaver; School for Debauchees; The Syracusans; The Trick Rider; The Wall-eyed Man; The Woman Drugged With Mandrake. Other titles bear the names of professions, mythological characters, and prostitutes.

EDITIONS—A. Meineke, Fragmenta Comicorum Graecorum, 1839–57, v 3; T. Kock, Comicorum Atticorum Fragmenta, 1880–88, v 2 and v 3; J. M. Edmonds, The Fragments of Attic Comedy, v 2 (Middle Comedy), 1959.

AMBROSE, Saint (Aurelius Ambrosius), bishop and Latin theologian, was born in about A.D. 339 and died in 397. We owe the facts of his career (as well as many legends that encrusted it) to a biography by his secretary Paulinus (422). The son of a man who occupied the powerful post of praetorian prefect at the imperial court at Treviri (Trier on the Moselle), Ambrose was educated at Rome and entered upon a legal career. Before long he obtained the rank of consul and the governorship of the northern Italian province of Aemilia, of which the capital was Mediolanum (Milan). On the death, in 374, of Auxentius, the bishop of that city, Ambrose was chosen to replace him by popular acclamation, though he had not been ordained or even baptized before his appointment.

As bishop, his aim was the creation of a wholly orthodox Catholic empire, from which heresy and paganism and Judaism should all be eradicated. By persuading the western emperor Valentinian II to reject the pleas of the Roman aristocracy for the re-erection of the Altar of Victory in the Senate house (384), Ambrose delivered a decisive blow to paganism. (The aristocracy was led by the distinguished scholar, statesman, and orator Symmachus, a zealous supporter of the ancient pagan religion.) Then, in 388, Ambrose compelled the emperor Theodosius I to cancel an order requiring the church of Callinicum on the Euphrates to rebuild a Jewish synagogue burnt down by fanatical Christians. In 390 he rebuked and imposed a penance on Theodosius for having ordered a punitive massacre at Thessalonica (Saloni- am′ brōz

SAINT AMBROSE

ca), and once again the emperor found it expedient to submit. Thus Ambrose's mounting influence over the court of the west reached heights unattained by any bishop before him. On occasion, he could behave like a domineering bully; but he had a high conception of his functions and carried them out with sound judgment and resolution.

Ambrose was a copious but not invariably interesting writer and preacher. In his funeral orations on the deaths of Valentinian II (392) and Theodosius I (395) he was at pains to present an ideal image of Christian emperors who, being obedient to the orders of Christ, paid dutiful attention to the counsels given them by their bishop.

He had also taken the trouble to master current Christian and pagan learning; and he dedicated this knowledge to expounding the allegorical significance of the Old Testament, for example in his *Hexaemeron (Six Days of Creation).* Moreover, sermons concerning the patriarchs, including tracts entitled *On the Goodness of Death* and *On Isaac and the Soul,* reveal his familiarity with Neoplatonic mysticism. By a further group of sermons, among which an *Exposition of St. Luke's Gospel* (A.D. 390) became especially well known, Ambrose acquired renown as a master of Latin eloquence and gained his most famous convert, Augustine. Some of these discourses, notably a group entitled *On Naboth,* denounced social

15

abuses. Other sermons sought and secured pardons for men who had been condemned to death. Still others advocated rigid asceticism. Parents were often reluctant to let their daughters listen to the addresses in which Ambrose eloquently urged the virtues of virginity. One famous treatise, *On Clergymen's Duties (De Officiis Ministrorum)*, provided a practical manual for churchmen, prescribing their behavior down to the smallest details. This work took the form of an ingenious revision of Cicero's *On Duties* and thus presented cultured speakers of Latin with a strongly classical version of Christianity.

Ambrose's remarkable hymns, however, which moved Augustine to tears, constitute his outstanding literary achievement. The best known of these pieces is *Aeterne Rerum Conditor (Eternal Lord the World That Made)*. Four other hymns generally regarded as authentically attributable to his authorship are *Veni Redemptor Gentium, Deus Creator Omnium, Iam Surgit Hora Tertia,* and *Splendor Paternae Gloriae;* and perhaps a dozen further productions, too, in the same iambic meter, may likewise have been by Ambrose's hand. They form the nucleus of what is called the Ambrosian hymnary. He was also believed to have introduced the Ambrosian chant, the form of plainsong that was sung in the diocese of Mediolanum and the churches under its influence (though discouraged by Charlemagne and others). However, this "chant" was in fact probably introduced by Ambrose's predecessor Auxentius, who had imported it from Antioch in Syria.

The influence of Ambrose's Roman education is apparent in his extensive reminiscences of leading classical writers—not only Latin authors, such as Cicero, but also Greek (notably Philo, Origen, Plotinus, and Basil). Ambrose's writings show a certain narrowness of outlook, and some of his enthusiasms—for example, his encouragement of the popular contemporary demand for martyrs' bones and relics—awake little respect in our own time. Nevertheless, there is much to praise in his conviction that the church possessed a responsibility to the community as a whole rather than merely to its own partisan interests. And, although he became so famous for imposing himself on emperors—thus foreshadowing medieval conflicts between church and state—he never thought of the church as a power that should dominate the state; his justification for seeking to augment his own authority was that not to do so would only mean that the pagan nobles, or Arian heretics, would seize power for themselves.

EDITIONS—J. P. Migne, Patrologia Latina, v 14–17; Corpus Scriptorum Ecclesiasticorum Latinorum, 10 vols. For translations *see* G. B. Parks and R. Z. Temple, The Literatures of the World in English Translation, v 1, p 244ff.
ABOUT—J. R. Palanque, Saint Ambroise et l'empire romain, 1933; F. Homes-Dudden, The Life and Times of St. Ambrose, 1935; G. Lazzati, Il valore letterario della esegesi ambrosiana, 1960; A. Momigliano, ed., The Conflict Between Paganism and Christianity in the Fourth Century, 1963; A. Paredi, St. Ambrose: His Life and Times, 1964; J. Répin, Théologie cosmique et théologie chrétienne, 1964; G. Gottlieb, Ambrosius von Mailand und Kaiser Gratian, 1973; P. Courcelle, Recherches sur Saint Ambroise, 1974; Y. M. Duval, ed., Ambroise de Milan: XVIe centenaire de son élection épiscopale, dix études (Ambrosius Episcopus), 1974; Atti del Congresso internazionale di studi ambrosiani (1974), 1976.

AMMIANUS MARCELLINUS, Latin historian of Greek origin, was born between A.D. 325 and 330 to a prosperous, semi-aristocratic Greek family of Antioch in Syria (Antakya in southeastern Turkey). As a young man, during the reign of Constantius II (337–61), he became an officer in the elite regiment of the household guards *(protectores domestici)*. In about 353 he was transferred to the staff of a senior Roman general, Ursicinus, at the frontier fortress of Nisibis (Nüsaybin, between the Euphrates and the Tigris). From there he accompanied his commander on a journey to Gaul in order to suppress the rebellion of Silvanus and stayed there to join the first German campaign (356) of the future ruler Julian. In the next year, however, Ammianus was recalled to the eastern frontier, where he took part in the emperor's campaigns against the Persians. In 359 he was a member of the besieged force in the frontier station of Amida (Diyarbakir). Next he seems to have held a post in the army supply service. In 363 he
am mi ä′ nus   mär kel lē′ nus

16

saw service in the eastern expedition of Julian, now emperor, who was fatally wounded in Mesopotamia. When Julian's successor Jovian retreated, Ammianus went with him as far as Antioch in Syria. Later, however, perhaps soon after 378, he settled in Rome, where he spent a large part of his remaining years, though he also returned to Antioch from time to time and traveled elsewhere. He probably died in about 395.

At Rome he recited passages of his major work, which dates from this later part of his life. It is a Roman history in Latin, probably entitled the *Book of Deeds (Rerum Gestarum Libri)*, perhaps with the addition of the words *From the Reign of Nerva.* The narrative covers the years from the accession of Nerva in A.D. 96 to the death of the eastern emperor Valens in 378. The first thirteen books, dealing with most of this period, are lost, but the last eighteen are extant. This surviving portion of the work—eighteen books—covers in great detail a period of only twenty-five years, starting with the latter part of the reign of Constantius II (353) and comprising the events of Ammianus' own lifetime. In Book 14, the first that we possess, attention is particularly directed toward Ammianus' commanding officer Ursicinus, whom he admired. The book begins, however, with the cruelties of the deputy emperor (Caesar) Constantius Gallus at Antioch and concludes with his death (354). Book 15 tells of the bloody aftermath of his downfall and describes the revolt of Silvanus in Gaul, where Julian was subsequently promoted to the high command in the western provinces, with the rank that Gallus had possessed in the east. Book 16 describes the only visit the emperor Constantius II ever made to Rome and recounts Julian's victories in the north culminating at Argentorate (Strasbourg) in 357 and followed, in the next book, by incursions across the Rhine and Danubian campaigns. Books 18 and 19 bring the account of operations against the Persians down to the siege of Amida. Book 20 describes how Constantius unfairly dismissed Ursicinus and tried to deprive Julian of his best troops, who thereupon hailed Julian as emperor, which he soon afterwards became, when Constantius died (361). The next four books deal with the reign of Julian,

known as the Apostate because he reverted from Christianity to paganism, and tell how he revived religious toleration, began to purge the administration of his capital, Constantinople, and made preparations at Antioch for a new Persian war. In Book 25 we learn how Julian met his death and how the brief subsequent reign of Jovian was followed by the elevation of Valentinian I to the throne. After a new preface to Book 26, indicating that he had originally intended to stop at this point, Ammianus tells of the division of the empire between Valentinian I and his brother Valens and the abortive revolt of Procopius against the latter. Books 27 and 28 give accounts of warfare on a number of different fronts and describe Valentinian's growing hostility toward the upper classes. The twenty-ninth book reports the trial and execution of the lawyer Theodorus, by Valens, for treason and magic, charges which also caused the ruin of many others. Book 30 describes Valentinian's Danubian campaigns and his death (375). The defeat and death of Valens in a battle with the Visigoths at Hadrianopolis (Adrianople, now Edirne) is the subject of Book 31.

A determination to tell the truth is voiced by Ammianus with an obsessive insistence that is, on the whole, convincing. Yet, in the sinister and oppressive atmosphere of the later Roman spy state, it was impossible for a writer to write with complete candor about everybody, and even Ammianus, who stopped his history at the point where he did in order to avoid delicate contemporary themes, cannot invariably live up to his ideal. Moreover, he tends to exaggerate the praises due Julian, though his admiration is not unmixed with criticism so that a balanced estimate of the emperor ultimately emerges.

Like Julian, but unlike all the other emperors of the age, Ammianus was a pagan. He was, however, unusually moderate and spoke up warmly for the toleration displayed by the Christian Valentinian. An arresting and complex picture of Valentinian and other emperors, as well as of lesser personages, emerges from Ammianus' work. His psychological studies are often admirable, for he possessed a special gift for the depiction of character. He also provides particularly valuable evidence for the process of transformation known as the Decline and Fall of the western empire. Although its termination lay only a century ahead, the empire still appeared very strong—so strong that Ammianus, despite all the contrary evidence he had amassed, was still optimistic about the future. For the oppressed lower classes he displays little sympathy, and he reserves many of his sharpest remarks for the arrogant idleness of the anti-intellectual nobility who perhaps did not give him the social welcome he hoped for at Rome. He also objects strongly to the immense bureaucracy of ignorant lawyers.

Ammianus, as is seldom recognized, is a historian of the caliber and stature of Tacitus, at the end of whose *Histories* he deliberately starts his own work. Both men are preoccupied with Rome, which Ammianus sees as glorious and eternal. Yet he concentrates far less than Tacitus upon the city's affairs, now that it was no longer at the center of events. This far wider canvas on which he chooses to paint enables him to embark on numerous interesting (though not always wholly relevant) geographical and ethnological digressions. He has a prejudice against the Germans, whom he tends to underestimate, but his treatment of Rome's eastern enemies, the Persians, is relatively generous and unbiased. Ammianus can tell as splendidly dramatic and exuberant a narrative as Tacitus. It is only because of his looser structure and occasionally turgid style that he takes second place.

Unlike earlier historians, Ammianus was not a partially Hellenized Roman but a Hellene who had absorbed the Roman and Latin tradition. Yet he remained consciously Greek, and phrases like *as we Greeks say* recur in his history. His vast curiosity and reading were also Greek: he uses a great variety of sources from many periods (often unidentifiable today) and quotes public archives and governors' reports, supplemented by the personal observations that he himself was able to offer as an important participant in the events of the day.

EDITIONS—C. U. Clark, 1910–15. *With translation:* J. C. Rolfe (Loeb ed.), 1935–39; W. Seyfarth (German), 1975, 1978.

ABOUT—P. de Jonge, Philological and Historical Commentary on Ammianus Marcellinus, 1935– (Bk. 17, 1977); E. A. Thompson, The Historical Work of Ammianus Marcellinus, 1947; J. Voigt, Ammianus Marcellinus als erzählender Geschichtsschreiber der Spätzeit, 1963; A. Demandt, Zeitkritik und Geschichtsbild im Werk Ammians, 1965; P. M. Camus, Ammien Marcellin, 1967; H. T. Rowell, Ammianus Marcellinus: Soldier-Historian of the Later Roman Empire, 1968; R. Syme, Ammianus and the Historia Augusta, 1968; M. Grant, The Ancient Historians, 1970; H. Drexler, Ammianstudien, 1974; J. M. Alonso-Nuñez, La vision historiografica de Ammiano Marcellino, 1975; R. C. Blockley, Ammianus Marcellinus: A Study of His Historiography and Political Thought, 1975; G. A. Crump, Ammianus Marcellinus as a Military Historian, 1975; A. Momigliano, Essays in Ancient and Modern Historiography, 1977; J. Szidat, Historischer Kommentar zu Ammianus Marcellinus (Books 20–31), v 1, 1977; G. Sabbah, La méthode d'Ammien Marcellin, 1978.

ANACREON, Greek poet, was born in about 570 B.C. at Teos (Sigalik) in Ionia (western Asia Minor). When his native country was threatened by the Persians (c. 545), he accompanied his compatriots who evacuated Teos and sailed to Thrace, where they founded the colony of Abdera. From there he was summoned to Samos by its autocrat or tyrant Polycrates (c. 539–522), after whose death he accepted an invitation from Hipparchus, who together with his brother Hippias had become the ruler of Athens. In about 514, however, after the murder of Hipparchus, Anacreon moved to Thessaly, where he was on friendly terms with the royal house. He subsequently went back to Athens, and there, when he was at an advanced age, he died when a grape seed stuck in his throat. A statue was erected in his honor on the Athenian Acropolis and another at his native Teos.

His poems, of which only fragments survive today, were arranged in three groups: lyrics, elegies, and iambics. The first group included hymns to Dionysus and Eros and Artemis, love songs to beautiful boys and women (notably the flute girls who were in attendance at banquets), and other convivial poems. Anacreon's elegant world is far removed from the hearty carousing of the earlier Lesbian lyricists such as Alcaeus. At

a nak' rē on

the glittering feasts he attends, he expresses distaste for any mention of conflict or fighting and instead pursues thoughts of his loves, which, while unromantic and untragic, are nevertheless too poignant to be wholly frivolous; not enough wine is drunk to intoxicate, but a shimmering, bitter-sweet intoxication gilds these bisexual amours.

His elegies are commemorative poems, dedications, and epitaphs. Some of them were written in his early days at Abdera. Although he found time to look at Thracian girls, he movingly mourns a young male friend who died in the fighting there. His iambic poems include a venomous attack on the nouveau riche Artemon, twirling his ivory parasol. Despite subject matter of this sort, Anacreon's reputation among the ancients was that of a poet exclusively devoted to love, wine, and song. This also had the curious effect of making him famous for lyrical pieces on these subjects written long after his death—known as Anacreontica, they continued to be composed right down to the Byzantine age. But many of these compositions are insipid, whereas Anacreon himself had contrived, with unerring grace, to display not only lightness but strength. His vivid and fanciful imagination is buttressed by an urbane, manneristic wittiness that prevents him from taking either himself or others too seriously, a new attitude in Greek literature.

EDITIONS—B. Gentili, Anacreonte, 1958; D. L. Page, Poetae Melici Graeci, 1962, and Epigrammata Graeca, 1976. Translations—J. M. Edmonds, Lyra Graeca (Loeb ed.), v 2, revised ed., 1931; M. Baumann, Die Anakreonteen in englischen Übersetzungen, 1974. ABOUT—C. M. Bowra, Greek Lyric Poetry, 2nd ed., 1962; D. A. Campbell, Greek Lyric Poetry, 1967.

ANAXAGORAS, Greek philosopher, the son of Hegesibulus, was born in about 500 B.C. at Clazomenae (Urla) in Ionia (western Asia Minor), and died in about 428. In c. 480 he came to Athens and was said to have been the earliest philosopher ever to reside there. Many years later (in 450 B.C.?), having become the teacher and friend of the Athenian statesman Pericles, he was prose-

an ak sag' ō ras

cuted by the latter's political enemies on charges of impiety and pro-Persian inclinations. However, with Pericles' help he escaped to Lampsacus (Lapseki) in the Troad (northwestern Asia Minor), where he established a philosophical school of his own and had become a widely respected figure at the time of his death.

Sharply conflicting testimonies and interpretations make the reconstruction of Anaxagoras' views almost impossible, but it may tentatively be agreed that he contributed several new conceptions to Greek philosophy. He developed the idea that matter is a continuum: "in one world, things are not cut off from one another by an axe." This enabled him to get around the attacks on Empedocles' pluralism (refusal to believe in the homogeneous unity of matter) made by Parmenides and Zeno of Elea, since his own view endowed both space and time with total indivisibility. In the beginning, Anaxagoras maintained, the world had been a mixture containing "seeds" (later known to the Aristotelians as homoeomeries) of every material substance. Thus, particles of every different kind were to be found in any object: "in everything there is a part of everything." These seeds took on their eventual, permanent quality from their quantitatively prevailing component. This is an explanation of growth that avoids assuming qualitative change, in pursuance of Parmenides' denial of any coming into being or passing away into nothing: in modern times the English philosopher and mathematician A. N. Whitehead has followed up this line of thought, which sees the world as process rather than matter.

It was under the impulsion of mind, according to Anaxagoras, that the seeds thus assumed their permanent configuration. His conclusive achievement was to devise a new formula for bringing mind and matter into relation with one another, the former being envisaged as the power that sets the latter in motion and as the animating principle of all animals and plants. By this formula he offered a new concept of mind and its place in the cosmic system, arguing that although all other things mix together, mind remains pure, the finest and purest of all substances, a uniquely unmixed and separate principle.

19

ANAXIMANDER

He did not, as Plato and Aristotle later noted with regret, actually define mind as Final Cause, since he still probably regarded it as material—a sort of fluid, the "thinnest" of all things. Nevertheless, he apostrophized mind in terms that show he saw it as the divine power. And thus he pointed the way, although he did not quite reach the destination himself, to a fundamental dualism of mind and matter which, after all, rejected Parmenides' unitary idea of nature.

In a wider sense, too, Anaxagoras interpreted mind as the basis of all movement throughout the cosmos. He believed it to have originated a movement of rotation which had gradually extended, separating out, in due course, the various seeds from each other: thus, stones were torn away from the circumference of the earth and became the heavenly bodies—the sun, red hot through motion, its light reflected by the moon. This view, formed or fortified by his knowledge of the fall of a meteorite, implied a denial that the heavenly bodies were divinities; and that is why he was prosecuted for impiety.

Like Milesian philosophers before him, Anaxagoras adopted prose (Ionic Greek) as the medium of his major philosophical work, later entitled *About Nature*. He influenced Plato and throughout antiquity enjoyed a massive reputation; Aristotle said he was like a sober speaker coming after babblers.

EDITIONS with translation—G. S. Kirk and J. E. Raven, The Presocratic Philosophers, revised ed., 1960; D. Lanza, Anassagora: Testimonianze e frammenti, 1966. ABOUT—F. M. Cleve, Anaxagoras, 1949; W. K. C. Guthrie, History of Greek Philosophy, v 2, 1965; U. Curi, Dagli Ionici alla crisi della fisica, 1974; C. Strong *in* R. E. Allen and D. J. Furley, eds., Studies in Presocratic Philosophy, v 2, 1975; J. Barnes, The Presocratic Philosophers, v 2, 1978.

ANAXIMANDER, Greek philosopher, was born at Miletus in Ionia (western Asia Minor) in about 610 B.C. and died shortly after 546. Thus he was roughly the contemporary of his fellow citizen Thales, whom later tradition maintained to have been his teacher. The tradition that he visited Sparta and took

a nak si man' dĕr

20

part in the foundation of Apollonia on the Black Sea shows him to have been a typical Ionian, taking an active part in public affairs. In about 546 B.C. he published what appears to have been the earliest philosophical treatise ever written in prose. In common with works by other philosophers, it was later given the name *About Nature*. It only survives in fragments preserved by later writers.

Like Thales before him, Anaximander speculated about the fundamental substance, but he did not agree that this was water, or, indeed, any other such ordinary material. Instead, he declared that the origin of all things was the Infinite, which he envisaged as both ruling and surrounding the universe; he described it as ageless and eternal, synonymous with the Divine. It was from this Infinite, he pronounced, that all things had come from the undefinable, inexhaustible basic stuff which was prior to any individual existence. This is the Unfathomable Deep of ancient Eastern speculation, converted, by the force of Greek language and thinking, into an abstract explanation of all being.

The worlds the universe contains, according to Anaximander, are innumerable, and he sees each of them as the product of pairs of conflicting opposites, such as hot and cold. These are separated from the Infinite and from each other, and "pay due compensation to one another." In stating this, Anaximander took the pioneer step of conceiving the universe as subject to the rule of law, extending this concept from human society to the physical world—a break with the more ancient view of a nature that is wholly capricious and anarchic.

He also revolutionized astronomy by his interpretation of the sun and moon, which he believed to consist of fire wrapped in vapor and to move in a circular path beneath the earth. He saw the visible sun as an opening in the vapor, about equal in circumference to the earth—a remarkable view, since even a hundred years later a great thinker such as Anaxagoras could still believe that the sun was only a little larger than the Peloponnese (the southern portion of Greece). No less precocious was Anaximander's construction of a model depicting the motions of stars and planets by means of wheels moving at different speeds, and he introduced another device, the sundial or gnomon, to measure these motions. He was also the first to draw a diagrammatic map of the earth. He showed its surface as a disk, for he believed the world to be shaped like a column (with its height equivalent to one-third of its diameter) standing freely in the precise center of the universe.

Although Anaximander did not agree with Thales' view that water is the basic substance, he agreed with him that the earth had originally come out of it. This view enabled him to construct an evolutionary theory of the origins of man, which holds that higher forms of life had evolved from lower forms. He envisaged life as having begun in the water, where human beings were at first a kind of fish. Later, on land, they shed their scales and adapted their way of living to this new medium.

His remarkable blend of scientific curiosity, poetic imagery, and provocative insight has caused Anaximander to be described as the world's first real philosopher.

EDITIONS with translation—G. E. Kirk and J. E. Raven, The Presocratic Philosophers, revised ed., 1960. ABOUT—C. H. Kahn, Anaximander and the Origins of Greek Philosophy, v 1, 1962; P. Seligman, The Apeiron of Anaximander, 1962; G. E. R. Lloyd, Early Greek Science: Thales to Aristotle, 1965; U. Hölscher, Anfängliches Fragen: Studien zur frühen griechischen Philosophie, 1968; D. J. Furley and R. E. Allen, eds., Studies in Presocratic Philosophy, v 1, 1970; X. Renou, L'infini aux limites du calcul: Anaximandre, Platon, Galilée, 1977; J. Barnes, The Presocratic Philosophers, v 1, 1978.

ANAXIMENES, Greek philosopher, was born at Miletus in Ionia (western Asia Minor) near the beginning of the sixth century B.C. and died between 528 and 525. Thus he was a little younger than his fellow citizen Anaximander, of whom, according to later tradition, he was a pupil. He wrote a philosophical treatise in Greek (Ionic) prose, of which fragments have survived.

In two respects, his theories seem to mark retrograde steps from Anaximander's views.

a nak si' me nēz

In the first place, his astronomical picture, in which the sky presses on the rim of the earth and the sun and moon run around the earth's disc at night, goes back to a more ancient Babylonian tradition. Secondly, he abandoned Anaximander's belief that the fundamental originative substance was something undefinable and indefinite and instead opted for a known material substance. In this he resembled their predecessor Thales, though Anaximenes decided that the substance was not water, as Thales had supposed, but air (aer)—not mist, as in Homer, but the normally invisible atmospheric air. This (he believed), the cosmos, in its unending cycle of movement, perpetually breathes. In consequence, he described it by the term infinite (which Anaximander, too, had applied to his primal source); and he regarded this basic, atmospheric material as divine.

Yet, in spite of the traditional aspects of this theory, there was also vital innovation in Anaximenes' endeavor to derive the universe from a substance whose ability to change its properties can be experimentally apprehended: for example, through changes in its temperature and humidity, air can even cease to be invisible—"All changes are condensation and rarefaction." When rarefied, according to Anaximenes, the air of which the cosmos is formed becomes fire; when condensed, it becomes—by a progressive series of changes—wind, cloud, water, earth, and stone. This process is rationally worked out in the course of an analysis which, by offering a purely physical account of the relation of things to their basic constituent and thus demonstrating that change in nature can be explained in mechanical terms, broke through some of the last surviving traces of myth.

Provided that we can believe our later sources, and in this case it may be supposed that we can, he saw even the human soul (pneuma) as part of the air. If so, although this view was partly suggested by the ancient equation of soul with breath, it forged a novel link between the microcosm of the individual human being and the macrocosm of the entire world and universe. Indeed, Anaximenes was probably proceeding by inference from the former to the latter, for his

21

deduction that air is the cosmic equivalent of the souls of human beings seems to have been an important motive behind his choice of air as the basic substance. Furthermore, the mention of the soul, apart from an alleged quotation from Thales that may well be of later origin, is the first Greek statement about psychology to have come down to us.

EDITIONS with translation—G. E. Kirk and J. E. Raven, The Pre-Socratic Philosophers, revised ed., 1960. ABOUT—W. K. C. Guthrie, History of Greek Philosophy, v 1, 1962; G. E. R. Lloyd, Early Greek Science: Thales to Aristotle, 1965; R. S. Brumbaugh, The Philosophers of Greece, 1966; D. J. Furley and R. E. Allen, eds., Studies in Presocratic Philosophy, v 1, 1970; J. Barnes, The Presocratic Philosophers, v 1, 1978.

ANDOCIDES, Greek orator, was born at Athens into a famous aristocratic family, in about 440 B.C., and died in about 390. His political sympathies, which were with the right-wing oligarchic movement, led him into an anti-religious free-thinking stance. This got him into trouble during the Peloponnesian War between Athens and Sparta, when, on the eve of the departure of the great expedition to Sicily in 415, the Athenians awoke one morning to discover that the statues of Hermes in the streets had been defaced. This act of blasphemy may have been committed either in an attempt to provide a bad omen which would postpone the expedition (Hermes being the god of travelers) or in order to show that law and order were in peril, so that an oligarchic coup would be justified. The leading politician Alcibiades was incriminated, and the young Andocides and his fellow members of an oligarchic club were arrested for having participated in the mutilations. Furthermore, it was said that they and Alcibiades had also performed parodies of the sacred rituals of Demeter and Persephone at Eleusis. Andocides escaped conviction, but only, it was afterwards maintained, by admitting his guilt (which he did, he said, to save his father) and by betraying his associates (which he denied). When, however, a decree soon afterwards forbade all who admitted sacrilegious guilt to enter temples or the Market-

an dŏ' ki dēz

place *(Agora)*, Andocides retired into exile in Cyprus and set himself up as a merchant. He also visited other regions of the Greek world and acquired considerable wealth. In 411 he provided oars at cost price to the Athenian fleet, but this attempt to rehabilitate himself failed because the oligarchic regime of the Four Hundred, which had just come into power, consisted of the very people whom his confession four years earlier had damaged, so he was put in prison at Athens. After his release, he withdrew for a second time to Cyprus, but there too, in the course of his trading, he fell foul of King Evagoras and was arrested for a second time. In 407 he appeared before the Athenian Assembly and in a speech called *On His Return* appealed to be allowed back—but in vain.

When the war was over, however, the amnesty of 403 permitted him to return. Nevertheless, three years later, his enemies, still unappeased, brought a charge of impiety against him on the grounds that in contravention of the above-mentioned decree of 415 (forbidding the sacrilegious to enter temples) he had attended performances of the Mysteries. His speech *On the Mysteries* rebutted this accusation successfully, and thereafter he regained some reputation at Athens. In about 392 he became a member of a deputation sent to Sparta to discuss the making of a fresh peace. On his return home his speech *On the Peace* advocated the acceptance of the terms that had been suggested. But the Athenians refused the terms, and the envoys were prosecuted for bribery and other alleged offenses. Andocides only escaped condemnation—which would have carried the sentence of death—by retiring into exile once again, and thereafter nothing more is heard of him.

When the ancient critics detected faults in Andocides' methods of rhetoric they were not wholly wrong, since his construction is often so loose and so encumbered with unmanageable parentheses that it becomes hard to discover what he is trying to say. Moreover, he found it difficult to stick to one point at a time. He was not a professional rhetorician, and his style lacked conscious rhetorical effects. All the same, in his own unorthodox way, he could compose a successful speech that flowed simply and conveyed an impression of spontaneous eagerness, which his natural gift for articulate narration reinforced.

WORKS—On His Return, On the Mysteries, On the Peace (already suspected in antiquity, probably without justification). A speech entitled Against Alcibiades has generally been regarded as spurious.
EDITIONS—U. Albini, On His Return, 1961, and On the Peace, 1964; D. Macdowell, On the Mysteries, 1962. With translation: G. Dalmeyda, Discours (Budé ed.), 1930; K. J. Maidment, The Minor Latin Orators (Loeb ed.), 1941; On the Mysteries in A. N. W. Saunders, Greek Political Oratory (Penguin ed.), 1970.
ABOUT—G. Kennedy, The Art of Persuasion in Greece, 1963; A. Anastassiou and D. Irmer, Kleine attische Redner, 1977.

ANDRONICUS, LIVIUS. See Livius Andronicus

ANTIAS, VALERIUS. See Valerius Antias

ANTIPHON of Rhamnus in Attica (c. 480–411 B.C.), Greek orator, was one of the most intelligent personalities in Athenian public life, although he remained in the background for most of his career. When consulted about cases in the law courts or the Assembly, he acted as legal adviser and speech writer for his clients; but he rarely spoke in public himself. He was, however, a well-known teacher of rhetoric; and it is believed that Thucydides may have been one of his pupils. In 411 B.C., when the Peloponnesian War against Sparta was entering upon its final phase, Antiphon suddenly attained power as the brain behind the right-wing, oligarchic putsch that temporarily overthrew the Athenian democratic government and replaced it by the rule of the Four Hundred. These oligarchs were divided into two schools of thought, the moderates under Theramenes, and the extremists, of whom Antiphon was the leader. He went with nine other delegates to Sparta in order to negotiate peace and obtain support for his regime. But the mission was unsuccessful, and soon

an' ti fon

afterward the Four Hundred fell. Most of them got away, but Antiphon and a colleague remained and were brought to trial, convicted, and put to death.

The earliest speeches attributable to Antiphon are three *Tetralogies* (groups of four orations) written in the late 440s or early 430s. They are concerned with cases of homicide, but the cases are imaginary. Each group of speeches includes two for the prosecution and two for the defense. They rely on argument from probability, and their demonstration of how such addresses should be composed throws useful light on the legal thinking of the time. For the most part they are in keeping with the teachings of the rhetorical handbooks and follow the prescribed patterns of judicial speeches, except that the customary narrative portions —a branch of his art at which Antiphon does not excel—are abbreviated or omitted altogether.

Of his three indubitably authentic speeches in real cases, again all relating to homicide, the earliest is probably *On the Chorus Singer* (419/18 B.C.?), in which he defends the financer of a chorus *(choregos)* who has unintentionally caused the death of one of his boy singers by giving him a drug to improve his voice. In *Against the Stepmother* (c. 416), which is generally but not universally regarded as belonging to an authentic court action, a woman is accused by her stepson of instigating a slave woman to poison his father. The speech *On the Murder of Herodes* (c. 414) tells of a voyage undertaken by Herodes in the company of the defendant. One night Herodes went ashore and was never seen again, and his companion was prosecuted for murder—possibly the case was brought in order to smear his father, who was unpopular at Mytilene in Lesbos for political reasons. We also have a papyrus containing some fragments of the speech Antiphon delivered in his own unsuccessful defense after the oligarchic coup of 411. When congratulated on its excellence he answered that he would rather have pleased one man of good taste than any number of unenlightened people.

At the time when Antiphon started to write, there was not yet a fixed tradition of prose in the Athenian (Attic) dialect, and the impact of the rhetoricians had not yet been felt in the city. Thus, he was free to experiment. The style he evolved, which in due course underwent rhetorical and sophistic influences, was regarded as austere, and he was compared in this respect to Thucydides, some of whose stylistic peculiarities can be ascribed to his use of Antiphon as a model. Antiphon's language, though sometimes crude, is always vigorous and exact. He liked neat balance and antithesis, and he used poetical words but avoided colloquialisms. He established a set structural form: introduction, narration (when included), evidence and proofs, peroration. His manner was dignified and elevated; he often appealed to divine law. He displayed fairness towards his opponents and for the most part avoided irrelevant personal abuse. His speeches show how the old methods of proof —oaths and examinations of slaves under torture—were being replaced by new methods of argumentation centered, in sophistic fashion, upon the establishment of probabilities. Yet, argument remains Antiphon's principal weakness; he does not handle it satisfactorily or fully exploit its opportunities, relying on general likelihoods as much as on the evidence of witnesses.

We also hear of another Antiphon—"the sophist." He was already distinguished from Antiphon "the orator" in ancient times, but it has been argued recently, with a good deal of probability, that they are one and the same man. Admittedly, one of the treatises of "the sophist" contains assumptions of the equality of all human beings, which seem very remote from the antidemocratic career of the orator; yet the difference may, perhaps, be accounted for by the nature and requirements of such essays. The treatise in question is *Truth,* in which Antiphon develops the doctrine of natural as opposed to man-made law. The surviving fragments of the essay entitled *On Working Together*— written in a different (and livelier) manner, which is not however sufficiently different to encourage the assumption of different authorship—displays a somewhat pessimistic attitude toward human affairs; yet it enlarges on the potentialities of education as a corrective.

WORKS—(1) *Speeches:* Later Greeks (the Alexandrians) knew of sixty of these, but twenty-five were already (rightly) dismissed as spurious by the first century B.C. (2) *Treatises:* (a) technical treatises *(Technae)* attributed to the orator were also rejected in ancient times, but a collection of commonplaces for beginnings and endings of speeches exists; (b) treatises of "the sophist": Against Alcibiades, On Dreams, and Politicus are doubtful.

EDITIONS—M. Untersteiner, The Sophists, 1954; A. Barigazzi, 1955; F. D. Caizzi, Antiphon's Tetralogiae, 1969; D. Ferrante, Antifonte; Peri tou Herodon Phonou, 1972; J. S. Morrison in R. K. Sprague, ed., The Older Sophists, 1972. *With translation:* L. Gernet, Antiphon: Discours (Belles Lettres), 1923; K. J. Maidment, Minor Attic Orators (Loeb ed.), v 1, 1941.

ABOUT—G. Kennedy, The Art of Persuasion in Greece, 1963; D. M. Macdowell, Athenian Homicide Law in the Age of the Orators, 1963; W. K. C. Guthrie, A History of Greek Philosophy, v 3 (The Fifth Century Enlightenment), 1969; C. J. Classen, ed., Sophistik, 1976.

ANTISTHENES of Athens, Greek philosopher, was born in about 445 B.C. of an Athenian father and a Thracian or Phrygian mother; he died in about 360. He was at first an adherent of the sophist Gorgias but later attacked him (in his *Archelaus*) after conversion to philosophy by Socrates, whose enthusiastic disciple he then became. Antisthenes also gathered his own followers around himself at the cosmopolitan Cynosarges gymnasium, which was connected, as its name indicates, with the Cynic school of philosophy. The true founder of that school was his most celebrated pupil, Diogenes of Sinope, but Antisthenes was sometimes believed in ancient times to have been its creator, and "the inaugurator of the Cynic way of life"; and he may fairly be regarded as the spiritual parent of the school. His cynic leanings are confirmed by the exaggerated stress he lays on Socrates' asceticism, though he did not carry this emphasis to the same length as later Cynics, and he differed from them by the interest he took in logic and literature, two studies which they held in contempt.

Antisthenes' asceticism was linked with an insistence on self-sufficiency. He welcomed his own poverty as a source of freedom and aimed at complete emancipation from passion and emotion, declaring that he

an tis' the nēz

would rather lose his wits than succumb to desire. Pleasures, he maintained, are generally treacherous and make no contribution to happiness—unless they are the result of hard work. To him, as to Socrates, happiness is based on virtue, which is the only good, as vice is the only evil. Virtue is founded on knowledge, which is teachable. The way in which it can be taught and learned, Antisthenes continued, is by investigating the meanings of words. He was very interested in definitions and believed that the man who discovers what a word means gains comprehension, at the same time, of what it denotes.

Yet he was more interested in practical ethics than in abstract speculation and did not hesitate to express himself in downright and violent terms against those who thought otherwise—including Plato, to whom, we are told, he devoted sharply caustic language in his three-book work *Satho*. Antisthenes liked to use mythology to illustrate his moral arguments, pointing to Heracles, as later Cynics also did, as the model for a life of laborious virtue; to Odysseus because of his superiority in intelligence to the other Homeric heroes; and (in an essay that may have been drawn upon by Xenophon) to the Persian King Cyrus as the ideal of a wise monarch.

Although his work is only preserved in fragments today, he was an enormously productive writer. We have the table of contents of a ten-book edition, including no less than seventy titles. Among these, the *Alcibiades, Aspasia,* and *Menexenus* were probably dialogues in the Socratic manner, while treatises on *Truth (Aletheia), Education,* and *Names* deal with themes that were also discussed by the sophists. In addition, Antisthenes produced two short declamations *(Ajax, Odysseus),* in which the heroes set forth their respective claims to the arms of Achilles; and he was also the author of further interpretations of Homer, which proved of interest to later commentators.

EDITIONS—F. D. Caizzi, Fragmenta, 1966; L. Paquet, Les cyniques grecs: Fragments et témoignages, 1975. ABOUT—D. R. Dudley, A History of Cynicism, 1937; R. Höistad, Cynic Hero and Cynic King, 1948; F. D. Sayre, The Greek Cynics, 1948; L. Radermacher, Artium Scriptores (declamations), 1951; W. K. C. Guthrie, History of Greek Philosophy, v 3, 1969.

APICIUS. See Caelius

APOLLINARIS, SIDONIUS. See Sidonius Apollinaris

APOLLODORUS of Athens, Greek chronicler, was born at Alexandria in about 180 B.C. and left in about 146/5 to go to Pergamum, later moving to Athens, where he died between 120 and 110. At Alexandria he worked under Aristarchus of Samothrace, and at Athens he studied with the Stoic Diogenes of Babylon.

Apollodorus was a many-sided scholar of great learning. His *Chronicle,* in four books, which is lost but can be partly reconstructed from many subsequent references, was written in verse (iambic trimeters) in order to help readers to memorize. Founded on the researches of Eratosthenes of Cyrene, the work covered the period from the legendary Fall of Troy down to Apollodorus' own day. It was originally dedicated to King Attalus II of Pergamum (160–138 B.C.), but Apollodorus then decided to carry the work on to about 120. In this *Chronicle,* when definite biographical dates were not available, it was his custom to fix upon a specific event in a man's life as his "prime" and then deduce that he had been born forty years previously. This method of calculation has exercised a bad effect on the many subsequent chronologies, ancient and modern alike. Another work of Apollodorus, once more surviving only in fragments, was a twelve-book *Commentary on the Catalogue of Ships in Homer's Iliad,* an important geographical study which was again partly based on Eratosthenes and contained many references to other authors as well. It was extensively drawn upon by subsequent geographers. Considerable use was also made, in later times, of his twenty-four works *On the Gods,* of which the fragments
à pol ō dō′ rus

suggest a rationalistic intention and a desire to be guided by the principle of development. In addition, Apollodorus compiled etymological studies, and commentaries on the poets Epicharmus and Sophron.

His name was also attributed to an account of Greek mythology known to the Byzantine world as the *Library (Bibliotheca);* this work is still partly extant. However, a comparison of this study with the fragments of *On the Gods* confirms the supposition that the two works are of different authorship. Furthermore, the *Library* cites a chronographer believed to belong to the first century B.C. Although it says nothing about Rome or Roman myths, the work could well have been written in the first or second century A.D. What the real name of its author was we do not know; he could have been called Apollodorus, which is common enough, or he may have masqueraded under the name so as to identify himself fraudulently as the celebrated writer of *On the Gods.* The surviving portion of the *Library* starts with the divine beginnings of the universe and then deals with various cycles of Athenian genealogical myths and legends. An epitome and fragments give some idea of the lost parts of the treatise.

Its composer was not endeavoring to write an artistic masterpiece; his desire was to inform rather than to embellish or amuse. His approach is uncritical. But he writes clearly and concisely, and he contrives to insert a comprehensive mass of mythical stories and personages into relatively few pages. Although Photius, in the ninth century A.D., is the earliest known writer to mention the *Library,* it still remains invaluable to students of mythology and, indeed, unsurpassed by any other single work in its contribution to our knowledge of this subject.

EDITIONS—(1) The Chronicle: F. Jacoby, Die Fragmente der griechischen Historiker, 2b, 244; (2) The Library: R. Wagner, Mythographi Graeci, v 1, 2nd ed., 1926. *Translations*—J. G. Frazer, Apollodorus: The Library (Loeb ed.), 1921; K. Aldrich, The Library of Greek Mythology, by Apollodorus, 1975; M. Simpson, Gods and Heroes of the Greeks: The Library of Apollodorus, 1976.
ABOUT—(1) R. Münzel, De Apollodori peri Theon Libris, 1883; F. Jacoby, Apollodors Chronik, 1902. (2) M.

van der Valk, Apollodori Bibliotheca (Revue des études grecques, v 71), 1958.

APOLLONIUS RHODIUS, Greek poet, was born in Egypt in about 295 and died in about 215 B.C. His birthplace was either Alexandria or Naucratis. In spite of conflicting evidence, it seems probable that he succeeded Zenodotus as director of the library at Alexandria in about 260 and occupied the post until the accession of King Ptolemy III Euergetes in 246. Apollonius quarreled violently with his fellow-poet Callimachus (c. 305–240), who had been his teacher but apparently became his subordinate at the library; Callimachus championed short poems against Apollonius' preference for epics, and, moreover, accused him of plagiarism. At first Callimachus got the upper hand in the dispute (though he apparently lost it in the long run), and Apollonius had to retire to Rhodes, thus gaining himself the designation of the Rhodian. Tradition, however, records that eventually the two men were reconciled and that they were buried beside one another.

Apollonius' *Argonautica,* in four books, celebrates the Argonauts who, under the leadership of Jason, sailed the ship Argo into the Black Sea and penetrated to its farthest shores, in order to seize the Golden Fleece from King Aeetes of Colchis. They had been sent by King Pelias of Iolcus in Thessaly, who, afraid that his nephew Jason would take his throne, dispatched him on this perilous adventure. In Book 1, Jason is appointed the leader of the expedition, whose members are enumerated. One of their number, Heracles, is left behind in Mysia, to search for his beloved boy Hylas, who had been abducted by a nymph. Book 2 recounts the various adventures and perils of the Argonauts' journey, including the passage through the Clashing Rocks (Symplegades) at the mouth of the Bosporus.

The third and most important book transfers the scene to Olympus, where the goddesses Athena and Hera (desirous of bringing doom to Pelias' house) visit Aphrodite to request the aid of her son Eros in

a po lō′ ni us   rō′ di us

bringing success to the Argonauts' mission; whereupon Aphrodite bribes Eros, by the promise of a ball of golden hoops, to launch an arrow into the breast of Medea, daughter of King Aeetes. When, therefore, the Argonauts arrive at their destination and enter the royal palace of Aeetes, Eros duly pierces her heart with passion for Jason. Aeetes gives him a bad reception, imposing terrible tests, but Medea selects a magic ointment that makes him invulnerable. With the aid of her magical gift, Jason surmounts his ordeals. Medea also manages to lull to sleep the giant serpent that guards the Golden Fleece, so that Jason is able to seize the fleece from the oak on which it hangs.

In the fourth book, the Argonauts start on their homeward voyage, pursued by a Colchian fleet but protected by Hera. At the mouth of the Danube, they are overtaken by the Colchians under Medea's brother Absyrtus; but Jason kills him. Then the Argonauts sail up the Danube to the sacred Amber Island at the mouth of the Eridanus (Po) and thence to the Rhone and down to its estuary (which is placed on the Tyrrhenian Sea)—and then on to Elba and Aeaea, the land of Aeetes' sister Circe. She drives them away, but with Hera's aid they escape the monsters Scylla and Charybdis and come to the Phaeacian island of Corcyra, where Jason and Medea celebrate their marriage. From Corcyra they are swept southward to the Syrtian Gulf of northern Africa, where they come to the Garden of Atlas and the Hesperides. Next they arrive on the shores of Crete and speed northward to Aegina, then home to Pagasae.

Apollonius, in depicting Medea's passion for Jason, became the first poet to use love as the central theme for an epic poem. With the single exception of Sappho, no other Greek poet has depicted the beginnings of love in a girl's heart with such sensitive sympathy or followed its subsequent stages with so much care. Apollonius achieves richly sensuous descriptions of nature and events and is capable of arresting similes. Moreover, he accomplishes a considerable feat by subtly adapting Homer's language to the new world of romantic sentiment he evokes.

Nevertheless, as an epic, *Argonautica* has to be adjudged a failure. It is lacking in structural unity, falling apart into a series of disjointed sections. Furthermore, Apollonius' characterization is feeble. Jason, who ought to be the hero, is totally unreal and uninspiring and conspicuously lacks all the qualities of leadership. Medea, too, fails to add up to a unified personality. Finally, the poet's attitude toward his epic theme is disconcerting to readers, since he approaches his task in a spirit of patronizing superciliousness.

On the other hand, Apollonius revels in the opportunities to display Alexandrian learning with which the subject of his epic provides him. For instance, he indulges particularly freely in etiology—the examination and explanation of the causes *(aitia)* of names, customs, relics, rituals, and so on. It is evident that he consulted a great many authorities in the course of his writing, and later commentators have indicated who some of these authorities were. In the light of his famous quarrel with Callimachus, it is noteworthy that Apollonius did in fact take whole extensive passages of Callimachus' poetry and retell them in his own style, just as Theocritus, in his turn, subsequently refashioned episodes from Apollonius' epic in the form of short separate poems—for example, the disappearance of Hylas, and the fight between Pollux and Amycus.

Latin writers drew extensively on the *Argonautica*. Varro of Atax (born 82 B.C.) translated or adapted the poem in his own *Argonautae*. In the *Aeneid* Virgil used the passion of Jason and Medea and echoed Apollonius' general conception of romantic love, in depicting the tragedy of Aeneas and Dido. The *Argonautica* of Valerius Flaccus, in the late first century A.D., is also indebted to Apollonius' poem, though without imitating it closely. Apollonius was also widely read and admired in late antiquity, and he is one of the few Hellenistic poets whose work was preserved in medieval manuscripts.

He also wrote other poems, now only surviving in fragments, about the Foundations (that is to say, origins, early history, and myths) of various cities (Alexandria, Naucratis, Rhodes, Caunus, and Cnidus, and possibly the communities of Lesbos). In addition, as the learned nature of such topics would suggest, and the erudition of many themes of his *Argonautica* confirms, he was a scholar of repute, compiling prose treatises on Hesiod, Antimachus, and Archilochus and writing an attack on Zenodotus, his predecessor at the library at Alexandria.

EDITIONS—Argonautica: G. W. Mooney, 1912; M. M. Gillies (Book 3), 1928; A. Ardizzoni (Book 3), 1958; Fragments: J. U. Powell, Collectanea Alexandrina, 1925. *Translations*—R. C. Seaton (Loeb ed.), 1912; G. Pompella (Italian, Books 3, 4), 1970; F. Vian and E. Delage (Budé ed.), 1974.
ABOUT—E. Delage, La géographie dans les Argonautiques d'Apollonios de Rhodes, 1930; P. Händel, Beobachtungen zur epischen Technik des Apollonios Rhodios (Zetemata, v 7), 1954; E. Eichgrün, Kallimachos und Apollonios Rhodios (Berlin, dissertation), 1961; H. Fränkel, Einleitung zur kritischen Ausgabe der Argonautika des Apollonios, 1964, *and* Noten zu den Argonautika des Apollonios, 1968; A. Köhnken, Apollonios Rhodios und Theokrit (Hypomnemata, v 12), 1965; A. Hurst, Apollonius de Rhodes: Manière et cohérence, 1967; D. M. Levin, Apollonius' Argonautica Reexamined, v 1: The Neglected First and Second Books, 1971; G. Paduano, Studi su Apollonio Rodio, 1972.

APPIAN (Appianos), Greek historian, was born in about A.D. 95 at Alexandria, where he held local office. After living through the Jewish revolt there, he obtained Roman citizenship and moved to Rome in 116 to become an advocate. He was a friend of the Latin orator Fronto, tutor of emperors. Subsequently Appian held an official position in the imperial service as *procurator Augusti,* probably in Egypt. It is not known when he died, but he lived at least until about 160, when he completed his *Romaica,* a history of Rome in twenty-four books, of which eleven have survived.

Arranged according to an ethnographic scheme, the work treats the successive Roman conquests one after another. After a preliminary three books about the early history of Italy, the scheme of the subsequent books is as follows: (4) Celts, (5) Sicily and islands, (6) Spain, (7) Hannibal, (8) northern Africa, (9) Macedonia and Illyria, (10) Greece and Asia (western Asia Minor), (11) Syria and Parthia, (12) Pontus (northern Asia Minor; the war against Mithridates VI); (13-17) civil strife (133-30 B.C.), (18-21) conquest of Egypt, (22) the first century

ap′ i ən

28

of the imperial principate, (23) Dacia, (24) Arabia. Books 6-8 survive complete, also the latter part of Book 9 and Books 11-17, so that Appian's entire treatment of the civil wars preceding the establishment of the principate is preserved. Other extant sections include the introduction to Book 4, a passage relating to Macedonia from 9, and a number of fragments from other books.

Appian derived his material from a variety of earlier writers, upon whom he drew without much critical penetration. He relied most heavily and directly, it would seem, upon the work of an early imperial annalist, now unidentifiable, whose writings he sought to adapt to the ethnic classification he had chosen for his work. The resultant, somewhat confused, picture gives an impression of isolated and haphazard Roman annexations, which, in its way, is as truthful as the pattern of organic inevitability envisaged by earlier historians. Yet Appian's approach also removes all sense of continuity and causes chronology to be neglected. However, for one important period of Roman history, the last century of the Republic, Appian abandons this ethnic division and concentrates upon the problems of Rome itself, to which he devotes five books (13-17, constituting 1-5 of the Civil Wars). Despite his incomplete knowledge of Roman institutions (which he found less interesting than wars), it is in these books that his greatest merit becomes most apparent. This is his political impartiality, particularly notable in his treatment of the Gracchi, where it creates a useful counterbalance to the biases habitually displayed by other sources.

Appian is an honest writer who tries to cram too much into too small a space. There is not much trace of any guiding personal conception. His style, on the whole, is plain and bare, though he is capable of raising its pitch when stimulated by exciting events. He also likes describing cunning tricks and stratagems; and, just occasionally, his imagination runs riot—for example, when he depicts Hannibal and Scipio Africanus engaging in a Homeric duel. He is loyal to Rome and an admirer of its imperialism, although not too obtrusively so: he writes as a Greek providing his fellow countrymen with information, in their own language, about the growth of the empire of which they form a part.

EDITIONS with translation—H. White, Appian: Roman History (Loeb ed.), 1912–13.
ABOUT—N. I. Barbu, Les sources et l'originalité d'Appien dans le deuxième livre des Guerres civiles, 1934; P. Melani, Il valore storico e le fonti del libro Macedonico di Appiano (Annali della Facoltà di lettere di Cagliari), 1955.

APULEIUS, LUCIUS, Latin orator, novelist, and philosopher, was born in about A.D. 123–25. It is not certain when he died. His birthplace was Madaurus in Numidia (now Mdaourouch in Algeria). He studied at Carthage and Athens and traveled in the east, where the mystery religions attracted his interest. At some stage in his early life he practiced as a rhetorician in Rome. Then he returned to northern Africa. In the course of a journey to Egypt, he fell ill on the way at Oea in Tripolitania, where he was nursed by a rich widow named Aemilia Pudentilla, whom he subsequently married at the suggestion of her son Sicinius Pontianus. This meant, however, that she had to jilt her brother-in-law, whose brother Sicinius Aemilianus prosecuted Apuleius on the grounds that he had won her love by magical means and that Pontianus, who was now dead, had been murdered by him for the sake of his fortune. The case was heard at Sabrata in about 155 by the proconsul of Africa, Claudius Maximus. Apuleius was acquitted, and he returned to Carthage. But he also traveled extensively around the other cities of Africa (c. 161), delivering numerous declamations after the manner of contemporary Sophists, which won him considerable fame as an orator and philosopher. Statues of him were set up at Carthage and Madaurus, and he became the high priest of the province.

The *Apologia* is the speech that he delivered at Sabrata in his defense against charges of magic and murder. The only Latin forensic speech to have survived from Roman imperial times, this flamboyant and dazzling production first disposes of the charge of magic by an overwhelming display

a pū lē′ yus

of erudition. The rest of the speech seeks to justify his marriage with Pudentilla and his dealings with her family.

The *Florida* (c. 180) (meaning anthology) is a selection (made by a later admirer) of excerpts from his declamations, which Apuleius himself had probably once published in full, though his original edition is now lost. Some of the excerpts are from speeches on public occasions; others have moral themes. Picturesque anecdotes and legends abound. The subjects encountered in the *Florida* include the flight of an eagle; the contest between Apollo and Marsyas; the flute-player Antigenidas; Indian gymnosophists (an ascetic sect); the artistic tastes of Alexander the Great; a comparison of Apuleius' own many-sided talent with that of the sophist Hippias of Elis; a discussion of parrots; the Cynic philosopher Crates of Thebes; Polycrates and Pythagoras of Samos; an argument between Protagoras and his pupil Euathlus about tuition charges; and the comic poet Philemon —this last piece being a particularly skillful display of artificial effects. Apuleius also wrote another elaborate declamation called *On the God of Socrates.* Probably basing it on a previous Greek treatise, he argues that the divine element *(daimonion),* to which Socrates in Plato's *Apology* had attributed the guidance of his actions, was one of the spirits who serve as intermediaries between the gods and human beings.

The *Metamorphoses* or *Golden Ass,* (c. 180 –190?), the work for which Apuleius is best known, forms eleven books and is ostensibly recounted in the first person by a young man named Lucius. Visiting Thessaly, he encounters two other travelers who tell him the story of a murder by a witch at Hypata, the town that is his destination. When he arrives there, he becomes the guest of Milo, whose wife Pamphile proves to be another witch. At a party given by a relative of Milo, Byrrhaena, Lucius hears another macabre tale about a witch and on his way home slays two bandits who turn out not to be human at all, but animated wineskins.

He makes love to the servant Fotis, who allows him to watch Pamphile transforming herself into an owl. Lucius wants to do the same, but owing to a mistake he becomes a donkey instead, though retaining his human faculties with the exception of his voice which has become an ass's bray. If he eats roses, he will regain his human shape, but before Fotis is able to bring him the flowers, robbers invade the house and carry him away. At their hideout, he listens to three stories about their profession and watches them bring in a beautiful girl, Charite, who had been kidnapped for a ransom on her wedding night. In order to comfort her, the robbers' old cook tells her the story of Cupid and Psyche (the "Fairy Bridegroom"), which forms a lengthy interlude in Apuleius' main narrative.

When the story of the *Metamorphoses* resumes, Charite is rescued by her lover, disguised as a robber. Subsequently he is assassinated by a rival, upon whom, however, she manages to take vengeance. Still in the shape of a donkey, Lucius witnesses the obscene orgies of Syrian priests and listens to four improper anecdotes: The Tale of the Tub, The Baker's Wife, The Lost Slippers, and the Fuller's Wife. Then follow three horror stories: The first describes the persecution of a poor family by an arrogant nobleman and the death of three brothers who try to help them; the second story is about a lecherous stepmother who tries to poison her unresponsive stepson; and the third is a tale of five murders committed by a sadistic woman. As part of her penalty, it is proposed to display her in public, making love to the donkey Lucius, who is so appalled by the prospect that he escapes from Corinth and flees to the neighboring town of Cenchreae. There he falls asleep on the seashore and dreams. In the last book of the *Metamorphoses,* the atmosphere is one of religious revelation. The Egyptian goddess Isis appears to the sleeping Lucius in all her glory, and amid resplendent pageantry he resumes his human shape. Vowing to dedicate himself to the savior goddess, he goes to Rome and receives initiation into the mysteries of Isis and Osiris.

The writings of Apuleius are pervaded by his personality. A rhetorician who professed to be a philosopher, he proudly displays in his work a whole armory of conceits and deploys a vast supply of superficial and undigested scholarship. But he was also, like many other people of his time, an ecstatic believer in pagan mystery religion. When he describes Lucius' initiation into the mysteries of the Egyptian goddess Isis and lavishes the wealth of his imagination on her glory, he seems to be recording a deeply felt experience of his own. All in all, he was a highly versatile representative of his age: novelist and sophist, lawyer and lecturer, poet and religious initiate.

The language of Apuleius, especially in the *Metamorphoses,* is startlingly extravagant and florid but often rises to a strange beauty all its own. It is a highly rhythmic diction, full of poetic color, and abounds in recondite words, and in Grecisms and archaic and colloquial usages. This stylistic exuberance has been ascribed to his African origin. His language, however, is the Latin of an epoch rather than a country. At a time when the classic Ciceronian grammar was rapidly breaking down, Apuleius managed to raise the "New speech"—the archaic and colloquial style of the orator Fronto—to an entirely new level of excellence.

The "Fairy Bridegroom," story of Cupid and Psyche imbedded in *The Metamorphoses,* was perhaps derived from a tale by an unknown Greek, Aristophontes of Athens; but whatever may have been the character of this earlier work, Apuleius adapted it so as to exhibit his own, highly original, storytelling skill in incomparable form. Apuleius' "Cupid and Psyche" incorporates a remarkable mass of traditional folktales. It also contains (though this remains a subordinate feature) an underlying allegory of the vicissitudes of the soul *(psyche),* the seat of the passions. It was with this thought in mind that Hellenistic art had often represented Psyche being tortured by Cupid. When, in the fourth century A.D., the search for such allegories became increasingly popular, the suggestion of allegory in Apuleius' tale was magnified into an elaborate construction, and Cupid and Psyche appear as spiritual symbols on early Christian sarcophagi. However, the Christian Fathers, in the course of prolonged discussion, were disposed to let Apuleius fall from favor. St. Augustine, for example, felt by no means certain that Apuleius himself had not actually been turned into a donkey, a victim of his own magic, and he warned his fellow Christians against those who were evidently praising Apuleius as a wonder-worker exceeding the power even of Jesus Christ himself.

The *Metamorphoses* was not unknown in the Middle Ages, as the existence of an eleventh-century manuscript testifies, but Apuleius' merits as a teller of stories only came into full recognition in the Italian Renaissance, when his gay spirit, his frank freedom, and his quick response to beauty were enormously admired. In 1427 Poggio Bracciolini discovered a second manuscript, which was published in Rome in 1469, only four years after printing had been introduced into Italy. The story of Cupid and Psyche became the most popular and influential part of the *Metamorphoses.* It was translated into English by William Adlington in 1566 (along with the rest of the work) and greatly appealed to Elizabethan and Jacobean exuberance. In the nineteenth century, English essayist and critic Walter Pater imitated the tale in *Marius the Epicurean,* a philosophical romance written in an ornamental style directly indebted to what Pater called the "perfumed personality" of Apuleius.

WORKS (not mentioned above)—Apuleius was the author of a translation of a passage from the Greek comic dramatist Menander. His authorship of the treatise On the Doctrine of Plato, an elementary and unperceptive exposition in two (originally three) books, is doubtful; and it is equally uncertain whether he is the writer of On the Universe, an inaccurate translation of a treatise erroneously attributed to Aristotle. Other works ascribed to Apuleius—Asclepius, The Art of the Physiognomist, The Botanist, Healthgiving Remedies—are spurious. *Writings authentically assigned to him, but lost,* include the following: Arithmetica, Astronomica, Convivial Investigations (Quaestiones Conviviales), Eroticus, Hermagoras (a romance), Historical Epitomes, Investigations of Nature, On Agriculture, On Fishes, On Proverbs, On the State, On Trees, a translation of Plato's Phaedo, poems, and speeches.

EDITIONS—Apologia *and* Florida: H. E. Butler and A. S. Owen, 1914; R. Helm, Verteidigungsrede: Blütenlese, 1977. Metamorphoses (Golden Ass): H. van Thiel, Der Eselsroman, 1971–72; J. C. Fredouille, Métamorphoses, 1975; A. Scobie, Book 1, 1975; B. C. Hijmans, R. T. van der Paardt, E. M. Smits, R. E. H. Westendorp Boerma, A. J. Westenbrink, 1977– . Cupid (Amor) and Psyche: L. C. Purser, 1910; R. Merkelbach and G. Binder, 1967; M. G. Balme and H. W. Morwood, 1976. *Translations*—Apologia *and* Florida: P. Vallette (Budé

ed.), 2nd ed., 1960. Metamorphoses: W. Adlington, 1566, revised by S. Gaselee (Loeb ed.), 1915; D. S. Robertson and P. Vallette (Budé ed.), 1940–45; L. MacNeice, 1946; R. Graves (Penguin ed.), 1950; J. Lindsay, 1960; J. G. Griffiths, The Isis Book (Book 11), 1975; Minor works: J. Beaujeu, Opuscules philosophiques, 1977.

ABOUT—P. Médan, La latinité d'Apulée dans les Métamorphoses, 1926; H. Riefstahl, Der Roman des Apuleius, 1938; H. Wittmann, Das Isisbuch des Apuleius, 1938; E. Paratore, La novella in Apuleio, 2nd ed., 1942; G. P. Golann, The Life of Apuleius and His Connection With Magic, 1952; J. O. Swahn, The Tale of Cupid and Psyche, 1955; E. H. Haight, Apuleius and His Influence, 1963 ed.; M. Bernhard, Der Stil des Apuleius, 2nd ed., 1965; E. Neumann, Amor and Psyche, 1966; B. E. Perry, The Ancient Romance, 1967; M. W. Sullivan, Apuleian Logic, 1967; A. Scobie, Aspects of the Ancient Romance and Its Heritage, 1969; P. G. Walsh, The Roman Novel, 1970; G. Bianco, La fonte greca delle Metamorfosi di Apuleio, 1971; G. C. Schlam, Cupid and Psyche: Apuleius and the Monuments, 1976; D. Fehling, Amor und Psyche, 1977; C. Moreschini, Apuleio ed il platonismo, 1978; J. Tatum, Apuleius and the Golden Ass, 1979.

ARATUS of Soli in Cilicia (near Mezitli in southeastern Turkey), Greek poet, seems to have lived from about 315 to about 240 B.C., though these dates are conjectural. It is possible that he was a pupil of the poet Menecrates of Ephesus. As a young man, however, he went to Athens, where he learned Stoicism from its founder, Zeno of Citium. Next, in about 277, he was invited by the Macedonian king Antigonus II Gonatas to his court at Pella. Later Aratus spent some time at the court of the Seleucid monarch Antiochus I in Syria, but eventually he returned to Macedonia where he died.

Many poems that he wrote are now lost, but his most famous work, written probably at the request of Antigonus, survives. It is an astronomical poem, the *Phaenomena,* consisting of 1,154 hexameters. After a prologue containing a dedication to Zeus and a reference to the poles, Aratus describes the fixed stars, the circles of the celestial sphere, and the stars' risings and settings. The remaining 421 lines of the poem, which comprise an account of weather signs *(Diosemeia),* were at one time treated, mistakenly, as a separate work.

Aratus was by no means the first to expound astronomy using the form of a poem,

a rä' tus

31

ARCHILOCHUS

ARATUS

and his *Phaenomena* did little more than versify a brief prose treatise by Eudoxus of Cnidus. Nor, as Cicero pointed out, was Aratus himself the possessor of any substantial astronomical knowledge; indeed, he not only followed numerous errors committed by Eudoxus but added others of his own. However, what prompted his choice of subject may well have been the growing fashion for astrology, largely imported from the east. His solemn introduction to the *Phaenomena* and the Stoic creed that pervades this and other parts of the poem suggest that he was a religious man who saw the heavenly bodies as imposing proof of the divine handiwork. Although the subject matter sometimes makes for difficult reading, Aratus' verses, modeled stylistically on Hesiod and linguistically on Homer, flow with a smoothness verging on monotony. Yet this sober pattern is relieved by occasional passages of a more elevated character, notably in the prologue, and poetical coloring is supplied by digressions—for instance, an account of the Golden Age of the past and descriptions of storms at sea.

The *Phaenomena* is constructed with an ingenious simplicity which shows the poet had a certain sense of form, but this in itself scarcely explains the ancient popularity of the work, which was enormous. It was praised extravagantly by Aratus' contemporary Callimachus and by Leonidas of Tarentum and had already been the subject of

several commentaries before the end of the second century B.C., since which time it has constantly been studied and adapted and imitated. St. Paul quoted the poem when he addressed the Athenians (*Acts* 17:28), and Aratus' portrait appeared on the coins of his native city. Moreover, the Romans particularly admired the *Phaenomena*. It helped to inspire Virgil's *Georgics,* and complete or partial translations were made by Varro, by Cicero (whose rendering influenced Lucretius), and by Germanicus, as well as by later men of letters, too, right up to the end of antiquity—and beyond, for Aratus also prompted the sky-map of Dürer in 1515. This extraordinary fame was to some extent due, at least initially, to the desire of the educated Hellenistic (Alexandrian) public to produce a great poet, whose subject must be the truth; and it was felt that, in the absence of the sublime truth of the supreme poets, the truth of scientific fact was as worthwhile an achievement as any other. But what seems to have been particularly popular was the poem's illustration of the Stoic doctrine of providence: Paul's motive in quoting from it, for example, was in order to appeal for Stoic sympathy for Christian providential belief.

WORKS—Phaenomena; also other poems (now lost) including Hymn to Pan (written for Antigonus II's wedding and victories over Celts); Dirges (Epicedeia), Elegies, Epigrams, Hymns, Trifles (Catalepton, after which the Catalepton attributed to Virgil took its name).
EDITIONS with translation—Phaenomena: G. R. Mair, Callimachus (Hymns and Epigrams) and Aratus (Loeb ed.), revised ed., 1955; J. Martin, Arati Phaenomena (French), 1956.
ABOUT—U. Wilamowitz-Moellendorf, Hellenistische Dichtung in der Zeit des Kallimachos, 1924, 1962; J. Martin, Histoire du texte des Phénomènes d'Aratos, 1956; H. J. Waschkies, Von Eudoxos zu Aristoteles, 1977.

ARCHILOCHUS, Greek poet, was born in (probably) about 710 B.C. (though his birth was sometimes placed nearly half a century later), and he may have lived to see the solar eclipse of 648. His birthplace was the island of Paros. He was the illegitimate son of Telesicles. His father came of a distin-
är ki′ lo kus

32

guished family, but his mother was a slave who may have come from Thasos, where Telesicles founded a Parian colony about 708. Archilochus himself took part in a later phase of the colonization of Thasos. He apparently went there—and elsewhere—as a mercenary soldier, a career that he had adopted because of a personal rebuff; a Parian named Lycambes had refused to let him marry his daughter Neobule, with whom Archilochus had fallen in love. According to a traditional tale (which is probably a fictitious deduction from his own words), the furious satires that the thwarted lover then composed against Lycambes and his daughter caused them both to hang themselves. Archilochus died in a battle between Parians and Naxians.

He is chiefly famous for his iambics, i.e. poetry written in meters based on the *iambus* (a short syllable followed by a long one). The earliest known use of the word *iambus* (which is probably of Asiatic origin) is, in fact, in his verse, where Archilochus seems to be referring to his employment of the iambic for satirical purposes. Aristotle indicated that the meter had first appeared (along with hexameters) in the *Margites,* a satirical epic, now surviving only in fragments, that was wrongly attributed to Homer. Archilochus owed a debt to the *Margites*—he even quoted one of its lines; but he evidently developed iambic satire in an original manner all his own, especially in order to express his likes and dislikes, which he did with such ferocity that Eustathius, a Byzantine scholar of the twelfth century A.D., described him as scorpion-tongued. In one fragment Archilochus attacks Lycambes, and in another he refers to Neobule whom he loved. Moreover, a recently discovered papyrus contains the last thirty-five lines of one of his poems (in addition to the first five lines of another) in which he has unpleasant things to say to an aging woman and describes his love-making to her younger sister.

Archilochus employs his iambuses in a variety of forms including the epode, a couplet in which a longer line was followed by a shorter—the epode was believed to be his invention. He also combined the iambic with other types of meter. For example, we find iambic lines linked with hexameters (as in

the *Margites*) in pieces comprising fables of traditional character about the relationship between the fox and the hedgehog, and the fox and the eagle, and the fox and the monkey; and among a wide variety of other meters he makes use of the trochaic to describe his own poetic skill, his personal misfortunes, the threat of war, and an eclipse of the sun.

Pindar ascribes to Archilochus songs of triumph sung by victors in the Olympic games. In addition, he composed elegiac epigrams—probably songs for singing after banquets, to the accompaniment of the flute —that infused subjects such as war and wine with a strongly personal character. These epigrams contain certain grammatical forms that are epic in origin, but for the most part Archilochus' diction is a colloquial brand of the Ionic dialect. The suggestion that such poems may have been oral compositions has not won general acceptance.

Archilochus displays an extremely changeable temperament, veering sharply from melancholy to enthusiasm to biting mockery, and often indulging in a self-exposure that seems positively embarrassing. Plutarch informs us that he was regarded as a major innovator; the meters, language, and subject matter found in the surviving fragments of his poetry confirm this reputation. In Roman literature, Catullus, Ovid, and Martial borrowed his meters. Horace claimed to have been the first to have introduced "Parian" (i.e. Archilochean) iambuses into Latin, a claim that is justified by the Horatian *Odes*—not so much perhaps by the precise meters they employ but by their general spirit.

EDITIONS—F. Lasserre and A. Bonnard, Archiloque: Fragments (Budé ed.), 1958; M. Treu, 1959; M. West, Iambi et Elegi Graeci, v 1, 1971; The new fragment: D. L. Page, Supplementum Lyricis Graecis, 1974. *Translations*—G. Davenport, Carmina Archilochi, 1964; H. Lloyd-Jones, Females of the Species, 1975; P. Green *in* Times Literary Supplement, March 14, 1975 (the new fragment).
ABOUT—C. M. Bowra, Early Greek Elegists, 1938; F. Lasserre, Les Épodes d'Archiloque, 1950; Archiloque (Entretiens Hardt, v 10), 1964; D. A. Campbell, Greek Lyric Poetry, 1967; J. Davison, From Archilochus to Pindar, 1968; J. Tarditi, Archilochus, 1968; T. Breitenstein, Hésiode et Archiloque, 1971; H. D. Rankin, Archilochus of Paros, 1978.

ARCHIMEDES, Greek writer on mathematics and science, was born at Syracuse in Sicily in about 287 B.C. The son of an astronomer named Phidias who belonged to a well-connected family, Archimedes probably studied at Alexandria. Subsequently he lived at the court of King Hiero II (269–215 B.C.) of Syracuse, where he was killed in 212 after the successful siege of the city by the Roman general Marcus Claudius Marcellus. Archimedes had postponed the capture of the city for two years by his efficient and ingenious catapults and grapnels. He was also the inventor of other engineering devices. These included "Archimedes' screw" for raising irrigation water (it can still be seen on Egyptian canals) and a compound pulley or windlass for the moving of heavy loads: "Give me a place to stand on," he said, "and I will move the earth." He also constructed a star globe and a planetarium worked by water; these were taken to Rome after his death. While trying to work out whether a crown made for Hiero was pure gold or alloyed with silver, he arrived at "Archimedes' principle" of specific gravity for the conduct of metallurgical tests: "Eureka" (I have found it), he was said to have exclaimed when he made this discovery in his bath by observing the water displaced by his body.

Archimedes reputedly refused to write a handbook about engineering, on the grounds that it was too practical and therefore too vulgar a subject; he wished his reputation to rest entirely on his contribution to pure theory. He was the greatest mathematician of antiquity, and one of the greatest of all time. He wrote extensively on the subject, not in the usual Greek of the age but in his native Doric dialect, though this has become somewhat watered down in the course of the transmission of his writings. He began with applied mathematics: his earliest known work, *Method of Mechanical Theorems,* dedicated to Eratosthenes, is a description of the system he had invented for finding out the areas and volumes of various figures (sphere, parabola, etc.). For the determination of these figures, he made use of rigorous techniques that anticipated the procedures of the integral calculus employed after 1600.

är ki mē′ dēz

The *Method* was rediscovered in 1907 at Jerusalem.

Archimedes soon moved on to more abstract problems. Some of these can be read about in his two-book essay *On the Sphere and Cylinder,* containing his formulas for calculating the surface area and volume of a sphere and its segments. A more important work that followed was *On Conoidal and Spheroidal Figures,* which shows his complete mastery of the doctrine of conic section; it calculates the volumes of segments of a number of solids formed by the revolution of a conic about its axis and discusses the already well-known problem of squaring the circle: Archimedes' tomb, which was designed in the form of a column by the future occupant himself and was seen by Cicero, displayed a sphere inscribed in a cylinder, a device that recalls his discovery of the relation between their volumes. Deeply interested in numeration (his work *On the Measurement of the Circle* gave an arithmetical approximation of the value of *pi*), he sought to find a better arithmetical method than the system generally employed by the Greeks, and this prompted him to write a popular treatise, the *Sand-Reckoner,* dedicated to Gelo, the son of Hiero II of Syracuse. Since the alphabetic notation used in current arithmetical calculations made the handling of large numbers especially difficult, Archimedes aimed at devising a scheme capable of expressing an enormous total conveyed in terms of the number of grains of sand in the entire universe: in effect, he employed a notation in which 100,000,000 is used as we use 10. The *Sand-Reckoner* displays a comprehension of numerical reckoning wholly unequaled by other writers of the ancient world. Its opening sections—one of the only two surviving portions of Archimedes' writings on astronomical themes—record its author's highly scientific efforts to make a more accurate determination of the angle subtended at the eye by the disc of the sun. He also wrote a two-book work on statics, entitled *The Equilibriums* (or *Centers of Gravity*) of *Planes,* in which, on the basis of preconceived definitions and axioms, he puts forward the theory of the lever. This superbly reasoned and greatly admired masterpiece illustrates his conception of science as an orderly series of deductions from a limited quantity of clearly understandable postulates, an idea that was prompted by his admiration for the logical consistency of geometry and caused him to set dynamics aside and concentrate on statics.

Thus, the whole science of hydrostatics was invented by Archimedes. In particular, he discovered and gave his name to the law of the upward force that a body experiences when it is immersed in a liquid; he deduced this law in his treatise *On Floating Bodies* (literally *On Things Carried*), using the same means by which he had demonstrated the law of leverability—that is to say, on the basis of rules he had already deduced. His rules are outdated today, but it was characteristic of Archimedes to use them as a starting point for highly sophisticated mathematical investigations.

Sixth century A.D. commentaries on several of his works survive, and when in the sixteenth century his complete works became known in western Europe, they exercised an overwhelming influence.

WORKS (in addition to those mentioned above)—Measurement of the Circle; On Spirals; Quadrature of the Parabola; Book of Lemmas (available only in Arabic and Latin translations); On the Heptagon in a Circle (Arabic and German translations).
EDITIONS—J. L. Heiberg, Archimedes: Opera Mathematica, 1910–15 (2nd ed., E. Stamatis, 1972–75). *With translation:* I. Thomas, The Greek Mathematicians (Loeb ed.), 1939, 1941; The Works of Archimedes, new ed., 1956; P. ver Eecke, Les oeuvres complètes d'Archimède (including Eutocius' Commentaries), 1961; C. Mugler, Archimède (Budé ed.), v 1, 1970–72.
ABOUT—E. J. Dijksterhuis, Archimedes, 1956; A. G. Drachmann, The Mechanical Technology of Greek and Roman Antiquity, 1961; M. Clagett, Archimedes in the Middle Ages, v 1, 1964; G. E. R. Lloyd, Greek Science After Aristotle, 1973.

ARCHYTAS, Greek scientist and philosopher, lived in the first half of the fourth century B.C. His birthplace was Taras (Tarentum, the modern Taranto) in southeastern Italy. He was several times appointed to the chief military command in his city and played an important part in the political affairs of the Greek cities in the region. He

är kī' tàs

was a close friend of Plato, who paid him a visit. Archytas was one of the first and most talented leaders of the philosophical school named after Pythagoras, the semi-legendary sage of the sixth century B.C., who had emigrated from Samos to Croton in southeastern Italy.

In the field of mathematics, Archytas distinguished harmonic from arithmetical and geometrical progressions and solved the geometrical problem of doubling the cube. He has also been described as the originator of mathematical mechanics. In acoustic theory, he argued that the sounds made by a stringed instrument were due to a movement or displacement of air. He also contributed to musical theory by working out the proportions underlying the relations of successive notes.

His mathematical writings were made use of by Plato. Fragments of them remain, but works attributed to him in other fields are for the most part unlikely to be authentic.

EDITIONS—H. Diels, Die Fragmente der Vorsokratiker, 11th ed., 1964; M. T. Cardini, I Pitagorici: Testimonianze e frammenti, v 2, 1958.
ABOUT—W. K. C. Guthrie, A History of Greek Philosophy, v 1, 1962.

ARCTINUS of Miletus (southwestern Asia Minor), Greek poet, lived in the seventh or sixth century B.C. His name is attributed to certain of the sequels to the *Iliad* and *Odyssey* known as the poems of the Epic Cycle. This group of early epics, independently composed at various dates by poets other than Homer and Hesiod, were later grouped together in an attempt to form an ordered series providing a history of the world in myth and legend, from the birth of the gods to the end of the Heroic Age. The poems themselves are now lost, but some fragments and abridged prose synopses survive. The quality of the originals was said to have been inferior to that of the Homeric poems. Aristotle condemned their lack of both dramatic movement and unity of action. In the course of time, however, these works came to be appreciated for their sequence of mythological narratives, which were drawn upon by

ärk tē' nus

35

later writers and especially by tragic poets in search of plots and themes for their choral lyrics.

The authors of the poems of the Epic Cycle are shadowy figures. The series includes six epics about the Trojan War, of which two, the *Aethiopis* and *Sack of Troy (Iliou Persis)*, tell of the legendary events occurring after the story of the *Iliad*. These, and another poem known as the *War With the Titans (Titanomachia)*, were sometimes attributed to Arctinus. The five books of the *Aethiopis* recounted the last exploits of Achilles: his killing of Penthesilea, queen of the Amazons (an alternative title of the poem is *Amazonia*) and of Thersites as well, for mocking when Achilles grieved for the queen; his purification from blood-guilt; his slaying of the Ethiopian prince Memnon, who was given immortality by Zeus; and the death of Achilles himself at the hands of Paris and Apollo, followed by his funeral, at which Odysseus and Ajax quarreled over his armor. An alternative version of the last line of the *Iliad* makes it lead on directly to the *Aethiopis*, which in consequence was sometimes ascribed to Homer himself. This attribution was not generally accepted; but the recurrence and repetition of many similar elements in the two poems suggest that their authors may have drawn on an identical earlier heroic tradition. However, the idea of purification that appears in the *Aethiopis* suggests to religious historians that it was written not earlier than about 700—that is to say, somewhat later than the final composition of the *Iliad*.

The two books that make up the *Sack of Troy* (sometimes also attributed to Lesches of Mytilene) consisted of a series of detached episodes, describing the introduction of the Trojan Horse within the walls of the city and the death of Laocoön, who suspected the strategem, followed by the capture of the city and the departure of the Greeks with their plunder while Athena planned their shipwreck as punishment for the rape of Cassandra at her shrine. This story of the entry into Troy overlapped with another poem of the Cycle, the four-book *Little Iliad* (variously ascribed to a number of poets other than Arctinus), of which the *Sack* may originally have formed part, becoming detached upon incorporation in the Cycle.

Later writers also provide a few scattered references to the *War With the Titans*. The two or more books that made up the poem evidently dealt with the offspring of Heaven and Earth and celebrated the accession of Zeus to the kingship of the universe. It was evidently one of numerous works on such subjects relegated to oblivion by the success of Hesiod's *Theogony*. The attribution of the poem to Arctinus was not unanimous; it was alternatively ascribed to Eumelus of Corinth.

EDITIONS with translation—H. G. Evelyn-White, Hesiod: The Homeric Hymns, Fragments of the Epic Cycle: Homerica (Loeb ed.), revised ed., 1936, with the addition of an Appendix by D. L. Page.
ABOUT—W. Kullmann, Die Quellen der Ilias, 1960; G. L. Huxley, Greek Epic Poetry, 1969. Proclus or Proculus, who died in A.D. 485, wrote a handbook (Chrestomachia) including epitomes of these poems, probably derived from an earlier synopsis. His work is lost, but parts of it were reproduced by Photius and other Byzantine writers (A. Severyns, Recherches sur la Chréstomathie de Proclus, v 4, 1963).

ARION, Greek poet, who worked towards the end of the seventh century B.C., came from Methymna on the island of Lesbos. He spent the greater part of his career at the court of Periander of Corinth (c. 625–585 B.C.). While returning there from a journey to Italy and Sicily he fell overboard and, according to a famous story told by Herodotus, was rescued and carried to land by a dolphin, a legend perpetuated on many ancient works of art (including a statue known by Herodotus himself at Taras, the modern Taranto). The dolphin was sacred to Apollo, the god of song, and this is one of many stories showing its friendliness to the human race.

Nothing now survives of Arion's work, but it seems to have been he who gave literary form to the type of poetry known as the dithyramb. This term, of oriental origin and uncertain meaning, was first used, as far as we know, by Archilochus, who recorded that it was a choral song to the god Dionysus. Herodotus' assertion that the di-

a rē′ ōn

36

thyramb was invented by Arion cannot be strictly accurate, since the term forms one of the most ancient titles of Dionysus, and the choral songs in his honor that bear this appellation may well likewise go back to an antique date. The lyric poet Pindar describes how these songs figured in processions, and the Suidas lexicon (tenth century A.D.) says that Arion was the first to compose a dithyramb, train a Corinthian choir or chorus to sing it, and give a title to what was sung. What he did, then, was to elevate the dithyramb to an artistic and elaborate form of choral chant conducted by regular choirs standing in a circle around the altar of the god and devoting their chants to some definite, named subject, apparently in the Doric dialect. The surviving fragments of later dithyrambic odes contain a large proportion of narrative, and this element too may have been introduced by Arion.

The Suidas also stated that Arion had his dithyrambs performed by satyrs reciting or singing in meter. This led the way to the satyr plays of the future and caused Arion's name to be associated at an early date with the birth of tragedy. Indeed, despite modern scepticism, it may well be true that this type of dithyramb, as evolved by the creative talent of Arion, contributed substantially to the subsequent development of the tragic drama. Aristotle, too, called the earliest tragedy "an improvisation by the leaders of the dithyramb," which seems to mean that the songs they sang to the gods on their way to the shrine of Dionysus played a part in its origins.

ABOUT—H. Patzer, Die Anfänge der griechischen Tragödie, 1962 (emphasizing the role of Arion as forerunner of the tragic poets); A. W. Pickard-Cambridge, Dithyramb, Tragedy and Comedy, 2nd ed. (revised by T. B. L. Webster), 1962; G. F. Else, The Origin and Early Form of Tragedy, 1965 (minimizing Arion's role).

ARISTARCHUS of Samothrace, Greek scholarly writer, c. 217–145 B.C., was a pupil of Aristophanes of Byzantium, whom he succeeded as director of the library at Alexandria, in about 153, under King Ptolemy

ar is tär′ kus

VI Philometor. Aristarchus was also the tutor of the king's son Ptolemy VII Philopator, but when Ptolemy VII was murdered in 145 and his successor began expelling Greek scholars from Egypt, Aristarchus left Alexandria for Cyprus, where he died almost immediately.

He was said to have written no less than eight hundred works. The most famous of them was an edition of the Homeric poems accompanied by a series of commentaries *(Hypomnemata),* the first full-scale commentaries on Homer that had ever been compiled. His commentary on the *Iliad* is in part preserved in marginal notes *(scholia)* by the Augustan scholars Didymus and Aristonicus on a Venetian manuscript. As to the epics themselves, it is Aristarchus' version, adapting the earlier texts of Zenodotus and Aristophanes of Byzantium, that is the basis of our modern editions. That does not necessarily mean, however, that our editions incorporate the readings which he himself preferred, since it was his practice to insert in his own text whatever reading the manuscripts at his disposal, or the best of them, might happen to offer, relegating to his bulky, elaborate commentaries his decisions (based on a meticulous concern for the best manuscript tradition) as to which versions were the correct ones and which were the products of interpolation, corruption, or unfounded guesswork. Owing to this approach, his work exercised comparatively little influence on the traditional text of Homer.

Aristarchus' conclusions were based on a careful study of Homeric language and meter. His impressive literary sense guided him to reliable judgments on matters of appropriateness and consistency, which he assessed on the basis of a determination to judge the poet by the poet's own usage. That is to say, in seeking the correct form (or meaning) of a word he followed the principle of analogy, collecting and comparing the various occurrences of the term in the text of his author according to the method which had been launched by Aristophanes of Byzantium and was defined by Aristarchus' assertion that an author is best explained from his own works. This procedure, however, involved him in strife with another

37

critic, Crates of Mallus, who argued that analogy sometimes caused Aristarchus to use force in order to adapt recalcitrant facts to the rules and types he had established, whereas the rival method of anomaly of the Stoic Chrysippus took note of the many manifestations of irregularity (anomaly) displayed by actual usage.

In addition, Aristarchus revised the system of marginal critical signs, his version of which can be reconstructed from the scattered portions and fragments of his commentaries that survive in medieval writings. Moreover, he supplemented his Homeric studies by separate treatises on specific matters—for example, the camp of the Greeks —and he wrote attacks on other Homeric scholars, including the *Chorizontes,* who denied the single authorship of the *Iliad* and *Odyssey.*

He also compiled commentaries on the Hesiodic poems, Archilochus, Pindar, Ion, Aeschylus, Sophocles, and the comic dramatist Aristophanes. His select lists of the best classical poets, together with the lists of Aristophanes of Byzantium, formed the basis of subsequent canonical classifications. Furthermore, he wrote a commentary on Herodotus, thus becoming, as far as we know, the first commentator ever to deal with a prose author.

Aristarchus was the greatest and most versatile of ancient scholars: he was known as *ho grammatikotatos,* the supreme critic, and as *ho mantis,* the seer. His researches, covering as they did an enormous grammatical, etymological, textual, and literary range, may be said to have marked the true beginnings of scholarship. Despite the difficulty people found in making use of his Homeric commentary, the school of philologists he inaugurated in Alexandria, the Aristarcheans, continued to flourish right on into the Roman imperial epoch, enrolling many distinguished scholars.

ABOUT—T. Heath, Aristarchus of Samos: The Ancient Copernicus, 1913, reissued 1966; J. E. Sandys, A History of Classical Scholarship, v 1, 3rd ed., 1921; A. Römer, Die Homerexegese Aristarchs, ed. by E. Belzner, 1924; M. van der Valk, Researches on the Text and Scholia of the Iliad, v 2, 1964; R. Pfeiffer, History of Classical Scholarship From the Beginnings to the End of the Hellenistic Age, 1965.

ARISTIDES, AELIUS, Greek speechwriter and man of letters, was born in Mysia (northwestern Asia Minor) in A.D. 117, of a land-owning family, and died in about 189. He was taught Greek literature by Alexander of Cotiaeum, who was also the teacher of Marcus Aurelius, and then studied rhetoric at Athens under the wealthy sophist Herodes Atticus, of whom he was the most eminent student. Subsequently Aristides' own lecture tours carried him through large regions of the Greek world and then to Rome, where, at the age of twenty-six, he was struck down by the first of a prolonged series of illnesses. These, probably psychosomatic in character, put an end to his public appearances and caused him to spend much time from then onward as a patient in the Temple of Asclepius (the god of healing) at Pergamum (Bergama) in his native country. But it was at Smyrna (Izmir) that he spent most of the rest of his life, and its people regarded him as their next most important citizen after Homer.

Throughout this period, lacking the capacity either to teach or to make extempore speeches, he devoted himself to writing orations, of which fifty-five (some in the form of letters), have come down to us, written in elegant, but somewhat bland, Attic prose. Like Isocrates, he claimed to incorporate the entire range of educational theory and practice in his speeches, and he sought in his essay *On Rhetoric* to prove the primacy of that art in contradiction to Plato, whose contemporary followers hastened to disagree. Furthermore, in his speech *On the Four,* Aristides criticized Plato's disparagement of four Athenian statesmen (Miltiades, Cimon, Themistocles, and Pericles). The same glorification of the history of Athens appears in another oration which he called *Panathenaicus* in imitation of Isocrates. An earthquake which severely damaged Smyrna in 178 prompted him to write his *Monody,* a short lament about the disaster, followed by *Palinode for Smyrna,* which urged the reconstruction of the city, *Smyrnaicus* expressing further hopes that the rebuilding would take place, and *Letter to the Emperor on Smyrna.* The *Monody* is one of a number of Aristides' orations which, al-

ar is ti′ dēz

though presented in prose, are of a semi-poetic nature—hymns, laments, and rejoicings, which treat of themes that would once have been dealt with in lyric verse. His *Addresses to the Gods,* again showing his desire to supersede the poets, were intended to serve as prologues to the great speeches in the same way as the Homeric hymns had introduced the performances of the ancient professional reciters *(rhapsodes).* Aristides' important speech *To Rome* (or *Roman Oration*) was delivered in 143, probably in the lecture-hall named the Athenaeum which Hadrian had built in that city. The speech is a eulogy of Rome (where his Greek friend Herodes Atticus was one of the consuls of the year) as seen by a provincial; the orator praises the blessings of universal peace and free communications, amid which the Greek city-states were able to prosper in a mighty world-state.

Aristides was an invalid; moreover, he was one of the greatest literary hypochondriacs of all time, and his six *Sacred Discourses* offer elaborate discussions of the treatment, by the healer-god Asclepius at Pergamum, of the illnesses from which Aristides had been suffering, or believed he had been suffering, for seventeen years. The *Discourses* narrate his long series of attempts to get healed by Asclepius and the interviews he had been accorded by the god in his dreams, and they reveal the advice he had thus received about medicines and cures. These descriptions are not only very illuminating in regard to the ancient practices of temple medicine but also provide the most comprehensive record of personal religious experiences that has come down to us from any pagan author. Aristides carries piety to the point of extreme superstition, combined with a vanity that convinced him that he had been singled out for special attention by the deity, who had restored his health and granted him fame.

EDITIONS—F. W. Lenz and C. A. Behr, P. Aelii Aristidis Opera Quae Extant Omnia, v 1, pt 1, 1976. *With translation:* J. H. Oliver, The Ruling Power, 1953 (Roman Oration), *and* The Civilising Power, 1968 (Panathenaicus); C. A. Behr, Aristides: Orations, v 1, Panathenaic Oration and In Defense of Oratory, 1973. ABOUT—G. Misch, History of Autobiography in Antiquity, 1950; A. J. Festugière, Personal Religion Among the Greeks, 1954; F. W. Lenz, Aristeidesstudien, 1964; J. Bleicken, Der Preis des Aelius Aristides auf das römische Weltreich, 1966; C. A. Behr, Aelius Aristides and the Sacred Tales, 1968; G. W. Bowersock, Greek Sophists in the Roman Empire, 1969; G. Kennedy, The Art of Rhetoric in the Roman World, 1972; G. Michenaud and J. Dierkens, Les rêves dans Les discours sacrés d'Aelius Aristide, 1972.

ARISTIDES OF MILETUS (southwestern Asia Minor), Greek short story writer, originated or developed around 100 B.C. a characteristic late Greek (Hellenistic) version of the short narrative that had enjoyed great favor from the time of Herodotus onward. These stories were the Milesian Tales *(Milesiaka),* named after Aristides' birthplace. Only one fragment attributable to his own authorship survives (it happens to be a brief passage about the *dermestes,* a skin-eating worm), but the principal features of the genre can be reconstructed to some extent from his imitators and adapters. The Milesian Tales presumably developed from the custom of storytelling as a social accomplishment in Hellenistic society, in which private and club dinner parties were entertained by the recitation of such tales. At times, they may possibly have included edifying stories of true love and innocent adventure, but the dominant type of anecdote was of a titillating, sexual character. Aristides of Miletus apparently incorporated a spicy selection of such narratives into a literary framework and became known to posterity as the most famous editor of such collections, although other collections, presumably of a similar type, also existed.

The erotic nature of Aristides' *Milesiaka* can be gauged by what we know of their Latin adaptations by the annalist Lucius Cornelius Sisenna in the early first century B.C., which greatly shocked the Parthians when they found copies in the baggage of captured Roman officers in 53. Further evidence can be gathered from the Milesian Tales inserted as separate short stories in the *Satyricon* of Petronius and the *Metamorphoses* of Apuleius, both in Latin—the most famous is Petronius' "Widow of Ephesus." The basic theme of such tales, developed
ar is ti′ dēz   mi lē′ tus

with thoroughgoing irony and cynicism, is that no man's honesty and no woman's chastity is proof against corruption and assault. But these points are only made after each story has begun against a background of true, chaste love which makes fun of the starry-eyed atmosphere of contemporary romantic novels. Then, as the plots develop, sex takes over; and it is often diversified by spooky magic and sorcery and by bizarre adventure. Thus the collections of Milesian Tales interwove several different threads of the various narrative techniques that had been handed down by the storytelling tradition.

A later work called the *Loves (Erotes)*, attributed mistakenly to Lucian, depicts its author as a listener to lubricious anecdotes narrated by others. From this it may be inferred that he was telling, in the first person, stories that he had allegedly heard from other narrators, and this may have been the practice of Aristides. In view of the generic name of Miletus, which was attached to these tales, we should perhaps assume that all or most of them were concerned with personalities or situations relating to that city. There seems no justification for supposing that Aristides combined his stories into full-length romances or novels.

ABOUT—S. Trenkner, The Greek Novella in the Classical Period, 1958; R. Reitzenstein, Hellenistische Wundererzählungen, 2nd ed., 1963; B. E. Perry, The Ancient Romances, 1967; P. G. Walsh, The Roman Novel, 1970.

ARISTOPHANES, Greek poet and comic dramatist, was born between 457 and 445 B.C. and died shortly before 385. He was the son of an Athenian, Philippus, who perhaps owned some property on the island of Aegina. The leading exponent of the Athenian "Old Comedy," Aristophanes spent two-thirds of his career as a dramatist under the shadow of the Peloponnesian War against Sparta (431–404), during which he wrote freely against leading members of the Athenian government and in support of the pacifist cause. In particular, he violently assailed the politician and demagogue Cleon,

ar is tof´ å nēz

who in retaliation prosecuted him, apparently without success, on charges of alien birth and high treason. Aristophanes continued his attacks and managed to survive two oligarchic revolutions and two restorations of democratic rule.

In the *Acharnians* (425), a character named Dicaeopolis (Good Government), a countryperson, is determined to force the Assembly of Acharnae (a place near Athens) to discuss negotiations with Sparta. Amphitheus offers to go there and make peace but is forcibly silenced. However, Dicaeopolis sends him to Sparta all the same to make a private peace for himself and his family. After Amphitheus has returned, Dicaeopolis is about to celebrate the vintage festival when he is attacked by a chorus of Acharnian charcoal-burners representing the war party. He wins half of them over, but the rest call in General Lamachus to lead them against him. The commander, however, cuts an unimpressive figure. Dicaeopolis offers to trade with anyone and everyone—with the single exception of the Spartans themselves—and men from Megara and Boeotia come to do business with him. Heralds now summon Lamachus to go to the war and invite Dicaeopolis to attend a wine party. At the play's end, Lamachus hobbles back wounded, and Dicaeopolis, having won a prize for drinking, staggers in with a pretty young woman on each arm.

In the *Knights* (424), the knights form the chorus of the play. Two slaves of crotchety old Demos (the people), masquerading as the Athenian generals Nicias and Demosthenes, complain of the nasty behavior of Demos' new favorite, a Paphlagonian tanner, who stands for the Athenian demagogue Cleon. But the generals, having learned from an oracle that the tanner will soon be supplanted as favorite by a sausage seller, sponsor a man of that profession whom they judge to be sufficiently ignorant and impudent to become a national leader. The sausage seller engages the tanner in a contest of abuse, appealing to the Council and trying to win Demos' favor by bribery. The tanner, like Cleon, claims credit for Athens' victory over the Spartans at Pylos, but the sausage seller (now named as Agoracritus, choice of the marketplace) finally triumphs. He rejuvenates Demos by stewing him in a pot, and the old man emerges determined to abolish innovations and restore old-fashioned ways, resisting the wiles of politicians who make cheap appeals to the people.

In the *Clouds* (423), old Strepsiades (Twister) is ruined by his son Pheidippides' passion for horse racing and proposes to send him to school next door, where Socrates and Chaerephon conduct a Phrontisterion (Think School). Here are taught various fantastic studies—in particular, two ways of thinking, a good way and a bad way, which can make false arguments sound plausible. This second line of thought so appeals to Strepsiades, who feels it will help him to cheat his importunate creditors, that he seeks admission to the school himself, in place of his son. Socrates, descending from a flying basket, enrolls him as a pupil, invoking the Ether and Clouds (the chorus), who are declared to be the only deities he recognizes. Strepsiades coaxes his son to come and study too, and Unjust and Just Reasoning engage in a dispute over which shall undertake the youth's teaching. The former wins, and equipped with her instruction, Pheidippides beats up his father, offering a "logical" justification; whereupon the indignant Strepsiades leads his slaves in attack on the School and sets it on fire.

In the *Wasps* (422), the old Athenian Philocleon (Cleon-Lover) is so fond of jury service that his son Bdelycleon (Cleon-Hater) has had to place him under detention in order to keep him away from the courts. After several unsuccessful attempts to break out, Philocleon tries to join the chorus of old jurymen, dressed as wasps, who denounce Bdelycleon as a blasphemer and a collaborator with the Spartan foe. Father and son engage in a farcical debate on the juror's role in society. Then the old man, deceived into voting for an acquittal for the first time in his life, collapses when he discovers the trick that has been played on him. Bdelycleon comforts him by promising that henceforward he will lead a life of pure pleasure, but Philocleon, at a banquet, behaves deplorably, getting drunk, insulting his fellow guests, and manhandling passersby on his way home. His son hustles him back into the house, but he reappears and breaks into a comic dance, in which the chorus join him.

The Peace (421), produced at a time when Athens and Sparta wanted to put an end to their conflict, begins with two slaves of Trygaeus feeding dung cakes to an enormous smelly beetle, on whose back, they explain, their master intends to climb to heaven in order to pray to Zeus for peace. Trygaeus himself appears, riding upon the beetle, on his way up to the mansion of Zeus, where Hermes informs him that the Gods have washed their hands of Greece, since its inhabitants repeatedly failed to seize the opportunities for peace that were offered them. War has shut Peace up in a cave, from which the chorus of farmers, egged on by Trygaeus, rescues her and her female attendants Harvest and Holiday. In the company of Harvest and Holiday, Trygaeus flies home. He is allotted the former as his bride, but the premarriage sacrifice to Peace is interrupted by a soothsayer who objects that the time for Peace to be set free has not yet come. He also tries to cadge some meat but is shooed away. A sickle maker is welcomed to the nuptial feast, but arms manufacturers are driven from the scene. Finally, all join in the wedding song.

The Birds (414) presents a chorus of jackdaws and ravens who guide Peithetaerus (The Persuader) and Euelpides (The Optimist) to find Epops, the hoopoe, in the hope that it will guide them to a better land than Attica, which has become intolerable. Peithetaerus forms a scheme for a utopian midair commonwealth of birds that will defy gods and mortals alike; their state is to be called Nephelococcygia (Cloudcuckooland). After would-be interferers from the earth—including a poet, some bureaucrats, and various other undesirables—have been hustled away, Poseidon, Heracles, and Triballus (a clownish barbarian) come as delegates from heaven. Peithetaerus agrees that the birds will cooperate provided he is given Basileia (Sovereignty) as his wife. His terms are accepted, and the play ends with a joyful marriage procession.

In *Lysistrata* (Disband-the-Army, 411), the main character has devised a plan to save war-torn Athens and summons, from all parts of Greece, women who want peace,

41

like herself. Her scheme is to deprive the men of sexual relations until the fighting is brought to an end. Some of the women seize the Acropolis, where a chorus of old men is prevented from smoking them out by a chorus of old women who arrive carrying water. A magistrate, who appears with four Scythian policemen to take money from the treasury for the sailors, is put to rout, but the women begin to weaken. However, the panting Cinesias is sexually teased and frustrated by his wife Myrrhine, and news of similar action is brought from Sparta by men who come as its envoys. Lysistrata scolds them and their Athenian counterparts for fighting among themselves when the armies of Greece's foreign foes are nearby; and she invites them all to the Acropolis to be entertained by the women. After they have eaten and drunk well, each man dances and sings with his wife to celebrate the restoration of peace.

The *Thesmophoriazusae* (the chorus of women at their private festival of Demeter and Persephone, 411) displays the tragedian Euripides in front of the house of his fellow poet Agathon, who is heard informing his old father-in-law Mnesilochus that these women are planning revenge upon him for his unflattering portrayals of the female sex. Agathon is thought suitable to spy on them because of his effeminate appearance, but he refuses to do so; Mnesilochus, however, obliges, in drag, and speaks up in Agathon's defense. Discovering Mnesilochus is really a man, the angry women deliver a vigorously feminist harangue, but Euripides, after the failure of several farcical attempts (which give Aristophanes the opportunity to comment on some of Euripides' dramatic techniques) manages to rescue the old man by promising the women he will not offend them again and then getting young women to lure the Scythian policeman who has taken Mnesilochus in charge. When the policeman realizes he has been tricked and starts in pursuit of the fugitives, the women give him misleading directions, showing that they now regard Euripides as their friend.

In the *Frogs,* which won the first prize at the Lenaean festival in 405, Dionysus, the patron god of drama, is on his way to the underworld, accompanied by his slave Xanthias, who is mounted on an ass. As Dionysus tells Heracles, at whose house he pauses for directions, the aim of his journey is to bring back Euripides, who has recently died. The ferryman Charon takes Dionysus across the infernal lake (making him row), but Xanthias, being a slave, has to walk around it instead. The Chorus of Frogs, offstage, keeps up a croak of "Brekekekek koax koax" but stops when Dionysus joins in. After they have disembarked, another Chorus of Dionysian initiates sings a hymn. After a series of comic and knockabout scenes Aeacus, the doorkeeper of Pluto's palace, takes Dionysus and Xanthias off to his master for interrogation.

In the *Ecclesiazusae* (Women Assemblymen, 392), the women have borrowed their husbands' clothes and put on false beards in order to go to the Assembly, where their leader Praxagora will propose that the government be handed over to women. Her husband Blepyrus, wearing a woman's dress because he cannot find his own clothing, is told by a neighbor that the Assembly has given in to the feminine coup but catches Praxagora stealing into the house; whereupon she outlines her projects for reform, according to which property of every kind, including spouses, must be held in common, and all men and women must make love to ugly partners before they are allowed attractive ones. Then, after the Herald has bidden everybody come to a public banquet, three old women try to enforce the new decree by fighting over a young man, whom one of them succeeds in tearing away from his girl. Finally, everyone flocks to the feast, dancing and singing.

In the *Plutus* (388), Chremylus, with his slave Cario, has consulted the Delphic oracle about how to make his son into a complete rascal so that he can be sure of getting on well in life. Told by the oracle to attach himself to the first person he meets after emerging from the shrine, he accosts a ragged old man who turns out to be the god of wealth, Plutus (blinded by Zeus—which is why good people are allowed to be poor, since he cannot identify them). Chremylus and a friend take Plutus to the Temple of the healing god Asclepius, driving away the huge, ferocious figure of Penia (Poverty), who complains that they are plotting to eliminate her, although she is really more useful than Plutus. The god regains his sight, declares that he will never leave the virtuous again, and enters Chremylus' house, which he fills with good things. In come a series of persons of different types, whose lives have been changed by this sudden influx of wealth, and the play ends with a procession to Athena's treasury on the Acropolis, where Plutus is henceforward to make his home.

Aristophanes, the only exponent of the Athenian Old Comedy who has left us complete plays, belongs to the later stages of the movement. In his day, comic plays were performed at Athens annually at the festivals of Dionysus, the great Dionysia and the Lenaea, at which occasions five poets competed, each producing a single play. Aristophanes' comedies normally contained (with some variation) the following parts: a prologue or exposition; the entry of the chorus *(parados);* a dispute *(agon)* between two characters constituting the principal theme of the play; a *parabasis* in which the chorus addressed the audience (the *parabasis* was composed of a number of sections, including a satiric speech on current affairs, known as the *epirrhema);* a number of further episodes separated by songs delivered by the chorus; and the concluding scene *(exodos),* in which the dominant note is one of rejoicing, generally leading up to a feast or a wedding or both.

The plots were built around a simple story or fable, imaginary, novel, entertaining, and satirical, involving a dispute on some subject of contemporary and current interest, in the course of which the dramatist made his own opinion known. In general, the characters tended to be little more than caricatures, or symbols, and were often actually described as personifications of abstract ideas. Yet some were taken from real contemporary life, and men prominent in the society of the day were selected for parody, ridicule, and vilification. The targets of Aristophanes' humor include notable politicians (Pericles, Cleon, Hyperbolus), poets (Euripides), philosophers (Socrates), scientists, and musicians. Aristophanes often makes fun of

cultural innovators (although the construction of his plays shows that he was one of them himself), whereas the characters with whom he expresses sympathy are usually people who just want to be left to enjoy themselves in traditional ways. Even they, however, are often depicted as self-seeking and ruthless.

Aristophanes' moral and social lessons are never clear-cut, since it was his purpose above all to stimulate and amuse, rather than to preach. Nevertheless, he clearly emerges as a supporter of the country party —the farmers and people on the land—and a vigorous adversary of the war policy from which they were the principal sufferers. The essential spirit of Old Comedy is the protest of ordinary men and women against all who are in some way stronger than they are. And, by this same token, the gods are treated with remarkable irreverence and often depicted as dishonest and ludicrous, although the reality of their power and the desirability that the community should give them due worship is assumed without question.

The acting parts in Old Comedy, both male and female, were taken by men, as in tragedy. The actors, who were normally four in number (sometimes there were supernumeraries), wore grotesque masks, and their padded robes included artificial exaggerations of stomach and phallus. The chorus, likewise masked and decked out in fantastic costumes, included twenty-four members, often divided into two semi-choruses (in some cases, one purporting to consist of men and one of women; though once again the performers were all, in fact, male). Although dances were an important element in their program, the chorus was also of primary importance in the plots of Old Comedy. In the central *parabasis* of Aristophanes' plays, the chorus, when it spoke directly to the audience, often maintained its own dramatic role and sometimes acted as mouthpiece for the poet. Its function, very often, was to excite and arouse the disputants rather than pacify them (which was what the tragic chorus often tried to do); but finally it sided with the "hero."

Aristophanes has an exceptionally keen ear for the absurd and pompous and displays a comic indecency, relating to sex and excretion, in which no holds are barred. Despite this, however, he is a master of lyrical poetry of every mood, solemn, delicate, or humorous; and his dialogue is vivid, colorful, and imaginative. A greater dramatist, evidently, than the other chief representatives of Old Comedy, Eupolis and Cratinus, he developed and intellectualized the genre, gradually transforming it into a new and brilliant art.

Moreover, Aristophanes' last two surviving plays, the *Ecclesiazusae* and *Plutus,* are generally regarded as specimens not of the Old but of the Middle Comedy, of which Antiphanes and Alexis were other exponents. In the Middle Comedy the *parabasis* disappeared, and the chorus gradually became totally different in character. Instead of the earlier choral lyrics composed by the playwright as integral parts of the play, pieces produced by other writers were employed. No attempt was made to preserve these pieces, and their place in the text was merely marked in manuscripts by the word *chorus.* Moreover, the Middle Comedy abandoned the tradition of boisterous attacks on politicians, and there is a new style of quiet, witty dialogue of the kind found later in the New Comedy of Menander, some of whose typical stock characters, too, were already anticipated in these last surviving plays of Aristophanes (and in others of even later composition that are not extant—for titles see below under WORKS).

Aristophanes' attacks on contemporary developments do not seem to have had much influence on the course of events, but his comedies were meticulously studied throughout the course of antiquity and became the subject of extensive ancient commentaries. They formed the foundation upon which the entire comic drama of Europe is based.

WORKS—Lost plays: Aeolosikon (two versions), Amphiaraus, Anagyrus, Babylonians, Banqueters, Centaur (or Dramas), Farmers, Friers, Gerytades, Heroes, Lemnian Women, Merchantmen, Phoenician Women, Polyidus, Rehearsal, Seasons, Seat Grabbers, Storks, Telemessias, Three-Phallus Man. There were also earlier versions of the Clouds and Plutus, and later versions of Peace and the Thesmophoriazusae. After 388, the Aeolosikon and Cocalus (foreshadowing Menan-

der) were produced by Aristophanes' son Aratus. Of doubtful authenticity are Dramas, Islands, Poetry, and Shipwreck of Dionysius.

EDITIONS—J. Van Leeuwen, 1893–1906. Wasps, Acharnians, Clouds: W. J. M. Starkie, 1897, 1909, 1911. Knights: R. A. Neil, 1901. Wasps: D. M. MacDowell, 1971. Peace: M. Platnauer, 1964. Frogs: L. Radermacher, 2nd ed., 1954; W. B. Stanford, 2nd ed., 1963. Ecclesiazusae: R. G. Ussher, 1972. Plutus: C. (K.) van Holzinger, 1940. Scholia: W. J. W. Koster, 1960–64. *Translations*—B. B. Rogers (Loeb ed.), 1924; M. Hadas, 1962; D. Barrett and A. H. Sommerstein (Penguin ed.), 1964, 1973; P. Dickinson, 1970; W. Arrowsmith, R. Lattimore, D. Parker (Mentor Greek Comedy), 1970, 1973. For translations of individual plays *see* A. M. W. Green, Classics in Translation: A Selective Bibliography (1930–76), 1976.

ABOUT—V. Ehrenberg, The People of Aristophanes, 2nd ed., 1951; T. B. L. Webster, Greek Theatre Production, 1956; H. J. Newiger, Metaphor und Allegorie, 1957, *and* (as ed.) Aristophanes und die alte Komödie, 1975; C. F. Russo, Aristofane autore di teatro, 1962; J. Taillardat, Les images d'Aristophane, 1962; L. E. Lord, Aristophanes: His Plays and His Influence, 1963; C. H. Whitman, Aristophanes and the Comic Hero, 1964; E. de Carli, Aristofane e la sofistica, 1971; K. J. Dover, Aristophanic Comedy, 1972; W. J. W. Koster and N. G. Wilson, Scholia in Aristophanem, 1975; R. von Scheliha, Die Komödien des Aristophanes in sieben Vorträgen interpretiert, 1975; C. W. Dearden, The Stage of Aristophanes, 1976; M. Landfester, Handlungsverlauf und Komik in den frühen Komödien des Aristophanes, 1977.

ARISTOPHANES OF BYZANTIUM,

Greek scholarly writer, was born in about 257 B.C. and died in 180. He studied in Alexandria and in 195 or 194 succeeded Eratosthenes as director of its library. His very extensive learning included textual criticism, grammar, linguistics, and literature, all pursued on a massive scale and with considerable thoroughness. It is in the career of Aristophanes that scholarship first has an autonomous existence, an activity no longer conducted by men who were poets or scientists at the same time but carried on solely in its own right.

His editions of the *Iliad* and *Odyssey,* though later eclipsed in their turn by his pupil Aristarchus, marked a substantial improvement upon the endeavors of Zenodotus and Rhianus and displayed a new degree of critical boldness and acuteness, even if the methods he used were still somewhat arbitrary. In criticizing the text, Aristophanes made use of symbols to indicate his doubts

ar is tof´ à nēz   bi zan´ ti um

concerning the authenticity of Homeric verses. He also wrote at least ten books containing editions and commentaries of the works of Hesiod, Alcman, and Alcaeus, although only relatively few fragments of his commentaries survive today. Moreover, Aristophanes produced the pioneer edition of Pindar—in whom the Alexandrians were deeply interested—collecting all his surviving poems into seventeen books, and producing in the process the first Greek lyric texts to be presented with their proper metrical divisions: though, on the debit side, he was probably responsible for the loss of the music that had accompanied this and other Greek poetry. He also wrote definitive works on Attic tragedy, which laid the foundations of all subsequent editions and commentaries. Like other Alexandrian scholars, he was able to comment on Aeschylus on the basis of a personal knowledge of almost all his plays, before serious textual losses had occurred. He also had at his disposal texts of 130 of the tragedies of Sophocles (of which 7 were reckoned spurious). He probably compiled a complete standard edition of Euripides' works as well, and the first critical edition of the Athenian comic poet Aristophanes. In addition, his commentaries on such plays were prefaced by introductions, now lost, on which were based the metrical introductory notes *(hypotheseis)* that have come down to us.

He also wrote a treatise about the New Comedy dramatist Menander, who was "imitated by life," he said, and was regarded by him, after Homer alone, as the greatest of all the poets Greece had ever produced. Moreover, the arrangement of the dialogues of Plato in trilogies is also attributed to Aristophanes, although he did not, as is sometimes believed, compose an edition of them. It would also seem that he inaugurated the lists of leading classical authors on which the classification of writers in the Alexandrian canon was founded. His *glossai* (or *lexeis*) were classifications of certain terms in Greek dialects, with examples of their literary usage; although, in common with his other works, they are now lost (except for a fragment), they exercised widespread influence on subsequent authors. In writing on grammatical matters Aristophanes (or possibly one of his fellow scholars) may well have encouraged the use of more punctuation than before, and it is also possible that he was responsible for two other innovations: the introduction of the accents and breathings still used in modern Greek and in ancient Greek texts, and the establishment (in his treatise *On Analogy*) of rules for declensions, on the basis of similarities of forms. This latter procedure contradicted the work *On Anomaly* by the Stoic Chrysippus, who had preferred to use visible manifestations of irregularity as a criterion; and owing to this difference of opinion a prolonged controversy was launched. Aristophanes was also one of a number of Alexandrian authors who collected proverbs for literary use, producing two books on the subject in verse and four in prose. This activity of proverb-collecting (paroemiography) went back to Aristotle, as did another, the study of out-of-the-way marvels (paradoxography), on which Aristophanes produced a work titled *On Animals* that survives in excerpts preserved by Byzantine scholars.

ABOUT—J. E. Sandys, A History of Classical Scholarship, v 1, 3rd ed., 1921; R. Pfeiffer, History of Classical Scholarship From the Beginnings to the End of the Hellenistic Age, 1968.

ARISTOTLE, Greek philosopher and scientist, was born in 384 and died in 322 B.C. His birthplace was the Ionian colony of Stagirus (later Stagira) in Chalcidice (Macedonia). The modern Stavros, on the Strymonic Gulf, may stand on its site. His father Nicomachus, who died when Aristotle was only a boy, belonged to the medical guild of the Asclepiadae and was the physician and friend of King Amyntas II of Macedonia. When he was seventeen, Aristotle was sent by his guardian, Proxenus, to study in Plato's Academy at Athens, where he remained for twenty years, first as a pupil and then as a researcher and teacher. In 347, however, he and Xenocrates, another leading member of the Academy, left Athens, either because the city was at war with Macedonia, then under the rule of Amyntas' son Philip II or because Speusippus, who had just succeeded

ar' is tot 'l

45

ARISTOTLE

ARISTOTLE

Plato as director of the school, seemed to them to be "turning philosophy into mathematics." The two men moved to the princedom of Atarneus in Mysia (northwestern Asia Minor), ruled by Hermias. In the town of Assos, Hermias presided over a small circle of Platonists, which Aristotle joined, marrying Hermias' niece and adopted daughter Pythias, who became the mother of his daughter and probably also of his son Nicomachus. He spent two years (345–343) at Mytilene on the neighboring island of Lesbos and then moved to Mieza, near the Macedonian capital Pella, to supervise the education of Philip II's thirteen-year-old son Alexander the Great. When Alexander became regent for his father in 340, Aristotle probably retired to Stagirus.

In 335, however, Aristotle returned to Athens. He began teaching, sponsoring research programs, and organizing collections and a library in the Lyceum, a grove sacred to Apollo Lyceius and to the Muses, in which there was a public gymnasium. His school (probably not established as a formal institution until after his death) was known as the Peripatetic School owing to the covered court *(peripatos)* that the building included. During Aristotle's period of residence in Athens, his wife died, and he took a mistress Herpyllis to live with him. At this time he enjoyed the friendship and protection of Antipater, whom Alexander, on departing for the East, had left as gover-

nor of Macedonia and Greece. However, after Alexander's death in 323, when the anti-Macedonian party at Athens regained the ascendancy, Aristotle was prosecuted on a charge of impiety and left the city, handing over the directorship of his school to Theophrastus. He then settled at Chalcis in Euboea, where he fell ill of a digestive complaint and died in the following year. He was described as a bald, thin-legged man with small eyes and a mocking expression. He was noted for the care with which he dressed.

His writings were of colossal range and dimensions. One of the many subjects to which he made great contributions was logic, which he did not regard as a science but as a general preparation for the study of all the sciences—designed for the purpose of attaining the truth. Aristotle's *Organon (Instrument, Tool)* is the most significant collection of writings on this subject that has come down to us from the ancient world. It consists of six treatises. *Categories* mainly comprises a discussion of the ten classes into which all predicables can be divided. *On Interpretation (De Interpretatione, Peri Hermeneias)* might more accurately be entitled *On Predication* since it deals with the nature of the affirmation of truths. The *Prior* and *Posterior Analytics,* the most important sections of the *Organon,* are both devoted to formal logic and the theory of knowledge. The analysis and discussion of a proposition are the themes of *Topics,* to which a monograph named *Refutations in the Manner of the Sophists (De Sophisticis Elenchis)* forms an appendix.

Researches on ultimate questions of existence were classified as primary philosophy by Aristotle himself, but his fourteen books of studies on these themes (including certain material that is probably of multiple authorship) were given the designation of *Metaphysica (After Physics)* by subsequent editors. Aristotle sees in the universe a hierarchy of existences, each imparting form and change to the one next below it. The prime Unmoved Mover at the apex is identified with God. His work *Physics,* which in ancient times was known as *Lectures on Nature,* examines the components of things that exist by nature (which he sees as "an innate impulse to movement"), discussing basic concepts such as matter, form, and time and space, and leading up to the same conclusions about the divinity as were reached in the *Metaphysics. On the Heavens,* in four books, deals with the movement of heavenly and sublunary bodies, while the two books that logically come next, *On Generation and Corruption,* describe the cyclical sequence of transformations that Aristotle detected in the evolution of the universe. *Meteorology,* in four books (the last of uncertain authenticity), deals mainly with atmospheric phenomena but also is concerned with meteors, comets, and the nature of the sea.

A series of works on biological themes includes the *History of* (or rather, *Inquiry Into*) *Animals,* in four books, a classification of facts regarding animal life; a four-book monograph *On the Parts (Members) of Animals;* five further books constituting *On the Reproduction of Animals;* and one book, *On the Locomotion of Animals.* An important three-book study *On the Soul* crowns the series by defining the internal vital principle that endows bodies with life. This element does not, in Aristotle's view, survive physical death, although a factor of active reason inherent in it is regarded by him as lasting and immortal. These psychological studies are pursued in further investigations grouped in a series known later as the *Parva Naturalia,* which includes *On Length and Brevity of Life, On Life and Death, On Youth and Old Age, On Perception and Perceptibles, On Memory and Recollection, On Sleep and Waking, On Dreams,* and *On Divination by Dreams.* There is also a treatise entitled *On Respiration.*

The work entitled *Politics* deals with political science, seen by Aristotle as the supreme practical study. It approaches the theme from the standpoint of the city-state, which he assumed to provide the fullest possible life for its individual citizens. The eight books of this work (of which the order is disputed) discuss the following topics: the definition and structure of the state and society; the ideal form of state; civic virtue, and a classification of constitutions; their various types, together with an assessment of their respective merits; revolutions and how to avoid them; democracies and oligarchies; education in the ideal state. Aristotle's view that morality is a branch of politics in the wider sense of the term is made explicit in the ten books of the *Nicomachean Ethics,* named after his son (who had perhaps edited his father's lectures). For the most part, this work is a study of the end (the Good) to which conduct should be directed; Aristotle identifies the end with the highest happiness, or rather well-being *(eudaimonia),* which he finds not in public activities after all but in the contemplative life. The shorter *Eudemian Ethics,* in seven books, covers a lot of the same ground, though with different emphases, and may represent an earlier edition of the same lecture-course compiled by his pupil Eudemus.

Aristotle's treatise *Rhetoric* deals with the means of persuasion. The first of its three books discusses the logical proofs based on dialectic, the second turns to proofs that make use of psychological and ethical factors, and the third presents a review of matters relating to style, arrangement, and figures of speech. *Poetics* is a study of poetry, the earliest surviving work of any writer devoted entirely to literary criticism. Originally, it dealt with epic, tragedy, and comedy, but the work as it has come down to us is mainly an analysis of tragedy, which Aristotle defines as "an imitation of an action that is serious, complete and of a certain magnitude...through pity and fear effecting the proper purgation [or purification] of the emotions."

Aristotle divided the sciences into three classes; the theoretical, aimed at knowledge of the truth; the practical, devoted to the conduct of the good human life; and the productive, dedicated to the making of useful and beautiful things. He wrote studies of exceptional and permanent value under each of these headings.

There has been a great deal of argument about the degree of Aristotle's opposition to Plato's thought and the extent to which, in the course of time, this opposition increased or diminished. The essential difference between the two thinkers lay in Aristotle's rejection of the Forms (Ideas) that according to Plato represented the unchanging reality behind the changing appearance of the world and its contents as perceived by our senses. Plato's fundamental distinction between what is perceived and what is real failed to appeal to Aristotle because of his predominant interest in concrete, individual objects that are in fact perceived through the senses. Aristotle was prepared to accept Forms as characteristics of what our senses perceive, but he refused to see them as separate, substantial, transcendental beings on their own account.

He was left, then, with the problem of defining what were the stable and unchanging realities existent in this world of change. It was in trying to answer that question that he arrived at the fundamental concepts of his philosophical system: Substance, Form and Matter, Act and Potency. A substance is simply a real thing that exists. Its form (used, as we have seen, in a sense different from Plato's) is its inward structure—the stable, permanent, knowable, definable element in things. A better name for what he called matter might have been Possibility, for this is the element that makes change possible, the factor of changeability in things: whereas Form is a thing's actuality, the Matter that has not yet taken on a particular Form is its potentiality. Everything (maintains Aristotle) that exists in the material, sense-perceived world not only is something in itself but that something has in it the possibility of becoming something else. This doctrine of actual and potential being—Act and Potency—is central to his thinking and capable of the widest application.

Like Plato, Aristotle wants to know both why and how things happen; however, he is more interested than Plato in the "how." He classifies these hows and whys into four categories (known somewhat misleadingly as the Four Causes), of which the last and most important is the Final Cause, the end or purpose for which something comes into being and the reason for its existence. He believed, as Plato had believed before him, that everything exists for an end, and a good one at that. In contrast to Plato, he saw a purposefulness in things and believed that a natural innate impulse prompts things to try to realize their Form as perfectly as possible. He also insisted that future events—including the actions of human beings—are not completely determined.

Aristotle envisaged the universe as a hierarchically ordered construction, containing at its middle point the spherical earth, the region of change and decay. Immediately surrounding the earth is the sublunary atmosphere, beyond which comes the vast machinery of the divine, celestial spheres that bring about the motion of the universe and form its most vital part. Following Plato, he held that these spheres rotate. But what is it that makes them rotate, what is the ultimate principle of movement and change? To answer this question is the duty of metaphysics, which studies the primary kinds of being. Aristotle does not seem to have felt that any supreme directing intelligence is involved in the universe; his thought is not God-centered, but cosmos-centered. He postulates as the cause and creator of the continuous, unending motion of the world a First Unmoved Mover and Creator, a substance that is eternal, immaterial, and unchanging. Yet this was not the only Unmoved Mover, for he believed that fifty-five others exist as well, producing the distinctive motions of the sun, moon, and stars and comprising in their entirety a single ordered hierarchy in which the First Mover stands at the apex.

In Aristotle's extremely important psychological analyses, the human soul, the microcosm, is seen as an ordered unity mirroring the macrocosm of the universe, with a transcendent intellectual principle standing at the summit of its structure. What he means by soul (in his treatise the *De Anima*) is the same as Form in things and is the principle of life and being, immaterial but intimately united with the material body, upon which it operates by means of its generative and life-giving heat *(pneuma)*. The three powers of the soul-in-body are nutrition, sensation, and thought. In moving from sense-perception to the formation of concepts by thought, Aristotle detected two intervening stages. The first is common or universal sense, which is sense-perception operating in a generalized way. The second (not always clearly distinguishable from the foregoing) is the image-making faculty which constructs mind-pictures *(phantas-*

mata) of the appearances revealed to us by the senses.

Passing from the mental to the moral processes of individuals, Aristotle sought in his ethical investigations to find out what human beings *are for*,—to identify the functions for which nature intends them. He traditionally assumed (though without satisfactory demonstration) that there is one ultimate end or good—synonymous with the Well-Being (or happiness) of humankind—which he sees as an activity of the highest or rational part of the soul, peculiar to human beings. This Well-Being can only consist of the highest kind of (or rational) activity of the mind, which is what Aristotle means by Contemplation. He hails it as the source of the greatest and purest pleasures, conferring a life more like that of the gods than of human beings (though his ideal, the Superior or Great-Souled Man, is likely to seem self-satisfied and pompous to modern readers). Aristotle interprets virtue or goodness, achieved by the deliberate choice of the will, as a mean, or middle course, but a mean that must be assessed in relation to ourselves—that is to say, not by any universal standard of mediocrity but by assessing the right strength and mixture of qualities that is suitable for each individual person.

Since he makes the individual human being the central feature of his philosophy, it is not surprising that Aristotle had a passionate interest in biology, which he made into his key science, as mathematics had been for Plato; and Aristotle was a biologist of marked originality and genius. Yet for him, as for Plato once again, the study of individuals is only part of the study of the society and community to which they belong. Thus, the classifications in his biological researches served to some extent as a model for his political thought; and, indeed, the whole field of ethics, as we have seen, is treated as a part and branch of Politics, the science governing the complete life of individuals living together in a city-state—which Aristotle still identifies (despite the transformation of the Greek world by Alexander the Great) as the natural and best form of self-sufficient society, containing everything needed to enable its citizens to lead the good life. In this ideal community, agricultural laborers and artisans are to be excluded from citizenship because manual labor makes a person banausic (vulgar) and leaves no time for a citizen's duties. All citizens must participate personally in the Assembly's lawmaking, must know each other personally, and must be able to hear the announcements of a single Assembly crier; so the state has to be small. It ought to combine features of oligarchy and democracy, keeping power in the hands of the stable, moderately well-to-do upper class. Extensive attention is devoted to the relations between slaves and their masters; and Aristotle declares that certain races are "natural slaves," although, in some slight measure of compensation, he does not regard it as justifiable that anyone at all *outside* this category should be reduced to slavery—nor may Greek enslave Greek.

He agrees with Plato that the citizen's education is of central importance. It is by this means that the city-state fulfills its proper function of making individuals good: they must be given an education that starts at birth or even before and that trains reason, emotions, and bodies alike. The purpose of this instruction should be predominantly ethical, directed at producing the very best type of citizen, excellent as ruler and subject alike.

The influence Aristotle's philosophy exerted on subsequent generations was incalculable, because of the instruments of inquiry he forged with such remarkable effectiveness and himself used in order to make enormous personal additions to knowledge, giving a decisive stimulus to the entire range of philosophical and scientific studies. Indeed, it seems likely that no other man has ever made and prompted important contributions to so many kinds of learning by his own single endeavors. His Peripatetic school evolved into a community of scholars and researchers stressing the naturalistic and scientific as opposed to the purely philosophical elements in his thought.

It was believed, until recently, that his major works remained unknown until the first century B.C., but this supposition has been weakened by recent studies, which have shown that borrowings of third century schools, Stoics and Epicureans, from

49

his system are more extensive than had been realized. The substantial Aristotelian element in later Platonism (in the time of the Roman empire) greatly influenced the earliest Christian thinkers. Subsequently, his teaching—made available through Latin versions of Arabic translations—became especially prominent in the works of the schoolmen, culminating in the lectures and *Summa* of St. Thomas Aquinas (c. 1225–74). Aristotelian philosophy was one of the principal subjects of medieval study; and later, too, Francis Bacon (1561–1626) adopted Aristotle's Four Causes. Very often, Aristotle's doctrines have percolated so thoroughly into our inherited ways of thinking that we adhere to them automatically and without recalling their source.

Moreover, his writings on literary and linguistic subjects had an after-life of their own. His study *Rhetoric* was long regarded as a major authority, and his *Poetics* attained great fame, exerting particular influence on the seventeenth century French classical playwrights, who believed that their doctrine of dramatic unities derived from Aristotle, though in fact this is due to a misunderstanding (since his treatise only insists on the necessity of the unity of action).

These were only a few of the multitudinous subjects illuminated by his passion for research. His intellect displayed a kind of inspired commonsense which rejects untenable extremes. He was also remarkable for a love of orderliness and tidiness, to which scientists and philosophers owe the classifications and definitions they are accustomed to using as the framework for their studies. Moreover, this orderliness was responsible for the development of a philosophical terminology which derives more from him than from anyone else—including, for example, the following antitheses: universal and particular, subject and attribute, premise and conclusion, potentiality and actuality.

WORKS—The Protrepticus, an exhortation to the study of philosophy, is lost, and so are extensive works apparently started by Aristotle and continued by his pupils and successors, including the Didascaliae (list of plays successful at the Dionysia and the Lenaea and a list of Olympic and Pythian victors), collections of treatises on rhetoric and other subjects, and a great collection of constitutions (of which only part of the Constitution of

Athens, written c. 329–328, survives). As stated above, some also regard parts of the Metaphysics as belonging to this category of multiple authorship; and the last book of Meteorology may not be by Aristotle at all. Other works wrongly attributed to him include: Magna Moralia (drawing on the Eudemian Ethics), Mechanica, Oeconomica, On Breath, On Colors, On Marvelous Reports, On Melissus Xenophanes [Zeno] and Gorgias, On Plants, On the Universe, On Uncuttable Lines, On Virtues and Vices, Physiognomica, Problems, Rhetorica to Alexander, Winds.

EDITIONS—Eighty are listed in the Oxford Classical Dictionary, 2nd ed., 1970, p 117ff. *Add:* R. Kassel, Ars Rhetorica, 1976. *Translations*—twenty-three volumes, by various authors, in Loeb ed., 1926–78, *and* twenty-seven in Budé edition. For other translations *see* A. M. W. Green, Classics in Translation: Selective Bibliography (1930–76), 1976. *Add:* J. Warrington, Politics and Constitution of Athens, reprint 1973; A. Zakro, Topics, 1974; J. Annas, Metaphysics (continued), 1976; R. Kassel, Ars Rhetorica, 1976.

ABOUT—H. Cherniss, Aristotle's Criticism of Plato and the Academy, 1944; F. Nuyens, L'évolution de la psychologie d'Aristote, 1948; T. L. Heath, Mathematics in Aristotle, 1949; M. E. Hamburger, Morals and Law: The Growth of Aristotle's Legal Theory, 1951; J. Lukasiewicz, Aristotle's Syllogistic From the Standpoint of Modern Formal Logic, 2nd ed., 1957; J. H. Randall, Aristotle, 1960; S. Mansion, ed., Aristote et les problèmes de méthode (Louvain symposium), 1961; P. Aubenque, Le problème de l'être chez Aristote, 1962, *and* La prudence chez Aristote, 1963; E. Berti, La filosofia del primo Aristotele, 1962; M. Grene, Portrait of Aristotle, 1963; J. Owens, The Doctrine of Being in the Aristotelian Metaphysics, 2nd ed., 1963; W. D. Ross, Aristotle, revised ed., 1964; R. Bambrough, ed., New Essays on Plato and Aristotle, 1965; M. Mignucci, La teoria aristotelica della scienza, 1965; La "Politique" d'Aristote (Entretiens Hardt, v 11), 1965; I. Düring, Aristoteles: Darstellung und Interpretation seines Denkens, 1966; G. Calogero, I fondamenti della logica aristotelica, 2nd ed., 1968; W. F. R. Hardie, Aristotle's Ethical Theory, 1968; G. E. R. Lloyd, Aristotle: The Growth and Structure of His Thought, 1968 *and,* with G. E. L. Owen (as eds.), Aristotle on Mind and Senses, 1978; J. M. E. Moravcsik, ed., Aristotle: A Collection of Critical Essays, 1969; D. J. Allan, The Philosophy of Aristotle, revised ed., 1970; M. Wieland, Die aristotelische Physik, 2nd ed., 1970; N. Gulley, Aristotle on the Purposes of Literature, 1971; J. Ferguson, Aristotle, 1972; J. P. Lynch, Aristotle's School, 1972; R. Stark, Aristotelesstudien, 2nd ed., 1972; J. L. Ackrill, Aristotle's Ethics, 1973; A. P. Bos, On the Elements: Aristotle's Early Cosmology, 1973; A. H. Chroust, Aristotle: New Light on His Life and on Some of His Lost Works, 1973; K. V. Erikson, ed., Aristotle: The Classical Heritage of Rhetoric, 1974; F. Grayeff, Aristotle and His School, 1974; J. Barnes, M. Schofield, and R. Sorabji, eds., Articles on Aristotle, v 1-4, 1925–78; S. R. L. Clark, Aristotle's Man: Speculations upon Aristotelian Anthropology, 1975; J. M. Cooper, Reason and Human Good in Aristotle, 1975; W. Fortenbaugh, Aristotle on Emotion, 1975; W. Leszl, Aristotle's Conception of Ontology, 1975; M. Mignucci, L'argomentativa dimonstrativa in Aristotele, 1975; J. M. Moore, Aristotle and Xenophon on Democracy and Oligarchy, 1975; A. Preuss, Science and Philosophy in Aristotle's Biological Works, 1975; W. N. Thompson, Aristotle's Deduction and Induction, 1975; D. Hamelin, Le système d'Aristote, 1976; S. Campese and others, Aristotele e la crisi della politica, 1977; D. Charles, Aristotle's Philosophy of Action, 1977; J. D. G. Evans, Aristotle's Concept of Dialectic, 1977; E. Hartmann, Substance, Body and Soul: Aristotelian Investigations, 1977; J. B. Morrall, Aristotle (Political Thinkers series), 1977; R. G. Mulgan, Aristotle's Political Theory, 1977; G. Vuoso, Aristotele e la pedagogia storistica, 1977; F. Brentano, The Psychology of Aristotle, 1978; A. Kenny, Aristotelian Ethics, 1978; H. Wijsenbeek-Wyler, Aristotle's Concept of Soul, Sleep and Dreams, 1978. (The Symposium Aristotelicum has met every three years since 1957, and a conference on Aristotle was held in August 1978 to celebrate the twenty-third centenary of his death.)

ARISTOXENUS, Greek writer on music and other subjects, was born at Taras (Taranto) in southeast Italy in about 370 B.C. Among his music teachers was his father. For a time he resided at Mantinea in Arcadia but later moved to Corinth, where he became friendly with the former King Dionysius II of Syracuse (who had been exiled since 343). They compared notes about the philosophy of Pythagoras, in which both were interested. Then Aristoxenus set up residence at Athens, where he transferred his allegiance from the Pythagoreans to Aristotle's Lyceum (the Peripatetic School). However, Aristotle passed him over for the succession to the directorship of the school in 322, and it is doubtful if Aristoxenus remained a Peripatetic thereafter. It is not known when he died.

A very prolific writer, he was said to have produced four hundred and fifty three book-rolls, of which the fragments bear witness to a large variety of themes. But no substantial part of his work has survived—only portions of three books about music. These passages, one of which is fairly large, probably come from two separate works that in combination are known as *The Principles and Elements of Harmonics* (or, more briefly *The Harmonics*), although the exact title is variously reported.

The first book discusses the general range of the subject and treats voice movements,

a ris tok' se nus

pitch, notes, intervals, and scales. The second (which is more disputatious) deals with similar topics but adds analyses of keys, modulation, and melodic construction. The third book comprises twenty-seven theorems on the appropriate combinations of intervals and tetrachords in scales. Although the surviving parts of the treatises do not offer a complete musical theory and, furthermore, show a conservative preference for old forms of composition, they improved in many important respects on their predecessors, notably the half-mystical Pythagoreans. In consequence they became highly influential, and they constitute our basic document for the study of Greek music.

Aristoxenus' powers of exposition and definition are seen to be worthy of his master Aristotle. Yet his emphasis on the ethical and educational value of music strikes an unfamiliar note today. And the personality that emerges from these writings is also strange, displaying a conceited, combative pride in his own achievement, reinforced by petty parades of logical scrupulousness and tediously triumphant vindications of the obvious. Aristoxenus also compiled a tractate, *The Elements of Rhythm,* of which we have a large fragment from the second book and a number of shorter passages or fragments quoted by later authors. The largest excerpt deals with the general character of rhythm, of which various aspects came under discussion, including matters relating to meter. Moreover, Aristoxenus was the author of a considerable number of other musical treatises, as well, of which little has survived.

Lost, too, are his abundant writings on other subjects. One of his interests was the field of biography, in which he inaugurated a long list of lives of famous men written by fellow members of the Aristotelian school, among whom St. Jerome considered, in retrospect, that Aristoxenus was "by far the most learned." Like his colleagues, Aristoxenus maintained that a man revealed his character through his actions. Nevertheless, he was by no means an orthodox Aristotelian biographer, since he was very fond of anecdote and prepared to offer individual and provocative views. Thus in his lives of Socrates, Plato, and Pythagoras he saw the first as a hot-tempered moneylender, the second as a plagiarist of the sophist Protagoras, and Pythagoras as a man of Etruscan origins who had learned his wisdom from Zarathustra. Aristoxenus also wrote a separate study of his own fellow citizen Archytas, a fourth century Pythagorean who was reputedly the founder of mechanics. Aristoxenus was attracted to him because of his lively interest in the Pythagorean way of life. In keeping with his musical interests, he seems to have adapted from later Pythagoreanism the view that the soul is a "tuning" of the body, an interpretation alien to Aristotle's thought.

WORKS—*On music* (partially extant): Principles and Elements of Harmonics, Elements of Rhythm. *Lost works:* On Music (at least four books), On Melody (at least four books), On Listening to Music, On Keys, On Auloi and Musical Instruments, On Aulos-Players, On the Boring of Auloi, On Tragic Poets, On Dancing in Tragedy. *Other works:* Lives of Men (the form of the title suggests that he planned a series of lives of women also); Educational Laws; Political Laws; Pythagorean Maxims (or, The Pythagorean Life); Historical Notes; Short Notes: Miscellaneous Notes; Scattered Notes.
EDITIONS—H. S. Macran, The Harmonics of Aristoxenus, 1902; R. da Rios, Aristoxeni Elementa Harmonica, 1954. Fragments of the remaining works *in* F. Wehrli, Die Schule des Aristoteles, v 2, 1945.
ABOUT—L. Laloy, Aristoxène de Tarente, 1904; C. A. Williams, The Aristoxenian Theory of Musical Rhythm, 1911; M. I. Henderson on ancient Greek music *in* The New Oxford History of Music, v 1; also, *see* other works on Greek music listed *in* Oxford Classical Dictionary, 2nd ed., 1970, p 712ff.; A. Momigliano, The Development of Greek Biography, 1971.

ARNOBIUS, Christian Latin theologian, was born in northern Africa in about A.D. 235 and taught rhetoric at Sicca Veneria in Numidia (El Kef in Tunisia). In about 295 he underwent a sudden conversion from paganism to Christianity, supposedly as the result of a dream. The bishop to whom he applied for admission to the church was suspicious, since Arnobius had previously been its vehement enemy. In order to prove his sincerity, he wrote a seven-book polemic *Against the Heathens (Adversus Nationes),* which survives in an imperfect copy. The first book appears to have been written in
är nō′ bi us

52

296/7, when he was still merely a neophyte and catechumen; composed in haste, but in a highly colored style, the work is directed against those pagans who maintained that Jesus Christ had only been a human magician and that ever since Christianity had made its appearance the world had been collapsing into ruin. *Against the Heathens* begins with a vigorous refutation of the latter charge, combined with the assertion that it had only been formulated by a few arrogant, frenzied intellectuals. It is rather with the pagans, declares Arnobius, that their own gods are angry, because of the repellent ideas their devotees hold about them and the disgusting rites with which they conduct their worship. Finally, in order to refute the objection that the Christians cut themselves off from their fellow countrymen's religion, the writer singles out for mockery the more outrageous of the myths and legends associated with the pagan cults; the remorseless attack which he delivers on polytheism (based on information ultimately descending from Varro and Lucretius and anticipating the subsequent onslaughts of St. Augustine) throws remarkable light on current and earlier religious practices in North Africa and elsewhere. Arnobius conducts his polemic with mordant wit and sarcasm, using his opponents' own weapons and turning against them the very same authorities whom they claimed as their own.

His supposition that the pagan gods "are angry" is strange doctrine for a Christian to hold: it presupposes that they possessed an authentic existence. And, indeed, Christianity, which he had now adopted as his own faith, seems much less familiar to him than his former pagan beliefs: he makes little use of the New Testament, and none of the Old. His view of God originates from Plato, who, he reminds his opponents, held theories very close to the Christian dogmas. Arnobius believed, in the Stoic tradition, that the soul must win its immortality by merit, somewhat superficially appending the hope that this merit will be acquired through Christ. Later thinkers and writers, especially in the sixteenth, seventeenth, and eighteenth centuries, have been greatly attracted by the style of his utterances, however much they sometimes seem to involve contradictions.

Arnobius' sonorous, easily flowing, colorful diction, embellished by a rich vocabulary and many literary reminiscences, draws on all the resources of the rhetoricians' schools, and the result is a mass of alliterations, antitheses, and rhetorical questions and exclamations.

EDITIONS—C. Marchesi, 1934; J. M. P. B. van der Putten, Arnobii Adversus Nationes v 3, 1-19, 1970.
ABOUT—A. J. Festugière, Arnobiana, 1952; P. Courcelle in A. Momigliano, ed., The Conflict Between Paganism and Christianity in the Fourth Century, 1963; P. Krafft, Beiträge zur Wirkungsgeschichte des älteren Arnobius, 1966.

ARRIAN (Flavius Arrianus), Greek historian, was born in about A.D. 95 into a prominent family at Nicomedia (Izmit) in Bithynia (northwestern Asia Minor) and died in about 175. He was a citizen not only of his own native city but also of Rome, and in its service he pursued a successful career, about which new inscriptions have come to light. In the 120s, during the reign of the philhellene Hadrian, he became consul, and then, in c. 130–37, imperial governor in Cappadocia (eastern Asia Minor), where he had to beat off an attack from German tribesmen, the Alans. He also traveled widely on imperial business, notably in the Danubian provinces Noricum and Pannonia. Later he retired to Athens, where he held civic office in 147–48. His own city honored him with a life priesthood.

Like many others, Arrian looked for a model in the classical past, half a millennium before. He found it, as he tells us more than once, in Xenophon, the historian. Like his forerunner, he took an interest in philosophy during his youth, when he listened to the Stoic philosopher Epictetus, an event to which we owe almost everything we know about that philosopher, for when Epictetus was dead and others began, without authorization, to publish the notes that Arrian had taken of his lectures, Arrian decided to publish them himself. They appeared in eight, or perhaps twelve, books of *Discourses (Diatribes),* out of which four survive, as well as in Arrian's brief synopsis or

ar' i án

Manual (Encheiridion) of his master's Stoic creed, dedicated to a certain Messalinus.

This was probably one of Arrian's earliest works. His first known composition, however, was a maritime guide, or circumnavigation, of the Black Sea, the *Periplus Ponti Euxini,* which he dedicated to Hadrian. It incorporated three reports that he had already written down in Latin, partly founded on an earlier authority but in one case on personal observations during his own Cappadocian governorship. In 136, while he still occupied the same post, he published his *Tactical Manual (Techne Taktike)* and *Order of Battle Against the Alans,* apparently an actual report to Hadrian on the dispositions to be made against that enemy, though additional material may have been inserted with a view to publication. After his retirement to Athens, Arrian devoted himself wholly to his literary career. His *Treatise on Hunting (Cynegetica),* which is still extant, repeats the title of a work attributed (dubiously) to Xenophon; and, like Xenophon once again, he practiced biography, writing lives (now lost) of Dion and Timoleon of Syracuse and, curiously enough, also of a notorious bandit named Tilloborus.

In the same period, Arrian also wrote the work about Alexander the Great that gave him permanent fame. He probably called it the *Anabasis* (expedition up from the coast) *of Alexander,* thus once again adapting a title of Xenophon (the *Anabasis of Cyrus*). Furthermore, he imitated Xenophon's seven-book structure as well, though he was also aspiring, by this time, to seek higher models, and to become the new Herodotus or Thucydides. Indicating Ptolemy I of Egypt and another of Alexander's officers, Aristobulus, as its sources, his *Anabasis* provides the best account that has come down to us of the events he describes. He was not entirely unbiased, it is true, since his authorities were Alexander's men. Nor was the work quite such good history as has sometimes been supposed, since Arrian, although capable of weighing a surmise and producing a second opinion, possessed no firsthand knowledge and was more of a practical soldier than a professional historian. Nevertheless, his account, written plainly and free of rhetorical frills, is a welcome corrective to the fog of fictional romance and slander that habitually obscured the image of Alexander, and it makes attractive reading.

He supplemented it by an *Indica,* a description of India going back to early Hellenistic sources including Megasthenes and Eratosthenes; and he also drew on Nearchus, whose circumnavigation of the coast from the Indus to the Tigris had been undertaken on Alexander's behalf. In this treatise, his desire to imitate Herodotus was indicated by the use of that historian's Ionic dialect, a touch that appeared again in the eight-book *Bithynica,* which narrated the history of his native land down to its annexation by Rome in 74 B.C. But the work is lost, as is his history of Parthia *(Parthica).* Of his ten-book history of Greece since the time of Alexander only a fragment remains.

EDITIONS—Epictetus: H. Schenkl, 2nd ed., 1916. *Translations*—W. A. Oldfather (Loeb ed.), 1925, 1928; J. Souilhé and A. Jagu (Budé ed.), 1943–66. Other treatises (with translations): E. I. Robson, Arrian: Anabasis of Alexander and Indica (Loeb ed.), 1929, 1933; P. Chantraine, Arrien: L'Inde (Budé ed.), 1952; F. Kiehle, Die Taktik des Flavius Arrianus, 1965; P. A. Brunt, Arrian: History of Alexander and Indica, v 1, 1976; A. de Selincourt and J. R. Hamilton, Arrian: The Campaigns of Alexander (Penguin ed.), 1976.
ABOUT—P. E. More, Hellenistic Philosophies, 1923; A. B. Breebaart, Enige historiografische Aspecten van Arrianus' Anabasis Alexandri, 1960 (with English summary); H. Montgomery, Gedanke und Tat: Zur Erzählungstechnik bei Herodot, Thukydides, Xenophon und Arrian, 1965; A. Bodson, La morale sociale des derniers stoiciens, 1967; M. Pohlenz, Stoa und Stoiker, 4th ed., 1970, 1972; F. H. Sandbach, The Stoics, 1975.

ARTEMIDORUS, Greek writer and soothsayer, lived in the second century A.D. He came from Ephesus in Ionia (Selçuk, western Asia Minor) but was generally known as Artemidorus of Daldis (Narli Kalesi), the Lydian birthplace of his mother.

Artemidorus wrote a monograph on the interpretation of dreams *(Oneirocritica),* in five books. This treatise, which has survived, provides illuminating insight into ancient beliefs and folklore on the subject. It is mainly a compilation from earlier writers, for dreams had attracted the attention of serious students as well as frivolous readers

är te mi dō' rus

ever since the Alexandrian (Hellenistic) age. A curious feature of the *Oneirocritica* is its detailed discussion of the dreams of athletes.

The work remained the model for future writers on dreams and attracted renewed attention in the sixteenth century, when a French translation was referred to by the satirist Rabelais; it was also epitomized in English, and a Spanish translation appeared as well.

Artemidorus also wrote works on augury *(Oinoscopica)* and palmistry *(Cheiroscopica).*

EDITIONS (of the Oneirocritica)—R. A. Pack, 1963; D. del Corno, 1975.
ABOUT—W. Reichardt, De Artemidoro Daldiano, 1894; R. Dietrich, Beiträge zu Artemidorus, 1910; H. A. Harris, Sport in Greece and Rome (Appendix), 1972; N. Lewis, The Interpretation of Dreams and Portents, 1976.

ASCLEPIADES, Greek epigrammatic poet, wrote between 320 and 290 B.C. He was also known as Sicelidas, under which name he is mentioned by Theocritus. His birthplace was the island of Samos, and he probably lived for a time at Alexandria.

Together with Callimachus, his rival and opponent, Asclepiades was the principal epigrammatist of the Hellenistic (Alexandrian) period. He appears to have been the leader of a group, or school, of writers of light verse working in Alexandria. They included Hedylus of Samos, one of whose epigrams, giving Asclepiades' name as Sicelidas, speaks of him as the model for poets of this type; and another of his associates was Posidippus of Pella, who along with Asclepiades was attacked by Callimachus for admiring the epic poetry of Antimachus of Colophon. Asclepiades, Hedylus, and Posidippus jointly published a collection of epigrams, the *Soros (Heap of Grain).*

Asclepiades specialized in the development of the love epigram, which he infused with a lively and passionate lyricism, in contrast to the more controlled and elevated manner of Callimachus. He also introduced to this genre such famous symbols as the boy Eros (Cupid) with his bow and arrows. Presenting himself as a hedonist preoccupied

as klē pi' á déz

54

with the love of women and boys alike, he writes in a spirit of considerable sexual frankness, though without the obscenity that later epigrammatists permitted themselves. Asclepiades aims at the honest depiction of personal feeling, employing a style that is simple, direct, and compact. His poems found their way into the Palatine Anthology (tenth century A.D.); one of them, a heartfelt tribute to the life of high emotion, declares that all the snow and hail and thunder and lightning that Zeus may ever send down upon the earth is not going to stop Asclepiades from enjoying the pleasures of love.

Asclepiades revived a lyric meter previously used by Alcaeus and Sappho, which became known as the Asclepiad, after him. Horace employed it extensively in his *Odes.*

EDITIONS—O. Krauer, Die Epigramme des Asklepiades von Samos, 1935; A. S. F. Gow and D. L. Page, Hellenistic Epigrams, 1965; D. L. Page, Epigrammata Graeca, 1976. *With translation:* W. R. Paton, The Greek Anthology (Loeb ed.), 1916–18; W. Wallace and M. Wallace, Asclepiades of Samos, 1941. For other translations of the Anthology *see* A. M. W. Green, Classics in Translation: A Selective Bibliography (1930–76), 1976; P. Waltz, G. Soury, F. Buffière, and R. Aubreton, Anthologie grecque (Budé ed.), 1974; H. Beckby, Anthologia Graeca (German), 1965.
ABOUT—L. A. Stella, Cinque poeti dell'Antologia Palatina, 1949; A. S. F. Gow, The Greek Anthology: Sources and Ascriptions, 1958, *and* (with D. L. Page) The Greek Anthology: Hellenistic Epigrams, 1965; L'épigramme grecque (Entretiens Hardt, v 14), 1968.

ASINIUS POLLIO, GAIUS. See Pollio, Gaius Asinius

ATACINUS, AULUS TERENTIUS VARRO. See Varro Atacinus, Aulus Terentius

ATHANASIUS, Saint,

Greek theological writer and bishop, was born in about A.D. 295 and died in 373. His place of origin was probably Alexandria. He became a deacon in 318 and a priest soon afterward, during the time when the doctrines of Arius ("the

ath a nā′ si us

Arian heresy"), against which he fought throughout his career, were at the height of their popularity, both in theological circles and among ordinary people. Arius, an ascetic Alexandrian priest, was accused of stressing the humanity of Jesus at the expense of his divinity. Alexandrian Greeks brought up in the classical philosophical tradition could not tolerate the duality of God the Father and Son (or the multiplicity of the Trinity), since it seemed to them that such pluralism infringed on the one-ness of God. These pluralist opinions culminated in the person of Arius, who concluded that Jesus, being the Son, derived his being from the Father and was therefore both inferior and younger: "there was when he was not." Athanasius made himself the leader of those who deplored these views as embodying a blasphemous depreciation of the Godhead of Jesus.

After attending the Council of Nicaea (Iznik) in 325, where it was asserted that the Son was equal in essence to the Father—a doctrine that compelled Arius to withdraw to Palestine—Athanasius became bishop of Alexandria, a post which he was to occupy for the next forty-five years, apart from five interruptions when he had to go into exile, owing to pressure from supporters of Arius and from other enemies. His first exile (335–37) was due to a successful attempt by Arius to rehabilitate himself, although death deprived him of his victory. Banished again almost immediately afterwards (337–45), Athanasius went to Rome to seek help from the pope and on the same occasion introduced Egyptian monasticism to the west. During his third exile (355–61) he took refuge with the Egyptian monks, but then, during a phase of attempted reconciliations, he returned to the center of events once more. In 362 Julian the Apostate forced "this notoriously troublesome man" into a further spell of banishment, but he came back again after that emperor's death, only to experience a fifth brief period of exile in 365–66. Seven years later he died, thus bringing to an end a stormy career as champion of orthodoxy. His death came too soon for him to see the final eclipse of the heresy he had always opposed; yet his career had exercised an incalculably vast influence on the future doctrine and development of the church.

Athanasius wrote a very large number of books, many of which underwent extensive revision almost at once owing to the mutually hostile editorial activities of his followers and opponents. Some of the most important of his writings were dogmatic statements of theology. His earliest extant work, *Against the Heathen (Contra Gentes),* dates from c. 318 and is divided into two parts, a refutation of pagan mythologies and an exposition of the doctrine of redemption *(The Incarnation of the Word of God),* which came to be recognized as a classic. But most of his theological books, as their titles show, were directed against Arianism, including an *Apology Against the Arians*—of historical importance because it incorporates the proceedings and decrees of church councils—and his three *Discourses Against the Arians,* which were written slightly later in about 358.

Particular interest, however, focuses on his *Letters.* Among his *Festal (Paschal) Epistles,* written to exhort his congregation in successive Lenten fasts, is a letter of A.D. 367 that first defines the canon of the New Testament in terms of the twenty-seven books that constitute its agreed content. Four *Letters to Serapion* are important for their exposition of the doctrine of the Holy Spirit. A number of official documents relating to Athanasius' episcopal duties include a *Letter to Paphnutius* written on a papyrus (now at the British Museum) that may be in the writer's own hand. Especial historical significance attaches to another work that bore his name and circulated by his initiative, though the extent of his personal authorship has been disputed: this was a life of St. Antony (c. 357), creator of Egyptian monasticism. This work established a new type of biography and contributed to the spread of the monastic ideal in the west, where it was extensively read in a Latin translation.

WORKS not mentioned above include: Treatise on the Synods of Rimini and Seleucia; doctrinal epistles: On the Teaching of Dionysius, On the Decrees of Nicaea, and several others relating to the Incarnation; On the Interpretation of the Psalms, a short discussion which must have been one of a considerable number of such exegeses; a number of monographs on virginity, wholly or partly preserved and of doubtful attribution—fragments of other essays on the same theme survive in Coptic, Syriac, and Armenian translations. A Coptic ascetic epistle, On Love and Self-Control, may come from an authentic original. But the Interpretation of the Creed, On the Unity of Christ, and a sermon On the Devil are not genuine; nor is the Latin Athanasian Creed *(Quicumque Vult),* though ascribed to him from the seventh century onward. In Latin, too, are the twelve books On the Trinity, derived in part from Athanasian models.

EDITIONS with translation—The Incarnation of the Word of God, 1944; R. T. Meyer, Life of St. Antony, 1950; C. R. B. Shapland, Letters Concerning the Holy Spirit, 1951; R. W. Thomson, Contra Gentes and De Incarnatione, 1971 (following an edition of the Syriac Athanasiana); C. Kannengiesser, Sur l'Incarnation du Verbe, 1973 (Italian ed., 1976).

ABOUT—H. A. Wolfson, The Philosophy of the Church Fathers, v 1, 1956; E. Schwartz, Zur Geschichte des Athanasius, 1959; J. Quasten, Patrology, v 3, 1960; H. Nordberg, Athanasius and the Emperor, 1963; D. Ritschl, Athanasius: Versuch einer Interpretation, 1964; E. P. Meijering, Orthodoxy and Platonism in Athanasius, 1968; J. Roldanus, Le Christ et l'homme dans la théologie d'Athanase d'Alexandrie, 1968; R. Graber, Athanase et l'Église de notre temps, 1973.

ATHENAEUS, learned Greek writer, was born during the second century A.D. at Naucratis (Nabira) in Lower Egypt. The only one of his writings that has come down to us includes some slighting remarks about Commodus, so that it cannot have been completed until after that emperor's death in 180. This work is his *Deipnosophistae,* sometimes translated as the *Sophists' Banquet* or *Learned Banquet,* though the term does not mean "the professors at dinner" but "the specialists on dining." What Athenaeus depicts is a banquet lasting over several days at the house of a distinguished Roman, Larensis (probably his patron). The dinner is attended by twenty-nine learned men of various backgrounds, including historical figures such as Galen and the grammarian Ulpian of Tyre as well as an undefined collection of philosophers, musicians, and others. Athenaeus pretends to record their conversation; thus, the work belongs to the familiar category of symposium literature, of which the most famous example had been the *Symposium* of Plato written over six centuries earlier.

As the party described by Athenaeus progresses, the diners converse on every topic

ath ə nē′ us

that could, by any stretch of the imagination, be thought of as relevant to the occasion: food (notably vegetables and fish); luxurious habits, especially those of earlier times; dinner guests, including professional parasites and flatterers; as well as a vast range of other subjects including literature, grammar, philosophy, history, law, medicine, and numerous antiquarian themes. Athenaeus, making appropriate use of the Library at Alexandria, preserved an enormous mass of varied information in the *Deipnosophistae* so that the work is not only a collection of entertaining anecdotes but also the most important single guide to ancient manners and tastes that has come down to us.

What adds greatly to its value is its author's mania for quoting. All the speakers he introduces are credited with prodigious powers of recollection, and they quote unceasingly from a multitude of authors in verse and prose. Among their favorite sources, for example, are Athenian dramatists of the Middle and New Comedy, whose works are otherwise lost; so it is to Athenaeus that we owe almost everything we know of them. Altogether he records passages from some 1,250 writers—of whom about 700 would otherwise have remained entirely unknown—and more than 10,000 lines of poetry. In addition, he records the titles of more than 1,000 plays, for he takes meticulous care to provide accurate references. He cannot himself, however, have read all the books from which he quotes, or even any considerable proportion of them. The order in which his excerpts are marshaled (as well as his tendency to lapse into anachronisms) suggests that he had been ransacking lexicons and may also have made use of the official records of Athenian dramatic performances.

Athenaeus' compilation, as it has come down to us, is in fifteen books, possibly out of an original thirty. The first two and part of the third, however, are preserved only in an epitome (and certain parts of the rest of the work, particularly the seventh book, are so formless as to suggest that they are extracts from what was once a fuller text).

WORKS—In addition to the Deipnosophistae,

Athenaeus wrote further works, now lost, of a historical nature but also, it would appear, including information on zoological subjects.

EDITIONS—Deipnosophistae: S. P. Peppink, 1936–39. *With translation:* C. B. Gulick (Loeb ed.), 1927–41; A. M. Desrousseaux, C. Astruc, and G. Rochefort (Budé ed.), 1956– .
ABOUT—F. A. Wright, History of Later Greek Literature, 1932; L. Nyikos, Athenaeus Quo Consilio Quibusque Usus Subsidiis Deipnosophistarum Libros Composuerit, 1941.

ATTICUS. See Cicero

ATTIUS, LUCIUS. See Accius, Lucius

AUFIDIUS BASSUS, Roman historian, wrote during the reigns of Tiberius, Gaius (Caligula), and probably also Claudius and died in the middle of Nero's reign (54–68). We are informed that he was old when he died and had never enjoyed good health.

According to the rhetorician Quintilian, he ranked as one of the major historians of the early Roman principate; yet, our knowledge of him remains tenuous, since no fragments of his lesser works survive and only two that can probably be attributed to his major publications. The first of these treatises, and almost certainly the earlier, was *On the German War (De Bello Germanico)*. The campaigns with which it dealt were probably those conducted by Tiberius during the reign of Augustus, from A.D. 4 onward. The theme offered ample opportunity to eulogize Tiberius, who was no doubt presented as the general who had restored the situation after the imprudent Varus had succumbed to the ambush of the German Arminius in A.D. 9. Varus became the scapegoat, and Tiberius was enhanced in contrast.

Next Aufidius Bassus composed a broad, full-dress, year-by-year (annalistic) *Roman History*. The work is likely to have been completed under Claudius (A.D. 41–54), although he had started work on it at some point during the preceding reigns, since it

ô fi' di us bas' sus

57

was cited by the elder Seneca, who did not live to see Claudius' accession. Since the surviving fragments that have been attributed to Aufidius' *History* form part of an obituary of Cicero, who died in 43 B.C., it has been suggested that the work may have covered events beginning with Caesar's death in the previous year. This cannot, however, be regarded as certain, since the fragments in question may instead be derived from some separate work, possibly a monograph or declamation about the last phase of Cicero's life.

The date at which Aufidius' history terminated must be regarded as equally unsure, since although Pliny the elder entitled his own book *From the End of Aufidius Bassus (A Fine Aufidii Bassi),* we do not know the chronological point at which he started his work. The form of Pliny's title, however, is thought to indicate that Aufidius cannot have brought his account to an end at the time of a change of emperors or he would have expressed himself differently: a historical treatment of any reign presented tricky diplomatic problems for a man writing while that emperor was still alive. A number of other dates have, therefore, been suggested. Nothing later than 55 is acceptable, however, since a passage in Pliny's history, quoted by Tacitus, refers to that year. Various junctures in Claudius' reign have been proposed. It may be tentatively supposed that Aufidius Bassus preferred to bring his work to a close with events that occurred well before the emperor's accession, perhaps at the fall of Sejanus in A.D. 31.

The manner of Aufidius' death—cheerful and unperturbed, as recounted by Seneca the younger—befitted his allegiance to the Epicurean school of philosophy. As to the qualities of his historical writing, there is nothing surviving to go on except the praise of Quintilian, who preferred him to Aufidius' contemporary Servilius Nonianus on the grounds that Aufidius' style was less diffuse. About the substance of his history there is once again no evidence to depend upon, except the belief of some modern scholars that the later Greek historian Dio Cassius regarded him with so much respect that he used him as his principal authority for his own work on the reign of Augustus; and this

view has a certain plausibility. There have also been suggestions that Tacitus made considerable use of Aufidius; and this, too, is probable enough, provided that we do not envisage him as the principal source employed for the period by Tacitus—who would clearly have preferred to rely for the most part on the testimony of a historian who was a senator, and there is no evidence that Aufidius possessed that rank or, indeed, that the state of his health permitted him to lead an active public life.

ABOUT—R. Syme, Tacitus, 1958 (Appendix 38).

AUGUSTINE, Saint (Aurelius Augustinus), theologian and bishop, who wrote in Latin, was born in A.D. 354 and died in 430. His birthplace was Thagaste (now Souk Ahras in Algeria). His father Patricius was a pagan of middle-class origins and his mother Monica a devout Christian who greatly influenced her son. He showed high academic promise, and his parents managed to pay for his education at Carthage, where he subsequently worked as a free-lance teacher of rhetoric. He also became a temporary convert to the dualist doctrines of the Manichees, who believed that the world, being evil, must have been created by a power other than God. He taught at Rome (383) and in the next year obtained an official professorship at Mediolanum (Milan). There he made an advantageous marriage (and gave up his concubine, the mother of his son, hoping by this means to obtain entrée into the literary elite. However, after meeting Bishop Ambrose, the most famous Christian of the day, he became a convert to Christianity and was baptized (387), adopting the Neoplatonic form of the faith that Ambrose favored. Subsequently he returned to northern Africa with his mother, who died at Ostia on the way. In 391, he was ordained priest at Hippo Regius and in 395 was appointed to the local bishopric, which he retained for the remaining thirty-five years of his life.

These years were lived out among the violent political and military convulsions that

ô' gus tēn (Engl. ô gus' tin)

were leading the western Roman empire toward its imminent ruin and transformation; Augustine's voluminous writings illustrate the process of decline at innumerable points.

His two most famous works are the *Confessions* (c. 397–400) and the *City of God* (413–26). The first nine of the thirteen books of the *Confessions* present a vivid, though highly selective and subjective, account of his life up to the year 388, detailing his intense spiritual and psychological struggles and depicting the successive transformations of his outlook. Book 1 tells of his infancy and youth, adding general thoughts on the education of children. Book 2 deplores the idleness and bad companions of his sixteenth year. In Book 3, he goes to Carthage, fornicates, reads Cicero, despises the scriptures, and joins the Manichaean sect. In Book 4 he becomes a professor, mourns the death of a friend, and embarks on his career as a writer. In the fifth book he moves to Rome and then to Milan, where he meets St. Ambrose. In the sixth he is neither a Manichee nor a Catholic. He tells how a wife was found for him, speaks of a brotherhood of friends, and discusses the immortality of the soul. Book 7 describes free will as the cause of sin, rejects astrology, and debates the relation of Platonism to Scripture. In Book 8 the problem of the will comes sharply into focus, as Augustine recounts his conversion, the difficulties that preceded it, and the conflict between his spirit and his flesh. In the ninth book he resigns his professorship, receives baptism, and grieves at his mother Monica's death.

But there are still four more books—no longer autobiographical—because for Augustine conversion was not enough: it was not so easy to cast off one's past identity. So he concludes with a confession to God, in the form of a passionate prayer. Book 10 sets forth the benefits that confession brings to the soul, giving a novel and unfamiliar dimension to such expressions of human weakness. Book 11 analyzes time in its relation to eternity, and Books 12 and 13 treat of the creation of the world and analyze the true meaning of the Scriptures. The remarkable spread of asceticism in the Latin world had given Augustine his readership for the

Confessions. He analyzes his feelings with fierce honesty, thus providing an intensely vivid self-portrait without illusions.

The City of God (De Civitate Dei) is a statement of Augustine's philosophy of history. It is a series of reflections on the huge topic of God's design for the salvation of mankind; his conception of the City sank deep into Christian consciousness. Originally prompted by the sack of Rome by the Visigoth Alaric in 410, this great work was written to answer the widely asked question: Why have things gone so disastrously with the empire ever since it became Christian? In reply, the first ten books turn their attention to the pagan deities, maintaining that they are no use in this life or any other: Book 1—They did not protect Rome; certainly, the Christians suffered along with their heathen compatriots, but the loss of worldly goods is not always a disaster. Book 2—The pagan gods have no moral teaching to offer, and their rites are obscene. Book 3—They failed to save either Troy or Rome, and the Romans fell into religious depravity. Book 4—The multiplicity of the pagan deities is ridiculous. Book 5—Astrology is fraudulent; Rome owed its success to Roman virtue. God helps the Christian emperors. Book 6—The gods of paganism cannot provide eternal life; indeed, even in this world, they are incapable of providing help. Book 7—Who are the gods that Varro, the scholar of the first century B.C., defines as principal or select? Is Jupiter supreme or is he not? Book 8—A short history of Greek philosophy: Platonists are declared to be near-Christians. Book 9—A discussion of demons and of Apuleius—the novelist of the second century A.D. who was believed to be a magician—and of the Neoplatonists. Book 10—The claims of theurgy (the pagan art of securing supernatural intervention) are false: the only true religion is the worship of the Christian God and Jesus.

The remaining twelve books of the *City of God* develop the concept of a divine social order and the coming millennium: Book 11—The truth of the Scriptures; wickedness is unnatural. Book 12—Evil is nonexistent; the cyclical idea of history is false; the world is not eternal. Book 13—The problems of the creation of human beings; death and resurrection. Book 14—The lives of the spirit and of the flesh; The Two Cities: a heavenly city comprising the righteous on earth and the saints in heaven and an earthly city perverted by worldly and selfish considerations and principles. Book 15—Humankind in the earliest times; the beginnings of the two cities. Book 16—From Noah to Judah. Book 17—The preparation for the Christ by scriptural prophecies (theology).

Book 18—The two cities down to the time of Jesus Christ. It is in this book that Augustine, commenting on the future of humankind, quotes Paul's assertion that "The Lord knows his own: for those whom he foreknew he also predestined to be fashioned in the likeness of His son," and he adds, "It follows that none of these can perish." This doctrine of predestination was evolved by Augustine as a belief in which every event was charged with a meaning as a deliberate act of God—an act of mercy for the elect, of judgment for the damned. Book 19—The supreme human Good is Peace, toward which everything is directed—even war. Book 20—The Last Judgment; Law and Order. Book 21—How is eternal punishment inflicted and what does the phrase mean? Does temporary punishment exist after death for some sinners? Book 22—The creation and resurrection; miracles still happen; the Vision of God.

Augustine wrote a vast number of other treatises as well—totaling more than a thousand books. Among his earliest writings were a few relating to the teaching duties he was engaged upon at the time, including the surviving six books, *On Music* (387–91), which deal with rhythm and meter. But most of his early works were of a philosophical nature. Thus, in retirement at Cassiciacum (Cassiago, near Lake Como in northern Italy?) in 386, he wrote three dialogues entitled collectively *Against Academics:* one, *On the Happy Life (De Beata Vita);* and two, *On Order (De Ordine).* These treatises offer criticisms of ancient philosophy from the Christian standpoint, setting forth the arguments against scepticism, outlining the means for attaining true happiness by the knowledge of God, and indicating the consequences of a doctrine of Providence. Somewhat later came the incomplete *Soliloquies* (387), in two books, which propose the

necessary qualifications for gaining the knowledge of truth and assert the immortality of the soul. This assertion is reiterated in two further tracts, the unrevised *On the Immortality of the Soul* (387), in which Augustine adopts the Platonic arguments for a future life, and *On the Magnitude of the Soul* *(De Quantitate Animae* (388), in which he distinguishes seven steps of the soul that enable it to climb to its perfection; the treatise is mentioned by Dante and affected him profoundly. The dialogue *On the Teacher* (389), the title of which is derived from a text in Matthew's Gospel, is a discussion with the youthful Adeodatus about the significance of words.

At about the same time, Augustine, in Rome, initiated his long succession of works on polemical theology; for, if there was a single purpose that dominated his mind, it was to defeat what he regarded as heresy. The long series of works devoted to this purpose began with a dialogue entitled *On Grace and Free Choice (De Gratia et de Libero Arbitrio)*—treating of the disputed question of divine foreknowledge—and an essay entitled *On the True Religion* (389–91), which he finished after his return to northern Africa. The beliefs of the Manichaeans are critically handled in these pieces and more amply denounced in a series of subsequent productions. In one of these, *On Two Souls* (c. 391), Augustine argues against the Manichaean belief that men and women have both a good soul and a bad one. Continuing his anti-Manichaean campaign, in 391 he wrote *On the Value of Believing* to his friend Honoratus (who had originally persuaded him to become a Manichaean). In the following year he held a public debate against another well-known Manichaean, Fortunatus—the *Acta seu Disputatio Contra Fortunatum.* Two or three years later he likewise attacked Mani's pupil Adimantus *(Contra Adimantum),* and in 397 he extended his onslaught to the publications of Mani himself *(Contra Epistulam Quam Vocant Fundamenti).* This denunciation was left incomplete but was followed soon afterward not only by criticisms of contemporary Manichaeans—Faustus (400), Felix (404), and Secundinus (405–6)—but also by a general assault on their basic tenets, the *De Natura Boni Contra Manichaeos* (405).

Augustine also devoted enormous attention to refuting the Donatists, the puritanical Church of the Martyrs, which had broken away from the main African church early in the fourth century, although it differed from Catholicism on matters of ecclesiastical discipline rather than doctrine. First he launched against them a psalm in accentual meter (the *Psalmus Contra Partem Donati* or *Abecedarium* (393–96), then a whole series of tracts. A note on a conference with these Donatist opponents *(Breviculus Collationis cum Donatistis)* was followed up by an address to them *(Ad Donatistas post Collationem,* 412), and then, after a pause, by a sermon *(Ad Caesariensis Ecclesiae Plebem)* and a report on a dispute with their bishop Emeritus (*Gesta cum Emerito,* 418). In the following year he wrote *The Soul and Its Origin,* in four books, to refute criticisms directed against him by Vincentius Victor, a young man who had been recently converted to Donatism.

From 412 onward, he mounted a strong attack in the form of a long series of sermons and treatises against the followers of the humanistic British (or possibly Irish) theologian Pelagius, who believed Augustine's doctrine of divine grace undermined free will and moral effort. A further work, entitled *On the Grace of Christ and Original Sin* (418), in two books, offers the first explicit statement of that doctrine in Christian literature, whereas a three-book study entitled *On the Merits and Remission of Sins and Infant Baptism* (412) had indicated the indispensability of infant baptism as a means of obtaining the divine Grace. *On Nature and On Grace* and *On the Perfection of Justice* followed in 415. *On the Actions of Pelagius* was sent to the Bishop of Carthage in 417, and in the next year Augustine wrote *Against Pelagius and Caelestius* (Caelestius was a supporter of Pelagius in northern Africa). In the two books of *On Marriage and Lust* (419–20) Augustine rejected the accusation that some of his views denied the holiness of marriage—a charge made by Julianus, the aristocratic Pelagian bishop of Aeclanum, who was also the target of a later six-book work and another left uncomplet-

ed. In 420 a further four-book monograph denouncing the Pelagians was produced on the suggestion of Pope Boniface.

Two further treatises denounced the Arians, who were said to minimize the divinity of Jesus. Late in life Augustine also wrote a general work, mainly of a derivative nature, *Against Heresies: For Quodvultdeus (De Haeresibus ad Quodvultdeum,* 428). In addition, he published a tract against the Jews *(Contra Judaeos),* in the following year.

In addition, he wrote a number of treatises intended to train his congregation in virtuous living. Among these were two works, *On Lying (De Mendacio,* 394; *Contra Mendacium ad Consentium,* 420), of which the second adopted a more rigorous view than its predecessor. *On Holy Virginity* (400 –401) attaches great significance to the virgin state, and, whereas the value of the married condition is fully accepted (*On the Good of Marriage: De Bono Coniugali,* also 400– 401), a widow is considered more praiseworthy if she does not remarry than if she does (*The Good of Widowhood for Juliana,* 414). Later, the *Mirror of Scripture (Speculum de Scriptura Sacra,* 421) selects a long series of Biblical texts supplying guidance on behavior.

When consulted about monastic conduct in Carthage, Augustine suggested in a report entitled *On the Work of the Monks* (400) that monks should not by the solicitation of alms make their profession an excuse for sponging. His teaching methods are explained in *On Cathechizing the Uninstructed* (also written in 400) and in *On Christian Doctrine* (397–426), which sets forth, in four books, a scheme of education based on the faith and is of great importance for assessing Augustine's attitude toward pagan cultures. He also composed vast collections of miscellanea (*De Diversis Quaestionibus LXXXIII,* 388–96; *Ad Simplicianum, De Diversis Quaestionibus,* 396; *De Octo Dulcitii Quaestionibus,* 423). His surviving letters are about 270 in number; his known sermons run into thousands.

The Biblical commentaries attributable to his authorship (some originally sermons) were numerous, detailed, and renowned. They deal with Genesis, selected portions from the first seven books of the Old Testa-

61

ment (*Quaestiones and Locutiones in Heptateuchum,* 419), Job (397–400), the Psalms (391–430), the Gospels of Matthew and Luke (*Quaestiones Evangeliorum,* 400, concentrating on difficult passages), the Sermon on the Mount (in two books 393–96), the Gospel and Epistle of John (416–17), the Epistles of James, and the Epistles of Paul to the Galatians and Romans (393–96). Augustine was also the author of a four-book work denying that the Gospels contradict each other (*De Consensu Evangelistarum,* 400), and he compiled brief handbooks on the Creed and on Christian faith, hope, and charity. He also wrote essays on demonology (*De Divinatione Daemonum,* 406–11), and on psychic research (*On the Attention to Be Devoted to the Dead: De Cura pro Mortuis Gerenda,* 421).

Not long before his death (426/7) he composed a critical bibliography of his own literary activity, the *Retractationes,* in two books. This gives a complete chronological catalog of his works, with an account of the circumstances under which each was composed, and thus provides a solid basis for establishing the chronology and authenticity of his almost incredibly numerous writings. Furthermore, in this same treatise, he enumerates the passages that his maturer judgment would have led him to omit or correct.

Catholic Christianity, for Augustine, was a wisdom that was at one and the same time guaranteed by heavenly authority and explorable by rational processes: the Divine Philosophy. He was a man of powerful creative intellect, wide literary erudition (despite poor Greek and nonexistent Hebrew), and strong practical sense combined with a vivid sensibility and an ardent, restlessly evolving religious faith, about which the somber, neurasthenic self-criticisms of the *Confessions* are intensely revealing. His mind is imaginative and passionate, daring but introspective, poetic and romantic. Stimulated by the successive changes in his career and circumstances and by an unending series of theological controversies into which he plunged with all the earnestness of his heart, he developed his ideas with a wholehearted verve and independence that sometimes left even his admirers aghast.

Although his early practice of rhetoric left its mark and endowed him with an easy supple style, seasoned with a variety of literary devices and conceits, his major works form successive landmarks in the gradual transformation of his classical ideals to suit his particular interpretations of Christianity. Above all, his early optimism was soon overshadowed by an increasingly radical doctrine of divine grace that seemed to his critics, notably the Pelagians, to leave human beings altogether too impotent. *The City of God,* addressing itself with timeless, poignant relevance to the reconciliation of the world of the spirit with the world in which we ourselves live, presented a definitive juxtaposition and contrast of Christianity and paganism.

In his final *Retractations,* Augustine indicated the confident belief that his literary output had progressively conformed to Catholic orthodoxy. But this was, to some extent, an illusion; and, in any case, it was a tragedy, with far-reaching consequences, that his anxiety to impose this orthodoxy on others led him to the conviction that, in order to achieve this aim and thus uphold the authority of the Catholic church, every possible means could be legitimately used, including even the use of coercion and persecution, in alliance with the imperial government.

Augustine has left us more knowledge about his real opinions than has any other historical character of equal renown. His writings, which convey his overwhelming consciousness of humankind's dependence on and reverence for the majesty and sovereignty of God, imposed a distinctive stamp upon many aspects of the Latin church and generally upon western Christianity. Strong as his influence was in his own epoch, it grew even stronger as time went on. The effect he exercised on the Middle Ages was vast (though in its later centuries there was a move away from the directness and simplicity that characterizes his own work). St. Thomas Aquinas (c. 1225 –74) put forward a strongly Augustinian version of the doctrine of Grace. Martin Luther (1483–1546) and John Calvin (1509–64) admired Augustine more than any of the early Fathers. In the seventeenth century St. Francis of Sales and Pascal and Bossuet, and in the twentieth century Jacques Maritain and Reinhold Niebuhr and Paul Tillich, all drew inspiration from his genius. In the history of Christianity he holds a place second only to St. Paul.

WORKS (other than those mentioned in the text)—On the Moral Behavior of Catholic Church and Manichaeans (388), On Genesis: Against the Manichaeans (388–89), On Two Souls: Against the Manichaeans (391–92); Faith and the Creed (393); On Continence (394–95); On Christian Combat (397); Against the Epistle of Parmenianus (three books, 400); On Baptism: Against the Donatists, and On the Unique Baptism (400); Faith in Things Unseen (400); Against the Writings of Petilianus (400–402); On the Unity of the Church (405); Against Cresconius (406); On the Spirit and the Letter (412); Epistle to Honoratus: On the Grace of the New Testament (412); Faith and Works (413); On the Trinity (fifteen books, 414); Against the Priscillianists and Origenists for Orosius (415); Against a Sermon of the Arians (415); On the Value of Fasting (c. 418); On Adulterous Marriages (two books, 419); Against the Adversary of the Law and the Prophets (two books, 420); On Admonition and Grace (426–27); Confrontation with Maximinus the Heretical Bishop of the Arians (427); On the Gift of Perseverance (428–29); On the Predestination of the Saints (428–29).

EDITIONS—J. P. Migne, Patrologia Latina, v 22-47; Corpus Scriptorum Ecclesiasticorum Latinorum (incomplete); E. Dekkers, Clavis Patrum Latinorum (Sacris Eruditi), v 3, 1951. Translations—J. Quasten and J. C. Plumpe, Ancient Christian Writers, 1946– ; J. H. S. Burleigh, A. C. Cutler, J. Burnaby, Library of Christian Classics, v 6-8, 1953–59. Confessions, City of God, and Select Letters: W. Watts, 1912; J. H. Baxter (Loeb ed.), 1953; G. E. McCracken, 1957. Confessions, City of God: R. S. Pine-Coffin, 1961; H. Bettenson (Penguin, Pelican ed.), 1972. For other translations see G. B. Parks and R. Z. Temple, The Literatures of the World in English Translation, v 1, 1968.

ABOUT—J. Burnaby, Amor Dei: A Study of the Religion of St. Augustine, 1938; P. Courcelle, Recherches sur les "confessions" de S. Augustin, 1950 and Les Confessions de S. Augustin dans la tradition littéraire: Antécédents et postérité, 1963; J. O'Meara, St. Augustine: Against the Academics, 1950 and The Young Augustine, 1954; R. W. Battenhouse, ed., A Companion to the Study of St. Augustine, 1955; F. G. Maier, Augustin und das antike Rom, 1955; H. I. Marrou, St. Augustine, 1957 and S. Augustin et la fin de la culture antique, 4th ed., 1958; E. Portalié, A Guide to the Thought of St. Augustine, 1960; J. G. Guy, Unité et structure logique de la Cité de Dieu, 1961; F. van der Meer, Augustine the Bishop, 1961; M. Pellegrino, Problemi vitali nelle Confessioni di S. Agostino, 1961; R. Holte, Béatitude et sagesse: S. Augustin et le problème de la fin de l'homme dans la philosophie ancienne, 1962; H. A. Deane, The Political and Social Ideas of St. Augustine, 1963; E. Lamirande, L'église céleste selon S. Augustin, 1963; J. E. Sullivan, Image of God: The Doctrine of St. Augustine and Its Influence, 1963; V. J. Bourke, Augustine's View of Reality, 1964;

G. L. Keyes, Christian Faith and the Interpretation of History: A Study of St. Augustine's Philosophy of History, 1966; A. H. Armstrong, St. Augustine and Christian Platonism, 1967; P. Brown, Augustine of Hippo, 1967; R. J. O'Connell, St. Augustine's Early Theory of Man, 1968; L. F. Pizzolato, Le "Confessioni" di S. Agostino: Da biografia a "confessio," 1968; G. Howie, Educational Theory and Practice in St. Augustine, 1969; E. A. Teselle, Augustine the Theologian, 1970; J. Château, Les grandes psychologies dans l'antiquité, 1978. Further studies of his individual works are listed in T. Gwinup and F. Dickinson, Greek and Roman Authors: A Checklist of Criticism, 1973. On the Pelagian controversy see R. F. Evans, Pelagius: Four Letters and Pelagius: Inquiries and Reappraisals, 1968.

AUGUSTUS (63 B.C.–A.D. 14), founder of the Roman principate (empire) and author of a public testament designated as his *Acts (Res Gestae),* was a member of the family of the Octavii from Velitrae (Velletri) in Latium; his original name was Gaius Octavius. Owing to the death of his father when he was four, he was brought up by his mother Atia, who was Julius Caesar's niece. In 46 he was in attendance at the Triumph of Caesar. In 45, despite the delicate health from which he suffered for much of his life, Octavius joined in Caesar's Spanish campaign. In the following year, Octavius, accompanied by his friend Agrippa, was sent to study at Apollonia in Epirus (now Albania), where he learned of Caesar's death. When the dictator's will was opened, it turned out that he had adopted the young man as his son, appointing him his principal heir. Octavius returned to Italy to avenge Caesar and claim his heritage. After fighting for the Senate against Antony at Mutina (Modena) in 43 B.C., he was recognized as Caesar's adopted son under the name of Gaius Julius Caesar Octavianus and was called Octavian. Very soon, however, he joined forces with Antony and Lepidus to form the dictatorial Second Triumvirate. They conducted savage proscriptions in which Cicero, among many others, met his death, and in the following year Antony and Octavian won the battle of Philippi against Caesar's assassins Brutus and Cassius, who then killed themselves. Antony assumed control of the east (in association with Cleopatra VII of Egypt, whom he preferred to Octavian's sister, his wife since the year 40), while Octavian controlled

ô gus' tus

AUGUSTUS

AUGUSTUS

the west, where in 36 he suppressed Pompey's surviving son Sextus in Italy and forced his fellow triumvir Lepidus into retirement. In 31 Agrippa, commanding Octavian's fleet, won the naval battle of Actium (northwestern Greece) against Antony and Cleopatra, both of whom committed suicide in the following year.

Octavian was now ruler of the entire Roman world, and in 27 B.C. he assumed the imposing name Augustus. During the more than forty years of his rule that followed—a rule that was tactfully disguised behind Republican institutions—he reorganized every aspect of Roman government and extended the frontiers at all points. He also composed a number of literary works, now all lost, including *Reply to Brutus on Cato* (unfinished), *Exhortations to Philosophy,* an autobiography (up to the time of the twenties B.C.), a hexameter poem on Sicily, some epigrams, and part of a tragedy (the *Ajax*), which he destroyed because he did not consider it good enough.

Although there could be, constitutionally speaking, no successor to his unprecedented powers, it became clear in A.D. 4 that Tiberius would succeed to them, which is indeed what happened when Augustus died in 14. The will he had deposited the previous year in the house of the Vestals included a summary of the military and financial resources of the empire, a document that has not survived, and his own record of his achieve-

ments, which is extant. The latter is known as the *Res Gestae Divi Augusti* or, more accurately, *Index Rerum Gestarum Divi Augusti.* It may have been written, in part, a good deal earlier and then brought up to date; in any case it was touched up in Augustus' last year or, possibly, after his death.

When Tiberius became ruler, copies of the *Res Gestae* were inscribed on stone tablets in many or all of the provinces, and the major part of the Latin text, together with a Greek translation, has been preserved at Ancyra (now Ankara) on the walls of a mosque that had been built as the Temple of Rome and Augustus. Known as the *Monumentum Ancyranum,* the inscription has a claim to be the most important document in all ancient epigraphy. Another much more fragmentary copy of both Latin and Greek texts has been discovered at Apollonia (Uluborlu) and a fragmentary copy of the Latin text at Antioch (Yalvaç)—both in Pisidia, central Asia Minor. Comparison of these three versions has enabled the words of Augustus to be preserved virtually in their entirety, apart from a few minor doubtful points.

The document comprises four parts: (1) a list of the public offices and honors received by Augustus, demonstrating his unique position in the state and his respect for Republican liberty; (2) a statement of the sums contributed by Augustus for public purposes from his private means; (3) his *Acts* (*Res Gestae),* a report on the victorious campaigns and conquests that formed one of the justifications of the special powers he held; (4) a statement summing up his position in the Roman state, combined with a repetition of his claim that he had restored Republican institutions and had been granted exceptional authority in consequence. Written in lapidary, triumphal style, the *Res Gestae* gives a remarkable indication of how Augustus wanted to be regarded and appreciated by his subjects—and of how good propaganda operates.

EDITIONS (of Res Gestae)—H. Volkmann, 1957; H. Malcovati, Caesaris Augusti Operum Fragmenta, 4th ed., 1962 (with bibliography); P. A. Brunt and J. M. Moore (Latin text), 1967; J. Gagé, revised ed., 1977. ABOUT—M. Durry, Les empereurs comme historiens d'Auguste à Hadrien (Entretiens Hardt, v 4), 1958; H. Bardon, Les empereurs et les lettres latines d'Auguste à Hadrien, 2nd ed., 1968.

AURELIUS, MARCUS (Marcus Aurelius Antoninus), Roman emperor and philosophical writer, was born in A.D. 121 of a family from southern Spain. He was taught by the foremost orator of his day, Fronto, to whom he wrote a series of somewhat formal letters, mainly in Latin, that have survived. Aurelius also gained the favor of the emperor Hadrian and after his death in 138 was adopted by Antoninus Pius as his son, together with the eight-year-old Lucius Verus. Thus, in 161, they came to the throne as Antoninus Pius' joint successors (Verus died in 169). From 166 onward, for the greater part of the fourteen years that remained to him, Marcus Aurelius was in the field, endeavoring to resist a grave military threat from the Germans against the northern frontiers of the empire. He planned the annexation of large areas of central Europe but died in 180 before these projects could be brought into effect, and his son Commodus, who succeeded him, abandoned his expansionist plans.

It was ironic that this deeply thoughtful man had to devote so much of his reign to fighting. In rare intervals of leisure he compiled a work of aphorisms and reflections in the Greek language, later entitled by editors "His Writings to Himself" but generally known as the *Meditations,* which were transcribed from his notebooks and published after his death. This masterpiece of self-scrutiny and self-admonition, although framed in literary form, possesses no systematic arrangement, with the partial exception of the first of its twelve books, which records his gratitude to his family, his teachers, and the gods.

The fact that the *Meditations* were designed purely for their author's private use and not for publication, makes them a dramatically intimate and personal document, of which the significance is enhanced, not indeed by any markedly original philosophical content since the work for the most part restates traditional Stoicism but by the impressive, superbly humane, personality of

ô rē′ li us

MARCUS AURELIUS

its author. By his writing of the *Meditations,* Marcus Aurelius became one of the few great rulers whose practical achievements have been eclipsed and outlived by what they wrote.

His doctrine, however, was an austere one, and provided little comfort—except what could be derived from putting its principles into practice. For, men and women must simply strive onward, Aurelius declares, and continue their laborious efforts as best they can, with patient, long-suffering endurance; only through turning inward and drawing upon their own inner resources will they find strength to carry on with their tasks, even if these, like his own, are almost intolerably burdensome. Life is a transient affair, according to Aurelius, a temporary visit to an alien land, and while it lasts all we can do is to confront its problems with all the courage and endurance we can muster. Many things, he believes in Stoic fashion, are predestined and cannot be altered; much else, however, can be altered and improved by the disciplined efforts of our own will power. Above all, we must treat our fellow human beings with unselfishness and decency, cleaving to the Stoic conviction that there is a spark of the same divinity in all of us. That being so, all other men and women are our brothers and sisters in the great cosmopolis of the universe, of which the Roman empire, for all its imperfections, seemed the nearest approximation upon this earth.

Marcus Aurelius set out to live up to these ideals by adopting an attitude of rigorous asceticism, characteristic of the times that were now beginning—an attitude that he displayed by harsh attacks on "the twitchings of appetite." Yet he was tortured, if not by such temptations—for of that we do not know—then by the grimness of his imperial responsibilities, from which his sensitive nature often shrank. He felt keen, self-searching, ever-recurrent doubts concerning his own personal adequacy, doubts which made him much more human than any other ancient Stoic. In terms of decent principles translated scrupulously into a consistent way of living, Marcus Aurelius' creed was the culmination of ancient paganism and of Rome.

EDITIONS—Letters: L. Pepe, ed., 1957. Meditations (with translation): C. R. Haines (Loeb ed.), 1915; A. I. Trannoy (Budé ed.), W. Theiler (German), 1951; A. S. L. Farquharson, 2nd ed., 1952; G. M. A. Grube, 1963; M. Staniforth (Penguin ed.), 1964.
ABOUT—G. Misch, History of Autobiography in Antiquity, 1950; A. Birley, Marcus Aurelius, 1966; A. Bodson, La morale sociale des derniers stoiciens: Sénèque, Épictète et Marc-Aurèle, 1967; R. Klein, ed., Marc Aurel, 1977.

AURELIUS VICTOR, SEXTUS. See Victor, Sextus Aurelius

AUSONIUS, Latin poet, was born at Burdigala (Bordeaux in southwestern France) in about A.D. 310 and died in about 395. His father was a well-known doctor. He was brought up by his grandmother and a maiden aunt and from 320 to 328 studied under an uncle at Tolosa (Toulouse), thereafter continuing his studies at Burdigala, where with some difficulty he learned Greek. Subsequently, he returned to Tolosa to become a teacher but then went back to his native town once again. There he taught for nearly thirty years, first at the secondary school level and then at the university level. In about 364 he was summoned to Treviri
ô sō′ ni us

(Trier on the Moselle) to become the tutor to Gratian, son of the emperor Valentinian I; he served on the imperial staff in campaigns against the German tribal group of the Alemanni (368–69). In 375 he held the minor office of quaestor, and then, after Gratian had ascended to the throne on the death of his father later in the year, Ausonius rose rapidly to the highest state posts, bringing in his wake his father, son, son-in-law, and nephew into official positions. In 378 he was made prefect of Gaul, and he became consul in the following year. When, however, the usurper Magnus Maximus killed Gratian in 383, Ausonius retired and lived quietly at Treviri. After Maximus had been overthrown in 388 Ausonius was too old for public employment and went to his estates near Burdigala, where he remained until his death, maintaining a correspondence with some of the most eminent men of his time.

Ausonius was an extremely prolific poet whose refined classicism was characteristic of fourth century upper-class culture in his native Gaul. He was an epicure, a loyal family man, an affectionate friend, and an amateur of the classics—but by no means a profound thinker. His principal gifts were for the ingenious handling of language and for the manipulation of verse in a variety of meters. Most of his works are little more than trifles, sometimes entertaining but more often tedious, though he more than once disarms criticism by apologizing for their worthlessness. To the historian, however, what he wrote is of considerable value, because, being profoundly self-centered, he reveals many things about himself and in the process adds a great deal of incidental information about the society in which he is living. Nominally he adhered to Christianity; as an occasional decorous prayer and hymn confirm. But in most of his works the Christian faith is quite unobtrusive, so that Ausonius may be regarded as the first Christian author whose writings do not center upon Christianity and as one of the forerunners of the secular literature of later Europe.

His *Ephemeris* (incomplete) is a versified account of his day from morning to night, quite humorous in parts. In the *Parentalia* he commemorates thirty of his own deceased relatives (including some whom he had never met), and in the *Commemoratio Professorum Burdigalensium* the same service is performed for his teachers at Burdigala (with results that are of interest for the history of ancient education). There are also thirty-five additional epitaphs and this suggests that Ausonius was in demand for obituaries of this kind. The *Eclogues* are thirty-six pieces on a variety of themes; one offers mnemonic aids to help in memorizing the details of the calendar. *Cupid Crucified,* inspired by a painting at Treviri, records a nightmare in which all the love-crossed heroines of mythology, reinforced by his own mother, threaten him with disciplinary retribution. His one hundred and twelve *Epigrams* include translations from the *Greek Anthology,* attempts at pornography, and praises of Bissula, a fair-haired, blue-eyed German given him as a share of the spoils in the Alemannic War. The *Ordo Nobilium Urbium* consists of addresses to twenty famous cities of the Roman world, beginning with Rome and ending with Burdigala; other poems of the same enumerative character feature the Seven Sages and the Twelve Caesars. Several poems in the *Domestica* enlarge on the writer's own consulship, which is also the theme of a grovelingly grateful prose letter addressed to Gratian.

Thirty-four *Epistles,* mostly in verse, and a number of contributions from his correspondents as well, are interesting because they feature distinguished figures of the time such as Symmachus (who rightly describes their exchange, however, as mutual backscratching) and Ausonius' own favorite pupil Paulinus of Nola (whose renunciation of his worldly responsibilities for a devout Christian life Ausonius finds incomprehensible). Other *Epistles* provide vivid pictures of his Greek bailiff and a neighboring squire. Utterly alien to the taste of today, though fashionable enough in Ausonius' own epoch, are the verbal tricks of such poems as the *Technopaegnion* (in which every line ends with a monosyllable), the *Griphus* (which elaborates the mystic number three with extraordinary ingenuity), and the *Nuptial Cento* (which cunningly rearranges parts of Virgilian lines to convey indecent meanings).

Far better than these third-rate works, at least to modern taste, is his poem of 483 hexameters in praise of the River Mosella (Moselle). The *Mosella* is carefully constructed in a series of rhetorically fashioned episodes. It begins with an itinerary of Ausonius' journey—probably undertaken in the course of the German war—from Bingen to Neumagen, where he first catches sight of the grassy-banked stream. Then we are given an account of its navigation and a description of the river bed, followed by an enumeration of the various fishes its waters contain. Next comes an eloquent word-picture of the vine-clad banks of the river, in a passage displaying a sense of natural beauty that seems halfway from classicism to medieval romance. We learn, also, of the pleasure that the stream gives the local inhabitants, and we are told of the country houses lining its banks and of the tributaries that increase its flow. And so Ausonius brings the Moselle to the Rhine.

EDITIONS with translation—H. G. Evelyn-White (Loeb ed.), 1919–21; M. Jasinski (French), 1935. *Translations* —J. Lindsay, 1930; H. Isbell, The Last Poets of Imperial Rome (Penguin ed.), 1971. The Mosella: C. Hosius, 3rd ed., reprint 1966; E. F. Corpet (Didot ed.), reprint 1972. ABOUT—M. J. Byrne, Prolegomena to an Edition of the Works of Ausonius, 1916; F. A. Wright, History of Later Latin Literature, 1931; F. J. E. Raby, History of Secular Latin Poetry, 2nd ed., 1957; J. Vogt, The Decline of Rome, 1967.

BABRIUS, Greek writer of fables, was probably an Italian—perhaps, to judge from his name, an Etruscan—who lived in Asia during the latter part of the second century A.D.: a papyrus containing part of his fables, is in handwriting that cannot be subsequent to 200.

He is the earliest Greek fabulist whose works survive. His fables, known as Aesopic *Mythiambi* after the half-legendary founder of the genre, are written in verse ("limping" iambics or scazons). The principal manuscript, discovered on Mount Athos in 1843 and now in the British Museum, contains 123 fables, many of them concerned with animals, arranged alphabetically in two

bä' bri us

67

books. The second book is incomplete, since the text breaks off at the letter *o.* Moreover, eighteen fables (including twelve from a Vatican manuscript and four from Palmyra wax-tablets) have been added; some are of doubtful authorship. Minoides Mynas, who discovered the Athos manuscript, later attempted unsuccessfully to insert ninety-four forgeries, probably written by himself. The two-book structure was known in the fifth century to the Roman fabulist Avianus or Avienus (not the same as the Etruscan poet Rufius Festus Avien[i]us). Originally, however, there may have been as many as ten books. The work is addressed to a son of "King Alexander" named Branchus, who has not been identified. The writer tells his fables succinctly and pleasingly, with a light and satirical touch that suggests city sophistication; the last two lines of a piece often conclude it with a punch line. Although Babrius is largely dependent on traditional Aesopic material for his subject matter, he does include narrative elements, from other sources, notably in the "Lying Arab" and "Priest of Cybele's Ass."

Babrius was very popular in ancient times, when the curriculum of the rhetorical schools regularly started with fables. In more recent epochs, the first critic who took a constructive interest in his work was Richard Bentley, in his *Dissertation Upon. . . the Fables of Aesop* (1697). In studying the prose fables attributed to Aesop, Bentley detected traces of versification and was thus able to isolate and reconstruct a number of verses that he reascribed to Babrius; and in the following century other scholars continued with this task of piecing together the metrical originals. It was only later that this approach was corroborated by the discovery of the Mount Athos manuscript.

EDITIONS with translation—D. B. Hull, Fables Told by Valerius Babrius, 1960; B. E. Perry, Babrius and Phaedrus (Loeb ed.), 1965.
ABOUT—R. C. D. Kovacs, The Aesopic Fable in Ancient Rhetorical Theory and Practice, 1950; B. E. Perry, Aesopica, 1952; M. Nøjgaard, La fable antique, v 2, 1967; L. Herrmann, Babrius et ses poèmes, 1973.

BACCHYLIDES, Greek poet, may have been born in approximately 524 or 521 B.C., or possibly a dozen or more years later. He died after 452. His birthplace was Iulis on the island of Ceos. His father's name was perhaps Midylus; his mother was the sister of the poet Simonides, whose personal follower he became, taking over his patrons. Bacchylides' earliest known literary activity may have been in Macedonia and Thessaly; he also undertook commissions from Aegina and Athens. In about 476 he accompanied Simonides to Sicily as the guest of King Hiero I of Syracuse. It is not known how long Bacchylides stayed on the island. Subsequently, he was exiled to the Peloponnese.

Our knowledge of his work was enormously increased by the discovery of two papyrus rolls in Egypt in 1896. They have subsequently been supplemented by additional finds; however, we still only have a small proportion of his work.

An important part of Bacchylides' work consists of Epinician Odes—that is to say, poems celebrating victories in the athletic and musical contests of the various Games. At least fifteen such Odes, attributable to Bacchylides' authorship, have survived in whole or part. In construction, they are comparable to the poems written by his contemporary Pindar for similar occasions: an elaborately recounted myth occupies the central position, around which the remaining parts of the ode form a frame. Bacchylides' pieces of this kind seem to have been composed in Thessaly (Ode 14) and Macedonia, and in about 485 he wrote Ode 13 for Pytheas of Aegina. Ode 10, of which the date is uncertain, was written in honor of an Athenian victor in the Isthmian Games. Ode 5 (476 B.C.) celebrated the victory of Hiero I of Syracuse in the horse race at Olympia, an event also commemorated by Pindar, who evidently took a jealous dislike to Simonides and Bacchylides during their subsequent visit to Sicily. Rivalry between Pindar and Bacchylides followed. In 470, where Hiero won his first chariot-race in the Pythian Games at Delphi, Pindar obtained the commission to compose the ode in the king's honor, and Bacchylides had to be

ba kil' i dēz

content with a brief congratulatory choral lyric (Ode 4). But when Hiero gained a similar victory at Olympia in 468, the positions of the two poets were reversed. Bacchylides also wrote at least five odes in honor of his fellow countrymen from Ceos who had won victories in the Games. Then, during his exile, he composed Ode 9 for Automedes of Phlius.

He also wrote a number of other pieces that can be roughly classified as hymns, including dithyrambs (originally songs in honor of Dionysus) and choral paeans, though the distinction between these two types of poetry had ceased to be clear. Extensive portions of half a dozen of his poems in this category survive. They include *The Sons of Antenor* (or *Demand for the Restoration of Helen*), describing the embassy of Menelaus and Odysseus to Troy; the *Heracles* (if that was its title), referring to the death of the hero at the hands of his wife Deianira; the *Youths (Eïtheoi)*, presenting the ship that carried the young Athenians to Crete as an offering to the Minotaur and showing how Theseus, as protector of one of the maidens destined for sacrifice, offered bold defiance to King Minos; the *Theseus*, in dialogue form, telling how Aegeus, King of Athens, heard news of the imminent arrival of the young hero—the performer of mighty deeds on the Corinthian Isthmus—but did not know him to be his own son; the *Io*, telling of Zeus's amorous intentions toward Io, the daughter of the king of Argos; and the *Idas*, in which the rape of Marpessa by Idas is described in a poem (now surviving in only a few verses) that was written for the Spartans, probably during the poet's period of exile. There is also some evidence for a *Philoctetes* and a *Laocoon,* both lost. In addition, Bacchylides wrote a panegyric *(encomium)* in honor of King Alexander of Macedon.

It was inevitable that Bacchylides should be compared with his competitor Pindar. The excellent critic known by the name of Longinus, who wrote the treatise *On the Sublime* in the first century A.D., duly contrasted them to the disfavor of Bacchylides, whom he assessed as smooth and equable but uninspired. It is true that Bacchylides with his well-trained, correct, and un-

profound simplicity is not in the same league as Pindar at all. Indeed, he more than once plagiarizes from that poet, so that he may well be the imitative "ape" to which Pindar makes a scornful reference. However, Bacchylides himself, tacitly allowing Pindar's claim to be considered an eagle, preferred to describe himself as the Cean nightingale. His particular talent was for narrative, presented with a light and polished clarity, enlivened by colorful epithets. Moreover, there are times when his rapid, sonorous flow raises him to the lyrical heights. Almost always he presents a lively stage, on which something bright and exciting and absorbing is happening.

EDITIONS—R. C. Jebb, 1905; A. Taccone, 1907; B. Snell (Teubner ed.), 10th ed., 1970. *Translations*—R. Fagles, 1961.
ABOUT—A. Severyns, Bacchylide, 1933; W. M. Calder III and J. Stern, eds., Pindaros und Bakchylides, 1970; E. Führer, Beiträge zur Metrik und Textkritik der griechischen Lyriker, 1976; M. R. Lefkowitz, The Victory Ode: An Introduction, 1976; A. Griffiths, Bacchylides, 1979.

BASIL, Saint (Basil the Great), Greek theologian, monastic organizer and bishop, was born at Caesarea in Cappadocia (Kayseri in eastern Asia Minor) in 329 to a rich, well-known Christian family. He was one of ten children; another of the five boys was St. Gregory of Nyssa, and one of his five sisters was St. Macrina the younger. Suffering from ill-health from the beginning, as he did all his life, Basil was brought up near Neocaesarea (now Niksar) in Pontus (northern Asia Minor) by his grandmother St. Macrina the elder and his mother St. Emmelia, daughter of a martyr. He received his education at Caesarea, Constantinople, and Athens, where be became acquainted with his fellow student the future emperor Julian the Apostate and gained the friendship of St. Gregory of Nazianzus (Basil, his brother Gregory of Nyssa, and Gregory of Nazianzus became known as the Cappadocian Trinity). In about 356 Basil returned home and practiced briefly as a rhetorician. Then, in 357, through the influence of his sister Macrina, he was converted to the monastic

baz′ il

movement, of which he gained firsthand experience by a tour of Egypt, Palestine, Syria, and Mesopotamia. Subsequently, he settled near his sister at Annesi in Cappadocia and organized with his brother Gregory the first large-scale, systematically planned monastery in Asia Minor; solitary asceticism, on the other hand, he discouraged. Ordained as a priest in 364, by Eusebius, bishop of Caesarea, Basil succeeded to that bishopric himself in 370 and until his death in 379 acted indefatigably in his efforts to oppose, and seek to win over, the adherents of Arianism, the form of Christianity that was favored by the eastern emperor Valens but that seemed to Basil and those who thought like him to relegate Jesus to inferiority in relation to God the Father. A stormy and sometimes headstrong controversialist, he nevertheless could, when he wished, bring great powers of tact, patience, and persistence to bear on the task of reconciliation.

Basil did much to give eastern orthodoxy its permanent form, and to the eastern church he is one of the Three Holy Hierarchs, the others being St. Gregory of Nazianzus and St. John Chrysostom. A sick man, Basil dreamed continually of a life of monastic solitude, devoted to reflection and creative work. Yet, as his activities in support of hostels and hospitals on the outskirts of Constantinople testified, he was above all else a practical organizer, therein resembling the western, Roman prelates (such as Pope Damasus with whom he corresponded) rather than the more philosophical and speculative eastern fathers: for Basil's genius lay in his administrative talent and found expression in his power not only to grasp the ideals of the growing church but to translate them into realistic effect. The *Longer* and *Shorter Rules,* which he composed for his monks with the help of St. Gregory of Nazianzus, exerted a decisive effect on the future of monasticism and were second only to the influence of the later *Rule* of St. Benedict, who owed a massive debt to Basil's principles and ideas.

Basil was also one of the first Greek theologians to insist on the essential value of the pagan classics for the education of Christian students. One of his surviving sermons, the *Address to Young Men on the Profitable Use of Pagan Literature,* puts forward, sometimes in rather prickly and defensive tones, his solution to this question, which is sometimes known as the theory of the honeybee: Christians must be as selective as bees, choosing from the pagan classics whatever is useful for their own purposes and rejecting the rest, so that in this fashion they can train their intellects until they are ready to comprehend the deeper sense of the holy scripture. Basil's advice, based on a remarkable combination of both cultures in his own person, affected generations of Christian leaders in the Byzantine empire and was widely read in Renaissance Italy.

Among his many theological studies, *On the Holy Spirit* was the first complete work ever to be devoted to that subject. It followed *Against Eunomius,* where Basil had already argued for the consubstantial nature of the Trinity, the terminology of which he did much to develop. His liturgical treatises, along with St. John Chrysostom's work, created the Byzantine liturgy which gradually superseded those of Alexandria and Antioch. The nine books of his *Hexaemeron,* or *Commentary on the Six Days of Creation,* illustrate his strongly marked rhetorical gifts. Basil's style, consciously archaistic in manner, greatly impressed the Byzantine scholar Photius, who described it as pure, persuasive, brilliant, and worthy of comparison with anything in Plato (from whom Basil often quotes) or Demosthenes. Historically speaking, however, the most significant portion of what he wrote consists of his letters, of which over three hundred authentic specimens provide a vivid and comprehensive picture of his daily activities.

EDITIONS with translation—Ascetic works: W. K. L. Clarke, 1925; M. M. Wagner, 1950. Letters: R. J. Deferrari (Loeb ed.), 1926–30; Y. Courtonne, Correspondance, 1957–66. On the Holy Spirit: B. Prucke, 1947; M. Blum, Über den Heiligen Geist, 1967. Address to Young Men on Greek Literature: R. J. Deferrari and M. J. P. McGuire (Loeb ed.), 1934; F. Boulenger, Aux jeunes gens sur la manière de tirer profit des lettres helléniques (Budé ed.), 1965; N. G. Wilson, Saint Basil on Greek Literature, 1975. Other works: G. Giet, On the Hexaemeron, 1950; A. C. Way, Exegetic Homilies, 1963; and for thirty-two homilies found at Stavronikita on Mount Athos, Symbolae Osloenses, v 51, 1976.
ABOUT—M. M. Fox, The Life and Times of St. Basil

the Great as Revealed in His Works, 1939; D. Amand, L'ascèse monastique de Saint Basile, 1949; A. Schmemann, The Historical Road of Eastern Orthodoxy, 1963; A. Angelis, Basilio di Cesarea, 1968; B. Savranis, Basileios der Grosse, 1972; Y. Courtonne, Un témoin du quatrième siècle oriental: Saint Basile et son temps d'après sa correspondance, 1973; P. Scazzoso, Introduzione all'ecclesiologia di S. Basilio, 1974.

BASSUS, AUFIDIUS. See Aufidius Bassus

BEDE. See *British Authors Before 1800* (H. W. Wilson, 1952)

BENEDICT, Saint, of Nursia (Norcia) in Umbria, abbot and Latin writer, was born in about A.D. 480 and died in about 543. All that we know about his life is derived from the *Dialogues* of Pope Gregory I (the Great, Pope from 590 to 604), who states that he was given his information by four of Benedict's disciples. Benedict was the son of prosperous parents who sent him to receive a secular education at Rome. Shocked, however, by the loose living in the city, he retired to Enfide (Affile) in the Simbruine Hills of Latium and later to a cave in the rocks above Sublaqueum (Subiaco) in the Abruzzi foothills, where he lived by himself for three years. As the fame of his asceticism spread, he was invited to become abbot of an adjoining monastery. He accepted the offer, but when his attempts to improve the institution stirred up ill will and a plot was even formed to poison him, he resigned and went back to his solitary cave. Once again disciples flocked to join him, and before long he established twelve small monastic institutions, each comprising twelve monks. Harassed, however, by the hostility of a neighboring priest, he decided to depart from the area and followed by his disciples settled at Monte Cassino in the Duchy of Benevento, where he founded and directed a monastery (c. 529) and won over the local population. His sister Scholastica came to live nearby as abbess of a nunnery, and in about 542 Benedict was visited by Totila, the Ostrogothic

ben′ ə dikt

king of Italy. His views on the monastic life are embodied in his *Regula Monachorum,* popularly known as the *Rule of Saint Benedict.* Composed, as Gregory the Great declared, in admirably lucid language and full of good sense, it supplies a brief but comprehensive series of directions for the administration and spiritual and material well-being of a monastery. Setting out, as its author puts it, to wage war against the Devil, the *Rule* demands the highest standard of conduct. It provides for a day divided as follows: five or six hours of prayer, four hours of reading the Scriptures and other religious writings, and five hours of some kind of manual activity. Each monk was to do the work for which he was most aptly fitted. Truly Roman in its orderly restraint, the *Rule* is always reasonable and temperate: to the vows of poverty, chastity, and obedience Benedict added the principle of stability. Extreme asceticism is not encouraged, and the abbot is warned not to overwork his monks, who are to be given an adequate quantity of food and allowed between seven and a half and eight hours of sleep. Their efforts are to be directed toward making their monastery self-sufficient and self-contained; and much time is to be spent not only in teaching the young but in copying manuscripts. The *Rule* drew on earlier sources, of which one of the most important seems to have been a longer and less incisive anonymous document known as the *Rule of the Master (Regula Magistri).*

After Benedict's death, his *Rule* was revised and amplified by a number of other hands, and it is supposed that the "final" text was established by Charlemagne in 787. By that time, the ideas contained in his *Rule* had gradually spread throughout western Europe, because of their excellence as a practical code. First Basil had adapted the monastic ideal to the world, and now Benedict had harmonized its eastern features to Roman law and industry, channeling the activities of monks and nuns into a disciplined, balanced, communal service of the Christian idea. And so, although he was, in his day, the founder of no order—the name Benedictine was not adopted until nearly 1400—it was from a Benedictine monastery in Rome that monks set out to convert England. In many other countries, too, the movement that Benedict had originated became so powerful and such an effective support to the papacy that the three hundred years after 700 have been named by historians the "Benedictine centuries." Benedict's *Rule* has been described as the central fact of western monastic history and, indeed, as the greatest single document of the entire Middle Ages.

EDITIONS (of the Rule), with translation—J. McCann, 1952; R. Hanslik, Benedicti Regula, 1960; D. H. Farmer, The Rule of St. Benedict, 1964; A. de Vogué and J. Neufville, La règle du Maître, 1972; G. Bellardi (Italian), 1975.
ABOUT—T. F. Lindsay, The Holy Rule for Laymen, 1947; T. Maynard, St. Benedict and His Monks, 1954; L. von Matt and S. Hilpisch, Saint Benedict, 1961; M. D. Knowles, Great Historical Enterprises, 1963: Regulae Benedicti Studia, v 1 (Erster Internationaler Regula Benedicti Kongress), 1972.

BION the Borysthenite, Greek popular philosopher and lecturer, was born in about 325 B.C. at Olbia, near the mouth of the River Hypanis (Bug) in southern Russia, not far from the estuary of the Borysthenes (Dnieper). His mother was a prostitute; his father, a fishmonger who had formerly been a slave, committed a fraud, which caused the whole family to be sold into slavery. However, Bion, who became the property of a rhetorician, received a good education. He was subsequently given back his freedom and inherited the fortune of his master. He proceeded to Athens and studied in the Aristotelian and Platonic schools (the Lyceum and the Academy) but was more strongly influenced first by the Cyrenaic creed that happiness is obtained by adapting oneself to circumstances and then more particularly by the school of the Cynics whose critical, caustic wit and anti-establishment way of life he admired. Yet he was not the adherent of any particular doctrines.

For a time Bion visited the court of the Macedonian king Antigonus II Gonatas; he survived Antigonus, who died in 239. But he spent most of his time wandering from city

bī′ ən

to city, lecturing for fees; he was one of the first of a long line of wandering professors who popularized philosophy and gave a special character to their age, like the wandering Christian preachers of a subsequent epoch. He was also credited with the foundation of the Greek *diatribe* (familiar conversation or address), which he converted from a popular variation of the academic lecture into a literary form. Thus Bion was described by Diogenes Laertius as "the first to tart up philosophy"—his term describes the gaudy embroidered clothes that prostitutes wore—by composing miscellaneous essays about such subjects as poverty, exile, death, and self-sufficiency and by cramming these pieces with mythical examples, erotica, quotations from poets, anecdotes, antitheses, personifications, and puns; the tone aimed at was *spoudogeloion,* a mixture of humor and seriousness. The connotation of abusiveness has only been imported into the term *diatribe* in modern times, but the few surviving titles and notes of Bion's compositions suggest that he prepared the way for this development by launching vituperative attacks on various kinds of passions and prejudices. Horace writes of sharply humorous satires as Bionian conversations *(Bionei sermones)* to which he acknowledges a personal debt; and, indeed, many passages of the Roman satirical poets are indebted for both theme and manner to the diatribes of Bion.

We also owe him a number of concepts and sayings that have passed into familiar usage: the idea of life as a feast from which one should eventually depart as a satisfied guest; the simile of the human being as an actor on the stage of the world; and the final words of the dying frog: "This may be fun for you, but it's death to me." Bion took great pride in his wit and was something of a charlatan; but he had his share of humane feelings. Moreover, he could compel men and women to listen to him; even in the Rhodian docks the sailors would stop to listen to his message: be content with very little, and face your fortune and your fate without flinching.

EDITIONS—C. Wachsmuth, Sillographorum Graecorum Reliquiae, 1885. *Translations*—L. Paquet, Les cyniques grecs: Fragments et témoignages, 1975; J. F. Kindstrand, Bion of Borysthenes: A Collection of the Fragments, 1976.

ABOUT—A. Oltramare, Origines de la diatribe romaine, 1926; D. R. Dudley, History of Cynicism, 1937; J. P. Sullivan, Roman Satire, *and* I. G. Kidd, The Impact of Philosophy on Greco-Roman Literature, *in* D. Daiches and A. Thorlby, eds., Literature and Western Civilization, v 1, The Classical World, 1972.

BOETHIUS (Anicius Manlius Severinus Boethius), c. A.D. 480–524, was a Latin philosophical and theological writer and state official. He belonged to the leading Christian family, the Anicii, one of whose members, Olybrius, had been emperor in 472, four years before the western empire came to an end. Boethius' father died when Boethius was still a boy and the lad was brought up by the senator and historian Quintus Aurelius Memmius Symmachus, great-grandson of the more famous Symmachus who had been the pagan opponent of Saint Ambrose. Boethius enjoyed the high favor of Theodoric the Great, the Ostrogothic king of Italy, becoming consul in 510 and director of the civil service *(magister officiorum)* some ten years later. But in 522–23, when a senator named Albinus was charged with plotting against the monarch in favor of the eastern (Byzantine) emperor Justin I, Boethius defended the accused man and thus incurred the anger of Theodoric, who imprisoned him and put him to death in 524, probably at Ticinum (Pavia), where his remains are buried. Boethius was posthumously revered as a martyr and a saint. Moreover, throughout the Middle Ages he exerted an enormous influence, because his writings preserved and handed on a very large part of the culture and civilization of later antiquity.

His theological works, the *Tractates,* five of which survive today, were valued particularly highly. They treat the Christian religion after the manner of Aristotelian philosophy, thus paving the way for St. Thomas Aquinas: for example, Boethius' essay *On the Trinity (De Trinitate)* offers a philosophical explanation, in Aristotelian

bō ē′ thi us

terms, of the paradox that God is both Three and One. *Against Eutyches and Nestorius* makes a similar attempt to define the double nature of Christ. Later scholastic philosophy owes as great a debt to him as to Augustine.

Boethius also wrote a number of works on the four arts of the medieval educational curriculum, the *quadrivium:* arithmetic, geometry, music, and astronomy. His treatises on arithmetic and music *(De Institutione Arithmetica, Musica)* have survived intact. Adaptations, in both cases, of Greek textbooks by Nicodemus of Gerasa, they draw on Archimedes for their mechanics and on the Pythagoreans in musical matters. This musical tractate was especially influential, receiving notable attention, for example, from Chaucer. Boethius also wrote a *Geometria,* now almost completely lost, in which he translated or elaborated upon the *Elements* of Euclid. His work on astronomy, founded on Ptolemy's, has completely disappeared.

On the other hand his very large output in the field of logic, which virtually created a new philosophical idiom, has survived almost in its entirety. Early on, he had declared it his intention to translate and write commentaries upon all the writings of Aristotle and Plato, so as to construct a harmony blending and reconciling the two. In this huge program his works include translations of Aristotle's *Organon, Prior Analytics, Topics, Sophistici Elenchi, Categories,* and *On Interpretation* (the last two accompanied by commentaries—in the latter case, by two), as well as a translation of Porphyry's *Isagoge* (once again with two commentaries), and an incomplete commentary on Cicero's *Topica.* Boethius also wrote a number of independent philosophical works of his own, devoted mainly to logical themes and derived for the most part from Aristotelian sources, employing the writers of Porphyry's school as intermediaries.

But Boethius' principal claim to fame as a writer and an independent philosopher is his *Consolation of Philosophy,* written in prison. In the five books of this work, which is conceived as a dialogue between himself and Philosophy, poems in a variety of meters—often of high quality—alternate with longer sections of prose. Although Boethius was a Christian, his book, being concerned with philosophy ("natural theology"), ignores the possibility of finding comfort in specifically Christian beliefs. After a first book in which Philosophy declares the world to be ruled not by chance but by the Divine Reason of God, the second deals with the vicissitudes of fortune, while the third describes the Supreme Good, the fourth justifies divine government, and the fifth discusses Free Will. Boethius was an accomplished Hellenist and draws freely on Greek and especially Neoplatonist sources. Written under sentence of death, the treatise is gallant and moving and majestically calm. It provided solace to innumerable readers throughout the Middle Ages, when it was more frequently rendered into European languages than any other book. In England its translators included Alfred the Great and Chaucer as well as Queen Elizabeth I in later times. It moved the historian Gibbon to declare: "The senator Boethius is last of the Romans whom Cato or Tully [Cicero] could have acknowledged for their countryman."

WORKS—(1) *Theological tractates:* De Trinitate; Utrum Pater et Filius et Spiritus Sanctus de Divinitate Substantialiter Praedicentur; Quomodo Substantiae, in Eo Quod Sint, Bonae Sint, cum non Sint, Substantialiter Bona; De Fide Catholica; Contra Eutychen et Nestorium. The Hebdomades is lost. (2) *Educational works:* See text of article above. (3) *Philosophical translations and commentaries:* See above; also perhaps parts of a commentary on Aristotle's Prior Analytics. (4) *Original logical works:* Elementary treatise on categorical syllogisms, partly in two recensions (Prolegomena, Introductio); De Syllogismo Hypothetico; De Divisione; De Differentiis Topicis.
EDITIONS—L. Bieler, De Consolatione, 1957; S. J. Tester, revised version of E. K. Rand's and H. F. Stewart's The Theological Tractates, and new translation of Consolation (Loeb ed.), 1973; O. Dall'Era, La Consolazione della filosofia, 1977. *Translations*—V. E. Watts (Penguin ed.), 1976.
ABOUT—H. R. Patch, The Tradition of Boethius, 1935; H. M. Barrett, Boethius, 1940; K. Dürr, The Propositional Logic of Boethius, 1951; P. Courcelle, La Consolation de philosophie dans la tradition littéraire: Antécédents et postérité de Boèce, 1967; E. S. Zalewski, Boethius' Commentary on Categories, 1969; L. Minio-Paluello, Boethius, *in* Dictionary of Scientific Biography, 1970, pp 228-36; H. Scheible, Die Gedichte in der Consolatio Philosophiae bei Boethius, 1972.

CAECILIUS STATIUS, Latin comic poet, was an Insubrian Gaul born in 223/2 B.C. at Mediolanum (Milan, at that time in Cisalpine Gaul). Brought to Rome as a slave between 200 and 194, he was freed later by his master Caecilius, whose name he assumed. According to St. Jerome—who seems to have obtained his information from Suetonius—Caecilius Statius was "famous" in 179 and died in 168 (if the reading is correct).

He had become a friend of his fellow poet Ennius, and it was possibly in order to avoid competition with him in other fields that Caecilius Statius concentrated on the *comoedia palliata,* comic drama dependent on Greek models (i.e. on the Athenian New Comedy of Menander). In this genre he was ranked comparable with Plautus and Terence. Varro recorded that the reputation of Caecilius Statius' plot-construction and emotional power was unequaled, and in c. 100 B.C. Volcacius Sedigitus placed him first in a list of ten writers of *palliatae,* with Plautus second and Terence sixth. Cicero, too, was quoted as ranking him at the top of all Roman writers of comedy. Since his plays, except for three hundred lines of fragments, have not survived, we cannot assess these judgments, but the extant passages show a free use of lyric which is characteristic of Plautus but hardly exists in Terence. Caecilius' broad humor also seems closer to the Plautine manner. On the other hand he resembled Terence in his serious-minded handling of his themes (noted by critics in the Augustan age) and in a taste for quotable, sententious turns of phrase and a close adherence to his Greek models, including the use not merely of Greek proper names but of words and whole phrases in Greek. It is also possible that Caecilius was the first poet to make use of prologues to express his own personal opinions, as Terence (who was believed to have received encouragement from him as a young man) did later. In the prologue to Terence's *Hecyra* the actor manager Lucius Ambivius Turpio observed that, although by presenting Caecilius' comedies repeatedly he had managed to make them popular, the plays had been severely criticized when they first appeared upon the stage. This may have been because

sē si′ li us st ā′ shi us

Caecilius had not yet gained complete mastery of the Latin language: even Cicero, despite his generally high opinion of his work, describes him as an inferior Latinist *(malus auctor Latinitatis)*.

Of his works we have forty-two titles, mostly in Latinized Greek, including *Hypobolimaeus (The Supposititious Child), Ex hautou hestos (Beside Himself, The Maniac),* and *Plocium (The Necklace).* It is not possible to reconstruct any of Caecilius' plots with completeness. But in the last-named play, adapted (not very closely) from the *Plokion* by Menander, the marriage plans of a young man and a young woman are upset when the young woman gives birth to a child of questionable paternity; her fiancé's mother suspects her own husband, but the matter is cleared up when a necklace supplies proof that the fiancé himself is the father after all.

Caecilius Statius was apparently the first of a series of eminent Latin authors who came from northern Italy, including, later, Catullus and Pliny the Younger.

EDITIONS—T. Guardi, Cecilio Stazio: I frammenti, 1974. *Translations*—E. H. Warmington, Remains of Old Latin (Loeb ed.), revised ed., 1956.
ABOUT—F. Arnaldi, Da Plauto a Terenzio, 1946–47; W. Beare: The Roman Stage, 3rd ed. revised, 1969; G. Williams *in* D. Daiches and A. Thorlby, eds., Literature and Western Civilization, v 1, The Classical World, 1972; J. Wright, Dancing in Chains, 1974.

CAELIUS, Latin writer, was the author of a cookbook whose style suggests it was written about A.D. 400. Entitled *Apicius, or the Art of Cookery by Caelius (Caelii Apicius de Re Coquinaria),* the work provides a large number of recipes, both ordinary and exotic. Among the subjects with which it deals are sauces and flavorings; methods of preserving meats, fruits, and olives; sausages and mincemeats; soups; vegetables; poultry, meat, and fish; and mixed dishes of poultry and meat, fish and vegetables. A special section is devoted to the dishes particularly favored by rich Romans.

We do not know who Caelius was. However, Apicius, after whom his book is called,

sē′ li us

had been the proverbial name of many Roman gourmets. Caelius' work was ascribed to at least three of these Apicii. The first flourished in the second or first century B.C. The second, who was born Marcus Gavius but took the name Apicius from his forerunner, lived under Augustus and Tiberius; he was the most famous of the three and left writings on cookery (in addition, perhaps, to erotic works). This second Apicius was referred to by a number of ancient writers; according to Seneca the Younger he conducted a cooking school but fell heavily into debt and killed himself, terrified that he would not have enough money to enable him to live in comfort. He invented various sorts of cakes and ragouts, and either he or one of the other Apicii also gave his name to several kinds of cakes.

The third man who bore or assumed the designation of Apicius lived in the second century A.D. He devised a secret method of preserving oysters, which enabled him to transport the delicacy to the emperor Trajan when he was far away in the east fighting a war against the Parthians.

How far the discoveries or writings of these three men were incorporated or adapted in Caelius' book is uncertain, but since the second Apicius is known to have been an author it is a particularly reasonable assumption that he was the man upon whom Caelius principally drew. If so, however, later material was also inserted in Caelius' work, since it refers to dishes named after the emperors Vitellius (A.D. 69) and Commodus (180–92).

EDITIONS—Martin Lister, De Obsoniis et Condimentis sive de Arte Coquinaria (de luxe edition, 125 copies), 1705; J. D. Vehling, Apicius: Cooking and Dining in Imperial Rome, 1936; B. Flower and E. Rosenbaum, The Roman Cookery Book: A Critical Translation of the Art of Cooking for Use in the Study and Kitchen, 1958; J. André, Apicius: L'art culinaire (Budé ed.), 1974.

CAESAR, GAIUS JULIUS, Roman conqueror, dictator, and Latin writer, was born in 100 B.C. He had connections with the general and political leader of the "popular" party Marius (d. 86), whose wife Julia was his aunt. In 84, Julius Caesar himself mar-

CAESAR

GAIUS JULIUS CAESAR

ried the daughter of Marius' associate Cinna. After serving with the army in Asia in 81, Caesar came to the public eye in Rome by conducting two (unsuccessful) prosecutions (77), after which he retired to the island of Rhodes to work under the Greek rhetorician Apollonius Molon. On the way to the island he was kidnapped by pirates, whom he subsequently captured and crucified. Returning to Rome, he was elected a priest *(pontifex)* in 73. In 70 he spoke in the Assembly in favor of granting an amnesty to the Marians whose enmity to the conservative dictator Sulla and his Senate party had caused them to be exiled, and in the following year he delivered the funeral speech for his aunt Julia, Marius' widow. Then, during his aedileship (superintendency of public works and archives) in 65, he restored the trophies of Marius—although, after his wife's death in 68, he had chosen Sulla's granddaughter as his new bride.

At this period, spending heavily and lacking resources of his own, Caesar was financed by the wealthy landowner Crassus, and there was a report, though it was probably without foundation, that the two men were involved in a plot to murder the consuls of 65 B.C. In 63 Caesar engineered the trial of Gaius Rabirius (allegedly a participant in the murder of the "popular" politician Saturninus in 100) as a demonstration against the practice, favored by conservative senators, of pronouncing emergency decrees; in the same year he achieved his first major political success by securing election as chief priest *(pontifex maximus)*. When Cicero, consul in 63, spoke in favor of executing the captured supporters of the conspirator Catiline, Caesar (who may, at an earlier stage, have been one of Catiline's backers) opposed the measure and gained only greater ill-will from right-wing senators, but was not successful. Then, after holding a governorship for a year in Farther Spain, he formed a close though informal, anti-conservative alliance with the Roman general Pompey (returned from eastern conquests) and Crassus, which was known as the First Triumvirate.

One of the principal results of this compact was his election to the consulship of 59. During his tenure in this office he satisfied the demands of Pompey and Crassus and secured his own subsequent appointment to a governorship comprising Illyricum (Dalmatia), Cisalpine Gaul (northern Italy), and Transalpine or Narbonese Gaul (southern France). This composite post served him as a springboard for the conquest of the remaining parts of Gaul (central and northern France), an enterprise which, preceded by the suppression of the German intruder Ariovistus, occupied the years 58–51 B.C. By 56 Caesar regarded the pacification of the country as complete. Meanwhile, however, the friendly relationships between the triumvirs were showing signs of strain, and in 55 the three men met at the Conference of Luca (Lucca) to plan the further fulfillment of their individual ambitions. Caesar then spent the campaigning seasons of 55 and 54 on a reconnaissance in Germany and on two expeditions to Britain. But now the scene darkened, for three reasons. First, Caesar's daughter, who was married to Pompey and had formed a bond between the two men, died; next, Crassus was killed fighting against the Parthians; and finally, two years of sporadic revolts in northern Gaul were followed in 52 by a general rising against Caesar in the central regions of the country under the leadership of Vercingetorix. Finally, however, the rebel leader was taken prisoner at Alesia (Alise-Sainte-Reine), and Gaul was reduced to dependent status, which was subsequently converted into formal annexation.

Caesar's relations with Pompey now deteriorated, and civil war between the two men broke out in 49. After capturing Italy and Spain, Caesar won the decisive battle of Pharsalus in Thessaly (48), and the defeated Pompey fled to Egypt where he was murdered. Caesar, living with the young queen Cleopatra VI in Alexandria, spent the winter fighting off their Egyptian enemies, and then, after a brief campaign in 47 against the king of Pontus in Asia Minor ("I came, I saw, I conquered"), overcame the armies of Pompey's sons and supporters at Thapsus (Ras Dimas) in northern Africa and Munda in southern Spain. During the intervals between these campaigns and in the one remaining year of his life after the fighting was concluded, he accomplished many outstanding administrative reforms—including a solution of the difficult debt question—and founded many settlements (Roman citizen colonies) for ex-soldiers and civilians alike. From 48 onwards he had held the dictatorship for varying periods, and early in 44 he became dictator for life *(perpetuo)*. This permanent curb on the freedom of the nobles, combined with the prospect of their subordination to his secretaries during his forthcoming eastern expedition, caused a group of them to plan his assassination, which they carried out on March 15th, at a Senate meeting in a hall attached to the Theater of Pompey.

Caesar's work *On the Gallic War (De Bello Gallico)* has survived. It consists of seven books, each covering a year from 58 to 52 (together with a final book down to 50, written by his officer Aulus Hirtius). Caesar also wrote three books entitled *On the Civil War.* These two compositions were entitled *Commentaries,* a term which deliberately falls somewhat short of *Histories,* denoting rather a set of commander's dispatches or memoranda, amplified partly by speeches (providing, as almost always in antiquity, the background rather than the exact words) and partly by informative material of other kinds. Caesar's powerful intellect and lucid, compact, nonrhetorical Latinity transform these ostensibly unambitious works into masterpieces. The author's unique inside knowledge as Roman commander-in-chief and the versatility of his talents confer extraordinary authority on what he writes, particularly on his expert descriptions of warfare and on the revelations of Roman efficiency and discipline that characterize the whole story. On the other hand the narrative is colored by his own personal preoccupations, most of all by his wish to refute his political enemies at Rome by displaying himself as the simple, straightforward patriot fighting necessary wars. His desire to create this largely erroneous impression sometimes induced him to magnify, minimize, and distort, but Caesar was too good a publicist to falsify the actual facts more than he deemed absolutely necessary.

On the Gallic War is the only contemporary narrative of a major Roman foreign war that has come down to us. It has been commended to students of war by generals of the caliber of Turenne, Napoleon, and Wellington. The ease and swiftness of Caesar's style (which has caused his *Commentaries,* rather curiously, to become required reading for generations of young school children) communicates a telling urgency to the whole account, and his deeds as he reports them, stirring and horrible alike, speak for themselves as freshly as when they were first written down. Apart from his own self-justifications, praise and blame are pared to a minimum—and so is information about individuals other than himself, including even his own principal subordinates. Nevertheless, the ferocious tale is varied by unexpected personal touches and insights that elevate it to unquestionable literary heights.

Each of the books that the *Gallic War* contains seems to have been completed at the end of the year with which it deals. These annual reports may have been sent, unofficially, one by one, to leading Romans (the men Caesar wanted to convince) in order to win their support in successive crises and elections. The work was published as a whole when the hostilities were well advanced or complete. The same is probably true of the *Civil War,* which covers the two initial years of that conflict: that the first annual instalment was at once made known to significant politicians is strongly suggested by its unusually emphatic, not to say strident, note of personal apologia. The argument, which Caesar constantly reiterates, is that the narrow, hate-ridden vendetta of his political enemies had forced on him a war he never wanted.

Caesar also wrote a number of other compositions, which have not survived. Beside some juvenile writings and a collection of sayings (which Augustus later suppressed as too trifling), he was the author of a study on grammar *(De Analogia),* which he dictated on his way across the Alps back to his province. This was dedicated to Cicero. But Cicero's praise of Cato the Younger, who killed himself after the battle of Thapsus, irritated Caesar so much that he answered it in a long and violent *Anti-Cato* (this did not, however, achieve the destruction of Cato's reputation). Then, on his way to Spain for the Munda campaign (45), Caesar composed a versified account of his journey *(Iter).* This was only one of a number of his poems (of which a few lines survive). They were not very highly regarded. But his oratory, which has likewise almost entirely disappeared, was second only to Cicero's.

WORKS—Supplementary books of the Civil War (on the Alexandrian, African, and Spanish wars) are by other writers. The author of On the Alexandrian War may have been Aulus Hirtius.
EDITIONS with translation—S. A. Handford, Caesar: The Conquest of Gaul (Penguin ed.), 1951; J. Pearl, Caesar's Gallic War, 1962; J. F. Mitchell, Caesar: The Civil War (Penguin ed.), 1967; E. Oddone, Cesare: La guerra civile, 1977.
ABOUT (the Commentaries)—K. Barwick, Caesars Bellum Civile: Tendenz, Abfassungszeit und Stil, 1951; M. Rambaud, L'art de la déformation historique dans les commentaires de César, 1953; D. Rasmussen, Caesars Commentarii: Stil und Stilwandel am Beispiel der direkten Rede, 1963; F. F. Adcock, Caesar as Man of Letters, 2nd ed., 1969; F. H. Mutschler, Erzählstil und Propaganda in Caesars Kommentaren, 1975; H. Gesche, Caesar, 1976; W. Richter, Caesar als Darsteller seiner Taten: Eine Einführung, 1977. General bibliographies in M. Grant, Julius Caesar, 1972, and Caesar, 1973.

CALLIMACHUS, Greek poet and scholar, was born in about 310–305 B.C. and died in about 240. He was a native of Cyrene (in Libya), the son of Battus, and a student of

ka li' mà kus

Hermocrates of Iasus. In his youth he moved to Alexandria, where he became a school teacher in one of its suburbs, Eleusis. Later, he was introduced to King Ptolemy II Philadelphus (283–246 B.C.), who gave him employment in the Alexandrian library. Callimachus conducted a vigorous literary feud with Apollonius Rhodius—first his pupil, but then his superior as the library director—who championed large poems against Callimachus' preference for small, highly polished pieces. Callimachus expressed his position in the phrase "a big book is a big evil." For a while, Callimachus was victorious, and Apollonius withdrew to Rhodes; but the taste for long poems prevailed in the end. The two poets were eventually reconciled, their burial places were side by side.

The only complete works of Callimachus that have survived are his *Hymns* and *Epigrams.* Of his six *Hymns,* the first four employ the epic dialect, the last two the Doric. All are in hexameters except the fifth which consists of elegiac couplets. Although modeled generally on the Homeric hymns, the hymns of Callimachus were never intended to be recited at festivals but are literary productions designed for recitation or reading to small audiences. Hymn No. 1, to Zeus, has a humorous undercurrent but also contains contemporary political allusions. So do hymns No. 2 and No. 4 to Apollo. The latter modernizes the Delian part of the Homeric *Hymn to Apollo,* whereas No. 2, together with No. 5 (The Baths of Pallas) and No. 6 (to Demeter), comprise a more original achievement by Callimachus, who vividly combines the techniques of lyric and dramatic mime, while also, in the Demeter hymn, showing himself by no means averse to the gruesome and macabre. His epigrams, which were extensively admired and copied, are represented by sixty-four examples today. Some are dedications and epitaphs; others express personal emotions or describe lovers' troubles.

Callimachus' longest and best known piece, of which only fragments survive, bore the name of the *Causes (Aitia).* It was a narrative of about seven thousand lines, divided into four books of elegiacs. The poem, in the form of a dream-journey from Libya to

Mount Helicon, where the Muses teach the poet many kinds of mythological learning, consisted of etiological myths (i.e. those indicating "causes" and origins) relating to Greek history, customs, and rituals. Praise of the early epic poet Hesiod is introduced both at the beginning and the end of the poem. We know of the subjects of Book 4, and to some extent those of Book 3, from fragments of three *Expositions (Diegeseis)* that have been found on papyri and apparently go back to a single lost original. From papyri, too, come the longest extant fragments of the *Aitia* itself; these relate to the cities of Sicily and the myths of Icus and of Acontius and Cydippe.

Callimachus published a second, revised edition of the *Aitia* that was subsequently included in his collected works. As a general foreword to this collection, or more particularly perhaps as an introduction to the *Aitia* itself, he wrote a *Retort to His Critics (Answer to the Telchines),* in which he sets out his final and most controversial views on how poetry ought to be written. Moreover, by way of a further answer to these critics, while deliberately refraining from the composition of large-scale epic works, he wrote a number of minor, shorter epics, including the *Hecale,* the most famous miniature epic *(epyllion)* in Greek literature. This poem, which was about a thousand lines in length, has vanished, but its subject is known to have been Theseus' conquest of the bull of Marathon, with emphasis on the nobility and hospitality of the poor old woman Hecale, who offered the hero a rustic meal while he was on his way to Marathon.

In its final edition the *Aitia* was followed by a book of poems in various iambic meters (i.e. based on the short-long iambic foot), in which Callimachus assumes the character of the satirical iambic poet Hipponax of Ephesus of the sixth century B.C. The collection amounts to about a thousand lines, divided into thirteen pieces—7–11 reminiscent of the *Aitia,* but 1–3 and 5 satirizing contemporary literary and moral attitudes and 4 and 13 responding to the critics of Callimachus' literary methods. The sixth piece describes Phidias' statue of Zeus at Olympia, and the twelfth celebrates the birth of a daughter to a friend Leon.

Of Callimachus' lyrics very little survives, but enough to show that he employed a considerable variety of meters, and used them to great effect; a surviving fragment of the *Divinization of Arsinoe (Ektheosis Arsinoes),* published after the death of that queen in 270 B.C., illustrates his skill as a court poet. So does another fragment from one of his elegiac pieces, the *Victory of Sosibius,* which commemorates a future minister of Ptolemy IV and shows that Callimachus was still writing significant poetry in the late 240s B.C. His *Ibis* delivers a mocking invective, in deliberately tortuous language, against his literary rival Apollonius Rhodius.

The Suidas (Suda) lexicon of the tenth century A.D. indicates that Callimachus also wrote tragedies, comedies, and satirical sketches. However, no passage from any of these works has come down to us.

Despite the ill-luck that has left us such a small proportion of his output, it is evident that Callimachus was a poet of very marked originality, whose verses (although their Alexandrian addiction to learning antagonizes modern taste), displayed bold experimentation, wide-ranging versatility, and an extreme degree of polished refinement, lightened by the interspersion of many lively realistic and personal touches.

His critics among contemporary poets, whom he continued to counterattack until the end of his life, included not only Apollonius Rhodius but Asclepiades of Samos and his collaborator Posidippus. To judge from the frequency with which Callimachus' poems were quoted by subsequent scholars and the unusually large number of papyri on which portions of his works appear, his reputation and popularity in the ancient world must have exceeded those of any other Hellenistic poet. Among Latin writers, too, he exercised a strong influence on the innovating poetical school of the first century B.C.; and Catullus, with whom the movement attained its climax, not only borrowed his lyric meters but closely adapted one of the sections of the *Aitia* in his "Lock of Berenice" (the model of Alexander Pope's "Rape of the Lock").

In the time of Augustus, Propertius declared himself, after his own fashion, the Roman Callimachus; and Ovid and the unknown author of *The Salad (Moretum)* admired and imitated his account of the country meal in the *Hecale*. Callimachus' epigram on his friend Heraclitus of Halicarnassus has been perpetuated by the translation: "They told me, Heraclitus, they told me you were dead" (nineteenth century English schoolmaster and lyric poet William Cory).

He was also a prose writer on a very extensive scale, though every one of these works is lost. They included his 120-volume catalog of the Alexandrian library; a study of the writings and language of the fifth century philosopher Democritus of Abdera; a *Chronological Summary of the Athenian Dramatic Poets;* collections of Paradoxes and Glosses; and a variety of encyclopedic studies on subjects including Winds, Rivers, Nymphs, Birds and Games.

Among his scholarly pupils were not only Apollonius Rhodius (who also wrote prose as well as verse) but Eratosthenes of Cyrene and Aristophanes of Byzantium.

EDITIONS—R. Pfeiffer, 1949–53; F. Bornmann, Calimachi Hymnus in Dianam, 1968; G. R. McLennan, Hymn to Zeus, 1977; F. Williams, Hymn to Apollo, 1978. *Translations*—A. W. Mair *in* A. W. Mair and G. R. Mair, Callimachus (Hymns and Epigrams), Lycophron and Aratus (Loeb ed.), revised ed., 1955; C. A. Trypanis, Callimachus: Aetia, Iambi, Hecale and Other Fragments, 1958; E. Cahen, Callimaque: Hymnes, Épigrammes, fragments choisis (Budé ed.), 1922, reprinted 1972.
ABOUT—E. Cahen, Callimaque et son oeuvre poétique, 1929; H. Herter, Kallimachos und Homer, 1929; H. Kranz, Kallimachos und die Sprache Homers: Eine Untersuchung der Hymnen auf Apollon und auf Delos (Vienna, dissertation), 1939; G. Schlatter, Theokrit und Kallimachos (Zürich, dissertation), 1941; C. M. Dawson, The Iambi of Callimachus, 1950; A. Körte and P. Händel, Die hellenistische Dichtung, 1960; E. Eichgrün, Kallimachos und Apollonios Rhodios (Berlin, dissertation), 1961; K. J. MacKay, Poet at Play (Mnemosyne, Suppl. v 6), 1962, *and* Erysichthon (Mnemosyne, Suppl. v 7), 1962; T. B. L. Webster, Hellenistic Poetry and Art, 1964; G. Capovilla, Callimaco, 1967; P. M. Fraser, Ptolemaic Alexandria, 1972; A. D. Skiadas, ed., Kallimachos, 1975; B. Lavagnini, Da Mimnermo a Callimaco, 1976; H. Reinsch-Werner, Callimachus Hesiodicus, 1976; R. Blum, Kallimachos und die Literaturverzeichnung bei den Griechen: Untersuchung zur Geschichte der Bibliographie, 1977.

CALLISTHENES, Greek historian and philosopher, was born in about 370 B.C. at Olynthus in Macedonia. He was a relative, probably grand-nephew, of Aristotle, whom he accompanied to Assos (northwestern Asia Minor) and to the Macedonian court, collaborating with him in the compilation of a *List of Pythian Victors* in 355 (though Aristotle remarked that the young man had no sense). Callisthenes also wrote a panegyric of Hermeias, tyrant of Atarneus and Assos, who was Aristotle's friend. These works, however, survive at best in fragments; and the same is true of all his other writings. They included *Hellenica* in ten books, covering the period 387–357—in which he flattered Alexander the Great by equating his travels with those of the Homeric heroes—and an account of the Third Sacred War (356–347). Later, Callisthenes accompanied Alexander on his Asian expedition, and wrote a biography of him, the *Deeds of Alexander*. Written, it was said, in a highflown style reminiscent of a declamation, this work, which was widely read and became the authorized version of Alexander's career, extolled the monarch (with an eye on the Greek opposition) as the champion of Pan-Hellenism and even utilized the pronouncements of certain oracles in order to declare him to be the son of Zeus.

In 327, at Bactra (Balkh near Bukhara), Callisthenes publicly brought forward this question of the divine descent of Alexander, from whom he hoped to secure the reconstruction of his own native city. He entertained an exaggerated sense of his own importance, displayed, it was said, by an assertion that Alexander's fame depended not on anything that he himself did but on what Callisthenes wrote. Inspired by the writer's references to his divine origin, Alexander decided to introduce the Persian custom of prostration *(proskynesis),* to be incumbent upon all who approached him. To Greeks this carried the implication that Alexander considered himself not merely the son of a god but an actual god himself. Supported, therefore, by other Macedonians, Callisthenes now opposed Alexander's intention and advised him to require the custom from Asiatics only. Shortly afterwards

kal lis' thə nēz

followed the conspiracy of the Pages (328), which involved Hermolaus whose tutor Callisthenes had been. Together with his pupil and the other youths involved, Callisthenes was put to death. Because of this, Alexander incurred the hostility of the school of Aristotle, whose pupil Theophrastus branded him a murderous despot; and from these attacks arose the portrait of Alexander as a tyrant whose achievements were due to good luck, an excess of which caused his downfall.

Being the earliest of all the writers about Alexander, Callisthenes was probably used by most of his successors. Owing to the fanciful way in which he wrote history, his name was erroneously attached to one of the earlier versions of the enormously popular *Alexander Romance* (apparently written in Egypt during the third century A.D. by someone unknown, who does not seem to have possessed any literary or constructional talent). The work is available only in editions of the later Roman empire; various Greek revisions exist as well, in addition to a Latin version written by Julius Valerius at the end of the third century A.D. Each of the texts has been expanded and altered by a later hand, and these manuscripts are often corrupt; the growth of this mass of material (including an important Armenian translation) has been complicated and abstruse, extending over a very long period. Yet, it still contains a small core of historical fact going back to within ten years of Alexander's death, an event, which is described in detail at the end of three of the texts. However, by far the greater part of the *Romance* is just that—a totally fictitious work, which takes Alexander, for example, to Italy and Sicily and northern Africa and makes him conquer all India and Tibet and China as well. The first edition also contained some forged letters to and from Alexander; and versions from Egypt and Persia (whose twelfth century poet Nizami wrote an epic work on the theme) trace his lineage from the ancient royal houses of those countries. In medieval French adaptations Alexander became a knight, and in Jewish versions he passed as a precursor of the Messiah. This whole folkloric assemblage bulked enormously in medieval European and other literature and exercised great influence on the writings of

periods to which Greek thought had become alien and exotic. It also established Alexander for evermore as a prime theme for imaginative literary entertainment. Because of the spread of the *Romance,* there are still Afghan chieftains today who claim to be his descendants.

EDITIONS—F. Jacoby, Die Fragmente der griechischen Historiker, 2b, 124.
ABOUT—F. Jacoby, *in* Real-Encyclopädie der Classischen Altertumswissenschaft, v 10, column 1674 ff.; L. Pearson, Lost Histories of Alexander the Great, 1960. *The Alexander Romance*—R. Merkelbach, Die Quellen des griechischen Alexanderromans, 1954; G. Cary, The Medieval Alexander, 1956; A. M. Wolohojian, The Romance of Alexander the Great (the Armenian version), 1969; H. von Thiel, Alexanderroman: Leben und Taten Alexanders von Makedonien, 1974.

CALPURNIUS SICULUS, TITUS, a Latin poet, wrote during the reign of the emperor Nero (A.D. 54–68). It is not known who he was. His family name may denote a relationship, perhaps that of freedman, to Gaius Calpurnius Piso, who was executed for plotting against Nero in A.D. 65; and this Gaius may also be the Calpurnius Piso celebrated in the *Praise of Piso (Laus Pisonis),* a panegyric in 261 hexameters sometimes, though inconclusively, attributed to Calpurnius Siculus. Also attributed to the poet were the contemporary Einsiedeln Eclogues (though they have also been ascribed to Gaius Piso and to Lucan). The poet's name *Siculus* could indicate that he was a Sicilian; but, alternatively, it may have been intended to signify his literary indebtedness to the Greek pastoral poet Theocritus of Syracuse.

The manuscripts of Calpurnius Siculus preserve eleven poems, four of which, however, have been correctly reassigned to a much later poet Nemesianus. Of the seven that remain attributed to Calpurnius, four (Nos. 2, 3, 5, and 6) are of the pastoral, bucolic, Theocritean type, with numerous debts also to Latin, Augustan poetry, and in particular to the *Eclogues* of Virgil, whom he praises. There is little evidence that he knew much more about the countryside than he could have obtained by reading Virgil, whom he uses as his model and whom he

kal pûr′ ni us si′ ku lus

exceeds in artificiality. Poem No. 2 is a singing match between a gardener and a shepherd. In No. 3, a shepherd complains of his mistress's infidelity. In No. 5, an old shepherd gives his flock to a young one, with instructions on how to care for it; No. 6 is a singing match broken off by a violent quarrel between the contestants.

Poems 1, 4, and 7, on the other hand, concentrate on courtly praises of the emperor, within a thin bucolic framework. In No. 1, shepherds find carved on a tree a prophecy of the return of the Golden Age, dawning under a ruler who will bring back peace and law and order and will refrain from persecuting the Senate. An oracle, the prophecy declares, has appeared in the sky; this indicates that the poem should be ascribed to A.D. 54, the year of Nero's accession. The shepherds set the oracle to music, hoping that a certain personage, given the traditional pastoral name of Meliboeus, will bring their work to the ears of the emperor. In No. 4, Meliboeus is described as a kind patron, a new and learned Maecenas (attempts have been made to identify him with Seneca, Gaius Piso, and others, but these efforts lack foundation). Meliboeus, we are told, has brought relief from poverty to the shepherd Corydon, who therefore joins his brother Amyntas, a promising young poet, in singing a duet to the emperor. In No. 7 Corydon (here evidently Calpurnius himself) has been to Rome and brings back an enthusiastic account of a spectacle in the amphitheater, with glowing praise of the "godhead" of the ruler.

The numbering of the poems is not chronological but architectural: Nos. 2, 4, and 6 are dialogue and are sandwiched between pieces that do not possess this form. The dialogue is skillfully contrived; for all his literary reminiscences and echoes Calpurnius, after borrowing a theme from Theocritus or Virgil, can enlarge upon it with some mild display of independence.

EDITIONS—C. Giarratano, Calpurnii et Nemesiani Bucolica (with Einsiedeln Eclogues), 1924, reprint 1951; C. Messina, Tito Calpurnio Siculo, 1975. *With translation:* J. W. Duff and A. M. Duff, Minor Latin Poets, revised ed., 1935; R. Verdière (French), T. Calpurnii Siculi De Laude Pisonis et Bucolica et M. Annaei Lucani De Laude Caesaris Einsidlensia Quae Dicuntur Carmina, 1954; D. Korzeniewski, Hirtengedichte aus neronischer Zeit, 1971.
ABOUT—E. Cesareo, La poesia di Calpurnio Siculo, 1931; E. Champlin, The Life and Times of Calpurnius Siculus (Journal of Roman Studies, v 68), 1978.

CAPELLA, MARTIANUS. See Martianus Capella

CAPITOLINUS, JULIUS. See Spartianus, Aelius

CARNEADES. See Sextus Empiricus

CASSIODORUS, FLAVIUS MAGNUS AURELIUS (Senator), c. A.D. 490–c. 583, Latin writer, statesman, and monk, was born into an important senatorial family, originally from Syria, that lived near Scylacium (Squillace) in Bruttium (southern Italy). He was quaestor (private secretary) to the Ostrogothic king of Italy, Theodoric, and in 523-26 was head of his civil service *(magister officiorum)* in succession to Boethius; he retained the post under the next king, Athalaric, who made him his praetorian prefect in 533. In 535 (under Athalaric's successor Theodahad) Cassiodorus tried to set up a theological college at Rome in collaboration with Pope Agapetus, but the project proved unsuccessful. Two years later (after Witigis had become king) he retired, and dedicated himself increasingly to religion and scholarship. In 540 he was taken prisoner by the troops of the eastern (Byzantine) empire and sent to Constantinople, where his learning earned him great respect, but in the 550s he returned to Italy after the Byzantine emperor Justinian had conquered the country from the Ostrogoths. Returning to his ancestral estates near Scylacium, Cassiodorus established two monastic foundations: a hermitage in the hills at Castellum and a less austere institution on his own estate, named

kas si ō dō′ rus

Vivarium after the neighboring fish ponds. Though Vivarium did not survive beyond the seventh century, it created a model of monastic life that subsequently influenced the Benedictine order; and it served as a nursery of literary monasticism, in which monks copied manuscripts day and night.

The numerous works Cassiodorus wrote during his very long life can be divided into two groups, one written before and the other after his retirement. The first is mainly of historical and political interest; the second, theological and grammatical. In the former category came the *Variae Epistolae,* published in 537 or soon afterward. These included his edicts as praetorian prefect and four hundred and sixty-eight official letters and documents that he had composed in the names of the Ostrogothic monarchs. Cassiodorus excelled at the honorific style, which was regarded as appropriate for royal correspondence, though some of his letters are considerably less solemn and more trivial. A discussion on the Soul, *De Anima,* published at almost the same time, was regarded by him as a supplementary book of the *Variae.*

His most important work is a twelve-book *History of the Goths.* This has only come down to us in an abridged version in Jordanes' *Getica,* which is our main source for the opinions about Gothic history current in the fourth and fifth centuries A.D. Written before 534 and revised in 551, Cassiodorus' *History* collected much important information about the Goths and Huns alike. Yet he was not averse to distorting historical facts to win the approval of his Ostrogothic rulers, of whom he also wrote panegyrics that survive in fragmentary form. Partiality to the Goths, whose origins Cassiodorus was proud to have placed within the framework of the Roman historical tradition, also appears in his extant *Chronica,* a summary of world history down to A.D. 519, the year of its publication. Based, not entirely accurately, on a number of earlier Roman historians, the work contains a list of Assyrian, Latin, and Roman kings, and of Roman consuls, over a period of 1531 years. Of another of his writings, the *Family History of the Cassiodori,* we only have a single fragment, known as the *Anecdoton Holderi.* Made up of a series of excerpts, it contains short ac-

counts of Cassiodorus himself, and of Boethius and Symmachus as well.

The most important of the works Cassiodorus wrote after his retirement was the *Institutes of Divine and Secular Literature (Institutiones Divinarum et Saecularium Litterarum),* intended to educate his monks in sacred (and pagan) scholarship. The first part discusses the study of the holy books, with observations on the Christian fathers and historians. Then follows a short survey of the liberal arts, providing a kind of summary of pagan learning. The latter section was used widely in the Middle Ages, in both shorter and longer versions. Various religious works also attributable to Cassiodorus include a commentary on the Psalms, and short notes on the letters of Paul and on the *Acts of the Apostles,* and *Revelation.* He also edited a Latin translation, made by others, of the *Jewish Antiquities* by Josephus, and entrusted to his friend Epiphanius the composition of a *Tripartite Church History (Historica Ecclesiastica Vocata Tripartita)* from Constantine the Great to Theodosius II, based on Latin versions of three Greek ecclesiastical historians (Sozomenus, Socrates, and Theodoretus). Finally, Cassiodorus was active in the grammatical field as well and in his ninety-third year wrote a treatise on spelling *(De Orthographia)* for the benefit of copyists, a compilation based on the works of eight grammarians.

He rendered an immeasurable service to posterity by preserving so much of ancient culture, both pagan and Christian, at a time when most of Italy was about to be submerged by alien forces. He provided one of the principal bridges from the ancient world to the civilization of the western Middle Ages.

EDITIONS—R. A. B. Mynors, Institutiones, 1937; M. Adriaen, Commentary on the Psalms 1958; J. W. Halporn, De Anima, 1960; L. Steinreuter, Historica Ecclesiastica Tripartita, 1977. *Translations*—T. Hodgkin, The Letters of Cassiodorus: A Condensed Version of the Variae Epistolae, 1886.
ABOUT—R. R. Bolgar, The Classical Heritage and Its Beneficiaries, 1954; A. Momigliano, Secondo contributo alla storia degli studi classici, 1960; P. Riché, Éducation et culture dans l'occident barbare, 1962; A. J. Fridh, Contributions à la critique et à l'interpretation des Variae de Cassiodore, 1968; U. Hahner, Cassiodors Psalmenkommentar, 1973.

CASSIUS DIO COCCEIANUS. See Dio Cassius

CATO, MARCUS PORCIUS (the Censor), public figure, agriculturalist, and Latin writer, was born of a farming family at Tusculum (near Frascati) in 234 B.C. and died in 149. He fought as a military tribune against Hannibal in the Second Punic War and was appointed quaestor in Sicily and northern Africa in 204, plebeian aedile (director of public works and archives) in 199, and praetor (governor) in 198 in Sardinia, from which he expelled the moneylenders. After holding the consulship in 195, he became governor of Spain. There he conducted extensive military operations and inaugurated the administration of Rome's recently annexed provinces in that country. Then he served with distinction in the war against the Seleucid monarch Antiochus III, fighting at Thermopylae (191); but soon afterward he led political attacks on Scipio Asiaticus (who had subsequently taken command in that war) and succeeded in hounding him out of public life, together with his brother Scipio Africanus, whose Hellenizing tastes and personality cult Cato deplored. In 184 he held the office of censor, which permitted him to put forward an austere policy of moral, social, and economic reconstruction, based on the traditions of ancient Rome. In carrying out his famous censorship, he displayed a strictness that has given the term *censorious* its meaning. In the years that followed, he pressed ahead with the same policy, involving himself perpetually in controversy and strife and carrying out his aims with ruthless ferocity and scathing wit. In 161 Cato was largely responsible for a decree expelling Greek philosophers and rhetoricians from Rome; and in 155 he insisted that a group of Greek philosophers visiting the city as envoys should leave as soon as their official business was completed. After a visit to Carthage in 153, he repeatedly demanded that the city should be destroyed *(delenda est Carthago),* a suggestion that became reality when, despite strong opposition from other senators,

kā' tō

Rome declared war against the Carthaginians in 150, thus launching The Third Punic War. Cato became a legend in his lifetime.

His policies found expression in a powerful literary talent that made him the outstanding pioneer of Latin prose writing. His only extant complete work is *On Agriculture (De Agricultura* or *De Re Rustica),* the oldest surviving prose composition in the language. Its theme is the cultivation for profit (in Latium and Campania) of vines, olives, and fruit, and the breeding of cattle. Asserting the advantages of agriculture over trading and banking, Cato goes on to discuss the best location of a farm, the duties of the owner and his steward, and various aspects of farm management. At the same time, he contrives to introduce much incidental information on such matters as medical and veterinary care, recipes for cooking, and religious and superstitious formulas. Written with straight-forward archaic vividness (though Cato's language has been somewhat toned down by later copyists), the book is singularly lacking in order or organization, but it was greatly valued and widely read in ancient times, as numerous quotations by other writers testify. To ourselves, it is of particular interest for its assessment, based on personal experience, of the new capitalist farming and for its extensive evidence relating to the Roman social scene; particularly striking, in this respect, is the writer's callous attitude toward wastage of slaves, though, for reasons of commonsense, he was against treating them too badly while they were still able to contribute work.

This was only one of a series of technical writings by Cato, the rest of which have not survived. They included a monograph *(commentarius)* on medicine, describing how he and his wife lived to a ripe old age and treated the ailments of their household staff. He also compiled a monograph on tactics *(De Re Militari)* and another on law; and for his son (the author of another legal treatise) he wrote a handbook of useful general knowledge including sections on medicine, agriculture, and rhetoric. This last section contained Cato's famous maxim "get the matter and the words will come" *(rem tene, verba sequentur),* and defined an orator as a good man skilled in speaking *(vir bonus dicendi peritus).* Cato also wrote a book on morality *(Carmen de Moribus)* and compiled a collection of aphorisms, though the extant book that purports to record his own sayings, very popular in the Middle Ages, dates from about the third century A.D.

The most important of his writings, however, was a historical work, the *Origins (Origines),* written between about 168 and 149, once again only surviving in fragments. The title was reminiscent of Greek treatises on the founding of cities, but Cato's scope (like theirs) was much wider, ranging over many matters besides the actual foundation stories. His first book dealt with Aeneas and Rome's early years and its kings, the second and third with the foundation traditions of other Italian cities, and the fourth with the Punic Wars down to the battle of Cannae (216 B.C.). The last three books brought the story of Rome down to Cato's own times. He drew upon earlier Roman historians writing in Greek (notably Fabius Pictor), as well as upon legendary and traditional material, and followed the Greek tradition by inserting speeches, including at least one oration of his own. The style, as fragments show, was somewhat uncouth but possessed a certain vivid force, at least in descriptive passages. Although Cato professed himself opposed to Hellenism, he made use of certain Greek rhetorical devices. He was, however, deeply proud of a feature of the Romans that he regarded as very un-Greek —the corporate nature of their achievement —and as a tribute to this he even declined to mention the names of victorious generals. The *Origins* seems to have been the first work of its kind in Latin, and it served as a model to later historians.

However, it was in his speeches that Cato most decisively influenced the development of Roman literature. He spoke his mind forcibly on every political issue for many years and acted as a protagonist in a remarkable number of political trials. Cicero knew as many as one hundred and fifty of these orations, and we have the titles of approximately eighty to which existing fragments can be assigned. They were considered rough but terse and torrentially vigorous; and they contained a great deal of amusingly sarcastic comment on Cato's contemporaries.

EDITIONS with translation (De Agricultura)—E. Bréhaut, Cato the Censor on Farming, 1933; W. D. Hooper and H. B. Ash, Cato and Varro: On Agriculture (Loeb ed.), 1935; R. Goujard, Caton: De l'agriculture (Budé ed.), 1975. *Fragments* (of other works)—H. Peter, Historicorum Romanorum Reliquiae, v 1, 2nd ed., 1914; H. Malcovati, Oratorum Romanorum Fragmenta, 1955; G. Calboli, Cato: Oratio pro Rhodiensibus, 1978.
ABOUT—R. Till, Die Sprache Catos, 1936; B. Janzer, Historische Untersuchungen zu den Redenfragmenten des M. Porcius Cato, 1937; D. Kienast, Cato der Zensor: Seine Persönlichkeit und seine Zeit, 1954; P. Fraccaro, Studi Catoniani, *in* Opuscula, v 1, 1956; E. Badian, The Early Historians *in* T. A. Dorey, ed., Latin Historians, 1966; F. della Corte, Catone censore, 2nd ed., 1969; W. A. Schröder, Marcus Porcius Cato: Das erste Buch der Origines, 1971; N. W. Forde, Cato the Censor, 1975; A. E. Astin, Cato the Censor, 1978.

CATULLUS, GAIUS VALERIUS, Latin poet, was probably born in about 84 and died in about 54 B.C. His birthplace was Verona in Cisalpine Gaul (northern Italy), where he belonged to a well-known local family. In about 62 he came to Rome and continued to live there for the rest of his life (although remaining in touch with his native region). In the capital he moved in smart and dissipated social circles and became deeply attached to the woman who appears as Lesbia in his poems. According to the novelist Apuleius, she was really called Clodia; and she has been plausibly identified, though without absolute certainty, as the beautiful woman of that name whom Cicero, the enemy of her brother Clodius, violently attacked for her loose living in his speech *In Defense of Caelius.* In 57, Catullus traveled to the province of Asia in the suite of the governor Gaius Memmius. His early death followed soon afterward.

By that time he had probably become permanently separated from Lesbia. But, before that, his love for her—punctuated by rifts and reconciliations, and finally by a fierce and desperately sad revolt against his enslavement to her charms—had inspired some of his most remarkable and bitter poems. By posterity it is as a poet of love that Catullus is specially admired: for not only is he a sympathetic narrator of the loves of others, in accordance with the Alexandrian tradition, but he is also uniquely able to

kȧ tul' lus

85

communicate his own passionate love, enlarging upon all the ecstasies and miseries by which it consumed his life.

In other short poems he displays a wide range of human responses: sorrow for the death of his brother, sympathy for a friend, mourning for his beloved's pet sparrow, a coarsely humorous lack of chivalry for a girl who does not attract him, mockery of vulgar contemporaries. His reactions are those of an individualist belonging to a young, sophisticated, privileged, intolerant clique. It is for the fellow members of this clique that he writes, and when he abuses Caesar and Pompey, as he does, his criticisms are not political but personal, prompted by distaste for the upstarts who had sprung up as the great men's satellites.

Writing in lyric, elegiac, and iambic meters alike, Catullus adapted his poetry to a remarkable variety of purposes and moods, and he himself, it is now believed, designed the order and arrangement of his poetic corpus to display these purposes and moods to the best advantage. Through his short poems he became the founder of a new form in Latin literature, the light, witty, brief piece of poetry that occupied a place between serious epic and tragedy on the one hand and humorous satire and comedy on the other. But it is a curious fact that in ancient times a literary critic such as Quintilian, while prepared to admit Catullus as a poet in the abusive iambic tradition, completely leaves him out of his survey of lyric poets, although to us he seems one of the greatest lyricists who has ever lived: this omission is at least partly due to the technical consideration that only five of Catullus' pieces were in meters regarded in antiquity as lyrical.

Several subsequent Latin poets, however, agreed that the right epithet to apply to Catullus was *doctus* (learned). This is in recognition of the scholarly concern for technical perfection that lay behind everything he wrote—short and long poems alike. He acquired it from the Latin Alexandrian movements of the Moderns *(Neoterici)*—as Cicero ironically called them—who, at the beginning of the first century B.C., had adapted the ideals of the Greek Alexandrians (led by Callimachus, c. 310/305–240 B.C.) to the task of raising Latin poetry to a new polish and refinement; the second generation of this movement, to which Catullus himself belonged, was especially associated with his own homeland Cisalpine Gaul.

The more artificial and erudite aspects of this Alexandrian heritage do not by any means dominate Catullus' writings as a whole. Yet in some of his longer poems they are abundantly apparent. In particular, the elegiac Lock of Berenice (*Coma Berenices* —No. 66) is a close adaptation of a poem by Callimachus himself. Catullus' No. 64, again, a hexameter poem on the mythical marriage of Peleus and Thetis (including a long digression on the stories of Theseus and Ariadne), owes its form as a "miniature epic" *(epyllion),* and much of its style and content as well, to Alexandrian models. Nos. 61 and 62 are Bridal Songs *(epithalamia),* the former in the meter named after Sappho (seventh to sixth centuries B.C.)—which recalls that Catullus is one of the very few poets who can stand beside Sappho for intensity of emotion. This intensity was not stifled by his access to the stylistic skill of the Alexandrians, but, quite on the contrary, became articulate through their influence. For example, the Alexandrians had inherited from their own predecessors a liking for hymns, and Catullus' poem No. 63 is a hymn to the Asian god Altis, whose cult was linked to that of Cybele, the Earth Mother. Catullus' invocation, remarkable for its ecstatic and uncontrolled feeling, is written in a racing, rhythmical meter (Callimachus' galliambic) that was particularly associated with this eastern cult.

Catullus exerted a profound effect on Virgil, who honors him with many verbal echoes; and these are heard again in the elegies of Tibullus, Propertius, and Ovid, the lyrics of Horace, and the satirical epigrams of Martial. After neglect during the Middle Ages Catullus' fame revived, and his influence reappears, for example, in Elizabethan wedding odes and in the works of Herrick and Ben Jonson. In the nineteenth century Byron translated two of his poems, and Landor, Tennyson, and Swinburne admired him greatly, to some extent on the grounds that he was a "spontaneous" writer—a belief that ignored the extreme technical skill displayed in all his work.

EDITIONS—W. Kroll, 2nd ed., 1929; M. Lenchantin de Gubernatis, 2nd ed., 1933, reprint 1953; C. J. Fordyce, 1961; H. Bardon (Latomus, v 112), 1970; K. Quinn, 1970; D. F. S. Thomson, 1979. *Translations*—F. O. Copley, 1957; R. A. Swanson, 1959; F. W. Cornish, *in* Catullus: Tibullus: Pervigilium Veneris (Loeb ed.), revised ed., 1962; P. Whigham (Penguin ed.), 1966; H. Gregory, 1972; J. Michie, 1972; R. Myers and R. J. Ormsby, 1972; F. Raphael and K. McLeish, 1978.
ABOUT—E. A. Havelock, The Lyric Genius of Catullus, 1939; K. P. Harrington, Catullus and His Influence, 1965; J. Granarolo, L'oeuvre de Catulle: Aspects réligieux, éthiques et stylistiques, 1967; R. G. C. Levens *in* Fifty Years (and Twelve) of Classical Scholarship, 1968; C. Witke, Enarratio Catulliana, 1968; K. Quinn, The Catullan Revolution, 2nd ed., 1969, *and* Catullus: An Interpretation, 1972; D. O. Ross, Style and Tradition in Catullus, 1969; T. P. Wiseman, Catullan Questions, 1969; H. Bardon, Propositions sur Catulle (Latomus, v 118), 1970; G. P. Goold, Interpreting Catullus, 1974; R. Heine, ed., Catull, 1975; F. della Corte, Personaggi catulliani, 2nd ed., 1976; F. Stoessl, C. Valerius Catullus: Mensch, Leben, Dichtung, 1977.

CELSUS, AULUS CORNELIUS, Latin writer and polymath, lived under the emperor Tiberius (A.D. 14–37). He was the author of an encyclopedia that covered agriculture, medicine, military science, and rhetoric, and probably jurisprudence and philosophy as well. Agriculture was the subject of the first five books, and eight books of medicine came next; apparently, philosophy was dealt with in six later books, in which Celsus summarized the history of the subject, revealing respect for the contemporary Stoic-Platonic school of the Sextii.

Apart from a few fragments from other sections, only the medical portion of the work survives. It begins with a brief but competent historical summary of the various schools of medical theory and practice, and goes on to discuss medical regimes according to differences of constitution, age, and season (Book 1). Then follow outlines of symptoms and methods of treatment (Book 2); illnesses affecting the whole body (Book 3), and only parts of it (Book 4); pharmacology (Books 5 and 6); surgery (Book 7); and various types of fractures and dislocations (Book 8). The first known mentions of

kel' sus

heart attack *(cardiacus)* and insanity *(insania)* are recorded; and the surgical section includes the earliest account of the employment of ligature.

A layman writing for other laymen, Celsus judiciously selects his material from various sources (he is most strongly influenced by the Greek doctor Themison of Augustan date), and it is largely through his work that we are able to reconstruct the medical doctrines of his time and the period that preceded it. Celsus himself emerges as a sensible, well-informed man of taste who dislikes extreme theories and treatments. Like Hippocrates, he lays stress on diagnosis and prognosis; he is also sound on anatomy and emphasizes its importance. He prescribes drugs more than Greek writers were accustomed to do but also strongly advocates personal hygiene and physical exercise, showing a Roman preference for sport as against gymnastics.

The encyclopedia of Celsus was soon regarded as a valuable work of reference. His younger contemporary Columella quoted its agricultural books no less than thirty times, in very respectful terms. The rhetorician Quintilian, too, while criticizing Celsus' treatise on rhetoric (as might be expected from a specialist) and describing him as a man of only moderate intellect *(mediocri vir ingenio)*, nevertheless called attention to the versatility of his knowledge.

On the whole, his work received little attention either in antiquity or in the Middle Ages. In the Renaissance, however, its medical section began to become very popular—because of his excellent literary style. Deprecating mere verbal cleverness but writing in lucid, agreeable language, with clear explanations of technical terms, Celsus came to be known as "the Cicero of the doctors" *(Cicero medicorum)*. In consequence, his medical treatise was published as early as 1478, thus becoming one of the first books in this field to appear in print; in 1539 it was translated into German. Moreover, it was an oblique compliment to Celsus that the sixteenth century Swiss physician and chemist who established the role of chemistry in medicine took the boastful name Paracelsus—by which he meant, superior even to Celsus.

87

EDITIONS with translation—W. G. Spencer, Celsus: On Medicine, 1935.
ABOUT—F. Marx, Corpus Medicorum Latinorum, v 1, 1915; J. Scarborough, Roman Medicine, 1969; H. Flashar, Antike Medizin, 1971.

CEPHALAS, CONSTANTINUS, Greek anthologist of the Byzantine epoch, lived in the ninth and early tenth century A.D. and was an official of the court at Constantinople. Shortly before 900 he compiled a large anthology of poetic epigrams derived from all previous periods of Greek literature and drawing upon the collections made in earlier epochs by Philip of Thessalonica, Strato of Sardis, Diogenianus of Heraclea, Agathias of Myrina, and others.

Cephalas endeavored to arrange his anthology according to subject matter but did not carry out this intention consistently. Moreover, he never completed the editorial preparation of the work, and it does not seem to have been published in the customary fashion. Like earlier collections, it failed to survive as a separate entity. However, a great many of the epigrams it contained were preserved in subsequent compilations, the Palatine and Planudean Anthologies (c. 980 and 1300). (For editions and modern studies of the Greek Anthologies, see the bibliographic material following the sketches of Asclepiades, Meleager, and Philip.)

CERCIDAS of Megalopolis in Arcadia, Greek poet, lived c. 290–220 B.C. During a period of tyranny in his native city (235) he may have lived in Crete. It was probably because of the part he played in restoring free government at Megalopolis that its citizens knew him as a lawgiver. Cercidas belonged to the circle of Aratus of Sicyon, general of the Achaean League, who sent him in about 226 to the king of Macedonia to request his intervention against Sparta. At the battle of Sellasia in 222 or 221, in which the Achaeans and Macedonians defeated the Spartans, Cercidas commanded a contingent of a thousand men.

ke′ fá làs
ker′ ki dàs

This lawgiver and warrior appears, despite some modern doubters, to be identical with the man of the same name who wrote popular, moralistic, quasi-satirical poetry, an identification already accepted by the Byzantine writer Stephanus who wrote of an "excellent lawyer and meliambic poet" (meliambic meters being iambics used for lyrical purposes). Some knowledge of his poetry can be built up from nine short fragments quoted in the literary sources, plus somewhat more substantial remains preserved by papyri and plausibly attributed to the same writer (though they have alternatively been identified as parts of an anthology of works by others, which Cercidas had collected). The poems are written in a forceful Doric dialect and in a variety of skillfully and originally manipulated meters, both lyrical and iambic (not only meliambic but also choliambic or "limping" iambic, already used by Callimachus).

Though himself a member of the upper class and a supporter of Aratus who fought hard to suppress social revolution, writing on behalf of the poor and oppressed Cercidas voices keen criticism of the social conditions of his day. Thus, the longest of his fragments warns the rich that unless they mend their ways they will be overtaken by revolutionary upheavals that will deprive them of their possessions. The same fragment questions divine providence, scolding the gods for their unjust distribution of earthly goods; Cercidas urges the poor not to wait for the vengeance of heaven to strike down the rich but to act themselves under the inspiration of a new triad of divinities: Paean, Sharing (Metados), and Nemesis. He also satirizes the habits of the avaricious and spendthrift alike. The prevailing tone of his message is moralistic sermonizing of a conversational kind, in the style of the popular lecturers of the day, with stress on the fatuity of lofty speculations and with censure of elaborate sexual self-indulgence as pointless.

At the end of the papyrus containing his principal surviving fragments he is described as Cercidas the Cynic, and this was no doubt the philosophical school with which he felt the greatest sympathy. For this allegiance, as well as for his blend of seriousness and jesting, he appears to have been indebted to Crates of Thebes (c. 365–285 B.C.), a pupil of Diogenes of Sinope (the founder of Cynicism) to whom Cercidas pays a heartfelt tribute. He also reflects the teaching of another poet, likewise influenced by Crates, namely Bion of Borysthenes, whose brisk, vivid "diatribe" he adapts, combining it with features from other literary forms, and adding skillfully selected quotations from Euripides, as well as from Homer, whom he was said to have warmly admired. Cercidas was echoed by Horace in a number of passages (though in more urbane and less aggressively Cynic fashion), and there is little doubt that his Greek verses should be classed among the forerunners of the whole Latin satirical tradition.

EDITIONS—L. Paquet, Les Cyniques grecs, 1975. *With translation:* A. D. Knox *in* J. M. Edmonds, Theophrastus: Characters, 1929, *and* A. D. Knox, Herodas, Cercidas and the Greek Choliambic Poets (Loeb ed.), revised ed., 1946.
ABOUT—A. Oltramare, Origines de la diatribe romaine, 1926; D. R. Dudley, History of Cynicism, 1937.

CHARITON, Greek novelist of the second century A.D., was from Aphrodisias (Kehre) in Caria (southwestern Asia Minor). His extant novel, *Chaereas and Callirhoe,* divided into eight books, is a romance based on the Athenian expedition against Syracuse in the fifth century B.C. According to Chariton's story Hermocrates, commander of the Syracusan forces, has a beautiful daughter Callirhoe, whom Chaereas, the son of a political opponent, loves at first sight and marries. Jealous rivals, however, succeed in making Chaereas suspicious of Callirhoe's fidelity; he kicks her into unconsciousness, which is mistaken for death, and she is carried to a tomb, where rich treasure is buried with her. Pirates who loot the grave discover she is alive and remove her, selling her as a slave to Dionysius, an Ionian prince. Dionysius respects her beauty and tragic history (as far as he knows it, for she fails to tell him she is married), and pays court to her in an honorable fashion. When she discovers she is two months pregnant, she decides, at her maid's suggestion, to marry Dionysius, hoping, that he will believe himself to be the

ka′ ri tōn

father of the child. However, Chaereas has now learned that his wife is still alive and sets out with a friend to get her back, but he is captured and sold as a slave to Mithridates of Caria. Mithridates, meanwhile, has seen Callirhoe and likewise fallen in love with her. He sends her letters both from Chaereas and from himself. Dionysius intercepts the letters and induces the Persian king Artaxerxes to summon Mithridates for trial. The king, however, makes advances to Callirhoe on his own account, to which she does not respond; and his decision as to which of her husbands she shall belong to is postponed for the time being, while Artaxerxes departs to put down a revolt in Egypt, placing Callirhoe in charge of his queen who accompanies him. Dionysius, who is serving in the Persian forces, deceives Chaereas into believing that Artaxerxes has awarded her to himself, and Chaereas in despair joins the rebellious army. Fighting with great success, he seizes an island where he captures the queen and her household, including Callirhoe, with whom he is thus reunited. Then he gives Artaxerxes back his queen, persuaded by Callirhoe to whom she had been kind; and the young couple sail back to Syracuse, where they live happily ever after.

Papyrus discoveries have revealed that *Chaereas and Callirhoe,* instead of belonging to the Byzantine age, as had sometimes been believed, must have been written not later than A.D. 200. Instead, therefore, of being one of the latest of the Greek novelists, Chariton emerges as the author of the earliest surviving work of this kind, though he was to a large extent the heir of earlier novelists such as the author of the *Ninus Romance,* which survives fragmentarily in two papyri of the first century A.D. (and was written some three centuries earlier than that).

Chariton's novel contains the intrigues, suspicions, perils, enslavements, shipwrecks, robberies, hairbreadth escapes, and mistaken reports of the heroine's death that will constantly recur in this romantic genre. Finally Fortune, the supreme goddess of later Greek times (whom the novelists imported to account for all implausibilities) brings the loving couple together; and Aphrodite (Venus) also plays her part.

CHRYSIPPUS

Though Chariton's style is comparatively unrhetorical—he sought to imitate the Attic historians Thucydides and Xenophon—melodrama and rich pageantry run high. The author himself declares that the trial scene will outdo anything to be seen on the stage. Moral virtue, too, is greatly to the fore: chivalry is much apparent, and constancy and chastity defeat every onslaught. The plot, for all its complications, goes ahead very rapidly—without too many irrelevances or digressions.

Some papyrus fragments indicate the existence of alternative texts, very different from the version that has come down to us; this may mean that, in medieval times, the novel became a chapbook or piece of popular literature, hawked around by peddlers. Later, in the Renaissance, the lucidity of Chariton's style was much admired.

CHRYSIPPUS

EDITIONS—A. Calderini, Le avventure di Cherea e Calliroe, 1913; W. E. Blake, Chariton's Chaereas and Callirhoe, 1938 (translation, 1939); K. Plepelits, Chariton von Aphrodisias: Kallirhoe, 1977; G. Molinié, Chariton: Le roman de Chéréas et de Callirhoé (Budé ed.), 1978.
ABOUT—B. E. Perry, The Ancient Romances, 1967; T. Hagg, Narrative Technique in Ancient Greek Romances, 1971; A. D. Papanikolaou, Chariton-Studien, 1973; G. L. Schmeling, Chariton, 1974; K. H. Gerschmann, Chariton-Interpretationen, 1975.

CHRYSIPPUS, Greek philosopher, was born in about 280 and died in 207/6 B.C. His birthplace was Soli (later Pompeiopolis, near the modern Mersin) in Cilicia (southeastern Asia Minor). He went to Athens in about 260 and studied under Arcesilaus and Lacydes at the Platonic (Middle) Academy, where he received training in logic and dialectic. He was converted to Stoicism by Cleanthes, whom he succeeded as head of the Stoic school in 232. He devoted the rest of his life to systematizing Stoic doctrine and defending it against attacks from the Academy.

More than seven hundred treatises are attributed to Chrysippus, but only fragments of them survive. In the course of this vast literary output, he remodeled and extensively developed the teaching of Zeno, particu-

krī sip′ pus

90

larly in the fields of logic and the theory of knowledge, in which he was probably the only Stoic to take a keen and knowledgeable interest. It was he who proceeded actively with the elaboration and classification of the various kinds of "indifferent" action (i.e. those irrelevant to the moral imperative), which came to be subdivided into preferred and deprecated and absolutely indifferent actions.

He also redefined Zeno's instruction "to live consistently," though he did so in order to bring out Zeno's intended meaning, rather than to alter it. According to Arius Didymus—a philosopher of the first century B.C.—Zeno's immediate successor Cleanthes had been the first to expand the phrase into the form "to live consistently with nature," whereas Chrysippus preferred the version "to live according to experience of what happens by nature"—meaning that consistency with nature can only be achieved through observation of nature's ways. Furthermore, Cleanthes was said to have interpreted "living consistently with nature" as meaning consistently with universal nature, whereas, according to Diogenes Laertius (third century A.D.), Chrysippus expanded the requirement to mean "consistently both with universal nature and in particular with human nature." But here again it does not seem probable that there was any real difference between these variously expressed doctrines. Chrysippus was not tampering with the pronouncement that life must be lived in harmony with universal nature; what he wanted to do was to add that such a life was also consistent with the natural behavior of human beings.

Chrysippus believed that the philosopher's primary concern is with his fellow men and women and with their improvement. A number of surviving fragments show that he maintained the tradition of the Cynic school (based on the doctrines of Diogenes, c. 400–325 B.C.) in challenging established conventions. For example, a passage from his treatise *On Appropriate Action* urges that the burial of one's dead parents is of no importance—indeed, their flesh can even be eaten, if that proves to be useful. But probably, like Zeno in his *Republic,* Chrysippus is here proposing hypothetical rules for a utopian society—not suggesting how people should actually behave in contemporary Greece.

He showed a willingness to grapple with the various difficulties to which Stoic doctrines gave rise, in the earnest hope of finding a solution for them—being a man, it was said, who was always ready to change his mind and correct himself, or to admit when he had been defeated in argument. The Stoic teaching that survived into subsequent epochs appeared largely in the form Chrysippus had given it, so that it was his philosophy that endured as canonical Stoic doctrine, obscuring the views of his predecessors.

However, he had a prolix and repetitive style, and, in particular, his writings on impulse and other psychological topics (from which most of the extant fragments are derived) were evidently turgid and poorly constructed. These defects, together with the sheer abundance of his writings, meant that briefer and clearer versions of Stoic beliefs had to be composed later on—and, indeed, it may be that some of the systematizations credited to Chrysippus were really of this subsequent origin.

EDITIONS—J. ab (H. von) Arnim, Stoicorum Veterum Fragmenta, 1902–5.

ABOUT—E. Bréhier, Chrysippe, 2nd ed., 1951; S. Sambursky, Physics of the Stoics, 1959; B. Mates, Stoic Logic, 2nd ed., 1961; G. Watson, The Stoic Theory of Knowledge, 1966; L. Edelstein, The Meaning of Stoicism, 1967; J. M. Rist, Stoic Philosophy, 1969, reprint 1977; J. B. Gould, The Philosophy of Chrysippus, 1970; M. Pohlenz, Stoa und Stoiker, 4th ed., 1970, 1972; A. A. Long, ed., Problems in Stoicism, 1971, *and* Hellenistic Philosophy, 1974; M. Frede, Die stoische Logik, 1974; F. H. Sandbach, The Stoics, 1975.

CHRYSOSTOM, JOHN, Saint. See John Chrysostom, Saint

CICERO, MARCUS TULLIUS, Latin orator, writer on oratory and philosophy, letter-writer, poet, and Roman statesman, was born in 106 and died in 43 B.C. His family, who were of respectable but not aristocratic status, came from Arpinum (Arpino) in central Italy, a place that had also been the birthplace of the soldier and political leader Marius (c. 157–86 B.C.), with whose family Cicero's grandmother had marriage connections. Cicero and his brother Quintus (b. 102) were sent by their father to receive an excellent education at Rome, where Cicero studied rhetoric and philosophy under Philo the Academic and Diodotus the Stoic and law under the two Scaevolas (making his debut in the lawcourts). Next, he moved to Athens, where he was the pupil of the head of the Platonic Academy, Antiochus of Ascalon, and then to Rhodes, where he was taught by the rhetorician Molo and the Stoic philosopher Posidonius.

Returning to Rome to pursue a public career, he was elected in 75 to the junior office of quaestor, which he served in western Sicily. Five years later, he established himself as lawyer and politician by his speeches against Verres, a dishonest governor of Sicily. In 66 Cicero obtained a praetorship, the second most important office in the state and in the course of this year he gave powerful public expression to his admiration for the rising politician Pompey. Then, in 63, he attained the top office of all by becoming consul, the first "new man" (i.e. a man lacking consuls among his ancestors) to achieve that distinction for many years past. During his consulship Cicero took the lead in averting a revolution fomented by the violent, anarchistic nobleman

CICERO

MARCUS TULLIUS CICERO

Catiline, whose aristocratic supporters he put to death; but his dream of the "harmony of the orders," reconciling the various discordant elements in the senatorial and knightly (equestrian) orders, was destroyed by the informal compact between Pompey, Caesar, and Crassus known as the First Triumvirate.

Cicero, who refused to join the Triumvirate, was exiled to Greece in 58–57 (for his execution of Catiline's supporters) and unwillingly went to govern Cilicia (southeastern Asia Minor) in 51–50. After hesitantly joining Pompey against Caesar in the subsequent Civil War (49), he acquiesced in Caesar's victory but subsequently applauded his murder (44), in which, however, the conspirators, fearing his indiscretion, had not invited him to participate. Soon, disgusted by the failure of the Republic to show any signs of revival, he gradually summoned the determination to attack the new autocrat, Antony. But Antony and his colleagues in the formal Second Triumvirate, Lepidus and the young Octavian (whose intentions Cicero had imprudently and patronizingly trusted), proscribed him and arranged his execution in the last month of that year.

Fifty-eight of Cicero's speeches have come down to us, in addition to considerable groups of philosophical and rhetorical treatises, many hundreds of surviving letters (together with some replies), and a small amount of poetry.

Cicero's earliest extant speech, *For Quinctius* (81), was concerned with a complicated suit arising out of a partnership in which Quinctius' dead brother had been involved. The outcome is unknown. In his oration *For Sextus Roscius Amerinus* (80) he successfully defended Roscius on a trumped-up murder charge and attacked the dictator Sulla's adviser Chrysogonus, who had bought up the estate of Roscius' proscribed father for a minimal sum. *For Roscius the Comic Actor* (77?) defends the celebrated actor of that name who had bought a half-share of a slave, now murdered, and was contesting with his copurchaser the division of the compensation offered by the murderer. In the fragmentary speech *For Tullius* (72–71?) Cicero defended a man with the same family name as himself in a boundary dispute with a veteran of Sulla's armies. The foundation of the orator's fame was laid by his speeches *Against Verres* (70) for maladministration in Sicily, in which he defeated the leading advocate of the day Hortensius. In the incomplete oration *For Fonteius* (69), on the other hand, he defended a man accused of similar offenses in Gaul. *For Caecina,* of the same year, suggests that improper force was used to oppose his client's occupation of a plot of land.

Cicero's praetorship (66) witnessed his first political speech, *On the Command of Cnaeus Pompeius* or *On the Manilian Law,* which he delivered in order to support Pompey's commission to command the operations against Mithridates VI of Pontus. *For Cluentius,* in the same year, defended a man of Larinum against his mother's charge that he had poisoned his stepfather—who had himself been convicted earlier of a similar offense. On becoming consul Cicero delivered three speeches *(On the Agrarian Bill* or *Against Rullus)* successfully attacking proposed land legislation as fraudulent. His speech *For Rabirius,* in defense of the man whom Caesar was accusing of the murder of an anti-senatorial politician thirty-seven years previously, was inconclusive. The height of Cicero's career, in his own view, was reached by his four speeches entitled *Against Catiline;* Cicero unveiled Catiline's conspiracy while serving as consul. In the same year, his oration *For Murena* defended one of the consuls-elect against a bribery charge. *For Sulla,* in 62, exonerated a kinsman of the late dictator on a charge of complicity in Catiline's plot.

For Archias, in the same year, spoke up for a Greek poet whose Roman citizenship had been disputed. *For Flaccus* (59) defended one of Cicero's supporters in the Catilinarian case on charges of extortion. In 57–56 Cicero delivered four speeches relating to his banishment during the previous year: these were *After His Return in the Senate, Before the People* (or *Thanks to the Senate* and *To the People*), *About His Home* (which had been demolished), and *About the Response of the Diviners* (whose omens had allegedly vetoed the restoration of his house). *For Sestius* (56) defended a man who had helped to get Cicero back from exile, on charges of violence brought by the orator's enemy Clodius; *Against Vatinius* assailed one of the witnesses who had tried to get Sestius convicted. *For Caelius* succeeded in acquitting a fashionable young friend on charges including not only the murder of an Egyptian envoy but also the attempted poisoning of Caelius' former mistress Clodia, the sister of Clodius.

Although greatly downcast by the formation of the First Triumvirate, Cicero capitulated to it in two speeches: *On Provincial Consulships,* advocating the prolongation of Caesar's Gallic command, and *For Balbus,* defending the citizenship that Pompey had procured for the rich Spaniard of that name. In 55, however, *Against Piso* was an attack on Caesar's father-in-law, who had been consul in the year of the orator's exile and who had recently criticized him in the Senate. *For Plancio* (54) rejected a bribery charge against a man who had befriended Cicero in exile. *For Rabirius Postumus* supported a henchman of Caesar accused of extorting money from the King of Egypt. In his speech *For Milo* (52), Cicero's plea of self-defense failed to prevent his client's conviction for the murder of his fellow gangster Clodius.

Later, after the Civil War, Cicero, reluctantly submitting to the dictatorship of Caesar, offered him three pleas for clemency on behalf of former supporters of Pompey: *For Marcellus, For Ligarius* (46), and *For King Deiotarus* (45), the last-named being a prince of Galatia (central Asia Minor) who was accused of trying to assassinate Caesar. After the successful attempt on the dictator's life in the following year, Cicero delivered fourteen violent attacks on the man who planned to succeed to his despotism, Antony (44–43). These orations, named the *Philippics* after Demosthenes' speeches against Philip II of Macedonia, contributed largely to the orator's death at the hands of Antony and his fellow triumvirs.

Cicero also wrote a number of analytical studies of his chosen art of public speaking. *On Invention* (c. 84), in two books, deals with the selection and arrangement of subject matter, defining the parts into which a speech should be divided, the various different types of speech, and the treatment appropriate to each type. *On the Orator* (55), in three books, is an attempt to answer the question how the perfect orator may be produced; the work is in the form of a discussion that supposedly took place in 91 B.C., featuring leading orators of the time. *The Divisions* or *Classification of Oratory (Partitiones Oratoriae,* c. 55) is a brief catechism of rhetoric for the instruction of Cicero's son Marcus and nephew Quintus. Only a fragment of *On the Best Kind of Orators* (c. 52) has survived. The *Brutus* (46), in which Brutus together with Atticus is ostensibly taking part in the discussion, supplies a critical history of Roman oratory from its beginnings down to the time of Cicero's own training and development. The *Orator,* of the same year and likewise addressed to Brutus, bears the alternative title *On the Best Kind of Speaking.* The last of Cicero's rhetorical monographs is the *Topica,* dealing with the choice and invention of arguments. The title is that of an essay by Aristotle, to which, however, Cicero's analysis bears little resemblance.

He also wrote two important treatises relating to political philosophy. *On the State* (54–51), in six books of which we only have portions today, is a fictitious dialogue between Scipio Africanus the Younger (Aemilianus) (c. 185–129 B.C.) and some friends. The discussion analyzes the Roman state and seeks to define the constitution and form of government that suit it best; the epilogue is a vision of the other world, the *Dream of Scipio,* in which Scipio Aemilianus is shown the heavenly habitation of great souls. Likewise incomplete is a monograph *On Laws* (52, 46–45), of which we have three books out of a probable five. The legal enactments described are those that would be introduced in Cicero's ideal state.

His remaining theoretical studies were popular, practical, philosophical essays, favoring Stoicism but modifying its rigidity by an infusion of the undogmatic approach characteristic of the current Platonic Academy under Antiochus of Ascalon. *Paradoxes (of the Stoics)* (46), dedicated to Brutus, consists of applications of the most familiar Stoic maxims to the purposes of oratorical delivery. The two following years, when Cicero was politically inactive, witnessed a remarkable efflorescence of his philosophical writing. *On the Chief Good and Evil (De Finibus Bonorum et Malorum),* in five books of dialogue, discusses the principal good that is the fundamental aim of human beings —the end to which lesser goods are only means. *Academics (Academica),* expanded from two books to four—of which we have Book 1 from the first edition and Book 2 from the second—presented the eminent statesmen Catulus (d. 87 B.C.) and Lucullus (d. 57), together with the orator Hortensius (d. 50) and the scholar Varro (d. 28), explaining the principal views and conflicting tendencies of the Academic School. Cicero's *Consolatio* (written to comfort himself for the death of his daughter Tullia), his *Hortensius* (in which that orator was cast as an opponent of philosophy), and his translation of Plato's *Timaeus* survive only in fragments. In 44, he completed *Discussions at My House at Tusculum (Tusculanae Disputationes),* in five books. This debates the essentials of happiness, under the following headings: (Book 1) the contention that death is not to be feared, (Book 2) the endurance of pain, (Book 3) the overcoming of grief, (Book 4) the alleviation of other mental disturbances, (Book 5) the sufficiency of moral goodness for the happy life. *On the Nature of the Gods,* in three books, sets forth the opinions of the Epicureans, Stoics, and Academics on this matter, through appropriate Roman spokesmen. Supplementary to this work are monographs entitled *On Fate* (part of which has survived) and *On Divination.*

In Cicero's famous essay *On Old Age (De Senectute),* Scipio Africanus the Elder (d. 129 B.C.) and his friend Laelius are found visiting Cato the Censor (d. 149), who explains why he finds old age not burdensome but pleasant. The treatise is dedicated to Cicero's friend, financial backer, and publisher Atticus, and he is also the addressee of *On Friendship (De Amicitia),* in which Laelius —who provided an alternative title for the work—discusses this concept with his two sons-in-law, with particular reference to the recent death of the elder Scipio. Cicero's last important philosophical composition was *On (Moral) Duties (De Officiis),* addressed to his son. It consists of three books, of which the first deals with the morally good, the second with the expedient, and the third with such conflicts between the two concepts, as may appear to arise.

From Cicero's correspondence between 67 and 43 B.C. (of which far the greater part comes from the later years of this period), 835 of his own letters survive, including 416 to Atticus *(Ad Atticum)* and 419 to more than ninety other friends, acquaintances, and relations *(Ad Familiares).* Each of these two collections is arranged in sixteen books. There are also 92 letters of which Cicero is the recipient, written by 31 different correspondents (including Pompey, Cato, Julius Caesar, Antony, and Brutus), and 20 exchanged between third parties (including reports to the government by Roman generals). A further 27 letters to his own brother Quintus Cicero *(Ad Quintum Fratrem),* in three books, date from the years 59–54 B.C. There are also 25 letters of a correspondence between Brutus and Cicero (with one letter from Brutus to Atticus, criticizing Cicero), all written in 43 B.C.

An extraordinary wealth of autobiographical and historical information is available in Cicero's letters, of which details were given above. It is largely as a result of this unique collection that we are so exceptionally well informed about his career and opinions. The correspondence constitutes our principal, and very often our only, source of knowledge for the events of this decisive period in the history of western civilization.

The letters vary greatly in style: some are careful and deliberate, others dashed off hastily in colloquial language. This provides exceptionally valuable evidence for the day-to-day speech of educated Romans, in which, evidently, the insertion of Greek words and quotations was frequent. Cicero evidently wrote his letters without any immediate thought of publication. When he first began to entertain such an idea—not, apparently, before 44 B.C.—he only envisaged a small collection of about seventy that were in the possession of his secretary Tiro, who augmented them with others provided by Atticus. After Cicero's death, Tiro published the *Letters to Friends,* but it is generally believed that the *Letters to Atticus* were not published until the time of Nero (A.D. 54–68).

Cicero also played a certain part in the history of Latin poetry. His best known poems, were autobiographical epics *On His Consulship (De Consulatu Suo),* 72 lines of which have been preserved, and *On His Life and Times (De Temporibus Suis),* of which only small fragments are extant. These pieces were derided in antiquity for their self-glorification. Cicero also wrote an epic *Marius,* of which one of the scanty surviving passages describes the seizure of a snake by an eagle. Another of his poetic works was a translation into hexameters of the *Phaenomena* of the Greek poet Aratus of Soli (c. 315–240 B.C.). 469 lines of Cicero's version have come down to us; and fragments from translations of Homer and the Greek dramatists are also available. Cicero's verse is of technical importance as a staging point between Ennius and Virgil, since he lightened the movement of the hexameter and enlivened it by rhetorical touches. His verse is facile and, although capable of powerful phrasing, remains on the whole workmanlike rather than inspired.

As a result of all his writings, we know this gifted, distinctive, and unique personage better than any other figure of the ancient world. It is true that much of this evidence is biased, since it comes from his own highly egotistical self, but in compensation he is self-revealing to an extraordinary degree.

The part he played as a politician emerges clearly from his speeches. It was, on the whole, an ineffective role. Like his contemporaries, he had no constructive ideas about how the reform of the state, which was so glaringly necessary, ought to be undertaken, but preferred to look back with nostalgic conservatism to a stable and balanced Republic that had never existed in such an ideal form. More seriously, Cicero lacked the ruthless toughness needed in a Roman politician of his time. Indeed, he was a timid man. For this reason he deserves all the more credit for having, on at least a few occasions in his career, screwed up his not usually very conspicuous courage to take a determined stand against the despotisms that he genuinely and invariably hated.

The last of these stands, the *Philippics* in which he so eloquently attacked Antony, eventually cost him his life. But twenty years earlier than that Cicero had already performed a wondrous deed—especially in his own eyes—by the part he played in suppressing the Catilinarian conspiracy. Modern readers are appalled by the loudness with which he blows his own trumpet in celebration of this achievement. Yet this was not sheer vanity, since Cicero, as his treatises and letters show, was in fact a relatively modest man (with an engaging tendency, even, to laugh at himself). His political boasting was due to the fear that people might think he had acted illegally and wrongly, a fear that proved all too amply justified. Moreover, as consul he suffered from a dearth of supporters because of the disadvantage of being a "new man"—a man, that is to say, whose ancestors had never held a consulship—so that, if there was a scarcity of people prepared to stand up for him, he had to stand up vigorously for himself.

There was only one single thing that made it possible for him to play a role on the competitive stage of Roman politics at all, and that was his genius as a public speaker. No activity reflected Roman ideals and aspirations more completely than oratory or was more highly valued for its practical effectiveness in law and politics. Greek textbooks in the art, of the Hellenistic age, abounded; but the most notable of all are their Latin coun-

95

terparts, or rather improvements on the same theme, by Cicero—which are of exceptional value, since it is rare for a first-rate exponent of any activity to describe it so admirably.

Cicero knew all the technicalities and could bring them into play with overwhelming effect. But he disdained to fit himself into any single rhetorical category, since he himself was capable of playing on virtually every human chord. He had impressive looks, a magnificent voice, and a keen awareness that audiences decided more problems by emotion than by reason: he acted upon this last with devastating effect. His gorgeous, ever-varying language—with its elaborate, resounding, meticulously exploited rhythms —has been almost universally described, in later ages, as the greatest Latin prose of all time; and he himself has been hailed as one of the most consummate prose stylists who has ever lived.

Cicero rose far beyond the rhetoricians' technical rules by insisting that an orator should possess an extremely wide range of knowledge; he worked incessantly to attain such knowledge himself. For one thing, he agreed with Aristotle that the famous, traditional conflict, or contrast, between rhetoric and philosophy was nonexistent and that the two arts should rather be regarded as inseparable: "to speak copiously and elegantly on the most important subjects is in itself the most important philosophy." And in consequence, since philosophy had long been predominantly ethical, this meant that the orator had to be not only a learned but a virtuous man—in the spirit of Cato the Censor, who had defined orators as "good men skilled in speaking." This meant that Cicero was profoundly conscious of the responsibility that orators wielded in Roman society; moreover he felt strongly that they were better equipped than anyone else to teach the good life.

It was only regrettable that the political conditions of the day and the exigencies of addressing refractory bodies such as the Senate, Assembly, and Law Courts quite often compelled him to fall, in practice, below his ethical ideals and to champion undesirable causes and personages for short-term political reasons. Nevertheless, his conduct remained at least as respectable as that of the best of his contemporaries. On his own behalf he also felt able to point out that if he himself ever lapsed into subjectivity or dishonesty, such lapses were at least never out of keeping with public opinion and never infringed, moreover, upon the rules of ordinary decency or upon the canons laid down by the Stoic philosopher Panaetius (c. 185–109 B.C.), of whom, as his own philosophical treatises show, he made a careful study.

What these treatises above all reveal is that Cicero, despite the defects and inadequacies of his own career, believed in individual human beings, that he was convinced of their rights and responsibilities and of their freedom to make decisions without detailed interventions from heaven or fate. This was a massive contribution to an age overshadowed by autocrats such as Sulla and Caesar. He explained his belief in terms of the Stoic doctrine that all human beings possess within themselves a spark of the divinity, the force that pervades the entire natural world. About further aspects of god or gods Cicero was a doubter, a man who, true to contemporary Academic principle, was not prepared to swallow dogmas. But one thing Cicero did persistently maintain was the Stoic belief that the universe had been created, and was governed, by a divine plan and that since this plan granted every individual the wonderful endowment of reason, humans must one and all do everything in their power to develop this higher faculty, which is what distinguishes them from animals. Moreover, as he went on to insist with unprecedented eloquence, our common possession of the divine spark binds us together with our fellow human beings with an indissoluble bond and demands that we should treat them decently. Of such decent behavior, in all its aspects, he is sure that there is an unchanging, objective standard. Right is right and wrong is wrong; and Cicero's declaration of this eternal, irrevocable distinction has reverberated down the ages.

Yet he was a practical man, and no original philosopher, as he himself was entirely ready to admit. What he learned in his readings from a wide, eclectically chosen variety of philosophical schools, he adapted to his Roman environment and his own views and tastes, the views and tastes of an experienced and sensitive person who enjoyed unequaled powers of self-expression and was pervaded by a keen and earnest sense of personal involvement. And in this task he immersed himself all the more deeply during the depressing dictatorship of Caesar, at a time, moreover, when the death of his beloved daughter Tullia had plunged him into a misery from which he urgently needed distraction.

But, over and above these considerations, it seemed to him a wholly worthwhile objective to Latinize, with additions and adjustments of his own, the various systems of Greek philosophy, presenting their most applicable portions for the benefit of his fellow Romans. The project was by no means an easy one (some told him it was impossible) because the Latin tongue had never hitherto been established as a medium for general ideas. But Cicero remedied this in no uncertain fashion, converting the language into a lucid and splendid vehicle for the conveyance of a massive range of abstract thought. In order to achieve this purpose, he had to create new ways of Latin thinking—and even invent a whole assemblage of new Latin words. Among the terms we owe him are the following: appetite, comprehension, definition, difference, element, image, individual, induction, infinity, instance, moral, notion, property, quality, science, species, and vacuum.

The influence of Cicero upon the history of subsequent European literature and ideas exceeds that of any other prose author in any language. His writings had their early critics, but Quintilian, in the first century A.D., was ready to canonize him as a model of superlative eloquence, character, and citizenship. The great Christian fathers, such as Jerome and Augustine, viewed his work with schizophrenic ambivalence, seeing him as the symbol of the pagan culture whose vanities Christianity had rejected and yet at the same time admiring him passionately, so that his work became an important ingredient in Christian doctrine and Scholastic logic; the *Dream of Scipio* (from *On the State*) particularly impressed Macrobius and Boethius, who lived at the watershed between the ancient and medieval worlds.

Pope Gregory the Great (A.D. 590–604), however, wanted to destroy Cicero's writings on the grounds that they diverted people's attention from the Scriptures. But, then, in the later Middle Ages the good sense in his writing, his public spirited portrayal of a civilized society, and his presentation and interpretation of earlier classical thought, appealed greatly to the rising urban communities of Europe. St. Thomas Aquinas could point to *On Duties* as advocating a life of civic responsibility, and Dante declared *On Friendship* his chief philosophical guide. This treatise, together with its sister volume *On Old Age,* won Cicero general renown as a good and wise man; and the same two works were the chief Latin sources for the thirteenth century *Roman de la Rose.* In the same period, Henry de Bracton (d. 1268), author of the first comprehensive English legal treatise, relied ultimately on Cicero's definitions of natural law.

The Italian Renaissance, a Renaissance of classical antiquity, owed an enormous amount to Petrarch's determination to use Cicero—of whose works he made important rediscoveries—as a guide toward the interpretation of his own age; for Petrarch saw him as a paragon of eloquence, an exemplar of an ideally civilized design for living, and, above all, a stimulating thinker on moral questions, though the political vacillation and inadequacy revealed in the *Letters* shocked him considerably. The next generation of Italians, however, was impressed by Cicero's patriotic Republicanism, which became the text for an ever-continuing analysis of the conflicts between freedom and despotism. Moreover, Cicero's ideal of the Whole Man, combining oratorical brilliance with a sense of public duty and a cultivated employment of leisure hours, became the basic education of the Renaissance upper class, notably in its academies at Ferrara and Verona.

From the sixteenth century onward these influences spread massively northward. *On Duties,* of which there were sixty-three editions between 1553 and 1610, seemed to Erasmus to embody every principle needed by an aspirant to public life. Martin Luther estimated Cicero's treatises as superior to Aristotle's, and Queen Elizabeth I had read nearly all his works by the age of sixteen. Yet the most truly Ciceronian phase in England is not the Elizabethan Age but the seventeenth century, in which the Authorized Version of the Bible showed many traces of his style, and John Milton and George Herbert and John Locke displayed massive debts to his prose and thought, and humanists, deists, believers in natural religion, rationalists, and free-thinkers alike all studied *On the Nature of the Gods*. In the eighteenth century, Diderot and Voltaire were among Cicero's admirers, and his manner is pervasively apparent in Samuel Johnson, Robertson, Gibbon, Burke, Sheridan, Fox, and the two Pitts. *On Duties* influenced philosophers such as Kant, Schiller, and Johann Herbart; and the impact of Cicero's political thinking both on the American and French Revolutions received emphatic acknowledgment from their leaders. In the nineteenth century, the German classical scholar and historian Theodor Mommsen's admiration for the Hohenzollerns caused him to deplore Cicero's Republican views, yet the Ciceronian *humanitas* remains a keyword for much that the western tradition of civilization seeks to preserve. The works in which he conveys his ideal have formed a major unifying force for Europe and America, serving as the supreme shaper of their civilized speech and the greatest of all transmitters of cultural values to their peoples.

WORKS that have vanished—In addition to his surviving 57 speeches, fragments of about 20 more are extant, the most important being from the two Cornelianae (Pro Gaio Cornelio *and* De Maiestate, 66 B.C.), the Oratio in Toga Candida (64 B.C.), and the Pro Aemilio Scauro (54 B.C.). We also know of 33 other speeches delivered by Cicero. In addition to these, he published orations in praise of Caesar (56), Cato the Younger (46), and Cato's sister Porcia (45), but these had never been delivered. His lost philosophical treatises included a monograph entitled On Auguries and translations of Plato's Protagoras and Timaeus (fragments) and of Xenophon's Oeconomicus; and fragments have survived of Consolation, Hortensius (45), On Glory (Books 1 and 2), and On Virtues (an appendix to On Duties, 44). A passage has also come down to us from a discussion entitled On the Best Kind of Orators; and we have a preface to his lost translations of the speech Against Ctesiphon by Aeschines (c. 397–322 B.C.) and of Demosthenes' reply. For Cicero's lost poems, see above, in the text of this article.

He also attempted certain historical compositions, of which, once again, only fragments are extant: Memoirs of His Consulship (Commentarius Consulatus Sui, in Greek), a Secret History (Anecdota), and Admiranda. Quintilian also mentions a collection of his jokes and puns (Liber Jocularis).

Speeches falsely attributed to Cicero include one entitled On the Day Before Going into Exile (Pridie Quam in Exsilium Iret) and an alleged reply (Responsio Ciceronis in Sallustium) to an attack on Cicero wrongly attributed to the historian Sallust (Invectiva Sallustii in Ciceronem). A letter addressed To Octavian found in a manuscript of some of Cicero's letters is also unauthentic. So is a didactic poem Orpheus (or, De Adulescente Studioso), which purports to have been written by Cicero for his son; and compositions entitled De Notis and Synonyma are equally spurious—the latter is the composition of an anonymous grammarian.

Another work wrongly attributed to Cicero in manuscripts is the Rhetorica ad Herennium, a not unimportant treatise on rhetoric in four books addressed to a certain Gaius Herennius. This Rhetorica seems to have been written in c. 86–82 B.C., and its author has been tentatively identified as Cornificius, a political supporter of Marius.

EDITIONS—*Listed in* Oxford Classical Dictionary, 2nd ed., 1970, p 238. *Add:* W. S. Watt, Letters to Quintus and Brutus, and Fragments, 1958; R. Kytzler, Cicero: Brutus, 1970; D. R. Shackleton Bailey, Letters to Atticus, 1970, *and* Letters to Friends (Ad Familiares), 1977; G. Puccioni, Ciceronis Orationum Deperditarum Fragmenta, 1974. *Translations*—numerous translators (Loeb ed.), 1954–77; M. Grant, Cicero on the Good Life (Penguin ed.), 1971, *and* Selected Works, revised ed., 1971, *and* Selected Political Speeches, revised ed., 1973, *and* Murder Trials, 1975; J. Soubiran, Cicéron, Aratea: Fragments poétiques (Budé ed.), 1972; *others listed in* A. M. W. Green, Classics in Translation: A Selective Bibliography (1930–76), 1976. Pseudo-Ciceronian Rhetorica ad Herennium: H. Caplan (Loeb ed.), 1964; G. Calboli (Italian, with commentary), 1969.

ABOUT—H. A. K. Hunt, The Humanism of Cicero, 1954; H. D. Meyer, Cicero und das Reich, 1957; L. Alfonsi and others, Marco Tullio Cicerone, 1961; J. C. Rolfe, Cicero and His Influence, 1963; K. Büchner, Cicero, 1964; T. A. Dorey, ed., Cicero, 1964; R. E. Smith, Cicero the Statesman, 1966; A. E. Douglas, Cicero (Greece & Rome: New Surveys in the Classics, no 2), 1968; G. Radke, ed., Cicero: Ein Mensch seiner Zeit, 1968; E. G. Sihler, Cicero of Arpinum, 1969; K. Bringmann, Untersuchungen zum späten Cicero, 1971; D. R. Shackleton Bailey, Cicero, 1971; D. Stockton, Cicero: A Political Biography, 1971; M. Gelzer, Cicero, 1972; G. Kennedy, The Art of Rhetoric in the Roman World, 1972 (including discussion and bibliography of the Rhetorica ad Herennium); G. V. Sumner, The Orator in Cicero's Brutus, 1974; M. Bellincioni, Cicerone politico nell'ultimo anno di vita, 1975; A. Heuss, Cicero's Theorie vom römischen Staat, 1975; A. Michel and R. Verdière, Ciceroniana (Hommages à K. Kumaniecki), 1975; E. Rawson, Cicero: A Portrait, 1975; S. L. Utčenko, Cicerone e il suo tempo, 1975; A. Desmouliez, Cicéron et son goût, 1976; W. K. Lacey, ed., Cicero and the End of the Roman Republic, 1978.

CINNA, GAIUS HELVIUS, Latin poet, lived in the first century B.C. and probably died in 44. He was born at Brixellum (Brescia) in Cisalpine Gaul (northern Italy) and was a pupil of Valerius Cato and a friend of Catullus, both of whom came from the same region. In 57, he was with Catullus in Bithynia (northwestern Asia Minor), in the entourage of the praetor Gaius Memmius. Plutarch and Shakespeare identified the poet Cinna, correctly, with Gaius Helvius Cinna, tribune of the people in 44, who carried one law and drafted another in pursuance of Julius Caesar's autocratic aims. After the assassination of Caesar, however, he was lynched by the dead man's supporters, since they mistook him for the praetor Lucius Cornelius Cinna who had expressed approval of the dictator's murder.

The poet Cinna belonged to the Latin movement, centered upon Cisalpine Gaul, whose members were known as New Poets or Neoterics. Their aim was to endow Latin verse with the technical polish and finish, the elaborate erudition, and the small-scale poetical genres that the Alexandrian school, led by Callimachus (c. 305–240 B.C.), had contributed to the literature of the Hellenistic Greeks. It is now believed that Cinna was the leader of this Latin Neoteric group.

His principal work, of which only three lines are extant, was a miniature epic, the *Zmyrna,* telling of the incestuous love of the girl of that name (otherwise known as Myrrha) for her father Cinyras, a theme that gave the poet an opportunity to develop the Alexandrian interest in psychological peculiarities. According to Catullus, the *Zmyrna* took nine years to write. It was evidently crammed with obscure learning, since before long it needed a commentary; and this, as we learn from the biographer Suetonius, was duly provided by a scholar named Lucius Crassicius. Cinna's choice of Zmyrna as his subject can be traced back to the Greek poet Parthenius of Nicaea, who had come to Italy as a prisoner of war in 73 B.C. and exercised a considerable influence on Cinna and other Neoterics.

Cinna also wrote a farewell poem *(Propempticon)* for the young Asinius Pollio (76 B.C.–A.D. 4)—later an eminent historian and

sin´ nä

statesman—who was about to start on a journey to Greece, perhaps in 56 B.C. In this piece the obscurities were largely of a geographical nature, but they, too, required a commentary, which was supplied by Augustus' scholarly librarian Hyginus. The *Propempticon* has not survived; nor have the lyric and erotic pieces, credited to Cinna, though one of his epigrams, an imitation of Callimachus, is extant.

He was a poet's poet whose work attracted impressive admirers. Catullus forecast, erroneously, that the *Zmyrna* would continue to be read until "Time itself grew gray." Virgil, in the *Eclogues,* considered Cinna too exalted a model for himself to endeavor to imitate, at least at that stage of his development. In the later first century A.D., Martial addressed an epigram to a man who believed that Cinna was a greater poet than Virgil—because he was more obscure.

EDITIONS—W. Morel, Fragmenta Poetarum Latinorum Epicorum et Lyricorum, 1927.
ABOUT—W. S. Teuffel, History of Roman Literature, 1900; M. Schanz and C. Hosius, Geschichte der römischen Literatur, v 1, 4th ed., 1927; C. J. Fordyce, Catullus: A Commentary, 1961; T. P. Wiseman, Cinna the Poet and Other Roman Essays, 1974; H. Dahlmann, Über Helvius Cinna, 1977; A. Kiessling, De Gaio Helvio Cinna Poeta, in Commentationes Philologicae in Honorem T. Mommsen, 1978.

CLAUDIAN (Claudius Claudianus), Latin poet, was born at Alexandria in Egypt in the late fourth century A.D. and probably died in about, or not long after, 404. At some time before A.D. 395 he had come to Italy, and it was in that year that he claims to have first drunk the stream of Latin song, when his Muse, deserting Hellas, assumed the Roman toga. Thereafter, he maintained an enormous output of poetry for nine years. Although he remained pagan while the imperial house was Christian, he became the court poet of the young western emperor Honorius (brother of Arcadius in the east) and of his regent Stilicho, whose enemies, notably in the eastern empire, Claudian savagely abused. A statue was erected to Claudian in the Forum of Trajan, bearing a

klô´ di ən

highly honorific inscription that still survives. After 404 no more is heard of him.

One group of his works consists of *Panegyrics* of men appointed to consulships. The earliest of these poems, honoring the youthful brothers Probinus and Olybrius who attained that office in 395, has the goddess Rome in person visit the emperors' father and predecessor Theodosius I in the hour of his victory over a usurper. Three other poems loyally celebrate consulates held by the nominal emperor Honorius himself (A.D. 396, 398, 404), to whom Claudius refrains from ascribing warlike prowess, which he clearly lacked, while fulsomely praising his birth, character, and good looks, and ingeniously introducing Honorius' eminent father to advise him on the duties of a ruler. The Manlius Theodorus whose consulship in 399 also inspired a poem by Claudian was apparently a lawyer and public official. According to the poet, Justice herself invites Theodorus to emerge from his retirement—which he agrees to do—and prepares to offer him the habitual lavish entertainments associated with the inauguration of consular tenures.

By far the longest of the consular *Panegyrics* was a three-book poem of 1,230 lines in honor of Stilicho himself, offering adulation of his military and statesmanlike achievements, with many echoes of the classical past that the hero is held to eclipse by his own deeds. There is also another panegyric that does not refer to a consulship but commemorates Stilicho's wife Serena (the adopted daughter of Theodosius), who selected a rich bride for Claudian. The emperor Honorius himself married Stilicho's daughter Maria, and Claudian wrote an *Epithalamium* (as well as four other shorter poems) for the occasion, manipulating all the traditional themes with considerable skill.

But the poet shows the vigor of his language to particularly great effect in his invectives against Stilicho's political enemies Rufinus and Eutropius, the successive chief advisers of the eastern emperor Arcadius. The criticism is unsparingly ferocious and introduces, with the aid of mythology, every conceivable form of unpleasant vituperation, however unjustified and tasteless. For example, the murder of Rufinus, which was almost certainly arranged by Stilicho, is described with great gusto, and the slave origin of the eunuch Eutropius is made a ground for imagining that he held a whole series of menial and disgusting occupations. Nevertheless, this political poetry contains important historical information, however distorted.

An incomplete poem of 526 lines—*War Against Gildo* (A.D. 398)—tells of the defeat of that rebel, who had led an uprising in Africa and threatened to starve Rome out by withholding its supply of grain. The slightly longer *Gothic War* (402) praises Stilicho for his defeat of the Visigothic King Alaric at Pollentia (Pollenza), although the result was by no means a decisive Roman victory despite the capture of Alaric's family. In addition to these poems, which could be described as epyllia (miniature epics), Claudian tried his hand at mythological epic on a larger, though still not full-length, scale. There is a 128-line fragment of a *War of the Giants (Gigantomachia).* But what seems today to be his finest work is *The Rape of Proserpine (De Raptu Proserpinae),* divided into four books, out of which 1100 lines have survived. The style of its descriptive narrative is richly lavish but elegant, and the familiar story of Pluto's capture of Proserpina on the flowery field of Enna is told by Claudian with compelling charm. He also wrote a group of *Carmina Minora,* or lesser poems, including an attractive *Phoenix* and a sympathetic study entitled *Old Man of Verona.*

Although his native language was presumably Greek, Claudian's command of Latin diction and technique and all the resources of versification warrants comparison with the poetic masters of the first century A.D. His talents gained him an unrivaled position among his contemporaries, so that he emerges as the last noteworthy representative of the classical tradition in Latin poetry, thus earning a pillar in Chaucer's House of Fame. In particular, he handled the difficult art of political poetry with remarkable and evidently heartfelt vigor, and it is not surprising that Stilicho, in whose favor he deployed this activity, made a collection of his poems on such themes and republished them separately (after 404). Yet

Claudian's flattery, as Gibbon declared, was deplorably servile, like that of so many of his pagan contemporaries, and could descend to nadirs of preposterous exaggeration from which his abundant store of mythological conceits could not rescue him. Moreover, his talents were further offset by an obsession for excessive elaborateness that lapses, from time to time, into the unintentionally ridiculous.

EDITIONS—J. B. Hall, De Raptu Proserpine, 1970; H. L. Levy, In Rufinum: An Exegetical Commentary, 1971; W. Simon, Claudiani Panegyricus De Consulatu Manlii Theodorii, 1975. *Translations*—M. Platnauer (Loeb ed.), 1922; V. Paladini, Claudianus Minor (Rape of Proserpine, Italian), 1952; H. Isbell, Rape of Proserpine and Epithalamium for the Marriage of Honorius *in* The Last Poets of Imperial Rome (Penguin ed.), 1971.

ABOUT—J. H. Creese, Claudian as an Historical Authority, 1968; O. A. W. Dilke, Claudian: Poet of Declining Empire and Morals, 1969; A. Cameron, Claudian: Poetry and Propaganda at the Court of Honorius, 1970; U. Keudel, Poetische Vorläufer und Vorbilder in Claudians De Consulatu Stilichonis, 1974; P. L. Schmidt, Politik und Dichtung in der Panegyrik Claudians, 1976.

CLAUDIUS, Roman emperor and writer in Latin and Greek, was born at Lugdunum (Lyon in France) in 10 B.C. and died in A.D. 54. He was the son of Nero Drusus (Drusus Senior) and of Antonia the Younger. Handicapped by constant illness and a physical handicap that was probably a spastic condition, Claudius obtained no government appointments from Augustus or Tiberius, but Gaius (Caligula), who was his nephew, gave him a consulship in A.D. 37. After Caligula's assassination in 41, the senior officers of the praetorian guard secured Claudius the throne, because his birth ensured dynastic continuity and because he was the brother of the popular general Germanicus. The Senate, which had not been consulted, was unenthusiastic, and a rebellion in Dalmatia and alleged conspiracies followed, together with a resumption of treason trials.

Meanwhile, however, the government of Claudius was active. His generals undertook the annexation of part of England (Britannia); and Claudius himself came to that

klô' di us

CLAUDIUS

country for the decisive capture of Camulodunum (Colchester), in A.D. 43. He displayed administrative talents at home and carried out his judicial duties with the utmost conscientiousness. His predecessor's employment of Greek or Hellenized freedmen as secretaries was continued and extended, but at this stage of his reign Claudius still kept even his most powerful secretaries, Narcissus and Pallas, under control. His young wife Messalina, who had borne him a daughter Octavia and a son Britannicus, was initially more interested in amusing herself than in exerting political authority. In 48, however, one of her lovers, Gaius Silius, was accused, of seeking the throne, and he and Messalina were put to death by the initiative of Narcissus.

Narcissus' moment of power, however, ended abruptly when Claudius married his own niece Agrippina the Younger in 49. During the five remaining years of his life the aging emperor, overworked, terrified of conspiracies, unhealthy, and alcoholic, partially lost his grip of affairs. Agrippina arranged that Nero, her own son by a former marriage, should be betrothed to Octavia (49). In the next year the youth was adopted by Claudius, evidently at Britannicus' expense; and when the emperor died—probably because Agrippina fed him poisoned mushrooms—Nero succeeded in his place.

When debarred from public life in his earlier years, Claudius had occupied himself

101

vigorously with scholarly activities. Pliny the Elder, who quotes him four times in his *Natural History,* ranked him among the hundred foremost learned writers of his day. Claudius' literary output was impressive, though virtually none of it survives today. Early on he composed a pamphlet in defense of Cicero, and the historian Livy himself, no doubt prompted by Augustus, recognized and encouraged the young man's inclination for historical studies. Claudius set to work on a Roman history, which he proposed to commence with the death of Julius Caesar. However, when his mother and grandmother, the daughter and widow respectively of Mark Antony who had succumbed to Augustus, protested to him that the civil wars at the outset of that period constituted a theme that was still too embarrassing, he abandoned the earlier part of the project and fixed the starting point of his work at the inauguration, in 27 B.C., of the New Order of Augustus, whom he greatly admired.

Claudius wrote forty-one books of his Roman history, presumably covering the forty-one years to Augustus' death in A.D. 14. He gave public readings of this work, though after he came to the throne he delegated this task to a professional reader (either because he was too busy, or because he stammered). He also wrote an eight-book autobiography, or memoirs *(Commentarii),* which seems to have covered his earlier life and the first years of his reign. The biographer Suetonius, who describes the work as "lacking rather in good taste than in style," may well have derived from it much of his detailed knowledge of the legislation and other events of the time. Claudius also wrote a treatise on dicing, of which he was fond, and a book on his theory of the alphabet, into which, after he became emperor, he introduced three new letters, though they were abandoned after his death. He also composed long and important works in Greek—namely twenty books of Etruscan history and eight of Carthaginian history—for which a new Museum of Claudius was established at Alexandria in order that these two works should be read aloud in their entirety, in alternate years. Their disappearance—especially that of the former, to which his first wife, of Etruscan blood, may have contribut-

ed original information—is one of the gravest of our losses in ancient historiography.

Claudius' diction has been preserved for us in a number of surviving edicts and official letters, among which a speech to the Senate, found at his birthplace Lugdunum, is of outstanding interest. These documents display good sense and far-sighted liberality, though their diction—when it preserves the emperor's own words—is idiosyncratic and tortuous. He was ready at all times to impart his erudition about Roman history or local antiquities to others or to calm superstitious fears by explaining, for instance, the natural causes of an eclipse. Letters were written to him, and works dedicated to him, by scientists and men of learning from many lands, including both Greek and Roman doctors such as Thessalus of Tralles and Scribonius Largus—and even by an Arabian chieftain Aretas.

EDITIONS (edicts and letters)—P. Fabia, La table claudienne de Lyon, 1929; E. M. Smallwood, Documents Illustrating the Principates of Gaius, Claudius and Nero, 1967.
ABOUT—A. Momigliano, Claudius: The Emperor and His Achievement, 1934, reprint 1961; H. Bardon, Les empereurs et les lettres latines d'Auguste à Adrien, 1940; V. M. Scramuzza, The Emperor Claudius, 1940, reprint 1971; M. Durry, Les empereurs comme historiens d'Auguste à Hadrien (Entretiens Hardt, v 4), 1958; R. Syme, Tacitus, 1958 (Appendix 40).

CLEANTHES, Greek philosopher, was born in about 331 and died in about 232 B.C. His birthplace was Assos (Behramkale) in the Troad (northwestern Asia Minor); his father's name was Phanias. Cleanthes moved to Athens, where he first studied under the Cynic philosopher Crates of Thebes and then became a pupil of Zeno, the founder of Stoicism. While pursuing his education, Cleanthes worked all night as water-carrier to a gardener, which earned him the nickname "drawer from the well." On the death of Zeno in about 262 B.C., Cleanthes succeeded him as leader of the Stoic School. Among his pupils was his own successor, Chrysippus of Soli, as well as Antigonus II Gonatas, king of Macedonia (284 –239 B.C.).

kle an' thēz

Cleanthes was said to have been slow of intellect, and the fragments of his work that survive suggest a certain philosophical woolliness. However, he was deeply sincere in his devotion to the novel doctrines of Zeno, and he wrote fluently, in an agreeable and easy manner. According to Arius Didymus (first century B.C.), it was Cleanthes who defined Zeno's instruction "to live consistently" as meaning "to live consistently with nature" (which was, in any case, what Zeno had intended). Cleanthes' ethical teaching, which was illustrated by vivid similes and examples, stressed the need for disinterested motives; he declared that to do good to others with a view merely to one's own advantage was no better than feeding cattle in order to eat them.

Evil thoughts, in his belief, were worse than evil actions, just as a tumor that bursts is less dangerous than one that remains intact. His principal contribution to Stoic theory, however, was his invention or development of the idea of tension as a force that is the cause of all durable, lasting conditions and things. This tension seemed to him the element that holds everything together, from the whole world down to its smallest object, so that it is also the factor that gives cohesion to the souls and bodies of individual beings.

Nine of the fragments of Cleanthes' writings are in verse, since he maintained that prose did not provide phrases capable of rising to divine greatness. His famous *Hymn to Zeus* has survived. In imposing language, it expresses the exaltation the poet felt as he contemplated the omnipotent power of Zeus —who is envisaged not as the anthropomorphic god of mythology but as the spirit that permeates and rules the universe. In his hymn, Cleanthes depicts the relationship of himself and other human beings to this all-powerful element: "We are of your race. Of all the animals that live and walk the earth, only we have a semblance of your reason. So shall I always hymn you and your power."

Other lines of the poem, later adapted by Seneca the Younger, illustrate one aspect of Stoicism that exerted widespread attraction: the idea that, since the whole world is ruled by God and every event that it experiences is an act of his will, individual human beings are obliged to accept all things that befall them, knowing that they are not only unalterable but the work of the perfect, infallible deity; and this unfailing acceptance will bring them peace of mind and protection against whatever sufferings they may have to undergo.

EDITIONS—A. C. Pearson, The Fragments of Zeno and Cleanthes, 1891; J. ab (H. von) Arnim, Stoicorum Veterum Fragmenta, 1920–25; J. U. Powell, Collectanea Alexandrina, 1925. *Translations* (Hymn to Zeus)—E. H. Blakeney (Texts for Students Series), 1921; J. Adam *in* W. J. Oates, ed., The Stoic and Epicurean Philosophers, 1940; M. Grant, Greek Literature in Translation, 1973.
ABOUT—S. Sambursky, Physics of the Stoics, 1959; F. Solmsen, Cleanthes or Posidonius? The Meaning of Stoicism, 1967; J. M. Rist, Stoic Philosophy, 1969, reprint 1977; M. Pohlenz, Stoa und Stoiker, 4th ed., 1970, 1972; A. A. Long, ed., Problems in Stoicism, 1971, *and* Hellenistic Philosophy, 1974; F. H. Sandbach, The Stoics, 1975.

CLEITARCHUS, Greek historian, of the late fourth and early third century B.C., lived in Alexandria. His history of Alexander the Great (d. 323) has not survived, but it seems to have been preserved in abbreviated form in Book 17 of the *World History (Bibliotheke Historike)* of Diodorus Siculus (first century B.C.).

Cleitarchus' history apparently contained not only a great deal of direct narrative, based on the Alexander historians who had preceded him, but also numerous passages of a spectacular and sensational nature; Cicero reported that he wrote "in rhetorical and tragic fashion." Cleitarchus' account of Alexander's reign was mainly responsible for establishing the popular, fictional tradition that surrounded the figure of his hero and was later reflected in the *History of Alexander* written by Curtius Rufus in the first century A.D., the *Philippic History* of Marcus Junianus Justinus in the second, and the *Anabasis Alexandri* and *Indica* of the Greek historian Arrian (c. 95–c. 175).

Although ancient critics took an unfavorable view of Cleitarchus' work, it was widely read in the early Roman empire and exer-

klī tär' kus

cised an influence on the development of the romantic novel.

EDITIONS—F. Jacoby, Die Fragmente der griechischen Historiker, 2b, 137.

ABOUT—F. Jacoby, in Pauly-Wissowa-Kroll, Real-Encyclopädie der klassischen Altertumswissenschaft, v 11, column 639; L. Pearson, The Lost Histories of Alexander, 1959; A. Momigliano, Alien Wisdom, 1976.

CLEMENT OF ALEXANDRIA, (Titus Flavius Clemens), Greek theological writer, was born of pagan parents in about A.D. 150, probably at Athens and died between 211 and 216. After studying rhetoric and philosophy, he became a convert to Christianity and traveled widely, attaching himself to Christian teachers and finally to Pantaenus, who presided over a school at Alexandria devoted to the instruction of converts. After receiving ordination as presbyter, Clement succeeded Pantaenus as director of the school sometime before 200 and held the office until about 202, when the emperor Septimius Severus' persecution compelled him to leave Alexandria and take refuge elsewhere. He may have been accompanied by his former pupil Alexander, who was bishop of Cappadocia (eastern Asia Minor) at that time, and later of Jerusalem. He may have died in Asia Minor.

He devoted his extensive writings to the defense of the Christian religion, thus justifying his own decision to abandon paganism in its favor. Pursuing and enlarging the tradition of Justin of Neapolis, who had made pioneering attempts to harmonize Christianity with pagan philosophy, Clement and his fellow Alexandrians collaborated with Aristotelian logicians in order to construct a complete and intellectually convincing Christian philosophy. Clement was not satisfied that faith alone was the proper basis of religion, preferring to regard it merely as a useful provider, in summary form, of urgent truths appropriate for people in a hurry. It was his ambition to place the New Testament on a logical, rational basis—in refutation of assertions that such a thing was impossible—and he believed this could be done by making use of the traditional pagan knowledge and learning as "an evident im-

age of the Truth, a divine gift to the Greeks." Like Justin (d. 165), he saw Jesus Christ as the final expression of the Hellenic Word of Divine Reason and Plato as the Attic Moses and forerunner of Jesus. True, pagan polytheism was, in Clement's view, an error, which had been falsely introduced by demons. Yet his own monotheism, too, remained more Hellenic than Hebrew in spirit.

The most important of his writings was a trilogy, which has survived almost complete. Its first part, *Exhortation to the Greeks (Protrepticus)* (c. 190), was intended to convert readers by proving the advantage of the Christian faith over pagan religions and philosophies. The second treatise, the *Tutor (Paedagogus),* offers instruction in the moral teaching of Christ, including detailed regulations on specific aspects of behavior. The third work in the trilogy, the *Miscellanies (Stromateis)*—probably written in about 200 or shortly afterward—is a collection of diffuse material describing the complete Christian ideal and pointing out, once again, its superiority to pagan philosophy. The *Miscellanies* comprise eight books, of which the last is a collection of somewhat uncoordinated notes relating to logic.

One of the manuscripts of the trilogy adds two other writings, both consisting of a brief series of notes: the *Excerpta ex Theodoto,* on the doctrines of the dualist (Gnostic) Theodotus, and *Prophetic Selections (Eclogae Propheticae).* Another tract, *Which Rich Man Can Be Saved?,* discusses the proper use of wealth and urges detachment from worldly goods. The *Outlines (Adumbrationes* or *Hypotyposes)* provided brief explanations of Genesis, Exodus, Psalms, Ecclesiastes, the Epistles of Paul, and the "Catholic Epistles" (James 1-2, Peter, Jude, and 1-3 John). Of his work on the epistles, however, only fragments are extant, preserved along with a Latin epitome of the Catholic Epistles (from which heterodox opinions, have subsequently been deleted). Fragments also survive of monographs entitled *On the Easter Season, On Providence,* and *Against the Judaizer,* the last-mentioned being dedicated to Clement's pupil Alexander. Essays on the prophet Amos, on fasting, and on malevolent gossip have not survived.

A man of elaborate education, thoroughly versed in the classics from which he quotes no fewer than 360 passages, Clement devotes charm, serenity, and jubilant hopefulness to his forceful and historic, though idiosyncratic, endeavor to reconcile Christianity and Hellenism. Particularly important is his attempt to harmonize Christian and Platonic teachings on the human body. While asserting that the body impedes the soul's clarity of vision—from which obstacle the soul is liberated by the body's death—he also declares that the soul is not good by nature, nor is the body necessarily evil, and he attacks the notion that evil characteristics are transmitted through sexual reproduction.

However, this explanation of sin as a result of free will—like his conviction that the spiritual elite in this world would remain elite in the world to come—was by no means universally acceptable among Christians. Cleanthes' writings were therefore declared to be heretically tinged with pagan humanism and in consequence doctrinally unsatisfactory. He was little read in medieval times, and only the *Outlines* were translated into Latin. The *Exhortation* and the *Tutor* survived in a single copy of A.D. 914 written by a Byzantine scribe, and the *Miscellanies,* too, were preserved in one manuscript only. In the west, however, Clement was long considered one of the saints; yet he was excluded from the Roman martyrology in 1586, a decision confirmed in 1748.

EDITIONS—O. Stähling, Die griechischen christlichen Schriftsteller, 1905–9 (index 1936).

ABOUT—E. F. Osborn, The Philosophy of Clement of Alexandria, 1957; B. Altaner, Patrology, 1960; H. Chadwick, Early Christianity and the Classical Tradition, 1966; O. Prunet, La morale de Clément d'Alexandrie et le Nouveau Testament, 1966; W. E. G. Floyd, Clement of Alexandria's Treatment of the Problem of Evil, 1971; S. R. C. Lilla, Clement of Alexandria: A Study in Christian Platonism and Gnosticism, 1971; T. H. B. Hamilton, The Early Greek Apologists and Greek Philosophy: Exemplified by Clement of Alexandria, 1973; J. Ferguson, Clement of Alexandria, 1974.

CLEMENT OF ROME (Clement I, Pope and Saint) was a Greek epistolographer. There was an ancient belief, difficult to accept, that he was the Clement mentioned in Paul's *Letter to the Philippians* and that he was consecrated by St. Peter. The second century Christian theologian Irenaeus identifies him as the third successor of Peter in the Papacy (bishopric of Rome), and Eusebius ascribes his tenure of that office to A.D. 92–101, while others prefer dates a year or two earlier. On the other hand, it has also been suggested that at this time monarchical bishops, or sole rulers of the local congregation, were still unknown in the church; and Clement himself sometimes seems to speak of bishops and presbyters as identical.

His name was that of a leading Roman nobleman Flavius Clemens, who was executed by the emperor Domitian in A.D. 96 for following Jewish (or, less probably, Christian) practices. The churchman may have been one of his slaves, who took his master's name after he had been freed (the tradition that he himself was Flavius Clemens is implausible).

In 1628 a fifth century manuscript of the Greek Bible—the Codex Alexandrinus presented by the Patriarch Cyril of Jerusalem to King Charles I of England—was found to contain two additional documents. One of them was the important *First Epistle* to the Corinthians *(1 Clement),* which proves to be the earliest extant example of Christian literature outside the New Testament. A manuscript including the epistle was published in 1633, and a complete text of the original came to light in 1875. On internal grounds, the letter may be ascribed to the period immediately following Domitian's persecution of the Christians and the emperor's death in A.D. 96. This *First Epistle* to the Corinthians may be regarded as one of the letters from his hand to which reference is frequently made in the works of early Christian writers, who honored them as Scripture up to the third and fourth centuries A.D., and even later.

News had reached Clement, at Rome, of disputes in the Corinthian church that had caused many there to repudiate the authority of the local leaders. It was his purpose in the letter to settle these dissensions, and to that end he contrasted the current disturbed state of the church with its past glories and, with the aid of Old Testament illustrations, deprecated discord and envy and pleaded for discipline, reconciliation, and love (while at the same time urging acceptance of the imperial system). Whatever Clement's exact position at Rome, the fact that its church thus assumed the responsibility of authoritative intervention in the domestic quarrels of the Corinthian church has figured largely in Roman claims to ecclesiastical primacy. Clement's letter, though diffuse and rambling, does not lose the thread of its central idea, which is the grievousness of the sin of pride: the jealous pride of a few self-seekers who have destroyed the peace of Corinth's Christian community.

The high regard in which Clement was held in the early church caused a number of other, later writings to be ascribed to his authorship. One of these was the second document attached to the Codex Alexandrinus, known as the *Second Epistle of Clement (2 Clement);* it is in fact, however, not a letter but a sermon, that discusses the moral combat in which the Christian has to engage as he faces the world. Although the attribution of this work to Clement was upheld in the fifth and sixth centuries A.D. by the Monophysites, who believed that its opening words "Brothers, we must think of Jesus Christ as of God" anticipated their own theology, the *Second Epistle* never became generally popular. Moreover, its genuineness had already been questioned by Eusebius and Jerome, and rightly so, since its substance and style alike favor a date not earlier than the middle of the second century A.D.

Also widely (but incorrectly) attributed to Clement were two other "epistles" entitled *On Virginity.* Though preserved in a Syriac manuscript of 1470—and one of them in Coptic fragments as well—they came from a Greek original, from which quotations appear in a collection of seventh century sermons. The two works were first mentioned in about A.D. 375 and were probably written slightly earlier in that century. Their aim was to denounce abuses of "spiritual" marriage and to censure lapses from asceticism; later, the Anabaptists quoted these treatises to justify the community of women.

Particularly influential were two other compositions that likewise bore Clement's name, the *Homilies* (preserved in the Greek original) and the *Recognitions* (extant in Latin and Syriac translations of about A.D. 400). Although these works may contain certain material, if not from the first century A.D., at least from the second and third centuries, they too were probably not written until the years immediately preceding 400. Their purpose was to glorify the eastern churches at the expense of Rome. They include a religious romance or novel telling of Clement's travels—in the company of Saint Peter—culminating in his recognition of his long-lost father, mother, and brothers at Aradus in Phoenicia. Use is made of themes relating to misunderstandings about relationships that were familiar from Plautus' *Menaechmi,* and later reappeared in Shakespeare's *Comedy of Errors.* A sinister appearance of Simon Magus in the *Recognitions* formed the basis of the medieval story of Faust. The work shows how these religious themes could combine edification with entertainment, while the *Homilies* also throw a good deal of light on varieties of Jewish-Christian belief during these centuries.

The *Homilies* and *Recognitions,* headed by an introductory letter purporting to have been written by Clement to Saint James, served as the starting-point for the False Decretals *(Decretals of Pseudo-Isidore)* of the ninth century, which were written as propaganda designed to free the church from interference by the state. The *Apostolic Constitutions,* the largest collection of liturgical and other ecclesiastical regulations that has survived from early Christianity, were more fully entitled the *Ordinances of the Holy Apostles Through Clement;* the work claims that it was drawn up by the apostles and then transmitted to the church by Clement's agency. However, it was, in fact, written in Syria in about A.D. 380, adapting a number of earlier works which were likewise largely Syrian in origin.

EDITIONS (First Epistle to the Corinthians) with translation—J. B. Lightfoot, The Apostolic Fathers, v 1, 1890; K. Lake, The Apostolic Fathers (Loeb ed.), v 1, 1912; L. Clarke, First Epistle of Clement to the Corinthians, 1937; M. Staniforth, Early Christian Writings (Penguin ed.), 1968; A. Jaubert, Épitre aux Corinthiens, 1971.

ABOUT—J. Quasten, Patrology, v 1, 1950; B. Altaner, Patrology, 1960; W. Jaeger, Early Christianity and Greek Paideia, 1962; K. Beyschlag, Clemens Romanus und der Frühkatholizismus, 1966; K. P. Donfried, The Setting of Second Clement in Early Christianity, 1974. On the Clementine literature: O. Cullmann, Le problème littéraire et historique du roman pseudo-clémentin, 1930; A. Stickler, Historia Juris Canonici, v 1, 1950; J. Quasten, Patrology, v 2, 1953; T. W. Crafer, The Second Epistle of Clement to the Corinthians, reprint 1958. Also see bibliographies in the Byzantinische Zeitschrift.

CLUVIUS RUFUS, Roman public figure and Latin historian, became consul before the death in A.D. 41 of the emperor Gaius (Caligula) and later became a friend of Nero, serving as herald for his theatrical performances and accompanying him on his artistic tour to Greece in 66. Galba, when he came to the throne two years later, appointed him his own successor as governor of Nearer Spain (Hispania Tarraconensis). In 69, the Year of the Four Emperors, Cluvius Rufus at first supported Otho but later joined the rival candidate Vitellius instead, bringing over the Spanish provinces to his cause. Nothing more is then heard of Cluvius. He seems to have been a rich and eloquent man, of considerable social attainments, but no great hand at warfare.

It is only from two notices in Tacitus' *Annals* and an anecdote in the younger Pliny that we know that Cluvius Rufus wrote a Roman history—if, that is to say, the public figure of whom we know and the writer whom they record were one and the same man, as is generally (though not always without hesitation) accepted to be the case. The history apparently began with Caligula and covered the reigns of Claudius and Nero, concluding either in the middle of 68, at Nero's death, or at the end of that year. It has sometimes been argued that Cluvius went on to write about the brief reigns of Galba, Otho, and Vitellius (A.D. 68–69), or at least about the first two of them, but this is by no means certain. It has also been put forward that the many features in common between Tacitus' *Histories* and Plutarch's Lives of Galba and Otho are due to their use of Cluvius' history as a common source. klōō' vi us rōō' fus

This, however, must be regarded as unproven.

What is unmistakable, however, is that the work's main part dealt with the reign of Nero and that its principal interest lies in the defense of that emperor that Cluvius evidently attempted, thus justifying, by implication, the part that he himself had played in Nero's principate. It also appears that Tacitus made some use of Cluvius' history in compiling his *Annals* (which twice mention Cluvius' name), though the extent to which he was one of its principal sources still eludes demonstration.

ABOUT—H. Furneaux, ed., The Annals of Tacitus, 1884; J. W. Duff, A Literary History of Rome in the Silver Age, 1927; R. Syme, Tacitus, 1958.

COLUMELLA, LUCIUS JUNIUS MODERATUS, Latin writer on agriculture in the first century A.D., was born at Gades (Cadiz) in Spain of a land-owning family. He served in the army as a young man in about A.D. 36; an inscription shows him as a tribune in the sixth legion *Ferrata* in Syria. After army service, he invested his fortune in Italian estates, notably at Ardea (not far from a property belonging to Seneca, whom he admired), and devoted the rest of his life to cultivating these properties, while writing about the subject in his spare time.

His work *On Agriculture (De Re Rustica),* in twelve books, completed in about A.D. 60, is the most comprehensive and systematic Roman treatise of its kind. The first book offers general advice on the selection of land, on water supply, on the planning of farm buildings, and on the distribution of tasks among the farm staff. Book 2 is concerned with ploughing and fertilizing, and Books 3-5, known as Surculares (from *surculi,* shoots), deal with vines, olives, and fruit trees (his wine calculations are the only detailed reckonings of return on agricultural investment in any surviving Roman source). The sixth and seventh books discuss animal husbandry, and the eighth deals with poultry and fishponds. Book 9 is on beekeeping. In Book 10 Columella breaks into verse (436 hexameters), to discuss gardening, in imita- ko lū mel' la tion of Virgil's *Georgics.* This poetic section was originally intended to be the conclusion and climax of the work, but on the insistence of the man to whom it was dedicated, a certain Silvinus, the author went on to write two further books as well: Book 11 discusses the tasks of a farm overseer, proposes a calendar for the various activities connected with farming, and adds a long section on gardening to supplement the verses in the previous book; the twelfth and last book prescribes the duties of the overseer's wife and contains recipes for making various kinds of wine and for pickling and preserving fruits and vegetables. A separate treatise by Columella *On Trees (De Arboribus),* dealing with the same subject matter as Books 3-5, represents part of an earlier and shorter treatment of the theme; it appears to have been the second of an original total of three books. A note at the end of Book 11 also refers to a study of arboriculture and viticulture dedicated to Eprius Marcellus that may be a lost work distinct from all the others, since this would bring his agricultural writings up to the total of sixteen books that Cassiodorus subsequently attributed to him. Lost, too, are treatises entitled *Against Astrologers* and *Concerning Lustrations and Other Rites on Behalf of the Earth (De Lustrationibus).*

Columella's prose style is neat, straightforward, and clear, without affectations or extravagances. He had been given rhetorical training in his youth but did not use it to indulge in misplaced fine writing, though he had a keen enough eye for landscape and color. His excursion into poetry in Book 10, however, is not a great success: his hexameters are careful and respectable but uninspired.

He writes as a large-scale farmer, conscious of the dignity and significance of his theme and aware of its social and moral implications. The decline of Italian agriculture causes him profound concern; he attributes it to the increase in fashionable country estates and absentee landlords, two factors that made Rome dependent on imported grain. What was needed, Columella maintained, was practical knowledge, hard work, and personal supervision. In addition to his own farming experience, Columella drew on a dozen literary authorities, Greek, Latin (including Cato, Varro, and Virgil) and Carthaginian (notably Mago).

A German translation of his work was made in 1491, but was not published. However, German, French, and Italian versions were printed during the following century.

EDITIONS—V. Lundström, Å. Josephson, S. Hedberg, L. Iuni Moderati Columellae Opera Quae Exstant, 1897–1968. *With translation:* H. B. Ash, E. S. Forster, E. H. Heffner, Columella: De Re Rustica (Loeb ed.), 1941–68; E. de Saint-Denis, Columelle: De Re Rustica, Livre 10 (De l'horticulture), 1969; K. Ahrens (German), 1972; M. Fernández-Galiano (Spanish), De Cultu Hortorum, 1975.
ABOUT—S. Hedberg, Contamination and Interpolation: A Study of the 15th Century Columella Manuscripts, 1968; K. D. White, Roman Farming, 1969, *and* Farm Equipment of the Roman World, 1975; W. Richter, Der Liber De Arboribus und Columella, 1972.

CONSTANTINE VII, Byzantine emperor, Greek writer, and patron of arts and letters, was surnamed Porphyrogenitus (born in the purple) because at the time of his birth (A.D. 905) his father, Leo VI, was the reigning emperor. From 913 Constantine was titular joint ruler as colleague—in succession—of his uncle Alexander, his mother Zoe, and of Romanus I Lecapenus. Romanus assumed precedence over Constantine but gave him his daughter in marriage. Romanus also crowned three of his own sons as joint emperors. In 944 they dethroned and exiled him, and in the following year Constantine VII, attracting public sympathy owing to the insults to which he had been subjected, gained sole control of the empire, raising his son Romanus II to imperial status beside him. Constantine died in 959.

As emperor, he adhered to his father-in-law's policies of safeguarding the soldiers' land allotments and legislating against the amassing of landed estates. He also continued the fighting against the Arabs in the Mediterranean, where one of his admirals failed to recapture Crete (949). However, Constantine's energies were principally devoted to the field of diplomacy. In 945, for example, negotiations were begun between the Byzantine government and the German emperor Otto who, like Berengar of Italy and Abd-el-Rahman of Cordova, sent en-
kon' stan tīn

CONSTANTINE VII

voys to Constantinople in 949. In 957 Constantine received a state visit from the Russian princess Olga, who had recently been converted to Christianity. Although Constantine was no soldier—he considered that an emperor in the field should be accompanied by a traveling library—the English historian Edward Gibbon's account of him as an ineffective, prejudiced, vindictive ruler who drank too much and was at the mercy of his intriguing wife Helen is unfair and one-sided.

In addition to extending very productive patronage to the visual arts—he was a painter himself—Constantine encouraged literature and scholarship on a prodigious scale. A number of manuscripts of classical Greek authors date from his reign and were produced under his sponsorship. Guided throughout by the assumption, universal in his day, that all wisdom resided in the past, he not only organized a considerable revival and expansion of the Byzantine educational system but also set on foot a huge program to extract excerpts from classical and later authors and then to collect them in an encyclopedic series of manuals. These manuals covered numerous aspects of life and administration, including strategy, agriculture, history, ethnology, archeology, law, topography, diplomacy, ceremonial, and horse breeding. In the field of historical studies in particular (of which the court became virtually an academy), he inspired

important compilations such as *History of the Emperors* by Genesius, *Historical Collection* in fifty-three books (of which only fragments are now extant), and *Continuation of Theophanes* (a historical writer who was his uncle). To this last work, which Constantine himself edited after Genesius had failed to perform the task adequately, he contributed a fifth book from his own hand, comprising the life of his grandfather the emperor Basil I, whose record he defended, glossing over the questionable features of Basil's career.

Constantine also produced three further works. One of them, *On the Themes (De Thematibus),* is a geographical and historical account of the Byzantine provinces; it is a youthful effort, consisting almost entirely of out-of-date information going back to the sixth century. On the other hand, his *Ceremonies of the Byzantine Court (De Ceremoniis Aulae Byzantinae)* is a monumental achievement, a handbook and codification of all the customs and practices of the court and church of Constantinople. Among its contents are descriptions of the procedures to be followed at every feast, reception, and investiture, as well as catalogs of tombs and robes and precious objects. This book of *Ceremonies* illustrates in luxuriant detail the gorgeous, ritualistic lives of the ruling potentates and their entourages. Constantine asserts that the imperial power, whose rhythm and order he sees as the earthly image of the divine harmony and order, shines in greater splendor and rises to greater dignity through noble ceremonials; and it is to his descriptions of them that our detailed knowledge of the Byzantine theory of empire is largely owed.

He also left a work that modern scholars have called *On the Administration of the Empire (De Administrando Imperio).* He himself, however, entitled the study "Constantine to His Son Romanus," to whom he dedicated it on the occasion of the boy's fourteenth birthday in 952. The emperor took an affectionate pride in Romanus, and his aim was to introduce him to the methods of government and to advise him of the most urgent problems, both domestic and external, that he would be likely to encounter. With this in mind, the emperor unearthed and reproduced an older and extremely informative treatise of his own that dealt with the origins of the foreign "nations" that lived all around the frontiers of the empire; onto this treatise he grafted an invaluable survey of the world situation as he saw it in 952, together with much wise advice. The survey includes sections on the imperial navy, upon which the dynasty so greatly depended, and on diplomacy. Detailed instructions are given about the ways in which one barbarous nation can be played off against another. Constantine's guiding principle, as set forth in *On the Administration of the Empire* is like that of other diplomats, to get as much as he could and give as little as possible in return. Above all, he says, there are to be no concessions to foreigners who come demanding marriage alliances, or hoping to acquire imperial crowns and robes, or trying to obtain Greek fire (the inflammable liquid, based on a secret formula, that won battles). Constantine also seizes the opportunity to blacken the reputation of his father-in-law Romanus I, under whose ill-treatment he had smarted.

With the exception of this last-mentioned, highly personal section, Constantine VII is to be regarded, in general, as a compiler rather than an author. Indeed, his writings were perhaps put together by assistants working under his supervision and with the help of his daughter Agatha who served as his private secretary. As a result, his works are too much of a patchwork to rank as literature. Constantine wrote in popular Greek, though he favored a brand of it slightly closer to ancient Greek than the language of his uncle Theophanes. His writing is relatively free of inaccuracies, but tends to be bombastic and obscure.

EDITIONS—A. Pertusi, De Thematibus, 1952. *With translation:* A. Vogt, Constantin VII Porphyrogénète: Le livre des cérémonies (Budé ed.), 1935–40; G. Moravcsik and R. J. H. Jenkins, De Administrando Imperio, 1949–62.

ABOUT—H. Grégoire *in* Cambridge Medieval History, v 4, 2nd ed., 1966; R. J. H. Jenkins, Byzantium: The Imperial Centuries: A.D. 610–1071, 1966; A. Toynbee, Constantine Porphyrogenitus and His World, 1973.

CORINNA, Greek lyric poet, of Tanagra in Boeotia, was believed in ancient times to have been an elder contemporary of her fellow Boeotian Pindar (518–438 B.C.), with whom a number of stories associate her (in particular, there were various anecdotes telling of their rivalry). On the other hand, her language, while containing elements drawn from the common stock of Greek poetical diction, has come down to us in the reformed Boeotian spelling, which was not current until the third century B.C. If, therefore, she had lived and worked two centuries earlier, as tradition maintains, we must conclude that her original writing was subsequently transliterated in order to be presented in the form in which we have it. However, it has been suggested, as an alternative, that her attribution to the fifth century is incorrect and that she lived in about 200 B.C. instead. In favor of the later date is the total absence of references to her (as far as we know) until the first century B.C.; the great Alexandrian grammarians say nothing about her. Yet there are also two factors that point in the opposite direction, militating against the radical redating. In the first place, although the ancient world was fond of inventing stories of rivalry between poets, it is difficult to imagine how the persistent tales of her competition with Pindar could have arisen if they had really failed to coincide by as much as two centuries. Secondly, the Latin poet Propertius describes Corinna as "antique," an epithet that, although not very exact, seems to suit the usage of the earlier period rather better than that of the later. Owing to these conflicting considerations, the dating of Corinna must still be regarded as unsolved.

Our fragments of her poetry have been augmented by a papyrus from Hermopolis (Esmunen) in Egypt, now at Berlin, that provides substantial remains of two poems. One is a singing contest between Cithaeron and Helicon, the personifications of the two mountains traditionally associated with poetry; the tradition behind such literary competitions goes far back to Sumerian and Babylonian times. The Muses invite the gods to decide who is the winner: the prize is awarded to Cithaeron, and an angry

kō rin' nà

shower of rocks rains down from Helicon. Its defeat may be intended to symbolize the inferiority of the Hesiodic school to Corinna's own.

The second work in the papyrus, however, is a catalog poem in the manner of Hesiod, indicating the mythological ancestries of local Boeotian heroes and personages. The prophet Acraephen, who is apparently in the service of Apollo, brings to Asopus joyful news about his daughter: she has been found worthy of the love of a god and great royal houses will be descended from her. The material included in the poem may go back to an epic tradition and is apparently based on colonization myths. Corinna also wrote narrative lyric poems for a circle of women of the Boeotian town of Tanagra, inspired, she declares, by the Muse Terpsichore who sponsors her work. The subjects, again, are Boeotian myths, including the Seven against Thebes, the slaying of the Teumessian fox by Oedipus, Iolaus the faithful helper of Heracles, and the return of Orion. There is also a poem on Orestes, who was not a figure of Boeotian mythology, but the last word of the fragment refers to seven-gated Thebes, the chief city of Boeotia, with which, therefore, the poem was somehow linked; it appears to be a choral hymn for a spring festival.

Corinna employed, for the most part, simple Ionian and Lesbian meters. Her name was added to the Alexandrian canon of lyric poets, and Ovid called the heroine of his love elegies after her.

EDITIONS—U. von Wilamowitz-Moellendorf *in* Berliner Klassikertexte, v 5, pt 2; D. L. Page, Poetae Melici Graeci, 1962. *Translations*—J. M. Edmonds, Lyra Graeca, v 3, revised ed., 1940.
ABOUT—P. Maas *in* Pauly-Wissowa-Kroll, Real-Encyclopädie der klassischen Altertumswissenschaft, v 11, columns 1393–97; D. L. Page, Corinna, 1953; A. Lesky, History of Greek Literature, 1966.

COSMAS INDICOPLEUSTES, Greek traveler, theologian, and writer, lived in the early Byzantine period, during the first half of the sixth century A.D. A merchant and sea captain from Alexandria, Cosmas made

koz′ mås in di kō ploōs′ tēz

journeys to the ports of the Red Sea, eastern Africa, and the Persian Gulf; despite the name *Indicopleustes* (Sailor to India or of the Indian Sea), which he received in about the eleventh century on the strength of his descriptions of India and the island of Ceylon, it is not known whether he ever visited these countries. On retirement from business, he withdrew to a monastery and wrote his *Christian Topography,* apparently between 535 and 547. These were memoirs of his commercial travels, in which he took the opportunity to attack Ptolemy's system of geography and astronomy, attempting to prove, in accordance with Christian scripture instead of pagan science, that the earth was rectangular and flat—not spherical—a theory he dismisses with scorn (like the idea that the Antipodes were populated). According to his design, the world resembles a ground-floor room with the sky as its ceiling and Heaven on the floor above, all bound together by side walls—the structure, he points out, that Moses had used for the tabernacle. The sun, Cosmas pronounced, is much smaller than the earth and is hidden at night by a lofty conical mountain at the earth's western extremity; the motive power for the heavenly bodies is provided by the angels. A careful student of biblical texts (a few fragments of his commentaries on the Psalms and the Gospels have survived), he was inclined to ask unexpected theological questions: why, for example, did God take six days to create the world? Cosmas' answer was that God wanted the angels to have time to gain a full understanding of his purpose, so that they should not fail in their service of the human race, despite all the disappointments its sinfulness and perversity had caused. His doctrinal sympathies are with Theodore of Mopsuestia, the theologian most highly esteemed by the Nestorians of Persia, with whom Cosmas had personal contact. He attacks, without mentioning him by name, the Monophysite John Philoponus, his contemporary at Alexandria.

Cosmas' idiosyncratic theoretical discussions on the form of the universe were not representative of the knowledge of his day and exerted little influence—partly perhaps because they are conducted in a ponderous and turgid style that is sometimes almost impossible to understand. His narrative and descriptive passages, on the other hand, are vividly written in a racy Greek owing more to the spoken tongue than to literary tradition. These sections of his work also contain ethnological and topographical information that has proved of use to subsequent geographers and makes valuable contributions to our understanding of early Byzantine commercial and foreign relations and to our knowledge of eastern history at that time. Moreover, Cosmas' survey of the far-flung expansion of Christianity paints an effective and striking picture: he attributed the prosperity of Byzantine trade to two causes, the Christian religion and the imperial coinage. He is a keen and inquisitive observer. On a southern journey, he reported sighting albatrosses; he was an eyewitness of an Axumite (Ethiopian) expedition against the Yemen; and in Ethiopia he copied inscriptions that he incorporated in the *Topography*. It is to his alertness that we owe our only record of the great expedition that the Egyptian king Ptolemy III Euergetes led into Asia in the 240s B.C.

The manuscripts of Cosmas' work, all probably imitated from a single original copy dating from the sixth century A.D., are adorned with two sets of illustrations: secular pictures executed in the classical style and religious designs displaying, by way of contrast, a monumental and Asiatic appearance.

EDITIONS—E. O. Winstedt, 1909. *With translation:* J. W. McCrindle, 1897, reprint 1964; W. Wolska-Conus (French), 1968–73.
ABOUT—W. Wolska-Conus, La topographie chrétienne de Cosmas Indicopleustès, 1962; L. Brubaker, The Relationship of Text and Image in the Byzantine Manuscripts of Cosmas Indicopleustes (Byzantinische Zeitschrift, v 70), 1977.

CRATES OF MALLUS (Karatas) in Cilicia (southeastern Asia Minor), Greek public figure and scholarly writer, was the first director of the library at Pergamum. In 168 B.C. he visited Rome as an envoy of the Pergamene king Attalus II Philadelphus. His stay in Rome was prolonged when he broke

krā′ tēz   mal′ lus

112

his leg in the Great Sewer (the Cloaca Maxima). The lectures he gave during his convalescence greatly influenced the development of Roman scholarship. His works are lost.

Crates was later described as a Stoic philosopher. He may not have adhered formally to the school; but it appears that in his philosophical and antiquarian writings on the poets (especially Homer, but also Hesiod, Euripides, Aristophanes, and Aratus), he utilized the same allegorical type of commentary that was assiduously employed by the Stoics in order to demonstrate that literature was an accurate reflection of divine and human truth. This allegorical method was different from the factual approach of the Alexandrian school. The geographer Strabo, in Augustan times, described Crates as the greatest "grammarian" or literary scholar next to his contemporary Aristarchus of Samothrace, who was head of the Alexandrian library. However, he and Aristarchus made use of widely different approaches. For one thing, Crates, as mentioned above, deviated from factual, pragmatic methods in his cosmological and geographical speculations, adopting, for example, the purely theoretical hypothesis that the four continents were distributed with geometrical regularity over the surface of the earth.

Their differences emerged more sharply still in the field of linguistics, since Aristarchus and the Alexandrian school favored the principle of analogy while Crates preferred to be guided by anomaly. That is to say, Aristarchus maintained that nouns and verbs are classifiable into regular declensions and conjugations on the basis of similarities of form, which he observed as yardsticks in trying to arrive at the correct text of an author, whereas Crates laid stress, instead, on the dissimilarities and irregularities that his practical observation of linguistic usage revealed to him—here, then, there was a reversal of position with Crates the more pragmatic of the two.

His teacher in this field was probably Diogenes of Seleucia in Babylonia, the writer of a Stoic grammar—it was an earlier Stoic, Cleanthes, who had described this unruly behavior of language as "anomaly." Adopting such ideas and applying them chiefly to the study of anomalous nouns, Crates dismissed the Alexandrian method of classification as mistaken in principle and futile in practice. In criticizing the Alexandrian reluctance to note discrepancies he was justified. However, his Pergamene school did not always carry out its stated aim of concentrating on usage, but sometimes tried, after all, to force it within the patterns of their own theories. Later the controversy spread to Roman scholars; it is reflected in Varro's *De Lingua Latina.*

ABOUT—H. J. Mette, Sphairopoiia: Untersuchungen zur Kosmologie des Krates von Pergamon, 1936, *and* Parateresis: Untersuchungen zur Sprachtheorie des Krates von Pergamon, 1952; J. Collart *in* Varron, Six exposés et discussions (Entretiens Hardt, v 9), 1963.

CRATINUS, Greek comic poet, c. 510?– after 423 B.C., was ranked by the ancients with Aristophanes and Eupolis as one of the principal writers of the Athenian Old Comedy. His productions, which gained him six victories at the festival of the City Dionysia and three more at Dionysius' other festival the Lenaea, can be traced from a date just before the middle of the fifth century to about 423 B.C. We have more than 460 fragments of his plays and 28 titles (some possibly spurious); it is clear from these that his subject matter was as varied as that of Aristophanes.

One of his comedies was called *Archilochus and His Companions* (the *Archilochoi* —a plural form of title characteristic of Cratinus). The play conjured up the ghost poet Archilochus (whose biting spirit was akin to that of the Old Comedy), possibly provided him with a chorus of "Archilochuses" (attendants of the same mind as himself), and engaged him in a literary contest with epic poets of the past. The *Archilochoi* was written not long after 450, since the death of the conservative Athenian leader Cimon, whom Cratinus supported, is mentioned as a recent occurrence.

Another play, the *Busiris,* was concerned with the mythical expedition of Heracles to Egypt. *Caught in a Storm (Cheimazomenoi)*

krä ti′ nus

won second prize to Aristophanes' *Acharnians* in the Lenaean Festival of 425. *Chiron and His Companions* (the *Cheirones*) supplied the centaur Chiron, who brought up Achilles, with a chorus of duplicates (in the manner of the Archilochuses). The play bemoans the corrupt times of Pericles—the favorite target of Cratinus, who called him onion-head because of the peculiar shape of his skull and was caustic about his mistress Aspasia. There is also a reference to a successful hunt organized to chase the various rascals of contemporary Athens. The *Cheirones,* which the playwright seems to have regarded as his favorite work, took him two years' hard work to complete.

Cleobulina and Her Companions takes its title, Plutarch tells us, from the pseudonym of a woman named Eumetis who was famous for her composition of riddles. The plot of the *Delian Woman* is unknown. The *Didascaliai* was perhaps about rehearsals. The plot of *Dionysus as Alexander* or *Paris (Dionysalexandros)* is summarized on a partially surviving papyrus: a combination of mythological burlesque and political allegory (such is not found in the extant work of Aristophanes); it attributed to the god Dionysus the fateful judgment among the three goddesses generally assigned to Paris. Dionysus runs away with Helen, but Paris catches them and is about to hand them over to the Greeks, when he is overcome by pity for Helen and makes her his wife. Dionysus, who is thus made to cause the Trojan War, stands for Pericles, who had started the Peloponnesian War (431), perhaps in the very year before the play was written. The play featured a chorus of satyrs, who addressed the audience about poets. The *Euneidae* or *Descendants of Euneus* (the son of Jason) contained two songs described by Aristophanes as popular. About the *Herdsmen (Boukoloi)* we know nothing. *Nemesis* concerns a local deity of the town of Rhamnus in Attica, who, after having intercourse with Zeus in the form of a bird, laid the egg from which Helen was produced. One fragment shows the egg being handed over to Leda (more generally regarded as Helen's mother), with instructions to sit on it until it hatches.

The Laws (Nomoi) perhaps presented personifications of the laws as old men, who sang as members of the chorus. The plot of *Odysseus and His Crew* (the *Odyssēs*) was the blinding of Polyphemus. At its start, the crew make their appearance in a model of Odysseus' ship (described as a new toy), and at the end they sail offstage again. This work was described by an ancient critic as representing a departure from Old Comedy, being anticipatory, rather, of the work of the Middle Comedians in its form owing to the absence of topical attacks on contemporary personages. *The Plutuses* probably had a chorus of wealth-giving spirits or "wealths" *(Ploutoi);* in a fairy-tale spirit, it surveyed examples of merited and unmerited prosperity in Athens by evoking a blissful Golden Age in which good food was freely available, already cooked. *The Pylaea* was presumably concerned with the meetingplace of the Amphictyonic League at Thermopylae.

The identities of the *Runaway Women (Drapetides)* is uncertain. *The Satyrs* came second to Aristophanes' *Knights* in the Lenaean Festival of 424. We do not know the subject of *The Seasons (Horai)*. The *See-All (Panoptae)* satirized contemporary sophists, in the person of Hippon of Rhegium. *The Men of Seriphos* was probably concerned with the myth of Perseus, who according to tradition was brought up on that island; one fragment offers directions for a journey to the "crooked profiteers" *(neoplutoponeroi)*. Another play was called *The Softies (Malthakoi)*. The *Thracian Women (Thrattai)* (?444–443), which probably concerned slave girls, was directed against foreign cults; it described Pericles as the squill-headed Zeus who wore the Odeon (a large domed building) on his head. The *Trophonius,* named after a hero who had an oracular shrine near Lebadea in Boeotia, represented this hero as the amusing villain or Master Thief of folktales.

The Wicker Wine Flask (Putine), probably the last play Cratinus wrote, makes comic use of his own notorious love of the bottle by showing him married to Comedy but chasing the idle girl Methe (Drunkenness) and the pretty boy Oeniscus (Little Wine). But the poet also expresses the conviction that a man who only drinks water will never create anything good. In the com-

petition of 423, the play defeated *The Clouds* of Aristophanes, who in his *Knights* had portrayed Cratinus as a discredited figure sunk in an alcoholic old age. In the *Wicker Wine Flask* Cratinus turned this weakness to dramatic advantage. In spite of the fragmentary survival of what he wrote—due to accident and to the ancient critics' arbitrary choice of only one comedian (Aristophanes) to read and study—it is fairly clear that he greatly influenced his fellow poet (Aristophanes commented on his torrential fluency and powerful expression) and that it was he himself who gave Old Comedy its characteristic shape and manner. His language was imaginative and succinct, though deficient, it was stated, in grace (and replete with obscenities); and his plots were criticized as inconsequential. Cratinus was the subject of commentaries in Hellenistic times, and a man of the same name, probably his descendant, was a writer of Middle Comedy. His is also mentioned in a fragment of a work on Old, Middle, and New Comedy *(On the Difference Between Comedies)* by Platonius, an ancient Greek writer of uncertain date.

EDITIONS—A. Meineke, Fragmenta Comicorum Graecorum, v 1, 1839–57; T. Koch, Comicorum Atticorum Fragmenta, v 1, 1880–88; J. M. Edmonds, Fragments of Attic Comedy, v 1, 1957.
ABOUT—A. Lesky, A History of Greek Literature, 1966; K. J. Dover *in* Fifty Years (and Twelve) of Classical Scholarship, 1968.

CREMUTIUS CORDUS, AULUS, Ro-

man senator and Latin historian, lived in the reigns of Augustus (31 B.C.–A.D. 14) and Tiberius (A.D. 14–37). He wrote a history that has not survived. It was perhaps known, in traditional fashion, as the *Annals (Annales)*. According to Seneca the Younger, the work comprised "the deeds of one epoch" *(unius saeculi facta);* that is to say, Cremutius dealt with the period from the Civil Wars until at least 18 B.C. and perhaps later. He refrained from showing any particular respect for Caesar or Augustus and censured the proscriptions—in which the young Octavian (Augustus) had played a prominent part—glorifying their victim Ci-
kre mū' ti us   kôr' dus

cero as well as Caesar's assassins Cassius, whom he decribed as "the last of the Romans," and Brutus.

The attitude of Augustus to the work is not clear. Later writers, Suetonius and Dio Cassius, assert that it was read by him, or to him, without incurring his disapproval. But it seems unlikely that one passage quoted by Suetonius, indicating that senators had to undergo a search before they were allowed to come into the imperial presence at senatorial meetings, could have reached his ears without eliciting a protest. Tacitus implies, probably with justification, that Cremutius' work was not published until the reign of Tiberius.

At that time, in A.D. 25, he incurred prosecution, partly, it would appear, for reasons that are unknown but also because of his eulogistic descriptions of Brutus and Cassius. The prosecutors were henchmen of the praetorian prefect Sejanus, who enjoyed the high favor of Tiberius. The emperor's attitude toward the trial (despite a reference by Tacitus to the grimness of his expression) remains obscure. Cremutius, according to the reports of his self-conducted defense (unless these were invented by Tacitus), protested that what he had written was not in any way directed against the emperor or his "parent" (adoptive father) the deified Augustus, who were protected by the treason law. His favorable attitude to Brutus and Cassius, he added, possessed precedents in the works of distinguished earlier historians, notably Pollio and Messalla, who had been allowed to praise the two assassins with impunity. And Cremutius went on to say that Caesar and Augustus had seen fit, on a number of occasions, to ignore even the most scathing slanders against themselves, adding that "this was a wise policy, since things unnoticed are forgotten, whereas resentment gives them status."

Nevertheless, Cremutius did not await the result of the trial but walked out of the Senate, returned to his home, and starved himself to death, thus anticipating, according to Seneca, the arrival of the men sent to arrest him. The Senate ordered his books to be burned by the aediles at Rome and by local officials in other cities as well, but copies were secretly preserved by his daughter

Marcia. Seneca's *Consolation to Marcia,* perhaps his earliest extant work, was written to condole on the death of her sons but was also, by implication, a defense of her father. It was probably written in A.D. 40, during the reign of Gaius (Caligula), who permitted the work of Cremutius and certain other writers of Republican inclinations to be brought out again and circulated and read, declaring his desire (so as to contrast himself with Tiberius) that everything that happened should be handed down to posterity. Owing to its author's dramatic fate, the *Annals* attracted a certain amount of public attention. In addition to Seneca, the elder Pliny made use of the work, and so also perhaps did the Greek historian Appian. Quintilian provided a select list of historians worth studying by orators; a name is missing in a hiatus of his text, and it may well be that of Cremutius.

ABOUT—B. Walker, The Annals of Tacitus, 1952; R. Syme, Tacitus, 1958.

CTESIAS, Greek historian, was born in the second half of the fifth century B.C. at Cnidus in southwestern Asia Minor. He was court physician to Queen Parysatis of Persia and was said to have lived at the court of her son, King Artaxerxes II Memnon (404–358 B.C.), for seventeen years. He also claimed, according to Xenophon, to have dressed the wound inflicted on that king by his brother Cyrus at the battle of Cunaxa between their two armies (401). In 398 Ctesias was sent as envoy first to Evagoras, king of Salamis in Cyprus, and then to the Athenian statesman Conon.

Not long afterward he wrote a twenty-three-book history in the Ionic dialect, the *Persica,* dealing with Assyrian, Median, and Persian history from the legendary king Ninus down to 398 B.C. We have a summary of a summary of the work, for it was epitomized by Pamphila, an erudite woman of the reign of Nero and in the ninth century A.D. Photius read her epitome and preserved the excerpts from it that have come down to us. Ctesias seems to have used the writings

kte′ si as

of Xanthus and Hellanicus, as well as the history of Herodotus whom he frequently and presumptuously criticized on the supposition that he himself was better informed. But although entertaining enough, Ctesias is an unreliable historian and, indeed, a fabricator of lies, especially when writing on anything of which he lacks personal knowledge. However, his facility for recounting anecdotes is valuable when it is applied to the royal Persian court, of which he had firsthand information. Subsequently, his *Persica* was revised and brought down to the 340s by Dinon of Colophon, who was the father of Clitarchus, the historian of Alexander the Great. The works of both Dinon and Ctesias were drawn upon to a considerable extent by writers of later generations.

It was recorded that Ctesias also wrote a treatise, *On the Tribute of Asia,* though it is possible that this formed part of his *Persica.* In addition, he was the author of a geographical work in three books, the *Periplus* or *Periodos,* from which certain extracts are preserved. He also composed the first known separate work on India, then an almost entirely unknown land to the Greeks, which offered ample scope for fantastic tales; an excerpt of this *Indica* was cited by Photius.

EDITIONS—J. Gilmore, Fragments of the Persica of Ctesias, 1888; F. Jacoby, Die Fragmente der griechischen Historiker, 3c, 688.
ABOUT—J. M. Bigwood, Ctesias of Cnidus (Harvard, dissertation): summary *in* Harvard Studies in Classical Philology, v 70, 1970, p 263 ff.

CURTIUS RUFUS, QUINTUS, Latin historian and biographer, wrote during the reign of an "emperor who shone out like a new star on the night which we believed to be our last"—sometimes identified as Augustus (31 B.C.–A.D. 14) but more probably Claudius (A.D. 41–54) or Vespasian (A.D. 69–79). Curtius' diction harmonizes with either of these last conclusions, since, although lucid and of virtually classical purity, it contains examples of the stylistic devices in which the Silver Latin writers of the mid-first century A.D. were accustomed to indulge.

kûr' ti us rōō' fus

He was the author of a history of Alexander the Great in ten books. Books 1 and 2 are lost, but the others, which survive (with certain gaps), show he preferred to concentrate on a relatively few dramatic episodes of Alexander's career to the neglect of other events. In Book 3 these showpieces include the numbering of the Persian army and a royal procession, the tale of Philip the doctor from Acarnania, and the battle of Issus between Alexander and the Persian King Darius III (333 B.C.). Book 4 is largely concerned with the siege of Tyre, the consultation of the oracle at Ammon, and the battle of Gaugamela (331). The highlight of Book 5 is the final period of the life of Darius III, who died in 330. Book 6 is constructed around other events of the same year: the Hecatompylus mutiny, the meeting with the Amazons, and the conspiracy of Philotas. The trial of Amyntas and the murder of Parmenio that followed are described in Book 7, which also gives an account of the march through the Sogdian desert (328). The predominant themes of Book 8 are the murder of Clitus, the conspiracy of the pages—followed by the death of Callisthenes—and the battle of the River Hydaspes (326). In Book 9 came the Hyphasis mutiny, the heroism of Alexander in the town of the Sudracae, and the journey through Gedrosia (325).

Curtius' concentration on a few episodes at the expense of other features of the story is detrimental to his value, both as a historian and as a biographer. Which of these two types of authorship (between which the ancients sharply distinguished) he should be regarded as practicing is not entirely clear. Probably, according to the classifications that were then in force, he should be treated as a historian. Nevertheless, his work displayed extensive biographical overtones (not least because the career of Alexander so completely dominated the history of the time); indeed, no other surviving Latin writer combined historical and biographical elements so ambitiously within a single work.

Although we do not know who Curtius was, his writings reveal his personal characteristics and prejudices very clearly. He shows a typical Roman contempt for foreigners, whether Greek or Egyptian or eastern, and he is equally contemptuous of the lower classes and of self-made careerists. Although, as a historian of Alexander, he offers a competent and conscientious military narrative—which very often gives us information that we otherwise would not possess—he cheerfully acknowledges that he sets down more than he believes to be true so as not to leave anything out. He displays a marked preference for the spectacular and sensational, akin to the semi-fictional biographical works that are fashionable today, and shows special skill in developing scenes of a strongly emotional character. He is also extremely fond of moralizing. This, to a larger or smaller extent, was the procedure of almost all ancient historians, but Curtius remorselessly carries the practice to exceptional lengths. Moreover, his moralizing utterances display a thorough saturation in rhetoric, which one encounters in many other features of his work, including the long pairs of carefully elaborated and balanced speeches, no doubt entirely fictitious, which he frequently inserts so as to present opposing points of view. As to his philosophical opinions, although like so many Romans he possessed at least a superficial interest in Stoicism, there is also one other fashionable concept of his day that recurs continuously in his work: the idea of Fortune as a guardian divinity watching over Alexander throughout his career.

In his assessment of that monarch, Curtius seems to have drawn upon the same authority, as yet unidentifiable, who had been utilized by the Greek historian Diodorus Siculus in his *Historical Library*. From this source Curtius derived a heroic interpretation of the king. At the same time his analysis does not ignore Alexander's all too human faults and vices. It has been complained that the resultant picture lacks consistency; but so, it might be replied, did the personality of Alexander himself. Curtius' own opinion seems to have been that the king had started off as a fine young man but subsequently became more and more corrupted by indulgent Fortune, until he finally degraded himself by copying the customs of the peoples he had conquered—a criticism that was widespread among historians of

Alexander. However, Curtius does at least allow the monarch to supply a justification of his endeavor to reconcile the conquered peoples—and a justification also of his marriage with the Persian Roxane, though the historian adds his own expression of distaste for the marriage.

Yet, despite all his flaws as an historian, the brilliant sequence of contrasting scenes by which Curtius builds up his picture of the mighty Alexander retains its power of fascination. Among the other ancient historians who tackled this theme and whose works have survived, such as Diodorus and Arrian, this dramatic presentation entitles Curtius to the first place from the standpoint of literary merit. In Roman historiography, however, his choice of theme set him apart from the main previous tradition; despite all the interest of the early empire in Alexander, he provides our earliest example of a Latin prose work not directly concerned with a Roman subject.

We have no clear evidence that Curtius exercised any effect on later Latin literature. He did, however, enjoy considerable popularity in the Middle Ages, as the abundance of his manuscripts proves. His fame rose to even greater heights in the Renaissance, when he was translated into Italian in 1438 (printed 1478), Spanish (printed 1481), German (1491; another version published 1538) and French (in 1540 and 1551).

EDITIONS with translation—J. C. Rolfe, Curtius: History of Alexander (Loeb ed.), 1946; K. Müller and H. Schönfeld (German), 1954; H. Bardon, Quinte-Curce: Histoire d'Alexandre (Budé ed.), 1961; A. Giacone, Quinto Curzio Rufo: Storia di Alessandro Magno, 1977.

ABOUT—A. Dosson, Étude sur Quinte-Curce, 1887; F. Wilhelm, Curtius und der jüngeren Seneca, 1928; D. Korzeniewski, Die Zeit des Quintus Curtius Rufus (Cologne, dissertation), 1959; E. I. McQueen, Quintus Curtius Rufus, *in* T. A. Dorey, ed., Latin Biography, 1967 (with bibliography of articles).

CYPRIAN, Saint (Thascius Caecilius Cyprianus), Christian churchman and Latin theological writer, was born in northern Africa in about A.D. 200, the son of rich parents who may have been of senatorial

sip′ ri ən

rank. He was a pagan at birth and received a classical education in rhetoric. As a young man, according to his own statement, he led a life of dissipation. When already of mature age, however, he became a convert to Christianity, adopting habits of total chastity and selling most of his property to help the poor. Soon afterward, he was ordained to the priesthood, becoming bishop of Carthage in A.D. 248. When, however, the persecution of Christians broke out under Trajanus Decius (250), Cyprian left Carthage and went into hiding, keeping in contact with his see by correspondence. His flight incurred criticism from the zealous, but he justified it on the grounds that it was for the good of his flock.

In 251–53 he supported Pope Cornelius in his dispute with the rigorous secessionist Novatian, the most famous of the Roman clergy of his day; but subsequently Cyprian's opposition to Novatian became less rigid. In 256–57, he is found vigorously criticizing Pope Stephen because of the latter's decision to recognize the baptism of Novatian's community. Under the emperor Valerian, in 257, a fresh persecution began, and Cyprian, although treated with the respect due to his class, was exiled to Curubis. In the following year, at Carthage, he was condemned to death and executed.

He produced a very large number of treatises and pamphlets on religious questions of the day, in which, despite the use of Stoic commonplaces, Christian sources completely replaced the pagan authorities of his upbringing. *That Idols Are Not Gods* is derivative from Minucius Felix and Tertullian, whom he admired and described as his teacher. In a little essay *To Donatus (Ad Donatum)*, probably a very early work, Cyprian sits with his friend Donatus in an agreeable arbor, recalls his own early moral delinquencies, and presents arguments (largely derived, once again, from Minucius Felix), calculated to attract a man of education to the church, enlarging upon the evil and turbulence of the pagan world. *Ad Demetrianum* refutes the widespread belief that these calamities from which the empire was suffering were due to the Christians. *On the Dress of Virgins* is a eulogy of virginity and a guide to the deportment of chaste young women, who are recommended to wear clothes lacking in adornment. *On the Lapsed (De Lapsis)* deals with the most pressing issue of his day, which was the question of how the faithful ought to regard those who had "fallen," that is to say, who had agreed, perhaps momentarily, to adopt outward conformity to paganism during the persecutions. Backsliders of this kind might fall into the category either of *sacrificati,* who under pressure had offered sacrifice to pagan deities, or of *libellatici* who had committed the less serious offense of buying a certificate *(libellus)* asserting their renunciation of Christian allegiance. While deploring all such actions and even censuring those who had just managed to lie low and escape notice, Cyprian advocates a sliding scale of severity and indulgence in proportion to the degree of collaboration and according to whether the lapsed had suffered torture or not.

Cyprian's most characteristic work, however, is *On the Unity of the Catholic Church (De Catholicae Ecclesiae Unitate),* an ideal which was particularly dear to his heart. *On the Lord's Prayer (De Dominica Oratione)* emphasizes the social and communal significance of praying. *On Mortality (De Mortalitate)* deals with an epidemic which had devastated Carthage for some years and had weakened the faith of many local Christians. In this work Cyprian endeavors to strengthen their endurance by arguments against the fear of death, arguments he derives from the Scriptures and from general considerations, and also from visions that he himself had experienced. Other treatises have self-explanatory titles: *On Works and Alms (De Opere Eleemosynis), On the Advantage of Patience (De Bono Patientiae),* and a sort of appendix to the latter, *On Envy and Jealousy (De Zelo et Livore),* that stresses the wickedness of these faults, which produce schism and dissension within the Church.

Cyprian also prepared two collections of "proof-texts," passages of Scripture demonstrating the principal points of the faith. One, *To Fortunatus on Exhortation to Martyrdom (Ad Fortunatum de Exhortatione Martyrii),* was probably occasioned by Valerian's persecution: it sets out the scriptural texts which denounce pagan images and their worship and cites others urging that persecution is not something that ought to be feared. A larger, three-book collection, *Testimonies (Testimonia),* was composed for a certain Quirinus described as his "dear son"—that is to say, a member of his congregation—after whom the work is sometimes called. It contains a large range of texts from both testaments, disposed under suitable headings. We also have eighty-one of Cyprian's letters that are concerned with questions of church policy and practice and throw valuable light on Christian life, especially in Carthage. Finally, a long document attached to his writings contains the views of the African bishops on the validity of heretical baptism.

Cyprian's prose style, seen perhaps at its worst in *To Donatus,* was verbose and naive, much inferior to that of the vigorous and temperamental Tertullian. An administrator rather than a thinker, Cyprian writes in the manner of a high functionary of Rome, insisting on proper procedure and obedience to his own authority. He speaks of bishops as judicial magistrates and in general uses the language of Roman jurists, thus permanently affecting the development of western Catholicism. It has been disputed whether his argument with Pope Stephen stemmed from a fundamental rejection of papal supremacy on Cyprian's part. Those who maintain that this was so have seen him as a champion of episcopalianism; but all, in fact, that he asserted was that the Christian community depended on "the concord of the bishops." Moreover, the Church, although it withheld its support from Cyprian in his quarrel with Stephen, did not subsequently hold his attitude against him, since he was named in the earliest list of feast days and in the Mass. His *Life* written by his deacon Pontius, the first of all surviving Christian biographies, seeks to show him as the equal of the martyr St. Perpetua, who was deeply revered in northern Africa.

WORKS—Twenty or thirty writings by others have come down to us under his name. They include a feeble attack on pagan deities (Quod Idola Dii Non Sunt—perhaps of his time, though not of his authorship) and six mediocre poems on various religious themes.
EDITIONS—W. von Hartel, Corpus Scriptorum Ecclesiasticorum Latinorum, v 3, 1868–71; L. Bayard, Letters, 1945; M. Bévenot, De Lapsis: De Ecclesiae Catholicae Unitate (Oxford Early Christian Texts, v 3) 1971 (with study of the transmission of manuscripts). ABOUT—E. W. Benson, Cyprian, 1897; A. Beck, Römisches Recht bei Tertullian und Cyprian, 1930; C. Saumagne, Saint Cyprien évêque de Carthage, "pape" d'Afrique, 1975. Also, *see* bibliography *in* B. Altaner, Patrology, 1960; M. M. Sage, Cyprian, 1975.

DAMASCENE, JOHN, Saint. See John Damascene, Saint

DEMETRIUS OF PHALERON, Greek statesman and philosopher, was born at Phaleron near Athens in about 350 B.C. He began his political life at that city in about 325 and was one of the city's annually elected generals during many of the years that followed. He escaped retribution as a supporter of Macedonia in 318 and in the following year was appointed by Cassander, one of the successors to Alexander's power, as governor *(epimeletes)* of Athens, where he remained in power for ten years, enjoying considerable freedom of action. His government mainly favored the upper classes, and he transferred from them to the state the heavy financial responsibility for such public functions as festivals, banquets, delegations, and repair of the fleet (services known as liturgies). On the other hand, he also attracted widespread support among other sections of the community: as lawgiver *(nomothetes)* in 317–315 he passed a wide variety of measures to restrict forms of extravagance—in funerals, in entertainments, and by women —and to reduce the period of military service. He also set up a committee to prevent undesirable legislation by the Assembly.

When Demetrius I Poliorcetes of Macedonia captured Athens in 307, Demetrius of Phaleron fled to Thebes. He later became a member of the court of Ptolemy I Soter at Alexandria, where he played a considerable part as adviser to the king, conducting the sponsorship of important scientific and cultural enterprises, notably the foundation of the Museum and Library. After the accession of Ptolemy II Philadelphus, who had been his pupil, he was ejected from the court

di mē′ tri us   få lē′ ron

and withdrew to Upper Egypt, where he died. The story that he persuaded Ptolemy II to commission the seventy-two translators of the Jewish Bible into Greek (the Septuagint) is apparently fictitious.

Demetrius of Phaleron was an outstanding orator, the last of his age thought worthy of remembrance by posterity, even though his soft and agreeable style was more suitable to theoretical than to practical themes. He also composed numerous treatises in various fields, of which only fragments survive. As a philosopher, he was a member of the Aristotelian school and a pupil of Theophrastus, who helped him to frame his legislative program and was in return helped by him to acquire property. Demetrius himself was the author of many philosophical works —sometimes employing the dialogue form —works that seem, in so far as we can judge them, to have been dilettante and superficial. They included an *Apology* dealing with Socrates' trial and a work on Fortune *(Tyche)*. He also composed a study of Athenian political organization and a chronological account of the constitutions of the city, written in the Aristotelian vein. In addition to a historical chronicle, the *Record of the Archons,* he produced a record of his own personal administration in monographs entitled *On the Ten Years* and *On the Constitution.*

A friend of the comic dramatist Menander, Demetrius was also active as literary critic and commentator. He wrote commentaries on the *Iliad* and *Odyssey* and organized readings of the Homeric poems at Games. He edited the oldest collection of Aesop's Fables that is known to us, as well as the maxims attributed to the Seven Sages. He compiled marginal notes *(scholia)* on Aristophanes, of which two fragments have survived, as have seven sayings *(Apophthegmata)* of his own.

WORKS—An alleged report that he wrote paeans to the god Serapis, for curing an illness of his eyes, has been doubted. The attribution of a monograph entitled On Style to Demetrius of Phaleron, by medieval writers, is erroneous; it appears instead to belong to the first century B.C. or A.D. and may have been written by Plutarch's friend Demetrius of Tarsus in about A.D. 80. A tractate entitled On Kinds of Letters, which has likewise come down to us under Demetrius of Phaleron's name, is spurious, dating from a period considerably later than his lifetime.
EDITIONS—F. Wehrli, Die Schule des Aristoteles, v 4: Demetrios von Phaleron, 2nd ed., 1967–69. *Translations* (On Style)—G. M. A. Grube, A Greek Critic: Demetrius on Style, 1961.
ABOUT—E. Bayer, Demetrios Phalereus der Athener, 1942, reprint 1969.

DEMOCRITUS, Greek philosopher, was born at Abdera in Thrace between 460 and 457 B.C., the son of a prosperous citizen, and reputedly lived to a very advanced age. He was said to have traveled to Egypt in order to learn geometry and to have visited Persia, the Red Sea, India, and Ethiopia. He himself recorded that he went to Athens, where the people ignored him ("no one knew me")— however, Demetrius of Phaleron, toward the end of the following century, refused to accept this story as authentic.

It has been argued that the date of publication of his most important work was 405 B.C. This was his *Little World System (Mikros Diakosmos),* clearly the counterpart of the *Great World System (Megas Diakosmos)* of another philosopher, Leucippus, who was stated to have been Democritus' teacher. Leucippus and Democritus together were reputedly the founders of the Greek atomic theory. Following up and amending the systems proposed by earlier, pre-Socratic philosophers they held that the components of real being, the elementary bodies that constitute the world, are the atoms, so-called because they are physically indivisible *(atomoi).* It has proved impossible to determine to what extent the authorship of this theory ought to be divided between the two men. However, there is some reason to believe that the essentials of the system were already found in Leucippus, and it is under his name, therefore, that it will be summarized in this book.

On the other hand, the psychological scheme deduced from the atomic theory may have been devised by Democritus, who evidently had a taste for the detailed observation of phenomena. According to this scheme the soul, which is the cause of life and sensation, consists of round and therefore highly mobile atoms. Perception is

de mok′ ri tus

effected through the impact made on the soul's atoms by films *(eidola),* thrown off by objects. A distinction is made between "true knowledge," by which he means a real understanding of the atomic structure, and "dark knowledge," which is knowledge of objects and their properties gained solely through the senses—and, in his view, only a matter of convention.

Through his psychology Democritus developed into a moralist, and it is with his ethics that most of our surviving fragments are concerned. They reflect an intellectual transition from the world of the pre-Socratics, with their predominantly cosmological concerns, to the preoccupation of Socrates (who was about ten years older than Democritus) with the good human life. Thus, Democritus' treatise *On Cheerfulness (Euthumia)* is based on the idea that the soul-atoms must be protected from violent upheavals and restless activity. This concept, while founded on the traditional Greek respect for moderation, is an early presentation of a type of argument that was to become characteristic of later philosophy, according to which peace of mind—an undisturbed calm derived from knowledge of the nature of the universe—is the goal to be aimed at by human beings. This goal is held to be achievable, for example, by eliminating the fear of death, an idea later developed strongly by the Epicureans. In contradistinction to the older concern with humans as part of the communal city-state, individuals are seen as a little cosmos in themselves, in which it is necessary to create and maintain law and order. Yet Democritus' view of social ethics was by no means wholly individualistic, since he appreciated that citizens must make a positive contribution to their society, which required a system of law to ensure its preservation. Democritus, whom certain fragments show to have been politically a democrat, based these views on a theory of the evolution of humankind from a primitive condition that is also found in Protagoras, to whom Democritus refers. (The tradition that Protagoras was his pupil is unlikely, since Protagoras was much the older of the two).

Thus, by communal and individual efforts alike, Democritus maintains, men and women can achieve peace of mind and happiness, which he defines as the total of all agreeable feelings. These feelings include, among other things, pleasure in what is beautiful. It is noteworthy that this exponent or cofounder of the materialistic theory of the atoms also declared that the highest happiness is pleasure in things not subject to mortality—a novel expression of praise for the wholly intellectual life. Democritus (like Socrates) was credited with the saying that to find out the cause of any single thing was of greater value than the entire kingdom of the Persians.

His literary output was vast; he must have been one of the most prolific of all ancient writers, although nothing remains today except for fragments—and already in the sixth century A.D. scholars were dependent on summaries. The emperor Tiberius' court astronomer Thrasyllus credited him with fifty-two separate works. These were divided into thirteen tetralogies, collected into the following groups or headings: ethics (2 tetralogies), physics (4), mathematics (3), music and literature and language (2), technical subjects (2). As a mathematician, Democritus earned a tribute from Archimedes (though in another passage he withdrew his favorable words). Aristotle often quotes him on biology. In a treatise on Homer, Democritus studies linguistic usages according to methods anticipatory of later Homeric philology. Thrasyllus lists separate memoirs by his hand *(Hypomnemata),* but some of these—for example, pieces dealing with travels in Chaldaea and Phrygia—do not seem to be genuine. On the other hand Thrasyllus omits apparently authentic essays entitled *Causes (Aitiai),* in which Democritus dealt with questions of a very varied character (the ninth was concerned with lodestones).

His surviving fragments are written in a terse, lucid, lofty, and colorful style. His enormous importance became obscured by the subsequent triumphs of other philosophical schools, notably those of Plato and Aristotle, whose eternal cosmos stood opposed to the perishable, materialistic universe of Democritus. However, his concept was revived by Epicurus, and by Lucretius who adapted Epicurus' thought to the Latin tongue. In Egypt, under Ptolemy II, Bolus of Mendes saw Democritus as the disciple of Persian sages and the repository of secret wisdom, an idea that was developed in the alchemical writings of later antiquity. The atomic science of modern times is a distant descendant of his own theories of structure.

EDITIONS—G. S. Kirk and J. E. Raven, The Presocratic Philosophers, revised ed., 1960.
ABOUT—S. Sambursky, The Physical World of the Greeks, 1956; W. K. C. Guthrie, History of Greek Philosophy, v 2, 1965; T. Cole, Democritus and the Sources of Greek Anthropology, v 2, 1967; D. J. Furley, Two Studies in the Greek Atomists, 1967; R. E. Allen and D. J. Furley, eds., Studies in Presocratic Philosophy, v 2, 1975; J. Barnes, The Presocratic Philosophers, v 2, 1978.

DEMOSTHENES

DEMOSTHENES, Greek orator, was born in 384 and died in 322 B.C. His birthplace was Athens, where his father, likewise called Demosthenes, was married to Cleobule (believed to be partly Scythian, i.e. from southern Russia) and was the owner of a factory that made swords and cutlery. He died, however, when his son was only seven, leaving the management of his estate to three guardians, Aphorbus, Demophon, and Therippides. Demosthenes later accused the three of misappropriating the property left in their charge with the result that at the age of eighteen he was left almost without funds. Prolonged legal wrangles ensued. In the course of these disputes, he benefited from the careful study of rhetoric and legal procedure he was pursuing under the orator Isaeus, and his cause eventually prevailed. There are many stories of the determined measures he took, during his early years, to overcome physical infirmity and poor delivery.

The reputation Demosthenes now began to make for himself in private cases brought him more and more frequent employment as an assistant prosecutor in public cases as well, and from about 355 onward he increasingly devoted himself to business of national importance. From 351, he began to be prominent as a politician, on the side of the opposition to the current Athenian government and in particular as the advocate of a

de mos' thə nēz

vigorous policy of resistance to the rising strength of King Philip II of Macedonia. However, the peace party, led by Eubulus, was in power at Athens, and its efforts to check Philip's advance proved entirely ineffective. In 347–346 it became necessary to negotiate terms with the monarch, and Demosthenes, like his fellow orator and political enemy Aeschines, was one of the negotiating team. The subsequent Peace of Philocrates did not curb Philip's territorial ambition, but now Demosthenes advised a cautious, unprovocative approach. However, Philip renewed his aggressions; and in 340 Demosthenes' party temporarily gained the ascendancy, which it lost, however, after the catastrophic defeat of Athens and Thebes by Philip at Chaeronea (338), where Demosthenes was fighting in the Athenian ranks.

Demosthenes remained in power after the battle, nevertheless, and was chosen to deliver the funeral oration. In 337–336 he held office, and Ctesiphon proposed that he should be awarded a gold crown for his services to the state and, in particular, for the measures he had taken to repair the city's fortifications. In 335 he helped the Thebans to revolt against Philip's successor Alexander the Great, who demanded that Athens should surrender Demosthenes into Macedonian hands, a fate that was only narrowly averted. In 330 he successfully resisted Aeschines' attack on Ctesiphon's complimentary proposal made six years earlier —an attack that amounted to an assault upon Demosthenes' entire public record.

The last phase of Demosthenes' career was clouded by the affair of Harpalus, a former treasurer of Alexander who fled to Athens in 324 with a mercenary force and a large amount of money. Failing to gain Athenian support, Harpalus left the city, but meanwhile about half the money had somehow disappeared, and Demosthenes was accused of taking part of it for himself; the charge was probably justified, although, if he took the sum, it is likely that he did so from patriotic or party motives rather than for his own personal enrichment. Found guilty, he escaped into exile. After the death of Alexander (323) he made his way back to Athens and whipped up opposition to the new Macedonian ruler Antipater. When, therefore, in the ensuing Lamian War, Athens and other Greek states had been defeated by Antipater at Crannon in Thessaly (322), the Athenians, under pressure from Antipater, condemned Demosthenes to death. He took refuge on the island of Calauria, near Aegina, where, pursued by an agent of Antipater, he poisoned himself.

We have between thirty-four and thirty-seven speeches that are correctly attributed to Demosthenes. His earliest forensic speech was *Against Androtion* (355), in which he raised objections (seconding a certain Diodorus) to Androtion's proposal that the usual crown be awarded the outgoing Councillors, citing as grounds the fact that the navy had not been augmented during the year. *Against Timocrates* (353) was again in support of Diodorus, this time in an embezzlement case. In these cases he remained in the background; his first personal appearance in a public case was on the occasion of the speech *Against Leptines* (355), in which he opposed Leptines' plan to abolish hereditary immunities granted to benefactors of the state. *On the Symmories* (Naval Boards, 354/3) argues against immediate war with Persia but urges a naval reform. *For the Megalopolitans* (353) advocates alliance with Megalopolis, a city recently founded in Arcadia, in order to check Spartan encroachments and gain friends for Athens in the region. *Against Aristocrates* (352) attacks the Athenian politician Charidemus for the part he played in the cession of the Chersonese (Gallipoli) to King Cersobleptes of Thrace. *On the Liberty of the Rhodians* (351) urged the Athenians to support the democratic party of Rhodes against its oligarchs backed by Queen Artemisia of Caria.

In the *First Philippic,* delivered in the same year, Demosthenes identified King Philip II of Macedonia as the true enemy and tried to arouse the Athenians to their danger. His three *Olynthiacs* (349) urged them, in vain, to prevent Philip from suppressing the Macedonian town of Olynthus, headquarters of the Chalcidic League of city-states. *On the Peace* (346), however, pointed out that the Peace of Philocrates recently concluded with Macedonia, however unfavorable it had proved to Athens, was nevertheless impossible to repudiate. Yet, in the *Second Philippic* (344), he argued that Philip's apparent goodwill toward Thebes, Messene, and Argos was merely a trick aimed to gain their support against the Athenians. *On the False Embassy* (343) declared that Demosthenes' rival Aeschines had been bribed to play into Philip's hands. *On the Chersonese* (341) is a plea not to repudiate Diopeithes who had taken settlers to that region in defiance of Macedonia; the *Third Philippic* (also 341) reiterates the same appeal and urges unity among the Greek states to meet the common menace. *On the Crown* (530), the last and greatest of his speeches, attempts a justification of the policy of the anti-Macedonian party over the whole period, including a fierce attack on Aeschines who had indicted Ctesiphon for proposing the award of a gold crown to Demosthenes.

Throughout the same period Demosthenes wrote and delivered a number of personal and nonpolitical speeches as well. In *Against Aphorbus* and *Against Onetor* (Aphorbus' brother-in-law) (363) he claimed recovery of his property from his guardians. He also spoke several times on behalf of a certain Apollodorus, supporting his demand to be awarded a crown in 359, although later, in *For Phormio* (350), he contested Apollodorus' claim for a sum of money allegedly owed to him by Phormio, who was chief clerk to the famous banker

Pasion. *Against Stephanus* (first speech, 349) attacks one of Phormio's witnesses for perjury. *Against Boeotus* (first speech, 348) seeks to prevent an illegitimate son from usurping the name of his legitimate half-brother. *Against Midias* (347), never delivered, denounces a personal and political opponent of Demosthenes who had slapped the orator's face while the latter was officiating at the festival of the Greater Dionysia.

Against Pantaenetus (346) is concerned with a damaged mine in which half a dozen owners, lessees, and mortgagees had a stake. *Against Nausimachus,* in the same year, tries to prevent certain orphans from reviving a claim against the heirs of their guardian. Another speech is *Against Eubulides* (345): at a time when the lists of Athenian citizens were under review, Eubulides had declared that the alleged citizen status of the plaintiff Euxitheus was spurious. *Against Conon* (341) brings a charge of assault. Two other orations are of uncertain date: *Against Callicles,* a case in which Callicles' father was charged with building a wall that caused the vineyard of a client of Demosthenes' to become flooded in wet weather; and *Against Spudias,* concerning a dowry dispute.

Demosthenes reached heights of eloquence unparalleled in the whole of classical antiquity. He prepared his speeches with a meticulous care that was considered extraordinary, and indeed blameworthy, by contemporary opinion. However, his persuasiveness could not fail to gain from this careful preparation, as it gained also from his passionate conviction in the rightness of his principal political cause. His reputation owes a good deal to this adamant determination and deep sincerity, but his claim to greatness also depends on his exceptionally lucid and crystal-clear exposition of his argument. He deliberately studied and exploited language as the instrument for convincing his hearers, of whose ignorance and weaknesses he was well aware and took devastating advantage, employing a wide range of skillful devices, including abundant metaphor, to sustain their attention and interest —and, when necessary, to mislead them. While flashes of humor are rare, Demosthenes often used bitter, scathing wit to discredit his opponents, and the ferocity of his

personal attacks was extreme, even by Athenian standards. Yet his style is of infinite variety and flexibility, and in his most solemn moments, for instance in the magnificent climactic passages of the *Second Olynthiac* and *Third Philippic,* he strikes an imposing note of stark plainness and moderation.

The contemporary orator Isocrates (436–338 B.C.) envisaged Philip II of Macedonia as the single champion who could rally the Greeks around his standard. Demosthenes totally disagreed; he saw Philip as the principal threat to the independence of the city-states, which must therefore resist him by every possible means. However, Demosthenes, despite his remarkable gifts, was unable to galvanize Athens into the action needed to take the lead in this anti-Macedonian policy, because the Athenians were both too weak and too self-seeking. Yet, whatever the flaws in Demosthenes' leadership or judgment, he was unmistakably a man of courage. Single-minded and consistent in his foreign policy (if occasionally disingenuous and dishonorable in his personal dealings), he wrestled manfully with a whole host of difficulties—the inertness and complacency of the Athenian Assembly; the criticisms of his acquaintances who (with some justification) found him tiresome, pompous, and self-righteous; the financial troubles that enveloped him after the early death of his father; and his own psychological and temperamental inadequacies, which included the lack of any outstanding abilities as a statesman. In the face of all these obstacles, it was a noteworthy achievement that, by sheer dogged persistence supported by remarkable eloquence, he was able to rouse a defeatist people into offering at least some sort of resistance to a force they could not hope to defeat.

Although Demosthenes had many rivals in his lifetime, subsequent Greek and Latin authors unanimously hailed him as the supreme orator of all time—the number of his papyrus fragments that have come to light is second only to Homer's—and he has maintained that reputation ever since. Cicero, his nearest competitor—who paid him the compliment of borrowing the name *Philippics* for his own speeches against Antony—wrote of this "one man's astonishing eminence in oratory" and dwelt on his variety, subtlety, and dignity. Subsequently, the critic who goes under the name of Longinus, in the first century A.D., laid special emphasis on his rugged sublimity and intensity. In 1470, Cardinal Bessarion published the *First Olynthiac* in Latin in order to stir up Byzantine enthusiasm for resistance to the Turks. In the days of Napoleon, Friedrich Jacob translated Demosthenes into German with a similar purpose in mind.

WORKS—Writings wrongly or dubiously attributed to Demosthenes include over thirty additional speeches. Among these are the Halonnesus and Fourth Philippic, ascribed to 342 and 341 respectively; other orations already reascribed in antiquity to the Athenian orator Hyperides and to Demosthenes' political ally Hegesippus; two fabrications by the historian Anaximenes of Lampsacus (c. 380–320 B.C.); six of the eight speeches delivered on behalf of Apollodorus; second speeches against Stephanus and Boeotus; an indictment of Theocrines (which must have been included in the corpus of Demosthenes' speeches by mistake, since it violently attacks him); a funeral oration (Epitaphius) that purports, falsely, to be the speech Demosthenes delivered over those who fell at Chaeronea (338); and a lover's address to a real or imaginary boy called Epicrates. All, or at any rate most, of the six letters ascribed to Demosthenes are likewise spurious.
EDITIONS—W. Wayte, Against Androtion and Against Timocrates, 2d ed., 1893; J. E. Sandys, various speeches, 1896– ; W. W. Goodwin, On the Crown, 1901, 1906, *and* Against Midias, 1906; W. Schwahn, Gegen Aphobos (Against Aphobus), 1929; P. Treves, L'orazione per la corona (On the Crown), 1933; J. J. Murphy, On the Crown: A Critical Case Study, 1967; H. Wankel, Rede für Ktesiphon über den Kranz (On the Crown), 1976. *Translations*—M. Croiset, G. Mathieu, O. Navarre, P. Orsini, J. Humbert, L. Gernet, R. Clavaud (Budé ed.), 1924–78; J. H. Vince, A. T. Murray, N. W. Dewitt and N. J. Dewitt (Loeb ed.), 1926–49; W. R. Connor, Greek Orations, 1966; J. A. Goldstein, Letters, 1968; J. R. Ellis and R. D. Milnes, The Spectre of Philip, 1970; A. N. W. Saunders, Greek Political Oratory (Penguin ed.), 1970, *and* Demosthenes and Aeschines, 1975.
ABOUT—A. W. Pickard-Cambridge, Demosthenes and the Last Days of Greek Freedom, 1914; E. Drerup, Aus einer alten Advokatenrepublik, 1916, *and* Demosthenes im Urteile des Altertums, 1923; C. D. Adams, Demosthenes and His Influence, 1927; P. Treves, Demostene e la libertà greca, 1933; P. Cloché, Démosthène et la fin de la démocratie athénienne, 1937; W. Jaeger, Demosthenes: The Origin and Growth of His Policy, 1938; G. Mathieu, Démosthène: L'homme et l'oeuvre, 1948; G. Ronnet, Étude sur le style de Démosthène dans les discours politiques, 1951; J. Luccioni, Démosthène et la panhéllenisme, 1961; C. D. Adams, Demosthenes and His Influence, 1963; U. Schindel, Demosthenes im 18.

Jahrhundert (Zetemata, v 31), 1963; H. J. Wolff, Demosthenes als Advokat, 1968; J. R. Ellis, Philip II and Macedonian Imperialism, 1976; L. Pearson, The Art of Demosthenes, 1976; G. E. Cawkwell, Philip of Macedon, 1978.

DEXIPPUS, PUBLIUS HERENNIUS, Greek historian, was born at Athens between A.D. 200 and 210 and lived until the reign of Aurelian (270–75) or perhaps Probus (276–82). Over successive generations, members of his family—a leading one in Athens—although possessing Roman citizenship, still preferred to become senators at Athens and to hold office there rather than at Rome. Dexippus himself occupied the most distinguished Athenian civic offices, priesthoods, and directorships of festivals. The most important event of his public life, however, was his confrontation of an invading German tribe, the Heruli, who assaulted, and for a brief period captured, the city in 267/8; Dexippus confronted the invaders with a rapidly collected force of two thousand men and forced them to retreat.

His first literary work was probably *Events After Alexander,* titled after a writing by Arrian from which it appears to have been adapted and excerpted. Like Arrian's history, Dexippus' treatise probably went on until 321/20 B.C. The few fragments that have been preserved, by the Byzantine scholar Photius, consist mainly of generalities, but they are sufficient to show that this was a book of considerable length and that it included a number of speeches by leading personages. However, it was evidently of an unoriginal and scholastic character.

Dexippus' next accomplishment, the most important of his career, was an annalistic *Chronicle* or *History,* in twelve books, that started in mythical times and continued until the reign of Aurelian. A description of his historical method provided by Eunapius, who wrote the sequel (Eunapius died c. 420), indicated that in this *Chronicle* Dexippus was no longer content to follow a single predecessor but employed a number of sources; he also gave consideration to the best method of indicating chronology, offering appropriate warnings about the uncer-

dek sip' pus

125

tainties of the earlier epochs. The surviving fragments attributed to the work include thirty-one relating to his own third century A.D., but we owe all except one of them to quotations in the unreliable *Historia Augusta;* consequently their authenticity cannot be regarded as certain. Nevertheless, it seems clear that the *Chronicle* formed an important bridge between the universal histories of Hellenistic times and the Byzantine chronicles that were to follow three and four centuries later.

Dexippus narrated the invasions of the empire by the Germans from A.D. 238 until at least 270. From a description by the fourth century monk Evagrius, and from a number of surviving fragments, it appears that the *Scythica* dealt mainly with the Greek east and represented the inhabitants of its cities as heroes of the resistance to the attackers, with little said about the part played by the Roman army, though two fragments concerning the emperor Aurelian do allude somewhat cryptically to its role. These and other excerpts raise difficult problems about the sources that may have been available to Dexippus in Greece, as he composed his historical works. There are also differences of opinion about his style, of which the praises offered by Photius have not been echoed by all modern historians. His style is best studied from the oration that Dexippus claimed he had delivered to his men before they repelled the German invaders. As a statement of the situation the speech is factual and accurate; but it is also laced with emotional appeals to Athenian patriotism and fortune and the divine will, framed in terms deliberately reminiscent of Thucydides.

EDITIONS—F. Jacoby, Die Fragmente der griechischen Historiker, 2a, p 452 ff.
ABOUT—E. Schwartz, Griechische Geschichtsschreiber, 1957; J. Stein, Dexippus et Herodianus Rerum Scriptores Quatenus Thucydidem Secuti Sint, 1957; F. Millar, P. Herennius Dexippus: The Greek World and the Third-Century Invasions (Journal of Roman Studies, v 69), 1969.

DICAEARCHUS, Greek philosopher and writer on many subjects, flourished during
di kĭ är′ kus

the last quarter of the fourth century B.C. and the beginning of the third century. He came from Messana (Messina) in Sicily but spent most of his life in the Peloponnese, especially at Sparta. He was Aristotle's most important pupil next to Theophrastus. We know from Cicero that Dicaearchus, whom he admired, did not agree with Theophrastus' preference for a life devoted to speculative thinking but attached more importance to the practical aspects of living.

Dicaearchus' works are now represented only by fragments. Among his philosophical writings was a treatise entitled *On the Soul,* which comprised a dialogue on the soul's nature and mortality, divided into two parts, *Lesbiakos* and *Korinthiakos.* His tractate entitled *On the Destruction of Human Beings* argued that humankind is more often destroyed by its own agency than by natural disasters. Dicaearchus also composed studies on prophecy and on the future; he was the author of *Descent Into the Cave of Trophonius* (a Boeotian oracular god), in which immoral behavior is ascribed to the priests of the shrine. He wrote a letter to Aristoxenus of Tarentum, a fellow pupil of Aristotle, as well as biographies of Plato and other philosophers and a life of the poet Alcaeus that was probably accompanied by a commentary. In the same field of literary history, he also compiled a number of works on Homer and *hypotheses* (introductory notes) to plays of Sophocles and Euripides, as well as a monograph on musical and poetic competitions *(Peri Mousikon Agonon).* These discussions of Greek poetry and drama by Dicaearchus contained valuable information, which was extensively drawn upon by later scholars.

Of particular significance were his three books, *Life in Greece (Bios Hellados),* which consisted of a number of essays dealing with points of cultural and antiquarian interest and may be described as the first attempt at a universal history of culture from earliest times onward. Dicaearchus was also especially interested in political and constitutional matters and wrote accounts of the constitutions of Sparta, Corinth, Athens, and Pellene. His *Tripoliticus,* perhaps cast in dialogue form, seems to have been an endeavor to portray a mixed constitution that included features taken from monarchic, aristocratic, and democratic systems alike. In addition, he composed orations for festivals (the *Olympiakos* and *Panathenaikos*) and a description of Alexander the Great's sacrifice before his victory over the Persians in the battle of the Granicus (334).

Dicaearchus was also a leading geographer, and later writers, greatly influenced by his work, declared him comparable in this field to Eratosthenes (d. 194 B.C.), the great mathematician and geographer. Dicaearchus' *Circuit of the Earth (Periodos Ges)*, which, like everything else he wrote, is lost except for scraps, was apparently a cartographic survey of the ancient world, probably accompanied by descriptive notes. It established a basic line of latitude extending from the straits of Gibraltar to the Himalayas and placed the eastern ocean on the further side of that range. The work may also have included estimated figures (in many cases exaggerated) for the heights of Greek mountains. This form of geographical research, a revival of the old Ionian tradition of such inquiries *(historie)*, was closely allied with the great voyages of discovery in the period, notably those of Pytheas, who sailed up the western coast of Europe to Britain and beyond.

Dicaearchus was not only prolific and versatile but a man of great learning whose approach was original and genuinely scientific. The disappearance of his writings is a particularly grave loss.

EDITIONS—C. Müller, Fragmenta Historicorum Graecorum, v 2, 1841–70, *and* Geographici Graeci Minores, v 1, 1855–61 (discusses the possibility that fragments of a work on Greek cities and their inhabitants may be attributable to Dicaearchus); F. Wehrli, Die Schule des Aristoteles, v 1, 2nd ed., 1967.
ABOUT—Pauly-Wissowa-Kroll, Real-Encyclopädie der klassischen Altertumswissenschaft, Suppl. v 11; J. O. Thompson, History of Ancient Geography, 1948; F. Lämmli, Homo Faber: Triumph, Schuld, Verhängnis?, 1968.

DIDYMUS, Greek scholar, writer, and compiler, was born in about 80 B.C. (or somewhat later) and died in 10 B.C. A teacher at Alexandria in Egypt, he was stated to

di' di mus

have written four thousand works; even if, as is probable, this estimate was exaggerated, his output was evidently so colossal that his nickname Bronze-Guts *(Chalkenteros)* was not undeserved. Another of his nicknames, however, was Book-Forgetter *(Biblio-lathas)*, because of occasional self-contradictions in his writings, owing to forgetfulness of what he had said on earlier occasions.

Didymus' importance for Homeric studies was especially great. In particular, his many treatises on that subject included works bearing on the Homeric researches of Aristarchus of Samothrace (c. 217–145 B.C.), to whose school Didymus belonged. By Didymus' time, Aristarchus' editions of Homer were apparently lost. However, Didymus reconstructed them as well as he could, by the examination of other surviving commentaries and monographs by Aristarchus and by following up clues provided by other critics (Aristophanes of Byzantium, Zenodotus). As a result of these investigations and of his own study of the Homeric texts, he went on to produce a very full commentary of his own. A later scholar, unidentified, compiled an epitome of this, from which two sets of extracts were subsequently made that constitute our principal source of information for Didymus' Homeric studies at Alexandria; their incorporation in the Codex Venetus of Homer ensured their survival. Didymus also wrote an essay about Homer's birthplace.

On other writers, too, he compiled immense and varied commentaries replete with information concerning biographical, historical, geographical, and mythological points. These writers included Achaeus, Aeschines, Aeschylus, Antiphon (Didymus was the first to offer the distinction, now doubted, between two authors of this name), Aristophanes (the comic poet), Bacchylides, Choerilus, Cratinus, Demosthenes (a papyrus fragment at Berlin illustrates Didymus's methods and offers valuable incidental information about Aristotle), Dinarchus, Eupolis, Euripides, Hesiod, Hyperides, Ion of Chios, Isaeus, Isocrates, Menander, Phrynichus, Pindar, Sophocles, and Thucydides (whose death, according to Didymus, took place in Athens, not in Thrace as was supposed by others). Many of the earliest scholia (marginal notes) to Aristophanes, Euripides, Pindar, and Sophocles are ultimately derived from Didymus' writings. He also composed a study entitled *On Lyric Poets* and one on Solon's laws *(On the Axones of Solon).*

Didymus' lexicographical works on tragic and comic drama, including a collection of rare or difficult words from tragedy, were extensively used by later scholars and lexicographers. His study, *On Proverbs,* was much drawn upon by the Alexandrian *paroemiographi* (collectors of proverbial sayings). In addition, he wrote separate tractates on corrupt, doubtful, and metaphorical expressions; on aspects of grammar (orthography, analogy, and inflection); and on various myths and legends *(Strange Stories: Xene Historia),* including the accounts of the death of Aeneas. Didymus was not an original researcher on his own account but a compiler of the views of others. However, he was an immensely hard-working, discriminating, careful, and versatile editor, not afraid of tackling problems of chronology and interpretation. Thus, he played an enormous part in the preservation and transmission of learning that would otherwise not have survived.

EDITIONS—M. Schmidt, Didymi Chalcenteri Grammatici Alexandrini Fragmenta, 1854. It is uncertain whether an attack on Cicero entitled On the State, which was answered by Suetonius, was written by this Didymus or by Claudius Didymus, a lexicographer of the first century A.D., whose works included an essay comparing Latin with Greek.
ABOUT—A. Ludwich, Aristarchs homerische Textkritik, 1884–85; H. Diels and W. Schubart, Didymus Kommentar zu Demosthenes, 1904; M. van der Valk, Researches on the Text and Scholia of the Iliad, v 1, 1963; L. D. Reynolds and N. G. Wilson, Scribes and Scholars, 1968.

DIO CASSIUS (Cassius Dio Cocceianus), Greek historian and Roman official, was born at Nicaea (Iznik) in Bithynia (northwestern Asia Minor) in about A.D. 163 or 164 and died some time after 229. He was the son of Cassius Apronianus, governor of Cilicia and Dalmatia, and may have been a

dī′ ō   kas′ si us

descendant of the Greek orator and philosopher Dio Chrysostom. Dio Cassius came to Rome at the age of sixteen or seventeen, in the early years of the reign of Commodus (180–92), under whom he subsequently became a member of the Roman Senate. During the brief principate of Pertinax (193) he was nominated to a praetorship, which he held in the following year after the accession of Septimus Severus. In 205 he served as consul, and during the reign of Severus Alexander (222–35) was appointed successively to the governorships of Africa, Dalmatia, and Upper Pannonia. In 229 he became consul again, as the colleague of the emperor himself. However, he did not spend his year of office in Rome, since the unpopularity of his strict discipline with the soldiers and praetorian guardsmen prompted the emperor to suggest that he should absent himself from the city. Leaving the public service, Dio withdrew to his native Bithynia, where he apparently remained.

He was the author of a Roman history in eighty books, extending from the beginnings to A.D. 229. Books 36-54 (68–10 B.C.) are preserved in their entirety and Books 55-60 (9 B.C.–A.D. 46) in abbreviated form, while Books 17 and 79-80 have survived in part. The portion of the work from Book 36 onward was summarized by the eleventh century Byzantine monk John Xiphilinus of Trapezus (Trabzon), whose epitome (lacking the reign of Antoninus Pius and the first years of Marcus Aurelius) is extant and provides a somewhat erratic and spasmodic selection of the original. Fortunately, it also preserves many passages in uncondensed form.

Extant, too, is the summary written by John Zonaras half a century later as part of his *Epitome of Histories.* Zonaras uses Dio's work for the period from the legendary arrival of Aeneas down to 146 B.C.—usefully preserving the structure of the original— and then again from the death of Julius Caesar onward. From the reign of Trajan onward, Zonaras merely excerpts Xiphilinus, but up to that point his précis is more coherent and intelligible than that of Xiphilinus and more successful in its efforts to abbreviate passages without losing their sense.

Dio's history took him ten years to prepare and twelve more to write. It was based on Republican and imperial historical traditions and particularly, for the appropriate periods, on Livy or the sources Livy had drawn upon. The structure of his history is annalistic, like that of many of his sources, yet within this framework he endeavors to establish a wider chronological basis. However, his handling of the period before the emperors is hampered by an inadequate knowledge of Roman Republican institutions and conditions and is colored by the view that detailed description is incompatible with the dignity of history. Thereafter, in his narration of events from the age of Augustus until his own time, Dio's treatment is impaired by an anachronistic projection of the monarchical conditions of his own day that prevents him from doing justice to the gradualness of imperial development. Thus, the speech of advice that Maecenas is made to deliver to Augustus anomalously mirrors the absolutist attitudes with which Dio himself was familiar. The principal value of the work lies in the period from A.D. 180 onward, during which time Dio's own official career enabled him, as an importantly placed eyewitness, to collect firsthand information.

His stylistic aim was Attic archaism, and his models, somewhat discordant with one another, were Thucydides (from whom he inherits a preference for political themes) and Demosthenes. Dio employs rhetorical artifices but seldom achieves a vivid narrative; yet he is not altogether averse to dramatization, as, for instance, in his narrative of Caesar's Gallic War. Though he aimed at an accurate and systematic reconstruction, with results that are in the main trustworthy, scientific criticism of the Republican annalists was beyond his powers, and he displays an excessive keenness for anecdotes. Yet the usefulness of his work remains very great, for Dio is the one historical writer of any significance whatever who enables us to build up a continuous and connected narrative of Roman history for the period from A.D. 70 onward. He is also a conspicuous example of a historian whose writings, insofar as they describe his own time, were largely based on personal participation in events at a high level. Final-

ly, our knowledge of the bilingual, bicultural Roman empire is considerably advanced by this phenomenon of a Greek who rose to high Roman office and wrote from the viewpoint of this dual experience, thus providing a vital link between the Hellenistic world of the past and the Byzantine civilization of the future.

Dio also wrote a biography of Arrian, and an account of the dreams and portents of Septimius Severus, but both these works are lost.

EDITIONS—P. U. Boissevain (German), 1895–1931 (5 v; new impression of first 4 v, 1954). *With translation:* E. Cary, Roman History (Loeb ed.), 1914–27.
ABOUT—F. Millar, A Study of Cassius Dio, 1964; G. T. Griffith, Fifty Years (and Twelve) of Classical Scholarship, 1968 (bibliography, p 223, note 123).

DIO CHRYSOSTOM (Dio Cocceianus), "the Golden-Mouthed" Greek orator and philosopher, also known as Dion of Prusa (Bursa) in Bithynia (northwestern Asia Minor), his hometown, was born in about A.D. 40 and died after 112. Entering upon the career of a rhetorician at Rome, Dio was at first critical of philosophy but became converted to Stoicism (with a Cynic tinge) by Musonius Rufus, Epictetus' teacher, who had been the target of a hostile pamphlet written by Dio at an earlier date.

In 82 Dio was exiled by the emperor Domitian as a result of a political intrigue, probably related to the fall of his patron Flavius Sabinus, and both Italy and his native Bithynia were closed to him. In consequence he spent the rest of Domitian's reign wandering through other parts of Asia Minor, and in Greece and the Balkans, as an itinerant lecturer on philosophical themes. During this period he was poor, and the sentiments he expressed were characteristic of a Cynic beggar-philosopher. Restored to favor by Nerva (A.D. 96–98), he became a friend of his successor, Trajan, but continued to travel widely and speak on his customary topics. Subsequently he retired to his family estates in Bithynia and became a leading figure in provincial affairs. All we know of his later years is that on one occa-

dī′ ō kri′ so stom

sion he was prosecuted in connection with a public building contract; this information comes to us from Pliny the Younger (111–12), whose letter to Trajan on the subject is preserved along with the emperor's reply.

Eighty speeches on a wide variety of themes have been attributed to Dio (although two of these should rather be ascribed to his pupil Favorinus, who affected a more artificial style). We learn from the Neoplatonist Synesius (d. 413), pupil of Hypatia and eventually a Christian bishop, that his sophistic pieces were the earliest and the political next, while the moralistic orations belong to the last phase of his career. One of the products of his first period is the long and literary *Trojan Oration,* which endeavored to prove that Homer was mistaken in believing that the Greeks captured Troy; this interpretation was presumably welcome to educated Romans, who traced the ancestry of their city back to Aeneas and the Trojans. The same speech also provides, in passing, a comprehensive exposition of the Homeric criticism of the day. Another of these early speeches deals with Socrates' debt to Homer; and there is also a comparison of the tragedies relating to the hero Philoctetes written by Aeschylus, Sophocles, and Euripides. In *On Training for Public Speaking,* a bibliography for some high official, Dio's liking for Plato and Xenophon is evident. In the same period he wrote a trifle entitled *The Praise of Hair,* and equally trivial eulogies of a parrot and a gnat, neither of which has survived.

His political speeches addressed to Greek cities, including Rhodes, Alexandria, Tarsus, Celaenae, and Borysthenes, provide valuable evidence for the life of the Greek east under Roman imperial rule. The earliest of these pieces is probably the long and carefully composed Rhodian oration, which by its polite remarks about Nero is shown to belong to the reign of the equally absolutist Domitian. In this speech Dio rebukes the people of Rhodes for their custom of altering inscriptions on old statues to meet the profitable demand for "new" honorary monuments. His address to the Alexandrians, while praising their cleverness, blames them for self-indulgence and flippancy. Speeches delivered before the Assembly and

Council at his hometown of Prusa deal with current local situations. In general, these discourses show Dio employing his prestige and good sense to warn the Greek cities against riotous and quarrelsome behavior and to persuade them to acquiesce in Roman rule as the best means of preserving their Hellenic way of life. The *Olympian Speech,* which belongs to the same period, puts forward a theory of art (with Phidias, the Greek sculptor of the fifth century B.C., as its mouthpiece) that pronounces poetry more effective than sculpture for the portrayal of character. The speech also contains interesting observations on the importance of art for the concept of deity.

Dio is at his best, however, in his moralizing treatises, which belong to his final period. The four *Royal Speeches,* probably addressed to Trajan, propose the Stoic-Cynic ideal of kingship, based on the requirement that the monarch should study and seek the welfare of his subjects. Two of these orations are cast in dialogue form, one between Philip II and his son Alexander the Great and the other between Alexander and Diogenes the Cynic. *Libyan Myth* uses the story of an enticing but cruel mermaid to offer a lesson on the control of the passions. Dio's most effective and admired oration is entitled *Euboicus (The Euboean).* The speech describes events, presumably fictitious, relating to a shipwreck off the island of Euboea. The narrator is rescued and looked after by a family of hunters whose idyllic, withdrawn life upon the island is depicted, with many of the techniques of the Greek romantic novel, to present a contrast with the corruption and restlessness of civilized urban life.

Chrysostom writes about the problems of the Greek society of his day with agreeable moderation and conviction—and an appealing blend of earnestness and humor. He is a Greek patriot, who idealizes the Hellenic past and its classical tradition but is at the same time by no means anti-Roman; as he grew older, his Stoic-Cynic philosophy divested itself of its radical character, though he continued to insist on the philosopher's right to criticize freely. Dio reflects the attitudes of the upper classes in the eastern provinces, who were beginning, at this time, to gain a share of political power. At the same time, he also takes an interest in the day-to-day life of less privileged human beings. Indeed, he is more enlightening than any other author about the ways in which people of this period lived and thought. He belongs to the Second Age of the Sophists but avoids their rhetorical excesses and aims at a relaxed and entertaining and at times almost conversational manner, offering the appearance of improvisation.

EDITIONS—H. von Arnim, 1893, 1896. *With translation:* J. W. Cohoon and H. L. Crosby (Loeb ed.), 1932–51; G. de Budé, Le Discours de Célènes, 1955; D. Ferrante, Dione Crisostomo, Peri Basileias (On Kingship), 1975.
ABOUT—H. von Arnim, Leben und Werke des Dio von Prusa, 1898; R. MacMullen, Enemies of the Roman Order, 1967; G. W. Bowersock, Greek Sophists in the Roman Empire, 1969; C. P. Jones, The Roman World of Dio Chrysostom, 1978.

DIO COCCEIANUS. See Dio Chrysostom

DIODORUS SICULUS, Greek historian, lived in the first century B.C. (until at least 21 B.C.) and came from Agyrium (Agira) in Sicily. He wrote a general history of the world from mythical times down to Caesar's Gallic War (54 B.C.), entitling it *The Library (Bibliotheke).* The first six of its forty books deal with legendary prehistory: Book 1 discusses Egypt; Book 2, Mesopotamia, India, Scythia, and Arabia; Book 3, northern Africa; Books 4-6, Greece and Europe. Then Books 7-17 cover the period from the Trojan War to Alexander the Great and Books 18-40 from Alexander's successors to Caesar. Books 6-10 and 21-40 survive only in fragments.

Diodorus professed a universal conception of history, though he felt obliged to insert a special history of his native island also. His principal aim, however, was to present a synchronized account of the histories of Greece and Rome, though the attempt to combine their chronologies resulted in considerable confusion. While the chronicle of Apollodorus of Athens, of

dī ō dō′ rus si′ ku lus

the second century B.C., provided his general framework, Diodorus used an extensive array of earlier sources in addition. For the classical period, however, he mainly employed the historian Ephorus; for the succeeding epochs he drew first upon Duris and Phylarchus and then on Polybius, followed by Posidonius. Other writers echoed in his work include Hecataeus, Ctesias, Theopompus, Aristobulus, Cleitarchus, Hieronymus, Diyllus, Philinus, Timaeus, and an early Roman annalistic historian. The public that Diodorus hoped to attract was broad and not very cultured; this is confirmed by his reactionary decision to give prominence to mythical prehistory, on which he derived his information from the treatises and handbooks of earlier mythological writers. His style rises and sags according to his sources, being florid and vivacious, for example, when the colorful Duris is being followed, although he also tones down the flamboyant character of certain of his sources, notably Agatharchides' monograph *On the Red Sea.* On the whole, however, Diodorus reflects his sources with a slavish lack of originality and distinction; he is valuable only for the light that he throws on authorities that are otherwise lost. While the nineteenth century English writer Thomas Babington Macaulay described Diodorus as "a stupid, credulous, prosing old ass," the *Bibliotheke* remains a rich mine of otherwise unavailable information.

EDITIONS—A. Burton, Book 1, 1973. *With translation:* C. H. Oldfather and R. M. Geer, Diodorus Siculus: Library of History (Loeb ed.), 1933–67; F. Chamoux, M. Casevitz, C. Vial, P. Goutkovsky, F. Bizière, Diodore de Sicile: Bibliothèque historique (Budé ed.), 1972– .
ABOUT—G. Perl, Kritische Untersuchungen zu Diodors römischer Jahrzählung, 1957; also *see* bibliography of articles *in* G. T. Griffith, The Greek Historians (Appendix), *in* Fifty Years (and Twelve) of Classical Scholarship, 1968, p 237.

DIOGENES LAERTIUS, Greek writer on philosophy, probably lived in the earlier part of the third century A.D. It is not known where he was born or where, or with whom, he studied or wrote. He was the author of a

dī oj′ e nēz lā ûr′ ti us

131

work in ten books entitled *Lives and Opinions of the Philosophers,* more generally known as *History of the Philosophers.* After a preliminary book dealing with non-Greek ("barbarian") philosophies and the half-legendary Seven Sages, Greek philosophy is presented in two sections that describe, in turn, an eastern (Ionian) and an Italian branch, with "successions" (schools) within each. Books 2-7 describe the principal Ionian or eastern philosophers, from Anaximander onward (Book 3, for instance, being devoted to Plato). Book 8 discusses the Italian schools, beginning with Pythagoras. Book 9 deals with the more important philosophers who did not found "successions." The whole of Book 10 is dedicated to a treatment of Epicurus—this is useful because of the original Epicurean documents it quotes that have not otherwise survived.

Indeed, the citation of original excerpts is a special feature of Diogenes' work. They vary from trivial gossip to summaries of philosophical doctrines that, when allowance is made for distortions, remain of considerable use. These excerpts, however, are often introduced at inappropriate points and fogged by the insertion of distracting marginal comments, so that it has been deduced that the *History of the Philosophers* is simply a first draft. Also, the excerpts are usually secondhand, being very often drawn from other compilers, among whom are Antigonus of Carystus, Apollodorus of Athens, Demetrius and Diocles of Magnesia, Favorinus, Hermippus, Pamphila, Sosicrates of Rhodes, and Sotion.

Diogenes gives the names of more than two hundred authors and more than three hundred writings, and his work varies in value from passage to passage in accordance with the quality of the source he happens to be using. His own personal philosophical predilections are hard to detect. He places admiring emphasis on Epicurus but praises the Cynics as well; he also addresses part of his book to a woman interested in Platonic doctrine. However, Diogenes seems to have felt a special affinity for the Sceptics, from one of whom, Sextus Empiricus, he may have inherited his general tendency to be impartial to all schools; and he describes one adherent of this school as "*our* Apollo-

nides," though it must be borne in mind that this assertion, like all others offering judgment about the philosophers, may be derived from one of his sources rather than from any personal preference of his own.

Diogenes was not a philosopher but a literary compiler; he was more interested in entertaining anecdotes than in doctrines. Yet, despite his faults, he knew the sort of facts that people wanted, and his summaries of Socrates, Plato, Aristotle, Zeno, and Chrysippus, for example, are competent. Moreover, he must be credited with the invention of the history of philosophy as a subject of study; and his book, which is the only work of its kind that has come down to us substantially intact, constitutes our most significant secondary source of information in this field. In consequence, its influence on the education of subsequent generations has been out of all proportion to Diogenes' intellectual abilities. In the sixteenth century, for example, it was carefully studied by Montaigne.

Diogenes also published a collection of *Epigrams.* This edition has not survived, but he quotes from the poems on more than twenty occasions in his extant works. They were evidently of very poor quality. Some of them described in various meters the deaths of famous men, except those of the philosophers, which he had inserted in his *History of the Philosophers.*

EDITIONS with translation—R. D. Hicks, Diogenes Laertius: Lives of Eminent Philosophers (Loeb ed.), 1925 (new ed. of v 1, 1938); M. Gigante, Diogene Laerzio: Vita dei filosofi, 2nd ed., 1975.

ABOUT—R. Hope, The Book of Diogenes Laertius, 1930; M. Dal Pra, La storiografia filosofica antica, 1950; A. Biedl, Zur Textgeschichte des Laertios Diogenes: Das grosse Exzerpt, 1955; J. Mejer, Diogenes Laertius and His Hellenistic Background, 1978.

DIONYSIUS OF HALICARNASSUS,

Greek rhetorician, literary critic and historian, was born in Halicarnassus (Bodrum) in Caria (southwestern Asia Minor) but came to Rome in about 30 B.C. and lived and taught there for at least twenty-two years, probably longer. We do not know when he died.

dī ō ni' si us   ha li kär nas' sus

His writings on literary criticism were included in a corpus generally known as the *Scripta Rhetorica.* One of its components was a work entitled *On Imitation,* in three books, of which fragments and excerpts survive. He also wrote a treatise *On the Ancient Orators,* of which the sections concerning Lysias, Isaeus, and Isocrates are extant. They offer, in each case, a short biography, critical observations, and specimen extracts, with special reference to the stylistic qualities, in which Dionysius was particularly interested. His introduction to *On the Ancient Orators* records distaste for rhetoric of the more florid character (known as Asianic), together with an expression of confidence that the good taste of the Roman ruling class will encourage a revival of the simpler (Attic) diction. Dionysius also composed a long discussion of the style of Demosthenes, sometimes regarded as a separate work *(De Admirabili Vi Dicendi in Demosthene).* The work offers a strong, well-reasoned eulogy of Demosthenes as the supreme master of oratory; and in Dionysius' *Letter to Pompeius Geminus* the point is pursued further, and Demosthenes is rated superior even to Plato. The *First Letter to Ammaeus* denies, on chronological grounds, that Demosthenes drew on Aristotle's *Rhetoric;* the *Second Letter to Ammaeus,* in response to a request, analyzes the style of Thucydides. An essay, *On the Peculiarities of Thucydides,* assesses that historian from a rhetorical point of view and concludes that he is inferior to Herodotus (who came from Halicarnassus, like Dionysius himself). *On Dinarchus* is a factual account of the orator of that name, appending a list of his speeches. Dionysius' most important work in the field of rhetoric, however—and the hardest to understand— is *On the Arrangement of Words.* The only surviving study of this subject, it discusses in detail the means by which prose could be rendered as attractive as poetry, analyzing, in the process, the structure of sentences and the choice and harmonious arrangement of words and discussing questions of rhythm and euphony. The treatise is also notable because it preserves two Greek poems of the first importance, Sappho's *Aphrodite* and the *Danae* of Simonides.

Dionysius is a judicious, knowledgeable,

and sensitive literary critic, and *On the Arrangement of Words* raises him almost to the first rank in this field. (*Handbook of Rhetoric,* formerly attributed to him, probably belongs to the third century A.D.). Furthermore, he was also the author of a large-scale historical work, *Roman Antiquities,* which began to appear in 7 B.C. Out of its twenty books, ten, and most of an eleventh, survive, in addition to passages from nine more. In its complete form, the work narrated Roman history from its mythical beginnings down to the First Punic War. Dionysius indicates that he learned Latin in order to tackle this book and devoted twenty-two years of research to its preparation, regarding it as his most important achievement. Yet it nowadays seems less successful than his essays in literary criticism. This is largely because the *Antiquities* contain so much moralizing, eulogy, and rhetoric. Moreover, in particular, Dionysius starts from the erroneous premise that the Romans, instead of developing from crude beginnings, had always possessed a high civilization, a flawless governing class, and elevated religion: he makes their heroes too heroic, shows naiveté about their politics, and misunderstands their institutions. Drawing upon the Roman annalists without any attempt at historical criticism, he tells many of the same stories as Livy at ten times the length and with one-tenth of the artistry. Nevertheless, Dionysius' prolix rehashes of the old tales are of value to the study of early Rome, since they preserve a good many interesting facts and details of an antiquarian nature that would otherwise be lost.

EDITIONS—C. Jacoby, Antiquitates, 1885–1925; H. Usener and L. Radermacher, Opuscula, 1899–1929; W. R. Roberts, Three Literary Letters, 1901, *and* On Literary Composition (On the Arrangement of Words), 1910; G. Marenghi, Dinarco, 1970. *With translation:* S. Usher, Critical Essays (Loeb ed.), 1974, 1977; W. K. Pritchett, Dionysius of Halicarnassus: On Thucydides, 1975; G. Aujac, Denys d' Halicarnasse: Les orateurs antiques (Budé ed.), v 1, 1978.
ABOUT—G. W. Bowersock, Augustus and the Greek World, 1965. *Literary criticism:* J. W. Atkins, Literary Criticism in Antiquity, 1934, 1952; S. F. Bonner, The Literary Treatises of Dionysius, 1939; G. M. A. Grube, The Greek and Roman Critics, 1965. *Antiquities:* A. Klotz, Livius und seine Vorgänger, 1941; E. Schwartz, Griechische Geschichtsschreiber, 1957.

DIONYSIUS THE AREOPAGITE. See John Scotus Erigena, Maximus Confessor, Proclus

DIONYSIUS THRAX, Greek grammarian, c. 170–90 B.C., was born at Alexandria; but he was called Thracian because his father Teres had come from that country. After attending the lectures of Aristarchus of Samothrace at Alexandria, he emigrated, probably when Ptolemy VIII Euergetes (Physcon) expelled many scholars from the city. Thereupon Dionysius moved to Rhodes, where he taught grammar and literature.

His only surviving work (his authorship of which was sometimes wrongly questioned in antiquity) is the *Art of Grammar,* the oldest grammatical treatise that has come down to us. It starts with a definition of the subject, goes on to classify accents, punctuation marks, letters, and syllables, and then deals with the eight parts of speech and their inflections. Syntax and style are not discussed. The work bears the stamp of the Alexandrian school but also shows awareness of other writers on the subject, notably the members of the Stoic school founded by Zeno of Citium.

The *Art of Grammar* was widely accepted as an elementary textbook and soon became known in Rome, probably through Dionysius' pupil Tyrannio the Elder, who was brought to the city in B.C. 72 as a prisoner by the general and statesman Lucullus in the Third Mithridatic War. Another student of Dionysius was Asclepiades of Apamea (Myrlea), who likewise worked for a time at Rome and produced a systematic study of philology. Dionysius' *Art of Grammar* served as a model for Latin grammarians, notably Remmius Palaemon in the first century A.D., and was still known by grammatical experts of later imperial times such as Apollonius Dyscolus and his son Aelius Herodianus. Later on, however, the work evidently gathered accretions, and vast commentaries grew up around the original text. The *Art* was used everywhere in the Greek world until the twelfth century A.D. Syriac

dī ō ni′ si us thraks

and Armenian translations are still extant, and, through Latin versions, most of the grammars in use in modern times are still dependent on Dionysius' work.

He also wrote commentaries on the Homeric poems and on Hesiod's *Works and Days* and was the author of a descriptive treatise on the island of Rhodes.

EDITIONS (The Art of Grammar)—K. Linke, Die Fragmente des Grammatikers Dionysios Thrax, 1977.
ABOUT—A. Hilgard, Scholia in Dionysii Thracis Artem Grammaticam, 1901; R. H. Robins, Ancient & Mediaeval Grammatical Theory in Europe, 1951; M. Fuhrmann, Das systematische Lehrbuch, 1960.

DIOSCORIDES, PEDANIUS, Greek physician and writer, lived in the middle of the first century A.D. He was born at Anazarbus (Anavarza) in Cilicia (southeastern Asia Minor) and served in the armies of Nero, presumably as a doctor. He traveled extensively before turning to literary activity.

His *Materia Medica* or *Pharmacology* in five books (with two further books serving as appendices) is the most important pharmacological work that has come down to us from ancient times. It describes the curative properties (e.g., as antidotes to poisons, *Alexipharmaca*) of some six hundred plants and nearly a thousand drugs of medicinal and dietetic importance, including not only vegetable but also animal and mineral products. Dioscorides is more interested in medicine than in botany. His observation is meticulous and his judgment reliable and unsuperstitious; his intention is to delineate a system of medicine, not merely to provide a list of drugs.

The *Materia Medica* superseded all previous writings and became a standard textbook in East and West alike. Jean de Rueil provided a Latin version in 1526, and translations into Italian, German, French, and Spanish followed during the next thirty years.

WORKS—Writings not certainly attributable to Dioscorides include a briefer Pharmacopoeia (Euporista) in two books. There are spurious monographs on poisons

dī os kor′ i dēz

and plant synonyms and one entitled De Herbis Femininis.

EDITIONS (of the Materia Medica)—M. Wellmann, 1907–14. *Translations*—R. T. Gunther, The Greek Herbal of Dioscorides, 1934.

ABOUT—L. Edelstein, Ancient Medicine, 1967; J. Scarborough, Roman Medicine, 1969; E. D. Phillips, Greek Medicine, 1974.

DIPHILUS, Greek comic poet and playwright, the son of a certain Dion, was born at Sinope (Sinop) in Pontus (northern Asia Minor) between 360 and 350 B.C. and came as a young man to Athens where he lived most of his life; he died early in the following century at Smyrna (Izmir) but was buried at Athens.

Together with Menander and Philemon, he was one of the principal playwrights of the Athenian New Comedy (his brother Diodorus was another). He wrote about one hundred plays, gaining three victories at the Lenaean festival of Dionysus. Only fragments of his comedies survive, but the titles that are known, about sixty in number, are mostly not uncommon in this type of comic drama. Nine are mythological, including the *Danaids, Peliads, Lemniae, Heracles, Theseus, Heros,* and *Hecate.* These plays seem to have varied in character; some may have been burlesque, whereas others took their names from the divine or heroic personage speaking the prologue, or from a man imitating or masquerading as a mythical figure, such as Heracles. A less familiar theme was also dealt with by Diphilus in his *Sappho,* one of the six plays on the subject that are known to us. In defiance of chronological accuracy he makes the poets Archilochus and Hipponax Sappho's lovers. Other historical characters, too, figure in the titles of his plays, including Amastris (wife of Xerxes) and Tithraustes (satrap of Lower Asia, 395). Another unusual theme is apparently presented by the *Wall-Stormer (Hairesiteiches),* perhaps referring to Demetrius Poliorcetes, one of the successors of Alexander the Great. The name of this play was changed to *The Soldier (Stratiotes),* when the play was rewritten, with a view to its revival on the stage.

dif' fi lus

Other plays by Diphilus are of special interest to students of Latin comedy because, although no longer extant today, they are known to have served as models for Roman dramatists. Thus his *Woman Assigned by Lot (Kleroumene)* was recast by Plautus in his boisterous *Casina;* Plautus also adapted Diphilus' *Suicide Pact (Synapothneskontes)* for his lost *Commorientes,* though omitting an early scene that Terence, however, was later to employ in his *Adelphi (Brothers).* Plautus may also have made use of Diphilus' *Schedia* for his *Tale of the Traveling Bag (Vidularia),* of which part survives; an unknown comedy of Diphilus (possibly *Pera*) was likewise the model for Plautus' exciting and romantic play *The Rope (Rudens).* Furthermore, it has been suggested that Plautus' *Braggart Warrior (Miles Gloriosus)* also goes back to a Diphilan original.

Although it is uncertain to what extent Plautus recast these models, it can be deduced that he derived certain qualities from Diphilus, notably a taste for vivid action and spectacle, a liking for strongly contrasted theatrical effects, and perhaps a preference for a less subtle form of characterization than was favored by Menander. Diphilus' imagery was vigorous; and signs of his overseas origin have been traced in his exotic vocabulary. Two of his fragments refer to Euripides, one in terms of parody and the other describing him as "gilded"; perhaps these allusions combine mild mockery with admiration.

EDITIONS—A. Meineke, Fragmenta Comicorum Graecorum, v 4, 1839–57; T. Koch, Comicorum Atticorum Fragmenta, v 2, 1880–88.
ABOUT—W. H. Friedrich, Euripides und Diphilos, 1953; T. B. L. Webster, Studies in Later Greek Comedy, 1953.

DONATUS, AELIUS, Latin rhetorician and grammarian, was active in the middle of the fourth century A.D. as a writer and teacher; one of his pupils was St. Jerome. Among Donatus' works was a school grammar, which has come down to us in two texts of different lengths. The shorter version, the *De Partibus Orationis Ars Minor,* was in-

dō nä' tus

tended for beginners and offers elementary instruction, of a strictly practical nature, concerning the eight parts of speech. The larger treatise, the *Ars Grammatica* proper —more than three times longer than the *Ars Minor*—pays more attention to syntax and less to accidence (inflection). It is divided into three sections and deals not only with the parts of speech and the elements of grammar but also with errors and beauties of language; the work concludes with a section on barbarisms, solecisms, the seventeen figures of speech, and the thirteen tropes (figurative use of words).

Although Donatus' has little claim to originality, his grammar was cited more often than any other before or since and became the subject of many commentaries; indeed, it formed the basis of all subsequent Latin grammars up to our own time. Initially, although Pope Gregory the Great regarded its teaching on barbarisms as too narrowly conservative, the book, especially in its shorter form, equaled the sixth century *Institutiones Grammaticae* of Priscian as the principal grammatical textbook of the Middle Ages, attaining such fame that a "Donat" in Chaucer's English is synonymous with a grammar lesson. In the sixteenth century, the religious reformer Melanchthon included Donatus among the few Latin writers whom he thought the average schoolboy should read; and in 1551 the first five of the seven classes in grammar at Jesuit colleges had a program requiring them to spend all their time on morphology and syntax, as laid down by Donatus and Despauterius (Jean Despautière, the Flemish grammarian of the late fifteenth and early sixteenth centuries).

Donatus' other writings included commentaries on Terence and Virgil, to which were attached *Lives* drawing upon those composed by Suetonius. The surviving version of the Terence commentary (in which the analysis of one play, the *Hautontimorumenos,* is missing) no longer retains its original form but appears to have been adapted in the sixth century A.D. from two original copies attached to manuscripts of Terence. The commentary is based on meticulous study of the dramatist and incorporates the work of reputable earlier com-

mentators such as Aemilius Asper of the second century A.D. (whose writings are otherwise lost). Donatus has interesting things to say about various aspects of Terence's work, including the staging of his plays and his relationship to his Greek originals.

Of Donatus' commentary on Virgil, apart from quotations, the only parts that are extant are the preface, a *Life* of the poet, and an introduction to the *Eclogues.* But a great deal of material derived from the work has also survived in the commentary by Servius; and in *Servius Danielis,* the longer version of Servius' work found in manuscripts originally published by Pierre Daniel in 1600, the supplementary material may comprise further portions of the commentary of Donatus that Servius himself had not incorporated. Donatus' commentary on the first six books of the *Aeneid* was annotated by the outstanding ninth century scholar Lupus of Ferrières. (This Donatus Aelius Donatus should be distinguished from Tiberius Claudius Donatus who wrote his *Interpretationes Virgilianae,* a commentary on the *Aeneid,* in the later fourth century A.D.)

EDITIONS—H. Keil, Grammatici Latini, 1864 (the Artes); P. Wessner (Teubner ed.), 1902–5); H. T. Karsten, 1912–13 (Commentary on Terence).
ABOUT—M. Schanz and C. Hosius, Geschichte der römischen Literatur, v 1 and v 2, revised eds., 1927, 1935; U. Schindel, Die lateinischen Figurenlehren des 5 bis 7 Jahrhunderts und Donats Vergilkommentar, 1975.

DURIS, Greek statesman and historian, lived from about 340 to about 260 B.C. He was the son of Scaeus of Samos and became ruler (tyrant) of that city.

Duris' principal historical work was his *Histories,* otherwise known as *Hellenica* or *Macedonica,* which may have been the original title. Comprising at least twenty-three books, Duris' work probably began with the death of King Amyntas III of Macedonia (370 B.C.), father of Philip II, and went on to the time of Pyrrhus of Epirus (c. 280), becoming increasingly detailed in the later periods. Only fragments survive, but they include an introductory remark that has at-

doo′ ris

tracted attention. In this passage the historian observes that his predecessors Ephorus and Theopompus had for the most part proved unequal to the events that they described, since in presenting them they made no attempt at dramatic "imitation" *(mimesis)* to make their narrative enjoyable ("to give it *hedone*") but concerned themselves merely with writing (or "with the formal aspects of writing"). Duris was a pupil of Theophrastus, the successor of Aristotle, and attempts have been made to link this theory of historiography with the Aristotelian school, which likewise made use of the term *mimesis* and produced certain manuals about history (notably those of Theophrastus and Praxiphanes). However, we know almost nothing of the contents of these manuals. Although it is probable enough that Duris employed the word *mimesis* because it was familiar to him from Aristotelian terminology, he himself seems to have used it in a nonphilosophical sense to mean a vivid, exciting, and sensational representation of events—the sort of "tragic history" that characterizes the extant fragments of his work.

Displaying a refusal to take an interest in style (for which he was criticized later by Dionysius of Halicarnassus), Duris aimed at dramatic emotional impact, often without regard for the truth. For instance, one fragment tells how the victorious Alcibiades sailed into Athens' port, the Piraeus, with purple sail hoisted, while Chrysogonus, victor in the Pythian Games, accompanied the oarsmen's strokes with his flute and Callippides, a tragic actor, called out the rhythm. Plutarch points out that this incident is not recorded by Xenophon or Theopompus or Ephorus and very probably never took place. Thus, Duris introduced a new element of poetical, fictitious reporting into history. His work greatly influenced the most important historian of the next generation, Phylarchus of Athens, though such methods continued to receive censure from historians such as Polybius who professed a dedication to accuracy.

Duris also wrote a *History of Agathocles,* tyrant and king of Syracuse (317–289 B.C.), in at least four books, and a work entitled *Chronicle of Samos,* in two books or more.

In addition, he composed various works on literature, music, and other forms of art (a work on toreutics, the chasing and embossing of metal, is mentioned), thus conforming with a tradition of anecdotal writing on such subjects which had then become established.

EDITIONS—F. Jacoby, Die Fragmente der griechischen Historiker, 2a, 76.
ABOUT—K. Fritz, Die Bedeutung des Aristoteles für die Geschichtsschreibung, *in* Histoire et historiens dans l'antiquité (Entretiens Hardt, v 4), 1956; L. Ferrero, Tra poetica e istorica: Duride di Samo (Miscellanea Rostagni), 1963; F. W. Walbank, Polybius, 1972; L. A. Okin, Studies on Duris of Samos (University of California [Los Angeles], dissertation), 1974; R. B. Kebric, In the Shadow of Macedon: Duris of Samos, 1977.

EGINHARD. See Einhard

EINHARD (Eginhard), Frankish statesman, scholar, and Latin biographer, was born on the banks of the River Main in about A.D. 770 and educated at the monastery of Fulda, where he was a fellow pupil of Hrabanus Maurus and became the abbey's notary. In the early 790s he joined Charlemagne's Palace School, where he was taught by Alcuin, the English leader of the Carolingian scholarly revival—thus receiving the best training available in his day. He became a prominent figure at court, and one of the emperor's principal advisers and envoys. Well versed in classical writings on architecture, especially Vitruvius, Einhard helped to plan the royal palace and church at Aachen (Aix-la-Chapelle), and it was reputedly at his suggestion that in 813 Charlemagne appointed Louis the Pious as his consort in the empire. After Louis became sole ruler in the following year, Einhard remained in the highest favor and was granted extensive estates and made abbot of four monasteries. Between 817 and 822 he directed the education of Louis' eldest son Lothair, but in 830, in order to dissociate himself from court intrigues, he retired to his abbeys and built a new religious foundation at Mulenheim (afterward Seligenstadt), where he died in 840.

in' härt

His most notable work is his *Life of Charlemagne,* which remains a primary source of information concerning the emperor's career. Einhard had read all the major Roman historians in the rich Fulda library, and above all he had devoted careful study to its manuscript of Suetonius' *Caesars,* perhaps the only copy still extant in western Europe, to which all our surviving manuscripts directly or indirectly go back. As a result, Einhard's style is characterized by the deliberate imitation of entire passages of Suetonius (especially from his Life of Augustus), sometimes to the detriment of the historical facts. Moreover, Einhard shows a manifest partiality toward Charlemagne, such as Suetonius had never shown to the subjects of his biographies. In order to emphasize the glories of the Carolingian Age, he presented, by way of contrast, a too unfavorable picture of the preceding Merovingian epoch and its rulers. Einhard's ability to follow classical models of expression, instead of adopting the *lingua mixta* that was the ordinary medium for writers of his time, was exceptional. While this reliance on the classical style made for a certain artificiality, his narrative is fluent, lively, and concise and remains a unique achievement of literary expression and historical exposition for its epoch.

In general arrangement, as in style, Einhard does his best to copy Suetonius, following his example, for instance, by departing from the purely chronological pattern adopted by annalists of his own time. Einhard begins with an account of the rise of the Carolingian dynasty to power and then, after saying he knows little about Charlemagne's youth, narrates the monarch's wars at some length. Next he gives a summary of countries conquered, treaties entered into, and major buildings constructed and then, after a passing reference to the emperor's patience in the face of his brother's provocation, proceeds to detailed accounts of his wife and children, his personal appearance, and his way of life (a very Suetonian section), and his religion. The *Life* concludes with descriptions of Charlemagne's tomb and epitaph and of his death (preceded by omens), together with details of his will.

Einhard has also left a series of seventy-one letters to various persons *(Einharti Epistolae),* which, insofar as they can be dated, extend from 814 to the year of his death. This correspondence provides a remarkable picture of the Carolingian empire of the early ninth century. Many other works, some of a religious nature, have also been attributed to him, often erroneously.

EDITIONS—Life of Charlemagne and Letters: P. Jaffé, Bibliotheca Rerum Germanicarum, v 4, 1867. Life: H. W. Garrod and R. B. Mowat, 1915. *With translation:* L. Halphen, Eginhard: Vie de Charlemagne (Belles Lettres), 1923, 1938. *Translations*—S. Painter, 1960; L. Thorpe: Einhard and Notker the Stammerer: Two Lives of Charlemagne (Penguin ed.), 1969; E. S. Firchow and E. H. Zeydet (German), 1972.

ABOUT—A. Kleinclausz, Eginhard, 1942; E. Auerbach, Literatursprache und Publikum in der lateinischen Spätantike, 1958; S. Hellmann, Ausgewählte Abhandlungen, 1961; G. B. Townend, Suetonius and His Influence, *in* T. A. Dorey, ed., Latin Biography, 1967; H. Beumann, Ideengeschichtliche Studien zu Einhard. . ., reprint 1969.

EMPEDOCLES, Greek poet, philosopher, statesman, scientist, doctor, and mystic, lived perhaps from about 493 to about 433 B.C. He was a citizen of Acragas (Agrigento) in Sicily, the son of Meton, and the grandson of the Empedocles who had won the horse race in the Olympic Games of 496. Much of the biographical information about Empedocles is legendary, fictitious, and miraculous; but there is probably some truth in the assertions that he was an ardent democrat, that he broke up an oligarchic organization known as The Thousand in his city, and that he was offered the kingship and refused it. He was evidently also a notable orator, who reputedly numbered Gorgias among his pupils, and was thus described as the forerunner of Sicilian rhetoric. His status as a physician, to which he himself seems to refer in a fragmentary passage, is confirmed by numerous references in subsequent medical writings: for example, Galen, one of the most famous physicians of antiquity, believed him to have been the founder of the Sicilian medical school. He also visited the Panhellenic colony of Thurii in southeastern Italy soon after its establishment (443 B.C.).
em pe' do klēz

There are many conflicting legends about his death, including the story (repeated in Matthew Arnold's *Empedocles on Aetna*) that he threw himself down into the volcano in order to strengthen the belief that he was a god.

Empedocles wrote two poems, entitled *Purifications* and *On Nature*. Together they totaled 5,000 hexameters, but only 100 verses of the former and 350 of the latter work have survived. *Purifications* illustrates his close relationship, at his hometown of Acragas, with the Orphic religious movement, which believed in the divine origin of the soul, its fall and successive reincarnations, and its final return to the company of the gods (the same scheme is found in Pindar's second Olympian ode, written in 476 B.C. for Theron of Acragas). According to the decree of Necessity, Empedocles declares, souls must wander for many eons from their blessed homes, being born into all manner of mortal bodies. Escape from this condition can be achieved by purifications, including abstention from the flesh of animals, which are our kinfolk.

Empedocles' thinking in his other poem, *On Nature*, seems at first sight surprisingly different. The work was written as a first "pluralistic" criticism of the philosophy of Parmenides, who had declared that real being is indivisible, imperishable, and motionless. That it is imperishable and permanent Empedocles agrees, but he rejects Parmenides' belief in its immobile unity. No such unity had ever existed, he says; there are, rather, four eternally distinct forms of matter—namely, Fire, Air, Earth, and Water—which he presents in divine, mythological guise as Zeus, Hera, Aidoneus, and Nestis (and which subsequently became the standard four elements of later Greek philosophy and led on to the multiple elements of the atomists Leucippus and Democritus). All things, Empedocles continues, consist of these four irreducible, indestructible elements, in various proportions, and they occupy the entire plenum or Sphere of the Universe, in which, therefore, there is no such thing as a nonexistent void. When we say that something "is born" or "dies," all that has really taken place is a reshuffling according to which one temporary combination of these elements has been dissolved and another has taken its place.

To account for the motions in space that produce such rearrangements, Empedocles discerned the existence of two motive forces —Love (or Aphrodite), the principle of unification, and Strife (or Ares), the principle of division—and he saw the cosmic process as a cyclical development in which each of these two forces predominates in turn. Originally, under the rule of Love, there had been perfect equilibrium of the opposing elements (a concept that later remained important in Greek medicine, as well as in ethics). Then, in a second and third stage, according to Empedocles, Strife had separated the elements and achieved control, during epochs that witnessed weird and incongruous combinations, until now we have reached the fourth and final stage, in which Love returns and Strife withdraws. It is at this point that a link becomes apparent between the ostensibly very different characters of this poem and *Purifications,* with its old-fashioned doctrines of transmigration; it was probably the cycle of the soul in *Purifications* that suggested to Empedocles the cosmic cycle in *On Nature.*

The final stage of the cosmic evolution, to which we ourselves belong, provides the scene for his observations on botany, embryology, and physiology, in all of which fields he made important contributions to Greek thought, displaying a keen interest in many aspects of the biological sciences. His views on sense-perception were particularly noteworthy. Parmenides had rejected the notion, but it could scarcely be thrown away by anyone embarking, like Empedocles, on physical and cosmological observations and speculations. It seemed to him that sense-perception, like growth and nutrition, operated on the symmetrical principle of like to like: that is to say, perception occurs when an element in the body of the perceiver meets with the same element outside. According to one fragment of his writings, all things that have come into existence are continually giving off effluences, and when these effluences are of the right size to fit into the pores of the sense organ, then the required meeting takes place and perception occurs. Thus, our powers of perception (and thinking) are held to depend on the constitution of our bodies. These doctrines of pores and effluences were later taken over and adapted in the biological doctrines of Plato and Aristotle.

Empedocles also launched ambitious (though less important) theories in the field of astronomy. For example, he explained day and night by the supposition that there are two hemispheres, one bright and one dark, revolving around the spherical earth.

EDITIONS with translation—G. E. Kirk and J. E. Raven, The Presocratic Philosophers, revised ed., 1960; C. Gallavotti, Empedocle: Poema fisico e lustrale, 1975. ABOUT—W. K. C. Guthrie, History of Greek Philosophy, v 2, 1965; J. Bollack, Empédocle, v 1, 1965, v 2 and v 3, 1969; U. Hölscher, Empedokles und Hölderlin, 1965, and Anfängliches Fragen: Studien zur frühen griechischen Philosophie, 1968; K. Reinhardt, Vermächtnis der Antike, 2nd ed., 1966; D. O'Brien, Empedocles' Cosmic Cycle, 1969; U. Curi, Dagli Ionici alla crisi della physica, 1974; R. E. Allen and D. J. Furley, eds., Studies in Presocratic Philosophy, v 2, 1975; N. van der Ben, The Proem of Empedocles' Peri Physeos (Amsterdam, dissertation), 1975; R. A. Prier, Archaic Logic: Symbol and Structure in Heraclitus, Parmenides and Empedocles, 1976; J. Barnes, The Presocratic Philosophers, v 2, 1978.

ENNIUS, QUINTUS, Latin poet, was born in 239 B.C. and died in 169. His birthplace was Rudiae, a small town in Calabria lying inland from Tarentum (Taranto) and Brundusium (Brindisi). This geographical origin gave him "three hearts," as he expressed it, meaning that he was familiar with three languages: his native tongue was Oscan (though he himself was a Messapian—that is to say, probably of Illyrian origin); he was educated in Greek, probably at Tarentum (which had formerly been the Greek city of Taras); and he wrote in Latin, which was the language of the army in which he served during the Second Punic War. When that war was ending, in 204 or 203, Ennius was in Sardinia, where he attracted the attention of Cato the Elder, who brought him back to Rome. There he gained the friendship of several of the leading Romans of the time, including Scipio Africanus and Marcus Fulvius Nobilior who, while consul in 189, took him to Greece on his campaign against the

en' ni us

140

Aetolians. Five years later Nobilior's son Quintus, as one of the commissioners for establishing Roman citizen colonies, arranged for Ennius to receive citizenship (it was probably on this occasion that he assumed the name Quintus), though he avoided, it would seem, the obligation to join one of the colonies, since we continue to hear of him at Rome. The living he earned as a teacher and poet was said to have been a modest one. However, he enjoyed a considerable reputation and had close connections with other poets and dramatists—Caecilius Statius was his friend and Pacuvius his nephew.

His principal work was an epic in eighteen books, the *Annals,* of which about one-twentieth, amounting to some six hundred lines, have survived. This was a versified chronicle of Rome from mythological times down to his own day. As the title suggests, it dealt with its theme year by year. The exact arrangement of the work is uncertain, but its main lines can be reconstructed. It opened with a dream in which the spirit of Homer declared Ennius to be his own reincarnation. Book 1 told the stories of the fall of Troy and the reign of Romulus, founder of Rome; the two next books dealt with the kings who came after him. Books 4-6 narrated the history of the Republic down to and including the war with Pyrrhus of Epirus (280–275 B.C.). The First Punic War was omitted, because Naevius had dealt with it in his epic poem entitled *Bellum Punicum;* the Second Punic War, comprising Hannibal's invasion of Italy, was the subject of the eighth and ninth books. Books 10-12 dealt with the subsequent Second Macedonian War against Philip V and Rome's pronouncement of the liberation of Greece (196 B.C.). Book 13 described the war against the Seleucid monarch Antiochus III the Great and the Aetolian League. It would appear that, with the victory of Ennius' patron Fulvius Nobilior over the Aetolians—to which the poet was eyewitness—the poem was at first intended to stop, but three more books were subsequently added, the latest datable reference being to the year 179.

The *Annals,* which owed various debts to the Alexandrian tradition, struck a modern note by their novel employment in Latin of the Greek quantitative hexameter, which from that time on, despite the great differences between the two languages, became the standard meter of the epic poetry that is one of the outstanding achievements of Latin literature. Inevitably, Ennius' handling of the meter seems clumsy and archaic in comparison with his Greek forerunners or with the subsequent Latin refinements of Virgil. Yet his language is often rhythmic and expressive and above all grand—and there is grandeur, too, in his handling of the massive historical theme, although its execution lacks unity and suffers from a somewhat incongruous blend of eyewitness history and myth. Nevertheless, this achievement by the "Father of Roman Poetry," as Ennius was declared to be, attracted immense subsequent admiration, notably from Cicero who, although he admitted the crudities of Ennius' diction and meter, was nevertheless his enthusiastic admirer.

Ennius also expressed his talent, and satisfied his patrons, by translating and adapting Greek plays. His tragedies were particularly important. Fairly numerous fragments have survived, and about twenty titles: *Achilles, Ajax, Alcmeo, Alexander, The Captive Andromacha (Andromacha Aechmalotis;* and perhaps a second play about her as well), *Andromeda, Athamas, Cresphontes, Erechtheus, Hector* (exact title uncertain, perhaps two plays?), *Medea in Exile (Medea Exsul;* and probably another play about her too), *Melanippa, Nemea, Phoenix, Telamo, Telephus,* and *Thyestes* (his last work, produced in 169).

A medieval glossary recorded that very many or most *(plurimae)* of the Greek tragedies translated or adapted by Ennius were plays of Euripides but that some *(nonnullae)* of his adaptations were based on plays by Euripides' little known contemporary Aristarchus of Tegea. We learn from the scholar Verrius Flaccus that Ennius' *Achilles* came from Aristarchus of Tegea, whose play thus becomes the only identifiable tragedy, other than those by Aeschylus, Sophocles, and Euripides that we know for certain to have been rendered into Latin. Other plays by Ennius—the *Ajax, Eumenides, Hector, Nemea,* and *Telamo,*—also do not seem to come from Euripidean originals. Probably

some of them, notably the *Eumenides,* were taken from Aeschylus. Ennius seems to have retained the structure of his Greek originals, and sometimes—for example, in the *Medea,* —he translated with a fair measure of exactness. On other occasions, however, he deviated from them quite considerably, even borrowing and inserting sections adapted from other tragedies as he went along. Moreover, his tone differs considerably from that of his models, replacing the more relaxed Greek by a rather high-flown formality, strong in rhetoric and pathos.

In addition to translations and adaptations of Greek drama, Ennius wrote original plays of his own, including one or more tragedies devoted to Roman themes, known as *fabulae praetextae* from the Roman purple-fringed costume that the principal characters wore. One such play was the *Sabinae,* which dealt with the legend of the rape of the Sabine women. It also appears that the *Ambracia* was a composition of the same Roman type. It presumably dealt with Fulvius Nobilior's campaign in Aetolia, which included his capture of the city after which the play was named. Ennius also wrote comedies, but apparently with less success; we know of two titles, but only four separate lines have survived.

His satire—*Satura* or *Saturae,* that is to say "Miscellanies"—inaugurated a kind of Latin literature that was to have a great future, though Ennius' own compositions evidently lacked the ferocious element subsequently introduced by Lucilius (d. 102/101). Written in four books, of which some seventy lines in a variety of meters survive, they treat a number of different subjects. The fragments that have come down to us deal (sometimes in dialogue) with the poet's personal habits and with ethical questions; one excerpt tells the fable of the crested lark and her young; another recounts a contest between Life and Death.

Ennius once remarked jokingly that he could only write poetry when he had gout, and indeed going out to dinner is one of his themes. Following the example of Archestratus of Gela, a Greek poet of the fourth century B.C., he wrote a separate *Art of Dining (Hedyphagetica)* in hexameters; the surviving fragment explains where to get the best fish of various kinds. Another poem was his *Sota,* named after the third century B.C. poet Sotades of Maronea, though fragments that are preserved do not reflect the indecency that was a feature of Sotades' verse.

Among Ennius' other writings was a panegyric in mixed meters on Scipio Africanus; a translation of a philosophical poem wrongly ascribed to the fifth century Sicilian poet-philosopher Epicharmus; and a philosophical poem of his own, the *Precepts (Protrepticon or Praecepta).* He also produced a prose work adapting the *Sacred Scripture (Hiera Anagraphe),* a famous Greek poem of Euhemerus (c. 300 B.C.) on the origin and nature of the gods. According to Euhemerus, the gods had originally been human beings, and it is remarkable to note, from the numerous fragments that have survived, that Ennius extended this notion of human origin to Jupiter, the supreme deity of the Roman state. It is one of our gravest losses that so relatively little of his vast, varied, and influential output has survived.

EDITIONS with translation—E. H. Warmington, Remains of Old Latin (Loeb ed.), 1935, 1956; J. Lembke, Bronze and Iron, 1973 (selections). Editions of Annals: L. Valmaggi, 1900; E. M. Steuart, 1925, 1945. Tragic fragments: H. D. Jocelyn, The Tragedies of Ennius, 1967.
ABOUT—S. Mariotti, Lezioni zu Ennio, 1951; O. Skutsch, The Annals of Quintus Ennius, 1953, *and* Studia Enniana, 1968; U. Knoche, Roman Satire, 1964; W. Krenkel, ed., Römische Satire, 1966; W. Beare, The Roman Stage, 3rd ed. revised, 1969; Ennius (Entretiens Hardt, v 17), 1972; M. Coffey, Roman Satire, 1976.

EPHORUS, Greek historian, lived from about 405 to 330 B.C. He was born at Cyme (Nemrutköy) in Aeolis (western Asia Minor) and was taught by Isocrates.

His *Histories* were of a comprehensive character, and Polybius, in the second century B.C., praised them as the first attempt at a universal history ever to be made—universal in that it sought to give an account of the Greek world from its earliest beginnings down to the writer's own time. Ephorus was also the earliest historian to divide his work into books, of which there were twenty-nine, preceded by a preface. As his starting point

e′ fō rus

142

he chose the return of the sons of Heracles to the Peloponnese, on the grounds that, as he overoptimistically believed, it was at this point that verifiable fact begins. The twenty-ninth book concluded with the siege of Perinthus by Philip II of Macedonia in 341 B.C.: Ephorus' son Demophilus added a thirtieth book, concerned largely with the Sacred War of 356–346.

Our information about Ephorus derives mainly from the fact that he was used as a principal source by Diodorus Siculus, the historian of the first century B.C., who followed him carefully, though with difficulty, for whereas Ephorus for the most part divided his material under various cities and countries (with digressions on geographical matters, to which his fourth and fifth books were devoted), Diodorus sought to amend this method to an annalistic, year by year treatment, thus introducing chronological errors.

Ephorus did make attempts to distinguish between myth and historical fact. Although these attempts were not invariably successful, he was at least duly suspicious of the apparently circumstantial detail with which mythical material had often been presented by his predecessors. Yet, at the same time, he often sacrificed veracity to rhetorical effect, or to his own personal opinions. Ephorus conformed with the tendency of Thucydides and Xenophon to concentrate on warfare; but Polybius, while admiring his accounts of fighting at sea, censured his descriptions of the land battles of Leuctra (371) and Mantinea (362) as displaying ignorance of military operations on land.

Ephorus combined the pan-Hellenism of Isocrates, which taught him the superiority of Greeks over barbarians, with the doctrine of Socrates and Plato that political judgments must be guided by morality; and he made use of the rhetorical powers he had acquired from Isocrates to glorify the supposed virtues of historical figures and exaggerate their vices. He consulted numerous earlier writers, but without much critical acumen; for example, the source he used for his narrative of the fifty years between the Persian and Peloponnesian wars was excessively pro-Athenian. Nevertheless, with the single exception of Xenophon, Ephorus was the most important historian of the fourth century B.C. His narrative was sober and rather colorless—Isocrates was believed to have said that, whereas his other pupil Theopompus needed the rein, Ephorus needed the spur—but perhaps it was this very lack of a markedly personal flavor, whether for praise or blame, which gained the confidence of later historians, because it seemed in conformity with the aims that universal history ought to fulfill. In any event, his *Histories* attained great and long-lasting popularity. Their extensive use by Diodorus Siculus is only one of the testimonies to this; later on, those who drew upon them included Strabo and Plutarch.

Ephorus wrote a number of other works as well, including an essay on style and a study of the history and antiquities of his native Cyme. Also attributed to him was a two-book treatise *On Discoveries* that sought to satisfy the then-popular demand for information on a variety of exciting subjects. However, this may have been a collection of excerpts from his *Histories* rather than a separate work on its own account.

EDITIONS—F. Jacoby, Die Fragmente der griechischen Historiker, 2a, 70.
ABOUT—G. L. Barber, The Historian Ephorus, 1935 (with bibliography); G. T. Griffith *in* Fifty Years (and Twelve) of Classical Scholarship, 1968 (bibliography of recent articles); F. W. Walbank, Polybius, 1972; A. Momigliano, Quinto contributo alla storia degli studi classici, 1976.

EPICHARMUS, Greek comic poet, was a Sicilian whose earliest activity can be ascribed to the last years of the sixth century B.C. or the first quarter of the fifth. Though he was said to have been born in Cos, he resided at Syracuse, with whose king Hiero I (478–467/6) many anecdotes associated him. He may still have been alive as late as 460; he was famous in antiquity for his longevity.

He wrote plays in the Sicilian Doric dialect of which a few fragments survive; thirty-seven of their titles, too, are known to us, partly from the recently discovered remains of a catalog and partly from other papyri, which have significantly increased our

e pi kär' mus

knowledge of his work. Titles and fragments alike testify to a most varied dramatic output. Epicharmus' plays may have been staged in connection with local festivals of the goddesses Artemis and Demeter; yet, somewhat strangely to our ideas, burlesques of myths evidently played an important part in these works. Odysseus is a favorite figure of Epicharmus: he wrote plays entitled *Odysseus Shipwrecked (nauagos)* and *Odysseus the Shirker (automolos)*. The latter work dealt with the hero's spying expedition to Troy and described how he tried to evade this hazardous task. In one passage, shown by lately discovered fragments to form part of a dialogue, he seems to be consulting a companion in order to devise a suitable explanation as to why the enterprise had failed. Another favorite character of Epicharmus is Heracles, who plays a prominent part in this playwright's mythological travesties: he is portrayed as a clumsy figure with prodigious gifts for sex, eating, and drinking; the *Marriage of Hebe* (in which Poseidon appears as a fishmonger), includes lists of the gastronomic delicacies Heracles enjoyed, and an eyewitness in the *Busiris* (or *Busirides*) tells with astonishment of Heracles' noisy appreciation of his food. Further titles are *Heracles' Journey to Fetch the Girdle of Hippolytus* and *Heracles' Visit to Pholus*.

A play called *Male and Female Reason* or *Mr. Argument and His Wife (Logos and Logina)* is shown by new fragments to belong to the same category of mythological plays. Papyrological discoveries have also revealed a *Medea;* and this makes Epicharmus the third poet known to have written a comedy on this theme, the others being a fellow Sicilian, Dinolochus, and Rhinthon of Taras. A papyrus has also preserved part of Epicharmus' *Prometheus and Pyrrha,* including a portion of a dialogue between Pyrrha and Deucalion about the ark that was to rescue them from the flood. It has been deduced from this fragment (and from a passage in another of Epicharmus' plays, the *Amycus*) that he brought three actors onto the stage, but this remains uncertain. It is also unknown whether his plays required a chorus, though a positive answer, at least as far as some of them are concerned, is

143

suggested by titles such as *The Victory Celebration (Epinikios)* and *The Festival (Heorta),* and perhaps also by plural titles such as *Envoys (Thearoi), Muses, Dionysoi, Dancers (Choreuontes), Revelers (Komastai;* its alternative name was the *Hephaestus), Sirens, Islands, Trojans, Persians,* and *Bacchants.* The two last-named look respectively like parodies of Aeschylus (whose tragedy the *Persians* was produced in Sicily) and Euripides, just as Epicharmus' *Philoctetes* may be a burlesque of Sophocles' play of that name. The use of set debates or altercations such as occur in *Earth and Sea* (in which Earth and Sea apparently argue over who is the richer) and the employment of such stock characters as the rustic in *The Rustic (Agroikos),* the parasite in *Hope or Wealth,* and braggarts and pedants in other pieces, offer analogies with Attic comedy, though there is no evidence that Epicharmus had any direct connection with this.

A lively and witty dramatist and a poet of colorful grace and considerable rhetorical skill, he used not only a wide variety of subjects but also a number of different meters. His tone, too, was equally varied. Heracles is presented in a spirit of ribald fun (not so obscene as in later Athenian comedy); a good deal is borrowed from the Doric popular farces of Sicily and from the mimes that were likewise so greatly favored in the Greek west; and Epicharmus speaks respectfully of a Sicilian predecessor, Aristoxenus of Selinus. But there are echoes of the ancient epic, too, and a humorous infusion of philosophy as well: for example, when a debtor and creditor try to cheat one another by asserting that they are not the same men as they were yesterday, Heraclitus' doctrine of flux is invoked. Moreover, Epicharmus indulges freely in philosophical moralizing, conveyed in concise, epigrammatical maxims. Because of his great prestige and influence, these maxims were later brought together into collections, so that the door was opened to extensive forgery. As a result, many philosophical and semi-scientific writings that included or extensively embroidered upon his genuine adages, came to be attributed to Epicharmus; indeed, one such, a collection of *Pseudepicharmeia* was already recognized as unauthentic as early as

the fourth century B.C. It was even claimed that Plato, who expressed a high opinion of Epicharmus, derived much material from him, but the allegedly Epicharmian passages in Plato seem to have been based on material composed later than the Sicilian poet's time. Ancient authorities also attributed works on medicine to Epicharmus, and Plutarch later reported a tradition, which may be true, that he became a follower of Pythagoras but was at odds with another philosopher, Xenophanes.

EDITIONS—G. Kaibel, Comicorum Graecorum Fragmenta, v 1, 1899; A. Olivieri, Frammenti della commedia greca e del mimo nella Sicilia e nella Magna Grecia, v 1, 1930.
ABOUT—A. W. Pickard-Cambridge, Dithyramb, Tragedy and Comedy, 2nd ed. (revised by T. B. L. Webster), 1962; L. Berk, Epicharmus, 1964.

EPICTETUS. See Arrian

EPICURUS, Greek philosopher and natural scientist, was born in 341 and died in 270 B.C. His birthplace was on the island of Samos, where his father, Neocles, an Athenian immigrant, taught in a school. His mother's name was Chaerestrate. As a boy, he was taught by the Platonist Pamphilus. In 323 he went to Athens, where he studied at the Academy, but soon afterward he rejoined his family, which in the meantime had moved from Samos to Colophon in Ionia (western Asia Minor). At this time or earlier, Epicurus' teacher was Nausiphanes of Teos (born c. 360 B.C.), who instructed him in the atomic philosophy of Democritus of Abdera. In 309 Epicurus himself went to teach at Mitylene on the island of Lesbos, and from there he moved to Lampsacus on the Hellespont (Dardanelles). Then in about 306 he settled at Athens, where he founded a teaching center of his own, giving his lectures in the Gardens *(Kepoi)* that gave the future Epicurean school its name. Since his students included women as well as men, the establishment attracted scandalous stories, but Epicurus earned great admiration for his exceptionally kind character. Apart from
e pi ku̅' rus

EPICURUS

occasional visits to Asia Minor, he remained at Athens until his death, at which time he left the Gardens and school in his will to Hermarchus of Mitylene.

Epicurus was credited by Diogenes Laertius (third century A.D.) with the authorship of three hundred rolls or volumes. Most of these are lost, but Diogenes' *History of the Philosophers* has preserved two of his open letters addressed to disciples—Herodotus (a summary of Epicurus' philosophy of nature) and Menoeceus (an elementary survey of his moral teaching)—and these constitute valuable summaries of the most significant parts of Epicurean doctrine. We also have a collection of forty short statements by Epicurus, known as the *Principal Doctrines* or *Sovereign Maxims (Kuriai Doxaí)*, which were intended as a practical manual of guidance for the benefit of those who had embraced the Epicurean doctrines. The *Vatican Sayings* or *Gnomologium Vaticanum* (so called because the work was found on a Vatican manuscript in 1888) comprises eighty-one similar short sayings. A large number of fragments from Epicurus' other works have also survived; some of them are of considerable importance. They include passages from his thirty-seven-book treatise *On Nature,* preserved on badly mutilated papyri from Herculaneum. However, our knowledge and appreciation of Epicurus' system mainly depends on the Latin poem of Lucretius *(De Rerum Natura),* which, al-

though written more than two centuries later, appears to add very little philosophical doctrine to what had actually been taught by Epicurus himself.

Like his contemporary Zeno, the founder of Stoicism, Epicurus is a thoroughgoing materialist in that he sees only material "bodies" as substantially real and capable both of acting themselves and of causing activity in other entities. In common with other Hellenistic philosophers, his principal aim is the search for imperturbability *(ataraxia),* the asset that renders the wise man entirely independent of the vicissitudes of fortune and, indeed, of all forces outside himself. Yet while the Stoics sought this ideal by self-identification with divine providence, Epicurus denied the existence of any such providence or fate and interpreted the sought-after tranquillity in a negative sense, as consisting of freedom from pain or trouble. It seemed to Epicurus that the worst of all pains and troubles was fear, and that the worst of all fears was the fear of death and of what might happen thereafter.

Epicurus agreed with the Stoics, however, in dividing philosophy into three parts: Canonic, Physics, and Ethics. The Canonic was concerned with the canons or criteria of truth: one of these, he maintains strongly, is sensation, which he regards as completely trustworthy (error only entering in when we make judgments about what our senses show us). His Physics (in which psychology and theology were included) was a repetition of the Atomism of the Greek philosopher-scientists of the fifth century B.C. Leucippus and Democritus, who had sought to demonstrate that all things consist of atoms moving perpetually in the void, in a multiplicity of worlds (in contrast with the unique divine universe of the Stoics). Epicurus departed from these older atomists when he introduced the new and remarkable doctrine of the Swerve *(parenklisis;* Latin, *clinamen).* According to this view, although the atoms of which the universe is composed normally fall downward in a straight line, under the impetus of their weight they sometimes act otherwise, swerving and slanting aside from their direct downward fall in an arbitrary, unpredictable, and random fashion. This was Epicurus' way of insuring

145

against the idea that everything happens by deterministic, ineluctable, rigidly mechanical necessity, for since the atoms, when they swerve, must inevitably collide with others, it follows that existence depends, in part, on undetermined movements. Consequently, actions of animals, including human beings, are not determined wholly by their genetic constitution and environment. In other words, free will can exist, and human actions can be prompted by its directions.

Epicurus' theology also appears to be original. In spite of his eagerness to exclude divine activity from the universe, he believed that the gods exist—on the grounds that men and women have distinct pictures of them in their minds and, when they are asleep, frequently see them in dreams. Since, however, these deities take no part in the affairs of the universe, he envisages them as living calmly in the serene spaces between the worlds, neither troubling human beings nor suffering trouble themselves.

One of the criteria of truth laid down by Epicurus—and indeed the ultimate criterion of his ethical system—consisted of feelings of pleasure and pain; it is these, he argued, that provide the test by which we determine what is good for us and what is bad. However, since absolute freedom from pain and unbroken tranquillity are what Epicurus understood by pleasure, he and his true followers lived a life of asceticism based on the reduction of their desires to the absolute minimum. This is in strange contrast to what is commonly understood by Epicureanism. The term owes its pejorative interpretation to the unpopularity and limited appeal of Epicurus' doctrines in the ancient world, where they ran counter to the development of later pagan religious thought, appealing only to a refined, exclusive minority who did not go out into the world but stayed in seclusion and felt for their austere master a devotion that amounted to reverence. In spite of the extraordinarily brilliant expression of Epicureanism by Lucretius, it was not until the seventeenth century that its doctrines became a serious candidate for the attention of philosophers.

(For further discussion of Epicureanism see the sketches on Diogenes Laertius and Lucretius.)

146

WORKS—Writings wrongly or dubiously ascribed to Epicurus include a letter to his pupil Pythocles on meteorology that is probably by a later member of the Epicurean school.

EDITIONS—H. Usener, Epicurea, 1887; C. Diano, Epicurus: Ethica et Epistulae, 2nd ed., 1974; J. Bollack, La pensée du plaisir: Épicure: Textes moraux, commentaires, 1975. With translation: C. Bailey, Epicurus: The Extant Remains, 1926; G. K. Strodach, The Philosophy of Epicurus, 1963; K. M. Geer, Letters, Doctrines and Parallel Passages, 1963; K. M. Geer, Letters, Principal Doctrines and Vatican Sayings, 1964; J. Bollack, M. Bollack, H. Wismann, La lettre d'Épicure, 1971; G. Arrighetti, Epicurus: Opere (Italian), revised ed., 1973.

ABOUT—E. Bignone, L'Aristotele perduto e la formazione filosofica di Epicuro, 1936; W. Schmid, Epikurs Kritik der platonischen Elementenlehre, 1936; O. Gigon, Epikur: Von der Überwindung der Furcht, 1949; N. W. De Witt, Epicurus and His Philosophy, 1954; A. J. Festugière, Epicurus and His Gods, 1956; P. Merlan, Studies in Epicurus and Aristotle, 1960; C. Bailey, The Greek Atomists and Epicurus, 2nd ed., 1964; B. Farrington, The Faith of Epicurus, 1967; D. J. Furley, Two Studies in the Greek Atomists, 1967; G. A. Panichas, Epicurus, 1967; P. Boyancé, Epicure, 1969; R. Müller, Die epikureische Gesellschaftstheorie, 1972; J. M. Rist, Epicurus: An Introduction, 1972, reprint 1977; D. Konstan, Some Aspects of Epicurean Psychology, 1973; D. Lemke, Die Theologie Epikurs, 1973; A. Manuwald, Die Prolepsislehre Epikurs, 1973; C. Diano, Scritti epicurei, 1974; A. A. Long, Hellenistic Philosophy, 1974; D. Pesce, Saggio su Epicuro, 1974; G. Rodis-Lewis, Épicure et son école, 1975; J. H. Nichols, Epicurean Political Philosophy, 1976; G. Reale, Storia della filosofia antica, v 3, 1976; J. Bollack and A. Laks, eds., Études sur l'épicurisme antique, 1977; J. Fallot, Il piacere e la morte nella filosofia di Epicuro, 1977; V. Goldschmidt, La doctrine d'Épicure et le droit, 1977.

ERASISTRATUS, Greek scientific and medical researcher, lived in the first half of the third century B.C. His birthplace was Iulis on the island of Ceos, but he lived in Alexandria, where he was a contemporary of another leading physician, Herophilus of Chalcedon. Both these scholars applied themselves particularly to the study of anatomy. Erasistratus, who preferred research to medical practice and pursued it indefatigably, displayed a special interest in comparative anatomy, on which he wrote books that were still read in the fourth century A.D. but have now disappeared. As a result of post mortem dissections, he was able to point to changes in the body due to disease. His physiological studies included investigation

e rà si' strà tus

into bodily growth and the process of digestion. Although careful not to neglect local variations of illnesses and the constitutions of individual patients, he concluded that all unhealthy conditions were due to digestive failures and to the "plethora" or overrepletion of the body that such failures caused. In consequence, he attached great importance to diet. Purgation, however, (like bloodletting) seemed to him to possess little therapeutic value.

Like Herophilus, he arrived at a clear distinction between the sensory and motor nerves. He utilized the concept of *pneuma*, the life-principle and motive-force, an idea that he adapted, indirectly, from pre-Socratic thinkers such as Empedocles. However, his notion that the arteries, as channels of *pneuma*, were separate from the blood-carrying veins delayed the discovery of the circulation of the blood.

Erasistratus had connections with the Peripatetic (Aristotelian) school through the physicians Metrodorus of Cnidus—who was his teacher—and (probably) Diocles of Carystus, as well as through Strato of Lampsacus who headed the school after Theophrastus (d. 287 B.C.).

EDITIONS—R. Fuchs, Erasistratea, 1892. *With translation:* J. F. Dobson (Proceedings of the Royal Society of Medicine, History of Medicine Section), 1927.
ABOUT—G. Spanopoulos, Erasistratos: Der Arzt und Forscher (Abhandlungen zur Geschichte der Medizin und Naturwissenschaft, v 32), 1939; L. Edelstein, Ancient Medicine, 1967; E. D. Phillips, Greek Medicine, 1974.

ERATOSTHENES, Greek polymath and poet, was born at Cyrene in about 275 B.C. (or a little earlier), and died in 194. He studied grammar at Alexandria and philosophy at Athens, where he came under the influence first of Zeno (founder of Stoicism) and then of Ariston of Chios (who formed an independent branch of the Stoic school leaning toward Cynic views) and Arcesilaus of Pitane (head of the Platonic Academy). In 246, at the invitation of King Ptolemy III Euergetes of Egypt, he became tutor to the king's family and the successor of Apollonius Rhodius as director of the Alexandrian

r ă tos′ thə nēz

library. Toward the end of his life he suffered from ophthalmia and became blind, and when he died it was said that he had starved himself to death.

Alexandrian specialists called him *beta,* probably meaning not so much that he was second-rate but that he did not become the leading authority in any field. However, he received another, more flattering, contemporary description, that of *pentathlos* (all-rounder), because he was the most versatile scholar of his age. Indeed, he took the whole of knowledge as his province, and actually invented the term *philologos* to describe himself, indicating not that he was a philologist in the modern sense but that his purpose was to handle and impart and elucidate facts of every kind.

Although not a mathematician of the highest caliber, Eratosthenes wrote works on arithmetic and geometry, including the *Duplication of the Cube* and *On Prime Numbers.* In *Platonicus,* he endeavored to arrive at mathematical definitions, in addition to establishing principles for music. His greatest achievement, however, was in the field of geography. In his treatise *On the Measurement of the Earth,* which shows him as a pioneer—indeed, the creator—of mathematical geography, he presents a calculation of the circumference of the earth that seems to have been impressively accurate, (although we do not know for certain the precise size of the *stadian,* the unit on which he based his conclusions). His calculations of the magnitude and distance of the sun and moon, are, however, less successful. Another of his contributions to astronomy was said to have been the compilation of the *Catasterismi,* a catalog of stars (including an account of their legendary origins). Of this last work we possess only an altered excerpt.

In the three books of his *Geographica* Eratosthenes gave a brief account of the history of the subject, dealing with it from the mathematical, physical, and ethnographical viewpoints alike. He was the first systematic exponent of geography—and may even have invented the term. His work was written in the new scientific spirit of his age, and with him the science of geography immediately reached a remarkably high standard, which it failed to retain for long; indeed, his praiseworthy rejection of all attempts to trace Odysseus' later wanderings is still not always listened to today. The great mathematician-astronomer Archimedes (d. 212 B.C.) evidently considered Eratosthenes his equal; he was often quoted by subsequent geographers, though not invariably with approval.

Another outstanding feat was his compilation the *Chronographies,* of which only a few fragments remain today. This treatise represented the first scientific attempt to determine the dates of political and literary events, from the Trojan War onward. Thus, Eratosthenes was virtually the inventor of scientific chronology, constructing a framework that Apollodorus of Athens could elaborate in the following century and that continued to prove its effectiveness through subsequent years. Among his other works were essays of a philosophical (perhaps ethical) nature, including a history of philosophy, but nothing is known of them. He also wrote on literary criticism, to which his major contribution was a study, *On Ancient Comedy,* in at least twelve books, following and fertilizing the researches of other writers on this subject—notably Lycophron of Chalcis and Alexander the Aetolian. This work dealt with etymological, historical, and antiquarian aspects of the comic drama, in addition to questions of authorship and theatrical production.

Eratosthenes also composed poems, of which fragments have survived. His short hexameter epic *Hesiod* (or *Anterinys,* from *Erinys,* Fury) describes the death of that poet and the punishment of his murderers. Another poem of the same genre, the *Hermes,* narrates the birth of the god, his exploits as a youth, and his ascent to the heavenly planets, which brought about the arrangement of the cosmos. The *Erigone,* written in the elegiac meter, tells the legend of the Attic peasant Icarius who was given the vine by Dionysus but then died at the hands of drunken peasants, whereupon his daughter Erigone, coming upon his corpse, hanged herself. As a poet Eratosthenes followed the precedent of Callimachus, but he showed little of the originality of his prose works.

EDITIONS—E. Hiller, Eratosthenis Carminum Reliquiae, 1872; E. H. Berger, Die geographischen Fragmente des Eratosthenes, 1880; I. Thomas, Greek Mathematical Works (Loeb ed.), v 1, 1939; F. Jacoby, Die Fragmente der griechischen Historiker, II b, 241. ABOUT—R. Pfeiffer, History of Classical Scholarship, v 1, 1968; P. M. Fraser, Eratosthenes of Cyrene (Proceedings of the British Academy, v 56), 1971.

ERIGENA (or **ERIUGENA), JOHN SCOTUS,** theologian, philosopher, and Latin writer, was born in about A.D. 810 and died in 877. He came from Ireland (Erin, hence his names Erigena and Scotus, since the Irish were at this time known as Scots). It was said, perhaps rightly, that as a young man John Scotus traveled in the east, where he obtained a knowledge of Greek, Chaldaean, and Arabic. In about 851 he was director of the palace school at the court of Charles II the Bald, king of the western Franks, who later became Holy Roman Emperor (875).

John addressed Greek verses to the king, and also wrote Latin poems. Moreover, at Charles's request, he translated the famous mystical works that had appeared in c. A.D. 500 under the pseudonym of Dionysius the Areopagite; John's versions acquainted the Christian west with many Neoplatonist beliefs. He also translated treatises by the eminent fourth century rhetorician Gregory of Nyssa and the seventh century theologian Maximus the Confessor and compiled commentaries on the prologue of St. John's Gospel and the *Opuscula Sacra* of Boethius, Roman philosophical and theological writer (c. A.D. 480–524).

John took part in the theological quarrels centering around the doctrines of the German Benedictine monk Gottschalk concerning predestination, and at the request of Archbishop Hincmar of Reims wrote a work entitled *On Predestination* (851), which was condemned, however, at the councils of Valence (855) and Langres (859). Subsequently, he produced his principal work entitled *On the Division of Nature,* a lengthy treatise that classifies the totality of things under four heads: nature uncreated and creating; nature created creating; nature created but not creating; and nature neither

e rij' e nà

created nor creating. The first and fourth are God, the second and third show creatures in their intelligible and sensible modes of existence. To John, since human beings are made in God's image, their innermost being shares in God's unknowability; they are the notion that God has of them, and the "link of the universe," since everything has been created in them and their idea. He sees creation and redemption as the two poles of the mighty human drama.

Although a layman, John was the outstanding theologian of his age, and unusually learned for those times. He was the greatest thinker since Boethius, the greatest theologian since Augustine, and the first important name in medieval western philosophy.

EDITIONS—J. P. Migne, Patrologia Latina, v 122. *Translations*—De Imagine of Gregory of Nyssa, 1965; I. P. Sheldon-Williams and L. Bieler, De Divisione Naturae, 1968.
ABOUT—H. Bett, Johannes Scotus Erigena, 1929; M. Cappuyns, Jean Scot Erigène, 1933; G. Bonafede, Saggi sul pensiero di Scoto Eriugena, 1950; M. dal Pra, Scoto Eriugena, 1951; P. Mazzarella, Il pensiero di Giovanni Scoto Eriugena, 1957; T. Gregory, Giovanni Scoto Eriugena, 1963; J. J. O'Meara, Eriugena, 1964, *and* (with L. Bieler, as eds.) The Mind of Eriugena (Dublin Colloquium, 1970) [1973]; B. Stock, The Philosophical Anthropology of Johannes Scottus Eriugena, 1967; Jean Scot Erigène et l'histoire de la philosophie (Colloque Laon), 1977; S. Gersh, From Iamblichus to Eriugena, 1978.

ERINNA, Greek poet, came from Telos, a small island belonging to Rhodes. According to the Suda (Suidas) dictionary (tenth century A.D.), she belonged to the time of Sappho (who died in the earlier part of the sixth century B.C.). But it is now widely agreed that Erinna lived instead in the late fourth or early third century B.C., since her work shows technical affinities with writers such as Theocritus (died c. 260); and her poems were apparently edited by Theocritus' contemporary Asclepiades of Samos.

Shortly before her death at about the age of nineteen, she wrote a poem known (in later times, though not apparently by herself) as the *Distaff (Elakate)*. In it she laments her friend Baucis, who had married

e rin′ nà

and then died. Minor passages of this piece, surviving from quotations, have recently been augmented by a papyrus of the first century B.C. that brings the total number of extant lines up to approximately three hundred. Many of them have only survived in a severely mutilated condition. Nevertheless, they are sufficient to reveal the skill and tenderness with which Erinna evokes the games and tasks and childish sorrows the two girls had shared. She shows a fondness for the depiction of little scenes, somewhat in the manner of the Hellenistic miniature epic.

Three other poems of her authorship were included in Meleager's anthology *The Garland*. Two are funeral epigrams in memory of Baucis, and the other praises a portrait painting of a girl.

WORKS—A lost poem lamenting the death of a friend's pet cicada and grasshopper was mentioned by Pliny the Elder. A poem wishing Baucis a successful journey (a form of poetry known as the Propempticon, or Escort), from which lines have survived, is unauthentic.
EDITIONS—E. Diehl, Anthologia Lyrica Graeca, v 1, 3rd ed., 1949; D. Page, Epigrammata Graeca, 1976.
ABOUT—K. Latte, Erinna (Nachrichten der Akademie, Göttingen, philologische-historische Klasse), 1953; F. Scheidtweiler, Erinnas Klage um Baucis (Philologus, v 100), 1956.

EUCLID, Greek mathematician of unknown origin, lived and taught at Alexandria in the time of King Ptolemy I (306–283 B.C.). He was the author of a great mathematical textbook, *Elements (Stoicheia),* in thirteen books. Books 1-6 are on plane geometry, 7-9 on the theory of numbers, 10 on irrational numbers, 11-13 on solid geometry. (Books 14 and 15 are by Hypsicles and a pupil of Isidore of Seville, respectively.) For this work Euclid drew upon scholars who had written works with the same title before him (Hippocrates of Chios, Eudoxus of Cnidus, Leon, Theudius of Magnesia) and made use of other mathematicians as well, especially Theaetetus. However, he added many features on his own account and introduced a novel arrangement, inventing fresh proofs when the earlier ones were no longer appropriate to his new plan. King Ptolemy was said to have

yū′ klid

protested about the length and difficulty of the work, to which Euclid supposedly replied that there could be a royal road in Egypt but not in geometry.

It is doubtful whether he was a mathematician of the same supreme quality as his younger contemporary Archimedes; Euclid's work is only first class when he has first-class sources at his disposal. However, he was a superlative teacher and expounder of mathematics, and his *Elements* have remained in use, almost unchanged, for more than two thousand years. Commentaries on the work were already being written in ancient times, by Hero and Pappus of Alexandria and by Simplicius and Proclus (whose notes on Book I are the most valuable of all). A revised version of the work published in c. A.D. 364 by the Platonist Theon of Alexandria, with textual amendments and some additions, became the basis of all subsequent texts until a better manuscript came to light in the early years of the nineteenth century. The *Elements* was frequently translated, into all the major languages, starting with Arabic (first done for Harun-al-Rashid, caliph of Bagdad, 786–809), Latin (initially from the Arabic, in the twelfth century), and Hebrew; the earliest European translation from the Greek appeared at Venice in 1505 and the earliest printed version, at Basel in 1533.

Euclid also wrote other works on elementary and higher geometry. In the former category is his *Data (Dedomena)*, which includes ninety-four propositions and demonstrates that, if certain elements in a figure are given, then other things, too, can be determined. The work is also significant for the development of algebra. A book *On Divisions (of Figures)*—in which the proofs of all but four of the propositions are missing—is extant only in an Arabic translation and a Latin adaptation. Another treatise, *On Fallacies (Pseudaria)*, apparently designed to warn beginners against various types of fallacious geometrical arguments, has not survived. In the field of higher geometry there are other lost works, including *Porisms (Porismata)* (perhaps the usual porism was "to prove that it is possible to find a point with such and such a property or a straight line on which lie all the points that satisfy

given conditions"—T. L. Heath), *Surface-Loci* (loci on or consisting of surfaces) in two books, and *Conics* (in four books later revised by Apollonius of Perge, who studied with Euclid's pupils).

Euclid's *Phaenomena,* an essay on the geometry of the sphere, designed for use by astronomers, is, however, still extant; and we have his *Optica* as well. (The *Catoptrica* is not by him but of a later date.) He also wrote on the elements of music: the *Sectio Canonis,* reproducing the Pythagorean theory of music together with some later additions, contains excerpts from his work in this field. (The author of the *Introductio Harmonica,* however, is not Euclid but Cleonides, a pupil of Aristoxenus.)

EDITIONS—Texts (with Latin translation), *in* I. L. Heiberg and H. Menge (Teubner ed.), 8 vols., 1883–1916; I. L. Heiberg and E. S. Stamatis, Elementa, revised ed., 1969–77. For other editions *see* A. Lesky, A History of Greek Literature, 1966, p 790, notes 3 and 4, *and* Oxford Classical Dictionary, 2nd ed., 1970, p 413. *With translation:* T. L. Heath, Elements, 2nd ed., 1925, reprinted 1956; I. Thomas, Greek Mathematical Works (Loeb ed.), 1939–41; J. Itard, Les livres arithmétiques d'Euclide, 1961; C. Thaer, Data (German), 1962; P. ver Eecke, L'optique et La catoptrique, 1938, reprint 1958. ABOUT—T. L. Heath, History of Greek Mathematics, v 1, 1921; A. Lejeune, Euclide et Ptolemée, 1948; O. Neugebauer, The Exact Sciences in Antiquity, 2nd ed., 1957; R. J. Forbes and E. J. Dijksterhuis, A History of Science and Technology, v 1, 1963; G. E. R. Lloyd, Greek Science After Aristotle, 1973.

EUCRATES. See John Moschus

EUDOXUS, Greek mathematician, astronomer, and geographer, was born in about 390 B.C. (or slightly earlier) and died in the 340s. His birthplace was Cnidus (near Reṣadiye) in southwestern Asia Minor. He was stated to have been a pupil of Archytas of Taras (Taranto) in geometry and of Philistion of Locri Epizephyrii in medicine, though this is uncertain, and it was also supposed that as a young man he was taught by Plato. At all events, Eudoxus seems to have come to Athens at the age of about twenty-three and then set out to travel. At some

yū dok′ sus

stage he went to Egypt, studying astronomy with the priests; he also visited the court of King Mausolus of Halicarnassus, near his hometown; and he founded a school of his own at Cyzicus (northwestern Asia Minor). Either before or after these events he lectured in the Platonic Academy at Athens, after which he returned to Cnidus and drew up laws for the city.

His contribution to mathematics was very important, largely because he gave a novel and useful definition of proportion that played a large part in ensuring that geometry would take the lead among mathematical subjects in Greece. Eudoxus also invented the method of approach to the limit (misleadingly described as the "method of exhaustion") that was adopted as the regular way of dealing with problems involving infinitely small entities. In that part of his theory of conic sections which dealt with the long-standing problem of the doubling of the cube, his pupil Menaechmus played a part as his associate.

In astronomy Eudoxus was the first to construct a mathematical scheme that endeavored to explain the motions of the heavenly bodies. This scheme took the form of an elaborate system of concrete celestial spheres with the earth at its center, which he illustrated by the construction of a model of twenty-seven spheres. By making use of this model, he hoped to describe the complex orbital movements of the planets in the sky, which he divided into spheres of longitude and latitude. Despite errors and discrepancies (since astronomical observation was still much inferior to mathematical theory), the brilliance of his procedures caused them to be adopted, in modified form, by Aristotle; and they had a long life thereafter. Eudoxus also wrote a description of the constellations that was published, with a calendar of their risings and settings, in two versions known as the *Enoptron* and the *Phaenomena*. This work improved on previous approximations of the length of the solar year and obtained widespread fame owing to its poetic adaptation in the *Phaenomena* of Aratus of Soli. Another of Eudoxus' writings on the calendar was the *Eight-Year Cycle (Octaeteris)*. (The essay known as the *Eudoxou Techne*, preserved on a papyrus, contains elementary information about the calendar and astronomy that is probably taken, for the most part, from his work). He also composed a descriptive *World Geography (Ges Periodos),* in a number of books, which set out to divide the earth into zones and contained a map of the known parts of the earth.

While Eudoxus was working at the Academy, he offered an explanation of the Platonic theory of Ideas (Forms) from a scientist's point of view. Furthermore, he argued that pleasure is the highest good; and this attracted the attention of Aristotle, who discussed his views in the *Nicomachean Ethics.*

EDITIONS—F. Lasserre, Die Fragmente des Eudoxos von Knidos, 1966.
ABOUT—T. L. Heath, History of Greek Mathematics, v 1, 1921; O. Neugebauer, The Exact Sciences in Antiquity, 2nd ed., 1957; G. E. R. Lloyd, Early Greek Science; Thales to Aristotle, 1970; E. Maula, Studies in Eudoxus' Homocentric Spheres, 1974; H. J. Waschkies, Von Eudoxus zu Aristoteles, 1977.

EUHEMERUS, Greek mythological romancer, lived at the court of Cassander, king of Macedonia, from 301 to 297 B.C. He was probably born at Messene in the Peloponnese, though his birthplace was also ascribed to Tegea in Arcadia and the island of Chios. Euhemerus was a supporter of the Cyrenaic school of philosophy, which maintained that the pleasures of the senses are the purpose of life.

He wrote a traveler's tale that has not survived, though its main features are known to us from fragments and an epitome. It described an imaginary journey to islands in the Indian Ocean, thus following the tradition of earlier writers who had invented similar Utopias. The work was called the *Sacred Record (Hiera Anagraphe),* after an inscription on a golden tablet the author professed to have found on an island named Panchaea. The inscription was alleged to have recorded the deeds of Zeus and his divine predecessors Uranus and Cronus at a time when they had been human beings and had reigned as great kings upon the earth. It was after their deaths, Euhemerus maintained, that they had first come to be wor-

yū hē' mēr us

151

shiped as gods by their grateful peoples. In other words, he explained, the gods—except when the word is used to personify some force of nature—are nothing but human heroes from the remote past, who earned the veneration of their subjects by their achievements as earthly rulers.

Thus the term *euhemeristic* came to be applied, as it still is, to interpretations of myth that suggest that gods were originally human beings. Euhemerus, however, was only developing much earlier traditions—found first in Asian lands and then among the Greeks, from Hecataeus and Stesimbrotus onward down to the sophists—that had blurred the distinction between gods and humans and had favored the rationalization of mythology. Such ideas were particularly relevant to Euhemerus' own day, when the powerful and remote monarchs who ruled the Hellenistic kingdoms claimed their subjects' worship.

In the first century B.C., Euhemerus' theory of the human origins of deities was taken up and incorporated by Diodorus Siculus in the sixth book of his *World History (Bibliotheke),* which is extant in fragmentary form. Among the Romans also, this interpretation proved particularly successful, because they too were disposed to accept the idea of the deification of their ancestors, including the mythical Aeneas and Romulus. The poet Ennius adapted the theory in his poem *Euhemerus,* which became well known, and there were many other Euhemerizing theories about Italian deities. The idea was also taken up by early Christians—in confirmation of their belief that the pagan gods were not true divinities at all. One such writer was Lactantius, who quoted Ennius extensively. In the eighteenth century, once again, Euhemerism was vigorously revived, particularly in France; and the English philosopher Herbert Spencer (d. 1903) was in sympathy with the same attitude.

EDITIONS—G. Nemethy, Euhemeri Reliquiae, 1889; G. Vallauri, 1956; F. Jacoby, Die Fragmente der griechischen Historiker, 63.
ABOUT—H. F. van der Meer, Euhemerus of Messene, 1948; J. W. Schippers, De Ontwikkeling der Euhemeristische Godencritiek in de Christelijke Latijnse Literatuur, 1952; H. Flashar, Formen utopischen Denkens bei den Griechen, 1974; J. Ferguson, Utopias of the Classical World, 1975.

EUPHORION, Greek poet, was born in c. 276/275 B.C. (or possibly a little later) at Chalcis in Euboea and studied at Athens. His mentor in poetry was Archebulus of Thera (Santorin). As far as we are aware, he never went to Alexandria, so that he was one of the few poets of this Hellenistic, "Alexandrian" age who possessed no connection with the court of the Ptolemies. In his later years, he was appointed librarian at Antioch in Syria by the Seleucid monarch Antiochus III the Great, whom he assisted at times as a propagandist. Hostile or envious gossip pronounced Euphorion to be a man of disagreeable appearance who had succeeded in enriching himself by an affair with an elderly widow.

To judge from his verses, which contain violent allusions to people who had defrauded him and stolen from him, he seems to have been a man of angry temperament, suffering from a persecution complex. His poem *Curses* or *The Man Who Stole a Cup (Poteriokleptes)* assembles a vast array of maledictions and warnings based on examples drawn from mythology directed against someone who had allegedly robbed him in this way. *Millennia (Chiliades),* in five books, also seems to prophecy misfortune for someone who had cheated him of money; the notion of inexorable but delayed punishments (fulfilled after the lapse of a thousand years), which the poet forecast in order to alarm his enemy, was later revived by Plutarch in his essay *On the Delay in Divine Retribution.* Euphorion's *Thracian (Thrax),* to which a number of recently discovered papyrus fragments seem to belong, likewise appears to have concluded its mythological narrations with a curse—in this case directed against Achilles (for murdering Trambelus because of the latter's violent courting of Apriate). Such cursing had become an established literary form in this later Greek (Hellenistic) age; although it is possible that the poet was intending to refer, as in *Millennia,* to some personal or topical happening. Another of Euphorion's poems that

yū fō′ ri on

may be about murder is *Hesiod,* which was also the subject of a piece of the same name by his contemporary Eratosthenes. Euphorion's *Mopsopia* or *Miscellanea (Atacta)* was a collection of the myths and legends of Attica, of which Mopsopia was an ancient name. Other mythological titles include *Hyacinthus, Inachus,* and *Philoctetes,* but these may have been parts of other, larger writings rather than separate works on their own account, since it was a common practice for sections of poems to be cited under titles of their own.

Euphorion also wrote a poetic epistle, *Replies to Theodoridas.* But in general the poems he liked to write were epyllia or miniature epics—narrative poems of from one hundred to six hundred hexameters, often on mythological themes. In other pieces, his aim was to bring together whole collections of myths, in what were virtually catalogs, with an inclination toward the more gruesome kind of story, and a preference for tasteless displays of sentiment and naive etymological explanations. Piling on detail in the most repetitive and far-fetched fashion, he deliberately sought obscurity of language, darkened further by numerous recondite mythological references. Euphorion derived much of his vocabulary from Homer, for whom he expressed appropriate admiration. Yet, at the same time, he was pointedly un-Homeric in his meticulous avoidance of a smooth flow of language and the broad epic sweep. Instead, he preferred to be an industrious and conscientious, indeed a shameless, follower and imitator, of the artificial, erudite methods of his immediate forerunners Callimachus and Apollonius Rhodius. This attitude appealed to the taste of subsequent epochs, so that Euphorion, beyond his merits, came to exercise considerable influence on later poets. Among these were not only Greeks (Nicander of Colophon, Parthenius of Cos, Nonnus of Panopolis) but also Latin writers, including Cornelius Gallus, who translated or imitated an epyllion of Euphorion about a cult of Apollo in Mysia; and Virgil, too, made use of the subject matter of his poems. Cicero, on the other hand, had criticized his partisans by implication, when he described them as "singers of Euphorion."

Euphorion was also the author of learned treatises in prose: *On the Aleuadae* (the leading aristocratic family of Thessaly), *On the Isthmian Games, About the Makers of Song.* These titles, which reveal his historical interests, were grouped together as *Historical Memoirs.* (The Euphorion who wrote a Hippocratic lexicon in six books may be someone else.)

EDITIONS—J. U. Powell, Collectanea Alexandrina, 1925; for additional papyri, *see* Oxford Classical Dictionary, 2nd ed., 1970, p 417; L. A. De Cuenca, Euforión de Calcis (Spanish), 1976; B. A. van Groningen, 1977. ABOUT—F. Skutsch, Euphorion (4) *in* Pauly-Wissowa, Real-Encyclopädie der klassischen Altertumswissenschaft, v 6, column 1174ff.; M. M. Crump, The Epyllion from Theocritus to Ovid, 1931; P. Treves, Euforione e la storia ellenistica, 1955; T. B. L. Webster, Hellenistic Poetry and Art, 1964.

EUPOLIS, Greek comic poet, was born at Athens in 446 B.C. and died in about 412. His first play was produced in 429, two years after the beginning of the Peloponnesian War, and during the next seventeen years, while the war continued, he won three victories at the Lenaean festival of Dionysus and at least one at the City Dionysia. We have over four hundred and sixty fragments from his comedies, including substantial pieces found on papyri, and nineteen of their titles.

One of his comedies was *Autolycus,* written in two versions. Autolycus was a champion athlete in 422, the lover of the rich Callias who was praised by Plato and Xenophon but who was attacked by Eupolis because of his immoral circle of friends. No doubt the play also contained allusions to Autolycus the famous trickster of mythology. The *Captains* (Taxiarchoi) apparently showed Dionysus looking for a good man to command the armies of Athens, but it is he himself, a cowardly figure, whom the leading general Phormio is seen trying to make into a soldier (Phormio had probably died shortly before the production of the play). *Cities* (c. 420) concerns itself with the relations between Athens and its subject cities, who provide the members of the chorus, individually characterized—and probably pleading for better treatment. The last of

yū′ po lis

153

EUPOLIS

Eupolis' plays, the *Demes* (c. 412), can be partially reconstructed from about two hundred surviving lines that show its principal character, an old Athenian citizen attending the festival of the *Anthesteria,* at which spirits of the dead were believed to walk abroad. By this device, great Athenians of the past are brought up from the underworld to offer topical counsel; the ghost of the soldier and statesman Aristides, known as "the Just," makes an appearance, and so does the shade of Nicias, recently killed in the Athenian expedition against Syracuse in Sicily; and Alcibiades, too, plays a prominent part. The character of Alcibiades also figures in *The Dippers (Baptai)* (after 424), in which, to the accompaniment of vigorous abuse, he was depicted performing the rites of the Thracian goddess Cotytto, probably in women's garb. (There was a story, not to be believed, that Alcibiades, on his voyage to Sicily, threw Eupolis overboard in revenge.)

Flatterers (Kolakes), which won the first prize at the City Dionysia in 421, deals, like the *Autolycus,* with the wealthy Callias, who is ridiculed for cultivating the society of sophists, who swarm like parasites round the dining table. Protagoras comes in for his share of mockery, and Alcibiades, the host's brother-in-law, is shown as a lecher. *Friends* contains some fun at the expense of Pericles' mistress Aspasia. *The Girl of Naxos* may be based on the story of Theseus' desertion of Ariadne. In the *Goats* the chorus seems to have been dressed as goats, and at one point they give a long list of the plants that they were accustomed to eat. *The Golden Race* seems to have had a chorus of blind cripples in rags; the title, referring to the legendary Golden Age, is presumably ironic. The play included mockery of the Athenian statesman Cleon (d. 422) and allusions to Odysseus and the Cyclops. *Helots* (of which *Laconians* may be an alternative title) apparently dealt with a rebellion of this social class against the Spartans who had reduced them to subjection. *Maricas (Homosexual,* 421) brings that charge against the demagogic politician Hyperbolus. The *People of Prospalta* makes fun of the inhabitants of the Attic deme (a unit of local government) of that name for their propensity for litigation and satirizes the Athenian lawcourts at the same time. About *Referee, Scoff-laws (Hubristodikai),* and *Shirkers (Astrateutoi)* or *Hermaphrodites (Androgynai)* we know nothing.

Aristophanes, Eupolis, and Cratinus were the three principal exponents of the Old Comedy at Athens. Eupolis, during his short life, was Aristophanes' most serious rival. At first they were on friendly terms, but later their relationship deteriorated when Eupolis claimed that he was the part-author of Aristophanes' *Knights* "and made a gift of it to bald-head," whereupon Aristophanes, in the *Clouds,* denounced his critic for having shamelessly plagiarized the *Knights* in his *Marikas* and went on to declare in his *Anagyros* that Eupolis had made himself three ragged garments out of Aristophanes' own mantle. In the competition of 421, Eupolis' *Flatterer* defeated the *Peace* of Aristophanes, who angrily contrasted his rival's dull coarseness with his own refinement and ingenuity. Another critic, the author of an anonymous *Life of Aristophanes,* saw Eupolis as "bitter and indecent." And indeed his style, insofar as we can reconstruct it from the longer fragments, does not quite compete with the genius of Aristophanes. Yet the grammarian Platonius (of uncertain date), in his treatise entitled *On the Difference Between Comedies,* may well have been justified in describing Eupolis as "rich in invention and sublime and attractive." He evidently brought a keen eye and a warm heart to bear on the life of his beloved Athens and directed his satirical fire with deadly accuracy wherever he saw perils threatening its welfare. For all his comic wit, he was a serious thinker and a strong political fighter, as caustic toward the novel tendencies of his age as Aristophanes and a good deal more warlike, being, above all, concerned to prevent lapses from military virtue. The disappearance of his plays is a serious loss.

EDITIONS—A. Meineke, Fragmenta Comicorum Graecorum, v 1 and v 2, 1839–57; T. Kock, Comicorum Atticorum Fragmenta, v 1, 1880–88; J. M. Edmonds, Fragments of Attic Comedy, v 1, 1957.
ABOUT—A. Lesky, History of Greek Literature, 1966.

EURIPIDES, Greek tragic dramatist, was probably born in 485 or 480 B.C. and died in 407 or 406. His home was at Phlya, east of Mount Hymettus near Athens. His father Mnesarchus (or Mnesarchides) belonged to a prosperous family that possessed a hereditary priesthood of Apollo Zosterios and owned a property on the island of Salamis that may have been Euripides' birthplace. He seems to have been a man of solitary habits, which gave him a reputation for unconvivial surliness (though the story that his two marriages brought him much domestic unhappiness may be legendary). He composed an ode to celebrate the victory of Alcibiades in the chariot race at the Olympic Games (416) but played no part in public affairs except to write an epitaph for the Athenians who fell in the disastrous expedition to Syracuse (415–413); however, it is also possible that he once went to Syracuse as a member of a delegation. In 408, at the very end of his life, he left Athens to go and live at the court of King Archelaus of Macedonia, a well-known patron of the arts. This decision may have been connected with the fewness of the victories Euripides had won at dramatic competitions—they only totaled four in his lifetime (and one after his death). The tale that he was torn to pieces by the Macedonian king's hounds is likely to be apocryphal.

He was said to have written eighty-eight or ninety plays, of which seventeen or eighteen tragedies and one satyr play survive. In his earliest surviving tragedy, *Alcestis* (438 B.C.), Apollo speaks the prologue telling how he had been banished for a time from Olympus and condemned to become a shepherd in the service of King Admetus of Pherae in Thessaly. Apollo came to love him and tricked the Fates into promising that, when his time came to die, Admetus might escape if he found a substitute who would volunteer to perish in his place. The only willing substitute Admetus could produce, however, was his own wife Alcestis. As the main part of the play begins, Thanatos (Death) comes to claim her. At this point the grieving household receives a chance visit from the boisterous god Heracles, who, discovering what has happened, goes off and

yū rip′ i dēz

rescues Alcestis from Death. She and Admetus, reunited, embrace; and Heracles goes on his way.

Medea was performed in 431 B.C. For the sake of her husband, Jason, leader of the Argonauts, Medea, daughter of King Aeetes of Colchis, has left her father, murdered her brother, robbed her family of the Golden Fleece, and contrived the death of Jason's uncle Pelias, King of Iolcus. Although she has been a faithful wife and has borne Jason two sons, he now proposes to cast her aside and marry the daughter of Creon, king of Corinth. Fearing her witchcraft, Creon orders Medea's exile from Corinth, but she induces him to let her stay in the city till the next morning; Jason, after trying to prove to her that he has acted for the best, retires discomfited before her withering invectives.

A chance meeting that same evening with Aegeus, king of Athens, enables Medea to provide a future refuge for herself. Now she proceeds deliberately to destroy not only Jason and her children by him but also his new love. The plot succeeds: first, Creon's daughter is destroyed by a corroding poison, and Creon with her; then Medea kills the children with her own hands. Jason rushes in, vowing vengeance, but as he tries to force the doors of the house, Medea suddenly appears above, a demonic figure, borne on a fiery chariot sent by her grandfather the Sun-god. She will bury the children herself, she says, in the precinct of the goddess Hera, where they shall receive worship in time to come. As the chariot moves out of sight, Jason is left vainly protesting against her cruelty.

The *Children of Heracles (Heracleidae, ?c. 429–427),* are hounded by King Eurystheus of Argos and Mycenae, as their father had been in his lifetime. They and Alcmena, Heracles' mother, have fled to the Temple of Zeus at Marathon, where an Argive emissary comes to seize them. Demophon, king of Athens, who has granted the children asylum, repels the emissary, who threatens war. An oracle, however, has revealed that Eurystheus can only be defeated if a noble maiden is sacrificed to Persephone, the goddess of the underworld. Heracles' daughter Macaria volunteers for the role and gives herself up to die. The Athenians defeat

Eurystheus and make him a prisoner. Alcmena demands his death, but the chorus of old men of Marathon pronounce it unlawful to kill a captive taken in war. Eurystheus refuses to beg for his life, declaring that, in accordance with an old oracle, his spirit will guard the city when the descendants of Heracles' children have turned against it. At Alcmena's continued insistence, he goes to his death.

In the *Hippolytus* (428 B.C.) Aphrodite, the goddess of love, expresses her anger with Theseus' son Hippolytus who has rejected her and instead honors only the virgin divinity Artemis. In revenge, Aphrodite causes Hippolytus' stepmother, Phaedra, to fall in love with him. Phaedra tries to starve herself to death but unwittingly reveals her shameful secret to her nurse. Discovering that the old woman has told Hippolytus what she has learned, Phaedra hangs herself —leaving, as an act of vengeance, an untrue report that Hippolytus had raped her. Theseus, praying for his son's death, sends him into banishment. On his journey, Hippolytus is dragged and mangled by his runaway horses; Artemis appears and discloses to Theseus the innocence of the youth, who dies reconciled with his father.

The *Andromache* (430–424 B.C.) tells how Hermione and her father, Menelaus, king of Sparta, are plotting to kill Molossus, her husband's child by the captured Trojan princess, Andromache. In the absence of Hermione's husband Neoptolemus, Andromache seeks refuge at the altar of the sea-goddess Thetis (the mother of Neoptolemus' father, Achilles). Hermione and Menelaus trick Andromache into leaving the sanctuary, and she and her child are condemned to die. However, Peleus, Neoptolemus' grandfather, arrives to save them; Menelaus decides to abdicate, and Hermione, now terrified of Neoptolemus' wrath, is prevented from committing suicide by her cousin Orestes. Orestes now plans the death of Neoptolemus, for whom Hermione had once jilted him. But the divine Thetis appears and prophesies a royal future for Andromache and her son and then, accompanied by Peleus, returns to the depths of the sea.

The *Hecuba* (c. 425–424 B.C.) begins with an appearance of the ghost of Polydorus, son of King Priam and Queen Hecabe (in Latin, Hecuba) of Troy. Murdered by Polymester of Thrace to whom he had been sent for safety, Polydorus reveals that the Greek fleet can only sail if his sister Polyxena is sacrificed on his grave and prophesies that on one and the same day Odysseus will lead Polyxena off to die and the captive Hecabe will see Polydorus' corpse. The prophecy comes true. In revenge for her daughter's death, Hecabe lures Polymestor to her tent, where she and her women (the chorus) put out his eyes and kill his two sons. Agamemnon declares that justice has been done; blind Polymestor, having foretold evil fates for Hecuba and Agamemnon, is put off on a desert island and stranded there.

In the *Suppliant Women* (c. 421 B.C.), the Thebans, having defeated Polyneices and his Argive allies have denied burial to the corpses of their enemies. The mothers of the fallen leaders (the Seven against Thebes), together with the defeated King Adrastus of Argos, father-in-law of Polyneices, as their spokesman, come to Attica imploring King Theseus of Athens to intervene with the Thebans. Theseus is hesitant but finally agrees to present their case to the Athenian Assembly: he sends a herald to demand the bodies of the slain from Thebes. The response to this demand, however, is a counterdemand that he expel Adrastus from Attic territory or face war. A battle ensues between Thebes and Athens that Theseus wins. The dead Seven are duly cremated, and Athena makes Adrastus swear that the Argives will never attack Athens again.

The *Heracles* or *Mad Heracles (Hercules Furens)* (c. 420), tells how King Lycus of Thebes plans to murder the family of the absent Heracles, burning them out of the sanctuary in which they have taken refuge. However, Heracles himself returns just in time and puts Lycus to death. Suddenly, Iris, messenger of the gods, makes her appearance, accompanied by Lyssa (Madness). They have been sent by the goddess Hera, Heracles' lifelong enemy, to drive him mad and make him kill his own wife and children: and they die at his hands. He would also have slain his father, Amphitryon, if Athena had not struck him unconscious with a stone. Heracles awakens, his sanity restored, and is dissuaded from committing suicide by Theseus, who offers him a haven at Athens.

Ion (421–408 B.C.) recounts the story of the son of the god Apollo and Creusa, an Athenian princess who gave birth to him secretly in a cave. Hermes takes the baby to be brought up by the priest of Apollo at Delphi, where the boy, when he has grown up, becomes a temple attendant. Now, Creusa and her husband Xuthus visit Delphi and unwittingly meet Ion. Xuthus hails him as the child he desires—because the oracle has told him that the first person he meets on leaving the temple will be his own son. Creusa, however, angered because a stranger (as she supposes) is being foisted on her, denounces Apollo and attempts, without success, to poison Ion. Then, the sight of the chest in which she had left him as a baby persuades her of his true identity; and Ion himself discovers from Athena that Apollo is his father. Athena orders him and his mother and stepfather to go to Athens, where Ion will become the ancestor of the Ionians, while the Dorians and Achaeans will be descended from Creusa and Xuthus.

In the *Trojan Women* (415 B.C.) Athena enlists Poseidon's help to wreck the fleet of the Greeks on the homeward voyage from Troy because both deities have grievances against the Greek army. The captive Queen Hecabe (Hecuba) and her women, who are her fellow prisoners and the chorus of the play, lament their downfall; and the Greek herald Talthybius comes to announce to them the names of the Greek leaders to whom each of them is to be enslaved. Hecabe's daughter-in-law Andromache, however, is also informed by the herald that her little son Astyanax has been condemned to death, and he is torn from her arms to be killed. Menelaus, king of Sparta, now appears on the scene to take back Helen, whose elopement with Paris had caused the war. Proclaiming her innocence, she returns with him to Greece. The women perform the funeral rites for Astyanax, and the city of Troy is engulfed in flames, into which Hecabe tries to hurl herself, although she is restrained. Finally, the captive women move down the beach to embark on the Greek ships, which face certain destruction by the gods.

The *Electra* (413) recalls events after the fall of Troy, in which Clytemnestra, aided by her lover Aegisthus, murdered the returning Agamemnon, because, at the outset of the expedition, he had sacrificed their daughter Iphigenia to the gods at Aulis, and now, ten years later, has brought back a captive mistress Cassandra to Argos. After the death of Agamemnon, his daughter Electra was compelled to marry a peasant. As the play opens, she is overheard bewailing her fate by her brother Orestes, who has returned home from exile in disguise with his cousin Pylades. An old servant recognizes Orestes, and brother and sister are joyfully reunited. The two young men slay Aegisthus at a banquet and return with his body. Clytemnestra, not knowing what they have done, arrives and tries in vain to justify Agamemnon's murder to Electra, who leads her into her hut to be killed by Orestes and Pylades. Both Orestes and Electra, however, are broken by what they have done. The Dioscuri (Castor and Polydeuces), the divine brothers of Clytemnestra, pronounce that her death was just but that Orestes ought not to have killed his mother. As punishment, he will be pursued for a long time by the Furies before his final acquittal.

In the prologue of the *Iphigenia in Tauris* (414–412) Iphigenia, dressed as a priestess and accompanied by a chorus of captive maidens, tells how she in fact escaped her fate at the hands of her father Agamemnon and was instead wafted away by Artemis to the kingdom of Thoas, where she has been allotted the duty of sacrificing to the goddess every stranger who visits the place. Her brother, Orestes (whom she believes to be dead), lands with Pylades, ordered by Apollo to steal the statue of Artemis for Athens. They are captured and finally recognized by Iphigenia. The three plan an escape. Iphigenia dupes King Thoas and they get away (with Artemis' statue). While Thoas is ordering their recapture, Athena appears and informs him that Poseidon himself has helped them to depart. She bids the fugitives make their way to Attica and instructs Thoas to release the captive maidens.

In the play *Helen* (412), the main character, Helen, explains that it was not she who was carried off to Troy by Paris as had generally been supposed but a phantom made of air fashioned by Hera, whereas she herself, the real Helen, had been sent with Hermes to Egypt. She is still there but has taken sanctuary at the grave of the Egyptian King Proteus to escape the lust of his son Theoclymenus. Her husband Menelaus, reported missing at sea, staggers onto the scene, shipwrecked and in rags, and finally accepts her identity when the other, unreal Helen he has brought with him evaporates into thin air. United at long last, Menelaus and the true Helen manage to escape by citing a fictitious Greek custom that a man lost at sea (in this case, Menelaus, of whose reappearance Theoclymenus knows nothing) must also be mourned at sea. By this ruse, Helen is able to borrow a ship. The king discovers the trick, but Helen's brothers, the divine Dioscuri Castor and Polydeuces, appear and order him to bow to fate, declaring that their sister is destined to become a goddess.

The aged queen Jocasta introduces the *Phoenician Women* (c. 410) by telling the story of the curse on the Theban royal family. Eteocles and Polyneices, sons of the self-blinded Oedipus and of Jocasta, have quarreled with one another, and Polyneices has enlisted an Argive army to join the attack of the Seven against Thebes. Jocasta fails to reconcile her two sons, but King Creon's son Menoeceus offers himself up as a sacrifice to the war-god Ares when it is announced that such propitiation is needed to save the city. Eteocles and Polyneices, however, slay each other in single combat, and Jocasta commits suicide. Creon condemns Oedipus to banishment so that the land may be freed of his curse and pronounces that whoever gives Polyneices burial rites shall be condemned to death; but Antigone declares that she will defy this edict. At the play's conclusion, Oedipus discloses a prophecy that he himself will finally find peace at Colonus near Athens. Then Antigone leads him out into exile.

In *Orestes* (408), having killed his mother Clytemnestra and her lover Aegisthus (because of their murder of his father Agamemnon) Orestes has been tortured by the Furies for six days, and the people of his city, Ar-

gos, have condemned him and his sister Electra to death. At this point, Agamemnon's brother Menelaus arrives on his way back to Sparta but is too cowed to help the pair. They plan to punish him for this failure to assist them by killing his wife Helen and seizing his daughter Hermione as a hostage. They threaten to kill Hermione, too, and burn the palace down, unless Menelaus agrees to intervene to save their lives. However, Apollo appears and snatches Helen away. He will effect a reconciliation between Orestes and the Argives and pronounces that Orestes, after suffering and banishment, is to be tried at Athens and freed by divine intervention; it is then his destiny to marry Hermione and become the ruler of Argos.

In the *Bacchants* (*Bacchae*, produced posthumously in 405), the god, Dionysus (Bacchus), who has returned from his triumphant progress through Asia to his native Thebes, speaks the prologue. His mother's sisters, including King Pentheus' mother Agave, had at first denied his divinity but, overcome by the Bacchic frenzy, are now on Mount Cithaeron, where he makes his way to join them. Then appear two half-comic old men: Cadmus, who is a zealous believer in the new god, and Tiresias the prophet, who considers it impolitic to oppose anything that bears the appearance of a supernatural power. The two old men intend to join the votaries on the hillside. A servant of Pentheus enters with a prisoner, who, though unrecognized, is Dionysus himself. Pentheus assails him and orders his imprisonment in the palace stables, but the palace crashes in ruins as though struck by an earthquake, and the captive, emerging, comforts the chorus (his Asiatic women companions) and replies calmly when Pentheus threatens further violence. A messenger then reports the miracles that have accompanied the revels of the women on the mountain; Dionysus persuades the king, who is at this point bemused, to disguise himself as a Bacchant and go to spy on them. Soon after Pentheus' departure, news is brought that under the leadership of his own mother Agave, who is out of her wits, the women have caught him and torn him to pieces. She enters, carrying his head, which in her madness she believes to be a lion's.

Cadmus brings her to her senses, and their laments are cut short by the appearance of Dionysus, who identifies himself and justifies his vengeance on those who had rejected him.

The *Iphigenia at Aulis* (produced posthumously in 406 or 405,) is staged at the Greek camp at Aulis, where the commander-in-chief Agamemnon emerges from his tent in distress, bearing a letter that is to be sent back to Argos. Earlier, he had written requesting his wife Clytemnestra to dispatch their daughter Iphigenia to Aulis, ostensibly to be married to Achilles but in reality to be slain as a human sacrifice, in response to an oracle, so that the Greek fleet will be able to sail. However, Agamemnon has changed his mind, and his brother Menelaus, after a dispute, agrees with his new decision that this abominable sacrifice cannot be performed. Iphigenia arrives with Clytemnestra, who is utterly appalled when she learns of the sacrifice that has been planned. Moreover, it now has to be carried through after all, in spite of Agamemnon's reluctance, because his army, he declares, will not allow him to abandon it. So Iphigenia goes to her death; a messenger appears to report that she has died with courage and dignity, but that, when the fatal blow was struck, she vanished, and all that was to be seen on the altar was a mountain doe, bleeding to death.

In addition to his tragedies, Euripides has also left us our only surviving example of the humorous satyric dramas (concerned with the satyr, half-men and half-goat, companions of Silenus in the woods and hills). These pieces were performed along with the tragedies at the annual festivals. This Euripidean satyr-play is the *Cyclops,* of uncertain date. The god Dionysus having been captured by pirates, Silenus has started out in pursuit, accompanied by his train of satyr companions, but has fallen into the hands of the Cyclops Polyphemus. Odysseus and his crew appear on the scene and bargain with Silenus for food in exchange for wine. But Polyphemus arrives and captures Odysseus and his men, whose subsequent escape, by blinding Polyphemus, is described in a plot that in general follows the Homeric *Odyssey* but is framed in comical terms, like satyr plays by earlier dramatists on the same theme that are lost.

Plays doubtfully attributed to Euripides include the surviving *Rhesus,* which belongs to the period of his early career but may not be the play of that name which he is known to have written. The scene is the Trojan camp during the Greek siege: King Rhesus of Thrace arrives with a large army to help the Trojans. He is reproached by Hector for his late arrival and killed during the night by Greek spies, Odysseus and Diomedes, who are captured after leading away his famous horses but escape. Rhesus' mother, the Muse Terpsichore, enters bringing her son's body and reveals who has killed him (thus exculpating the Trojan hero Hector, whom the dead man's charioteer had accused of the murder). She declares that Rhesus will not descend to the underworld but is destined to become an oracular spirit in a remote cavern. Hector secures the king's shield and leads out his troops to what he proclaims will be the conclusive victory.

One of Euripides' peculiar contributions to Athenian tragedy was a new interest in human character. At the height and turning point of Athenian imperialism, the collective values of society were being called more and more into question, and the experience of the individual spirit was coming to assume ever greater importance. Euripides knew the deadly forces always ready to constrain the individual and felt compassion for the strivings of men and women to resist these coercive elements. According to Aristotle, pity and fear were the emotions properly stimulated by tragedy, and, therefore, in his view the most tragic of poets was Euripides. Some of his plays, it is true, have happy conclusions of a kind, but others end with no consolation or comfort for the afflictions that abound. Instead, the demonic forces of which human beings are the helpless victims cause a chaos of events that reveals no moral meaning or rational pattern.

All but the earliest plays of Euripides were written against the background of the Peloponnesian War (431–404 B.C.), in which Athens suffered grievously and deteriorated sharply in moral behavior and decency. Looking at these events with grimmest realism, the dramatist felt appalled by the senseless devastation of warfare. In consequence, the legendary "heroes" who caused all the miseries of the Trojan Wars emerge in his dramas as highly unattractive figures. Among Euripides' women, too, are a number of notably horrible figures (who caused him, not quite fairly, to be regarded as a woman-hater); the lofty-spirited Alcestis is a rarity beside the hate-consumed Medea and the no less murderous Electra.

Likable or not, these leading characters are fully endowed with psychological interest. Yet their humanity is curiously diluted by the fashionable sophistic arguments and hair-splittings in which Euripides reveled. For the dramatist has a critical and clinical eye for the seedy, calculating, profit-and-loss attitude that had become so prominent in his own time, and he delineates its manifestations in displays of unscrupulous, didactic, almost forensic advocacy. True, no one was more aware than he of the perils of this contemporary "art of over-subtle words," as he himself called it. Yet he also loved to recast the traditional stories into just this sort of disputatious form. After all the prosy argumentation that this predilection produced, the marvelous poetry of his choral lyrics provides a strangely contrasted beauty and relief—and they were accompanied, it appears, by music of the latest and most original kind.

Euripides retains the gods as dramatic entities but not as deities in any theological sense. They appear variously as profound psychological forces, shady seducers, or figures of fun. His approach to their existence, or nonexistence, reflects an attitude of investigative questioning that the comments of his *dramatis personae* often make even plainer. Not unnaturally, many contemporaries thought of such a destroyer of illusions as nothing short of impious, like Socrates, who was his friend and admirer; and that may have been another of the reasons why, at the end of his life, Euripides went to live in Macedonia. Yet, he was not so much impious as an inquirer who disbelieved in easy or complete solutions. The consequent discordance, or irresolution, of his thought is illustrated by a strange feature of certain plays; the *deus ex machina,* the god or goddess who intervenes at the end,

and clears up all the embarrassing or unresolved situations of the plot. Announcing the future destinies of the characters—very often to the overlong accompaniment of erudite detail involving antiquarian traditions —he or she resolves the action with abruptness, providing a semblance of a happy ending for those who prefer one and adding a bit of extra spectacle as well.

Another feature of which Euripides showed great fondness was the prologue or introduction. Usually in the form of a monologue but occasionally a dialogue, this served a purpose similar to that of the modern printed program, which sets forth the situation and states the facts the audience needs to know. The dramatic structure favored by Euripides is looser and more episodic than the tight constructions of a Sophoclean play, and his clear, natural diction is closer to that of ordinary life. The same is true of the situations he chooses to depict; although they generally involve violent stress and passionate, conflicting impulse, their treatment is essentially realistic.

Euripides' literary methods were subjected to vigorous criticism by the contemporary comic dramatist Aristophanes, who employed him as a leading character in his plays and built up several farcical scenes from quotations taken from his tragedies. Nevertheless, as a number of Plutarch's anecdotes illustrate, he enjoyed great renown even while he was still alive and continued to be enormously popular after his death. Subsequently, he became the most admired of the tragic poets, and his plays were constantly revived. He also exercised profound influence on the plots of the New Comedy of Menander. In the third century B.C., Satyrus included a Life of Euripides among his collection of biographies.

WORKS—*Lost plays:* Aegeus, Aeolus, Alcmene, Alcmaeon in Corinth, Alcmaeon in Psophis, Alexander, Andromeda, Antigone, Antiope, Archelaus, Auge, Autolycus, Bellerophon, Busiris, Cadmus, Cercyon (or Alope), Chrysippus, Cresphontes, Cretan Women, Cretans, Danae, Dictys, Epeos, Erechtheus, Eurystheus, Glaucus (or Polyidus), Hippolytus Veiled, Hypsipyle, Ino, Ixion, Lamia, Licymnius, Melanippe Captive, Melanippe the Wise, Meleager, Mysians, Oedipus, Oeneus, Oenomaus, Palamedes, Peleus, Peliades, Phaethon, Philoctetes, Phoenix, Phrixus (two versions), Pirithous, Pleisthenes, Protesilaus, Reapers, Rhadamanthus, Sciron, Scylla, Scyrians, Sisyphus, Stheneboea, Syleus, Telephus, Temenidae, Temenus, Theseus, Thyestes.

EDITIONS—F. A. Paley, 2nd ed., 1872–80; H. Weil, Sept tragédies d'Euripide, 3rd ed., 1905; A. Nauck, Tragicorum Graecorum Fragmenta, 1964 (supplement by B. Snell on Euripides); C. Austin, Nova Fragmenta Euripidea in Papyris Reperta, 1968. For lists of commentaries on individual plays *see* Oxford Classical Dictionary, 2nd ed., 1970, p 421; Encyclopaedia Britannica, 1971, v 8, p 835; T. B. L. Webster, Greek Tragedy (Greece & Rome: New Surveys in the Classics, no 5), 1971. *Add:* C. Collard, Suppliant Women, 1975; K. H. Lee, Trojan Women, 1976. *Translations*—A. S. Way (Loeb ed.), 1912; P. Vellacott (Penguin ed.), 1953, 1972, 1974; D. Grene and R. Lattimore, eds., The Complete Greek Tragedies, 1958–60; translations of individual plays listed *in* A. M. W. Green, Classics in Translation: A Selective Bibliography (1930–76), 1976. *Add:* P. Roche, Three Plays, 1974; W. S. Merwin and G. E. Dimock, Iphigenia in Aulis, 1978; R. E. Braun, Rhesos, 1979.

ABOUT—G. Murray, Euripides and His Age, 2nd ed., 1946; R. P. Winnington-Ingram, Euripides and Dionysus, 1948; E. R. Dodds, The Greeks and the Irrational, 1951; L. H. G. Greenwood, Aspects of Euripidean Tragedy, 1953; G. Norwood, Essays on Euripidean Drama, 1954; G. Zuntz, The Political Plays of Euripides, 1955, revised reprint 1963; H. Strohm, Euripides, 1957; Euripide: Sept exposés et discussions by J. C. Kamerbeek and others (Entretiens Hardt, v 6), 1960; A. Spira, Untersuchungen zum Deus ex Machina, 1960; R. Goossens, Euripide et Athènes, 1962; G. M. A. Grube, The Drama of Euripides, 1964; A. Lesky, Tragische Dichtung der Hellenen, 2nd ed., 1964; D. J. Conacher, Euripidean Drama, 1967; T. B. L. Webster, The Tragedies of Euripides, 1967; E. Segal, ed., Euripides: A Collection of Critical Essays, 1968; S. A. Barlow, The Imagery of Euripides, 1971; A. P. Burnett, Catastrophe Survived: Euripides' Plays of Mixed Reversal, 1971; A. Rivier, Essai sur la tragique d' Euripide, 2nd ed., 1975; P. Vellacott, Ironic Drama, 1975; C. H. Whitman, Euripides and the Full Circle of Myth, 1975; P. T. Stevens, Colloquial Expression in Euripides, 1977; W. Sale, Existentialism and Euripides, 1978.

EUSEBIUS, Greek ecclesiastical historian, was born in about A.D. 260 and died in about 340. His native city was Caesarea Maritima in Syria Palaestina (near Sdot Yam in Israel). He was educated in the Alexandrian tradition of Christian learning by Pamphilus, who was martyred in 310 during the Great Persecution of Diocletian and Galerius, the last persecution of the Christians under the Roman empire. In about 314 Eusebius was appointed bishop of Caesarea. He tended to support the theologian Arius (whose view of

yū sē' bi us

Christ stressed that the Son was distinct in essence from the Father) but when Arius was condemned for his doctrines at the Council of Nicaea (325), Eusebius acquiesced in the Council's action. He also attended the Council of Tyre in 335, which condemned Arius' opponent Athanasius. That same year he delivered a speech celebrating the thirtieth anniversary of the reign of Constantine the Great, with whom he was closely associated.

Eusebius wrote voluminously as apologist, chronographer, historian, exegete, and controversialist and was credited with forty-six theological works. Fifteen have survived, plus incomplete versions of four others and translations in Syriac, Armenian, and Latin. Among his earlier writings were *Preparation for the Gospel* and *Proof of the Gospel,* in fifteen and twenty books respectively. The first of these works demonstrated that Greek philosophy at its best coincided with or derived from Christian doctrine; the second (of which little more than half is preserved) showed how all previous history, and especially Jewish prophecy and experience and thought, had constituted preliminaries to the Christian revelation. The same argument is maintained in Eusebius' commentaries on the books of the Bible—those on *Isaiah, Psalms,* and *Luke* have partly survived. He also compiled *Chronological Tables (Chronica)* based on the *Chronography* of a Christian philosopher Julius Africanus of Jerusalem and epitomizing the principal happenings in the histories of the world's chief nations. Juxtaposed with one another, these events relating to different civilizations brought the pagan and Hebrew past into a firmer time-relationship; they also have contributed to our knowledge of Greek and Roman dates. Another work, *Against Hierocles,* endeavored to refute the views of a man who was one of the bitterest opponents of Christianity and who, as governor of Bithynia and Egypt, had played a significant part in the Great Persecution. Eusebius also wrote a biography of his patron Pamphilus, who had been one of the persecutors' victims; and he composed a eulogy, *Martyrs of Palestine*—a longer version of this has survived in a Syriac translation.

Eusebius' most important work was his

History of the Church or *Ecclesiastical History.* Divided into ten books, it offers an account of Christianity from its beginnings up to the early fourth century A.D. Eusebius first announces his general aim: to describe the apostolic succession, the principal landmarks of the history of the Church, its outstanding leaders and "heretics," the disasters that befell the Jews after they had crucified Jesus, and the deaths of the Christian martyrs. The main narrative opens with an account of Jesus and his contemporaries (Book 1), followed by a narration of the deeds of the apostles up to the deaths of St. Peter and St. Paul (Book 2) and then by a discussion of the adversaries within the church and of its earliest persecutors (Book 3). Books 4 and 5 deal with the persecutions and martyrdoms under Marcus Aurelius (A.D. 161–80) and the heresies of Marcion and Montanus. Book 6 describes the persecutions of Septimius Severus (193–211) and Trajanus Decius (249–51) and tells of the careers and literary activities of the Alexandrian Christians Clement and Origen. Book 7, after discussing further heresies, narrates the worsening of the persecution under Valerian (253–60)—the victims included Cyprian of Carthage—and goes on to tell of the more relaxed policy toward Christians that prevailed under Valerian's son Gallienus. The climax of Christian martyrdoms is reached in Book 8, which describes the Great Persecution, one of whose instigators, Galerius, recanted on his death-bed in the year 311. However, as Book 9 describes, his successor Maximinus II continued to pursue anti-Christian measures until his death two years later. The last book celebrates the Peace of the Church established when Constantine the Great and his eastern colleague Licinius published the Edict of Milan (313), guaranteeing the tolerance that (in spite of Licinius' subsequent reluctance) soon made Christianity the official religion of the state.

Eusebius' *History of the Church* inaugurated ecclesiastical history and served as a model for all subsequent church historians. One of its most valuable aspects is the inclusion of nearly two hundred and fifty verbatim quotations, including numerous official documents, whose authenticity has been corroborated by inscriptional evidence.

Moreover Eusebius, whose learning was extensive, cites or summarizes letters or edicts from more than a hundred books. In assembling this material, he occasionally sounds a note of judicious caution about its veracity, but he does so as an apologist for the Church rather than as a secular historian; and this stance causes him to neglect or distort worldly truth. Furthermore, his slovenly diction shows a sharp decline from classical standards: moreover, the structure of his narrative is shallow and uninspired—and planned on muddled and haphazard lines, so that even the most exciting events become shrouded in an atmosphere of monotony. There is a great contrast, then, between the grandeur and significance of Eusebius' task and the abilities he was able to devote to it, which were slight, despite his undoubted industry and enthusiasm.

After Constantine's death in 337, Eusebius wrote his *Life* (its authenticity has been questioned, probably without justification, by some modern scholars). Once again, the work is not so much biography as panegyric or encomium. Of the darker sides of the emperor's career no trace is to be seen; to Eusebius Constantine appears as a man of superhuman qualities who received visions and signs from God, upon which he nobly acted, ruling the empire with a virtue fully in keeping with this divine guidance. Adapting old pagan philosophies of kingship to Constantine, Eusebius praised his autocracy as the earthly mirror of the rule of God, who had united Church and State and made each indispensable to the other.

EDITIONS—Most of his works *in* Griechische christliche Schriftsteller, 1902–56, including Church History by E. Schwartz, 1903–09. *Translations* (of Church History)—K. Lake (v 1), H. J. Lawlor and J. E. L. Oulton (v 2) (Loeb ed.), 1926–32; G. del Ton, Storia ecclesiastica e i martiri della Palestina, 1964; G. A. Williamson (Penguin ed.), 1965. Tricennial Orations: H. A. Drake, In Praise of Constantine, 1976. For editions and translations of other works *see* Oxford Classical Dictionary, 2nd ed., 1970, p 423ff; *add* J. Sirinelli and E. des Places (v 1), G. Schröder (v 2), La préparation évangélique (The Preparation for the Gospel), 1974–75.
ABOUT—R. Laqueur, Eusebius als Historiker seiner Zeit, 1929; A. Alföldi, The Conversion of Constantine and Pagan Europe, 1948; R. L. Milburn, Early Christian Interpretations of History, 1954; B. Altaner, Patrology, 1960; D. S. Wallace-Hadrill, Eusebius of Caesarea, 1960; J. Sirinelli, Les vues historiques d'

Eusèbe de Césarée durant la période prénicéenne, 1961; F. Winkelmann, Zur Geschichte des Authentizitäts-problems der Vita Constantini, 1962, *and* (as ed.), Eusebius: Über das Leben des Kaisers Konstantin, 1975; A. Dempf, Eusebios als Historiker, 1964; R. Farina, L'impero e l'imperatore cristiano in Eusebio di Cesarea, 1966; C. Sant, The Old Testament Interpretation of Eusebius of Caesarea, 1967; R. P. C. Hanson, Biblical Exegesis in the Early Church, *in* Cambridge History of the Bible, v 1, 1970.

EUTROPIUS, Latin historian of the 4th century A.D., is almost certainly (despite modern doubts) to be identified with a high functionary, probably a native of Burdigala (Bordeaux), who received a rhetorical or sophistic education, became secretary to the emperor Constantius II (who died A.D. 361), accompanied his successor Julian (A.D. 361–63) on his Persian expedition, and held very important offices under the eastern emperor Valens (364–78): secretary of petitions (*magister memoriae*) in 369, proconsul of Asia in 371–72. Thereafter, he was accused but acquitted of treason, visited Gratian's court and Rome (c. 379), became prefect in Illyricum (380–81), and gained the consulship as the colleague of Valentinian II in 387. The eminent Symmachus, whose allegiance to paganism Eutropius evidently shared, wrote him a letter that same year; in 390 Eutropius seems to have been the man, high in the emperor's confidence, to whom another letter was addressed by the Greek rhetorician Libanius. Eutropius owned estates in Asia Minor and restored buildings at Magnesia on the Maeander. He was also interested in medicine.

His history was a survey of the story of Rome *(Breviarium ab Urbe Condita)* in ten short books, commissioned by Valens, to whom it was dedicated, and datable to approximately A.D. 370. Starting with the legendary origins of the city under Romulus, the work reached the Civil War between Sulla and the Marians by the end of Book 5 and described the death of Julius Caesar in Book 6. Books 7-10 cover the entire period of the emperors down to the death of Jovian (364). Eutropius employs a conventional but practical system of chronology, based on a two-fold method of dating derived partly

yū trō′ pi us

from the foundation of the city (on the year of which, however, he vacillates) and partly from consular years. For the republic and empire alike he draws upon one of those abridgments of Livy that largely replaced the original work, whereas his other material for the imperial epoch is derived from an enlarged adaptation of Suetonius, supplemented apparently by a lost imperial history written by an unknown author, of whom another historian, Aurelius Victor, also made use.

The need that was evidently felt for these abbreviated, meager histories betrays the low standard of historical knowledge and curiosity at that time. Eutropius' work, like others by Aurelius Victor and Festus, is scrappy; yet it sometimes fills gaps left by more impressive historians. Moreover, in writing of the final period, Eutropius was able to bring to bear his own personal knowledge and experience of events. In general, he shows reasonably good judgment and balance: although his humanity is tempered by a one-sided conviction of the rightness of Roman domination, his brief characterizations of individual emperors are just; and, in particular, his summings-up of rulers of his own day, Constantine and Julian, display commendable impartiality.

These qualities, and above all the practical, down-to-earth character of Eutropius' summary, reflected in a clear and·unpretentious style, ensured its popularity from the outset. Not only the author or authors of the largely fraudulent *Historia Augusta* but also the great historian Ammianus Marcellinus made use of the *Breviarium* at least twice: it was translated into Greek by Paeanius (c. 380), and it was adapted in the same language by Capito of Lycia (sixth century), whose version has been preserved almost complete. In the fifth century the Spanish ecclesiastic Orosius, drew on Eutropius' work, as did Saint Jerome, one of the early Doctors of the Church. The English scholar, historian, theologian Bede (673–735) did likewise. And, in the eighth century it served the Lombard historian Paul the Deacon as the basis of his much longer *Historia Miscella;* and in about 1000 it was again enlarged by Landulfus Sagax. It was translated into Spanish in 1561 and into English, by Nicholas Haward, three years later. For many generations of students Eutropius has served as an introduction to Latin prose.

EDITIONS—H. Droysen, 1878, 1879; C. Wagener, 1884; F. Ruehl, 1887, reprint 1975.
ABOUT—J. Sorn, Der Sprachgebrauch des Historikers Eutropius, 1892; M. Galdi, L'epitome nella letteratura latina, 1922; R. Syme, Ammianus and the Historia Augusta, 1968; A. H. M. Jones, J. R. Martindale and J. Morris, The Prosopography of the Later Roman Empire, v 1, 1971, p 317; W. den Boer, Some Minor Roman Historians, 1972; M. Capozza, Roma fra monarchia e decemvirato nell'interpretazione di Eutropio, 1973.

FABIUS PICTOR, QUINTUS, historian of Rome who wrote in Greek and was a member of the famous and powerful Roman patrician family of the Fabii, served his country in battle, politics, and religion; a recently published inscription shows that his father's name was Gaius. Quintus took part in the Second Punic War (218–202 B.C.) and was chosen to consult the Delphic oracle after the disastrous defeat at Cannae (216 B.C.).

Toward the end of the war he published, in Greek, a *History of Rome,* the first such history ever to have been written. His work dealt fairly substantially with the earliest period (from Aeneas onward—a period that had already been studied by Greeks of antiquarian inclinations); then discussed subsequent happenings at lesser length. The scale was once again extended as he approached the contemporary scene, until the work became a detailed narrative of the events of the third century B.C., notably of the First Punic War (264–261). Fabius struck a balance between the annalistic, year-by-year, method that was to become characteristic of Roman senatorial historians and the wider sweep of their Greek, Hellenistic, predecessors. He indicated the consuls for each year, at least in the more detailed sections of his work, but he dated by Olympiads (four-year periods), thus following recent Greek attempts to establish a chronology that would be universally understandable.

Fabius' choice of the Greek language as
fā′ bi us   pik′ tôr

his medium has led some to conclude that he wrote primarily for a Greek public, whom he intended to make aware of the history and institutions of Rome. No doubt there is some substance to this view, since he adopted a powerfully chauvinistic standpoint (to which Polybius called attention), which suggests that he is attempting to assure the Greeks of Rome's power and endurance and good faith. In any case, however, he had little alternative, for the Latin tongue was not yet suited to the composition of literary prose, and indeed such a thing had never been attempted. Furthermore, Fabius' work was similar to other histories written in Greek by foreigners about their own lands (Babylonia, Egypt, etc.). These works, however, were certainly comprehensible to cultured Romans—senators like Fabius himself—and the same was true of his own treatise. For example, he recounts anecdotes about his family that were surely intended for Roman consumption. Since, therefore, there were many features of his history that would interest not only leading Romans but Greek-speaking foreigners as well, it seems probable that he was writing for the educated world as a whole—for Greeks and Romans and members of other nations alike.

Fabius' viewpoint was not only nationalistic but also strongly conservative. His readers, wherever they may have been, were intended to appreciate the wise prudence with which the Senate had conducted Rome's affairs, in contrast to the foolish self-assertions of the Assembly and its popular demagogues. Prominent in his eulogy of the Senate were praises of his own house of the Fabii, which enable us to arrive at a terminal date for his narrative. Since the greatest of his kinsmen, Quintus Fabius Maximus Cunctator, achieved glory in the years immediately following the disaster of Trasimene in 217 (with which the latest surviving fragment of the history is concerned), whereas after 209 he was eclipsed by Scipio Africanus, the account may well have ended at about that juncture.

Fabius Pictor, though writing in Greek, was the virtual creator of Roman historiography, and he guided it into a special channel in which it would long remain. Fabius meant history-writing to be an honest inquiry into the past, yet an inquiry that was morally and politically committed, suitable reading for many but not least for the leading figures of Roman life. And so in his selection of material, especially in the earliest part of his work, he took decisive steps toward the forming of that mass of national legend and myth that so enormously influenced the psychology and education of future Romans. This mythological corpus had been gradually evolving for more than a century past, and now it took manifest shape—colored strongly by Fabius' sympathetic attitude to his own senatorial class.

EDITIONS—H. Peter, Historicorum Romanorum Reliquiae, v 1, 2nd ed., 1914; F. Jacoby, Die Fragmente der griechischen Historiker, 3c, 845ff.
ABOUT—P. Bung, Der erste römische Annalist (Cologne, dissertation), 1950; A. Alföldi, Early Rome and the Latins, 1964; M. Gelzer, Kleine Schriften, v 3, 1964; E. Badian, The Early Historians, in T. A. Dorey, ed., Latin Historians, 1966; M. Grant, Roman Myths, 1971; F. W. Walbank, Polybius, 1972; L. Pepe in Gli storiografi tramandati in frammenti, 1975; A. Momigliano, Essays in Ancient and Modern Historiography, 1977.

FABIUS RUSTICUS, Latin historian, wrote in Rome in the first century A.D.; since the fact that Britain is an island, demonstrated by Agricola's fleet in A.D. 84, was unknown to him, he apparently had completed at least part of his work before that year. If he was the Fabius Rusticus referred to in an inscription, he was still alive in 108. The historian came from Spain and does not seem to have been a senator—i.e., he was not one of the "senatorial historians," senators who had established a tradition of keeping historical writing in their own hands.

His history, of which only fragments have survived, dealt with the reign of Nero (A.D. 54–68) and perhaps with the civil war year A.D. 69 as well. He was hostile to Nero (blaming him for incestuous overtures to his mother Agrippina) and showed favor to his own compatriot and patron Seneca the Younger (d. A.D. 65). Fabius Rusticus is generally identified with a historian highly praised, though not named, by another

fā′ bi us   rus′ ti kus

Spaniard, the celebrated rhetorician Quintilian; if that is correct, his work had evidently won recognition before the death of Domitian (A.D. 96). Moreover, Fabius was explicitly named by the great historian Tacitus as a prose stylist of the same eminent caliber as the early historian Livy, who was much esteemed by his contemporaries. But the degree to which his work was utilized by Tacitus, either directly or through intermediaries such as Pliny the Elder, cannot be determined with any certainty.

EDITIONS—Fragments in H. Peter, Historicorum Romanorum Reliquiae, v 2, p 112ff.
ABOUT—R. Syme, Tacitus, 1958.

FAVORINUS, Greek rhetorician and philosopher, was born in about A.D. 81/2 at Arelate (Arles in southern France) and died in about 150. He learned Greek very early and went to Massilia (Marseille) to receive a Greek education—later supplemented, perhaps, by attendance at the lectures of Dio Chrysostom at Rome. Favorinus himself then carried out lecture tours to Athens and Corinth and the cities of Ionia. Subsequently, at Rome, he enjoyed the favor of the emperor Hadrian (A.D. 117–38) and became a knight and provincial high priest. In about 130, however, he fell into disgrace and was exiled to Chios, being supplanted in the imperial circle by his rival Polemo of Laodicea (d. 144). Antoninus Pius (138–61), however, allowed him to return to Rome, where he regained his former position and continued to live until his death. Plutarch was one of his friends, and his pupils included Herodes Atticus, Fronto, and Aulus Gellius. From birth, Favorinus had been a eunuch.

Apart from maxims preserved in collections of such material, few remains of his many writings have come down to us, but the titles of nearly thirty of them are extant. His works included two massive compilations reflecting his extensive reading: *Memoirs (Apomnemoneumata),* largely consisting of anecdotes about philosophers, and the *Miscellaneous History (Pantodape Historia),* an encyclopedic work in twenty-four books anticipating subsequent miscellanies by

fav ō rī′ nus

Aelian and Athenaeus. *On Exile*—portions of which have been found on a papyrus—and *Corinthian Affairs (Corinthiaca)* were autobiographical. The latter, in addition to an essay entitled *On Chance,* was formerly attributed to Dio Chrysostom, whose relatively simple style, however, is quite different from the artificial manner of Favorinus, which is laden with many figures of speech, quotations, and rhythmical effects.

A number of his works on philosophical themes showed his sympathy with the Sceptics; these included a treatise in ten books, *The Pyrrhonian Modes* (named after Pyrrho, the founder of the school). In this treatise Favorinus discussed the modes (grounds for suspense of judgment) propounded by another Sceptic, Aenesidemus of Cnossus, who had lived in the first century B.C. Galen, in his *De Optimo Dicendi Genere,* criticized Favorinus for supporting an inconsistent variety of scepticism.

EDITIONS—E. Mensching, Favorin von Arelate (Texte und Kommentare), 1963–; A. Barigazzi, Favorino di Arelate: Opere, 1966.
ABOUT—W. Schmid *in* Pauly-Wissowa-Kroll, Real-Encyclopädie der klassischen Altertumswissenschaft, v 6, column 2078; T. Colardeau, De Favorini Arelatensis Studiis et Scriptis (Grenoble, dissertation), 1903; B. Häsle, Favorin: Über die Verbannung (On Exile; Berlin, dissertation), 1935; C. Mensching, Favorin von Arelate (Berlin, dissertation), 1963.

FELIX, MARCUS MINUCIUS. See Minucius Felix, Marcus

FIRMIANUS LACTANTIUS, LUCIUS CAELIUS (or CAECILIUS). See Lactantius

FIRMICUS MATERNUS, JULIUS, Latin writer on astrology and theology, lived in the fourth century A.D. and came from Syracuse in Sicily.

In about A.D. 334–37, he wrote an eight-book treatise on astrology entitled *Learning*

fûr′ mi kus   må tûr′ nus

(Mathesis), a not uncommon name for this enormously popular pseudoscience that claimed to represent knowledge par excellence. The first book defends these claims, particularly against the criticisms of Carneades (head of the Platonic Academy in the second century B.C.). Elsewhere in the first book Firmicus boasts that it was he himself who introduced astrology to the Romans, an assertion which the prior existence of Manilius' *Astronomica* (first century A.D.) shows to have been unjustified. There are, in fact, considerable resemblances between portions of the two works, which may have drawn upon the same sources—perhaps a comprehensive treatise of the second century B.C. that we know to have been produced under the Egyptian pseudonyms *Nechepso* and *Petosiris.* Alternatively, Firmicus may have known the poem of Manilius, in which case he is one of the very few writers to have made use of it.

At any rate, despite little technical knowledge and modest protests that his talents fall short of so momentous a theme, Firmicus utilized his heavy dependence on earlier authorities to amass a great deal of knowledge on astrology—on which, indeed, *Learning* is the most comprehensive, if not the most intelligent, textbook. In order to avoid possible unfavorable repercussions from the court of Constantine the Great, during whose last years he was writing, he specifically exempted the emperor from the influence that the stars exert on ordinary human beings, on the grounds that he was a divinity.

Firmicus entertained an exalted conception of the calling of astrologers, from whom he demanded a rigorous code of moral integrity: they must lead a godly life because their concern is with the gods, and they must help those who consult them, not only with technical interpretations of the stars but with friendly advice as well. Astrologers, according to Firmicus, must also avoid certain things: nocturnal rites; the Circus (so that no one should think the results of contests were due to their presence); awkward questions about paternity; and perilous requests for the horoscopes of third parties.

The last two books of *Learning* list the constellations that determine how a person's life and career are going to turn out. This would seem to require thoroughgoing doctrine of predestination, but, the conflict between fate and free will is settled by Firmicus on Stoic lines, according to which the soul, being divine, is capable of triumphing over the stars, since their decrees, however formidable, may be overcome by prayer and worship of the gods. Although Firmicus is useful because he preserves information that is not otherwise accessible and although he does his best to embellish the *Learning* by an ornate form of diction, it remains a very dull work. Nevertheless, to judge by the many manuscripts that have come down to us, it appears clear that, despite ecclesiastical denunciations from time to time, the work was widely and eagerly read for centuries after its appearance.

After writing this pagan work, Firmicus, in his earnest quest after a satisfactory way of life, became a convert to Christianity—and a very enthusiastic one at that—as he showed by the composition of a further treatise, *On the Error of Profane Religions (De Errore Profanarum Religionum).* This polemic, which appeared between 343 and 350, in the reign of Constans and Constantius II, is much more vigorous and lively than *Learning*, and, although it has only survived in a battered and incomplete condition, it offers, in particular, many valuable details about the pagan cults and mysteries, which incur Firmicus' violent denunciation as the works of the devil; and he calls upon the emperors to wipe them out.

EDITIONS—Learning: W. Kroll, O. Skutsch, and K. Ziegler (Teubner ed.), 1897–1913. *With translation:* J. R. Bram, Ancient Astrology, Theory and Practice: The Mathesis of Firmicus Maternus, 1975. On the Error of Profane Religions: G. Heuten (German), 1938; K. Ziegler (German), 1953; A. Pastorino (Italian), 1969. An anonymous work entitled Consultations of Zacchaeus and Apollonius was ascribed to Firmicus by Dom G. Morin (1935 ed.). It is of interest to specialists in the text of the Latin Bible.
ABOUT—M. Hadas, History of Latin Literature, 1951; W. Gunkel and H. G. Gunkel, Die astrologische Literatur in der Antike, 1967.

FLACCUS, GAIUS VALERIUS. See Valerius Flaccus, Gaius

FLACCUS, QUINTUS HORATIUS. See Horace

FLORUS, LUCIUS ANNAEUS (one manuscript calls him Julius), Roman historian, lived in the second century A.D.: he is generally, though not always, identified with a poet named Florus who exchanged jocular verses with the emperor Hadrian (A.D. 117–38), or with another Florus, named Publius Annius, who wrote a dialogue on the well-debated (though to our minds, somewhat curious) issue of whether Virgil should be defined as an orator or a poet *(Vergilius Orator an Poeta).* The latter work, of which part of the introduction is extant, describes its author as an African who competed without success in the Capitoline literary competition under Domitian (A.D. 81–96) and then went to live at Tarraco (Tarragona) in Spain but returned to Rome in the reign of Hadrian.

The historical treatise that bears the name of Florus is an *Epitome of All Wars During Seven Hundred Years (Epitome Bellorum Omnium Annorum DCC).* The first of its two books sketches the rise of Rome's military strength and includes the wars of conquest down to 50 B.C. The second deals with what the writer regards as the period of decline, covering the civil wars from the time of the Gracchi in the second century B.C. down to the campaigns of Augustus, who receives praise for bringing peace to the world. The writer's statement that he is writing "not much less than two hundred years" after could be understood as referring to the political emergence of the future ruler Augustus in 43 or to his crowning victory in 31 B.C. The authorities whom Florus occasionally draws upon or echoes include Julius Caesar, Sallust, Seneca the Elder, and Virgil (and perhaps Lucan and Mela and Pliny the Elder), but above all Livy. Indeed, one of Florus' manuscripts describes his work as an abridgment of Livy's history. (In fact, however, he sometimes displays deviations from that source.) Nevertheless, the *Epitome* resembles Livy in its ecstatically patriotic tone, which results in Florus' description of

flō′ rus

the foreign powers Rome attacked during the republic as rebels—an anachronistic Florus interpretation of events. The *Epitome* contains topical references, including analogies to the wars of conquest of Trajan (A.D. 98–117), whose achievements he presents very favorably, though not without occasional implied criticisms—for example, the suggestion, "it is more important to keep a province than to conquer it."

All in all, he was a mediocre historian, whose narrative, although efficiently constructed and not without a certain vigor, was marred by repetitiveness, a rhetorical taste for exclamation, and a liking for epigrams that degenerate into obscurity. Although he consulted certain authorities, there are serious flaws in the chronology and geography cited in the *Epitome,* and his descriptions of individuals are faulty: for example, his indication of Marius' humble origins is incorrect. Yet, a convenient, rapid, emotionally nationalistic sketch of this kind met a characteristic need of his age and continued to be widely read from that time onward as the demand for such summaries increased still further. The *Epitome* influenced Rufius Festus and Ammianus Marcellinus in the fourth century, Orosius in the fifth, and Jordanes in the sixth; it remained influential in Byzantium, where John Malalas made use of the work; and it was apparently translated into Greek. In the medieval west, too, Florus' manuscripts multiplied, and he was quoted in the twelfth century by John of Salisbury. Moreover, his popularity continued throughout the Renaissance: the great humanist Joseph Scaliger (1540–1609) described him as "a very fine writer" *(un très bel auteur),* and new editions proliferated—in the Netherlands alone there were six between 1638 and 1674.

EDITIONS—E. Malcovati, 2nd ed., 1972. *With translation:* E. S. Forster, Florus (with Cornelius Nepos) (Loeb ed.), 1929; also Florus' poems *in* J. W. Duff and A. M. Duff, Minor Latin Poets, 2nd ed., 1935; P. Jal, Florus (Budé ed.), 1967.
ABOUT—J. W. Duff, A Literary History of Rome in the Silver Age, 1927; S. Lilliedahl, Florusstudien, 1928; W. den Boer, Some Minor Roman Historians, 1972.

FORTUNATUS, VENANTIUS. See Venantius Fortunatus

FRONTINUS, SEXTUS JULIUS, Roman official and Latin writer on military matters and hydraulic engineering, was born in about A.D. 30 and died in about 104. In 70 he was city praetor and held his first consulship in c. 74. Immediately afterward, he became governor of Britain (74–78), where he gained important successes against the Silures of southern Wales; and it was probably he who established the legionary camp at Isca (Caerleon on the Usk). In 83 he seems to have performed further military service in Germany with Domitian. That emperor's successor, Nerva, appointed him superintendent of Rome's aqueducts or water commissioner *(curator aquarum)* in 97. In the following year Frontinus served as consul for the second time and then, on a third occasion, in 100, as colleague of the next ruler Trajan.

He wrote a theoretical essay on Greek and Roman military science *(De Re Militari),* which was used by the military expert Vegetius in the fourth or fifth century B.C. It has not survived, but we possess its sequel, the *Stratagems (Strategemata).* Written in the reign of Domitian, this is a practical manual for the use of officers; it illustrates strategies or *ruses de guerre* by examples selected from Greek and Roman (mainly republican) history. The first of its four books deals with matters to be attended to before battle, the second discusses the battle itself, and the third is concerned with stratagems relating to the siege and defense of towns. The fourth book is of a different character, illustrating military management and concerning itself, also, with psychological and ethical questions and matters of morale; nor is its style quite the same. Owing to these divergences (and certain repetitions) from the earlier books, Frontinus' authorship of this final book has been questioned. The problem is complicated by the likelihood that the first three books, as we have them, contain later interpolations, some of which were perhaps inserted by the author of the
fron tiˊ nus

fourth book (if indeed he was a different person).

In his introduction to the *Stratagems* Frontinus claims to be the only writer who has ever provided a systematic treatment of military science. His work is a collection of anecdotes told one after another without intermission. Presented in a concise and straightforward style, they describe many interesting episodes of ancient history and make good reading. Numerous sources are drawn upon, especially Caesar, Sallust, and Livy, but this source material is freely rehandled—indeed sometimes too freely, since on occasion Frontinus' borrowings are inaccurate. Certain of his examples taken from military history are well abreast of modern ruthlessness, though it is curious to read that he sees no likelihood of existing engines of war ever being improved upon. In the Middle Ages, the *Stratagems* were excerpted by Sedulius Scotus and quoted by John of Salisbury. Petrarch possessed a copy, or had read one. Translations were made into French in 1430 and into English by William Caxton (from the French) in 1489; in the following century Spanish, German, and Italian versions appeared.

Frontinus also wrote a two-book treatise entitled *On Land-Surveying* (likewise published under Domitian), of which only fragments survive. But we still have his work entitled *On the Water Supply of Rome (De Aquis)*, which he began when he assumed the water commissionership under Nerva and completed during the reign of Trajan. On appointment to this position, believing that any decent man entrusted with an office should not be content with delegating everything to his staff, he set about collecting all the information that would help him in his duties, both for his own personal guidance and for the benefit of his successors. The result is a plain, competent, well-informed description of the aqueducts, indicating their history, the methods by which they were constructed, and the ways in which they were utilized for public reservoirs and other state needs, as well as for private purposes. In addition to investigating on his own, Frontinus consulted not only earlier authorities but engineers' reports, official documents and plans, and senatorial decrees on such subjects as the conservation of the water supply and ways of measuring the flow. A manuscript of *On the Water Supply* was discovered in Monte Cassino library in 1429 and was used as a practical textbook by the engineers who restored the old Roman aqueducts and built new ones. The work remains of great value today, not only for its technical information but because of the light it throws on an efficient, honest, Roman public servant carrying out his public functions.

EDITIONS—Stratagems: G. Gundermann, 1888; On the Water Supply: F. Krohn, 1922. *Translations*—C. E. Bennett and M. B. McElwain, Frontinus: Stratagems, Aqueducts (Loeb ed.), 1925, 1950; P. Grimal, Frontin: Les aqueducs de la ville de Rome (Budé ed.), 1944–61. On Surveying: Fragments *in* C. Lachmann, Römische Feldmesser, 1848.

ABOUT—C. Herschel, The Two Books on the Water Supply of Frontinus, 2nd ed., 1913; E. B. van Deman, The Building of the Roman Aqueducts, 1934; T. Ashby, Aqueducts of Ancient Rome, 1935; C. G. M. Bendz, Die Echtheitsfrage des vierten Buches des frontinschen Strategemata, 1938, *and* Textkritische und interpretatorische Bemerkungen zu den frontinschen Strategemata, 1943.

FRONTO, MARCUS CORNELIUS, Latin orator and philologist, was born in about A.D. 100 and died in 166 or soon afterward. His native city was Cirta in Numidia (Constantine in Algeria). He was educated at Carthage and probably Alexandria, where he formed numerous friendships; his teachers included the philosopher Athenodotus and the orator Dionysius. Moving to Rome, Fronto rapidly acquired a reputation as a barrister during the reign of Hadrian (117–38), whose successor Antoninus Pius appointed him tutor in Latin rhetoric to his adopted sons the future emperors Marcus Aurelius and Lucius Verus, with whom Fronto remained on intimate terms for the rest of his life. Fronto also passed through the successive stages of the Roman official career and became consul in 143. Ten years after that he was appointed governor of Asia but was unable to take up the post owing to the gout from which he persistently suffered during his later years. Moreover, his happy family life was shattered by the successive

fron' tō

deaths of five of his six daughters, in addition to that of the son of the only daughter who survived. When he himself died, Marcus Aurelius, who had become emperor with Lucius Verus as his colleague, set up his statue in the Senate and placed his bust among his own household gods.

Fronto was the leading orator of the day; later writers ranked him with Cato the Censor, Cicero, and Quintilian. Yet the few excerpts and titles of his speeches that have survived do not permit us to determine to what extent this reputation was deserved—or how far his practice corresponded with his theory. Of that theory we know a great deal, owing to the discovery in the early nineteenth century of palimpsests (at Milan and Rome) containing his letters (mainly addressed to Marcus Aurelius and Lucius Verus) together with a number of replies, among which Antoninus Pius is represented. These letters, although they show an increasing preoccupation with Fronto's health, throw useful light on the Antonine age and the quiet home life of its imperial circle. They display a genuine, and evidently mutual, affectionate relation with Marcus Aurelius, although Fronto was obviously disappointed that the young man preferred philosophy to rhetoric.

But, above all, the letters illustrate Fronto's views about the Latin tongue, the all-absorbing interest of his life. He firmly rejected the prevailing Silver Latin style and sought to reinvigorate the language—for example by a meticulous selection of vocabulary and by the lavish employment of similes. He also deplored the conventional purism that sought to restrict literary Latin to the words used in Cicero's speeches; he himself, instead, gave impetus to a movement already in existence by preferring the use of archaic words that he had found in early writers. He also added diversity to his style by the insertion of words current in popular speech. The composite form of diction that he thus created was known as the *elocutio novella.* In Fronto's own hands, as far as we can judge, it was lifeless, pedantic, flat, and dull. Nevertheless, it gained him a following, the *Frontoniani;* and it sprang to a fresh and extraordinary life when it was adapted by the genius of Apuleius (b. A.D. 123/25).

Some of Fronto's epistles are covering letters to rhetorical exercises that are mostly in Latin: *In Praise of Smoke and Dust,* for example, and *In Praise of Carelessness.* Other exercises, however, are in Greek, such as *The Erotic Discourse,* which resumes the arguments about homosexual love in Plato's *Phaedrus.* These essays are superficial and feeble, like his *Arion,* which narrates a myth already told by Herodotus without even a touch of Herodotus' freshness. Otherwise, Fronto's letters deal with commonplace matters between friends and are laced heavily with hypochondria.

EDITIONS—M. P. J. van den Hout, v 1, 1954; F. Portalupi, 1974. *Translations*—C. R. Haines, Fronto: Correspondence (Loeb ed.), revised eds., 1928, 1929.
ABOUT—M. D. Brock, Studies in Fronto and His Age, 1911; R. Marache, La critique littéraire de langue latine et le développement du goût archaisant au deuxième siècle de notre ère, 1952; P. Portalupi, Marco Cornelio Frontone, 1961.

GAIUS, Roman jurist, composed treatises on the law between the years 130 and 180 A.D. His other names are unknown, but some scholars have identified him with a jurist named Gaius Cassius Longinus, who was exiled by Nero in A.D. 65 and was recalled by Vespasian (69–79). If this identification is correct, the extant writings associated with Gaius' name cannot be in the form in which he wrote them, but must be later adaptations (by unknown authors), since they contain references to subsequent periods. Gaius Cassius Longinus was a pupil of the great jurist Masurius Sabinus and succeeded him as head of the school named after him, the Sabinian school, to which the works of Gaius also show allegiance. The fact that there are no contemporary notices of Gaius' life or literary activity, may be attributed partly to his relative insignificance, but can also be regarded as evidence that he lived and wrote somewhere in the provinces—an impression that is confirmed by the provincial preoccupation detectable in his writings, which make special reference to conditions in Asia Minor.

gā′ yus

This interest is particularly apparent in his monograph *Ad Edictum Provinciale,* the only known commentary on the Provincial Edict—that is to say, the edict published by governors of provinces to define the procedures they intended to follow during their period of office. Gaius also wrote a number of other monographs including a *Commentary on the Twelve Tables* (Rome's earliest juridical pronouncement, of the fifth century B.C.); the fragmentary remains of this commentary add something to our knowledge of Roman law.

His most important treatise, however, the *Institutiones* (Institutes), has been reconstructed almost in its entirety in the years since 1816 when the texts existing at that time, which were imperfect and had been contaminated by external elements, were supplemented by the discovery of a manuscript (probably of the fifth century A.D.) at Verona; the subsequent find of a fragmentary papyrus of the fourth century has filled certain gaps in the Verona text. The *Institutes* is a manual for beginners, divided into four books: (1) on persons and their different legal statuses; (2) on things and the modes by which rights over them may be acquired; (3) on intestate succession and obligations; (4) on actions and their forms. This arrangement, with the further subdivisions it entailed, may have originated not from Gaius himself but from some later editor, but owing to its simplicity it has exercised enormous influence on subsequent legal thought.

So too has the manner of Gaius' writing, for he offers an agreeably clear and economical form of exposition. Another of his merits is an unusual perseverance in attempting historical explanations. However, they are by no means always correct. Indeed, Gaius is rarely profound in any way whatever. To judge from his literary endeavors that have come down to us, he was a jurist of only the third or fourth rank, yet an enormous number of quotations from his works (as well as an imitation of the general plan of his *Institutes*) are to be found in the *Institutes* of Justinian I (A.D. 527–65). Yet those echoes in themselves can be of only limited use in any attempt to reconstruct Gaius' writings, owing to the ever-present dangers of distortion between his and Justinian's times. In consequence, the independent survival of the manuscript directly reproducing Gaius' *Institutes* is of exceptional value for our understanding of Roman legal development; and, in particular, our knowledge of Roman civil procedure relies almost entirely on what the work tells us.

EDITIONS—P. Krüger and G. Studemund, 7th ed., 1923; J. Reinach, 1950; M. David and H. L. W. Nelson, 1954– ; M. David, 2nd ed., 1964; E. Seckel and B. Kübler, 1969. Also, *see* Corpus Iuris Civilis: Digesta (extracts). *With translation:* F. de Zulueta, 1946–53.
ABOUT—A. M. Honoré, Gaius: A Biography, 1962; Gaio nel suo tempo (Atti del Simposio romanistico internazionale), 1966; W. Kunkel, Introduction to Roman Legal and Constitutional History, 1966; R. G. Boehm, Gaiusstudien, v 1-16, 1972–75.

GALEN (Galenos), Greek physician, anatomist, physiologist, psychologist, philosopher, and literary critic, was born in about A.D. 129 and died in about 199. His birthplace was Pergamum (Bergama) in Mysia (northwestern Asia Minor). At an early age he studied the Platonic, Peripatetic, Stoic, and Epicurean schools of philosophy. In 146, however, he began to learn medicine and after two years went to Smyrna to study under the eminent physician Pelops. Then he set out on extensive educational travels in Asia Minor, Greece, Cyprus, Phoenicia, Palestine, and Alexandria, where he visited the famous medical school. In 157 he returned to Pergamum to become a doctor attending gladiators. He moved to Rome about five years later, where he won a considerable reputation as a physician and gained many distinguished pupils and friends. In 166 he returned to Pergamum but three years later was recalled by the emperor Marcus Aurelius to serve in the German wars. This, however, Galen contrived to avoid, securing instead the appointment of medical attendant to Aurelius' son and heir Commodus. About the rest of his life little is known. Apparently he was in the capital in 191, when part of his library was burned in the fire that ravaged the city. He was still giving lectures there in the reign of Pertinax (193) but was apparently in Sicily at the time of his death.

gā′ len

His own bibliography, written in his later years and dedicated to a certain Eugenianus, was called *On the Order of His Own Works* —that is to say, the order in which they should be read. In it Galen enumerated 153 works he had written, contained in 504 books. Even so the list was not comprehensive, for much that has survived finds no place in it. The extant medical works attributed to his authorship (filling twenty volumes of Kühn's edition) number more than 150, complete or preserved in large part, of which nearly a hundred are evidently authentic; eighteen further monographs survive only in fragments; and others have come down to us in Latin or Arabic translations.

As anatomist and physiologist alike, Galen not only gathered together and amended the results achieved by earlier generations of researchers but added many new facts on his own account. His anatomical studies were unequaled in the ancient world for their thoroughness and accuracy. His principal works in this field are *On the Use of the Parts of the Human Body* and *On Anatomical Procedure*. These treatises deal effectively with the skull, the vertebral column, the ribs, the breastbone, and the bones of the limbs. Although Galen's dissections were largely performed on animals, much accurate information relating to human muscles and bones is also incorporated in his writings.

Galen's physiological researches, which were likewise of pioneering character, are represented by his essay entitled *On the Natural Faculties*. His views on the origin and flow of the blood and on the septum of the heart, and his hypothesis of three types of spirit *(pneuma)*, dominated medical studies for many centuries. In the field of epidemiology, he concluded that three factors were involved in the causation of epidemics: (1) an alteration in the balance of body humors; (2) a nonspecific external factor; (3) a specific external factor, dependent on the weather. As an experimental physiologist, he produced cerebral lesions in animals and did work on the function of the spinal cord not fully appreciated until the nineteenth century. His acumen in the field of neurology is particularly impressive.

On the subject of pathology he left a six-book work entitled *On Affected Places (De Locis Affectis)*, giving an authoritative account of inflammation and describing malaria, bronchitis, empyema, and hydrophobia. His treatise *On Tumors* put forward views on the nature of external swellings that remained unassailed for a millennium. His researches in pathology were founded on the doctrine of the Four Humors that went back to the school of Hippocrates of Cos, the founder of Greek medicine in the fifth century B.C., whom Galen held in particular esteem.

On therapeutics Galen's principal treatise is *Therapeutical Method*. He also wrote many pharmacological studies, including a piece entitled *About the Mixing and Efficacy of Drugs;* he was indefatigable in his search for new drugs in the course of his travels. In the field of diagnostics, *On the Diagnosis of Different Pulses* not only displays his mastery in diagnosis and prognosis but gives valuable autobiographical information as well. His treatise entitled *On Medical Names* survives in an Arabic retranslation of a Syriac version.

He also left several psychological studies of considerable interest. The *Protrepticus,* supplemented by *Students' Guide to Medical Sects,* is an attempt at the popularization of medicine in which he recommends its study to the young, arguing with urgent sincerity that professional studies of one kind or another are the only suitable occupation for people whose minds are above the animal level. In addition he wrote commentaries on no fewer than nineteen texts of the Hippocratic corpus and an important work entitled *On the Doctrines of Hippocrates and Plato,* in nine books. Galen rejected specialization, characteristic of his time, as undesirably narrow and instead set himself the gigantic ambition of covering practically the entire field of medicine. He was familiar not only with the Hippocratic tradition but with all the other principal medical systems as well. Nor was his practical understanding of medicine inferior to his theoretical knowledge; he appreciated with special clarity that the subject can never find full expression in general statements, since the physician's concern is always with separate individuals.

Galen believed that every physician ought to equip himself with an adequate education before he began to study medicine at all. To this end he wrote extensive nonmedical works, of which only fragments survive. Of his grammatical and rhetorical writings we know little more than the titles. Many of them bear witness to a detailed preoccupation with the vocabulary of the Attic prose authors; and he wrote a monograph, *Noteworthy Attic Words*. In addition, he compiled five studies on ancient comedy. In particular, however, his bibliography of his own works mentions no less than one hundred and twenty-four philosophical treatises (in addition to his comparative analysis of Hippocrates and Plato), including commentaries on Plato's *Timaeus* and *Philebus* and on Aristotle's *Categories* and *Analytics*. Galen's own position is that of a well-read eclectic who is prepared to give credit to all schools except Epicureanism and Stoicism. And, in particular, he held Plato and Aristotle in very high respect.

He also occupies a significant place in the history of religion. Like many of his contemporaries, he possessed a firm monotheistic belief in a supreme creator of the entire universe. As a determinist, he believed that Providence had disposed the bodily organs in such perfect relation to their functions that no superior arrangement could possibly be imagined. But he goes farther, asserting that God's purposes can be discovered in full detail from the examination of his works. This was an attitude that foreshadowed the Middle Ages. Incidentally, Galen makes several mentions both of Judaism and of Christianity, though his opinion of neither religion was high.

The tone of his writings suggests that he was not an easy person to get along with. He indulges in copious and aggressive vituperation directed against men whose opinions have incurred his disapproval; and at all times he seems thoroughly pleased with himself, not to say boastful. In the fourth century A.D. his follower Oribasius declared that he ranked first among the great physicians, declaring him "supreme among all those who have written about the same subject, since he employs the most exact methods and definitions, as one who follows the Hippocratic principles and opinions"—a statement that illustrates the widespread belief that Galen faithfully represented the original tradition of Hippocrates, though this ignores the many centuries of development that had intervened.

Galen's monotheism no doubt contributed to his enormous popularity among medieval scholars, on whose conception of the nature of life he exercised a decisive effect. His writings were translated first into Arabic; in about the eleventh century certain Latin versions were in circulation; and after 1400 the canon of his original Greek writings was gradually restored. While Andreas Vesalius, the founder of modern anatomy, subjected his medical methods to attack in 1543 (as some had ventured to do earlier), nevertheless, Galen's influence persisted throughout all this period—and even in later centuries—on a scale comparable only to that of Aristotle. He was revered not only for his massive scientific achievements but, above all, for his establishment of common concepts of medicine that rise above all sectional differences and provide common ground where all scientists can meet and agree.

WORKS (spuriously or dubiously attributed to Galen)—In the corpus of more than 160 Galenic works 45 are falsely ascribed to him and 19 are of doubtful authenticity.

EDITIONS—C. G. Kühn, 20 (22) volumes, 1821–33, gradually being superseded by Corpus Medicorum Graecorum (Teubner ed.), 1914– ; J. Marquardt and others, Claudii Galeni Pergameni Scripta Minora (Teubner ed.), 1884–93. Lists of works *in* Corpus Medicorum Graecorum and *in* K. Deichgräber, Deutsche Akademie der Wissenschaften (Altertumswissenschaft, v 8), 1957. Lists of commentaries and translations *in* A. Lesky, History of Greek Literature, 1966, p 897, and *in* Oxford Classical Dictionary, 2nd ed., 1970, p 455; translations after 1954 *also in* J. Scarborough, Roman Medicine, 1969, pp 165-66. *Add*: L. H. Duckworth, On Anatomical Procedures: The Later Books, 1962; J. S. Kieffer, Institutio Logica, 1964; B. Alexanderson, On Crises (De Crisibus), 1967; M. T. May, On the Usefulness of the Parts of the Body, 1968; N. Marinone, La dieta dimagrante, 1973; R. J. Durling and F. Kudlien, Galenus Latinus, 1976, 1978; R. B. Edlow, On Language and Ambiguity (De Captionibus), 1976; R. Siegel, On the Affected Parts (De Locis Affectis), 1976.

ABOUT—R. Walzer, Galen on Jews and Christians, 1949; G. Sarton, Galen of Pergamon, 1954; R. E. Siegel, Galen's System of Physiology and Medicine, 1968, *and* Galen on Sense Perception, 1970, *and* Galen on

GALLICANUS

Psychology, Psychopathology, and Function and Diseases of the Nervous System, 1973; H. Flashar, ed., Antike Medizin, 1971; L. G. Ballester, Galeno en la sociedad y en la ciencia de su tempo, 1972; C. R. S. Harris, The Heart and the Vascular System in Ancient Greek Medicine, 1972; G. E. R. Lloyd, Greek Science After Aristotle, 1973, and Hippocratic Writings (Penguin ed.), 1978; E. D. Phillips, Greek Medicine, 1973; O. Temkin, Galenism, 1973; V. Nutton, Galen, 1979.

GALLICANUS, VULCACIUS. See Spartianus, Aelius

GALLUS, GAIUS CORNELIUS, Roman governor and Latin poet, was born at Forum Julii (Fréjus in southern France) in 69 B.C. and died in 26. He was perhaps of Gallic descent. In 41, during the civil wars, he held some responsibility for the settlement of ex-soldiers in Cisalpine Gaul (northern Italy) and was said to have prevented Virgil's farm from being confiscated for this purpose. After the victory of Octavian (the future Augustus) over Mark Antony at Actium, Gallus, a senior officer in Octavian's service, took over Antony's forces in Cyrenaica and advanced to Alexandria, where he helped to arrange the capture of Cleopatra. He was subsequently made the first governor *(praefectus)* of the new Roman province of Egypt, directly dependent on the ruler himself. In this capacity, he crushed local revolts and advanced south beyond the First Cataract, receiving the king of Ethiopia into clientship with Rome. Then he proceeded to commemorate these feats in a bombastic trilingual inscription at Philae (29 B.C.) and in further inscriptions upon the pyramids; he also set up his own statues in numerous places. For this reason, and possibly for others unknown, the emperor recalled him and renounced his friendship, allowing a charge against him, probably for treason, to come before the Senate; whereupon Gallus committed suicide.

His poetry included four books of elegies entitled *Loves (Amores)*, addressed to his mistress (formerly Antony's), the actress Volumnia, who bore the stage name of Cytheris but was called Lycoris in his po-

gal' lus

174

ems. Only one line of all these writings survives, but Virgil, in his tenth *Eclogue* in which Gallus himself appears, includes passages and lines based on his poetic works. These poems by Gallus were quite widely read; they belonged to what was later regarded as the standard type of Latin elegiac verse, consisting of a series of brief poems treating of the poet's relationship with a single woman. Indeed, this was a poetic form that seems to have been inaugurated by Gallus himself; if so, Lycoris was the forerunner and model of the literary "mistresses" of Tibullus, Propertius, and Ovid. In the words of the last-named, "Gallus and Propertius succeeded Tibullus; I myself was the fourth in order of time." Some of Gallus' elegies were based on short prose outlines (still extant) of love-stories adapted from Greek originals by his friend the poet and elegist Parthenius of Nicaea, who had come to Italy in 73 B.C. and dedicated his book on unhappy love affairs to Gallus.

In addition to elegies, he also wrote epyllia (miniature epics), including a poem (of which only a single line survives) about the shrine and grove of Apollo at Gryneium in Aeolis (western Asia Minor). His model for this piece was Euphorion, the Greek poet of the third century B.C., who, although he did not go to Alexandria, was one of the leading practitioners of the Alexandrian, Hellenistic tradition; in Latin literature Gallus was likewise one of the principal exponents of Alexandrianism.

ABOUT—R. Syme, The Roman Revolution, 1939; V. Ehrenberg and A. H. M. Jones, Documents Illustrating the Reigns of Augustus and Tiberius, 2nd ed., 1955, p 58 (No 21, texts of the Philae inscription); H. Bardon, La littérature latine inconnue, v 2, 1956; J. P. Boucher, Gaius Cornelius Gallus, 1966; G. Luck, The Latin Love Elegy, 2nd ed., 1969; D. O. Ross, Backgrounds to Augustan Poetry: Gallus, Elegy and Rome, 1975.

GELLIUS, AULUS, Latin encyclopedic writer, was born in about A.D. 130—it is not known where—and died in about 180, or perhaps somewhat earlier. He studied at Rome, learning literature from Gaius Sulpicius Apollinaris of Carthage and rhetoric from Antonius Julianus; he was also ac-

gel' li us

quainted with Fronto. Continuing his education at Athens, he attended the lectures of Calvena Taurus and was entertained by Herodes Atticus. On returning to Rome he served for a time as a judge dealing with private cases and fulfilled his duties with meticulous devotion. He was married and had children.

He wrote the *Attic Nights (Noctes Atticae)* in twenty books, so called in memory of the happy time he spent at Athens. The work is an enormous collection of anecdotes about people he had known—rhetoricians, grammarians, and philosophers—as well as great personages of the past. In this museum of curiosities Gellius roves over a wide range of subjects, including law, religion, and history, but his principal concern is with literature: textual, biographical, and philological questions and various aspects of criticism receive attention, but above all the correct use of words, phrases, and idioms. No fewer than 275 Greek and Latin authors, past and present, are mentioned by name, and they are cited abundantly in quotations which fill many gaps in our knowledge. As a friend of the archaizer Fronto, Gellius pays particular attention to the older literature of the Roman Republic, and his own style is a curious mixture of purity and archaism. Many of these older sources were evidently available to him from his own extensive library, whereas his acquaintance with others was only secondhand, though it is difficult to determine the authorities from whom he obtained them.

Although he himself does not appear to have possessed specialized competence in any of the fields in which he dealt, Gellius is on the whole conscientious and accurate. The arrangement of his work, he tells us, is deliberately haphazard. Still, individual chapters are constructed with care and frequently brightened by picturesque imaginary settings. A section often begins with a conversation with some learned personage and continues with a quotation from some book that throws light on the problem under discussion. Gellius' manner has an undoubted charm, and he seems to have been an amiable and modest man with a deep respect for scholarship.

Moreover, the things that caught his eye have a way of being interesting. In the fourth century he was used by the lexicographer and grammarian Nonius Marcellus and earned Augustine's praise; then Macrobius drew upon him for his *Saturnalia.* Gellius' medieval popularity is displayed by his appearance in anthologies of the twelfth century, when John of Salisbury also studied his work. Petrarch possessed, or had read, a copy of the *Attic Nights,* and it was subsequently one of the earliest Latin works ever to be printed. Among his later admirers was Erasmus.

EDITIONS—J. M. Hornsby, 1936 (Book 1 only); F. Weiss, 1975. *Translations*—J. C. Rolfe (Loeb ed.), 1927, revised ed. of v 3, 1952; R. Marache, Aulu-Gelle: Nuits attiques (Budé ed.), 1967–78.
ABOUT—M. D. Brock, Studies in Fronto and His Age, 1911; R. Marache, La critique littéraire de la langue latine et le développement du goût archaïsant au deuxième siècle de notre ère, 1952; L. Gamberale, La traduzione in Gellio, 1969; B. Baldwin, Studies in Aulus Gellius, 1975.

GEORGE THE MONK (otherwise known as the **Archimandrite** or as **Hamartolus,** the Sinner), Greek historian of the Byzantine epoch, lived during the reign of Michael III (the Drunkard) (A.D. 842–67), but nothing else is known about his life.

He was a writer of a *Concise Chronicle (Chronicon Syntomon),* which was a four-book universal history covering the period from Adam to the death of the Byzantine emperor Theophilus in 842. His authorities are diverse and not always identifiable, including ecclesiastical histories that are now lost; but the early part of his work is mainly compiled from the chronicle of John Malalas (died c. 578) and from Theophanes Confessor (died 817). However, he deals with his sources very uncritically, and it is only the last part of his *Chronicle*—covering the earlier years of his own ninth century—that possesses significant value as a historical source. It is, indeed, our only contemporary chronicle for the period. For the events of his own time, George makes use of the oral accounts of contemporaries in addition to his own personal observation and offers a vivid account of the topics and problems that preoccupied Byzantine monks of the epoch, including the threatening expansion of Islam. Greek mythology, too, is a subject of interest to him.

George's style is simple and popular; in his own words, "It is better to stammer in company with the truth than to Platonize with falsehood." He also claims in his introduction that his sole purpose is to narrate such things as are "useful and necessary," with strict adherence to the truth. However, his aim is, in fact, not the objective truth but a narrowly ecclesiastical and edifying version. His concept of historical causation is entirely theological. He is a violent opponent of the iconoclastic "heresy" that had until recently prevailed at court and he praises the restoration of icons by Theophilus' widow Theodora (843).

The *Chronicle* of George the Monk was drawn upon by the excerptors employed by Constantine VII Porphyrogenitus (913–59), and the work formed the basis of many Byzantine attempts at universal history. As a result of this popularity, however, his manuscript tradition was altered and embroidered on numerous occasions and has come down to us in an insolubly complicated form. The *Chronicle* also exercised great influence on the early stages of Slavonic literature, having been translated into Old Slavonic in the tenth or eleventh century and fulfilling an important role in the beginnings of Russian historical literature. Moreover, an illustrated manuscript of one of the Russian translations contains 127 miniatures that are of importance to the study of that country's thirteenth century art. The *Chronicle* was also translated into Georgian, perhaps in c. 1100.

A continuation of the *Chronicle* carried the historical narrative up to 948. Its writer, who is known as Georgius Continuatus, was more interested in political history than his predecessor, and his strong bias against Constantine VII and the Macedonian dynasty suggests that he was a supporter of the deposed emperor Romanus I Lecapenus (919–44); he has been believed by some to be the historian Symeon Magister, whose own identity, however, is the subject of much discussion. Subsequently, Georgius Continuatus was reedited with substantial additions taken from the *History* of Joseph

Genesius. This work, like the original *Chronicle,* was extensively used by later Byzantine scholars and was translated into Old Slavonic.

EDITIONS—J. P. Migne, Patrologia Graeca, v 110; C de Boor, Georgius Monachus, Chronicon, 1904; V. M. Istrin, The Chronicle of George Hamartolus in Its Old Slavonic-Russian Version, 1974.
ABOUT—D. Ainalov, Compte-rendu du deuxième Congrès international des études byzantines, 1927; G. Moravcsik, Byzantinoturcica, 2nd ed., v 1, 1958. On Georgius Continuatus: see bibliography in A. A. Vasiliev, History of the Byzantine Empire, 1961 ed., v 1, p 365, note 170.

GEORGE THE PISIDIAN, Greek poet of the Byzantine epoch, lived in the first half of the seventh century A.D. and was born in Pisidia (central Asia Minor). In the reign of the emperor Heraclius I (610–41), he became deacon and archivist *(chartophylax)* of the Church of the Holy Wisdom (Hagia Sophia) at Constantinople.

His works include important historical poems. *On the Expedition of Heraclius Against the Persians* was apparently an eyewitness account. It consisted of nearly eleven hundred iambic verses; his other pieces were shorter. The *Avarica* was a description of how the attack on Constantinople by the group of central European barbarian peoples known as the Avars, in 626, was defeated by the intercession of the Holy Virgin. The *Heraclias* is a panegyric on the emperor Heraclius on the occasion of his final victory over the Persian king Chosroes II in 628. There is also a brief piece on Heraclius' recovery of the cross. *The Six Days (Hexaemeron)* alludes to the six-year war in which the emperor had defeated the Persians. But this poem's principal subject was the creation of the universe *(Cosmourgia),* a favorite subject of Christian writers. It was later translated into Armenian and Old Slavonic. George the Pisidian also wrote a poetic treatise on the vanity of life, in the manner of *Ecclesiastes,* as well as a poem on the resurrection of Christ and an attack on the heretical Severus, bishop of Antioch. In addition, he was the author of epigrams, some

pi sid' i ən

of inordinate length, on religious and historical themes of the day.

But George's style is lucid and pure, and sometimes achieves grandeur. His vocabulary is extensive and judiciously employed, and his imagery can be imposing. He knew the Greek tragedians well, yet he did not echo them slavishly. But his main achievement was technical and metrical. He ingeniously combined the laws of classical meter, based on quantity, with new, Byzantine, metrical principles, based on numbers of syllables and patterns of stress accent. He thus became the perfecter, if not the originator, of the twelve-syllable meter used by subsequent Byzantine poets as late as the fourteenth century. As these imitations testify, George the Pisidian was much respected by his compatriots in ancient times: the famous eleventh century scholar Michael Psellus was even asked: "Who was a better writer of verse, Euripides or George of Pisidia?" Modern opinion finds this question surprising, since nowadays George's verses, despite their merits, seem to fall a good deal short of the great tragedians. Nevertheless, he was the best secular poet the Byzantine empire ever produced; and, in particular, his historical poems are still, as they have always been, an important source for the campaigns of the age.

EDITIONS—J. P. Migne, Patrologia Graeca, v 92; A. Pertusi, Giorgio di Pisidia, Poemi, v 1: Panegirici epici, 1960 (with Italian translation).
ABOUT—K. Krumbacher, Geschichte der byzantinischen Literatur, 2nd ed., 1897; F. Dolger, Die byzantinische Dichtung in der Reinsprache, 1948.

GERBERT, Latin scholar and writer, who became Pope Silvester II, was born in the Auvergne (central France) in about A.D. 950 and died in 1003. He studied at the Benedictine monastery of S. Géraud at Aurillac under abbot Raimund. Then, in 967, he was brought to Spain to study mathematics by Borel, count of Barcelona, who entrusted his higher education to Hatto, bishop of Ausonia (Vich). In 970 or 971 Gerbert accompanied these two dignitaries to Rome, where his knowledge of music and astronomy
zher bâr'

prompted Pope John XIII to recommend him to the German emperor Otto I as tutor to his sons. In about 972, however, he returned to France where he lectured for many years at the cathedral school at Rheims. There, despite clashes with rival scholars such as Otric of Saxony (against whom, by order of Otto II, he conducted a formal disputation at Ravenna in 980) he won far-reaching fame as both a scholar and a teacher, and he played a prominent part in extending the study of logic and reviving the knowledge of Greek thought. The works he wrote, and his methods of teaching, and the pupils he taught—who included Robert Capet, the future king of France, and the chronicler Richer of Chartres, and Fulbert the future bishop of the same town—played a preeminent role in the advancement of learning in northern Europe during the next two generations.

In about 982 Gerbert was made abbot of Bobbio and prince of the empire by Otto II, on whose death in the following year, however, he returned to his studies at Rheims. There, on the death of the archbishop, Gerbert (after an initial disappointment amid numerous intrigues) was appointed to the office in 991. When, however, confirmation of the appointment was withheld from Rome, he proceeded there in order to attempt to obtain it and was present at the coronation of the young emperor Otto III (996), who fell under his influence. Otto, whose vision of a restored Holy Roman Empire was said to have been largely Gerbert's idea, secured for him first the archbishopric of Ravenna (998) and then in the next year the papacy, to which he succeeded as Silvester II. Gerbert's ambitious, universal, plans for the advancement of the church and empire, in partnership, were terminated by the deaths first of Otto (1002) and then of himself.

He was not only the leading statesman of his time but also its most eminent scholar; he transformed the current educational thought by demanding that the various disciplines aim at covering the whole of experience. We know from his learned pupil Richer how, at Rheims, he taught the *Trivium* (grammar, rhetoric, dialectic)—composing a series of model speeches for his pupils to imitate—and, in addition, the more advanced *quadrivium* (arithmetic, astronomy, geometry, and music). He was responsible for a revival of mathematics: to assist his courses in this subject, he borrowed from the Saracens—and thus reintroduced to the West—the ancient calculating board known as the abacus, which he constructed with twenty-seven divisions and a thousand counters. For his astonomy lectures he made elaborate celestial and terrestrial globes; he also devised a remarkable clock or sundial at Magdeburg. Music, however, was apparently the subject in which he was particularly expert, and his inventions in this field included an organ and other instruments. Probably his most lasting achievement, however, and a task to which he devoted great attention and expense, was his collection of ancient manuscripts of the rapidly vanishing pagan classical writers.

Gerbert's extant writings include mathematical works *(On the Use of the Abacus, On the Division of Numbers,* and *Geometry)* and philosophical treatises, including a discussion of the question whether the employment of reason can properly be described as an attribute of the responsible human being *(De Rationali et Ratione Uti)*. Less technical and more stylish are his official reports. However, particular value attaches to his letters, of which more than two hundred have survived, mostly concerned with ecclesiastical and political affairs but many also treating of personal and domestic matters.

Gerbert's renowned erudition and portentous versatility caused a large number of miraculous (and sometimes erotic) legends to accumulate around his career; in particular, it was widely supposed, notably by William of Malmesbury, that he must have been a magician who derived his learning from the devil, to whom he had sold himself.

EDITIONS—J. P. Migne, Patrologia Latina, v 139; J. Havet, Lettres de Gerbert, 1889; N. Boubnov, Gerberti Opera Mathematica, 1899. *With translation:* H. P. Lattin, The Letters of Gerbert . . . , 1961.
ABOUT—M. Manitius, Geschichte der lateinischen literatur des Mittelalters, 1911–31; J. Leflon, Gerbert d'Aurillac: Humanisme et chrétienté au dixième siècle, 1946; K. Strecker, Introduction to Medieval Latin, 1957; G. Cremaschi, Guida alla studio del latino medi-

oevale, 1959; P. Wolff, L'éveil intellectuel de l'Europe, 1971; K. F. Werner, Zur Überlieferung der Briefe Gerberts von Aurillac, 1974.

GERMANICUS (Nero Claudius Germanicus), Roman imperial prince and Latin poet, the elder son of Nero Drusus (Drusus the Elder) and Antonia (the Younger), was born in 15 B.C. and died in A.D. 19. In A.D. 4 he assumed the names Germanicus Julius Caesar upon his adoption by the future emperor Tiberius (himself Augustus' adopted son), under whom he served in Pannonia (Middle Danube) and in Germany. After holding the consulship in A.D. 12, Germanicus became the principal commander in Gaul and Germany, where he dealt with a mutiny on the Rhine and conducted three spectacular but unproductive campaigns in the heart of "free" Germany, for which Tiberius, now emperor awarded him a Triumph in the year 17. He was then appointed to an overall command in the eastern provinces instead but died mysteriously at Antioch, his death being blamed, probably without justification, upon the governor of Syria, Cnaeus Calpurnius Piso, with whom his relations had been seriously strained. His widow, Augustus' granddaughter Agrippina the Elder, who had borne Germanicus nine children, survived.

Germanicus was affable and attractive, and these qualities, which were in marked contrast to the grim reserve of Tiberius, gained him great popularity among his soldiers and supporters. Moreover, he was studious and eloquent, achieving a considerable reputation as an orator. He also composed Greek comedies, which have vanished, though his brother Claudius staged one of them after his death. In addition, he wrote epigrams in elegiac couplets, Greek and Latin alike; a few of these poems have been preserved, including a Latin piece about a boy who met with a fatal accident on the ice.

Germanicus is also generally regarded as the author of the hexameter adaptation of a Greek poem by Aratus of Soli (d. 240/239) B.C.), the *Phaenomena.* The Latin version of

jûr man' i kus or gār mä' ni kus

GERMANICUS

this work contains nine hundred lines of which seven hundred are devoted to astronomical matters and the remainder to weather forecasts *(Diosemeia)*. It has come down to us under the unspecific name of Claudius Caesar, but the fourth century writer Lactantius quotes a verse from "Germanicus Caesar in his Aratean poem," and the attribution to his authorship is confirmed by internal evidence. Astronomy formed part of the liberal Roman education, and the blend of astronomy and mythology favored by Aratus had remained popular; an earlier Latin version had been produced by Cicero. Germanicus is both a better poet and a better astronomer than Cicero had been; indeed, his verses are as poetical as those of Aratus—or, rather, no more unpoetical. He paraphrases his Greek original rather than translating it exactly, correcting errors in the light of later knowledge and inserting passages of his own composition. He is also slightly apologetic about the veracity of some of the myths he introduces, prefacing them with rationalistic reservations such as "if an old story may find favor."

EDITIONS—D. B. Gain, The Aratus Ascribed to Germanicus Caesar, 1976; A. Le Boeuffle, Germanicus: Les phénomènes d'Aratos (Budé ed.), 1975.
ABOUT—W. F. Akveld, Germanicus, 1961; R. Seager, Tiberius, 1972; A. Garzetti, From Tiberius to the Antonines, 1974 (bibliographies on p 572ff. and p 734ff.); B. Levick, Tiberius the Politician, 1976; C. Santini, Il segno e la tradizione in Germanico scrittore, 1977.

GORGIAS, Greek rhetorician and sophist or itinerant lecturer, was born in about 483 B.C., or slightly earlier, and died in about 376. His birthplace was Leontini (Centini) in Sicily, where he was said to have been a pupil of the philosopher-scientist Empedocles. He also appears to have come under the influence of two other Sicilians, Corax and Tisias, joint authors of the first textbook on rhetoric, the second of whom accompanied him when he visited Athens as an envoy of his hometown in 427. The date is remembered as an important one in the history of rhetoric, for, from this time onward, Athenian poets and orators and historians began to model their styles on Gorgias. Little is known about the rest of his travels; he appears to have given lectures in Thessaly, and he erected a statue of himself at Delphi, where the base of another of his statues, set up by a descendant, has also been found.

His philosophical background, reflecting western Greek schools, was displayed by his work entitled *On Not Being* or *On Nature,* which has not survived, though we can obtain some idea of its character from a subsequent reference and from a treatise of unknown authorship with the title *On Melissus, Xenophanes and Gorgias.* In *On Not Being* Gorgias is said to have made three points: nothing exists; if it did, we could not know about it; and finally, even if it did exist and could be known, it could not be communicated. As a rhetorician, Gorgias was to some extent out to shock his audience, or at least to show them how arguments could be pursued to extreme and sometimes paradoxical conclusions. But this was also his way of warning people against excessive pretensions to positive knowledge. For he preferred probability to certainty, regarding absolute truth as undiscoverable—and perhaps inexpressible as well.

As the key to the discovery of the probable, Gorgias, even more than other sophists, stressed the potency of oral communication, seeing rhetoric as "the mistress of persuasion," the title coined for it by his fellow

gôr′ ji ǎs

Sicilians. He studied and applied the best ways of making prose impressive and interesting, consciously and deliberately exploiting the sound of the spoken word for oratorical effect. To this end, he made use of quasi-poetic figures of speech that, although not entirely new, he himself developed so elaborately that they became known as Gorgian figures *(schemata Gorgieia)*. In particular, he constantly arranged his language and thought alike in a series of balancing and often rhyming parallelisms and antitheses, heightened by continuous verbal assonances and framed in a highly ornate form of Attic diction.

Gorgias probably felt equally at home delivering both prepared and extemporaneous orations. A considerable section of the *Funeral Speech (Epitaphios)* that he wrote for the Athenian dead in the Peloponnesian War (431–404 B.C.) is extant: it asserts that victories of Greek over Greek can only merit lamentation. There is also record of a speech entitled *In Praise of Elis* and of another entitled *Pythian Address* that was delivered from the steps of the Delphic altar when his statue was dedicated there.

Two further compositions by Gorgias have survived complete—they constitute the earliest rhetorical declamations to have come down to us. One, *In Praise of Helen,* defends the heroine from the many criticisms directed against her; it employs every rhetorical device and contains a significant eulogy of "the word," reflecting his belief in the preeminent importance of language. The *Defense of Palamedes*—according to the legend Palamedes was put to death by the Greeks before Troy as a supposed traitor—is another protest against unjust condemnation. In both pieces Gorgias argues his case on the basis of probability, but in the concluding passage of the *Helen* he admits that he is writing with tongue in cheek. He also shows awareness that his rhetorical technique borrows some of its methods from the poets, declaring that oratory resembles poetry in that both can exercise complete mastery over the soul.

Gorgias' methods were echoed by the orator Antiphon and the historian Thucydides; his views also colored the styles and methods of a number of his own pupils. These included the tragic poet Agathon (whose speech in Plato's *Symposium* is a parody of Gorgias), as well as the philosopher Antisthenes, until the latter attached himself to Socrates instead. But Gorgias' influence appears at its strongest in Isocrates, whose teacher he became in Thessaly.

EDITIONS (of Fragments)—O. Immisch, Gorgiae Helena, 1927; H. Diels, Fragmente der Vorsokratiker, 5th ed., 1934; L. Radermacher, Artium Scriptores, 1951; W. Vollgraff, L'oraison funèbre de Gorgias, 1952. *Translations*—R. K. Sprague, The Older Sophists, 1972.
ABOUT—M. Untersteiner, The Sophists, 1954; G. Kennedy, The Art of Persuasion in Greece, 1963; R. S. Brumbaugh, The Philosophers of Greece, 1964; W. K. C. Guthrie, History of Greek Philosophy, v 3, 1969; R. Vitali, Gorgia: Retorica e filosofia, 1971; H. J. Newiger, Untersuchungen zu Gorgias' Schrift über das Nichtseiende, 1973; C. J. Classen, ed., Sophistik, 1976.

GOTTSCHALK (Fulgentius Godescalchus), German theologian and Latin poet, was born in about A.D. 805 or 810 and died in 867 or 870. He came of an aristocratic Saxon family. As a child, he became an oblate (dedicated to the monastic or religious life) at the monastery at Fulda, where Hrabanus Maurus was abbot. But Gottschalk decided to seek relief from his vows and in 829 obtained a dispensation from the synod of Mainz. However, this displeased Hrabanus, who after carrying the case to the emperor had the dispensation revoked and compelled Gottschalk to enter another monastery at Orbais. There he got to know the works of Saint Augustine. After a few years he emerged from Orbais as a traveling preacher, delivering sermons at Rheims (where he was irregularly ordained a priest) and in the Verona and Friuli regions of northern Italy (c. 845–46); at one point he also visited the Balkans.

His theological message was largely concerned with double predestination—that is to say, the doctrine that an omniscient and omnipotent God foreordains not only the salvation of certain souls but also the damnation of certain others. He also maintained that the divine will to grant salvation was of limited extent and that Christ's redemption

gôt' shälk

only benefited the elect. These teachings evoked protests from the bishop of Verona, and in 848 Hrabanus Maurus, who had become archbishop of Mainz, summoned him before his court, censured him for heresy, and had him flogged. Then Gottschalk was transferred to the supervision of Hincmar, archbishop of Rheims. At first, though kept in close confinement, he was still permitted to write. But when, in the following year, even though his books had been burned, he still refused to abandon his heresies and continued to write in the same vein as before, he was deprived of his priesthood and detained in the monastery of Hautvilliers. Meanwhile the controversy continued. In a number of pamphlets and at synods (853 and 860) Hincmar set out an opposite view of predestination, but a number of other eminent theologians, including the delegates at the synod of Valence who had no love for Hincmar, supported doctrines similar to Gottschalk's. He, himself, however, remained in detention and died still refusing the absolution that was promised him if he recanted.

Gottschalk, as a theologian, was a determined, tragic, and tormented figure, and his sadness is reflected in his extant verse. It displays deep feeling and remarkable metrical and rhythmic subtlety and has been described as the most musical poetry to have been written in Europe for centuries. Yet, according to his own account, he had spent only one year studying poetry, probably at Orbais where he wrote his first poems.

EDITIONS—Monumenta Germaniae Historica, Poetae, v 3, 4, and 6; C. Lambot, Oeuvres théologiques et grammaticales de Godescalc d'Orbais, 1945; K. Langosch, Lyrische Anthologie des lateinischen Mittelalters, 1968. (The attribution of the Theodolus Eclogue to Gottschalk is upheld by its editor Osternacher and denied by K. Strecker.)
ABOUT—H. Waddell, The Wandering Scholars, 1927; K. Vielhaber, Gottschalk der Sachse, 1956; J. Jolivet, Godescalc d'Orbais et la Trinité, 1958.

GREGORY OF NAZIANZUS, Saint,

Greek theologian, was born in about A.D. 329 and died in about 389. His birthplace was Nazianzus (Gelveri) in Cappadocia
na zi an' zus

(central Asia Minor), where his father was bishop. At Caesarea (Kayseri), the capital of the region, and at Athens, Gregory was a fellow student and friend of Basil of Caesarea, another member of what became known as the great Cappadocian trinity of theologians (the third was St. Gregory of Nyssa). The Nazianzene Gregory was induced by Basil to join him in monastic seclusion in Pontus (northern Asia Minor). In about 361, after many doubts, he received ordination as his father's assistant and gained a reputation as a preacher. Then, in 372, in order to support Basil's appointment to the Caesarean see, he allowed himself to be persuaded to become bishop of Sasima, but he never took up the office. After his father's death two years later, he assumed charge of the church of Nazianzus. Later, however, he went into retreat. These last events took place in the reign of the eastern emperor Valens (364–78), who belonged to the Arian church or heresy that regarded Christ as distinct from God and inferior, a doctrine Gregory deplored. But when Valens died, Gregory was summoned by his successor Theodosius I to Constantinople (379). There, in the following year, he became head of the Church of the Holy Wisdom (Hagia Sophia).

He was appointed bishop of the city in 381 at the instance of the Council of Constantinople (later recognized as the second Ecumenical Council), for its members approved Gregory's anti-Arian measures, which called for a judicious reform of current orthodoxy, modified by scholarly Hellenistic philosophy. Although he hoped that his "gentleman's religion" would contribute to ecclesiastical unity, it lacked the practical qualities to achieve this aim and brought a storm of personal attacks upon his head. Too sensitive to stand up to this criticism, he resigned his bishopric before the year was over and lived for the rest of his life in Nazianzus—temporarily administering the see when a vacancy occurred—or on his nearby estate.

Gregory has left four hundred and fifty-eight Homilies or sermons, including five Theological Orations delivered at Constantinople and a speech entitled On the Love of the Poor that showed his concern for the underprivileged. His discourses on the Trinity earned him the title of The Theologian. He also composed violent invectives against Julian the Apostate, whose death in A.D. 363 caused him delight. Of his *Letters* designed for publication, two hundred and forty-three have come down to us; they include a series defending the full humanity of Christ against the heretical sect of Apollinaris (bishop of Laodicea; c. A.D. 310–90), who seemed to deny it. Although Gregory's writing gives the impression of naturalness and wit, his prose style is highly polished and florid and filled with neat turns of phrase, rhetorical figures of speech, and allusions to the classics; he was regarded as a decisive authority by Byzantine theologians of subsequent centuries.

Many of his poems have also survived. Some are concerned with theological questions—for example, the *Evening Hymn* and *Admonition to Virginity* (both pioneer examples of accentual rather than quantitative verse). But others are autobiographical, including a piece of nearly two thousand iambic lines entitled *On His Own Life* and shorter compositions such as *Dirge on the Suffering of His Own Soul.* These autobiographical poems have often been compared to Augustine's *Confessions,* owing to the self-revelations they offer. Two hundred and fifty-four of Gregory's epigrams have also come down to us. His poetry, however, though it shows as good a knowledge of classical models as that possessed by any other writer of the time, pagan or Christian, is not particularly distinguished.

EDITIONS—J. P. Migne, Patrologia Graeca, v 35-38; A. J. Mason, Five Theological Orations, 1899; Library of Christian Classics, v 3, 1954 (Theological Orations and Letters); P. Gallay, Lettres (Budé ed.), 1964; A. Knecht, Gregor von Nazianz: Gegen die Putzsucht der Frauen (with translation), 1972; C. Jungck, Gregor von Nazianz: De Vita Sua, 1974. The attribution to Gregory of Nazianzus of the long tragedy Christus Patiens, made up of lines of Euripides, is erroneous, since the play dates from several centuries later.
ABOUT—P. Gallay, La vie de Saint Grégoire de Nazianze, 1943; M. M. Hauser-Meury, Prosopographie zu den Schriften Gregors Nazianzen (Bonn, dissertation), 1960; B. Wyss, Gregor von Nazianz, 1962; J. N. D. Kelly, Early Church Doctrines, 3rd ed., 1965; J. Mossay, La mort et l'au delà dans Saint Grégoire de Nazianze, 1966; F. Rudasso, La figura di Cristo in S. Gregorio Nazianzeno, 1968; R. R. Ruether, Gregory of Nazianzus, 1969; T. Spidlik, Grégoire de Nazianze, 1969; F. Trisoglio, San Gregorio di Nazianzo in un quarantennio di studi (1925–1965), 1974; J. J. Rizzo, The Encomium of Gregory Nazianzen by Nicetas the Paphlagonian, 1976.

GREGORY OF NYSSA, Saint, Greek philosophical theologian, was born in about A.D. 335 in Cappadocia (central Asia Minor) and perhaps died soon after 394. His elder brother was Basil of Caesarea, to whom he acknowledged a great debt. Gregory embarked on a church career but abandoned it temporarily for the rhetorical profession owing to a psychological crisis (apparently marrying a girl called Theosebeia). Then he accepted an invitation from Basil, by this time bishop of Caesarea, to assume the bishopric of the little town of Nyssa (near Sereflikoçhisar). Gregory accepted reluctantly and carried out his duties with such tactless incompetence that Basil had to remonstrate with him on several occasions. Pressure from the government of the eastern emperor Valens, who as an Arian disliked the orthodoxy of the two brothers, caused Gregory to be exiled in 376, but when Valens was killed two years later, he returned. In 381 he attended the Council of Constantinople and was nominated by the orthodox emperor Theodosius I as a model for the guidance of the churches of Pontus (northern Asia Minor). But he continued, at times, to visit the capital, attending a Council there in 394.

Gregory of Nyssa, and his brother Basil, and Gregory of Nazianzus, form the great Cappadocian triad of theologians. Although Gregory of Nyssa lacked the statesmanlike wisdom of Basil and the eloquence of the other Gregory, he possessed the acutest intellect of the three. His writings were abundant and varied. In 329 he wrote two essays in memory of his beloved elder sister Macrina, abbess of a nunnery near their home: the *Life of Macrina* and the *Dialogue on the Soul and Resurrection,* the latter being a Christian adaptation of Plato's *Phaedo.* Gregory also honored Basil by a eulogistic funeral oration and wrote commentaries in support of his *Hexaemeron.* In these and

nis' så

other works, he used his text as the starting point for allegorical interpretation, a procedure he likewise followed in his commentaries on books of the Bible; these describe the mystic ascent of the soul in terms adapted from Plato and Plotinus to his Christian purpose. The manner of the argument is highly characteristic of Gregory's thought, which likes to carry a line of pagan philosophical reasoning up to the point where it might interfere with Christian orthodoxy, but then to drop it, for fear of deviating into heresy.

Indeed, in other treatises he strongly defends the orthodox position. Such is the theme of two attacks on Basil's opponent Eunomius and of a speech entitled *On the Divinity of the Son and the Holy Spirit*, a subject which frequently engaged his attention in further works, notably a tract on the different names and conceptions of the Trinity. But the culmination of his writings in this field is the *Great Catechism*, in which he outlines the principal dogmas of Christianity. He also delivered and published numerous sermons on the feast days of the church and a panegyric, full of miraculous folktales, on a man he admired and sought to model himself on, Gregory the Wonderworker (Thaumaturgus) of Pontus (c. A.D. 213–75). In addition, Gregory of Nyssa addressed letters to a number of men in order to warn them against specific heresies; his training in rhetoric helped him to gain a hearing from people of varied attitudes and temperaments. His main preoccupation, throughout, was the indefatigable search for perfect Christianity and for the sort of life best calculated to achieve it. This was the explicit purpose of his treatises, *What Is the Name and Profession of Christian* and *On Perfection and What the Christian Ought to Be;* and in his monograph entitled *On Virginity*, speaking as a married man himself, he commends the unmarried state as best for the weak-minded.

EDITIONS—J. P. Migne, Patrologia Graeca, v 44-46; W. Jaeger and others, Gregorii Nysseni, Opera, 1952– ; M. Aubineau, Grégoire de Nysse: Traité de la Virginité, 1966; V. W. Callahan, Ascetical Works, 1967; J. Daniélou, Grégoire de Nysse: La vie de Moïse (Sources chrétiennes, 1) 1968; J. Barbel, Die grosse katechetische Rede, 1971; R. E. Heine, Perfection in the Virtuous Life (De Vita Moysis), 1975; also, *see* other editions and translations listed *in* G. P. Parks and R. Z. Temple, The Literatures of the World in English Translation, 1968, and *in* Encyclopaedia Britannica, 1971 ed., v 10, p 907. ABOUT—W. Volker, Gregor von Nyssa als Mystiker, 1955; W. Jaeger, Early Christianity and Greek Paideia, 1962; A. S. Dunstone, The Atonement in Gregory of Nyssa, 1964; W. Jaeger, Gregor von Nyssas Lehre vom Heiligen Geist, 1966; E. G. Konstantinou, Die Tugendlehre Gregors von Nyssa, 1966; E. Mühlenberg, Die Unendlichkeit Gottes bei Gregor von Nyssa, 1966; R. Staats, Gregor von Nyssa und die Messalianer, 1968; D. S. Wallace-Hadrill, The Greek Patristic View of Nature, 1968; J. Daniélou, L'être et le temps chez Grégoire de Nysse, 1970, *and* Orientations actuelles de la recherche sur Grégoire de Nysse, 1971; P. Zemp, Die Grundlagen heilsgeschichtlichen Denkens bei Gregor von Nyssa, 1970; L. Gallinari, L'istituto cristiano di Gregorio di Nissa e il suo significato educativo, 1974.

GREGORY OF TOURS, Saint, Latin historian and religious writer, was born in about A.D. 539 at Arvernus (Clermont-Ferrand in central France) and died in 594. He belonged to an eminent Gallo-Roman family. He was baptized Georgius Florentius but on ordination as a deacon in 563 changed his name to Gregorius. Ten years later he was elected to the bishopric of Turonum Civitas (Tours), of which thirteen out of the previous eighteen incumbents had been his own ancestors or kinsmen. One of the most important dioceses in western Europe, it was constantly fought over by the successors of the Merovingian Clovis, and consequently its population was subject to continual chaotic violence. During Gregory's episcopacy the place came under the often disagreeable governors of no less than four kings; of these monarchs Chilperic I seemed to him the worst, though he detested his queen Fredegund even more.

During his career Gregory produced many works, of which his *History of the Franks,* in ten books, is the most notable. In form, at least, it is a universal history. The first book, sometimes entitled *First Book of the Ecclesiastical History,* starts with the Creation, surveys Old Testament and New Testament times, and continues up to the death of St. Martin of Tours in A.D. 397. Books 2, 3, and 4 carry the account onward to the murder of the Merovingian king, Sigibert, in 575. Books 5 through 10 provide toor a detailed account of contemporary history down to 591. Gregory continued to work on the enterprise until his death. It is possible that he composed considerable portions of Books 5-10 before Books 2-4. The work is written in the Latin of the period, substantially different from the classical language. Although generally undramatic and unadorned, his narrative style makes its points and depicts personal characters with considerable effect. Gregory also has a wry sense of humor.

He quotes numerous sources, inserting the texts of seven documents in his two final books. For the whole of this last period his personal experiences and observations, and oral information he received in the course of them, figure largely in the account. Indeed, he himself appears in no less than 67 out of the 265 chapters in the last six books—and in many of these events he is playing a vital part; yet he remains remarkably modest about his own role. Although rather garrulous, he was clearly a man of high ideals and strong courage, holding the fort to the best of his considerable ability in extraordinarily difficult and bloodthirsty times.

On the whole, he is a careful and reliable recorder of events: and the brutality of the Merovingian secular power, on which he expatiates, cannot be denied. Nevertheless, he tends to view the regime exclusively from the viewpoint of the church, of which he was an extremely zealous adherent, and he never tires of describing miracles and martyrdoms and denouncing heresies. Still, if his facts are occasionally wrong, it is surprising, given the anarchic circumstances of the epoch, how rarely such errors occur. He has been blamed for including masses of trivial detail, but for the historian these form a treasure house of information. Indispensable (and often uncheckable from other sources), for many of the events described, Gregory's *History* is a unique achievement.

WORKS—In addition to those indicated above, Gregory wrote: On the Martyrs, On the Martyrdom and Virtues of Saint Julian, On the Virtues of Saint Martin the Bishop, On the Lives of the Fathers, On the Glory of the Confessors, On the Miracles of the Apostle St. Andrew, The Martyrdom of the Seven Sleepers at Ephesus (a translation), The Movements of the Stars, Commentary on the Psalms (mostly lost), and a treatise on the

offices of the church (On the Masses of Sidonius Apollinaris).

EDITIONS—Historia Francorum: W. Arndt and B. Krusch, Monumenta Germaniae Historica, Scriptores Rerum Merovingicarum, 1884–85; F. Thürlemann, Das historische Diskurs bei Gregor von Tours, 1974. *Translations*—O. M. Dalton, The History of the Franks by Gregory of Tours, 1927; L. Thorpe, Gregory of Tours: The History of the Franks (Penguin ed.), 1975; R. Latouche, Grégoire de Tours: Histoire des Francs, 1963–65.

ABOUT—Introductions to the editions mentioned above; *also* J. M. Wallace-Hadrill, The Long-haired Kings and Other Studies in Frankish History, 1962; E. Auerbach, Literary Language and Its Public in Late Latin Antiquity and the Middle Ages, 1965; K. Langosch, Profile des lateinischen Mittelalters, 1967; B. Smalley, Historians in the Middle Ages, 1974.

GREGORY THE GREAT, Saint, Pope and Latin theological writer, was born in about A.D. 540 and died in 604. He came of a noble and wealthy Roman family. Embarking on a political and administrative career, in 573 he became prefect of the city. However, desiring instead to adopt a monastic life, he resigned from this office, allocated his extensive estates in Sicily and on Rome's Caelian hill to the endowment of seven new monasteries, and became a Benedictine monk in his own new foundation of St. Andrew in Clivo Scauri. Subsequently he was appointed as one of the seven regional deacons *(regionarii)* of the city and was sent by Pope Pelagius II as Papal Nuncio *(apocrisiarius)* to the Byzantine emperor at Constantinople (579). Some years later he returned to Rome to become abbot of the monastery of St. Andrew and after a tenure of five years was elected to the papacy. Owing to ill-health and a preference for the contemplative life, he only accepted the elevation with reluctance.

He became pope at the time when Italy was being overrun by the Lombards and the Byzantine province (exarchate) of Ravenna was proving itself powerless to withstand them. Although he recognized the authority of the Byzantine emperor in temporal matters, Gregory's far-reaching feats of reform and diplomacy ensured that the papal see became the dominant secular, as well as ecclesiastic, power of the country; and he was able to arrest the advance of the Lombards (598) and reintroduce a measure of stability. He paid attention to every aspect of the life of the church and its foundations and organized far-reaching systems of poor relief for the many destitute and displaced persons of the time. He was also active in the missionary field, dispatching Augustine, a Benedictine monk of his own monastery of St. Andrew, to undertake the conversion of Anglo-Saxon England. After Gregory's death he was canonized and was known as Saint Gregory the Great.

He wrote a large number of theological works. His *Dialogues,* composed in Rome during the earlier part of his papacy, were intended to entice readers away from pagan classics by providing even more fascinating stories of the Christian faith. They profess to report discussions between Gregory and a certain deacon Peter. The discussions particularly center upon the lives of the Italian saints, the second book being entirely devoted to St. Benedict, among whose followers Gregory was the first to attain the papacy. Special attention is paid to miracles associated with the careers of these saints, in accordance with the work's original title (later subtitle) *On the Life and Miracles of the Italian Fathers and the Immortality of the Soul.* There are also discussions on prayer and predestination. The *Dialogues* were excellently received and their popularity extended to Lombardy, where Queen Theudalinda became one of their admirers (moreover, Gregory sent her valuable silver treasures for her new church at Monza). The treatise was summarized and translated first into Greek and then from Greek into Arabic; in due course Old French and Old English translations also appeared.

Gregory's tract entitled *On Pastoral Care (Liber Regulae Pastoralis)* gave meticulous instructions about the spiritual and administrative life and calling of a Catholic bishop —with stress not merely, as in the past, on doctrinal orthodoxy but on moral integrity as well—and became a standard work of reference for the medieval episcopacy. His *Morals,* started in Constantinople and finished in Rome, formed a voluminous, allegorical commentary on the Old Testament book of Job, directed toward right living; it was written for the benefit of St. Leander of Seville. Gregory also wrote other Bible commentaries (under the influence of Origen's *Homilies*) and composed liturgical works; the term *Gregorian chant* testifies to beliefs of uncertain justification, current from the ninth century onward, that the chanting practiced in the city of Rome at that time— soon to become a model for other western churches—was devised on his initiative. His eight hundred and fifty-four letters are of particular historical interest. Collected in fourteen books, they cover the fourteen years of his papacy, providing a vast amount of valuable information on ecclesiastical matters, and about the political situations with which he was called upon to deal.

Despite his unavoidable involvements in secular affairs, Gregory's great intellectual powers were so heavily concentrated upon the church and its concerns and doctrines that little time was left for other interests. Nonreligious kinds of culture seemed to him a waste of energy, at least for a bishop: such matters as grammar, along with its most eminent practitioner Donatus, received his indignant condemnation. As for Gregory himself, he glories in the rusticity of his own literary style. In practice, however, he did not carry this support of Christian illiteracy to excess, writing in a clear, trim Latin without many grammatical deviations, but he made the point in order to emancipate his Christian readers from dependence on the classical past. This placed him in a different category from the great, classicizing, Romans of the previous generations, such as Boethius and Cassiodorus. Whereas they formed bridges between the ancient and medieval worlds, Gregory, by his enormous contributions and activities, must be regarded as one of the principal founders of the Middle Ages. Although his reputation did not immediately rise to great heights and the first account of his life (written by a monk of Whitby) was a trivial composition, the imposing nature of his achievements caused him to be known to posterity as The Great.

EDITIONS—Morals *in* Library of the Fathers, 1844–50; Letters *in* P. Ewald and L. Hartmann, Registrum Epis-

HADRIAN

tolarum, 1887, 1891; On Pastoral Care *in* Ancient Christian Writers, v 11, 1950.

ABOUT—F. Holmes-Dudden, Gregory the Great: His Place in History and Thought, 1905; E. Spearing, The Patrimony of the Roman Church in the Time of Gregory the Great, 1918; E. K. Rand, Founders of the Middle Ages, 1928; P. Batiffol, Saint Gregory the Great, 3rd ed., 1929; N. Sharkey, Saint Gregory the Great's Concept of Papal Power, 1950; W. Ullmann, The Growth of Papal Government in the Middle Ages, 1955; C. Chazottes, Grégoire le Grand, 1958; G. Sanderlin, St. Gregory the Great: Consul of God, 1964; G. Dufner, Die Dialoge Gregors des Grossen im Wandel der Zeiten und Sprachen, 1968; J. P. MacClain, The Doctrine of Heaven in the Writings of St. Gregory the Great, 1972; C. Dagens, Saint Grégoire le Grand: Culture et expérience chrétienne, 1977; H. B. Sol, ed., La Vie du Pape S. Grégoire: Huit versions françaises médiévales de la légende du bon pêcheur, 1977.

HADRIAN

HADRIAN (Publius Aelius Hadrianus), Roman emperor and Latin poet, was born in A.D. 76, probably at Italica (Santiponce near Seville) in the south of Spain. He died in 138. He was of Romano-Spanish descent, and his paternal grandfather had married the aunt of the emperor Trajan (A.D. 98–117), another Romano-Spaniard. In Trajan's reign, Hadrian held a series of important military and administrative offices, culminating in a first consulship in 108 and the post of governor of Syria (virtually chief of the imperial staff) in Trajan's eastern expedition (114). Whether the dying Trajan designated him as heir, as was afterward stated, remains uncertain, but with the aid of Trajan's widow Plotina, Hadrian duly became his successor. In the following year, however, the alleged Conspiracy of the Four Consulars was suppressed, to the accompaniment of executions by his praetorian prefect, an event from which Hadrian's reputation with the Senate never fully recovered.

Unprecedentedly, he spent more than half his reign traveling in the provinces, to inspect the army and organize administrative reforms, and to see life in the provinces. Thirteen of his surviving *Remarks* illustrate picturesque encounters on the way. Under the impulse of his own personal interest, his reign also witnessed important advances in the law, particularly in the appointment of judges. On the northern frontier of Britain

hā′ dri ən

he constructed what is known as Hadrian's Wall from Tyne to Solway (122–26). In Judaea, his Romanizing and Hellenizing policy precipitated the large-scale Second Jewish Revolt or Second Roman War (132–35). His wife, with whom his relations were mediocre, was Sabina; his special devotion was reserved for the youth Antinous, who was drowned in 130.

Hadrian was not only the sponsor of huge, enlightened, and innovative architectural schemes (among them, his villa in Tibur and the reconstructed Pantheon in Rome) but was also a learned devotee of literature, Greek and Latin alike, and encouraged its cultivation in the great educational centers—Rome and Athens and Alexandria—by stimulating many literary activities and dispensing endowments. He himself was an accomplished speaker, and twelve of his orations were published. Portions of the addresses he gave on five successive days to his troops at Lambaesis (Lambèse) in Numidia, have survived on an inscription. Another inscription has preserved thirty-seven lines of a funeral oration he pronounced for Trajan's niece Matidia. We also have fragments of a speech, including material of an antiquarian nature, that he delivered to the Roman Senate in support of the claim of his native city Italica to colonial status *(De Italicensibus).*

In many other branches of Latin letters, too, he was very eager to excel. Among his compositions was a work on grammar, consisting of at least two books, of which a single fragment survives; his literary taste was archaistic, exhibiting a preference for Ennius over Virgil, Cato over Cicero, Coelius Antipater over Sallust, and Antimachus over Homer. Unfortunately his autobiography is another of his numerous prose writings that has not come down to us. A further work attributable to his authorship, though it is not certain whether it was written in prose or verse, was his *Miscellany* or *Catachannae,* a rustic term for a tree upon which a variety of alien stocks have been grafted.

As to his verse compositions, the obituary hymns he wrote to Trajan's widow Plotina have likewise failed to survive, but other poems of his are extant. They include the dedication of a bearskin to the temple of Eros (Cupid) at Thespiae in Boeotia (central Greece); an epitaph on a Batavian cavalryman inscribed on his Danubian tomb; another epitaph on his own favorite horse (Borysthenes) that died at Apta (Apt) in southern France; and Greek verses written for a statue of a certain Lucius Catilius Severus at Ephesus and for Arete the wife of Parthenius who taught Virgil Greek. A few of Hadrian's epigrams have also been preserved, their chief feature being a certain dexterity in capping lines written by others. On the whole, his verses are the technically competent but undistinguished performances of a distinctly minor poet. Yet, one last poetic endeavor has rightly won the attention and admiration of the world. It comprises five haunting, delicate, plaintive, melodious lines addressed to his own soul *(animula, blandula, vagula),* when he was just about to die.

EDITIONS—*texts in* E. M. Smallwood, Documents Illustrating the Principates of Nerva, Trajan and Hadrian, 1966; *translations in* B. W. Henderson, The Life and Principate of the Emperor Hadrian, 1923. *Translations Lambaesis addresses in* A. H. M. Jones, A History of Rome Through the Fifth Century, v 2, 1970.
ABOUT—B. W. Henderson, The Life and Principate of the Emperor Hadrian, 1923; W. den Boer, Religion and Literature in Hadrian's Policy (Mnemosyne, v 8), 1955; M. Durry. (Entretiens Hardt, v 4), 1959; S. Perowne, Hadrian, 1960; R. Syme, Hadrian the Intellectual *in* Les empereurs romains d'Espagne, 1965; H. Bardon, Les empereurs et les lettres latines d'Auguste à Adrien, 2nd ed., 1968; A. Garzetti, From Tiberius to the Antonines, 1974.

HAMARTOLUS (the Sinner). See George the Monk

HECATAEUS, Greek geographer, mythologist, and forerunner of the historians, must have been born before the last quarter of the sixth century B.C., since his work was known to Heraclitus who seems to have written in about 500. It is not known when he died. His birthplace was Miletus in Ionia (western Asia Minor). The son of Hegesander, who belonged to the local aristocracy, Hecataeus was one of the men who unsuccessfully advised the Greek cities of that region not to undertake their revolt against the Persians (500–494). After the uprising ended in defeat he was one of the envoys who helped to persuade the Persian satrap to restore the local constitutions.

Hecataeus was the writer of two works, extant only in isolated passages. One, of which the surviving fragments number three hundred, was the *Journey Around the World (Periegesis Ges);* in spite of ancient and modern doubts, it should still be attributed to his authorship. Divided into two books, this treatise consisted of itineraries and notes, describing first Europe and then Asia, which was held to include Africa as well. The work offered a survey of the countries and peoples to be encountered on a voyage around the coasts of the Mediterranean and Black seas, with detours into the interior, as far as Scythia and Persia and India. Hecataeus inserted into his narrative careful observations —often based on his own travels—on peoples, place-names, local historical and religious peculiarities, and fauna and flora. Although later generations found him too uncritical for their taste, he appears to have been the first writer ever to note and record systematically the topography and traditions of the cities throughout the Greek world; and in launching this pioneer activity he made geography into a more serious study than it had ever been before. His work

hek à tē′ us

was illustrated by a map that was probably an adaptation and improvement of the map made by his compatriot Anaximander, from whom he took the oriental concept of the Ocean flowing around a disklike world divided into four neat quadrants. The historian Herodotus ridiculed this idea, but made use of Hecataeus' work, all the same, on quite an extensive scale, though he never mentions him by name and acknowledges his existence only when he wants to complain of him.

Hecataeus also held that human development should be seen in its chronological as well as its environmental perspective, and to this end, perhaps some years after his *Journey,* he wrote his *Genealogies,* otherwise known as *Histories* (i.e. *historiai,* inquiries) or *Heroology* (work about heroes or demigods). The surviving fragments, fewer in number than those of his other work, show that he was tracing back to mythological times the lineage of families that claimed divine or heroic origin—including, evidently, his own. The work is notable for its introductory statement: "What I write here is the account I believe to be true. For the stories that the Greeks tell are many, and in my opinion ridiculous." This praiseworthy spirit of scepticism was a decisive contribution to the future writing of Greek history. However, it did not mean that Hecataeus was always able to emancipate himself from gullibility in matters of mythical material: indeed, even his contemporary Heraclitus classed him among learned men who lacked common sense—because he could not see the universe whole. The method Hecataeus applied to the myths was a mixture of acceptance and rationalistic criticism. He was apparently the first to attempt to reconcile mythology and history in this way—that is to say, one of the first of the "logographers," the writers who attempted history before the historians. Thus, if Herodotus is the father of history, Hecataeus is its grandfather. He also pointed the way for future historians by writing in prose. By this departure from the earlier, traditional verse compositions in favor of the medium employed by Milesian philosopher-scientists such as Anaximander, Hecataeus confirmed his devotion to

188

factual inquiry. His language is spare but vigorous and elegant.

EDITIONS—F. Jacoby, Die Fragmente der griechischen Historiker, v 1, 2nd ed., no. 1; G. Nenci, Hecataei Milesii Fragmenta, 1954.
ABOUT—L. Pearson, Early Ionian Historians, 1939; D. Prakken, Studies in Greek Genealogical Chronology, 1943; F. Jacoby, Griechische Historiker, 1956; K. Latte, Die Anfänge der griechischen Geschichtsschreibung (Entretiens Hardt, v 4), 1956; P. Tozzi, Ecateo di Mileto, *in* Athenaeum (Italy), 1963–66; F. H. Diamond, Hecataeus of Abdera: A New Historical Approach (University of California [Los Angeles], dissertation), 1974.

HELIODORUS, Greek novelist from Emesa (Homs) in Syria, was, as recent discoveries of papyri show, active as an author at a later date than his fellow romancer Achilles Tatius. Heliodorus' exact dating, however, is a matter of dispute, and alternative arguments have been offered in favor of the second, third, and fourth centuries A.D., the third century perhaps being the most widely accepted.

Heliodorus wrote the longest of extant Greek novels, the ten-book *Aethiopica,* or *Work (Syntagma) About the Ethiopian Events Relating to Theagenes and Chariclea.* As a baby, Chariclea was cast out and exposed by her mother, the queen of Ethiopia, who feared retribution from its black king because her daughter was white. Rescued by a Greek priest, the girl grew up at Delphi, where she and Theagenes, a noble Thessalian, fell in love. Accompanied by Calasiris, an Egyptian sage whom the queen has dispatched in search of her child, they set out for distant lands, where the Delphic oracle has pronounced that they would find happiness. After numerous adventures they come to the shores of Egypt as prisoners of a band of pirates. Separated from one another and then reunited, they are finally brought by their captors to Meroe, Ethiopia's principal city. Just in time to preserve them from dying as sacrificial victims, their parents recognize them. The royal blessing is accorded to their marriage, and priesthoods are bestowed upon them both.

The *Aethiopica* plunges straight into its

hē li ō dō′ rus

tale of sensations, and the story proceeds briskly at high tension. Heliodorus constructs his plot skillfully, and the conventional oracles, oaths, soliloquies, desperate suicide plans, and pretended deaths are given richly melodramatic treatment in a series of vigorous episodes containing clever characterization and some humor.

The writer shows himself abreast of current tastes by his extensive infusions of fictitious geography and ethnology, which readers of these romantic travelers' tales expected. Although he himself is Syrian, his patriotism extends also to Egypt; Ethiopia, too, receives sympathetic treatment, although white people are shown as superior to black, and Greek to non-Greek. Another of Heliodorus' specialities is love, to which he devotes a novel sort of treatment. The innovation is the resourceful lead taken by Chariclea in her relationship to her lover who, although brave, is inferior to her both in endurance and in inventiveness: consequently the work was even sometimes entitled simply *Chariclea*. Unusual, too, is the uninhibitedly, violently, emotional nature of her love and loyalty toward Theagenes. But Heliodorus is also at pains to show the heavenly guidance directing their loves and adventures, frequently ascribed to the acts of Providence and divine justice, for the *Aethiopica* is more deeply preoccupied with religion than any other extant Greek romance. Despite every setback on the way, the gods are helping and guarding their special charges. The novelist wants to unify myths and cults and to trace them back to their eastern origins. And in particular he reveals a veneration for the cult and universality of the Sun, with whose Syrian cult his forebears had been associated, as his name bears witness.

Owing to this religious emphasis, Byzantine tradition inaccurately classified Heliodorus (like Achilles Tatius) as a Christian convert and dignitary, in order to make his novel suitable reading for the monks, who found it enjoyable, justifying their enjoyment by the interpretation of erotic intrigues as ethical lessons. Tasso, Cervantes, and Raphael bear witness to the popularity of the work during the Renaissance, when its French and English translations (1547, 1587) were constantly reprinted. Racine, too, admired Heliodorus greatly.

EDITIONS—R. M. Rattenbury and T. W. Lumb, with French translation by T. W. Lumb (Collection des Universités de France), 1935–43; A. Colonna, 1938; English translation by M. Hadas, 1957.
ABOUT—V. Hefti, Zur Erzählungstechnik in Heliodorus Aethiopica (Basel, dissertation), 1950; R. Helm, Der antike Roman, 2nd ed., 1956; É. Feuillâtre, Études sur les Éthiopiques d'Héliodore, 1966 (favors second century A.D. date); R. Keydall *in* Polychronicon für F. Dölger, 1966 (favors fourth century); B. E. Perry, The Ancient Romances, 1967; A. Scobie, Aspects of the Ancient Romance and Its Heritage, 1969.

HELLANICUS, Greek chronicler and mythographer, was perhaps born in the 480s B.C. and died not earlier than 406. A citizen of Mytilene, the chief town of the island of Lesbos, he was said to have resided for some time at the court of Macedonia, but he died at Perperene in northwestern Asia Minor. Fairly substantial fragments have survived from his works, of which twenty-four titles are known.

Among them are a number of monographs on the local histories of various countries of the world, in which both ethnology and mythology played important parts. Some of these treatises were concerned with foreign peoples, such as the *Aegyptiaca, Cypriaca, Lydiaca, Persica,* and *Scythica.* Others dealt with regions of Greece itself, notably the *Aeolica, Lesbiaca, Argolica, Boeotica, Thessalica.* This group of writings also included an *Atthis,* a history of Attica and Athens. In its first form, the *Atthis* came down to the year 411. Later, Hellanicus continued the narrative to 404. The work inaugurated a whole genre of patriotic Athenian local history, whose practitioners, known as Atthidographers, became especially popular in the following century (from Cleidemus, c. 350, onward). Although the *Atthis* contained too liberal a proportion of myth to be regarded as scientific, it did tackle a basic historical problem: the reconstruction of a factual chronicle of the past, with the inadequate help of genealogies, surviving laws, oral traditions of the great families, and the lists of the annual Athenian ar-

hel la' nē kus

chons, whose years of office formed the subdivisions of the work. This form of chronological structure found widespread acceptance among historians of the time. Furthermore, two of his later treatises, in the form of lists, *Victors at the Carnean Games (Karneonikai)* and *Priestesses of Hera at Argos,* helped to establish a firm framework of dates for the use of later historical writers, though eventually a different kind of reckoning, according to the years of Olympic Games (based on a list of their victors compiled by Hippias of Elis), became the normal practice.

Hellanicus also wrote more general works on quasi-historical, ethnographic matters. His *Foreign Customs (Barbarika Nomima)* —a title which reminds us that he was a contemporary of Herodotus—was evidently related to his essays on individual foreign lands. However, unlike Herodotus, he never attained the concept of a single, universal current of events exceeding purely local spheres of activity. Other titles that have come down to us include *On Peoples (Peri Ethnon), On the Names of Peoples,* and *On the Foundings of Cities and Peoples,* but these three may all be different names for the same monograph. The *Founding of Chios,* however, was probably a separate composition. Further works by Hellanicus are concerned entirely with mythology; in them he sought to reconcile the contradictions in mythology, though with greater credulity and less rationalization than Hecataeus or Herodotus had applied to the task. Hellanicus employed genealogy as his principal instrument for introducing order into the myths, reckoning three generations to a century—this later became standard practice. The titles of his writings in this mythological field resemble those of epic poems, from which, indeed, they may be derived. In the *Phoronis,* covering the period up to the return of the children of Heracles, a number of Peloponnesian families were traced back to the supposed first man, Phoroneus. The *Atlantis, Asopis,* and *Deucalionea* were similar. The *Troica* carried the tale of the Trojan War beyond the fall of the city, up to the coming of Aeneas to Italy. These works were drawn upon considerably by later writers with an interest in such subjects, notably Dionysius of Halicarnassus and Apollodorus of Athens.

EDITIONS—F. Jacoby, Die Fragmente der griechischen Historiker, v 1, 2nd ed., no 4, pp 104-52; 3b, pp 40-45, and suppl. pp 1-57; 3c, pp 1ff., 190, 412-14.
ABOUT—L. Pearson, Early Ionian Historians, 1939, *and* The Local Historians of Attica, 1942; F. Jacoby, Atthis, 1949, *and* Griechische Historiker, 1956.

HERACLIDES PONTICUS, Greek philosopher and scientist, lived in the fourth century B.C. and died after 322. He came of a rich and noble family from Heraclea (Ereğli) in Pontus (northern Asia Minor) and moved to Athens, where he attended the Academy of Plato, who temporarily entrusted to him the directorship of that institution during his own absence on his third journey to Sicily (361–360). Later, Heraclides was a pupil of Plato's successor Speusippus, after whose death (328) he himself stood for the leadership of the Academy. Defeated in the election by a few votes, he returned to Heraclea, where he may have founded a school of his own.

Heraclides' writings, only a few fragments of which survive, covered an extremely wide field. In physics, he attempted to account for change by a theory of molecules, which was probably evolved from Plato's *Timaeus* and bore a similarity to atomism. In the field of astronomy, he argued for the axial rotation of the earth and may have proposed a theory that Venus and Mars revolve around the sun, and the sun around the earth. He was also interested in occult phenomena, which he employed to illustrate reincarnation, the existence of the gods, and their intervention in worldly affairs, thus foreshadowing the more supernaturalistic features of Neoplatonism.

He also composed a work on the legendary Persian sage, Zoroaster. His colorful treatment of other quasi-legendary figures such as Empedotimus, Abaris, Empedocles, and Pythagoras contributed to the development of the semi-fictional kind of biographical writing. Heraclides was also the author of treatises on literary criticism, musicology, ethics, logic, metaphysics, rhetoric, and

her à klī′ dēz   pon′ ti kus

grammar. Most of his writings were cast in the form of dialogues, which were notable for their elaborate introductions and attractively presented anecdotes and myths. Heraclides exercised an influence on both Cicero, whose *Dream of Scipio* (in *On the State*) is partly based on his account of the vision of Empedotimus, and Plutarch's treatise entitled *On Music* drew extensively on his works. The extent to which Heraclides was an original thinker is disputed, but what admits of no doubt is his considerable literary talent, which was fertilized by contact with the leading intellectuals of his day.

EDITIONS—F. Wehrli, Herakleides Pontikos (Schule der Aristoteles, v 7), 1953.
ABOUT—O. Voss, De Heraclidis Pontici Vita et Scriptis (Rostock, dissertation), 1896; F. A. Steinmetz, Die Freundschaftslehre des Panaitios, 1967 (Appendix); W. K. C. Guthrie, History of Greek Philosophy, v 4, 1975 and v 5, 1978.

HERACLITUS, Greek philosopher, was born at Ephesus in Ionia (western Asia Minor), probably not long after 550 B.C. and was at the height of his activity in about 500. His father, Bloson, came of a family of "kings," that is to say, was a member of the highest local aristocracy, but Heraclitus renounced his hereditary class privileges in favor of a brother. Solitary and critical by nature, he despised and kept aloof from other human beings, describing them as "asleep"; and he felt alienated from other Greek philosophers and poets.

The surviving fragments of his work—brief, abrupt, and peremptory—may reproduce what had originally been oral pronouncements but were apparently gathered together (by someone else) in a treatise deposited in the Temple of Artemis in Ephesus. The original title of the work is unknown; it was subsequently given various designations, including the name traditionally attached to such writings, *On the Nature of the World*. Like his fellow Ionian Anaximander before him, Heraclitus saw the universe and its continual change and decay as ceaseless conflict and tension between opposites, so that the saying *panta rhei—all*

her à klī' tus

things are in a state of flux—was subsequently attributed to him. However, the doctrine he stressed with even greater emphasis was that of an ultimate, all-embracing unity, in which the opposites, in spite of their apparent conflict and contradiction, are in fact linked together, by a hidden attunement and connection, into a single coherent system.

All this Heraclitus maintains with a wealth of trenchant, cryptic paradoxes, fully justifying his reputation as obscure (*skoteinos*); his aim, he said, was "neither to say nor conceal but to indicate" the truth. Plato and Aristotle and the Stoics, when they sought to explain him, often seem on the wrong track, and many of his views still remain highly controversial. Yet, he himself declares that this vast overall scheme is possible for human beings to understand, although he maintains that they had failed to do so. His name for the scheme was *the Word (Logos),* by which he meant the great transcendental governing principle of the universe, in accordance with which every event in nature takes place and has its being: The Word is the divine order from which all human laws proceed, the one and only wisdom, which may be called Zeus—or may not.

This order is equated with an ever-living Fire that fills the sky as *ether* (shining upper air). Sometimes, the fire turns into sea and sometimes (through the sea) into earth; sea and earth revert to fire, which is how the unity persists throughout every change. Heraclitus is not just following in the steps of his Ionian predecessors, such as Thales and Anaximenes, by pronouncing the existence of a single basic universal stuff. His Fire is endowed with Reason and sometimes seems virtually synonymous with the Logos and God. In his fire imagery Heraclitus seeks to express not only the tensions that lead to ultimate harmony but the violent energy that flows through the universe. In human beings, he said, "the dry soul is wisest," because it is closest to the divine fire. His challenge to men and women is to learn to grasp the discourse of nature, to know the "natural" way to think and speak and act. This wisdom, he insists, lies not in erudition but in the awakening of the spirit from the sluggish slumber of its private knowledge and desires to awareness of the universal, macrocosmic, pattern.

EDITIONS—G. S. Kirk, Heraclitus: The Cosmic Fragments, 1954; P. Wheelwright, 1959; G. S. Kirk and J. E. Raven, The Presocratic Philosophers, revised ed., 1960; J. Bollack and H. Wismann, Héraclite ou la Séparation, 1972; B. Snell, Heraklit: Fragmente, 6th ed., 1976; E. Bodrero, Eraclito: Testimonianze e frammenti, 1978.
ABOUT—P. Wheelwright, Heraclitus, 1959; E. Zeller and R. Mondolfo, La filosofia dei greci, v 1, 4, 1961; W. K. C. Guthrie, History of Greek Philosophy, v 1, 1962; M. Marcovich, Pauly-Wissowa-Kroll, Real-Encyclopädie der klassischen Altertumswissenschaft, Supplement v 10, 1965; K. Reinhardt, Vermächtnjs der Antike, 2nd ed., 1966; U. Hölscher, Anfängliches Fragen: Studien zur frühen griechischen Philosophie, 1968; D. J. Furley and R. E. Allen, eds., Studies in Presocratic Philosophy, v 1, 1970; M. C. West, Early Greek Philosophy and the Orient, 1971; R. Mondolfo and L. Taran, Eraclito: Testimonianze e imitazioni, 1972; M. C. Stokes, One and Many in Presocratic Philosophy, 1972; R. A. Prier, Archaic Logic: Symbol and Structure in Heraclitus, Parmenides and Empedocles, 1976.

HERMAGORAS, Greek rhetorician, lived in about the middle of the second century B.C. His hometown was Temnos in Aeolis (western Asia Minor), but it is supposed that he taught rhetoric in some larger center. He was the author of an elaborate discussion of the parts of rhetoric, a work we know from a few quotations and from comments by later writers, especially Cicero, Quintilian, and Hermogenes. Its structure was a modified version of the system that had been well known since the time of Aristotle. The discussion of *heuresis*—the rhetorical employment of an unproved thesis in order to stimulate intellectual discovery—was the most important feature of the treatise and came first. The task of the orator, maintained Hermagoras, was to provide as persuasive a treatment as possible of the "political question," by which he meant anything that involved the citizen in a more or less practical fashion. These questions were divided into two classes: first, limited themes involving definite persons and specific situations *(hypotheses);* and, second, themes of an unlimited or general nature *(theses).* By including the latter category the

hûr mag' ō ràs

192

author indicated that he was writing for students rather than people concerned with practical problems of litigation. Such theses were already employed as exercises in the philosophical schools, but Hermagoras may have been the first to present them to students of rhetoric; by doing so, he helped to widen the range of rhetorical education to include questions of ethics and philosophy.

Also significant was his treatment of "stances" or issues *(staseis)* by which the orator may deal with a problem. The term had already been used in this rhetorical sense by earlier writers, but Hermagoras produced a more elaborate analysis. He seems to have distinguished between four such kinds of issues: (1) conjecture *(stochasmas)*—did A kill B?; (2) definition *(horos)*—was it murder?; (3) contingency *(kata sumbebekos)* or quality *(poiotes)*—when the parties involved agreed about what had been done but disagreed about its importance, justice, or utility (for example, when the defense claimed mitigating circumstances); (4) objection *(metalepsis,* Latin *translatio)*—where the defendant argues that the prosecutor or court has no reason or right to proceed. Each of these four categories of *stasis* was discussed in considerable detail by Hermagoras, and subcategories were established.

After this lengthy treatment of invention, he turned to economy *(oikonomia),* which he dealt with under the headings of judgment, division, order, and style. His analysis was employed as a model by later authors. He also discussed style, but this was said not to have been his strongest point.

Hermagoras' methods were highly systematic and brought the traditional system of ancient rhetoric almost to its fullest development. Such classifications were useful training and helped readers understand how a great orator proceeded, though they also could, and did, lead to sterile and oversubtle complexities. However, for hundreds of years to come, Hermagoras exercised far-reaching influence on Greek and Latin rhetoricians, and probably on Roman lawyers as well. As an innovator of advanced instruction, Quintilian declared that he "made a path of his own, which many have followed."

EDITIONS—D. Matthes, Hermagorae Temnitae Testimonia et Fragmenta, 1962.
ABOUT—D. Matthes, Hermagoras von Temnos 1904–1955 (Lustrum, v 3), 1958; R. Nadeau, Classical Systems of Stasis in Greek: Hermagoras to Hermogenes (Greek, Roman and Byzantine Studies, v 2), 1959; G. Kennedy, The Art of Persuasion in Greece, 1963.

HERMOGENES, Greek rhetorician, was born in about A.D. 161. The date of his death is uncertain. He came from Tarsus in Cilicia (southeastern Asia Minor). At the age of fifteen, he gained the admiration of Marcus Aurelius (d. 180) as an orator, but in this capacity he failed to fulfill his early promise and instead became a writer on rhetorical topics.

In his work entitled *On Issues (Peri Ideon)* he analyzed classical models, especially Demosthenes, from a stylistic viewpoint, in order to provide a systematic discussion of the various forms and categories of speech. This he did by defining seven qualities of style, all of which he identified as ingredients in Demosthenes' achievement. This classification was derived, to a considerable extent, from Dionysius of Halicarnassus (first century B.C.), and ultimately from Aristotle's successor Theophrastus (d. 288/5 B.C.).

Hermogenes also owed a good deal to his older contemporary Aelius Aristides of Mysia. Yet, although so largely derivative, he himself displayed discerning taste and judgment of his own; indeed, he was the most important rhetorical writer of the entire Roman imperial age. His influence became dominant in late antiquity, and remained powerful in the Byzantine epoch, when an extensive corpus of *Commentaries on Hermogenes* came into existence. A number of manuscripts of his works, and of others that were attributed to him (see below), were to be seen in fifteenth century Italian libraries, and an Italian translation dates from 1597.

WORKS—Monographs On Invention and On Aids for a Vigorous Style, attributed to him, are spurious, though he wrote treatises on these subjects that are now lost. Preliminary Exercises (Progymnasmata) which were also ascribed to him and were recast by the rhetorician Aphthonius of Antioch in the fourth century in a form which became very popular in the Byzantine Age, may or may not have been his work.
EDITIONS—H. Rabe, Rhetores Graeci, v 6, 1913. *Translations*—Progymnasmata: C. S. Baldwin, Medieval Rhetoric and Poetic (to 1400), 1928.
ABOUT—G. Kowalski, Hermogenes De Statibus, 1947; M. Patterson, The Renaissance: Seven Ideas of Style, 1970; G. Kennedy, The Art of Rhetoric in the Roman World, 1972; G. Lindberg, Studies in Hermogenes and Eustathios, 1977.

HERO (Heron), Greek writer on mathematics and science, evidently lived in or after the first century A.D., since he referred to a lunar eclipse visible in A.D. 62 at Alexandria, which was his native city.

Four of his works on mechanical subjects survive. The *Pneumatica,* in two books, describes the structures of devices operated by compressed air, steam, and water, including a fire engine, a water organ, and "penny-in-the-slot" machines. The *Peri Automatopoietices (On the Making of Automata)* is mainly concerned with mechanical toys that purported to perform miracles in temples. A small automatic theatre is also described. A third work, the *Belopoeica,* deals with ballistic engines of war.

The *Mechanics,* in three books, is extant only in an Arabic version; among other subjects it describes the construction of various types of engines, and discusses mechanical problems encountered in the course of daily life.

A number of geometrical treatises, preserved in their Greek originals, are also attributed to Hero. The most important is *Metrica,* in three books, on the measurement of surfaces and bodies. *Definitions* is concerned with geometrical terms and concepts. *Geometrica, On Measures,* and *Stereometrica* all deal with mensuration and are of importance as our main authorities for practical mathematics in the Greco-Roman world. *On the Dioptra* is an impressive treatise on land surveying, named after a sighting instrument used for the same purposes as the modern theodolite (the appendix to the work describes an automatic hodometer or road-measuring instrument). The *Catoptrica,* on reflecting surfaces, is only preserved in a Latin translation.

hûr moj′ e nēz

hēr′ ō

Hero was an expert mathematician and a master of applied mechanics, and his writings supply wide-ranging reviews of the progress that had been attained in those fields. However, these surveys do not achieve a great deal of originality in themselves, relying extensively on his predecessors such as Archimedes (third century B.C.) and Ctesibius (second century B.C.).

WORKS (that have not come down to us)—Commentary on Euclid (Arabic excerpts survive); the Baroulkos (on a weight-lifting machine) of which portions are incorporated in the Mechanica and Dioptra; on Water-Clocks, in four books; and perhaps Cheiroballistra (an artillery weapon). The Geodaesia and Liber Geoponicus are later compilations based largely on Hero's writings.
EDITIONS—Bibliography in Encyclopaedia Britannica, 1971, v 11, p 437ff.
ABOUT—R. J. Forbes and E. J. Dijkterhuis, History of Science and Technology, v 1, 1963; also see bibliography in Encyclopaedia Britannica, 1971, v 11, p 437ff.

HERODAS (Herondas, Herodes), Greek poet, probably lived in the reign of Ptolemy III Euergetes of Egypt (246–221 B.C.)—if, that is to say, an allusion to a good king refers to that monarch, as seems probable. The background of his writings is sometimes the island of Cos, where he may have been born.

A papyrus acquired by the British Museum in 1889 was found to have seven of Herodas' mimes, together with the first three lines of an eighth. Additional fragments subsequently came to light. Mimes are short, pithy, pungent, realistic verse sketches that were written in the "limping" iambic (choliambic) meter of scazons (iambic trimeters ending in a spondee) and were consequently described as *mimiambi.* They were probably intended for recitation by a speaker who personified the various characters by skillful variations and gestures. The first mime is *The Procuress,* named after a certain Gyllis, who visits a young woman named Metriche and suggests that she should give up waiting for her lover or husband Mandris, who has been away for ten months in Alexandria, and should transfer her affections to a young athlete named

he rō' dás

194

Gryllus. Metriche rejects the idea but has a drink with Gyllis, who then goes off to find Gryllus another mistress instead. *Battarus,* perhaps the best of Herodas' creations, is named after a villainous, unctuous brothel-keeper who complains in court that the grain merchant Thales has broken down his door and abducted one of his girls. *The Schoolmaster* portrays the visit of the voluble Metrotime who has brought her incorrigible son to be whipped, a task which he willingly undertakes. *The Women Worshippers* presents two women who come, accompanied by their maid, to deposit a humble offering at Asclepius' shrine of Cos—the bad-tempered Cynno and the naive Cocale; they admire the artistic treasures of the temple and encounter a sanctimonious sacristan. *The Jealous Woman* tells of Bitinna, who, outraged by the infidelity of her lover Gastron with her slave-girl, orders him to be scourged and branded, but at the end the slave-girl Cydilla begs him off, at least for the present. Slaves were also scolded in another mime, *Having Breakfast,* of which only a fragmentary introduction survives. *The Private Conversation* is an obscene discussion between two women, Metro and Coritto, about a dildo the cobbler Cerdon has made for them. *The Cobbler* shows Cerdon himself, oily and offensive, displaying smart shoes to haggling customers whom Metro has brought to his shop. In the fragmentary eighth mime, *The Dream,* a farmer tells how he dreamt that his goat was torn limb from limb by devotees of Dionysus and how, in the singing competition that followed, he himself won the prize. The farmer is evidently Herodas himself, who seems to be referring to the severe treatment his works had received from critics and wants to express the hope that he will nevertheless achieve literary success in the end.

When the London papyrus was first discovered, the appearance of so unmitigated a realist, writing so crudely about the sordid side of life, was greeted with enthusiasm as a refreshing change from traditional classical decorum. Subsequently, however, critics became less generous, pointing out, for example, that this "realism" is conveyed in an entirely artificial dialect and larded heavily with erudite allusions. Nevertheless, Herodas does achieve lifelike reality by setting the varied characters of his miniature dramas in relentlessly sharp focus—which must have given the reciters of these pieces excellent opportunities to show their virtuosity.

EDITIONS—W. Headlam and A. D. Knox (with extensive commentary and translation), 1922; G. Puccioni, Herodae Mimiambi, 1950; Q. Cataudella, Eroda: I mimiambi, 1968; I. C. Cunningham, Herodas: Mimiambi, 1971; V. Schmidt, Herondae Mimiambi, 1979. *Translations*—A. D. Knox, Herodes, Cercidas and the Greek Choliambic Poets *in* J. M. Edmonds, The Characters of Theophrastus (Loeb ed.), 1929.

HERODIAN, Greek historian, was a Syrian, probably originating from Antioch. He held a post in the Roman imperial administration and died after A.D. 238.

He was the author of a historical work in eight books entitled *Histories of the Empire After Marcus,* covering events from the death of Marcus Aurelius in A.D. 180 to the accession of Gordian III in 238. Although Herodian's account partly deals with contemporary events and is thus based, to some extent, on personal knowledge, he himself played such a minor part in the happenings of his time that his narrative cannot compete with the account of the same period by Dio Cassius, who was at the center of events. Despite some awareness of the long Greek historiographical tradition behind him, Herodian offers a conventional moralistic and rhetorical version of Roman history; he is also pompous, repetitive, and evidently derivative (though his sources remain obscure). A series of fabricated speeches aping the Thucydidean manner fails to dissipate the general dullness of the writing, only relieved, on occasion, by fairly lively accounts of spectacular events such as murders.

Though Herodian, perhaps for puritanical reasons, ignores the sexual habits of the emperors, which had fascinated so many other historians, his narrative method is mainly of a biographical character. However, he does not maintain this approach in a systematic fashion or with any success or distinction, since his subjects are portrayed with a curiously flat, monotonous sameness of character, and any situation requiring the

slightest complexity of treatment, as well as any effective discussion of causes or motives, is beyond his powers. His geography, too, is vague and inaccurate. Nevertheless, what he has to record is sometimes of value, especially when Dio Cassius is only available in an epitome or not at all. For example, Herodian is our best authority for the war between the generals Septimius Severus and Pescennius Niger (193–96) to determine which would be emperor.

The *Histories* was employed as a source by the writers of the Historia Augusta (late fourth century A.D.). During the Renaissance, he was again keenly studied, and at the request of Pope Innocent VIII the Italian humanist Politian prepared a very competent Latin version of the work, published at Bologna and Rome in 1493.

EDITIONS with translation—E. C. Echols, 1961; C. R. Whittaker (Loeb ed.), 1971; F. Cassola (Italian), 1968. ABOUT—F. Millar, A Study of Cassius Dio, 1964; R. Syme, Ammianus and the Historia Augusta, 1968, *and* Emperors and Biography, 1971; F. Kolb, Literarische Beziehungen zwischen Cassius Dio, Herodian und der Historia Augusta, 1972; G. W. Bowersock *in* D. Kagan, ed., Studies in the Greek Historians, 1975.

HERODOTUS, Greek historian, was born in about 480 B.C., or perhaps earlier, and died in about 425. His birthplace was Halicarnassus (now Bodrum) in Caria (southwestern Asia Minor), at that time under Persian rule. He was the son of Lyxes, who came of a distinguished local family, and his uncle was the epic poet Panyassis. When Panyassis was killed by the ruler of the city, Lygdamis, in a civil war (461), Herodotus withdrew to the island of Samos. By 454/3 Halicarnassus had got rid of Lygdamis and was a member of the Delian League, dependent on Athens. At this juncture, Herodotus may possibly have returned home for a time, but, if so, he did not stay but remained an exile and traveled extensively (as he may already have before). He also gave lectures in many places.

His visit to Athens—where he was paid an unprecedentedly large sum for reciting—and exposure to its advanced intellectual culture decisively influenced his life and outlook. Later, however, he began to travel again, joining and becoming a citizen of a new Panhellenic settlement that was founded under Athenian inspiration at Thurii on the Gulf of Taras (Tarentum, Taranto in southeastern Italy, 444/2). Herodotus may have returned to mainland Greece for a brief period at the end of his life; but his tomb and epitaph were shown at Thurii, and it was probably there that he died.

Herodotus' *History* has an episodic appearance because it was written to be read aloud. This accounts for the recurrence of associative connecting links—and for the inclusion of so much material calculated to keep the audience amused. The division into nine books was probably first made long after Herodotus' death, by a scholarly editor at Alexandria. The task was skillfully done, for each of the books is arranged so as to have a leading theme. However, the *History*, as Herodotus himself had planned the work, is divided into two main parts. The first part, or Prelude, tells of the origins of the quarrel between east and west, the rise of the Persian empire, and the historical background, with special reference to Athens and Sparta. The second, and main, part concentrates on the Persian Wars—the invasions of Greece by the Persian armies of Darius I and Xerxes I. These campaigns seemed to Herodotus the outstanding feature of world history: they had united the Greeks, opened up vast areas for exploitation, and given a decisive turn to the whole story of the western world. Thus, Herodotus was the prototype of all historians who have made war their central theme. Yet he also cherished the wider and more general aim of "putting on record the astonishing achievements both of our own and of the barbarian [Asian] peoples."

The plan of his *History* is as follows:

A. Prelude

Book 1. The history of Croesus, King of Lydia (c. 560–546 B.C.), with a glance at the early history of his country (including the legend of Gyges and Candaules); the story of the alleged relations of Croesus and the Athenian Solon; the conquest of Lydia (western Asia Minor) and the creation of the Persian empire by Cyrus I the Great, King of Persia (549–530), with an account of his country, and of Babylon, and of the Greeks in Asia Minor.

Book 2. A description of Egypt.

Book 3. The conquest of Egypt by the Persian king Cambyses (530–522); the story of the false Smerdes, who tried to seize the Persian throne; the rise of Darius I to power (521–486).

Book 4. The expedition of Darius against the Scythians (southern Russia) and Libyans (northern Africa), with an account of both these peoples.

Book 5. The operations of Megabazus with a division of the Persian army against the Thracians, and an account of that people; the Ionian revolt (western Asia Minor), and the burning by the rebels of the local Persian capital Sardes (498).

B. The Persian Wars

Book 6. The suppression of the Ionian revolt by the Persians; the march of the Persian general Mardonius to Macedonia and the wreck of the Persian fleet off Mount Athos; the expedition under Datis and Artaphernes, and the battle of Marathon (490 B.C.).

Book 7. The death of Darius; the preparations of Xerxes I (486–465) to invade Greece, and his carrying out of the project in 480; the battle of Thermopylae.

Book 8. The battles of Artemisium and Salamis, and the withdrawal of Xerxes from Greece.

Book 9. The battle of Plataea (479), and the retreat of the Persians; the sea battle of Mycale; the liberation of Sestos (Gallipoli peninsula) by the Athenian fleet.

In the end, we are provided with what is virtually a continuous history of Greek lands from the mid-sixth century onward. It comes to us, however, in an oblique manner, through a vast range of material that reflects, with remarkable fullness, the complexity of the historical scene. And indeed—though this remains conjectural—the whole work may originally have been intended to be geographical, a "Journey," on the lines of an earlier work of that kind by the geographer and proto-historian Hecataeus of Miletus (c. 500). Then Herodotus, probably under the influence of the contacts he made at Athens, gradually evolved from a traveler telling tales to an artist employing subtler techniques to convey important truths. The extent to which this change of plan involved rewriting what he had already written has been widely discussed and disputed. Much of his geographical data must have been collected before 444/3. But if the final version of his *History* came from something like a single act of composition, this cannot have taken place earlier than the first years of the Peloponnesian War (431–404), to which there are references in the text; moreover, a joke made by the comic dramatist Aristophanes in 425 seems to allude to the work. The *History* ends with a story about Cyrus I, founder of the Persian empire —an unexpected and enigmatic termination —which may mean that Herodotus died before he had applied the finishing touches.

His *History* is written in a literary form of the Ionic dialect and deals extensively with his native Ionia, to whose philosophers, with their passion for inquiry and explanation, he owes many debts—including the already mentioned debt to the Ionian Hecataeus, which is not concealed by the criticisms Herodotus subjects him to. He was also Ionian in his deep indebtedness to the Homeric poems. Herodotus took from these epics the basic theme of a struggle between east and west, now revived (it seemed to him) in the contrast between Greek freedom and Persian despotism. Moreover, the numerous speeches inserted in his *History*—inaugurating a custom that persisted throughout ancient historiography—are another Homeric feature. They do not claim to reproduce what was actually said but serve to illustrate viewpoints and patterns of behavior and the backgrounds to situations. It is probable, too, that Herodotus' general approach was influenced by another epic poet of his own time, his own elder kinsman Panyassis, who shared the Homeric desire to shed glory on the past.

The most glorious of all the deeds that had ever happened, Herodotus believed, was the salvation of Greece from Persia, begun in 490 and completed in 480/79; the historian particularly admires this successful act of resistance because it was a striking example of pan-Hellenic collaboration. Nevertheless, he believed that the Athenians had played the leading part—no wonder his lectures and recitations at Athens earned unprece-

dented fees. And from the same city, too, he derived numerous written and oral sources of information. They left him with a strong bias in favor of the system of the Athenians, whose moderate democracy, even when it was under the guidance of a single, quasi-autocratic personage such as Pericles, he saw as the best of all constitutional devices —provided always that the laws protecting individual freedom were not infringed. While Herodotus gives credit to Sparta as well as Athens for the victories over the Persians, his pro-Athenian attitude prevents him from doing the Spartan effort full justice. But he was writing in the early years of the Peloponnesian War, at a time when Spartan armies were ravaging Attica regularly, and it is hardly surprising that he showed special sympathy for Athens in his *History*.

Like the contemporary Athenian tragedians, whose poetic methods he adapted to prose (among them, Sophocles, who wrote an ode in his honor), Herodotus was preoccupied with the divine background of cause and effect. He felt a conviction that prosperous men, like the kings Croesus and Xerxes, must eventually provoke the gods to bring them down in ruin. He knew that the ways in which the divine power chooses to inflict suffering are often inconsistent and amoral. Yet, however blind the stroke, at least it restores the balance. Besides, suffering is not always undeserved, for the kings who succumbed did so not only because they were prosperous but because they were often arrogant and guilty of many excesses as well.

However, Herodotus was living at a time when the old religious attitudes at Athens were becoming overlaid (under Ionian influences) by new scientific attitudes. In this changed climate he discreetly modified the divine pattern by modern, rational explanations of cause and effect (carefully distinguishing between immediate and permanent causes). However, despite these incursions into rationalism, he remains a thoroughgoing believer in divine intervention, and particularly reveres the sanctity of oracles. Human decisions, to Herodotus, are hampered by fate—and by accident as well. Nevertheless, the force and importance of such decisions must not be underestimated, for, he is convinced, individuals, and particularly important individuals, are the driving force of history—an attitude that foreshadows the art of historical biography. His biographical studies are also strongly tinged by a moral and didactic view of events that he bequeathed to almost all subsequent ancient historians.

Nevertheless, he was tolerant. Despite his continual contrasts between Greeks and "barbarians," he specifically praised certain Persian customs (thus earning himself the later epithet of pro-barbarian). He was, in fact, a cheerfully broadminded man, whose overriding stimulus was nothing other than the spirit of inquiry *(historie)* that has given "history" its modern meaning. Moreover, his interest and curiosity were combined with an inexhaustible flair for spicy anecdotes and piquant digressions of all shapes and sizes, which makes him the most amusing of all historians and provides an enormous mass of information, true and mythical alike—but very often true, since his determination to get at the truth was outstanding and prompted him to make almost incredibly extended journeys. Through the evidence he collected on these, he became the pioneer not only of history but also of anthropology, ethnology, and archeology. Many of his descriptions have been confirmed by modern excavators and researchers. And he is no less interested in agriculture and geology as well.

His sources for all this material were very mixed: personal observation, hearsay and oral tradition, literary sources and documents. Oral evidence, if possible collected from eyewitnesses, he regarded as a paramount requirement. The literary authorities available to him, on the other hand, were relatively sparse—eastern inscriptional records, archives of various kinds, official chronicles, and the documents of land surveyors—yet all of these, in combination, enabled him to achieve a relative chronology. When it came to the Persian Wars, events were already a generation past, and hard facts about them were desperately few, which made the writing of their history an extraordinarily difficult task. It is scarcely surprising, therefore, that Herodotus' accounts of happenings (for instance, battles)

were often patchy and contained a number of mistakes. Furthermore, he is too credulous about what his friends have told him, and, in the interests of a complete record and a worthwhile story, he is prepared to include a good deal against his better judgment. Divine causation also gets in the way —although, with few exceptions, he refuses to accept the physically impossible. On the whole, he seems to realize with remarkable acuteness when the information he has received is inadequate. His intelligent and observant approach to his material led the way for the entire succession of the world's future professional historians.

Herodotus outstripped and transformed the diction of his forerunners and made Greek prose into a fine art. The principal features of his style are speed and an expansive, comfortable directness raised to the point of genius. Not only does he display perfect control of the language and provide absorbing entertainment but he is also a deep and powerful thinker, behind whose cheerful humor lies a certain fundamental pessimism and sadness.

Subsequent writers—Ctesias, Aristotle, Manetho—criticized his methods. But in Hellenistic times he was one of the very few prose writers honored by the Alexandrians with a commentary, and in the first century B.C. his compatriot Dionysius properly appreciated his merits as a marvelous storyteller. Later, however, Plutarch and Lucian called Herodotus a liar; it seemed to them that his breadth of knowledge must mean that, if he was not plagiarizing, he was inventing. It was in the fifteenth and sixteenth centuries that Herodotus truly came into his own; and, in the eighteenth, his vast sweep appealed to the French political philosopher Montesquieu and the English historian Edward Gibbon. In our own time, his stupendous originality and endearing character have once again been appreciated.

EDITIONS—W. W. How and J. Wells, 2nd ed., 1928; A. B. Lloyd, Book 2, Introduction, 1975. *Translations*—A. D. Godley (Loeb ed.), 1920–24; H. Carter, 1962; A. de Sélincourt (Penguin ed.), 2nd ed., 1971; P. E. Legrand (Budé ed.), 1932–34.
ABOUT—T. R. Glover, Herodotus, 1924; M. Pohlenz, Herodot, 1937; J. E. Powell, The History of Herodotus, 1939, reprint 1967; J. L. Myres, Herodotus: Father of

History, 1953; P. E. Legrand, Hérodote, 2nd ed., 1955; J. Wikarjak, L'histoire générale d'Hérodote, 1961; A. de Sélincourt, The World of Herodotus, 1962; F. W. Walbank, Speeches in Greek Historians, 1965; H. R. Immerwahr, Form and Thought in Herodotus, 1967; K. A. Riemann, Das Herodoteische Geschichtswerk in der Antike, 1967; H. F. Bornitz, Herodot-Studien, 1968; W. Aly, Volksmärchen, Sage und Novelle bei Herodot und seinen Zeitgenossen, 1969; S. Bernardete, Herodotean Inquiries, 1969; M. Grant, The Ancient Historians, 1970; J. Cobert, Herodots Exkurse und die Frage nach der Einheit seines Werkes, 1971; C. W. Fornara, Herodotus: An Interpretative Essay, 1971; K. H. Waters, Herodotus on Tyrants and Despots, 1971; F. Solmsen, Two Crucial Decisions in Herodotus, 1974; A. Masaracchia, Studi erodotei, 1975; P. Hohti, The Interrelation of Speech and Action in the Histories of Herodotus, 1976; R. Tölle-Kastelbein, Herodot und Samos, 1976.

HERONDAS. See Herodas

HEROPHILUS, Greek physician, lived in the first half of the third century B.C. He was born at Chalcedon (Kadiköy in northwestern Asia Minor) and, after studying under Praxagoras of Cos, worked at Alexandria. His writings have only survived in fragments.

His most important researches were anatomical studies based upon the study of human corpses. Herophilus was one of the first to perform postmortem examinations, and these earned him the reputation of the first and greatest anatomist of his epoch. Particularly admired were his descriptions of the ventricles of the brain, which he regarded as the organ of the soul and recognized as the center of the nervous system (thus superseding Aristotle's notion of the heart as the central organ).

Herophilus also investigated the eye and its cataracts, the liver, the pancreas, the salivary glands, and the sexual organs. Working from the observations of Praxagoras, he discovered—and formulated a law for—the rhythm of the pulse; and he distinguished between sensory and motor branches of the nerve trunks. He devoted careful attention to prognostics and laid emphasis on the curative powers not only of drugs but of dietetics and gymnastics. He also wrote

he rof' i lus

commentaries on the writings of Hippocrates, in addition to a monograph on the causes of sudden death and a handbook for midwives.

Although tradition unanimously classified Herophilus as a supporter of the dogmatic school of medicine, his writings were primarily guided by the practical tasks and questions facing a physician. He became the founder of an Alexandrian school of anatomy that was still in existence and active at the beginning of the Christian era and that gave birth, in its turn, to the Empirical School, with its tendency to greater scepticism.

EDITIONS with translation—Fragments: J. F. Dobson (Proceedings of the Royal Society of Medicine, History of Medicine Section), 1925.
ABOUT—L. Edelstein, Ancient Medicine, 1967; E. D. Phillips, Greek Medicine, 1973; also bibliographical note in Oxford Classical Dictionary, 2nd ed., 1970, p 510.

HESIOD, Greek poet, seems to have composed his poems shortly before 700 B.C.; Aristarchus of Samothrace was probably right in regarding him, against opposing views, as living later than Homer (the story of the competition between the two poets is probably mythical). Hesiod himself states that his father, a merchant of Cyme (Namurtköy) in Aeolis (western Asia Minor) was compelled by poverty to migrate to Ascra in Boeotia (central Greece), where Hesiod was born and worked as a farmer. On his father's death the division of the estate between himself and his brother Perses gave rise to long-drawn-out disputes. On one occasion, Hesiod tells us, he took part in a poetic contest at Chalcis in Euboea and won a prize with a hymn. According to Plutarch and others, he was murdered at Oenoe in Locris (central Greece) by the brothers of a woman whose seduction he had either accomplished himself or helped another to perform. His tomb was shown at Orchomenus in Boeotia.

Hesiod was the founder and principal exponent of the second great epic tradition, the

hē' si od

tradition that stems not from Homeric Ionia but from the Greek mainland. Two of his major poems have survived, the *Works and Days* and the *Theogony*.

The *Works and Days* starts with an invocation to the Muses to sing the praises of Zeus and with a promise that the poet will tell his brother, Perses, something that is true; and he urges Perses to a reconciliation of the quarrel between them, pointing out that although emulation of another man is good, to carry it as far as strife is evil. It is the will of the gods, or of Zeus, that livelihood is hard to come by. The fall of humankind was caused by the curiosity of a woman, Pandora, who opened the jar in which all evils were kept, so that only Hope remained, caught under its lid. The poem goes on to enumerate the five ages of humanity: Gold, Silver, Bronze, the Age of Heroes, and the present Iron Age, which is unpleasant and will grow steadily worse.

A hawk said to a nightingale that lamented because it was caught: "Why do you grieve? Might is right." But men and women should pursue righteousness, for heaven sends prosperity to the righteous but ruin to the wicked. Zeus not only sees everything for himself but has innumerable unseen envoys watching over all the deeds that are done on the earth. One of these envoys is Justice, who notes whenever she is abused and reports the offense to Zeus. Animals and birds may devour one another, but Zeus had made justice the special attribute of human beings. The following things are wrong: idleness, dishonesty, unkindness to strangers, violation of a brother's bed, ill-treatment of orphans, harsh words to parents, bad relations with neighbors.

Next comes a long section laying down the stages of the farmer's year and describing the hard work he will have to perform at different tasks in different seasons. A calendar is provided for his benefit, diversified by a description of a summer picnic and a digression on navigation. Then follow precepts on a number of different subjects: the right age for marriage, prudence in family and money affairs, decent manners. Finally, *Works and Days* ends with an indication of which days are lucky and which are not.

The *Theogony* is unique in providing a systematic account of the gods of Greece and their genealogy from the time of Chaos down to the creation of a permanent divine hierarchy. The poet begins by announcing that he is prompted by the Muses and inspired by them to tell the truth. First of all was Chaos, then Earth, Tartarus, and Eros (Love). Earth brought forth Uranus (Heaven) and bore him the Titans, who, under the leadership of Cronus and the instigation of their mother, rose against their father and castrated him, whereupon the foam around his severed genitals gave birth to Aphrodite. To Cronus, Rhea bore divine children, whom he ate as soon as they were born, with the single exception of Zeus, who was taken off to Crete and kept in safety. Zeus later rose up and conquered his father Cronus, who spewed up the offspring he had eaten earlier. One of the Titans, Prometheus, deceived Zeus in his division of a sacrificial victim between gods and men and stole fire for mankind that had been deprived of it; whereupon Zeus bound him to a rock, where an eagle ate his liver every day, and had the first woman, Pandora (though she is not named here), created to plague men.

War broke out between the children of Cronus and the Titans, whom Zeus' allies hurled down to Tartarus; and when Typhoeus, whom Earth had borne to Tartarus, likewise revolted, he too was cast down to the same depths by Zeus' thunderbolts. Next, after all his enemies had been overcome, Zeus was chosen by the gods to be their king. He took a series of divine wives, one after the other; the last of them was Hera. Her daughter Hebe married Heracles, who after his earthly life became a god himself. Next the poet names the sons borne by goddesses to other mortal men, and the *Theogony* closes with an appeal to the Muses to sing of women as well.

The *Works and Days* represents an old, traditional genre in Near East literatures, but in Greek there is no known precedent. Hesiod was the first Greek poet to seek his main subject outside the realms of mythology (however, myths are also included). The poem reflects the harsh circumstances of his own life and, incidentally, provides a unique source for social conditions in early archaic Greece. It summons its listeners and readers not to Homeric glory but to hard work, honesty, sobriety, and thrift, in a world where life was grim and ridden with extortion and in which the human spirit had degenerated. It offers the experience of a surly, conservative countryman—schooled in adversity, circumspect, grumbling but courageous—who feels a profound sense of human misery and injustice in a tyrannical age and is deeply conscious of the gods' presence lying heavily around him.

Hesiod was no lover of women, as is shown by his inclusion of the myth of Prometheus in both poems. In the *Theogony,* Zeus punished humankind—because it had received Prometheus' gift of fire—by creating the first woman, the root of all evils. In the *Works and Days,* her name, Pandora, is added, and it is said that "into her heart the god Hermes put lies, and wheedling words of falsehood, and a treacherous nature, to be a sorrow to men who eat bread." The poem, as we have it, is likely to contain some later interpolations.

The *Theogony* (the attribution of which to the same poet as the *Works and Days* has sometimes been unjustifiably doubted—notably by Pausanias in the second century A.D.) is entirely mythological in theme. The poem is of immense importance as a very early statement of Greek stories about the creation and other religious themes, and some of the tales display strong connections with various beliefs held in countries farther to the east, notably among the Hurrians and Hittites of Asia Minor and its borderlands. The *Theogony* concentrates extensively, in stories that have attracted keen interest from anthropologists, upon the supremacy that Zeus has ferociously acquired and the destructive weapons afforded him by his power over physical forces. By this means one rebel after another is shattered. Their heroic but vain uprisings, as depicted by Hesiod, kindled the imagination of many subsequent poets, notably Milton, in whose *Paradise Lost* the downfall of Satan incorporates many details from the *Theogony.*

Like Homer, and many later poets, Hesiod begins his poem with an invocation to the Muses. But his invocation is one of the most elaborate and heartfelt of all; and it constitutes the first literary manifesto in western literature. The poet indicates his belief that there is factual as well as artistic matter in poetry and that it is his duty to communicate such facts truthfully. He is *engagé* and didactic, employing his myths in order to edify, in the manner of a priest or a prophet such as the Hebrew Amos, who lived at almost the same time.

Hesiod's hexameters are written in a language that is for the most part the Ionian of Homer but contains a certain admixture of Boeotian dialect as well. Although not free from stylistic awkwardness, his poetry is capable of rising to impressive solemnity and power and includes vivid descriptive passages, illustrating the very distinctive personality of the poet. Living, apparently, at the time when Greek writing had just been introduced, Hesiod either wrote his poems down himself or dictated them to scribes.

WORKS (wrongly attributed to Hesiod, or rightly attributed to him but now lost)—In the former category is the Shield (of Heracles), a short narrative poem about Heracles' fight against Cycnus; it reveals analogies with art of the period c. 580–570 B.C., thus confirming the conclusion of the commentator Aristophanes of Byzantium (c. 257–180) that the work was not by Hesiod. This poem still survives, but only fragments of the others that have likewise been falsely ascribed to Hesiod's authorship. These include the Catalog of Women or Eoeae (Ehoiai) in five books, a continuation of the Theogony (which had ended with an appeal for a poem on women). This catalog, like the Shield, does not seem to antedate the sixth century.

Poems apparently written by Hesiod that have not come down to us include a genealogical piece of a similar kind known as the Great Eoeae and the Melampodia in three books, comprising stories of famous diviners and prophets. Among his other mythological poems were the Marriage of Ceyx (who was turned into a bird, along with his wife Alcyone); the Idaean Dactyls; the Aegimius, in at least two books (ascribed by some ancient writers to Cecrops of Miletus); didactic pieces including the Precepts of Chiron (addressed to Achilles), Astronomy (the risings and settings of stars), the Great Works, and Divination by Birds (attached to the Works and Days in some ancient manuscripts); and a poem known as the Caminus or Kerameis, which some authorities ascribed to Hesiod, according to Pollux in the second century A.D.

EDITIONS—M. L. West, Theogony, 1966, *and* Works and Days, 1977; C. F. Russo, Shield of Heracles, 2nd ed., 1965; R. Merkelbach and M. L. West, Fragmenta Hesiodea, 1967. *Translations*—H. G. Evelyn-White, Hesiod: The Homeric Hymns, Fragments of the Epic Cycle: Homerica (with Appendix by D. L. Page), revised ed., 1936; N. O. Brown, Theogony, 1953; R. Lattimore, Works and Days, Theogony, Shield of

Heracles, 1959; D. Wender, Theogony, Works and Days; Elegies of Theognis (Penguin ed.), 1973; C. J. Rowe, The Essential Hesiod, 1978.
ABOUT—G. Steiner, Der Sukzessionsmythos, 1958; Hésiode et son influence (Entretiens Hardt, v 7), 1962; H. Schwabl, Hesiods Theogonie: Eine unitarische Analyse, 1966; P. Walcot, Hesiod and the Near East, 1966; T. Breitenstein, Hésiode et Archiloque, 1971; G. P. Edwards, The Language of Hesiod in Its Traditional Context, 1971; E. Simon, Pergamon und Hesiod, 1975; P. Pucci, Hesiod and the Language of Poetry, 1976; M. E. Pelikaan-Engel, Hesiod and Parmenides, 1977.

HIERONYMUS, Greek officer, high official, and historian, was born in about the middle of the fourth century B.C., or shortly afterward, and died in about 260 or 250 at Cardia on the Thracian Chersonese (Gallipoli peninsula). He entered the service of his fellow townsman Eumenes of Cardia, a military and political leader who took an active part in the wars between the successors *(Diadochi)* of Alexander the Great. Hieronymus fought for Eumenes against Perdiccas, formerly Alexander's second-in-command, and against Antigonus I the One-eyed until in 316 the latter defeated Eumenes at the battle of Gabiene (south of Isfahan in Iran) and put him to death. Hieronymus then became a follower of Antigonus and was present at the battle of Ipsus in Phrygia (Asia Minor), where Antigonus was defeated and killed by Lysimachus and Seleucus I (301). The dead man's son Demetrius Poliorcetes, on becoming king of Macedonia, gave the governorship of Boeotia in central Greece to Hieronymus, who also became a friend of Demetrius' successor Antigonus II Gonatas (284/3–239).

He wrote a *History of the Successors* that probably continued down to the death of King Pyrrhus of Epirus in 272. Only a very few fragments survive, and consequently the arrangement of the subject matter cannot be determined. Nevertheless, certain conclusions can be drawn about the *History,* owing to its extensive employment by later writers; for example, it was the most significant source used by Diodorus Siculus and Arrian in their descriptions of the period. Pompeius Trogus, too, drew upon the work for the

hi ēr on' i mus

account of Macedonia in his *Philippic Histories,* as did Plutarch in his biographies of Eumenes, Demetrius Poliorcetes, and Pyrrhus.

Hieronymus' account was evidently a major work of first-class reliability and importance (modern attempts to contradict this view have not, on the whole, gained credence). Dating events by campaign years, like Thucydides, and exhibiting an unusual degree of accuracy when he quotes figures, Hieronymus devoted himself to telling the truth as he saw it—in contrast to the often fictitious sensationalism of his contemporary Duris of Samos. Furthermore, it is clear that he could not only tell a story but also depict characters. For instance, the fact that we know so much about the personality of Demetrius Poliorcetes today must in part be owed to Hieronymus, who first portrayed him; and if this is so, he was an innovator, since most Greek writers were content to interpret character as fixed and static. Hieronymus based his portrayal of Demetrius, and of other figures of the time as well, on intimate personal knowledge, since he himself played an active and prominent part in the happenings he narrated, thus illustrating the subsequent dictum of Polybius that in Greece only men of action could become competent historians.

According to Dionysius of Halicarnassus, writing in the first century B.C., Hieronymus was the first author to deal with the early history of Rome. However, he can scarcely have done more than touch briefly on Rome's conflict with King Pyrrhus (280–275), and his contemporary Timaeus can more accurately be described as the first historian of Rome.

EDITIONS—F. Jacoby, Die Fragmente der griechischen Historiker, 2b, 154.
ABOUT—T. S. Brown, Hieronymus of Cardia (American Historical Review, v 52), 1946–47; W. W. Tarn and G. T. Griffith, Hellenistic Civilisation, 3rd ed., 1952; R. H. Simpson, Abbreviation of Hieronymus in Diodorus (American Journal of Philology, v 80), 1959.

HIERONYMUS, EUSEBIUS, Saint. See Jerome, Saint

HILARY (Hilarius), Saint, was born in about A.D. 315 at Pictavi (Poitiers in western France). He died in 367. His parents were pagans, and he was taught Neoplatonism in the course of his higher education. As a young man, however, he became a convert to Christianity and was elected bishop of his hometown in about 353. He became a champion of Catholic orthodoxy against the Arian belief, which pronounced the Son to be distinct and inferior to the Father. However, the emperor Constantius II was sympathetic to Arianism, and Hilary's resistance to its Gallic exponent, Saturninus of Arelate (Arles), caused him to be banished to Phrygia in Asia Minor, where he spent several years (356–60). He employed this period of exile to increase his knowledge of Greek literature. He also continued to defend and propagate orthodox doctrine, so that the local Arians pronounced him "the mischief maker of the east." Eventually, despite his appeals to the emperor, it was arranged that he should be removed from Phrygia and recalled to Gaul. There he went back to Poitiers, and in 361, the year of Constantius' death, secured the condemnation of his opponent Saturninus. Indeed, his influence became so strong that in 364 he was summoned to Mediolanum (Milan) to examine the orthodoxy of its bishop, Auxentius. He was later described as the "Athanasius of the west," because of the unceasing opposition to Arianism that the two men shared.

Hilary was the author of numerous theological works that were clearly the products of a daring speculative mind but that found expression in a difficult and personal style. The most effective of these writings was a treatise entitled *On the Trinity,* in twelve books, the first Latin work to treat this theme on so comprehensive a scale. He also wrote a *Commentary on Matthew,* which was likewise the first of its kind in the West, and was the author of a *Commentary on the Psalms* as well. His *Tractatus Mysteriorum* dealt with typology, the doctrine that the Old Testament must be interpreted in terms of the New, which it was believed to prophesy and prefigure; for instance, Hilary pronounced that proclamations of Christ were

hil´ á ri

to be found in the Old Testament books. Thus, posterity should be enabled to contemplate the present in the past and venerate the past in the present. This sort of interpretation, with the many allegories that accompanied it, became exceedingly popular when taken up by Saint Ambrose and others and considerably retarded the progress of historical criticism of the Bible.

Hilary also wrote a work entitled *On Synods or on the Faith of the Peoples of the East (De Synodis seu de Fide Orientalium)* in which he tried to persuade the easterners why they should rally round his orthodox views and, at the same time, explained the history of the dispute between the Church and the Arians for the benefit of his Gallo-Roman colleagues. The knowledge he had acquired of Greek as well as of his native Latin equipped him excellently to perform this double task, and his performance of its second aspect showed how well he had learned to expound a complicated controversy to the comparatively uninformed Latin world. Because of its careful definition of all the disputed terms and its description of the various creeds issued by successive church councils, *On the Synods* remains a valuable source of knowledge for the ecclesiastical history of the period.

Taking the idea from eastern practice, Hilary also wrote three Latin hymns, the earliest that have come down to us (the hymn written for the Epiphany is in rhyme). The hymns are not very poetic or skillful, but they were pioneer attempts; and as a result of them the triumphs of Ambrose in this field became possible shortly afterward.

Hilary was the most eminent writer in Gaul of his generation—and indeed the greatest western theologian of the age. His works were read by Jerome, one of the best known of the Christian Fathers, who found his reasonable and philosophical presentation of Christian doctrine very persuasive.

EDITIONS—J. P. Migne, Patrologia Latina, v 9 and v 10; also list *in* Encyclopaedia Britannica, 1971, v 11, p 491.
ABOUT—A. S. Walpole, Early Latin Hymns, 1922; P. Smulders, La doctrine trinitaire de S. Hilaire de Poitiers, 1944; C. Borchardt, Hilary's Role in the Arian Struggle, 1966; N. J. Gastaldi, Hilario de Poitiers, 1969; J. Doignon, Hilaire de Poitiers avant l'exil, 1971.

HIPPARCHUS

HIPPARCHUS, Greek astronomer and geographer, was born in about 190 B.C. at Nicaea (Iznik) in Bithynia (northwestern Asia Minor) but spent much of his life on the island of Rhodes, as well as some time at Alexandria. One of his observations of the heavens seems to have been carried out in 127; it is not known how long afterward he died. He wrote numerous works, of which all but one have disappeared, though we know about those that are missing from Strabo and Ptolemy. His only extant writing is an early treatise, *Commentary on the Phaenomena of Eudoxus and Aratus,* in three books. A young friend had written to Hipparchus asking for information about the accuracy of Aratus' famous poem the *Phaenomena.* Hipparchus, in reply, points out that Aratus (d. 213 B.C.) had depended on facts provided by the astronomer Eudoxus (died c. 340 B.C.)—whom he then proceeds to criticize; his analysis yields useful information about his own star coordinates.

It is known that Hipparchus wrote an extremely important work that cataloged the stars—the first such catalog ever to be completed. He listed more than eight hundred fixed stars, dividing them into categories of magnitude and brightness, and gave some record of their appearances, so that future astronomers might be able to detect changes. This catalog, in spite of incorrect hypotheses and inadequate instruments, was for its period an extraordinary achievement. "He made the heavens a legacy to all humankind," said Pliny the Elder, "if only anybody could have been found capable of claiming the inheritance."

Possessing access, evidently, to Babylonian eclipse records, Hipparchus was the first astronomer to construct a theory of the movements of sun and moon that was properly based on observational findings. He got the sun's movement right but found it impossible to determine the motion of the moon—and accordingly, in the true scientific spirit, left the solution of this problem to his successors. Another of his works entitled *On the Displacement of the Solstitial and Equinoctial Points* reflected his most famous discovery, the precession of the equinoxes (the changes of the measured positions of

hip pär′ kus

the stars that result from the movement of the points of intersection of the eclipse and of the celestial equator). In this book, he stated that the precession is not less than one degree in a century; his subsequent researches led him to a figure of 1 degree, 2 minutes and 20 seconds, a figure from which the modern estimate departs by only 10 seconds.

Hipparchus' discovery of precession enabled him to lay down, in his monograph entitled *On the Length of the Year,* more accurate values for the tropical year (the period of the sun's apparent rotation from the equinox to the same equinox again)—his figure is only six and one-half minutes too large. He retained the erroneous geocentric theory (that the sun and stars revolved around the earth) in preference to the heliocentric discovery of Aristarchus, which meant that when he attacked the problem of the relative size and distance of the sun and moon his figures were inaccurate. Here again, however, as in his study of the motion of the moon, he realized to his credit that his results were unsatisfactory. All in all, he was a pioneer astronomer of extraordinary merit, improving observational techniques out of all recognition and showing a remarkable capacity to select the data that were relevant to his purposes.

In the field of mathematics, too, Hipparchus was a major innovator. The discovery of stereographic projection was probably his work. He was also the first person, as far as we know, to make systematic use of trigonometry. His researches on the trigonometry of the sphere guided his series of geographical studies that took the form of a three-book work criticizing the procedures of Eratosthenes. Hipparchus' own chief contribution to the subject was his endeavor to apply rigorous mathematical principles to the determination of location; he seems to have been the first scholar to employ the modern practice of specifying longitudes and latitudes. In order to get these established, he even mobilized the cooperation of different observers all over the world, though the political situation then made this even more difficult to achieve than it is today. His work on mathematical geography played an important part in the development of that subject, since it established the necessary observational rules on a scientific foundation.

EDITIONS—K. Manitius, Commentarius in Aratum, 1894; D. R. Dicks, The Geographical Fragments of Hipparchus, 1960.
ABOUT—O. Neugebauer, Notes on Hipparchus, in Studies Presented to Hetty Goldman, 1956, and The Exact Sciences in Antiquity, 2nd ed., 1957; G. E. R. Lloyd, Greek Science After Aristotle, 1973.

HIPPIAS, Greek sophist, popular philosophical lecturer, and polymath, was a younger contemporary of his fellow sophist Protagoras and lived from about 485 to 415. He came from Elis in the Peloponnese and was the principal Peloponnesian representative of the sophistic movement. Hippias traveled widely in the Greek world, serving as the envoy of Elis and delivering lectures from which he earned large sums. He even spoke at the Olympic Games near his native city, wearing a magnificent purple robe. He often demonstrated a series of mnemonic tricks that he described as an "art of memory" in a sort of quiz program he had invented—for Hippias was the most impressive exponent of that section of the sophists whose members aimed at exhibiting competence throughout the whole field of human knowledge. He himself claimed to know about rhetoric, dialectic, grammar, poetry, legendary prehistory, mathematics, astronomy, and music—the essential elements that were later brought together more formally as the components of an encyclopedic education. He was also a master of various handicrafts and asserted that everything he wore on his person, including his ring, was made by his own hands. Our information about his teaching and writing is extremely inadequate. The *Hippias Minor* of Plato and the *Hippias Major* (which is less certainly attributed to Plato) depict him vividly, though with an element of pejorative caricature that overstresses his glibness and may fail to do full justice to his unusual ability.

Hippias also produced a massive output of writings. In his capacity as a mathematician, he discovered the first curve other than the circle to be recognized by Greek math-

ιπ′ πι ας

ematicians, namely the *quadratrix*, which can be used for dividing an angle into any number of equal parts; he himself may have trisected angles by this means and may have employed the same method to square the circle. According to Plato, Hippias was also the author of poetry of widely diverse kinds, including epic, tragic, and choral (dithyrambs); we have the title of one of his elegies, about the deaths of a chorus of boys from Messenia who were drowned. Moreover, he and other sophists provided the first known studies of earlier poets.

Among Hippias' numerous prose works was a treatise, *The Names of Peoples,* and a work entitled *Collection (Synagoge),* which no doubt contained a miscellany of antiquarian material; and he may have been the first doxographer (author of studies on the doctrines of philosophers). He also wrote a *List of Victors at the Olympic Games,* which proved a vital contribution to the establishment of Greek chronology, since later historians used it as the framework of their narratives.

If Plato, in his *Protagoras,* is offering an accurate quotation—the context and tone indicate that he intends to—Hippias prefaced an address by the words: "kinsmen, men of like feelings, fellow citizens by nature [phusei] rather than by law and custom [nomo]." The address goes on to declare that nature binds like and like together, while law and custom, like tyrants, often exercise forms of coercion that are contrary to nature. This antithesis, which was soon to become the subject of extensive discussion, cannot be found in the works of any other writer earlier than the middle 320s B.C., when Antiphon had a lot to say about the matter. When he did so, he was probably echoing Hippias. If so, it may well be that Hippias was the first, or one of the first, to argue against the primacy of the national, city-state ties created by law and custom—thus, he invented, in effect, the concept of cosmopolitanism.

EDITIONS—H. Diels, Die Fragmente der Vorsokratiker, v 2, 7th ed. (ed. by W. Kranz), 1954; R. K. Sprague, The Older Greek Sophists, 1972.
ABOUT—M. Untersteiner, The Sophists, 1954; W. K. C. Guthrie, History of Greek Philosophy, v 3, 1969. On

HIPPOCRATES

Plato's Hippias dialogues: R. Robinson, Plato's Earlier Dialectic, 1953; M. Soreth, ed., The Greater Hippias, 1953 (defending its authenticity); R. K. Sprague, Plato's Use of Fallacy, 1962; W. K. C. Guthrie, History of Greek Philosophy, v 4, 1972; M. Leminta, Il problema della bellezza autencità e significato dell'Ippia Maggiore di Platone, 1974. On Hippias and Antiphon: F. Heinimann, Nomos und Physis, 1965.

HIPPOCRATES, Greek physician, was approximately contemporary with Socrates (469–399 B.C.), or slightly younger. His birthplace was the island of Cos (off the west coast of Asia Minor) where there was already an important medical school (another was at Cnidus, opposite, on the mainland). The son of the physician Heraclides and a member of the guild or association (or perhaps family) of physicians known as the Asclepiadae, he seems to have pursued his early medical studies in the temple of Asclepius (the god of healing) at Cos. His teachers were said to have been his father, his gymnastics teacher, Herodicus of Selymbria (who wrote on dietetics), the sophists Gorgias and Prodicus, and the philosopher Democritus. Thereafter, Hippocrates himself taught medicine (for fees) and practiced it at many centers including, reputedly, Athens, Delos, Thrace, and Thessaly, where he died (at Larissa) at an advanced age. He was a man of diminutive stature.

Hippocrates very rapidly became a well-known doctor; but the famous medical oath associated with his name does not seem, in its present form, to have dated before the fourth century B.C. (moreover, it was apparently limited to a special group of practitioners). According to Plato, Hippocrates considered the body as an organism and based his medical practice on the linkage of all the scattered particulars relating to the body into a single, coherent concept. Meno, a pupil of Aristotle, recorded that he attributed diseases to indigestion, which in his view caused air excreted from the remains of food to invade the body, thus infecting it with illness.

It is by no means certain, however, that Hippocrates ought to be included in the

hi pok′ rȧ tēz

present volume at all. About a hundred and thirty writings have come down to us in his name, but approximately half of these can be rejected immediately as late forgeries, and it is not certain that any of the others should be ascribed to his authorship. The *Corpus Hippocraticum* that they comprise consists of 58 works in 73 books, some taking the form of carefully composed lectures, others addressed to a general audience. They deal with methods of treatment, preservation of health, surgery, general pathology and the pathology of particular conditions, diagnosis and prognosis, physiology, gynecology and embryology. The *Corpus* is evidently the work of a large number of medical writers belonging not only to the school of Cos but to other groups or schools as well—including, apparently, that of the physicians of Cnidus.

Most of the treatises were compiled between 430 and 330 B.C. (some are later), but none of them can be attributed to Hippocrates himself with any confidence. However, two other pieces could conceivably be by his hand, since their style shows that they date from his lifetime. One is entitled *On Airs, Waters and Places,* or, as it is often called today, *On Environment.* This monograph is divided into two parts: the first discusses the effect of various environmental conditions on human beings; the second, following the tradition of earlier Ionian ethnology, compares and contrasts the soils, climates, and demographic situations of Europe and Asia. The other early work is entitled *On the Sacred Disease* and deals with epilepsy. In this treatise the author, while conceding that in the last resort everything comes from a divine origin, demonstrates clearly that epilepsy is not more holy than any other illness. The argument is accompanied by attacks on demonology and other superstitions. A further group of writings, including *Epidemics* (Books 1 and 3) and the *Prognosticum,* may conceivably have been written, not indeed by Hippocrates himself, but at least under his direct influence.

However, the collection of so-called Hippocratic writings *(Corpus Hippocraticum)* as a single, united entity, cannot be traced back earlier than the first commentators and lexicographers of the third century B.C. By that time the fame of Hippocrates, as the founder of medical science, had eclipsed that of all other early doctors, and he was attracting the same sort of legendary reverence as Pythagoras and Plato. But the character of his fame varied greatly from place to place and from time to time, since he came to stand for whatever any particular writer happened to consider most valuable in early medicine. He was idealized—for example, by Galen, in the second century A.D.—both as a doctor and as a medical and biological theorist. From the ninth to the twelfth centuries, Arabic scholars studied, translated, and adapted the Hippocratic writings, and before and after 1100 Latin versions were made, from the Arabic and perhaps also from the original Greek. From the fourteenth century onward, Hippocrates and Galen were prominent in European university curricula, and many new translations followed; the decline of Galen's reputation in the sixteenth century left the fame of many Hippocratic theories untouched. The *Corpus* remains of great value today for the light it throws not only on early medicine but on early Greek science as a whole and for the vital issues it raises about medical ethics and the doctor's responsibility to his patient and the community.

EDITIONS (of Hippocratic Corpus)—E. Littré, Oeuvres complètes d'Hippocrate, 1839–61; I. L. Heiberg, H. Grensemann, H. Diller *in* Corpus Medicorum Graecorum, 1927, 1968, 1970; W. Putzger, Letters, 1914; F. C. Unger, The Heart, 1923; K. Deichgrüber and E. Schwytzer, The Body (Peri Sarkon), 1935; H. Grensemann, The Sacred Disease, 1968; I. M. Lonie, The Seed, The Nature of the Child, 1979. *Translations* —W. H. S. Jones and E. T. Withington (Loeb ed.), 923–31; J. Chadwick, W. N. Mann, E. T. Withington, M. Lonie *in* G. E. R. Lloyd, eds., Hippocratic Writings (Penguin ed.), 1978; R. Joly (Budé ed.), 1967–78; A. Roselli, La chirurgia hippocratica, 1975.

ABOUT—M. Pohlenz, Hippokrates, 1938; W. A. Heidel, Hippocratic Medicine: Its Spirit and Method, 1941; L. Edelstein, The Hippocratic Oath, 1943; C. Lichtenthaeler, La médecine hippocratique, 1948–60; L. Bourgey, Observation et expérience chez les médecins de la collection hippocratique, 1953, *and* with J. Jouanna, eds., La collection hippocratique, 1975; R. Joly, Le niveau de la science hippocratique, 1966; L. Edelstein, Ancient Medicine, 1967; F. Kudlien, Der Beginn des medizinischen Denkens bei den Griechen, 1967; H. W. Nörenberg, Das Göttliche und die Natur in der Schrift "Über die heilige Krankheit," 1968; H. Flashar, ed., Antike Medizin, 1971; K. Deichgräber, Hippokrates de Humoribus in der Geschichte der griechischen Medizin, 1973; E. D. Phillips, Greek Medicine, 1973; J. Jouanna, Hippocrate: Pour une archéologie de l'école de Cnide, 1974; H. Grensemann, Knidische Medizin, v 1, 1975; La Collection hippocratique et son rôle dans L'histoire de médecine (Actes du Colloque hippocratique de Strasbourg, 1972), 1975; Corpus Hippocraticum (Actes du Colloque hippocratique de Mons, 1975), 1977; E. Hussey, Four Hippocratic Texts, 1979.

HIPPONAX, Greek poet, was born in the earlier part of the sixth century B.C., probably to aristocratic parents; it is not known when he died. His birthplace was Ephesus (Selçuk) in Ionia (western Asia Minor), from which he was banished; he then moved to another Ionian city, Clazomenae (Urla). There he lived in great misery and poverty, as he tells us in his own poems, written perhaps in about 550. Only fragments of these pieces exist; they are mostly composed in a meter he himself was said to have invented, the limping iambic (choliambic or scazon), in which the iambic trimeter terminates not with an iambus (a short and then a long syllable) but with a spondee (two long syllables). The surviving excerpts show him as a spokesman of the underprivileged, deploring their lot with satirical, venomous scurrility. In one poem he complains of the blind, arbitrary behavior of Plutus, the god of wealth, and prays to another deity, Hermes, for a coat and warm boots, since he is desperately cold and frostbitten. Another fragment tells of a quarrel with the painter Mimnes (Hipponax is interested in painting and writes elsewhere of an artist who has painted a snake on the side of a ship so that it seems to be biting the helmsman). More famous, however, was his legendary disagreement with the sculptor Bupalus, whose brother Athenis was also said to be involved. According to a later tale they made a statue caricaturing the features of Hipponax and were so distressed by the ferocious verses this action evoked in return that they both committed suicide. This story, however, is not likely to be true—first, since no portrait statue of such a kind could have been made in the sixth century B.C.; and, secondly, because, as Pliny the Elder demonstrated, the

hip pō′ naks

brothers were still producing sculptures after the date of the quarrel. More probably, as other fragments suggest, the dispute of the two brothers with Hipponax was over a woman of the name of Arete. In another fragment the poet tells us how he drank with her, taking turns with a single bowl, since the cup had been broken by a slave. Nevertheless, his opinion of the female sex, as of much else, is fiercely cynical: a woman, he says, gives her husband pleasure on only two occasions, the day they marry and the day he buries her.

Hipponax was later credited with the invention of parody, and it is likely enough that he developed this genre, since his fragments include the beginning of a mock-heroic poem in Homeric verse that leads a certain gluttonous Eurymedontiades through an Odyssey of grotesque adventures. Elsewhere, when Hipponax pleads for a bushel of barley, the high tone he adopts contains an element of burlesque. He is also capable of unrestrained obscenity.

Indeed, his language is, in all respects, trenchant and laced not only with contemporary Greek slang but with foreign terms taken from Lydian and Phrygian everyday speech. Hipponax is, above all else, the poet of realism, his sufferings relieved only by his wit. The leading poet of the Hellenistic age, Callimachus, admired his earthy verses and declared that all writers of the same limping iambic meter took their inspiration from this Ephesian source—one of these writers was, in fact, Herodas, whose mimes owe Hipponax a substantial debt.

EDITIONS—A. D. Knox, The Greek Choliambic Poets, 1929; W. de S. Medeiros (Coimbra, dissertation), 1961; O. Masson, Les fragments du poète Hipponax, 1962; M. L. West, Iambi et Elegi Graeci, v 1, 1971.
ABOUT—W. de S. Medeiros, Hipponactea, 1969.

HOMER. The poems attributed to Homer, the *Iliad* and *Odyssey,* seem to have been sung in their final form during about the eighth century B.C., although contradictory Greek traditions offered many alternative datings. A number of cities asserted that they were the poet's birthplace, but the strongest claims were those of the island of Chios, off the west coast of Asia Minor, and the city of Smyrna (Izmir) on that coast. The internal evidence of the poems on the whole supports the belief that this was the region of the Greek world from which he came. The tradition that he was blind is not implausible, since the bards who earned a livelihood by singing at Greek courts were often blind.

The *Iliad* tells of a brief and late stage in the siege of Troy near the Hellespont (Dardanelles, northwestern Asia Minor) by the armies of the various Greek states, led by Agamemnon of Mycenae (near Argos). Together with his brother Menelaus of Sparta, he had induced the Greek leaders to join an expedition against the Trojan King Priam, because Paris, one of Priam's sons, had abducted Menelaus' wife, the beautiful Helen. The Greek forces have for nine years been encamped beside their ships on the shore near Troy but have not succeeded in reducing the city, though they have captured and looted a number of towns in Trojan territory, under the dashing leadership of Achilles, prince of the Myrmidons, the most redoubtable and most unruly of Agamemnon's princely supporters. The success of these raiding parties leads to a feud between Achilles and his commander-in-chief. Agamemnon has been allotted the captured girl Chryseis as his prize, and he refuses to give her up to her father, Chryses, a local priest of Apollo, even though Chryses has come to the camp with a ransom for her release. The priest prays to his god, a plague ensues, and Agamemnon is forced to surrender the girl in order to propitiate the angry divinity. In his frustration, Agamemnon recompenses himself by confiscating one of Achilles' own prizes, a girl named Briseis. Achilles, in great anger, refuses to fight any more and withdraws the Myrmidon force from the battlefield.

After an abortive truce, intended to allow Menelaus and Paris to settle their quarrel by single combat, the two armies join battle again, and, as a result of Achilles' absence from the field, the Greeks, who have hitherto kept the Trojan forces penned up in Troy or close to its walls, find themselves on the defensive. They are even forced to dig a trench and build a rampart around their hips and huts. But these defenses are eventually stormed by the son of King Priam of Troy, Hector, who succeeds in setting fire to one of the Achaean ships. At this point Achilles, who has remained obdurate to all entreaties, yields to the extent of permitting his friend Patroclus to lead the Myrmidon force to the rescue of the hard-pressed Greeks. Patroclus brilliantly succeeds in this mission, but he pushes ahead too far and is killed under the walls of Troy by Hector.

This disaster brings Achilles to life. In an excess of rage and sorrow, he reconciles himself with Agamemnon, takes the field once more, hurls the panic-stricken Trojans back into their city and finally kills Hector—savagely maltreating his corpse. Hector's father, King Priam, in his grief, is inspired by the gods to visit Achilles in his camp by night, in order to request the return of his son's body. Achilles relents. The *Iliad* ends with an uneasy truce for Hector's funeral.

Archeology confirms that the city of Troy was destroyed in about 1250 B.C.—very possibly by representatives of the Greek-speaking Mycenaean civilization on the mainland, though this is not certain. Shortly afterward the Mycenaean civilization itself was destroyed—perhaps by Dorian invaders from the north, though this too has been questioned. As the Greek world, in the form to which we apply the term, began to take shape, the Homeric poems took on something like their present appearance, toward 750 or 700 B.C.

During the intervening period, the bards had been unlettered, but epic poems in some form or other had been orally transmitted from one to another, with their stock formulas (themes, word-groups, and phrases) as mnemonic guides for impromptu singing. In the 28,000 lines of the *Iliad* and *Odyssey* there are 25,000 repeated phrases (including "wine-dark sea," "rosy-fingered dawn," etc., etc.), and clauses, and sentences. Handed down through the generations by such methods, the *Iliad* not only contains certain references to Mycenean objects and institutions dating from a time half a millennium earlier but also incorporates more extensive allusions reflecting the circumstances of the eighth century in which the poem was completed, together with numerous accretions

of subject matter from the centuries between —all cast into a balanced and harmonious unity by the genius who gave the poem its final form. Whether he himself made a single epic out of the numerous and perhaps relatively short lays that he inherited or whether this amalgamation had already, in whole or part, been gradually evolved by previous singers—perhaps over a long period—cannot now be determined.

Probably he accompanied his own recitation of the poem with a lyre or baton, and he may similarly have directed the performances of others. Such performances are likely to have taken place at a great festival, perhaps the Pan-Ionian festival at Mount Mycale (western Asia Minor). The *Iliad* could be recited in fifteen two-hour sessions, that is to say, in the course of two or three days. The eighth century was about the time when, as inscriptions show, the Phoenician (Semitic) alphabet was being adapted by the Greeks. That meant that the poem could be copied down—probably not by Homer himself, though not long after his day. The *Iliad* and *Odyssey* are the products of the impact of literate on illiterate culture. Once composed, the poems became the property of a guild or clan, the Homeridae, who "published" them by recitation. Perhaps Pisistratus, the tyrant (autocratic ruler) of Athens (560–527 B.C.), arranged for them to be cast into their final form. The present division into twenty-four books may date from the third century B.C.

Homer possessed an exceptionally powerful and imaginative visual sense, which prompted Voltaire to define him as a "sublime painter." The color, vividness, and tenderness of his similes, for example—drawn as they are from an extensive range of nature and life—convey the pictorial and emotional appeal of everyday scenes and doings with deep sympathy and intuitive power. The rapidly moving, picturesque, imaginative diction in which the poet enlarges on these and many other themes is always suited to its various subjects.

Homer's unique descriptive talent enables him to present each personage as a strongly differentiated individual. The most formidable in the *Iliad* is Achilles. Savage, sulky, and vindictive, at times, but also the most

209

handsome, eloquent, courteous, generous, wise, and cultured of all the heroes, possessing in extreme degree all their virtues and faults. He is by turns lustful for imperishable fame, valorous in battle, and furiously sensitive to insults—in short, he is the most nearly complete exponent of the Homeric code of honor, which, for good or evil, is one of the *Iliad's* outstanding contributions to the social history of the world.

A hero, as Homer imaginatively reconstructed this archetypal figure from past history and legend, used his superior birth, wealth, and military and athletic prowess in order to win renown, which he confidently pursued with violently competitive vigor. In his effort to excel and win applause—the task that was the driving force and aim of his existence—the hero converted his whole life into an unremitting struggle for the first prize among his peers. The glory conferred on him by success was the quality by which he could become not wholly unlike the gods. The heroes, although human, seemed in some sense to live in a half-way state between human beings and the gods. They could rise to their greatest heights by battle: fighting was the Homeric hero's prime occupation. Yet, in the *Iliad,* an atmosphere of tragedy also surrounds these mighty warriors. There is pathos in their struggle, which is not only against their own rivals but against destiny itself, and against the formidable, sporadic interventions of the amoral, anthropomorphic, often unedifying Olympians. A hero finally fulfills himself in death itself, the last and most searching ordeal, the ultimate test of merit. Achilles knows he is soon to die: and in his meeting, at the poignant end of the poem, with the aged Priam, whose son Hector he has killed, the roar and exultation of battle has given way to sorrow and compassion.

His enemy Hector, too, had been a noble fighter, but a less ferociously whole-hearted man of blood than Achilles—a good son, husband, father, champion, and patriot, in whom the martial and elegiac moods meet and are blended. The most interesting among the other heroes are all Greeks. Their supreme commander Agamemnon is physically brave, but anxious, truculent, greedy, lying, boastful, tactless, and deficient in

moral courage, veering rapidly between pig-headed overconfidence and pessimistic despair. His brother Menelaus is brave enough, but cuts an unlucky figure as the cuckolded husband. Ajax is beefy and thick-witted and is victimized by the cleverness of Odysseus, who is not only overwhelmingly intelligent but at the same time the complete man of action, unromantically yet lovingly delineated by the poet.

There are real women, too, in the *Iliad.* True, a woman is a mere chattel. For instance, in the wrestling contest between Odysseus and Ajax in the funeral games of Patroclus, she is the prize of the loser, whereas the winner got a tripod. Yet, it was only because of Paris' love for Helen that the war was ever launched: and such was her beauty that the Trojan elders had only to gaze upon her to see how it had happened. The wives of other heroes, too, play their parts with sensitive poise, responsibility, and good taste. In particular, the last meeting of Andromache with her doomed husband Hector is almost unbearably tragic. Such compassionate chords complete the profound humanity of the *Iliad.* The Homeric view of all these personages is impersonal and disengaged. Yet the poet's interpretation of character is both lively and understanding, tolerant but never indifferent, passionate but nobly balanced.

The myths and legends this epic enshrines did a great deal to furnish the Greeks with their abundant and abiding concern for human dignity. In classical times the Trojan story was everywhere: one-fifth of all Aeschylus and Euripides is derived from it, and two-fifths of Sophocles. The *Iliad* had already begun to attract commentators from the sixth century B.C. onward. For the entire millennium of Greco-Roman antiquity this poem was the greatest unifying, civilizing factor in the classical world, forming the indispensable basis of its educational system and exerting a thousand effects on its literary, moral, social, and political thinking. Throughout subsequent ages, too, the influence of the *Iliad* on writers and painters has been immeasurable.

The *Odyssey* tells the story of the return home of Odysseus from the Trojan War. His wanderings lasted ten years, but the action of the *Odyssey* covers only the final six weeks of this period. The poet brings in the earlier part of the story by means of flashbacks. When the poem opens Odysseus is a castaway, in the island paradise of the goddess Calypso, who has kept him there as her lover for nearly eight years, though he longs to go back to his home in Ithaca. There, meanwhile, his son Telemachus is almost a grown man and his home is overrun with unwanted guests, the suitors of his wife Penelope. Feasting at the house's expense, they continually press her to marry again and, after being fobbed off for years, finally insist that she must make her choice.

Odysseus' plight is due to the hostility of Poseidon, father of the Cyclops whom the hero blinded early in his wanderings. In Poseidon's absence the other gods are persuaded by Athena to take pity on Odysseus and help him, and so the plot is set in motion. Athena prompts Telemachus to visit Pylos and Sparta in search of news of his father, and Zeus orders Calypso to let Odysseus go. He builds a raft and sets sail; Poseidon raises a storm and he is shipwrecked but eventually cast up on the shore of Scheria, inhabited by the estimable and civilized Phaeacians. Here he meets the princess Nausicaa, whose parents entertain him royally in their splendid palace. During the feasting Odysseus describes his adventures ever since he left Troy. He tells of many strange and perilous encounters: with the Lotus-Eaters; with cannibals, monsters, whirlpools, and clashing rocks; with Aeolus, god of the winds, the enchantress Circe, the ghosts of the dead, and the cattle of the Sungod; and he describes how at the last, he had come to the island of Calypso, the sole survivor of the raft's crew.

When his tale has been told, the Phaeacians transport him to Ithaca (thus incurring the anger of Poseidon). There, in the guise of a beggar, he learns about the behavior of Penelope's suitors. Athena brings Telemachus back from Sparta, and father and son, reunited at last, plan how to destroy them. At Odysseus' house, no one recognizes him except his faithful dog and his aged nurse; but when Penelope proposes a final contest in archery for the suitors before making her choice, no one but he can

string the great bow. The suitors are slaughtered, Penelope is convinced of her husband's identity, and Odysseus is established in his kingdom once more.

The *Odyssey* is cast in the form of an epic, but its basis is a common folk story: that of the man who is so long absent that he is given up for dead and yet finally, after prolonged and varied adventures and journeys, regains his home and is reunited with his faithful wife. This main story, in the *Odyssey*, has drawn to it a great many other ancient and ageless folktales, ingeniously converted and united into one of the most exciting and readable of all poems. The bard who achieved this unifying feat of transformation has added numerous elements of his own, thus stamping his own indelible mark on the whole, for his Odysseus is the product of unequaled narrative genius. And the poet who created him belongs to a calling that was held in deep respect—indeed, he himself, in the course of the poem, on more than one occasion explicitly ensures that the importance of his profession should not be forgotten.

After centuries of vigorous controversy, it cannot be proved that the ancients were wrong in supposing that the *Iliad* and *Odyssey* were the work of the same poet. What must be said, however, is that the spirit of the two poems is different and that the *Odyssey* seems to be the later of the two—perhaps by something like a generation, bringing it to the end of the eighth century, just before the recently developed Greek alphabet created literary and historical records; indeed, Odysseus' Voyage to Hades bridges the previous and subsequent epochs by contradictorily placing his destination at the End of the World, on the one hand, and the Underworld of King Minos on the other, representing an earlier and a later range of ideas respectively.

Like the *Iliad,* the *Odyssey* praises courage, physical prowess, and resourcefulness. But there has been a move away from joyful and tragic heroism and doom-laden passion, toward calmer and more cautious virtues such as endurance, self-control, forbearance, and acceptance. Although a savage delight in bloodshed is still apparent—for example, in the mass-execution of the girls

211

who had been the suitors' concubines—there is a shift, at the same time, in favor of other kinds of values, so that men and women look at life in a new way: courtliness begins to take precedence over chivalry, and love of wife and home seems more important than love of comrades and honor.

There is a newly enhanced interest, too, in the social backgrounds of the aristocratic rulers and their households. Hospitality, friendship, respect for good breeding, and attention to decorous formality have become very prominent qualities: beneath the narrative of the excitements and wonders we can discern the pattern of a class managing its fixed residences and estates. There is also an unfamiliar kind of sentiment, for example in the description of Odysseus' old dog, lying on his dungheap and recognizing his returned master just before he dies. Like the *Iliad,* this picture echoes both earlier and contemporary ways of life at one and the same time, but the emphasis has now shifted in the direction of the latter; and the novel scene is acutely and truthfully observed.

The character that towers over the poem is that of the heavy-jawed, beetle-browed Odysseus himself. His enduring, unconquerable heart, ferocious but amazingly resourceful, drives him on to overcome fantastic obstacles. He is for all time the type of man who has striven against the storms and vicissitudes of life and has conquered them. He is also immeasurably clever—cleverer by far than any hero of the *Iliad.*

A subtle balance is struck between his sturdy, savage independence and the protection he needs and receives from his divine patron Athena. As the poem proceeds, she intervenes more and more on his behalf, treating him with a humorous, admiring familiarity. Ridicule of the Olympians, as in the *Iliad,* was still by no means impossible in the *Odyssey,* which contains, for example, the famous tale of Aphrodite caught in bed with her lover Ares by her husband Hephaestus. Yet while a goddess could still be made fun of, the poet for the first time endows his female characters with full, human personality: that of Penelope, in particular, is delineated with considerable subtlety. Nausicaa, too, is brave, sensitive, and re-

sourceful; and the enchantments woven by the two witches, the predatory Circe and the affectionate Calypso, leave lasting impressions on the listener's and reader's mind. (Many scholars have tried to identify the islands on which they lived and lurked, but without success, for, as the geographer Eratosthenes of Cyrene pointed out in the second century B.C., it was not Homer's intention that we should be able to locate all these wanderings on the map.)

The Greeks of the classical age were of two minds about whether Odysseus represented a noble ideal or was too tricky by half. In Rome the more critical view tended to prevail, although one of its earliest literary achievements was Livius Andronicus' *Odyssia Latina.* And yet, throughout the ages, the hero has caught the imagination of innumerable people as the supreme searcher who against all odds reaches his goal. After the classical age, his first great portrayal was in Dante's *Inferno,* where his cunning and greediness to learn are presented with respect. Odysseus became a sympathetic figure to the Renaissance, when it was no longer found difficult to blend the warrior and the man of craft in one personage. Tennyson saw him as reflecting his own need "to follow knowledge, like a sinking star, beyond the utmost bound of human thought." The *Ulysses* of Irish writer James Joyce (1922) used the hero's wanderings as a cosmic framework for the wanderings of Bloom over a single square mile of Dublin. Greek poet George Seferis (1931) saw Odysseus as one whose stormtossed exile is never quite over, his past and present coexisting in our thoughts; and his compatriot Nikos Kazantzakis wrote an immense *Odyssey* (1938) loaded with symbols of contemporary aspirations and perplexities.

The *Iliad* and *Odyssey* tell their stories with pellucid simplicity, dramatic directness, and, above all, unswerving speed, and in their climactic moments contain some of the most moving poetry that has ever been written. Their rich, traditional language, consisting of various dialectical forms in which Ionic elements predominate, is capable of rising to every emotion and mood and occasion—an instrument utilized to particular effect being the simile, which is a cunning means of conjuring up a whole world of often humble people and things, lying outside the main story. In the subsequent centuries of ancient Greece, the epics formed the basis of all education and were universally esteemed as a source of general wisdom, providing an unending mine of quotations and attracting a lengthy series of meticulous commentators. In the fifteenth century, they were the first important works printed in Greek, their first edition appearing at Florence in 1488, produced by the immigrant scholar Chalcondylas, who taught Greek in Italy.

WORKS—Writings wrongly attributed to Homer (in addition to other ascriptions, possibly right or wrong) include a number of the epic poems (now lost) subsequently collected in the Epic Cycle—notably the Thebaid, Epigoni, Cypria (covering the mythical period from the Judgment of Paris to the War); Aethiopis (about Achilles' slaying of Penthesilea the Amazon, Thersites, and the Ethiopian Memnon, followed by his own death); the Margites, a satirical epic, the hero of which is a fool *(margos);* Nostoi (returns of the heroes); and Batrachomyomachia (Battle of the Frogs and Mice), a parody of an epic poem.

Certain of the surviving Homeric Hymns have also been ascribed to Homer. These have come down to us in a form that is literary rather than devotional; their main content is the narration of myth. Some of the pieces seem to belong to the eighth century B.C., but others are later. The earliest hymns, at least, seem to belong to the tradition of Ionia rather than of the mainland (but see No. 3 in following paragraph). They appear to have been sung by professional bards *(rhapsodes),* in competitions held at festivals or thanksgiving ceremonies or funeral games. Some of the shorter hymns may have been written as invocations introducing the recitation of the Homeric epics.

The Hymns are not, as far as we are aware, mentioned as a collection until the first century B.C. Some survive only in fragments: (1) Of the first Hymn, to Dionysus, only 21 lines survive, dealing with the god's birthplace and the establishment of his festival. (2) The Hymn to Demeter (495 lines) is a fine miniature epic narrating the story of the sufferings of the goddess. Written in the late seventh or early sixth century, when the influence of Homer was still fresh, it is our earliest source of information on Eleusis and its mysteries. (3) The Hymn to Apollo (546 lines), is divided into parts dealing with Delos and Delphi. The former was assigned to Homer by Thucydides and Aristophanes of Byzantium; the latter seems to belong to the mainland rather than the Ionian tradition. (4) The Hymn to Hermes (580 lines) gaily describes the roguery and inventiveness of the infant god. (5) Hymn to Aphrodite (293 lines) enlarges on her sensual power and describes how Zeus caused her to love a mortal, Anchises. (6) This likewise is a hymn to Aphrodite (21 lines). (7) Hymn to Dionysus (59 lines) tells how the god was seized by pirates and performed miracles. (8) Hymn to Ares (15 lines) is Orphic and astrological. The remaining hymns are successively addressed to Artemis, Aphrodite, Athens, Hera, Demeter, the Mother of the Gods, Heracles the Lion-Hearted, Asclepius, Castor and Polydeuces (the Dioscuri), Hermes, Pan (No. 19, an original sort of piece describing his woodland sports), Hephaestus, Apollo, Poseidon, Zeus, Hestia, the Muses and Apollo, Dionysus, Artemis, Athena, Hestia, the Earth Mother, Helios, Selene, and the Dioscuri.

EDITIONS (Iliad and Odyssey)—W. Leaf, Iliad, 1900–02, reprint 1960; W. B. Stanford, Odyssey, 2nd ed., 1959. *Translations*—G. Chapman, 1611, 1616; A. Pope, 1715–20, 1725–26; A. T. Murray (Loeb ed.), 1919, 1924–25; E. V. Rieu (Penguin ed.), 1945, 1950; R. Lattimore, 1951, 1967; R. Fitzgerald, Odyssey, 1962; E. Rees, 1977. (For other translations see G. B. Parks and R. Z. Temple, The Literatures of the World in English Translation, v 1, 1968; A. M. W. Green, Classics in Translation: A Selective Bibliography, 1930–76, 1976.) Poems of the Homeric Cycle: G. W. Kullmann, Die Quellen der Ilias, 1960; G. Schoeck, Ilias und Aithiopis, 1961; W. C. Lawton, The Successors of Homer, 1969. *Homeric Hymns:* H. G. Evelyn-White, Hesiod: The Homeric Hymns—Fragments of the Epic Cycle: Homerica (with appendix by D. L. Page), revised ed., 1936; C. Boer, 1970; T. Sargent, 1973; N. J. Richardson, The Hymn to Demeter, 1974, reprint, 1979; F. Cassola, Inni omerici (Italian), 1975; A. N. Athanassakis, 1976.

ABOUT—*Iliad and Odyssey:* A. Lang, Homer and the Epic, 1893, reprint 1970; C. M. Bowra, Tradition and Design in the Iliad, 1930, *and* Heroic Poetry, 1952, *and* Homer and His Forerunners, 1955, *and* Homer, 1972; W. J. Woodhouse, The Composition of Homer's Odyssey, 1930; R. Carpenter, Folk Tale, Fiction and Saga in the Homeric Epics, 1946, reprint 1958; H. L. Lorimer, Homer and the Monuments, 1950; B. Marzullo, Il problema omerico, 1952; H. Schrade, Götter und Menschen Homers, 1952; H. T. Wade-Gery, The Poet of the Iliad, 1952; A. Heubeck, Der Odyssee-Dichter und die Ilias, 1954; W. B. Stanford, The Ulysses Theme, 1954; D. L. Page, The Homeric Odyssey, 1955, *and* History and the Homeric Iliad, 1959, *and* Folktales in Homer's Odyssey, 1973; F. Buffière, Les mythes d'Homère et la pensée grecques, 1956; Homer über die Dichtung, 1957; J. L. Myres, Homer and His Critics, ed. by D. H. F. Gray, 1958; T. B. L. Webster, From Mycenae to Homer, 1958; C. H. Whitman, Homer and the Heroic Tradition, 1958, reprint 1965; A. B. Lord, The Singer of Tales, 1960; A. Lesky, Göttliche und menschliche Motivation im homerischen Epos, 1961; G. S. Kirk, The Songs of Homer, 1962 (abridged as Homer and the Epic, 1964), *and* (as ed.) The Language and Background of Homer, 1964, *and* Homer and the Oral Tradition, 1977; A. J. B. Wace and F. H. Stubbings, A Companion to Homer, 1962; J. A. Scott, Homer and His Influence, 1963; G. F. Else, Homer and the Homeric Problem, 1965; A. Hoekstra, Homeric Modifications of Formulaic Prototypes, 1965; J. A. K. Thomson, Studies in the Odyssey, 1966; F. Matz and H. G. Buchholtz, eds., Archaeologica Homerica, 1967–77; C. R. Beye, The Iliad, the Odyssey and the Epic Tradition, 1968; J. B. Hainsworth, The Flexibility of the Homeric Formula, 1968, *and* Homer (Greece & Rome: New Surveys in the Classics, no 3), 1969; C. E. Nelson, ed., Homer's Odyssey: A Critical Handbook, 1969; A. Dihle, Homerprobleme, 1970; P. Vivante, The Homeric Imagination, 1970; A. Parry, ed., The Making of Homeric Verse by Milman Parry, 1971; H. Eisenberger, Studien zur Odyssee, 1973; A. Heubeck, Die homerische Frage, 1974; J. V. Luce, Homer and the Heroic Age, 1975; M. N. Nagler, Spontaneity and Tradition, 1975; S. Shannon III, ed., Oral Literature and the Formula, 1976; M. I. Finley, The World of Odysseus, revised ed., 1977; C. M. Moulton, Similes in the Homeric Poems, 1977; C. A. Trypanis, The Homeric Epics, 1977; O. Tsaragakis, The Nature and Background of Major Concepts of Divine Power in Homer, 1977. *About the Homeric Hymns*—E. Heitsch, Aphroditehymnus, Aeneas und Homer, 1965; N. J. Richardson, The Homeric Hymn to Demeter, 1974; J. Schroeder, Ilias und Apollonhymnos, 1975.

HORACE (Quintus Horatius Flaccus), Latin poet, was born in 65 and died in 8 B.C. His birthplace was Venusia (Venosa) in Apulia (southeastern Italy), where his father, a collector of payments at auctions, had acquired a small estate. He gave his son the best education of the day, first at Rome under the famous grammarian Orbilius Pupilius and subsequently at Athens. There Horace was persuaded by Brutus, who had recently assassinated Julius Caesar, to serve under him as an officer *(tribunus militum)* in his Republican army trying to resist the Second Triumvirate (Antony, Octavian—the future Augustus—and Lepidus). However, Brutus and his partner Cassius were killed at the battle of Philippi (42 B.C.), about which Horace wrote that he himself ran away (though here he may just be following a literary convention). After the defeat, he returned to Italy, only to find his father's house and land lost in the triumvirs' confiscations. But he himself was pardoned and managed to purchase a civil service job concerned with the keeping of records for the quaestors *(scriba quaestorius)*. However, according to his own account (in what may be, once again, a traditional and semi-jocular device), poverty impelled him to start writing verse, and in about 38 B.C. he was introduced by his fellow poets Virgil and Varius Rufus to Octavian's adviser Maecenas, the leading literary patron of the day, of whose literary circle Horace subsequently became

an increasingly important member. Maecenas gave him a farm in the Sabine country, in the valley of the river Digentia (Licenza), and presented him to Octavian. Although Horace tactfully declined Octavian's later offer of a secretaryship, after the death of Virgil in 19 B.C., he became the principal poet of Rome and the imperial court, so that when the ruler decided in 17 B.C. to revive the traditional and sacred Secular Games it was Horace who was requested to write the hymn for the occasion. He outlived Maecenas by a few months only.

Horace remained unmarried throughout his existence. His *Life* by Suetonius describes him as short and stout. He speaks of himself as prematurely grey and rather bald, fond of sunshine, and quick tempered but easy-going.

Horace's *Satires* are two books of hexameters, the first of which includes ten poems completed in about 35 B.C. and the second, made up of eight pieces, was published in about 30. The first book contains statements put forward by the poet himself; in the second, all but one of the poems are presented in dialogue form. The *Satires* express Horace's rejection of public life and the need to aim at wisdom through serenity. He discusses ethical questions: the race for wealth and position, the folly of extremes, the need for mutual tolerance, and the undesirability of ambition. But the essential feature of the collection is the fullness with which, by the aid of humorous anecdotes (and self-mockery), he seems to reveal every aspect of his own life and beliefs (though, as we shall see later, such an impression may be something of a delusion).

This ostensibly autobiographical method goes back to the tradition of Lucilius, the satirist of the second century B.C., whom Horace acknowledges as his model for the genre he was following. His dependence on Lucilius even extended to specific subjects, such as the Journey to Brundusium, which echoed the earlier poet's Sicilian journey. In other respects, the two writers are extremely different. Unlike Lucilius, Horace does not indulge in savage personal attacks, and the hexameter that he employs, the product of careful and deliberate artistry, is far more capable of great flexibility and diversity than that of Lucilius, standing midway between epic stiffness and conversational informality.

The *Epodes,* which were started in about 40 B.C. and published some ten years later, consist of seventeen poems, in iambic or partly iambic (based on the *iambus* or short-long foot) meters, for which Horace claims that his model is Archilochus of Paros, the Greek iambic and elegiac poet of the seventh century B.C. The iambic was traditionally employed for personal invective and ridicule, and the mockery in the *Epodes* is less gentle than that of the *Satires.* Yet, even here, Horace prefers to attack social abuses rather than individuals. The somewhat tense and strained tone of some of the *Epodes* reflects his anxious mood during the difficult years before Octavian (Augustus) brought peace to the distracted Roman world by defeating Antony at Actium in 31 B.C.

The *Odes* are divided into four books. The first three were published as a single unit in about 23 B.C. and the fourth about ten years later. Books 1-3, addressed to Maecenas, comprise eighty-eight poems, most of which are from 16 to 50 lines long. Horace asserts that Alcaeus and Sappho, the early Greek lyric poets of Lesbos, are his models: he claims to be the first Roman to introduce their manner and their various meters (Alcaic, Sapphic, Asclepiad, etc.) into Latin— although his debt to the polished techniques of the Greek Alexandrian poets of much later times is also very great. However, after all debts have been considered, Horace's end-products remain entirely original.

The subject matter of the *Odes* covers a very extensive range. The dominant formal theme of more than a third of them is friendship; indeed, a friend is normally their addressee, to whom Horace offers counsel, encouragement, or philosophical comment. Nearly another third of these pieces deals with love, a subject on which Horace strikes a novel note, signalized by a considerable degree of detachment and displaying emphasis on the irony, pathos, and charm that can be extracted from some typical amorous situations; although by no means homosexual, he seems more genuinely devoted to his male friends than to the women of whom he writes. Other poems deal with the practice

of poetry; one of Horace's specialities is the *recusatio,* the polite refusal to tackle this or that type of verse that someone has requested him to write—in particular, the grand sort of national epic; although, at the same time, a very notable group of Horace's *Odes* do in fact devote themselves to patriotic themes and, in their own way, glorify the Augustan regime (though with a severe dignity that never falls into adulation). The best of these poems, notably the six *Roman Odes* at the beginning of Book 3 (in which Horace appears as a Roman reincarnation of the stately Greek lyricist Pindar, of the fifth century B.C.), are perhaps the greatest political poetry ever written. After Virgil's death, Horace, as we have seen, had become the national poet, and that was how he was commissioned by Augustus to write the choral lyric, the *Secular Hymn (Carmen Saeculare),* for the solemn Secular Games that the emperor celebrated to give religious sanction to his new imperial system. And it was once again at Augustus' suggestion that a fourth short book of *Odes* was added in 13 B.C., including some additional pieces in praise of the imperial house. This fourth book was addressed to Paullus Fabius Maximus, a close friend of the emperor. The brilliant language of Horace's *Odes* is close-knit and succinct. The English nineteenth century poet Alfred Lord Tennyson called their lines ". . . Jewels five-words long,/that on the stretch'd forefinger of all Time/sparkle for ever."

The *Epistles* of Horace were written in hexameters, like the earlier *Satires,* which they somewhat resemble, but they reveal a more mature, profounder approach. The first book, containing twenty of these poetic "letters," was published in about 20 B.C. Latin letters in verse had been written before, notably by Lucilius, but Horace made an original creation out of the form, employing it as a framework for informal and conversational discussion that could be adapted to any topic whatever that the poet wished to discuss from a personal point of view. In the first of these pieces he half-jokingly informs Maecenas that he has given up poetry in favor of the more important study of philosophy. Yet the "philosophy" that he puts forward, while inimitably ex-

215

pressed, is of a somewhat traditional, moralizing form, praising the excellence of the simple life, warning against the dangers of avarice, and so on.

Subsequently, Horace set to work on further literary letters—much longer than any in the first book—relating in different ways to poetic activities and literary criticism. Two such pieces make up the whole second book of the *Epistles.* The first epistle, written after 17 (and probably after 15) B.C., surveys earlier Latin literature in its relationship to society, asserting the merits of contemporary poetry against all such previous endeavors. The second epistle, addressed to a certain Florus, returns to Horace's reasons for concerning himself with "philosophy" rather than lyric poetry. And there is also a third of these long epistles, not belonging to either of the two books, which is known as the *Ars Poetica (Poetic Art).* Addressed to a Roman nobleman named Piso and his sons, probably in about 19 or 18 B.C., this poem consists of some thirty maxims for the guidance of young poets, concentrating largely on the traditional literary genres of epic and drama and containing many memorably expressed judgments.

Horace's renown rests to a considerable extent upon the likable personality revealed in his own writings. Autobiographical touches abound in his poetry; he seems to tell far more about himself, his temperament, his development and his manner of living than any of the other leading poets of antiquity, and this proliferation of personal material gives us the impression that we know quite a lot about him. Yet such self-revelations are not factual but literary—a cunning, illusory feature of his technique for creating an intimate atmosphere. Even his actual beliefs are difficult to pin down with any certainty, since his assertions of them often seem little more than devices, not necessarily sincere, to introduce a theme or mood. His attitude toward love is characteristic: he likes to portray himself in conventionally literary situations, often involving a measure of self-ridicule, but without in fact really telling the reader anything at all about his love life. Yet Horace's claim that the views and criticisms he inserts in his poetry are intended for the good of society does

seem to be seriously intended, for it appears that he believed more and more that the good poet must, above all, be a good man and useful to the community as an educator and civilizing influence. Goodness meant, in particular, moderation; he is always deploring excess and refusing, deprecating, dissuading from extreme courses of action.

Despite his smoke screens, some aspects of his detached and evasive personality can finally be detected from his poetry. The man who emerges is kindly, humane, and tolerant, though capable of strength; above all, he is a mocker both of himself and of others, lighthearted yet astringent and standing no nonsense. While certain of his later admirers see Horace as the poet of the lighter side of life, others (particularly in our own century and in the English-speaking world) less admiringly interpret him above all as the poet of imperial Rome and Augustus. Both are equally right, for this balance and diversity were the very essence of his poetical nature: wholeheartedly supporting the autocratic Augustan regime—seeing that it had put an end to decades of destructive civil disturbance and strife—Horace nevertheless adheres to a firm, though tactful, assertion of his own personal independence.

From the time of his *Secular Hymn* onward, his works were known and appreciated by all educated Romans; in fact, before he was dead his *Odes* were suffering from the fate for which he had ruefully destined them: they had become a textbook for the use of the schoolroom. Such was their inimitable quality that they had few successors in lyric poetry, until some early Christian writers sought to adapt his forms and meters to their own different requirements. Thereafter, the Middle Ages had little use for the *Odes,* the cynical aspects of which conflicted with the piety of the times, although Horace's *Satires* and *Epistles* continued to be read because of their predominantly moralistic tone: indeed, it is as "the satirist" that Dante values Horace. The lyrics came into their own again in the Renaissance, when the French poet Ronsard, for example, admired them more than any other poetry he knew. In the seventeenth century, the English poets Ben Jonson, Andrew Marvell, and William Collins were deeply Horatian;

moreover, the *Ars Poetica* was regarded, erroneously, as a complete guide to poetry, and its translation by the French critic and poet Nicolas Boileau (1636–74) exercised an enormous influence on classical French drama. The *Satires* lived again in the adaptations by Jonathan Swift and then by Alexander Pope; to the eighteenth century, Horace's urbanity and philosophy of moderation exerted a special appeal. Above all, however, it is the many-faceted intricacy of the *Odes* that has challenged translators of all periods; the renderings that have been attempted throughout the centuries run into thousands.

EDITIONS—J. Gow, 1896, 1901–09; E. C. Wickham, revised by H. W. Garrod, 1912; A. Kiessling and R. Heinze, 9th and other eds., 1957. Odes and Epodes: H. Darnley Naylor, 1922; F. Plessis, 1924; M. Hubbard and R. G. M. Nisbet, Odes, Book 1, 1970, *and* Book 2, 1978. Satires and Epistles: P. Lejay, 1911. Epistles: A. S. Wilkins, 1892. Art of Poetry: A. Rostagni, 1930, reprint 1946. *Translations*—H. R. Fairclough, Satires, Epistles, Ars Poetica (Loeb ed.), revised ed., 1929; J. P. Clancy, Odes and Epodes, 1960; Lord Dunsany and M. Oakley (Everyman ed.), 1961; J. Michie, Odes (Penguin ed.), 1967; C. E. Bennett, Odes and Epodes (Loeb ed.), revised ed., 1968; G. Williams, Odes, Book 3, 1969; S. P. Bovie, Satires and Epistles, 1959; N. Rudd, Satires of Persius and Horace (Penguin ed.), 1973; T. S. Dorsch, Art of Poetry, *in* Classical Literary Criticism (Penguin ed.), 1965; D. A. Russell and M. Winterbottom, eds., Art of Poetry, *in* Ancient Literary Criticism, 1972.
ABOUT—J. F. D'Alton, Horace and His Age, 1917, reprint 1962; G. C. Fiske, Lucilius and Horace, 1920; G. Pasquali, Orazio lirico, 1920; E. Stemplinger, Horaz im Urteil der Jahrhunderte, 1921; G. Showerman, Horace and His Influence, 1922, reprint 1963; T. R. Glover, Horace: A Return to Allegiance, 1932; Orazio nella letteratura mondiale (bimillenary), 1936; R. Heinze, Vom Geist des Römertums, 1938, reprint 1960; A. Noyes, Horace: A Portrait, 1947; L. P. Wilkinson, Horace and His Lyric Poetry, 2nd ed., 1951; E. Fraenkel, Horace, 1957; N. E. Collinge, The Structure of Horace's Odes, 1961; S. Commager, The Odes of Horace: A Critical Study, 1962; C. O. Brink, Horace on Poetry: Prolegomena to the Literary Epistles, 1963, *and* The Ars Poetica, 1971; J. Perret, Horace, 1964; N. Rudd, The Satires of Horace, 1966; C. M. Goad, Horace in the English Literature of the Eighteenth Century, 1967; D. West, Reading Horace, 1967; A. La Penna, Orazio e la morale mondana europea, 1968; M. R. Thayer, The Influence of Horace on the Chief English Poets of the Nineteenth Century, 1968; G. W. Williams, Tradition and Originality in Roman Poetry, 1968; N. A. B. Hunt, Horace the Minstrel, 1969; M. J. McGann, Studies in Horace's First Book of Epistles, 1969; K. J. Reckford, Horace, 1969; H. Oppermann, ed., Wege zu Horaz, 1972; H. P. Syndikus, Die Lyrik des Horaz, 1972; G. D. N. Costa, ed., Horace, 1973; H. Hierche, Les Épodes de Horace, 1974; J. V. Cody, Horatian and Callimachean Aesthetics, 1976; F. Cupaiuolo, Lettura di Orazio lirico, 1976; C. MacLeod, Horace's Epistles, 1979.

HRABANUS MAURUS, MAGNENTIUS,

Frankish churchman and Latin theologian and poet, was born in A.D. 780 at Mainz. His name also appears as Rabanus (the Raven) and Rhabanus. He went to school at Fulda, the monastery of which possessed the greatest library in Germany, and then studied at Tours under the leading Carolingian scholar Alcuin, who declared him to be his best pupil and named him Maurus after the favorite disciple of St. Benedict (Hrabanus preserved the notes of Alcuin's lectures for his own use). Returning to Fulda he was appointed abbot in 822 (in which capacity he objected strongly to the heterodoxy of his student Gottschalk). He retired from that office twenty years later for political reasons and in order to devote himself to study. In 847, however, he became archbishop of Mainz, where he died in 856.

The leading cultural personality of the second Carolingian generation, Hrabanus was an exceptionally voluminous author; in the standard edition his prose writings fill seven thousand closely printed pages. They reveal him to be a more able thinker than his master Alcuin, whom he excelled as an organizer as well. Nevertheless, he made no claim to originality in all this activity. Haunted by the spectacle of a civilization that seemed to be crumbling around him, his overriding aim was to preserve and disseminate whatever seemed worth preservation. He was content, therefore, to expend his gifts in the task of expounding and collating the work that had been done by others. In doing so, he became one of the principal founders of German education, earning the title *praeceptor Germaniae;* and Fulda became the rival of Tours.

Characteristic of his aim was the compilation of an encyclopedia entitled *On the Universe (De Universo,* or *De Naturis Rerum),* in which, basing himself closely on the labors

rä bä' nus mou' rus

217

of Isidore of Seville, he created a compendium of received knowledge, expounding the nature of the universe in terms of history and of mythology. Like Alcuin, he emphasized the value of the seven liberal arts of the secular teachers and sought to justify the study of pagan writers, as an aid to the understanding of Christianity. Thus he continued Alcuin's task of rescuing philosophy from its eclipse during the previous centuries; in the poetic field, the models he recommended seem to us strange: Juvencus, Sedulius Scotus, Arator, Alcimus, Paulinus of Nola, and Venantius Fortunatus.

Hrabanus also wrote more specialized educational monographs, including the *De Compito* on calculations of the calendar; and he composed a brief treatise entitled *On the Invention of Languages* (or *of letters*). This reflects his interest in runes, ciphers, and the like, an interest that he also displayed by copying down the sixteen-letter alphabet of the Viking Age (this manuscript is preserved in a ninth century manuscript at St. Gallen. Also, his essay entitled *On the Teaching of the Clergy (De Clericorum Institutione),* became a model for subsequent generations. His formidable output of theological works included commentaries on Biblical books, and essays on the enrollment of boys as oblates (i.e., dedicated to monastic life; the *De Oblatione Puerorum*), on marriages between blood relatives *(De Consanguineorum Nuptis),* and on the reverence of sons toward their fathers *(De Reverentia Filiorum erga Patres).*

Hrabanus also wrote a substantial amount of verse, though the hymn *Veni Creator Spiritus,* for which he became famous, cannot be ascribed to his authorship. One of his poems, the *Altus Prosator,* an extensive treatment of the Catholic faith based on Irish models, does not obey the classical rules of quantity (long and short syllables) but is composed in rhyming verse; however, Hrabanus' remaining poetic works were written in the quantitative verse he learned from Alcuin. They include poems on theological subjects, composed in a spirit of simple and severe piety, though Hrabanus was also able to unbend sufficiently to commend to the attention of King Lothair II a sort of mnemonic parody, the *Feast of St. Cyprian,*

based on St. Zeno's first communion addresses. His poem *De Laudibus Sanctae Crucis* contains what, to modern taste, is a deplorable conceit, namely, verses superimposed on a drawing so that the letters that emerge along its outline can be seen to form further words or sentences. He also wrote poems comprising the sort of correspondence with archbishops and bishops and other friends that forms so large a part of monastic literature. One or two rise to the level of fresh, direct observation; and others, for all their traditional foundations, come close to impressive poetry—notably, a scholar's declaration of his faith: "The written word alone flouts destiny, revives the past and gives the lie to death."

EDITIONS—J. P. Migne, Patrologia Latina, v 107–12, poems *(carmina)* ed. by E. Dummler, *in* Monumenta Germaniae Historica: Poetae Latini Aevi Carolini, v 2, 1884; A. Knöpfler, ed., De Institutione Clericorum, 1900; E. Heyse, De Institutione Clericorum, 1901; E. M. Almedingen (with translation), The Lord's Passion, 1938; Hrabanus Maurus Enzyklopädie De Rerum Naturis, 1969.
ABOUT—F. A. Wright and T. A. Sinclair, History of Later Latin Literature, 1931; R. R. Bolgar, The Classical Heritage and Its Beneficiaries, 1954; P. Lehmann, Erforschung des Mittelalters, v 3, 1960; P. Wolff, L'éveil intellectuel de L'Europe, 1971.

HROSWITHA (Hrotswitha, Hrosvitha, Roswitha), writer of Latin comedies and narrative poems, was born in about A.D. 935 and died in about 1000. She came of an aristocratic Saxon family. At the age of twenty-three, she entered the important Benedictine nunnery at Ganderheim (near Hildesheim in Germany), where she apparently spent the rest of her life. She learned Latin from the abbess Gerberga, niece of the emperor Otto I; and she corresponded with leading figures such as the Italian prelate and historian Liutprand of Cremona.

Hroswitha's six moralizing comedies are based, in form, on the plays of Terence (second century B.C.) but are written in a rhythmic and partly rhyming Latin prose and derive their plots from legends about the saints. These plays were designed to provide edification for the·nuns, whom Hroswitha

hrōs vē′ tä

urged not to prefer the empty pleasures of secular writings to the sterling value of sacred literature: "If you do not much like my efforts," she wrote to the bishops who were to judge them, "at least they have pleased myself." Three of the plays deal with the conflict between Christianity and paganism. *Gallicanus* is about a pagan general of Constantine the Great who claims the emperor's daughter in marriage. The emperor at first delays his reply, knowing that the girl is vowed to virginity, but then sends chaplains who convert Gallicanus to the Christian faith: whereupon the general sadly abandons his marriage plans, so that the young woman may remain a virgin. *Dulcitius* begins almost as a farce. The work takes its name from one of the emperor Diocletian's provincial governors, who imprisons three Christian virgins in his kitchen. When night falls he pays them a visit with lustful intentions; in the darkness, however, he embraces the round pots on the wall, mistaking them for the maidens' swelling bosoms, a mishap which makes him so grimy that his own soldiers fail to recognize him and drive him away. But then the drama turns to a graver theme, since the virgins, still refusing to renounce Christianity, suffer tragic deaths for their faith. *Sapientia (Wisdom)* concerns a foreign woman of that name who has come to Rome in the reign of Hadrian, accompanied by her three daughters, Faith, Hope and Charity; she launches a campaign to persuade Roman wives to deny sex to their husbands. Alerted by a complaint, Hadrian summons the visitors and cruelly puts the girls to death, whereupon Sapientia, after an eloquent speech, falls lifeless beside them.

The three remaining pieces deal with conflicts between the spirit and the flesh. *Calimachus* tells of the love of a youth of that name for Drusiana, who is so holy that she even refuses her husband's embraces. She is so shocked by Calimachus' overtures that she prays to die, and does. He, however, with necrophilous intentions, visits the tomb but is slain by a monstrous serpent, along with the servant set to guard the place (whom he had bribed). However, the Apostle John brings both Calimachus and Drusiana back to life, though the servant, who refuses to repent, is handed back to his

master Satan. *Pafnutius* is about a schoolteacher. Asked by his students why he looks so unhappy, the teacher explains that this is because of the people who commit offenses against God; and he particularly has in mind a whore named Thais. Disguised as a prospective client, Pafnutius pays her a visit and converts her to repentance; she obediently follows him to a convent to which, three years later, he himself returns, in order to be at her side as she breathes her last. *Abraham* concerns a hermit in the desert, whose niece Mary is lured away as a child, only to become, as he later learns, a prostitute in a neighboring city. After long searchings, Abraham succeeds in discovering where she is, and after a vivid recognition scene, she repents of her way of life, goes back with him to the desert, and finds happiness.

These plays, with their fast-moving dialogue and precipitous action, were evidently intended to be read and not acted. Their Latin style and technique display the crudities (from a classical point of view) typical of the period. In addition, their author is in certain respects ludicrously naive. However, her characters talk to one another in quite a realistic fashion, and the stark simplicity of Hroswitha's language achieves emotional effects that usually manage to avoid mawkishness. Indeed, not only her moral tone but also her insight into character often compare favorably with the achievements of the two great writers of comedy Plautus and Terence. Furthermore, Hroswitha's love scenes offer an occasional hint that she herself had not been wholly unfamiliar with emotional experiences before her convent days.

She was also the author of a series of narrative poems on a variety of themes, mostly written in hexameters containing internal rhymes, although some in the elegiac form are also included. One set of pieces is devoted to the Christian martyrs. The story of Theophilus, the priest who made a compact with the devil, is the earliest known poetic handling of the Faust legend, and Hroswitha enriches the traditional material by numerous touches of her own. She also wrote about a certain Pelagius, living in Cordoba in her own time, who rejected the homosexual advances of the Caliph Abderrahman;

whereupon the young man had been executed, allegedly to the accompaniment of a variety of miracles.

Finally, Hroswitha wrote two long chronicle poems in hexameters, one containing a history of the Gandersheim nunnery from its foundation in c. 856 down to the year 919 *(De Primordiis et Fundatoribus Coenobii Gandersheimensis),* the other recounting, in epic style, the feats of the emperor Otto I *(Carmen De Gestis Oddonis).*

Hroswitha is generally regarded as the first German woman poet.

EDITIONS—P. von Winterfeld, 1902. *With translation:* C. St. John, The Plays of Roswitha, 1923; H. J. W. Tillyard, 1923; M. G. Wiegand, The Non-dramatic Works of Hrosvitha, 1936; M. G. Bergman, 1943 (chronicle poems).

ABOUT—J. Schneiderhan, Roswitha von Gandersheim: Die erste deutsche Dichterin, 1912; J. Preissl, Hrotsvith von Gandersheim und die Entstehung des mittelalterlichen Heldenbildes, 1939; K. Langosch, Profile des lateinischen Mittelalters, 1967; B. R. Reece, Learning in the Tenth Century, 1972.

HYGINUS, GAIUS JULIUS, Latin scholar and writer, was born in (perhaps) about 64 B.C. His place of origin was variously described as Spain or Egypt (Alexandria); from one or the other of these countries he went to Rome as a slave or prisoner of war and was subsequently freed by Augustus. A pupil of Cornelius Alexander, whose erudition earned him the name of Polyhistor, Hyginus became a friend of the historian Clodius Licinus and was also well acquainted with the poet Ovid, who addressed a poem to him in A.D. 10/12. He was made director of the Palatine Library by Augustus; in addition, he was a teacher and one of the greatest scholars of his time. He may have died in about A.D. 17.

Hyginus' literary output, now lost, covered a very extensive range and displayed a wide knowledge of Greek and Latin literature alike. Among these works was a treatise on agriculture, including, or perhaps separate from, a study on bees *(De Apibus).* He also wrote a commentary on Virgil, cited later by Gellius and Servius, and another on a poem (the *Propempticon*) written in 56

hi ji' nus

B.C. by Gaius Helvius Cinna, who was an older contemporary of Virgil. But Hyginus was particularly prolific in monographs of an antiquarian and topographical nature. One was *On the Lives and Affairs of Eminent Men (De Vita Rebusque Inlustrium Virorum)* and another, related in subject, was called *Precedents (Exempla)*—it probably recounted the sayings and doings of distinguished personages. A book *On Trojan Families* provided a description of the Roman houses that claimed to be descended from Aeneas and his companions. Another study was entitled *On the Origin and Topography of Italian Cities (De Origine et Situ Urbium Italicarum).* He was also the author of studies on religious cult and history, including an essay on the ancient Di Penates and a discussion entitled *On the Characteristics of the Gods,* the only certainly identifiable fragment of which refers to the proper sacrifices that ought to be made to various deities, including the stars.

Other manuscripts headed by the name of Hyginus cannot be attributed to Gaius Julius Hyginus, since they seem to fall too short of his standard of erudition and quality (nor are they the work of two other men of the same name who wrote books on land surveying in the second and third centuries A.D. or of another Hyginus, of the third century, who wrote on camp fortification). One of these writings is a collection entitled *Genealogies* or *Tales (Fabulae),* mainly mythological in character, which probably belongs to the second century A.D. We have selections from this treatise—made by some unidentifiable excerptor—that show its author was both fatuous and ignorant of Greek. Nevertheless, the work is of some value, since it draws upon plays by Greek tragedians that are now lost. The first printed edition of 1535 (Basel) is our only authority for the text. An elementary piece on astronomy *(De Astronomia,* generally known, without justification, as the *Poetica Astronomica),* may perhaps be by the same hand; it depends for the most part on Eratosthenes, though not, it appears, directly.

EDITIONS—B. Bunte, De Astronomia, 1875; H. Funaioli, Grammaticae Romanae Fragmenta, v 1, 1907; Historicorum Romanorum Reliquiae, v 1, 2nd ed., 1914. Pseudo-Hyginus: A. Grillone, Hyginus Gromaticus: Liber de Metatione Castrorum, 1977; M. Lenoir, Les fortifications du camp (Budé ed.), 1978.

ABOUT—H. J. Rose, Handbook of Latin Literature, 1966. (Rose also wrote a critical edition of the Genealogies by the later Hyginus, Hygini Fabulae, 1934.)

HYPERIDES, Greek orator, was born in about 389 B.C. at Athens; his father was Glaucippus, who belonged to a wealthy family. Hyperides (like another orator, Lycurgus) was reputed to have been a pupil both of Plato and of Isocrates. He became a professional speech writer but dabbled in politics as well. From 346 until some time before 324 he supported Demosthenes in the struggle to maintain the independence of their city and of Greece against Macedonia. In pursuance of this policy, after the defeat of the city-states by the Macedonian king Philip II at Chaeronea (338), he proposed vigorous measures for the public safety, including the freeing of slaves, which earned him an impeachment for illegality. While he had proposed a decree to honor Demosthenes, he later was one of ten prosecutors who charged him with receiving a bribe; perhaps the reason for his change of attitude was the growing conviction that his fellow orator was not taking a strong enough line against Philip's successor, Alexander the Great. During the Lamian War, however, which Athens and its allies waged against the Macedonians after Alexander's death (323/2), Demosthenes was again in alliance with Hyperides, who became the leader of the war party and pronounced the funeral oration over the Athenians who had fallen in the disastrous campaign. When the victorious Macedonian leader, Antipater, demanded his surrender, he fled but was captured and put to death.

In ancient times, seventy-seven speeches were ascribed to Hyperides, of which fifty-two were considered authentic. Papyrus finds in the nineteenth century have produced imperfect but extensive remains of six of them. One of the best-preserved is *Against Athenogenes*, which appears on a papyrus of the second century B.C. and is therefore one

hī per ī′ dēz

of the most ancient classical manuscripts to have survived. Hyperides' client, in an attempt to free a slave boy he loved, had bought a perfume business from the tricky Athenogenes, only to find that it was burdened with debts for which he had now become responsible. We do not know whether Hyperides' appeal to the judges to punish the rascal on general grounds, even if the legal basis for the specific charge was weak, may have brought him victory in the case. *For Euxenippus* defends a man who had been bidden to sleep in the shrine of Amphiaraus so that the god-sent dream he might have there would determine the assignment of a piece of land disputed between two tribes: he was accused for reporting his dream falsely. Hyperides' client Lycophron, in the speech named after him, is an aristocratic cavalry commander accused of adultery—there is also a question of property rights involved, and the prosecution hoped to introduce political considerations as well. The *Funeral Speech,* given after the Lamian War, tries to introduce an original note into the customary commonplaces.

Against Philippides, indicting a man who proposed a decree in honor of Philip of Macedonia, has survived in battered condition; *Against Demosthenes,* in fragments, and *Against Philocrates* (343), not at all. The last-mentioned was an attack on the Athenian politician who had negotiated peace with Philip in 348/6. Another of Hyperides' speeches that has likewise not come down to us was *For Phryne,* in defense of a prostitute (also a model of the sculptor Praxiteles) who had found herself charged with impiety. As the climax of his oration, Hyperides dramatically bared the breasts of his client to impress the jurymen with their beauty. He also wrote two speeches (again lost) denouncing his own mistress Aristagora. He was famous, as many contemporary jokes recorded, for keeping three women simultaneously, one of them the most expensive in Greece. Apart from women, his principal enthusiasm was gastronomy, including a special taste for fish.

Hyperides showed a remarkable lack of discrimination in the choice of cases he undertook; he seemed prepared to write or deliver speeches against anyone, even his oldest friends, on charges of any and every kind. He had been a student of Isocrates, whose teaching can be detected in the high-flown *Funeral Speech,* but for the most part he is closer to the less elaborate style of Lysias. He borrowed terms and phrases from the comic dramatists in order to bring his diction within range of everyday speech, and this helps to achieve a clever natural-ness, which often gives the appearance of extemporization; his language has been studied in connection with the rise of the common language of later Greek times, the *koine.* The later literary critic whom we know as Longinus, author of the treatise en-titled *On the Sublime,* called him a pentath-lete, that is to say, an all-round performer, one who makes a good showing in every aspect of his art but is first-class, it is im-plied, at none of them. However, the same critic does not fail to call attention to Hype-rides' light persuasive touch and his suave wit. Witty he certainly was; and, unlike so many other speakers of the day, he avoided becoming abusive and offensive. He was one of the ten orators whose biographies, uncer-tainly attributed to Plutarch, have come down to us; ancient opinion ranked him as second only to Demosthenes.

EDITIONS with translation—J. O. Burtt, The Minor Latin Orators (Loeb ed.), v 2, 1954; G. Colin, Hypé-ride: Discours, 1946. *Translations*—Funeral Speech: W. R. Connor, Greek Orations, 1966.
ABOUT—D. Gromska, De Sermone Hyperidis, 1927; U. Pohle, Die Sprache des Redners Hypereides in ihrer Beziehung zur Koine, 1928; G. Kennedy, The Art of Persuasion in Greece, 1963; A. Anastassiou and D. Irmer, Kleine attische Redner, 1977.

IAMBLICHUS, Greek philosopher and writer on the supernatural, was born in about A.D. 250 at Chalcis (Mejd el Anjar) in Syria (now Lebanon). After the death of Plotinus, the founder of Neoplatonism, he studied in Rome and Sicily under his succes-sor Porphyry but later returned to Syria, where he founded his own school, perhaps at Apamea (Qala'at el Mudig). He died some time during the reign of Constantine the Great (306–37).

Iamblichus' extant works include five su-

i am' bli kus

perficial studies comprising a sort of popu-lar, encyclopedic collection of Pythagorean dogmas as the title of one of them, *On the Pythagorean Life,* indicates. One of the other studies, the *Exhortation to Philosophy (Pro-trepticus),* is a compilation of extracts from previous writers and has some value as a source book. The other treatises in the same collection are *On the Common Mathemati-cal Science*—in which he explores the ap-plications of mathematics to science—and *The Technological Principles of Arithmetic,* and *On the Arithmetic of Nicomachus,* a mathematician and Neopythagorean from Gerasa (Jerash in Jordan) who lived be-tween A.D. 50 and 150. These studies, how-ever, are by no means representative of the body of Iamblichus' thought. More signifi-cant is *The Reply of Abammon to Porphyry's Letter to Anebo* (Abammon purporting to be an Egyptian priest), a work more generally known as *On the Mysteries (De Mysteriis),* which, despite arguments to the contrary, can legitimately be attributed to his hand. Although written deplorably badly, it in-troduces one of the most significant defenses of spiritual religion from the pen of any pa-gan. Indeed, it is one of the most important religious documents of late antiquity, since its defense of ritualistic magical practices is significant evidence for the attitudes of the very large number of people who shared these views.

Among Iamblichus' other writings, which have not come down to us, was an elaborate account of the theology of the Chaldaeans in which he draws on a poem edited or com-posed by Julianus the Chaldaean in the previous century that was regarded as an inspired scripture by the Neoplatonists of Iamblichus' time. He also wrote commen-taries, warped and one-sided in character, on Plato and Aristotle and essays such as *On the Gods* and *On the Soul,* of which frag-ments are still extant.

Iamblichus did more than any other philosopher to develop and at the same time transform the Neoplatonism of Plotinus, which he built up into an immensely elabo-rate, complicated, and abstruse system. Above all, he superseded the spiritual, intel-lectual, nontheological mysticism of Ploti-nus by throwing the door wide open to miracles, magic, superstitions, and demonological practices, often imported from eastern religious traditions.

Although Iamblichus was a philosopher who led the way to the speculations of the later Athenian school, he was also a guru of charismatic power; so that his career and writings display a fascinating combination of mystic and rationalist. Moreover, he cherished a far-reaching aim—to supply the speedily disintegrating paganism of the ancient world with a comprehensive, coherent, rigid, and watertight theology such as it had never possessed before. Yet he and his fellow Neoplatonists lacked Plotinus' sense of the living order and harmony of the universe, which they split up into subheadings with such feverish determination that their divisions and classifications become abstract and unreal. To Iamblichus, it has been said, "belongs the honor or reproach of being the first scholastic."

EDITIONS—B. D. Larsen, Jamblique de Chalcis: Exégète et philosophe, 1972; V. de Falco, Theologumena Arithmeticae, and N. Festa, De Communi Mathematica Scientia, and H. Pistelli, In Nicomachi Arithmeticam Introductionem, all three in corrected editions by U. Klein, 1975. On the Mysteries: É. Des Places, Jamblique: Les mystères d' Égypte, (Budé ed.), 1977. Commentaries on Plato: J. M. Dillon, Iamblichi Chalcidensis in Platonis Dialogos Commentariorum Fragmenta, 1973.
ABOUT: A. H. Armstrong, ed., Cambridge History of Later Greek and Early Medieval Philosophy, 1967; F. W. Cremer, Die chaldäischen Orakel und Jamblich De Mysteriis, 1969; R. E. Wallis, Neoplatonism, 1972; H. Dörrie and others, De Jamblique à Proclus (Entretiens Hardt, v 21), 1975; B. D. Larsen, Iamblique de Chalcis: Exégète et Philosophe, 1976; S. Gersh, From Iamblichus to Eriugena, 1978.

IBYCUS, Greek poet, lived in the later 6th century B.C. He was a native of the Aeolian-Dorian colony of Rhegium (Reggio Calabria) in southwestern Italy; his father's name may have been Phytius. He had the opportunity to become the autocratic ruler (tyrant) of his city, but he declined and had to go into exile. He settled at the court of Polycrates, tyrant of Samos (c. 535–522), and addressed to a certain Euryalus a poem flattering a young man called Polycrates

ib' i kus

who was probably the tyrant's son. According to a legend, Ibycus met his death at the hands of robbers near Corinth. As he was fighting for his life, it was said, a flock of cranes was passing overhead and Ibycus cried "Those cranes will avenge me." Later, one of the robbers saw the cranes over the city and said to his companion, "There go the avengers of Ibycus." This was overheard, and the murderers were arrested and brought to justice. The story provided Friedrich von Schiller with the subject of his poem *Die Kraniche des Ibykus.*

Ibycus' poems were collected in seven books, from which only fragmentary passages survive. They seem to have been largely choral in character. He began his career by composing lyrical narratives in the manner of Stesichorus of Mataurus, who had been active in the sixth century B.C. Fragments indicate that Ibycus' subject matter included the Birth of Athena, Meleager's Calydonian Boar Hunt, Ortygia (the island on which the colony of Syracuse was founded), and other Sicilian themes. Some of the most arresting passages, however, are in poems that belong to his Samian period, including panegyrics, verses deploring the approach of old age, personal love songs, and the piece noted above mentioning the son of the ruler Polycrates (this poem has been interpreted as a metaphorical leave-taking of the poet's earlier literary manner for the erotic style that was fashionable at Samos).

Ibycus wrote in a wide variety of meters and displays a rich and scintillating style and a vivid, forceful imagination. Particularly notable was his talent for depicting the emotion of love; and he describes nature beautifully as well.

EDITIONS—D. L. Page, Poetae Melici Graeci, 1962 and Supplementum Lyricis Graecis, 1974; F. Mosino, Ibico: Testimonianze e frammenti, 1966; J. P. Barron in Bulletin of the Institute of Classical Studies, v 16, 1969 (pp 119-49). Translations—J. M. Edmonds, Lyra Graeca (Loeb ed.), v 2, revised ed., 1931; O. Marx and E. Morwitz, Poems of Alcman, Sappho and Ibycus, 1945. ABOUT—C. M. Bowra, Greek Lyric Poetry, 2nd ed., 1962; A. Lesky, History of Greek Literature, 1966; D. A. Campbell, Greek Lyric Poetry, 1967.

IGNATIUS, Saint, bishop and writer of Greek epistles, was born during the first century A.D. at Antioch in Syria (now Antakya in southeastern Turkey) and died between 107 and 110. Of his origin, birth, and early life, we know nothing with certainty, but as his name indicates (it is the same as the Latin Egnatius), he presumably came from a non-Jewish family. Phrases in his letters suggest that it was pagan, and that, after youthful dissipations which he later regretted, he became a convert to Christianity. He was described, thereafter, as Theophoros, a term that had previously, as far as we know, only been employed in connection with pagan worship. In application to himself, it could either mean "God-borne" or "God-bearer"—probably the latter, used to define his new character as a Christian.

Subsequently, Ignatius became bishop of Antioch; the recorded date for his appointment is A.D. 69. If that is correct, he remained in office for thirty-eight years, during which time nothing is known of what happened to him. But in about 107, during a persecution of the Antiochene church, he was arrested—for reasons we do not know —and sentenced to death and conducted to Rome under military guard. During this journey, in the course of a prolonged stop at Smyrna (Izmir) in Ionia (western Asia Minor), he wrote to the churches of Ephesus, Magnesia on the Maeander, and Tralles, from which deputations had come to visit him; and he also wrote a letter to the church at Rome. Later on, too, while at Alexandria Troas (near Troy), he sent further epistles to the Christian communities of Philadelphia and Smyrna, together with a personal letter to Polycarp, bishop of Smyrna. Then he was taken to Rome and put to death; according to tradition he was thrown to wild beasts in the Colosseum.

His seven Greek letters have all survived (a theory that our texts are only later expansions of Syriac originals has been adequately refuted). They provide a vivid picture of Christian life, organization, and doctrine and convey something of the character of their author as well. Above all, they show his deep preoccupation with the struggle to restore unity to the divided church, a cause

ig nā′ shi us

he served by launching relentless attacks against heresy. The sect he was particularly concerned to refute was that of the Docetists, who, influenced by Greek and Asian beliefs in the worthlessness of everything material, pronounced that Christ had not really possessed a human body while on earth, but only the appearance *(dokesis)* of one. Another group censured by Ignatius was the Jewish Christian community (or perhaps, in particular, a Christianized section of the Essenes, whose Jewish forebears have been identified with the former brotherhood of Qumran on the Dead Sea). He objected to the discord between their Old Testament allegiances and the new teachings about Jesus.

Another way in which Ignatius sought to fight against Christian fragmentation was by insisting on the local episcopacies as focuses of unity: in every one of his letters to the churches (with the exception of the epistle to Rome) his farewell message counsels obedience to episcopal authority. "Do nothing," he ordered, "without the bishop," whom he regarded as the earthly counterpart of the heavenly monarch so that "we ought to regard him as the Lord himself." This was not the sum total of Ignatius' teachings on the subject, however, for he also envisaged a threefold ministry of bishop, presbyters, and deacons as a practical measure to stop and prevent the disruption of churches by internal rivalries and dissensions.

Yet what made the profoundest impression on later Christians was not his life but his death, for he exulted in the prospect of martyrdom; and, when he wrote to Rome, he even urged its congregation not to take any step that would prevent him from attaining this glorious end. There was an ancient Hebrew tradition of self-sacrifice for the faith, and Ignatius, fortified by the examples of Jesus and Peter and Paul, passionately declared it to be the supreme prize and goal. This exercised a profound effect on the imagination of Christian posterity.

EDITIONS with translation—R. M. Grant, The Apostolic Fathers, v 4, 1966. *Translations*—E. J. Goodspeed, The Apostolic Fathers, 1950; M. Staniforth, Early Christian Writings (Penguin ed.), 1968; J. A. Fischer, Schriften des Urchristentums, v 1, 1976.

ABOUT—F. A. Schilling, The Mysticism of Ignatius of Antioch, 1932; T. Ruesch, Die Entstehung der Lehre vom Heiligen Geist bei Ignatius von Antiochia, 1952; A. Omodeo, Ignazio di Antiochia e l'episcopato monarchico, 1958; V. Corwin, St. Ignatius and Christianity in Antioch, 1960; W. Telfer, The Office of a Bishop, 1962; M. P. Brown, The Authentic Writings of Ignatius, 1963; W. H. C. Frend, Martyrdom and Persecution in the Early Church, 1965; E. J. Goodspeed and R. M. Grant, A History of Early Christian Literature, 1966; H. Chadwick, The Early Church, 1967; H. Paulsen, Studien zur Theologie des Ignatius von Antiochien, 1978.

INDICOPLEUSTES. See Cosmas Indicopleustes

IRENAEUS, Saint, Greek theologian, was probably born in about A.D. 130 and died in about 200. His birthplace was Smyrna (Izmir) in Ionia (western Asia Minor). At some stage he went to Gaul as a missionary. From there, having become a priest, he was dispatched as an envoy to Eleutherius, bishop of Rome (Pope), taking a letter having to do with the disruptions from which the church in Gaul was suffering. On his return he was elected to the bishopric of Lugdunum (Lyon), which was vacant owing to the execution of his predecessor by the Roman authorities. In about 190 he wrote to Pope Victor, who had tried to compel the Gallic church to abandon its traditional but unorthodox date for Easter; Irenaeus supported the Roman interpretation but urged an attitude of tolerance. He apparently remained at Lugdunum until his death.

He was particularly concerned to refute the dualists or Gnostics, who by declaring that the world, containing evil, could not be God's creation, seemed to diminish His omnipotence and thus conflict with the thoroughgoing monotheistic faith that Christianity had inherited from Judaism. Irenaeus' major work, in five books, entitled *Against Heresies (Adversus Haereses),* of which only part has survived in the original Greek (though a complete Latin version is extant), argued strongly against the dualistic view that the existence of an additional or intermediary power has to be accepted in

ī re nē′ us

order to explain the origin of evil. He also differed with those who maintained that Adam, by his Fall, had caused all future human beings to fall in his wake. Humankind, according to Irenaeus, is God's raw material still in the process of creation: He is continually working His purpose out, toward the supreme future good that was foreshadowed by the Apostles. This millennium that lies ahead Irenaeus envisaged in a literal, earthly sense that did not commend itself to the Greek east (although Epiphanius of Salamis transcribed part of his work in 374/5)—which is why it is only in Latin versions that most of his treatises have survived. In the west, during the generation after him, both Hippolytus of Rome and Tertullian of Carthage freely drew upon his writings. Two centuries later, however, their optimism was effectively superseded by St. Augustine's contrary, Pauline doctrine of the Fall that is shared by every human being, so that all alike are plunged into helpless sin from which only divine grace can rescue them.

Irenaeus, whose work also included a *Demonstration of Apostolic Preaching* (found in an Armenian translation in 1904), helped to elevate Christianity to a new intellectual status. He also reveals the development of the authoritative New Testament canon. He is the first writer to assert that there are, and can only be, the four Gospels, to which he assigns the traditional authorships. He also makes frequent mention of what he calls the Rule of Truth and recounts the principal articles of belief in a manner suggestive of the Apostles' Creed—this seems to indicate that a baptismal creed was already in existence, intended to ensure the avoidance of heresy.

Irenaeus also provides important evidence for the organization and claims of the early Church, though varying deductions have been drawn from his words. Clement of Rome had laid down the doctrine of the apostolic succession of church officers. By A.D. 185 this doctrine and the concept of a single bishop in a church were effectively combined by Irenaeus. With the support of this double argument, the major bishoprics began to emerge. Irenaeus particularly emphasized the Roman church, allegedly founded by the two chief apostles Peter and Paul, as the conspicuous and most venerable exemplar of episcopal authority. His emphasis on Rome represents an early but important stage in the evolution of the papacy; and to Catholic historians it has been seen as a landmark in the unfolding of the principle of papal primacy. Irenaeus has also been hailed as one of the founders of medieval political thought in the West, because he argued that secular government is unavoidable and necessary owing to the vices and shortcomings of the human race.

EDITIONS—Against Heresies: A. Rousseau and others, Irénée Contre les Hérésies, 1952–69; W. W. Harvey, 1957. *English translations—In* J. Quasten and J. C. Plumpe, eds., Ancient Christian Writers, 1946– ; C. C. Richardson and E. R. Hardy, eds., Library of Christian Classics, 1953–61.
ABOUT—J. Lawson, The Biblical Theology of Saint Irenaeus, 1949; A. Houssian, La christologie de Saint Irénée, 1955; C. Wingren, Man and the Incarnation: A Study in the Biblical Theology of Irenaeus, 1959; A. Benoit, Saint Irénée: Introduction à l'étude de sa théologie, 1960; R. A. Norris, God and World in Early Christian Theology, 1965; G. Jossa, Regno di Dio e Chiesa, 1970; H. B. Timothy, The Early Christian Apologists and Greek Philosophy: Exemplified by Irenaeus . . ., 1973; R. Tremblay, La manifestation et la vision de Dieu selon Saint Irénée de Lyon, 1978.

ISAEUS, Greek speech writer, was born in about 420 or 415 B.C., and died in about the middle of the fourth century. He was variously stated to have come from Athens or Chalcis in Euboea; perhaps his birthplace was Chalcis, but he went to live in Athens. The fact that he never delivered speeches, but only wrote them for delivery by others, has suggested to some that he never obtained Athenian citizenship. However, this cannot be regarded as certain. At all events he was a professional speech writer. It was recorded that he had been taught by Isocrates, but this may only mean that he was impressed by him as a youth (his work shows little trace of Isocratic influence). Isaeus himself was said to have taught Demosthenes, whose style owed so much to him that the story is not improbable.

His *Life,* dubiously attributed to Plutarch, states that sixty-four speeches were ascribed

ī sē′ us

226

to him, of which fifty were regarded as authentic. Eleven and a considerable part of a twelfth have survived. The eleven all deal with cases of succession, on which Isaeus was an expert. Each one of these speeches had a title beginning with the words *On the estate of . . .*, and in all of them a will is directly or indirectly at stake. Six of the orations, and notably *On the Estate of Cleonymus,* are concerned with disputed claims to an inheritance. Three more deal with prosecutions for false witness in testamentary suits. Another involves an action brought to make a man discharge the obligations he has assumed as surety in connection with a will. The eleventh relates to the prosecution of a guardian for ill-treating his ward. Only the twelfth speech, which is incomplete, deals with matters other than inheritance. It bears the name of Euphiletus, who is appealing against the decision of his community (deme) of Erchia to have him struck off its roll.

Isaeus, evidently, devoted most of his attention to testamentary lawsuits, and no such case, however unpromising, seems to have been too great a challenge for him to undertake. Many of the issues were extremely complex, and it is easy to understand why the litigants required the services of a professional to write their speeches. The juries could not be expected to concentrate very intensely or retain many of the facts in their minds. A general impression of convincing righteousness, lasting for just a few minutes, was what was required from the speech writer, and this Isaeus provided admirably, with an abundant appearance of sweetly reasonable, earnestly businesslike lucidity, even when his client was deeply in the wrong. Unlike his contemporary Lysias, he did not seek to adjust his style to the personalities of the clients who were going to deliver the speeches but adopted a standard technique directed solely toward developing the most persuasive arguments possible. The literary critic Dionysius of Halicarnassus remarked that Lysias (and Isocrates) created an impression of simple honesty even in bad cases, whereas the tricks of Isaeus (and Demosthenes) aroused suspicion even when their cases were strong. In other words, Isaeus was sly. Evidently, he was also extremely successful.

Perhaps his most important innovation was his method of presentation, which, while ignoring the subdivisions prescribed by the rhetoricians, concentrated on building up his case point by point by logical argument—with frequent repetitions and a final recapitulation as well, in order to make sure that the jury would understand what he was trying to say. He took particular care to avoid long, unbroken recitations of fact, which would be difficult to absorb all at once, by interweaving passages of anecdotal narrative. Isaeus resembled Lysias in the simplicity and clarity of his diction, but he added a few touches of his own. In particular, he frequently indulged in rhetorical questions; and it was his habit to imagine the objections that his opponents were raising and set them down, one after another, for refutation.

EDITIONS—W. Wyse, 1904. *Translations*—E. S. Forster, Isaeus (Loeb ed.), 1927; P. Roussel, Isée: Discours (Budé ed.), 1922.
ABOUT—G. Kennedy, The Art of Persuasion in Greece, 1963; R. F. Wevers, Isaeus: Chronology, Prosopography and Social History, 1969; A. Anastassiou and D. Irmer, Kleine attische Redner, 1977.

ISIDORE OF SEVILLE, Saint (Isidorus Hispalensis),

Latin encyclopedist, historian, and theologian, was born in about A.D. 560 or a little later. He probably came from Carthago Nova (Cartagena) in Spain, but in about 600 or 602 he became the successor of his brother Leander as archbishop of Seville. In 633 he presided over the Synod of Toledo. Three years later he died.

His most important work was the *Etymologies* or *Origins,* now divided into twenty sections or books. It provided a summary of all the world's knowledge that he had been able to amass. Except in the tenth book, which is in dictionary form, Isidore does not follow an alphabetical arrangement but usually gathers related subjects together. Starting with three books about the liberal arts, *Etymologies* goes on to deal with the world in general, its cosmology and peoples and languages, human psychology, the liberal arts and sciences (with particular concen-

tration on medicine, anatomy, and natural history), geography, architecture, navigation, astronomy, and agriculture; and these discussions extend over the widest variety of subjects, from prodigies to food and drink.

Written at a time when secular learning was rapidly vanishing, the *Etymologies* utilize the works of previous encyclopedists, notably Cassiodorus, and directly or indirectly call upon a wide sweep of earlier authorities, ranging from Pliny the Elder and Suetonius down to Lactantius (whose conclusion that all the Greco-Roman deities were originally human beings is repeated). On some subjects Isidore was very well informed. For example, he evidently borrowed from a good textbook on minerals and precious stones (unless he was drawing on personal knowledge). And he was aware, to take another instance, that in the original Hebrew the *Book of Job* was almost wholly in poetic form. However, amid correct facts of this kind are the most glaring mistakes, especially in the field of etymology, which, as the title of the work suggests, Isidore believed to be the most fundamental of all subjects, to which everything else could be traced back.

Nevertheless, the *Etymologies* attained enormous fame. As the existence, to this day, of almost a thousand medieval manuscripts testifies, the work remained one of the most widely consulted and imitated books of reference for seven centuries. It comprised one of the principal links between classical learning and the Middle Ages and earned its author the appellation of *el gran doctor de las Españas.*

Isidore wrote separate monographs, too, about many of the matters treated in his encyclopedia, including linguistics (*Differentiae,* in two books, and perhaps *Synonyma),* cosmology (*De Natura Rerum),* and natural science (*De Ordine Creaturarum).* He also devoted much attention to national historical studies, compiling histories of German peoples, the Vandals, the Suevians, and the Goths, in whose (Visigothic) kingdom he was living; the work survived in two editions. Furthermore, he composed a continuation of the treatise, *On Illustrious Men,* written by Jerome and Gennadius and compiled an expanded and updated version of

Jerome's *Chronicle,* known as the *Chronica Majora.*

Isidore was also an extremely prolific writer on biblical and theological matters. In this field he wrote *Old Testament Studies (Quaestiones in Vetus Testamentum),* polemics against the Jews *(De Fide Catholica contra Judaeos)* and against heretics *(De Haeresibus),* directions concerning liturgy and the monastic life *(De Ecclesiasticis Officiis, Regula Monachorum),* and a collection of maxims *(Sententiae)* that bore witness to the authority and influence of St. Augustine but drew particularly on the *Moralia* of Gregory the Great and were intended to serve as a religious and ethical handbook. Furthermore, he compiled biographies of eighty-six personages of the Bible *(De Ortu et Obitu Patrum).*

It is not certain whether the first edition of the *Hispana,* an unofficial collection of ,anon law that came to be accepted everywhere in Spain, was in fact produced by Isidore, though it was sometimes called by his name *(Collectio Canonum Isidoriana)* and appears to date from his time. Other writings of which any attribution to Isidore is palpably erroneous are the *False Decretals,* which professed to be a collection of decrees of church councils and decretals of popes of the first seven hundred years. First used at councils subsequent to A.D. 800, they were sometimes known as the *Collection of Isidore Mercator* because they begin with the words *Isidore the merchant, a servant of Christ, greets the reader (Isidorus Mercator, servus Christi, lectori salutem).* The inclusion, however, of spurious material (alongside authentic) in their contents was demonstrated in 1628 by David Blondel (Reformed theologian, 1591–1655); the *False Decretals* were a creation of the lower clergy of France, seeking to protect themselves against their local lay and clerical masters.

EDITIONS—J. P. Migne, Patrologia Latina, v 81–84. Etymologies: W. M. Lindsay, 1911; portions translated *in* E. Brehaut, An Encyclopedist of the Dark Ages: Isidore of Seville, 1912. De Natura Rerum: G. Becker, 1857. History of the Goths, Vandals and Suevians: translated by G. Donini and G. B. Ford, 1966. Chronica: T. Mommsen, Monumenta Germaniae Historica (Auctores Antiquissimi), Chronica Minora, 1894. De Fide Catholica: K. Weinhold (editing early German translation), 1874. De Haeresibus: A. C. Vega, 1940. Letters: G. B. Ford, The Letters of St. Isidore of Seville, 2nd ed., 1970.

ABOUT—J. Fontaine, Isidore de Séville et la culture dans l'Espagne visigothique, 1959; F. Sánchez Faba, San Isidoro: Cientifico, 1970; H. J. Diesner, Isidor von Sevilla und das westgotische Spanien, 1977.

ISOCRATES, Greek writer and educationalist, was born in 436 B.C. and died in 338. He was the son of Theodorus of Athens, a flute manufacturer who was wealthy enough to undertake expensive state services and to give his sons a good education. Isocrates' teachers were said to have included the rhetorician Tisias, the rhetorician-sophists Prodicus and Gorgias, and the moderate oligarchic statesman Theramenes. He was also acquainted with Socrates. His family property was wiped out during the Peloponnesian War, and after the final defeat of Athens in 404 he began to earn his living by writing speeches for delivery by litigants in the lawcourts. They included: *On the Team,* written for the son of the famous Alcibiades, whom it mentions favorably many times; the *Aegineticus,* a speech before a court of law at the island city of Aegina about a dispute regarding an inheritance; the *Trapeziticus* on behalf of a resident alien who was reclaiming a deposit from Pasion the banker; and three prosecutions, including an oration entitled *Against Euthynous,* a case that attracted attention because neither side could produce any witnesses.

In about 392 B.C., however, Isocrates abandoned this kind of work and turned to an educational career, opening his own school of rhetoric, first at Chios and then, perhaps two years later, at Athens. In this enterprise he achieved enormous success; he trained only a few young men at a time, but among them were a considerable number of the most distinguished personalities of the age. Throughout his long life, he took the keenest interest not only in education but in the internal and external politics of Athens and made indefatigable efforts to bring his influence to bear on these varied problems. He gave his views on them in numerous speeches—or rather, essays cast in the form

ī sok′ rȧ tēz

of speeches, though they were not intended to be delivered in public but to be privately read. The first of these orations to be published after the opening of his school included the *Busiris* (on a mythological king of Egypt, c. 390) and the *Helen* (390/80), familiar themes that Isocrates cast into the form of eulogies but that were designed to advertise his literary views. *Against the Sophists,* composed at about the same time, is a more overt defense of his principles and objectives and is directed against philosophers, the supporters of more extemporaneous methods, and professors of forensic oratory.

His first major political discourse, which took him ten years to complete, was the *Panegyricus* (380). Its theme, a conventional one, was the desirability of the Greek city-states uniting under the joint leadership of Athens and Sparta. The opening sections skillfully draw an elaborate picture of the mighty achievements of Athens, not only in warfare waged for the salvation of Greece but in the spheres of peace and culture as well. The speech contains the significant assertion that the name *Greek* describes partnership in Hellenic civilization rather than mere kinship of blood. After Thebes seized and destroyed Plataea on the borders of Attica in 373, Isocrates wrote his *Plataicus,* in which the speaker, a Plataean, brings an action against the attackers and urges the Athenian assembly to retaliate. *To Nicocles* (c. 372) shows that he had some connection with the ruling house of Cyprus, whose young monarch is given a long lecture on the duties of kingship; another rhetorical exercise of the same kind is the *Nicocles* (c. 368), in which the prince addresses his own subjects; the *Evagoras* (c. 365) is in praise of the prince's father. The *Archidamus* (c. 366) is supposedly delivered by the future King Archidamus III of Sparta, whose comments on conditions of peace offered by Thebes revert to the theme of its aggressive power. In his oration *On the Peace* (c. 356) Isocrates, prompted by Athens' failure in the Social War and by the financial stringency that now prevails in the city, demands the abandonment of belligerent imperialism among Greeks in favor of a universal Greek peace combined with the solution of economic problems by the colonization of Thrace. The *Areopagiticus,* (c. 354?), in pursuance of a long literary tradition, advocates the revival of the venerable Council of the Areopagus to give spiritual and educational leadership to the citizens of Athens.

In the *Antidosis* (353), which is the principal source of our knowledge about Isocrates' educational theories, he contrasts the prosaic practicality of other orators' speeches with the more elevated tone of his own, which were dedicated to the common interest. In 346 he published his most important political manifesto, the *Philip,* in which he called upon the King of Macedonia to unite the Greeks under his own leadership and lead them in the great national struggle against the Persians. And finally the *Panathenaicus,* begun when he was ninety-four and completed in 339 when he was ninety-seven, provides a long, rambling encomium of Athens—which is compared very favorably to Sparta—combined with an explanation and defense of his own theories on writing and teaching.

Such are Isocrates' orations that survive today; some four, or perhaps seven, others seem to be lost; the speech to *Demonicus* is rejected as spurious. Nine *Letters* bearing his name, which, like the speeches, though in briefer form, advertise his opinions on current affairs, have also been handed down. Once again, however, their genuineness has been questioned. One letter, however, addressed to Philip, appears to be authentic—and perhaps another as well.

Despite startling vacillations in regard to particular matters, Isocrates adhered consistently enough to his dominant political theme—the policy of unifying his countrymen for the purpose of a war against their natural enemy, Persia. Having failed to persuade Athens and Sparta to take the lead together, he turned instead, in succession, to a series of individual autocrats to provide the leadership, including finally Philip II of Macedonia. To those like Demosthenes, who regarded Philip as the greatest enemy and menace to the Greeks, Isocrates' policy seemed traitorous collaboration. He himself and his supporters, however, saw it as the only logical way to bring the Greek city-states together at long last and put an end to their catastrophic dissensions. Despite the fact that among his pupils were leading Athenian politicians, including Timotheus, Isocrates' practical influence on the course of political events does not seem to have been very extensive.

In the history of education, on the other hand, he played a highly influential and significant part. With contemporary rhetoricians he would have nothing to do, since he maintained that their purely practical techniques and sets of rules possessed no educational value, in contrast to his own broader and more liberal and humane system, which he regarded as universally relevant and which he defined as the true philosophy. Education was the dominant concept that provided the guidelines of Isocrates' entire activity and thought; and in this respect Isocrates was a representative spokesman of his age. For him, education preeminently means the ability *to speak,* a talent that distinguishes humankind from the animals: and here we have the prototype of the humanism, based on eloquence, that Cicero developed and handed on to late antiquity and Petrarch and the Renaissance.

In view of this belief in the spoken word, it is not surprising that one of Isocrates' major achievements was the highly artistic form he gave to his writings. His speeches, at least until his declining years, display the most meticulously planned structure and style and represent Attic prose in its most elaborate form; he seems to have lavished more attention on the details of verbal expression than any Greek writer before or after him. His periods display a consummate rhythmic balance; careful avoidance of hiatus and roughness produces a smoothly harmonious, continuous flow. This could be monotonous—as he himself realized, for he warned those who were reciting his compositions only to read as much as would not tire their listeners out. The influence of his style on future writers was extensive among Greeks and Romans alike.

EDITIONS—G. Norlin and L. R. van Hook (Loeb ed.), 1928–54; G. Mathieu and E. Brémond, Isocrate: Discours, 1928–62. Aegineticus: F. Brindesi, Isocrate: Eginetico, 1971. Busiris: L. Giovannacci, Isocrate: Busiride, 1955. Panegyricus: E. Buchner, Der

Panegyrikos des Isokrates, 1958; Panegyricus and Philip (translation): A. N. W. Saunders, Greek Political Oratory (Penguin ed.), 1970.
ABOUT—W. W. Jaeger, Paideia: The Ideals of Greek Culture, 1944; E. Mikkola, Isokrates: Seine Anschauungen im Lichte seiner Schriften, 1954; D. L. Clark, Rhetoric in Greco-Roman Education, 1957; M. A. Levi, Isocrate: Saggio critico, 1959; P. Cloché, Isocrate et son temps, 1963; G. Kennedy, The Art of Persuasion in Greece, 1963; K. Bringmann, Studien zu den politischen Ideen des Isokrates, 1965; G. M. A. Grube, The Greek and Roman Critics, 1965; F. Seck, ed., Isokrates, 1976.

ITALICUS, TIBERIUS CATIUS SILIUS. See Silius Italicus, Tiberius Catius Asconius

JEROME, Saint (Eusebius Hieronymus), was born between A.D. 340 and 348 and died in 420. His birthplace was Stridon on the northwestern border of Dalmatia (Yugoslavia), where his family were prosperous Christians. His earliest education took place at home, but at the age of about twelve he went to Rome, where he studied rhetoric, grammar, and philosophy as a pupil of Aelius Donatus, the most famous teacher of the age. Toward the end of his student life in Rome he was baptized (c. 366), though this step did not deter him, according to his own account, from leading an immoral life. Subsequently he moved for more studies to Treviri (Trier) on the Moselle (western Germany) and then back to Stridon and finally to Aquileia (northern Italy). At this stage of his life he became strongly attracted to the ascetic and monastic way of living.

Next he set out upon a journey to the east—apparently a pilgrimage to Jerusalem —and on arriving at Antioch (374) spent his time there improving his theological learning and his knowledge of Greek. He suffered a nearly fatal illness in the following year. Then he spent two or three austere years in the desert of Chalcis in the Syrian frontier land, where, with considerable difficulty, he learned Hebrew. However, finding himself persecuted for alleged theological heterodoxy, he returned to Antioch. There, while attending lectures and continuing to be involved in religious controversies, he was or-

je rōm' (Brit. jer' um)

dained a priest by one of the contenders for the bishopric of the city—a conferment that he accepted on the condition that he should not be forced to undertake priestly duties, since his aspirations were primarily monastic. Thereafter, in the course of a visit of almost three years to Constantinople, he became a keen disciple of St. Gregory of Nazianzus and got to know St. Gregory of Nyssa as well.

The most important influence on Jerome's middle life occurred on his return to Rome, where during the years 382–85 he was the secretary of Pope Damasus, who urged him to embark on the Latinization of the Bible. Jerome also became the spiritual adviser of a coterie of fashionable Roman widows and unmarried women, for whom he held classes in one of their homes. These relationships, however, together with his vituperative attitude toward such matters as hypocritical virgins, lax Roman clergymen, and self-indulgent monks, aroused several storms of angry protest, against which, after the death of Damasus, he found himself unable to oppose an effective resistance—especially as he himself was suspected of hoping to become pope in Damasus' place.

So Jerome decided to get away from Rome and accompanied by two women, Paula and Eustochium, returned to the east. There he visited Antioch, Jerusalem, and Egypt and finally settled at Bethlehem (386), where he founded a monastery for men, a convent for women (under Paula), and a hostel for pilgrims. There he continued to live, apart from brief travels, until his death more than thirty years later.

Jerome's writings, which fill nine volumes of Migne's *Patrologia Latina,* may be divided into seven categories: (1) translations of the Bible into Latin from Hebrew, Greek, and Chaldaean; (2) biblical Commentaries; (3) other works on biblical subjects; (4) Controversy; (5) Biography; (6) History; (7) Letters.

In the first category his outstanding feat, one of the greatest literary achievements of antiquity, was his new Latin translation of the Bible called the Vulgate (following upon revisions of existing renderings of the New Testament that he had undertaken earlier). This took him twenty years to complete and

became, subsequently, as revised by Clement VIII (anti-Pope of the Avignon line, 1423–29), the authorized version of the Catholic Church. The second category comprised at least sixty-three books of commentaries on various books of the Bible—with special attention to the prophets, and including four New Testament Epistles. Some of Jerome's commentaries were original, while others were translated from the Greek of Origen (c. A.D. 185/6–254/5). The third category included Latin adaptations of numerous homilies by Origen, notably fourteen each on Jeremiah and Ezekiel, nine on Isaiah, two on the Song of Songs, and thirty-nine on the Gospel of St. Luke. In the fourth we find that as a theological controversialist Jerome is violent and vituperative, preferring withering abuse to the original exposition of doctrine. *Against Vigilantius* ("Wakeful," described by Jerome as "Soporific," *Dormitantius*) is a ferocious onslaught on a man who criticized the veneration of the tombs of martyrs. *Against Helvidius,* whom he describes as a disagreeable idiot, is the first Latin treatise on Mariology (the veneration of Mary), supporting the doctrine of the perpetual virginity of Mary. *Against Jovinian,* wherein Jovinian's theological deviations are attributed to disgusting personal habits, contests the opinion that virgins and widows and married women have equal merit and that the devil cannot lead baptized persons into sin. In comparison, the *Dialogues Against the Pelagians* is surprisingly moderate; these hated heretics (the opponents of Augustine's doctrine of Grace, which seemed to them to destroy free will) are even allowed their own spokesman. *Against Rufinus* is Jerome's self-defense on charges that he himself was tainted with various heterodoxies for which Origen was censured.

In the fifth category romance, biography, and edification are blended in an account of three ascetics, Paullus and Hilarion (both hermits) and Malachi. To this, Jerome later added a Latin rendering of the Rule of the Egyptian monastic pioneer Pachomius, together with a version of his letters. *On Illustrious Men (De Viris Illustribus)* comprises a series of brief descriptions of eminent writers from Peter to Jerome himself, mostly Christians (though including certain heretics), so that the work is virtually a history of Christian literature; a few non-Christian authors are included too, notably Philo Judaeus, the Jewish theologian of Alexandria. Title and plan are taken from the Latin biographer Suetonius, whose Christian counterpart Jerome endeavored to be. Out of the 135 sections of the treatise, the first 78 depend closely on the fourth century religious historian Eusebius of Caesarea—so closely, indeed, that Eusebius' mistakes are meticulously reproduced. For the rest of the work, Jerome continues independently, and the information that we possess about Christian authors such as Tertullian, Minucius Felix, Cyprian, and Novatian is owed largely to the descriptions with which we are provided here.

In category (6) Jerome's *Chronica* (379/80) once again draws extensively on Eusebius, of whose *Chronological Canons* (not extant in its original form) he provides a virtual translation. But in the later part of Jerome's treatise, which carries the history from Constantine (Eusebius' finishing point) down to the death of Valens (378), he adds a good deal of material from what he has read himself—inserting, for instance, valuable and otherwise unavailable extracts from Suetonius on Latin literature, though his selection of these borrowings is somewhat hasty and arbitrary.

In category (7) 154 of Jerome's letters have come down to us, written between the years 370 and 419. They are of enormous interest as Christian and sociological documents, even comparable in importance to the correspondence of Cicero himself, and infinitely superior to the tired classicizing productions of contemporaries. Some of these so-called letters are really treatises in epistolary shape; others are pictures of the world Jerome saw around him. They include vigorous eulogies of the saintly women Marcella, Blaesilla, and Fabiola; two discussions on female education; admonitions to widows and divorced women; and a series of epistles laying down codes of behavior for virgins, monks, and secular clergy. On this last class, Jerome is witheringly satirical. Indeed, his satire flashes over a wide range of society, with devastating effect. His letters, in all

their vivid diversity, display him as one of the most shattering and effective satirists of all time.

Jerome possessed an ardent and passionate temperament, which is reflected in his tender affection for his friends; his combative hatreds pursued, even at long distance, with remarkably bitter abusiveness; his vituperative disgust for those he regarded as hypocrites and heretics; and his equally unsparing readiness to pronounce violent condemnation against himself.

Psychologists have good reason to study the advocacy of extreme asceticism that he directed toward Roman ladies of high birth, eventually resulting in the scandal that caused him to leave Rome; and painters—for example, Bellini, Mantegna, Dürer, Van Dyck—have excelled themselves in depicting the sensual dreams that beset him in his desert retreats.

Jerome's spirit was deeply divided between the claims of austerity and the enticements of classical literature. He would fast and then read Cicero afterward—and, in a feverish vision, while sick at Antioch, he heard God, at the Judgment Seat, pronouncing him a Ciceronian and not a Christian. He had absorbed Cicero, Virgil, Horace, and other Latin authors so deeply that constant echoes of their writings appear in his works, and of all Christian Latin writers it is he whose style, although direct and popular, most nearly approaches classical purity. His reputation is primarily due to the enormous services his scholarship rendered to the study of scriptures in the West, most of all by the Vulgate, which, in spite of an initially hostile reception, became the authorized text of the Catholic Church. From the thirteenth century onward, he was pronounced one of the Four Doctors of the Church.

EDITIONS—J. P. Migne, Patrologia Latina, v 22–30; J. Haussleiter, I. Hilberg, S. Reiter, *in* Corpus Scriptorum Ecclesiasticorum Latinorum, v 49, 54–56, 59, 1866–1913; G. Morin, Corpus Scriptorum Christianorum (Series Latina), v 78, *and* Anecdota Maredsolana, v 3, 1895–1903. *Translations*—W. H. Fremantle, Letters and Select Works *in* A Select Library of the Nicene and Post-Nicene Fathers, v 6, 1912; Ancient Christian Writers, v 33, 1963; Fathers of the Church, v 18, 53, 57, 1964, 1965, 1966. *Translations* (of individual works)—F. A. Wright, Select Letters, 1933; also list *in* G. B.

Parks and R. Z. Temple, The Literatures of the World in English Translation, 1968.

ABOUT—L. Huizinga, Hieronymus, 1946; M. de Ferrara, Life of St. Jerome, 1949; F. X. Murphy, ed., Monument to St. Jerome, 1952; C. C. Mierow, St. Jerome: The Sage of Bethlehem, 1959; J. Steinmann, St. Jerome and His Times, 1960; D. S. Wiesen, St. Jerome as a Satirist, 1964; Y. Bodin, S. Jérôme et l'église, 1966; P. Antin, Recueil sur S. Jérôme, 1968; M. Testard, S. Jérôme: l'apôtre savant et pauvre du patriciat romain, 1969; D. Adams, The Populus of Augustine and Jerome, 1971; I. Opelt, Hieronymus' Streitschriften, 1973; J. N. D. Kelly, Jerome: His Life, Writings and Controversies, 1975; P. Rousseau, Ascetics, Authority and the Church in the Age of Jerome and Cassian, 1978.

JOHN CHRYSOSTOM, Saint, patriarch and Greek theological writer, was born in about the middle of the fourth century A.D. at Antioch in Syria (Antakya, southeastern Turkey). He died in 407. His father, who was a general, died soon after he was born, and he was brought up by his mother Anthusa. After attending the school of Libanius, who trained him in rhetoric and law, and completing his education by attending the local lawcourts, John embarked on the legal profession. After embracing Christianity and receiving baptism in about 368, he abandoned this career and became a pupil of Diodorus, bishop of Tarsus, in order to learn the techniques of biblical research. He also adopted the practices of asceticism in the Syrian desert. This self-denial, however, shattered his health and compelled him to return to Antioch, where he was ordained presbyter in 386 and started upon a far-famed career as a preacher, in which he so greatly excelled that he earned his nickname *Golden-Mouthed*—he often had to rebuke his congregations for applauding. In 398 he was summoned by the emperor Arcadius to Constantinople to become its bishop. In this office he showed an urgent concern for the poor and underprivileged—a concern he manifested in such uncompromising terms that he caused offense not only to the clergy and the rich but also to the empress Eudoxia, who took his attacks on luxurious living as a personal affront. The Asiatic bishops, too, resented his endeavors to extend the authority of his see in order to control

kri′ so stom

their actions. Before long, therefore, Theophilus, bishop of Alexandria, some of whose dissident monks John had harbored, came to Constantinople and summoned the unofficial Synod of the Oak (403), which placed John on trial and deposed him. He went into exile, but popular pressure resulted in his immediate recall. Then, however, he once again insulted Eudoxia, even more gravely than before, and was banished for a second time in 404—this time to Cucusus in Armenia. His appeal to Pope Innocent I (as well as to the bishops of Milan and Aquileia) met with a highly sympathetic response that did not, however, succeed in securing his recall. Yet, helped by the deaconess Olympias, a widow related to the emperor Theodosius, John maintained a large and unrepentant correspondence, which prompted the government to order his removal to an even remoter spot. On the way there, however, at Comana (Tokat), he died.

He was the author of a great many works on religious themes. His *Dialogue on the Priesthood,* in six books, describes his early life. His first writings, dating from about 375, include the *Parallel Between a King and a Monk* and *Against the Opponents of the Monastic Life,* in which he criticized fathers of families who did not want their children to become monks or nuns. After he became priest, he wrote *On Compunction,* addressing it to two monks, and gave sympathetic counsel to two others, Theodore and Stagirus, who were passing through a vocational crisis. He also wrote: *To a Young Widow, On Second Marriages, On Virginity* (and *How to Practice Virginity*), and *On Suspect Cohabitations.* In 386 and 387 John delivered five vigorous and imposing sermons, *On the Incomprehensibility of God* or *On the Anomians* (an extreme form of Arianism that believed the Son inferior to the Father). From then onward, his writings concentrated more closely on his pastoral duties: they included *Baptismal Catechisms* (now supplemented by recent discoveries), treatises on the feasts and fasts of the Church and on the commemorations of the martyrs, and the strangely named *Vainglory and Children's Education* (393?), in which he reprimands the pious for concentrating on their devo-

233

JOHN CLIMAX

tions to such an extent that they neglect the upbringing of their children.

But, above all, John was the leading exponent of the Antiochene school of researchers on the Bible, producing a massive array of tracts and sermons on a wide range of books and themes of the Old and New Testament alike (altogether, in his works, he makes seven thousand quotations from the former, and eleven thousand from the latter). His greatest admiration, however, was reserved for St. Paul, on whom he pronounced five orations that form a compendium of Pauline teaching; he also delivered fifty-five homilies on the Acts of the Apostles, comprising its only complete commentary during the whole of the first millennium of our era. In the Byzantine empire his works (together with others whose attribution to him is not authentic) came to be regarded as a major authority.

EDITIONS—J. P. Migne, Patrologia Graeca, v 47–65; On the Priesthood: G. Neville, Six Books on the Priesthood, 1977; Baptismal Catechisms: A. Wenger, Huit catéchèses baptismales inédites, 1957; A. M. Malingrey, Lettre d'exil à Olympias et à tous les fidèles, 1964; J. Dumortier, À Théodore, 1966; R. Caligari, Dall'esilio, 1976. *Other translations—Listed in* G. B. Parks and R. Z. Temple, The Literatures of the World in English Translation, v 1, 1968.
ABOUT—D. Attwater, St. John Crysostom: Pastor and Preacher, 1959; C. Baur, John Chrysostom and His Time, 1959–60; S. Verosta, Iohannes Chrysostomus: Staatsphilosoph und Geschichtstheologe, 1960; C. Fabricius, Zu den Jugendschriften des Johannes Chrysostomus, 1962; S. Neill, Chrysostom and His Message, 1963; L. Schläpfer, Das Leben des Heiligen Johannes Chrysostomus, 1966; M. G. Fouyas, The Social Message of St. John Chrysostom, 1968; A. M. Malingrey, La littérature grecque chrétienne, 1968 (list of his works on the Bible); Studies on St. John Chrysostom (Thessalonike symposium), 1973; J. M. Leroux, S. Jean Chrysostome et le monarchisme, 1975; J. N. D. Kelly, Golden Mouth; the Life of St. John Chrysostom, 1978. Unauthentic works: J. A. de Aldama, Repertorium Pseudochrusostomicum, 1965.

JOHN CLIMAX (Climacus), Saint, was a Greek theologian of the Byzantine epoch, c. A.D. 550–649. After some years in Egyptian monasteries, notably St. Catherine's on Mount Sinai (c. 600), he spent forty years as a hermit on the mountain itself, subsequently returning to St. Catherine's to become

klī' maks

234

abbot. However, he went back to his hermitage shortly before his death.

He was the author of the *Climax (Scala Paradisi, Ladder to Paradise),* which gave him his name (his alternative designation *Climacus* is a Latinization of the genitive of the word). Summing up the teaching of the desert fathers, the thirty chapters or "rungs" into which the work is divided form a treatise on the spiritual development of the ascetic, from the renunciation of worldly life on the first rung of the ladder up to the attainment of faith, hope, and charity on the thirtieth and topmost rung.

The work exercised profound influence on Byzantine monastic life for many centuries. It was also translated into Syriac, Georgian, Arabic, Slavonic, and modern Greek, and, in addition, attracted wide attention in the medieval West, where Latin, Italian, and French versions appeared. Many manuscripts include a series of miniature illustrations of religious and monastic life, which are of considerable artistic importance.

John Climax also compiled the *Liber Ad Pastorem,* a handbook for the guidance of abbots of monasteries.

EDITIONS—J. P. Migne, Patrologia Graeca, v 88. *Translations*—F. Robert, The Holy Ladder of Perfection, 1858; L. Moore, The Ladder of Divine Ascent, 1959.
ABOUT—J. R. Martin, The Illustration of the Heavenly Ladder of John Climacus, 1954; D. Bogdanovic, Jean Climaque dans la littérature byzantine et la littérature serbe ancienne, 1966; W. Völker, Scala Paradisi: Eine Studie zu Johannes Climacus, 1968.

JOHN DAMASCENE, Saint, Greek theologian of the Byzantine epoch, was born in about A.D. 675 and died in about 749. His birthplace was Damascus in Syria, where his father Sergius, a Christian, known in Arabic as Mansur (victorious), was a senior financial officer at the Moslem court of the Ummayad Caliphs. Sergius was said to have searched all Persia for a teacher who would not inspire in his son a passion for hunting, or archery, or athletics, or soldiering. John succeeded his father in his post but soon resigned it and entered the monastery of Mar Saba, ten miles from Jerusalem. He

dam' à sēn

spent most of the rest of his life studying, preaching, writing, practicing a regime of rigorous asceticism, and acting as theological adviser to successive patriarchs of Jerusalem; one of whom ordained him as a priest. He served the patriarchs of Antioch in a similar capacity.

Before entering the church, he had already written three treatises collectively entitled *Against Those Who Depreciate Holy Images* (730). The Byzantine emperor Leo III the Isaurian (717–41) was a strong supporter of the Iconoclastic policy, which sought to eradicate religious effigies, but John Damascene, living in Moslem territory, was out of his reach and became the principal defender of their worship in the Orthodox Church. Curiously enough, it appears that the Ummayad caliph Yazid II (720–24), three years before the date of Leo's decree, had ordered the destruction of all icons in the Christian churches of his empire. Yet, as far as we know, John Damascene was not hampered in his literary endeavors to defend their veneration.

The most significant of his voluminous writings is the *Fountain of Knowledge* or *Of Wisdom (Peri Gnoseos),* an extensive, soberly written didactic treatise in three parts, the first of which deals with philosophical problems and terminology; the second describes and refutes a hundred and three heresies; and the third—to which the two foregoing had served as introductions—is a systematic exposition of the Orthodox Faith. The *Fountain* is based upon the Bible, the church councils, and the eastern Fathers, from many of whom the author draws much of his material, so that his survey comprises a personal synthesis of their writings and thus offers a sort of compendium of previous Christian literature. The work has been described as the dogmatic handbook of the Middle Ages, throughout which its popularity remained enormous, as can be seen from the five hundred and fifty Greek manuscripts that still survive today—in addition to one hundred and fifty copies of the twelfth century Latin version of Burgundio of Pisa that greatly influenced western scholasticism.

John also wrote a number of monographs on particular theological themes; tracts on moral and ascetic problems; criticisms of the Iconoclasts and other sections of Christian belief denounced as heretical; biographical and eulogistic accounts of saints; and a series of long hymns or Canons, of a type particularly associated with this Iconoclastic period. A series of homilies and biblical commentaries was also ascribed to his hand, but not all of these are authentic. Doubts have also been voiced (though not necessarily with justification) about his authorship of the *Sacred Parallels,* an anthology of more than five thousand biblical and patristic texts (many of the latter from works that have not come down to us) arranged under ethical categories. It is usual nowadays to reject the ascription to John of the enormously popular and extensively translated work of edification *The Story of Barlaam and Joasaph,* a Christianized Greek version, via Persian, Arabic, and Georgian intermediaries, of the story of Buddha. (Probably an original Buddhist text was adapted to the purposes of Manichaean apologia in central Asia, and this Manichaean version was translated into our present Greek text by Euthymius the Athonite, who died in 1028).

Although he contributes a personal touch to the treatment of theological themes, John Damascene disclaimed originality for himself, declaring: "I will say nothing of my own." This is accurate, for the most part, since what he mainly did was to compile from others. As a compiler he was impressive, because of his magisterial command of previous Christian literature, which he coordinated and systematized on a majestic scale, although, living when he did, he inevitably lacked the range of its earlier masters. He was also familiar with pagan writings insofar as these were filtered through the writers of late antiquity.

EDITIONS—J. P. Migne, Patrologia Graeca, v 94–96; B. Kotter, Die Schriften des Johannes von Damaskos, v I, 1969. *Translations*—The Fountain of Knowledge: F. H. Chase, *in* Fathers of the Church, v 37, 1958. Against Those Who Depreciate Images: M. H. Allies, On Holy Images, 1898. Barlaam and Joasaph: Translation by G. R. Woodward and H. Mattingly (Loeb ed.), 1914 (with new introduction by D. M. Lang, 1967).
ABOUT—G. Richter, Die Dialektik des Johannes von Damaskos, 1964; A. Kallis, Der menschliche Wille in seinem Grund und Ausdruck nach der Lehre des Johannes Damaskenos (Munster, dissertation), 1965; B.

JOHN MOSCHUS

Studer, Jean Damascène ou de Damas, *in* Dictionnaire de Spiritualité, v 8, 1972, pp 452–66.

JOHN MOSCHUS (Eucrates), Greek writer on the monastic life in the Byzantine period, was born in about the middle of the sixth century A.D. and died in about 619. His birthplace was apparently in Palestine; he visited monastic settlements and hermitages in that country and in Egypt, Sinai, Syria, Asia Minor, and the islands of the eastern Mediterranean, including Cyprus and Samos. Finally, in 614, he went to Rome, where he stayed until his death.

During these numerous and extensive journeys he had taken notes, and after he was dead his friend and traveling companion Sophronius, a poet and theologian from Damascus who subsequently became patriarch of Jerusalem, collected and edited them to make a book, *The Spiritual Meadow (Pneumatikos Leimon, Pratum Spirituale)*. The work contains a great deal of vividly presented topical information about the journeys they had made together, and the institutions they had visited. It also contains a lot of biographical detail about the monks whom they encountered and heard about, often conveyed in the form of edifying but spicy anecdotes heavily interlarded with marvels.

Written in language close to the vernacular, *Spiritual Meadow* offers a great deal of information about the life in the monastic establishments at the end of the sixth century and beginning of the seventh. It throws extensive light on both the spiritual ideals and ascetic practices of the inmates and is, in general, a valuable document for the social and economic conditions of the age and for the history of civilization.

The *Meadow* became a favorite book of subsequent Byzantines, and an Old Slavonic translation was widely read in Russia. There was also an Arabic rendering, and a Latin version achieved considerable popularity in the West.

EDITIONS—J. P. Migne, Patrologia Graeca, v 87; P. Pattenden, 1979. *Translations*—D. C. Hesseling, Morceaux choisis du Pré spirituel de Jean Moschos, 1931;

mos' kus

M. J. Rouët de Journel, Le pré spirituel, 1946; B. P. Dubrovina, Pratum Spirituale (in Russian), 1967.
ABOUT—N. H. Baynes, Byzantine Studies and Other Essays, 1955; E. Mioni, Jean Moschus *in* Dictionnaire de Spiritualité, v 8, 1973 (pp 632–40).

JOHN SCOTUS ERIGENA. See Erigena, John Scotus

JORDANES, Latin historian of German origin, lived in the middle of the sixth century A.D. He himself states that he was a Goth, but since he also remarks, somewhat ambiguously, that he will not show partiality to that race, "on the ground that *[quasi]* I myself am sprung from it," it has been thought that he may have been of mixed blood or perhaps a member of one of the Balkan tribes of the lower Danubian region that were loosely described as Gothic. Jordanes also records that, following in the footsteps of one of his forebears, he became secretary or notary to a German military chieftain Gunthigis Baza, the son of Andag. Gunthigis has been conjecturally identified as the son of the Andag whom Jordanes describes as the slayer of Rome's ally, the Visigothic king Theoderic I, in the battle of the Catalaunian Plain (near Châlons-sur-Marne in France) against Attila in 451.

Jordanes indicates that he held this secretaryship "before my conversion," which has been generally supposed to refer to a conversion from Arianism (the branch of Christianity adopted by the Goths) to Catholicism—or conceivably, from lay status to holy orders or to the monastic life.

His major work, now lost, was the *Getica*, a summary of the twelve-book history of the Goths written by the Roman statesman and writer Cassiodorus (c. A.D. 490–583). Jordanes composed his abridgment in 551, using a manuscript that came from the household of Cassiodorus himself. He reports that he was able to borrow the work from Cassiodorus' steward for only a few days, though this assertion has been doubted by modern scholars. However, it is probable that Jordanes does not reproduce the actual words of the original, though he claims to

jôr dā' nēz

offer a faithful representation of its substance and spirit. He also professes to have made certain additions on his own account, including the prologue and epilogue. This statement, however, has been regarded with some suspicion, owing to the close resemblance of his prologue to a translation from Origen by Rufinus of Aquileia.

Such additions to Cassiodorus as Jordanes inserted are likely, for the most part, to have been geographical details taken from other authors, together, perhaps, with a heightening of the heroic legends associated with the Goths. For example, he praises the Visigoth Alaric, declaring that when that monarch sacked Rome in 410 he did not allow the shrines of the saints to be insulted or burned. Here Jordanes is echoing Cassiodorus, who was himself a senator of the Ostrogothic kingdom. But he breaks away from Cassiodorus when he censures the Gothic faith of Arianism. Moreover, he may perhaps be striking out on his own once again in his final chapters, when he offers hopes of a permanent reconciliation between the Gothic and Byzantine thrones. Jordanes writes in a feeble style and is neither scholarly nor shrewd; yet, though his original has not come down to us, we owe him some vivid historical incidents that would otherwise be lost.

It is uncertain whether the *Getica* were written at Rome, or in some Balkan monastery, or at Constantinople; and the same applies to Jordanes' other work, a summary of Roman history known as the *Romana,* which is now lost. This, too, was composed in 551; it was started, apparently, before the *Getica* and concluded shortly after the latter's completion. It was undertaken at the request of his "most noble brother" Virgilius, who has been identified with the man of that name who was Pope from 537 until 555. The best manuscript of the work describes the author as *episcopus,* and it has been suggested, with a good deal of probability, that the Jordanes who was bishop of Croton (Crotona) in southern Italy was the same man. The *Romana,* which dealt briefly with the history of all the principal known peoples and empires from the Creation onward, drew material from a number of earlier writers but relied especially upon the lost history of Quintus Aurelius Memmius Symmachus, who was executed by Theodoric the Ostrogoth. The book was used as a compendious work of reference in later times.

EDITIONS (of the Getica)—T. Mommsen, 1882; also *in* Monumenta Germaniae Historica, 1941–49; C. C. Mierow, Jordanes: The Origin and Deeds of the Goths, 2nd ed., 1915, reprint 1960 (with translation); E. C. Skrzhinskaia, 1960 (in Russian).
ABOUT—W. Wattenbach and W. Levison, Deutschlands Geschichtsquellen im Mittelalter, v 1, 1952; E. S. Duckett, Italy: The Gateway to the Middle Ages, 1960; J. Svennung, Jordanes und Scandia, 1968; E. Bartolini, ed., I barbari, 1970; O. Giordano, Jordanes e la storiografia del sesto secolo, 1973; I. Korkkanen, The Peoples of Hermanaric, 1973; B. Smalley, Historians of the Middle Ages, 1974.

JOSEPHUS, FLAVIUS, Jewish notable and Greek historian, was born in A.D. 37 or 38 and died after 94/5. In Hebrew he was Yoseph ben Matatyahu, the son of Matthias, a well-known member of the priestly aristocracy of Jerusalem; and his mother was related to the former royal house of the Hasmonaeans (Maccabees). Josephus' native language was Aramaic, but he received an excellent Hebrew education. As a youth, he espoused in turn the three principal versions of Judaism, successively becoming an adherent of the Sadducees, the monastic Essenes, and the Pharisees, in whose ranks he then enrolled permanently, joining the priesthood at Jerusalem. In about A.D. 64 he went to Rome in order to intercede for a fellow priest who had been arrested, and through the help of Alityrus—a Jewish actor in the entourage of Nero (54–68)—and of the empress Poppaea, his mission was successful.

Josephus returned to Rome to find that the First Jewish Revolt against the Romans (to the Jews, the First Roman War) had become imminent. The Jewish leadership, however, was sharply divided, and Josephus was one of those who felt such an insurrection could not succeed. Nevertheless, when the rebellion began in 66, a moderate group of Jewish leaders who were temporarily in charge of Jerusalem sent him to take command of the troops in Galilee. But a number

jō sē′ fus

237

of local Jews opposed him and, as the Roman governor of Syria, Vespasian, who had been entrusted with the suppression of the rising, approached with an army, Josephus withdrew inside the fortified town of Jotapata. When, however, this fortress had been under siege for nearly seven weeks and the defenders, in desperation, pledged themselves to a suicide pact, Josephus evaded the pact and went over to the Romans.

Kept prisoner at first, he was released because he seemed useful as a collaborator—and also because he prophesied that Vespasian would become emperor, a prediction that came true in 69. During the siege of Jerusalem he earned additional hatred from his countrymen by acting as interpreter to the Roman commander, the new ruler's son Titus, whom subsequently, after the capture of the city, he accompanied to Alexandria and then to Rome. There he was awarded Roman citizenship and assumed the imperial family name of Flavius; and he received a residence and a pension as well. His three successive wives were all Jewish; they were: first, a woman of Caesarea Maritima in Judaea, whom he married at the request of Vespasian; then, while he was in Alexandria, a woman from that city; and finally, at Rome, an aristocratic heiress from Crete.

It was during his residence in Rome that he became a writer. His first work, the *History of the Jewish War,* completed in 77 or 78 was divided (though not necessarily by the author himself) into seven books. In accordance with a well-worn tradition, the preface describes the war he has chosen for his subject as the greatest conflict of all time. The rest of the first book surveys the history of the Jews from the time of Judas (Yehudah) Maccabaeus (d. 160 B.C.) down to the time of Herod the Great (37–4 B.C.), whose reign is then surveyed. Book 2 continues with an account of Herod's sons and of the periods of Roman annexation (A.D. 6–41, 44–6) that finally led to the outbreak of the First Revolt; and we learn of Josephus' appointment in Galilee. The third book records the southward advance of Vespasian and Titus and tells of the author's own resistance and subsequent capitulation; there are also descriptions of various regions of Palestine and an account of the Roman

army. Book 4 records the rival Jewish factions in Palestine and the atrocities that they were said to have committed against one another and reports the accession of Vespasian to the imperial throne. The next two books narrate the siege and capture of Jerusalem and the fire that destroyed the Temple. The final book summarizes the subsequent mopping-up operations in other parts of the country, notably at Masada on the Dead Sea, which did not fall for another three years.

Our Greek text is not the original, which was in Aramaic, and was intended for the Jews of the eastern Dispersion (Diaspora); whereas the Greek version that has come down to us was composed "for the sake of such as live under the government of the Romans." Josephus, whose Greek was shaky, employed helpers to assist him with the translation—or rather, the adaptation or paraphrase—and the numerous references to classical literature must be peculiar to the Greek edition. What the Aramaic original was called we do not know, but the Greek title *History of the Jewish War* (rather than Roman War) shows a pro-Roman bias that is apparent throughout, not only in his adulation of his captors but in the conviction that Roman might was too unassailable to be worth resisting. About his own role, which seemed so inglorious to his compatriots, he writes with a curious blend of damagingly candid admissions and fulsome conceit. Except, however, on the somewhat numerous occasions when self-justification seems to him to be required, he is generally a reliable narrator and, indeed, at times a first-class historian. He is also virtually our only source for an extremely important chapter of history.

Josephus tells us that the *Jewish War* was the offshoot of a much larger project, a general history of the Jews. Subsequently, this massive enterprise took shape as his second major work, published in about 93/4. It is known to us as the *Jewish Antiquities,* though he himself called it the *Archaeologia.* Written in Greek and surveying the story of the Jewish people from the Creation down to the outbreak of the revolt, it fills twenty books—the same length as the entire canon of the Old Testament, which is closely copied by the first ten books of Josephus' work, down to the conquest of Babylonia and Assyria by the Persian king Cyrus (539). The ensuing period of three centuries and a quarter, down to the death of Judas Maccabaeus, is compressed into Books 10 and 11. The fourteenth and fifteenth books bring us as far as Pompey's sack of Jerusalem (63 B.C.), the assistance given to Caesar by the Jews, and the rise of Herod, whose reign is described in the next two books, in greater detail than had been provided in the *Jewish War*. Book 18 opens with the Roman annexation of Judaea, and Books 19 and 20 describe the deterioration of the province culminating in its rebellion.

Jewish Antiquities is dedicated to a certain Epaphroditus (who may perhaps be identified with a learned Greek grammarian of that name, a former slave who lived at Chaeronea in Greece and possessed a library of thirty thousand volumes). Its composition was an act of piety toward Judaism, to which Josephus did not feel, as so many others did, that he was a traitor or renegade. Moreover, although professing a desire for reconciliation, the *Antiquities* asserts the superiority of the law and historiography of the Jews over those of other peoples. Josephus is weak on biblical interpretation and comparative religion and misleads by adjusting the occasional point or fact to suit Roman susceptibilities; but the postbiblical parts of the work, the later sections of which are based on the lost writings of Nicolaus of Damascus, are often of great value because they deal with events of which no record has otherwise come down to us. The *Antiquities* attained great fame because of its supposed references to Jesus. But these are insertions by a later hand, and other passages relating to his brother James and to John the Baptist are also suspect, at least in parts.

In 73 Josephus' life in Rome had been disturbed when a fellow Jew, Jonathan of Cyrene, denounced him to Vespasian as one of the instigators of the rebellion. This and other attacks were duly warded off, but a further and more deadly blow, launched in the reign of Titus' suspicious brother Domitian (81–96), could not be similarly ignored. This was in a polemic (now lost) by Justus of Tiberias, a participant like himself in the revolt, who repeated the accusation of complicity in its outbreak and conduct. Very soon, therefore, after completing the *Antiquities* Josephus decided to publish a supplementary essay, or epilogue, which he entitled his *Life*, although, in fact, nine-tenths of it is a defense of his conduct in Galilee in the single year 67. Josephus declares that it was not himself but Justus, who fomented the insurrection in the Galilean town of Tiberias. The *Life* is written in a somewhat unpolished style and apparently without the aid of helpers.

It was followed, perhaps almost immediately, by another treatise, answering further attacks, which this time had been directed against his eulogies of the Jews in the *Antiquities*. Manuscripts call this essay *Concerning the Antiquities of the Jews: Against Apion*, but it is generally known as *Against Apion*, because the second of its two books contains refutations of a Greco-Egyptian grammarian of that name who had joined in protests against the Jews submitted to the emperor Gaius (Caligula) (A.D. 37–41) and had published widely read pamphlets attacking them. Josephus also takes the opportunity to rebut other anti-Semitic writers as well, ranging from the early third century B.C. down to his own day. His monograph was intended to be read not so much by pagans as by the Jews of the Dispersion, to prevent their faith from becoming undermined by the hostile barrages of their enemies; and it has attracted a great deal of attention in subsequent epochs.

Whereas the Jews hated Josephus as a traitor to their cause, adherents of Christianity enjoyed reading him for that reason, as well as for the extensive information he provided about Palestine (which, as we have seen, was augmented by fictitious interpolations about Jesus and others). The destruction of Jerusalem, of which Josephus gave so long and terrible an account, was interpreted by Christians as a fulfillment of New Testament prophecies. Between the fourth and sixth centuries, therefore, at least three Latin translations were published. Greek epitomes made their appearance as well; new and expanded passages relating to Christianity were preserved in an Old Slavonic text of complex origins that survives in seventeen different manuscripts. An early Syriac version of the sixth book of the *Jewish War* became part of the Peshitta, the Syriac Bible. In southern Italy, too, during the tenth century A.D., there came into being a free Hebrew paraphrase known as the *Yosippon,* which was translated subsequently into Arabic and Ethiopic. The first printed Latin text was published at Augsburg in 1470, and the first edition of the Greek original at Basel in 1533. French and Spanish translations, also, had already made their appearance before 1500.

EDITIONS with translation—H. St. J. Thackeray, R. Marcus, A. Wikgren, L. H. Feldman (Loeb ed.), 1926–65; T. Reinach and L. Blum (Budé ed.), 1900; A. Pelletier (Budé ed.), 1975. *Translations*—G. A. Williamson, Josephus: The Jewish War, 1959.
ABOUT—H. St. J. Thackeray, Josephus: The Man and the Historian, 1929; F. J. Foakes Jackson, Josephus and the Jews, 1930; R. J. H. Shutt, Studies in Josephus, 1961; L. Feldman, Scholarship on Philo and Josephus 1937–62, 1963; M. Grant, The Ancient Historians, 1970 *and* The Jews in the Roman World, 1973; A. Schalit, ed., Zur Josephusforschung, 1973; O. Betz, K. Haacker, and M. Hengel, Josephus-Studien, 1974; E. M. Smallwood, The Jews Under Roman Rule, 1976.

JULIAN THE APOSTATE (Flavius Claudius Julianus),

Roman emperor and Greek writer, was born at Constantinople in A.D. 332 and died in 363. He was the son of Julius Constantius (half-brother of Constantine the Great), and of Basilina, daughter of a governor of Egypt. His mother died soon after his birth, and his father was lynched in 337 in a mutiny fomented by the new emperor Flavius Julius Constantius (Constantius II). In 341 Julian and his half-brother Constantius Gallus were sent to a remote region of Cappadocia (central Asia Minor), where they continued to receive a strictly Christian education. Returning to Constantinople six years later, in about 351, Julian came under the influence of the pagan philosopher Maximus of Ephesus, perhaps secretly abandoning Christianity at this time. Twice summoned west to Mediolanum (Milan), on the second occasion he was proclaimed Caesar by Constantius II, which meant that he became the heir to the throne. Julian then conducted successful campaigns in Germa-

jōōl′ yən   à päs′ tāt

JULIAN THE APOSTATE

ny, winning a decisive victory at Argentorate (Strasbourg) in 357. When, however, Constantius II jealously tried to deprive him of some of his best units, the army at Lutetia (Paris) mutinied and declared Julian emperor (360); and he ascended the throne in the following year without fighting, since Constantius, who had intended to suppress him, fell ill and died.

Julian now decreed general religious toleration. But, in fact, he showed marked favor to paganism, to which he openly declared his personal adherence; a deeply superstitious man, he was also dedicated to a rigorous, indeed unkempt, personal asceticism. Julian anticipated the Byzantine rulers of the future by his blend of opportunism, preciosity, and sense of divine mission. He was also an immensely hard-working and conscientious ruler, who showed his administrative common sense by imposing drastic cuts on the palace staff and bureaucracy. In 362 he moved to Antioch in Syria to plan a major campaign against the Persians. In the following year, during the invasion, his march to join up with a relief force met with continual harassment, in the course of which he received a severe wound that proved fatal.

Julian's numerous literary works are written in Greek. While Constantius II was alive, he had to write two orations in praise of him—concealing his real feelings of detestation—in addition to a more sincere eulogy of Constantius' first wife Eusebia. He also composed a *Commentary* on his own German campaigns, which has not survived. After he came to the throne, his writings were devoted to the propagation of his personal ideas. Thus his subsequent orations include a prose hymn to the sun-god Helios, dedicated to Sallustius, the principal contemporary theologian of paganism, who is also the subject of Julian's *Consolation to Himself on the Departure of Sallustius from Gaul*. Another composition is addressed to the Mother of the Gods, and two others *(Against Uneducated Dogs*—that is to say, Cynics—and *Against the Cynic Heraclius)* are concerned with the Cynic school of philosophy; its contemporary adherents met with his disapproval, since he found them too similar to the Christians and excessively far removed from the original Cynicism of Diogenes. Julian's *Beard-Hater (Misopogon)* or *Antiochicus* is a satirical onslaught upon the people of Antioch, who laughed at his beard and his pagan austerity and devoted their lives to frivolous pleasures. The work contains important autobiographical material. *The Caesars* is another satire in which Romulus, the mythical founder of the city, is represented as receiving various outstanding emperors of the past, from Augustus to Constantine, who set forth their rival claims to distinction; Marcus Aurelius wins the competition, while Christianity is mocked for its easy absolution of sins, however frequently repeated. Julian's famous anti-Christian work *Against the Galileans*, which owes a good deal to another enemy of that faith, Porphyry, has not survived except in extensive excerpts quoted in a retort by Cyril of Alexandria (died A.D. 444); the original essay itself was destroyed by the pious Christian emperor of the east, Theodosius II (408–50).

The most comprehensive sources of information regarding Julian's career and beliefs are his *Letters*. Some are of a personal nature and others, more formal. In the latter category is an epistle to the sophist Themistius and an autobiographical message, *To the Athenians*, intended to justify his acceptance of the title of Augustus while he was in Gaul. A letter entitled *To the Community of the Jews* assures them freedom from hostile discrimination and promises to rebuild their Temple, a project that was conceived with an anti-Christian purpose but never came to fruition. A fragmentary epistle entitled *To a Priest* encourages pagan priests to emulate the Christians in their teaching of morality. However, many of Julian's letters (and epigrams) raise problems of authenticity, since forgeries were concocted on a substantial scale.

Julian and his brief career attracted lasting attention. He was, indeed, one of the most versatile and gifted of Roman emperors. The belief that, on receiving his fatal wound, he cried, "Thou hast conquered, O Galilean," even if the story is apocryphal, accurately represents the restoration of official Christianity that followed; and consequently Julian remained not only one of the last ancient champions of non-Christian Hellenism but also an obvious target for censure and abuse. Indeed, he became a demon of the medieval Church; but, later, a tragic hero of the Renaissance, a man of reason to the eighteenth century, and a romantic rebel to the nineteenth, when he fascinated authors as diverse as the Norwegian poet and dramatist Ibsen and the French novelist Anatole France—as in our own time he has attracted the novelist Gore Vidal.

EDITIONS—J. Bidez and F. Cumont, Juliani Imperatoris Epistulae Leges Poemata Fragmenta Varia, 1922; B. A. van Groningen, Juliani Imperatoris Epistulae Selectae, 1960. *With translation:* W. C. Wright (Loeb ed.), 1913–23; J. Bidez, G. Rochefort, C. Lacombrade, L'empereur Julien (Budé ed.), 1924–64; L. Goessler, Kaiser Julian der Abtrünnige, 1971; I. Labriola, Giuliano l'Apostata: Autobiografia, Messaggio agli Ateniesi, 1975.
ABOUT—J. Bidez, La vie de l'empereur Julien, 1930; W. E. Kaegi, Research on Julian, 1945–1964, in Classical Weekly, v 58, 1965; N. A. S. Levine, The Caesares of Julian: A Historical Study (Columbia, dissertation), 1968; L. Goessler, Kaiser Julian der Abtrünnige, 1971; R. Browning, The Emperor Julian, 1977; D. Bowder, The Age of Constantine and Julian, 1978; G. W. Bowersock, Julian the Apostate, 1978.

JULIANUS, SALVIUS (Lucius Octavius Cornelius Publius Salvius Julianus Aemilianus), Roman public official and jurist, was born in about A.D. 100 and prob-
jōō li ä nus

241

ably died in about 169. His birthplace was near Hadrumetum (Sousse in Tunisia), perhaps at the village of Pupput, where an inscription was discovered recording his distinguished and varied career. After serving on the staff of the emperor Hadrian (A.D. 117–38) as quaestor—he was given twice the customary salary because of his learning—he held the praetorship and became director of both the national and military treasuries. Next he became consul in the reign of Antoninus Pius (148) and was subsequently appointed to the governorship of Lower Germany followed by similar posts in Nearer Spain and then Africa under Marcus Aurelius and Lucius Verus (168–69). He was a member of the imperial council from the time of Hadrian onward. As a lawyer, Salvius Julianus was probably the last and certainly the most distinguished director of the Sabinian school, which took its name from the jurist Masurius Sabinus of the early first century A.D. (The school is also sometimes named Cassian, after Sabinus' successor Gaius Cassius Longinus; it was the rival to the school of the Proculians, named after Sempronius Proculus).

Salvius' principal monument was his *Digest (Digesta)*, in ninety books, much of which was preserved in the sixth century *Digest* of the Byzantine emperor Justinian; even more numerous citations are owed to subsequent authors. The work amounts to a systematic treatise on the entire field of the law. Salvius' pupil Sextus Caecilius Africanus also collected the views and rulings *(Responsa)* of his master. In addition to these activities as a respondent jurist, Salvius, while still relatively young, had been entrusted by the emperor Hadrian (who was deeply interested in legal matters) with the collection and revision of the successive edicts that the annually elected praetors had for centuries pronounced at the outset of their years of office. Salvius' achievement meant that from then on the edicts would be recognized as permanently valid and unalterable; although the poor *(humiliores)* were discriminated against in the courts in comparison with the more privileged *honestiores,* at least Julianus' publication of the edicts diffused among them a far clearer understanding of the legal safeguards to which

242

they were entitled than had ever been available to them before.

Roman law, under the initiative of Hadrian, was entering upon the most creative and philosophical period of its Golden Age; and in this development Salvius took the lead. Indeed, he is perhaps the outstanding figure in all Roman jurisprudence and legal science. Moreover, no other jurist ever exercised a more abiding influence on its shape and scope: The frequent allusions to his *Digest* by later lawyers of the time of Septimius Severus (A.D. 193–211) make it abundantly clear how many points his opinions had settled. These Severans—Papinian, Ulpian, and Paulus—outdid Salvius in the volume of their encyclopedic writings, but it seems probable that he equaled or even exceeded them in originality and creative force.

EDITIONS—Corpus Iuris Civilis: Digesta (extracts). ABOUT—L. Boulard, Salvius Julianus, 1902; W. Rechnitz, Studien zu Salvius Julianus, 1925; O. Lenel, Edictum Perpetuum, 3rd ed., 1927, reprint 1956; A. Guarino, Salvius Julianus: Profilo bibliografico, 1946, reprint (Labeo, v 10), 1964; F. Serrao, La jurisdictio del pretore peregrino, 1954, reprint 1968; E. Bund, Untersuchungen zur Methode Julians, 1965; W. Kunkel, Introduction to Roman Legal and Constitutional History, 1966.

JUSTIN MARTYR, Saint, Greek theological writer, was born in about A.D. 100 of pagan parentage and died between 163 and 167. His birthplace was Flavia Neapolis (Nablus on the west bank of the Jordan). Wandering from place to place and familiarizing himself with the various philosophical schools he encountered—Stoics, Aristotelians, Pythagoreans, and finally Platonists—he concluded that they were all unsatisfactory, and after meeting by chance an elderly Christian at Ephesus, he became a convert to that faith, inspired by the courage that had been shown by its martyrs. He continued his travels, with his philosopher's cloak on his back, and during the reign of Antoninus Pius (138–61) moved to Rome, where he lectured to small classes on Christian themes. A denunciation of his proceedings reached the authorities; it was said to have come from an adherent of Cynicism named Crescentius, who disapproved of his teaching. At all events, he was arrested and executed, as the *Acts* of his martyrdom record.

His surviving works include two *Defenses (Apologiae),* nominally addressed to the emperor but aimed at a wider public. The first was composed in Rome in about 155. It begins by defending his fellow Christians against the current calumnious charges of atheism and disloyalty to the Roman state. In the course of these arguments, the author presents a positive justification of his faith, paying special attention to rituals of worship and providing the fullest accounts of baptism and the Eucharist that we possess from this period. The work ends with an allusion to Hadrian's decree of about A.D. 125 granting toleration to the Christians. Like Bishop Melito of Sardis a generation later, Justin takes a relatively hopeful view of relations between state and church. His *Second Apologia,* a kind of postscript to the first, cites the recent trials and executions of three Christians by the prefect of Rome under Marcus Aurelius, arguing that the prosecutors themselves proved the innocence of their victims.

The *Dialogue With Trypho,* whether based on an actual disputation or not, purports to provide an account of Justin's conversation (over a period of two days) with an erudite Jew and is valuable as the first known example of anti-Jewish theological argument by a Christian. The dialogue is also significant because it recognizes Greek philosophy, and especially Platonism, as a preparation for the truths of the Christian religion; although no great philosopher himself, Justin was the first in the long line of those who sought to harmonize and reconcile the two ways of thinking. He knew, as yet, of no fixed canon of New Testament writings, but it is possible that the "Memoirs of the Apostles" to which he refers were the Synoptic Gospels. Various other writings ascribed to Justin *(Treatise on Monarchy, Oration to the Greeks, Exhortation to the Greeks)* are of other authorship and much later in date.

EDITIONS—J. P. Migne, Patrologia Graeca, v 6; J. C. T. Otto, ed., 1876–81. The Apologiae: A. W. F. Blunt, 1911 (with commentary); E. Goodspeed, 1914. Dialogue: G. Archambault, 1909 (with French transla-

tion). *English translations*—T. B. Falls, Fathers of the Church, v 5-6, 1949; G. Coxe, 1950.
ABOUT—E. R. Goodenough, The Theology of Justin Martyr, 1923; J. Daniélou, Message évangelique et culture hellénique, 1961; H. Chadwick, Early Christian Thought and the Classical Tradition: Studies in Justin, Clement and Origen, 1966; L. W. Barnard, Justin Martyr: His Life and Thought, 1967.

JUSTIN THE PHILOSOPHER. See Justin Martyr, Saint

JUSTINIAN. See Gaius; Julianus, Salvius; Papinian; Paulus; Ulpian

JUVENAL (Decimus Junius Juvenalis), Latin satirical poet, was born some time between A.D. 50 and 70 and died after 127. He may have come from Aquinum (Aquino) in central Italy. The ancient "biographies" purporting to give accounts of his life contain improbable statements that are merely based on conjectures from his own poems. However, according to the least untrustworthy of these Lives, he was the son or ward of a rich freedman (a class he attacks in his writings) and practiced declamation until middle age—which seems likely enough in view of the characteristics of his literary style. Like his friend Martial, who praised his eloquence, Juvenal was for some time extremely poor and lived at Rome as a dependent of wealthy men; but in due course he acquired a small property at Tibur (Tivoli). Several ancient sources state that he was banished for a time for causing offense to the actor Paris, a favorite of the emperor Domitian (81–96). The banishment was said to have taken the form of a military appointment to Egypt, where he died. None of these details, however, are certain, although the knowledge of Egyptian customs he displays in his writings makes it probable that he had a personal knowledge of the country.

Juvenal left five books of hexameter satires, comprising sixteen poems. The first book contains five of these pieces. The first, by way of an introduction, asserts that the

jōō′ ve n'l

243

poet, when he gazes upon Rome, cannot keep himself from writing satire about its deplorable condition but adds that, for safety's sake, he will not attack the living but the dead. The second satire assails men who cloak vice under the appearance of philosophy and develops into an attack on homosexual practices. In the third Juvenal's friend Umbricius declares that he is going to depart from the capital because honest people cannot make a living there and because poverty involves continuous degradation and danger. The fourth poem tells how the late emperor Domitian (A.D. 81–96) summoned his obsequious council to deliberate on the cooking of a giant turbot. The fifth gives the story of the dinner a client attended at the home of his patron, where he was subjected to every sort of humiliation.

Book 2 consists of a single poem, which is a remorseless onslaught on the whole female sex, with special denunciation of immoral and tiresome wives. Book 3 comprises three satires (poems 7–9): one praises the current emperor Hadrian (117–38) as a supporter of literature but enlarges on the wretched prospects of writers who have the misfortune to lack generous patrons; another rebukes noblemen who consider aristocratic blood more important than virtue; the last is a discussion by a male prostitute of the difficulties of conducting his profession.

Book 4, which like its successor is a good deal gentler in tone than the others, again includes three poems (poems 10–12). The first deplores the foolishness of humankind in wanting harmful things instead of settling for courage and soundness of body and mind; the next, which takes the form of an invitation to dinner, pronounces that neither ancient austerity nor contemporary extravagance is right or appropriate but that sensible, decent moderation is what is required; the third poem narrates a friend's rescue from shipwreck, which gives the opportunity for a discussion of true and false friendship.

The remaining four satires (poems 13–16) are grouped in the fifth book. The first is an ironical consolation to a friend who has been cheated out of some money. The second relates the bad effects that the faults of parents, especially that of greed, can have on their children. The third describes, in detail, an incident involving mass violence and cannibalism in Egypt, illustrating the inhumanity human beings are capable of displaying to one another. The last poem, of which the latter and larger part is missing, deplores the unfair privileges enjoyed by soldiers.

This poetry is forcible, imposing, realistic, and violent. Like the satirists such as Lucilius and Horace, to whom he owes many debts, Juvenal employs the epic hexameter meter, but in contrast to these models he invests the medium with torrential epic vigor and power. Each hexameter is a fresh hammer blow. He employs the diction of the Silver Age with conciseness and vigor and above all makes brilliant use of its rhetoric: its exploitation in his hands leads to fantastic exaggerations, of which, however, he retains full control. His satires abound in relentless, unrelaxing abuse, crushing epigrams, and brutal parodies: he emerges as a man with a ferocious sense of unfairness and failure. Arrangement and characterization scarcely concern him, but he has a remarkable talent for presenting a scene from Roman life in a few graphic strokes. Above all he revels in savage caricatures: his mockery is not humorous but stormy and grim, and its fierceness gives some plausibility to his asseveration (traditional though it is) that "even if nature denies the gift, indignation produces the verses."

Although Juvenal declares that, owing to the danger of launching attacks on those who are still alive, he will concentrate on assailing the dead, it is evidently his own time that he always has in mind. To a poor and embittered man the Rome of the second century A.D. was doubtless not quite the haven of enlightenment that other writers (such as Pliny the Younger) display to us. His indignation was no doubt whipped up by the personal disappointments that he himself had experienced. But it was based, in addition, not only on the doctrines of the Stoics and other philosophical schools but on a strongly held moral ideal of Juvenal's own—old-fashioned, traditional and narrow, incapable of distinguishing among sins the grave from the trivial.

Yet this morality is expressed with a nobility that subsequent epochs have found arresting. It is true Juvenal was scarcely known before the fourth century A.D., when Lactantius mentioned his name and Ausonius and others imitated him. But then, in the latter half of that century, his poems were edited and published with a commentary and immediately became popular. All through the Middle Ages, readers derived a powerful moral uplift from the *Satires:* thus Chaucer, for example, more than once appeals to his authority. During and after the Renaissance, Juvenal became the model for many satirists, and indeed it was he, more than any other ancient writer, who gave satire to the world. On the whole, once the medieval period was over, it was his bitter eloquence rather than his moral tone that impressed itself on the western world. His influence on seventeenth century France, spread by the critic and poet Boileau, was enormous. In England, John Dryden translated his poems and in 1681–82 adapted him in three great satires of his own: *Absalom and Achitophel, The Medal,* and *Mac Flecknoe.* The satirist Jonathan Swift and the poet Alexander Pope, in their distinctive ways, followed the same tradition. Furthermore, Samuel Johnson's *London* and *Vanity of Human Wishes* owe a great deal to the third and tenth poems of Juvenal respectively.

EDITIONS—J. E. B. Mayor, revised eds. (omitting satires 2, 6, 9), 1880–81, 1889; L. Friedländer, 1895; J. D. Duff (expurgated, and omitting satires 2 and 9), 1898. *Translations*—J. Dryden (satires 1, 3, 6, 10, 16), 1693; G. G. Ramsay, Juvenal and Persius (Loeb ed.), revised ed., 1940; R. Humphries, 1958; H. Creekmore, 1963; J. Mazzaro, 1965; P. Green (Penguin ed.), 1967. ABOUT—P. de Labriolle, Les satires de Juvénal, 1950; G. Highet, Juvenal the Satirist, 1954, reprint 1962; A. Serafini, Studio sulla satira di Giovenale, 1957; R. E. Colton, Juvenal and Martial, 1959; W. Krenkel, ed., Römische Satire, 1966; U. Knoche, Roman Satire, 1975; M. Coffey, Roman Satire, 1976; J. Gérard, Juvénal et la réalité contemporaine, 1976.

LABEO, MARCUS ANTISTIUS, Roman jurist and Latin writer, was born in (perhaps) about 50 B.C. and died in about A.D. 10 or 11. He came of a distinguished family from Samnium (central Italy). The son of a

lab' e ō

friend of Brutus, the assassin of Julius Caesar, he adhered firmly to the same Republican views, even after Augustus had become the supreme ruler. He insisted inconveniently on the senatorial rights of the disgraced former triumvir Lepidus and implied ridicule of a proposal that a bodyguard of senators should keep watch outside the emperor's bedroom. As a result of this attitude Labeo, after becoming praetor, never rose to the consulship, though whether this was due to his own or the emperor's wish is uncertain. Instead, he concentrated on jurisprudence. His teachers had included not only his father, who was likewise a lawyer, but other prominent jurists, among them Cicero's protégé Trebatius Testa.

Labeo was accustomed to spend six months of each year teaching at Rome and the rest of the time writing in the country. He was an immensely prolific author, whose books, now all lost, were said to have numbered as many as four hundred; they exercised an influence almost unparalleled for its profound and long-lasting effects. This was particularly true of his commentaries on the annual edicts which the praetors were accustomed to issue at the outset of their annual terms of office; quotations from his commentaries continued to turn up repeatedly in the works of later jurists. Labeo was particularly well informed about the archaic Roman period, which he studied in writings on the laws of the Twelve Tables and the college of priests *(pontifices)*. He also published a series of cases *(Epistulae* and *Responsa)* and compiled *Pithana (Persuasive Arguments),* a collection of axiomatic legal definitions and decisions. His *Libri Posteriores,* a systematic exposition of the law in at least forty books, was published after his death. These are known from an extensive and widely used epitome made by a jurist of the first century A.D., Javolenus Priscus, and further citations come from later authors, whose frequent reference to the work shows Labeo's enormous prestige.

He was the contemporary of another prominent jurist, Ateius Capito, who adopted a more cooperative attitude to the regime of Augustus (thus gaining the consulship Labeo missed); and the political and personal animosities between the two men led to the establishment of two rival legal schools, the Proculian (named after Sempronius Proclus, a follower of Labeo) and the Sabinian (named after Masurius Sabinus, a follower of Capito). The remains of Labeo's legal works show him to have been a man of progressive outlook. Moreover, he possessed a broad range of knowledge concerning matters far outside the law, including the history of Greek philosophy, dialectic, and rhetoric and extending to Latin language and grammar as well—this last interest being exemplified by numerous etymological explanations that often look startlingly wide of the mark today but were in keeping with the linguistic science of his time.

EDITIONS—Corpus Iuris Civilis: Digesta (extracts). ABOUT—L. A. A. Pernice, Marcus Antistius Labeo: Das römische Privatrecht im ersten Jahrhunderte der Kaiserzeit, 1873–1900 (v 2 in 2nd ed., reprint), 1963; O. Lenel, Edictum Perpetuum, 3rd ed., 1927, reprint 1976; W. Kunkel, Introduction to Roman Legal and Constitutional History, 1966.

LACTANTIUS, LUCIUS CAELIUS (or **CAECILIUS) FIRMIANUS,** Latin writer, was born between A.D. 240 and 250 and died in about 320. His birthplace was in northern Africa, where he studied under the eminent teacher of rhetoric Arnobius, at that time a pagan. In about 290 Diocletian summoned Lactantius to his capital Nicomedia (Izmit, northwestern Asia Minor) to teach rhetoric. Subsequently, following in the steps of Arnobius, he became a convert to Christianity; this step must have been taken before 303 since, when the Great Persecution began in that year, he lost his post. Leaving Nicomedia two years later, he moved to the West, and in about 317 became the tutor of Constantine the Great's eldest son Crispus at Treviri (Trier on the Moselle).

Lactantius seems to have produced a number of writings before his conversion, including a *Symposium* and a versified account of his journey to Nicomedia; but they have not been preserved. (It is uncertain if another poem, the *Phoenix,* is by his hand.) His earliest extant work, written in 303/4, is entitled *On the Handiwork of God (De* lak tan′ ti us

Opificio Dei), in which, following Cicero and Varro, he argues—against certain philosophical schools—that the human body, with its admirably efficient organization, could only have been created by God ("How appropriate is the padded flesh of the buttocks for sitting!"). His next, and most important, publication was the *Divine Institutions.* Written by him between 305 and 313 (doubts on his authorship are unjustified) and dedicated to Constantine, the *Institutions* seeks to justify Christianity to educated minds, refuting each and every opposite argument that had been or could be put forward; the work constitutes the first systematic presentation of Christian thought and the first construction of a Christian ideal of happiness that had ever been attempted in the Latin language. It is divided into seven books, which may originally have formed separate studies. The first and second books *(On False Religion* and *On the Origin of Error)* refute polytheistic religion, and the third *(On False Philosophy)* criticizes Roman philosophers. From that point onward Lactantius turns from criticism to construction, though without abandoning polemics completely. Book 4 *(On True Philosophy and Religion)* demonstrates the unbreakable union of those two fields of study in the Christian faith; Book 5 *(On Justice)* discusses personal morals and social justice; and Book 6 *(On True Worship)* links Christian ethics with their divine origin. *On the Happy Life (De Vita Beata),* which comprises the seventh and last book, deals with the purpose of creation and of humankind, expounds the immortality of the soul, and concludes with an exhortation to rise to the Christian challenge. In this climax of his task, Lactantius exerts all his efforts to point a favorable contrast between Christianity and current pagan doctrines and to provide practical guidance to an integrated Christian life. (Later, he produced an epitome of the whole work.)

His next treatise, *On the Wrath of God (De Ira Dei),* takes issue with the Stoics and Epicureans and argues that anger is a necessary element in the character of God, who must arm Himself by such means against those who do evil, since otherwise there can be no divine jurisdiction or providence. The effects of this divine wrath are demonstrated in the publication entitled *The Deaths of the Persecutors (De Mortibus Persecutorum)*, written in about 318. This tract describes, in passing, Constantine's famous vision before the battle of the Milvian Bridge, but its main purpose is to provide a long list of the gruesome fates that supposedly fell upon those who persecuted Christianity, particularly in Lactantius' own time. This is a savage and vengeful pamphlet, diverging from Lactantius' usually more temperate manner.

Although Lactantius possessed little philosophical knowledge or ability, his Latin was, for the most part, tasteful, harmonious, and oratorical. He drew extensively upon earlier Latin authors; indeed, he was the most classical of all the early Christian writers and became known to the Renaissance as "the Christian Cicero." It is noteworthy that, by way of contrast, he quotes the Scriptures very sparsely, refraining, for example, from the usual practice of citing the Old Testament prophets as guarantors of the truth of Christianity and substituting the Sibylline oracles and his own millenarist deductions in their place.

EDITIONS—S. Brandt and G. Laubmann, Corpus Scriptorum Ecclesiasticorum Latinorum, v 19 and v 27. On the Handiwork of God: M. Perrin, Lactance: L'ouvrage du Dieu Créateur, 1974 (with translation). Divine Institutes: M. F. McDonald, Fathers of the Church, v 49 and v 54, 1964 (translation); H. W. A. van Rooijen-Dijkman, De Beata Vita: Het zevende Boek van de Divinae Institutiones van Lactantius, 1967. Epitome: E. H. Blakeney, 1950 (translation). On the Wrath of God: H. Kraft and A. Wlosok, De Ira Dei, 1957. On the Deaths of the Persecutors: J. Moreau, Sources chrétiennes, 1954 (with translation). Phoenix: M. C. Fitzgerald, De Ave Phoenice, 1933 (with translation).
ABOUT—R. Pichon, Lactance, 1901; A. Alföldi, The Conversion of Constantine and Pagan Rome, 1948; A. Wlosok, Laktanz und die philosophische Gnosis, 1960; J. Wojtczak, De Lactantio Ciceronis Aemulo et Sectatore, 1969; R. MacMullen, Constantine, 1970; J. Holland Smith, Constantine the Great, 1971; J. Fontaine and M. Perrin, Lactance et son temps (IV Colloque Patristique, 1976), 1978; R. M. Ogilvie, The Library of Lactantius, 1979.

LAMPRIDIUS, AELIUS. See Spartianus, Aelius

LEO VI, THE WISE

LEO VI, THE WISE or **THE PHILOSOPHER,** Byzantine emperor, Greek scholar and legal compiler, was born in A.D. 866 and died in 912. His parents were the emperor Basil I the Macedonian and his second wife Eudocia Ingerina. Leo was made joint emperor with his father in 870, at the age of four, and succeeded Basil in 886. He lacked the taste and ability for soldiering, but while his reign was marked by grave military reverses at the hands of both Bulgarians and Saracens, the adverse results of these setbacks did not prove permanent, with the exception of the final loss of Sicily to the Saracens in 902. After a threatening expedition against Constantinople by the Russians in about 905, a trade agreement and a commercial treaty were signed (907, 911). Leo's reputation has suffered unduly from the hostility of a historical work of the time *(The Chronicle of the Logothete)* toward his family; in addition, by marrying four times in order to produce an heir (Constantine VII), he incurred the grave disapproval of the church. Meanwhile, however, he carried out major administrative reforms designed to strengthen the themes (administrative division of the Byzantine empire) and render them more defensible against enemy invasion.

Although given to fits of ungovernable anger and disliked for dynastic reasons by members of his own house, Leo inspired and retained the loyalty of people of widely different opinions, even when they did not approve of his policies, and this helped him to pass a great deal of legislation—113 decrees *(novels)* covering a wide range of ecclesiastical and secular problems in the empire. He was above all a scholar and an apt pupil of the great Photius, who had created an intellectual atmosphere at Constantinople that Leo did everything he could to maintain. He himself, though not an author of exceptional talent, wrote a funeral encomium of his father Basil I; a manual of tactics; various religious and secular poems; and a book of sermons. (A collection of oracles circulating in the fourteenth and fifteenth centuries was attributed to him falsely.) He also extended favor and protection to men of learning and letters, so that his palace, people said, had virtually taken on the appearance of an academy.

His father's achievements in the legal field made it possible for Leo to publish the *Basilica* (term derived from the Greek word *basileus,* monarch), which forms the most comprehensive and complete digest of Byzantine or Graeco-Roman law. Through the efforts of a commission of jurists appointed and directed by the emperor, all parts of the sixth century code of Justinian I were reshaped, supplemented by more recent material, and combined into a single code, written in Greek. Basil I had laid the foundation for this enterprise, when he selected and revised the laws he proposed to retain. He may have divided the resultant corpus into forty books; Leo's further adaptation amounted to sixty books, in six volumes, and was consequently described as the *hexabiblos.*

No single manuscript has preserved the whole vast bulk of the *Basilica,* but a number of different manuscripts have preserved more than two-thirds of its contents; and the *Tipucitus,* a treatise of the twelfth century ascribed to the Byzantine jurist Patzes, has recorded Leo's chapter headings and rubrics. In the West, however, no part of the code seems to have attracted attention until its importance for the study of Roman law came to be appreciated in the sixteenth century.

EDITIONS—J. P. Migne, Patrologia Graeca, v 107; R. Vari, Leo VI: Tactica, 1917–22; A. Vogt and A. Hausherr, Leo VI: Panegyric of Basil I, 1932; A. Dain, Leonis VI Sapientis Problemata, 1935; L'extrait tactique tiré de Léon le Sage, 1942; P. Noailles and A. Dain, Les novelles de Léon VI, le Sage (with French translation), 1944.

ABOUT—C. A. Spulber, Les Novelles de Léon le Sage, 1934; A. A. Vasiliev, History of the Byzantine Empire, v 1, 1952; H. G. Beck, Kirche und theologische Literatur im byzantinischen Reich, 1959; D. M. Wood, Leo VI's Concept of Divine Monarchy, 1964; H. Grégoire *in* Cambridge Medieval History, v 4, pt 1, 1966; R. Jenkins, Byzantium: The Imperial Centuries, A.D. 610–1071, 1966.

LEONIDAS, Greek epigrammatic poet, was born in the later years of the fourth century B.C. and died in about 260. His birthplace was Taras (Tarentum, now Taranto in southeastern Italy). He left his home and wrote patriotic poems, first for King Neoptolemus of Epirus (northwestern Greece) and later for his murderer and successor, Pyrrhus (307–272 B.C.). After Pyrrhus' attempted invasion of Italy and Sicily had been driven off by the Romans (275), he led the life of a restless itinerant poet in the countries of the eastern Mediterranean.

Leonidas was one of the earliest Hellenistic epigrammatists. About a hundred of his pieces have come down to us; all except two of them are in the Palatine Anthology, compiled in the tenth century A.D. Many of these poems echo the hard conditions of their author's life. He writes in a vein of intense pessimism, as an impoverished, hungry poet who expects to die far from his home, and finds his only consolation in the gift of the Muses. Of his own career he says little; but he shows great sympathy with others who are in distress, and some of his most appealing compositions are a series of epigrams about fishermen, peasants, and other poor people. The epigrams elevate their hard daily tasks into poetry—they are shown, for example, dedicating the tools of their trades to the gods of the district in which they work. The spirit of these poems is akin to that of contemporary Hellenistic sculptors who made statues of impoverished workmen and decrepit old women. There is a gentle and resigned pathos in Leonidas' epitaphs

lē on' i dàs

on humble people, though their deaths he professes to commemorate are often manifestly invented—fictitious excuses for his nostalgic thoughts—as when, for instance, a dead shepherd begs his surviving companions to do their work near his tomb so that he may listen to the familiar rustic sounds. Yet the poet is not always sad—for instance, in one poem he joyfully makes Priapus, the god of the harbor (as well as of fertility and gardens), announce the revival of sea travel at the start of the delightful season of spring. Leonidas is also capable of launching a fierce onslaught on those he believes to be his enemies, and sometimes his epigrams end in a sharp point, which at this period of literary history was unusual.

His preference is for the elegiac meter, though he also writes sometimes in iambics. His is a highly finished style, in which the extravagance of his compound words and a taste for odd, complex sentences laden with technical terms contrast strangely with the stark realism of some of his themes. Although he was little more than a skillful versifier, his popularity was enormous. For generations after his death, epigrammatists continued to copy his manner and compose variations on his epigrams. Antipater of Sidon, and the woman poet Nossis from Locri in southern Italy, and a little-known poet named Ariston, all imitate him in a very direct fashion; another of his admirers was the Latin poet Propertius. About twenty of the epigrams attributed to Leonidas are by an inferior namesake.

EDITIONS—J. Geffcken, 1897; A. Veniero, I poeti dell'Antologia Palatina, 1905 (with translation); A. S. F. Gow and D. L. Page, Greek Anthology: Hellenistic Epigrams, 1965; D. L. Page, Epigrammata Graeca, 1976. *With English translation:* E. Bevan, 1931.
ABOUT—J. Geffcken, Leonidas von Tarent, 1896; L. A. Stella, Cinque poeti dell'Antologia Palatina, 1949; A. S. F. Gow, The Greek Anthology: Sources and Ascriptions, 1958; C. Gallavotti, Planudea, v 2 (Accademia dei Lincei), 1960; T. B. L. Webster, Hellenistic Poetry and Art, 1964.

LEONTIUS, Greek bishop and writer about the saints in the Byzantine epoch, was born in about A.D. 600 and died in about 650 lē on' ti us

or a little later. He became bishop of Neapolis in Cyprus. Leontius was a friend, and eulogistic biographer, of a fellow Cypriote, St. John the Almsgiver or Merciful *(Eleemon)*, who was archbishop of Alexandria and who died in 619. His Life by Leontius provides valuable evidence for the social and economic history of the period (including a reference to trade between Egypt and Britain); and he paints vivid pictures of life in the Egyptian capital. Above all, page after page is filled with stories illustrating John's endless acts of charity, which poured forth "like a second Nile." Some of the anecdotes indicating this passion for social justice assume miraculous forms, but many others seem circumstantial and convincing: for example, his assistance to refugees from the Persian invasion of Syria, his foundation of hospitals and poorhouses, and his insistence that fraudulent weights should not be employed.

Leontius also wrote a Life of St. Symeon the Foolish *(Salos)* of the great Christian center Edessa in Mesopotamia (Urfa in southeastern Turkey). This work, however, contains a greater legendary element and less historical information. Symeon, who lived in the sixth century A.D., was an ascetic of the eastern, non-Greek type. He and his friend John lived in the desert, subsisting on plants and roots and whatever else they could find and believing that they were carrying out the will of God. On return to urban society, they seemed to behave like idiots, but this, the author wants us to know, was in order to avoid being honored by people who did not understand their marvelous powers.

In the strange tales of Symeon's wonderful deeds, as well as elsewhere in Leontius' writings, we encounter many words and expressions reflecting the strong influence of the popular language, which was tending toward modern Greek. Leontius, unlike the great majority of Byzantine writers about the saints, composed his Lives for the less privileged sections of the population. In his theology, he was anxious to dissociate himself from the opinion, destined to prevail at Constantinople in the Iconoclastic controversy of the following century, that the devotion paid to images was idolatrous;

indeed, he suggested that the practice be extended to the pictures of saints. "The image of God is man," he declared, "and especially such a man as has received the indwelling of the Holy Spirit. I therefore justly honor and worship the image of God's servants and glorify the house of the Holy Spirit."

EDITIONS—J. P. Migne, Patrologia Graeca, v 86 and v 93; A. J. Festugière and L. Ryden, Leontios de Neapolis: Vie de Syméon le Fou et Vie de Jehan de Chypre, 1977. Life of John: H. Gelzer, ed., Leontios von Neapolis: Leben des heiligen Johannes des Barmherzigen Erzbischofs von Alexandrien, 1893; E. Dawes and N. H. Baynes, Three Byzantine Saints, 1948 (slightly shortened translation). Life of Symeon: L. Ryden, Das Leben des heiligen Narren Symeon, 1963.
ABOUT—G. Gelzer, ed., Ausgewählte kleine Schriften, 1907; D. Stiernon, Léonce de Neapolis in Dictionnaire de Spiritualité, v 9, 1976 (pp 666-70).

LEONTIUS OF BYZANTIUM, Greek theologian of the Byzantine age, was born at Constantinople. He died in about A.D. 545. He was trained as a lawyer and became a monk at Jerusalem, thus earning the two additional designations of Scholasticus and Hierosolymitanus.

Leontius' writings were especially directed against the Monophysites, who were accused of teaching that in the person of Jesus Christ there was one nature rather than two natures, divine and human, as had been declared at the Council of Chalcedon (451). At the same time, he himself, while insisting on the doctrine of the two natures, nevertheless accepted the Monophysite emphasis on the essential unity of Jesus Christ; and he took part in a conference of Orthodox Chalcedonians and Monophysites at Constantinople in 531.

Two other so-called heresies likewise attracted his opposition. One was at the opposite pole to Monophysitism, namely the sect of the Nestorians (named after Nestorius, patriarch of Constantinople, who died after A.D. 451), which stressed the independence of the two natures so sharply as to suggest that they were virtually two persons. Leontius wrote a tract attempting to refute this opinion *(Tractatus Adversus Nestorianos)*. His other target was the Eutychian sect,

lē on' ti us bi zan' ti um

named after Eutyches, an archimandrite of Constantinople and a contemporary of Nestorius, who had presented a somewhat confused view, at one point pronouncing in favor of one nature of Christ but also frequently affirming "two natures before, one after the incarnation." Leontius wrote a book *Against Nestorians and Eutychians,* in which he developed the concept of *enhypostasia,* the inseparable union of human nature and divine person in Christ. He also composed sermons and other works.

Leontius' writings show how Plato's influence on the Church Fathers was already beginning to give way to Aristotle; his introduction of Aristotelian distinctions into theology entitles him to be regarded as one of the precursors of medieval scholasticism.

WORKS erroneously attributed to Leontius of Byzantium—An extensive monograph On Sects (De Sectis) is by another and later writer, although perhaps founded on his notes.
EDITIONS—J. P. Migne, Patrologia Graeca, v 86. *Translations* (of sermons)—M. Aubineau, Hésychius de Jérusalem, Basile de Seleucie, Jean de Béryte, Pseudo-Chrysostome, Léonce de Constantinople, Homélies Pascales, 1972.
ABOUT—F. Loofs, Leontius von Byzanz, 1887; W. Rugämer, Leontius von Byzanz, 1894; E. R. Hardy, ed., Christology of the Later Fathers, 1954; D. B. Evans, Leontius of Byzantium, 1970.

LIBANIUS, Greek rhetorician and popular lecturer, was born in A.D. 314 and died in about 393. His birthplace was Antioch in Syria (Antakya in southeastern Turkey). The son of rich pagan parents, he received the earlier stages of his education at home and subsequently continued his studies at Athens (336–40). In 342 he opened a rhetorical school at Constantinople but was compelled to abandon it four years later owing to the intrigues of rivals. After a period spent teaching at Nicomedia (Izmit), he was recalled to Constantinople by Constantius II, whose offer of a chair of rhetoric, however, he chose to decline. Instead, he accepted a similar post at Antioch (354), where he remained for the rest of his life. His pupils included many men who later attained distinction, including eminent Christians such

li bā' ni us

as John Chrysostom and probably Basil of Caesarea and Gregory of Nazianzus. In his later years, Libanius became a famous educational and literary figure, acquainted with many of the leading personages of the day. The central fact in his life was his friendship for the pagan emperor Julian the Apostate, whose death in 363 was not only a bitter personal loss but a blow to the Hellenism they both admired. Nevertheless, in spite of his paganism, Libanius subsequently retained high favor under the pious Christian emperor Theodosius I (378–95), who conferred upon him the honorific title of praetorian prefect.

Libanius has left sixty-four orations. Some were not written for public delivery but to be read. Many are purely imaginative exercises (for example, *An Apology for Socrates*) or deal with broad ethical themes (greed, boasting, wealth) in the manner of Dio Chrysostom and the Cynics. Seven speeches relate to Julian, including a *Monody* and a funeral oration that strikes a note of strong personal affection. Even under a strongly Christian administration sixteen years after Julian had died, Libanius was still prepared to hint that Christians had been indirectly responsible for his death. Yet, despite his desire to preserve the pagan classicism of the past, he was a model of religious tolerance himself and was glad to help Christian as well as pagan friends. What he objected to, as his speech entitled *On Sanctuaries* showed, was the barbarization of culture, which seemed to him the effect of the more ascetic versions of Christian practice.

He composed an autobiographical oration and another oration in praise of his native Antioch, which was delivered at the Olympic Games held in that city and contains interesting historical material. Many of his other speeches, too, deal with various aspects of contemporary affairs, casting extensive light on the urban life of the day, and on emperors of the east and their regimes.

One of the most important sources of information on the period is provided by Libanius' sixteen hundred surviving letters, the largest corpus of this kind that has come down from antiquity (four hundred Latin letters, however, are spurious). Addressed to almost all the important personages of the day—Christian as well as pagan—who considered it a prize to receive one of these epistles, such was Libanius' contemporary renown, they thank, praise, intercede, recommend, and condole. Among his other publications are many pieces related to his rhetorical teaching—notably fifty-one declamations on mythological, historical, or dramatic themes—and a hundred and forty-three *Practice Models (Progymnasmata)*—including presentations of dramatic situations—which he wrote for his pupils. His *Hypotheses* (arguments) to Demosthenes' speeches were composed for the proconsul Montius, who was one of Libanius' admirers.

He emerges from his writings as a pedantic antiquarian, seeing the world through a snobbish, literary purism. Yet warmth and sincerity break in from time to time; moreover, he is free from vindictiveness and unusually willing to fight against social injustice. In matters of diction, he particularly admired Aelius Aristides, the sophist of the second century A.D. but at the same time wanted to adhere to the great ancient models as far as he could. He worked exceptionally hard at his style, which frequently becomes tortuous and difficult. Nevertheless, it was greatly respected in Byzantine times.

EDITIONS—R. Foerster, 1909–27. *With translation:* G. Downey, Oration in Praise of Antioch (Oration 11) *in* Proceedings of the American Philosophical Society, v 103, no 5, 1959, *and* Orations 5 and 10 *in* A History of Antioch in Syria, 1961; M. Crosby and W. W. Calder, On the Silence of Socrates (Greek, Roman and Byzantine Studies, v 3), 1960; A. F. Norman, Libanius: Autobiography, Oration 1 (Loeb ed.), 1965, *and* Selected Orations (Loeb ed.), v 1, 1969, v 2, 1978, *and* Selected Letters, 1978; B. Schouler, Discours moraux 6, 7, 8, 25 (Budé ed.), 1973; J. Martin and P. Petit, Autobiographies (Budé ed.), v 1, 1978.

ABOUT—G. R. Sievers, Das Leben des Libanius, 1868; R. A. Pack, Studies in Libanius and Antiochene Society Under Theodosius, 1935; L. Petit, Libanius et la vie municipale à Antioche au quatrième siècle après Jésus-Christ, 1956, *and* Les étudiants de Libanius, 1957.

LIUTPRAND (LIUDPRAND), Italian diplomat and Latin historian, was born in

lē′ ŏŏt pränt

about A.D. 920 and probably died in about 972. His birthplace was Pavia in northern Italy; he came of a rich and noble Lombard family with a tradition of imperial service. After his father's death, Hugh of Provence (or of Arles), king of Italy, took him, at the age of seven, into his household, where he served as a singing page but also studied assiduously and became a deacon at Pavia. When Hugh fell from power, Liutprand passed into the service of Berengar II, who sent him on a courtesy mission to the imperial court at Constantinople. While there, however, he was compelled to make the customary gifts to the Byzantine emperor at his own expense without his employer's help. Because of the avarice and greed of Berengar and his wife Willa, Liutprand later left them to go into voluntary exile. He found refuge with the German emperor Otto I the Great (936–73), who, as a reward for his services, appointed him bishop of Cremona in northern Italy in about 961 and made him one of his principal counselors and envoys. In 968 Liutprand was again sent to Constantinople to request the hand of a Byzantine princess for the German emperor's son (the future Otto II), but the mission was a failure, and when Liutprand, on his departure, reached the frontier of the Byzantine empire, its customs officials confiscated the purple silk he had bought for himself at Constantinople.

Considerably the longest of his writings is the work entitled *To Everyone His Due* or *Tit for Tat (Antapodosis)*. It is a history of Italian affairs from 887 to 949, the last three of its six books being concerned with events that took place in his own time. The work owes its singular title to Liutprand's open intention of getting his own back on Berengar and his wife, who is described as a Jezebel and a vampire. The *Antapodosis* is historical in form, but it also contains numerous passages of original verse, and the author is not only free with classical quotations but frequently interlards his Latin with Greek phrases. He also has a strong taste for picturesque and spicy anecdotes, which brings his work into the category of historical romance rather than plain historiography.

Liutprand's *Deeds of Otto (Gesta* or *His-*

toria Ottonis) likewise has a special purpose. Indeed, its title is misleading, since it is very brief and only deals fully with a single incident in the reign of Otto I, namely his removal from office of Pope John XII in 963, an act that Liutprand is at pains to defend. After a short description of the coronation of Otto as German (Holy Roman) emperor in the previous year, the principal episode is dealt with in some detail. The account closes with the reinstatement of Otto's own nominee Leo VIII (who had been Pope before John), which gave rise to the highly controversial "Ottonian Privilege," requiring popes to take an oath of obedience to the emperor before their consecration.

The bias of Liutprand's other treatise is directed sharply against the Byzantine government. Its subject is his unsuccessful and humiliating embassy to Constantinople in 968 *(Relatio de Legatione Constantinopolitana)*. This description, although crammed with virulent hostility, is a unique and masterly piece of contemporary reporting. He provides a vivid picture of life in the greatest city in the world. He also shows clearly how and why mutual misunderstandings of every kind bedeviled its contacts with the West. For although Liutprand had learned Greek as a young man, his account shows a cordial dislike of the way of life of the Byzantines, a dislike accentuated by their allegedly insulting behavior toward him: for example when they placed him and his companions lower than the Bulgarian envoys at a dinner. In his indignation he goes so far as to describe their emperor Nicephorus II Phocas not only as a fox and a perjurer but as a foul-smelling boor.

EDITIONS—I. Bekker, Liudprandi Episcopi Cremonensis Opera (Scriptores Rerum Germanicarum in Usum Scholarum), 1915. *Translations*—F. A. Wright, 1930. ABOUT—M. Lintzel, Studien über Liutprand von Cremona, 1933; W. Baum, Die politischen Anschauungen Liutprands von Cremona, 1936; W. Wattenbach-R. Holtzmann, Deutschlands Geschichtsquellen im Mittelalter: Deutsche Kaiserzeit, v 1, and v 2, 1948; R. W. Southern, The Making of the Middle Ages, 1953; H. Grégoire *in* Cambridge Medieval History, v 4, pt 1, 1966.

LIVIUS ANDRONICUS, Latin poet and translator of Greek origin, was born early in the third century B.C. at Tarentum (the Greek Taras, now Taranto) in southeastern Italy, and died in about 204. When the Romans captured that city in 272, they brought him as a prisoner of war to Rome, where he was later freed by his owner, a member of the Livian house, whose family name he added to his original name Andronicus. He earned his living as a teacher of Greek literature and was apparently the first, or one of the first, who ever engaged in such an occupation.

His writings, of which only fragments have survived, broke entirely new ground. His main work was the *Odusia,* an adaptation into Latin of Homer's *Odyssey,* apparently intended as a schoolbook; forty-six scattered lines are still extant. As far as we are aware, no such renderings of Greek literature into Latin had ever been attempted before. The meter (Saturnian) was heavy in comparison with the flow of the original Homeric hexameter, and Cicero and Horace subsequently regarded the whole production as crude—but they were writing in terms of later literary conventions. The *Odusia* was evidently a work not only remarkably original in concept (and in execution, too, since it included a good deal of material inserted on Livius' own account) but carried out with skill and force.

Livius also led the way in another epoch-making development. For, at the Roman Games (Ludi Romani) of 240 B.C., at the request of the official (aedile) in charge, he composed the first Latin play or plays ever to be staged at Rome, a tragedy and perhaps also a comedy, once again adapted from Greek models that he had probably seen performed at Tarentum. After this inauguration of Roman drama, he continued to write and produce tragic and comic plays alike from 235 onward, in competition with the poet Naevius. Forty lines of his tragedies have survived, and eight of their titles. They are *Achilles, Aegisthus, Ajax the Whip-Bearer (Mastigophorus), Andromeda, Danae, Hermione, Tereus,* and *The Trojan Horse.* The *Ajax* is based on Sophocles' play; the others go back to Sophocles or Euripides, or

liv' i us an drō nī' kus

dramatists of later date. The *Trojan Horse* echoes the special interest the Trojan legends held for the Romans, who liked to believe that their race had originated from Troy. Fragments of the play suggest that Livius dispensed with the Greek choral odes but increased the number of chants or *cantica* interspersed with the actor's speaking parts, so that Roman tragedy had moved in the direction of modern opera. Livius skillfully adapts the Greek iambic (short-long) and trochaic (long-short) meters, perhaps drawing on popular borrowings of an earlier date. His plays continued to be performed for many years, though remarks by Cicero indicate that, by his time, only erudite people still knew them at first hand. Livius' comedies do not seem to have enjoyed the same success. The titles which have come down to us, *The Swashbuckler(?) (Gladiolus)* and *The Gambler (Ludius)* suggest that he was adapting models of the Athenian New Comedy of Menander and others.

Although many of the anecdotes relating to Livius are unreliable, it is possible to accept the report that he acted in his own plays to begin with, but subsequently, after his voice had failed, employed a boy hidden behind the scenes to pronounce the lines, while he himself provided an accompaniment in the form of gestures.

In 207 B.C., during the latter stages of the Second Punic War, Livius also wrote a hymn that is now lost. The occasion arose when the priestly college, after consulting the Sibylline Oracles, decreed that in order to ward off menacing omens a procession of twenty-seven maidens should chant a hymn praying for divine intercession; and the poet commissioned to compose the work was himself. Although the historian Livy (c. 59 B.C.–c. A.D. 12), in later and more sophisticated days, dismissed this poem as rough and uncouth, it was evidently much admired in his own day. Indeed, from that time onward, the temple of Minerva on the Aventine Hill was set aside as the place where writers and actors could hold meetings and present votive dedications. And so, through the achievement of Livius Andronicus, who had made such an enormous pioneer contribution to Latin literature, poetry itself received official recognition from the Roman authorities.

EDITIONS—O. Ribbeck, Scaenicae Romanorum Poesis Fragmenta, v 1 and v 2, 1897, 1962; A. Klotz, Scaenicorum Romanorum Fragmenta, v 1, 1953. *With translation:* E. H. Warmington, Remains of Old Latin, v 2, 1936.
ABOUT—E. Fraenkel, *in* Real-Encyclopädie der klassischen Altertumswissenschaft, Suppl. v 5, columns 598ff.; S. Mariotti, Livio Andronico e la traduzione artistica, 1952; W. Beare, The Roman Stage, 3rd ed. revised, 1969; G. Broccia, Ricerche su Livio Andronico epico, 1974; J. Wright, Dancing in Chains, 1974; M. Verrusio, Livio Andronico e la sua traduzione dell' Odissea omerica, 1977.

LIVY (Titus Livius), Latin historian, was probably born in about 59 B.C. and died in about A.D. 12, though it is sometimes supposed that both these dates should be brought forward by five years. His birthplace was Patavium (Padua) in northern Italy (Cisalpine Gaul). Very little is known about his life, but it is evident that he moved at an early age to Rome, where he gave readings of his work that gained him a large reputation in literary circles. Augustus showed an interest in his historical project and allowed him to encourage the future emperor Claudius in his historical studies.

The enormous dimensions of Livy's *History of Rome* must have meant that he spent most of his life at his desk, either at the capital or at Patavium. His renown is illustrated by the story of a man who came all the way from Gades (Cadiz) in Spain in order to see him. According to Quintilian, Livy had a son, who may perhaps be identifiable with a geographer cited by Pliny the Elder; if the Titus Livius mentioned on an inscription of this period from Patavium is the historian, he was the father of a second boy as well. Seneca the Younger states that he also had a daughter, who was married to a rhetorician named Lucius Magius. Livy died at his native Patavium.

The *History of Rome* comprised 142 books: 35 survive, namely 1-10 and 21-45, covering the periods 753–243 B.C. and 219–167 B.C. respectively. Of the lost books we have fragments and excerpts; and there are

liv' i

also two sets of résumés (epitomes). Parts of the work were roughly divided into groups of ten books—called decades—each of which subdivided in turn into two halves or pentads.

The preface declares the grandeur of the subject, expresses diffidence about the author's ability to handle it, laments the decline of Rome in its most recent period, and offers a warning about the unverifiable character of its earliest history. Book 1 deals with the mythical story of Aeneas and the epoch of the Roman kings (traditionally 753 –510 B.C.), culminating in the establishment of the Republic. Book 2 (509–477 B.C.) tells the legendary sagas of the early Republic, describes the first resistance of the plebeians to patrician rule, and reports Rome's defeat by Veii on the River Cremera. Book 3 records the Law of the Twelve Tables (451– 450) and the fall of its promoters (the decemvirs), notably Appius Claudius, who was guilty, according to the myth of the rape of Virginia. Book 4 narrates the death of the would-be tyrant Maelius and the seizure of the town of Fidenae from Veii. In the following book the town succumbs to the Romans though Rome shortly afterward fell briefly to the Gauls under Brennus. Books 6 and 7 continue the tales of internal social and constitutional struggles and external Italian wars, until, in Book 8, Rome finally defeats the Latins (338). The wars against the Samnites of central Italy form a main theme of Books 7-10.

The lost second decade of the work (Books 11-20) was divided into two halves. The first pentad reached the termination of the war against King Pyrrhus of Epirus (272), and the other covered the First Punic War (264–241) and the events leading up to the Second (218–201), which forms the theme of the third decade. At the beginning of Book 31 Livy inserted a new preface, necessitated by Rome's imperial expansion now opening up before him. This pentad and the two that follow cover the wars of the early second century B.C., down to 192, 179, and 167 respectively. Of the portions of the *History* that dealt with later periods, nothing has survived, except in the epitomes; but it appears that the arrangement by decades and pentads was now modified in some parts of his narrative. The destruction of Carthage (146) was recorded in the fifty-first Book; Tiberius Gracchus' attempts at constitutional reform in the fifty-seventh; Marius' defeat of the German Cimbri and Teutones in the sixty-eighth; and the beginning of the Marsian or Social War (Italian revolt) in the seventy-first. Marius was the central figure of three books, and Sulla of the two that followed. The division into decades was reasserted by their deaths, which were recorded in Books 80 and 90 respectively. But thereafter, a less symmetrical arrangement was reverted to, and events were dealt with in greater detail. Julius Caesar's career, from his first consulship in 59 B.C. until his death fifteen years later, occupied Books 103-16, with his defeat of Pompey at Pharsalus in the hundred-and-first book, and the murder of Pompey in the hundred-and-twelfth. Books 109-16 were at some point given the separate title of the *Civil Wars*.

The next five books were limited to the twenty months following the assassination of Caesar. The victory of Octavian (the future Augustus) over Antony and Cleopatra at Actium (31 B.C.) was described in Book 133. The next book seems to have contained an indication that everything that came afterward was supplementary to Livy's original intention. Books 136 and 137 (of which the abridgments are missing) appear to have dealt chiefly with military operations on the imperial frontiers, conducted in large part under the leadership of Augustus' stepsons, Tiberius and Nero Drusus (Drusus the Elder), whose death in 9 B.C. was related in the final book, 145.

Livy quotes his sources more often than most Greek or Roman historians; and when he makes an assertion, he often adds a qualification, so that it shall not be too sweeping and misleading. He frequently shows a healthy distrust of dubious evidence and tries to select material that is plausible and appropriate. For all these reasons, Dante called him "Livy who errs not."

Dante's verdict seems a false one today; and some might agree instead with the emperor Caligula's assessment of the historian: "Long-winded and careless." Furthermore, his unremitting literary activity precluded any practical experience of public life, so

that his knowledge of Roman institutions was patchy. Livy's first ten books, at least, are not history at all but myth—a fact of which he was not altogether unaware. To many readers, this section of his history seems its very best part, because Livy's gifts were essentially of a romantic and poetic nature; he is not so much a historian as an epic poet in prose. He is also a moralist: the demands of history, as we understand them, are thwarted by his strong adherence to the ancient custom of seeing history in moralistic terms. Indeed, his main aim—served, for example, by the insertion of numerous, eloquent, fictitious speeches—is to draw moral lessons from the past to serve the present. These lessons, however, are of a specialized nature, harnessed to an overriding purpose. This purpose was the greater glory of Rome (its early brutalities being glossed over) and the glory of Italy too (now taking shape as an emotional concept). It is as the panegyrist of Rome and Italy that Livy finds his most memorable expression. He himself, coming from northerly Patavium, felt all the patriotic emotions characteristic of a frontiersman, and when the contemporary historian Pollio (76 B.C.–A.D. 4/5) sneered at him for *Patavinitas* he meant that Livy seemed to him provincial.

His books concerning the time of Augustus are lost, but, as we can detect from allusions and foreshadowings earlier in the work, the emperor evidently won his admiration. Yet Livy's preface shows a remarkable detachment from Augustus' current reforms, and he is known to have written respectfully even of Brutus and Cassius, who had fought on the other side at Philippi and who had killed the deified Julius Caesar, the adopter of Augustus. An anecdote records that Augustus half-jokingly called Livy "Pompeian"—a backer of Caesar's enemy Pompey. All the historian's reverence for the Republic and its protagonists was permissible, because Augustus himself claimed not to be an autocrat but the restorer of the Republic.

Livy's *History of Rome* adds up to an imaginative achievement of great grandeur, nothing less than the reconstruction of eight centuries of Rome's greatness. He carried this enormously ambitious project to a successful conclusion because he was a supreme master of the Latin language. His prose was worthy of Cicero's but more subtle, more malleable, and more lyrical. In the course of a powerful eulogy, Quintilian speaks of the "milky abundance" of the Livian style, *milky* indicating not only richness but purity; and he even asserts Livy's equality with the Father of History, Herodotus himself. Other writers of the early empire, too, expressed their admiration for his massive feat. But it is significant that the poet Martial declares that he had not room for the whole work in his library: It was because of its immense size that skeleton summaries or epitomes began to be published, with the result that large parts of the original work could, after a time, no longer be found. In the fourteenth century Petrarch managed to collect twenty-nine of its books; the five others that we possess were not rediscovered for nearly another two hundred years.

Machiavelli (d. 1527) wrote *Discourses on the First Decade of Livy;* and his account of the youthful Roman Republic was a favorite sourcebook of the French Revolution. A selection of speeches in Livy's *History,* translated by Rousseau, served as models for the orators of the day. Moreover, his classic, legendary heroes took on a new lease of life once again in Thomas Babington Macaulay's *Lays of Ancient Rome* (1842); and nineteenth century educationalists, concerned with the training of an elite, found him fascinating. Throughout all these centuries, he has been Europe's principal textbook to Roman history and principal guide to how the Romans thought and acted and accomplished their enormous feats.

EDITIONS—W. Weissenborn, H. J. Müller, and O. Rossbach, 2nd ed., 1880, reprint 1962; R. M. Ogilvie, Books 1-5, 1965; J. Briscoe, Books 31-33, 1973; *also* editions of individual books. *Translations*—B. O. Foster, F. G. Moore, E. T. Sage, A. C. Schlesinger (Loeb ed.), 1919–67; A. de Selincourt (Penguin ed.), Books 1-5, 1960, Books 21-30, 1965; H. Bettensen, Books 31-45, 1976; J. Bayet, G. Baillet, R. Bloch, G. Vallet, A. Hus, P. Jal (Budé ed.), 1940–76.
ABOUT—H. Hoch, Die Darstellung der politischen Sendung Roms bei Livius, 1951; I. Kajanto, God and Fate in Livy, 1957; P. G. Walsh, Livy: His Historical Aims and Methods, 1961, *and* Livy (Greece & Rome: New Surveys in the Classics, no 8), 1974; R. Bloch, Tite-Live et les premiers siècles de Rome, 1965; M.

Mazza, Storia e ideologia in Livio, 1966; E. Burck, ed., Wege zu Livius, 1967; D. W. Packard, Concordance to Livy, 1968; E. Pianezzola, Traduzione e ideologia: Livio interprete di Polibio, 1969; M. Grant, The Ancient Historians, 1970; T. A. Dorey, ed., Livy, 1971; G. Wille, Der Aufbau des livianischen Geschichtswerks, 1973; L. Bessone, La tradizione liviana, 1977; T. J. Luce, Livy: The Composition of His History, 1977; H. Tränkle, Livius und Polybios, 1977.

LONGINUS is the name traditionally assigned to the Greek literary critic who wrote the treatise entitled *On the Sublime (Peri Hupsous),* of which about two-thirds have survived. The first surviving manuscript, of the tenth century A.D., headed the work "Dionysius Longinus," and the earliest printed editions, from 1554 onward, followed the same attribution. However, the index to the manuscript had read "Dionysius *or* Longinus." That caused the writer to be identified either with Dionysius of Halicarnassus, of the Augustan period, or with Cassius Longinus (c. A.D. 213–73), the rhetorician and philosopher who was chief adviser to Queen Zenobia of Palmyra. But both these identifications are incorrect, the former on grounds of style and substance alike and the latter because the treatise answers a work on the same subject by the freedman Caecilius of Kale Acte (Caronia) in Sicily, who lived in the Augustan epoch. It must be concluded, therefore, that the author of *On the Sublime* lived in the earlier part of the first century A.D.; but we cannot say who he was.

The word in his title translated as *sublime* denotes the expression of a great spirit, the distinction and elevation which enable authors to win justified fame. Longinus regarded as inadequate Caecilius' treatment of sublimity as primarily stylistic in character. Moreover, Caecilius had dealt with the concept by a purely technical set of rules, failing, for example, to give weight to the emotional factor.

After a formal preface, Longinus launches straight into an attack on what he describes as false and pretentious sublimity: within this category he includes everything that is merely bombastic, or sentimental, or
lon jĭ′ nus

frigid, or based on fatuous and pedantic conceits. Then comes the main body of the essay, which identifies five sources of what is authentically sublime. Two of these are mainly innate. The first and foremost is grandeur of thought, the power to form noble conceptions, which is conferred by qualities of soul and character; Longinus offers illustrations from Homer and the Book of Genesis, thus becoming the first pagan to quote the Old Testament (which he may have learned about from Caecilius, who was of Jewish extraction). The second of his sources of sublimity is vehement and inspired emotion, a theme which Longinus does not develop, promising to deal with it more extensively in a separate work (though he probably said something more about it in the sections of *On the Sublime* that are missing). His remaining three sources depend on skill: the effective employment of stylistic and rhetorical figures, fine diction and phrasing, and impressive composition: that is to say, the most appropriate arrangement of words, the apt use of rhythm and euphony, and the preservation of organic unity.

The author of *On the Sublime* is a critic of exceptional caliber. His one and only criterion is excellence—and by this he means the excellence of gigantic, mighty rivers, not of diminutive streams. In identifying its elements and communicating his keen enthusiasm to his readers, he shows outstanding acumen, casting abundant light on what constitutes literary merit. Moreover, his skillful choice of quotations from classical literature, together with the penetration and concreteness of the analyses to which he submits them, place him in the forefront of practical as well as speculative critics. He is also deeply concerned with the moral and social functions of literature. Is the contemporary dearth of sublime writers, he asks, due to the autocratic political system of the Roman empire? He answers that it is not but is due to the desire for money and to the pursuit of popularity that comes all too easily and cheaply.

The treatise received no mention, as far as we are aware, from any subsequent writer of the ancient world; it was far ahead of its time. But ever since it was first printed in 1554, and especially since it was translated into French by the critic and poet Nicolas Boileau in 1674, it has probably proved the most influential single work of literary criticism of all time. John Dryden, seventeenth century poet laureate and historiographer, became its first popularizer in Britain; it received high praise from the eighteenth century English historian Edward Gibbon; and its writer's understanding of the values of great poetry makes a direct appeal to the modern mind.

EDITIONS—D. A. Russell, 1965. *Translations*—W. Rhys Roberts, 2nd ed., 1907; G. M. A. Grube, 1957; T. S. Dorsch, Classical Literary Criticism (Penguin ed.), 1965.
ABOUT—J. W. H. Atkins, Literary Criticism in Antiquity, 1934; T. R. Henn, Longinus and English Criticism, 1934; S. H. Monk, The Sublime, 1935; M. H. Abrams, The Mirror and the Lamp, 1953; J. Brody, Boileau and Longinus, 1958; H. D. Blume, Untersuchungen zu Sprache und Stil der Schrift Peri Hupsous, 1963; W. Buhler, Beiträge zur Erklärung der Schrift vom Erhabenen, 1964; G. M. A. Grube, The Greek and Roman Critics, 1965; J. M. Crossett and J. A. Arieti, The Dating of Longinus, 1975.

LONGUS was a Greek novelist. Comparisons based on the symmetry and other devices of his style suggest that he lived early in the third century A.D. To judge from his descriptions of the island of Lesbos, that was probably his place of origin.

His only extant work, *Daphnis and Chloe,* is a pastoral romance. The hero and heroine (like many real children in the ancient world) were exposed to die by their parents at birth, but they were discovered and adopted by foster parents, whose flocks they tended together throughout their childhood. The customary novelistic themes of piracy, warfare, unwanted suitors, and fierce kidnappers are duly introduced into the plot, but with a difference from other romancers: in Longus' story they rank only as secondary issues, impinging in incidental fashion upon a world that is fundamentally bucolic and idyllic. The boy and girl are in love with one another; but they do not know what this means and have no idea what to do about it. In due course, however, Daphnis is instructed in the necessary sexual techniques by an older woman. Finally he and his beloved

long' gus

257

Chloe are reunited with one another and with their respective parents, who turn out to be rich citizens of Mitylene, the principal town of Lesbos. They marry—and presumably live in happiness ever afterward.

Daphnis and Chloe, entitled by one manuscript "the Pastorals of Lesbos," is the only surviving pastoral prose romance from the ancient world, and many believe that it was the first ever written. Like the pastoral poets Theocritus and Virgil, who preceded him, Longus approaches the countryside in a sophisticated spirit of nostalgia; indeed, he himself proclaims this artificiality at once by defining his scene as the literary pendant of a painted picture. This elaborate Arcadian background, only briefly intruded upon by the events of the narrative, is a kind of laboratory, far away from the world, in which the hero and heroine can be observed, under the guidance of the rural divinities who preside over this Golden Age.

The insipidity inherent in this approach is avoided by the introduction of a certain ironic tang: an implied contrast between the idyllic rusticity and the world outside. The rococo Arcadia, while seen as a gracious ideal, is also looked upon as something of a joke. Longus continues to mock gently at the conventions he has chosen to adopt. His romance of true love's springtime is pseudo-naive and sometimes flippant; its detailed account of the hero's and heroine's ignorance of how to make love is written with a certain prurience.

Despite the satire in *Daphnis and Chloe,* there is a serious religious or philosophical undercurrent, for Longus sees Plato's Love (Eros) as the supreme cosmic force behind events, so that he even, as one of the characters is made to assert, "possesses greater power than Zeus himself." Thus, the plot unfolds in an atmosphere in which seriousness and levity are piquantly blended. Throughout, lapses into the ludicrous are avoided, a note of sincerity rings through the sentiment, bold realism is effectively introduced from time to time—all, thanks to Longus' gifts as a careful, graceful stylist.

During the centuries after its first appearance, *Daphnis and Chloe* came to be regarded as a romantic masterpiece. Monks indulged in surreptitious readings—one medieval manuscript of discreetly miniature size begins and ends with religious texts to facilitate rapid concealment—and the Byzantine scholar Michael Psellus found it necessary to advise novices to read more serious, classical works instead. Longus' work exercised great influence on the pastoral tradition of the Middle Ages. Furthermore, he enjoyed special favor among sixteenth century writers and courtiers, notably the English poet, statesman, soldier Sir Philip Sidney, whose *Arcadia* owes him many debts. Among his subsequent admirers were the eighteenth century French philosopher Jean Jacques Rousseau and the German poet Johann Wolfgang von Goethe (1749–1832).

EDITIONS—G. Dalmeyda, Longus: Pastorales (Budé ed.), 2nd ed., 1960; O. Schönberger (German), 1960. *English translations*—G. Moore, The Pastoral Loves of Daphnis and Chloe, 1924; M. Hadas, Three Greek Romances, 1953; P. Turner (Penguin ed.), 1956; P. Sherrard, 1965.
ABOUT—E. Rohde, Der griechische Roman und seine Vorläufer, 3rd ed., 1914, 1960; L. Castiglioni, Stile e testo del romanzo pastorale di Longo, 1928; F. A. Todd, Some Ancient Novels, 1940, 1968; B. Lavagnini, Studi sul romanzo greco, 1950; R. Helm, Der antike Roman, 2nd ed., 1956; B. E. Perry, The Ancient Romances, 1967.

LUCAN (Marcus Annaeus Lucanus), Latin poet, was born at Corduba (Cordova in southern Spain) in A.D. 39 and died in 65. His father, who was the brother of the younger Seneca, moved to Rome when his son was less than one year old. There Lucan received the best education, including rhetoric, at which he excelled, and philosophy, which he studied under the Stoic Cornutus. He went on to Athens to complete his studies but was recalled by Nero (A.D. 54–68), who gave him the office of quaestor and admitted him to his inner circle of personal friends. In A.D. 60, at the inaugural celebrations of the Neronian games, he won a prize with a poem in praise of the emperor. Subsequently, however, their relations became strained, until in 65 Lucan took part in a serious plot against Nero, generally known as the conspiracy of Piso. When the plot was

lū' kån

detected, Lucan was obliged to commit suicide. It was alleged that he had joined the conspirators from motives of embitterment because Nero had forbidden him to give public recitations of his poetry. But it is also probable that his Republican feelings had become outraged by the ruler's increasingly autocratic behavior.

Lucan wrote extensively, mainly in verse but also in prose, and the titles of many of his works have been preserved. However, only a few fragments remain of them, with the exception of the single extant poem on which his reputation is founded. This is the *Civil War (Bellum Civile)* generally known as the *Pharsalia* (after the decisive battle fought at Pharsalus in Thessaly), though the latter title is based on a misunderstanding of one of the poem's lines. The work deals with the war between Caesar and Pompey (49–48 B.C.) and carries the story down to Caesar's arrival in Egypt; then the poem abruptly stops, in an unfinished condition.

Beginning with an invocation, Book 1 assesses the characters of Caesar and Pompey and records the panic and portents at Rome at the outset of the war. Book 2 describes the character of Cato and the capture of Corfinium (Corfinio) by Caesar, followed by Pompey's evacuation of Italy from the port of Brundusium (Brindisi). In Book 3 we hear of Caesar's visits to Rome and Massilia (the Greek Massalia, now Marseille), and in Book 4, of his victorious campaign in Spain and the failures of Gaius Antonius and Curio in Illyricum and northern Africa respectively. The highlight of Book 5 is Pompey's farewell to his wife Cornelia. Book 6 narrates the campaign that followed around Dyrrhachium (Durrës in Albania), and Book 7 recounts Caesar's crowning victory at Pharsalus. The theme of Book 8 is Pompey's flight to Egypt, his assassination, and burial. Book 9 describes the march of his ally, Cato, through the deserts of northern Africa and records the arrival of Caesar in Egypt, where Pompey's severed head was delivered to him. Book 10 continues the story of Caesar's Alexandrian interlude with Cleopatra, until the poem breaks off.

Lucan's epic, unlike Virgil's, has a subject taken from authentic history—history that for its author had a fairly recent date. Unlike Virgil again, he deliberately dispenses with the gods and their interventions in human affairs, which had formed the traditional machinery of the epic. His chief historical source was apparently Livy (whose own books relating to this period are now lost); but Livy's already high coloring is heightened still further for purposes of dramatic presentation and Stoic-Republican moralizing. In particular Lucan abandons continuous narrative in favor of episodes and speeches selected for their impressive and illustrative character (occasionally they are pure inventions—for instance, a speech delivered on the eve of Pharsalus by Cicero, who was not even there. These episodes are frequently depicted with a harrowing, morbid, macabre ultrarealism that is reminiscent of the tragedies of the writer's uncle Seneca the Younger.

From the outset, critics noted that Lucan, who had received a rhetorician's education, wrote poetry of a markedly rhetorical character. The *Civil War* displays every possible rhetorical firework—in fact, this element is so strongly marked that Quintilian saw Lucan as a model for orators rather than poets. Lucan is outrageously spectacular; and at first reading his palpable exaggeration, untimely philosophizing, ponderous didacticism, and taste for massive digressions distract attention from his formidable merits. Yet, his rhetoric, despite the remark of Quintilian, is often elevated to the level of poetry. His abundant epigrams show all the incisive punch that the Latin language is capable of. His hatred of autocracy and its archpractitioner Caesar—a feeling that becomes more and more pronounced as the poem proceeds—is expressed with eloquence. If his poem has a hero, however, it is scarcely the man against whom Caesar was pitted on the battlefield, the unheroic Pompey, though the contrast between his services to Rome and his miserable end on an alien shore is brought out with fierce passion and grandeur. Lucan's hero, however, is rather the arch-Republican Cato, even if the portrayal of this inflexible, unflinching Stoic evokes admiration—not sympathy—from most readers.

Lucan's epic is today sometimes estimated a magnificent failure; but it has not been judged a failure throughout the centuries. In the Middle Ages the work enjoyed a mighty reputation—partly because it served as a historical textbook. The *Civil War* was often imitated by the early heroic poets of France, and more often still by the classical French dramatists. It also exerted great influence on the elevated diction of Elizabethan England. In the nineteenth century, the poet Shelley saw Lucan as a genius transcending even Virgil, an opinion he changed later, although he remained an admirer of Lucan's burning force and his hatred of tyrants.

WORKS—The titles of lost writings include: Iliaca, dealing with the death and ransoming of Hector (a juvenile work); Medea, a tragedy (left unfinished); Catachthonia, a description of Hades; Silvae *(Rough Drafts),* in ten books; fourteen *salticae fabulae* or libretti for the use of dancers *(pantomimi);* a poem in honor of Nero (see above); an extempore poem on Orpheus for a competition; epigrams; and at least three speeches, one on the Great Fire of Rome and two comprising an imaginary accusation and defense in a murder case of A.D. 58.

EDITIONS (of the Civil War)—C. E. Haskins (with introduction by W. E. Heitland), 1887. *With translation:* J. W. Duff (Loeb ed.), 2nd ed., 1969; W. Ehlers (German), 2nd ed., 1977.

ABOUT—P. Tremoli, M. Anneo Lucano, v 1: L'ambiente familiare e letterario, 1961; J. Brisset, Les idées politiques de Lucain, 1964; M. P. O. Morford, The Poet Lucan: Studies in Rhetorical Epic, 1967; D. Gagliardi, Lucano: Poeta della libertà, 1968; B. Marti, ed., Lucain (Entretiens Hardt, v 15), 1970; W. Rutz, ed., Lucan (Wege der Forschung, v 235), 1971; O. A. W. Dilke, Lucan's Political Views and the Caesars *and* Lucan and English Literature, *in* D. R. Dudley, ed., Neronians and Flavians, v 1, 1972; F. M. Ahl, Lucan: An Introduction, 1976; D. Gagliardi, Lucano poeta della libertà, 1976; W. D. Lebek, Lucans Pharsalia: Dichtungsstruktur und Zeitbezug, 1976.

LUCIAN, Greek satirical writer, was born c. A.D. 120–25 at Samosata in Commagene (Samsat in southeastern Turkey) and died after 180. Such information as we have about his life comes from his own writings and cannot always be taken literally. It appears, however, that his parents, who were not well off, apprenticed him to a sculptor, but that he soon quit sculpture in favor of rhetoric (though retaining an unusually keen eye for art). Although his mother-tongue was probably Aramaic, he spent

lū′ shən

some years in Ionia improving and perfecting his Greek and gaining a thorough familiarity with the principal Greek authors. He also studied rhetoric and subsequently adopted the profession of a rhetorician, becoming first a lawyer and then a successful traveling lecturer. He also visited Italy and held a lucrative teaching post in Gaul. At about the age of forty, however, although not abandoning the practice of public recitation, he began to concentrate on the brand of popular philosophy for which he became famous. During this time he made his home in Athens. In his later years, he accepted a senior post in the imperial administration in Egypt.

About seventy prose works (in addition to about ten regarded as spurious) are attributed to Lucian. They can be roughly divided into the following categories:

(1) *Rhetorical exercises.* These include two speeches named after Phalaris, tyrant of Acragas (Agrigento in Sicily) in the sixth century B.C.; in the first he sends his famous bronze bull to Delphi, and in the second a Delphian urges the people to accept the gift. Lucian also wrote a *Tyrannicide, Disinherited* (or *The Disowned Son*), *Praise of a Fly* and *A Slip of the Tongue in Making a Greeting,* this last being a mock-serious defense of a gaffe by which he had said "good-bye" to an official instead of "good-day." Most of these pieces are by no means dissimilar to the essays in popular philosophy ascribed to other writers (sophists) of the day, except that Lucian's pieces are rather more skillful.

(2) *Writings on Literary Subjects.* The *Trial Before the Vowels* and *Lexiphanes* both make fun of authors who affect an extreme Attic, archaic style; in particular, the latter piece ridicules those who have a taste for obsolete words, which they use in unnatural senses. *How to Write History,* though still jocular, offers criticisms of rhetorical and unoriginal historians and provides newcomers in this field with excellent advice. The *True Story* (which Lucian at the outset declares to be entirely untrue) is an entertaining parody of the very popular genre of travelers' tales and, in particular, of voyages to Utopia.

(3) *Popular Philosophy.* This category includes some of Lucan's best and most char-

acteristic work. Many of these pieces are in dialogue form, including the *Cock,* in which Micyllus the shoemaker is instructed, to his surprise, by his own bird, who in a former existence had been the philosopher Pythagoras; in passing, this piece directs criticism against the rich and their ways. This same distaste for the pointlessness of worldly wealth and pride recurs in many of the famous little sketches known as *Dialogues of the Dead.* In the same vein is *Charon,* about the ferryman of the River Styx, who offers his comments on the peculiar carryings-on of human beings; the *Descent Into the Lower World,* which describes a boatload of the dead and their reception in Hades; and the *Menippus* (or *Necromancy*) in which the Gadarene philosopher of that name (a Cynic philosopher who lived in the early third century B.C. and is often echoed by Lucian) has paid a visit to the underworld and describes what he saw there. The *Demonax* is a life of a contemporary Cynic philosopher, who is praised for his tough and austere virtue. Other sketches, however, are a good deal less patient with schools of philosophy and their adherents. The *Icaromenippus* stresses the fatuity of many philosophical disputes, the *Hermotimus* mocks the pretensions of all schools, especially the Stoics; the *Fisher,* however, explains that it is not the schools themselves but only their unworthy representatives who are being taken to task. In the *Philopseudes* the philosophers are maliciously made to narrate fabulous ghost stories. *The Ship* laughs at the folly of human wishes. In a number of these dialogues Lucian himself appears in thin disguise, as Lycinus or the Syrian.

(4) *Other Satires.* Another set of satires is directed against other people besides philosophers: for instance, The *Illiterate Book-Buyer* ridicules false pretensions to scholarship; the *Dependent Scholar* tells (like Juvenal) of the degradations suffered by hangers-on of the rich. *Dialogues of Prostitutes* are sketches containing numerous reminiscences of comic drama.

(5) The *Cross-Examination of Zeus* brings out the incompatibility of the doctrines of fate and free will. *Dialogues of the Gods* and *Dialogues of the Gods of the Sea* hold up to scorn some aspects of conventional myth-

ology, and *The Syrian Goddess* (written in the Ionian dialect and its authenticity not entirely certain) seems to be a parody of popular accounts of divine miracles. *The Liar, Alexander the Oracle-Monger* (Alexander of Abonuteichus in Pontus, a famous religious quack), and *Peregrinus* use greater virulence in attacks on contemporary religious aberrations and the charlatans who led them.

(6) *Miscellaneous Works.* The list of these attributed to Lucian includes a short novel *Lucius and the Ass,* which it may be right to ascribe to his authorship. The piece is evidently an abbreviated form of a Greek comic romance, probably entitled the *Metamorphoses,* of which an otherwise unknown Lucius of Patrae (in Greece) was either the writer or the narrator; Apuleius' story of the same name developed a fuller version in Latin. Lucian also wrote verse, including two burlesque tragedies (or two parts of a single one), *Tragic Gout (Tragicopodagra)* and *Swift-foot (Okypus),* a parody of Oedipus (Swollen-foot).

Lucian not only draws on the literature of the past but is a beguiling illustrator of the life and manners of his own age; his satirical handling of many contemporary but traditional ideas is neat, apt, and funny. He has no claim or desire to be regarded as a deep thinker—indeed, he holds no consistent philosophical position—but is concerned above all to make amusing points that will appeal to comparatively unreflective minds of the leisured classes. Yet he possesses a rich imagination and a bright and agile wit that are amply and adroitly displayed by the satirical dialogue form and style he invented or developed.

Ever since the Renaissance Lucian has considerably influenced many important European writings, including the *Praise of Folly* and *Colloquies* of the Dutch scholar Erasmus (who translated him extensively), the *Utopia* of English statesman and writer Saint Thomas More, the *Gargantua* and *Pantagruel* of the French humorist and satirist Rabelais, the English satirist Swift's *Gulliver's Travels,* and the works of French writer Voltaire.

EDITIONS—J. Sommerbrodt, 1886–99; N. Nilén,

261

LUCILIUS

1907– ; A. M. Harmon, K. Kilburn, M. D. Macleod (Loeb ed.), 1913–67. *Translated selections*—P. Turner, True History and Lucian or the Ass, 1958, *and* Lucian: Satirical Sketches (Penguin ed.), 1961; B. P. Reardon, Selected Works, 1965; L. Casson, Selected Satires, 1968; H. L. Levy, Lucian: Seventy Dialogues, 1977; M. Matteuzzi, Luciano: Racconti fantastici, 1977; C. Robinson, Lucian, 1979.

ABOUT—J. Bompaire, Lucien écrivain: Imitation et création, 1958; F. G. Allinson, Lucian: Satirist and Artist, 1963; H. Homeyer, Lucian: Wie man Geschichte schreiben soll, 1965; J. Schwartz, Biographie de Lucien de Samosate, 1965; G. W. Bowersock, The Sophists in the Roman Empire, 1969; B. P. Reardon, Courants littéraires grecs des deuxième et troisième siècles après J.-C., 1971; B. Baldwin, Studies in Lucian, 1974; V. Andò, Luciano critico d'arte, 1975; G. Anderson, Lucian: Theme and Variation in the Second Sophistic, 1976, *and* Studies in Lucian's Comic Fiction, 1976.

LUCILIUS, GAIUS, Latin satirical poet, was born in the earlier part of the second century B.C. at Suessa Aurunca (Sessa), a small town in Latium, near its border with Campania. He came of a wealthy and prominent family of Roman citizens. His brother was a Roman senator, his father may also have been one, and he himself was the great-uncle of Pompey. He was well informed in Greek philosophy and one of the best educated men of his time; he seems to have spent some time at Athens, where Clitomachus, director of the Academy (c. 126–110 B.C.), dedicated a book to him. At Rome Lucilius, enjoying the income from substantial estates, had friends and enemies among the best-known figures in the city's political life; he belonged to the circle of the politician and general Scipio Aemilianus, with whom he served in the cavalry at the siege of Numantia in Spain in 134–33. He retired to Neapolis (Naples) in 105 and was living there when he died; its people honored him with a public funeral, probably because he had supported Scipio against encroachments by the tribune Tiberius Gracchus' land commissioners on the rights of the Italians to occupy public land.

Lucilius put his opinions on a vast range of subjects into thirty books of verse, fragments of which survive, amounting to about thirteen hundred lines but not containing a single substantial passage. Turning to satire

lū si' li us

after his return from Numantia, he published what is now contained in Books 26-30 after 125 B.C. and Books 1-21 at some subsequent date—Books 22-25 being added to the complete edition after his death.

Book 1 included the description of a mock-heroic assembly of the gods called to decree the death of a certain Lucius Cornelius Lentulus Lupus, leader of the Senate (131), because of his shady and extravagant behavior. Book 2 presented a parody of the trial of Quintus Mucius Scaevola for extortion (119) and made fun of Titus Albucius who loved to speak Greek on every occasion. The third book gave details of a journey to Rhegium (Reggio Calabria) and provided the model for Horace's *Journey to Brundusium*. Book 4 seems to have included a contrast between urban luxury and rustic simplicity. Book 5 was in the form of a letter to a friend who had failed to visit Lucilius when he was ill. The sixth book was apparently the prototype of Horace's satire entitled *The Bore*. One of the subjects dealt with in Books 7 and 8 was sex. Book 9 not only raised literary and grammatical questions but also described the sights to be seen while walking in Rome. Book 10, which inspired Persius (c. A.D. 62) to embark on satirical verse, discussed literary composition, described a stormy wartime naval landing, and delivered a number of personal attacks against individuals. The eleventh book supported Scipio against a tribune who had prosecuted him in 140. Book 13, followed by Book 20, attacked excessive gastronomy (as did Horace in a later satire), and Books 14 and 16 continued to advocate simple living. The fifteenth book, after some discussion of horses, showed how philosophy can cure both superstition and avarice. Book 17, perhaps parodying Homer's *Odyssey*, praised Penelope and other beautiful epic heroines. Book 21 (not Book 16, as was claimed) was known as Collyra, the name of Lucilius' real or fictitious mistress. Books 22-25, in elegiacs, consisted, at least in part, of epitaphs for Lucilius' freedmen and slaves. Books 26-30, written earlier than the rest, are represented by a proportionally larger number of fragments. The twenty-sixth book opened with a dialogue in which he first defended his satiric poetry and then went on to satiize Quintus Metellus Macedonicus, a political opponent of Scipio; there is also a burlesque of tragic poetry probably directed against the early Roman poet and playwright Lucius Accius. Book 28 described a banquet of Athenian philosophers and the adventures of a Roman lover. The thirtieth and last book contained varied material, including the fable of the fox and the lion, a portrait of a hen-pecked and cuckolded husband, an attack on a writer of comedy, and praise of a general who was a "friend of the people" and is probably identifiable with Scipio.

Lucilius was apparently the inventor of poetical satire: that is to say, he was the first poet to offer the distinctive type of comment on manners, politics, and literature that the word *satire* still denotes. A ruthless and outspoken critic of every extreme, every sham, every crookedness that he could discern on the Roman scene, he was declared by Horace to have "rubbed the town down with salt." His onslaughts, by their very freedom, created a profound impression, though it is evident that sheer vituperation played only a minor part in Lucilius' conception of satire, which ranged over a far wider field. His work was intended to cater, he said, to readers who were neither too learned nor too ignorant.

Although he wrote in various meters, it was the hexameter, in particular, which he established as the characteristic meter of the new type of verse. This was the comparatively rough and uncouth sort of line already employed by Ennius. Lucilius, too, wrote unevenly and carelessly, and crudely—as Horace, despite all his debts to him, later pointed out. Yet Lucilius understood the Hellenistic, Alexandrian rules of diction, and his own personal contribution was a style that, for all its faults, was both powerful and flexible. In the first century A.D., Quintilian recorded that some of his contemporaries preferred Lucilius not only to all other satirists but to any other poet whatever. He was a writer on a massive, forceful scale—little short of a genius—and the disappearance of most of his work is one of the most lamentable losses in Latin literature.

EDITIONS—F. Marx, 1904–5; E. H. Warmington, Remains of Old Latin (Loeb ed.), v 3, revised ed., 1967; W. Krenkel, Lucilius: Satiren (with German translation), 1970; J. Lembke, Bronze and Iron (translation of selections), 1973; F. Charpin, Lucilius: Satires (Budé ed.), v 1, revised ed., 1978.
ABOUT—C. Cichorius, Untersuchungen zu Lucilius, 1908; N. Terzaghi, Lucilio, 1934; M. P. Piwonka, Lucilius und Kallimachos, 1949; I. Mariotti, Studi luciliani, 1960; V. Knoche, Roman Satire, 1964; M. Coffey, Roman Satire, 1976.

LUCRETIUS (Titus Lucretius Carus), Latin poet and philosopher, probably was born in 99 B.C. and died in 55, though St. Jerome favored dates some four or five years later. Almost nothing is known about his life. The only ascertainable fact is that he "hoped for the friendship" of the Memmius to whom he dedicated his poem—probably Gaius Memmius, praetor in 58 B.C., the son-in-law of Sulla and patron of the northern Italian poets Catullus and Gaius Helvius Cinna. It is uncertain whether Lucretius belonged to the aristocratic Lucretian clan (according to one theory, he was a landowner in Campania), or whether he may not have been, instead, a freedman who took his name from it. Jerome states that he became mad from an aphrodisiac and, after writing some books in lucid intervals, which Cicero later "emended," or edited for publication, eventually committed suicide. The story may, however, have been invented by hostile Christian writers who noted, and misinterpreted, the term *furor* (frenzy) applied to Lucretius in the first century A.D. by the poet Statius.

Lucretius was a convinced and ardent devotee of the Epicurean philosophy, which his poem entitled *On the Nature of the Universe* or *The Way Things Are (De Rerum Natura)* sets out to describe in six books.

Book 1, after an introductory invocation to nature's creative force Venus, sets forth the atomic doctrine of Epicurus, which alone, it is maintained, provides a satisfactory explanation of phenomena. Lucretius argues that the atoms of which the universe consists are solid, indivisible, and eternal and that they and space together make up the totality of what exists. Book 2 begins with an encomium of the blessings of
lū krē′ shi us

philosophy and goes on to deal with the motions of the atoms, reproducing Epicurus' theory that, instead of inevitably moving in a straightforward and downward direction, the atoms sometimes manifest a swerve or slant—which offers the possibility of human free will. After dealing with the shapes and other qualities of atoms, the book goes on to outline the Epicurean view that there is not one single world but many and then concludes with an account of the creation and annihilation of the atoms.

Book 3, after a preliminary panegyric of Epicurus, is concerned with the human soul, which is envisaged as material (though composed of extremely rarefied elements) and mortal, dying at the same time as the body. The greater part of the book is devoted to demonstrating this mortality and enlarging upon the folly of the fear of death. Book 4, opening with a picture of the Epicurean message that Lucretius hoped to propagate, is mainly concerned with the psychology of sensation and thought. The poet demonstrates that sight is effected by means of "images" coming from things and entering the eye. He discusses the nature of sensation and thought and deals with false inferences of the mind based on sensation—which is, in itself, infallible. At the end of the book he analyzes certain functions of the body, especially the passion of love—which he violently condemns.

Book 5 is devoted to the phenomena of our world. After another hymn of praise to Epicurus, and an attack on theology, Lucretius shows that the world had a beginning and will have an end. He describes its formation and discusses certain problems of astronomy. He then describes the origin of vegetable and animal life, the creation of humankind, and the early development of civilization.

Book 6, the preface of which is, once again, a eulogy of Epicurus, deals with miscellaneous phenomena—celestial and terrestrial. Among the former, Lucretius discusses thunder, lightning, thunderbolts, waterspouts, clouds, and rain; among the latter, earthquakes, volcanoes, the Nile, lakes and hot springs, the magnet, pestilences, and in conclusion the famous plague at Athens.

Although his Greek master, Epicurus,

had been calm and retiring, Lucretius is th[e] most fanatical of ancient philosophical writ[ers]. He contrives to present the doctrine [of] materialism, and of reliance upon the sense[s] not only with extraordinary dramatic powe[r] but also in verse that is a poetical and de[scriptive] achievement. Epicurus' unimpre[s]sively presented arguments concerning th[e] structure of the universe and his protest against fear of death and of the gods ar[e] converted by Lucretius into forceful on[slaughts] slaughts against those who cherish or en[courage] courage belief in such unwarranted terror[s] for dying, the poet declares, is irrelevant—i[t] brings no pain but is eternal sleep. Neverthe[less], less, he expresses the pathos of death in [a] passage that has awakened many subsequen[t] echoes; such are the touches of genius b[y] which he rescues and transforms the Epicu[rean] rean doctrine from drabness and aridity.

According to Lucretius, without reason which inspires Epicureanism and eliminate[s] the need for these pointless fears, all huma[n] activity and bustle is devoid of purpose. Ye[t] he is far from contemptuous of humanit[y] and its potentialities. Indeed, it is with [a] superb exaltation that he shares an[d] reaffirms the confidence of Epicurus in th[e] achievements and destiny of humankind[.] Lucretius' masterful restatement of the be[lief] lief that atoms do not always move along [a] predetermined course dramatically empha[sizes] sizes the possibility of freedom in a world [of] necessity. Lucretius also presents a highl[y] arresting reconstruction of the early histor[y] of humankind, told in terms of its wonderf[ul] achievements and giving highly articulat[e] expression to the humanism that had bee[n] inherent in the prose of Epicurus.

Instead of writing pedestrian Greek lik[e] his master, Lucretius creates Latin poetry [of] the noblest quality. Despite the power an[d] grasp of his scientific, inquiring intellect— an intellect without parallel among Roma[n] writers—he prefers to shelve careful philo[sophical] sophical argumentation in favor of vivi[d] concrete pictures presented in prodiga[l] abundance. He is an inspired poet who de[nounces] nounces with great violence what he doe[s] not like. Yet, like the Hebrew prophets, wh[o] do the same, he does not only denounce bu[t] pities as well: his great range includes no[t] only anger and irony but tenderness. More[over]

ver, his matchless eloquence compels per-
uasion for his beliefs, plausible and im-
lausible alike. Lord Tennyson reported
atherings to read the poetry of Lucretius at
hich everyone present was "carried away
nd overwhelmed by its poignant force."

Although Lucretius seems, at first sight,
) stand apart, he was not exempt from the
ifluences of his time—that is to say, he duly
rofited by living in an age when Hellenistic,
Alexandrian techniques were transforming
ie Latin language. His own majestic, sono-
)us hexameters were as far removed from
ie polite intricacies of the Alexandrians as
iey were from the later technical perfection
f Virgil. However, Virgil's debt to him was
ery considerable and seems to be acknowl-
lged in a fine tribute in the *Georgics*. Ci-
ero, too, praised both his genius and his
rtistry. In the first century A.D. Statius,
s we have seen, wrote of the towering
frenzy" of Lucretius; yet in ancient times,
s a whole, he made comparatively little
lark; and in the Middle Ages he was almost
ompletely forgotten.

Then, however, after the Italian humanist
oggio Bracciolini had acquired a manu-
cript of *On the Nature of the Universe* in
417, Lucretius' belief in humankind won
ie attention and admiration of Renaissance
umanists. In subsequent centuries, too,
1any passages of his poem, including par-
cularly his account of the beginnings of
ivilization, have attracted keen interest. In-
eed, it is he, not Epicurus, who has handed
own to the world the ancient atomic theo-
ies that are the forerunners, in a sense, of
ie atomic knowledge of today.

DITIONS—C. Bailey, revised reprint, 1950; K. Müller,
975; E. J. Kenney, Book 3, 1977. *Translations*—R.
atham (Penguin ed.), 1951; A. D. Winspear, 1955; R.
eer, 1965; J. H. Martinband, 1965; R. Humphries,
968; M. F. Smith, 1969; W. H. D. Rouse (Loeb ed.),
evised ed. by M. F. Smith, 1975; C. H. Sisson, 1976;
. O. Copley, 1977.
 BOUT—G. D. Hadzsits, Lucretius and His Influence,
935, reprint 1963; E. E. Sikes, Lucretius: Poet and
hilosopher, 1936, reprint 1971; G. J. Sullwood, Lu-
retius' Imagery, 1958; H. L. Bergson, Philosophy of
oetry: The Genius of Lucretius, 1959; U. Pizzani, Il
roblema di testo e della composizione di De Rerum
latura di Lucrezio, 1959; P. Boyancé, Lucrèce et
'épicurisme, 1963; L. W. A. Crawley, The Failure of
ucretius, 1963; A. D. Winspear, Lucretius and Scientific Thought, 1963; D. R. Dudley, ed., Lucretius, 1965;
R. Minadeo, The Lyre of Science: Form and Meaning
in Lucretius' De Rerum Natura, 1969; L. Perelli,
Lucrezio: Poeta dell'angoscia, 1969; D. A. West, The
Imagery and Poetry of Lucretius, 1969; P. H. Schrij-
vers, Horror ac Divina Voluptas: Études sur la poétique
et la poésie de Lucrèce, 1970; H. Ludwig, Materialis-
mus und Metaphysik, 1976; J. H. Nicholas, Epicurean
Political Philosophy: The De Rerum Natura of Lucretius, 1976; B. P. Wallach, Lucretius and the Diatribe
Against the Fear of Death, 1976; D. J. Furley and
others, Lucrèce (Entretiens Hardt, v 24), 1977; E. J.
Kenney, Lucretius (Greece & Rome: New Surveys in
the Classics, no 11), 1977; J. D. Minyard, Mode and
Value in the De Rerum Natura, 1977; M. Serres, La
naissance de la physique dans le texte de Lucrèce:
Fleuves et turbulences, 1977; M. Bollack, La raison de
Lucrèce, 1978.

**LUPUS OF FERRIÈRES (Lupus Ser-
vatus)**, Latin scholar and writer, was born in
A.D. 800 and died in 863. His birthplace was
near Sens in France; he was educated first at
the monastery of Ferrières and then at Fulda in Germany, where he became a pupil of
the Frankish scholar and theologian Hrabanus Maurus. He returned to Ferrières in
836. Four years later, through the intervention of Judith, wife of the emperor Louis I
the Pious, Lupus was made its abbot by their
son Charles II the Bald, king of the western
Franks (840–77), who became Holy Roman
Emperor in 875 and whose adviser in ecclesiastical and literary matters Lupus now
became. He accompanied Charles on an expedition to separatist Aquitaine, reformed
the monasteries of Burgundy, and was sent
as envoy to the pope.

His writings include biographies of saints,
a theological treatise, and a series of letters.
These sometimes launch into discussions on
grammar, metrics, and semantics; but they
also include some of the most entertaining
literary productions of the age. Lupus' letters display him as an ardent collector of
manuscripts; but he appears, in addition, as
a capable and courageous man of affairs,
capable of writing to the king in firm language when the interests of his abbey are at
stake and considering no detail too humble
for his personal attention. He also, on occasion, reveals a sly humor, for example when
he asks Abbot Marcward to send him two
loo′ pus fe ryâr′

265

blue cloaks and two white ones, but adds "if this request seems too steep, I shall not turn up my nose at half; for I possess enough of the world's wisdom to ask invariably for more, and hope for less, than I receive."

EDITIONS—J. P. Migne, Patrologia Latina, v 119; L. Levillain *in* Les classiques de l'histoire de France au Moyen Age, 1923– .
ABOUT—F. A. Wright and T. A. Sinclair, History of Later Latin Literature, 1931.

LYCOPHRON, Greek poet and dramatist, was born in about 320 B.C. at Chalcis in Euboea; we do not know when he died. He was the adopted son of Lycus of Rhegium, a historian. As a young man he was in touch with the philosopher Menedemus of Eretria (also in Euboea), who presided over symposia for poets and musicians. In about 285/3 Lycophron went to Alexandria, where King Ptolemy II Philadelphus entrusted him with the arrangement of the comic plays selected for the library. Ovid in his poem *Ibis* seems to imply that he was killed by an arrow.

He was regarded as one of the Pleiad, the name given by later Alexandrian scholars to the seven most eminent tragic poets of the time of Ptolemy Philadelphus. It was recorded that he wrote either sixty-four or forty-six tragic dramas, of which the names of twenty have come down to us. Fragments are extant of the *Menedemus,* a satyr-play (a form apparently favored by the Pleiad) that depicts the blend of elevated thinking and unseemly behavior that prevailed in the circle of his teacher Menedemus. Four lines from the *Children of Pelops (Pelopidae)* have also been preserved. Another of Lycophron's tragedies, *The People of Cassandreia (Cassandreis),* must have dealt with contemporary history, since the town of Cassandreia (the former Potidaea) in Macedonia was not founded until about 316 B.C. The play apparently dealt with the sufferings of the local populace under revolutionary leadership.

What has survived, however, is an iambic poem of 1,474 lines, the *Alexandra.* It is in the form of a messenger's speech reporting

ĭ' kō fron

266

to King Priam of Troy the prophecies of Cassandra (for whom the name *Alexandra* is a synonym) on the day that Paris set out for Sparta to seize Helen; her predictions cover a period down to six generations after Alexander the Great. The work is one of the most preposterous curiosities in the whole of ancient literature. This is due partly to the recherché material and partly to the mixing of many incompatible myths, but above all to the complexity of the language. Out of about three thousand words used in the *Alexandra,* more than five hundred are found nowhere else, and another hundred and seventeen appear there—as far as we know—for the first time. Moreover, every line of the poem is crammed with obscurities. Human beings and divinities and places alike are almost never called by their habitual, well-known names but are referred to instead by the most abstruse, remote, and far-fetched allusions. The amount of erudition and ingenuity lavished on this composition was enormous, and the fact that such a task could have won Lycophron a considerable reputation casts a significant light on the rarefied, erudite taste of the time.

The poem is valuable because its author shows considerable interest in the west, including Rome, about which he perhaps learned from the historian Timaeus (d. 260 B.C.). Indeed, the references to Rome's power are so explicit that some have felt that the poem, or at least these passages, belong to a period a good deal later and were written by a namesake or descendant of the tragedian Lycophron. Such conjectures seem unnecessary, however, since the tragedian was likely to have been aware of the Roman delegation that visited Ptolemy II in response to an embassy he had sent to Rome in 273.

WORKS—The titles of Lycophron's lost tragedies are as follows: Aeolides (or Aethalides?), Aeolus, Andromeda, Aletes (the Wanderer), Cassandreis, Chrysippus, Elephenor, Heracles, Hiketae (The Suppliants), Hippolytus, Laius, Marathonii, Nauplius (a revised version), Oedipus (two versions), Orphanus (The Orphan), Pentheus, Pelopidae, Symmachi (The Allies), Telegonus.
EDITIONS (of the Alexandra)—L. Mascialino, 1964. *With translation:* C. von Holzinger (German), 1895; G. W. Mooney, 1921; A. W. Mair *in* A. W. Mair and G.

R. Mair, Callimachus, Lycophron and Aratus (Loeb ed.), revised ed. 1955.
ABOUT—K. Ziegler *in* Pauly-Wissowa-Kroll, Real-Encyclopädie der klassischen Altertumswissenschaft, v 13, columns 2316-81; G. Walter, De Lycophrone Homeri Imitatore (Basel, dissertation), 1903; S. Josifović, Lykophron-Studien, 1957.

LYCURGUS, Greek statesman and orator, was born in Athens in about 390 B.C. and died in 324. He was a member of the ancient family of the Eteobutadae. Isocrates and Plato were dubiously asserted to have been among his teachers.

Lycurgus supported Demosthenes in resisting the expansion of Macedonia under Philip II but he himself only became prominent after Philip's defeat of Athens and other Greek states at Chaeronea in 338. During the twelve years that followed, while holding a variety of different offices, he controlled the entire finances of Athens, either directly or through his nominees, and managed to double the state's revenue. During the same period he carried through an extensive building program, reconstructed the docks, and enlarged the navy. He also passed a measure requiring that official copies of the plays of the great Athenian tragic poets, Aeschylus, Sophocles, and Euripides, should be made and preserved.

Lycurgus felt himself guided by a mission to improve the level of public and private morality in the city. A religious man of the loftiest standards, he demanded the same standards unremittingly from others. In support of this cause, he brought a number of indictments against persons whom he believed to have failed in their duty toward the gods and the state. These prosecutions were, in part, motivated by his political views, for he retained his strongly anti-Macedonian stance. (Indeed, he was one of the men whom Alexander the Great at first ordered to be handed over because of their hostility, though this was not done.) Lycurgus launched an attack against Lysicles, one of the generals at the disastrous battle of Chaeronea. He brought charges against others as well who had shown signs of defeatism after the engagement, including a charge of

lī kûr′ gus

treason against Leocrates in 331/30. Out of the fifteen speeches ascribed to his authorship in antiquity (all but one of them personal indictments of men supposed to have failed in their national obligations) this is the only example that has survived. Leocrates was a prosperous Athenian blacksmith of reputable family who, on hearing the news of Chaeronea, had panicked and fled to Rhodes in the company of his mistress. Subsequently, he moved to Megara, where he spent about five years working in the grain trade. Then, believing that the circumstances of his withdrawal from Athens should by now have been forgotten, he made his way back to the city. He had apparently broken no law by living away from Athens (true, he was said to have exported grain illegally, but no legal issue was made of this). Nevertheless, Lycurgus accused him, considering it his duty to prosecute for treason a man who had preferred to become expatriate when his country was plunged into crisis. While the first third of the speech, then, is devoted to proving the facts of the charge—no very difficult matter, since Leocrates was apparently quite candid about his flight—the remainder, couched in moralizing, patriotic terms, asserts the gravity of such behavior, citing abundant precedents from history and even more copious quotations from the poets (quotations that have preserved for us important passages we should not otherwise possess). It is a curious commentary on the ethics of the time that a man of such uncompromising rectitude as Lycurgus should rely on these extralegal, rhetorical methods to press his case. His sincerity and strength command attention, but his style, although distantly based on Isocrates, is inartistic and haphazard.

After his death, Lycurgus was accused of having left a financial deficit, which his sons were ordered to repay; when they failed to do so, they were cast into prison but subsequently released after Demosthenes had interceded for them. Within two decades of his death, however, his services to the state had received abundant recognition.

EDITIONS—A. Petrie, Lycurgus: The Speech Against Leocrates, 1922; P. Treves, Licurgo: L'orazione contro Leocrate, 1934. *With translation:* J. O. Burtt, Minor

LYSIAS

Attic Orators (Loeb ed.), 1954; F. Durrbach, Lycurgue: Contre Léocrate, fragments (Budé ed.), 1932; E. Malcovati, Lycurgus: Orazione contro Leocrate e frammenti, 1966.

ABOUT—G. Kennedy, The Art of Persuasion in Greece, 1963; A. Anastassiou and D. Irmer, Kleine attische Redner, 1977.

LYSIAS

LYSIAS, Greek speechwriter, c. 459(?)–c. 380 B.C., was the younger son of Cephalus of Syracuse in Sicily, a resident foreigner (*metoikos,* metic) of Athens who had settled there at the invitation of Pericles (d. 429 B.C.) and was portrayed by Plato in the *Republic.* After his father's death Lysias went with his elder brother Polemarchus to the new Greek colony of Thurii in southern Italy (founded in 443 B.C.). There he studied for a time under the Syracusan rhetorician Tisias; then he proceeded, according to Cicero, to teach rhetoric for a time. In the late 420s (rather than 413 or 412 as has been supposed) the brothers returned to Athens, where they conducted a successful business at the Piraeus as manufacturers of shields. But when Athens, defeated in the Peloponnesian War, succumbed in 404 to oligarchic revolutionaries (the Thirty), Polemarchus and Lysias were proscribed and arrested on account of their democratic sympathies and their wealth; Polemarchus was executed, but Lysias escaped and fled to Megara, though his property was confiscated. In exile, he backed the other banished democrats, and when their party returned to power in 403 he came back too. At the instance of the democrats' leader Thrasybulus, he was awarded full Athenian citizenship. Owing to a technical irregularity, however (the measure had not been presented to the Council before the Assembly), the conferment was declared invalid, and thenceforward, not being a citizen (though he remained in a favored category of resident foreigners), Lysias was disqualified from delivering public speeches in person. He decided, therefore, to make a profession of writing them for delivery by others instead; and between that time and his death it was believed that he composed more than two hundred orations (the attribution of lis' i ás

over four hundred was recognized to be exaggerated).

Thirty-four speeches survive: (1), *On the Murder of Eratosthenes:* Euphilus defends himself on a charge of killing his wife's lover for adultery (before performing the act she had locked her husband up in his room); (2), *Funeral Oration (Epitaphios),* for the Athenians who were killed in the Corinthian war against Sparta (395–386 B.C.). Since, however, Lysias was not a citizen at this time, he cannot have delivered this speech himself, and if its authorship was his (as, despite earlier doubts, now seems likely), it may have been a purely literary composition. (3), *Against Simon,* and (4), *On a Wound by Premeditation,* are both concerned with acts of violence performed in the heat of amorous rivalry for the possession of young slaves, a boy and a girl respectively. The narrative portion of the latter piece is lost. (5), *For Callias,* is a fragment of a speech defending a man of that name, a resident alien like Lysias himself, on a charge of sacrilege. (6), *Against Andocides For Sacrilege,* is probably not by Lysias and is not a speech but a pamphlet compiled by a democrat in response to Andocides' self-defense entitled *On the Mysteries* (399 B.C.) (7), *On the Sacred Olive:* a rich Athenian indignantly defends himself before the Areopagus court on the charge of uprooting the stump of a sacred olive on his farm, an offense punishable by banishment and confiscation of property. (8), *Accusation of Calumny Against Fellow Members of a Society,* is almost certainly not by Lysias. (9), *For the Soldier,* is also of doubtful authenticity; a certain Polynaeus defends himself against a charge of nonpayment of a fine. (10) and (11, which summarizes its contents) are *Against Theomnestus,* who is accused of having slandered the speaker by charging him with parricide. (12), *Against Eratosthenes* (not the same man as in speech 1), was Lysias' most important speech; he delivered it in person in 403, during the brief period when he was, or believed himself to be, an Athenian citizen. Eratosthenes, a member of the Thirty, is accused of having caused the death of Lysias' brother Polemarchus. The outcome of the case is not known. (13), *Against Agoratus,* likewise deals with the wrongdoings of the Thirty, for whom this man was an agent and informer; Agoratus is accused of responsibility for the murder of Dionysodorus, whose cousin and brother-in-law had been the actual killers. (14) and (15), *Against Alcibiades,* indict the son of the well-known politician and general of the same name (d. 404 B.C.) for desertion and evasion of military service. In (16), *For Mantitheus,* the young man of that name denies the charge that he served in the cavalry under the Thirty and says it would be unfair if his elegant clothes and manner were to be held against him. (17), *On the Property of Eraton* (c. 397), is a claim against the treasury by a creditor of Eraton, whose property has been confiscated by the state. Of (18), *On the Confiscation of the Property of the Brother of Nicias,* only the peroration has survived. Nicias was the Athenian general who was killed at Syracuse in 413 B.C. His brother, Eucrates, had been put to death by the Thirty, and his sons and nephews protest against the confiscation of his property. In (19), *On the Property of Aristophanes* (not the comic poet), the dead man's brother-in-law protests against a charge that part of the property had been withheld from the confiscators. (20), *For Polystratus,* is a defense of a man by one of his sons against some charge arising from an office he held under the oligarchic Four Hundred (411). Lysias may not be the author. (21) is the concluding (and only surviving) part of a *Defense Against a Charge of Taking Bribes.* (22), *Against the Grain Dealers,* is composed in the interest of the wholesaling community and attacks certain resident foreigners who as middlemen had bought wheat over the legally permissible quantity. (23) is *Against Pancleon,* who, when faced with prosecution, had claimed that he was a Plataean and not a resident foreigner of Athens—that is to say, not under Athenian jurisdiction. The speech argues that he was a runaway slave. (24), *For the Cripple,* perhaps Lysias' masterpiece, is a cunning and amusing defense put into the mouth of a dubious character charged with collecting a disability pension to which he was not entitled. (25), *Against a Charge of Subverting the Democracy,* denies that the speaker was involved in the misdeeds committed by the Thirty. (26), *On the Scrutiny of Evandros,* a speech made during an inquiry into Evandros' qualifications for an official post, seeks to incriminate him for participating in the Thirty's evil actions. (27)-(29), *Against Epicrates, Against Ergocles,* and *Against Philocrates,* are recapitulations of speeches prosecuting these men for the embezzlement of public funds. (30), *Against Nicomachus,* charges him not only with exceeding the time he had been allotted in order to undertake the revision of certain religious laws, but also with refusing, apparently, to render an account of how he had conducted his job. (31) is *Against Philon,* who, like Evandros in speech 26, is being scrutinized for public office. (32) is part of a speech entitled *Against Diogeiton,* that charges him with acting dishonestly to his ward. (33), *The Olympic Oration,* was delivered in person by Lysias at Olympia (where he was allowed to speak, as he could not at Athens) during the Olympic Games of 388. Unique among Lysias' speeches for its concern with international policy, it is an attack on Dionysius I of Syracuse, whose deputation was present. (34) is a fragment of a speech entitled *Against the Subversion of the Ancestral Constitution of Athens,* written after the reconstruction of democracy in 403 B.C. It denounces a proposal that the rights of citizenship should be restricted to those who possessed landed property. In addition to all these surviving speeches, a papyrus also provides fragments of another oration, *Against Hippotherses,* showing that Lysias himself was still involved, for years, in legal cases about his lost fortune.

The political attitudes of Lysias' speeches vary; although a confirmed democrat by conviction, he sometimes wrote for oligarchs as well, since as a professional speechwriter he felt entitled, within limits, to accept whatever commissions were offered him. He wrote beautiful, limpid, Attic Greek, with equal mastery over short sentences and long periods. He made no attempt to vary this diction to suit the different characters and conditions of the people for whom his speeches were going to be delivered. However, he varied their substance and manner enormously, to serve just this purpose; indeed, his most remarkable characteristic was his ability to shape these orations in just this way. Moreover, it is he (together with Demosthenes) who provides our fullest and most intimate insight into Greek private life and Athenian law.

Lysias was also said to have composed a number of pieces, now lost, which were not forensic speeches but academic rhetorical models *(For Socrates,* and *Technical Writings).* He also wrote literary letters, mainly of an erotic nature (compare an erotic piece in Plato's *Phaedrus* that purports to be Lysias' work). These minor efforts probably belonged to his earlier period as a teacher of rhetoric.

EDITIONS—C. D. Adams, Lysias: Selected Speeches, 1905, reprint 1970; M. F. Galiano, v 1, 1953; U. Albini (with Italian translation), 1955. *Other translations*—W. R. M. Lamb (Loeb ed.), 1930; A. N. W. Saunders, Greek Political Oratory (Penguin ed.), 1970; L. Gernet and M. Bizos, Lysias: Discours (Budé ed.), 1924–26; M. Bizos, Lysias, Quatre discours, 1967; L. Dal Santo, Lisia: Contro Ergocle, 1967; L. Rojas Alvarez, Lysias: Contro Eratóstenes, 1976; D. Alasia, Per l'invalido (For the Cripple), 1977.
ABOUT—F. Ferckel, Lysias and Athens, 1937; G. Kennedy, The Art of Persuasion in Greece, 1963; K. J. Dover, Lysias and the Corpus Lysiacum, 1968; A. Anastassiou and D. Irmer, Kleine attische Redner, 1977.

MACER, GAIUS LICINIUS, Roman politician and Latin historian, belonging to
mà' kĕr

a great and ancient clan, was born in the last years of the second century B.C. His powers as an orator secured him early admission into politics, and he became tribune of the people in 73. In this capacity he performed two actions that showed his strong partisanship for the cause of the *populares*—the politicians who were prepared to go straight to the Assembly and by-pass the Senate—against the pro-senatorial *optimates* who had the support of the dictator Sulla. First, Macer brought a charge against Gaius Rabirius, who had been responsible for the assassination of the *popularis* Saturninus in 100; next, he delivered a speech *In Defense of the Etruscans (Pro Tuscis),* the surviving fragment of which shows that it deplored the hardship caused to these people by Sulla's settlements of ex-soldiers on Etruscan lands. Macer became praetor in about 68 but then in 66, after governing a province, he was accused of extortion before a tribunal presided over by the praetor Cicero. He died suddenly in the following year, presumably by his own hand.

Macer wrote a history of Rome, in at least sixteen books, of which only fragments remain. The work began with the origins of the city, and the latest extant reference in the work is to king Pyrrhus of Epirus (297–272 B.C.). It has been supposed that Macer had brought his narrative beyond the third century B.C. at the time of his death. He not only shows himself a determined supporter of all the past actions performed by members of his clan and by its political allies—actions he was prepared to magnify and amend by gross fabrications—but he also shapes his whole history in order to extrapolate the current political tensions from even the remotest periods of Roman history, to the advantage of the *populares.* His philosophy centered on the sovereignty of the people; to him, the Senate was merely a deliberative council with a certain prestige, not the powerful instrument of government that Sulla had intended it to be.

It is clear that Macer's history was highly rhetorical; Cicero regarded him as a very competent orator, but too slick—and no great researcher. Nevertheless, as quoted by Livy, Macer made the interesting assertion that he had read and used certain ancient

Roman records, written on linen *(libri lintei),* that evidently gave lists of ancient state officials, including those of early Republican times. Modern opinions on the existence of these linen books have differed, some historians supposing that they were an authentic and important source, others maintaining that Macer's reference to them was a fraudulent fabrication and that they never existed at all. Perhaps the most probable conclusion is that the books existed and that Macer saw them but that instead of their being ancient records they were not compiled until the mid-second century B.C. when the use of personal last names *(cognomina)* that were quoted as part of their contents had become habitual.

EDITIONS—H. Peter, Historicorum Romanorum Reliquiae, v 1, 2nd ed., 1914; L. Pepe, Gli storiografi latini tramandati in frammenti, 1975.
ABOUT—R. M. Ogilvie, A Commentary on Livy, Books 1-5, 1965; P. G. Walsh, Livy: His Historical Aims and Methods, 1967.

MACROBIUS, AMBROSIUS THEODO-SIUS,

Latin scholar and prose writer, has been identified with the Macrobius who was governor-general of Spain in A.D. 399, and with the proconsul of Africa of the same name in 410, and with the imperial grand chamberlain of 422—or perhaps they were all the same man. The writer did not come from Italy, since he apologizes for a lack of Roman stylistic elegance; he may have been African. There is no evidence to suggest that he was a Christian.

The longer of his two extant works is the *Saturnalia,* in seven books, which has come down to us nearly complete. During the December feast of Saturn (the Saturnalia), a number of men of distinction and learning meet and talk at a dinner given by the Roman patrician Vettius Praetextatus, an antiquarian of repute. His guests include Servius, the commentator on Virgil; Rufius Festus Avienus (or Avienius) who wrote an adaptation of the *Phaenomena* of Aratus; Avienius (or Avianus), author of a Latin metrical version of Aesop's *Fables;* two members of the house of Albinus, notable

må krō′ bi us

for their worship of Virgil; Quintus Aurelius Symmachus, champion of conservatism and classical literature; Flavian the Younger, another public figure; and Evangelus, whose rough uncouthness serves as a foil to the urbanity of the others. At the dinner, their discussion covers a gigantic range of subject matter, so that the work falls into the tradition of earlier miscellanea such as those of Athenaeus and Gellius. Philology, history, antiquarianism, and science are ransacked to provide this mine of varied knowledge, much of it inaccessible to us from any other source.

Book 1 begins with a discussion of the Feast of Saturn and goes on to talk about slaves—who enjoyed special license on these occasions—and the calendar. Book 2 consists chiefly of a collection of witty remarks, ascribed for the most part to Cicero, Augustus, and Augustus' daughter Julia. The third book is concerned with various aspects of Roman religion and also discusses the luxury of earlier generations, especially in the gastronomic field. Books 4 through 6 form an important corpus of Virgilian criticism, foreshadowing the medieval conception of the poet as an infallible, omniscient figure (the fourth book dwells on his pathos, the fifth compares him with Homer, and the sixth lists his borrowings from earlier Latin poets, notably Ennius and Lucretius). Book 7, after a digression on jokes, turns to a series of questions relating to natural science —for example, are women by nature warmer than men? The answer is in the affirmative: They must be, because they wear less clothing.

Macrobius also wrote commentaries on the *Dream of Scipio,* the only part of Cicero's *Republic* that was known until nineteenth century discoveries. These commentaries depend for the most part, directly or through intermediary writings, on Porphyry's commentary on Plato's *Timaeus,* and they exerted a strong influence on philosophical studies in the Middle Ages. Macrobius also wrote a work of a grammatical nature, *On the Differences and Similarities of the Greek and Latin Verb (De Differentiis et Societatibus Graeci Latinique Verbi),* of which only fragments remain.

EDITIONS—F. Eyssenhardt, 2nd ed., 1893. Saturnalia (with translation): P. V. Davies, 1969; H. Bornecque and F. Richard (French), 1937; N. Marinone (Italian), 1968. Commentaries on Dream of Scipio: W. H. Stahl, 1952. On the Differences: H. Keil, Grammatici Latini, v 5, 1961.

ABOUT—T. Whittaker, 1923; K. Mras, Macrobius' Kommentar zu Ciceros Somnium, 1933; H. de Ley, Macrobius and Numenius, 1972; M. Bevilacqua, Introduzione a Macrobio, 1973; J. Flamant, Macrobe et le néoplatonisme latin à la fin du quatrième siècle, 1977.

MALALAS, JOHN, Greek historian of the early Byzantine age, was born c. A.D. 491 and died in 578. He was probably of Syrian origin and a native of Antioch and has been conjecturally identified with John III, Patriarch of Constantinople (565–77), who was of Antiochene origin. The name *Malalas* means rhetorician in Syriac.

Malalas wrote a universal *Chronicle (Chronographia)* in eighteen books, of which only a single continuous manuscript (of twelfth century date, now at Oxford) has survived, evidently in slightly abbreviated form. The work begins with the time of the Creation and ends with the reign of Justinian I (527–65). The original narrative may have come down to Justinian's first year; but then a continuation was added by the author himself—or perhaps by another hand, since Book 18 shows a curious shift from allegiance to the Monophysites (who believed that Jesus Christ had only one nature instead of two, human and divine) to more orthodox sympathies. Malalas is also a strong, if somewhat naive, supporter of the Byzantine monarchy. His work ranges widely, comprising Biblical history, Greek mythology, and accounts of Asian peoples, in addition to the political history of the Greeks, Romans, and Byzantines.

The *Chronicle* is a lowbrow production written for popular consumption. It throws important light on the interests of the semi-educated public for which it was designed. Confused in arrangement and content, it freely inserts remarkably absurd errors and introduces many transparent fictions, describing, for example, the personal appearances of wholly mythical figures. Nor does Malalas attempt to distinguish between im-

má la' làs

portant and trivial matters; yet he report them all alike with graphic verve. N. F Baynes set down a few of the *Chronicle* themes as journalistic headlines: Wonderfi Display of Shooting Stars: What Does I Portend?; Italian's Marvellous Performin Dog; Horrible Scandal in the Churcl Shocking Charges Against Well-Know Bishops; Audience With an Abyssinia King: Weird Etiquette of an Oriental Couri The White Slave Traffic in Constantinopl Royalty Intervenes; The Law's Delays: Ex emplary Punishment of Corrupt Barrister: Expulsion of Ballet Dancers: Special Favou Shown to Alexandria's Corps de Ballet.

Malalas was also very much concerne with the local traditions and happenings a Antioch, accounts of which play a leadin part until the transition in the last bool Indeed, local chronicles of the city were evi dently among his principal sources. He mus also have drawn upon official records, a well as on earlier general histories and an nals; and, consequently, the *Chronicle,* de spite its ludicrous weaknesses, yield significant information, providing man curious facts that would otherwise have re mained unknown. It was the first work o any significant dimension, as far as w know, to be written in the spoken Greel tongue, widely current in the East; this vul gate provided a vivid, racy medium for th preposterous effusions of Malalas, who als interlards it with many eastern and Lati terms.

Owing to its obvious appeal to popula taste, the *Chronicle* exercised a massive in fluence upon Byzantine, Asian, and Slavoni historiography. The large number of Slavon ic translations are of great assistance in re storing the original Greek text.

EDITIONS—J. P. Migne, Patrologia Graeca, v 97; A Schenk von Stauffenberg, Römische Kaisergeschicht bei Malalas (Books 9-12), 1931; Books 8-18 (Slavoni version), translated by M. Spinka and G. Downey 1940.

ABOUT—K. Krumbacher, Geschichte der byzantini schen Literatur, 2nd ed., 1897; G. Moravcsik, Byzan tinoturcica, v 1, 2nd ed., 1958; G. Downey, History o Antioch, 1961; K. Weierholt, Studien im Sprachge brauch des Malalas, 1963.

MANILIUS, MARCUS, Latin poet, lived and wrote, as his own allusions show, during the reigns of Augustus (31 B.C.–A.D. 14) and Tiberius (A.D. 14–37). About his life nothing known.

He is the author of the *Astronomica,* which sets out to explain the theory of astrology in Latin verse. The work contains 4258 lines but was probably intended to be longer, since the last of its five books breaks off abruptly. (Not only does it contain references to passages that cannot be found, but also the extant order of lines and passages sometimes seems incorrect and provisional, and important aspects of the subject, such as the movement and the influence of the planets, are omitted altogether.

Book I tells of the creation of the universe and the origins of astrology and describes the configuration of the heavens and the zones and circles into which they are divided; a survey of comets is appended. Book 2 analyzes the signs of the zodiac, their relationships to the gods and to the various parts of the human body, the loves and hatreds the signs were supposed to govern, and the different methods for subdividing them into categories. The third book gives a list of the twelve practical units *(athla, sortes)* that correspond to the twelve signs and that are the criteria for finding out how the signs apply to the lives of human beings. Next, Manilius sets out the rules by which horoscopes are determined, by discovering the position of the most significant points in a nativity; then he indicates the signs that govern each year, month, and day, listing the number of years of life each sign is able to provide, and records the four "tropic" (equinoctial and solstitial) signs. Book 4 notes what character traits are given by each sign and then embarks on details concerning their fractions and the effects of each. Then comes a digression on the different parts of the earth governed by each sign, followed by a section on the effects of eclipses. The book concludes with a defense of the hypothesis that it is possible to predict the future: human beings are related to the heavens and can decipher the implications of this relationship. Book 5 begins with an account of the signs that arise outside the zodiac, then turns to the number

ă ni′ li us

and differing magnitudes of the stars, at which point the poem abruptly closes.

Manilius writes with enthusiasm on his subject, astrology, in which such huge numbers of the ancients firmly believed. His purpose is to make converts and to provide practical instruction. His astronomy, however, is often inaccurate, and it is clear that he frequently misunderstands his sources (what these sources were, however, we do not know, though it is noteworthy that much of what he tells us is not to be found elsewhere). As a Stoic, he emphasizes the providential government of the universe and the operation of divine reason. He is by no means a major poet, though his verses do rise on occasion from banality to forcefulness. Unfortunately, he also takes pride in a curious capacity for versifying astronomical calculations, a practice in which he indulges to excess. However, the general reader can find something to admire in the prefaces to the various books and can enjoy Manilius' occasional showpieces and illustrations from daily life. His work has become widely known to classical students because it engaged the attention of three of the greatest Latinists—J. J. Scaliger, R. Bentley and A. E. Housman.

EDITIONS—A. E. Housman, larger ed. (5 columns), 2nd ed., 1937, *and* smaller ed. (text and critical notes only), 1932; F. Serra, 1975. *Translations*—G. P. Goold (Loeb ed.), 1978; Book 2 with notes: H. W. Garrod, 1911.

ABOUT—W. Gunkel and H. G. Gunkel, Die astrologische Literatur in der Antike, 1967.

MARCUS AURELIUS. See Aurelius, Marcus

MARIUS MAXIMUS. See Spartianus, Aelius

MARO, Publius Vergilius. See Virgil

MARTIAL (Marcus Valerius Martialis),
Latin poet and epigrammatist, was born at
Bilbilis (Calatayud) in Spain in about A.D.
40 and died in about 104. After receiving his
education in Spain, he came to Rome at the
age of twenty-four, where, apart from a brief
visit to Cisalpine Gaul (northern Italy) in
88, he made his home for the next thirty-
four years.

When he first arrived in the city, he hoped
for the protection of his fellow Spaniards—
the younger Seneca, Lucan, and other members of their family; but this connection
was almost immediately cut short by their
involvement in the Pisonian conspiracy
against Nero, for which Lucan and Seneca,
among others, were executed. Subsequently,
Martial's life in the capital was for the most
part poverty-stricken, involving dependence
on patrons whose generosity does not seem
to have been outstanding. He was able, however, to acquire a small farm at Nomentum,
a few miles from Rome, and in due course
received an honorary appointment to a senior army post (the military tribunate) and
secured other privileges. Moreover, he was
acquainted with a broad spectrum of Roman
society, including emperors, the leading literary personages of his day, and men and
women from many different social groups.
After the accession of the emperor Nerva
(A.D. 96–98), the younger Pliny paid for
Martial's return to his birthplace, where he
lived on an estate presented to him by his
Spanish friend Marcella.

Martial wrote fourteen books of poetry,
comprising 1,561 pieces (1235 of them in the
elegiac meter). His first publication known
to us is the *Book of Spectacles (Liber Spec-
taculorum),* which was written to commemorate the opening of the Colosseum in
A.D. 80 by the emperor Titus. About five
years later the *Xenia* and *Apophoreta* (now
Books 13 and 14) appeared: the former comprises 127 mottoes meant to accompany presents sent on the occasion of the Festival of
Saturn *(Saturnalia),* and the latter contains
223 more for gifts received and taken home
at the same season. Most of these pieces are
light and ephemeral.

The twelve books of the *Epigrams* proper,
which are his major contribution, were pub-
mär′ shəl

lished at intervals of about a year from A.D.
86 onward. Four of these books are intro
duced by prose prefaces. Some of these po
ems are epigrams according to the primar
meaning of the term—that is to say they ar
like inscriptions on graves or works of ar
Others are amusing anecdotes or caricature
—for example, the one about a man wh
wanted to borrow Martial's poems but di
not care to buy them. He excels at depictin
timeless and easily recognizable characte
and types: the fussy shopper, the dilettant
the philosophical servant, the flatterer, th
barber, the doctor, the collector of antique
the man who tries to hide his bald patch, th
woman whose hair is dyed or artificial. Ma
tial also produces some extreme obscenitie
—adding the traditional disclaimer tha
even if his writing is lecherous, his life i
clean. His subject matter is extremely va
ied, but perhaps its keynote, and his favorit
effect, is surprise: a stimulating confronta
tion with the unexpected.

Martial was the greatest epigrammatist o
the ancient world; and it was he who intro
duced to the form the point and wit tha
have given the term *epigram* its habitual an
current meaning. He takes pains to differen
tiate the genre from other forms of poetr
and claims that, for all its lightness and flip
pancy, it is capable of quality and merit fa
in excess of mere frivolities. Martial write
with pungency, ingenuity, facility, and pol
ish. His keen eye for the ridiculous enable
him to puncture social shams and make
him a formidable witness to his age. Al
though the epigram was admirably suited t
the contemporary Silver Age of Latin
which was so devoted to sparkling effect
Martial is the only poet of that age who i
wholly exempt from its rhetorical tenden
cies.

Many of his epigrams have an immediat
and direct sting. For example, like othe
writers of the day, he execrated Domitia
(81–96), when that emperor was dead; how
ever, until then he had treated him to ful
some flattery. A couplet directed against
certain Sabidius has achieved wide fame i
our own language in Thomas Brown's trans
lation written at Oxford in the seventeent
century: "I do not love you, Dr. Fell . . .
Other pieces combine abuse with unre

trained obscenity. But many more of his poems show that Martial was fundamentally a kind-hearted man with simple tastes, who appreciated natural beauty and possessed a sensitive insight into human behavior.

To call him the laureate of triviality, therefore, is not enough; but Hadrian's adopted son Aelius Caesar (d. 138) may have gone too far in the other direction (and was no doubt joking) when he described him as his Virgil. Yet Martial's influence on subsequent European literature has been enormous. The quality of his work was felt and acknowledged by the English seventeenth century poets Ben Jonson, Milton, Herrick, and Cowley. Moreover, his thirteenth book, comprising single couplets entitled *Xenia* (presents for guests) served as a model for the eighteenth century German poets Goethe and Schiller, who wrote similar *Xenien* to mock their literary enemies.

EDITIONS—L. Friedländer, Martialis Epigrammaton Libri, 1886. *Translations*—A. L. Francis and H. F. Tatum, Martial's Epigrams: Translations and Imitations, 1924; R. Humphries, Martial: Selected Epigrams, 1963; W. C. A. Ker, Martial: Epigrams (Loeb. ed.), revised ed., 1968; J. Michie, The Epigrams of Martial, Selected and Translated, 1972.

ABOUT—A. G. Carrington, Aspects of Martial's Epigrams, 1960, *and* Martial *in* D. R. Dudley, ed., Neronians and Flavians: Silver Latin, v 1, 1972; R. E. Colton, Juvenal and Martial, 1969; C. Salemme, Marziale e la poetica degli oggetti, 1976; E. Siedschlag, Zur Form von Martials Epigrammen, 1977.

MARTIANUS CAPELLA (Martianus Minneus Felix Capella), Latin writer, was living in northern Africa before its Roman government was overthrown by the Vandals in A.D. 429. He was a lawyer at Madaura (Mdaourouch in Algeria) and proconsul at Carthage; he does not seem to have been an adherent of Christianity, which he does not mention.

In his old age he wrote, and dedicated to his son, a work in mixed prose and verse, *On the Marriage of Mercury and Philology (De Nuptiis Mercurii et Philologiae).* The first two of the nine books present a story, in allegorical form, of the wedding of Mercury to a nymph called Philology. When Mer-

när ti ā′ nus kà pel′ là

cury, after deciding he wanted a wife, had considered and rejected a number of candidates (Sophia, Mantice, Psyche), he took the advice of Virtue and consulted Apollo, who recommended Philology, a "young woman of great learning." The bride is duly carried up to heaven, where each of the nine Muses welcomes her with a song; then, with Prudence, Justice, Temperance, and most of the other virtues in attendance, she appears before the celestial Senate and is raised to divinity. Procedures for obtaining this award and gaining Jupiter's consent are elaborately described. Apollo brings forward seven maidens, who are Mercury's present to his bride; they are personifications of the Seven Liberal Arts (the familiar curriculum of the schools)—Grammar, Dialectic, Rhetoric, Geometry, Arithmetic, Astronomy, and Music. The remaining seven books of the work present the long discourses that these bridesmaids deliver successively, in explanation of their respective specialities.

This allegorization is often carried to the point of absurdity and beyond. For example, Athanasia (Immortality), who is entrusted with the task of elevating Philology to heaven, is unable to do so until she has removed a burden from her stomach by disgorging a parcel of various books, which the Muses gather up. The purpose of this weird allegorical framework was to make the compendium of information that is the rest of the work more interesting—a worthy enough purpose since the facts that emerge from the lips of the Liberal Arts are little more than dry enumerations of technical details, mostly presented in elementary and superficial terms. Yet this mass of facts has value all the same, because in assembling it Martianus drew on a variety of sources, not all of them any longer fully available today, including Pliny the Elder, Solinus, Aquila, Romanus, perhaps Aristides Quintilianus, and Labeo or Varro or both. For instance, from one of the two last-named comes a rare piece of Etruscan lore that describes the sixteen parts of the heavens to which Jupiter sent his invitations to the wedding party.

Martianus believed that the written language should maintain an academically classical standard, although his own prose is pedestrian, involved, and verbose. Yet his book, however second-rate, was an encyclopedia of the culture of his time and a principal avenue for the transmission of that culture to future generations, for this far-fetched and heavy-going treatise became, startlingly enough, one of the half dozen most widely circulated books in the Middle Ages (from which many manuscripts survive) and contributed enormously to the shaping of European education. Upon it was founded the curriculum of the Seven Liberal Arts: once a medieval scholar had learned Latin from Donatus, Martianus was the principal, or only, school text. Mentioned by the Latin scholar Fulgentius (480–550), the *Marriage* was revised about a century after its appearance by the Christian rhetorician Memor Felix; it greatly appealed to the later Carolingians, became a sourcebook for logic, medicine, rhetoric, and allegory and was the subject of commentaries by the medieval philosopher and theologian John Scotus Erigena (ninth century) and others. In the twelfth century the work found favor with the School of Chartres, a major center of learning, and was recommended by leading scholars.

EDITIONS—A. Dick and J. Préaux (Teubner ed.), revised ed., 1978; J. Willis, 1979. *Translations*—W. H. Stahl, R. Johnson with E. L. Burge, 1971, 1977.
ABOUT—H. W. Fischer, Untersuchung über die Quellen der Rhetorik des Martianus Capella, 1936; F. May, De Sermone Martiani Capellae (ex libris 1 et 2) Quaestiones Selectae, 1936; R. R. Bolgar, The Classical Heritage and Its Beneficiaries, 1954; W. H. Stahl, Bibliography *in* Speculum, 1965, p 102ff.

MAXIMUS, MARIUS. See Spartianus, Aelius

MAXIMUS, VALERIUS. See Valerius Maximus

MAXIMUS CONFESSOR, Saint, Greek theologian and mystic of the Byzantine age, was born at Constantinople in A.D. 580 to a
mak′ si mus

noble family and died in 662. At the age of thirty he was appointed principal secretary to the emperor Heraclius (610–41), but subsequently led a monastic life at Chrysopolis (Üsküdar, Scutari), and later at Cyzicus (Bal Kiz), both in northwestern Asia Minor. After the Persian invasion of that area in 626, he moved to northern Africa, where he became the leading figure among the opponents of the Monothelites who maintained that although there were two activities in Christ—human and divine —there was only a single will. The emperor Constans II (641–68), however, was one of the adherents of this sect, and when Maximus moved to Rome he was arrested, tried and banished to Thrace (653). Later, in 662 he was put on trial again and sentenced to have his tongue cut out and his right hand amputated. After the sentence was carried out, he was exiled to Skhemaris in Lazica, at the southeastern end of the Black Sea, where he died shortly afterward.

The works of Maximus, written in lucid, flowing Greek, with very little attempt at unnecessary ornamentation, cover almost every main branch of theology; but he is particularly notable for his mystical writings, which provided the foundation for most subsequent Byzantine religious mysticism and contribute enormously to our understanding of Byzantine spirituality. Particularly admired was his *Four Centuries on Love* or *Charity (agape),* in which Maximus explains the multiple divine energies by which God is made communicable to men and reveals himself in creation. The work is divided into four "centuries," each consisting of one hundred paragraphs which range from two or three to twenty lines or more. It blends the dry speculative mysticism of Dionysius the Areopagite (Christian writer of the fourth century) with the practical requirements of the contemplative ascetic life. He also wrote a *Book on Asceticism (Liber Asceticus)* and other treatises on the same subject. His *Mystagogia* is an interpretation of the symbolic actions in the liturgical rites of the church; the *Ambigua,* an exposition of the teaching of St Gregory of Nazianzus, illustrates the author's complete command of the works of the principal fathers, among whom he was especially familiar with St. Gregory of Nyssa and Athanasius. Other writings by Maximus included the *Quaestiones ad Thalassium* (sixty-five answers to difficult questions of Scripture), commentaries on biblical texts, and a long series of essays on questions of dogma—all of these works demonstrating his trenchant powers of logical argument and his polemical debating skill. He has also left a large number of interesting letters.

Maximus has been described (not quite fairly, perhaps, to some of his successors) as the last truly independent thinker in the eastern church. Certainly, the influence of his writings was not restricted to the East, since the ninth century western thinker John Scotus Erigena translated the *Ambigua* and declared that he himself owed his own understanding of the influential works that go under the name of Dionysius the Areopagite (c. A.D. 500) to the expositions of Maximus, whom he described as the most eminent of teachers and as a philosopher who was all wise and divine.

EDITIONS—J. P. Migne, Patrologia Graeca, v 90-91. *With translation:* E. Kadloubovsky and G. E. H. Palmer, Four Centuries on Love (from the Russian text), *in* Early Fathers from the Philokalia, 1954; P. Sherwood, The Ascetic Life and The Four Centuries on Charity, 1956; A. Argyrion and I. H. Dalmais, Le mystère du salut, 1965.
ABOUT—A. Brilliantov, The Influence of Eastern Theology upon Western as Evidenced by the Works of John the Scot Eriugena (in Russian), 1898; S. Epifanovich, The Blessed Maximus Confessor and Byzantine Theology (in Russian), 1915; P. Sherwood, An Annotated Date List of St. Maximus, 1955; I. Thunberg, Microcosm and Mediator: The Theological Anthropology of Maximus the Confessor, 1965; W. Völker, Maximus Confessor als Meister des geistlichen Lebens, 1965; V. Croce: Tradizione e ricerca: Il metodo teologico di San Massimo il Confessore, 1974; A. Riou, Le monde et l'église selon Maxime le Confesseur, 1974.

MELA, POMPONIUS, Latin geographer, was born at Tingentera (Algeciras?) in southern Spain and wrote during the reign of Gaius (Caligula, A.D. 37–41) or early in the reign of Claudius (41–54). He seems to have had a rhetorical education.

His surviving work is a geographical survey of the world, *De Chorographia* or *De Situ*

mē′ lä

Orbis. The first of its three books describes the earth's division into hemispheres (north and south) and into five zones (two of which are temperate and habitable, but only the northern zone is known, the southern being an island of Antichthones or Antipodeans). Then follows an account of the relative positions and boundaries of the continents, of which Mela identifies three: Europe, Asia, and Africa. These continents, Mela maintains, are separated from one another by four seas—the Mediterranean, the Red Sea, the Persian Gulf, and the Caspian (mistakenly believed by him to possess a link with the northern regions of the ocean)—which in turn are arms of a greater ocean that entirely surrounds the land masses.

Following the tradition of Greek geographical works, Mela went on to describe the shores of the various seas—the interiors of the continents for the most part are neglected—indicating their cities and other principal features. He presents these in the order in which a traveler would come to them if he began from the Straits of Gibraltar (near Mela's home), sailed east along the shores of northern Africa, and then northward to the coasts of Asia Minor and the Black Sea. Europe is the subject of the two books that follow. Book 2, starting with Scythia, deals with the various countries bordering on the Mediterranean, proceeding westward from Thrace to Spain and then describing the Mediterranean islands. The third book considers the coastlands of the countries facing the outer Ocean: Spain, Gaul, Germany, lands farther north, and eastern Asia; the British isles and mysterious Thule; India, the Persian Gulf, and the Red Sea; Ethiopia and western Africa—Africa south of the equator is omitted.

More than fifteen hundred geographical names are recorded, and particulars of natural and climatic characteristics and local and regional customs are sometimes included; moreover, a short phrase is often added to indicate the special interest of the places mentioned. Mela's work is well arranged; his aim is to provide a popular, concise, readable summary, adorned by occasional excursions into rhetoric (in which he was trained) but making no claim to geographical originality or expertise. Indeed, his information is often palpably obsolete, ignoring facts that had been demonstrated generations before and must have been known to almost every educated person. For example, he gives the Danube a mouth on the Adriatic as well as on the Black Sea—in other words, he has never apparently heard of the empire's Danubian frontier and the immensely important territories that bordered upon the river. He must have depended exclusively on literary sources, and out-of-date ones at that; he cites no one later than Nepos (died c. 24 B.C.), and echoes of the geographical passages of Sallust (died c. 35 B.C.) are also to be found. Nevertheless, Pliny the Elder made use of Mela's work and so, occasionally, did later writers. The *Chorographia* was translated into Italian in 1557 and into English in 1585, by Arthur Golding, whose version influenced Shakespeare.

EDITIONS—G. Ranstrand, Pomponii Melae De Chorographia Libri Tres, 1971.
ABOUT—J. O. Thompson, History of Ancient Geography, 1948; M. Cary and E. H. Warmington, The Ancient Explorers, revised ed., 1963; P. Parroni, I barbari in Pomponio Mela, 1977.

MELEAGER, Greek epigrammatic poet, anthologist, and philosopher, came from Gadara in Syria (now Umm Keis in Jordan). He was born in about 140 B.C. and died in about 70. He lived at Tyre in Phoenicia (now Sur in Lebanon) and, in his later years on the island of Cos. It appears, from what he writes about himself, that he was trilingual, speaking Greek and Latin and Phoenician.

In about 100 B.C. he collected an anthology of poetic epigrams that served as a treasure house for later anthologists. Compilations of such a kind had been made before, but Meleager's was the first substantial endeavor to make a critical selection. It contained works by more than forty poets, named in a preface still extant today. In the preface each poet is compared to a flower or a plant, and the anthology as a whole was entitled the *Garland (Stephanos)*. The earliest poet included was Archilochus (seventh century B.C.); most of the contributions were in elegiac couplets, and all were short, averme le ā' gĕr

aging eight lines in length. It was suggested in ancient times that Meleager arranged these epigrams alphabetically by the initial letter of the first line, but it is now regarded as more probable that he grouped them by authors and subjects.

He included in the *Garland* a considerable number of his own poems, of which about a hundred examples have survived in the Palatine and Planudean Anthologies of Byzantine date, which are, in fact, based on his and other such compilations. Nearly all of Meleager's own epigrams are about love. While continually quoting and adapting his predecessors, he supplements the traditional forms of epitaph and dedication by a special individual emphasis on erotic emotion. This sentiment, while sometimes achieving an authentic note, is never very profound or original and displays little variety. Meleager reveals marked tendencies toward narcissism, preciosity, and sugary mawkishness. His style, too, is affected by the flamboyant rhetoric of the day. Yet, it also shows considerable ingenuity and verbal flair; the structure of the poems is taut and adroit, and his exploitation of meter, scrupulously precise.

Meleager also wrote satires in prose mixed with verse after the manner of his fellow townsman Menippus, of the third century B.C. But these pieces have not survived.

EDITIONS—A. Presta and G. Perrotta, Antologia Palatina, 1957; A. S. F. Gow and D. L. Page, Anthologia Graeca: The Greek Anthology, Hellenistic Epigrams, 1965; D. L. Page, Epigrammata Graeca, 1976. *Translations*—W. R. Paton, The Greek Anthology (Loeb ed.), 1916–18; P. Whigham and P. Jay, The Poems of Meleager, 1975; A. Oehler, Der Kranz des Meleagros, 1920; R. Aubreton, Anthologie grecque (Budé ed.), v 13, Appendice planudéen, 1979.
ABOUT—K. Radinger, Meleagros von Gadara, 1895; A. Wifstrand, Studien zur griechischen Anthologie, 1926; L. A. Stella, Cinque poeti dell'Antologia Palatina, 1949; A. S. F. Gow, The Greek Anthology: Sources and Ascriptions, 1958; T. B. L. Webster, Hellenistic Poetry and Art, 1964; L'épigramme grecque (Entretiens Hardt, v 14), 1968.

MELISSUS, Greek philosopher, was born early in the fifth century B.C. and came from the island of Samos. He is known to have me lis' sus commanded a Samian fleet during the island's revolt against the Athenians in 441–440 B.C.

His work entitled *On Nature* can be partly reconstructed from the fragments that survive. He emerges as the last significant follower of the Eleatic school of philosophy, of which Parmenides had been the founder and the most important representative. For the most part, Melissus' philosophy consisted of a defense of Parmenides' doctrine that reality is a changeless, single, undifferentiated whole. Seeking to refute those who denied this (Anaximenes in the sixth century, Diogenes of Apollonia and Empedocles in the fifth, and others), Melissus elaborated the Parmenidean doctrine by advocating the eternity, infinity, and unity of being: Parmenides had implied that indeterminacy involved infinity, and Melissus' aim was apparently to carry this implication to its logical conclusion. Melissus' rejection of the void can probably be interpreted as a criticism of earlier Pythagoreans rather than of the atomists (Democritus, Leucippus), whose doctrines Melissus' formulation may, according to this interpretation, be held to have preceded.

EDITIONS—G. Reale, Melisso: Testimonianze e frammenti, 1970.
ABOUT—G. S. Kirk and J. E. Raven, The Presocratic Philosophers, 1960; W. K. C. Guthrie, History of Greek Philosophy, v 2, 1965; R. Vitali, Melisso di Samo sul modo o sull'essere, 1978.

MENANDER, Greek poet and comic dramatist, was born in about 342 B.C. and died in about 292. An Athenian of prosperous family, he became a pupil of the philosopher Theophrastus, the successor of Aristotle. One of Menander's fellow pupils and friends was Demetrius of Phaleron, whose expulsion from the governorship of Athens in 307 brought Menander into danger of prosecution. Menander was said to have declined invitations to visit Macedonia and Egypt. He met his death by drowning while he was swimming at the Piraeus.

Menander wrote over a hundred comedies. Following remarkable discoveries of

me nan' dĕr

MENANDER

papyri in recent years, there are now ten of which we have substantial passages or fragments.

The earliest of his plays, datable to 317 B.C., seems to be the *Dyskolos (Bad Tempered Man* or *Curmudgeon),* which has come down to us almost complete. In this comedy, the rich young Sostratus, out hunting, sees Myrrhine and falls in love with her but is warned off by her morose father Cnemon. At the suggestion of Daos, however, who is the slave of Cnemon's stepson and neighbor Gorgias, Sostratus pretends to be a poor farmer and goes to dig on Gorgias' land. Cnemon repels various visitors rudely but then falls into his own well and is so impressed when Gorgias goes to his rescue that he adopts him as his son. He also asks Gorgias to find a husband for Myrrhine: Gorgias puts forward the name of Sostratus, who in gratitude gives Gorgias his own rich sister in marriage. The ensuing celebrations are at first shunned by Cnemon, but finally, after much pestering, he is dragged onto the dance floor to join in the festivities.

The *Epitrepontes (Arbitrants),* apparently a late play, written after 304, is likewise sufficiently well preserved for a reconstruction of its plot to be possible. An Athenian Charisios (Charming) has married Pamphile (Lovely), daughter of Smicrines (Small-minded). Only five months after the wedding, however, Charisios discovers, apparently from his slave Onesimus (Profitable),

279

that Pamphile has given birth to a child, which he believes cannot be his. In distress, he vainly seeks consolation with a harp-girl Habrotonon. When two countrymen request Charisios to arbitrate a dispute over the possession of identity tokens found on an exposed child, Onesimus recognizes one of these objects as a ring of his master's. It comes to light that the baby is the child that had been borne by Pamphile and that the father is, after all, Charisios himself, who had seduced her at a festival before their marriage, neither knowing who the other was. Thus when Smicrines comes to insist that his daughter leave her husband, because of the quarrel that had arisen between them, he finds that all is well after all and that the couple are reconciled and happy.

We also have about 450 lines of the approximately 1000 in the *Perikeiromene (The Unkindest Cut)*. A poverty-stricken merchant, Pataecus, had exposed his twin infants, Moschion and Glycera. Moschion was later adopted by the rich Myrrhine, who then became the wife of Pataecus. In consequence, Pataecus adopted Moschion, not knowing that the youth was his own son. Glycera, brought up in poverty, had become the mistress of the soldier Polemo, but when Polemo catches her kissing Moschion (whom she now knows to be her brother, although he is unaware of this), he jealously cuts off the girl's hair (hence the title of the play), whereupon she flees to the house of Pataecus and Myrrhine. However, her birth tokens convince Pataecus that she is his daughter, and Moschion, eavesdropping, discovers that he himself is her brother. Polemo, who has planned to assault the house, repents and is forgiven by Glycera, and they prepare to get married to each other.

A considerable part of the *Samia (Woman from Samos)* has survived. The lost beginning probably told the following story: Demeas, a rich bachelor, was unable by law to marry the Samian woman Chrysis, with whom he was living, because her parentage was unknown. At the same time, Demeas' beloved adopted son Moschion (who is the natural son of Chrysis) has fallen in love with Plangon, but the affair is a secret because Plangon cannot provide a dowry.

While Demeas is away, Chrysis has borne him a child, but the child has died (for some reason that we cannot reconstruct, Demeas had ordered that if she bore a baby it would have to be exposed). Plangon, too, has had a child by Moschion, which Chrysis now brings up. She tells Demeas on his return that Plangon's infant is a foundling she is anxious to keep. Demeas plans that Moschion should marry Plangon. The surviving portion of the manuscript begins with preparations for the wedding banquet. Now, however, Demeas suspects that Chrysis has seduced Moschion and drives her out of the house with her child, whom Demeas later suspects to be a premarital offspring of Moschion and Plangon. Subsequently Moschion, in despair, decides to go abroad as a soldier. Presumably, however, there is a happy ending; though it has not been preserved.

Substantial portions of the *Aspis (Shield)* have also come to light. The plot depends on a feature of the Athenian law of inheritance: if an unmarried girl was left as heiress to an estate, her closest male relative was entitled to marry her—indeed, if her inheritance was small, the law *compelled* him to marry her, or, if not, to subsidize her from his own property. In the *Aspis*, the slave Daos reports the death of his young master Cleostratos on military service; the avaricious Smicrines plans to take advantage of the law and marry the dead man's sister (who is rich). But, we learn from the goddess Luck that Cleostratus is, in fact, still alive—and about to return home. Meanwhile, the resourceful Daos seeks to deter Smicrines' marriage plans. At this juncture, in the fourth act, Cleostratus returns, but how the fifth and last act was worked out to the appropriate happy ending we cannot tell, since it is missing. However, the *Aspis* is of historical significance because of the character of Daos: for this is the only substantially surviving play to present the character of the helpful and cunning slave who is guide, philosopher, and friend—a personage often encountered in the shorter fragments.

The *Hero*—apparently titled after a household deity, some famous ancestor—has survived in only one fragment of any size. This is part of the prologue, which takes the form of a discussion between Daos, a slave of Laches, and another slave named Getas. Although the rest of the comedy is lost, the outline of its plot has survived: an unmarried girl of the name of Myrrhine, seduced by Laches, gave birth to twins, a boy and girl, and exposed them at birth. They were discovered by a farm manager, Tibeius, who brought them up himself. Subsequently, Myrrhine became Laches' wife. Tibeius later dies, owing money to Laches, and in order to pay the debt off the boy whom Tibeius had adopted, Gorgias, goes with his sister Plangon to work on Laches' estate, not knowing (any more than Laches did) that they were both Laches' children. Daos falls in love with Plangon, his supposed fellow slave, and when a neighbor, Pheidias, seduces her, wants to take the responsibility upon himself. Finally, Laches recognizes his children from tokens left with them when they were exposed as infants; and Pheidias and Plangon duly marry.

The staging of *Georgos (Farmer)* requires two houses. In one lives a widow named Myrrhine; by her late husband, a poor man, she has a son, who is away working with a farmer called Cleaenetus. Still living with her, however, is her daughter, whose father is Cleaenetus (with whom Myrrhine had had a premarital affair long ago—an affair that had left Cleaenetus with such a bad conscience he never married). In the second house on stage lives a rich man who has a son by his first marriage and a daughter, Hedeia, by his second. The rich man's son has made Myrrhine's daughter pregnant and wants to marry her, but his father has arranged for him to marry his own half sister Hedeia instead. In the first extant scene of the play the rich man's son comes out of his father's house and addresses the audience in great distress. There are also five other surviving fragments, but they do not show clearly how the plot developed or was resolved.

A recently discovered fragment is of a comedy called the *Man* [or *Men*] *from Sicyon*. This, as far as we can tell, is a different sort of comedy altogether, mainly consisting not so much of moralizing or social comment as of narrative. Parts of a prologue and of a long messenger's speech are extant.

Stratophanes is a young soldier who has just come back to Athens from military service in Asia Minor. He believes his hometown to have been Sicyon (on the Gulf of Corinth); but the woman he supposes to be his mother lives in Athens. On arriving there, he sends his slave Pyrrhias ahead to give her advance information of his safe return. But Pyrrhias comes back to him with the news that his mother has died; and he brings her will and a letter and parcel (containing tokens of identity) that she has left for Stratophanes. From these the young man learns that he is not the dead woman's son after all, and not a Sicyonian but an Athenian. Moreover, the girl he is in love with, Philumene, who had been captured by pirates in her infancy and sold in Asia Minor, fortunately turns out to be a freeborn Athenian as well, so that the legal objection that they had supposed to be a fatal obstacle to their marriage does not exist after all.

We know of the *Kolax (Flatterer)* only from the *Eunuchus* of the Roman playwright Terence (c. 195/185 B.C.–159 B.C.), which was partly based on it. Menander's play evidently portrayed the arrogance, thickheadedness, and vulgarity of a Greek professional soldier, together with his habit of exaggerating his warlike exploits. In Terence's adaptation, a henchman of the soldier pronounces a monologue describing his own technique of flattery; and then the soldier arrives, and delivers a speech which illustrates his talent for boasting. A more sympathetic military figure is Thrasonides in the *Misoumenos (The Hated One* or *The Man She Loved to Hate*, a play written late in Menander's career). After the fortunes of war have brought him a young girl as a prisoner of war, Thrasonides falls passionately in love with her, but, when she shows distaste for him, chivalrously refrains from laying a hand on her and frees her without ransom when her father comes to claim her.

A papyrus discovered in 1968 contains parts of Menander's *Dis Exapaton (A Double Deceit)*, which is evidently the original of a passage adapted by the Roman dramatist Plautus (c. 254/250 B.C.–184 B.C.) in his *Bacchides*. In Menander's plot, Mnesilochus, while absent in Ephesus to collect a debt owing to his father, has fallen in love

281

with a prostitute, Bacchis, who is about to be taken to Athens. He writes to his friend Pistoclerus in Athens, asking him to try and find the girl. Pistoclerus succeeds but himself falls under the spell of her twin sister, likewise known as Bacchis. Mnesilochus learns of this and mistakenly believes that Pistoclerus' affections have fallen on the sister whom he himself loves. The plot is concerned with the clearing up of this imbroglio.

The plays of Menander's New Comedy seem to have had a fixed structure, comprising five acts, of which the first contained the exposition of the theme, the second and third its development, the fourth the principal climax, and the fifth the clearing up of outstanding situations and problems. The breaks between the acts were filled by choral interludes, presented by young revelers *(komoi)*. (The text of these interludes has not been preserved; Menander may not ever have written them down).

No scene of Menander's needs more than three speaking actors at a time. However, if the actors were in fact limited to three, major parts must, on occasion, have had to be shared between two of them: so that it is not inconceivable that there was sometimes a fourth. The scene is generally a town street, backed by two or three houses in which, by a conventional coincidence, some or all of the principal characters of the play have their homes. In some plays, however, one of the houses may be replaced by a temple and the street by a seaside path or country lane.

These comedies are set in contemporary Greece, usually Athens or Attica. Although the characters show a certain awareness of the outside world, the plays are not concerned with the bloodlettings, famines, and political convulsions that characterized Athens in the fourth century B.C. In contrast to the Old Comedy of Aristophanes (but in pursuance of a shift in emphasis begun by the Middle Comedy of Antiphanes and Alexis), the New Comedy turned its attention to the private domestic problems of a relatively prosperous nonpolitical dream world, and in particular to a certain range of situations that were now becoming an established theatrical tradition: foundling children and their recognition tokens,

kidnapped daughters, clever scheming slaves, extramarital pregnancies, expensive entanglements with prostitutes, and the loss of merchant ships carrying family fortunes.

Ranging right across the whole of society, Menander's characters have moved a good distance from the more or less caricatured types of Middle Comedy; they assume the three-dimensional shapes of individual human beings. Although not portrayed in any psychological depth, they are depicted credibly enough and often stray quite sharply away from the types they might be expected to represent: nor is it always clear to the reader whether Menander intended them as serious or comic. They seemed very lifelike to the ancients, and their creator was praised by the scholar Aristophanes of Byzantium for representing life in such faithful terms: "O Menander and Life," he asked, "which of you imitated the other?"

His plays always included a love interest, though it is not always the central theme. To deduce Menander's own views from those expressed by his characters would not be legitimate; yet his own personality does unmistakably emerge from his overall treatment. Although not primarily a serious social critic but a playwright who sets out to entertain, he appears to admire altruistic friendship and approves particularly of benevolence that cuts across the barriers of class and wealth. He feels a sense of duty and sympathy toward his fellow human beings, especially those whom fortune has worsted; and he sees the family as a protection against the jolts of an unkind world. These vicissitudes inspire him with a certain melancholy pessimism, and yet at the same time he feels a certain hope that things may change for the better.

His view of the gods, although somewhat difficult to assess owing to the incomplete survival of his works, seems to be fairly typical of educated Athenians of the time. That is to say, he does not believe very seriously in the principal Olympian divinities but on the whole prefers to speak more vaguely of "the divine power" or "the gods" or "god." Yet he recognizes the existence of unseen forces and exploits their power with considerable dramatic skill, particularly through the deities and personifications (Chance, Ignorance, Pan, etc.) who speak his prologues.

Menander was an ingenious constructor of plays, well acquainted with the techniques for creating surprise and variety. It is remarkable how his vivid details, short speeches, and passages of dialogue manage to serve a number of different purposes at one and the same time, how skillfully his characterization is coordinated with the development of his themes. The plots move along with pleasing continuity and flow, displaying a concern with symmetry and balance. Menander also makes effective use of devices that not only link one scene to the next but also conceal those elements—such as threadbare plots and improbable coincidences—that would otherwise have destroyed the illusion of realism.

Realism is also fostered by his handling of language. Menander employs as verse form the iambic trimeter (varied, in the early plays at least, by another meter, the rhythmical trochaic tetrameter), which although basically artificial and unrealistic, does provide a sort of semblance of the currently spoken tongue. And while his characters, of whatever personality or class, all normally speak the same dialect—a largely colloquial though grammatical late Attic—a considerable number of these men and women are also endowed with distinctive modes or habits of speech, which are presented with subtle variations of rhythm. Menander's smart, sententious sayings—like "Those whom the gods love die young" (in the *Double Deceit*)—became famous. But the collections that were subsequently made of these epigrams give an exaggerated impression of their frequency, since Menander produced them only at special junctures in his plays in order to serve some specific dramatic purpose or make an ironical point.

Naturally, he was influenced by his dramatic predecessors, although it is not easy to offer reliable generalizations about this. For one thing, the history of many of his stereotypes can easily be traced back to the Athenian Old Comedy of Aristophanes; indeed, if we can judge from the anonymous *Life* of the latter, Aristophanes' last play, the *Kokalos* (which is lost), prefigured numerous Menandrian features. Menander also owed a great deal to the tragedies of Euripides, whose *Ion*, for example, anticipated a whole series of New Comedy situations and whose *Orestes* provided a scene that Menander substantially recreated in his *Man* [or *Men*] *from Sicyon.* Moreover, Menander's general ideas of economical, highly organized plot structure may also be derived from Euripides. His friendship with two Peripatetics (Aristotelians), Theophrastus and Demetrius of Phaleron, has been cited by modern scholars as evidence of Aristotelian doctrines in his plays; however, if such ideas are present in them at all, which is doubtful, they are deeply interwoven into his own highly original fabric.

In his own day Menander was a less successful writer than such fellow playwrights as Philemon (c. 368/60–267/63 B.C.), and he won only eight victories at dramatic festivals. After his death, however, he soon became famous, and by later agreement, voiced by Quintilian, he was regarded as the leading practitioner of the New Comedy. His plays ranked high among those selected for Latin adaptation by Plautus in the third century B.C. and Terence in the second. Through these Roman intermediaries he deeply affected the dramatists of later Europe, including Molière in the seventeenth century and Sheridan in the eighteenth. His direct influence, however, was eliminated by the disappearance of his plays during the seventh and eighth centuries A.D., and it is only in quite modern times that important papyrus discoveries are partially retrieving this position.

WORKS—Comedies lost or only surviving in short fragments include the following: Anger, Bridesmaid, Brothers (two plays), Brothers Who Love Each Other, Carthaginian, Changeling (or Rustic), Charioteer, Coppersmiths' Holiday, Cousins, Doorkeeper, Drunkenness, Eunuch, False Accuser, False Heracles, Fishermen, Flute-Girl (or Robe-Bearer), Ghost (of which a summary has survived), Girl Twins, Handkerchief, Heiress, Hired Mourner, Hirer of Mercenaries, Hymnis, Imbrians, Man of Ephesus, Marriage-Broker, Mistress, Necklace, Noise-Fearer, Nurse, Phanium, Pilots, Pitcher, Possessed Women, Priestess, Promiser, Ring, Self-Tormentor, Shipowner, Slave, Sold, Soldiers, Stable-Boy, Superstitious Man, Thais, Thrasyleon, Treasure, Trophonius, Widow, Woman of Andros,

Woman of Boeotia, Woman of Cnidus, Woman of Leucas, Woman of Olynthus, Woman of Perinthus, Woman-Hater, Woman Possessed, Woman Set on Fire, Woman Slapped, Women's Lunch. A considerable number of fragments have survived from plays that cannot be identified.

EDITIONS—A. W. Gomme and F. H. Sandbach, 1972–73. Individual plays listed *in* W. G. Arnott, Menander, Plautus, Terence (Greece & Rome: New Surveys in The Classics, no 9), 1975; *add* E. W. Handley, Dis Exapaton, 1975. *Translations*—L. A. Post, Epitrepontes, Perikeiromene, Samia (undated); W. G. Arnott, Dyskolos, 1960; W. E. Blake, Dyskolos, 1966; L. Casson, Aspis, Dyskolos, Epitrepontes, 1971; E. G. Turner, Samia, 1972; P. Vellacott (Penguin ed.), 2nd ed., 1973; The Lost Beginning of Menander: Misoumenos, 1978; K. Martin, L'atrabiliaire (Dyskolos), 2nd ed., 1972; J. M. Jacques, Le dyscolos (Budé ed.), revised ed., 1976.

ABOUT—Menandrea (Miscellanea Philologia, Genoa), 1960; F. Stoessl, Personenwechsel in Menanders Dyskolos, 1960; A. Theuerkauf, Menanders Dyskolos als Bühnenspiel und Dichtung, 1960; T. B. L. Webster, Studies in Menander, 2nd ed., 1960, *and* Art and Literature in Fourth Century Athens, 1969, *and* Studies in Later Greek Comedy, 2nd ed., 1970, *and* An Introduction to Menander, 1974; A. Barigazzi, La formazione spirituale di Menandro, 1965; A. Schäfer, Menanders Dyskolos: Untersuchungen zur dramatischen Technik, 1965; F. Zucker, ed., Menanders Dyskolos als Zeugnis seiner Epoche, 1965; P. Flury, Liebe und Liebessprache bei Menander, Plautus und Terenz, 1968; E. W. Handley, Menander and Plautus: A Study in Comparison, 1968; Ménandre (Entretiens Hardt, v 16), 1970; H. D. Blume, Menanders Samia: Eine Interpretation, 1974; W. G. Arnott, Menander, Plautus & Terence (Greece & Rome: New Surveys in the Classics, no 9), 1975; A. G. Katsouris, Linguistic and Stylistic Characterisation: Tragedy and Menander, 1975, *and* Tragic Patterns in Menander, 1975; E. J. H. Greene, Menander to Marivaux: The History of a Comic Structure, 1978.

MENANDER PROTECTOR, Greek historian of the Byzantine age, lived in the later part of the sixth century A.D. and perhaps in the early years of the seventh. Born at Constantinople, he first studied and practiced law and subsequently became an army officer *(protector)* attached to the court of the Byzantine emperor Maurice (582–602).

At Maurice's suggestion, he wrote a history of the empire that began in 558, where the work of Agathias (Scholasticus) had left off. The surviving text, which has been preserved in considerable excerpts by Constantine VII Porphyrogenitus and the Suidas or Suda lexicon (an encyclopedia compiled at the end of the tenth century A.D.), carried on

me nan' dĕr prō tek' tōr

the narrative until at least 582. Relying on eye-witness accounts and official documents, of which he quotes a considerable number, Menander surpasses Agathias in detailed accuracy and provides a uniquely valuable source for the last ten years of Justinian I and the reigns of his immediate successors Justin II and Tiberius II. The work is particularly rich in geographic and ethnographic material.

Subsequently, Menander's work was continued by the historian Theophylactus Simocatta, an Egyptian, up to the murder of Maurice and his children by Phocas in 602.

EDITIONS (of fragments)—L. Dindorf, Historici Graeci Minores, v 2, 1871; U. P. Boissevain, Excerpta de Sententiis, 1906. *With translation:* I. P. Cory, The Tyrian Annals *in* Ancient Fragments . . ., 1828, reprinted 1876; E. Doblhofer, Byzantinische Diplomaten und östliche Barbaren; aus den Excerpta de Legationibus des Konstantinos Porphyrogenitos ausgewählte Abschnitte des Priskos und Menander Protektor, 1955. ABOUT—O. Veh, Beiträge zu Menander Protector . . ., 1955; G. Moravcsik, Byzantino-turcica, v 1, 2nd ed., 1958; R. Browning, Justinian and Theodora, 1971.

MENIPPUS, Greek popular philosopher and satirical writer, lived in the first half of the third century B.C. He began life as a slave in Pontus in northern Asia Minor, perhaps at Sinope (Sinop) but then made a fortune by money-lending, purchased his freedom, and became a citizen of Thebes. There he was taught by Metrocles, a pupil of Theophrastus converted to the Cynic school of philosophy; and he may also have been influenced by Metrocles' better-known brother-in-law and mentor Crates of Thebes (c. 365–285 B.C.). According to one report, Menippus was robbed of his money and hanged himself in despair.

Although his writings are lost, it is clear from his imitators that he pioneered some remarkable novelties. For one thing, he created the seriocomic type of literature *(spoudogeloion),* the style of earnest jesting that sought to give humorous expression to philosophical views. His second innovation

me nip' pus

was to intermingle prose with poetry (whether the poems were original pieces or quotations is unknown); this was a Semitic literary form that he presumably learned at his birthplace. Moreover, he appears to have aimed his philosophical ideas at a wider section of the population than had ever hitherto been the targets of such literature.

His works, which filled thirteen books, directed mordantly mocking attacks, in the Cynic manner, not only against the systems of the philosophers but against many other foolish human institutions, concepts, and conventions. These satires were presented in a wide variety of arresting and unfamiliar settings. Thus, *Necyia (Descent Into Hades),* one of the numerous offspring of Book 2 of the *Odyssey,* followed Crates by criticizing the fatuity of traditional representations of life after death; the *Arcesilaus* made fun of the luxurious living at the Academy; the *Birth of Epicurus* ridiculed the personality cult maintained by the followers of that philosopher. Menippus also wrote a *Symposium, Auction of Diogenes,* and theological parodies.

He seems to have been the most caustic of the Cynic philosopher-satirists; and it is to this that he owed his enduring reputation, as shown by numerous adaptations of *Descent Into Hades, Symposium,* and *Auction.* Marcus Aurelius saw him as "a mocker of man's ephemeral existence"; and to Lucian he was "a frightening dog [the word from which the Cynics derived their name] with a treacherous bite." Particularly influential was his mixture of prose and verse given the name of "Menippean satire." This was recognized as a distinctive literary form by Quintilian and was imitated not only by Meleager and Lucian in Greek but by Latin authors including Varro, Seneca, Petronius, and Martianus Capella—and much later, in 1594, there was a famous French political pamphlet in a satirical vein, the Ménippée.

EDITIONS—C. Wachsmuth, Syllographi Graeci, 1885; L. Paquet, Les cyniques grecs: Fragments et témoignages, 1975.

ABOUT—R. Helm, Lucian und Menipp, 1906; D. R. Dudley, A History of Cynicism, 1937.

MIMNERMUS, Greek poet, was said to have flourished during the years 632–629 B.C., which is possibly a little too early since he engaged in political exchanges with the Athenian statesman Solon, who first appeared on the political scene in about 600. Mimnermus is usually thought to have been born in Colophon in Ionia (western Asia Minor), though his birthplace was alternatively stated to be Smyrna or Astypalaea. By profession he was a flute player, which at that time and place did not rank high in the social scale.

His poems were elegies (i.e., in the elegiac meter, composed of couplets of a hexameter and pentameter), and were collected in two books, of which only fragments survived. At a later date, when it had become customary to attach titles to poetical works, one of the two books was named after the flute-girl Nanno, whom he was believed to have loved —her name, which is not Greek but eastern, exemplifies the mixed nature of the Ionian civilization at that time. The book of Nanno seems to have been a work of some length, offering a contrast to Mimnermus' shorter poems; if so, we are perhaps at the origins of narrative elegy. To what extent, however, the girl provided the book with a unifying theme, remains uncertain. While it is true that the Roman elegist Propertius appears to have regarded Mimnermus as primarily a poet of love, it is also clear that the character of Nanno did not by any means monopolize her book, for certain passages attributed to it deal instead with a variety of subjects: the early history of Colophon; mythological themes (notably the story of Tithonus); and the nightly movement of the sun-god around the stream of Ocean on his magic golden bowl, which journey the poet describes with great charm. Another passage tells how Jason stole the Golden Fleece from Aea on the Ocean shore, where the sun-god resided in his palace. Clearly, mythology, as well as love, played a considerable part in Mimnermus' poetry. He also respected warlike

mim nûr' mus

qualities, praising a warrior, for example, who had fought bravely in the war against King Gyges the Lydian; the passage may come from a piece called the *Men of Smyrna (Smyrneis)*.

However, Mimnermus' dominant preoccupation is pleasure—above all else the carefree pleasure of youth contrasted with the hateful discomforts of old age. The large majority of the fragments that have come down to us are made up of gloomy reflections on the brevity of life—he quotes the verse of the *Iliad* that compares human beings with fallen leaves—and dwell on its miseries once youth is over. Indeed, the poet prayed for a painless death at the age of sixty, for which the more cheerful Solon sharply took him to task.

Mimnermus' remarkable command of language and meter gained him a place in the Canon of elegiac poets drawn up in Hellenistic times. His employment of the elegiac couplet shows the sensitiveness of a musician, and his images are brilliantly conceived and well rounded. The emotional impact made by his verse is fresh and compelling.

EDITIONS—T. Bergk, Poetae Lyrici Graeci, v 2, 1915; M. L. West, Iambi et Elegi Graeci, v 2, 1972.
ABOUT—T. Hudson-Williams, Early Greek Elegy, 1925; C. M. Bowra, Early Greek Elegists, 1938; D. A. Campbell, Greek Lyric Poetry, 1967; B. Lavagnini, Da Mimnermo a Callimaco, 1976.

MINUCIUS FELIX, MARCUS, Latin Christian author, probably wrote during the decades after A.D. 197, since he seems to have been aware of two works by Tertullian published in about that year. To judge from further internal evidence, he came from northern Africa, or at least had close connections with that region, but lived for a considerable part of his life at Rome.

His *Octavius* is a dialogue between the pagan Caecilius Natalis (perhaps identical with a man mentioned in inscriptions from Cirta [Constantine], c. A.D. 210–17) and his visitor Octavius Januarius who refutes him in the interests of Christianity to which he himself has been converted; they discuss the

mi nū′ ki us fē′ liks

subject as they are strolling on the beach near Ostia, with Minucius himself, another convert, acting as umpire. As they pass a statue of the Graeco-Egyptian god Sarapis, Caecilius offers it a formal salute, whereupon Octavius deplores this sign of baseless superstition. Caecilius replies with a criticism of Christianity, expressing pained surprise that his friend could adhere to so ridiculous a system of belief. He points out that since everything concerning the supernatural remains entirely obscure and since the philosophers have not succeeded in illuminating these questions, scepticism is the only reasonable position to assume. This being so, he continues, it is best to go on subscribing to the traditional cults, which have given Rome its greatness and which, therefore, should not be subjected to vilification by the Christians. As for them, he continues, not only do they commit the absurdity of worshiping a man who has died a common criminal's death, but they indulge in horrible practices, such as killing and eating babies as part of their initiation rites; they indulge in sexual abominations; and they keep themselves apart in miserable secrecy and ignorance, incapable of meeting the demands of this life upon earth and manifestly unqualified to predict the life beyond the grave. Octavius, however, replies (at somewhat greater length), refuting these slanders. The Christians may not be rich, he adds, but should not be denied their fair share of natural intelligence. Their belief in a single divine ruler is in accordance with the statements of poets and philosophers alike, who agree that this God is the father of the human race and that he is One. This is a truth, declares Octavius, against which the insubstantial myths of the pagans, their ridiculous worship of deified persons, and their grotesque and vicious rituals carry no weight. Even animals and birds, he points out, can see that pagan statues are not gods. Pagan Rome's triumphs are based not on piety but on aggression and violence; demons, not gods, are behind the oracles hostile to the Christians, who avoid pagan shows and activities not from any desire to be separate but because such performances are impious and cruel. And so, the adherents of Christianity do not deserve the sufferings inflicted on them—yet they endure them heroically. After pondering, Caecilius declares he is convinced and accepts the Christian faith, like his friends.

The *Octavius* is well stocked with a variety of classical learning. The pagan case is founded on an attack on Christianity by Fronto (c. A.D. 150), now lost, while the Christian argument makes special use of Stoic material taken from Cicero's *On the Nature of the Gods* and from Seneca; other arguments are derived from the Greek Christian apologists. But the work is so skillfully designed that its polemical theology does not intrude unduly—even the name of Christ is not specifically mentioned—and neither side appeals to revealed authority. There is little originality in the treatise. But of all the apologies offered by the ancients for Christianity it was the least likely to provoke or offend an open-minded, educated pagan.

EDITIONS—J. van Wageningen, 1923; M. Pellegrino, 1963; C. Becker, 1967. *Translations*—J. H. Freese, 1920; G. H. Rendall *in* T. R. Glover and G. H. Rendall, Tertullian: Apology, De Spectaculis, and Minucius Felix: Octavius (Loeb ed.), 1931; R. Arbesmann *in* Fathers of the Church, v 10, 1951; J. Beaujeu (Budé ed.), 1964; B. Kytzler (German), 1965; E. Paratore, 1971. ABOUT—C. Becker, Der Octavius der Minucius Felix, 1967.

MOSCHUS, Greek poet and grammarian, was described as a pupil of Aristarchus, and since this was probably Aristarchus of Samothrace (c. 217–145 B.C.), director of the Alexandrian library, Moschus must have worked in about the middle of the second century B.C. He came from Syracuse in Sicily and was said to be a grammarian like Aristarchus; he may, perhaps, be identifiable with a man of the same name described as the writer of a treatise entitled *On Rhodian Words,* which has not come down to us.

The extant works of Moschus, however, are not grammatical but poetical. He is the author of a miniature epic (epyllion) of one hundred sixty-six hexameters that narrates the well-known story of the rape of Europa by Zeus in the form of a bull. A distinctive feature of the poem, characteristic of this

mos′ kus

highly polished type of Hellenistic poetry, is a twenty-five-line passage describing the golden basket of Europa and the mythological pictures inlaid in its surface. As Zeus swims with his bride across the sea, its inhabitants gambol around him and celebrate his wedding with a triumphal procession, and Europa herself dreams prophetically that she will be the cause of a clash between two continents, the Trojan War.

Three extracts are also preserved from Moschus' *Bucolica,* a title which recalls that he was known as one of three Greek bucolic or pastoral poets, of whom the others were Theocritus and Bion. These extracts from *Bucolica* are of thirteen, nine, and eight hexameters, each probably comprising a complete poem in itself. The first contrasts the pleasant life of the countryman with the fisherman's hard lot and tells eloquently of the flashing sea and of the safety of the land that the raging gale attacks in vain. The other two excerpts, however, are erotic pieces that seem to have little or nothing to do with pastoral themes. The same poet has left us, in addition, an epigram entitled *Eros as Ploughman* and a piece of twenty-nine lines, *The Runaway Love,* describing Aphrodite's search for the escaped Eros—this latter piece was imitated by the seventeenth century English poet and dramatist Ben Jonson. Attributions to Moschus, however, of two further poems, the *Lament for Bion* and the *Megara* (a tearful duet between the wife and mother of Heracles bemoaning his prolonged absence) are unlikely.

Although occasionally cloying, Moschus uses comparatively simple vocabulary for a Hellenistic poet and reveals an attractive sensitivity to nature.

EDITIONS—W. Bühler, Die Europa des Moschus; Text, Übersicht und Kommentar, 1960. *With translation:* J. M. Edmonds, The Greek Bucolic Poets (Loeb ed.), revised ed., 1928; A. S. F. Gow, The Greek Bucolic Poets, translated with brief notes, 1953; P. Legrand, Bucoliques grecs, v 2: Pseudo-Théocrite, Moschos, Bion, divers, 2nd ed., 1953; H. Beckby, Die griechischen Bukoliker: Theokrit, Moschos, Bion, 1975; Megara: J. W. Vaughn, 1976. ABOUT—T. Breitenstein, Recherches sur le poème Mégara, 1966; A. J. Boyle, ed., Ancient Pastoral, 1975.

MOSCHUS, JOHN. See John Moschus

MUSAEUS GRAMMATICUS, Greek poet, should be attributed to the later fifth or early sixth century A.D., since his use of meter and language shows his dependence on the fifth century Greek epic poet Nonnus, and he was known to the sixth century Byzantine Greek writer Agathias, who died in about 580. Scholars and poets were entirely mistaken in their belief that he had written half a millennium earlier and was the Musaeus described in mythology as a pupil of Orpheus.

He is the author of an epyllion (miniature epic) of three hundred forty hexameters, *Hero and Leander.* Leander dwelt at Abydus on the Asian side of the Hellespont (Dardanelles) and Hero, at Sestus on the European bank, where she lived in a tower outside the town with one old servant and tended a shrine of Aphrodite and of her son Eros. She herself did not escape Eros' shafts, for at a festival of Adonis she met Leander, and they fell in love. Hero told him where to find her home, and he swore that he would swim to her by night; she must light a lamp to guide his journey. And so he came to her often, and they made love through many summer nights. But when summer gave way to winter, and the sea grew stormy, she ought to have stopped lighting her lamp. However, love and fate compelled her, and the fatal night arrived. Leander struggled with the waves, but his strength failed him— and Hero's lamp was blown out by the wind. When morning dawned and there was still no sign of him, she went out to search and finally found his body, shattered by the rocks, lying at the foot of her tower. And so she hurled herself from the heights, to meet death with her lover.

The story may have been a comparative latecomer to classical mythology, but it was not new, since ten lines of a version preserved on a papyrus are of Hellenistic date; and the tale had been told again by epigrammatists and by Virgil and Ovid and was depicted on wall paintings, mosaics, reliefs, and coins of the cities that claimed to have

myū zē′ us grà mat′ i kus

been the birthplaces of the tragic pair. The poem in which Musaeus repeats their legend is a gracefully proportioned piece combining classical form with profound and sensitive human sympathy. He feels for young beauty and love; and a taste for certain affectations does not spoil his lucid brevity and appealing directness nor his understanding of the remorseless grandeur of the sea.

His poem was deeply admired by subsequent generations. In the Middle Ages it formed part of the repertory of the troubadours and was reproduced in hundreds of the popular pamphlets known as chapbooks. Echoed in the works of the poets Dante, Chaucer, and Tasso, Musaeus received acclaim from the sixteenth century Italian classical scholar Julius Caesar Scaliger, who considered him superior to Homer, and the story of Hero and Leander was splendidly retold in the same century by the English dramatist Christopher Marlowe and often referred to by Shakespeare. In the nineteenth century, Austrian playwright and poet Franz Grillparzer wrote a tragedy around it. Earlier, in the eighteenth, the German poet and playwright Schiller composed a ballad; and in the nineteenth, the English poet Keats wrote a sonnet.

EDITIONS—K. Kost, Musaios: Hero and Leander, 1971. *Translations*—T. Gelzer, ed. and C. H. Whitman, tr., appended to C. A. Trypanis, Callimachus: Aetia, Iambi, Hecale (Loeb ed.), 1974; P. Orsini, Musée: Héro et Léander, 1968.
ABOUT—M. Grant. Myths of the Greeks and Romans, 1962; D. Bo, Musaei Lexicon, 1966; K. Kost, Kritische-exegetische Kommentar zu Musaios, 1966; Musaeus: Hero und Leander, 1971.

NAEVIUS, CNAEUS, Latin dramatic and epic poet, c. 270–201 B.C., was a native of Capua (Santa Maria Capua Vetere) in Campania, of Italian stock and the possessor of Roman citizenship. He served in the First Punic War (264–241 B.C.). Then, in 235 (only five years after the first play had been performed at Rome), he started his career as a dramatist, which he pursued for thirty years. In a number of his comedies he made outspoken comments about leading Roman politicians. He told, for example, how the

nē′ vi us

father of Scipio Africanus dragged his son from the arms of his mistress. More famous, however, was his attack on the noble family of the Caecilii Metelli: his suggestion that they had gained their consulships by "fate," that is to say, by their social position rather than through merit—the reference was to Lucius Caecilius Metellus, consul in 206—resulted in his imprisonment in c. 204. Later he resided at Utica in northern Africa (now Henchir bou Chateur in Tunisia), where he died.

He wrote tragedies, comedies, and an epic poem. Of his tragedies, all based on Greek models, we have sixty lines and seven titles. *Hector's Farewell* may conceivably come from a Greek play by Astydamas (fourth century B.C.). Two other titles *(Danae and The Trojan Horse)* correspond with the names of plays by Livius Andronicus, which makes it probable that Naevius was deliberately challenging comparison with this older contemporary by employing the same Greek originals. Naevius also invented a new type of drama by writing at least two plays on national Roman themes *(fabulae praetextae)*, the *Romulus* (perhaps the same as *Lupus, the Wolf*), telling of the twins Romulus and Remus and the origin of the city, and the *Clastidium,* describing the victory of Marcus Claudius Marcellus in single combat against the Gallic chieftain Viridomarus in 222 B.C., which was probably produced at Marcellus' funeral games in 208. But this Roman type of play never became popular and had very few successors (the *Octavia,* wrongly attributed to Seneca the Younger, is one famous example).

But Naevius evidently achieved greater success with his comedies, of which twenty-eight titles are known to us. Only insubstantial fragments survive, yet it is clear, even from these, that he greatly outshone Livius Andronicus in this field and should be regarded as the inaugurator of the forceful and colorful comic style that was soon to reach its zenith under Plautus (254–184 B.C.). Naevius adapted his Greek originals with considerable freedom, exchanging passages from one play to another and transforming dialogue into song when he felt inclined. It was in these plays, too, that he offered con-

temporary references and political comments, such as the epigram which so greatly irritated the Metelli. A Roman critic of about 100 B.C., Volcacius Sedigitus, somewhat surprisingly placed Naevius as high as third among Latin writers of comedy, after Caecilius Statius (223/2–168 B.C.) and Plautus (254 or 250–c. 184 B.C.) but ahead of Terence (195 or 185–159 B.C.).

In his old age, Naevius wrote a national epic poem in a native Italian meter (the Saturnian), which later scholars regarded as his most important work. It was, indeed, an entirely original venture for a Roman writer. This was *The Punic War (Carmen Belli Poenici),* which was subsequently divided into seven books, though only sixty lines are extant. The title refers to the first of the wars against the Carthaginians, in which Naevius himself had fought: his selection of this contemporary theme shows awareness of Hellenistic models. But the work also dealt, perhaps in a series of long digressions, with earlier history and legendary origins; for example, he brought Aeneas and his fellow Trojans to Carthage to meet Dido and part from her, thus providing a mythical antecedent for the Punic Wars and bequeathing Virgil's *Aeneid* one of its principal themes.

Naevius' style clanks prosily but maintains a grand and archaic solemnity. Cicero, although he gave priority to Ennius as a national epic poet, nevertheless expressed respectful admiration of the *Punic War,* comparing it to a statue by the sculptor Myron—lacking polish but affording pleasure all the same.

WORKS (of which fragments survive)—*Tragedies translated or adapted from the Greek:* Andromacha (?), Danae, Hector's Farewell (Hector Proficiscens), Hesiona, Iphigenia, Lycurgus, The Trojan Horse. *Tragedies on Roman themes:* Clastidium, Romulus or The Bringing Up of Romulus and Remus (Alimonium Romuli et Remi), The Wolf (Lupus; if this is not an alternative title for the Romulus). *Comedies include:* Agitatoria (from *agitator,* charioteer), Astiologa, The Branded One (Stigmatias), The Charcoal-Woman (Carbonaria), The Circumcised (Appella), The Clever One (Technicus), The Comedy of Masks (Personata), Commotria, Demetrius, The Flatterer (Colax), The Flirt (Tarentilla), The Game (Ludus), The Garlands (Corollaria), Glaucoma, Gymnasticus, Lampadio, The Lion (Leo), The Madmen (Dementes), The Mistress (Paelex), Nagido, Nervolaria, The Potter (Figulus), Projectus, The Quadruplets (Quadrigemini), The Sailors (Nautae), The Sleepless Ones (Agryphontes), The Soothsayer (Hariolus), Speared (Acontizomenos), Stalagmonissa, Tribacelus, The Trick (Dolus), Triphallus, Tunicularia. *Epic poem:* The Punic War (Bellum Poenicum).

EDITIONS (Fragments)—Plays: A. Klotz, Scaenicorum Romanorum Fragmenta, 3rd ed., v 1, 1953; O. Ribbeck, Scaenicae Romanorum Poesis Fragmenta, v 1 (Teubner ed.), 3rd ed., 1962. Epic: W. Morel, Fragmenta Poetarum Latinorum (Teubner ed.), 2nd ed., 1927; E. V. Marmorale, Naevius Poeta, 2nd ed., reprint 1967. *With translation:* E. H. Warmington, Remains of Old Latin (Loeb ed.), v 2, 1936; J. Lembke, Blood and Iron, 1973.

ABOUT—E. Fraenkel *in* Pauly-Wissowa-Kroll, Real-Encyclopädie der klassischen Altertumswissenschaft, Suppl. v 6, 1935, columns 622ff.; L. Strzelecki, De Naeviano Belli Punici Carmine Quaestiones Selectae, 1935; S. Mariotti, Il Bellum Poenicum e l' arte di Nevio, 1955; W. Richter, Das Epos des Cnaeus Naevius, 1960; M. Barchiesi, Nevio epico, 1962; W. Beare, The Roman Stage, 3rd ed., 1969; J. Wright, Dancing in Chains, 1974.

NAMATIANUS, CLAUDIUS RUTILIUS. See Rutilius Namatianus

NASO, PUBLIUS OVIDIUS. See Ovid

NEMESIANUS, MARCUS AURELIUS OLYMPIUS, Latin poet, lived late in the third century A.D., if we can judge from his praises of the emperors Carinus and Numerian, who reigned jointly from 283 to 284. His place of origin was Carthage.

He wrote four short *Eclogues,* pastoral or bucolic pieces totaling three hundred nineteen lines in all; they closely follow the framework of Virgil's poems of the same title; and whole lines are also taken from Calpurnius Siculus, the pastoral poet of Nero's time (A.D. 54–68), to whom the writings of Nemesianus were formerly attributed. In the first of these poems the shepherd Timetas sings a dirge for Meliboeus (this name is sometimes held to be a pseudonym for the poet's own teacher) reminiscent of the eulogy of Daphnis in Virgil's fifth *Eclogue.* The second poem is a rehash of three of Calpurnius Siculus' pieces, and the third also draws on him freely: the song requested from Pan in this poem also echoes a similar demand from Silenus in the sixth *Eclogue* of Virgil. The ultimate source of the theme, however, is no doubt a poem from the Hellenistic age, and Nemesianus' fourth and last piece, too, repeats descriptions of magic that Virgil had earlier derived from Theocritus.

In addition, three hundred twenty-five lines have survived of Nemesianus' verses *On Hunting (Cynegetica),* dated to 283/4 by the above-mentioned reference to the imperial couple, to whose warlike achievements the writer, in a long-winded introduction, promises that he will devote his next work. Meanwhile, he justifies the choice of his present subject on the grounds that mythological themes have been worked to exhaustion. Then follow sections on dogs and on horses and a passage about nets and other hunting equipment that is only extant in fragments. The main theme is believed (though this is disputed) to be derived from the *Cynegetica* of the poet Grattius, of the Augustan age, with reminiscences also of Virgil's *Georgics.*

Two fragments of a poem entitled *On the Trapping of Birds,* amounting to twenty-eight lines altogether, are also attributed to Nemesianus; but they may belong not to a separate piece but to the *Cynegetica.* Furthermore, we learn from the dubious authority of the *Lives* of Carus, Carinus, and Numerian, in the *Historia Augusta,* that he also wrote *On Fishing (Halieutica)* and *On Seamanship (Nautica).*

Nemesianus was a diligent versemaker, who adhered to correct classical techniques (except in certain quantitative details in which he reflected his own period). He wrote with melodious smoothness, but his diligence was that of the schoolroom and relied excessively on conventional forms and images and, indeed, on plagiarisms as well. His principal interest is historical, since he was writing Latin poetry at a time when there were few other practitioners of the art.

EDITIONS with translation—J. W. Duff and A. M. Duff, Minor Latin Poets (Loeb ed.), revised ed., 1935; P. Volpilhac, Némésien: Oeuvres (Budé ed.), 1976. Eclogues: C. H. Keene, The Eclogues of Calpurnius and Nemesianus, 1887; C. Giarratano, Calpurnii et

ne me si ä' nus

Nemesiani Bucolica, 1924, reprint 1951; D. Korzeniewski, Hirtengedichte aus spätrömischer und karolingischer Zeit, 1976. Cynegetica: D. Martin, 1917; P. van de Woestijne, 1937.
ABOUT: J. Hubaux, Les thèmes bucoliques dans la poésie latine, 1930; P. Verdières, Prolegomènes à Némésien, 1974; A. J. Boyle, ed., Ancient Pastoral, 1975; D. Korzeniewski, ed., Bucolica Aetatis Romanae Posterioris et Aevi Carolini, 1976.

NEPOS, CORNELIUS, Latin biographer and historian, was born in about 99 B.C. and perhaps died in about 24. He came from a rich family in Cisalpine Gaul (northern Italy), the country of his friend Catullus; perhaps his hometown was Ticinum (Pavia). As a young man, he moved to Rome, where he formed friendships with many of the principal public figures of the time. He did not take part in politics, but devoted himself to writing and publishing instead. He remained in Rome until he died.

With the exception of a collection of love poems, he wrote exclusively in prose. Among his works were the *Chronica,* an outline history of the world in three books; a treatise on geography, cited by Mela and Pliny the Elder but regarded as too loosely constructed and uncritical; a collection of anecdotes *(Exempla)* in at least five books; and full-length biographies of Cato the Elder (the Censor) and Cicero, the latter written as an act of respect after the orator's death.

These writings have not come down to us, but what has survived is a portion of his work entitled *On Famous Men (De Viris Illustribus).* This composition, in sixteen books, contained lives of Romans and foreigners alike from many different professions. It is certain that kings, generals, poets, and historians were represented; fragments suggest that a section on orators may have been included; and so also, perhaps, were statesmen, philosophers, and grammarians. *On Famous Men* was dedicated to Atticus, a wealthy and influential Roman knight who was a friend of Cicero and had long been a close associate of Nepos as well. The first edition came out while Atticus was still alive; after his death in 32 B.C. Nepos published a revised edition, including lives of persons who were not Greeks. It is to this
nē′ pos

second edition that the fragments we have belong. The greater part consists of a single book, which includes accounts of Greek generals (the *Epaminondas* and *Agesilaus* resemble eulogistic orations), the Persian commander Datames, a number of Greek and Persian kings (in a brief section), and the Carthaginians Hamilcar and Hannibal. Parts of another book also survive, containing biographies of Cato the Younger (of Utica) and of Atticus himself; this last is an expanded version of what had evidently appeared in the original edition.

Although biography already had a considerable pedigree in Greece, it was of recent development in Rome, and Nepos is the earliest Latin writer from whom specimens of this genre have come down to us. He probably derived the idea of including biographies of foreigners from the *Imagines* of his older contemporary Varro, who was reputed to have been the first Roman biographer. Nepos cites numerous other sources but does not often use them at first hand. Although he makes an attempt to avoid monotony by varying the structure of his Lives, and although he diversifies his prose by colloquialisms and adornments (often illjudged), his style remains meager and tedious. As a historian, he is of little importance —indeed, history is not what he is trying to write. His principal desire is to offer praise— most of all in the ridiculously fulsome biography of Atticus. Moreover, he scarcely ever loses sight of a strongly moral purpose, based on the most banal ethical generalizations. This high-principled tone, together with his relatively easy language, earned for his biographies an ample future as a schoolbook; it formed part, for example, of the curriculum of English and Scottish schools from the early years of the eighteenth century.

WORKS—The surviving lives are of Miltiades, Themistocles, Aristides, Pausanias, Cimon, Lysander, Alcibiades, Datames, Epaminondas, Pelopidas, Agesilaus, Eumenes of Cardia, Phocion, Timoleon, followed by Persian and Macedonian kings and the successors of Alexander the Great and then by accounts of Hamilcar, Hannibal, Cato the Younger, and Atticus.
EDITIONS—K. Nipperdey, 12th ed. (revised by K. Witte), 1962; M. Ruch, Cornelius Nepos: Vies d'Hanni-

NERO CLAUDIUS GERMANICUS

bal, de Caton et d'Atticus, 1968; L. Agnes, Cornelius Nepos: Opere, 1977; P. K. Marshall, Cornelius Nepos: Vitae cum Fragmentis, 1977. *Translations*—J. C. Rolfe *in* E. S. Forster and J. C. Rolfe, Florus: Cornelius Nepos (Loeb ed.), 1929; A. M. Guillemin (Budé ed.), 1923.
ABOUT—D. R. Stuart, Epochs of Greek and Roman Biography, 1928; E. M. Jenkinson *in* T. A. Dorey, ed., Latin Biography, 1967; P. K. Marshall, The MS Tradition of Cornelius Nepos, 1978.

NERO CLAUDIUS GERMANICUS. See Germanicus

NICANDER, Greek didactic poet and scholar, was a native of Colophon (Değirmendere) in Ionia (western Asia Minor). Although there is a good deal of confusion about his chronology, his dedication of a hymn to King Attalus III of Pergamum (138–133 B.C.) suggests that other information ascribing him a much earlier date is either erroneous or refers to a former poet of the same name (whose existence is known from an inscription).

Two hexameter poems by Nicander have survived. One, the *Theriaca (Treatise on Beasts,* in this case, noxious beasts), devotes nearly a thousand lines to describing various snakes and other poisonous creatures and indicates the best remedies for their bites. The other piece, the *Alexipharmaca (Curative Herbs)* describes animal, vegetable, and mineral forms of poison and lists their antidotes. Nicander derived his material from a prose treatise on poisons by Apollodorus the Iologus, who lived in the early third century B.C. Being careless and no sort of scientist, Nicander often reproduces his facts incorrectly and records many blatant superstitions. Occasionally he enlivens his writing by the insertion of an episode or anecdote, mythological or otherwise, but his main stylistic concern is to employ the obscurest possible language and overload his lines with curiosities, difficult technical terms, altered meanings of words, and forced grammatical constructions.

Indeed, he is no more a poet than a scientist, his chief purpose being to force out-of-

nī kan' dēr

the-way erudition into verse of a pedestrian character. Nevertheless, his recondite material has a good deal of interest for the historian of medicine and its folklore, and in antiquity he was sometimes quoted as a reputable source. More often, however, he attracted the notice of ancient professional scholars by the tortuous character of his language and style. Works of his that are now lost included a separate poem on snakes, the *Ophiaca* (apparently in the elegiac meter); a *Prognostica,* versifying a treatise on the same subject wrongly attributed to Hippocrates; and a *Collection of Cures (Iaseon Sunagoge).*

These poems, however, have not survived. Nor have Nicander's epics, the *Thebaica, Oetaica, Sicelia, Cimmerii,* and perhaps a *Europia* as well. (His *Aetolica* may have been written in prose; also commemorations of his home town, namely a *Colophoniaca* and a treatise entitled *About Poets*—that is to say, poets from Colophon.) Another of his compositions of which we have virtually nothing is a five-book poem *On Changes of Shape (Heteroioumena),* which told stories from Greek mythology of miraculous transformations. Excerpts of this work made by Antoninus Liberalis, a Greek mythographer of the second century A.D., who based his own writings on this work, show that Nicander attempted to link the tales together by ingenious devices—like Ovid, who borrowed the idea for his *Metamorphoses.* Nicander's poem entitled *On Farming (Georgica)* was praised for its stylistic qualities by Cicero, and its title was taken over by Virgil, who may also have used Nicander's piece entitled *On Bee Farming (Melissurgica)* as a source book.

The Byzantine lexicon known as the Suda (Suidas) describes Nicander as "a grammarian, poet and doctor." The belief that he was a doctor is perhaps merely a deduction from the subject matter of some of his poems; the view that he was a grammarian may likewise be founded on the learned comments on Homeric and other early terms and phrases with which he interlarded his verses—indeed, he proudly described himself as Homeric. The Lexicon adds, however, with insight, that Nicander was, essentially, a man who was prepared to convert into verse any topic that came to hand.

EDITIONS with translation—A. S. F. Gow and A. F. Schofield, Nicander: The Poems and Political Fragments, 1953.
ABOUT—H. Schneider, Vergleichende Untersuchungen zur sprachlichen Struktur der beiden erhaltenen Lehrgedichte des Nikander, 1962; M. Geymonat, ed., Scholia in Nicandri Alexipharmaca, cum Glossis, 1974.

NICOLAUS OF DAMASCUS, Greek statesman, historian, and philosopher, was born in about 64 B.C. and died some time after the year 4. His parents were rich citizens of Damascus in Syria, and his father, Antipater, served frequently as an official and an envoy of that city. After receiving a complete liberal education, culminating in philosophical studies, Nicolaus assumed the duties of tutor of the children of the Roman general Mark Antony and Queen Cleopatra VII of Egypt—a boy and girl who were born in 40 B.C. and another boy born in 36—and then, probably before the deaths of those rulers in 30, became minister and intimate adviser and representative of King Herod the Great of Judaea (37 B.C.–4 B.C.). When, in 30, Herod transferred his allegiance to Antony's conqueror Octavian (the future Augustus), Nicolaus no doubt did the same. In 14 B.C. he traveled with Herod along the coast of Asia Minor and negotiated with Greek city-states in an endeavor to persuade them to give better treatment to the Jewish sections of their population. During the struggles between Herod's sons and potential heirs, he took sides against one of them, Antipater, whom he denounced at Rome in 12 B.C. In the year 8 he was sent to Rome again to patch up a rift between Augustus and Herod, and in 5 he proceeded to Syria to deliver a further attack on Antipater. Then, in the following year, when Herod died after appointing another son, Archelaus, as his principal successor, Nicolaus went to Rome once again, to undertake the delicate task of convincing Augustus of the wisdom of the choice. After that he appears to have retired.

Nicolaus was a voluminous writer. His most important work was a 144-book *Universal History,* substantial passages of which have come down to us in the form of adaptations by the Jewish historian Josephus (who

ni kō lā′ us

mentions him on no less than thirty-three occasions—and his debts go much farther than that). There are also excerpts preserved by the Byzantine emperor Constantine VII Porphyrogenitus and others. Nicolaus' history started with the earliest times and continued in a narrative that used an extensive number of Greek historians and some Roman as well. After devoting seven books to the Graeco-Persian war and, in a later part of the work, fourteen to Rome's war against Mithridates VI of Pontus, the history carried on down to the death of Herod the Great, about whose reign the surviving extracts provide useful and vivid information —in spite of a strong tendency to defend the record of the monarch, of whose memoirs Nicolaus made use. "What he produced," remarked Josephus, "was not a history for others but a work meant to help the king." At the same time Nicolaus has to justify his own career in Herod's service, a task of self-defense he pursued further in his own autobiography. In this work, which was principally designed for a Greek public, the accusations he felt obliged to answer included charges that, while at Rome, he had consorted with the common people instead of restricting his social contacts to the powerful and rich and that he had behaved in a friendly fashion toward slaves.

He also acted as Augustus' literary agent among the Greeks and wrote a eulogistic biography of that emperor's first forty years or so. The surviving fragments are valuable because they are evidently based, to a large extent, on the lost autobiography of Augustus himself, which was probably composed in about 25 B.C. and may have been followed soon afterward by the publication of Nicolaus' work. His other writings included a collection of ethnological information and various philosophical and scientific treatises in the Aristotelian tradition. He was also the author of comedies and tragedies, an activity that may have contributed to the theatrical nature of his historical writings, although that also owed much to the dramatic techniques that had been popularized by the historian Ctesias of Cnidus in the fifth century B.C.

NONIUS MARCELLUS

EDITIONS—F. Jacoby, Die Fragmente der griechischen Historiker, 2a, 90.
ABOUT—B. Z. Wacholder, Nicolaus of Damascus, 1962; G. W. Bowersock, Augustus and the Greek World, 1965; A. Schalit, König Herodes, 1969; M. Grant, Herod the Great, 1971.

NONIUS MARCELLUS, Latin lexicographer and grammarian, is probably to be identified with the Nonius Marcellus Herculius, who, according to an inscription of A.D. 326/33, was a citizen of Thubursicu Numidarum (Khamissa in Tunisia). Manuscripts describe the author as a roving Thubursican *(peripateticus Tubursicensis).* He was the compiler of a sort of lexicon *(De Compendiosa Doctrina per Litteras ad Filium;* this title, however, only belongs properly to the three longest chapters in the work). There are altogether twenty chapters (of which the sixteenth is lost), and the treatise falls into two parts, of unequal length. The first and longer section, comprising the first twelve chapters, deals with points of grammar, including the meanings, inflections, and genders of words. The second portion groups words according to the nature of what they refer to. Thus, chapter 13 gives the names of different kinds of ships; chapter 14 enumerates different kinds of clothing; chapter 15 lists the varieties of vases and cups; the lost chapter 16 reverted to matters of costume (including the names of shoes); and chapter 17 deals with fruits and other foodstuffs. Within chapters words are arranged alphabetically. Each successive topic is illustrated by quotations, excerpted from a wide range of writers, including many poets of the Roman Republican epoch. The writers quoted appear invariably in the same sequence throughout different chapters—which was evidently the order in which he found them in his sources: First is Plautus, followed by Lucretius; then come a number of writers whose works have not survived in substantial form, so that for many of them, notably Lucilius (second century B.C.) and Varro (first century B.C.), Nonius is our principal authority. It is probable, however, that he did not consult them direct but through contemporary reference books. In

nō′ ni us mär sel′ lus

general, he avoids specifying the sources he is using, so that the second century (A.D.) encyclopedist Gellius, for example, whom he copies with great frequency, nevertheless receives no mention at all. Another model seems to have been Flavius Caper, a grammarian of the late second century A.D.; and a variety of encyclopedias and lexica are also drawn upon. Nonius' use of these works often shows grave lacks of judgment, understanding, and accuracy—on one occasion, for example, he takes Marcus Tullius and Cicero for two different authors—but his work was consulted subsequently by a number of scholars, including Priscian (sixth century A.D.) and Fulgentius (fifth century A.D.).

EDITIONS—W. M. Lindsay (Teubner ed.), 1903.
ABOUT—W. M. Lindsay, Nonius Marcellus' Dictionary of Republican Latin, 1901; M. Schanz, C. Hosius, and G. Krüger, Geschichte der römischen Literatur, v 4, 1920; F. della Corte, La poesia di Varrone Reatino ricostituita, 1938; A. H. M. Jones, J. R. Martindale, and J. Morris, The Prosopography of the Later Roman Empire, v 1, 1971, p 552.

NONNUS, Greek poet, lived during the fifth century A.D. He came from Panopolis —known earlier as Chemmis—(the modern Akhmim) in Egypt, but his name is Celtic.

He wrote a very long epic poem, the *Dionysiaca,* which narrated, in forty-eight books of hexameters, the earthly career of Dionysus (Bacchus). The work deals chiefly with the god's role as conqueror of the East, telling of his invasion of India and his battles against King Deriades, a mythical theme that reflected the historical expeditions of Alexander the Great. Furthermore, the poem contains a complete account of the rest of Dionysus' legendary history. In ample introductory sections the happenings before the god was born are recounted. The entire cosmos is Nonnus' stage, and he presents it in a state of upheaval: Typhoeus has seized the power of lightning and is threatening Zeus with destruction. But Cadmus of Tyre, the founder of Thebes, will be the savior; his daughter Semele is destined to give birth to Dionysus. In Book 8, Nonnus tells of Dionysus' birth, then gives an account of

non′ nus

his youthful years. This brings us to the thirteenth book, which starts with the preparations for the Indian expedition, culminating in the downfall of Deriades in Book 40. Numerous adventures ensue during Dionysus' homeward march, including striking demonstrations of his power, such as the punishment of Pentheus, who had failed to acknowledge Dionysus as a deity; finally he is admitted to Olympus.

The poem displays a lavish profusion of material. No piece of anecdote or astral legend or mythological tale that could by any manner of means be dragged into the story is omitted, so that the narrative is heavily cluttered by innumerable digressions. Yet Nonnus possesses an extraordinarily fertile imagination and remarkable powers of fantastic description, which often suggest the influence of the Greek novel. Moreover, he displays an overwhelming command of all the resources of Greek poetical diction. However, this mastery is highly idiosyncratic, revealing itself in an abundance of inflated, unfamiliar language, in which ornamental epithets, daring metaphors, elaborate riddles, and incantatory formulas recur and proliferate. Although Nonnus enjoys a consummate knowledge of Greek literature of all periods, his bombast and frenzy should scarcely be judged by classical standards. And yet, in strange contrast to this absence of restraint, the metrical structure of his hexameters displays rigorous strictness, even at a time when the quantitative differences of Greek vowels were already beginning to vanish.

Nonnus became a convert to Christianity, but it seems right to suppose (despite arguments to the contrary) that the *Dionysiaca,* preoccupied as it is with astrology and magic, was written while he was still a pagan. After his conversion, however, he composed a further, shorter, hexameter poem, comprising a paraphrase *(Metabole)* of the Gospel according to St. John. This shows all the extravagance of the *Dionysiaca,* but this time, the colorful invention and descriptive fantasy are dimmed. There were a few poetical followers of Nonnus' style later in the fifth century, including the epic writers Triphiodorus and Colluthus, but then the long life of hexameter verse came to an end.

EDITIONS—Dionysiaca, with translation: W. H. D. Rouse, H. J. Rose, and L. R. Lind (Loeb ed.), 1940; R. Keydell (German), 1959; F. Vian and P. Chuvin (Budé ed.), 1976. Metabole of St. John's Gospel: A. Scheindler (Teubner ed.), 1881.

ABOUT—R. Keydell *in* Pauly-Wissowa-Kroll, Real-Encyclopädie der klassischen Altertumswissenschaft, v 7, columns 904-20; J. Golega, Studien über die Evangeliendichtung des Nonnos, 1930; G. d'Ippolito, Studi nonniani, 1964; B. Abel-Wilmanns, Der Erzählaufbau der Dionysiaka des Nonnus von Panopolis, 1977.

NOTKER BALBULUS, the Stammerer, monk, teacher, musician, and Latin author, was born in about A.D. 840 and died in 912. He entered the Benedictine monastery of St. Gall (Switzerland), where he studied music under Ratpert (the historian of the institution), Iso, and the talented Irish musician and scholar Marcellus (Moengal). In 890 Notker became the librarian of the monastery, greatly enlarging its stock of books; subsequently he became master of the school attached to the place. He possessed some knowledge of pagan literature—though, when writing a book of instruction for Salomon, a future abbot, he sought to dissuade him from reading non-Christian authors. Notker was said to be a shy and gentle man.

He found it hard to remember the passages, full of long vowels, comprising the Alleluia Jubilus, a prolonged melodic extension that followed the final *a* of the Alleluia and was divided into parts known as Sequences. As a mnemonic aid to the singing of these Sequences, it had become customary, in the ninth and tenth centuries, to set them to words, the texts in question being known as Proses. In 862 a French monk from Jumièges arrived at St. Gall bringing an antiphonary containing specimens of such Proses, whereupon Notker decided to improve on these versions by writing a Prose in which a single syllable should correspond to each note in the melody; and he also designed a new composition which included the entire melody of the Alleluia and remodeled its central portion, while retaining the original Jubilus at the beginning and end. The initial result of this project was his *Psallat Ecclesia,* a *vers libre,* or rhythmical prose poem, for the dedication of a church. Notnōt′ kĕr bal′ bū lus ker's endeavors led to the establishment of the most famous of the schools of Sequences; later writers and composers added assonance and then rhyme, until something like the modern rhymed hymn came into existence.

Notker the Stammerer also seems to have been the author of other works, if, as is probable, he was the same person as a monk at St. Gall (born in the Thur valley, near Lake Constance) who wrote a book of anecdotes between 884 and 887 for the emperor Charles the Fat (the great-grandson of Charlemagne) and compiled his life as well. Notker Labeo of St. Gall (c. 950–1022), on the other hand, and Notker Bishop of Liège (c. 940–1008), are distinct personages.

EDITIONS—Hymns and Sequences: J. P. Migne, Patrologia Latina, v 171; P. de Wintereld, Carmina, 1890. Life of Charlemagne: G. Meyer von Knonau, Monachus Sangallensis (Notker Balbulus) De Carolo Magno, 1918. *Translations*—L. Thorpe. Two Lives of Charlemagne (Penguin ed.), 1969; W. Wittenbach, Notkeri Gesta Karoli, ed. by R. Rau (German), 1962.
ABOUT—J. Werner, Notkers Sequenzen, 1901; H. Waddell, The Wandering Scholars, 1927; F. A. Wright and T. A. Sinclair, History of Later Latin Literature, 1931; T. Siegrist, Herrscherbild und Weltsicht bei Notker Balbulus, 1963; E. Lechner, Vita Notkeri Balbuli, 1972.

OCTAVIAN. See Augustus

OLYMPIODORUS, Greek historian and poet, was born in about A.D. 380 and died after 425. His birthplace was Thebes in Egypt, but he went to live at the court of the eastern emperor Theodosius II (A.D. 408–50) at Constantinople. There, although a pagan, he became one of the first recognizable members of the great Byzantine diplomatic profession. In 412 he was sent on a mission to the Huns; in 415 he stayed at Athens; later, he traveled to the remotest parts of Upper Egypt; and in 425 he made his only known journey to the West, visiting Rome. For twenty years he kept a pet parrot which, he claimed, could not only call its master's name but could sing and dance as well.

Although Olympiodorus stated that poetry was his métier, he is known to us instead from his history, or memoirs, in twenty-two books, covering the period from A.D. 407 to 425. This work, which was dedicated to Theodosius II, has disappeared; it was, however, used by Sozomen and Philostorgius not long after its publication, as well as by the Greek historian Zosimus (c. 500). It was also summarized in the ninth century by Photius, patriarch of Constantinople, in a piece known as *The Forty-Six Fragments of Olympiodorus*. Filled with erudite digressions, Olympiodorus' work was particularly valuable because of its detailed descriptions of contemporary Roman and German life; and his treatment of this wide field, while based on a certain range of literary sources, gained added authority from the personal experiences and prolonged personal researches he was able to draw upon. He was a witness to the decline of the western empire, which he attributed to a combination of bad luck and incompetence. But he pinned his hopes on the political unity reintroduced by the eastern ruler Theodosius II when he placed Valentinian III on the throne of the western empire in 425. In welding all this material into a fluent and coherent narrative, he occupied a place of his own in the tradition of Greek writing about Roman affairs.

Olympiodorus of Thebes has to be distinguished from the two philosophers named Olympiodorus who were natives of Alexandria, one a Peripatetic of the fifth century A.D. and the other a Neoplatonist of the sixth century A.D. Olympiodorus the Alchemist, writer of a treatise entitled *On the Sacred Art of the Philosopher's Stone,* is variously identified with the historian of Thebes and the Neoplatonist of Alexandria.

EDITIONS (of the History of Olympiodorus of Thebes)—K. Müller, Fragmenta Historicorum Graecorum, v 4, 1851; L. Dindorf, Historici Graeci Minores, v 1, 1870. *With translation:* C. D. Gordon, The Age of Attila, 1960. Edition of Olympiodorus the Alchemist: M. Berthelot, Collection des alchimistes grecs, 1887–88.
ABOUT—W. Haedicke *in* Pauly-Wissowa-Kroll, Real-Encyclopädie der klassischen Altertumswissenschaft, v 18, no 1, 1939, columns 201–7; G. Moravcsik, Byzantinoturcica, v 1, 2nd ed., 1958; J. F. Matthews, Olympiodorus of Thebes and the History of the West (Journal of Roman Studies, v 60), 1970.

ō lim pi ō dō′ rus

ORIBASIUS, Greek medical writer, was born in about A.D. 320 and died at a date not earlier than 396. His birthplace was Pergamum (Bergama) in Mysia (western Asia Minor) (not, apparently, Sardes, as was alternatively stated). His parents, who were prosperous pagans, sent him to Alexandria to study medicine under the eminent physician Zeno of Cyprus. Subsequently, Oribasius himself practiced in Asia Minor. Then he became a close associate of the future emperor Julian who, on being named Caesar (heir to the throne) in 355 at the age of twenty-three, made him his chief librarian and took him to Gaul as his personal physician. There Oribasius encouraged Julian's secret reversion to paganism. He was closely involved in his proclamation as emperor (361) and remained in Julian's company until the latter's death in Mesopotamia two years later. Then, however, he was banished to Gothic territory by the new rulers Valentinian I and Valens, who were Christians. Before long, Valens recalled him and restored his property, and he resumed the practice of his profession. He took as his wife a rich and well-known woman who subsequently bore him four children.

The first of Oribasius' compilations, which only survives in fragments, was a selection or epitome of the voluminous writings of Galen (A.D. 129–c. 199), the renowned physician and philosopher who came from the same town. Oribasius' epitome was written on the instructions of Julian; and so was his principal work, which came next. This was his vast *Medical Collection,* an encyclopedia of medicine in seventy (or seventy-two) books, of which twenty-three (or twenty-five) have been preserved in their entirety, along with excerpts from others. In his preface to the work, he explains to Julian that his plan is to produce an even more comprehensive compendium than his earlier endeavor, which had been based on Galen alone. Now, he declares, he will draw on "all the best physicians"—though still allotting the first place to Galen, who seemed to him the truest representative of the Hippocratic tradition. To judge from the extant books of the *Medical Collection,* Galen is in fact still Oribasius' principal source, though the

o ri ba' si us

work provides a massive array of excerpts from other medical writers ranging from Alcmaeon of Croton, at the end of the sixth century B.C., to his own contemporaries Adamantius and Philagrius.

The missing portions of the *Medical Collection* can be partly reconstructed from abbreviated versions made by the author himself, including a *Synopsis* in nine books addressed to his son Eustathius and a sort of domestic pharmacopoeia in four books that was known as the *Euporista* or *To Eunapius* (to whom it was dedicated).

Oribasius was as determined an adherent of paganism as his patron Julian, and his encyclopedia was in keeping with Julian's efforts to retain and reconstruct the classical heritage. The significance of the work lies in the numerous extracts from earlier writers that it offers. For subsequent generations, the *Collection* served as model and source alike; Byzantine medical writers drew on it continually for quotation and summarized it in numerous epitomes. The *Synopsis* and *Euporista* were twice translated into Latin in the fifth or sixth century, and in the ninth century Arabic versions of both works were composed, in addition to a Syriac rendering of part of the *Collection.* These and other Arabic and Syriac versions played an enormous part in the communication of Greek medicine to the Islamic world, from whence it later passed back to the West.

EDITIONS—J. Rader, Corpus Medicorum Graecorum, v 6. *Translations*—C. Daremberg and U. C. Bussemaker (French), 1851–76, reprint 1962.
ABOUT—H. O. Schröder *in* Pauly-Wissowa-Kroll, Real-Encyclopädie der klassischen Altertumswissenschaft, Suppl. 7, columns 797ff.; H. Morland, Die lateinischen Oribasiusübersetzungen, 1932; E. D. Phillips, Greek Medicine, 1973.

ORIGEN (Origenes Adamantius), Greek theologian, was born in A.D. 185 or 186 and died in 254 or 255. His birthplace is likely to have been Alexandria, and his parents were variously reported to be of Christian or pagan origin. They were probably Christians; at all events, his father Leonides was one by the end of his life, since he perished in the

ō' ri gen

persecution of Septimius Severus (202). After Leonides' death, Origen provided for his mother and six younger brothers by becoming a teacher of grammar. Subsequently, however, he studied in the catechetical school at Alexandria under Pantaenus and Clement, whom he succeeded, first informally and then officially (203), as director of the institution. He also attended the lectures of the Alexandrian Platonist Ammonius Saccas and visited Antioch, Palestine, Arabia, and Rome. It was said that in order that his female pupils should not distract his attention from his work, he castrated himself.

His activity as a teacher was interrupted for a time by the emperor Caracalla's massacre of the Alexandrians in 215, which caused him to move to Palestine. Later, the bishop of Alexandria, Demetrius, called him back; and Origen came to be a well-known figure in the eastern church, traveling widely in response to numerous invitations. On one such journey, however, in about 230, he allowed himself to be ordained a presbyter at Caesarea Maritima in Palestine, an action which, together with heterodox elements in his teaching, caused Demetrius to take away his job and drive him out of Alexandria. This verdict was ignored in Palestine, where Origen went to live, settling at Caesarea and attracting many pupils; he also continued to travel. When the emperor Trajanus Decius launched his persecution of the Christians in 250, Origen was imprisoned and tortured. He survived, with weakened health, but died a few years later at Tyre (Sur).

Origen was a pioneer writer in a variety of fields, and on an enormous scale. One of his principal tasks was biblical criticism, for he felt it essential for Christians to be able to argue with Jews on the basis of a generally recognized text of the Scriptures. He therefore compiled a huge synopsis of the various versions of the Old Testament. This work, begun in 231 at the earliest and finished in 244/5, was entitled the *Hexapla* (sixfold), because it placed in six parallel columns the Hebrew text, a transliteration of it into Greek characters, and the four main Greek versions. (For the *Psalms,* he added two further translations, one of which came from a manuscript he had found in a jar in the Jordan valley). His main purpose was to ensure

greater accuracy for the Septuagint, which was the accepted version of all the Greek churches. His critical activity, however, led him into sharp controversy with an older Christian scholar, Julius Africanus, who pointed out Origen's error in regarding the *History of Susanna* as an original part of the Book of Daniel.

However, Origen regarded the exegesis of the Bible as his principal task, and the greater part of his writings consists of commentaries, sermons, and marginal notes (scholia) on books of the Old and New Testament. None of his commentaries has survived complete, partly because they were not always orthodox enough to win approbation but also because of their great length, which made it very difficult to copy them. Certain of these commentaries, however, were drastically abbreviated and paraphrased by his contemporary Rufinus of Aquileia. And Rufinus, together with Jerome, preserved many of his sermons, in their original form or in Latin translation.

Rufinus also translated into Latin an important doctrinal work by Origen, *On First Principles (De Principiis),* frankly admitting, however, that he had inserted adjustments in the interests of orthodoxy; however, considerable passages of the original Greek survive. *On First Principles* was a systematic and thoughtful statement of Christian doctrine, based on the hypothesis that whereas every member of the Church is committed to the rule of faith laid down by the Apostles, the informed believer is also free, over and above this commitment, to put forward whatever speculations he himself may wish to offer.

One of Origen's most famous writings was entitled *Against Celsus (Contra Celsum),* a vindication of Christianity against pagan criticism. Celsus was a Platonist who, in about A.D. 176, had composed the *True Word (Alethes Logos),* an elaborate denunciation of Christianity. In c. 248/9 a certain Ambrose, a rich friend and patron of Origen who paid stenographers to record his sermons, persuaded him to reply to this onslaught; Origen's treatise answered Celsus point by point, bracketing successive quotations from the *True Word* (otherwise no longer extant) with arguments of his own, so that we are given the opportunity of hearing both sides of the debate. Celsus' sharp attack on Christianity as a naive and barbarous denial of the values and traditions of classical civilization provokes Origen into arguing that any person with a philosophically trained intellect is fully justified in thinking within a Christian framework and that Christian belief is neither irrational prejudice nor the mere eccentricity of social dissidents.

He also wrote devotional works, *On Prayer (De Oratione)* in about 231 and an *Exhortation to Martyrdom* of about 235, addressed to Ambrose and another friend Protoctetus, both of whom suffered in the persecution under the emperor Maximinus I (235–38).

In his lifetime Origen was already the target for numerous attacks, on the grounds that he was polluting Christianity with infusions of pagan philosophy. After his death, although he had powerful defenders (including the Cappadocian Fathers Gregory of Nazianzus and Basil, who jointly made a collection of excerpts from his works, the *Philocalia*), opposition steadily mounted, culminating in his denunciation as a heretic by the Byzantine emperor Justinian I. These controversies continued almost without cessation in and beyond Renaissance times, eastern writers generally showing a more critical attitude than those of the West. The numerous accusations against Origen included complaints that he made the Son inferior to the Father, reduced the Resurrection of the Body to unreality, denied the existence of hell, and eliminated the historical basis of the Redemption by reducing everything to allegory. Nevertheless, it remains difficult to deny the assertion of Jerome that, after the Apostles, he was the greatest of all the teachers of the early church. Yet "Who," as Jerome observed, "could ever read all that Origen wrote?" Because of his endless labors, he was nicknamed Adamantius, the iron man.

EDITIONS—C. de la Rue, Opera Omnia, 1733–59, reprinted *in* J. P. Migne, Patrologia Graeca, v 11-17; P. Nautin, Origène, v 1, 1977. *Individual works:* F. Field, Hexapla, 1875; H. Görgemanns and H. Karpp, Vier Bücher von den Prinzipen (On First Principles), 1976.

Selections from the Commentaries and Homilies: R. B. Tollinton, 1929. *With translation:* M. Simonetti, I principi, Contra Celsum e altri scritti filosofici, 1975; Contra Celsum: H. Chadwick, 2nd ed., 1965; On First Principles: G. W. Butterworth, 1936; On Prayer, Exhortation to Martyrdom, Dialogue With Heracleides: J. E. L. Oulton and H. Chadwick, 1954; On Prayer, Exhortation to Martyrdom: J. J. O'Meara, 1954; On Prayer: E. G. Jay, 1954; Philocalia: G. Lewis, 1911. ABOUT—E. de Faye, Origène: Sa vie, son oeuvre, sa pensée, 1923–28; D. Daniélou, Origen, 1955; R. P. C. Hanson, Allegory and Event, 1959; H. Crouzel, Origène et la connaissance mystique, 1961; J. M. Rist, Eros and Psyche: Studies in Plato, Plotinus and Origen, 1964; H. Chadwick, Early Christian Thought and the Classical Tradition: Studies in Justin, Clement and Origen, 1966; W. Gessel, Die Theologie des Gebetes nach dem De Oratione von Origenes, 1975; N. R. M. de Lange, Origen and the Jews, 1977; L. Rougier, Celse contre les chrétiens, 1977.

OROSIUS, PAULUS, Spanish theologian and historian who wrote in Latin, was born in about A.D. 380 and died in about 420. He was probably born at Bracara Augusta (now Braga in northern Portugal), where he entered the priesthood. After the invasion by the Suebi and Vandals, he moved, in about 414, to Hippo Regius (now Annaba in Algeria), in order to become a pupil of St. Augustine. On arrival in northern Africa, he wrote *Instruction on the Erroneous Beliefs of the Followers of Priscillian and Origen (Commonitorium De Errore Priscillianistarum et Origenistarum),* which prompted Augustine to write a tract in support. In 415, despite his ignorance of the Greek language, he was sent by Augustine to Jerome in Bethlehem to help him refute Pelagius, whose doctrines supposedly did too little justice to the divine grace. Orosius engaged in a public debate with Pelagius in Jerusalem and further explained his case in a monograph *(Liber Apologeticus Contra Pelagianos).*

Early in the following year he returned to northern Africa, where Augustine induced him to write a history of the world from the Christian point of view, his *History Against the Pagans.* The first of its seven books deals with events from the creation of the world down to the founding of Rome. Books 2-6 relate the history of what were regarded as the four principal world states: the Babylonian, Macedonian, Carthaginian, ō rō' si us and Roman. The seventh and last book is concerned with the Roman imperial epoch down to the writer's own time, with particular reference to the story of the Christian church.

Orosius draws special attention to the disasters that had overtaken humankind before the coming of Christianity, in an effort to contradict the frequent pagan accusation that the contemporary misfortunes of the Roman empire were due to its conversion to the Christian faith. The structure of his treatise is founded on Augustine's providential theory of history, which assumed that God's plan had included the destinies of the leading pagan states as well as of the Jewish and Christian communities. Orosius' chronology was based on Jerome's version of Eusebius' *Chronicle*. As regards his other sources, he did not bother to consult at first hand the leading historians of Greece or Rome or, of course, of the East but made use of secondhand Latin summaries of their works. However, Orosius is much more socially conscious than the majority of Greek and Roman historical writers, showing keen awareness, for example, of the horrors that warfare brought to the poorer sections of the population, however exciting it may have been for the nobles. He also shows an awareness, equally rare among writers of his age, that he was living in a transitional epoch; and, for events of his own lifetime, his alertness and enthusiasm are infectious. Yet his history suffers from grave faults. For one thing, his choice of the world states to be discussed is incomplete and his treatment of them, sketchy in the extreme. Moreover, the remorseless bias of his work, ascribing an unrelieved record of catastrophes to the pre-Christian world, reveals little more than his own preconceived opinions and rules him out of account as a significant historical writer. Furthermore, his work is not only written in a dull and unattractive style but shows abundant signs of haste and carelessness; it does not, for example, inspire confidence to find Caesar's *Commentaries* attributed to Suetonius. Nevertheless, his history became the standard manual on ancient pagan world history during the Middle Ages—as the survival of more than two hundred manuscripts testifies.

300

EDITIONS—G. Schepps and K. Zangemeister, Corpus Scriptorum Ecclesiasticorum Latinorum, v 5 and v 18. *Translations* (of the History)—I. W. Raymond, 1936; R. J. Deferrari, 1964.
ABOUT—J. Svennung, Orosiana, 1922; J. Ferguson, Pelagius, 1957; A. Antonaci, Paolo Orosio apologeta, 1961; A. Momigliano, Conflict Between Paganism and Christianity in the Fourth Century A.D., 1963.

OVID (Publius Ovidius Naso), Latin poet, was born in 43 B.C. and died in A.D. 17. His birthplace was Sulmo (Sulmona) in the territory of the Paeligni, east of Rome, where he came of a family of knightly (equestrian) rank. He learned rhetoric at Rome from Arellius Fuscus and Porcius Latro, the foremost rhetoricians of the time. He also studied at Athens and visited Asia Minor and Sicily. Then, for a time, he held minor judicial posts at Rome. Subsequently he abandoned the legal career for poetry, becoming a member of the circle of the statesman and literary patron Messalla, like his fellow poet Tibullus. Ovid's literary activity gained him a considerable reputation among the fashionable Roman upper class. He married three times; it was probably his second wife who bore him a daughter (unless the girl was a stepdaughter); his third was related to Paullus Fabius Maximus, a close friend of the emperor Augustus.

In A.D. 8, however, when Ovid was the leading poet of the capital, Augustus suddenly banished him to Tomis on the Black Sea (now Constanţa in Rumania). The reasons for the imperial decision are not fully known, but Ovid himself described his offenses as a "poem" (perhaps the *Art of Love*) and an "indiscretion" *(error):* possibly he was an accomplice in the adultery of the emperor's granddaughter Julia, who was exiled at the same time, for adultery. At Tomis, a small, superficially Hellenized place on the extreme fringe of the empire, perilously subject to barbarian attacks, Ovid remained: neither Augustus (d. A.D. 14) nor his successor Tiberius (14–37) ever recalled him.

Ovid is the poet of the middle and later years of Augustus. He was younger than the other leading elegists (Propertius and Tibullus) and long outlived them. Much of his

ov' id

work belongs to a different era from theirs and displays a different character as well, for he was born too late to feel any emotional commitment to the Augustan regime. He belonged to a new, smart, sophisticated society, less serious in its interests, that now flourished in the capital. His verse reflects his elaborate rhetorical education. It moves lightly and speedily, exploiting to perfection the elegiac meter that Ovid employed for all his major works (except the *Metamorphoses*) and transformed into the scintillating instrument of a novel refinement. The elegy was traditionally "tearful": but he calls it "festive" instead.

Thus, when Ovid published the first edition of his *Loves (Amores)*, an epoch ended and another began. Its original edition, in five books, appeared in about 20 B.C., whereas what we possess today is a revised three-book edition issued some two decades later. Most of the poems in the *Amores* are studies or sketches of love in a variety of moods, ranging from the seducer's approach to that of the simple, faithful lover. The principal figure of many of the pieces is a girl named Corinna, a name that sounds like a pseudonym, though whether she really existed or not we cannot tell. At all events, this is love poetry of an unfamiliar sort, as flippant as Horace's but adding a fresh ingredient—an absorption in female psychology that had been made fashionable in Greek literature by the Hellenistic poets of Alexandria. Ovid is understanding about the woman's point of view. Yet, this is not subjective, introspective love poetry, about passions deeply felt by the poet himself; it comes from a light heart and is infused with mockery and humor. Only occasionally, in the *Amores,* is a deeper chord struck, for example when he writes of Tibullus who had been his friend.

Another collection sometimes regarded as Ovid's second endeavor (though attribution to a later date in his career is also a possibility) was known as the *Heroines (Heroides)* or *Letters of Heroines (Heroidum Epistulae).* These pieces take the form of twenty poetic love letters (for a twenty-first, see below, under WORKS) purporting to have been addressed by mythological women to their absent lovers or husbands and including, in three cases, replies from the addressees. The women's complaints of unhappy love are rhetorical and ingenious, and Ovid imparts to them a glittering tone of adventurous excitement. But these pieces, like the *Amores,* are not real, earnest, love poetry at all. Although sensitive to the plight of his romantic heroines, who are updated into contemporary ladies of Roman fashion, the poet views them with a dispassionate and almost clinical detachment.

Ovid's incomplete poem entitled *On Taking Care of a Woman's Face (Medicamina Faciei Femineae),* of which about one hundred lines survive, was probably published during the last years of the first century B.C. It contains recipes for the care of the female complexion. His *Art of Love (Ars Amatoria),* issued not before 1 B.C., is a didactic poem on the arts of seduction and intrigue. Of its three books, the first two, intended to be read by men, comprised the original poem, whereas the third, for perusal by women (who are in turn instructed in how to become seducers), was added, we are told, in response to a woman's request. While pretending to deal with lovemaking as a science, Ovid succeeds in making fun of love poetry, didactic verse, and the literature of moral uplift at one and the same time. The poem also exemplifies its author's remarkable talent for telling stories, to which his sparkling versification was ideally adapted; its vivid sketches of contemporary Roman society—at circus, theatre, and banquet—and its many flashes of satire and vivacious wit give it a unique position in ancient literature. The *Art of Love,* however, caused sufficient sensation among at least some of its readers to call for a conciliatory sequel, *The Cures of Love (Remedia Amoris).* This eight-hundred-line mock recantation, full of clever and unexpected variations, contains an interesting justification of the poet's outspokenness. But the piece was too flippant to have appeased puritanical disapproval.

When Ovid was exiled in A.D. 8, he had completed the most substantial and influential of his writings, the *Metamorphoses,* composed, unlike his other works, in hexameters. This long poem, in fifteen books, tells of miraculous changes of shape. It begins with the transfiguration of Chaos into the ordered universe. Then, after a succession of Greek mythological themes, it passes to Aeneas and Dido and moves onward down to the death and deification of Julius Caesar in 44 B.C. Although this is an epic poem in meter and form, the tales do not constitute any traditional, serious kind of epic plot and are, indeed, only very loosely connected one with another. Their unity lies in the common theme and in the atmosphere with which Ovid's narrative gift envelops the entire work. In spite of many verbal echoes of Virgil, his hexameter is something quite different, wholly lacking in the older poet's sonorous profundity, avoiding also the conversational tone of Horace's poems in the same meter.

Like the Alexandrian Greeks, who had revived interest in erudite topics, Ovid was learned. Yet he carries his learning very lightly and gives new life to the principal myths and legends of ancient Greece and Rome. The legendary figures are modernized, as are the gods and goddesses, whose presentation is flavored with a mocking lack of reverence. There is also tenderness in the *Metamorphoses,* for example in the depiction of young people, of whom Ovid is fond; and he loves to portray natural scenery and coloring.

Ovid had also half finished his *Fasti* at the time when the blow of banishment fell. This collection of elegiac poems in six books, which were to have been expanded to twelve before his exile caused the work to be laid aside, was designed, in the spirit of the *Causes* of Callimachus (c. 305–240 B.C.), as a study of the Roman calendar in the light of the old stories and records; it sought to show which events are commemorated on which days and what the origins of the various rituals may have been. The mass of religious lore that Ovid thus manages to include and the numerous descriptions of festivals, rites, and historical events that he inserts along the way, give him an opportunity to retell once again, in his own inimitable manner, a wide range of the Greek and Roman myths and legends, offering at the same time digressions on a multitude of different themes. His older contemporary Propertius had also turned his attention to the romantic charm of these antique customs and had handled them with power, but Ovid is more

inclined to use them as a stimulating source book for his special narrative gifts and as a field for the accomplishment of his metrical *tours de force.* The *Fasti,* published after his death, made him a national, patriotic poet in the manner of so many of his predecessors, giving him a broad popularity he never enjoyed during his lifetime.

The poems he continued to write at Tomis inevitably lack the gaiety of his earlier work and display a certain failure of dignity and fortitude. They are, however, still extremely skillful poetry and gain added value, as far as we are concerned, from the biographical and personal notes they contribute about Ovid himself. The *Lamentations (Tristia),* in five books that were written during the early years of his banishment (A.D. 8–12), are mostly in the form of poetic "letters" to his wife and unnamed friends and comprise many complaints about his punishment and hopes for its mitigation. Book I includes a poem giving an account of the last night he had spent before his departure from Rome; the remaining pieces were written in the course of his long voyage to Tomis and enlarge upon the storms and hardships he experienced during the journey. Book 2 is a single piece, consisting of a protest that his sentence is disproportionate to his fault. The piece has been regarded by some as a sort of manifesto of the "alternative culture," not blessed by the imperial approval, for which he himself stood.

The *Ibis,* published in about A.D. 11 (and, despite views that have been expressed to the contrary, acceptable as a work of Ovid's authorship), is a curse directed against an unnamed personal enemy. The object of this attack may have been a man mentioned several times in the *Tristia,* but the *Ibis,* full of rhetorical fireworks and recondite mythological erudition, reads more like an artificial literary creation than a genuine polemic. Its idea and title were borrowed from an attack by Callimachus on his rival Apollonius Rhodius.

Ovid's *Letters from Pontus (Epistulae ex Ponto),* in four books, were composed in the later years of his exile, the last of his life (c. A.D. 12–16). These pieces are similar to the *Tristia* except that he now names the supposed recipients; many of his friends and acquaintances figure among them, including public figures and poets and rhetoricians. His continued hopes that his banishment will be rescinded are now largely centered on Tiberius' adopted son Germanicus, who is mentioned or addressed in various passages. In others, we hear of Ovid's attempts to learn the local Getic language and of the kindness of his barbarian hosts, although he continues to find the environment of his forced residence loathsome.

His reputation throughout the centuries has been incalculably large and pervasive. Quotations from the *Art of Love* are found on graffiti at Pompeii; and Ovid's powers of storytelling greatly influenced later Latin writers, who freely imitated and borrowed from his poems and benefited from his presentation of the world of Greek and Roman myths and legends. In medieval times, too, he was extensively read, quoted, and adapted. The *Metamorphoses,* in particular, fostered the concept of knightly romantic love, and the *Loves* and *Heroines* contributed to the same ideal: indeed, at times, their "letters" were even believed to be real. There was truly an "Ovidian period" in the Middle Ages, when he was the favorite author of the time. Thus in the fourteenth century, the English poet Chaucer knew Ovid much better than he knew any other Latin writer, and he paid special tribute to the *Metamorphoses*.

The work provided an inexhaustible reservoir of stories—and of themes for paintings as well, since its great word pictures were a major source of inspiration to Renaissance artists. Because of his supreme narrative gifts, and the wit and grace with which he exercised them, Ovid, far more than any other ancient poet, was the model of the European Renaissance and the English Elizabethan and Jacobean ages: the translation of the *Metamorphoses* by Arthur Golding (1565–67) made a decisive impact on Shakespeare's mind (*Midsummer Night's Dream* is in part inspired by Ovid's work). Later, too, the heroic couplets of Dryden, Matthew Prior, and Pope are thoroughly reminiscent of Ovid; and Wordsworth, Shelley, and Keats—despite their apparently un-Ovidian outlooks—continued to betray his influence.

WORKS—Lost writings include a tragedy, the Medea, highly praised by Quintilian and Tacitus; only two lines survive. Among poems wrongly attributed to Ovid are the Halieutica in hexameters (of which we likewise only have a fragment) on the marine creatures of the Black Sea, the Nut (Nux) that purports to be a complaint by a nut tree, and the Consolation to Livia (Consolatio ad Liviam) or Dirge for Drusus (Epicedion Drusi) on the death of Nero Drusus (Drusus Senior), the son of Livia and stepson of Augustus. One of the poems of the Heroides, purporting to be a declaration by Sappho, is of doubtful authenticity.

EDITIONS (of individual works)—*Listed in* Oxford Classical Dictionary, 2nd ed., 1970, p 765. *Add:* W. S. Anderson, Metamorphoses, Book 6-10, 1972; F. Capponi, Halieuticon, 1972; J. B. Pighi, Fasti, 1974; E. de Saint-Denis, Halieutiques, 1975; A. S. Hollis, Ars Amatoria, Book 1, 1977; A. Metzger and H. Kugler, Metamorphosis, 1978. *With translation:* G. Showerman, J. H. Mozley, F. J. Miller, J. G. Frazer, A. L. Wheeler (Loeb ed.), 1914–39; M. M. Innes, Metamorphoses (Penguin ed.), 1955; R. Humphries, Metamorphoses, 1957 *and* The Loves, The Art of Beauty, The Remedies for Love, The Art of Love, 1957; H. Gregory, Love Poems of Ovid, 1964; G. Lee, Ovid's Amores, 1968; P. Turner, The Techniques of Love: Remedies for Love, 1968; L. R. Lind, Tristia, 1975; F. Bömer, Fasti (German), 1957–58; F. W. Lenz, Remedia Amoris (German), 1960; F. Munari, Amores (Italian), 2nd ed., 1964; E. Zinn, Ars Amatoria and Remedia Amoris (German), 1970. For earlier translations *see* J. C. Thornton and M. H. Thornton, Ovid: Selected Works, 1939.

ABOUT: H. Fraenkel, Ovid: A Poet Between Two Worlds, 1945; L. P. Wilkinson, Ovid Recalled, 1955 (abridged as Ovid Surveyed, 1962); N. I. Herescu, ed., Ovidiana, 1958; Atti del Convegno internazionale ovidiano, 1959; E. K. Rand, Ovid and His Influence, 1963; H. T. Sorley, Exile: A Study in Three Books, 1963; J. C. Thibault, The Mystery of Ovid's Exile, 1964; E. Zinn and M. von Albrecht, Ovid, 1968; W. Stroh, ed., Ovid im Urteil der Nachwelt, 1969; B. Otis, Ovid as an Epic Poet, 2nd ed., 1970; J. W. Binns, ed., Ovid, 1973; D. R. Dudley and T. A. Dorey, eds., 1973; O. S. Due, Changing Forms: Studies in the Metamorphoses of Ovid, 1974; H. Jacobson, Ovid's Heroides, 1974; H. Doerrie, P. Ovidius Naso, 1975; C. G. Galinsky, Ovid's Metamorphoses, 1975; H. Froesch, Ovid als Dichter des Exils, 1976; A. F. Sabot, Ovide: Poète de l'amour dans les oeuvres de jeunesse, 1976; N. Scivoletto, Musa Iocosa: Studi sulla poesia giovanile di Ovidio, 1976; S. Viarre, Ovide: Essai de lecture poétique, 1976; K. Morgan, Ovid's Art of Imitation: Propertius in the Amores, 1977; J. Barsby, Ovid (Greece & Rome: New Surveys in the Classics, no 12), 1978; R. Syme, History in Ovid, 1978.

PACUVIUS, MARCUS, Latin tragic poet, 220–c. 130 B.C., was born at the Roman
pà kū′ vi us

colony of Brundusium (Brindisi) in south-eastern Italy. His mother was the sister of the poet Ennius, who had claimed to combine the Oscan, Latin, and Greek cultures; and Pacuvius' name was Oscan. As a young man he followed Ennius to Rome and subsequently became a friend of the younger Scipio Africanus. He was still at Rome at the age of eighty but was at Tarentum (Taranto) when he died.

He was well known as a painter; as a writer, unlike his versatile uncle Ennius, he restricted himself to tragedy. About four hundred lines of his plays have survived, and thirteen of their titles. Twelve of these are adapted from Greek models. The *Antiopa* was based on the *Antiope* of Euripides; its fragments include a debate on the relative merits of the artistic and the practical life. The *Atalanta* shares its name with a tragedy by Aeschylus, although there is nothing to show whether Pacuvius copied him directly. *The Award of Armor (Armorum Judicium)* is likewise an Aeschylean title. In the *Chryses,* a character jeers about divination in a manner reminiscent of Euripides' *Chrysippus;* but the title corresponds with one of Sophocles' plays. So does the name of another of his plays, *The Foot-Washing (Niptra)*—the washing of the feet of Ulysses (Odysseus) by his old nurse—in which, Cicero informs us, the wounded Ulysses bore his pain with greater fortitude than in the corresponding Sophoclean passage. The plot seems to have included an unusually long succession of incidents, suggesting that Pacuvius may have amalgamated two separate Greek plays. His *Hermiona* is suggestive of the *Andromache* of Euripides, though to what extent it was modeled on that play is not clear. *Iliona* was named after a daughter of Priam, to whom, in a pathetic scene, the ghost of her murdered son Deiphilus appeared in a vision. The *Medus,* which took its name from Medea's son who killed his uncle Perseus and became the ruler of Media, evidently had a very complicated plot. The *Pentheus* was perhaps taken from Euripides' *Bacchae.* The *Periboea* may have treated the same story as Sophocles' *Hipponus,* in which a mythical personage sent his pregnant daughter to Oeneus of Calydon to be killed; but Oeneus married her instead. *Slave-*

Orestes (Dulorestes) apparently recounted an unfamiliar version of the myth in which Orestes, in order to carry out his task of murdering his mother and her lover, disguised himself as a slave. *Teucer* dealt with the return of that hero from Troy to his native Salamis in Cyprus, from which his father Telamon then proceeded to expel him because he had failed to bring back his half brother Ajax. Other fragments suggest that Pacuvius wrote still more plays after Greek models, plays of which we have no knowledge. Furthermore, like his uncle Ennius, he embarked on the type of tragedy that celebrated Roman themes, the *fabula praetexta;* for instance, this was the character of his *Paullus,* which evidently commemorated the victory of Lucius Aemilius Paullus over King Perseus of Macedonia at the battle of Pydna in 168 B.C.

Pacuvius' style was notable for descriptive power, philosophical speculation, and exuberant inventiveness, all of which enabled him to strike out quite independently from his Greek originals. His plots were ingenious and learned, and his style displayed bold verbal innovations, including compound adjectives of remarkable length. When he was eighty, before he finally left Rome, one of his rivals in a dramatic competition was Accius, who was only thirty at the time. In subsequent epochs the merits of the two playwrights were variously compared. Varro and Cicero considered Pacuvius the foremost of Latin tragic poets. Later, the Augustans considered him equal with Accius; indeed, Quintilian, though he admired Pacuvius' forcefulness, regarded Accius as the greater of the two.

EDITIONS with translation—E. H. Warmington, Remains of Old Latin, v 2, 1936.
ABOUT—M. Valsa, Marcus Pacuvius: poète tragique, 1957; I. Mariotti, Introduzione a Pacuvio, 1960; W. Beare, The Roman Stage, 3rd ed., 1969; G. A. Tourlides, Meletai peri ton Pakoubion, 1975.

PANAETIUS, Greek philosopher, was born in the period 185–180 B.C. and died in about 109. His birthplace was the island of Rhodes, where his father Nicagoras was a

på nē' ti us

Stoic philosopher. Panaetius was sent to Pergamum to attend the lectures of Crates of Mallus, the first director of the Pergamene library. Later, he moved to Athens and studied at the Stoic school, first under Diogenes of Babylon (died c. 152 B.C.), then under Antipater of Tarsus, Diogenes' disciple and successor as head of the school. At some period between 170 and 150 Panaetius must have returned to Rhodes, at least for a brief stay, since he occupied a priesthood at one of its towns, Lindos. In about 144, however, he moved to Rome, where he became a member of the literary circle of Scipio Africanus the Younger (Scipio Aemilianus), whom he subsequently accompanied on travels in the East (c. 140–138). Thereafter Panaetius resided alternately at Rome and at Athens but finally settled at the latter city, succeeding Antipater in 129 as head of the Stoa and retaining that position until his death.

His writings, which do not seem to have been extensive, have survived only in fragments. They reveal a change in direction from the Stoic orthodoxies of previous directors of the school, from Chrysippus (c. 280–207 B.C.) onward. Panaetius abandoned the theory of a periodic conflagration of the universe in favor of the Aristotelian doctrine of its eternity, and his treatise entitled *On Providence* totally rejected the claims of astrology, which other Stoics had attempted to harness to their doctrines. His known literary activity, however, was mainly on ethical themes, addressed to practical problems of conduct. One monograph was concerned with cheerfulness, or being of good heart, and another dealt with political activity.

The work that we know most about was entitled *On Appropriate Action;* this can be reconstructed to a large extent from Cicero's adaptation in his *De Officiis (On Duties).* According to Panaetius' treatise, human beings are distinguishable from animals by their possession of reason, their desire to learn the truth, their ambition to become preeminent, their unwillingness to take orders except for their own good, and their sense of order and propriety. From these roots, he maintained, originate the four cardinal virtues (already established by the philosophers), each connected with the others but also possessing a special field of its own: wisdom that consists in knowing the truth (the only theoretical quality of the four); justice, the virtue that arises from the social instincts (forbidding injury to other persons and promoting the active beneficence that is society's bond); bravery or perhaps "greatness of spirit" (as the Romans called it later) that springs from the desire for preeminence; and *sophrosyne,* the quality of temperance or keeping one's head—associated by Panaetius with "propriety," the Latin *decorum*—that demands the appetites be controlled and limited by reason.

Certain aspects of this classification seem to be novel and, indeed, original. In the first place, Panaetius derives all the virtues from innate instincts, rather than from conceptual knowledge as his predecessors at the Stoa had been accustomed to do. Secondly, he seems to have evaded, or quietly dropped, the orthodox Stoic view that no one is good but the person who is *perfectly* wise. Instead, he preferred to emphasize that all men and women should have their own personal ideals, appropriate in each case to the individual's capacities. Thirdly, he laid stress on the positive, active features of justice and bravery—in contrast with early Stoic emphasis on the more negative virtues of *not* doing wrong and *not* allowing danger to disturb one. This type of emphasis was appropriate for a citizen of Rhodes, a proudly independent city-state with a tradition of service and welfare. More important, however, was that Stoic philosophy now became applicable, indeed appealing, as a code to Romans in public life: as a result of Panaetius' doctrines, Stoicism became, to a large extent, the philosophical basis of Roman political activity, so that Augustus, for example, was publicly presented in 27 B.C. with a golden shield on which the names of the four cardinal virtues were inscribed.

EDITIONS—M. van Straaten, Panaetii Rhodii Fragmenta, 2nd ed., 1962.
ABOUT—B. N. Tatakis, Panétius de Rhodes, 1931; L. Labowsky, Die Ethik des Panaetius, 1934; M. van Straaten, Panétius: Sa vie, ses écrits et sa doctrine, avec une édition des fragments, 1946; L. Edelstein, The Meaning of Stoicism, 1967; F. A. Steinmetz, Die Freundschaftslehre des Panaitios, 1967; J. M. Rist, Stoic Philosophy, 1969; M. Pohlenz, Stoa und Stoiker,

4th ed., 1970, 1972; H. A. Gärtner, Cicero und Panaitios, 1974; A. A. Long, Hellenistic Philosophy, 1974; F. H. Sandbach, The Stoics, 1975.

PANYASSIS, Greek poet, was born early in the fifth century B.C. and died in about 454. He came from a family of Halicarnassus (Budrum) in Caria (southwestern Asia Minor) and was either the cousin or the nephew of Herodotus; his name is not Greek but Carian. He became involved in local political quarrels and was put to death by Lygdamis, the autocratic ruler (tyrant) of his city. He was said to have been a skilled interpreter of signs.

His two known poems have survived only in fragments. One was the *Heracleias,* in fourteen books of hexameters, an epic description of the adventures of Heracles in various countries. Three long fragments can be ascribed to Panyassis' poem. In one of them, Eurytus urges Heracles not to drink too much (a theme to which the poet reverts on another occasion). Further passages from the *Heracleias* dealt with the struggle for the Delphic tripod between Apollo and Heracles, who seized it and, as a punishment, was made a slave of Omphale in Lydia, an incident which Panyassis particularly enjoyed because it showed the hero in menial subservience to a woman of Asia, whence he himself came. He also described how, when Heracles fell ill in Lydia, he was cured by the healing waters of the rivers Hyllus and Achelesius—an idea which had already appeared, though not necessarily in the same form, in the work of a seventh century epic poet, Pisander of Rhodes.

The full description of the twelve labors of Heracles provided by Panyassis apparently differed in a number of respects from the versions given in the Homeric poems. A fragment referring to the life of the goddess Demeter upon earth may have formed part of an account of Heracles' initiation into her Eleusinian mysteries. Because of his origin and background, Panyassis showed a special interest in the peoples and topography of Asia Minor; certain of his fragments reveal differences of opinion from Herodotus. Cle-

på ni as' sis

ment of Alexandria accused Panyassis of plagiaristic borrowing from the *Sack of Oechalia* written by another epic poet, Creophylus of Samos, but this may merely mean that both men treated the same subject in the same sort of traditional epic language.

Panyassis' second poem was the *Ionica,* perhaps written in the elegiac meter. Reputedly seven thousand verses long, this work gave an account of the establishment and settlement of the Ionian colonies in western Asia Minor. Although not a single quotation from the *Ionica* can be derived with certainty from any ancient writer, there is one fragment that is more likely to belong to this poem than to the *Heracleias.* It tells the story of Myrrha (or Smyrna) and her son Adonis, and is perhaps intended to explain the non-Greek origins of the city of Smyrna and the Adonis cult.

Panyassis knew all the customary epic techniques but was also fond of strange and unusual stylistic features. Moreover, he enjoyed embroidering his stories to make them especially quaint and recondite and liked to indulge in protracted bouts of moralizing. Although not greatly appreciated in his own time, he was rated very highly indeed by later Roman critics, such as Dionysius of Halicarnassus (his own city) and Quintilian —who ranked him with Homer, Hesiod, Antimachus, and Pisander in the canon of the epic poets and declared him superior to Hesiod in his selection of subject matter and to Antimachus of Colophon in the arrangement of his material. Panyassis was the last important epic poet of archaic Greece, and the almost-complete disappearance of his poetry is a major loss.

EDITIONS—V. J. Matthews, Panyassis of Halicarnassus, 1974.
ABOUT—G. L. Huxley, Greek Epic Poetry, 1969.

PAPINIAN (Aemilius Papinianus), Roman jurist, was born in about A.D. 140 and died in 212. It is uncertain whether he came from Syria or northern Africa, but Emesa (Homs) in the former country may have been his birthplace. In any case, he moved to Rome, where the eminent lawyer Quintus Cervidi-

på pi' ni an

us Scaevola was apparently his teacher. After serving as an imperial secretary *(a libellis)* of Marcus Aurelius, he was promoted in 203 by Septimius Severus (likewise a pupil of Scaevola) to the prefecture of the praetorian guard, in which two other leading jurists, Paulus and Ulpian, served as his assessors. In 212, however, Papinian was killed by the guardsmen, apparently on the instigation of Severus' son Caracalla, either because of his insufficiently keen partisanship against the latter's murdered brother Geta or because his nonmilitary background had made him unpopular with the soldiers.

His principal writings, like those of Paulus and Ulpian, were collections and summaries of cases, presented according to various different methods. The *Quaestiones* in thirty-seven books, completed before 198, supplements such reports by doctrinal discussions, and the nineteen-book *Responsa,* not completed until after 204, includes rulings by other lawyers and decisions pronounced by emperors and their prefects. Papinian also wrote a monograph entitled *On Adultery (De Adulteriis)* and compiled a collection of definitions *(Definitiones).* Independent of mind and always prepared to change his opinion if he thought fit, he formulated solutions and comments which are original, closely reasoned, and of incomparable precision. He was prepared to generalize rather more than his contemporaries; and in his deliberations he allowed ample scope for equity, morality, and humaneness. Papinian's intellect was critical and judicial, and his comments deliberate, moderate, and unbiased; he applied the law with unfailing responsibility and an acute instinct. His style is characterized by an almost archaic but not inelegant terseness, as he unswervingly relates the facts to the legal principle involved and isolates the essential points.

Although Papinian was the author of no comprehensive systematic treatise, the quality of his writings, together with his undeniable moral presence and the halo of his martyrdom, made him the most famous name in the whole history of classical jurisprudence. Notes on his works were ascribed to Paulus and Ulpian (though Constantine did not always accept the validity of these notes), and his reputation continued to soar.

Special deference was accorded to his opinions by the Law of Citations (regulating the forensic use of legal literature in A.D. 426), which singled him out as the decisive casting vote whenever other writers disagreed. In the law schools of the Roman empire his authority was definitive; and third-year students were known as *Papinianistae.* Moreover, the emperor Justinian I declared that his brilliance entitled him to the first place among all jurists. Nowadays, however, despite all his merits, a deeper insight into the history of Roman law suggests that the great jurists of preceding imperial times, and indeed of the later Republic as well, had exceeded him in fertility and creativeness.

EDITIONS—Corpus Iuris Civilis: Digesta (601 extracts). ABOUT—Bibliographies *in* W. Kunkel, Introduction to Roman Legal and Constitutional History, 1966, and *in* Oxford Classical Dictionary, 2nd ed., 1970 (*see under* Jurisprudence and *under* Law and Procedure, Roman).

PAPINIUS STATIUS, PUBLIUS. See Statius, Publius Papinius

PARMENIDES, Greek philosopher, was born probably in about 515 B.C.—an alternative ancient tradition that would make him about twenty-four years older seems less acceptable. The date of his death is uncertain. He was a citizen of Elea (the Roman Velia, now Castellamare di Bruca) in southwestern Italy and was said to have composed laws for his city. He attached himself for a time to the aristocratic brotherhood that Pythagoras had founded at Croton.

Parmenides embodied his philosophical views in a short poem *On Nature,* of which about one hundred and sixty incisive but not very poetic hexameters have survived. The piece begins with an allegorical introduction, in which the poet describes how he himself, borne in a chariot and accompanied by the daughters of the Sun, journeyed from darkness into light and was conducted to the Sun's gates, which are guarded by Justice. There he received a revelation of truth from a goddess (we do not have his own name for

pär men' i dēz

307

her, but she is variously identified with Wisdom, or Nature, or Themis). It is she who is made the speaker in the rest of the poem; and she begins by declaring to him that he must learn all things, not only truth—which is certain and "well-rounded"—but also "the opinions of human beings in which there is no true belief at all"—which require study to determine their worth. This introduction, drawn from the literature of oracles and mysteries, is designed to have all the gravity of a religious revelation; and it is also intended to forestall criticisms from his fellow Pythagoreans.

The second and most important part of the poem is entitled *The Way of Truth;* representative portions survive. In it the goddess assures him that there are only three conceivable ways of inquiry or philosophical methods: One can maintain that the reality under study necessarily exists, or necessarily does not exist, or both exists and does not exist (i.e., comes into being and changes and perishes). But the last two of these three hypotheses, she concludes, have to be rejected, because nothing except what exists can be known. The goddess then proceeds to define what exists: something that has always existed and remains forever unchangeable and immobile. It cannot increase or diminish or be divided. It is whole and homogeneous and continuous, and balanced in perfect equilibrium, and nothing can come out of it. That which exists is limited and spherical but occupies the whole of space, for there can be no void.

With these concepts, Parmenides stands at the opposite pole from his Pythagorean mentors, who believed that in addition to substance there was void. He is also opposed to Heraclitus, who saw flux as the essence of the universe. He likewise differs from others who believed that the plurality our senses demonstrate to us is real. Thus, those things that human beings imagine to have reality are, in fact, subject to generation and change and destruction and are, therefore, mere words, existent only in name, delusions—in short, nonbeing, which thought cannot follow because nonexistence is unthinkable. Only that which can be thought is reality—which is what thought and reasoning are all about.

By means of these arguments, Parmenides presented the problem of the One and the Many in its sharpest and most dramatic shape for the consideration of later philosophers. He was a thinker of startling originality. Indeed, he may be described as the first Greek philosopher who employed reasoning—who founded his universal picture on rational, logical argument, based on a rigorous analysis of the meaning of the term *to be:* his enumeration of the three conceivable ways of inquiry is the earliest discussion of philosophical method. Moreover, his differentiation between what is believed and what is known drew a distinction between philosophy and science. Plato, in his *Parmenides* and *Sophist,* made dialectical use of Parmenides' analysis of reality in support of his own doctrine of Ideas. And Aristotle, too, saw him as one of the principal founders of metaphysics, one of the first men—perhaps the first—to adopt the metaphysical as opposed to the physical method of theorizing: for that is what Aristotle meant when he wrote of "the science of truth as it was inaugurated by the school of Anaxagoras and Parmenides."

After these outstanding achievements in the second part of his poem, it is highly disconcerting and indeed not readily explicable to find that the final and longest portion of the work reflects an entirely different attitude. Not a great deal of this section is preserved, but what survives shows that Parmenides is now speaking as though the plurality revealed by the senses, which he has just previously rejected in so uncompromising a fashion, is valid as reality after all. This section, entitled *The Way of Opinion,* describes this multiplicity of things, not as they *exist* (since, as we have seen, they do not exist at all!) but as they *appear:* "mortal beliefs in which there is no true faith." Now the poet makes the goddess unfold a long and traditional account of the origins of the universe. At the same time, in spite of the illusory character of plurality, he also takes the opportunity to reject the "monism" according to which his Ionian predecessors had seized upon one single element (water or air or fire) as the basic constituent of the universe. Instead, Parmenides derives the world's apparent phenomena, as the senses comprehend it, from the polarity of two opposite "forms," Light and Dark. Yet, once again, we are warned that they, too, only have a nominal, specious existence. The whole of this line of thought, we are presumably meant to understand, is an exploration of unreality and error, using the terms and methods that other philosophers erroneously employed in order to get as near to reality as their inadmissible postulates allow. This final section of *On Nature,* then, is an attempt to analyze how other people see things: they are wrong, Parmenides says, but this is the best that can be made of their unreal beliefs.

EDITIONS—M. Untersteiner, Parmenide: Testimonianze e frammenti, 1967. *With translation:* F. M. Cornford, Parmenides' Way of Truth and Plato's Parmenides, 1939; L. Tarán, Parmenides, 1965; G. S. Kirk and J. E. Raven, The Pre-Socratic Philosophers, revised ed., 1966.
ABOUT—K. Deichgräber, Parmenides Auffahrt zur Göttin des Rechts, 1959; J. Mansfeld, Die Offenbarung des Parmenides und die menschliche Welt, 1964; J. Beaufret, La poème de Parménide, 1965; W. K. C. Guthrie, History of Greek Philosophy, v 2, 1965; A. P. D. Mourelatos, The Route of Parmenides, 1970; K. Bormann, Parmenides: Untersuchungen zu den Fragmenten, 1971; M. C. Stokes, One and Many in Presocratic Philosophy, 1972; A. A. Long, The Principles of Parmenides' Cosmogony, *in* R. E. Allen and D. J. Furley, eds., Studies in Presocratic Philosophy, v 2, 1975; J. Jantzen, Parmenides zum Verhältnis von Sprache und Wirklichkeit, 1976; M. E. Pelikaan-Engel, Hesiod and Parmenides, 1976; P. Somville, Parménide d'Élée: Son temps et le nôtre, 1976; K. Reinhardt, Parmenides und die Geschichte der griechischen Philosophie, 3rd ed., 1977; J. Barnes, The Pre-Socratic Philosophers, v 1, 1978.

PARTHENIUS, Greek poet, lived during the first century B.C. and was born at Nicaea (Iznik) in Bithynia (northwestern Asia Minor). Taken prisoner by the Romans during their third war against King Mithridates VI of Pontus, he was sent to Rome and became the slave of a certain Cinna, who probably belonged to the family of the Helvii, since Helvius Cinna, a prominent member of the "new" (Neoteric) school of Latin poets, was under Parthenius' literary influence. Parthenius was subsequently freed and lived first at Rome and then at Neapolis (Naples),
pär thē′ ni us

where it was said that he became the teacher of Virgil.

Although only fragments of his poetry survive today, his output is known to have been voluminous, and in antiquity he enjoyed a considerable reputation that has scarcely been appreciated until recently. In particular, he was hailed as the prophet, at Rome, of the Alexandrian school of Callimachus (died c. 240 B.C.); and, indeed, Pollianus, in the Palatine Anthology, considered Parthenius the equal of Callimachus. Parthenius' best-known poems, including his *Metamorphoses (Transformations),* were in elegiac couplets. He also wrote other mythological pieces, including *Iphitus* and *Heracles;* and papyri have yielded fragments of two dirges, one for his wife Arete—on whom he also wrote an encomium, in three books of verses—and the other for a certain Timander. Other friends to whom he dedicated poems included a younger contemporary and fellow poet, Crinagoras of Mytilene, who was born in about 70 B.C. Parthenius has been described as the last of the Greek Alexandrians; his poetry was later read with admiration by the emperors Tiberius and Hadrian.

He also compiled a prose collection of *Sorrowful Love Stories (Erotika Pathemata),* which have been preserved. Their intention is to narrate, in the easiest possible form, unfamiliar tales of well-known mythological personages, generally presenting them against a background of warfare. The collection is dedicated to the Latin elegiac poet Cornelius Gallus (d. 26 B.C.), with the intention that Gallus should rewrite and adapt this material in verse. In contrast to the style of his own poetry, which is scrupulously correct, Parthenius, in the *Love Stories,* allows himself an occasional colloquialism; and his anecdotes display all the exalted sentiment, strong emotion, and vigorous dramatization so typical of the three previous Hellenistic centuries. The *Stories* resemble miniature novels, and are of significance to the study of the Greek prose romance, with which they display numerous connections.

EDITIONS—E. Martini, Mythographi Graeci, v 2, fasc. 1 (suppl.), 1902 (for additions *see* A. Lesky, History of Greek Literature, 1966, p 756, note 2); A. Meineke,

Analecta, Alexandrina, 1843, reprint 1965. *With translation:* S. Gaselee *in* J. M. Edmonds and S. Gaselee, Daphnis & Chloe . . . Parthenius, The Love Romances, and other fragments (Loeb ed.), 1916.
ABOUT—B. Lavagnini, Studi sul romanzo greco, 1950; E. Rohde, Der griechische Roman, 4th ed., 1960; W. V. Clausen, Greek, Roman and Byzantine Studies, v 5, 1964; B. E. Perry, The Ancient Romance, 1967.

PATERCULUS, GAIUS VELLEIUS. See Velleius Paterculus, Gaius

PAUL THE DEACON (Paulus Warnefridus Diaconus), Latin historian, religious writer, grammarian, and poet, was born in about A.D. 725 and probably died in 799. He came of an aristocratic Lombard family of Friuli (northeastern Italy), where his father Warnefrid was a man of some eminence. Paul was educated at the royal court of the Lombards at Pavia, which he served as a page. Subsequently he became the teacher and intimate friend of Adelperga, the daughter of Desiderius, king of the Lombards, and apparently accompanied her to Benevento after her marriage to its duke (757). There he remained until the fall of Desiderius to Charlemagne in 774, whereupon, after implication in a conspiracy against the victor, he retired to the monastery of Monte Cassino. In 782, however, he joined Charlemagne's court and became a leading figure in the Carolingian cultural revival before returning to Monte Cassino (787), where he lived for the rest of his life.

Paul's major literary work, written during his last years at Monte Cassino, was his *History of the Lombards (Historia Langobardorum),* carrying the narrative down to the death in 744 of Liutprand, king of the Lombards. Founded on written and oral sources alike, the *History* is our most important authority for Lombard history. Composed in a pious, patriotic, heroic vein, it is not only lucidly written but full of vivid and entertaining material, including a remarkable diversity of piquant anecdotes, ranging from cheerful to macabre. Other historical writings by Paul included the *Historia Romana (Miscella)*—an expansion and sequel to the history of Eutropius (fourth century), down

to the reign of Justinian I—as well as a *Life of Gregory the Great* and the *Record of the Bishops of Metz.* Paul also wrote a commentary on the Rule of St. Benedict and a voluminous series of homilies for the various stages of the ecclesiastical year, largely based on the writings of the early Church fathers. His grammatical works included an epitome of the second century grammarian Sextus Pompeius Festus, himself the epitomizer of Verrius Flaccus (late first and early second century).

In addition, Paul composed a substantial amount of occasional poetry, including some fine lines on Lake Como and a moving epitaph on a little girl. He may also be the author of a hymn to John the Baptist that is famous because, in the eleventh century, Guy of Arezzo adopted the first syllables of the words at the beginning and middle of the first three lines of its first stanza as the notes in the musical scale.

EDITIONS—Histories: L. Bethmann and G. Waitz, *in* Monumenta Germaniae Historica . . . Scriptores Rerum Langobardicarum, v 2, 1878; Historia Romana: A. Crivellucci, 1914. Poems: K. Neff, 1908. *Translations*—Histories: W. D. Foulke, 1907; Historia Romana: K. Langosch, Lyrische Anthologie des lateinischen Mittelalters, 1968. Other works: M. Manitius, Geschichte der lateinischen Literatur des Mittelalters, v 1, 1911.
ABOUT—F. A. Wright and T. A. Sinclair, History of Later Latin Literature, 1931; D. Bianchi, L'epitafio di Ilderico e la leggenda di Paolo Diacono, 1956; L. J. Engels, Observations sur le vocabulaire de Paul Diacre, 1961; G. de Rosa, Questioni e problemi della dominazione longobarda in Italia, 1966; K. Langosch, Profile des lateinischen Mittelalters, 1967.

PAUL THE SILENTIARY, Greek poet of the early Byzantine period, was chief usher *(silentiarius,* whose primary function was to procure silence at court ceremonies) at the courts of Justinian I (A.D. 527–65) and Justin II (565–78) at Constantinople. The dates of his birth and death are unknown.

Eighty-one of his epigrams are in the Greek Anthology; no doubt they were collected by his son-in-law and fellow epigrammatist Agathias. Between them, the two men revived this sort of poetry to a late moment of distinction. Forty of Paul's pieces, displaying a precise versification influenced by the fifth century Greek poet Nonnus, deal with amorous themes, to which he devotes a vivid, sophisticated prurience, displayed in extensive anatomical detail. He does not seem seriously inhibited by his membership in the Christian Church. Paul also wrote twenty short poems commenting on works of art with appealing sensitivity and relish. This type of poetry, which was not uncommon in the Anthology and enjoyed favor in Constantinopolitan cultural circles, went back to a well-known kind of prose writing, the *ekphrasis,* one of the types of rhetorical exercise *(progymnasmata).*

But Paul also wrote three longer poems in the same descriptive manner. The best known of them was a piece consisting of about a thousand hexameters, in which he celebrates the reconstruction and reopening of the Church of the Holy Wisdom (Santa Sophia) by Justinian in 363; the work was written for recitation, at the emperor's command. Its principal interest lies in its accurate depiction of the architectural features of the marvelous building. But the author, despite learned, conventional mannerisms, also achieves memorable poetry: for example, when he tells of the brilliant windows of the soaring dome at night, blazing a comforting light over the city and its harbor and welcoming the sailor as he moves from the stormy Aegean or Black Sea into the final hazards of his homeward journey. And here Paul does not omit to strike a religious note, for he not only envisages Santa Sophia as a Pharos (lighthouse) guiding the returning traveler but also sees it pointing the way to the living God.

He also wrote *Ambo (Pulpit),* a three-hundred-line description of the pulpit in Santa Sophia; he declaimed the piece shortly after his recitation of the longer poem about the same church. And he was the author of *The Hot Pythian Springs,* composed for Justinian's empress, Theodora, of whose entourage Paul was a member when she went to take the cure at the warm baths in Bithynia.

EDITIONS with translation—A. Veniero, Paolo Silenziario, 1916; G. Viansino, Paulus Silentiarius: Epigrammi, 1963.
ABOUT—P. Friedländer, Johannes von Gaza und Paulus Silentiarius, 1912; A. Cameron's references *in* Journal of Hellenic Studies (v 86, p 210ff), 1966.

PAULINUS OF NOLA, Saint (Meropius Pontius Anicius Paulinus), Latin poet and letter writer and bishop, A.D. 353–431, was born at Burdigala (Bordeaux in southwestern France) of a patrician Gallo-Roman family; his father was wealthy and powerful. Paulinus, brought up as a Christian, was dedicated to St. Felix, whose tomb at Nola in Campania (southwestern Italy) was on one of his family's estates. After studying under the poet Ausonius, he embarked on an official career, becoming a Roman senator and subsequently consul (378) and governor of Campania. Returning to Gaul, he married a Spanish woman named Therasia, in whose company he moved to Spain in 389, receiving baptism at about this time, at the age of forty-six. After the death of their only child in 392, they decided to abandon the world and sold their Gallic and Spanish possessions. Then, after Paulinus had been ordained a priest, they went to settle at Nola, where they led a life of asceticism and charity. In about 409 he became the bishop of Nola and remained there for the last twenty-two years of his life.

Thirty-three of his poems have survived. Fourteen of these, including some of his best work, are birthday pieces written each year for the festival of St. Felix. These are early examples of the verse eulogies of saints and martyrs that later figured so largely in Christian literature; they present a vivid picture of the popular religion of the age. One poem, for instance, describes the countryfolk gathering in their brilliantly illuminated church to celebrate the festival; in another, Paulinus hails the spring, with a plea that he may be inspired to sing like the nightingale that pours forth its melody from the depths of the wood. Another poem is a wedding song to Julianus and Titia—the first Christian epithalamium. He also wrote the earliest Christian elegy, a long poem about the death of a boy named Celsus written to console his parents: Paulinus reminds them that his own child, too, has died re-

pô lī′ nus nō′ lȧ

cently. In addition, he conducted a poetical correspondence with Nicetas, apostle to the Dacians, wrote paraphrases of the Gospels and Psalms, and compiled descriptive verses about church paintings.

Paulinus contributed greatly to the Christianization of poetry. Of particular interest is his tenth poem, written in a mixture of elegiac and lyric and hexameter meters, in which he tries to explain his abandonment of worldly and literary interests. He addresses his explanation to Ausonius, to whom this transformation of his favorite pupil came as a great puzzle and shock. Paulinus' verses are correct and classical; upon occasion, the sincerity of his feelings raises them to the level of authentic poetry. They do provide a portrait of the poet's character, which seems attractive but not particularly strong (except when he made his fateful decision).

His character is once again reflected in his fifty-one surviving letters. Written from the year 393 onward, they are of considerable historical interest, because he corresponded with some of the most eminent men of his day, including Augustine and Jerome. In some of these letters, Paulinus gives a vivid picture of Christian friendship; in others, he conveys the spirit of a tranquil monastic existence—yet at the same time he satirizes those who do not understand the merits of such a life of renunciation. Rather often, he descends to trivialities and pedantries, but when he does so, he disarms his critics by freely admitting that he is capable of becoming tedious. The style of these epistles is often exuberantly rhetorical, and, although they abound in biblical quotations, they are also as full of classical references as any letters penned by his pagan contemporaries. In one passage, he discusses the proper use to be made of pagan literature by a Christian and concludes that its copiousness of language and elegance of expression are fully deserving of imitation, provided that readers do not allow themselves to be captivated by its pernicious charm.

EDITIONS—W. von Hartel, Corpus Scriptorum Ecclesiasticorum Latinorum, v 29-30, 1894; P. G. Walsh, Letters of Paulinus of Nola in Ancient Christian Writers, v 35-36, 1967.
ABOUT—P. Fabre, Essai sur la chronologie de l'oeuvre de Saint Paulin de Nole, 1948 and Saint Paulin de Nole et l'amitié chrétienne, 1949; J. A. Bouma, Het Epithalamium van Paulinus van Nola, 1968; W. H. C. Frend, Paulinus of Nola and the Last Century of the Western Empire in Journal of Roman Studies, v 59, 1969; R. P. H. Green, The Poetry of Paulinus of Nola, 1971; W. Erdt, Christentum und heidnische antike Bildung bei Paulin von Nola, 1976; J. T. Lienhard, Paulinus of Nola and Early Western Monasticism, 1977.

PAULINUS OF PELLA, Latin poet, lived in the fifth century A.D. He was the grandson of the Gallo-Roman writer Ausonius but was probably born at Pella in Macedonia at a time when his father was governor of that country. Paulinus was educated at Burdigala (Bordeaux) and became a convert to Christianity at the age of forty-six. After the comfortable beginning to his life, misfortunes of all sorts continually descended upon him, ranging from legal depredations, on the death of his father, to the abundant political catastrophes of the western Roman empire and the gradual dismemberment of Roman Gaul into "barbarian" German states.

Paulinus describes this disastrous career in the six hundred sixteen hexameters of his *Eucharisticus (Thanksgiving),* which he produced in his eighty-fourth year; he professed to discern in all that happened the beneficent hand of God toward His unworthy servant. This unusual poem provides an interesting contemporary sidelight on the collapse of the western empire and its ruling class, though Paulinus does not fully perceive the enormous implications of what he is recording. His writing, too, is somewhat awkward and inarticulate; and indeed, although he has read Virgil, Ausonius, and Paulinus of Nola, he is aware of his intellectual limitations. He is also somewhat humorless or ingenuous; for example, in describing his youth he takes credit for satisfying his sexual inclinations with his mother's maids rather than going to bed with women of good social class.

EDITIONS—W. Brandes, Corpus Scriptorum Ecclesiasticorum Latinorum, v 26, Poetae Christiani Minores, Pt 1, 1888. *With translation:* H. G. Evelyn-White, Paulinus Pellaeus: The Eucharistics, in Ausonius

pô li' nus pel' lä

With an English Translation, v 2, 1961; H. Isbell, The Last Poets of Imperial Rome (Penguin ed.), 1971.
ABOUT—H. G. Evelyn-White, Paulinus Pellaeus: The Eucharisticos, *in* Ausonius With an English Translation, v 2, 1961; H. Isbell, The Last Poets of Imperial Rome (Penguin ed.), 1971; P. Tordeur, Concordance de Paulin de Pella, 1973.

PAULUS, JULIUS, Roman jurist, was active in the early years of the third century A.D. It is not known when or where he was born or died. After studying under Quintus Cervidius Scaevola, he adopted the career of an advocate and then, with Ulpian as his colleague, was appointed to the office of assessor to Papinian while the latter was prefect of the praetorian guard (A.D. 203–12). Paulus subsequently became the senior imperial secretary *(magister memoriae)* and a member of the imperial council of the emperor Septimius Severus (d. 211) and of his son Caracalla (d. 217). He was sent into exile by Elagabalus (218–22), but Severus Alexander (222–35) recalled him to be a member of his imperial council and praetorian prefect. He probably held this office jointly with Ulpian, though it may be surmised that they were not on good terms, since in all their extensive surviving writings they never refer to one another at any point.

Paulus' works were more voluminous than those of any other Roman lawyer, amounting to nearly three hundred and twenty treatises. They included a large number of systematic studies, the longest of which was an eighty-book commentary on the praetorian edict that had been revised by the well-known jurist Salvius Julianus in about 130 A.D. on the orders of Hadrian. Paulus also composed a sixteen-book exposition of the civil law, in the form of a commentary on the first century jurist Masurius Sabinus, after whom the Sabinian school for jurists was named; and he wrote commentaries on earlier Roman jurists as well. His other works included notes on Papinian, twenty-six books of cases *(Quaestiones)*, and twenty-three forming a collection of *Rulings (Responsa)*—he evidently enjoyed a great reputation as a jurist. He was also a teacher; and his *Institutiones* and *Regulae* were written
pô' lus

ten as textbooks. In addition, he was the author of analyses of various types of enactments (laws, senatorial decrees, imperial "constitutions") and wrote on numerous other topics relating to many different branches of the law.

A work called *Opinions (Sententiae),* which is preserved in part, enjoyed a great reputation in later antiquity, and Constantine the Great ruled that special weight should be attached to it. Some modern scholars deny Paulus' authorship of the work, and others detect no less than six distinct chronological layers in its composition. In all probability, it was a compilation or anthology of his writings, originally put together in the early fourth century A.D. and subsequently reedited on more than one occasion.

Because of these processes of reediting, the views and style of Paulus are so difficult to disentangle from later interpolations that he has been subjected to very diverse judgments, including estimates that fall far short of the high esteem in which he was held in ancient times. He has been charged, for example, with an excessively doctrinaire rigidity—and, somewhat contradictorily, with giving too free rein to his fancy. He has also been accused of being reluctant to acknowledge his debts to earlier authorities and of having too many such debts—in other words, he has been labeled as a mere unoriginal compiler. A compiler and a synthesizer he is, but neither unoriginal nor uncritical. It is inevitable to compare him with his contemporary Ulpian, after whom he is the author most frequently excerpted in Justinian's sixth century *Digest,* which, among other tasks, codified the works of classical jurists; and from this comparison it emerges that Paulus, without possessing Ulpian's precise clarity, excelled him in independence, breadth of interest, abstract reasoning power, and penetrating criticism of other experts' opinions. The two jurists expressed somewhat different points of view about the Roman monarchy: whereas Ulpian was conscious of cases in which the emperors' exemption from the laws was absolute, Paulus commented: "It is befitting to the imperial majesty to live according to the laws from which the emperor himself seems to be exempt."

EDITIONS—Corpus Iuris Civilis: Digesta (2,081 extracts).
ABOUT—Bibliographies *in* W. Kunkel, Introduction to Roman Legal and Constitutional History, 1966, and *in* Oxford Classical Dictionary, 2nd ed., 1970 (*see under* Jurisprudence and *under* Law and Procedure, Roman). *Add:* E. Levy, Pauli Sententiae: A Palingenesia, 1945; H. Schellenberg, Die Interpretationen zu den Paulus-sentenzen, 1965; R. Syme, Emperors and Biography, 1971.

PAULUS DIACONUS. See Paul the Deacon

PAUSANIAS, Greek travel writer, lived in the second century A.D.; the latest event referred to in his work is the invasion of Greece by the Costoboci in 175. He came from somewhere near Magnesia (Manisa) in Lydia (southwestern Asia Minor), beneath Mount Sipylus. He is not identifiable with any other known man of the same name.

Pausanias is the author of a *Description (Periegesis) of Greece,* in ten books, which takes the form of a tour of Greece, starting from Cape Sunium, not far from Athens. Book 1 covers Attica and Megara; Book 2, Corinth and the Argolid (including Argos, Mycenae, Tiryns, and Epidaurus); Book 3, Laconia (Sparta); Book 4, Messenia; Books 5 and 6, Elis (Olympia); Book 7, Achaea; Book 8, Arcadia; Book 9, Boeotia; and Book 10, Phocis (Delphi). The ten books appear to have been written in the order in which they are now placed, and the whole work seems to have taken about a decade and a half to complete.

Its sections usually begin with a sketch of a history of the most important cities and the topography of the territories surrounding them. But the narrative also contains all manner of myths and legends and folktales and historical disquisitions. Not much is said about the scenery, but digressions describe natural phenomena (not all of which were known to him from personal observation)—for example, the icebound seas of the

pô sa′ ni às

north, the noonday sun toward the equator, and the signs heralding an earthquake. There are occasional glimpses of the daily lives and activities of the various peoples. Greatly attracted to the ancient glories of Greek history, Pausanias tells of his visits to the battlefields of Marathon and Plataea, reports on his inspection of the memorials of treaties and victories at Olympia, and writes of the trophies and shields he saw at the Delphic shrine and the laws and monuments of famous men and events which were on view at Athens. Olympia and Delphi and Athens move him for another reason also: because he is deeply concerned with religion, especially in its primitive and obsolete forms, he takes great trouble to record religious buildings and works of art. Indeed, his descriptions of these are still indispensable today; we owe him details of many Greek statues and paintings of which no other account exists. Without embarking on art criticism—although his own preference is for the work of the fifth and fourth centuries B.C.—he notes down what seems to him to be worth seeing, explains how to find it, and then leaves the reader to form his personal artistic judgment.

During his travels Pausanias utilized the services of guides *(exegetai)* and was able to observe personally many of the places he describes. When based on his own observations, the locations he gives for the objects and buildings have proved very exact and reliable—for example, the Hermes of Praxiteles was found just where he said it was. When, however, he follows earlier authorities, as he often does—when reproducing, for instance, the inscriptions on monuments —he decides his construction and arrangement for himself, and inaccuracies creep in.

To call him "the Baedeker of Antiquity," as has sometimes been done, is misleading, since he is writing not for travelers but for readers. For their sakes, he endeavors to avoid monotony, not only by including a wide diversity of material but by varying his patterns of composition and word order and employing paraphrases, rhetorical artifices, and Herodotean archaisms. These efforts to achieve diversity cannot be regarded as successful, since his style remains almost wholly without distinction. Nevertheless, the

314

book is extremely well adapted to the requirements of the armchair tourist, who will be further pleased because Pausanias airs few personal prejudices about politics or philosophy.

EDITIONS—P. S. J. Levi, 1979. *With translation:* J. G. Frazer, 1898; W. H. S. Jones, H. A. Ormerod and R. E. Wycherley (Loeb ed.), 1918, 1935 (revised ed. of v 5, 1955). *Translations*—P. Levi, Pausanias: Guide to Greece (Penguin ed.), 1971; E. Meyer (German, abridged), 1954; N. D. Papahadzis (modern Greek), 1963, 1965.
ABOUT—W. Gürlitt, Über Pausanias, 1890; R. Heberdey, Die Reisen des Pausanias, 1894; T. R. Glover, Prince of Digressors *in* Springs of Hellas and Other Essays, 1946; O. Strid, Über Sprache und Stil des Periegeten Pausanias, 1976.

PELAGIUS. See Augustine

PERSIUS (Aulus Persius Flaccus), Roman satirical poet, A.D. 34–62, was born of a wealthy family of knightly rank at Volaterrae (Volterra) in Etruria. After the death of his father when Persius was six, followed by the death of his stepfather a few years later, he went to Rome at the age of twelve to study under two renowned teachers, the grammarian Quintus Remmius Palaemon and the rhetorician Verginius Flavus. Four years later, he became the pupil and friend of the Stoic philosopher and rhetorician Lucius Annaeus Cornutus, a freedman of Seneca; and Persius later met Seneca himself but did not greatly take to him. Persius was described as a good-looking, gentle, and modest young man, who was very fond of his mother and sister and aunt. When he died at the age of twenty-eight, he left these relatives a substantial fortune. Cornutus, who admired him as a writer, went through his poems, introducing minor revisions, eliminating below-standard juvenile pieces, and then handed the rest over to Caesius Bassus, a lyric poet, to be edited for publication.

Persius' output amounted to no more than six satires, totaling only six hundred fifty hexameters and prefaced by a brief,

per' si us

ironic prologue, in scazons or choliambics ("limping iambics"). The first piece, couched as a dialogue between Persius and a friend, attacks the deterioration of the literature and the literary taste of Rome, as displayed by a liking for decadent, trashy poetry that seems to symbolize the corruption of morals. Satire No. 2 raises the question of what we may legitimately ask from the gods and derides those who pray for material possessions rather than virtue. Satire No. 3 again censures moral inertia and mistaken desires, diagnosing, in medical language, the harm done to sick souls by sluggishness and vice. The fourth satire enlarges on the unfitness for a career in public office of a certain young Alcibiades, whose ideals are immature and inadequate to guide his fellow citizens and the state. Satire No. 5 begins with a eulogy of Cornutus and goes on to expound the Stoic paradox that all men are slaves—with the exception of the wise Stoic. Satire No. 6 is an explanation of why money should be spent sensibly, without covetousness.

Persius' style is individual and exceptionally difficult—obscure, abrupt, contorted, digressive, heavily laden with cryptic allusions, and crammed with jarring colloquialisms, forced images, and metaphors. In his own words, his work has "the taste of bitter nails." Yet his use of sound and rhythm are masterly, and his portraits of people are vivid, sometimes even eloquent. He borrows a lot from Horace, but they are extremely different writers in character, and what Persius says is worth hearing entirely on its own account. His moral tone rises far above the personal attacks or light-hearted mockery of earlier satirists and is equally far removed from the rhetorical indignation of his successor Juvenal.

His attitude to Nero, in whose reign he was writing, has called for attention. In the first satire, the poetry that Persius derides bears a resemblance to the emperor's own productions; and it was said that Cornutus, when looking at the poems after the poet's death, changed "King Midas has donkeys' ears" to "Who has not donkeys' ears?," in order that Nero should not take offense. And in Satire No. 4, the unsatisfactory young leader Alcibiades again invites comparisons with the youthful emperor.

Persius' work subsequently gained the esteem of Quintilian and Martial. And he was employed as a model by the English poet John Donne (1573–1631).

EDITIONS—W. V. Clausen, 1956; N. Scivoletto, 1956; D. Bo, 1969. *Translations*—G. G. Ramsay, Juvenal and Persius (Loeb ed.), revised ed., 1940; A. Cartault (Budé ed.), 3rd ed., 1951; W. S. Merwin (with W. S. Anderson), 1961; N. Rudd, The Satires of Horace and Persius (Penguin ed.), 1974.
ABOUT—F. Villeneuve, Essai sur Perse, 1918 *and* Les satires de Perse, 1921; E. V. Marmorale, Persio, 2nd ed., 1956; R. G. M. Nisbet *in* J. P. Sullivan, ed., Critical Essays on Roman Literature: Satire, 1963; C. S. Dessen, Iunctura Callidus Acri: A Study of Persius' Satires, 1968; E. Paratore, Biografia e poetica di Persio, 1968; S. Grimes, Structure in the Satires of Persius *in* D. R. Dudley, ed., Neronians and Flavians: Silver Latin, v 1, 1972; J. C. Bramble, Persius and the Programmatic Satire, 1974.

PETRONIUS, Latin novelist, wrote in the first century A.D., although the date of the *Satyricon,* his chief work, and the identity of its author have been the subjects of controversy since the Renaissance. Nowadays, however, scholarly opinion agrees with the traditional ascription of the work to a date in the reign of Nero (A.D. 54–68) (rather than in the third century A.D., as has also been suggested) and accepts the identification of the author with a certain Petronius described by the historian Tacitus and mentioned more briefly by Pliny the Elder and Plutarch as well. Tacitus names him Gaius, but the other two writers are more likely to be correct in calling him Titus instead, since the man seems to be identifiable with Titus Petronius Niger, who held a consulship in about A.D. 62. Tacitus describes the Petronius to whom he refers as "arbiter of elegance" *(elegantiae arbiter)* at Nero's court, and nearly all the manuscripts of the *Satyricon* (as well as the late Roman writers Macrobius and Marius Victorinus) give its author the designation of *Arbiter.* The term seems to be a sort of nickname such as members of clubs and societies invented to describe one another.

Tacitus depicts Petronius, the arbiter of

pe trō′ ni us

elegance, as a man of sophisticated and luxurious tastes, lazy and inert in his ordinary life but capable of energy in public affairs. He incurred the jealousy of Tigellinus, the joint commander of the praetorian guard, who falsely denounced him as the friend of a conspirator, so that Petronius, on receiving an ominous command from the palace not to move from the house in which he was staying at Cumae, was compelled to take his own life. He died with easy panache, after first writing out a full list of Nero's sexual irregularities, with names attached, and making sure that the document was duly sent to the emperor under seal.

The first surviving scene of the *Satyricon* involves the youths Encolpius (Into-the-Crotch) and Ascyltus (Tireless, i.e. sexually), who happen to be staying at a seaside inn with Encolpius' beautiful male lover Giton (Neighbor, again in a sexual sense). In hope of cadging a meal, Encolpius and Ascyltus are visiting a school of rhetoric run by the brothers Agamemnon and Menelaus. Meanwhile Encolpius engages Agamemnon in discussion about the reasons for the current deterioration of oratory. Encolpius thinks this decline is the fault of the teachers, because they never come to grips with the facts of everyday life. Agamemnon, however, shifts the blame from the teachers to the pupils' parents, who are excessively ambitious, he believes, to give their offspring a "proper" education, with disastrous results; and he caps his argument by expressing his own educational ideals in hackneyed, heavily moralistic verses about the need for frugality, etc.—ideals that come strangely from the self-indulgent hypocrite that the versifier is seen to be.

Next follow a series of comic episodes. Mistaking the direction to his lodgings, Encolpius is guided instead to the local brothel, where he finds that Ascyltus has already found his way separately. Together they return to their lodging house, where Giton awaits them, complaining of an attempt on his virtue by Ascyltus. The two competitors for the young man's affections, Encolpius and Ascyltus, face up to one another for a battle—in which the weapons are to be wholly rhetorical; subsequently, Encolpius resumes his cozy intimacy with Giton, but this is rudely broken when Ascyltus lays into his rival with a strap. A farcical encounter then takes place in the market, involving the ownership of a stolen coat with money hidden in the seams. Subsequently the young men go back to their house where the priestess of the obscene god Priapus—a certain Quartilla, who swears she cannot remember ever having been a virgin—takes them to witness the "marriage" her seven-year-old maid Pannychis (All-Night) is going to celebrate with Giton.

Then comes the famous center piece of the work, the dinner given by the wealthy upstart Trimalchio. As the party progresses, this buffoon, in his endeavors to display gentlemanliness and affluence, commits breaches of taste—on a colossal scale—in behavior, clothing, conversation, and ludicrously over-lavish food; and he inflicts preposterous practical jokes on his guests. These diners, all carefully characterized, are sensible enough in their own ways, and make a number of shrewd observations, but when they try to make cultured, upperclass conversation, their vulgarity equals Trimalchio's. During a pause in the dinner, the host, in a morbid, pompous mood of booziness, gives an account of the design of his tomb and the grandiose epitaph he has arranged to have inscribed on it. In the end, as the party is getting out of hand, Trimalchio, now lachrymose, calls for an immediate rehearsal of his own funeral. The trumpets of the funeral march, however, are mistaken for a fire alarm, and the arrival of the fire brigade extinguishes the entertainment and drives the guests away.

Later, Giton deserts Encolpius for Ascyltus, whereupon his abandoned lover, after sulking for three days, sallies forth to seek vengeance, from which, however, he is comically deterred by a passing soldier. After expressing his bitter mood in verses deploring the hollowness of friendship, Encolpius visits a picture gallery, where he meets Eumolpus (Good Singer). This man, a shallow and fatuous poet with a chip on his shoulder, breaks into denunciations of greed and the decay of erudition and illustrates a painting by reciting a long iambic poem of his own composition about Laocoön and the Wooden Horse of Troy. Those who hear this effusion begin to throw stones at the poet, and the two men leave together for the public baths. Now, Encolpius deserts his new friend in favor of the penitent Giton, and the two of them return happily to their lodging. Eumolpus, however, makes his appearance in order to try to gain the favors of Giton for himself and, locking Encolpius up in his room, he takes the boy away with him. In despair, Encolpius thinks black thoughts of suicide. Subsequently, however, he has the satisfaction of seeing Eumolpus beaten up; then peace is restored, and he, Eumolpus, and Giton embark together on a voyage to Tarentum.

As Encolpius tries to sleep on board the ship, he hears voices on deck, which he recognizes as those of his worst enemies, the stern puritan Lichas (Cruel) and the more luxuriously inclined lady Tryphaena (Extravagance). A battle develops, but it is broken off for a meal, at which Eumolpus tells the prurient story of the Widow of Ephesus. Lichas is shocked by its obscenity. Moreover, he becomes more furious still when he learns that Encolpius and Giton have had their hair cut—an action that, according to a current superstition, was likely to cause bad weather at sea. Lichas and Tryphaena agree that Giton must be executed. A storm comes just in time to prevent this action, and Lichas is washed overboard. Encolpius and Giton, however, are saved by fishermen, and they manage to rescue Eumolpus, who is still scribbling verses when they find him.

Next, the trio proceed to Croton (southeastern Italy), planning a scheme to attract and rob legacy-hunters. On the way to the city, Eumolpus offers reflections on the true nature of poetry and delivers an epic poem of his own on the civil war between Caesar and Pompey. In the following scene, the young men have their first encounter with the legacy hunters, but what happens then cannot be reconstructed from the few fragments that remain of this section.

Then comes the climax of the novel. The maid Chrysis approaches Encolpius on behalf of her mistress Circe, to whom he attempts to make love without success, owing to an embarrassing attack of impotence. Circe has him flogged and thrown out. A visit to the priestess of Priapus, Oenothea, fails disastrously to remedy his condition, but the disability is eventually cured by Mercury (Hermes), the divine patron of thievish adventurers. The last extant scene shows Eumolpus, apparently on his deathbed and surrounded by the legacy hunters, insisting that his heirs shall only inherit his property if they agree to devour a portion of his corpse in public. The ending of the novel may have come soon afterward; probably the "heroes" somehow made their escape from Croton.

As a story of adventurous wanderings, Petronius' novel owes formal debts to the Hellenistic "travelers' tale." But he is also much concerned with love (of a kind); and in this respect he is the heir of the Greek romantic novelists. They, however, unlike Petronius, had not intended to be funny, and their high-flown heroes and heroines are conspicuously absent from Petronius' narrative. All his main characters are disreputable—which makes the *Satyricon* a major ancestor of the picaresque novel of Europe.

In the Menippean tradition, named after Menippus of Gadara—a serio-comic Greek poet of the third century B.C.—and adapted to Latin literature by Varro (116–27 B.C.), Petronius' prose is interlarded with poems in various meters and on various topics. Yet while Menippus' writings were described as satire, the same label can scarcely be attached to Petronius' work, since it contains not the slightest trace of ethical uplift or of any sort of moral. The *Satyricon* does display an affinity with the amoral stage shows known as mimes; and a strong element of parody is apparent. Indeed, one of its major components is a parody of "the wrath of the gods"—a traditional theme of the Homeric and Virgilian epic, here redirected toward the phallic god Priapus. Although gross indecency is one persistent element in Petronius' novel, it also contains a good deal of literary criticism, both direct and oblique, in which mockery of overstatement and bombast is prominent. Moreover, the two longest surviving poems incorporated in the work, the *Sack of Troy* and the *Civil War,* appear to be intended as aspersions on contemporary writers (Lucan has been mentioned as a possible target, since his major

poem was on the Civil War, but Petronius does not seem to be parodying him directly).

The *Satyricon* also includes various short stories, including two notable flesh-creepers, and some Milesian Tales—spicy, sexy, anecdotes belonging to a genre invented by Aristides of Miletus (in about 100 B.C.) and adapted to Latin by Sisenna not long afterward; Petronius' best example of this genre is the "Widow of Ephesus." The longest and most notable of these self-contained sections of the work is his riotous account of the dinner of the vulgar millionaire Trimalchio. This vaguely draws upon a number of literary traditions but transforms them into something wholly original. Trimalchio is regarded by some as the greatest comic character in all ancient literature. As for the guests, their utterances in richly varied idioms provide rare (if somewhat selective) examples of uneducated colloquial Latin speech. And the contents of their observations are of considerable value to students of Roman social history. Indeed, beyond its function as entertainment, the *Satyricon* as a whole gives a detailed and dramatic picture of certain sections of life in the Roman empire of Nero's era.

The novel seems to have been very little known in ancient times. Tacitus does not even see fit to mention it—or any other literary activity—in his obituary of Petronius, and we can only find bare allusions in the second century grammarian Terentianus Maurus and the fifth century poet Sidonius Apollinaris. It seems probable that separate fragments of the work were arranged by a Carolingian scholar; and John of Salisbury (d. 1180) had some knowledge of its existence. However, it was not until the discovery of a manuscript (the Codex Traguriensis) in the mid-seventeenth century that substantial portions of its contents became known. Thereafter Petronius played a great and varied part in the mixed development of modern fiction.

In addition to this novel, Petronius has left a small selection of lyric and elegiac poems, some of which are highly evocative and successful.

EDITIONS—K. Müller, revised ed. of text, 1965. Dinner of Trimalchio: W. B. Sedgwick, 2nd ed., 1950; E. V.

Marmorale, 2nd ed., 1961; P. Perrochat, 3rd ed., 1962; M. S. Smith, 1975. Civil War Poem: G. Guido, 1976. *Translations*—P. Dinnage, 1953; W. Arrowsmith, 1959; J. P. Sullivan (Penguin ed.), 1965; M. Heseltine *in* M. Heseltine, Petronius *and* W. H. D. Rouse, Seneca: Apocolocyntosis, revised ed., 1969; A. Ernout (Budé ed.), 4th ed., 1958.
ABOUT—G. Bagnani, Petronius: Arbiter of Elegance, 1954; V. Ciaffi, La struttura del Satyricon, 1955; B. E. Perry, The Ancient Romances, 1967; J. P. Sullivan, The Satyricon of Petronius: A Literary Study, 1968; P. Corbett, Petronius, 1970; P. G. Walsh, The Roman Novel, 1970; H. von Thiel, Petron: Überlieferung und Rekonstruktion, 1971; O. Pecere, Petronio: La novella della matrona di Efeso, 1975; P. Grimal, La Guerre Civile de Pétrone dans ses rapports avec la Pharsale, 1977; J. Gruber, ed., Petron, 1977; G. L. Schmeling and J. H. Stuckey, A Bibliography of Petronius, 1977.

PHAEDRUS, Latin writer of verse fables, was born during the principate of Augustus, probably in about 15 B.C. and lived at least until the reign of Claudius (A.D. 41–54). His birthplace was in Pieria (Macedonia), and his parents were Thracian slaves—his mother seems to have been the wife, or possibly the servant, of a schoolteacher. At an early age he went to Italy (where it has been conjectured that his father opened a school) and received a good education, not only in Greek but also in Latin, of which he may not have possessed a thorough knowledge before. He became a freedman—apparently in the house of Augustus himself—and a friend of other freedmen who were apparently of some importance, to whom he offers literary dedications (Eutychus, Particulo, Philetus). But subsequently something that he wrote caused offense to Tiberius' minister Sejanus, and as a result Phaedrus was prosecuted and incurred some unknown punishment.

The five books of his poems that have survived, together with additions preserved in the epitome of Perotti (c. 1465), comprise more than a hundred pieces of his authorship. Others are known from prose paraphrases bearing the name of a writer called Romulus, perhaps of Carolingian date. Phaedrus' poems are mainly fables, many of them relating to animals, though others are anecdotes, short stories, or jokes. Greek fables had long been collected under the name of Aesop (sixth century B.C.), and earlier

fē′ drus

Latin poets, too, including Ennius, Lucilius, and Horace, had adopted some of them for insertion in their own poems. But Phaedrus was apparently the earliest writer to render whole books of fables into Latin.

He employed iambic verse, exercised considerable originality in his adaptations, and took himself very seriously as the founder of a new literary genre, in which he endeavored to combine entertainment with ethical uplift, for he frequently and conscientiously introduced a moral. The moral is often forced and misplaced, but the entertainment is there without a doubt: such stories as "the Wolf and the Lamb" and "The Fox and the Sour Grapes" are eternally familiar. Moreover, spice is added by various allusions to contemporary society, and Phaedrus expressed himself with succinct and pithy simplicity, of which he was proud.

Later Roman critics paid him little or no attention, and indeed the first certain allusion to his work is by the fabulist Avienus (or Avianus) nearly four hundred years later. In the Middle Ages, Avienus was more widely read than Phaedrus. The latter's fables, however, were printed in 1596; the seventeenth century French fabulist La Fontaine made good use of them (to serve his own much superior talents), and the eighteenth century German dramatist and critic Lessing, though his appreciation of Phaedrus was not unqualified, composed German versions.

EDITIONS—L. Havet, 1895, with notes, 1923; L. Herrmann, 1950; F. Serra, 1975. *With translation:* B. E. Perry, Babrius and Phaedrus (Loeb ed.), 1965; A. Brenot (Budé ed.), 1924.
ABOUT—L. Hervieux, Les fabulistes latins, v 1 and v 2, 2nd ed., 1893–94; C. Zander, Phaedrus Solutus, 1921; M. Nøjsgaard, La fable antique, v 2, 1967; G. Pisi, Fedro traduttore di Esopo, 1977.

PHILEMON, Greek comic poet and dramatist, was born between 365 and 360 B.C. and died in 264 or 263. He came from Syracuse in Sicily but moved to Athens, where he acquired Athenian citizenship in 307/6. For a time, he left Athens and went to Egypt, at the invitation of the Ptolemaic court; there were many anecdotes about his

fi lē′ mon

return journey, on which his ship was supposed to have been driven ashore by a gale in the territory of King Magas of Cyrene, whom Philemon had earlier derided for deficiencies in his culture; but Magas, the story went, treated him kindly. He was at Athens, a very old man, when he died; he was reading a book at the time, while his audience was waiting for him to give a recitation.

One of the principal playwrights of the Athenian New Comedy, he was ranked equal by his contemporaries to Menander, whom he defeated in a number of dramatic competitions; Philemon gained his first victory at the Dionysia in 327 and won three times at the Lenaean festival as well. He wrote approximately ninety-seven plays, of which something over two hundred fragments survive. We also have sixty of his titles. Most of them are typical of New Comedy in general, but two, the *Myrmidons* and the *Palamedes,* are suggestive of mythological burlesque; and one existing fragment parodies the story of Medea. Other titles indicate that Philemon adopted a strongly moralistic tone, praising peace and justice and advocating humane treatment for slaves. Philemon frequently attempts to achieve epigrammatic effects, but the results display a platitudinous flatness that falls short of Menander's efforts. Moreover, his characters, who are made to speak in literary Greek, fail to maintain Menander's illusion of real-life talk.

Further and more positive qualities can be detected by examining three plays by the Roman comic dramatist Plautus. For these, as Plautus himself asserts, were modeled on originals by Philemon, now lost: his *Mercator, Trinummus,* and *Mostellaria* (perhaps) were adapted from Philemon's *Merchant (Emporos), Treasure (Thesaurus),* and *Phasma (Ghost)* respectively. These works suggest that Philemon was a master of dramatic technique, with a particular taste for surprise effects, including exciting and sensational endings. The Roman novelist Apuleius, in the second century A.D., praised him for his keen wit and realistic characterization (despite the literary language in which his characters speak) and for his neat and lucid plots. Nevertheless, Apuleius was among those who reversed the

verdict of the dramatist's contemporaries by placing him below Menander, and this was also the opinion of other critics of Roman imperial times. (Philemon of Soli in Cyprus is a different poet.)

WORKS—Plays included: The Changeling, The Claimant, The Doorkeeper, The Ghost, Kidnapped, The Merchant, The Myrmidons, Naera, Palamedes, The Pancratiast, The Soldier, The Stateless Man, The Suicide Pact, The Treasure.

EDITIONS—T. Kock, Comicorum Atticorum Fragmenta, v 2 and v 3; A. Meineke, Fragmenta Comicorum Graecorum, v 4; J. Demiańczuk, Supplementum Comicum, 1912; D. L. Page, Select Papyri (Loeb ed.), v 3, revised ed., 1942.

ABOUT—E. Rapisarda, Philemone comico, 1939; B. Krysiniel-Józefowicz, De Quibusdam Plauti Exemplaribus Graecis, 1949; T. B. L. Webster, Studies in Later Greek Comedy, 2nd ed., 1970; F. H. Sandbach, The Comic Theatre of Greece and Rome, 1977.

PHILETAS (or **PHILITAS**), Greek poet and scholar, the son of a certain Telephus, was born not later than 320 B.C.; it is not known when he died. He came from the island of Cos, off southwestern Asia Minor. King Ptolemy I Soter of Egypt (d. 283/2 B.C.) invited him to Alexandria to become the tutor of his son, who later became Ptolemy II Philadelphus. His other pupils included the poets Hermesianax, Theocritus —who was probably taught by him in 275–71, and who acknowledged him as his master—and the librarian and scholar Zenodotus. Philetas seems to have been buried at Cos.

Five titles of his poems are known as well as a scant array of some fifty fragments, cited by various later authors from these works. One of the pieces was in hexameters, a miniature epic entitled the *Hermes.* This introduces an amorous theme into the story of Odysseus by telling of his love for Polymele, a daughter of Aeolus, to whom the hero relates the story of his wanderings, though in a different order from the *Odyssey.* Philetas' other recorded poems are in elegiac couplets, and it is for his skill in the use of this meter that he was principally admired. The most important of these pieces was apparently the *Demeter,* which narrated the wanderings of the goddess, in the course of which she probably visited the poet's native

fi lē′ tàs

island Cos. The *Telephus* included an allusion to the wedding of Jason and Medea; the title probably refers to a mythical king of Mysia rather than to Philetas' father of the same name. *Paignia (Playthings)* and *Epigrammata* are listed as separate works, but it is possible that these are alternative titles for a single collection. Hermesianax and Ovid record that in some work or other, perhaps the *Paignia,* Philetas wrote in praise of a certain Bittis, his wife or mistress; and the people of Cos later set up a statue of him singing her charms.

His inclusion of this love interest has invited surmises, in modern times, that Philetas (in addition, perhaps, to other Hellenistic writers) had already invented the personal love elegy that later appears fully developed in Latin literature; and, indeed, Philetas was included in the canon of elegists, being generally regarded, according to Quintilian, as second only to Callimachus; and Propertius and Ovid identify him as their elegiac model. Yet there is no trace in the fragments of Philetas of any material prefiguring the manner or method of the Latin writers with any exactitude, so that to credit the foundation of the love elegy to him, rather than them, is probably incorrect.

In any case, whatever his role in the development of elegy, Philetas may be considered the founder of the Alexandrian school of poetry. He was also the first of the Alexandrian poet-scholars, since his writings included a prose lexicon of *Unclassifiable (?) Glosses (Ataktoi Glossai),* consisting of technical terms, words used in various dialects, and rare words from Homer. This work moved the Homeric scholar Aristarchus to write a polemic *Against Philetas;* but Philetas' treatise also earned much admiration and played a pioneer role in the establishment of literary scholarship. It also figured largely in educational anthologies; however, only some thirty fragments survive today. Another monograph, entitled *Hermeneia* (which perhaps means *Interpretation*), was also ascribed to his authorship.

EDITIONS—J. U. Powell, Collectanea Alexandrina, 1925; A. Nowacki, Philitae Coi Fragmenta Poetica, 1927; G. Kuchenmuller, Philetae Coi Reliquiae, 1928; E. Diehl, Anthologia Lyrica Graeca, v 6, 3rd ed., 1949–52.
ABOUT—A. A. Day, The Origins of Latin Love-Elegy, 1938; A. Rostagni, L'influenza greca sulle origini dell'elegia erotica latina *in* Entretiens Hardt, v 2, 1953; R. Pfeiffer, History of Classical Scholarship: From the Beginnings to the End of the Hellenistic Age, 1968; G. Luck, The Latin Love Elegy, 2nd ed., 1969.

PHILIP, Greek anthologist and epigrammatic poet, was writing in about A.D. 40. He came from Thessalonica (Salonica) in Macedonia (northeastern Greece) but lived at Rome, where he may have worked as a rhetorician. On internal evidence, it appears that he sought or enjoyed patronage at the imperial court.

He collected a *Garland (Stephanos)* —likening each poet to a flower—containing Greek epigrams that had been written since the first major Greek Anthology (also called Stephanus) had been brought together by Meleager in about 100 B.C. Philip's collection, of which the introductory list of poets included is extant, displays some evidence that he was one of the members of a literary school. However, the pieces he included are, for the most part, less distinguished than those Meleager had gathered, since so much of the best work in Philip's time was no longer being done in Greek, but rather in Latin. Nevertheless, his collection was largely incorporated in the anthologies of the Byzantine era, notably that of Cephalus (eighth century A.D.) and the Palatine and Planudean Anthologies (c. 980 and c. 1300, respectively).

Eighty-nine surviving epigrams are ascribed to Philip's own authorship. Eighty of them appear in his *Garland.* The Palatine Anthology includes seventy-eight; the Planudean omits fifteen of these, includes four without Philip's name, and adds eleven on its own account. Philip's pieces are most commonly concerned with the following themes: dedications, mostly literary and fictitious; strange occurrences and experiences, again largely fictitious; literary exercises on historical or literary or mythological subjects; and descriptions of works of art. A few of these poems are of adequate quality, especially two on convivial topics;

but most are dull and uninteresting, and some sink to fatuous banality.

Philip's diction, however, is generally efficient, and occasionally skillful. Its only peculiarity is a taste for new, and preferably compound, word-formations. He is a plagiarist on a considerable, if not shameless, scale, who borrows extensively from well over a dozen different models.

EDITIONS with translation—W. R. Paton, The Greek Anthology (Loeb ed.), 1916–18; A. S. F. Gow and D. L. Page, The Greek Anthology, v 2: The Garland of Philip and Some Contemporary Epigrams, 1968; for other English translations of the Anthology see A. M. W. Green, Classics in Translation: A Selective Bibliography (1930–76), 1976. Translations (into other languages)—P. Waltz, G. Soury, F. Buffière, R. Aubreton, Anthologie grecque (Budé ed.), 1974– ; H. Beckby, Anthologia Graeca (German), 1965.
ABOUT—A. S. F. Gow, The Greek Anthology: Sources and Ascriptions, 1958; L'épigramme grecque (Entretiens Hardt, v 14), 1968.

PHILISTUS (or PHILISCUS), Greek historian, c. 430–356 B.C., was a native of Syracuse in Sicily. As a boy he witnessed his city's successful defense against the Athenian expedition (415–413) and in 405, after helping Dionysius I to seize power as tyrant of Syracuse, he became his principal adviser and governor of the citadel. Later, however, Philistus fell from favor, owing to his support of the tyrant's brother Leptines, and was sent into exile, residing mainly in Epirus. Recalled at the instance of the courtiers of Dionysius' son and successor Dionysius II, he acted as the agent of the new ruler in the expulsion of Plato's patron Dion (366) and held a leading command in Dionysius' forces during the civil war that Dion subsequently launched. Serving first in the Adriatic and then at home, Philistus failed to stop Dion's invasion from Greece (357) and in the following year suffered a naval defeat. Shortly afterward he committed suicide.

He had begun to write his *History of Sicily (Sicelica),* of which only fragments are now extant, during his period of exile in Epirus. Its two parts were later regarded as separate works, but originally they had belonged to a
fi lis' tus

single, unitary history. The first part, the initial seven of its thirteen books, narrated the history of the island from the earliest times down to 406 B.C. The second part, in six books, described contemporary events down through Dionysius I and the early years of Dionysius II (367–363).

Very extensive use was made of Philistus by later historians; indeed, he became the principal authority for the affairs of the western Greek world during the fourth century B.C. Ephorus drew on him heavily for the Sicilian sections of his *History,* and he was also one of the main sources employed by Timaeus, who disapproved, however, of his favorable attitude toward the Syracusan tyrants. Philistus was subsequently described by Cicero as "almost a miniature Thucydides," at a time when histories of the cool, Thucydidean type were fashionable, in reaction against the more melodramatic Hellenistic historians. Echoing the assertion that Philistus was an imitator of Thucydides, Dionysius of Halicarnassus, who agreed with Timaeus that he groveled excessively to the rulers of Syracuse, commented that he copied all his model's worst points and coordinated his material ineffectively. In the second century A.D. the Alexandrian rhetorician Theon accused Philistus of plagiarizing Thucydides and drawing on his account of the Athenian expedition almost verbatim. The surviving fragments are too sparse for us to make our own estimate regarding such charges. But, whatever the answer, Philistus' history was competent enough to become a standard work—and to inspire another Syracusan historian, Athanis or Athanus, to take up the narrative at the point where he left off.

EDITIONS—F. Jacoby, Die Fragmente der griechischen Historiker, 3b, 556 and perhaps 577 (fragments 1 and 2).
ABOUT—R. Lauritano, Ricerche su Filisto, in Kokalos (v 3), 1957; G. de Sanctis, Ricerche sulla storiografia siceliota, 1958.

PHILO (often known as PHILO JUDAE-US), Greek writer on Hebrew religion and philosophy, was born in about 30 B.C. and
f ī' lō joo dē' us

probably died in the early 40s A.D. He was a member, and eventually head, of the large Jewish community of Alexandria, where his brother Alexander was an important tax official *(alabarchos)*. The only event in Philo's life of which anything is known—since he himself left a full account of the incident —was his participation in a Jewish mission to Rome in A.D. 39–40, sent to try to persuade the emperor Gaius (Caligula) to withdraw his insistence that the Jews must worship him as a god.

Philo's writings were very numerous and extensive. Two of his earliest compositions (preserved in an Armenian version) take the form of dialogues between himself and his nephew, called Alexander. In the first of these pieces, named after his interlocutor, they discuss whether animals possess reasoning powers; the second, *On Providence,* consists of two books and deals with Stoic beliefs on that subject. Philo was also the author of two further monographs (the authenticity of which has been doubted, probably without justification)—namely, *On the Indestructibility of the Universe,* which defends this thesis against Stoic objections, and *On the Contemplative Life,* about the semimonastic sect of the Therapeutae. In addition, he wrote *On Nobility* and *On Dreams;* the latter piece examines the various kinds of dream images in the light of the Bible.

More than three-quarters of the confusingly large number of titles of Philo's monographs probably do not, in fact, stand for independent works but represent sections of larger compositions. These included three major commentaries on the Pentateuch (the first five books of the Old Testament), a subject to which he devoted a great part of his literary career. Pride of place among his works on this theme goes to the most important of all his writings, the *Allegorical Expositions of the Holy Laws,* a vast collection of essays dealing with individual passages of Genesis for the benefit of his fellow Jews. *Questions and Solutions* is a somewhat shorter exposition of Genesis and Exodus, in the form of queries and answers; only fragments (numerous but brief) of the Greek text are preserved, but about half the work survives in an Armenian translation, and a Latin fragment also exists.

Philo also wrote a group of compositions setting out the Hebrew Law of Moses (Torah) for the benefit of pagans. The work has three principal divisions: (1) *On the Creation of the Universe,* which is interpreted in a philosophical and partly Platonic fashion; (2) *Biographies of the Wise*—that is to say, of Abraham, Isaac, and Joseph, who are declared to have displayed the excellence of the law by the excellence of their lives (another biography, the *Life of Moses* is more akin to pagan biographies of Greek philosophers); and (3) the Law itself, comprising a four-book treatise entitled *On the Decalogue* —the ten principal chapters of the Law— and further books entitled *On the Individual Laws,* which these chapters comprised. The lost *Apology* (or *On the Jews*) was once again probably intended to justify the Jewish faith in pagan Gentile circles.

Two of five books by Philo on Alexandrian Jewry have been preserved. One, *Against Flaccus,* tells how Aulus Avillius Flaccus, prefect of Egypt under Gaius (Caligula), allowed the local Greeks to persecute Judaism but was soon afterward banished and died a miserable death, thus demonstrating the Providence that watches over the Jews. The second, imperfectly preserved, work, entitled *On the Embassy of Gaius,* describes the persecution following upon the demands of that emperor for divine honors and tells the story of the harrowing experiences of the Alexandrian Jews sent to Rome in A.D. 39 to ask him to modify his request: A lost, final, part of the work probably dealt with Gaius' downfall, representing it, once again, as an act of divine retribution.

In both these treatises, Philo is eager to indicate that God is mindful of his Jewish people and brings death upon those who persecute them (a view that Lactantius later adapted for Christian use in his treatise entitled *On the Death of the Persecutors*). Yet Philo himself was very far from being an enemy of the Roman system or of Hellenistic civilization. Indeed, the latter was a far more prominent influence on his work than Judaism (whether of the Alexandrian or any other variety. His very endeavors to show that Greek and Jewish doctrines closely resemble each other demonstrate how Greek he was. His principal sources were

Plato, Aristotle, the Stoics (especially Posidonius), and the Neopythagoreans. Philo seems to have been outstanding among the Jewish philosophers of the Alexandrian school and has been described as "the first theologian."

He felt difficulty in bridging the gulf between the world of God and the world of matter, since, if the latter were created by God, it seemed to him impossible to explain the existence of evil; in consequence, like so many dualists after him, he introduced an intermediary, which he called the Logos. At the same time, Philo did not exclude the possibility of making direct contact with the divinity; in his view human beings are able to obey the will of God, not only by following his ordinances but also by discovering and seeing him in a communion he describes as "ecstasy." Yet, he maintains, this they cannot achieve without the grace of God, upon which their souls are ultimately dependent. This view was to have great influence on the development of the mysticism that became such an important feature of the religious thought in subsequent centuries, culminating in the Neoplatonism of Plotinus. Philo's thinking on God and matter also exercised a considerable effect on Augustine's distinction between the Two Cities in the *City of God*. For these and other reasons Philo, though not an original philosopher himself, played a very significant part as a link between the Greek philosophies he inherited and Neoplatonism and Christianity alike.

WORKS (wrongly attributed to Philo)—Essays on Samson and on Jonah (both preserved only in Armenian). EDITIONS—H. Cohn, P. Wendland, S. Reiter, H. Leisegang, 1896–1930 (smaller edition, 1896–1915). *Translations*—F. H. Colson, G. H. Whitaker, R. Marcus (Loeb ed.), 1929–62; C. Mondésert, J. Pouilloux, M. Petit (French), 1961–75; L. Cohn and J. Heinemann (German), 1909–38, reprint 1960. *Individual Works*: M. R. James, Biblical Antiquities (from Latin), 1917, reprint 1971; F. W. Tilden, On the Contemplative Life, 1922; H. Box, In Flaccum, 1939; R. Cadiou, The Migration of Abraham (French), 1957; E. M. Smallwood, Legatio ad Gaium, 1961, *and* with A. Pelletier (French), 1972; M. Alexandre, De Congressu Eruditionis Gratia (French), 1967; A. Mosès, De Specialibus Legibus (French), 1970; E. Starobinski-Safran, De Fuga et Inventione (French), 1970.
ABOUT—J. Drummond, Philo Judaeus, or the Jewish Alexandrian Philosophy, 1888; N. Bentwich, Philo Judaeus of Alexandria, 1910; T. H. Billings, The Platonism of Philo Judaeus, 1919; H. A. A. Kennedy, Philo's Contribution to Religion, 1919; I. Heinemann, Philons griechische und jüdische Bildung, 1932 (later reprint with appendices); E. R. Goodenough, By Light, Light: The Mystic Gospel of Hellenistic Judaism, 1935, *and* The Politics of Philo Judaeus, 1938, *and* An Introduction to Philo Judaeus, 1940; A. Meyer, Vorsehungsglaube und Schicksalsidee in ihrem Verhältnis bei Philo von Alexandrie, 1939; S. Belkin, Philo and the Oral Law, 1940; H. Leisegang *in* Pauly-Wissowa-Kroll, Real-Encyclopädie der klassischen Altertumswissenschaft, v 20, 1941; M. Pohlenz, Philo von Alexandria, 1942; H. H. Wolfson, Philo: Foundations of Religious Philosophy in Judaism, Christianity and Islam, 1948; M. Pohlenz, Les idées philosophiques et réligieuses de Philon d'Alexandrie, 3rd ed., 1950; J. Daniélou, Philon d'Alexandrie, 1958; A. Maddalena, Filone Alessandrino, 1970; B. L. Mack and E. Hilgert, ed., Studia Philonica, 1972, 1973; G. D. Farandos, Kosmos und Logos nach Philon von Alexandria, 1976; E. M. Smallwood, The Jews Under Roman Rule, 1976; V. Nikoprowetzsky, Le commentaire de l'écriture chez Philon d'Alexandrie, 1977.

PHILOCHORUS, Greek historian, antiquarian and critic, was born slightly after the middle of the fourth century B.C. and died in about 260. He was an Athenian of distinguished family and held official positions as interpreter of sacrifices and as diviner *(mantis)*. He took an active part in the last attempts to recover for Athens the independent political position it had lost to Macedonian domination, and when Ptolemy II Philadelphus of Egypt (289/88–246 B.C.), in alliance with Sparta and Athens, endeavored to break the power of the Macedonian kingdom in the Aegean region, it was Philochorus who led the anti-Macedonian faction among the Athenians. When, however, the subsequent Chremonidean war ended with the capitulation of Athens in 262, he attracted the hostility of the Macedonian monarch Antigonus II Gonatas, who apparently had him kidnapped and murdered.

His principal work lay in the field of Atthidography, a type of literature dealing with the history, mythology, ancient religion, and political institutions of Attica and Athens. The genre had become popular since the middle of the fourth century B.C., and Philochorus became its most distin-

fi lo' kō rus

guished practitioner. His *Atthis (History of Attica)* was in seventeen books, apparently compiled in the late 290s and 280s B.C. Unlike most other writers in this field—and perhaps because they had handled this material at such exhaustive length—Philochorus dealt fairly briefly with the earlier periods of Athenian history in the first two books. In the next four books he recounted events up to the battle of Chaeronea (338), perhaps even to the rise to power of Demetrius of Phaleron (308/7). The eleven remaining books, with increasing detail, surveyed contemporary history "as far as Antiochus of Syria"—either the second king of that name (261–246) (taking in his accession), or more probably the first (292–261), if, as seems likely, he chose to end his work at the Chremonidean War.

The *Atthis* was arranged in chronological, annalistic order; the fragments that remain bear witness to a simple style, lacking rhetorical adornment. Philochorus must be regarded as a historian of note: first, because he possessed a scholarly interest in accurate research and, secondly, because he was an eyewitness of many of the events he describes. Very little, however, has survived from the last seven books, since subsequent writers were chiefly interested in his descriptions of the earlier Attic orators and in consequence preserved fewer passages from the later sections.

He was also the author of at least twenty-six other works, from which scarcely anything has come down to us. Many of them were specialized pieces relating to the same themes as his *Atthis,* for which they may have served as preliminary studies: among these are *Attic Inscriptions* (the first collection of the sort of which we have any knowledge), *On Contests in Athens, On the Mysteries of Athens, On the Tetrapolis* (Marathon and three other towns of northern Attica), *On the Foundation of Salamis,* and *On Delos* (a dependency of Athens until 314). It is also to be supposed that his other treatises—among them *Festivals, Days* (of religious celebration), *Sacrifices, Divination,* and *Purifications*—were also related to Athenian practices.

Philochorus also wrote a good deal of literary criticism. In this category were several studies of tragic poetry, including monographs entitled *On Tragedies* and *On the Themes of Sophocles,* two essays on Pythagorean topics *(On Symbola* and *Pythagorean Women),* and a treatise entitled *On Inventions* that seems connected with subjects favored by the Aristotelian school.

EDITIONS—F. Jacoby, Die Fragmente der griechischen Historiker, 3b, 328, *and* Suppl. 1, p 235.
ABOUT—L. Pearson, The Local Historians of Attica, 1942; F. Jacoby, Atthis: The Local Chronicles of Ancient Athens, 1949; J. H. Oliver, The Athenian Expounders of the Sacred and Ancestral Law, 1950.

PHILODEMUS, Greek philosopher and poet, c. 110–c. 40 B.C., came from Gadara in Syria (now Umm Keis in Jordan). He went to Athens to become a pupil of the Epicurean philosopher Zeno of Sidon but in about 75 B.C., in the aftermath of Rome's first war against King Mithridates VI of Pontus, moved on to Italy. There he became a prominent member, and, in due course, one of the leaders of the local Epicurean movement, the headquarters of which were at Neapolis (Naples) and Herculaneum. During the disturbed period of civil war after Julius Caesar's death, Philodemus vigorously opposed the policies of Antony and encouraged Republican feelings among his associates, who apparently included Virgil and Horace.

On arrival in Italy he had become the friend and philosophical counselor of the rich and powerful Lucius Calpurnius Piso Caesoninus, consul in 58 B.C. and father-in-law of Caesar; and it was probably Piso who gave him the house at Herculaneum in which he spent much of his time. But outside the same town another, very large, residence that probably belonged to Piso himself is also associated with Philodemus. The mansion is known as the Villa dei Papiri because its excavation provided an enormous haul of over eighteen hundred carbonized papyri (in addition to yielding a major collection of sculpture). Out of those papyri that it has so far proved possible to decipher—less than four hundred in number—two-thirds have proved to be philosophical monographs written by Philodemus,

fi lō dē′ mus

325

who thus becomes one of our principal sources of evidence for the Epicurean school.

The recovered papyri, it is true, give only a limited impression of his voluminous output. Nevertheless, they include works on logic, ethics, theology, rhetoric, and music (on these last two subjects, he attacked the views of the Stoic Diogenes of Babylon). The treatises also include some intended for a wider audience, for example a general outline of the history of Greek philosophy viewed from the Epicurean viewpoint, in ten or more books. His prose style is earnest, pedestrian, and uninspired. Special interest, however, attaches to his theory of art, which he believed to be an independent field of intellectual activity, distinct from morality and logic and assessable by purely esthetic values. Cicero, although he disliked Piso, and in consequence wrote of Philodemus in a somewhat facetious fashion, knew the latter's philosophical writings well and employed them as an authority for Epicurean doctrine. He described Philodemus as a writer of "reams of verse to Piso and about Piso" but also suggested that certain of his poems were both "witty, neat and elegant." Twenty-five of these erotic epigrams have survived. They are often very funny in a lecherous way; and they rival in point and ingenuity the similar work of his older contemporary, Meleager. These verses of Philodemus bear no perceptible relation at all to his philosophical treatises, and it has been suggested that he wrote the poems when he was young and the philosophy when he was older. However, this remains a mere conjecture.

EDITIONS—For a list of partial and separate editions of his prose works *see* P. Treves *in* Oxford Classical Dictionary, 2nd ed., 1970, p 818ff. *Translations*—H. M. Hubbell, The Rhetorica, 1920 (abridged paraphrase); P. H. DeLacy and E. A. DeLacy, On Methods of Inference: A Study in Ancient Empiricism, revised ed., 1978. Epigrams: G. Kaibel, 1885; D. L. Page, Epigrammata Graeca, 1976.
ABOUT—C. Cichorius, Römische Studien, 1922, reprint 1961; A. Rostagni, Scritti minori, v 1, 1955 (theory of art); A. J. Neubecker, Die Bewertung der Musik bei Stoikern und Epikureern: Eine Analyse von Philodems Schrift De Musica, 1956; W. Liebich, Aufbau, Absicht und Form der Pragmateiae Philodems, 1960;

F. Sbordone, ed., Ricerche sui papiri ercolanesi, v 1, 1969.

PHILOPONUS, JOHN, Greek theologian and philosopher of the early Byzantine age, was born in about A.D. 490 and died in about 570. He came from Caesarea Maritima in Palestine (near Sdot Yam in Israel) and moved to Alexandria to study under the Greek philosopher Ammonius Hermiae, one of the most influential Aristotelian commentators. He seems to have succeeded Ammonius as director of the Alexandrian school, and under his direction it became Christian. Philoponus belonged to the Monophysite branch of Christianity, which taught that Jesus Christ possessed one nature—rather than two, divine and human—and this belief brought him into conflict with the Council of Chalcedon in 451. To support this Monophysite position, he attacked (in a work now lost) the decisions of that Council, making use of arguments from Aristotle. His own conception of the Trinity, outlined in the *Arbiter* (which is preserved complete in Syriac and in fragments in the original Greek), laid him open to charges of a heretical belief in three deities instead of one. He also wrote about the Resurrection and composed a long commentary on the biblical narrative of the Creation *(De Opificio Mundi),* in the hope of making it comprehensible in terms of Aristotelian physics and metaphysics.

As an Aristotelian and a Christian, Philoponus found himself at odds with the rival school at Athens, which was still pagan and attached to Platonism. Thus Philoponus, in a pamphlet that has not survived, denounced the Neoplatonist Iamblichus for his idolatrous attitude to images. When the emperor Justinian I closed down the Athenian school in 529, he wrote an additional polemic entitled *On the Eternity of the World (De Aeternitate Mundi),* censuring the view of another Neoplatonist, Proclus, that the heavens exist timelessly and are imperishable and arguing instead that the world was created by God and will one day come to an end. In another monograph on

fi lo' po nus

the same lines, now lost, Philoponus criticized Aristotle for supporting the view that the (circular) movement of the heavens is eternal; unlike most other Aristotelians of the age he was prepared to disagree with his master.

This independent attitude, which earned him a fierce retort from the Aristotelian commentator Simplicius, gave a special character to his own commentaries on several treatises of Aristotle; these commentaries—*Meteorologica, De Generatione, De Anima, Analytica, Categories,* and *Metaphysics*—were mainly written in his early years (and taken, in many cases, from the notes of his teacher Ammonius) and earned him the surnames *Philoponus* (industrious) and *Grammaticus.* Although prolix, his notes often show acute penetration and draw vividly on contemporary technological knowledge for illustrative purposes; they greatly influenced later Aristotelian commentators, particularly in the twelfth century. Philoponus played a major part in synthesizing pagan and Judaeo-Christian thought: a characteristic example of this activity was his endeavor to harmonize the Book of Genesis with Greek cosmological theories—attacking Theodore of Mopsuestia's (A.D. 350?–428?) unsophisticated employment of the Bible as a scientific authority and provoking a somewhat confused refutation from Cosmas Indicopleustes, sixth century Egyptian priest. Nor were these scandalized critics without their supporters, for to the Orthodox church Philoponus was a heretic, so that his writings were only read gingerly—and quoted without acknowledgment; indeed, in 680, they were officially condemned as heretical.

EDITIONS—Commentaria in Aristotelem Graeca, v 13–17, 1887–1909; G. Reichardt, De Opificio Mundi, 1897; H. Rabe, De Aeternitate Mundi, 1899; A. Sanda, ed., Opuscula Monophysitica, 1930.
ABOUT—B. Altaner, Patrology, 1960; S. Sambursky, The Physical World of Late Antiquity, 1962.

PHILOSTRATUS, FLAVIUS, was a Greek sophist, or popular philosopher. Although great confusion arises from the prob-

fi los' trà tus

able existence of no less than four writers of this name, living at different dates, it seems likely that Flavius Philostratus was born in about A.D. 170 and died in the reign of Philip the Arabian (244–49). He was the son of a sophist named Philostratus Verus, none of whose writings survive. Flavius Philostratus' birthplace may have been on the island of Lemnos, but he studied at Athens and elsewhere; his teachers included notable orators such as Damianus of Ephesus and Antipater of Hierapolis, who was also the tutor of Caracalla and Geta, the sons of the emperor Septimius Severus (193–211). Philostratus moved to Rome where, probably at the instance of Antipater, who was the emperor's secretary, he was introduced into the court circle of the empress Julia Domna, a cultured Syrian. After her death in 217 he seems to have returned to Athens to work as a sophist, though he may also have lived for a time at Tyre in Phoenicia.

His most famous work was the *Life of Apollonius of Tyana* (in Cappadocia, central Asia Minor), an ascetic Neopythagorean preacher of the first century A.D. to whom numerous miracles and prophecies, and some letters of doubtful authenticity, were attributed. Apollonius was revered by the emperor Caracalla, who stopped at Tyana in 215 in the company of his mother Julia Domna and ordered the construction of a shrine in the preacher's honor; thereafter the sage continued to assume a more and more important role in pagan theology, figuring extensively in the struggle against the Christians. His "biography" by Philostratus no doubt helped in establishing his influence: Philostratus deliberately elevates Apollonius from a mere magician into a holy and venerable wonderworker, so that his treatise is comparable to the *Acts of the Pagan Martyrs* (produced by nationalists of Alexandria in Egypt in the second and early third centuries A.D.) and foreshadows the lives of Christian saints. At the same time the work is an elaborate and sensational novel and travel romance, dazzlingly furnished with the exotic, oriental touches that would appeal to Philostratus' imperial patron and her circle. He quotes "the notebooks of Damis" —allegedly a contemporary of Apollonius— but they may be fictitious. However, the four

327

books written about the sage by a certain Moeragenes, which he also cites (but claims to have deliberately ignored), are independently attested.

This same Philostratus also wrote *Lives of the Sophists,* addressed either to Gordian I or Gordian II (before they became joint emperors in 238). These Lives describe both the original philosopher-rhetoricians in the fifth century B.C. and the members of the so-called second sophistic movement, which flourished in the second century A.D.: it is for its treatment of these later figures that the work is chiefly interesting. Another of Philostratus' writings was the *Gymnasticus,* an essay on athletic contests and training methods; and he was also the author of the *Heroicus,* a dialogue about the local cult of the mythical Protesilaus, in which the speakers are a winegrower of the Thracian Chersonese (Gallipoli) and a traveler from Phoenicia. He may also have written a dialogue entitled *Nero* (wrongly attributed to Lucian), in which the Stoic philosopher Gaius Musonius Rufus describes that emperor's tyrannical behavior. In addition, the name of Philostratus is attached to a collection of letters surviving in three versions, although the authenticity of some of them is dubious. The collection includes a number of erotic pieces, but particularly noteworthy is an epistle defending the sophists before Julia Domna; this seems correctly attributed to the man who wrote the *Life of Apollonius,* and the same applies to at least a few of the other letters.

There were also, it appears, two subsequent writers of the same name, his son-in-law and his grandson. A treatise on *Images (Eikones),* much admired by the German poet Goethe (1749–1832), which discusses sixty-five real or imaginary wall paintings in a colonnade at Neapolis (Naples), consists of two series, one of which may be the work of the first of these later Philostrati and the other (much inferior) a composition of the second. To the former is also attributable a treatise on epistolary style *(Dialexis 1)* addressed to Aspasius of Ravenna, imperial secretary *(ab epistulis)* and professor of rhetoric at Rome. The authorship of the second *Dialexis,* which attempts to settle the opposition between nature and law, is uncertain.

EDITIONS with translation—F. C. Conybeare, W. C. Wright, A. Fairbanks (Loeb ed.), 1912 (revised ed. 1950), 1921, 1931; A. R. Benner and F. H. Fobes, Letters of Alciphron, Aelian and Philostratus (Loeb ed.), 1949; C. P. Jones (ed. and abridged by G. W. Bowersock, with bibliography), Life of Apollonius (Penguin ed.), 1970.
ABOUT—F. Grosso, La vita di Apollonio di Tiana come fonte storica, in Acme (v 7), 1954; G. W. Bowersock, Greek Sophists in the Roman Empire, 1969; F. Lo Cascio, La forma letteraria della Vita di Apollonio Tianeo, 1974; J. Palm, Om Filostratos och hans Apollonios-biografi, 1976.

PHOTIUS, Greek scholar and churchman of the Byzantine epoch, c. A.D. 820–91, was appointed professor of philosophy at the imperial school of Constantinople by Theoctistus, the principal adviser of Theodora who acted as regent (842–56) for her son Michael III the Drunkard (842–67). Assisted by the marriage of his brother to Theodora's sister, Photius became chief of the imperial chancery and a member of the Senate. In 858, upon the forced resignation of the patriarch Ignatius during a political upheaval, Photius, although ordained a priest only six days previously, was appointed to succeed him. This act unleashed the fiercest ecclesiastical upheaval of the century: Pope Nicholas I, siding with the vigorous partisans of Ignatius, condemned Photius to excommunication (863), thus incurring a violent protest from Michael III. Under Michael's successor Basil I (867–86), Photius became patriarch again (877) but had to resign once more after Basil's death. He died, however, in the monastery of Gordon in 891, in communion with Rome. The relations between the Greek and Roman churches during this disturbed period, and the part that these events played in their eventual formal separation, have been endlessly discussed. During his patriarchate, Photius extended Byzantine religious influence in Moravia, Bulgaria, and Russia.

It is, however, as a prolific writer and a scholar of enormously wide range that he is chiefly remembered. His principal work, written at some date before 858, is the *Library (Bibliotheca or Myriobiblon),* an account of two hundred and eighty books

fō′ ti us

perused by a reading group under Photius' direction and recorded for the benefit, and at the request, of his brother Tarasius. Each item is accompanied by a summary and critical assessment of the work under discussion, often backed up by extensive excerpts. Though poetry and philosophy are almost wholly omitted, the works included are by writers in many different spheres, in which theology and history predominate. The *Bibliotheca* is of considerable intrinsic value, because Photius' criticisms are not only frequently acute in themselves but throw significant light on the critical methods of this period, when a revival of Byzantine learning was taking place after a period of eclipse. But the treatise is also of special value because more than half the writings described, pagan and Christian alike, including sixty relating to nontheological matters, do not survive today.

Further lost works are referred to in an earlier compilation by Photius, his *Lexicon* of rare words and expressions encountered in classical literature, a complete manuscript of which was found in Macedonia in 1959. The principal sources of this dictionary included the *Lexicon of Plato* by a scholar of the fourth century A.D. named Timaeus, and, more particularly, another encyclopedic collection, likewise of late antique date, known as the *Lexica Segueriana* (after the name of its former owner). Ostensibly, though indirectly, the authorities employed in Photius' *Lexicon* are Aelius Dionysius, Diogenianus, and Pausanias.

He also wrote nineteen *Homilies,* some of which, particularly an oration referring to the Russian attack on Constantinople in 860, are of notable historical significance. Photius' other contributions to theological literature included the *Amphilochia* (replying to some three hundred questions on matters of religion), commentaries on the New Testament (now surviving only in fragments), a polemic against the Manichaeans, and a treatise on the procession of the Holy Spirit (the *Mystagogia*). In addition, he has left more than two hundred and fifty letters, including official documents, which throw light on numerous aspects of the intellectual and social life of the time. Many spurious works have also become attached to his name.

EDITIONS—J. P. Migne, Patrologia Graeca, v 101-4; S. A. Naber, Lexicon, 1864–65; B. Laourdas, Homiliai, 1959; R. Henry, Bibliothèque (Budé ed.), 1959–78. *Translations*—J. H. Freese, The Library (v 1 only), 1920; C. Mango, Homilies, 1958.
ABOUT—E. Orth, Photiana, 1928; F. Dvornik, The Photian Schism: History and Legend, 1948, *and* The Patriarch Photius in the Light of Recent Research, 1958; R. Jenkins, Byzantium: The Imperial Centuries, 1966; J. Alexiou, The Great Photius (in Greek), 1968; P. Lemerle, Le premier humanisme byzantin, 1971; T. Hägg, Photios als Vermittler antiker Literatur, 1975.

PHRYNICHUS (1), Greek tragic poet, worked in the later years of the sixth century B.C. and the first quarter of the fifth. He was an Athenian and won his first dramatic victory in the City Dionysia between 511 and 508.

His plays, of which a few fragments remain, include the following titles: *Actaeon; Alcestis* (perhaps a satyric drama rather than a tragedy, from which, we are told, Euripides made certain borrowings); *Antaeus; The Daughters of Danaus* and *The Egyptians* (these are also the titles of two of the plays in a subsequent trilogy of Aeschylus, of which only the *Suppliants* survives); *Tantalus; Troilus;* and *Women of Pleuron,* about the Calydonian boar hunt and the fatal enmity between Meleager and his mother Althaea.

Phrynichus was particularly noteworthy for his two tragedies on contemporary historical themes. The first of these was the *Capture of Miletus,* which described the sack of that city by the Persians in 494, after Athens had failed to respond to appeals by the leaders of the Ionian revolt. When this play was acted, according to Herodotus, the whole audience burst out weeping and the Assembly sentenced Phrynichus to a thousand-drachma fine for reminding them of something they did not want to hear about; and a law was even passed that the piece should never be staged again. His second topical venture was more successful. This was the *Phoenician Women (Phoenissae),* which, like the *Persae* of Aeschylus, cele-
fri' ni kus

329

brated the Greek naval victory over the Persians off Salamis in 480. The scene of Phrynichus' play was set in Persia. It opened with a eunuch preparing seats for a meeting of the Persian councillors; and the news of the disaster was announced. The Phoenician women were the members of the chorus; they may have been temple slaves or, conceivably, widows of men who had died in the engagement.

It seems possible that the statesman Themistocles backed both these plays in turn: not only was he the state official (archon) of 493–492 to whom Phrynichus submitted the *Capture of Miletus* but he was also the architect of the victory of Salamis which was the theme of the *Phoenician Women.* Indeed, the text of an inscription (that we owe to Plutarch) dedicated by Themistocles in gratitude for a victory in the tragic competition of 476 surely refers to the latter play. The Suidas Lexicon also records a play of Phrynichus known as *The Just Men,* or *Persians,* or *Partners (Sunthokoi);* it has been suggested that these may be alternative titles for the *Phoenician Women,* but that does not seem very probable.

Coming chronologically after Thespis in the early history of Attic tragic theater, Phrynichus was apparently the earliest of its practitioners whose work was still preserved to a substantial extent in later antiquity. He was said to have been the first to display female masks—that is to say, to introduce female characters into his tragedies. Aristophanes, who presented him as a good-looking dandy, greatly admired his work, especially dwelling on the honeyed sweetness of his lyrics; spoken, lyrical, lamentations seem to have been among his principal innovations. Plutarch noted the numerous varieties of dance that he invented. One form of his father's name, Polyphradmon, was Ionian, and his own choice of language shows Ionian features, so that he has been seen, with some plausibility, as representing the elegant, Ionian element in the Athenian cultural synthesis.

EDITIONS—A. Nauck, ed., Tragicorum Graecorum Fragmenta, revised ed., 1964.
ABOUT—A. Peretti, Epirrema e tragedia, 1939; A. W. Pickard-Cambridge, Dithyramb, Tragedy and Comedy, 2nd ed. (revised by T. B. L. Webster), 1962.

PHRYNICHUS (2), Greek comic poet and playwright, lived in the fifth century B.C. His birthplace was Athens. He was a playwright of the Old Comedy, of which his contemporary Aristophanes was the most famous representative. Phrynichus probably produced his first play in 434 B.C. and won his first victory in the competition of the Lenaean festival in 429. He gained one further success at a subsequent Lenaea and was also victorious at the Dionysia some time after 420.

We have eight titles of Phrynichus' comedies and nearly a hundred fragments. His play *The Solitary Hermit (Monotropos),* about a man who rejected contemporary civilization, placed third at the Lenaean festival in 414, when Aristophanes' *Birds* came second. Phrynichus' *Muses* (about a contest betweeen Sophocles and Euripides) came second to Aristophanes' *Frogs* in 405.

In each of these plays of Phrynichus' there is a notable similarity to topics favored by Aristophanes—political satire, metrics, and music. Indeed, in the *Frogs* Aristophanes accuses him of using stale comic tricks.

WORKS—Other titles include Cronos, Herb-Gatherers, Incubus, Initiates, Satyrs, Tragedians. Two other plays, Revelers (Members of the Comus) and Connus, should probably be attributed to another dramatist, Ameipsias, who won first and second prize respectively with them.
EDITIONS (of fragments)—T. Kock, Comicorum Atticorum Fragmenta, 1880–88; J. Demianczuk, Supplementum Comicorum, 1913.

PHYLARCHUS, Greek historian, worked in the second half of the third century B.C. It is not certain whether he came from Athens, or from Sicyon in the Peloponnese, or from Naucratis in Egypt.

Among a number of other writings, he was the author of *Histories,* in twenty-eight books, covering the period between the death of King Pyrrhus of Epirus in 272 and

frī′ ni kus

fi lär′ kus

the victory of Antigonus III Doson of Macedonia over Cleomenes of Sparta in 222. Only fragments of the work have survived, and its arrangement cannot be reconstructed; but the plan does not seem to have been chronological.

Phylarchus' moralistic excursuses and prejudices against Macedonia lessened his trustworthiness. The historian Polybius (second century B.C.) made some use of his work but disliked him. This was partly because of the sympathy Phylarchus expressed for both revolutionary Sparta and the sufferings experienced by the men who had rebelled against the Achaean League, of which Polybius was an adherent. But Phylarchus was also criticized by Polybius on general grounds: for the cheap emotional sensationalism of his style. This was a feature he adopted in imitation of Duris of Samos, who had dealt with the preceding period in the same colorful, tragic, dramatic manner. At a later date, in the second century A.D., another writer who took exception to Phylarchus' methods was Plutarch. But this did not prevent Plutarch from making extensive use of his work, for Phylarchus was evidently the most important historian for the century in which he lived.

EDITIONS (of fragments)—F. Jacoby, Die Fragmente der griechischen Historiker, v 2.
ABOUT—T. W. Africa, Phylarchus and the Spartan Revolution (University of California Publications on History, v 68), 1961; F. W. Walbank, Polybius, 1972.

PINDAR, Greek lyric poet, was born in about 518 and died in about 438 B.C. His birthplace was Cynoscephalae, a village near Thebes in Boeotia. The name of his father was variously recorded as Daiphantus, Scopelinus, and Pagondas (or Pagonidas): a reference in one of Pindar's own poems to the aristocratic house of the Aegeids may indicate that he belonged to that family, though this is uncertain. His mother was called Cleonice. Anecdotes identifying the Boeotian woman poets Myrtis and Corinna as his teachers may be legendary; but he learned music from an uncle and continued his studies at Athens under Apollodorus
pin' dĕr

and Agathocles, who also taught Damon (one of the earliest writers on musical themes). Pindar himself gained a considerable reputation as a poet at a very early age. He appears to have cherished a special connection with Delphi, where the shrine of Apollo was the object of his particular devotion. In the Persian Wars of 480–479 he did not reject the Theban policy of neutrality, though later he duly greeted the Greek victories at Salamis and Plataea with applause. It is generally believed that in 476 he went to Sicily at the invitation of Hiero I, king of Syracuse, and stayed there for about two years. Thereafter, he had patrons in many parts of the Greek world but wrote in especially warm praise of Athens. He died at Argos—according to one story, in the arms of his male lover Theoxenus.

In ancient times Pindar's poems were collected in seventeen books. From this corpus there survive, more or less intact, four books of Epinician Odes—that is to say, choral songs composed in honor of athletic and musical victories in the major contests, the Olympian, Pythian, Nemean, and Isthmian Games. Each of the four books of Epinicians is concerned with one of these festivals.

The fourteen Olympian Odes celebrate victories in the Olympic Games, founded in 776 B.C. in honor of Olympian Zeus and held every four years; crowns of wild olive from the god's temple precinct were the prizes. The victors honored by Pindar are the following: Hiero I of Syracuse, in the horse race of 476 B.C., won by his horse Pherenicus; and Theron of Acragas (Agrigento) in the chariot race of the same year (two poems); Psaumis or Samios in the chariot race of 452 and mule-car race of 448 (two poems; the authenticity of the latter is questioned); Hagesias of Syracuse in the chariot race of 472; Diagoras of Rhodes in the boxing match of 464; Alcimedon of Aegina in the boys' wrestling match of 460; Epharmostus of Opus in the wrestling match of 468; Hagesidamus of Locri Epizephyrii (southern Italy) in the boys' wrestling match of 476 (two poems); Ergoteles of Cnossus (Crete)—who had settled at Himera in Sicily—in the long foot-race of 472; Xenophon of Corinth in both the short foot-race (the *stadium*) that always remained the

331

principal event of the Games and the pentathlon of 464; Asopichus of Orchomenus in the boys' short foot-race, perhaps in 488.

Pindar's twelve *Pythian Odes* commemorate victories in the Pythian Games that were held in honor of Apollo at Delphi. These contests had been reorganized in 582 on a four-year instead of an eight-year basis; the prizes were crowns of bay leaves plucked in the valley of Tempe. Pindar celebrates the following victors: Hiero I of Syracuse in the chariot race of 470, for another success not in the Pythian games but probably in the Theban Iolaia (468?), and in the Pythian horse races of 482 and 478, won by his horse Pherenicus (the first three odes); King Arcesilaus IV of Cyrene in the chariot race of 462 (the next two odes); Xenocrates of Acragas (modern Agrigento) in the chariot race of 490 (his son Thrasybulus was the driver); Megacles of Athens in the chariot race of 486; Aristomenes of Aegina in the boys' wrestling match of 446; Telesicrates of Cyrene in the race in full armor in 474; Hippocleas of Pelinna (Thessaly) in the boys' double-stadium race (800 yards) of 498; Thrasydaeus of Thebes in the boys' foot-race, probably in 454 (rather than 474, as has also been suggested); Midas of Acragas in the flute-playing competition of 490 (the musical competitions always held the first place in the Pythian Games).

The eleven *Nemean Odes* commemorate the following victories won in the games held in each alternate year at Nemea in the Peloponnese in honor of Nemean Zeus, with crowns of wild celery as the prizes: Chromius of Etna (Sicily) and formerly of Gela, the brother-in-law of Hiero I, in the chariot race of 476; Timodemus of Acharnae (near Athens) in the pancratium (a combination of boxing and wrestling), possibly 485; Aristocleides of Aegina in the pancratium, perhaps 474; Timasarchus of Aegina in the boys' wrestling match, perhaps 473; Pytheas of Aegina in the boys' pancratium, possibly 485; Alcimidas of Aegina in the boys' wrestling match, possibly 461; Sogenes of Aegina in the boys' pentathlon, perhaps 467; Deimias of Aegina in the long (double-stadium) race, perhaps 459. The last three Nemean Odes celebrate victories unconnected with the Nemean Festival: by Chromius of

Etna in the chariot race at Sicyon in the Peloponnese, perhaps in 473; by Theaeus of Argos in the Hecatomboea (Festival of Hera) at that city, perhaps in 464; and the final poem is an installation ode honoring Aristagoras of Tenedos on his assumption of office as president of his local Council in about 446.

The Isthmian Games were athletic competitions held at Corinth every second year in honor of Poseidon, the prizes being wreaths of pine branches. Pindar's eight *Isthmian Odes* commemorate the following victors: Herodotus and Zenocrates of Aegina in chariot races (perhaps both written in 470); Melissus of Thebes in the pancratium of the Isthmian Games and chariot race of the Nemean Games, perhaps both of 476; Phylacidas of Aegina in the pancratium, perhaps in 480 and 484 respectively; and Strepsiades of Thebes and Cleandros of Aegina in pancratia, perhaps in 454 and 478 respectively.

The literary form known as the Epinician Ode had taken shape in the sixth century B.C. Although the structure of such poems is not fixed, it is governed by rules, and there is a certain degree of uniformity in the content. A reference to the victor is required and to the place and nature of his victory; allusions to other victories won on earlier occasions by his relations may be added, as may compliments to his trainer. Generally, too, a fairly elaborate myth is inserted, more or less relevant to the occasion, though Pindar tends to emphasize selected highlights in a mythical narrative and even to alter it to suit his own purpose, instead of describing the victor's triumph in a straightforward fashion. His Odes, between twenty-five and two hundred lines in length, also include wise moral maxims and sage reflections on life; some of these sayings are derived from ancient authority, while others originate from the poet himself, who speaks at times in his own person—often with insight and brilliance. Despite the formality of his patterns, Pindar varies his arrangement by placing these ingredients as his fancy directs him, often with changes of theme that seem to us sharp and abrupt and need close inspection before we can detect what his overall purpose may be.

His dominant preoccupation is with that part of experience in which mortal persons are raised up or illuminated by a divine force. When this happens, he believes the human spirit experiences the same noble enhancement of consciousness that athletes and musicians enjoy at the moment of their triumphs: and that in this climactic manifestation of their excellence *(areta)* they are enveloped, temporarily, in a happiness like that of the gods themselves. To Pindar, this life-enhancing, divine effulgence, which from time to time descends on fortunate mortals, is the ultimate justification of human existence.

Moreover, he considers himself uniquely qualified to seize upon these extraordinary moments and immortalize them by his poetic talent. He displays a profound sense of his lofty mission as a poet, and a soaring confidence in the inborn genius that lifts him above those pedestrian figures who are his competitors.

Pindar's ethical and social beliefs are far removed from those of contemporary Athens, in which novel and disconcerting explorations of thought proliferated. The values that Pindar prefers are entirely different: they are those of an old-fashioned, conservative aristocracy that maintained an archaic admiration of physical prowess and harbored a corresponding suspicion of intellectuals—that valued hereditary aristocracy and family tradition with a wholehearted snobbishness and respected the opportunities for display and self-expression conferred by inherited riches. Yet success, in Pindar's view, could not be achieved without labor and dangerous endeavor and enterprise. The powerful man must also be courteous and magnanimous, and he must use his authority in the cause of peace and order—after the manner of Zeus himself.

Pindar is, above all else, a religious poet, as his other poetical works showed no less clearly. They consisted of paeans, dithyrambs (originally the term had referred to songs to Dionysus), procession songs, maiden songs, songs to accompany mimic dances *(hyporchemata),* panegyrics *(encomia),* and dirges. These pieces have only survived in fragments, though sometimes of considerable size; but substantial new passages of the paeans and dithyrambs have come to light on papyri. They do not show marked differences from the Epinician Odes in thought and style.

Pindar's language displays a grandeur that rises at times to a sublimity almost unequaled in the world's poetry; and it is magnificently adapted to his soaring imagination and exalted emotion. The diction he uses is an international literary form, based largely, though not exclusively, on the Doric dialect; it could be understood everywhere in the Greek world. He employs two different types of lyric meter (and sometimes a third) with a flexibility that is masterly.

Pindar's glory was not universally accepted, and he was deeply sensitive to the opposition he encountered. His poems contain passages that have been rightly interpreted as polemics against his contemporary literary rivals, including Simonides and Bacchylides, who grudged him his poetic successes in Sicily (and in some cases scored successes against him on their own account). Pindar was also attacked as a friend of tyrants and denounced as a neglector of his own homeland; but in a poem of 474 he seems to be defending himself against Theban charges of undue favor toward Athens. Still later, after 460, Athenian imperialist policies caused him dismay.

Amid the rapid developments of the classical epoch, a writer of his type was doomed to be soon regarded as old fashioned, and this was the fate that at first befell him. Nevertheless, Hellenistic (Alexandrian) scholarship took a keen interest in Pindar, in the first place because he was difficult and allusive, and secondly because he had such a strong sense of his poetic vocation. Subsequently, in Rome, he was particularly admired by Horace, who chose him as the model for his patriotic Odes but claimed to believe he could never reach comparable heights himself. In later Europe, a Pindaric Ode came to mean a poem that echoed Pindar's lofty, free-ranging imaginative vigor, and among those he inspired were the French poet Ronsard and the English poets Milton, Dryden, Gray, Shelley, Wordsworth, and Gerard Manley Hopkins.

EDITIONS—B. L. Gildersleeve, Olympian and Pythian

PLATO

Odes, 2nd ed., 1890, reprint 1965; J. B. Bury, Nemean Odes, 1890, *and* Isthmian Odes, 1892, reprint 1965; W. Christ, 1896. *Translations*—L. R. Farnell, 1930–32; J. E. Sandys (Loeb ed.), revised ed., 1937; C. A. P. Ruck and W. H. Matheson, Selected Odes, 1968; C. M. Bowra (Penguin ed.), 1969; G. S. Conway, 1972; R. A. Swanson, 1974; R. Lattimore, 2nd ed., 1976.
ABOUT—F. Dornseiff, Pindars Stil, 1921; H. Gundert, Pindar und sein Dichterberuf, 1935; G. Norwood, Pindar, 1945; J. H. Finley, Pindar and Aeschylus, 1955; E. L. Bundy, Studia Pindarica, v 1, v 2, 1962; R. W. B. Burton, Pindar's Pythian Odes, 1962; C. M. Bowra, Pindar, 1964; W. Schadewaldt, Der Aufbau des pindarischen Epinikion, 2nd ed., 1966; M. A. Grant, Folktale Motifs in the Odes of Pindar, 1967; J. Davison, From Archilochus to Pindar, 1968; D. C. Young, Three Odes of Pindar (Mnemosyne, Supplement, v 9), 1968, *and* Pindar Isthmian 7: Myth and Exempla, 1970; W. M. Calder III and J. Stern, eds., Pindaros und Bakchylides, 1971; R. Hamilton, Epinikion: General Form in the Odes of Pindar, 1974; L. F. Guillen, Pindaro: Estructura y resortes del quehacer poetico, 1975; M. R. Lefkowitz, The Victory Ode: An Introduction, 1976.

PLATO

PLATO, Greek philosopher, was born in about 429 and died in 347 B.C. He came of an Athenian family that was aristocratic on both sides. He began his literary career by writing poetry but after meeting Socrates— probably in about 407—became one of his disciples and turned to the study of philosophy. It appears that Plato twice attempted to enter Athenian political life: first under the "Thirty" who briefly achieved an oligarchic revolution (404) and again when democracy was restored shortly afterward. After Socrates' execution in 329, Plato and some of his fellow pupils took temporary refuge with the philosopher Euclides at Megara. During the next twelve years he apparently traveled extensively. In about 387 he paid visits to Italy and Sicily, where he met King Dionysius I of Syracuse and became a close friend of Dionysius' brother-in-law Dion; he also got to know the Pythagorean philosopher and mathematician Archytas of Taras (Tarentum). On his return journey to Greece, he may have been taken prisoner at Aegina and released on payment of a ransom.

He began teaching at Athens, near the tomb of Academus outside the city, from which his Academy took its name; and it was to this occupation that he devoted most of the last four decades of his life. However, plā' tō

he also paid two further visits to Sicily. On the death of Dionysius I in 367, Dion summoned him to try to make his nephew, the young Dionysius II, into the ideal philosopher-king; but Dionysius grew jealous of the friendship between the two older men and compelled Dion to leave Syracuse. Apparently, Plato then returned to Athens. He paid a longer visit to the city in 361—probably to secure better treatment for Dion— but on this occasion Dionysius sequestered Dion's funds and even detained Plato himself as a prisoner until the influence of Archytas the philosopher and mathematician secured his release. (Four years later, Dion expelled Dionysius by force but was subsequently murdered.)

Plato's death was variously reported to have taken place at a wedding party or while he was engaged in writing. He was buried in the Academy.

The earliest of his works present Socrates as the principal figure and are intended to demolish the views of those who had accused him of corrupting Athenian youth and impiously promoting the worship of new gods. The *Apology* purports to be the speech made by Socrates at his trial for impiety, at which Plato was apparently present. In the *Crito,* Socrates' friend of that name comes to see him in prison, where he is awaiting his death, but Socrates rejects the idea that he should escape. In the *Charmides* (named after Plato's right-wing uncle), the

Laches (after a general), and the *Lysis* (a handsome young man) Socrates is presented as discussing temperance, courage, and friendship respectively. In the *Hippias Major,* of doubtful authenticity, the sophist (popular philosopher and lecturer) Hippias of Elis, who was Socrates' older contemporary, is presented as knowing many things but failing to understand the nature of the good. The *Hippias Minor* makes the paradoxical point that a person who intentionally does evil is less to blame than someone who does it unintentionally.

In the second group of Plato's writings Socrates is still the central figure, but the doctrines put forward in these dialogues must be regarded as originating not so much from Socrates as from Plato himself. The *Gorgias,* named after the rhetorician and sophist Gorgias of Leontini (c. 483–376 B.C.), argues that rhetoric is an art of flattery, directed at pleasure, in contrast with the higher, Socratic form of statesmanship. The *Protagoras,* introducing the fifth century sophist Protagoras of Abdera and two of his colleagues, Hippias and Prodicus of Ceos, is a vigorous interpretation of the Socratic teaching on virtue. The group debates whether political science can be taught and reaches the conclusion that all the excellences reduce themselves to one, which is knowledge. The *Euthydemus* is a broad satire on the role of the sophists. The *Cratylus* (named after a philosopher of the school of Heraclitus) is about the origin of language and leads up to the Platonic theory of Forms (the designation *Ideas,* taken from the original Greek word, is misleading) by his insistence on the existence of certain realities that lie behind words and alone are the true objects of knowledge. The *Phaedo* recounts how Socrates met his death and presents his last dialogue with his friends, in which arguments for and against the immortality of the soul are considered.

The declared subject of the *Republic,* which is from Plato's middle period, is Justice, but the theme is enlarged so as to comprehend the whole of society and humankind's place in it, as well as the destiny of the human soul in the afterlife. In Book 1 the sophist Thrasymachus of Chalcedon, who envisages justice as the ad-vantage of the stronger, is refuted by Socrates. In Books 2-4, Socrates himself attempts to define justice, by constructing a model state under a highly trained ruling class known as the Guardians, who possess no private property of their own. Justice is found to consist in the performance by each class of citizens of its own distinct and proper functions, just as each of the three parts of every individual's soul, likewise, has its own particular functions to perform.

Book 5 indicates that women and children are to be held in common and that sexual relations ought to be carefully regulated to improve the stock. Book 6 enumerates the qualities needed in the philosopher-king; society requires an intellectual discipline leading to pursuit of the Form (Idea) of the Good, which is the aim and unifying principle of all knowledge. Book 7 begins with an allegory of a cave, in which human beings live chained in their seats so that they can only see mere shadows of reality projected on a wall; people need education to enable them to escape from the prison of the senses.

Book 8 describes the cycle of political evolution and indicates the deterioration of character that accompanies each successive downward step from one type of constitution to another. Book 9 explains how persons of the tyrannical type are essentially unhappy, whereas the just man achieves happiness. Book 10 attacks poetry as an art of illusion, the goal of which is pleasure and not truth; it also sets out the scheme of divine retribution in the Vision of Er, a mythical hero, who was slain in battle but returned to life after twelve days and recounted what he had seen in the other world.

The *Meno* (named after a Thessalian general) reverts to the question of whether virtue can be taught and suggests that knowledge is latent in the immortal soul and in fact comprises reminiscence, which it is the purpose of teaching to elicit. The *Menexenus,* not always attributed to Plato, consists largely of a funeral oration supposedly written by Pericles' mistress Aspasia and apparently satirical in purpose. In the *Phaedrus,* Socrates discusses rhetoric with his young friend of that name, distinguishing between true and false kinds and illustrating his argument by speeches on the subject of love composed in either style. In the *Symposium,* which takes its title from a party supposedly held at the house of the poet Agathon, each of the guests offers a discourse on the theme of love. Socrates claims he has learned from Diotima, a priestess of Mantinea in Arcadia, that love may possess a nobler, intellectual aspect; and then the young Alcibiades, slightly drunk, offers a racy testimonial to Socrates himself, giving an account of his extraordinary character.

The *Theaetetus* (named after an Athenian mathematician), is Plato's principal work on the theory of knowledge; it is also the last of the dialogues to give prominence to Socrates, who compares himself to a midwife bringing to birth the thoughts of others. The difficult *Parmenides* is named after the great pre-Socratic philosopher Parmenides of Elea, who attacks certain ways of presenting the theory of Forms (Ideas) and is allowed to do this so convincingly that Plato himself, it appears, has changed some of his own views.

In Plato's third group of writings Socrates plays a lesser part or none at all, and, although these works formally retain the dialogue structure, they are often not far from continuous monologues. The *Sophist* is a sequel to the *Theaetetus,* once again satirizing sophists as deceivers; it goes on to inquire, in terms important to the history of logic, whether deception involves the existence of Non-Being. The *Politicus (Statesman)* examines the character of the true king or leader, concluding that, in the absence of the ideal monarch, the best course is for the citizens to frame the laws of their city with great care—and then to ensure that they are inviolable.

The *Timaeus* (he was a Pythagorean philosopher) continues a theme in the *Republic,* the beginnings and structure of the universe, and also discusses the origin of sensations and diseases, the three kinds of human soul, and what happens to human beings after death. One of the participants in the *Timaeus* was an uncle of Plato's named Critias, leader of the oligarchic Thirty, for whom a sequel is named. This *Critias* includes the legend of the Athenian victory

over the people of the lost island of Atlantis, in a battle that was believed to have been fought nine thousand years previously. The *Philebus,* returning to practical morality (with Socrates making his last appearance in one of these dialogues) is Plato's final discussion of the relations of knowledge (identified with happiness) to the good: knowledge and the good have to be mixed, but knowledge comes first.

The Laws is the latest and longest of Plato's works, in which the *Republic* is amended and restated in more practical and practicable terms, to the accompaniment of a good deal of unmitigatedly authoritarian detail. For example, heretical beliefs are to be made criminal, although the rulers themselves are not envisaged as believing their own tenets but are required to enforce them as political discipline. The authenticity of the *Epinomis* (or *Supplement to the Laws*) has been questioned. So, too, has that of many or all of the thirteen *Epistles,* though at least the seventh, defending Plato's conduct at Syracuse, seems to be genuine.

Socrates had taught, or, rather, had tried to show—by the dialogue method to which he devoted his life—that virtue is knowledge: that is to say, there is such a thing as moral goodness, it is the same for everyone without exception, and only by really knowing it could men and women become good. He had not attempted, however, to define in detail what sort of thing this goodness was or what sort of soul becomes good by understanding it.

Plato's first task, then, was to try to arrive at these answers. This was a task in which he was helped by his contacts with the Pythagoreans, the followers of the semi-legendary Pythagoras of Samos (sixth century B.C.), who apparently wrote nothing but founded a religious society in southern Italy (of which Philolaus and Archytas, of the fifth and fourth centuries respectively, were distinguished later adherents). The conviction of the Pythagoreans that there is a divine, unchanging reality transcending our senses impressed Plato greatly. So, too, did their argument that it is possible to express this reality in terms of mathematics (number, geometrical pattern, and harmony); this in consequence became the key science of

Plato's philosophy. He also adopted the Pythagorean belief that the soul is a fallen deity that is imprisoned in the body but capable, eventually, of realizing its divine character and returning to its proper place after death.

By combining these earlier elements with Socrates' moral doctrine, Plato was able to formulate the various aspects of his doctrine of Forms (Ideas). These forms constitute a realm of eternal realities, entirely distinct from the changing world perceived by our senses and knowable only by the mind and pure reason; yet they exist quite independently of the minds that know them. The supreme Form is that of the Good, on which are ultimately founded all the others. There are Forms, according to Plato, that correspond to every universal or general concept that we are capable of imagining. Plato, in his early and middle dialogues, vividly portrays the world of Forms as a domain of radiant perfection. Although his doctrines evolved throughout his career, he never wavered in his conviction that the Forms provide the eternal and objective norms by which men and women must govern their lives—and he continued to regard the world of these Forms as comprising the ground of all authentic knowledge about everything that there is. Thinking about them, he insisted, is the only kind of thinking that can grasp the truth, for they constitute the whole of reality.

Yet they do have one partner in reality, and that is Soul. Soul is the knower and the Forms are the known. Soul itself is a Form, yet also something more than a Form, being the single transcendent reality of absolute perfection comprising the ultimate cause and explanation of the universe and synonymous with the God who is its director. To Plato, the soul of an individual human being is far more real than the body, being not only the personality, as interpreted by Socrates, but also the divine spirit of the Pythagoreans, a being immortal in its own right that has always existed (before entering into any body) and will continue to exist after it has gained release from its long series of incarnations in bodies. The soul cannot acquire any knowledge of the Forms through its bodily senses but has known them in its divine existence before coming

into a body. When the soul is contained in a body, Plato's doctrine of Recollection (Anamnesis) tells us that it is "reminded" of the Forms.

Within the human soul, he discerned three parts, the proper functioning of which, in unison, constitutes virtue. These parts are: the natural appetites; the resolution that we can summon up, if we so choose, to resist the appetites; and the reason that determines when we shall resist. Reason is the ruler of this tripartite entity, just as Eros or Desire is the driving force behind it.

The process of learning about the complex world of Forms and about the relationship of one Form to another, is what Plato calls dialectic. The *Republic* sets out a hierarchy of Forms through which the mind rises to the ultimate and universal Form, the Good, which is seen not as a remote abstraction but as an immensely rich and potent reality. In subsequent writings Plato sought repeatedly to answer the criticism that he seemed to have placed an unbridgeable gulf between the world of Forms and the world we are aware of by sense perception (in which, indeed, he came to show increasing interest). What bridged this gulf for him was the intermediary of the Soul, which he came to see not only as the self-moving principle but as the intelligent directing power of the material universe.

The divine Craftsman of the *Timaeus,* who creates this universe, symbolizes Soul performing its cosmic function, not omnipotent but devoting to its task as much perfection as is permitted by the rather refractory material in which it has to reside—a material displaying an unending flux of shifting qualities in perpetual, disorderly, irrational motion. Yet, despite these imperfections that the rational Soul must overcome in its search for the transcendent World of Forms, the existing universe, being the only extant copy of a unique Form, remains a necessity: since it is the best and most beautiful universe that is possible.

Plato inherited from his Pythagorean predecessors the conviction that the earthly body is only a prison and that a life of contemplation is the noblest activity for the human spirit. Yet he never sought to impose the asceticism of the early Pythagoreans on

337

his pupils, and he displayed (and tried to put into practice in Sicily) what might seem to some a contradictory insistence on the duty of the philosopher to direct the community, to seek to persuade it to live by the dictates of Reason. However, Reason can never rule by sheer brute force but must rely on persuasion, nor can it, on its own account and unaided, govern a human personality but has to work in association with the higher emotions. It is in view of this necessity that Plato sees the training of the emotions as one of the most important functions of education, a process in which art, music, and poetry are clearly of preeminent importance. It is for this reason that, among various other controls that seem to us incomprehensible and alarming, he insists on the cultural censorship that has so particularly shocked so many readers of Plato.

The rule of Reason—the contemplation of the moral Forms—is what constitutes Virtue, and, since Virtue is essentially indivisible, Plato makes no very firm distinction between the particular virtues (including the cardinal four—Prudence or practical wisdom, Justice, Courage, and Temperance). Nor does he distinguish between ethics and politics; his teaching about the latter is simply an extension and elaboration of his views about the former. His political philosophy is that of a Greek city-state aristocrat, with a contempt for manual labor and a distaste for what he regarded as the extreme democracy into which Athens had plunged.

However, it is for the most part because of other characteristics that Plato has exercised such enormous influence on philosophic and religious thought: that is to say, because of his idealism and his belief in an invisible, eternal world behind the shifting unrealities of the world and the senses and because of his conception of God and his insistence on the connection between religion and morality. With him begins the great central tradition of metaphysics, which has continued without a break ever since his day. Nearly seven centuries after him, this long history of Platonism produced the extraordinary figure of the Roman philosopher Plotinus (c. A.D. 205–70). Moreover, though Plotinus' Neoplatonic followers were deeply opposed to Christian-

ity, they helped unwittingly to shape it; so that, through these intermediaries as well as directly, the influence of Plato exerted great force on Christian thinkers such as St. Augustine. Although Plato himself was the least systematic of philosophers, he is an infinitely fertile source and originator who, throughout the ages, has compelled those who want to discover what is worth looking for and how it can be found to return to him again and again.

He also has a strong claim to be regarded as the greatest writer of Greek prose. Whether in the pure dialogue form of his earlier works or in the continuous expositions that almost monopolize the later treatises, his style possesses almost endless variety, ranging from graceful and humorous narrative to passionate solemnity and religious fervor. His language is full, lavish, powerful, and flexible, packed with vivid metaphors and rising to poetic lyricism, notably in the elaborate mythical and allegorical narratives to which he has recourse in order to illuminate otherwise scarcely expressible profundities of thought and intuition.

WORKS (attribution to Plato, dubious)—As mentioned in the text: the Hippias Major, Menexenus, Epinomis, the Clitopho, and many of the Letters. *Spurious Works* —Alcibiades I and 2, Amatores, Axiochus, Definitions, Demodocus, Eryxias, Hipparchus, Minos, On Justice, On Virtue, Sisyphus, Theages.

EDITIONS—J. B. Skemp, Plato (Greece & Rome: New Surveys in the Classics, no 10), 1976 (supplements lists in Oxford Classical Dictionary, 2nd ed., 1970, p 842 *and* in Encyclopaedia Britannica, 1971 ed., v 18, p 36). Translations (general)—H. N. Fowler, W. R. M. Lamb, P. Shorey, R. G. Bury (Loeb ed.), 1914–55; F. M. Cornford, J. McDowell, D. Gallop, J. C. B. Gosling, C. C. W. Taylor (Clarendon ed.), 1941, 1973, 1975, 1975, 1977 respectively; W. Hamilton, H. Tredennick, H. D. P. Lee, W. K. C. Guthrie, T. J. Saunders (Penguin ed.), 1951 and 1960 and 1973, 1954, 1955 and 1971, 1956, and 1970 respectively; B. Jowett, 4th ed., revised by D. J. Allan and H. E. Dale, 1953; A. E. Taylor, J. Warrington, M. Joyce with M. Oakley and J. Warrington (Everyman ed.), 1960, 1961 and 1963, 1964, respectively; E. Hamilton and H. Cairns, eds. (Bollinger ser. 71), 1961, 1975. For other recent translations of individual dialogues *see* A. M. W. Green, Classics in Translation: A Selective Bibliography (1930–1976), 1976.

ABOUT—A. E. Taylor, Plato: The Man and His Work, 2nd ed., 1927; J. Burnet, Platonism, 1928; R. S. H. Bluck, Plato's Life and Thought, 1949; G. C. Field, The Philosophy of Plato, 1949, reprint 1969; G. M. A. Grube, Plato's Thought, revised ed., 1958; H. J. Krämer, Arete bei Platon und Aristoteles, 1959, *and* Die Ursprung der Geistesmetaphysik, 1964; R. S. Brumbaugh, Plato for the Modern Age, 1962; N. Gulley, Plato's Theory of Knowledge, 1962; W. G. Runciman, Plato's Later Epistemology, 1962; I. M. Crombie, An Examination of Plato's Doctrines, 1962–63 (abridged as Plato, the Midwife's Apprentice, 1964); K. Gaiser, Platons' Ungeschriebene Lehre, 1963; R. W. Hall, Plato and the Individual, 1963; E. A. Havelock, Preface to Plato, 1963; H. D. Rankin, Plato and the Individual, 1963; T. L. Thorsen, ed., Plato: Totalitarian or Democrat?, 1963; R. E. Allen, ed., Studies in Plato's Metaphysics, 1965; R. Bambrough, ed., New Essays on Plato and Aristotle, 1965, *and* Plato, Popper and Politics, 1967; J. E. Raven, Plato's Thought in the Making, 1965; E. W. Schipper, Forms in Plato's Later Dialogues, 1965; G. Ryle, Plato's Progress, 1966; M. J. O'Brien, The Socratic Paradoxes and the Greek Mind, 1967; J. B. Skemp, The Theory of Motion in Plato's Later Dialogues, 1967; H. Thesleff, Studies in the Style of Plato, 1967; P. Shorey, The Unity of Plato's Thought, 1968; P. Friedländer, Plato: The Dialogues, 1969; K. M. Sayre, Plato's Analytic Method, 1969; T. M. Robinson, Plato's Psychology, 1970; E. N. Tigerstedt, Plato's Idea of Poetical Inspiration, 1970, *and* Interpreting Plato, 1977; G. Vlastos, Plato, 1971, *and* The Philosophy of Socrates, 1971, *and* Platonic Studies, 1973, *and* Plato's Universe, 1975; P. M. Huby, Plato and Modern Morality, 1972; J. C. B. Gosling, Plato, 1973; J. N. Findlay, Plato: The Written and Unwritten Doctrines, 1974; A. D. Winspear, The Genesis of Plato's Thought, 3rd ed., 1974; R. Barrow, Plato: Utilitarianism and Education, 1975; A. W. Gouldner, Enter Plato, 1975; A. Graeser, Platons Ideenlehre, 1975; W. K. C. Guthrie, History of Greek Philosophy, v 4, 1975 and v 5, 1978; D. Roloff, Platonische Ironie, 1975; F. Sarri, Socrate e la genesi storica dell'idea occidentale di anima, 1975; R. Barrow, Plato and Education, 1976; F. Chiereghin, Implicazioni etiche della storiografia filosofica di Platone, 1976; R. Hackforth, The Authorship of the Platonic Epistles, 1976; W. Scheffel, Aspekte der platonischen Kosmologie, 1976; J. B. Skemp, Plato (Greece & Rome: New Surveys in the Classics, no 10), 1976; W. H. Werkmeister, ed., Facets of Plato's Philosophy, 1976; N. P. White, Plato in Knowledge and Reality, 1976; H. Gundert, Studia Platonika, 1977; T. H. Irwin, Plato's Moral Theory: The Early and Middle Dialogues, 1977; M. Mader, Das Problem des Lachens und der Komödie bei Platon, 1977; H. F. North, ed., Interpretations of Plato (Swarthmore Symposium), 1977; W. S. Sahakian and M. L. Sahakian, Plato, 1977; E. N. Tigerstedt, Interpreting Plato, 1977. For studies of individual dialogues *see* T. Gwinop and F. Dickinson, Greek and Roman Authors; A Checklist of Criticism, 1973. On epigrams misattributed to Plato *see* D. L. Page, Epigrammata Graeca, 1975. The periodical Phronesis, published since 1955, is to a large extent concerned with Platonic studies.

PLATO (Comicus),

PLATO (Comicus), Greek comic poet, worked in the later part of the fifth and ear-

plā' tō ko' mi kus

lier years of the fourth century B.C.; his first play was probably produced in 427, and his last in 387. He was an Athenian and belonged to the Old Comedy of which Aristophanes, approximately his contemporary, was the protagonist.

Thirty titles of plays attributed to Plato Comicus have survived (though these attributions are not always correct), and two hundred seventy fragments. Some of the titles, notably *The Troubles of Zeus* and *The Long Night* (dealing with the begetting of Heracles), were evidently intended to burlesque mythological themes. The *Phaon* was concerned with a fabulous phallic demon that made women go mad—a figure related here, somewhat unexpectedly, to the circumstances of the death of Sappho. The *Sophists* made fun of artistic innovations of the time and perhaps mocked novel philosophical tendencies as well. Most of Plato's comedies seem to have been strongly political. The *Hellas* (or *Island*) dealt with general questions relating to Greek politics, but other plays were devoted to personal attacks on contemporary public figures. One of these was Hyperbolus, assailed in *The Sufferer (Perialges*, ?420); another, Diitrephes, was denounced in *The Festivals* (*Heortai*, ?414). In other cases, for the first time, comedies are actually named after the statesmen they were attacking: notably *Pisander* (of uncertain date) and *Cleophon* (405).

WORKS—Titles other than those given above include Adonis, Daedalus, The Envoys, Laius, The Property Dresses.
EDITIONS (of fragments)—T. Koch, Comicorum Atticorum Fragmenta, 1880–88.

PLAUTUS, TITUS MACCIUS (?),

PLAUTUS, TITUS MACCIUS (?), Latin poet and dramatist, was born perhaps in about 254 or 250 B.C. and died in about 184, according to Cicero (though Jerome, less probably, attributes his death to 200). Jerome and Sextus Pompeius Festus, a scholar of the second century A.D., say that he was born at Sarsina (Mercato Saraceno) in Umbria; doubts whether this is true, on the grounds of the backwardness of the region, are probably unjustified. It was record-

plô' tus

ed by Aulus Gellius (c. A.D. 130–c. 180) that Plautus supported himself as a stage carpenter and as a laborer in a flour mill, writing his plays during his time off from his duties, but these assertions may be fictitious.

Some one hundred thirty comedies were attributed to him in antiquity; there were also alternative lists of forty and one hundred. However, the scholarly Varro, in the first century B.C., drew up a list of twenty-one plays that were generally ascribed to Plautus' authorship, and these have all survived, with the exception of one which is fragmentary.

In the *Amphitryo* Jupiter, desiring to seduce a mortal woman, Alcmena, has assumed the appearance of her husband Amphitryo of Argos, who is away fighting a war. Mercury, too, has taken on human form, in the shape of a slave Sosia (who is also absent). Alcmena is tricked by the two impostors. Amphitryo, on his return, quarrels violently with his wife, and an arbitrator cannot tell which of the two Amphitryos is the genuine one. Finally the voice of Jupiter from the heavens declares that he is the guilty lover and that one of the twin boys to whom Alcmena subsequently gave birth, Hercules, is his child, whereas the other, Iphicles, is the son of Amphitryo.

The *Asinaria (Comedy of Asses)* presents the henpecked Demaenetus, who wants to give financial help to his son Argyrippus for a love affair with a prostitute Philaenium. Demaenetus arranges that a sum of money, brought to his wife's steward Saurea in payment for donkeys, should be transferred to a slave of his own, Leonida. The money is duly passed on to Philaenium, who consequently allows Demaenetus himself to go to bed with her. A rival for Philaenium's affections gives Demaenetus away to his wife, who arrives in a fury and drags him out of the brothel.

In *Aulularia (Pot of Gold)* miserly old Euclio's household god shows him a hidden pot full of gold, which will enable his daughter Phaedria to have a suitable dowry to marry Lyconides, who has seduced her; but instead of giving her the gold, Euclio hides it away. Now, Lyconides' uncle, the rich Megadorus, wants to marry Phaedria himself, and Euclio agrees provided that no

dowry is required. However, before he can smuggle the pot out, the hiding place is detected by Lyconides' servant Strobilus, who steals the treasure. Finally, however, Lyconides, by whom Phaedra is pregnant, announces that he is going to marry her, disclosing that Megadorus is willing to step aside in his favor.

The *Bacchides* are two sisters named Bacchis who are prostitutes. One of them, Bacchis of Samos, is loved by Mnesilochus. In order to free her from the soldier Cleomachus, who has brought her to Athens, the other sister (Bacchis the Athenian) mobilizes Mnesilochus' friend Pistoclerus, who loves Bacchis of Samos but is accused, falsely, of going to bed with the Athenian sister instead. Mnesilochus' resourceful slave Chrysalus clears up the confusion and arranges for a sum of money belonging to his master's father Nicobulus to be diverted to Mnesilochus. Nicobulus and the father of Pistoclerus try to invade the brothel to put a stop to their sons' matrimonial plans but are met by the two sisters who entice them inside, whereupon they give in to the young men's wishes.

In the *Captivi (Prisoners of War)* Philopolemus, one of the sons of the Aetolian Hegio, had been taken prisoner at Elis; the other, Tyndarus, was stolen and sold by a runaway slave when only four years old. In his anxiety to ransom Philopolemus, Hegio buys up Elean captives to offer in exchange; one is a certain Philocrates and the other, his slave, happens to be Tyndarus. But Tyndarus pretends to reverse roles with Philocrates, who is consequently released (as being a mere slave) and goes away. However, he eventually returns, bringing with him not only Philopolemus but the slave who had originally stolen Tyndarus—whose identity is thus dramatically disclosed.

Casina is a sixteen-year-old slave girl desired by both her master Lysidamus and his son Euthynicus; the two men both plan to marry her off to their own slaves, Olympio and Chalinus respectively. Lots are drawn and Olympio wins. Both he and Lysidamus try to go to bed with Casina but are beaten up, because the supposed girl is really Chalinus in disguise. Lysidamus' wife Cleostrata, who has arranged the trick, forgives him, and Casina proves to be a freeborn Athenian and is thus able to marry Euthynicus.

In the *Cistellaria (Casket-Comedy)*, Selenium, a girl of Sicyon, and Alcesimarchus of Lemnos are in love, but, because she is only the humble daughter of the procuress Syra, Alcesimarchus' father has chosen him another bride, and the young man is in despair. However, Syra drunkenly reveals that Selenium was really a foundling whom she had given to her prostitute friend Melaenis to bring up as her own, and it emerges that her father was the freeborn Demipho of Lemnos. And so she is able to marry Alcesimarchus after all.

Curculio (The Weevil, the name of a parasite in the play) tells how Curculio goes to Caria to raise some money for his master Phaedromus, who wants to buy his beloved, Planesium, from her slavemaster, the procurer Cappadox. Curculio fails to get the money but manages to steal the signet ring of a soldier, Therapontigonus, who claims to have bought Planesium for himself. Curculio gains possession of her by means of the ring, which also proves that she and the soldier are sister and brother; so Phaedromus is able to marry her, and Cappadox has to give her purchase price back as the penalty for having sold a freeborn woman.

The *Epidicus* concerns the slave of that name belonging to Periphanes. Periphanes' son Stratippocles, leaving for the wars, has asked Epidicus to trick his father into buying the music girl Acropolistis, whom the young man loves. Epidicus manages this by telling Periphanes that Acropolistis is his own long-lost daughter Telestis. Meanwhile, however, Stratippocles has bought a second girl, a captive from the wars, once again with the help of Epidicus, who has raised the money from Periphanes by a further lie. The second captive turns out, in fact, to be his own sister Telestis, whom he therefore cannot marry. This revelation causes joy to Periphanes, and Epidicus, in trouble because his fabrications have come to light, gains his pardon.

The *Menaechmi (The Two Menaechmuses)* deals with the twin sons of a Syracusan merchant, one of whom, Menaechmus, was abducted and taken to Epidamnus. After his father's death, the grandfather gives the name of Menaechmus to the second boy as well. This youth, when he grows up, goes with his slave Messenio to Epidamnus, where he is mistaken for his brother by the latter's mistress, and wife, and father-in-law, while servants and parasites add to the comedy of errors. Finally, Messenio guesses how the confusion has occurred. The puzzle is cleared up, and the two brothers return to Syracuse together.

The *Mercator (Merchant)* tells about the young Athenian Charinus, sent by his father Demipho on a business trip to Rhodes in order to get him away from prostitutes, procurers, and moneylenders. While there, Charinus falls in love with a slave girl, Pasicompsa, and brings her back home to Athens. Demipho, however, who is told only that the girl has been brought as a maid for his wife, becomes fond of her himself and gets his friend Lysimachus to buy her and install her in his own house; whereupon Charinus, on discovering that she has been sold, decides in despair to leave the country. When, however, Demipho learns that his son is in love with Pasicompsa, he graciously gives her up to him.

The *Miles Gloriosus (Braggart Warrior),* concerns Pyrgopolynices of Ephesus, who has carried off the girl Philocomasium from Athens and who also seizes Palaestrio, her lover Pleusicles' slave, who has given chase. Pleusicles manages to meet his beloved by clambering through a secret passage, and Palaestrio concocts elaborate schemes to get them all free of their kidnapper and bring about his ruin. Finally, Pyrgopolynices is beaten up by slaves; and, when he discovers how thoroughly he has been tricked, he is sorry for the way he has behaved.

The *Mostellaria (Ghost)* sets forth the tricks employed by a slave, Tranio, in order to keep his master Theopropides, unexpectedly returned from Egypt, from entering his own house, where a rowdy mixed dinner-party is being given by his son Philolaches; the young man has also bought the slave girl Philematium, whom he loves, by means of a moneylender's loan. Among other things, Tranio tells Theopropides that the house is haunted by the ghost of a murdered man and has been vacated. The slave's deceptions are finally exposed, but Theopropides pardons Tranio and is reconciled with Philolaches.

In the *Persa,* the slave Toxilus loves a prostitute Lemniselenis, but her brothelkeeper Dordalus refuses to release her without payment. Toxilus plans to raise the funds by "selling" Dordalus another young woman, masquerading as a captive Persian —and by arranging that his own confidant, the parasite Saturio, should subsequently claim her as a girl of free birth. The scheme, elaborately worked out, is successful, and Dordalus is jeered at for losing both girl and money.

The *Poenulus (Little Carthaginian)* relates the story of Agorastocles, who was kidnapped at the age of seven and taken to Calydon, where he became a rich man's heir and fell in love with a girl named Adelphasium. She is really his cousin, a fact they did not know at the time, since she was working as a prostitute for the procurer Lycus. The young man's slave Milphio endeavors to outwit the procurer with the support of the girl's father. Lycus, threatened with prosecution for kidnapping, gives in, and Agorastocles and Adelphasium are able to marry.

Pseudolus is about a slave who employs his wiles to free Phoenicium, the girl friend of his young master Calidorus. The deed is successfully managed, to the discomfiture, first, of Ballio, the procurer who owns her; then of a Macedonian soldier to whom Ballio sells her; and, finally, of Calidorus' father Simo, who accuses his son of fraud, but is later won over and rewards Pseudolus for the successful swindle he has practiced on Ballio.

In the *Rudens (Rope),* the fisherman Gripus recovers from the sea a wicker chest containing objects that confirm the identity of the slave Palaestra, whose owner Labrax had attempted to carry her off to Sicily when the ship in which they were traveling was wrecked. Gripus hauls the chest up from the sea in his net with the help of a rope, the other end of which is seized by Trachalio, the slave of Plesidippus, who is Palaestra's lover. Trachalio demands that the chest be returned to Palaestra. An investigation of its contents enables Palaestra to be identified as the long-lost daughter of Gripus' master

Daemones, who agrees willingly to her marriage to Plesidippus.

In the slender plot of the *Stichus* (named after a slave who is one of the characters), Panegyris and her sister are married to two brothers who have been away for three years. The women are being pressed by their father Antipho to remarry, though they do not want to do so. The husbands return from abroad loaded with wealth, and farcical scenes of merrymaking follow, in which Stichus, who has come back with them, celebrates drunkenly, in the company of both his girl friend and a rival for her affections.

In *Trinummus (Three-Dollar Day)* Charmides, on going abroad, has left his friend Callicles in charge of his affairs, with particular instructions to guard a treasure that is hidden in the house and intended as a dowry for his daughter. In his absence, his son Lesbonicus squanders all his father's fortune and even sells his house—which Callicles himself buys. Lysiteles, a rich friend of Lesbonicus, wishing to do him a kindness, proposes to marry his sister without taking a dowry. But Callicles, though approving of the match, thinks she ought to have a dowry from the still-hidden treasure —though he must not disclose its existence. In consequence, by the payment of a certain sum (the *trinummus*) he hires an unscrupulous character who is to pretend to come to Lesbonicus, bringing a letter from his father and a thousand gold pieces to be used as the girl's dowry; whereas, this money is in fact going to be taken from the treasure. But Charmides himself unexpectedly arrives and exposes the trick. He upbraids Callicles but, on learning the facts, thanks him for his fidelity instead, gives his daughter to Lysiteles with a dowry, and forgives the now penitent Lesbonicus.

In the *Truculentus,* the grasping prostitute Phronesium is loved by three men: a young Athenian, Diniarchus, whom she has virtually ruined; a country boy, Strabax, whose infatuation disgusts his ill-tempered slave Truculentus; and a Babylonian soldier Stratophanes, from whom she decides to extort money by pretending that a borrowed baby is his. The three men are demoralized by her unscrupulousness; in the end Strabax and Stratophanes are left to outbid one another for her favors until she agrees to a solution: that she will accept both of them as lovers.

Only about a hundred lines of the *Vidularia (Tale of a Traveling Chest)* have survived, but the plot seems to have been somewhat similar to that of the *Rudens.* The young Nicodemus, in a shipwreck, has lost the chest containing his tokens of identity and is reduced to working as a farm laborer for the kindly landowner Dinia. When the chest is recovered, the contents not only establish Nicodemus' identity but also prove that Dinia is his long-lost father.

Plautus borrowed the plots of his plays from the Athenian New Comedy, the leading exponent of which had been Menander. In the spirit of the Hellenistic Age that it foreshadowed, the New Comedy dealt with the personal preoccupations of ordinary men and women: their private lives, and their love affairs and tender sentiments— Plautus, in adapting these plays, employs a style that is far more rapid and racy, and far less introspective. In the process, he manages to convert the still relatively primitive Latin language into an instrument of an altogether new vividness and pliancy. He also played a decisive part in the adaptation of Latin literature to Greek metrical procedures, performing the extraordinarily difficult task of importing from the Greek quantitative scansions—i.e. meters depending not on the beat but on the quantity (long or short) of syllables. These were habitual in Greek but did not come naturally to Latin. Although Plautus used colloquial language, this metrical decision eventually divorced poetical Latin from the spoken tongue. However, it also infused the crudities of the current Latinity with much needed Greek discipline, grace, and rhythm.

Unlike Menander's sophisticated Athenian audiences, Plautus' Roman spectators wanted action, force, puns, and quick and coarse repartee, all of which his versatile and resourceful talents were able to give them. His New Comedy plots are highly complex and elaborate, consisting largely of numerous confusions, misunderstandings, surprising turns of fortune, and, above all, a great deal of amusing and cynical trickery. Clever slaves play a particularly prominent part, and the ingenious tricks are usually theirs. This was a holiday atmosphere of fantastical reversal, a turning upside down of social norms with the underdog coming out on top, although Plautus (despite topical Roman allusions) is careful to plant his action in the Greek milieu of New Comedy rather than in Roman Italy, so that his mocking of the conventions should not come into conflict with government censorship, which was vigilant.

Censorship was only one of the hazards that made Plautus' success all the more remarkable. Another was the absence of any permanent theatre at Rome at the time. Moreover, as part of the program of the Games, theatrical performances were sandwiched between chariot races and other nonliterary attractions, such as boxing matches and ropedancing. The poet Horace adds that one advantage of the iambic (short-long) metrical structure favored by Plautus for his vigorous dialogues and monologues was that it could be heard above the clamor of the audience.

Yet Plautus achieved immense popularity as a playwright, and repeatedly brought his spectators to their feet in enthusiastic applause. His comedies were revived time after time during the subsequent centuries of antiquity. The earliest, though incomplete, manuscript of his surviving plays is a text of the fourth century A.D. (overwritten by a Latin version of the Book of Kings). More than a millenium later, he became the inspiration for modern comic drama in almost all its aspects—farce, burlesque, romantic and domestic comedy, and comedies of manners and ideas. In English drama, for example, his powerful influence can be traced in the sixteenth century theatre of Nicholas Udall and John Lyly, and then in Shakespeare's *Comedy of Errors,* as well as in many of the plays of Ben Jonson (whose braggart soldier Bobadil is Plautine) and in the *Amphitryon* of Dryden.

WORKS—Lost comedies figuring in the larger lists of Plautus' plays that circulated in ancient times included a number that may possibly have been authentic. Among these were the Bacaria, Blind Man, Bondsman, Flatterer, Lipargus, Nervolaria, Rustic, Saturio, Strait, Woman Banker, Woman of Boeotia.
EDITIONS—J. L. Ussing, 1875–92, reprint 1972. For list

of commentaries on individual plays *see* W. G. Arnott, Menander, Plautus, Terence (Greece & Rome: New Surveys in the Classics, no 9), 1975; *add* G. Maurach, Poenulus, 1975; W. T. MacCary and M. M. Willcock, Casina, 1976. *Translations*—P. Nixon (Loeb ed.), 1916 –38; G. E. Duckworth, 1942; E. F. Watling (Penguin ed.), 1964, 1968; C. W. Parry (three plays), 1954; E. Segal, 1963, 1978; P. Roche (three plays), 1968; B. R. Reece, Epidicus, 1972; J. R. Poynton (five plays), 1973; C. E. Passage and J. H. Mantiband, Amphitryo, 1974. ABOUT—G. E. Duckworth, The Nature of Roman Comedy, 1952; E. Fraenkel, Elementi plautini in Plauto, 1960 (enlarged ed. of Plautinisches im Plautus, 1922); G. Norwood, Plautus and Terence, 1963; F. della Corte, Da Sarsina a Roma, 2nd ed., 1967; P. Flury, Liebe und Liebessprache bei Menander, Plautus und Terenz, 1968; E. W. Handley, Menander and Plautus: A Study in Comparison, 1968; E. Segal, Roman Laughter: The Comedy of Plautus, 1968; W. Beare, The Roman Stage, 3rd ed. revised, 1969; L. Braun, Die Cantica des Plautus, 1970; V. Pöschl, Die neuen Menanderpapyri und die Originalität des Plautus, 1973; J. Wright, Dancing in Chains: The Stylistic Unity of the Comoedia Palliata, 1974; W. G. Arnott, Menander, Plautus, Terence (Greece & Rome: New Surveys in the Classics, no 9), 1975; J. D. Hughes, A Bibliography of Scholarship on Plautus, 1975; G. Petrone, Morale e antimorale nelle commedie di Plauto: Ricerche sullo Stichus, 1977.

PLINY THE ELDER (Gaius Plinius Secundus), Roman official and Latin historian and scientist, was born in A.D. 23 or 24 and died in 79. His birthplace was Novum Comum (Como in northern Italy), where his father was a knight of some means. He went to Rome at an early age and embarked on an official career in 46 or 47, spending most of the ensuing decade in military service in Germany, where one of his posts was the command of a squadron of horse; he was also, for a time, a fellow officer of the future emperor Titus, the son of Vespasian. On retirement from the army, as we learn from his nephew Pliny the Younger, he practiced as a lawyer. After the accession of Vespasian (69), he served as imperial representative *(procurator)* in nearer Spain, in two Gallic provinces, and in Africa (Tunisia). He became a close associate and counselor of Vespasian, who appointed him commander of the Roman fleet at the principal naval base of Misenum in Campania, at the northwestern end of the Bay of Naples. When, shortly after the accession of Titus in 79, the great eruption of Vesuvius occurred, he set

pli′ ni

sail to the southern end of the bay—as his nephew, the younger Pliny, recorded in a letter to the historian Tacitus—in order to assist people who were in danger; the next morning, at Stabiae (Castellamare di Stabiae), asphyxiated by the fumes, he collapsed on the beach and died.

His nephew recorded a list of his voluminous writings in chronological order; all but one of them has disappeared. The lost works are as follows: (1) *On Throwing a Javelin from Horseback (De Iaculatione Equestri),* in one book, written when he was in command of a cavalry squadron; (2) *Life of Pomponius Secundus,* a friend and patron who had been his commanding officer in Germany and was also regarded as an outstanding tragic poet of his day; (3) *History of the Wars in Germany (Bella Germaniae),* in twenty books, a history of all Rome's campaigns, perhaps up to the year A.D. 47. Pliny asserted that the project had been suggested to him by the ghost of Drusus the Elder (died 9 B.C.), the leader of Rome's armies in major German wars and father of Germanicus and of the emperor Claudius (A.D. 41–54); (4) *The Students (Studiosi),* in three books, a technical training manual for young men learning oratory; (5) *Linguistic Queries (Dubius Sermo),* in eight books, written in the later years of Nero's reign (A.D. 54–68) when this seemed a safe subject for perilous times; (6) *A Continuation of the Roman History of Aufidius Bassus.* This treatise, in thirty-one books, was written between A.D. 71 and 77—and perhaps went down as far as 71, but the date at which it began cannot be fixed because we do not know the point at which Aufidius had terminated his work (perhaps some time during the reign of Tiberius (A.D. 14–37). Tacitus refers to Pliny's *History* more than once, in somewhat derogatory terms, though he evidently made very extensive use of it; and though the work must have been credulous, biased, and overburdened with detail, its disappearance is one of our major historical losses.

Pliny's seventh work, the *Natural History,* published in 77 and dedicated to the future emperor Titus, has been preserved in the massive entirety of its thirty-seven books (he may have intended it to be even longer). Book 1 comprises a general introduction, followed by a table of contents of the following books. The subjects of Book 2 are the physics and component elements of the universe. Books 3-6 are devoted to the geography and ethnology of Europe, Asia, and Africa. Book 7 describes the physiology of human beings. Books 8-11 handle zoological themes, dealing with land and sea animals, and birds and insects. Books 12-19 are concerned, for the most part, with botany, including forestry and agriculture (Book 18). Books 20-27 cover medicinal botany, while Books 28-32 summarize the cures to be derived from animal sources. The remaining books treat metallurgy and minerals, including an account of the uses to which they have been put in the arts: Book 33 discusses gold and silver; Book 34, bronze—and its statuary—and iron and lead; Book 35 the materials used for paintings; Book 36, various stones with reference to their uses in construction and sculpture; and Book 37, precious stones and gems.

In the introductory section a list of authors consulted enumerates 146 Roman and 327 foreign authors. However, Pliny estimates that he drew particularly upon one hundred of these and upon two thousand of their works, from which he asserts that he accumulated twenty thousand facts. His work remains an immense and invaluable storehouse of information, much of it (notably the facts he supplies on sculpture and painting) inaccessible from any other source. He provides us with innumerable fascinating incidental details; his curiosity and thirst for knowledge, his energy and industry, were boundless. No wonder that he had little time for sleep, as we are told, and dictated or had books read to him even in his bath. In many matters he is up-to-date and enlightening. Yet he did not have nearly enough time to research with scientific care the whole of the enormous field he attempted to cover; nor had he the training. The work is therefore not only unsystematically and indiscriminately arranged but heavily loaded with gross mistakes, impossibly tall stories, misreadings, superficialities, and anachronisms. Moreover, Pliny's style oscillates strangely between arid, crabbed abruptness and prolixity or affected mannerism.

He was an enthusiastic admirer of nature and believed, after the fashion of the Stoics, in a beneficent deity or pantheistic spirit pervading all of its works. Of contemporary humankind, on the other hand, he was vigorously critical, deploring its folly, selfishness, ingratitude, and luxury. He also maintained a very Roman distaste for the Greeks and their influence.

The *Natural History* was found indispensable by later writers such as the Latin grammarian and writer Solinus in the third century, the compiler of the *Medicina Plinii* in the fourth, and the Spanish prelate and scholar Isidore of Seville in the seventh, who abridged it, often with imperfect understanding and unhappy results. A notable translation of the whole work into English was made in 1601 by Philemon Holland, the classical scholar known as Translator General.

EDITIONS—D. Detlefsen, 1866–73. *With translation:* H. Rackham, W. H. S. Jones, D. E. Eichholz, E. H. Warmington (Loeb ed.), 1938–78; J. Beaujeu, L. Robert, J. Desanges, R. Schilling, A. Ernaut, E. de Saint-Denis, R. Pépin, J. André, H. Le Bonniec, G. Serbat, H. Zehnacker, H. Gallet de Santerre, J. Croisille, R. Bloch (Budé ed.), 1950–77; K. Jex-Blake, The Elder Pliny's Chapters on the History of Art, ed. by E. Sellers, 1896; K. C. Bailey, The Elder Pliny's Chapters on Chemical Subjects, 1929–32; Inventorum Natura; The Wonderful Voyage of Pliny, illus. by U. Woodruff, 1979.
ABOUT—F. Münzer, Beiträge zur Quellenkritik der Naturgeschichte, 1897; H. N. Wethered, The Mind of the Ancient World: A Consideration of Pliny's Natural History, 1937; H. Le Bonniec, Bibliographie de l'histoire naturelle de Pline l'ancien, 1946; A. Önnerfors, Pliniana, 1956; R. Syme, Tacitus, 1958; M. Chibnall *in* T. A. Dorey, ed., Empire and Aftermath (Silver Latin, v 2), 1975.

PLINY THE YOUNGER (Gaius Plinius Caecilius Secundus), Roman official, Latin writer, and orator, was born in A.D. 61/62 and died in 111 or 113. His father, Lucius Caecilius, a rich landowner of Novum Comum (Como) in northern Italy, died when he was young, and he became the ward of the eminent former consul Lucius Verginius Rufus. Moving to Rome, the younger Pliny studied under the Greek rhetorician Nicetes Sacerdos and was taught law by the Roman rhetorician Quintilian. He was,

pli' ni

however, principally looked after by his mother's brother Pliny the Elder, with whom he and his mother were staying at Misenum in 79 at the time when the eruption of Vesuvius caused the older man's death. Gaius, adopted in his will as his son, took his family name. Soon afterward, he began his career as a lawyer and entered the Senate. Following a brief interlude in the army as a military tribune, he did well in the civil courts and also began to make a name in the political court that conducted trials of provincial governors and other officials on charges of extortion. In 93, the emperor Domitian supported his election as praetor, at an early age for the office, and then made him prefect of the military treasury (94–96). When, however, Domitian was murdered in 96, Pliny aligned himself with the general senatorial hatred of the dead emperor by vindicating the cause of men he had executed. Under Trajan (98–117), Pliny, while continuing to prosecute provincial functionaries charged with extortion, became director of the national treasury (98–100), chairman of the drainage board (104–6), and in 109—or perhaps 111—imperial governor of Bithynia-Pontus (northwestern Asia Minor), with special powers to deal with the financial and political disorganization into which the province and its cities had fallen. He was still there, apparently, when he died.

Ten books of Pliny's letters have survived. The first nine seem to have been issued singly or in groups of two or three, at intervals between the years 100 and 109. Addressed to a most varied group of correspondents and covering an extremely wide range of the themes of interest to Pliny in his personal, professional, and literary capacities, the letters display Roman society in all its diversity. They are neither imaginary, sermon-like epistles like Seneca's, nor truly authentic, unaltered letters like those of Cicero, but something in between. That is to say, they are genuine in the sense that they were written communications addressed and dispatched to their recipients, but each, all the same, was a carefully constructed and elaborately posed composition, dealing with a single, selected theme and intended for publication—they read like carefully revised versions of what may have been less polished

originals. Pliny developed the literary letter into something new in Latin literature, rather like the occasional poems of his contemporary Martial, but quite without his scathing obscenity. Judging from his correspondence, we find Pliny a highly amiable figure, conscious of his position, complacent in his references to appreciative words received from others, pleasantly willing to do good, and happy to tell you when he has done it. His style, varying from brevity to diffuseness according to the topic, shows all the tricks of intricate arrangement and balance that were characteristic of contemporary rhetoric. But Pliny also has an unusually keen eye for human nature, and a gift for describing it. The letters also contain some attempts at versification, which are only mediocre.

The tenth book of the series is entirely different from the others. Collected and published after his death, it contains a selection of his correspondence with Trajan, together with the emperor's replies, all written while he held his special commission in Bithynia-Pontus during the last two years of his life. To us it seems that he refers an excessive amount of business to the emperor, but perhaps the disorganized state of the cities in his province left him no alternative; only once does Trajan show a sign of mild impatience at his fussiness. Of particular historical interest is their famous exchange about the methods of dealing with the local Christian communities, in which Pliny seeks the emperor's guidance and is advised not to seek them out for punishment but to punish them if they are brought before him and their "guilt" is proved.

Additional light on the regime of Trajan is provided by our only surviving example of Pliny's oratory, the *Panegyricus,* which he pronounced in the Senate on entering upon his consulship in A.D. 100. Like his letters, this is a highly wrought piece of literature, but in contrast to their more delicate touch it is vigorous and even passionate in tone. The *Panegyricus* is particularly concerned to contrast the evil-doings of the late Domitian, whose patronage Pliny tried to forget that he had ever received, with the scintillating merits of Trajan, who is praised in a manner that seems to modern taste excessive and groveling.

EDITIONS—A. N. Sherwin-White, The Letters of Pliny: A Social and Economic Commentary, 1966; M. Durry, Pline le jeune: Panégyrique de Trajan, 1938. *Translations*—B. Radice, Pliny: Letters and Panegyricus (Loeb ed.), 1969; A. M. Guillemin, Pline le jeune: Lettres et Panégyrique (Budé ed.), 1959; F. Trisoglio, Opere di Plinio Cecilio Secondo, 1973; C. Grieg, A Selection of His Letters, 1979.
ABOUT—A. M. Guillemin, Pline et la vie littéraire de son temps, 1929; S. E. Stout, Scribe and Critic at Work in Pliny's Letters, 1954; L. Vidman, Études sur la correspondance de Pline le jeune avec Trajan, 1960, reprint 1972; P. V. Cova, La critica letteraria di Plinio il Giovane, 1966; B. Radice *in* T. A. Dorey, ed., Empire and Aftermath (Silver Latin, v 2), 1975; G. Picone, L'eloquenza di Plinio: Teoria e prassi, 1978.

PLOTINUS, Greek philosopher, A.D. 205–70, was born at Lycopolis in upper Egypt; in spite of his Roman name, he was Greek in culture and background. We know the main features of his career from his pupil Porphyry. At the age of twenty-eight he turned to the study of philosophy and worked for the next eleven years under the Platonist Ammonius Saccas at Alexandria. In 242/3 Plotinus joined the military expedition of the emperor Gordian III against the Persians, with the intention of studying Persian and Indian philosophy; but, when Gordian was murdered in Mesopotamia in 244, he retired to Antioch, the capital of the Roman province of Syria, without having made any of the contacts he had wanted. Later in the year he moved to Rome, where in time he achieved renown as a teacher of philosophy and leader of an intellectual circle. At one point, he endeavored to gain the support of the emperor Gallienus (253–68) for a plan to establish a Platonic community on the site of an abandoned Pythagorean center in Campania. He died after a prolonged and painful illness that he evidently endured with great courage. Plotinus was an outstanding spiritual director—himself a troubled and urgent personality, he was also a man of attractive character, who showed a great deal of practical kindness.

He began writing at the age of fifty, after ten years at Rome. His philosophical essays
plō tī′ nus

arose directly out of the discussions at his teaching seminars and were intended primarily for the use of his students. They were collected and published during the first years of the fourth century by Porphyry, who classified them roughly according to their subject matter and grouped them in six *Enneads,* or groups of nine. With the exception of politics, of which nothing is said, Plotinus' treatises cover the entire range of ancient philosophy. The first *Ennead* is concerned mainly with ethics and esthetics; the second and third, with physics and cosmology; the fourth, with psychology; and the fifth and sixth, with metaphysics, logic, and epistemology. Although Plotinus had not planned his talks as a systematic survey (and Porphyry's arrangement of them is somewhat artificial) the *Enneads* comprise—next to the works of Aristotle—our most comprehensive corpus of ancient philosophical teaching, a wide-ranging structure of thought that includes in its majestic scope both the macrocosm of the world and the microcosm of the human soul.

Plotinus saw the living universe as a complex and ordered process of continuous and unending descent from the transcendent One, the First Principle, in an unbroken series of successive stages. This Principle, the sole source of all existence and all values, pours itself out in an everlasting downward rush of generation that brings into existence all the different levels, layers, and living forms of our world. But this downward impetus has a complementary, reverse counterpart. For in the never-ending dance of the universe there is always an upward surge as well, an ascent toward identification and amalgamation with the One.

This First Principle, as Plotinus envisaged it, is outside the range of human thought or verbal definition, inexpressible in terms of space or time or number. Looked at in a different way, it comprises the whole of superabundant reality and is synonymous with pure and absolute goodness. Unlike the God of the Jews and Christians, however, the First Principle is not a power that directs the people and things on the earth; rather it remains wholly external to them and does not impinge on them. As the creator of all things

347

in the universe, it links every level of the cosmos with every other.

The structure of every human being mirrors the structure of the First Principle itself, with which men and women have the capacity to reunite themselves: their whole existence, like the existence of everything else in the universe, can take the form of an upward craving impulse, an urge to reascend to the summit and mingle with the One. In this potential union between the One and the human body, Plotinus saw two intermediaries, of which the higher is Mind and the lower is Soul. On the cosmic scale, Mind is the perpetual thought-force of the universe and Soul the activity that emanates from Mind's working. Mind and Soul are not only universal entities but are also present and operative within all human beings, who are microcosms of the larger structure. Our mortal bodies, Plotinus felt, like other thinkers of his age, are poor degraded things. Yet the souls and minds of individual human beings provide the means by which they are able to rise to the heights.

Indeed—and here is the mystical centerpiece of Plotinus' teaching—humans have the power, though only on the rarest occasions, to take the supreme step: to obtain a brief view of the One itself, and even to merge with it. This they can accomplish by turning their gaze within themselves. Contemplation had often been urged by philosophers before, but it was Plotinus who made it into the potent device for thinking away into insignificance the restrictions of body and time and space, until we are able to achieve union with the highest reality itself. As we learn from magnificent passages in the *Enneads,* he was convinced that he himself, on a very few occasions, by the exercise of the sternest discipline, had experienced this mystic union, in which his personality became awakened to what it truly was.

The whole of Plotinus' philosophy endeavors to animate our dulled sense of the supernatural and bring us a way to reach our true nature and source. With this new and dynamic version of more than six centuries of Platonic teachings, he became the western world's pioneer in mysticism. Plotinus possessed a remarkable power to communicate the luminous splendor of what he called the "blessed fullness"; and so he brought pagan spirituality to its culmination, at a time of profound political, social, and economic despair. At the same time, he made vital contributions to psychology and esthetics, and to the theory of the nature and origin of evil.

Although Plotinus was the greatest of all the philosophers of the Roman age and one of the most remarkable mystical thinkers in the history of the world, his doctrines did not achieve popularity in his own time: for one thing, they were couched in an allusive, condensed, and individual style (his bad eyesight preventing revision); and then, in addition, they were deliberately written to appeal to a spiritual and intellectual elite. Yet soon after his death this Neoplatonism, of which he was the supreme exponent, became the dominant philosophy of Graeco-Roman civilization—and subsequently exercised a profound influence on the Christian fathers. Through St. Augustine, St. Basil, St. Gregory of Nyssa, and the anonymous writer whose works went under the name of Dionysius the Areopagite, the *Enneads* of Plotinus profoundly affected the thought of the Middle Ages and the Renaissance. He still remains today the supreme text for those who yearn for spiritual exaltation.

EDITIONS with translation—S. MacKenna and B. S. Page, 3rd ed., 1962; A. H. Armstrong (Loeb ed.), 1966– ; E. Bréhier (Budé ed.), 1924–38.
ABOUT—A. H. Armstrong, the Real Meaning of Plotinus' Intelligible World, 1949; H. R. Schwyzer *in* Pauly-Wissowa-Kroll, Real-Encyclopädie der classischen Alterthumswissenschaft, v 21, columns 471-592, 1951; J. Trouillard, La purification plotinienne, 1955, *and* La procession platonienne, 1955; E. Bréhier, The Philosophy of Plotinus, 1958; Les sources de Plotin (Entretiens Hardt, v 5), 1960; P. Hadot, Plotin ou la simplicité du régard, 1963; J. N. Deck, Nature, Contemplation, and the One, 1967; J. M. Rist, Plotinus: The Road to Reality, 1967; A. Graeser, Plotinus and the Stoics: A Preliminary Study, 1972; J. Igal, La cronología de la Vida de Plotino de Porfirio, 1972; R. Wallis, Neoplatonism, 1972; G. J. P. O'Daly, Plotinus' Philosophy of the Self, 1973; D. J. O'Meara, Structures hiérarchiques dans la pensée de Plotin, 1975; R. B. Harris, ed., The Significance of Neoplatonism, 1976; J. M. Charrue, Plotin: Lecteur de Platon, 1978.

PLUTARCH (Lucius Mestrius Plutarchus), Greek biographer and philosopher, ploo' tärk was born before A.D. 50 and died after 120. He belonged to a well-known family at Chaeronea in Boeotia (central Greece) and spent most of his life in his native city, for which he felt great affection. Nevertheless, he also went on fairly extensive travels. In A.D. 66 he was in Athens, studying physics, natural science, and rhetoric—though the subject which held the greatest interest for him was ethics. Not long afterward, he was sent on a political mission to Rome, where he got to know a famous rhetorician, Favorinus of Arelate, and added to his large circle of Greek friends many influential figures in Roman life. These included Lucius Mestrius Florus (consul 72), whose name he adopted, no doubt because he had received Roman citizenship at Florus' hands; at one point, the two men visited the civil war battlefield of Bedriacum together. During his stay in Rome, Plutarch lectured on philosophical and rhetorical subjects—delivering his lectures in Greek since he never mastered Latin completely. He paid a further visit to the city in the early nineties, when his reputation attracted substantial audiences. He also visited Asia Minor and Alexandria and traveled to various parts of his native Greece, where he was given honorific positions by Trajan and Hadrian. Athens granted him citizenship, and in the nineties a life priesthood was bestowed on him at Delphi.

His biographical writings mostly seem to belong to the years between 105 and 115, though some of them may be earlier or later. Most of these *Lives* of soldiers and statesmen were grouped in pairs, one Greek and one Roman, linked by a comparison between the two. Twenty-three pairs of *Lives* have come down to us. The Greek series begins with ten Athenians, three Spartans, a Syracusan, and a Theban. Next comes Alexander the Great, and the list continues as far as the Spartan reforming monarchs of the third century B.C., concluding with Philopoemen of Megalopolis (d. 182 B.C.), leader of the Achaean League. The Roman biographies start with the first two mythical or legendary monarchs, Romulus and Numa, and conclude with eleven personages of the first century B.C., of whom the last is Mark Antony (d. 30). Four separate *Lives* outside the parallel series also survive: Artaxerxes II Mem-

non of Persia, Aratus of Sicyon who built up the Achaean League, and the Roman emperors Galba and Otho (A.D. 68–69). The biography of the emperor Vitellius is missing, as are those of the divine Heracles, six Greek poets and statesmen, Scipio the Younger, and a pair comprising Epaminondas and Scipio the Elder—it was Epaminondas whose spectacular military career had inspired Plutarch to write the *Lives* in the first place.

His use of parallelisms between Greeks and Romans, a common exercise of the rhetorical schools, while permitting Plutarch the introduction of contrasts as well as similarities, was not a very effective device for casting light on the characters of his subjects. The parallelisms do, however, illuminate Plutarch's own public and literary careers, because these aptly epitomize the coming together of the Greek and Roman cultures in the imperial world of his day. Although he is, for the most part, impartial in his comparisons between the representatives of the two cultures, his initial intention in launching the series was probably to show that Greece, in the past, had produced men as great as the greatest Romans; indeed, two-thirds of the material in his *Lives* and other writings relate to Greece. Devoting himself to his country's service from a mixture of patriotic, antiquarian, and religious motives, Plutarch perfectly embodies the upper class, conservative, Greek attitudes of his time. As he supports the authoritarian elements in past history, so also, in the politics of his own day, he is loyal to the Romans, recognizing and urging that it was useless to attempt to do anything else.

Plutarch's interpretation of life and of history is determinedly moral; he supports the traditional view that we must study the past in order to derive ethical uplift. Classical biographers had traditionally tended to produce eulogies of their subjects, exhorting readers to imitate their excellent qualities; and Plutarch elevates this tendency into a deliberate philosophical purpose. He is a hero-worshiper, who looks at great men as a race apart (though, in the process, he throws in just a few bad examples, as deterrents, namely Demetrius I Poliorcetes of Macedonia [d. 283 B.C.] and his Roman counterpart Antony). He selects precisely the material that will illustrate moral character—including the little peculiarities that seem to him to be revealing—with a consequent diminution of emphasis on the actual events of a man's career. Like other ancient writers, he has little idea of dynamic biography, remaining convinced that characters are fixed at birth and do not change: at most, following an Aristotelian tradition, he is sometimes prepared to concede that *acquired* characteristics may undergo modification.

Yet his patterns of investigation are by no means fixed: The range of human actions he is prepared to consider is wide—and it includes sayings as well as doings. The scheme is flexible, and each biography comprises a unity of a different kind. The introductions that precede the biographies are likewise cleverly diversified; and Plutarch, who was writing for the most part for people of leisure, indulges in spacious digressions, containing abundant material of curious and antiquarian interest. His unique talent lies in the selection of significant anecdotes, in which he shows an expert ability to catch and keep his reader's interest. Many of these stories are frivolous, but some are solemn and somber; it is in terms of a great play, acted out in a huge theatre, that Plutarch sees both life and the lives of his characters. He wants us to enter into the hearts and emotions of these people and skillfully provides us with the illusion that that is what we are doing. At the same time, however, his historical sense is markedly defective. Not possessing the slightest idea how to interpret his sources, he sees everything in terms of his own times and attitudes, and so anachronisms abound. Indeed, the concept of change scarcely enters into his thought processes at all: one would deduce from his *Lives* that there had not been any social developments whatever during the whole of the previous millennium—in his defense, however, in the almost unbroken tranquillity of the Pax Romana, it may not have seemed, even to a thinking person, that the next millennium would provide any either.

Plutarch was a strongly religious man, most knowledgeable about cults, deeply devoted to the Delphic oracle, and a slave to numerous superstitions. Nevertheless, at times he was fired by scientific curiosity, and displayed eagerness to reconcile ancient beliefs with up-to-date thinking. This he set out to do by a conscientious, though somewhat gingerly, process of rationalization, reassuring himself that such inquiries were a positive assistance to the best sort of religion. As to his general reliability, not only were his religious, moral, and social preoccupations, and his lack of historical sense, bound to lead to distortion, but his factual accuracy was far from reliable. However, at least he knew—for he tells us so—that it is not always easy to discover what is true and what is not, and occasionally, in the course of his reading from an enormous range of sources (including local chronicles), he bestirred himself to decide between rival versions. In the process of his research, he became a keen collector of oral traditions, taking careful notes and, above all, making an effort to see a great deal for himself.

The *Lives* remained comparatively little known until the first quarter of the fifteenth century, when no less than eight manuscripts were recorded as appearing in important libraries. Before 1450, there were Latin translations, one of which was published in Rome in 1472 or 1473. The French translation by the great classical scholar Jacques Amyot (1559) created a fashion for Plutarch's work, and for collective and comparative biography in general; Thomas North's 1579 English rendering of Amyot's version exercised a profound influence on English literature and style. The English poet John Dryden edited a new translation that was first published in 1683–86, and through the eighteenth century Plutarch's influence remained enormous.

But these *Lives* were only a small part of his literary output, for an ancient catalog of his works lists no less than two hundred twenty-seven items. His surviving writings on ethical, religious, physical, political, and literary topics are collectively known as the *Moralia* (in Greek, *Ethica*) and amount to more than sixty treatises (besides those that are doubtful and spurious), including lectures and speeches and debates, of varying degrees of formality, and essays cast in the form of question and answer. One group is marked off by its rhetorical character: written mostly at an early stage in Plutarch's career—he evidently did not have enough success as a rhetorical performer to persist in this activity—these pieces show him declaiming on various subjects, including, for example, Fortune, and its role in the life of Alexander the Great and in the histories of Rome and Athens. The *Moralia* also included popular philosophical monographs on such topics as marriage and peace of mind; and there are further treatises in which Plutarch, who was a Platonist, attempts serious philosophical discussion, notably a tractate on the doctrine of the soul in Plato's *Timaeus,* three polemics against the Stoics, and three more against the Epicureans. Plutarch also wrote on the psychology and intelligence of animals and argued against the eating of meat, in the manner of the Pythagoreans who insisted on abstention from this practice.

In the sphere of religion, which meant so much to him, he wrote several works, including *On Isis and Osiris* (on the form and decline of the Delphic oracles) and *On God's Late Judgment* (a discussion, staged at Delphi, that deals with the problem of divine justice). These religious writings are pious, warm, and sincere, but lacking in depth. On the other hand, such works as his antiquarian miscellanea, *Greek and Roman Questions,* are mines of information about religious antiquities. Plutarch's taste for didactic, pedagogical themes emerges strongly in those sections of the *Moralia* that deal with politics: for example, in a list of instructions he drew up for prospective statesmen. He also occupied himself, in a somewhat dilettante fashion, with scientific inquiries, for instance in a study entitled *On the Face of the Moon.* Treatises on womanly virtue and laconic sayings give scope for his delight in anecdote, and the *Table-Talk of the Seven Sages* and the nine-book *Symposiaca* are crammed with an almost overwhelming diversity of contents. All these works are liberally spiced with quotations, particularly from Greek poetry.

Introduced into Italy by Byzantine scholars in the fifteenth century, the *Moralia* was published at Venice in 1509; and Amyot's French version (1572) exercised a strong effect on the *Essais* of Montaigne (1533–1592) in the following decade. A famous English translation by Philemon Holland appeared in 1603. It was not, of course, the *Moralia* but the *Lives* which brought Plutarch his principal fame, though recent scholarship takes a different line, regarding the former work, with its philosophical and religious speculations, as the most noteworthy monument to this versatile representative of second century intellectual life.

EDITIONS with translation—B. Perrin, F. C. Babbitt, W. C. Helmbold, P. H. De Lacy, B. Einarson, P. A. Clement, H. B. Hoffleit, E. L. Minar, F. H. Sandbach, H. N. Fowler, H. Cherniss (Loeb ed.), 1914– . *Translations*—Lives: (Penguin ed., selections) I. Scott-Kilvert, The Rise and Fall of Athens, 1960, *and* Makers of Rome, 1965, *and* The Age of Alexander, 1973; Moralia: (Penguin ed., selections) R. Warner, Moral Essays, 1971; On Isis and Osiris: J. G. Griffiths, 1970.
ABOUT—A. Lesky, History of Greek Literature, 1966 (List of Moralia on pp 826-28); R. H. Barrow, Plutarch and His Times, 1967; A. J. Gossage, Plutarch, *in* T. A. Dorey, ed., Latin Biography, 1967; D. Babut, Plutarque et le Stoicisme, 1969; C. J. Gianakaris, Plutarch, 1970; C. P. Jones, Plutarch and Rome, 1971; D. A. Russell, Plutarch, 1974; A. Wardman, Plutarch's Lives, 1974; F. F. Brenk, In Mist Appareled: Religious Themes in Plutarch's Moralia and Lives, 1977; J. Vernière, Symboles et mythes dans la pensée de Plutarque, 1977.

POLLIO, GAIUS ASINIUS, Roman statesman and Latin historian, was born in 76 B.C. and died in A.D. 4 or 5. He came of a leading family of the Marrucini, a people on the Adriatic coast of central Italy. After entering public life at Rome in the fifties and incurring the displeasure of Pompey, Pollio fought on Caesar's side in the civil war, serving in Africa and Greece, and in Spain, where he held a command. After Caesar's death he governed Cisalpine Gaul (northern Italy) on behalf of Antony. While serving as consul in 40 he helped reconcile Antony with Octavian. In the following year he defeated the Parthini, an Illyrian tribe, and was awarded a triumph. In the final clash between Antony and Octavian (31) he refused to take part and subsequently withdrew from public life, appearing as an advocate, supporting literary causes—he founded Rome's first public library from his

pol' li ō

351

Illyrian spoils—and introducing the custom of an author's holding public or semi-public recitations of his own writings. In his youth he was a friend of Catullus (with whom he found fault later on), and he subsequently formed friendships with Horace, who praised his Illyrian victory, and Virgil, who dedicated his Fourth Eclogue to him after Pollio had saved his northern Italian estate from confiscation.

Pollio's own most important literary achievement was his *Histories.* In this work, which he started to write soon after 35 B.C., he undertook the hazardous task of narrating Roman history during a near contemporary and convulsed period: he began his story with the year 60 B.C., the date of the formation of the First Triumvirate, which according to his estimate (sometimes contested by modern scholars) inaugurated the prolonged period of civil warfare that followed. He may have concluded his narrative with the year 42 B.C., when the Republicans Brutus and Cassius died at the battle of Philippi—to deal with the years after that would have been too politically embarrassing.

Only one fragment of any substance has survived; but it is clear from other evidence that the *Histories* were trenchantly analytical and independent. Indeed, despite the autocracy now established by Octavian (Augustus), Pollio was prepared to praise Brutus as an emblem of the Republican "freedom" to which he held tenaciously as an ideal.

Cicero, however, he blamed for lack of fortitude in adversity, while recognizing, nevertheless, that his literary and oratorical achievements had won everlasting renown (though Pollio had less kind things to say about his style elsewhere). Caesar's *Commentaries,* on the other hand, he censured as careless and biased, and he condemned Sallust (perhaps in a separate treatise, but also in a letter) for his use of archaisms and Livy, who came from Patavium (Padua), for his *Patavinitas,* by which he probably meant provincialism. Evidently Pollio was determined not to be overshadowed by anyone else. His own style seems to have been not too unorthodox or unrhythmical but somewhat jerky and rugged. The *Histories* must

have been full of vital information—incisive and well-informed, if somewhat sour, judgments—and their disappearance has left one of the largest of all the gaps in our knowledge of Latin historiography. They are sometimes believed to have been an important source for Plutarch, though this has been much disputed.

Pollio's poetry, like his other works, is lost. It was apparently too old-fashioned for the taste of the day. We are told that it included some minor erotic pieces, and that he also wrote tragedies, of which Virgil and Horace thought highly. But he gave up writing serious verse when he took to history. He also enjoyed a very considerable reputation as an orator whose speeches displayed meticulous composition and a spare elegance of style.

ABOUT—E. D. Pierce, A Roman Man of Letters, 1922; J. André, La vie et l'oeuvre d'Asinius Pollion, 1949; R. Syme, Tacitus, 1958. On his relation to Appian: E. Gabba, Appiano e la storia delle guerre civili, 1956; E. Badian's comments *in* Classical Review (v 8, no 2, pp 159-62), 1958.

POLLIO, MARCUS VITRUVIUS. See Vitruvius

POLLIO, TREBELLIUS. See Spartianus, Aelius

POLLUX, JULIUS (Julius Polydeuces), Greek rhetorician and scholarly writer, lived in the later second century A.D. Leaving his home, Naucratis in Egypt (not before 178), he was appointed to the chair of rhetoric at Athens.

His *Onomasticon* is a compendium of Greek terms (mostly rare). The work was dedicated to the emperor Commodus (d. 192), to whom introductory epistles at the beginning of each of the ten books are addressed. Arranged not in alphabetical order but according to topics, the *Onomasticon* amasses technical, rhetorical terms covering an extremely wide range (for example,

pol' luks

thirty-three terms of abuse to apply to a tax collector), illustrating their meaning by numerous literary quotations. Among the subjects he covers is that of the Athenian constitution; and music, dancing, and the theatre (including its ancient history) are interestingly prominent. At one point Pollux replies to criticisms from a rhetorician named Phrynichus, who had been his unsuccessful rival for the Athenian chair. This Phrynichus was a strict Atticist, whereas Pollux was more interested in technical terminology than in linguistic orthodoxy—although he did not escape criticism from his contemporary Lucian for Atticism and other fashionable literary vices.

The original version of the *Onomasticon* is now lost, but copies were made of an early epitome that belonged to Arethas, archbishop of Caesarea, in about A.D. 900, and our existing manuscripts are based on these copies. The popularity of the work is illustrated by the numerous processes of abbreviation and interpolation that the copies underwent and by the presence of more than half a dozen of the manuscripts in fifteenth century Italian libraries.

EDITIONS—W. Dindor, 1824; E. Bethe *in* Teubner's Lexicographi Graeci, 1900–31, v 9.
ABOUT—F. von Stojentin, De Iulii Pollucis in Publicis Atheniensium Antiquitatibus Enarrandis Auctoritate, 1875; E. Zarncke, Symbolae ad J. Pollucis Tractatum De Partibus Corporis Humani, 1885; J. E. Sandys, History of Classical Scholarship, 3rd ed., 1921.

POLYBIUS, Greek historian, was born in about 200 and died after 118 B.C. His birthplace was Megalopolis in Arcadia (Peloponnese, southern Greece), where his father, Lycortas, was a rich landowner, a prominent member of the Achaean League, and the friend of its leader Philopoemen. Polybius himself carried the ashes of Philopoemen to burial in 182. In 180 he was appointed to a delegation going to Egypt, a mission that was canceled, however, because of the sudden death of the Egyptian king Ptolemy V Epiphanes. In 170–169 B.C. Polybius served as cavalry commander (hipparch) of the Achaean League. When Rome became in-

pō li′ bi us

POLYBIUS

volved in war against King Perseus of Macedonia, Polybius and a cavalry force were sent by the League to help the Roman cause. But the Romans, suspicious of the League's attitude, rejected the offer and, after their victory at Pydna (168 B.C.), deported to Italy a thousand Achaeans, of whom Polybius was one, detaining them for political investigation without trial.

At Rome, Polybius was chosen as the tutor to the sons of the eminent Aemilius Paullus. The younger son, Scipio Africanus the Younger (Scipio Aemilianus), became his close friend and enabled him to stay on in the city when the other Achaean internees were distributed around the Italian towns. In 151 B.C. he probably accompanied Scipio to Spain and northern Africa. During the following year, he was one of three hundred survivors of the deported Achaeans who were allowed to return home. However, when the Third Punic War broke out, he joined Scipio at Carthage and witnessed that city's siege and destruction by the Romans in 146. Subsequently, he took part in an Atlantic voyage of exploration.

Meanwhile hostilities had broken out between Rome and the Achaean League. In Greece shortly after the sack of the League's capital Corinth, Polybius was entrusted by the Romans with the reorganization of the area. About the last two decades of his life little is known. For much of this period, he must have been occupied in literary work.

353

However, he also visited Alexandria in Egypt and Sardis in Asia Minor, and, since he wrote a history of the Numantine War, in which Scipio finally defeated the Spanish rebels, he may also have been present at the capture of Numantia in 133. His death was caused by falling from a horse.

Out of the forty books of Polybius' *Histories,* only Books 1-5 have come down to us complete; excerpts, some of substantial size, survive from the others. Books 1-2 provide an introduction dealing with the years from the beginning of the First Punic War (264), at which the Sicilian historian Timaeus (c. 356–260 B.C.) had ended his work, down to 220, just before the Second Punic War began.

Then follows the main part of Polybius' work, in which he had originally intended to tell the story of the fifty-three years from 220 down to the Roman victory over King Perseus of Macedonia at Pydna (168), which almost completed Rome's mastery of the Mediterranean world. Subsequently, Polybius revised his plan, extending it to describe how the Romans exercised their supremacy down to 146. The events of this later period, discussed more and more from a Roman point of view, were told in Books 30-39 (Book 34 being a digression on geographical themes). Book 40 comprised a general survey and recapitulation.

As his central theme, Polybius chose the expansion of Roman power throughout the entire Mediterranean world, because he saw this as a process of unprecedented importance. He contributed significantly to human thought by realizing that this virtual unification of the known world under Rome made a new genre of historiography both possible and necessary and called for a universal, synoptic method of approach. Although Polybius praises the historian Ephorus (c. 405–330 B.C.) as a partial forerunner in such an approach, he also claims that no one before himself had attempted a world history on a truly systematic scale. Such a project he regards as infinitely superior to specialized studies, which seemed to him to encourage sensational exaggerations that the perspective of a wider canvas would avoid. Polybius greatly admired the old, indomitable Roman spirit—and the traditional Roman immunity to bribes—and was enormously impressed by the leading Romans of his own time, such as his friend Scipio Aemilianus. However, he identified the key to Rome's success as its "mixed" constitution, the special excellence of which he attributed to its perfect balance of the monarchical, aristocratic, and democratic elements (Book 6).

Nevertheless, Polybius announced that he would adopt an objective attitude toward the Roman achievement—since he was not disposed to regard ultimate success as the sole criterion of history. As a result, he treats Hannibal, for example, with a fairness notably deficient in the tradition generally accepted by the Romans. In accordance with the same principle, his observations about Roman policy in the 160s and 150s, although for the most part not unfavorable, contain a good many censorious remarks. In his account from 150 onward, it is true, Polybius seems increasingly pro-Roman. Yet, before the Third Punic War, he still openly sets out the arguments put forward on the Carthaginian side.

Although Polybius himself deplored the hostility that the Achaean League showed toward the Romans at this stage, the annihilation of the League at Rome's hands and the destruction of its capital Corinth must have come as a terrible shock. However, this was partly assuaged by his appointment by the Romans to organize the subsequent settlement. By agreeing to do this, Polybius foreshadowed the phenomenon of Greek literary figures—men such as Dionysius of Halicarnassus and Plutarch—who chose to collaborate with the conqueror. Yet at the same time he never forgot he was a Greek; his work shows a strong bias toward his native Arcadia, toward the Achaean League, and toward prominent members of it whose policies agreed with his own views. The Achaeans, in return, recognized his sympathy and assistance by erecting numerous statues and monuments in his honor.

Polybius echoed with approval Thucydides' claim that he was writing history of practical value, and he emphasized continually that this was true of his own work as well and that he was guiding public figures toward right actions. Unlike Thucydides, however, he wrote in a Greek that is flat, prosy, and verbose. He excused his style on the grounds that he is not out to amuse but to teach and, in particular, to give the true causes of events—an effort he defends with the Thucydidean claim that his method is based on the consistent application of a scientific and technical point of view. This claim notwithstanding, he realized that it would be fallacious to attribute everything that happens in history to scientifically identifiable causes, and, in consequence, he appealed repeatedly to the concept of Chance, which he maintained to be as integral a part of every human being's destiny as his or her looks or intellectual gifts. The rise of the Romans to power, however, did not seem to him an event attributable to Chance, since there were also perfectly rational, identifiable causes for the emergence of the empire. Indeed, sometimes (he believed), Chance may merely be another name for Providence: and, in particular, Rome's ascendancy could only be described as providential (which was, perhaps, some comfort to the humiliated Greeks). As for religion in general, however, Polybius saw it in the light of a political convenience—indispensable because the masses are so unstable that they need all the paraphernalia of cult to give them some sense of direction.

When Thucydides had written about the Peloponnesian War between Athens and Sparta (431–404 B.C.), he had devoted all his great investigatory talent to the examination of the various kinds of causes of that conflict; Polybius, in the *Histories,* imitates him by inquiring into the causes of the Second Punic War, in which the Romans finally defeated their greatest enemy Hannibal in 202. However, while borrowing Thucydides' distinction between immediate and ultimate causes of hostilities, he added a third element as well, the "first overt act." Yet, in spite of this additional refinement, he still falls considerably below the subtlety of his model.

Polybius repeats, with even greater emphasis, Thucydides' stress on the need for truthfulness, extending this doctrine to the speeches he quotes, which in Thucydides and other early historians had often been more or less imaginative recreations. The speeches reported by Polybius, on the other hand, of which about fifty appear in the surviving portions of his work, purport to be accurate reproductions of what had been said—although he admits that some of them are abbreviated versions and that others have been worked over to a certain extent.

Polybius agrees with Thucydides that the only events worth writing about are contemporary or near-contemporary history. Moreover, he regards it as essential that the historian should have taken part personally in the events he narrates—as he himself (even more than Thucydides) had done. Two elements in Polybius' own experience proved particularly valuable to him as a historian. First, he had personal knowledge of military affairs—and indeed he was the author of a tactical handbook (now lost)—that helped him in his account of the Roman army. Secondly, he had traveled very widely —as we have seen, he even made a voyage of discovery into the Atlantic—which enabled him to write such works as his study entitled *On the Habitability of the Equatorial Region.* He was very proud of his extensive travels and was so keen to be regarded as the second Odysseus that he fiercely attacked the geographer Pytheas (fourth century B.C.) as a possible rival for the honor. Polybius' geographical knowledge, it must be conceded, was not entirely up-to-date, but his insistence in writing about the subject in a clear and comprehensible way deserves praise.

So too does his use of written records— archives and documents—whenever he could get access to them, chiefly in Rome but also elsewhere. The vastness of his *Histories* required him to employ literary sources as well. In making use of these, he claims to adopt, in general, a sympathetic and deferential attitude to earlier authorities. However, he completely fails to live up to this declared aim, indulging instead in resentful abuse and self-justification at the expense of his sources. A particularly prolonged and savage onslaught is directed against Timaeus, who is stigmatized as a credulous, prejudiced, womanishly sensationalist armchair historian. Polybius is especially irritated by Timaeus' old-fashioned incomprehension of

355

federal institutions such as the Achaean League.

Nevertheless, despite all such unfairnesses, Polybius was a diligent researcher and a shrewd observer, and his admiration for the truth, to which reference has been made above, was sincere, indeed passionate. He did not enjoy favor among the Roman historians of the later Republic, because they found his style boring and preferred romancers of the stamp of Timaeus, whom he was so eager to attack. Cicero, however, borrowed his concept of the "mixed" (balanced) constitution, and Livy, too, owed Polybius a great deal of material. He was also studied and imitated by Byzantine writers of the twelfth and thirteenth centuries, and, indeed, we owe his survival to Greek-speaking readers of the Byzantine age. Subsequently, the mixed constitution became the accepted creed of Machiavelli (d. 1527), and also left its mark on the thought of John Calvin (1509–1564). John Locke (d. 1704) and Montesquieu (d. 1755) were likewise profoundly affected by the *Histories* but saw the Roman system as one of mutual checks and balances rather than as a union of different types of political organization. Through their interpretations, Polybius inspired political attitudes in the new United States of America—where he was constantly quoted by John Adams—and it is largely due to his influence that the American constitution is today the example *par excellence* of separated powers held together by an equipoise of checks and counterchecks. In the nineteenth century, Theodor Mommsen declared: "His books are like the sun." People have never read Polybius a great deal, but his influence has been strikingly disproportionate to his readership.

EDITIONS—F. W. Walbank, A Historical Commentary on Polybius, v 1-3, 1957, 1967, 1978. *Translations*—E. S. Shuckburgh, 1889, reprint 1962; W. R. Paton (Loeb ed.), 1922–27; M. Chambers (selections), 1964; J. de Foucault, P. Pédech, R. Weil (Budé ed.), 1960–77. ABOUT: K. von Fritz, The Theory of the Mixed Constitution in Antiquity: A Critical Analysis of Polybius' Thought, 1954; P. Pédech, La méthode historique de Polybe, 1964; F. W. Walbank, Speeches in Greek Historians, 1965; K. F. Eisen, Polybiosinterpretationen, 1966; G. A. Lehmann, Untersuchungen zur historischen Glaubwürdigkeit des Polybios, 1967; E. Graeber, Die Lehre von der Mischverfassung bei Polybius, 1968; K. E. Petzold, Studien zur Methode des Polybios und zu ihrer historischen Auswertung, 1969; M. Grant, The Ancient Historians, 1970; J. A. Foucault, Recherches sur la langue et le style de Polybe, 1972; F. W. Walbank, Polybius, 1972; Polybe (Entretiens Hardt, v 20), 1974; K. Meister, Historische Kritik bei Polybios, 1975; A. Momigliano, Essays in Ancient and Modern Historiography, 1977.

POMPEIUS TROGUS. See Trogus, Pompeius

POMPONIUS MELA. See Mela, Pomponius

PORPHYRY, Greek philosopher and student of religion, was born in A.D. 232/4 and died in about 305. He came from either Tyre in Phoenicia (now Sur in Lebanon) or Batanaea (near the southern frontier of Syria). He originally bore the Syrian name Malchus (king), which appeared in Greek as Porphyrios (purple, like a king's robes). After studying under the eminent philosopher and orator Cassius Longinus at Athens, Porphyry went to Rome in 262 or 263 and became a dedicated follower of Plotinus, the founder of Neoplatonism, with whom he spent five decisive years. Then, owing to a nervous breakdown, he left the school and spent a long time in Sicily, before eventually returning to Rome. Made his literary executor by Plotinus, who died in 270, Porphyry published the master's *Enneads* in about 301, accompanied by an introductory biography of Plotinus that stands out among lives of ancient philosophers for its reliability and factual accuracy. He also wrote, on his own account, very numerous and extensive works, the titles of seventy-seven of which are known.

Porphyry's philosophical and religious writings may be divided into two categories, those written before and those written after he attached himself to Plotinus. In the first group is an essay entitled *On the Philosophical Benefit of Oracles,* considerable passages of which are extant. Written while Porphyry

pôr′ fi ri

was still in Syria, this monograph is pervaded by a belief in demons and in magical means of controlling the actions of the gods and may be the same as a composition referred to frequently by Augustine as *On the Return of the Soul.* Another of Porphyry's early works seems to have been a *History of Philosophy* down to the time of Plato, from which the surviving *Life of Pythagoras* was probably an excerpt. Later, he also wrote another work, a four-book presentation of Neopythagorean themes entitled *On Abstinence*—that is to say, vegetarianism—deriving his material from Theophrastus and others. He was the author of an inquiry entitled *On the Images of the Gods,* extant only in fragments.

After joining Plotinus in Rome, he wrote many treatises that reflect this new discipleship. Those that have survived in whole or part include a collection of philosophical aphorisms *(Aphormai)* borrowed or adapted from Plotinus and a *Letter to Anebo,* an Egyptian priest, in which he expressed himself scathingly about bogus priestly miracles. One particularly attractive piece is his *Letter to Marcella,* his wife (the widow of a friend), to whom he writes with warm eloquence about the Plotinian attitudes to belief and reverence and truth. Extracts from a work entitled *Various Investigations (Summikta Zetemata)* have also come down to us. As a historical document, however, his most important work must have been his fifteen-book tract entitled *Against the Christians.* From the numerous passages preserved by the Church Fathers it seems clear that this was a thorough, scholarly, and legally based onslaught on Christian faith and practices, employing modern methods of historical criticism. This polemic was condemned to be burned, by imperial order, in A.D. 448.

Porphyry also compiled numerous philosophical commentaries on Plato, Aristotle, Theophrastus, and Plotinus. They have not, for the most part, come down to us, but we have the foreword *(Eisagoge)* to his commentary on Aristotle, which subsequently, in a Latin translation by Boethius (480?–?524), played an important part in the cultural tradition of the Middle Ages. Porphyry also wrote treatises on rhetoric and grammar and literary criticism, including two studies on Homeric questions, one of which adopts the method of allegorical interpretation. A *Life of Homer,* falsely included in the writings of Plutarch, is also sometimes ascribed to Porphyry. Technical subjects, too, came within his purview and are represented by two studies of Ptolemy—an introduction to his *Tetrabiblos* and an incomplete commentary on his *Harmonica.* In addition, Porphyry is now regarded as the writer of a work on embryology that used to be attributed to Galen; it is dedicated to a certain Gaurus.

In the main, Porphyry is uncritical and unoriginal: everything he wrote was derived from other authorities—whom, happily, he is scrupulous to mention by name. But his polymath learning was formidable; he was the last imposing scholar that paganism produced. He was also a characteristically complex figure of this later pagan age, since his abundant scholarship did not prevent him from indulging in mysticism; moreover, he preached the ascetic life and was fascinated by oracles.

EDITIONS—There is no complete edition of the works of Porphyry. For editions and translations of individual works *see* Oxford Classical Dictionary, 2nd ed., 1970, p 865 *and* Encyclopaedia Britannica, v 18, 1971, p 251. *Add:* W. Pötscher, Pros Markellan, 1969; A. R. Sodano, Quaestionum Homericarum, Book 1, 1970; J. Bouffartigue and M. Patillon, De l'abstinence (Budé ed.), 1977, 1979.
ABOUT—J. Bidez, Vie de Porphyre, 1913, reprint 1964; Porphyre (Entretiens Hardt, v 12), 1966; A. H. Armstrong, ed., Cambridge History of Later Greek and Early Medieval Philosophy, 1967; R. Wallis, Neoplatonism, 1972; A. Smith, Porphyry's Place in the Neoplatonic Tradition, 1974.

POSIDONIUS, Greek philosopher, historian, and scientist, was born in about 135 B.C. and died in about 50. He came from Apamea (Qala'at el Mudig) in northern Syria but made his home at the leading cultural center of Rhodes, where he was a pupil of the Stoic philosopher Panaetius. At Rhodes he enjoyed the rights of a citizen, occupied high office, and was a famous figure, around whom something like a school began to assemble. He was also well
po si dō′ ni us

POSIDONIUS

POSIDONIUS

known at Rome, where he had easy access to the great houses. He was sent there in 87 to ingratiate the Rhodians with the Roman military and political leader Marius, for whom, however, he formed a profound dislike. In 78 Cicero attended his lectures in Rhodes and became one of his admirers, although Posidonius later refused to compose a eulogy of the orator's political achievements. However, he was prepared to write enthusiastically in support of Pompey, who came to see him before leaving on his successful expedition to the east, and again on his return in 62. Posidonius paid a second visit to Rome in 51, when its government renewed its treaty with the Rhodians. He was one of the most remarkable travelers of antiquity, journeying to Sicily, the eastern shores of the Adriatic, Spain, Liguria, and outside the Roman frontiers into Gaul.

Posidonius' works are only preserved in the quotations that later writers provided from them, but the score of recorded titles confirms that he was an author and thinker of breathtaking versatility. In addition to studying the nature of the universe and the gods and the soul and life after death and producing further researches in astronomy and epistemology and ethics, he wrote extremely influential monographs on meteorology, geography, and ethnology; devoted his attention to literary criticism, rhetoric, lexicography, and ethics; and composed a fifty-two book history of eastern and

western peoples with whom Rome had come into contact, from about 146 to the eighties B.C.

Owing to the almost total disappearance of this enormous corpus of writings, which represents one of our most serious literary losses from the ancient world, the most diverse opinions have been entertained about the character and quality of Posidonius. He was unquestionably a man of inquiring and wide-ranging intellect, who followed up the ideas of others with a sweeping flair that almost amounted to originality. And there was a unifying thread that ran through all his writings: his vision that everything in existence was interconnected, by a process of general "sympathy." The world and universe, that is to say, seemed to him to be a harmonious whole, of which all the parts were related; and since this was so, he saw it as his duty to throw down the barriers between science and philosophy, politics and ethics, earth and heaven, human beings and the gods, and different races and classes of society. Pursuing an eclectic philosophical course based on an idiosyncratic form of Stoicism, he followed that school in envisaging an ideal cosmopolis ruled over by divine providence, in which all peoples and persons have a share. The earthly reflection of the cosmopolis seemed to him the commonwealth of nations embodied in the empire of Rome. However, he lived in constant fear that moral decline was sapping the social order on which this achievement was based.

To demonstrate his dominant thesis—that the same laws and processes are at work in humankind and in nature—he felt it essential to observe and record facts in a variety of scientific fields, although he was only an amateur in the field of science himself (and unduly addicted to curiosities and wonder). In this cause, he worked out the circumference of the earth, constructed a sphere and a map, demonstrated the dependence of the tides on the phases of the moon, and fitted meteorological studies, too, into the general, harmonious, universal system he was eager to demonstrate.

And he apparently wrote well and entertainingly: this was one reason why his work appealed so greatly to posterity. For example, Cicero based a number of his moral treatises on Posidonius' views and expounded Posidonius' doctrines of the afterlife in the *Dream of Scipio* (in Book 5 of the *Republic*); Sallust was impressed by his conception of history; Tacitus depended on his ethnology of the Gauls and the Germans; a whole array of historians imbued with the idea of the Roman cosmopolis derived it, directly or indirectly, from what he had written; and he was quoted as an authority on astronomy, meteorology, and seismology. True, he did not exert much effect on the Stoic school, partly because few of its later members (except Seneca) were interested in the world of nature; and later attention by the Neoplatonists and Church Fathers is unproven. Nevertheless, all in all, his was the most influential brain of the two centuries his lifetime spanned.

EDITIONS—L. Edelstein and I. G. Kidd, v 1, 1972.
ABOUT—I. Heinemann, Poseidonios metaphysische Schriften, 1921; K. Reinhardt, Poseidonios, 1921, *and* Kosmos und Sympathie, 1926, *and* Poseidonios über Ursprung und Entartung, 2nd ed., 1966; P. Schubert, Die Eschatologie des Poseidonios, 1927; S. Sam?bursky, The Physics of the Stoics, 1959; M. Laffranque, La philosophie de Posidonius d'Apamée, 1964; J. M. Rist, Stoic Philosophy, 1969; A. A. Lang, Problems in Stoicism, 1971 *and* Hellenistic Philosophy, 1974; F. H. Sandbach, The Stoics, 1975.

PRATINAS, Greek dramatist from Phlius in the Argolid (northeastern Peloponnese), was born in the sixth century B.C. and died before 467. He is recorded as a participant in the dramatic contest of 499/6 at Athens, in which, as an author of tragedies, he competed against Aeschylus. He was said to have written eighteen tragedies and was one of the earliest tragedians after Thespis. Thirty-two "satyr plays" were also ascribed to Pratinas, and he was believed to be the inaugurator of this type of drama. Owing to their link with horse-eared Silenus, who came to be regarded as foster-father of the god Dionysus, the satyrs (mythological creatures of the wild country, part human and part horse or goat—subsequently the latter connection prevailed) became associated with the Dionysiac cult and dramatic festival. Satyr plays of a primitive and
prà' t'n ás

embryonic kind had presumably existed long before Pratinas, but it seems to have been he who transformed them from a shapeless kind of harlequinade into the regular dramatic form found in the subsequent Attic theatre. Since satyrs, with horsetails and horse ears, but in increasingly humanized form, figure frequently in the paintings on Athenian vases from about 520 B.C. onward, the evolution of satyr plays in Pratinas' hands may perhaps be dated shortly after that time. In the subsequent period of the great Attic drama, it was customary for each playwright to submit for competition a tetralogy consisting of three tragedies and one satyric piece. But there is no evidence that the situation was formalized in this fashion as early as Pratinas. Indeed, the high numerical ratio of his satyr plays to his tragedies suggests the contrary; one possibility that has been conjectured is that his satyric works may have been intended for performance in conjunction with tragedies written by others. Aristotle's theory that the satyr drama was one of the precursors of tragedy seems to be based on a misunderstanding of Pratinas' achievement.

The longest surviving fragment of his plays, which evidently comes from one of these satyric works, deals with a dispute between satyrs and flute players over different types of music. The increasing predominance of the flute accompaniment over the words, at this time, comes under hard-hitting and boisterous criticism from Pratinas. In a passage showing abundant verve and command of language the chorus of satyrs declares that the god Dionysus belongs to them alone: let the flute content itself with the role of subordinate to the singing (the instrument under attack is compared with a toad, *phryneos,* a pun on the name of his rival Phrynichus.) It appears likely that, by introducing this essentially artistic argument into his plays, Pratinas is here reflecting the struggle he himself had to carry on in order to establish his own form of drama. He may have had considerable difficulty in doing this: it was reported (though this cannot be regarded as certain) that he only scored a single victory in the entire course of his career. After he was dead, however, his son Aristias won a further prize with three

359

of his father's plays, the tragedies *Perseus* and *Tantalus* and a satyric drama *The Wrestlers* (467 B.C.); it is not known whether there was a fourth play to make up a tetralogy.

EDITIONS—A. Nauck, Tragicorum Graecorum Fragmenta, revised ed., 1964.
ABOUT—M. Pohlenz, Das Satyrspiel und Pratinas von Phleius, 1926; F. Brommer, Satyrspiele, 1959; A. M. Dale, Words, Music and Dance, 1960; A. W. Pickard-Cambridge, Dithyramb, Tragedy and Comedy, 2nd ed. (with T. B. L. Webster), 1962; T. B. L. Webster, Greek Tragedy, *in* Fifty Years (and Twelve) of Classical Scholarship, 1968.

PRISCIAN (Priscianus), Latin grammarian, was born in the fifth century A.D. and died in the sixth; he dedicated a poem to the Byzantine emperor Anastasius I (493–518). His hometown was Caesarea in Mauretania (now Cherchel in Algeria), but he moved to Constantinople where he became a teacher.

The most important of his writings was the *Grammatical Foundations (Institutiones Grammaticae),* a systematic exposition of Latin grammar and the most extensive work ever written on the subject in that language. It consists of eighteen books, the first sixteen of which (known as *Priscianus Major*) are mainly concerned with sounds and word formations and inflections; the last two, constituting nearly a third of the entire treatise, discuss syntax. Priscian's principal sources were grammarians of the second century A.D.: in Latin, his chief guide was Flavius Caper, but he possessed a good knowledge of his other important Latin grammatical forerunners as well and was also able to supply apt quotations from the leading Republican and Augustan authors of Rome, thus preserving many passages that would otherwise have been lost. He was very well acquainted with Greek literature, too, and cited freely, if not always felicitously, from its writers, relying especially on Apollonius Dyscolus ("the difficult") of Alexandria and, to a lesser extent, on his son Herodianus. The employment of both languages gave *Grammatical Foundations* some of the characteristics of a comparative grammar. However, the work as a whole not only fails

pris' ki ản or prish' ən

to achieve a rational historical treatment but perpetrates a number of the wildly erroneous etymologies common in the ancient world.

Despite these shortcomings, however, Priscian was the best known of all Latin grammarians, exercising, along with Donatus, an overwhelming influence on the teaching of Latin grammar in Europe, where he was esteemed for centuries as the principal authority on correct Latinity. He was especially valued by such medieval English scholars as Aldhelm, Alcuin, and Bede, whose first language was no longer Latin. *Grammatical Foundations* also provided the basis for the study of the logic of language, which began in the thirteenth and fourteenth centuries A.D., and it was only in 1366 that Priscian's work was dropped from the Paris arts course to be replaced by more recent texts, the versified *Doctrinale* (c. 1199) and the *Grecismus,* which takes Priscian to task for not indicating the reasons for the usages he mentions. Nevertheless, his work survives in more than a thousand manuscripts.

Priscian's minor works included *On Noun, Pronoun and Verb; On Numerical Symbols (De Figuris Numerorum); On the Meters of Terence; On Accents* (of doubtful attribution); *On the Parsing of the First Twelve Verses of the Aeneid;* an adaptation of Greek rhetorical exercises for Latin readers *(Praeexercitamina Rhetorica);* and a verse-translation in 1,087 hexameters of a tedious poem *(Periegesis)* by a writer of the second century A.D., Dionysius Periegetes (the Guide). Three of these treatises were dedicated to Quintus Aurelius Memmius Symmachus, consul in 485. Priscian also wrote a three-hundred-line panegyric of the emperor Anastasius I, which touches the rock bottom of groveling servility.

EDITIONS—H. Keil, Grammatici Latini, v 2 and v 3, 1855, 1859.
ABOUT—A. Luscher, De Prisciani Studiis Graecis, 1912; J. E. Sandys, History of Classical Scholarship, v 1, 3rd ed., 1921, reprint 1967; R. R. Bolgar, The Classical Heritage and Its Beneficiaries, 1954.

PROCLUS, Greek philosopher and poet, was born in A.D. 410 or 412 and died in 485. His birthplace was Constantinople, but when he was still an infant his father and mother, Patricius and Marcella, took him back to their native city Xanthus (Kinik) in Lycia (southern Asia Minor), where he received his first education. He then moved to Alexandria, where he trained to become an advocate and learned Latin. After a visit to Constantinople with one of his teachers, a sophist named Leonas, he returned to Alexandria in order to study philosophy, as a pupil of the Aristotelian Olympiodorus. He also worked at mathematics under a certain Heron. While still in his teens, he departed for Athens, where he studied first under a certain Plutarch, founder of the Athenian Neoplatonic School (neither Plutarch nor Heron are the famous men of those names) and then under the next director Syrianus, who particularly influenced his thought. After the death of Syrianus and a brief subsequent tenure by Domninus, Proclus was promoted to the directorship of the school, a post he retained until his death. We owe the facts of his career to a eulogistic biography by his successor Marinus.

Proclus' huge output of writings may be divided into four groups: philosophical, religious, scientific, and literary. His original works in the field of philosophy included *The Elements of Theology,* a concise analysis of Neoplatonic metaphysics in two hundred and eleven propositions, and *The Platonic Theology,* an even more elaborate exposition in six books. *Ten Doubts Concerning Providence, On Providence and Fate and Free-Will: To Theodore the Mechanist,* and *On the Existence of Evil* are extant in Latin translations (to which it is now possible to add portions of the original Greek); *On How to Live,* in two books, has not come down to us at all. In addition, he wrote a series of commentaries on Plato's dialogues: five are recorded but lost; however, those on the *Parmenides, Republic, Alcibiades I, Cratylus* (in part), and *Timaeus* are preserved. In still another treatise Proclus tried to meet Aristotle's objections to the *Timaeus.* Proclus was also the author of *Clarification of Inquiry into Plato's Doctrines* (written against prok' lus

his predecessor Domninus), which has disappeared, and of *Commentary on the Enneads of Plotinus,* fragments of which have survived.

His religious writings included *The Hieratic Art,* which begins with the defense of theurgy—the superstitious art of guiding the workings of the supernatural—and then discusses how the gods can be reached by such means. This treatise may be part of a larger work, perhaps entitled *On Mythical Symbols.* Mention is also made of lost works entitled *On the Mother of the Gods* and *On the Theology of Orpheus.* In this category, too, may be placed *Eighteen Arguments in Favor of the Eternity of the World and Against the Christians,* the greater part of which is reproduced by his critic John Philoponus (died c. 570). Proclus' argument is here directed against the Christian doctrine of the world's creation. There is also a fragment of a commentary on the Chaldean Oracles, a theme to which he subsequently returned in a ten-book work in which he argued that Orpheus, Pythagoras, and Plato were substantially in agreement about the validity of these prophecies. This treatise was probably completed by Proclus after Syrianus had written the first draft.

Proclus' scientific works included several studies on mathematical topics, notably commentaries on Euclid, on Nicomachus of Gerasa (a second century Neopythagorean arithmetician), and on the *Tetrabiblos* of the mathematician, astronomer, and theologian Ptolemy. He also wrote an outline of astronomical theory, the *Hypotyposis,* as well as the *Sphaera,* a short elementary treatise on the same subject. A monograph, *On Eclipses,* only survives in two separate translations; the *Uranodromus,* of which only two fragments remain, seems to have been an essay on the stars and the zodiac. *Elements of Physics,* based on Aristotle's theory of motion, takes the form (like *Elements of Theology*) of a series of propositions (fifty-two in number) and proofs. Proclus' lost letter to a certain Aristocles apparently contained a discussion of the four elements and other physical doctrines.

He was a poet of some stature. A famous and moving *Hymn to the God,* formerly ascribed to St. Gregory of Nazianzus, has been reassigned to Proclus, though without any measure of certainty. (However, his biographer Marinus asserts that he wrote numerous hymns). At least six that are certainly of his authorship (though they reveal the influence of Nonnus) have come down to us, addressed one each to the Sun (or Apollo), the Muses, All the Gods, and Hecate, and two to Aphrodite. (A seventh, to Athena Polymetis, is of doubtful attribution). The fervor of Proclus' hymns provides impressive testimony to the best type of paganism in this age. He also wrote brief epigrams and an epitaph, as well as commentaries on Homer (and, in addition, a monograph entitled *On the Gods in Homer,* begun by Syrianus) and on Hesiod (the introduction to which survives). It is questionable whether the *Chrestomathy,* the extant outline of which classifies the different kinds of poetry, was written by Proclus or by some previous scholar.

Although the most noteworthy representative of the Athenian Neoplatonic school, he does not appear to have been as original a thinker as has sometimes been claimed. However, he was a remarkable systematizer, the last man to bring together the Greek philosophical inheritance, and his encyclopedic achievement in this field became the principal vehicle for diffusing Platonic and Neoplatonic ideas throughout the worlds of Byzantium and Islam. The process started very early on, for within a generation of his death some unknown person rewrote his *Elements of Theology* in Christian terms, presenting it as the work of the very popular mystical writer who assumed the pseudonym of Dionysius the Areopagite; and so it was under Dionysius' name that Proclus' work attained its greatest popularity. His vogue spread to the medieval west, and lasted into the Renaissance, when the *Sphaera* was translated into Italian (three times) and into English and French in the middle years of the sixteenth century. It has been said that Proclus' metaphysics are closer in spirit and method to Hegel than to Plato. Samuel Taylor Coleridge declared that *The Platonic Theology* embodied "the most beautiful and orderly development of philosophy."

EDITIONS—List *in* Encyclopaedia Britannica, v 18, 1971, p 586ff. *Translations*—List *in* G. B. Parks and R. Z. Temple, The Literatures of the World in English translation, v 1, 1968, p 160ff. *Add:* J. Trouillard, Éléments de théologie, 1965; G. R. Morrow, Proclus: A Commentary on the First Book of Euclid's Elements, 1970; D. Isaac, Proclus: Trois études (Budé ed.), v 1, 1977; L. G. Westerink and H. D. Saffrey, Proclus: Théologie platonicienne (Budé ed.), v 3, 1978. ABOUT—L. J. Rosán, The Philosophy of Proclus, 1949; E. R. Dodds, Introduction to his edition of Elements of Theology, 2nd ed., 1963; A. Severyns, Recherches sur la Chréstomathie de Proclos, 1963, 1977; F. J. Leroy, L'homilétique de Proclus de Constantinople, 1967; P. Bastide, Proclus et le crépuscule de la pensée grecque, 1969; J. Trouillard, L'un et l'âme selon Proclos, 1972; R. Wallis, Neoplatonism, 1972; S. E. Gersh, Kinesis Akinetos: A Study of Spiritual Motion in the Philosophy of Proclus, 1973; L. G. Westerink, Proclus on Plato's Proofs of Immortality, 1973; J. A. Coulter, The Literary Microcosm: Theories of Interpretation of the Later Neoplatonists, 1976; H. Dörrie and others, De Jamblique à Proclus (Entretiens Hardt, v 21), 1977.

PROCOPIUS, Greek historian of the early Byzantine period, was born in about A.D. 500 and probably died in 565, the same year as the emperor Justinian I. He came from Caesarea Maritima (Sdot Yam) in Syria Palaestina. After moving to Constantinople as a lawyer and rhetorician, he became the adviser to Justinian's leading general Belisarius, whom he accompanied on his campaigns against the Persians and the Vandals in northern Africa and then against the Ostrogoths in Italy (527–40). He was still with Belisarius, it appears, when the latter subsequently visited Constantinople and returned to the eastern front. In 542, however, Procopius was back in the capital, since he witnessed and described the plague which devastated the city in that year. In 560 a title of nobility *(illustris)* was conferred on him, and he was appointed Prefect of Constantinople in 562. It seems likely that he outlived Justinian by a few months.

Three works by Procopius have survived. His *History of the Wars,* in eight books, is divided, after the model of Appian, between theatres of warfare. Two books each deal with the Persian and Vandal Wars of Justinian, and three with the war against the Ostrogoths in Italy. After these sections had been completed up to the year 552, a further book was added to cover the events on all

prō kō' pi us

fronts up to 554. The work also contains many important digressions on political and other events at Constantinople, notably the plague and the formidable Nika insurrection of 532.

Thus, what Procopius provides, in effect, is a general history of the first two-thirds of the reign of Justinian; and for this period he remains our principal authority.

Indeed, he is a historian of the first order, comparable to the greatest of his forerunners. Benefiting from his eyewitness position at the center of events and employing Greek, Latin, and Syriac written sources, including the official archives to which he had easy access, he displays a sober and finely balanced judgment and a keen regard for the accuracy of what he narrates. Germans and Slavs are among those who have gathered from him much invaluable information about their early histories. Although his adherence to the classical language of his predecessors produces a certain artificiality, his style remains lucid, vigorous, and compelling.

Procopius' hero in his *History* is Belisarius; for Justinian and his wife Theodora he has only lukewarm praise. This is rectified in his second work entitled *On Buildings*. The principal object of this treatise is to give an account up to the year 560 of the numerous buildings in every part of the empire erected by the initiative of Justinian—the greatest of all imperial sponsors of architecture. Procopius surmounts the difficulties of architectural description with considerable skill, and his essay is a mine of artistic, geographical, and topographical information. Presumably, it was written at the request of Justinian; at all events it eulogizes him with pompous and fulsome adulation—perhaps in order to counterbalance the poor impression that had been left by the absence of flattery from his earlier work.

Neither the *History* nor *On Buildings* prepares us for the third of his compositions, the *Secret History (Historia Arcana)*. This professes to be a continuation of the first seven books of the *History*. But it is, in fact, something quite different, namely a virulent, ferocious, and scurrilous attack on the emperor—and on the empress, too, who is assailed in obscene terms; and joining them, as targets for abuse, are Belisarius and his wife, and other leading officials as well. No wonder the work was known as the "Unpublished" *(anecdota),* for it could not possibly have been issued, or even shown to anyone at all, while Justinian was still alive. So extraordinary does the difference from Procopius' earlier works appear that some have hesitated to regard him as the author of the *Secret History.* Yet its author he clearly was, though the style shows some signs that the work was left incomplete or unrevised.

The psychological and historical causes of this *volte-face* remain a mystery; perhaps Procopius had written his *History* in the only way possible for publication in an autocratic state, taking care not to say anything that was untrue, but at the same time passing over the unsayable in silence; whereas his conscience (or perhaps some burning personal grudge—or was he a pagan?) thereafter compelled him to redress the balance in the *Secret History,* for the benefit of posterity. As to the accuracy of this work, there was certainly a great deal amiss in the reign of Justinian; yet it remains true, despite it all, that the empire revived its greatness under his guidance, whereas Procopius' exposures are too indiscriminating and merciless to be entirely convincing. With these reservations, however, the *Secret History* can be used as a valuable source for the internal affairs of the empire during this period.

EDITIONS—J. Haury, 1905–13. History: M. Craveri, Le guerre persiane, vandalica, gotica, 1977; F. M. Pontani, Le guerre, 1977. On Buildings: O. Veh, Die Bauten, 1977. Secret History: F. Ceruti, Storia inedita, 1977. *With translation:* B. H. Dewing and G. Downey, History of the Wars: Secret History (Loeb ed.), 1914–40. *Translations* (of Secret History)—R. Atwater, 1927, reprint 1961; G. A. Williamson (Penguin ed.), 1966; F. Ceruti, Storia inedita, 1977.
ABOUT—B. Rubin, Prokopios von Kaisareia, 1954; R. Browning, Justinian and Theodora, 1971; J. A. S. Evans, Procopius, 1972.

PRODICUS, Greek sophist (popular philosopher and lecturer), was approximately contemporary with Socrates (469–399 B.C.), who was his friend. His birthplace was

pro' di kus

363

PROPERTIES

Iulis on the island of Ceos (off the Argolid, southeast of Athens). The lectures he delivered at Athens and elsewhere won him an impressive reputation and considerable fees. He was employed by the Ceans on diplomatic missions, which gave him opportunities to further his professional interests as a teacher. In Plato's *Protagoras* he is a character who appears carefully wrapped up in blankets, conducting a class from his bed. The implication was that he did not seek the limelight with the same determination as his colleagues; but in any case his voice was not strong enough to carry effectively. He never extemporized but only gave well-prepared lectures.

Prodicus defined the sophist as a being halfway between philosopher and politician. But he himself approached his task largely from the point of view of a linguist, discussing the right use of words and proposing meticulous discriminations between the different shades of meaning of terms that seemed more or less synonymous. His work *The Horae* has not survived, but its contents can to some extent be reconstructed. The Horae, the goddesses of the seasons in Greek mythology, were apparently interpreted by Prodicus as fertility goddesses, since agriculture as the foundation of civilized life was a principal theme of his treatise. He seems to have argued that religion came into existence as the response of human beings to their environment; at first, he said, people had regarded the powers and gifts of nature as divine and subsequently, by analogy, had elevated to divine status inventors who had contributed to human progress—a rationalistic explanation of the origin of the gods that anticipated the doctrines of Euhemerus of Messene (c. 300 B.C.). It is not surprising to learn that Prodicus was regarded, in some quarters, as an atheist.

The *Horae* included an allegorical story of the Choice of Heracles, who was confronted, according to this tale, by Virtue and Vice in the shape of two women of contrasting appearance and dress, between whom he had to make his choice. This allegory of the dividing of the ways, which is partially reminiscent of the description of the two ways of life in the poet Hesiod's ancient *Works and Days*, symbolized the need for men and women to commit themselves morally, to stand up and be counted. The story became very well known and exercised prolonged and persistent influence.

WORKS dubiously attributed to Prodicus' authorship included—*On Nature* or *On the Nature of Man*.
EDITIONS—H. Diels and W. Krantz, Fragmente der Vorsokratiker, 11th ed., v 2, 1964; M. Untersteiner, sofisti: Testimonianze e frammenti, v 2, 1967. *Translations*—K. S. Guthrie, The Choice of Heracles, 1925; R. K. Sprague, The Older Sophists, 1972.
ABOUT—M. Untersteiner, The Sophists, 1954; G. Kennedy, The Art of Persuasion in Greece, 1963; W. K. C. Guthrie, History of Greek Philosophy, v 3, 1969; C. J. Classen, ed., Sophistik, 1976.

PROPERTIUS, SEXTUS, Latin poet, was born in about 50 B.C. and died in about 16. He belonged to a leading and prosperous family of Asisium (Assisi) in Umbria. However, his father died when he was young, and the family property was among the estates confiscated by Octavian (the future Augustus) in 41/40 B.C. for the settlement of veterans. Propertius was able to receive a good rhetorical education at Rome. His relatives' intention was to prepare him for the law, but he directed his interest toward writing poetry (and making love) instead. Propertius was pale, thin, delicate, morbidly overemotional, and excitable—and very careful about his clothes and deportment. In his poetry the woman to whom he was obsessively devoted appears under the pseudonym of Cynthia, but according to Apuleius (writing in the second century A.D.) her real name was Hostia. Propertius presents her with such startling force that she cannot be a literary fiction but must surely have existed. Their stormy affair seems to have started in about 29 and evidently lasted for some five years.

He published only four books of elegies (the second is divided by some editors into two). One modern theory regards the first three books as comprising a single unitary plan, but this idea is not generally accepted. The publication in not later than 28 B.C. of his first book secured him admission to the poetic circle of Maecenas, the adviser of Augustus and patron of letters. This book,

prō pûr' shi us

364

which contains much of Propertius' best work, concentrates, as the title implies, largely upon his passion for Cynthia and was described in some manuscripts as "Propertius in a single volume" (*Monobiblos*). In his second book, she continues to be the main subject, but there are also proud references to the poet's association with Maecenas. Propertius in his third book begins by adopting the pose of the Roman counterpart to the leading Hellenistic poet Callimachus (c. 305–240 B.C.), a conceit that caused irritation to Horace (although Propertius invested his claim with a considerable element of irony). Some of the poems relating to Cynthia in this book are as good as ever, but others are less effective. At the conclusion of the book he sadly renounces his love for her. Nevertheless, she recurs in two powerful poems in the fourth book: in one, as a violent gate-crasher at a party where Propertius is entertaining other girls, and in the other, written after her death, as a ghost who visits him in a dream.

This fourth book, however, consists mainly of a group of poems on antiquarian and legendary subjects, anticipatory of Ovid's *Fasti*—a new archeological variant of the patriotic verse that Propertius had at first avoided. In one piece, the spirit of a certain Cornelia is depicted consoling her widowed husband. The latest events referred to in Books 2, 3, and 4 relate to the years 26, 23, and 16 B.C. respectively.

Propertius veered rapidly, evidently at Cynthia's whim, from ecstasy to wild, self-pitying depression. The self-abasement, in which he so often wallows (though mitigating its monotony by strong flashes of rueful wit) owes something to the same Alexandrian convention that gave him his self-conscious artistry and taste for learning. The neuroses, however, are very much his own; they have earned him comparisons with the English poets John Donne (1573–1631) and Rossetti (1828–1882).

Inspired by his love, Propertius' visual and tactile imagination achieves very powerful expression, through his variation of the elegiac meter, in which the second verse of the couplet, the pentameter, is invested with a novel strength and emotional force; in Propertius' hands meter and feeling, subject and

form have attained perfect integration. His language is enriched by a sensuously romantic evocation of Hellenic names. It also shows a marked tendency to abrupt transitions—and has often been regarded as obscure and puzzling. But the apparent confusions often resolve themselves once the implied setting and dramatic development of his poems are understood—though this task is rendered difficult by the poor manuscript tradition.

Propertius' writings mark the culmination of the Latin elegy. They also signal the end of a historical epoch, for this is one of the last collections to retain a personal and individual character, outside the orbit of the emperors whom future poets became increasingly reluctant to ignore—although, under the patronage of Maecenas, Propertius attempted to rectify this neglect in his last book. His work was quite widely read in ancient literary circles; yet the critics, while respecting his grace and charm and his technical skill, were inclined to withhold wholehearted admiration from a poet who so thoroughly deviated from classical austerity. There was a tendency to prefer the far less powerful but smoother Tibullus (d. 19 B.C.).

Propertius left little mark on medieval poetry but was imitated by the Italian poets Petrarch, Tasso, and Ariosto. His elegies produced an "agitation" in the soul of Goethe, whom Schiller hailed as Tibullus' German counterpart. To the modern reader, acquainted with Freud and his successors, Propertius' self-revelations are of peculiar interest; and they inspired Ezra Pound to some remarkable adaptations.

EDITIONS—H. E. Butler and E. A. Barber, 1933; W. A. Camps, 1961–67; L. Richardson, 1977; P. G. Enk (Book 1), 1946; R. A. Buttimore and R. Hodge, Monobiblos (Book 1), 1977; J. C. Giardina (Book II), 1977. *Translations*—H. E. Butler (Loeb ed.), 1912; S. G. Tremenheere, 1931; C. Carrier, 1963; A. E. Watts (Penguin ed.), revised ed., 1966; J. P. McCulloch, 1972; R. Musker, 1972; J. Warden, 1972. On Ezra Pound's adaptations *see* J. P. Sullivan, Ezra Pound and Sextus Propertius, 1965.
ABOUT—D. R. Shackleton-Bailey, Propertiana, 1956; G. Luck, The Latin Love Elegy, 2nd ed., 1969; M. Hubbard, Propertius, 1974; W. Eisenhut, Properz, 1975; J. P. Sullivan, Propertius: A Critical Introduction, 1976; M. Bigaroni and F. Santucci, eds., Colloqui-

um Propertianum (Assisi, 1976), 1977; A. La Penna, L'integrazione difficile: Un profilo di Properzio, 1977; E. Wistrand, Miscellanea Propertiana, 1977.

PROTAGORAS, Greek thinker, teacher and writer, was born in about 490 and died after 421 B.C. (or possibly a decade later). His birthplace was Abdera in Thrace (northeastern Greece). He was the earliest and most famous of the Greek sophists. The word *sophistes* originally denoted a wise man *(sophos)* or expert, but by the fifth century B.C. the term had come to denote simply a professional teacher, usually itinerant, who gave instruction in a variety of subjects in return for fees, thus filling the gap left by the absence of an adequate school system. For forty years Protagoras practiced this occupation, with great success. His widespread travels included a visit to Sicily, and he probably went often to Athens. In the course of these travels, he delivered both carefully prepared orations and improvised addresses, sometimes lecturing in public but more often conducting private courses. Like other sophists, however, he did not employ his oratorical talents to impart a philosophical system but rather to convey techniques that would enable his listeners to succeed in their lives.

Protagoras' particular claim was that he could teach the art of politics; and, as a friend of the leading statesman Pericles (who died in 429), he became influential at Athens. When the Panhellenic colony of Thurii was founded by Athenian initiatives in 444, he was chosen by Pericles to draw up its code of laws. It was said that at Athens a certain Pythodorus, who represented the conservative, oligarchic reaction to the sophists, threatened to prosecute Protagoras for impiety; his books, according to this tradition, were publicly burned, and he himself only escaped legal action by setting sail again for Sicily; but his ship was wrecked on the way and he was drowned. These stories about his downfall and death have sometimes been regarded as inventions by later writers; but they may be well founded.

The importance of the spoken word in the

prō tag′ ō ràs

teaching of Protagoras and other sophists did not prevent them from publishing books about their doctrines: most of these works have now disappeared, however, largely because enemies of their movement were able to suppress them. Diogenes Laertius, biographer of the third century A.D., lists numerous monographs ascribed to Protagoras' authorship, though it is likely that some of these titles refer not to independent writings but to self-contained sections of his larger works. *On the Gods* was said to be the first of his treatises that he read in public. It began with the following words: "I know nothing about the gods, either that they are or that they are not, or how they are shaped. For many things prevent sure knowledge— the obscurity of the subject and the brevity of human life." This does not necessarily mean that Protagoras was a thoroughgoing atheist, for he may well have shrunk from such a far-reaching deduction: but the statement shows that he must at least have been an agnostic and explains why he was accused of impiety in later years (or why subsequent authors imagined that such a charge must have been made). The list of his writings also includes a study entitled *On Hell*, which was probably intended to dispel the traditional terrors of the afterlife as unfounded.

Protagoras also laid down his principles as a political educator in an essay entitled *Truth or Refutations*. It began with the epoch-making statement: "The human individual is the measure of all things: of things that are, that they are; and of things that are not, that they are not." This is an assertion of total relativism and subjectivity in regard to all human value judgments. His radical followers took this theory to its logical and practical conclusion by insisting that every kind of orthodoxy, including all traditional authority, must be subject to continual reexamination.

Protagoras himself confronted some of the consequences of his doctrine in a monograph entitled *On the Original Condition of Mankind* (the principal features of which are given, apparently in a reliable form, in the dialogue by Plato that is named after him). In this work, Protagoras offered a story *(mythos)*—so-called in order to dis-claim the authority of a reasoned statement or *logos*—in which he outlined an account of the origin of civilization: since primitive human beings were less well equipped than wild animals in the struggle for survival, Zeus ordered Hermes to bring them morality and a sense of justice, which opened the way to political and cultural evolution. Unlike Hesiod, whose *Works and Days* had drawn a picture of incessant degeneration in the world, the sophists felt an optimistic assurance of progress. Nevertheless, although Protagoras believed that a moral sense had thus been implanted in each of us, he also maintained that this innate virtuous tendency has to be reinforced and developed by education. Indeed, that was the conviction that inspired and justified his whole career—and enabled him, in practice, to make his peace, at any rate for most of his life, with the established order that his other theories seemed to undermine.

He also wrote a work known as the *Antilogiae (Contradictions),* in two books. According to Diogenes Laertius, he suggested that on every topic there are two potential arguments, one for and one against. This doctrine of "speech both ways" mirrored a general belief that humankind lives in a world full of such antithetical possibilities. But it could also reflect the suggestion that a speaker has it in his power to make the weaker statement the stronger—and, moreover, proceeding to a more cynical conclusion still, to make the worse case the better. Once again, Protagoras himself, being basically less radical in his political and social attitudes than his theoretical thinking would suggest, did not carry this doctrine to its ultimate nihilist conclusions: but, in this respect too, his followers did not hesitate to do just that.

EDITIONS—H. Diels and W. Krantz, Fragmente der Vorsokratiker, 11th ed., v 2, 1965; M. Untersteiner, I sofisti: Testimonianze e frammenti, v 2, 1967. *Translations*—R. K. Sprague, The Older Sophists, 1972. ABOUT—M. Untersteiner, The Sophists, 1954; A. Capizzi, Protagora, 1955; G. Kennedy, The Art of Persuasion in Greece, 1963; W. K. C. Guthrie, History of Greek Philosophy, v 3, 1969; C. J. Classen, ed., Sophistik, 1976; K. M. Dietz, Protagoras von Abdera, 1976. Also, *see* editions of Plato's Protagoras.

PRUDENTIUS, Latin poet, was born in A.D. 348 in Nearer Spain, probably at Caesaraugusta (Saragossa). He died sometime after 405. In his youth, he studied rhetoric, but, according to his own account, devoted his time largely to dissipation. Then he practiced at the bar and then became the governor of two successive provinces. Subsequently the emperor Theodosius I (A.D. 379–95) gave him a post at court. Tiring of worldly life, however, in about 392, he turned to writing poems on Christian subjects, publishing a collection of them in 405 with an autobiographical preface in which he announced his intention of dedicating himself henceforward to the service of God.

His poetry was of various types. The *Cathemerinon* (Hymns for the Day) are twelve substantial lyric poems. Although extracts from them have found their way into modern hymnals and his "Hymn for the Burial of the Dead" has attracted particular admiration, these pieces, which contain substantial extracts and paraphrases from the Bible, are too long to have been designed for congregational singing. Prudentius' aim, one of considerable originality, was to divorce the hymn from a purely liturgical purpose and transform it into a work of literature. The *Peristephanon* is a collection of fourteen long pieces composed to celebrate the martyrs of his native Spain and those of northern Africa and Rome, to whom, between 401 and 403, he paid the visits that inspired the composition of these poems. The writing is vivid but lapses from time to time into passages of polemical rhetoric and tasteless ghoulishness. The *Peristephanon* is important because it describes the guidelines of the martyr cult. It is also significant from a literary point of view, because its amalgamation of epic and lyric foreshadows the ballad.

The *Cathemerinon* and *Peristephanon* are written in a variety of lyric meters. The remaining five poems of Prudentius, however, are in hexameters; and their character is didactic. The *Apotheosis,* more than a thousand lines long, is concerned with the divinity of Christ and the nature of the Trinity; it assails in succession the views of various Christian sects denounced as heretical and

prōō den' shi us

367

condemns the beliefs of Jews and Manichaeans as well. The *Birth of Evil (Hamartigenia)* is an attack on the second century Gnostic theologian Marcion who had evolved the dualist doctrine of two Gods, one the Creator and Judge, the other the deity revealed by Jesus. *The Soul's Conflict (Psychomachia),* a Virgilian epic of the struggles between personified Virtues and Vices, is the least successful of Prudentius' works as a literary achievement—but also the most influential, for it was the first poetical Christian allegory and became enormously popular in the Middle Ages, serving the artists of the period as a much-used source book. Another work of reference medieval painters found useful was the *Dittochaeon* (the authorship of which has sometimes been disputed), a collection of forty-nine pieces, consisting of four hexameters each, which set out to explain the wall paintings in a Roman church, including twenty-four themes from the Old Testament and twenty-five from the New; the treatise is valuable for art historians and students of Christian iconography.

Prudentius' work entitled *Against Symmachus,* in two books, was written in refutation of the demands by the Roman senator Quintus Aurelius Symmachus, a zealous proponent of paganism, that the altar of Victory should be restored to its traditional place in the Senate house (384), a key issue in the continuing struggle between Christianity and paganism. *Against Symmachus* was written nearly twenty years after this event; Book I is an attack on the pagan religion, including its polytheism, its myths, its astrology, and the worship of the Sun. Symmachus himself receives respectful treatment, but the second book addresses itself to a refutation of his appeal, on grounds as patriotic as Symmachus' own: Change, maintains Prudentius, does not mean the denial or downfall of the genius of Rome. In this work, he probably comes nearer than any other ancient writer to achieving an authentic symbiosis between the two conflicting ideals; just as the literary form he adopts, though abounding in echoes of the pagan poets, gives equal space to biblical allusions and clothes Christian material in classical literary form.

368

EDITIONS—J. Bergman, Corpus Scriptorum Ecclesias ticorum Latinorum, v 61, 1926; M. P. Cunningham Aurelii Prudentii Clementis Carmina, 1966. *With trans lation:* H. J. Thomson (Loeb ed.), 1953; M. Lavarenn (Budé ed.), 1943–51.

ABOUT—M. Laverenne, Étude sur la langue du poèt Prudence, 1933; A. Salvatore, Studi prudenziani, 1958 K. Thraede, Studien zu Sprache und Stil des Prudent us, 1965; R. Hertzog, Die allegorische Dichtkunst de Prudentius, 1966; M. M. van Assendelft, Sol Ecce Su git Igneus: Commentary on the Morning and Evenin Hymns of Prudentius, 1976; M. Smith, Prudentiu Psychomathia: A Reexamination, 1976.

PTOLEMY (Claudius Ptolemaeus), Gree astronomer, mathematician, and geogra pher, was born in Ptolemais Hermiou in Up per Egypt. Some of his astronomica observations were carried out between A.D 127 and 145/8, and on the strength of a Arab tradition that he lived to the age of 7 it has been tentatively suggested that he wa born in about 100 and died in about 178. H lived in Alexandria.

The most famous of Ptolemy's writing was his astronomical work the *Mathemati cal Collection (Mathematike Syntaxis),* late known as *The Great Astronomer* to distin guish it from a collection of other as tronomical works described as *The Littl Astronomer.* It is, however, to its later de scription by Arabian astronomers as *megist* ("the greatest") that this treatise owes it more generally employed title, the *Almages* The work contains thirteen books and run to over twelve hundred pages in the moder Teubner edition. Book I outlines the geocen tric system of the universe, which Ptolem inherited from Hipparchus (whose views ar chiefly known to us through this work) an rejects the heliocentric theory of Aristar chus, which was not revived until the tim of Copernicus (1473–1543). After an essa on spherical trigonometry, the next Book discuss the motions of the sun and moo (pointing out discrepancies between the ac tual positions and those assumed by the cur rent theories) and the lengths of the year an month. Instructions are also provided fo the construction of an astrolabe. Book treats of eclipses of the sun and moon, an Books 7 and 8 deal with the fixed stars. Th

tol' e mi

ast five books discuss the planets. Despite his thoroughgoing geocentric viewpoint, Ptolemy related their motions to that of the sun, which thus appears as something more than a body rotating around the earth, among six other bodies.

The most comprehensive astronomical treatise that has come down to us from antiquity, the *Almagest* is a lucid and well ordered synthesis, compiled by a practicing astronomer who knew how to make good use of both his own observations and the conclusions reached by other astronomers before him. It rapidly became a standard work and was made the subject of numerous commentaries and translations, retaining this preeminent position for more than a millennium in the Byzantine empire, the Islamic world, and medieval Europe. The first edition of the Greek text was published at Basel in 1538.

Ptolemy also wrote a number of other monographs on astronomical themes. These included a general description of his system, a series of astronomical tables (surviving only in a revised version), a list of constants (*Canobic Inscription*), an essay in two books (of which only one is extant) on the times of the risings and settings of important fixed stars (together with weather indications), and descriptions of the theoretical bases of the astrolabe *(Planisphaerium)* and sundials *(Analemma)*. Another work provided a scientific foundation of astrology (the *Apotelesmatika* or *Tetrabiblos*); it may be regarded as a sort of appendix to the *Almagest* —and it became almost as famous.

Ptolemy was also a geometrician of impressive caliber; the theorem named after him, which deals with a quadrilateral inscribed in a circle, is once again based on researches by Hipparchus, but Ptolemy presents them and refines them with admirable lucidity and conciseness. Early commentators also credit him with another geometrical essay, *On Dimension,* which sought to prove that there cannot be more than three spatial dimensions; and in addition he apparently wrote three works on mechanics, of which one title, *On Balancings,* has come down to us. In the field of music, a work entitled *Harmonica,* in three books, expounds the mathematical theory of harmo-

ny. Of Ptolemy's *Optics* we have only Books 2-5 in a Latin version translated from the Arabic; the treatment shows a considerable advance on Euclid.

Equal in fame to the *Almagest* is Ptolemy's *Guide to Geography (Geographike Huphegesis),* divided into seven books. The first of them, after a general introduction, offers amendments, based on astronomical observations, to the findings of Marinus of Tyre, who lived earlier in the second century A.D. A discussion of maps follows, with instructions on how to make them. The remaining six books offer a list of places, tabulated by longitude and latitude, and are accompanied by Ptolemy's famous maps (Book 8). First (Book 2) come Europe and the Mediterranean, then Africa and Asia. References are given to no less than eight thousand locations, but only a small proportion of these data is founded on exact observation, and the work includes many fundamental mistakes, as well as a number of internal contradictions; then, too, Ptolemy's treatment of many matters (including rivers and mountain ranges) is negligent and careless. Nevertheless, no one in the ancient world ever wrote a geographical survey that achieved greater accuracy, or a more comprehensive one either; and in consequence the work remained canonical until modern times. Moreover, one of Ptolemy's errors, his belief that Asia stretched much farther eastward than is in fact the case, exercised remarkable influence, since it encouraged Christopher Columbus' conviction that China could be reached more easily by sailing toward the west.

EDITIONS—J. L. Heiberg, 1898–1907. Catalogue of Stars: E. B. Knobel and C. H. F. Peters, 1915. Optica: A. Lejeune, 1956. Guide to Geography: C. T. Fischer and C. Müller, 1883–1901. *With translation:* Almagest: R. C. Tagliaferro and C. G. Wallis (with versions of Copernicus and Kepler), 1952; G. J. Toomer, 1978; K. Manitius (German), revised ed., 1963. Tetrabiblos: F. E. Robbins *in* W. G. Waddell and F. E. Robbins, Manetho, Aegyptiaca and Ptolemy, Tetrabiblos (Loeb ed.), 1940.
ABOUT—P. Luckey, Das Analemma von Ptolemäus, 1927; T. L. Heath, Manual of Greek Mathematics, 1931, reprint 1963; J. O. Thomson, History of Ancient Geography, 1948; W. H. Stahl, Ptolemy's Geography: A Select Bibliography, 1953; O. Neugebauer, The Ex-

act Sciences in Antiquity, 2nd ed., 1957; G. E. R. Lloyd, Greek Science After Aristotle, 1973.

PUBLILIUS SYRUS, composer of Latin mimes, was born a slave in the first century B.C. His native land was Syria, as his name shows, and his hometown may have been Antioch. He came to Rome, where he obtained freedom from slavery and in about 46 B.C. started his career as a producer of Latin mimes—sketches or playlets, of Greek origin, in which the actors used their voices, features, and gestures to present short and frequently indecent scenes from daily life or mythology, accompanied by farcical imitations and spectacular dances and acrobatics. The actors did not wear masks, and (unlike performers in other forms of drama) women played the female parts. The mimes associated with the name of Publilius—that is, those produced under his management and partly (at least) of his authorship—were of the kind that depended less on literary composition than on improvisation and clever acting. His one rival was an older man, Laberius. Julius Caesar once compelled the two playwrights to compete on the stage. This gave Publilius the advantage, because the performance, being extemporaneous, was better suited to his talents than to those of his rival, who preferred more careful preparation; and, in addition, Laberius felt humiliated by the occasion because he was a Roman knight.

We know the titles of two of Publilius' mimes, *The Pruners (Putatores)* and the *Myrmidon.* The improvised character of their plots and speeches made it difficult to preserve them with any completeness, although numerous attempts were made to do so, and versified aphorisms early began to circulate under his name. Their terse neatness (praised by Aulus Gellius in the second century A.D.) often serves merely to convey a platitude, but at other times it confirms the elder Seneca's observation that their author could express some thoughts better than any other dramatist (a verdict that did not receive the agreement of Cicero, who regarded mimes as tedious).

If there was a message in the mimes of

pub li′ li us si′ rus

Publilius, it was that people should see to their own self-interest before anything else. But in spite of this anti-social attitude, and in spite also of a rich infusion of pornography, selections of his epigrams were brought together in order to provide proverbial wisdom for schoolchildren; St. Jerome remembered one of them from his schooldays in the fourth century A.D. Lists were made of these sayings in alphabetical order; and Publilius was one of the authors quoted by the English ecclesiastical leader and classical scholar John of Salisbury in the twelfth century and by the Welsh ecclesiastical scholar Giraldus Cambrensis not long afterward. Editions, of which there have been many, muster some seven hundred lines, though a number of them may be later interpolations.

EDITIONS—R. A. H. Bickford-Smith, Publilii Syri Sententiae, 1895. *With translation:* J. W. Duff and A. M. Duff, Minor Latin Poets (Loeb ed.), revised ed., 1935. ABOUT—O. Skutsch, Pauly-Wissowa-Kroll, Real-Encyclopädie der klassischen Altertumswissenschaft, v 23, 1959, columns 1920–29; F. Giancotti, Mimo e gnome: Studi su Decimo Laberio e Publilio Siro, 1967; W. Beare, The Roman Stage, 3rd ed., 1969.

PYRRHO. See Sextus Empiricus

PYTHAGORAS. See Archytas; Plato

PYTHEAS, Greek explorer and geographer, was active at the end of the fourth century B.C. His birthplace was Massalia (Marseille, in southern France). At about the time when Alexander the Great was conquering Asia (334–323), Pytheas made a remarkable journey all over northwestern and northern Europe, circumnavigating Britain and even reaching the borders of the Arctic zone. Ancient authorities (notably Polybius and Strabo) doubted the feat, regarding it as incredible.

His treatise entitled *On the Ocean* is lost, but some impression of its contents can be derived from later geographers, who use it extensively; however, it remains impossible

pith′ ē ås

to say how the work was constructed—or to give particulars of the extent of Pytheas' travels. It is clear, nevertheless, that he described the inhabitants and climate of Britain, that he reported on the island of Thule (variously identified with Norway and, less probably, Iceland), and that he referred to an island rich in amber, which may be Heligoland.

Pytheas closely calculated the latitude of Massalia and gave estimates for the parallels of other places he passed in his journey. He was able to deduce that the moon affects the tides and made notes (not always easy to understand) on the varying lengths of the longest day, and he calculated the ratio of the hand of a sundial to its shadow at the summer solstice. He also provided a number of careful observations on regional customs, such as the use of threshing barns and the composition of local drinks made of cereals and honey. If his measurements of distances were shaky, and if, as his ancient critics remarked, he believed far too readily in fables, such as the story of a Stagnant Sea at the northern extremity of the world, he nevertheless laid a powerful foundation for geographers of future times.

ABOUT—M. Cary and E. H. Warmington, The Ancient Explorers, 2nd ed., 1963; C. F. C. Hawkes, Pytheas: Europe and the Greek Explorers, 1975. Also *see* bibliography *in* Oxford Classical Dictionary, 2nd ed., 1970, p 904.

QUINTILIAN (Marcus Fabius Quintilianus), Latin educationalist and literary critic, c. A.D. 35–c. 100, was born at Calagurris (Calahorra) in Spain. In his early years he went to Rome, where at least part of his training was undertaken by the advocate Cnaeus Domitius Afer (d. 59). At some period, he returned to Spain but joined the entourage of the new emperor Galba in 68 and, in his company, went back to Rome again. There he became a well-known and prosperous teacher of rhetoric and was probably the first professor of the subject to receive a salary from public funds, supplied by Vespasian (69–79). At the same time, Quintilian practiced advocacy in the law

kwin til' yən

courts. In about 88, he retired to devote himself to writing. Domitian subsequently made him tutor to his two grandnephews, who were at that time prospective heirs to the throne; and he was awarded the consular insignia. His later years were darkened by the deaths first of his eighteen-year-old wife and then of their two young sons.

His great work was *The Education of an Orator (Institutio Oratoria),* composed and probably published before Domitian's death in 96. Its twelve books seek to provide a comprehensive educational program from first steps until maturity. After a long introduction, Book I starts with the pupil in his infancy and goes through his childhood education, taking a sensible and humane line that still seems valid and convincing today. The book concludes with a careful discussion of grammar and language. In Book 2 the boy is admitted to the school of rhetoric, which Quintilian sets out to justify as a science and fine art fit to serve as the basis of Roman education, defining its aims, discussing suitable exercises, and delivering a famous definition of what constitutes a good schoolteacher. The third book gives an account of the origins of rhetoric and indicates its subdivisions and their functions. The structure of speeches is analysed in Books 4 to 6, the last of which also includes interesting sections on how to appeal to the listener's emotions and sense of humor. Book 7 deals with arrangement, and Book 8 with style, the discussion of which continues in Book 9, where analyses of figures of speech and structure and rhythm are offered. The tenth book, the most famous in the eyes of posterity, offers a review of a wide range of Greek and Latin authors. Quintilian's comments are always well worth noting; some strange emphases and omissions are accounted for by the particular purpose of this reading list, which is specifically designed as a contribution toward the training of an orator. The eleventh book emphasizes the powers of memory the orator needs to possess and adds a disquisition on delivery, clothing, and gestures. Book 12 assesses the ethics of the profession and accepts Cato the Elder's definition of the complete orator as "a good man, skilled in speaking"—a person, that is to say, who does not only know how to speak, but possesses the loftiest character and ideals—in short, the best possible type of Roman.

Quintilian is competent and discriminating; and his humanity and sincerity are apparent throughout his work. While depending extensively on his numerous forerunners, he contributes a consistent individuality that is his own. His style, while displaying many traits of the Silver Latin of the age, is practical, lucid, and firm. A sensible and moderate summing-up of the system of classical education, the *Institutio* transmitted a tradition that was not seriously modified for hundreds of years to come.

In the twelfth century, Quintilian appeared in the reading lists of English classical scholars Alexander Neckam and John of Salisbury. But the period of his greatest influence still lay ahead. Petrarch's copy, though incomplete, appealed to its owner's interest in the training of a dominant elite; and in the Renaissance the *Institutio* became the standard textbook of pioneer humanist schools and literary academies. The work was first printed in 1470 at Rome, and greatly influenced the Dutch scholar Erasmus (1466?–1536).

Quintilian also wrote a treatise on the causes of the decline of oratory, and a speech in defense of the Jewish queen Berenice (the mistress of the emperor Titus) on some unknown charge; another speech defended a woman charged with forging her husband's will. These, however, are now lost. Two volumes of rhetorical exercises *(Declamationes)* that survive may be transcripts of his lecture courses, since these, as he tells us himself, were published by his pupils without his authorization; and, if such is their origin, they do not necessarily reflect his views.

EDITIONS—L. Radermacher and V. Buchheit, 1959; Corpus Iuris Romani Publici, 1977. *With translation:* H. E. Butler (Loeb ed.), 1920–22; H. Rahn (German), 1972–75; J. Cousin (Budé ed.), 1975– ; G. Garuti (Italian), 1977.
ABOUT—J. Cousin, Études sur Quintilien, 1936, 1975; G. G. Bianca, La pedagogia di Quintiliano, 1963; R. Farandra, ed., Quintiliano: L'Istituzione oratoria, 1968; G. Kennedy, Quintilian, 1969 *and* The Art of Rhetoric in the Roman World, 1972; M. Winterbottom, ed., Problems in Quintilian, 1970 *and* Quintilian, *in* T. A. Dorey, ed., Empire and Aftermath (Silver Latin, v 2), 1975; F. R. Varwig, Der rhetorische Naturbegriff bei Quintilian, 1976; O. Seel, Quintilian oder Die Kunst des Redens und Schweigens, 1977.

RABANUS. See Hrabanus Maurus, Magnentius

RATHER (Ratherius), Latin churchman and scholar, was born at Liège (Belgium) in A.D. 890, received his education at Lobbes, where he learned good Latin and became abbot, moved to Italy with Bishop Ildoin, and was appointed by Hugh of Arles to the bishopric of Verona (at a moment when Rather was apparently dying of a grave illness). However, he subsequently turned against Hugh to support Arnold of Bavaria, whereupon, after Arnold's defeat, he was arrested and exiled to Pavia. Reappointed to the Verona see, he proved an unpopular choice and had to retire hastily for a second time. Next he joined the household of the Saxon prince (and later saint) Bruno, brother of the emperor Otto I the Great; when Bruno became archbishop of Cologne (Köln), Rather was made bishop of his own hometown Liège. Once again, however, his subordinates revolted, and he had to withdraw, receiving the bishopric of Verona (at the hand of Otto) for the third time and for the third time suffering ejection soon afterward. Henceforward, he seems to have been without a see.

During his period of banishment at Pavia, Rather wrote the *Meditations of the Heart* (or *Praeloquia* or *Agnosticum*), which sets out rules for living to men and women in a great variety of occupations and social levels. The first of its six books covers nineteen different trades, beginning with the soldier and concluding with the beggar. The second considers the various stages of life—father, mother, grandparent, husband, wife, and so on. The next two books provide a lengthy discussion on the duties of monarchs, after which similar treatment is accorded to ecclesiastics, and especially bishops. Rather expresses a low opinion of his Italian col-

rä′ ᵗʰēr

leagues, whom he regards as extravagant and frivolous.

Similar invectives occur in his other works as well. These include the *Phrenesis;* essays entitled *On Idle Talk* and *On Discord;* the *Dialogus Confessionalis,* which is a lucid and pitiless examination of his own conscience; a small number of epistles that constitute an intimate, vituperative journal rather than actual correspondence; and thirteen *Sermons,* crammed with varied material, to which he apparently dedicated his last years. At Verona, Rather came upon a manuscript of Catullus (first century B.C.) and played an important part in the establishment of the poet's medieval reputation—and that of the historian Livy (B.C. 59–17 A.D.) too. He also enjoyed reading Plautus, the great Roman writer of comedy. Indeed, although he wrote Latin in a tortuous, crabbed style and devoted much of his energy to endless, intemperate strife with his superiors and subordinates alike, he was one of the major scholars of his age.

EDITIONS—J. P. Migne, Patrologia Latina, v 139; F. Wiegle, Letters, 1949; P. L. D. Reid, Opera Minora, 1976.
ABOUT—R. R. Bolgar, The Classical Heritage and Its Beneficiaries, 1954; V. Cavaliari, Raterio e Verona, 1954; H. M. Klinkenberg, Versuche und Untersuchungen zur Autobiographie bei Rather von Verona, 1956; B. R. Reece, Learning in the Tenth Century, 1972.

RHABANUS. See Hrabanus Maurus, Magnentius

RHIANUS

RHIANUS, Greek poet and scholar, was born in the first half of the third century B.C. He came from some place in Crete—either Bene or, less probably, Ceraea. Born a slave, he had a job in a wrestling school but succeeded in obtaining an education and adopted a literary career, probably at Alexandria.

Rhianus became best known as a writer of epics, now only surviving in fragments. One such poem was the *Heracleias,* describing, in fourteen books, the feats of Heracles. Four other pieces were named after Greek territories, the *Thessalica* (in sixteen books), rī ā′ nus

Achaica, Eliaca, and *Messenica.* The last-named, dealing with Sparta's Second Messenian War of the seventh century B.C., took the Spartan Aristomenes as its hero and provided romantic accounts of his escape from prison and of a love affair that brought disaster to the Messenians.

Rhianus' longest surviving fragment, which may perhaps be a separate and complete piece, comprises twenty-one strongly composed, unadorned hexameters about the folly of mankind. He was also active as a dramatist and wrote a number of epigrams, a dozen or so of which have been preserved in the Greek Anthology. They are well written but deal with no more than conventional love themes, displaying a special interest in the love of boys.

He also produced an edition of the *Iliad* and *Odyssey* that was, to judge from the forty-five surviving excerpts, of competent quality, though somewhat conservative.

EDITIONS—J. U. Powell, Collectanea Alexandrina, 1925; F. Jacoby, Die Fragmente der griechischen Historiker, 265; A. S. F. Gow and D. L. Page, The Greek Anthology: Hellenistic Epigrams, 1965.
ABOUT—C. Mayhoff, De Rhiani Studiis Homericis, 1870; J. Kroymann, Pausanias und Rhianos, 1943; M. M. Kokolakis, Rhianus the Cretan (in Greek), 1968.

RHINTHON

RHINTHON, Greek comic playwright, was active in about 300 B.C. He was the son of a potter from Taras (Taranto) in southeastern Italy.

His speciality was the "merry tragedy" *(hilarotragoidia)* or phlyax play (from *phluax, phluaros,* silly talk), a genre so closely associated with his name that the Romans called it the *fabula Rhinthonica.* These compositions were farces in the Doric dialect, performed by a small company. They presented ludicrous, versified scenes from daily life; and vases and statuettes depicting the characters from these phlyax plays show that travesties of myth also comprised a favorite theme. The performers, who were masked, wore enormous phalli and costumes grotesquely padded in stomach and buttocks. The stages on which these displays rin′ thon

373

were enacted seem to have been platforms put up specially for the occasion.

Nossis, a poet from Locri in southern Italy, was a contemporary of Rhinthon. She wrote his epitaph, describing him as a man of Syracuse—which presumably means that he resided at that city at some time—and praising him for the innovation of "tragic phlyakes." That is to say, he evidently endowed a crude dramatic form with a somewhat more literary and cultural character than it had possessed before, raising the tone by the use of tragic themes as the targets of his parody. Out of thirty-eight pieces ascribed to his authorship extremely few fragments survive. However, nine titles are known: among them *Heracles, Iphigenia in Aulis, Iphigenia in Tauris, Medea,* and *Orestes.* In all of these cases, it is evident that the tragedian selected for parodying is Euripides, whose popularity was so great in Hellenistic times. Rhinthon also composed an *Amphitryon.*

There must have been a good deal of similarity between the themes of these phlyax sketches and those of formal comedy; the two genres also had a lot in common with the various sorts of mime, to which, indeed, they probably owed many features of their development. Epicharmus, the Sicilian comic dramatist of the fifth century B.C., has also been supposed to have exercised a strong influence on the phlyax plays. They were particularly popular at Taras but also flourished in southern Italy (notably at Posidonia or Paestum) where they may have played a part in the evolution of the native Italian farce, the *fabula Atellana.* But they also appear to have been performed at Alexandria, where Sopater of Paphos is mentioned as one of their authors; a passage from his work *The Gauls*—our longest surviving phlyax fragment—shows a process of development from buffoonery to a more philosophical type of satire.

EDITIONS—E. Völker, Rhinthonis Fragmenta, 1887; G. Kaibel, Comicorum Graecorum Fragmenta, 1899; A. Olivieri, Frammenti della commedia greca e del mimo nella Sicilia e nella Magna Grecia, v 2, 2nd ed., 1947.
ABOUT: A. D. Trendall, The Phlyax Vases (Bulletin of the Institute of Classical Studies, Suppl. Paper 8), re-vised ed., 1967; M. Gigante, Rintone e il teatro in Magna Grecia, 1971.

ROMANUS THE MELODE, Greek hymn writer of the early Byzantine period (early 6th century A.D.), was born of Jewish parents at Emesa (Homs) in Syria and became a deacon at Berytus (Beirut in Lebanon). In the reign of Anastasius I (493–518), he moved to Constantinople, where he served as a priest at one of the churches and later composed a great number of hymns, said to have totaled more than a thousand; approximately eighty of these, mostly dating, it would appear, from the reign of Justinian I (527–65), have survived (although there are many arguments about authenticity).

Their subjects cover an extensive range, including the life of Joseph and other Old Testament stories, as well as episodes from the New Testament, such as Judas' Betrayal, the Denials of Peter, and Mary at the Cross. Romanus also wrote hymns about the careers of prophets and saints and in celebration of Easter and Christmas. Christmas inspired his famous piece "Today the Virgin Brings Forth the Supersubstantial." (The Akathistos Hymn, the most famous hymn of the Greek church, written for the feast of the Annunciation, has also been ascribed to his authorship—but without any certainty).

Romanus was the supreme master of the most characteristic achievement of Byzantine hymnography, the *kontakion.* The earliest form of Byzantine hymn had been the *troparion,* a short stanza of rhythmic responses, inserted after each of the last six (or three) verses of a psalm. The *kontakion* was an expansion of the *troparion* and consisted of twenty or more stanzas, each a self-contained unit of sense and melody and accentual rhythm (although images are ingeniously pursued from one stanza to another), including acrostics and passages of colloquial, vivacious dialogue. The *kontakion,* as developed by Romanus, reflected the influence of the church of his native Syria, where Saint Ephraim, in the fourth century, had dramatized Bible stories in his Syriac hymns and introduced vigorous dialogues that pro-
rō mä' nus me lōd'

foundly influenced Romanus' usage.

Romanus has been described as the outstanding poet of the Byzantine epoch, "the Dante of the neo-Hellenes," and the greatest Christian hymnographer of all time. The powerfully dramatic structure of his long hymns was reinforced by profound feeling and by language that, although lucid and simple, makes extensive use of assonance, wordplay, and rhyme. But Romanus also indulged in substantial dogmatic digressions (notably on Jewish history and the ethical conditions of the east), and engaged in prolonged polemical onslaughts on pagans and heretics (Monophysites and Nestorians); these are features that tend to distract modern readers from his poetic gifts. His poetry aside, it is impossible to judge his achievement as a hymnographer with any degree of accuracy, since the music has not come down to us. Their oratorio-like content suggests that they were rendered in a sort of recitative, in which the congregation joined.

EDITIONS—N. B. Tomadakis, 1952–61; P. Maas and C. A. Trypanis, 1964 (dubious and spurious hymns in 1970). *With translation* (of some hymns): J. M. Neale, Hymns of the Eastern Church, 2nd ed., 1863; H. J. W. Tillyard, Byzantine Music and Hymnography, 1923; J. Grosdidier de Matous (French), 1964–66.
ABOUT—G. Cammelli, Romano il Melode, 1930; E. Mioni, Romano il Melode, 1937; E. Wellesz, A History of Byzantine Music and Hymnography, 3rd ed., 1962; C. A. Trypanis, Romanos the Melodist: The Orthodox Ethos, 1966; K. Mitsakis, The Language of Romanos the Melodist, 1967; M. Carpenter, The Kontakia of Romanus, Byzantine Melodist, 1972; E. Topping, the Apostle Peter, Justinian and Romanos the Melodos (Byzantine and Modern Greek Studies, v 2), 1976.

ROSWITHA. See Hroswitha

RUFUS, LUCIUS VARIUS. See Varius Rufus, Lucius

RUFUS, QUINTUS CURTIUS. See Curtius Rufus, Quintus

RUTILIUS NAMATIANUS, Latin poet, was born in the latter part of the fourth century A.D. in southern Gaul, probably at Tolosa (Toulouse). It is not known when he died. He was a member of one of the rich Gallo-Roman land-owning families that played a preeminent part in the western Roman empire during these final decades of its existence. Rutilius himself, although a pagan, held the highest offices under the emperor Honorius, who made him one of his principal secretaries of state *(magister officiorum)* (412) and prefect of the city of Rome (414), a post his father Lachanius had held before him. Two years later he left Rome to return to estates in Gaul that had been pillaged by German invaders. From his own words it seems that he was very reluctant to leave Rome, so that it may be conjectured that he had fallen into imperial disfavor.

Since the overland route had become perilous owing to the invasion of the Goths, he decided to travel by sea; and he has left us a description of his journey, *The Return Home, or The Gallic Journey (De Reditu Suo sive Iter Gallicum).* Written in the elegiac meter, it consists of six hundred forty-four lines of a first book and the abruptly cut-off beginning of a second (a new fragment of which has recently come to light). The poem is in the form of a journal covering a two-month period starting in September or October A.D. 416. In his introduction Rutilius offers a stirring farewell to Rome, which he continues to praise for a hundred lines, eulogizing its temples and aqueducts and engineering feats and calling upon it to arise and strike down the Goths (who had sacked the city in 410) as it had struck down the Gauls when they, too, had come on a raid eight hundred years earlier. After proceeding to the port of Rome near Ostia, where he sadly parts from his friends, Rutilius takes ship and sails up past the shore of Etruria, the coastal scenery of which he depicts with rhetorical vividness.

The stages of the voyage are Centumcellae (Civitavecchia), Portus Herculis (Port'Ercole), and an anchorage at the mouth of the river Umbro (Ombrone). The sight of the island of Ilva (Elba) inspires him to expatiate on the virtues of the iron it pro-
rōō ti′ li us nȧ má ti ä′ nus

375

duces, which seems to him more beneficial than gold. At Faleriae (the medieval Porto Falese), the traveler's arrival coincides with a festival of Osiris, during which his annoyance at an avaricious Jewish innkeeper prompts the poet to attack the rituals and beliefs of that faith.

At the port of Populonia, the passengers receive news from Rome, and on the fifth day of their journey they catch sight of Corsica and, half way between Corsica and the mainland, glimpse the isle of Capraria (Capraia), whose monks Rutilius castigates for living dreary and useless lives. At Vada Volterrana he calls on his friend Albinus and describes the working of the salt pans nearby. The ship passes Gorgon Island (Gorgona), which has unhappy memories for Rutilius because a young nobleman had recently gone there to lead the existence of a hermit. At Pisae (Pisa) he visits a friend, sees a statue of his own father, and takes part in a boar hunt; and Book 1 concludes with an account of a storm. The fragmentary second book takes him only as far as Luna (Luni), where he describes the local marble quarries, adding a general account of Italy's salient geographical features and inserting an attack on the emperor's former minister Stilicho (d. 408).

Rutilius is an accomplished poet with a sharp eye and a keen interest in all he encounters; and his likes and dislikes are strong. Written in Latin of unusual purity for the period, *The Return Home* throws a vivid light on the thoughts and emotions of the men who were in charge of the speedily disintegrating western empire. His eloquent and heartfelt paean to Rome is all the more arresting for its having been written amid the city's catastrophic decline and its empire's radical metamorphosis, the implications of which are beyond his comprehension.

EDITIONS—R. Helm, 1933; E. Merone, 1955; E. Doblhofer, 1972, 1977. *With translation:* J. W. Duff and A. M. Duff (Loeb ed), revised ed., 1935; J. Vessereau and F. Préchac, Rutilius Namatianus: Sur son retour (Budé ed.), 1933; E. Castorina, Claudio Rutilio Namaziano: De Reditu, 1967.
ABOUT—O. Schissel-Fleschenberg, Claudius Rutilius Namatianus gegen Stilicho, 1920; J. Cirino, L'idea di Roma negli scrittori latini e particolarmente in Rutilio Namaziano, 1934; I. Lana, Rutilio Namaziano, 1961; F. Paschoud, Roma Aeterna, 1967; R. Mellor, Dea Roma, 1976. For the new fragment of the second book *see* M. Ferrara, Atene e Roma (v 18, New Series), 1973, *and* Italia medioevale e umanistica (v 16), 1973.

SALLUST (Gaius Sallustius Crispus), Latin historian, was born in about 86 and died in about 35 B.C. His birthplace was Amiternum (San Vittorino) in the Sabine country (Abruzzi) northeast of Rome, where his family presumably belonged to the local upper class. There are stories of his youthful debauchery but they may to some extent be legendary. Sallust was elected to the junior office of quaestor at Rome in 55. Then, as tribune of the people in 52, he was one of those who, against Cicero, charged the right-wing political gangster Milo with murdering his radical counterpart Clodius. In 50 Sallust was one of a number of people expelled from the Senate by the censors. It was alleged that he had committed adultery with Milo's wife, but, whether this was true or not, his anti-conservative stance during his tribunate had no doubt gained him a number of political enemies. In the Civil War between Caesar and Pompey (49), Sallust again opposed the conservatives (Pompey's allies), siding with Caesar, who made him quaestor for a second time, thus restoring his membership in the Senate. In 48 he commanded a legion in Illyricum (now Yugoslavia) without much success and failed to suppress a mutiny in Campania in the following year. Nevertheless, on appointment as praetor in 46, he took part in Caesar's campaign in northern Africa that culminated in the victory at the battle of Thapsus and this earned him the subsequent appointment as first governor of the new province of Africa Nova (Numidia, now eastern Algeria). On his return to Rome, however, he was prosecuted for extracting illegal gains from his province; and although not brought to trial by Caesar, he retired permanently from public affairs.

He spent the remaining decade of his life on the large estates he had acquired, including the magnificent Sallustian Gardens at Rome, which later became the residence of

sal' ust

emperors. Although, in his writings, he expresses a lofty distaste for public life—explaining that the writing of history is a greatly preferable activity—more oblique remarks suggest that he bore a grudge against Antony, Octavian, and Lepidus (the members of the Second Triumvirate established in 43 B.C. after Caesar's death) for making no move to revive his official career.

His first historical work, probably written shortly after the triumvirs had defeated their Republican enemies at Philippi, was the *Catilinarian War (Bellum Catilinae),* generally known as the *Catiline,* giving an account of the conspiracy launched by that violent aristocrat against the Roman government, more than two decades earlier in 63 B.C. In his introduction, Sallust explains that he is selecting this theme because Catiline's crime had faced the Republic with a threat of an unprecedented kind, coming from inside its own ranks. A description of Catiline's personality follows, and then a summary of Rome's early history and a survey of its subsequent ethical deterioration. Next comes an account of Catiline's alleged (but dubiously historical) first attempts at revolution (66–65 B.C.); and we are given a character sketch of the immoral noblewoman Sempronia, who became one of his followers.

After his defeat in the consular elections in 63, Catiline's projects assumed an unmistakably subversive character, and we learn from Sallust how he began forming private armies in various parts of Italy and plotting arson and assassination in the capital itself. Taxed with these intentions by Cicero, who was one of the consuls in that year, Catiline walked out of the Senate and left Rome to join his rebel camps at Arretium (Arezzo) and Faesulae (Fiesole). Sallust describes Italy's miserable condition—which had won many adherents to this dissident cause. At this point, the conspiracy was revealed to Cicero by Gallic tribesmen on a visit to Rome who reported that the plotters attempted to undermine their loyalty to the government.

Five leading Roman noblemen were found to be implicated and were placed under arrest. The Senate then discussed what was to be done with them; and the main speeches during the debate are reported by Sallust at length. Caesar argued against the infliction of capital punishment, suggesting that instead the conspirators should be kept in confinement in the towns of Italy. Cato the Younger, on the other hand, demanded that they should be put to death, and his view prevailed. The characters of Caesar and Cato, regarded by Sallust as the outstanding personalities of the day, are described and contrasted. The consul Cicero duly arranged the execution of the five plotters, and at the beginning of 62 B.C. at Pistoria (Pistoia) in northern Etruria, Catiline himself was cornered with his army and killed.

The title of Sallust's second historical study, written in c. 41/40 B.C., is the *Jugurthine War,* Rome's war of 111–105 B.C. against Jugurtha, the King of Numidia (Sallust had served as Rome's first governor there). He points out, once again, that his theme is of special significance, first because of the hard-fought military operations and their fluctuating fortunes and secondly because the war involved the first challenge by Romans to the supremacy of their own governing class.

The historian begins by describing Jugurtha's early life and rise to power and his acts of defiance toward Rome. When the Romans finally retaliated by declaring war against Jugurtha, we are told how the corrupt behavior of their own senior officers caused the military operation to peter out. After the king's visit to Rome (in the year 110) to plead his case had failed, Metellus Numidicus, an aristocrat who belonged to the great Caecilian family, was appointed to take the command against him. Metellus gained victories but proved unable to bring the war to an end. In spite of aristocratic opposition, Metellus' lieutenant Marius, a "new" man, gained the consulship and was appointed commander-in-chief in Metellus' place. After Marius had worn Jugurtha down in three campaigns (107–105 B.C.), his second-in-command, Sulla (the future dictator) arranged for the king to be ambushed and betrayed into Marius' hands. The work ends with Marius' reelection as consul in order to deal with the menace from the German Cimbri and Teutones beyond Italy's northern borders.

In about 39 B.C., Sallust started on the composition of his *Histories,* his most important literary achievement. Regrettably, the work only exists in fragments, including four speeches, two letters, and about five hundred short passages. The *Histories* consisted of five books (the last of which was probably left incomplete), covering a period of recent history extending from 78 B.C. to the early sixties. Sallust may have intended to add further books bringing the story down to 60, or possibly even to 51 or 50. But, if so, his death prevented the completion of the plan.

From the fragments, we know that the work began with a prologue on earlier Roman history, in which Sallust argued that the stability of the Republic had disappeared when there was no longer anything to fear from Carthage (destroyed in 146 B.C.), and that then came the beginning of internal party politics, with all their attendant dishonesty and corruption. The first book went on to deal with the year 78 B.C., in which the consul Marcus Lepidus (father of the triumvir) had staged an abortive revolt against the conservative political system established by the dictator Sulla. Sallust makes Lepidus deliver a violent speech against Sulla at a time when the latter had resigned his dictatorship but was still alive. The rest of the book was about Sertorius, the heroic adherent of the Marian party who raised the greater part of Spain against Sulla and the government that succeeded him. Book 2, after reporting the death of Lepidus in Sardinia (77), told how Pompey—who evidently figured as the major character throughout the *Histories*—was sent out to Spain to fight against Sertorius. The third book told the stories of Sertorius' downfall and death (72), the dispatch to the east of Marcus Antonius (father of the triumvir) with a special command against the pirates (74), the beginning of the slave revolt under Spartacus (73/72), and the initial military victories of the pro-senatorial general Lucullus against Mithridates VI of Pontus (northeastern Asia Minor). Book 4 continued the story of Lucullus' successes. The last book, or what was written of it, began

with the first setbacks Lucullus suffered and went on to describe the debates in the capital that gave Pompey the command in his place (67), against strenuous senatorial opposition.

In the last convulsive years of the Republic, Pompey, Crassus, and Caesar claimed to stand for the "popular" cause—represented by those politicians who were prepared to appeal to the people over the heads of the Senate. However, there was never this simple dichotomy, but rather a constantly shifting pattern of loose alliances. In any case, says Sallust, the ambitions of every Roman politician—whether a noble or a "new man" —were entirely selfish, and their utterances fraudulent eyewash. The historian himself, for all his wealth, was a "new" man and felt a particular distaste for the hereditary governing class. Moreover, his feeling was strengthened by an unusual appreciation of the miseries of the poor. At the same time, he was by no means wedded to the popular cause: in his view, there was nothing much to choose between the various political factions, seeing that each exploited any advantage with equal ruthlessness.

In Sallust's pages, Caesar, who had claimed to be the most "popular" of all, is juxtaposed and contrasted with the ultraconservative Cato. The gifts of these two protagonists, felt Sallust, were all the more conspicuous amid the surrounding ruin of the Republic; and the two men both stood, in their different ways, for an old order that had already disappeared at the time when Sallust was writing. The sharply contrasting orations ascribed to Caesar and Cato during the Catilinarian debate are presented in a style too thoroughly Sallustian to be anything like what either speaker can actually have said. Sallust treats their speeches as the highlights of the crisis and says little about Cicero's part—in remarkable contrast to what the orator proclaimed about himself.

Censorious, biting, and disillusioned, Sallust detected Chance at work everywhere— a capricious symbol of life's unfairness. Yet, whatever his own ethical failings may have been, he was as intensely moralistic as any historian before him, seeing all political and economic issues alike in terms of morality. However, like Thucydides, he also laid great stress on intellect: the Roman "virtue" that constituted his ideal was a matter of brain no less than of character. The conception pervaded Sallust's portrayals of individuals, and through them he made an important contribution to the art of biography. His character studies are built up by a series of swift, incisive sketches, displaying persons gripped by strong passions and involved in violent conflicts. Very often, however, these pictures are, in fact, biased and inaccurate—and the same applies, indeed, to his entire method, or lack of it, for Sallust, throughout his writings, perpetrates gross, chronological distortions, admits an abundant crop of unproved rumors and vague and irrelevant generalizations, displays a sweeping carelessness about geography and numbers, and offers a whole series of historical judgments that are inept and misguided.

And yet his literary gifts were outstanding. Roman history at last had a practitioner whose style was capable of doing justice to his theme. Sallust declared that a historical writer ought to achieve *both* accuracy *and* stylistic excellence, and though the former aim was beyond him, he composed literary masterpieces that have captivated the world. His work is a series of brilliantly described incidents, dramatically illustrating and exploiting his historical themes, and linked together into elegant, closely knit structures (books), each of which leads steadily and irresistibly to a powerful conclusion and climax. Narratives and descriptions move with what Quintilian called Sallust's "immortal speed." Yet this is not achieved by straightforward simplicity, which indeed the historian deliberately avoids, striving instead for an archaic, epigrammatical abruptness, often carried to the point of obscurity. This method was an implied criticism of the smooth amplitude of Cicero; Sallust's preference went back to the earliest of the Latin historians, Cato the Censor (whose criticisms of the senatorial class was another feature that he enjoyed). Above all Sallust wanted to be the Roman equivalent of the Greek historian Thucydides, whose style he deliberately echoed in his old-fashioned severity of diction.

Yet it seems overpatriotic of Quintilian to have placed Sallust on the same level as Thucydides; the latter's historical analyses were far beyond his Roman imitator's powers. Nevertheless, the Latin epigrammatist Martial took the same view as his contemporary Quintilian, declaring Sallust to be, by the general consensus of men of learning, "the foremost among Roman historians," and later Tacitus also spoke very highly of his gifts. In late antiquity and the Middle Ages this admiration persisted; and the Dutch scholar Erasmus recommended him for schools, in preference to Livy or Tacitus, in the year 1511. In eastern Europe he ranks particularly high today, because of his disillusionment with the traditional governing class.

WORKS (wrongly attributed to Sallust)—Two Letters to Caesar in His Old Age (Epistulae ad Caesarem Senem) appear anonymously in a Vatican manuscript that also includes Sallust's authentic writings. These letters were allegedly written in about 50 and 46 B.C. but are almost certainly rhetorical pieces *(suasoriae)* of imperial date. Invectives against Cicero—ostensibly datable to 54 B.C. —were attributed to Sallust in the manuscript tradition and accepted by Quintilian; however, they are probably the work of a rhetorician of later, Augustan, date.
EDITIONS—R. Jacobs, 11th ed. (H. Wirz and A. Kurfess, eds.), 1922. Catiline: K. Vretska, 1975; P. McGushin, 1977. Jugurtha: W. C. Summers, 1902. Invectives and letters (of uncertain authenticity): K. Vretska, Invektive und Episteln, 1961. *Translations*—J. C. Rolfe (Loeb ed.), revised ed., 1931; S. A. Handford (Penguin ed.), 1963; I. Scott-Kilvert, 1963; J. M. Carter, Fragments of the Histories and Letters to Caesar by Pseudo-Sallust, 1970; A. Ernout, Salluste, 1941, *and* Pseudo-Salluste: Lettres à César, Invectives (Budé ed.), 1962.
ABOUT—R. Syme, Sallust (including Appendix 2, The False Sallust), 1904; E. Bolaffi, Sallustio e la sua fortuna nei secoli, 1949; L. O. Sangiacomo, Sallustio, 1954; E. Skard, Sallust und seine Vorgänger, 1956; W. Steidle, Sallusts historische Monographien, 1958; K. Büchner, Sallust, 1960; D. C. Earl, The Political Thought of Sallust, 1961; G. M. Paul *in* T. A. Dorey, ed., Latin Historians, 1966; A. La Penna, Sallustio e la rivoluzione romana, 1968; E. K. H. Wistrand, Sallust on Judicial Murders in Rome, 1968; E. Pasoli, Problemi delle Epistulae ad Caesarem sallustiane, 1970; J. Malitz, Ambitio mala: Studien zur politischen Biographie des Sallust, 1976.

SALLUSTIUS (Saloustios), Greek philosopher, wrote during the reign of the emperor Julian the Apostate (A.D. 361–63). It was believed until recently that he was Julian's friend Saturninus Sallustius Secundus, but it

sal lus′ ti us

379

now seems that he should rather be identified with a high official of the same period named Flavius Sallustius, who was praetorian prefect of the Gauls in 361–63 and consul in 363.

Sallustius' work entitled *On the Gods and the Universe (De Deis et Mundo)* is a brief handbook of the Neoplatonic doctrines of which Plotinus (d. 269/70) had been the most original and famous exponent. He echoes the language and ideas of another Neoplatonist, Iamblichus of Chalcis (who died c. 325) and also reproduces the views of Julian himself. However, Sallustius' own formulations are often of interest. After a general discussion of beliefs, he remarks: "Of the gods and of the universe and of human affairs this account will be enough for those who are neither able to be steeped in philosophy nor suffer from an incurable sickness of the soul."

Like the philosophers before him and the Christians of his own time, he believed that the world we see around us is insubstantial: "The universe itself can be called a myth, since bodies and material objects are apparent in it, while souls and intellects are concealed." And he once again had in mind the Christian position—with its insistence on the permanent validity of Jesus' experience —when he interpreted the passion and resurrection of pagan gods (notably Attis, Adonis, and Osiris) as events that take place anew every year and only in a secondary sense as things that had happened once only, on a single definitive occasion. It would be wrong, however, to regard his work as primarily a commentary on Christianity for by this time pagan thought had, in his hands and those of his contemporaries, become organized, articulate, and polemical in its own right.

EDITIONS with translation—A. D. Nock, Sallustius, 1926; G. Rochefort, Saloustios: Des dieux et du monde (Budé ed.), 1960.
ABOUT—A. D. Nock, Conversion, 1933; G. Murray, Five Stages of Greek Religion, 1951; A. H. Armstrong, ed., Cambridge History of Later Greek and Early Medieval Philosophy, 1966.

SALVIAN, Latin theological writer, was born in about A.D. 400 and died after 470. His birthplace was probably Treviri (Trier on the Moselle), where he experienced the assault of the Franks in 418. In 425, with the agreement of his wife, he joined the monastery established by Honoratus on the Mediterranean isle of Lérins opposite Cannes and about fourteen years later became a priest (presbyter) at Massilia (Marseille), where he remained until his death.

The only surviving examples of his voluminous literary output are nine letters, *Timotheus to the Church*—a four-book tract against avarice in which Timotheus is a pseudonym for himself—and the far more important eight-book treatise, *On the Government of God (De Gubernatione Dei),* published in about 440. As the western Roman empire, overrun and suffering from innumerable internal ills, was disintegrating, Christian people raised the question of why their faith did nothing to help them amid the widespread hardship and oppression, whereas the pagans of the past had lived in a happier world. Was God, then, indifferent to their own misfortunes and had He given up the task of governing the earth? This is the problem to which Salvian addresses himself in order to justify the acts of God as ruler and judge. We suffer these evils, he claims, because we deserve them for living in wickedness and heresy as we do. If, guilty of these sins, we had ever been permitted to flourish, then indeed it might have been right to charge God with failing to govern.

Nor, Salvian observes, is it valid to take comfort in the fact that at least we as Christians adhere to the right religion, whereas the barbarians, who are allowed to conquer us, remain heretics or pagans. Heretics and pagans they are, replies the author, and they possess many vices as well, but so do we— and in many respects they are our betters. Here, like Tacitus in the *Germania,* Salvian uses the barbarians as foils to the overcivilized Romans. Uncouth and imperfectly organized though these invaders are, Salvian draws a favorable contrast between their morality, social solidarity, and sense of justice, and the far-reaching corruption of Roman society. Moreover, although his

sal' vi ăn

motives in writing *On the Government of God* were ethical and rhetorical, this point of view did in fact help him to develop an unusually constructive attitude toward the Germanic peoples. Unafraid to look ahead, and seeing beyond the hidebound xenophobic conservatism of many of his Roman contemporaries, he succeeded in detecting not only what was novel and important in this phenomenon of the invading Germans but also what might have led to a fruitful collaboration between the barbarians and the Roman educated class—though the collaboration, in fact, abysmally failed to materialize.

Salvian's particular importance lies in his unusual and comprehensive denunciation of the treatment of the poor by the rich in the western Roman empire. He describes the numerous abuses with abundant detail, sparing neither the landowners nor the governors of provinces, nor even the unfortunate city councillors who were obliged to act as the governors' agents. Although rhetorical exaggeration is part of his technique, the general picture is convincing, and Salvian must be seen as an invaluable source of information for the social history of the period.

Because of this general moral and social deterioration of the empire, of which he finds so much evidence, he is scarcely surprised that imperial defense has foundered to the extent that cities are left unguarded—their inhabitants preferring to watch the games or gaze at indecent plays—even when the barbarians are almost in sight. One would have supposed, he observes, that these townsmen, like other people, did not want to die; and yet none of them make the slightest attempt to save themselves from death. Most of the people of the western world, he discerningly adds, lacked the imagination to realize the supreme peril that confronted them—or, if they realized it, they lacked the nerve to do anything to defeat it. For such reasons the empire was breathing its last, or was dead already. These comments are far more realistic and perceptive than the blinkered, traditionalist complacency displayed frequently by so many of Salvian's contemporaries. It is,

however, scarcely surprising that his gloomy work does not seem to have been popular.

EDITIONS—P. Pauly, Corpus Scriptorum Ecclesiasticorum Latinorum, v 8; G. Lagarrigue, Oeuvres, 1971, 1972, 1975. *With translation:* E. M. Sanford, On the Government of God, 1930; J. F. O'Sullivan, Writings (Fathers of the Church, v 3), 1947.
ABOUT—A. Schaefer, Römer und Germanen bei Salvian, 1930; M. Pellegrino, Salviano di Marsiglia, 1940; E. A. Isichei, Political Thinking and Social Experience: Some Christian Interpretations of the Roman Empire from Tertullian to Sabrian, 1964; F. Paschoud, Roma Aeterna, 1967; M. Grant, The Fall of the Roman Empire, 1976.

SALVIUS JULIANUS. See Julianus, Salvius

SAPPHO, Greek poet, was born in the later seventh century B.C. We do not know when she died. Like Alcaeus, who was approximately her contemporary, she lived on the island of Lesbos; she may have been born at Eresus, one of its towns. The name of her father was Scamandronymus, and her mother was Cleis. As a child, at some date between 604 and 595 B.C., she was taken to exile in Sicily, presumably owing to political disturbances at Lesbos. However, she returned to spend most of the rest of her life at Mytilene, the chief city of the island. She had three brothers, Larichus, Charaxus, and Erigys: Larichus, she tells us, poured the wine at council banquets and Charaxus, a merchant, sailed with a cargo of wine to Naucratis in Egypt, where he managed, to his sister's disapproval, to involve himself expensively with a local woman, Doricha.

Sappho herself was married to Cercolas, a rich man from the island of Andros, and they had a daughter who was given her grandmother's name, Cleis. Some of the new discoveries of papyri, which have extended our fragmentary knowledge of Sappho's poetry, record her relations with her daughter. One passage advises Cleis how to do her hair and discusses her desire for a brightly colored hat from Lydia. Elsewhere, Sappho speaks lovingly of her daughter's beauty. She herself, however, according to tradition,

saf' ō

was short and sallow. The famous story that she jumped to her death from the promontory of Leucas was probably a myth.

One important group of her poems consisted of wedding songs *(epithalamia)*, which were, in origin, the pieces chanted by young men and young women in front of the bridal chamber, in order to celebrate the good fortune of the bridegroom and the beauty of the bride. Sappho composed her *epithalamia* for performance by a chorus. The meager fragments that survive show her remarkable capacity for elevating this traditional form to finished poetry without any sacrifice of spontaneous charm. One passage contains a nostalgic farewell to virginity; another is humorous and shows the young women sneering at the large feet of the youth who has been set to guard the door of the house where the bride has been taken, in case the women try to rescue her from her husband.

Sappho's favorite poetic form was the individual song to the lyre, describing the feelings of her own heart. It seems that in Lesbos at this period the women who could afford to do so gathered together in more or less informal groups and spent their days in pleasant occupations, including the composition and recitation of poetry; Sappho herself expresses jealousy or contempt for rival groups, such as those of Archenassa and Gorgo. Some of the members of her own female circle are named by her, but more often those she sings about are left anonymous. Much of her poetry revolves around the loves and hatreds that flourished in this hothouse atmosphere. The famous twenty-eight line *Prayer to Aphrodite,* which is the only one of her poems to have survived intact, calls on the goddess, in verses of magical beauty and passion, to help her in her pain of unsatisfied longing. In another piece, of which sixteen lines survive, Sappho declares that godlike happiness is the lot of the man who sits quietly opposite a young woman and just listens to her talking and laughing; however, the poet, as she herself declares, is completely overcome by a glimpse of the young woman's face.

Many of the other fragments, too, tell in similar terms of her loves for the young women around her; in one of them, she

speaks of one who is now far away in Sardis, where she outshines the women of Lydia as the moon outshines the stars—and there follows an incomparable description of a moonlit night. The term *lesbian* is derived from the way in which Sappho writes about her female companions. In surviving fragments, there is no reference to any physical relationships, but her feelings for her own sex were evidently intense. This intensity of feeling emerges with burning directness from the verbal melodies of her candid and simple language. And while she has the power to stand back and recollect her agonies and ecstasies, she makes an unprecedentedly intimate contact with her listener or reader.

Sappho wrote in various meters, some probably of her own invention; an especially graceful type of four-line lyric stanza was given her name. Her influence on later poets, including Anacreon, Ibycus, and eventually Theocritus, was extensive, and Catullus produced a Latin version of her poem describing her reactions at the sight of the young woman she loved. Much of her work survived until the end of antiquity, but by the eighth or ninth century A.D. nothing was left except quotations by subsequent authors; these were all we possessed until additional fragments were discovered on papyri during the past eighty years.

EDITIONS—E. Lobel and D. L. Page, Poetarum Lesbiorum Fragmenta, 2nd ed., 1963; E. M. Voight, 1971. *Translations*—M. Barnard, 1958; D. L. Page, Sappho and Alcaeus, 2nd ed., 1959; W. Barnstone, 1965; G. Davenport, 1965; S. Q. Groden, 1966; E. Mora (French), 1966; M. Treu (German), 3rd ed., 1976. ABOUT—M. Fernández Galiano, Safo, 1958; D. M. Robinson, Sappho and Her Influence, 1963; M. Treu, B. Gentili and G. Lanata, *in* Quaderni Urbinati di Cultura Classica, v 2, 1966; H. Saake, Zur Kunst Sapphos, 1971, *and* Sappho-Studien, 1972; G. M. Kirkwood, Early Greek Monody, 1974; G. A. Privitera, La rete di Afrodite: Studi su Saffo, 1974.

SATYRUS, Greek historian-biographer, worked either in the third or in the second century B.C. His birthplace was Callatis Pontica (Mangalia in Rumania), but he wrote mainly in Egypt, at Alexandria and at

sa′ ti rus

Oxyrhynchus, a town favored by scholars and writers.

He wrote biographies, of which only fragments have survived, but they are sufficient to show that some of the studies, remarkably enough, were in dialogue form. Their subjects comprised famous men of all types, for Satyrus included men of action such as Philip II of Macedonia and Dionysius the Younger of Syracuse, in addition to intellectual figures such as Pythagoras, Demosthenes, and Sophocles.

Four pages of a life of Euripides have also been discovered on a papyrus at Oxyrhynchus. It is clear from this and other fragments that Satyrus made ample and uncritical use of anecdotic and legendary material—for example, he deduced many of his biographical details from the text of Euripides' own tragedies. This utilization of the works of the author whose life he is writing is in keeping with the practice of biographers belonging to the Peripatetic (Aristotelian) school, whose interest in literary history he further reflected by pointing out how Euripides in some respects foreshadowed the New Comedy of Menander.

EDITIONS (of fragments)—K. Müller, Fragmenta Historicorum Graecorum, v 3, 1883.
ABOUT—A. Dihle, Studien zur griechischen Biographie, 2nd ed., 1970; A. Momigliano, The Development of Greek Biography, 1971.

SCYLAX, Greek explorer, geographer, and biographer, was active in the first half of the sixth century B.C. He came from Caryanda in Caria (southwestern Asia Minor). By order of King Darius I of Achaemenid Persia, he was sent in about 515 B.C. to explore the course of the River Indus down to its mouth (starting from a town near the modern Attock) and then to coast along the shores westward and sail around unknown Arabia into the Red Sea. After two and a half years he returned by sea to Heroonpolis on the Isthmus of Suez. This journey has been queried but need not be doubted.

The prose work he wrote about the journey, quoted by Hecataeus and attested by other Greek writers, is lost except for fragments. It appears, however, to have been a very early example of the *Periplus*—a literary genre comprising the description of the coast seen from ships in the course of their voyages. The scanty remains of the work of Scylax demonstrate the breadth of his geographical and ethnological interests but at the same time (for example, in his account of India) indicate the admittance of an element of fable or fiction. Nevertheless, the fact that he wrote, for the most part, on travels that had actually taken place represented a significant step forward; and the fact that the travels had been undertaken by himself foreshadowed the art of autobiography.

Scylax also appears to have been an important pioneer of biographical writing. According to the report by the medieval Suidas (Suda) Lexicon, he wrote a biography of Heraclides, a contemporary autocratic ruler of Mylasa in Caria who played an important part in the revolt against the Persians (498) and possibly took part in the subsequent Persian War as well. The character of this work, however, is unknown, but it seems to have been used, at the end of the third century B.C., by the historian Sosylus of Sparta.

WORKS—A Periplus that has been preserved under the name of Scylax—our earliest surviving specimen of this genre—cannot be his work but is a collection of material of various dates brought together in about 350 B.C.
EDITIONS (of fragments)—F. Jacoby, Die Fragmente der griechischen Historiker, 1 a, Nachträge 10, 2nd ed., and 3 c, 709. Pseudo-Scylax, Periplus: K. Müller, Geographi Graeci Minores, v 1, 1855.
ABOUT—J. O. Thomson, History of Ancient Geography, 1948; A. Diller, The Tradition of the Minor Greek Geographers, 1952; M. Cary and E. H. Warmington, The Greek Explorers, 2nd ed., 1963; A. Momigliano, The Development of Greek Biography, 1971.

SEDULIUS SCOTUS (or **SCOTTUS**), Latin poet and scholar, worked in the middle of the ninth century A.D. He was born in Ireland (described as Scotia at this time) in the 840s, and his last identifiable date is 874. Early in his life he had arrived with two storm-tossed companions at Liège (Belgium), where the scholarly Bishop Hartgar appointed him as a functionary *(scholas-*

skī' laks or sī' laks

se dū' li us skō' tus

383

ticus) in the cathedral school. Sedulius also won the favor of Hartgar's successor Franco and of Iado, archbishop of Milan; in addition he sought assistance from a certain Count Robert, finally gained the favorable attention of Charles II the Bald, king of the western Franks and subsequently emperor, and of his wife Irmingarde. Sedulius had hitherto been the typical impoverished scholar—always thirsty and usually short of funds—but with such patrons at hand and with the aid of his own serious learning—which included a profound knowledge of music—he earned himself a position and assumed, in the process, some of the decorum of a court official.

Sedulius' poems are mostly in classical Latin meters. To the earlier stages of his career belong pieces that to some extent foreshadow the satirical (goliardic) songs of a later medieval epoch. His lodgings at Liège, he tells us, although they availed to shelter poor Irishmen from the cold, possessed neither windows nor door fastenings; and the beer was disgusting. He vigorously flatters Count Robert, in the hope of some wine, a hundred flagons of which are then forthcoming; and further versified pleas, including a poem that begins with lyrical praise of spring, sought to extract food and liquor from Bishop Hartgar as well. Another ingenious elegy, on the death of Hartgar's ram, makes a comparison, in dubious taste, of the "martyred" animal with the Christian symbol of the Lamb of God. Sedulius also described Jesus Christ as a more gracious Apollo, son of Zeus and god of light, and he tells the story of the Nativity, with many echoes of classical literary and mythological traditions. Other poems include panegyrics honoring Charles II the Bald, the emperor Lothar (840–55), and Hartgar, on whom he enjoins his Muse, the Naiad Egla, to implant a kiss with her red lips.

One of Sedulius' later works is a treatise in very pure Latin entitled *De Rectoribus Christianis (On Christian Rulers),* an early example of the medieval type of literature that sought to provide guidance, or "mirrors," for princes. Each of the twenty chapters deals with a virtue appropriate to a Christian ruler; and each is written for the most part in prose but concludes with a pas-

sage of verse. In the twelfth century, Sedulius' poetry was copied onto a manuscript that is now at Brussels.

He also worked on a Greek text of the Bible. A number of Greek biblical manuscripts, with interlinear Latin translations, are ascribed to his circle, and one of them, the Greek text in the Berne Epistles of St. Paul, may well be of his own authorship; in its margin are the names of the Irishmen belonging to his circle.

EDITIONS—J. P. Migne, Patrologia Latina, v 103 (*see* v 19 for Carmen Paschale by Coelius Sedulius, who is not the same person); L. Traube, Monumenta Germaniae Historica: Poetae Aevi Carolini, v 3; S. Hellmann, De Rectoribus Christianis, 1906; H. J. Frede, Des Sedulius Scottus Collectaneum in Apostolum, *in* Pelagius: Der Irische Paulustext, Sedulius Scottus, 1961; D. Brearley, Commentarius Seduli Scotti in Donati Artem Majorem, 1975; B. Löfstedt, Commentarius Seduli Scotti in Donati Artem Minorem, 1977. ABOUT—H. Pirenne, Sedulius of Liège, 1882; L. Traube, Sedulius Scottus, 1892; H. Waddell, The Wandering Scholars, 1927; J. F. Kenney, Sources for the Early History of Ireland, 1929; F. A. Wright and T. A. Sinclair, History of Latin Literature, 1931; R. Düchting, Sedulius Scottus: Seine Dichtungen, 1968; W. Huber, Heliand und Matthäusexegese, 1969.

SEMONIDES, Greek iambic and elegiac poet, probably lived in the seventh and sixth centuries B.C. His birthplace was Samos, but his name is particularly associated with another island, Amorgos, on which he founded a Samian colony.

His longest surviving fragment consists of one hundred and eighteen lines of his *Iambus on Women.* Semonides offers comparisons of different sorts of women with various types of animals, in a coarsely unchivalrous manner that is reminiscent of the anti-feminism of Hesiod (eighth century B.C.) and shows the influence of the mutual vituperation of the sexes that was a common feature of folktales. From these lines Semonides emerges as a tough and unregenerate satirist, to whom rhetoric came naturally in an epoch when it had not yet been discovered as an art. The piece is also of considerable historical importance as the longest specimen of this type of early iambic satire that

sē mŏn' i dēz

has come down to us; and its literary merit received new appreciation in recent studies.

Another iambic fragment dwells on the illusions and uncertainties of life, and although Semonides declares that one must make the best of things, he says this in a tone not far removed from despair. A passage from an elegy contains similar ideas of the futility of human hopes, combined with a lame appeal to enjoy oneself all the same. Semonides was also said to have written two books of elegiacs on the history of Samos.

EDITIONS—M. L. West, Iambi et Elegi Graeci, v 2, 1972. *With translation:* H. Lloyd-Jones, Females of the Species, 1975.

SENECA THE ELDER (Lucius Annaeus Seneca), Latin historian and writer on rhetoric, was born in about 55 B.C. and died between A.D. 37 and 41. He came from a family of knights at Corduba (Cordoba) in Baetica (southern Spain). He made a lot of money and may have held an official post in Spain or conducted profitable trading operations. He was in Rome as a young man, when he studied rhetoric under a teacher named Marullus, and he went there again after his marriage; his knowledge of the city's affairs suggests lengthy periods of residence. His wife Helvia, a fellow Spaniard, bore him three children: Novatus who took the adoptive name Gallio, by which he was described in the *Acts;* Seneca the Younger; and Marcus Annaeus Mela, the father of the poet Lucan.

In the semi-retirement of his later years, the elder Seneca composed two works describing his own times. In the historical field, he wrote a history of Rome from the beginning of the civil wars almost up to the time of his own death. Unfortunately, scarcely a trace of it has survived. But Suetonius records one detail from the account of the death of Tiberius (A.D. 37); and Lactantius reported that Seneca divided the history into stages derived from human life —infancy under Romulus, childhood from King Numa Pompilius to Servius Tullius, adolescence from Tarquinius Superbus to

sen′ ə kå

the end of the Punic Wars, vigorous adulthood to the end of the Republican conquests, old age from the beginning of the civil wars, and senile decrepitude under the empire.

He also wrote a work consisting of extracts from the Roman and Greek declaimers—orators speaking in imaginary cases—whom he had heard during his life, together with observations and digressions of his own. This compilation, dedicated to his sons, was entitled *Oratorum Sententiae Divisiones Colores—sententiae* are brief and pointed utterances by the imaginery speakers; *divisiones* are the logical divisions of these utterances into their principal issues; and *colores* are the twists or slants imposed by the declaimers on the facts in order to create extenuation or insinuation. Originally, the whole work consisted of ten books of *controversiae* (fictitious lawsuits argued on both sides before an imaginary jury), each book being introduced by a foreword), and at least two more books of *suasoriae* (in which historical or mythological personages are given advice on how to act in a particular situation). Only five books of the *controversiae,* however, and only one of the *suasoriae,* have come down to us, in a somewhat incomplete form.

The declamatory exhibitions that are quoted range over a period of sixty years from the period preceding Augustus' sole rule down to the reign of Tiberius. Seneca's long career and phenomenally retentive memory make his compilation an invaluable source for our knowledge of the educational system and cultural standards of the early imperial epoch. Moreover, in addition to the abundant quotations that form the core of his work, he offers the benefit of his own shrewd observations, put forward in an easy but succinct style of prose that is halfway between Ciceronian and Silver Latin. As his son the younger Seneca recorded, he is suspicious of novelty and Hellenism and bemoans contemporary social decline; however, his judgments are conscientiously fair, and not without a certain caustic humor.

It is uncertain to what extent the work was utilized by subsequent authors. Like his history, it appears to have been deliberately held back for posthumous publication—

SENECA THE YOUNGER

conceivably because an element of Republicanism in its tone might have made it unpalatable to the imperial authorities in his lifetime.

EDITIONS with translation—M. Winterbottom, Seneca the Elder: Declamations (Loeb ed.), 1974; H. Bornecque, Sénèque le Rhéteur: Controverses et suasores, 1932; M. Bonaria, Seneca il vecchio, 1972. Suasoriae only: W. A. Edward, 1928.
ABOUT: H. Bornecque, Les déclamation et les déclamateurs d'après Sénèque le père, 1902; H. Bardon, Le vocabulaire de la critique littéraire chez Sénèque le rhéteur, 1940; S. F. Bonner, Roman Declamation in the Late Republic and Early Empire, 1949; G. Kennedy, The Art of Rhetoric in the Roman World, 1972.

SENECA THE YOUNGER (Lucius Annaeus Seneca, generally known as just "Seneca"), Roman statesman and philosopher, Latin tragic poet and satirist, was born in about 4 B.C. and died in A.D. 65. His birthplace was Corduba (Cordoba) in Baetica (southern Spain). He was the second son of Seneca the Elder, the rhetorician, and his mother was Helvia, whose sister brought him to Rome when he was still a child. There he studied grammar and rhetoric but soon turned to philosophy, which he studied under teachers belonging to various schools. At some stage, he joined his aunt in Egypt, where her husband was the provincial governor, and she nursed Seneca through an illness. Returning to Rome in A.D. 31, he held the junior office of quaestor, became a speaker at the bar, and was admitted to the Senate. But in 39 he incurred the disfavor of the emperor Gaius (Caligula); and after the accession of Claudius (41), he came under suspicion of adultery with the new emperor's niece Julia Livilla and was exiled to Corsica. In 49 Seneca obtained his recall, at the instance of Agrippina the Younger—whom Claudius had just married—and became tutor to her son Nero. He also gained the office of praetor.

When Nero became emperor in 54, Seneca and the praetorian prefect Burrus virtually controlled the empire for eight years. They may also have been accomplices in Nero's murder of Agrippina in 59; at all events they covered up for him afterward.

sen' ə kå

SENECA THE YOUNGER

When Burrus died in 62, Seneca virtually withdrew from public life and in 65, accused of participation in the unsuccessful Pisonian conspiracy against Nero, he was compelled to commit suicide.

Seneca was a writer of extraordinarily versatile literary gifts. His surviving prose works include ten ethical treatises. Perhaps the earliest of these pieces are three *Consolations,* datable to the period 40–43. One of these, *To Marcia,* is addressed to the daughter of the historian Cremutius Cordus to comfort her for the loss of her son; *To Helvia* is addressed to Seneca's mother, to console her for his own condemnation to exile in Corsica; *To Polybius (Ad Polybium De Consolatione)* is a groveling appeal to a powerful freedman of the emperor Claudius to secure his recall from banishment. Among his other essays, *On Anger,* in three books, was dedicated to Seneca's brother Novatus (who adopted the name Gallio) as was another essay, *On the Happy Life,* which is Stoic in tone and consists, in part, of an apology for the writer's own career.

Three further works are addressed to Annaeus Serenus, the commander of Nero's Watch *(vigiles).* In one of them, *On the Constancy of the Wise Man* (written after 47), Seneca declares that a man of true wisdom cannot suffer wrong or insult. *On Tranquillity of the Soul* is concerned with the pursuit of peace of mind amid the troubles of life, and *On Leisure (De Otio)* advocates the devotion of leisure hours to contemplation. *On Shortness of Life* (c. A.D. 49), addressed to Seneca's father-in-law Paulinus, urges the importance of using time wisely and not wasting it on vicious pursuits. The seven books of *On Benefits* (c. A.D. 54 and later), addressed to Aebutius Liberalis, seek to discover what *benefit* really means and discuss gratitude and ingratitude. *On Clemency* (55/6), in three books (of which the first and the beginning of the second survive), is presented to the young Nero and recommends mercy as the quality of a ruler. *On Providence,* which argues that no evil can befall the good man, is dedicated to a friend of Epicurean leanings, Lucilius Junior.

Lucilius is also the recipient of Seneca's *Investigations of Nature (Naturales Quaestiones)* (after 62/3), which are planned less from a scientific than from a Stoic and ethical standpoint. Out of the original books, probably eight in number, seven have survived, in somewhat disorganized shape. Book 1 describes fire and related subjects; Book 2 deals with air (including thunder and lightning); Book 3 discusses water in various forms; Book 4 deals with the rise of the Nile and snow; and Book 5 presents information about atmospheric movements including wind. The subjects of Books 6 and 7 are earthquakes and comets respectively.

The longest of Seneca's prose works is his series of one hundred twenty-four *Moral Letters (Epistulae Morales),* likewise dedicated to Lucilius. These do not form part of an authentic correspondence but are essays on various aspects of life and morality. Of a very different character—though it is wrong to deny its attribution to Seneca—is the *Pumpkinification (Apocolocyntosis)* or *Joke About the Death of Claudius (Ludus de Morte Claudii),* written at some point in the reign of Nero in cruel mockery of the deification of his predecessor: on the proposal of Augustus, Claudius is ejected from heaven to the underworld, where he is made clerk to one of his own freedmen. The work is a medley of prose and verse in the style known as Menippean satire, so-named after its Greek inventor Menippus of Gadara (third century B.C.).

The principal poetic works of Seneca are nine tragedies. The *Mad Hercules (Hercules Furens)* is largely based on Euripides' play of the same name, though instead of menacing the children of Hercules with death, Lycus demands his wife in marriage; and Hercules' assassination of her, together with their children, forms part of the stage action. *The Trojan Women (Troades)* is again adapted from a similarly entitled play of Euripides, to which, however, it adds the sacrifice of Polyxena (an event taken from Euripides' Hecuba). Seneca's *Medea,* too, is derived from a Euripidean forerunner: in this Latin version, Medea herself requests that her children should accompany her into exile, and when Jason objects because he wants to keep them himself, she sees where he is vulnerable and kills them in vengeance for his faithlessness. The *Phaedra* is founded on the *Hippolytus* of Euripides, but in Seneca's version it is Phaedra in person, not her nurse, who discloses her love to her stepson; who slanders him to Theseus; and who (instead of the goddess Artemis) announces what she has done before she dies.

The *Oedipus* is taken from Sophocles' *Oedipus the King.* Seneca adds to his version a long description of the Theban plague and an account of necromantic rites; and Jocasta's suicide is shown on the stage. The *Phoenician Women (Phoenissae)* seems to blend a situation from Sophocles' *Oedipus at Colonus* (the blind Oedipus guided by Antigone) with material from other sources (Antigone is now at Thebes with Jocasta, who tries in vain to reconcile her sons Eteocles and Polyneices); but the play only survives in a mutilated condition, and the surviving portions may be fragments of two separate tragedies. The *Hercules Oetaeus,* a long play (portions of which may be spurious), is on the general theme of Sophocles' *Trachinian Women* but presents Deianira, not as the gentle and attractive figure of the Sophoclean play but as a jealous and terrifying personage; and a new scene is added, describing Hercules' death and deification on Mount Oeta in northern Greece.

The dependence of Seneca's *Agamemnon* on Aeschylus' play of the same name may only be indirect and secondhand. In this version, Aegisthus, urged on by the ghost of Thyestes, takes the initiative in inducing Clytemnestra to murder her husband Agamemnon: Cassandra, the prisoner and mistress Agamemnon has brought from Troy, does not die with him, as in the Aeschylean tragedy, but later on; Orestes' sister Electra makes an appearance and enables her brother to escape. Seneca's *Thyestes,* for which no Greek original is extant, tells how Atreus, whose wife Aethra had been seduced by his brother Thyestes, took vengeance by killing Thyestes' children and serving them up to him at dinner.

Although ideas taken from philosophers were always of interest to Seneca's lively mind, he was not himself primarily a philosopher but a public figure and a rhetorician. He delivers passionate attacks on those who criticize philosophers for not living up to their ideals; but his own grasp of philosophical principles is only superficial. Yet his particular brand of Stoicism, modified by infusions from other sources and mellowed by personal experience and common sense, displays an enlightened humaneness and tolerance. His purpose is above all practical, subordinating philosophical theory to moral exhortation, so that his treatises, whether in the form of letters or essays, are in effect disquisitions on various conventional themes relating to ethics: the nature of happiness and the supreme good, the perils of wealth and power and luxury, the pointlessness of fearing death, and so on.

However, Seneca also adds certain original touches of his own—for example, in his careful attention to problems of will and of conscience and in his conviction that a proper attitude to life cannot be obtained without a certain scientific understanding of the physical world we see around us. This sermonizing is rendered all the more attractive and persuasive because Seneca is engagingly frank and modest about his own moral performance. He displays astute and caustic gifts of psychological observation, and his persuasiveness comes over with all the force that a skillful rhetorician can muster, enhanced by many a cunning anecdote disclosing sidelights on contemporary society and on his own career.

His extraordinary diction represents the Pointed Style of the Latin Silver Age in all its aspects. Seneca aims at the ultimate ex-

tremes of vividness and ingenuity, achieving his neat and brilliant effects by every sort of verbal trick and device—rhythmical wordplay, alliteration, exaggeration, antithesis, and paradox. Brevity is preferred to Ciceronian rotundity, staccato abruptness to smooth continuity; every phrase is an epigram with a punch line.

Seneca's tragedies contain the same features as his prose works, including Stoic emphasis on the blinding effects of passion and the ineluctability of Fate. But to Seneca the dramatist this passion is an independent force that fights against reason and perverts it to its own ends; and Fate, or Providence, is a blind and hostile power. Hecuba, Medea, Phaedra, and Hippolytus are vigorously depicted, but not very subtly. His characters are not so much human beings as simplified, moralistic exponents of emotions and vices.

Seneca's plays are characterized by much sparkling declamation, mythological erudition, and clever argument; but the agony is piled on by an accumulation of ghoulish horrors that often becomes bizarre and grotesque. In substance and manner, he deviates markedly from his Greek originals, yet he adheres to them by retaining the conventional structure, comprising dramatic episodes interspersed by odes for delivery by a chorus. However, although the possibility of private stage performances cannot be altogether excluded, it seems possible that he intended his tragedies to be declaimed privately rather than acted. These are not plays of action, but plays that weave words to create the illusion of action and to present dramatic tension with the miminum of visual aid.

The groveling flatteries in which Seneca indulged to secure his return from exile, his mockery of the late Claudius' physical disabilities in the *Pumpkinification,* the vast wealth he acquired as Nero's minister, and the crimes in which he must have connived while occupying that office are disconcerting. Yet as a public official he deserves great credit for the good administration of Nero's early years. Struggling with ill-health and confronted by all the perils that contemporary court and society had to offer, he did at least always try to accept the least of possible evils; and he would have been a worse and unhappier man without the philosophy that buoyed him up.

His literary achievements attained enormous popularity among the young, for his manner and method were perfectly in harmony with his time. However, his flashy style was sneered at by the emperor Gaius (Caligula, A.D. 37–41) and deplored as a bad influence by Quintilian, who dismissed him as an inadequate philosopher (but did admire his "castigation of moral failings"). On the other hand, Seneca's treatises won the approval of early Christian apologists, and a collection of letters purporting to be his correspondence with his contemporary St. Paul came into circulation, although it has now long since been recognized as a forgery. The Italian poet Petrarch studied his moral essays in the fourteenth century, and they were known also to the English poet Chaucer. Queen Elizabeth I "did much admire Seneca's wholesome advisings"; and her age, and the ensuing Jacobean period, witnessed a reaction against ornate, formal manners of writing toward the brevity and point of Seneca's diction. Sharp controversy on this linguistic aspect continued; but his prose style became associated with a smart, advanced intellectual independence of outlook and left a permanent mark. His tragedies, too, were fervently admired in the Italian Renaissance and also left their stamp on the Tudor and Jacobean epochs of England, when they influenced, in particular, the "learned" type of tragedy. Then, too, stock characters in the romantic plays of Shakespeare, such as the ghost, the nurse, and the barbarous villain, came to him from Seneca the Younger.

WORKS wrongly attributed to Seneca include a tenth tragedy, the Octavia, about Nero's murder of his wife of that name in A.D. 62—important because it is our only surviving example of the *praetexta,* comprising tragedies on Roman historical themes. Of the seventy-seven epigrams ascribed to Seneca not more than three have a claim to authenticity. Reference to portions of his play the Hercules Oetaeus, which may be spurious, and to his fictitious correspondence with St. Paul have been made above.

EDITIONS—*Prose works:* Dialogues: J. D. Duff (10-12) 1915; P. Faider, C. Favez, P. van de Woestijne, De Clementia, Book I, 1928, Book II, 1950; C. Favez (6 and 12) 1929, 1918; H. Dahlmann (10) 1949; P. Grimal

(2 and 10) 1953, 1959; L. D. Reynolds, 1965, 1978; M. Rosenbach, Epistulae Morales, I, 1974; C. Scarpat, Epistulae Morales, I, 1975. Apocolocyntosis: O. Weinreich, 1923. *Tragedies:* F. Lea, 1878–79, reprint 1963; H. Moricca, 1947; D. N. Costa, Medea, 1973; C. Ballaira, Pseudo-Seneca: Octavia, 1974; R. J. Tarrant, Agamemnon, 1977. *Translations*—Prose works: J. Bascoe, R. M. Gummere, T. H. Corcoran (Loeb ed.), 1928–72; R. Campbell, Letters from a Stoic: Epistulae Morales ad Lucilium (Penguin ed.), 1969; P. Meinel, To Helvia, 1972; R. Waltz, F. Préchac, A. Bourgery, P. Oltramare, H. Noblot (Budé ed.), 1921–64. Apocolocyntosis: J. P. Sullivan (Arion, v 5), 1966, (Penguin ed.) 1977; A. Athanassakis, 1973. Tragedies: F. J. Muller (Loeb ed.), 1917, 1929; M. Hadas (three plays), 1955, 1956, 1957; L. Herrmann (Budé ed.), 1924–27. ABOUT—B. Axelson, Senecastudien, 1933, *and* Neue Senecastudien, 1939; J. H. L. Wetmore, Seneca's Conception of the Stoic Sage as Shown in His Prose Works, 1935; C. W. Mendell, Our Seneca, 1941, reprint 1968; W. Cornwallis, Discourses upon Seneca the Tragedian, 1952; T. P. Hardeman, The Philosophy of Lucius Annaeus Seneca, 1956; J. F. Brady, A Study of the Stoicism in Senecan Tragedy, 1958; R. M. Gummere, Seneca the Philosopher and His Modern Message, 1963; C. J. Herington, Senecan Tragedy (Arion, v 5), 1966 *and* Seneca's Tragedies (Arion, v 7), 1968; F. L. Lucas, Seneca and Elizabethen Tragedy, 1969; A. L. Motto, Seneca Sourcebook, 1970, *and* Seneca, 1973; W. Wili, Seneca morale, 1970; J. N. Sevenster, Paul and Seneca, 1971; J. Ferguson and H. M. Currie, *in* D. R. Dudley, ed., Neronians and Flavians: Silver Latin, v 1, 1972; E. Lefèvre, ed., Senecas Tragödien, 1972; C. D. N. Costa, ed., Seneca, 1974; J. Dingel, Seneca und die Dichtung, 1974; K. Heldmann, ed., Untersuchungen zu den Tragödien Senecas, 1974; A. Traina, Il stilo drammatico del filosofo Seneca, 1974; U. Knoche, Roman Satire, 1975; H. Loewenstein, Seneca: Kaiser ohne Purpur, 1975; G. Maurach, ed., Seneca als Philosoph, 1975; S. Walter, Interpretationen zum römischen in Senecas Tragödien, 1975; F. Bruckner, Interpretationen zur Pseudo-Seneca-Tragödie Octavia, 1976; M. T. Griffin, Seneca: A Philosopher in Politics, 1976; G. Scarpat, Il pensiero religioso di Seneca e l'ambiente ebraico e cristiano, 1977; F. P. Waiblinger, Seneca's Naturales Quaestiones: Griechische Wissenschaft und römische Form, 1977; L. Bocciolini Palagi, Il carteggio apocrifo di Seneca e S. Paolo, 1978; P. Grimal, Sénèque ou la conscience de l'empire, 1978.

SERVATUS, LUPUS. See Lupus of Ferrières

SERVIUS (his full name was believed, from the ninth century A.D. at least, to be **Marius** or **Maurus Servius Honoratus**), Latin commentator and grammarian, was perhaps born in about A.D. 360/5; he appears as a

sûr′ vi us

389

young man *(adulescens)* in 384 in the *Saturnalia* of Macrobius, who makes him offer a series of erudite comments on Virgilian questions. The date of his death is uncertain. It is evident from his writing that he is a pagan.

His most important work is a commentary on Virgil; doubts regarding its authorship need not be accepted. Being intended for schools, the commentary is concerned chiefly with stylistic matters and concentrates particularly on grammatical and linguistic points. For the most part, Servius' notes describe the meanings of difficult words or explain unusual forms and constructions; some notes are devoted to the naming and elucidation of rhetorical figures. Nevertheless, about one-third of his commentary relates to subject matter, on which Servius sometimes displays a competent level of learning, providing a good deal of miscellaneous information that we should not otherwise possess. His knowledge and expository talent do not, it is true, extend to the wider problems of esthetics and literary form; yet he quotes from a variety of Latin authors other than Virgil: notably Cicero and Sallust among prose writers, Terence among dramatists, and other poets including Lucan, Statius, and Juvenal. His principal source, however, is Aelius Donatus, the most famous of the grammarians of the fourth century A.D.—although Servius mentions his name only in order to refute him. While Servius is not afraid to record conflicting views or to see his way through them to a firm opinion of his own, his guiding principle is to praise and justify Virgil, whom he regarded as the repository of the supreme truth. The commentary was employed extensively as a medieval textbook, exercising an influence, for example, on Irnerius and Bernard of Chartres.

A longer version of the work became known when it was published by Pierre Daniel in 1600. This enlarged text has been given the name of Servius Danielis or Servius Auctus. Its basis is the original work by Servius (somewhat altered), but this has been supplemented by a series of important additions. They evidently come from a commentary based on erudition greatly superior to that of Servius and are mostly concerned with Virgil's subject matter—and particularly with points of mythology and other antiquarian questions. That this additional material is not by the same hand as the briefer commentary is demonstrated by the frequency with which contradictions occur between the two. It is generally beieved that the supplementary portions may be from parts of the Virgilian commentary of Aelius Donatus, other than those Servius himself originally incorporated.

A number of other treatises by Servius have also survived. They include a commentary on the grammer of Aelius Donatus and a survey of various meters *(De Centum Metris)*. Servius' name is also associated with a monograph on the meters of Horace and with a study of accents and final syllables *(De Ultimarum Syllabarum Natura* or *De Finalibus)*.

EDITIONS—G. Thilo, 1881–87, 1902; E. K. Rand, J. J. Savage, H. T. Smith, G. B. Waldrop, J. P. Elder, B. M. Peebles, A. F. Stocker *in* Servianorum in Vergilii Carmina Commentariorum Editionis Harvardianae volumen, v 2, 1946, *and* A. F. Stocker, A. H. Travis, H. T. Smith, G. B. Waldrop, R. T. Bruère, v 3, 1965.
ABOUT—E. Thomas, Essai sur Servius et son commentaire sur Virgile, 1880; R. R. Bolgar, The Classical Heritage and Its Beneficiaries, 1954; E. Fraenkel, Kleine Beiträge zur klassischen Philologie, v 2, 1964 (reprinting articles from Journal of Roman Studies, 1948, 1949); C. E. Murgia, Prolegomena to Servius, v 5, 1976 (The Manuscripts).

SEXTUS EMPIRICUS, Greek philosopher and doctor, can be dated to about the end of the second century A.D. from his medical quarrels with Galen of Pergamum, who may have died in about 199. Sextus was a Greek—he writes of the Greeks as "ourselves"—but we do not know where he came from. He probably spent some time at Rome, since he was taught medicine by a certain Herodotus, who practiced there.

In philosophy, he belonged to the school of the Sceptics, who denied the possibility of knowledge, or withheld judgment on the subject. Greek Scepticism had been founded by Pyrrho of Elis (c. 365/60–c. 275/70 B.C.); his doctrines were introduced by Arcesilaus of Pitane (316/15–242/1 B.C.) into

seks' tus em pi' ri kus

the Platonic Academy, where (especially under Carneades, who like Pyrrho left no writings) they formed the foundation of teaching (often in a more academic and theoretical form than Pyrrho's original doctrine) until the early first century B.C. Then, while Sceptical views fell into disfavor in the Academy, they were revived outside it in the original, stronger, Pyrrhonian version. An important teacher in this tradition was Aenesidemus of Cnossus, in the mid-first century A.D., who opposed the Academy because of its defection from Sceptical ideas and has been called the last original thinker of antiquity. His work is known to us from the *Life of Pyrrho* by the third century biographer Diogenes Laertius and from the writings of Sextus Empiricus, who was Diogenes' follower.

Sextus recorded the general history of Scepticism from the time of Pyrrho onward. Thus, his surviving *Outlines [Hypotyposes] of Pyrrhonism,* in three books, founded on a work of the same title by Aenesidemus, offers a complete summary of Pyrrhonian doctrines and their relationship to Academic Scepticism and other schools. Another treatise *Sceptica* is divided into two parts: the first, composed of six books is entitled *Against the Professors (Mathematici)* and successively criticizes grammarians, orators, geometricians, arithmeticians, astrologers, and musicians. The second part, in five books, is entitled *Against Dogmatists* and assails logicians, natural philosophers, and teachers of ethics. All proponents of dogmas are shown by Sextus to display abundant self-contradictions; and he argues that neither speculation nor sense perception serve any purpose whatever as guides to truth or as aids to the differentiation between good and evil. Although Sextus is for the most part a compiler, and his own contribution amounts to very little, he is capable of following and expounding an argument and provides a good deal of useful information.

As a doctor, Sextus belonged to the school of the Empiricists, as his second name indicates. The Dogmatist school of doctors argued that knowledge of the human constitution and of the causes of illnesses is indispensable to medical practice and that experience must therefore be supplemented by reasoning and conjecture. On the other hand, Sextus and the Empiricists claimed that speculation on such matters is neither necessary nor desirable. In this matter they were following the later Sceptic position, according to which the denial, by earlier members of their school, that knowledge was impossible could not be accepted, because such a denial is in itself a dogmatic assertion, so that on this point, as on all others, the Sceptic must refrain from offering judgment.

EDITIONS with translation—R. G. Bury (Loeb ed.), 1933–49; P. P. Hallie and S. G. Etheridge, Scepticism, Man and God (selections), 1964; A. Russo, Sesto Empirico: Contro i logici, 1975.
ABOUT—E. Bevan, Stoics and Sceptics, 1913; V. Brochard, Les sceptiques grecs, 2nd ed., 1923, reprint 1959; M. Patrick, The Greek Sceptics, 1929; K. Deichgräber, Die griechische Empirikerschule, 1930; K. Janácek, Prolegomena to Sextus Empiricus, 1948; C. L. Stough, Greek Scepticism, 1970; J. C. Berberelli, The Greek Sceptics and Sextus Empiricus (Columbia, dissertation), 1974.

SICELIDAS. See Asclepiades

SICULUS, TITUS CALPURNIUS. See Calpurnius Siculus

SIDONIUS APOLLINARIS, Saint, Latin poet and letter writer, Gallo-Roman landowner, and bishop, was born in A.D. 430/1 and died in the 480s. His birthplace was Lugdunum (Lyon) in Gaul, and he came of a family with important political connections. Through his wife Papianilla, he acquired the property of Avitacum in the land of the Arverni (Auvergne); and when her father Avitus was proclaimed the western Roman emperor in 455, Sidonius accompanied him to Rome and pronounced his panegyric in verse. However Avitus was dethroned almost immediately afterward, and Sidonius associated himself with a dissident movement at Lugdunum. But then he became reconciled with the new emperor Majorian, whom he also honored with a
si dō′ ni us à pol li nä′ ris

391

panegyric (458) and under whose administration he subsequently held a post. When Majorian, in his turn, was overthrown and lost his life (461), Sidonius withdrew once again to Gaul but in 467 led a Gallo-Roman delegation to congratulate the next emperor but one, Anthemius. He became prefect of the city of Rome, but, encountering fresh political difficulties, returned in 469 to Gaul, where he entered the priesthood and was appointed bishop of Arverna (Clermont Ferrand). In this unfamiliar capacity he confronted an invasion of the Visigoths with stubborn resistance that terminated only when the western empire ceded them the entire region of the Auvergne in 475. Sidonius was arrested by the Visigoths and detained, in mild conditions, in the fortress of Liviana (near Carcassone). He was released in the following year and permitted to resume his episcopal duties, which he continued to carry out until his death; at this point he held his office as a subject of the Visigoths, on whose monarch Euric he lavished the same tactful praise as he had formerly dedicated to three Roman emperors.

To modern taste, these panegyrics to various monarchs, modeled on those of Claudian, seem fulsome and inaccurate. But Sidonius has also left twenty-one other pieces of verse, in a variety of meters. They include two wedding poems, or *Epithalamia,* crammed with literary, philosophical, and mythological lore. In one of them, celebrating the marriage of philosopher Polemius and Araneola, the poet describes a temple of philosophy, in which the past practitioners of the art and the Seven Sages receive veneration. Another poem is a detailed account of a great feudal castle in Gaul, the Burgus of Leontius. This description, which displays Sidonius' sharp eye for external details, is of considerable value to social, economic, and architectural historians—and, indeed, the poems of Sidonius in general throw a great deal of light on current Gallic conditions. In particular, their mixture of courtliness, pedantry, and triviality, even conveyed as it is in verse that is woolly and bombastic and turgid, illuminates all too clearly the foolish mutual admiration society constituted by the late Roman and Romano-Gallic upper class—although

Sidonius still stands out among his peers for his enterprising resistance to invasion at Arverna.

His nine books of letters, addressed to many friends and relations, fill out and amplify the picture very informatively. Modeling himself on Pliny the Younger and always keeping one eye on his readership, he offers a lavish display of his own genial, generous, and vain personality, always fatuously eager for applause. Many of the letters are purely frivolous, and in some cases by no means unfunny; but a number of others are serious, and indeed deeply religious. Yet Sidonius reveals a basic narrowness in matters of religion and race, disliking the Jews (although he likes a member of their faith) and greatly despising the coarse habits of the heretical Germans despite his fulsome compliments to their monarch.

EDITIONS with translation—W. B. Anderson, W. H. Semple, and E. H. Warmington, Poems and Letters (Loeb ed.), 1936, 1965; A. Loyen, Poèmes, Lettres (Budé ed.), 1960, 1970.
ABOUT—C. E. Stevens, Sidonius Apollinaris and His Age, 1933; A. Loyen, Sidoine Apollinaire et l'esprit précieux en Gaule aux derniers jours de l'empire, 1943.

SILIUS ITALICUS, TIBERIUS CATIUS ASCONIUS, Latin poet, c. A.D. 26–101, may have been born at Patavium (Padua), but this is uncertain. He made a successful career as a lawyer and became a senator but earned an unsavory reputation as an informer under Nero, in whose last year (68) he became consul. Although Silius supported the emperor Vitellius in 69, it was Vitellius' successful rival Vespasian who subsequently gave him the governorship of Asia (c. 77), the duties of which he performed successfully. Thereafter, however, he withdrew into a prosperous, cultured retirement in Rome and Campania, where he spent his time writing and engaging in learned discussions with his literary friends. A man of considerable wealth and a connoisseur of works of art, he bought a number of fine country houses, including the Tusculan villa of Cicero, whom he greatly revered. He also felt a special veneration for Virgil, whose tomb at Neapolis (Naples) he acquired and restored; and the
si' li us i ta' li kus

Stoic Cornutus dedicated to Silius a commentary on Virgil. Another Stoic with whom he was also acquainted was Epictetus, who was said to have respected him as a philosopher. Silius, too, was an adherent of Stoicism and displayed this by the manner in which he died: when he discovered he was suffering from an incurable tumor, he starved himself to death.

His only known work is an epic known as the *Punica,* a poetic history of the Second Punic War (218–201 B.C.), in which Hannibal's Carthaginian army invaded Italy. The *Punica* was planned by A.D. 88 but not completed until after 96; it is the longest poem in Latin literature, comprising 12,200 hexameters in seventeen books. Book 1 tells how the goddess Juno egged Hannibal on to strike against Rome by besieging Saguntum, which he captures in Book 2. The third book describes Hannibal's parting from his wife and child and the crossing of the Pyrenees, the Rhone River, and the Alps by the Carthaginian army. Book 4 records the battles of the Ticinus and Trebia, and Book 5 the even worse Roman disaster at Lake Trasimene. Book 6 is a digression about the Roman general Regulus who had bravely gone to his death in the First Punic War, and Book 7 returns to the second war to tell of Fabius, who planned to save Rome by his delaying tactics. The eighth book leads up to the battle of Cannae, which is described in the two books that follow. Book 11 brings Hannibal to Capua, where the demoralization of his army begins; and in Book 12 he appears outside Rome. The thirteenth book tells, amid digressions, how Capua was brought back into Roman hands and how Scipio, after the deaths of his father and uncle in Spain, visits the Underworld. In Book 14 Marcellus recaptures Syracuse, and Book 15 narrates the appointment of Scipio to the Spanish command and his capture of Carthago Nova (Cartagena). Book 16 describes Scipio's Games to honor the dead and reports his request to the Senate to be allowed to transfer the war to northern Africa, where, in the last book, he wins the decisive victory at Zama.

Silius is capable at times of a good straightforward narrative and vivid simile, yet he clings with slavish faithfulness to the traditional epic machinery and mythology, so that Scipio hardly ever comes alive, though Hannibal shows signs of doing so, at least in an occasional scene. In general, the story told so stirringly by Livy becomes merely tedious and ridiculous. There is endless tautology and overelaboration, and far too much rhetorical oratory and tiresome learning, derived, as far as geography and topography are concerned, from the scholars Varro (second century B.C.) and Hyginus (first century B.C.), and in ethnological matters from the eminent historian, scientist, and philosopher Posidonius, directly or through intermediaries. Silius also has a taste for the macabre and likes dwelling on ghoulish, morbid incidents.

A manuscript of the *Punica* was rediscovered in 1416 or 1417, and it was twice printed and published in 1471.

EDITIONS with translation—J. D. Duff (Loeb ed.), 1934; P. Miniconi and G. Devallet (Budé ed.), 1979 (Books 1-4).
ABOUT—J. W. Duff, Literary History of Rome in the Silver Age, 1927; J. Nicol, The Historical and Geographical Sources Used by Silius Italicus, 1936; L. Håkanson, Silius Italicus: Kritische und exegetische Bemerkungen, 1976.

SIMEON. See Symeon

SIMONIDES, Greek poet, c. 556–468 B.C., was born (like his nephew and fellow poet Bacchylides) at Iulis on the Ionian island of Ceos (Kea), the nearest of the Cyclades to Attica. After studying music and poetic composition at home, he went away as a young man to reside at Athens. There he became one of the literary figures at the court of Hipparchus, who, together with his brother Hippias, had succeeded their father Pisistratus as the joint rulers (tyrants) of the city. However, when Hipparchus was murdered in 514, Simonides left for Thessaly, where he gained the patronage of local autocrats, Scopas of Crannon and the Aleuadae of Larissa. By the time of the Persian Wars he was back in Athens, where the epitaph he wrote for the men who had fallen at Mara-
sī mōn′ i dēz

thon (490) was preferred to that of Aeschylus; and after the invasion by Xerxes (480), he enhanced his reputation by a number of additional epitaphs, as well as a dirge for the Spartan dead at Thermopylae and choral lyric odes commemorating the seafights at Artemisium and Salamis. Adaptable and progressive by temperament, Simonides was well equipped to express the Panhellenic spirit evoked by the Persian wars. Moreover, at this time he was closely associated with the celebrated Athenian general and statesman Themistocles, the architect of the combined Greek military effort; and he launched an attack against Themistocles' critic Timocreon of Rhodes. In about 476 Simonides went to Syracuse in Sicily as the guest of its ruler Hiero I, whom he succeeded in reconciling with his enemy Theron of Acragas; it was at Acragas that Simonides was buried.

He was said to be unattractive in appearance but an excellent business man—the first Greek poet, it would seem, to make substantial profits from his writings. These have only come down to us in fragments; they evidently included poems of various kinds. His dirges won great renown. In addition to those celebrating the men who had fallen in battle, there was one written for an occasion when, at a banquet given by the Scopades, rulers of Thessaly, the palace collapsed and buried the members of the family; Simonides compares this sudden reversal of human fortunes to the speed with which a fly buzzes from one spot to another. And elsewhere he declares that not even Heracles, the son of a god, was granted a life free of disasters; nothing is exempt from mortality—not even, finally, posthumous fame. The transitory nature of everything belonging to this world is a familiar Greek theme, but no poet expresses it with such uncompromising emphasis.

Simonides also wrote religious poems, for which he won no less than sixty-five prizes; these were dithyrambic odes, presented by male choirs in annual competitions at the festivals of Dionysus. It was also said that he wrote tragedies, but this may have been an incorrect inference from the dialogues that this dithyrambic poetry incorporated. Another sort of poem that brought him a great

reputation was the victory ode *(epinikion)* acclaiming the winners of athletic contests; it was Simonides who first established this type of choral lyric as an art form and thus created the Games' historic connection with poetry. His younger contemporary Pindar developed the genre more elaborately, and his victory odes, unlike those of Simonides, have come down to us intact; but it is clear from the latter's fragments that his poems displayed a much lighter touch than Pindar's.

He also wrote drinking songs, the surviving passages of which breathe a spirit of philosophical moderation, combined with a gentle scepticism regarding the ethical capabilities of human beings. One such poem, for example, addressed to Scopas of Crannon, offers the opinion that moral excellence is difficult to attain and impossible to keep, so that it is wiser to set a more unpretentious standard and to praise anyone who does not voluntarily do evil. A particularly impressive piece of poetry, of which we do not know the context, is the "Danae fragment," the song of Danae, daughter of Acrisius, king of Argos, over her child as they are locked together in a wooden chest and tossed on the stormy sea.

Simonides' epigrams and epitaphs gained him special renown. However, the authenticity of the pieces that have come down to us is often very doubtful, because the inscriptions, carved into stone surfaces, did not include the name of the writer; nor was any attempt made to collect those composed by Simonides before the fourth century B.C. The few epigrams that can with any probability be ascribed to his authorship (recent editors regard only one of them as certain) are filled with a grave intensity of feeling that is dramatically conveyed by the impersonality and brevity of the verses. A collection of trenchant sayings, or apothegms—ostensibly addressed to Hiero, Themistocles, and others—was also associated with his name, since he was almost more famous as a man of wisdom than as a poet.

EDITIONS—Lyric poems: D. L. Page, Poetae Melici Graeci, 1962. Epigrams: E. Diehl, Anthologia Lyrica Graeca, v 2, 1925.

ABOUT—A. Hauvette-Besnault, De l'authenticité des épigrammes de Simonide, 1896; U. von Wilamowitz-Moellendorf, Sappho und Simonides, 1913; G. Christ, Simonidesstudien (Zurich, dissertation), 1941; C. M. Bowra, Greek Lyric Poetry, 2nd ed., 1961; W. Kierdorf, Erlebnis und Darstellung der Perserkriege, 1966; D. A. Campbell, Greek Lyric Poetry, 1967.

SIMPLICIUS, Greek philosopher of the Byzantine epoch, lived in the sixth century A.D. and came from Cilicia (southeastern Asia Minor). He studied under Ammonius at Alexandria and under Damascius at Athens, and the influence of both men—representing different branches of Neoplatonism—is apparent in Simplicius' work. When the school of philosophy at Athens had been suppressed by the emperor Justinian I (529), Simplicius, together with Damascius and others, decided in 531 or 532 to emigrate to the Persian (Sassanian) court of King Chosroes (Khosrau) I. Within two years, however, they returned, and Simplicius applied himself to literary activity.

His most important writings comprised commentaries on works by Aristotle *(Physics, Categories, On Heaven,* and *On the Soul).* These commentaries display both erudition and judgment and are of importance because they contain many valuable excerpts not only from Simplicius' immediate predecessors but also from earlier philosophers, going back to the pre-Socratics. He is particularly concerned to demonstrate that Aristotle had always been in agreement with Plato and that any apparent discord between them arises only from the imperfect understanding, by subsequent writers, of what Aristotle was trying to say. Simplicius also compiled a commentary on the *Enchiridion (Manual)* of Epictetus.

EDITIONS—Commentaria in Aristotelem Graeca, v 7-11, 1892–1907. *Translations*—Commentary on Manual of Epictetus: G. Stanhope, Epictetus His Morals, with Simplicius His Comment, 1694, reprinted to 1750. ABOUT—P. Hadot, Le problème du néoplatonisme alexandrin: Hiéroclès et Simplicius, 1978.

sim pli' ki us

SISENNA, LUCIUS CORNELIUS, Latin historian and translator of fiction, lived in the early first century B.C. He was a partisan of the dictator Sulla (81), became praetor in 78, and then held the governorship of the province of Sicily. A friend of the conservatives Lucullus and Hortensius, he supported the latter in his defense of Verres, charged by Cicero with misdeeds in Sicily (70). After serving as a legate under Pompey's supreme command, Sisenna died in Crete in 67.

He wrote a history of his own times, only fragments of which now exist. It comprised at least twelve books (or possibly twenty-three) and perhaps continued the work of another historian, Sempronius Asellio (second century B.C.). After an allusion to Rome's origins (unless this was part of a digression in a later section of the work), Sisenna's treatise dealt with the Social or Marsian war (the revolt of the Italian allies, 91–87 B.C.) and then narrated the civil war won by Sulla, with whose final victory in 82 the work possibly concluded; though it may, alternatively, have continued until Sulla's abdication at the end of 81, or his death and funeral in 78.

Cicero described Sisenna as "a man of scholarly training who was dedicated to liberal studies," and continues: "He spoke pure Latin, knew a good deal about state affairs, and was not without wit; but he did not take sufficient pains and lacked practical legal experience. His talents can best be seen in his *History,* which, while easily surpassing all our other historians up to the present time, nevertheless reveals the imperfections of historiography in Latin literature, in which, hitherto, inadequate efforts have been made to cultivate the art." Cicero's reference to Sisenna's lack of pains is intended to apply to his literary endeavors as well as his public life. Elsewhere, the orator repeats his judgment (with Atticus as his mouthpiece), adding that "Sisenna, in his historical writing, has an almost childish purpose in view, for it seems that Cleitarchus is absolutely the only Greek author whom he has read, and that his sole desire is to imitate him." Cleitarchus was a romanticizing historian of the early third century B.C., who, although much despised by scholars, had at least tried

si sen' nà

to make his work readable, as apparently Sisenna also did. But the latter's style was described as diffuse and redundant, a verdict confirmed by extant fragments. Moreover, his viewpoint exhibited a strong political bias in favor of Sulla. Even Sallust, who in his *Jugurthine War* declared Sisenna to have been the best and most accurate of the historians of Sulla, had to admit that his judgment of the dictator had been altogether too favorable.

Sisenna also translated the *Milesian Tales* of Aristides of Miletus (c. 100 B.C.) into Latin, thus bringing these popular, erotic, short stories into fashion at Rome. Ovid remarks on this enterprise in terms that suggest Sisenna turned from his serious occupation of writing history to this lighthearted and salacious type of literature as a form of relaxation.

EDITIONS—H. Peter, Historicorum Romanorum Reliquiae, v 1, 2nd ed., 1914; F. Buecheler and W. Heraeus, Petronii Saturae, 4th ed., 1922; G. Calboli *in* Gli storiografi latini tramandati in frammenti, 1976.
ABOUT—E. Badian, Studies in Greek and Roman History, 1964; R. Syme, Sallust, 1964; P. G. Walsh, The Roman Novel, 1970.

SOCRATES. See Plato

SOLON, Greek statesman and poet, was born in about 640 B.C. and perhaps died soon after 561. He was the son of Execestides, an Athenian nobleman, but was not a rich man; he may have been a merchant in the earlier part of his life. After winning a reputation as a patriot in Athens' war with the city-state of Megara over the possession of Salamis (c. 600), he became the city's chief archon (senior official of the administration), for the year 594–593. As archon he was granted special legislative powers to deal with grave economic distress and political conflict due largely to the reduction of many poor persons to serfdom owing to their failure to pay their debts.

It is to this year that most scholars attribute his principal laws, which were published
sō′lon

on at least sixteen wooden tablets *(axones);* however, we cannot now disentangle Solon's original wording from subsequent amendments and additions. His measures included the "shaking off of burdens" *(seisachtheia),* an annulment of all debts for which land or personal liberty formed the security and the restoration of freedom of those who had been sold into slavery; it was a sweeping measure, although not sweeping enough for those who had hoped for a wholesale redistribution of land. It was probably in 592/1 that Solon received a further appointment as "reformer of the constitution," once again with full legislative authority. Acting under these powers, he altered the qualification for public office from one based on birth and wealth to one based on wealth only, without regard to birth, thus breaking the power of the hereditary nobility; and he also divided the citizens into four census classes based on their annual production of grain, oil, and wine, the first two of which were to provide holders of the principal offices. Moreover, alongside the ancient conservative Council of the Areopagus, he instituted a new Council, four hundred strong, of which the main function was to prepare business for the Assembly. He also made the Assembly into a judicial panel, under the name of the Heliaea —another important innovation, since for the first time the people, or their representatives selected by lot, were to act as jurors and judges.

Then Solon withdrew from Attica for ten years and devoted himself to travel, visiting Egypt and Cyprus and elsewhere but returning in time to set up impassioned but ultimately unsuccessful resistance to the plans of Pisistratus to establish an autocracy or "tyranny" (561). Solon does not seem to have survived this event for very long, if at all.

He used verse freely to express his ideas, and it is of great value to hear this leading personage in the Athenian state explaining his political actions. In one long poem, he unfolds the philosophy of life that lay behind these actions, speaking first of the gods' care for the Athenians, and then pointing to the social discontent of the people themselves as the greatest peril facing their city; and he closes with a eulogy of Good Order *(Eu-*

nomia). A fragment of another poem, in which Solon tries to explain the eternal conundrum of why the wicked prosper, reverts to his determination to justify the ways of heaven. At the end, he stresses another basic element of his moral and political thinking—namely, wise moderation and the golden mean: there are limits in all things. What he has done, he tells us elsewhere, is to unite power and justice with a strong hand. In a number of poems, he takes stock of his various achievements as a statesman, displaying an imposing blend of justified pride, vigorous piety, high-minded superiority to personal ambition, and vigilant determination to repel the internal foe. As for external enemies, there is a fragment of a famous poem of his earlier days which, according to a later story, he recited publicly under the pretense that he was mad, thus arousing the Athenians to go to war against Megara and seize Salamis. In another piece, which has come down to us, he divides human life into ten sections of seven years each, the purpose of this arrangement, as we learn from a further elegy, being to counter Mimnermus, who said that he himself wanted to die when he reached sixty; Solon feels that a man ought to be glad to live until the age of eighty, provided he still continues to learn as he grows old.

With this love of discovering new things and his delight in the works of Dionysus, Aphrodite, and the Muses, Solon is the first discernible representative of the characteristic spirit of Athens. He is also the city's first poet—not a great poet, however, though he is capable of rising above commonplace levels and has the power to clothe his sane and intelligent talent in not unworthy language. And it has been suggested, too, that he influenced the history of Attic literature in another fashion as well, by decreeing the systematic reading of Homer at the Panathenaic Festival. In the subsequent traditions of Athens, Solon was regarded as one of the Seven Sages and invested with almost superhuman stature. Plato quoted an assertion that he was not only the most outspoken of poets but also the wisest of men, thus implying that his reforms, however far-reaching, were nevertheless sensible enough not to pander to the mob.

EDITIONS—E. Diehl, Anthologia Lyrica Graeca, 1949; M. L. West, Iambi et Elegi Graeci, v 2, 1972. *With translation:* J. M. Edmonds, Greek Elegy and Iambus (Loeb ed.), v 1, 1931.
ABOUT—K. Freeman, Work and Life of Solon, 1926; C. M. Bowra, Early Greek Elegists, 1938; W. J. Woodhouse, Solon the Liberator, 1938; A. Masaracchia, Solone, 1958; G. Ferrara, La politica di Solone, 1964; E. Ruschenbusch, ed., Solonis Nomoi, 1966; V. L. Ehrenberg, From Solon to Socrates, 1968; A. Martina, Solon: Testimonia Veterum, 1969; G. Pfohl, Die griechische Elegie, 1972.

SOPHOCLES, Greek poet and tragic dramatist, was born in about 496 B.C. and died in 406. His birthplace was Colonus near Athens. He was the son of Sophilus, a wealthy arms manufacturer. In the course of a good education, he was taught music by Lampros, the best-known musician of the day and perhaps studied tragedy under Aeschylus, whom he subsequently defeated in the dramatic festival of 468, thus gaining his first victory at these competitions. In 433–442 Sophocles acted as Hellenotamias, the chairman of the board that collected tribute from the subject-allies of Athens. Then, in 440, he was elected one of the ten Athenian generals *(strategoi)* under the chairmanship of Pericles and in this capacity shared the command in the war against rebellious Samos. Later he again became a general under Nicias and after the failure of the Athenian expedition to Syracuse (413) was appointed one of the special commissioners *(probouloi)* to deal with the emergency. He also served as a member of delegations to foreign states. He was a priest of Amynos (or Alcon or Halon), a god of healing, and offered his own house as a place of worship for the healing deity Asclepius until his temple was ready. In addition, he founded a literary and musical society.

Sophocles was handsome, rich, courteous, and versatile. He married first Nicostrate and then Theoris of Sicyon, each of whom gave him sons, Iophon (a tragedian) and Agathon (father of a tragedian, the younger Sophocles) respectively. Unlike his rival Euripides, he had very early acquired a favorable public; Sophocles outlived Euripides by

sŏf′ ə klēz

397

a few months, dying just before the catastrophic end of the Peloponnesian War.

A hundred and thirty plays were attributed to him, (seven of which were subsequently reckoned spurious). In the dramatic competitions he probably won twenty-four victories—that is to say, twenty-four of his tetralogies (each comprising three tragedies and a satyr play) were successful. Seven of his tragedies have survived.

The plot of the *Ajax* (written before 441 B.C.) centers upon the bestowal of the arms of the dead Achilles. Ajax claimed them, on the grounds that he was the bravest man in the Greek army before Troy, but they were awarded instead to Odysseus, upon whom Ajax vowed vengeance, as well as on those who had chosen Odysseus as the recipient of the arms. However, the goddess Athena, patron of Ajax but angered by his arrogant assertion that he had no need of divine aid, deludes him with hallucinations so that he identifies sheep and cattle as his enemies; and at the beginning of the play she promises Odysseus to show him his mad adversary attacking the harmless animals. Ajax recovers from his madness and declares that only suicide can wipe out his shame. Tecmessa (his captive and concubine) and the chorus composed of his sailors from Salamis endeavor to dissuade him, but he refuses to abandon his purpose and sends for his son Eurysaces. After Eurysaces has arrived, Ajax leaves final instructions for his brother Teucer, bids farewell, fetches his sword from his tent, and goes forth to die. Then a messenger from the camp arrives to report a pronouncement by the seer Calchas: Ajax is in danger from Athena for one day only, and all will be well if he stays in his tent for the duration of that time. But it is already too late; and Tecmessa finds his dead body. Menelaus, backed by Agamemnon, refuses a burial for the corpse, but Teucer opposes them, and Odysseus finally persuades them to relent. Ajax is carried by his Salaminians to his tomb.

At widely different dates, Sophocles also wrote three great tragedies about the Theban mythology. In the first of these plays the *Antigone* (441), Creon, ruler of Thebes, has forbidden anyone on pain of death to bury the body of Oedipus' son Polyneices, one of

the Seven Against Thebes, who, with the help of Argos, had attempted to capture the city. But Polyneices' sister Antigone resolves to defy the edict and perform his funeral rites. She is caught, however, and brought before the infuriated king, to whom she justifies her act by virtue of the overriding divine law. Creon, unrelenting, condemns her to be walled into a cave alive. Her sister, Ismene, who has refused hitherto to take part in the defiant deed, now claims a share in the guilt and the penalty. Haemon, Creon's son, who is betrothed to Antigone, pleads in vain with his father, then goes out, warning his father that he will die with her. The blind seer Tiresias threatens Creon with the fearful consequences of flouting the sacred law. Creon, at last moved, sets out hurriedly for the cave where Antigone has been immured. He finds Haemon clasping her dead body, for Antigone has hanged herself. Haemon thrusts vainly at Creon with his sword, and then he, too, commits suicide. Creon returns to the palace, to find that Eurydice, his wife, in despair, has taken her own life.

The *Oedipus the King* (written soon after 430) refers to an earlier stage in the history of the family. In this play Oedipus has ruled the city for a number of years, having left his home in Corinth to escape the fulfillment of an oracle that said he would kill his father and marry his mother. He now has to investigate the murder of the previous king, Laius, who has been slain at a country crossroads by persons unknown. Step by step he discovers that he himself was the killer of Laius, that Laius and not, as he believed, the king of Corinth was his father, and that his wife Jocasta is also his mother. The oracle has after all been fulfilled. Jocasta commits suicide; Oedipus blinds himself, takes leave of his two daughters, and is led away.

The *Oedipus at Colonus,* Sophocles' last play performed in 401 after the dramatist's death, contains a minimum of plot. It describes how the aged Oedipus, a blind, helpless, and squalid beggar, arrives at Colonus near Athens after years of wandering; how he is received there, in a series of encounters involving the recapitulation by Oedipus of his tragic career; and how, finally, summoned by peals of thunder, he leads the way with majestic confidence to the spot where his mysterious apotheosis takes place, witnessed by no one but Theseus, the Athenian king. A messenger reports his passing; Theseus returns to the city with the two mourning daughters of Oedipus, and agrees to convey them home to Thebes.

In Sophocles' *Electra,* performed at some date between 418 and 410 (whether before or after the *Electra* of Euripides is disputed), Orestes, accompanied by Pylades, is making his way to Mycenae to carry out the command of the Delphic oracle that he should avenge the death of his father Agamemnon at the hand of Queen Clytemnestra. The two young men plan to disguise themselves and seek an interview with the queen, pretending that Orestes is dead and that the urn they are bringing her contains his ashes. Orestes' sister Electra enters bewailing her unmarried lot and cursing the murderers of her father; her milder sister Chrysothemis rebukes her. Clytemnestra and Electra assail one another with reproaches but break off when a messenger brings false news that Orestes is dead. Chrysothemis, however, returns from the tomb and declares to Electra that flowers and a lock of hair she had seen there must have been left by Orestes; her sister does not believe her. Then Orestes and Pylades carry out their murderous plan, and Clytemnestra's death shriek is heard. Next, her lover Aegisthus, who has been sharing the throne with her, appears on the scene and departs again, whereupon he too is struck down. The chorus of Mycenaean women hail the usurper's death, which they hope will bring the curse on the royal house of Atreus to an end.

The *Trachinian Women,* perhaps first performed in the early 420s B.C., takes its name from the members of its chorus. At the beginning of the play we find Deianira at her house at Trachis, in central Greece. Worried by the long absence of her husband, Heracles, she decides to send their son Hyllus to search for him. A messenger then arrives to report that Heracles is well and on his way home. The good news is soon confirmed by his herald Lichas, who reveals that after the performance of mighty deeds the hero is visting the island of Euboea, and consecrating an altar to Zeus as a thank offering. From the town of Oechalia, which Heracles has enslaved, Lichas has brought several women prisoners, and Deianira discovers that one of them, Iole, has attracted Heracles' love. Deianira determines to win his affections back by sending him a robe smeared with a love charm bequeathed to her by the dying centaur Nessus. But the supposed charm is in reality a deadly poison, and Hyllus comes to report that Heracles, after he has put on the robe, is dying in agony. Deianira kills herself, and Heracles bids Hyllus burn his body on a pyre at Mount Oeta and take Iole for himself. At the end, Hyllus assails the gods, who load even the noblest man with sorrows and then view the result with indifference.

The *Philoctetes* dates from 409 B.C. Nine years before the action of the play begins the hero of that name, on his way to the Trojan War, had been left behind on the island of Lemnos, afflicted by a grievous snakebite. He has with him, however, the bow and arrows of Heracles, and without these, a seer has declared, Troy cannot be taken by the Greeks. So Odysseus has been commissioned to sail to Lemnos, pretending that he is on his way back to Greece, and get hold of the weapons. He takes with him Neoptolemus (the son of Philoctetes' dearest friend Achilles), who reluctantly consents to accompany him and deceive the stricken man. Racked with pain, Philoctetes entrusts his bow and arrows to the care of Neoptolemus, who regrets the trick, however, and confesses it to the sick man in remorse. Odysseus now appears and claims the bow; and Neoptolemus intervenes to prevent Philoctetes from killing Odysseus. Neoptolemus now agrees, unwillingly, to take Philoctetes back to Greece: but at this juncture Heracles, who has now become a god, appears with orders from Zeus that they should both instead return to Troy, where the bow will bring about the fall of the city and Philoctetes will be cured.

Sophocles was an innovator in tragic construction. He introduced the third actor, which made it possible, since the actors could double, to develop plots and situations of a much more elaborate character than those of his forerunner Aeschylus. Moreover, Sophocles, although like his predecessors he had to offer four plays (three tragedies and a satyr play) at each dramatic competition, abandoned the practice of presenting connected trilogies or tetralogies; instead he made each play an artistic whole in itself. Unity is determined not by events outside the play but by the experiences the characters undergo and the catastrophes that befall them. His plots are delineated with all the force and wealth of a supremely eloquent and flexible style that commands the entire massive range of dramatic diction.

Aristotle handed *Oedipus the King* down to posterity as the model of what a tragedy should be. Its continual imagery of blindness, light, and darkness leads to a supremely dramatic, harrowing conclusion. Yet the audiences attending Sophocles' plays were not surprised by the course of events, for they knew the myths on which the plots were based. Therefore, since the spectators are all in the secret and only the actors are not, the whole progression of events is a cumulation of the "tragic irony" especially associated with Sophocles' name. In this process his choruses (increased from twelve to fifteen) play an indispensable part, for he is the tragic poet who most closely integrates the choric pronouncements with the dramatic purpose of his plays. Rising above the role of a mere mouthpiece of the poet or a sympathetic onlooker of the action, the chorus gives organization and background to Sophocles' version of the traditional myths, helping him to use them as arresting symbols of human hatreds and aspirations.

Oedipus is the most famous of all searchers for truth: the supreme moments are those involving the passage from ignorant confidence of guiltlessness to recognition, appalling knowledge, and despair. Sophocles is less interested in morality than in the human personalities. Yet in the rapid movement of his dramas the characters are not depicted in subtle psychological detail but drawn in boldly contrasted, starkly powerful lines, so that all attention is concentrated upon the moral qualities that prompt their decisions. At one remove, as it were, from the ordinary human lot, these personages work out their crucial dilemmas, determining—as Sophocles and his compatriots had

to determine for themselves in an era of rapid change and constant questioning—what they owed to the gods, and to their city-state, and to their families, and to the promptings of their own hearts and minds.

Among these demonic, iron-willed and hot-tempered sufferers of Sophoclean drama, Oedipus stands out as the self-taught, self-made autocrat, who unaided has risen to mastery over adversaries hitherto believed invincible. It was Aristotle's theory expressed in his *Poetics,* that, in tragedy misfortune should fall on a prominent figure because he or she is tainted by an "error" or defect of character *(hamartia).* It may be a moral fault or frailty, such as greed or excess ambition; or it may be a hereditary quasi-physical curse or blight (familiar from the story of the house of Agamemnon as told by Aeschylus); or perhaps it is an intellectual error of judgment. This last was Deianira's flaw in the *Trachinian Women,* since she did not understand that the supposed love charm was a poison, whereas Oedipus' "error" stems from his ignorance of material facts and circumstances, his misconception which prompts the overconfidence the Greeks called *hubris* and touches off the series of events that lead to disaster. Yet the utter ruin that overcomes him, involving a classic reversal of his circumstances, is incurred in the conduct of an investigation that he had believed to be his duty, and an unpleasant one at that.

Downfalls such as that of Oedipus are caused by the gods, to whom all things are easy, and come when the divine order has somehow been breached. We cannot always detect when a breach has occurred, or why the divine purpose works as it does, or make the catastrophe that follows harmonize with our own understanding of what is just and what is not. The men or women fate strikes down are victims of the unpredictability of events, which their own injudicious actions often involuntarily assist in bringing about. Sophocles viewed this suffering, and the evil it caused, as beneficial, because it was educative. In comparison with (and confrontation with) a god or the gods—he uses both terms—human beings are of no account; they must humble themselves before the will of the divine power, which, however dreadful inexplicable, and unbearable its manifestations may be, cannot ever be condemned as wrong, because it embodies the natural order of events. Yet even in the utter appalling crash of the mortal victim, there remains a splendid heroism. And there also remains hope, for the *Oedipus at Colonus* displays a sublime reconciliation in which the solemn and mysterious ways of heaven are made to seem, after all, less unrelenting to humankind.

The *Antigone* takes up the Theban story after the blinded Oedipus has departed from the city. In this play the purpose of the speeches is not so much to develop argumentative theses (as in the *Ajax* and *Trachinian Women*) as to illustrate the character and principles of the speakers and the remorseless development of the action. The plot centers wholly around a bitter and fatal conflict between two passionately held principles, with widely reverberating repercussions: the collision between private conscience and public authority, between the divine law on which Antigone founds her case and those human laws that the man of state, Cleon, sets against her. Antigone is harsh and stubborn, but as the play runs rapidly on its doom-laden course, we see how her voluntary, courageous, almost ferocious self-sacrifice stems from an inner necessity, with no reward to herself but the cold comfort of knowing she could not do otherwise and no fulfillment except in self-destruction. Creon, speaking for the world, the state, and expediency, has a respectable and reasonable case to present. But his conception of duty stands lower than Antigone's. Flawed by that special, classic *hubris* that makes important personages do wrong, he dies trying to correct a moral standard that lies beyond his control.

The high estimation in which Sophocles was held in antiquity has been shared in later ages. In the seventeenth century the French dramatic poet Racine was among its spokesmen, and in the eighteenth the German dramatist and critic Lessing. In the nineteenth the English poet and critic Matthew Arnold saw him as one "who saw life steadily and saw it whole," though that century tended to overstress the tranquil sereneness of Sophocles' piety and to say too little

of the painful torment that his meditations about the ways of the universe seem to have caused him. In our own century, one of the offspring of Sophoclean drama was Sigmund Freud's Oedipus Complex, the theory that love of mother and jealousy of father provided the most powerful of all instinctive drives. But Sophocles' clashes of authority, divine and human, have also prompted much other heartfelt interpretation during the political and moral crises of our own time.

A substantial portion of another play of authentic Sophoclean authorship has also come down to us. This is not, however, a tragedy but one of the lighthearted satyr plays, a dramatic genre shaped by the playwright Pratinas (sixth century B.C.). Satyr plays, all having to do with the adventures of the satyrs and of the convivial god Silenus who was their master, figured as accompaniments of the three tragedies each playwright presented at a festival. Sophocles' satyr play, the *Ichneutae (Searching Satyrs)*, of which a considerable part has survived, involves the theft by Hermes, soon after his birth, of the cattle of Apollo. Silenus offers his services and those of his sons, the chorus of satyrs, to recover the cattle, in exchange for the promise of a golden wreath and of freedom from servitude. Owing to an indiscretion by the mountain nymph Cyllene, the satyrs get on the track of the lost animals, and in the missing part of the play Apollo apparently confronted Hermes and was won over by the gift of his lyre (as in the Homeric Hymn to Hermes); whereupon he rewarded the satyrs for their discovery.

WORKS (now lost) include the following plays: Acrisius, Admetus, Aegeus, Aegisthus, Ajax of Locris, Alcmaeon, Aleadae, Aletes, Alexander, Amphiaraus, Amphitryon, Amycus, Andromache, Andromeda, Antenoridae, Assembly of the Achaeans, Athamas (two), Atreus, Banquet of the Achaeans, Camicians, Captive Women, Cedalion, Cerberus, Chryses, Clytemnestra, Colchian Women, Creusa, Daedalus, Danae, Dionysiskos, Dolopes, Epigoni, Erigone, Eriphyle, Eris, Ethiopians, Eumelus, Euryalus, Eurypylus, Eurysaces, Helen Claimed, Helen Seized, Heracles, Heracles at Taenarum, Herakleiskos, Hermione, Hippodamia, Hipponous, Hybris, Iambe, Iberians, Image Bearers, Inachus, Iobates, Iocles, Ion, Iphigenia, Ixion, Judgment, Laconian Women, Laocoon, Larissaeans, Lemnian Women (two versions), Lovers of Achilles,

Madness of Odysseus, Marriage of Helen, Meleager, Memnon, Minos, Momus, Muses, Mysians, Nauplius the Fire-Kindler, Nausicaa, Niobe, Odysseus Akanthoplex, Oeneus, Oenomaus, Palamedes, Pandora, Peleus, Pelias, Phaeacians, Phaedra, Philoctetes at Troy, Phineus (two), Phoenix, Phrixus, Phrygians, Phthian Women, Polyides, Polyxena, Priam, Procris, Root-Cutters, Salmoneus, Scyrians, Scythian Women, Shepherds, Sinon, Sisyphus, Tantalus, Tereus, Teucer, Thamyras, Theseus, Thyestes (three), Triptolemus, Troilus, Tympanists, Tyndareus, Tyro (two), Voyage of Nauplius, Water-Carriers. A few of these plays may be of other authorship, and some of the titles may be alternative designations of the same play.

EDITIONS (of plays)—Recent commentaries include: J. C. Kamerbeek, Ajax, Trachinian Women, Oedipus the King, Electra, 1953, 1959, 1967, 1974; W. B. Stanford, Ajax, 1963; T. B. L. Webster, Philoctetes, 1970; P. L. Easterling, Trachinian Women, 1971; J. H. Kells, Electra, 1973; A. Colonna, Ajax, Electra, 1975; M. dos Santos, Phoenician Women, 1975; S. Radt, ed., Tragicorum Graecorum Fragmenta, v 4, 1976. *With translation:* R. C. Jebb, 1883–1902, reprint 1952; F. Storr (Loeb ed.), 1912–13; E. F. Watling (Penguin ed.), 1947, 1953; F. L. Lucas, Greek Drama for the Modern Reader, 1954, *and* Greek Drama for the Common Reader, 1967; T. H. Banks, Three Theban Plays, 1956, *and* Four Plays by Sophocles, 1966; P. Roche, The Oedipus Plays of Sophocles, 1958; D. Greene and R. Lattimore, eds., The Complete Greek Tragedies, 1959; H. D. F. Kitto, Three Tragedies, 1962; Fragments: A. C. Pearson, 1917; S. Radt, Tragicorum Graecorum Fragmenta, v 4, 1977. *Translations* (of individual plays) —List *in* G. B. Parks and R. Z. Temple, The Literatures of the World in English Translation, v 1, 1968; A. M. W. Green, Classics in Translation: A Selective Bibliography (1930–76), 1976; *add* J. Ferguson and P. Berthoud, Two Oedipus Plays, 1976; S. Berg and D. Clay, Oedipus Tyrannus, 1978; C. K. Williams and G. W. Dickerson, Women of Trachis, 1979.

ABOUT—C. M. Bowra, Sophoclean Tragedy, 1944; F. R. Earp, The Style of Sophocles, 1944; J. T. Sheppard, The Wisdom of Sophocles, 1947, *and* Aeschylus and Sophocles: Their Work and Influence, 1963; C. H. Whitman, Sophocles: A Study of Heroic Humanism, 1951; A. J. A. Waldock, Sophocles and Greek Pessimism, 1952; F. J. H. Letters, The Life and Work of Sophocles, 1953; V. Ehrenberg, Sophocles and Pericles, 1954; S. M. Adams, Sophocles the Playwright, 1957; G. M. Kirkwood, A Study of Sophoclean Drama, 1958; W. N. Bates, Sophocles, 1961; T. B. L. Webster, An Introduction to Sophocles, 2nd ed., 1961, *and* Greek Tragedy (Greece & Rome: New Surveys in the Classics, no 5), 1971; B. M. W. Knox, Heroic Temper: Studies in Sophoclean Tragedy, 1964; A. Lesky, Greek Tragedy, 1966; W. Walter, The Plays of Sophocles, 1966; T. M. Woodard, ed., Sophocles: A Collection of Critical Essays, 1966; H. Musurillo, The Light and the Darkness: Studies in the Dramatic Poetry of Sophocles, 1967; A. A. Long, Language and Thought in Sophocles, 1968; M. J. O'Brien, Twentieth Century Interpretations of Oedipus Rex, 1968; H. Lloyd-Jones, The Justice of Zeus, 1971; S. Melchinger, Sophocles, 1974; G. F. Else, The Madness of Antigone, 1976; K. Rein-

hardt, Sophokles, 1977; H. M. Harvey and E. D. Harvey, Sophocles, 1978.

SOPHRON, Greek writer of mimes, lived in the fifth century B.C. and was a Syracusan.

In Greece, as elsewhere, mimetic dances had been popular from very early times; solo performers, and later small companies whose members belonged to the same social category as acrobats, offered imitations on the stage, employing voice, gesticulation, and facial expression—the ancients made a distinction between spoken and sung mime (mimody). Such performances were closely associated with the city-state of Syracuse; Xenophon tells of a mime danced there by a boy and a girl at a private dinner party to the accompaniment of music; the girl performed also as a sword dancer and was the mistress of the Syracusan who produced the turn. The theme of the piece Xenophon describes was mythological, "Dionysus and Ariadne," but others dealt with topics taken from daily life. The language of the mimes was colloquial and included many proverbial and traditional sayings.

It appears likely that Sophron, under the influence of his fellow Sicilian Epicharmus, was the first to give literary form to these pieces. One substantial papyrus fragment from his works is extant and about a hundred and seventy brief quotations, mostly preserved by later scholars to illustrate features of the Doric dialect, which was Sophron's medium; he employed very irregular verse or rhythmical prose, probably the latter. Either he or his ancient editors divided up his mimes into women's and men's, according to the sex of the majority of the characters. The largest surviving fragment belongs to the former category, being entitled *The Women Who Say They Will Drive Out the Goddess.* The goddess may be Hecate, who was associated with the world of ghosts and the uncanny; the passage contains a performance of popular magic, in which a group of female sorcerers try to drive out a spirit by which someone is possessed. Other "female" pieces by Sophron

sō′ fron

included *Women Watching the Isthmian Games, Women at Breakfast (Sunaristosai), The Bridesmaid (Numphoponos), The Mother-in-law (Penthera),* and *The Seamstresses (Akestriai).* Among the titles of his "male" mimes are *The Messenger, The Tunny-Fisherman,* and *Fisherman Versus Peasant.*

Sophron's mimes were kept by Plato under his pillow. Later, they were in particular favor with the realistically minded literary circles of the third century B.C.: the pastoral poet Theocritus and apparently also Herodas, a writer of mimes, owed him substantial debts, and Rhinthon of Taras gave literary form to the phlyax plays or "merry tragedies" that were a branch or offshoot of such mimes. In the following century Apollodorus of Athens, author of a commentary on Epicharmus, wrote another on Sophron. Sophron's sketches remained in popular favor throughout the whole of antiquity. Another writer of mimes was his son Xenarchus, about whom hardly anything is known.

EDITIONS—G. Kaibel, Comicorum Graecorum Fragmenta, 1899, reprint 1958; A. Olivieri, Frammenti della commedia greca e del mimo nella Sicilia e nella Magna Grecia, v 3, 1930. For the longer fragment *see* D. L. Page, Papyri (Loeb ed.), v 3, 1942.
ABOUT—H. Reich, Der Mimus, 1903; M. Bieber, The History of the Greek and Roman Theater, 1939.

SOTADES, Greek poet, lived in the time of King Ptolemy II Philadelphus of Egypt (289/8–246 B.C.). His home was at Maronea in Thrace (northeastern Greece). One of his poems was addressed to Belestiche, Ptolemy's mistress, but his criticisms of Ptolemy's incestuous marriage to his sister Arsinoe impelled one of the royal governors to put him to death at Caunus (now Dalyan) in Caria (southwestern Asia Minor).

His poems, of which very few survive, were in iambics. In addition to its use in tragedy, there had been a long tradition of iambics being employed for satirical and scurrilous purposes; in the Hellenistic age this type of iambic vituperation was revived. Sotades, who belonged to this movement,
sō' tả dēz

invented a meter of his own known in his honor as Sotadean. Based on the minor ionic (two short and two long syllables) and capable of a wide range of variations, it was adapted by him for spoken verse and used in his travesty of the *Iliad.* He also wrote *Amazon, Adonis, Descent Into Hades,* and a poem to the flute player Theodorus in this meter.

He was noteworthy for the remarkable impropriety and foulness of his verse, which caused him to be classified among "cinaedologic" poets (from *kinaidos,* a male prostitute). In this connection, his piece called the *Priapus* created a special obscene poetic genre, the *Priapeia,* poems in honor of the fertility god Priapus, whose symbol was a grotesquely large phallus. Originally worshiped at Lampsacus (Lapseki) on the Hellespont (Dardanelles), Priapus became increasingly popular in the Hellenistic age, especially as a god of gardens where his phallic statues, fulfilling the dual role of patron deity and scarecrow, were inscribed with jocular verses, varying from lighthearted wit to extreme crudity. These verses are best known from Latin collections, but Sotades' *Priapus* inaugurated their conversion into a literary form, for which a special meter was devised by Aristarchus' teacher Euphronius, who came from the Chersonese (Gallipoli peninsula) nearby.

A collection of wise sayings ascribed to Sotades, which may have been composed for the education of Greek children in Egypt, is evidently not from his hand; and certain other titles assigned to his authorship have to be reattributed to an Athenian comic playwright of the fourth century B.C. who bore the same name.

EDITIONS—J. U. Powell, Collectanea Alexandrina, 1925; E. Diehl, Anthologia Lyrica Graeca, v 2, 3rd ed., 1949–52.
ABOUT—H. Herter, De Priapo, 1932.

SPARTIANUS, AELIUS, is one of the six ostensible authors of a collection of Latin biographies of Roman emperors, princes and usurpers, now known as the *Historia Augusta* though its original title is uncertain. The biographies, extending chronologically
spär ti ä' nus

403

from Hadrian (A.D. 117–38) to Carinus and Numerianus (283–84), have survived, with the exception of a gap from 244 to 259. The other alleged authors are named Julius Capitolinus, Vulcacius Gallicanus, Aelius Lampridius, Trebellius Pollio, and Flavius Vopiscus. But there is every reason to suppose that all these six names are invented and that the *Historia,* which displays considerable stylistic uniformity, is instead the work of a single, unidentified writer. The work is professedly written in the reigns of Diocletian (284–305) and Constantine I the Great (306–37), to each of whom certain of the biographies are dedicated; internal evidence, however, proves that these dedications are fictitious and that the actual period of composition is a good deal later. After extensive investigation and controversy, a date near the end of the fourth century is now generally preferred, on the grounds of certain echoes and imitations of writers of that time.

The *Historia Augusta* has to be given serious attention because it is frequently our only surviving source of information for the period that it covers. The work also has to be used with extreme caution. Its first part, from Hadrian to Caracalla (211–17), includes a good deal of authentic and knowledgeably presented material, much of which may be derived (as frequent references suggest) from Marius Maximus who wrote a series of biographies of emperors from Nerva (96–98) to Elagabalus (218–22) (in continuation of Suetonius' *Lives*). However, the second part of the *Historia Augusta* is far less reliable. Although there still remains a thin substratum of fact, most of the numerous quotations from documents are palpable forgeries, many of the proper names included are equally spurious, and even the events the author describes are often suspect to the highest degree.

The ancient world has left us a number of such pseudepigrapha—writings that are not the work of the authors whose names are attached to them—and the purposes of these false ascriptions are various. The aim of the *Historia Augusta* has been extensively disputed. Its author reveals pro-senatorial sympathies, does not approve of hereditary monarchy (though he favors the supposed

descendants of Claudius II Gothicus, 268–70) and deplores the army's interventions in politics. According to one modern theory, he concealed his identity and date in order to place himself in a safer position to attack Christianity and present paganism in a favorable light; at all events, the work stands in the tradition of imperial biography as this was envisaged by cultivated pagans in the later fourth century A.D. Possibly, however, all that he was trying to do was to entertain like-minded readers by spicy and unscrupulous sensationalism. He is also an erudite fancier and collector of archaic, flowery, and precious words. But his writing is slapdash and hasty and his style flat and monotonous; though he is not without a certain sly, tongue-in-cheek humor, and the barefaced effrontery of his fraudulent fabrications may well have raised laughs among his readers.

The first known use of the *Historia Augusta* was by Quintus Aurelius Memmius Symmachus, consul in A.D. 485 and the father-in-law of Boethius. Later, the work became very popular in the Middle Ages, and no less than seventeen manuscripts (widely varying in accuracy and completeness) have been preserved, all ultimately derived from the ninth century Codex Palatinus from Fulda, now in the Vatican. The first printed edition was published at Milan in 1475.

EDITIONS with translation—D. Magie, Scriptores Historiae Augustae (Loeb ed.), 1922, 1924, 1932. *Translations* (partial)—A. Birley, Lives of the Later Caesars (Penguin ed.: Hadrian to Elagabalus), 1976.
ABOUT—N. H. Baynes, The Historia Augusta: Its Date and Purpose, 1926; W. Hartke, Geschichte und Politik im spätantiken Rom (Klio, Beiheft 45), 1940; J. Straub, Studien zur Historia Augusta, 1952; H. Stern, Date et destinataire de l'Histoire Auguste, 1953; A. Momigliano, An Unsolved Problem of Historical Forgery: The Scriptores Historiae Augustae, 1954, reprinted *in* Secondo contributo alla storia degli studi classici, 1960; Atti del Colloquio Patavino sulla Historia Augusta, 1963; J. Straub, ed., Historia-Augusta-Colloquia Bonn, 1964–75; A. R. Birley, The Augustan History, *in* T. A. Dorey, ed., Latin Biography, 1967; R. Syme, Ammianus and the Historia Augusta, 1968, *and* Emperors and Biography: Studies in the Historia Augusta, 1971; A. Chastagnol, Recherches sur l'Histoire Auguste, 1970; F. Kolb, Literarische Beziehungen zwischen Cassius Dio, Herodian und die Historia Augusta, 1972; T. D. Barnes, Sources of the Historia Augusta, 1978.

STATIUS, CAECILIUS. See Caecilius Statius

STATIUS, PUBLIUS PAPINIUS, Latin poet, c. A.D. 45–96, was born at Neapolis (Naples). His father was a schoolteacher, but also a poet, and trained his son in poetic techniques. Statius moved to Rome, where he achieved a considerable reputation. Although not a rich man, he was sufficiently well off to be able to buy a small estate at Alba Longa, where his father was buried; the house was provided with running water by the emperor Domitian (81–96), who had built a palatial villa nearby. Statius became court poet of Domitian, whom, perhaps unavoidably, he flattered in the most extravagant fashion. In about 89 he was a prizewinner at the annual poetry competition instituted by Domitian at Alba; much to his disappointment, he was unsuccessful in the quinquennial Capitoline contest that was held in about 94. Shortly after this setback, and perhaps to some extent as a result of it, he returned to Neapolis, where he died. His health had not been good, and he was nursed through one serious illness by his wife Claudia, to whom he was happily married; they had no children, though she had brought one from a former marriage, and they adopted a son, who died young. Statius was an amiable character, but a great snob; he knew most of the leading personages of his day and tells us so with undisguised satisfaction.

His principal epic poem was the *Thebaid,* which was published in about 91; it was the outcome, he informs us, of twelve years' work. Its twelve books tell of the quarrel between Eteocles and Polyneices of Thebes, who, after their father Oedipus had blinded himself, agreed to reign in alternate years; but when, at the end of the first, Eteocles refused to give up the throne, Polyneices returned with the Seven Against Thebes, and the two brothers fought and killed each other. Book I, after compliments to Domitian, tells how Oedipus invokes the Fury against his sons for insulting him, and Polyneices leaves for Argos where he mar-

stā′ shi us

ries the daughter of King Adrastus. In Book 2 the ghost of Laius (whom Oedipus had murdered and succeeded) warns Eteocles that his brother is going to attack him, and in the next book Polyneices' wife persuades Adrastus to help her husband. The fourth book catalogs the Argive invaders, who reach Nemea, where the slave-nurse Hypsipyle guides them to a stream; but while she is doing so her charge Opheltes is bitten by a snake and dies, and Book 6 recounts his funeral and its games. In Book 7, the army arrives at Thebes and begins fighting, but one of its leaders, Amphiaraus, is swallowed up in the earth with his chariot. His reception in the underworld is described in the eighth book, which continues up to the death of another of the Seven, Tydeus. Book 9 tells of the exploits of Hippomedon, one of the seven chiefs, and Book 10 recounts the sensational ends of Menoeceus, son of Creon, and Capaneus, another of the Seven. In Book 11 Eteocles and Polyneices fight their fatal duel, and in Book 12 Creon succeeds to the throne, only to be slain by the Athenian Theseus; whereupon peace is made.

The subject of the *Thebaid,* in broad outline, is the eventual triumph of right over wrong. But, as is clear from the foregoing summary, one of Statius' major weaknesses is lack of structure; and he lacks a hero as well. The poem is at its best in individual episodes, which are often recounted in flashing phrases and presented with a lively sense of drama. For the rest, the *Thebaid* shows all the cultured artificiality and elaborate mythological apparatus of Silver Latin epic. Statius' own contribution is a peculiar, contrasting blend of gloomy and gruesome macabre with a Virgilian sympathy for human suffering that often, however, overflows into mawkish sentimentality.

His second epic was the *Achilleid,* which remained incomplete: only one book and the start of a second, totaling about eleven hundred lines, were ever written. Once again there is an invocation to Domitian, after which comes the story of how the young and handsome Achilles was hidden by his mother among the maidens at the court of Lycomedes, king of the island of Scyros, because she knew that if he joined the Trojan expedition he would never return. But the seer Calchas reveals his whereabouts to the Greeks, who send Ulysses (Odysseus) and Diomedes to fetch him. The youth is identified by a ruse of Odysseus and cannot evade going to Troy. Before his departure he marries the princess Deidamia, with whom he has fallen in love. The poem, as it stands, concludes with Achilles' entertaining account of the educational methods of his teacher, the centaur Chiron. In contrast to the morbidity of the *Thebaid,* the tone of the *Achilleid* is bright; it paints the joy of youth in radiant colors. But the epic remained unfinished, either because Statius' death intervened or perhaps because the poet (as he seems to suggest in one passage) felt that his inspiration was flagging. Once again, his literary abilities are more perceptible in the small-scale effects he attempts than in his endeavors to compose on a larger canvas.

This being so, it is understandable that his *Silvae* are generally regarded as more successful than his epics. There are thirty-two of these short poems (all but six in hexameters) in five books, the first of which was published shortly after the *Thebaid,* the next three later in his life, and the fifth after his death. *Silva* (forest) indicates raw material, implying a modest apology for hasty drafts that could be elaborated later, though in fact these pieces, like his others, flow smoothly and are highly polished. Indeed, they mostly appear artificial and exaggerated and inordinately long, though one poem, "Sleep," lacks all these faults and has won widespread admiration for its haunting, romantic insight into nature, revealed in the brief span of nineteen graceful lines. Other poems offer picturesque descriptions of the mansions and gardens of the poet's friends. An ode for the birthday of the poet Lucan has good passages; and verses dealing with family affection or bereavement give the appropriate impression of coming from the heart. Five other pieces are devoted to eulogies of Domitian and his advisers; another makes its contribution to social history by listing the gifts and entertainments the emperor provided for the Roman public at the Saturnalia.

In the fifth century A.D. the early Christian prelate, writer, and politician Sidonius Apollinaris knew the *Silvae,* but thereafter they were forgotten and remained more or less unknown until a manuscript was rediscovered in 1417. The epics, on the other hand, had been greatly admired in medieval times, when the *Thebaid* was interpreted allegorically as a *psychomachia,* or war for the soul between the good and evil powers; the English ecclesiastical leader and scholar John of Salisbury quoted it extensively, and the *Achilleid* as well. The Italian poet Dante, who appreciated Statius' sensitivity to human suffering, classed him as a Christian and ranked him, as a poet, with Ovid, Virgil, and Lucan, assigning him a prominent role in the *Purgatorio.* In England, Chaucer and Lydgate, his disciple, were influenced by the story of the *Thebaid,* and expressed their admiration for its rendering by Statius.

EDITIONS—Thebaid: J. B. Poynton, 1971, 1975; Achilleid: O. A. W. Dilke, 1954; Silvae: F. Vollmer, 1898. *With translation:* J. H. Mozley (Loeb ed.), 1928; H. Frère and H. J. Izaac, Les Silves (Budé ed.), 1961; J. Méheust, Achilléide (Budé ed.), 1971.

ABOUT—W. Schetter, Untersuchungen zur epischen Kunst des Statius, 1960; H. Cancik, Untersuchungen zur lyrischen Kunst des P. Papinius Statius Silvae, 1965; B. A. Wise, The Influence of Statius Upon Chaucer, 1967; L. Håkanson, Statius' Silvae: Critical and Exegetical Remarks With Some Notes on the Thebaid, 1969, *and* Statius' Thebaid: Critical and Exegetical Remarks, 1972; A. J. Gossage *in* D. R. Dudley, ed., Neronians and Flavians (Silver Latin, v 1), 1972; D. Vessey, Statius and the Thebaid, 1973.

STESICHORUS, Greek poet, was a contemporary of Sappho and Alcaeus. His dating has been much disputed, but it seems likely—from recent comparative studies of vase painting—that he was born (as the Suidas or Suda lexicon of about the tenth century A.D. suggested) in the third quarter of the seventh century B.C. and died at an advanced age in the middle of the sixth. His real name was probably Tisias—*Stesichorus,* meaning chorus-master, described his occupation. He came from Mataurus, a colony of Locri Epizephyrii in southern Italy but lived for the most part at Himera (Imera) in Sicily. According to one report, he tried to prevent the establishment of a tyranny at another Sicilian city, Acragas (Agrigento): the fact that his intervention evidently

ste si' kō rus

failed, gives some plausibility to an assertion that at one time he was in exile in Arcadia (central Greece). But, if so, he returned to Sicily to die and was buried at Catana (Catania).

His poems were choral lyrics, mostly in a simple type of dactylic meter (i.e., based on the dactyl, or long-short-short foot). His work was said to have been collected in no less than twenty-six books, out of which only a few score fragments survive. In his poetry, mythical narrative is dominant; that is to say, his themes are the same as those of the earlier epics, and Quintilian, therefore, describes him as the lyric continuator of these epics. Most of his myths are taken from the sequels to the Homeric poems known as the Epic Cycle. For example, Stesichorus was the author of *Sack of Troy (Iliu Persis)*, the story of Epeus, who built the Wooden Horse, and he composed a narrative, the *Returns (Nostoi)*, dealing with the return of the Greek heroes from the Trojan War; the latter poem, as a papyrus fragment shows, contains echoes of the *Odyssey*. In his *Funeral Games of Pelias* he drew on the saga of the Argonauts. He also wrote several poems about Heracles: the *Cerberus*, which told how he dragged away the warder of Hades; the *Cycnus*, which was named after a robber, the son of Ares, whom Heracles slew; and the *Geryoneis*, which recounted his quest of the cattle of Geryon and described the magic cup of the Sun, which he borrowed for his journey. The last-mentioned poem reveals a knowledge of the silver mines of Tartessus in Spain. Stesichorus' *Boar-Hunters* seems to have been about the Calydonian hunt; the Theban cycle was the basis of his *Europea*, recounting the foundation of Thebes and telling the story of Eriphyle, the unfaithful wife who was punished by her son Alcmaeon.

In *Helen*, his first poem on this subject, he seems to have followed the usual tale of her seduction by Paris, which she willingly accepted, but in a second piece, his famous *Palinode*, he declared himself prompted by Helen herself to declare that what he had said before was untrue, a fiction spread by Homer, and that Helen had never gone to Troy at all (then in a second *Palinode* he put the blame on Hesiod). These recantations gave rise to a legend that Helen blinded Stesichorus for his initial impiety but was moved by his change of mind to restore his sight. His retraction may, in fact, have been due to a desire not to offend those who revered Helen as a goddess. She was venerated, for example, at Sparta, where Stesichorus' *Oresteia* (in two books), which located the death of Agamemnon at that city, may have been written to be sung at a spring festival.

Although Claudius Aelianus, a Roman rhetorician who wrote in Greek in the third century A.D., pronounced that Stesichorus was also the founder of pastoral poetry, this claim may merely come from the fact that one of his themes was the unhappy love and death of the shepherd Daphnis, who was loved by a nymph but was blinded because his affections strayed. However, in other respects, Stesichorus was a pioneer on a remarkable scale. For one thing, he was the first great literary representative of western Greece or Magna Graecia (southern Italy and Sicily). Moreover, he created a bridge between epic and lyric poetry; he gave new life and vigor to the heroic mythology and made it available for the tragedians of later generations. He also seems to have explored the tragic implications of love in a way that no one had before him.

In subsequent times, Stesichorus was spoken of with great respect, not only as a canonical authority on myths and legends but as a writer whose plots and characterizations were notable for their grandeur. That was the verdict of Dionysius of Halicarnassus, and Quintilian praised him for the moral elevation *(dignitas)* with which he invested his heroes and heroines.

WORKS (wrongly attributed to Stesichorus)—Certain poems that anticipate the romantic poetry of Hellenistic times, including the *Rhadine* about a girl who was killed by the tyrant of Corinth to whom she was betrothed, are more likely to have been written by a later Stesichorus of Himera, who wrote poetry in the fourth century B.C.

EDITIONS—D. L. Page, Poetae Melici Graeci, 1962, *and* Supplementum Lyricis Graecis, 1974.

ABOUT—J. Würtheim, Stesichoros' Fragmente und Biographie, 1919; C. M. Bowra, Greek Lyric Poetry, 2nd ed., 1962; G. A. Campbell, Greek Lyric Poetry, 1967; J. G. Griffith, Early Greek Lyric Poetry, *in* Fifty Years (and Twelve) of Classical Scholarship, 1968.

STRABO, Greek historian and geographer, was born in about 63 B.C. and lived until at least A.D. 21. He came of an eminent Greek family, partly Asian in origin, living at Amaseia (Amasya) in Pontus (northern Asia Minor). He went with his family, first to Nysa in Caria (southwestern Asia Minor), where he studied under the rhetorician Aristodemus (who held the curious view that Homer had been a Roman), and then to Rome, where one of his teachers was a well-known grammarian, Tyrannio the Younger. Strabo was also acquainted with the philosopher-historian Posidonius—whose Stoicism he adopted after a period as an Aristotelian. He seems to have stayed at Rome until his ·middle thirties. He was very proud of his extensive travels, which, although they included little of Italy and Greece (it is even uncertain whether he visited Athens), covered a wide range of countries. He resided for a long time at Alexandria and in about 25 B.C. was a member of the entourage of Aelius Gallus, the second Roman governor of Egypt, who led an expedition into Arabia. But it seems likely that Strabo returned, eventually, to his native city, where he spent the last two or three decades of his life.

Strabo was the author of *Historical Sketches (Historika Hupomnemata)* in forty-seven books, a continuation of the work of Polybius, (d. after 118 B.C.), whose writings had influenced him profoundly. The work took up its narrative with 146 B.C., where Polybius' had ended, and went on at least until the death of Julius Caesar. The *Sketches* are lost except for a few minor fragments, but we can deduce from Strabo's own observations elsewhere that they were composed for the benefit of men in high public office (such as his patron Aelius Gallus). Moreover, Strabo shared the Stoic conviction of Posidonius that Rome fulfilled a beneficent and necessary role as the unifier of the earthly world-state, which, according to followers of this new persuasion, reflected the heavenly cosmopolis.

This same view reappears in his extant work, the *Geography,* which resembled the *History* in purpose, and was designed as its complement, on the assumption that history and geography belonged together as philo-

strā′ bō

sophical (and political) subjects. The *Geography* was substantially completed by about 7 B.C., although a few additions were made in c. A.D. 18–19 (a reference to an event of c. A.D. 23 may have been inserted subsequently by an editor). The work is in seventeen books. The first two provide a general introduction, in the course of which Homer is defended as a geographer, but Eratosthenes (whom Strabo brings up to date) and Polybius are criticized. Books 3–10 deal with the geography of Europe, concluding with Greece, which is treated in a very old-fashioned and mythological manner. The subject of Books 11–16 is Asia, with an entire book (including some historical and mythical digressions) dedicated to Strabo's native Asia Minor; and the last book discusses the lands of Egypt, Ethiopia, and northern Africa.

Strabo's *Geography* is of very great importance because it is the only general study on the subject that has come down to us from the ancient world. Moreover, his work is a storehouse of information and ignores neither the philosophy nor the history of geography. He also emphasizes every geographer's need for mathematical and scientific knowledge, although he himself does not, in fact, possess this, or seek to deploy it, to any great extent—marking a decline in this respect from the standards of his Hellenistic predecessors and sources such as Pytheas, Hipparchus, Eratosthenes, Polybius, and Posidonius.

Nevertheless, for all his careful notes, his critical employment of these sources is inept; and they themselves, for all their merits, had become very out of date. Nevertheless, it is for his sources that we value him: without Strabo we should scarcely have the slightest idea how ancient geography developed. Moreover, his entertainment value is considerable; no such work since Herodotus had been so crammed with readable, intriguing, picturesque lore. In his own day he exercised little or no influence; but by early Byzantine times the *Geography* was already a standard work, and it retained this position for centuries.

EDITIONS—W. Aly, Books 1–6, 1962; F. Sbordone, Books 1–6, 1963–70. *With translation:* H. L. Jones

(Loeb ed.), 1917–35; F. Lasserre, G. Aujac, R. Baladié (Budé ed.), 1966, 1978.

ABOUT—G. Sarton, History of Science: Hellenistic Science and Culture in the Last Three Centuries B.C., 1959; G. W. Bowersock, Augustus and the Greek World, 1965; G. Aujac, Strabon et la science de son temps, 1966; C. S. Floratos, Strabon über Literatur und Poseidonios, 1972.

STRABO, WALAHFRID. See Walahfrid Strabo

STRATO (Physicus), Greek philosopher, died in 270/269 B.C. His birthplace was Lampsacus (Lapseki) in the Troad (northwestern Asia Minor). After the death of Theophrastus in the early 280s, he had become head of the Aristotelian (Peripatetic) School.

Strato wrote on physics, cosmology, zoology, logic, and psychology, but only fragments of his works have survived. He followed Aristotle's lead in pronouncing the universe to be unique, uncreated, and geocentric. However, as can be inferred from the introduction to the Pneumatica of Hero of Alexandria (a work of the first century A.D.), Strato evidently contradicted Aristotle by pronouncing that void exists in the cosmos. When he went on to declare that the processes of nature are to be explained by natural and not divine causes, he was likewise rejecting Aristotle's postulation of the divine unmoved mover. However, the main thrust of his arguments was directed against the Stoics.

Strato was the last director of the Peripatetic School to produce important work, and his writings continued to exert considerable influence on later writers, notably Erasistratus (third century B.C.) and Hero (first century A.D.).

EDITIONS (of fragments)—F. Wehrli, Die Schule des Aristoteles, v 5, 1950; H. B. Gottschalk, Strato of Lampsacus: Some Texts (Proceedings of the Leeds Philosophical and Literary Society, Literary and Historical Section, v 11), 1965.

ABOUT—G. Rodier, La physique de Straton de Lampsaque, 1890; A. Schmekel, Die positive Philosophie, 1938.

strä′ tō

SUETONIUS (Gaius Suetonius Tranquillus), Latin biographer, was born in about A.D. 70 and died some time after 130. His family, which was of knightly rank, probably came from Hippo Regius (Annaba in Algeria). Suetonius may have taught literature at Rome for a time. He also seems to have practiced law and then to have served on the staff of Pliny the Younger—who had earlier helped to secure him a small property in Italy—when Pliny was governor of Bithynia-Pontus (northern Asia Minor) in c. A.D. 110–12. Subsequently, Suetonius occupied a succession of posts at the imperial court. First he held the "secretaryship of studies" (a studiis), the precise functions of which are uncertain. Then he became director of the imperial libraries and was finally placed in charge of the emperor's correspondence. Probably he occupied the first two of these three offices under Trajan (98–117); the last and most important appointment dates from Hadrian (117–38). In 122, however, he seems to have been dismissed from his post for disrespectful behavior toward the empress Sabina. If, as is sometimes suggested, one of his lost treatises entitled On Public Offices, was the last of his works to be written, this choice of subject, made at a time of administrative reforms by Hadrian, suggests that he may have enjoyed at least a partial return to imperial favor. The younger Pliny describes him as a quiet and studious man, devoted to writing—the sort of professional scholar that flourished in the second century A.D.

In the reign of Trajan Suetonius wrote his first series of biographies, The Lives of Illustrious Men. In pursuance of a Greek tradition, these were brief biographical sketches of Roman literary personalities—about twenty-one grammarians and sixteen orators (De Grammaticis et Rhetoribus), thirty-three poets (De Poetis), and six historians. Only a few fragments of this work have survived. In the orators' section, a brief abstract of the life of Passienus Crispus (who was the stepfather of Nero) has come down to us. Of the poets' biographies we have Terence, Virgil, Horace, and (in part) Lucan. Brief studies of Tibullus and Persius may also belong to the collection, though it seems likely that

sū e tō′ ni us

they have been edited and abbreviated by later hands. The accounts of the historians have disappeared entirely, except for a fragmentary one of Pliny the Elder.

The *Lives of the Caesars* are biographies of the Twelve Caesars, from Julius to Domitian (d. A.D. 96). The work is preserved, except for a few chapters of Julius' life. These biographies are dedicated to Gaius Septicius Clarus, who became prefect of the praetorian guard in 119 and was dismissed along with Suetonius himself three years later; perhaps the last of the biographies in the work formed a supplement, published later than the rest. Apart from the undistinguished historical writer Cornelius Nepos (d. 24 B.C.), Suetonius is the first Latin biographer whose writings have come down to us. He was aware that he must strike out in a different direction from the writers of history (which was regarded as a different and superior genre). This notion seemed all the more important for Suetonius because the contemporary historical work of Tacitus was too overpowering to be competed against. In consequence, he abandoned the chronological method his Greek fellow biographer Plutarch tended to favor and adopted a method—occasionally employed in Greek and Latin before—whereby the straight narrative was interrupted by material that was classified according to subject matter and that dealt successively with the different characteristics his personages displayed; in this procedure it may be possible to detect the expert on grammar and grammarians.

Suetonius' principal contribution lies in his relatively high degree of objectivity. With him we have moved away from the traditional eulogistic treatment altogether and have entered a much more astringent atmosphere, in which the men he is describing are looked at with a cool and disenchanted eye. Owing to our losses in earlier literature, it is impossible to state with any assurance whether, or to what extent, such an objective approach had been achieved by previous writers. But at all events Suetonius innovated by selecting the rulers of Rome as targets for this examination. He has gathered together, and freely inserts, information both for and against his subjects, usually without adding any personal judgment—and above all without introducing the moralizing that had so frequently pervaded Greek and Roman biography and history alike. Occasionally, conflicting statements are weighed, but generally the presentation does not discriminate among them. This has the result—since he loved an entertaining story—of leaving the subject's eccentricities rather than his virtues in the reader's mind. Indeed, in all this collection of weird and fascinating material there appears to be little effort on the part of Suetonius to reach a decision about the personalities he is describing or to build up their characteristics into a coherent portrait. Perhaps he may have felt that accuracy required no more, that people possess discordant elements that do not in fact add up to a harmonious unity. The best quality of his work, however, is his power to create rapid, dramatic, and often moving narrative, including, at times, impressive set-pieces, among which the death of Nero is especially notable.

Suetonius' stories are generally told in a clear and straightforward manner, though his disjointed and staccato diction sometimes leads to obscurity. An unusual, and perhaps unprecedented, feature is his willingness to quote verbatim from his sources, offering literary citations from imperial letters and public and private records alike. This use of documentary material, however, is almost entirely limited to the biography of Augustus: so it was probably after writing it (the second of the twelve) that he was dismissed from court and consequently lost access to the archives. His employment of literary authorities is hard to reconstruct, because, like so many other authors, he is reluctant to cite them by name. He twice quotes Pollio (who died in A.D. 4), however, and once Cremutius Cordus (who died in A.D. 25)—and he echoes the *Acts* of Augustus on at least four occasions.

EDITIONS—De Grammaticis et Rhetoribus: F. della Corte, 1968; De Poetis: A. Rostagni, 1956. For editions of individual lives of the Caesars *see* Oxford Classical Dictionary, 2nd ed., 1970, p 1021; *add* B. H. Warmington, Nero, 1977. *With translation* (all works): J. C. Rolfe (Loeb ed.), 1914 (v 1, revised ed., 1951). *Transla-*

tions (of Caesars)—R. Graves (Penguin ed.), revised by M. Grant, 1979; H. Ailloud (Budé ed.), 1931–33. ABOUT—D. R. Stuart, Epochs of Greek and Roman Biography, 1928; W. Steidle, Sueton und die antike Biographie, 1951; G. d'Anna, Le idee letterarie di Suetonio, 1954; F. della Corte, Svetonio: Eques Romanus, 2nd ed., 1967; G. B. Townend *in* T. A. Dorey, ed., Latin Biography, 1967; M. Grant, The Ancient Historians, 1970; C. Grassi, Svetonio, 1972; P. Venini, Sulla tecnica compositiva Svetoniana, 1975; E. Cizek, Structure et idéologie dans les vies des douze Césars de Suétone, 1977; H. Gugel, Studien zur biographischen Technik Suetons, 1977.

SULPICIA, Latin poet, lived in the time of Augustus. She was the daughter of the nobleman Servius Sulpicius Rufus and the niece by marriage and ward of the leading statesman, soldier, and patron of letters Marcus Valerius Messalla Corvinus (64 B.C. –A.D. 8).

Six short poems of her authorship, totaling forty lines in all, have come down to us in the collection of poems written by Tibullus (d. 19 B.C.) and others and known as the *Corpus Tibullianum,* in which they figure as the seventh to the twelfth poems of the fourth book. These pieces deal with her passionate love for a young man in her own circle, who appears under the pseudonym Cerinthus. Poem No. 7 announces joyfully the consummation of their love, which she is proud to proclaim to the world. No. 8 describes her forthcoming birthday as a hateful occasion, because although Messalla has planned for her a special trip to the country it will keep her away from her lover; but No. 9 happily reports that the treat has been called off, so that she and Cerinthus can be together after all. In No. 10, however, she is deeply unhappy and her pride is shattered, because she believes him to have been unfaithful to her with a prostitute. In the eleventh piece she is ill but only wants to get better if she can be sure that he is moved by her troubles. In No. 12 she apologizes for leaving him alone on the previous night: she only did so, she declares, because she was afraid to reveal how much she cared for him.

Sulpicia displays a frank directness that is not to be found elsewhere in Latin elegiac love poetry. Like Sappho, one of the leading

sul pish' i a

writers of Greek lyric poetry, before her, she uses her own name without dissimulation or fear; and, like her again, she writes with unaffected, full-blooded sincerity and passion—a gift for social historians concerned with the position of women at Rome.

In the same Tibullan corpus appear five further elegies, "The Garland of Sulpicia," which were written about her and her lover Cerinthus by someone else—a sympathetic poet and friend, who has resisted attempts at identification. The group of poems is introduced by verses supposedly accompanying a present given to Sulpicia on the festival of the Matronalia. Another of these pieces presents her concern when her lover has gone on a boar hunt. In the next she is ill, and Cerinthus prays for her recovery; the last two are written for birthdays, presenting his loving thoughts on her anniversary, and hers on his. The poems are neatly and gracefully written, but they lack the authentic, firsthand feeling that emanates from Sulpicia's verses, to which they form a kind of poetic commentary.

The Sulpicia to whom a satire of seventy lines has been attributed is, in fact, another and later woman poet (the wife of a certain Calenus), who wrote in order to complain of the expulsion of philosophers by Domitian (A.D. 81–96).

EDITIONS (of the earlier Sulpicia)—Generally with the poems of Tibullus; *also* J. G. Taiphakos, Sulpicia's Elegidia, 1974. *Translations*—J. P. Postgate *in* F. W. Cornish, J. P. Postgate, J. W. Mackail, Catullus: Tibullus: Pervigilium Veneris (Loeb ed.), revised ed., 1962; P. Dunlop, The Poems of Tibullus, With the Tibullan Collection (Penguin ed.), 1972.
ABOUT: G. Luck, The Latin Love Elegy, 1969. The later Sulpicia is discussed by H. Fuchs, Das Klagelied der Sulpicia über die Gewaltherrschaft des Kaisers Domitian, 1968.

SULPICIUS SEVERUS, Latin historian, was born between A.D. 353 and 360 and died in about 420. There is a brief account of his life by a biographer named Gennadius (c. 500). The birthplace of Sulpicius was in Aquitania (southwestern France), where he belonged to a well-known family. He studied law at the distinguished school of Burdigala

sul pi' shi us se vē' rus

(Bordeaux) and was converted to Christianity in about 389, together with his friend Paulinus of Nola, to whom he wrote thirteen extant letters. Sulpicius' wife, who came of a noble house, died early. After her death, under the influence of Saint Martin of Tours, he gathered his friends together in a kind of monastic community upon his own estates, where he arranged for churches to be built and spent much time writing. His activities were supported financially by his mother-in-law Bassula of Treviri (Trier). As a priest, however, Sulpicius earned the disfavor of the orthodox. Indeed, in his later years he seems to have come under the influence of the followers of the British monk and theologian Pelagius, who were accused of depreciating the divine grace because they complained that Saint Augustine's dependence on its total efficacy undermined human willpower and moral effort. Nevertheless, both Augustine and Jerome referred to Sulpicius in friendly terms.

His best known literary work was the *Vita Sancti Martini,* a life of Saint Martin of Tours who had been his mentor and guide. This treatise, which was already in draft before Martin's death in 397, is not so much a biography as a fictional encomium. Crammed with wonders, it provides a vivid picture of the saint's struggles with the Devil, his miraculous acts of healing, his visions of the imminent end of the world, and finally his resurrection from the dead. Sulpicius' purpose throughout is to defend the practices of asceticism. He writes in an attractive manner that owes something to the historians Sallust and Tacitus; Edward Gibbon, eighteenth century English historian, expressed surprise that "facts adapted to the grossest barbarism should be narrated in a style not unworthy of the Augustan Age." The *Life* enjoyed fame in the medieval period, when it became the principal source of the legends surrounding St. Martin.

It was supplemented by three letters by Sulpicius about Martin's miracles and death and by a series of *Dialogues.* These, published in 404, comprise a discussion, presided over by Sulpicius, in which the deeds of Martin are compared with those of the hermits of Egypt, whose merits are weighed up against his own by one of his monks, speaking with a traveler recently returned from the Egyptian deserts. This, too, is a very skillful piece of writing.

Sulpicius also wrote a universal *Chronicle (Chronica)* in two books, extending from the Creation down to A.D. 400 and published in about 402/4. This is an epitome of scriptural history, omitting the Gospels. It concludes with a brief survey of the ten persecutions of the Church by the Roman imperial regime and a discussion of the beliefs of Arius and Priscillian, which were regarded as heretical. Arius (d. 336) had been accused of the heterodox view that God the Son was subordinate to, and distinct in essence from, the Father. Priscillian, a Spanish layman, who preached a mystical and ascetic form of Christianity, had been denounced as a magician and put to death on the orders of the usurper-emperor Magnus Maximus' praetorian prefect (385), thus becoming the first Christian martyr to die at Christian hands; his execution aroused protests from St. Martin and was also deplored equally by Sulpicius Severus. His account of this tragic event is a valuable historical contribution; and his *Chronicle* contains others as well, while its general plan constitutes an interesting attempt to summarize history from the point of view of a Christian. He makes use of St. Jerome and other Christian chroniclers, and of pagan authors as well.

EDITIONS—C. Halm, Corpus Scriptorum Ecclesiasticorum Latinorum, v 1, 1866; Life of Martin: J. Fontaine, 1969. *Translations*—A. Roberts, 1894; B. M. Peebles, 1949.
ABOUT—P. Hylten, Studien zu Sulpicius Severus, 1940; S. Prete, I Chronica di Sulpicio Severo, 1955; J. Fontaine *in* Mélanges C. Mohrmann, 1964; G. K. van Andel, The Christian Concept of History in the Chronicle of Sulpicius Severus, 1976.

SYLVESTER II, Pope. See Gerbert

SYMEON THE NEW THEOLOGIAN (or SYMEON THE YOUNGER), Saint, Greek churchman, theological writer, and mystic of the Byzantine age, was born in A.D. 949 and died in 1022. Originating in
sim' ē ən

Paphlagonia (northeastern Asia Minor) of an aristocratic family, he moved in early boyhood to Constantinople. There, in 977, he entered the monastery of Studius (later known as the Studion), but since the abbot objected to his reforming projects, he transferred almost immediately to the neighboring foundation of St. Mamas, of which he became abbot in 980. There, however, he encountered the displeasure of the patriarch and had to leave for the Asiatic shore of the Bosporus, where he devoted his care to the monastery of St. Marina near Chrysopolis (Üsküdar). In due course, his quarrel with the patriarch came to an end; but he still would not return to Constantinople.

Symeon became a famous and popular figure and earned a reputation in the outside world as a reasonable man; for example, he gave a visitor some pigeon's meat to eat on a day of fasting—because the man was dyspeptic and needed it. Our knowledge of Symeon's career is owed to a biography by the eleventh century writer Nicetas Stethatus, who conscientiously quotes earlier authorities. Symeon may owe his designation "the New Theologian" to a desire to distinguish him from the earlier "theologians" held in special reverence by the Orthodox Church: the Apostle St. John the Evangelist and the fourth century St. Gregory of Nazianzus.

His extensive and numerous writings comprise hymns and prose works, including sermons. His fifty-seven *Hymns of the Divine Loves,* which are written in fifteen-syllable accentual verse, describe ecstatic religious experiences. Among the sermons are thirty-four *Catecheses,* originally preached to the community of St. Mamas and later revised and combined with further compositions by Symeon to provide a popular edition *(the Capita).* Aided by earlier authors, including the so-called Dionysius the Areopagite (c. A.D. 500) and Maximus Confessor (d. 662), Symeon built up a comprehensive theoretical and practical system of mysticism, available to clerics and laymen alike. Drawing upon the religious events of his own life, he dedicates his highly individual, direct, and unpretentious insight to the mystical experience, concentrating upon the various means by which it can be attained—and of these

means the foremost are obedience and tears. He sees the experience as union with God, Christ (or, sometimes, the Trinity) being the necessary medium. Symeon's work provided a vital link between the mystics of the past and those of the future; indeed, it created the framework within which all subsequent Byzantine mysticism developed.

WORKS—Listed by B. Krivochéine *in* Orientalia Christiana Periodica, v 2, 1954.
EDITIONS—J. P. Migne, Patrologia Graeca, v 120 (some works, mostly in Latin translation only); J. Koder and others, Hymns v 1-3, 1969–73; A. Kambylos, Hymnen, 1976. *With translation:* J. M. Hussey, The Hymns, 1961; J. Darrouzès, Chapitres théologiques, gnostiques et pratiques (the Capita), 1957, *and* Traités théologiques et éthiques, v 1, 1966 and v 2, 1967; B. Krivochéine and J. Paramelle, Catéchèses, 1963, 1964.
ABOUT—I. Hausherr, Syméon le nouveau théologien, 1928; J. M. Hussey, Church & Learning in the Byzantine empire, 867–1185, 1937; D. I. Stathopoulos, Die Gottesliebe bei Symeon dem Neuen Theologen, 1964; D. Moosdorf, Symeon der Neue Theologe, 1974; W. Völker, Praxis und Theoria bei Symeon dem Neuen Theologen, 1974.

SYMMACHUS, QUINTUS AURELIUS, Roman official, Latin orator, and man of letters, was born not long after A.D. 340 and died in about 402. He came of a noble and wealthy pagan Roman family and after training by a Gallic rhetorician went through all the stages of an official career in the western empire. He was with the emperor Valentinian I in Gaul (369–70), where he formed a close friendship with the poet Ausonius (c. A.D. 310–95.) In 373 Symmachus became governor of Africa. When, in 382, Gratian, under the influence of Ambrose, bishop of Mediolanum (Milan), ordered the removal of the pagan statue of Victory from the Senate house at Rome, Symmachus was chosen by the Senate to go to Mediolanum to urge the emperor to cancel the edict, but Gratian refused to receive him. Under the next ruler, Valentinian II, Symmachus, on becoming prefect of Rome, renewed his plea, but the power of Ambrose ensured its failure once again. Symmachus regained much of his influence, however, when Valentinian II was driven out of Italy in 387 by Magnus Maximus, to whom, as
sim′ mà kus

413

leader of the Senate, he offered the congratulations of that body. After Maximus' downfall, therefore, he fell into disgrace. However, he delivered an apology and a panegyric before the victorious Theodosius I, who forgave him and made him consul in 391. Under the pro-pagan regime of Eugenius (392–94) he became even more prominent; when it was overthrown, he lost his power once again, but still managed to survive.

Symmachus is chiefly notable as the leading opponent, in his epoch, of the established Christian religion. An enormously rich man, owning three houses in Rome and fifteen properties in Italy, Sicily, and Mauretania, he was also a strong believer in the merits of high birth: "good blood tells," he declared, "and never fails to recognize itself." His culture was wide, but artificial and uninspired. During his lifetime, he won a considerable reputation as the most distinguished orator of the day; fragments of eight of his speeches have survived. So have ten books of his letters, addressed to the principal personages of the empire. The letters are, for the most part, consistently banal, being concerned very largely with the achievement of elegant and melodious expression; each verbose conceit in turn is repeated in a monotonous succession of minor variations. "The luxuriancy of Symmachus," wrote English historian Edward Gibbon, "consists in barren leaves without fruit and even without flowers."

Like Pliny the Younger three centuries earlier, he wrote his letters for publication, composing them with great care; and he deliberately imitated Pliny by arranging them in ten books, nine of which were private and the tenth, official correspondence. This tenth book, comprising forty-nine dispatches *(relationes),* is of considerable historical value. Of particular interest is the third piece, which consists of his unsuccessful appeal to Valentinian II for the restoration of the altar of Victory in the Senate house, which he combined with a request for the public maintenance of the Vestal Virgins. This plea earned replies from Ambrose and (nineteen years later) from the poet Prudentius. Both praised its eloquence, which, in Prudentius' view, even exceeded that of

Cicero; if only its author would become a Christian, he added, his words would deserve to be written in gold. Symmachus' letters were heavily purged by his son, for political reasons, when he edited them after his father's death.

Symmachus also displayed his devotion to the classical tradition by working for the preservation of literary texts—particularly that of the historian Livy. In 401 he gave a friend a complete transcript of Livy's work, which had been made by Victorianus (editor of a Latin translation of Philostratus' *Life of Apollonius of Tyana*) under the sponsorship of Symmachus' family.

EDITIONS—O. Seeck *in* Monumenta Germaniae, v 6, p 1, 1883. *With translation:* R. H. Barrow, Prefect and Emperor: The Relationes of Symmachus, 1973.
ABOUT—H. Bloch, The Pagan Revival in the West at the End of the Fourth Century, *in* A. Momigliano, ed., The Conflict Between Paganism and Christianity in the Fourth Century, 1963; R. Klein, Symmachus; eine tragische Gestalt des ausgehenden Heidentums, 1971; M. T. W. Arnheim, The Senatorial Aristocracy of the Later Roman Empire, 1972.

SYNESIUS, Greek Neoplatonist, scientist, writer, and bishop, was born in about A.D. 370 and died between 412 and 415. His birthplace was Cyrene (now in Libya), where he came of a pagan family that claimed descent from the children of Heracles at Sparta. In his homeland he lived the life of a hunting country gentleman. Moving to Alexandria, however, he studied philosophy, mathematics, and astronomy under the Neoplatonist Hypatia, daughter of the philosopher-mathematician Theon. Synesius' wife and brother were Christians, and he himself embraced that faith—probably before a visit he paid to Constantinople in 399 in order to plead for tax remission for Cyrenaica. In view of this service to his homeland and because of his successful organization of resistance to brigands who threatened it, he was elected bishop of the Cyrenaic Five Cities (Pentapolis) at Ptolemais (Barca) in 410; however, he only accepted this office with reluctance, laying down the condition that he should remain at liberty to retain his own philosophical opin-

si nē' si us

ions. Thereafter, he attempted to conduct his episcopacy according to the best standards of Christianity and paganism combined, and his efforts were evidently successful.

We learn of these matters, and of his tolerant, charitable, independent character, from his one hundred fifty-six letters, which provide us with a virtual autobiography. One of the friends to whom they are addressed is his teacher Hypatia, and another recipient (of an open letter) is his brother, to whom he discloses his heart-searchings about the acceptance of the bishopric of Pentapolis. A further letter describes his voyage home from Constantinople.

Synesius also wrote a considerable number of more formal prose works. *The Egyptian Tale,* or *On Providence,* describes the experiences of his patron Aurelianus and allegorizes contemporary historical events, under the guise of the mythical struggle between the gods Osiris and Typhon, into the conflict between good and evil. Another treatise, *Dion,* which he sent to Hypatia with a covering letter, is named after Dio Chrysostom of Prusa, the Greek orator and philosopher of the first and second centuries A.D. Taking Dio as his model, he attacks all the credulous, degrading fanaticisms held by contemporary superpagans and Christian monks alike. His *Praise of Baldness* is a jocular trifle prompted by Dio's *Praise of Hair. On Dreams* argues in favor of their role as a means of establishing relationship with the gods. *On Kingship,* delivered in the presence of the eastern emperor Arcadius in 399, displays a praiseworthy freedom from the customary adulation and presents a criticism of the segregation of the sovereign's person from his subjects. *On the Gift* refers to one of his scientific activities; he was the designer of a celestial map, a conical projection of the sphere of the stars. He also designed an aerometer (hydroscope), with a weighted float that could measure the specific gravity of fluids.

In these prose treatises, Synesius' aim was to write pure Attic Greek, but his nine hymns, written in ancient meters, adopt a Doric coloring. Inspired by the poems of Mesomedes, a Cretan freedman of the emperor Hadrian (A.D. 117–38), they combine Neoplatonic and Christian elements to express an authentic religious emotion. Synesius himself points out that he is using these time-honored forms not, like his pagan forerunners, in order to celebrate pretty girls or adolescent youths but in the service of God and divine wisdom; he claims to have been the first man to compose Christian hymns for accompaniment by the lyre. The third of these pieces, composed on his return from Constantinople, describes how he spent his time there on visits to martyrs' shrines, while reiterating pleas to God for the grace of baptism, which he did not receive, it was said, until after he had been elected to his bishopric.

EDITIONS—N. Terzaghi, Synesii Cyrenensis Opuscula, 1944; K. Treu, Synesios von Kyrene: Ein Kommentar zu seinem Dion, 1958. *With translation:* A. Fitzgerald, The Letters, 1926, *and* The Essays and Hymns, 1930; C. Lacombrade, Le discours sur la royauté de Synésios de Cyrène (On Kingship) (Budé ed.), 1951, *and* Hymns, 1970; S. Nicolosi, Il De Providentia di Sinesio di Cirene, 1959; K. Treu, Synesios von Kyrene, Dion Chrysostomos oder Vom Leben nach seinem Vorbild, 1959; A. Dell'Era, Sinesio di Cirene; Inni, 1968; A. Casini, Tutti le opere di Sinesio di Cirene, 1970; C. Lacombrade, Synesius de Cyrène, Hymnes (Budé ed.), 1979. ABOUT—A. Gardner, Synesius of Cyrene: Philosopher and Bishop, 1886; N. Crawford, Synesius the Hellene, 1901; H. I. Marrou, Synesius of Cyrene and Alexandrian Neoplatonism, *in* A. Momigliano, ed., The Conflict Between Paganism and Christianity in the Fourth Century, 1963; A. Casini, Sinesio di Cirene, 1969; J. A. Bregman, Synesius of Cyrene: A Case-Study in the Conversion of the Greco-Roman Aristocracy (Yale, dissertation), 1974.

TACITUS, PUBLIUS CORNELIUS, Latin historian, orator, and public official, was born in A.D. 56 or 57 and died shortly before or after 117. His family, which probably came from Narbonese Gaul (southern France) or Cisalpine Gaul (northern Italy), may not have been of wholly Italian ancestry. His father may perhaps have been an imperial representative *(procurator)* at Augusta Trevirorum (Trier) or Colonia Agrippensis (Cologne) in Lower Germany and paymaster general for the armies of the Rhine. In c. 74/5, during the reign of Vespasian, Tacitus studied rhetoric at Rome under leading practitioners of the subject, tas' i tus

Marcus Aper and Julius Secundus, and subsequently he himself became one of the best known speakers of his time (however, none of his speeches have survived). In about 76 or 77 he served as a legionary officer (military tribune) and in 77 married the daughter of the eminent Cnaeus Julius Agricola, who was consul in that year. In one of the first two years of Domitian's reign (81–96), Tacitus held office as quaestor, a post which carried with it admission to the Senate. In 88 he obtained the more impressive office of praetor and in the same year became a member of the prestigious priestly college that had the duty of preserving the Sibylline books (the *quindecimviri sacris faciundis*). Not long afterward, he departed for a four-year period in the provinces, during which he may have commanded a legion. He was still away from the capital when Agricola died in 93 but returned to witness Domitian's ferocious treatment of the Senate during the last years of his reign.

Either Domitian or his successor Nerva (96–98) designated Tacitus to the consulship, which he held in 97. In the same year he pronounced the funeral oration over a distinguished personage, Verginius Rufus; and in 100, after Trajan had come to the throne, he joined Pliny the Younger in prosecuting a sinister former governor of Africa, Marius Priscus, on a charge of extortion. During the years 112–13 Tacitus held one of the two highest governorships in the senatorial career, the proconsulate of Asia (western Asia Minor). Unlike the highest figures of the day, however, he was never awarded a second consulship. Whether he lived to see the accession of Hadrian in 117 is disputed.

The five works of Tacitus that have survived are the *Germania, Agricola, Dialogue on Orators, Histories,* and *Annals.* In A.D. 98 he completed his monograph *On the Origin, Geography, Institutions and Tribes of the Germans,* generally known as the *Germania.* This geographical and ethnological survey of the peoples of central Europe contains certain traditional moralistic contrasts, both stated and implied, between the degeneracy of Rome and the simple vigor of the teeming tribesmen beyond the Rhine, feckless and drunken though they were. Writing at a

time when the emperor Trajan, in the year of his accession to the throne, was engaged in important military operations against the Germans, Tacitus shows prophetic foresight in describing these people, despite their relatively rudimentary organization, as a serious potential menace to Rome, even more serious than the Parthian kingdom in the east.

The *Agricola* was published in the same year; it is the earliest of his writings with a largely historical content. However, like the *Germania,* it contains much geography and ethnology, relating, this time, to Britain, where the author's father-in-law Cnaeus Agricola had served as Domitian's governor from 78 to 84. The main purpose of the work, whose Latin title is *De Vita Julii Agricolae,* is to sing Agricola's praises, in the familiar Graeco-Roman tradition of the semi-biographical, moralizing encomium, which Tacitus endows with novel artistry and flexibility. At the same time every rhetorical resource is devoted to attacking Domitian's record of tyranny. The infusion of history into the monograph is deliberate, since the *Agricola* is announced as an introductory installment of the *Histories.*

The *Histories,* however, was not the next work that Tacitus completed. For not very much later, primed by his rhetorical education and experience, Tacitus composed a treatise on the subject of public speaking. In this *Dialogue on Orators,* four historical characters—the poet Curiatius Maternus (at whose house the discussion is staged), the leading speakers Marcus Aper (d. A.D. 85) and Julius Secundus, friend of Quintilian—under both of whom Tacitus himself had studied—and a nobleman Vipstanus Messalla—are discussing the claims of oratory against other branches of literature; and they debate the reasons why eloquence has declined since Cicero's death and the transformation of the Republic into the Principate or Empire. The *Dialogue* claims to be reporting a discussion that took place in about A.D. 75. It is dedicated to Lucius Fabius Justus who was consul in 102 and was probably published in that year or shortly afterward. Doubts regarding Tacitus' authorship of the *Dialogue* appear to be unjustified.

In the years that followed, excerpts may

have been recited, or even published separately, from Tacitus' first major publication, completed in about 109. The manuscripts bear no title, but we know the work as the *Histories*. Originally divided, perhaps, into twelve books, its contents covered the period of Roman history during Tacitus' later adolescence and early manhood—that is, from the Year of the Four Emperors (68–69) to the death of Domitian (96). The first four books and part of the fifth are all that have come down to us. Book 1 describes the situation at the death of Nero and the accession of Galba, and deals with the first part of the following year, including Galba's death and the proclamation of Otho, and the march from the Rhine toward Italy of the generals supporting his rival Vitellius. The second book tells of the first battle of Bedriacum (near Cremona in northern Italy) where the Vitellian commanders defeated those of Otho, who committed suicide in April 69; Vitellius crossed the Alps and proceeded to Rome, but meanwhile Vespasian was declared emperor by legions serving in the east. Book 3 describes the second battle of Bedriacum in October, in which Primus, who had advanced into Italy as the partisan of Vespasian, defeated the Vitellians. Primus then marched on the capital, and Vitellius was put to death in December. The fourth book records the revolt on the northern frontier by Civilis, a German (Batavian) who was supported by Gallic chiefs. Reference is also made to omens announcing the imperial destiny of Vespasian. The surviving portion of Book 5 offers a brief general description of the Jews, whose First Revolt (called by their descendants the First Roman War) had been crushed by Vespasian and his son Titus, the conqueror of Jerusalem in 70. Reference is also made to the suppression of Civilis' revolt by the Roman general Cerialis, in the same year.

All the rest of the *Histories* is lost, but the contents of the missing parts can conjecturally be restored. Books 5 and 6 probably brought the story down to Vespasian's death (69), thus completing a group of six books *(hexad)*. The second hexad (Books 7–12) can then be regarded as having covered the reigns of Titus (A.D. 79–81) and, at much greater length, Domitian (81–96), culminat-

ing in the latter's military failures and political purges.

Tacitus' last and greatest masterpiece, the *Annals,* was published shortly before (or possibly after) the end of the reign of Trajan (98–117). For this work, he chose to go back to the years preceding the events narrated in the *Histories.* The *Annals* described events from A.D. 14, the beginning of the reign of Tiberius, the successor of Augustus, to some point in 68, the year of the death of Nero, the last emperor of Augustus' Julio-Claudian dynasty. Tacitus himself seems to have called his work "From the Death of the Divine Augustus." Of the eighteen books that it apparently contained, we have most of Books 1–6 and Books 11–16. The extant account ends at A.D. 66.

The first six books covered the reign of Tiberius (A.D. 14–37), dividing it into two equal parts. The second of these two sections, covering the time when the emperor had finally shown his true colors, displays a more mournful picture than the first. Book I opens with a sketch of previous Roman history and provides a summary of Augustus' reign, including a survey of people's opinions about the future. The remaining portion of the book is mostly concerned with mutinies on the northern frontiers and with the first German campaigns of Tiberius' popular nephew and adopted son Germanicus (A.D. 15). Book 2 continues the account of these wars until Germanicus' transfer to the east and his death at Antioch in 19. Book 3 covers the trial and suicide of Germanicus' enemy Cnaeus Piso, who was suspected of having murdered him and was being investigated by the Senate. A serious rebellion took place in Gaul (21). The fourth book refers to the sinister ascendancy of Tiberius' chief minister Sejanus and the outbreak of the first treason trials, while the fifth tells of the death of the emperor's mother Livia (29). Sejanus' downfall and death in the year 31 are missing. Book 6 recounts the aftermath, emphasizing the glumness and debauchery of Tiberius, who was now in retirement at Capreae (Capri), and the violent ends of other imperial personages, followed by the death of the emperor himself.

The middle portion of the work, now

417

missing, described the eccentric regime of Caligula (37–41) and the first year of the reign of Claudius (41–54). The surviving part of Book 11 describes the excesses and downfall (48) of Claudius' wife Messalina. The twelfth book, which covers the events of six years, tells how he married Nero's mother Agrippina the Younger and how she arranged his death by poisoning.

The final part of the *Annals* covered the reign of Nero (54–68). The thirteenth book indicates the weakening of Agrippina's influence and Nero's murder of his stepbrother Britannicus (55). The historian then passes on to the campaigns of Corbulo in the east (58). The highlights of Book 14 are the assassination of Agrippina by her son, Nero, his public exhibitions as a charioteer, the revolt of Boudicca (Boadicea) in Britain (61), and the initiation of a reign of terror including the murder of Claudius' daughter Octavia. She was succeeded as Nero's wife by Poppaea. The fifteenth book resumes the account of the distinguished general Domitius Corbulo's eastern campaigns and describes the Great Fire of Rome (64)—for which Nero blamed the Christians—and the conspiracy against the emperor in the following year by Gaius Calpurnius Piso, who had been robbed of his wife by Caligula and banished from Rome. In Book 16 a series of persecutions leads up to the death of the Roman senators who led the Republican, philosophical opposition to the regime, Thrasea Paetus and Barea Soranus (66). With the suicide of Thrasea the *Annals* break off.

Tacitus' diction shows an overwhelming contrast to the flowing, rotund manner of Cicero or Livy. As it reaches its climax in the *Annals,* his prose, having absorbed all the pointed, dramatic effects of Silver Latin, has become a style of intense individuality. His short, abrupt sentences, varying sharply in tone according to the significance he attaches to each episode, abound in staccato, trenchant epigrams, utilizing a vivid and often poetic vocabulary; never has Latin literature been so far removed from the spoken tongue. Moreover, his treatment of his theme is no less arresting than his language. He is the supreme artist among ancient historians and blends into a single unique

framework all the features he inherited from his forerunners. The antique title *Annals* suggests that Roman traditions are not forgotten; and the Greeks are drawn upon for ethnological and biographical methods, stock rhetorical types and situations, frequent incursions into moralizing, and a variety of emotional effects.

Tacitus writes that he has been unmoved by indignation or partisanship, since in his case "the customary incentives to these were lacking"—in other words, he had nothing to gain from indulging in one bias or another. But such protestations were conventional, and Tacitus notably fails to live up to them. His studies of the emperors are unforgettable, but they can scarcely claim to be free from hatred and partiality. In particular, Tiberius (A.D. 14–37), a gloomy but apparently honest ruler with whose reign the *Annals* commence, is presented by Tacitus as the stock tyrant of ancient literature, unjust, ruthless, suspicious, cunning, and lecherous. It has often been suggested, with considerable plausibility, that this adverse picture is influenced by the experience of Tacitus himself as a participant in the last years of the somber Domitian's reign, when senators were intimidated and terrified—that is to say, Tacitus reinterpreted Tiberius as a proto-Domitian. Moreover, the memory of Domitian may have affected the historian in another way as well, for he had accepted high public office under that emperor and must have been obliged to acquiesce in the purges inflicted upon his own colleagues and friends.

Such may have been the traumatic events that apparently encouraged him to see not only Tiberius but also the other early emperors as the tyrants that, in reality, they scarcely were. Tacitus' narrative is so enthralling, so convincing as a work of art, that it pulls the wool over the reader's eyes. Indeed, it all but carries conviction as history—especially as there is very rarely a better literary authority from which we can check what he chooses to tell us. Moreover, the actual facts that he places on record cannot usually be faulted in respect of accuracy. Yet the manner of their presentation, designed with the utmost care, is often highly invidious. The historian makes a great display of judicious selection from his sources (which are often not identifiable), but this selective process frequently proves to be yet another way of inserting a sinister hint, a damning insinuation—and such hints and insinuations, often highly unfair, form a vital element in the unforgettable psychological pictures he provides for us.

And fairness is further sacrificed to the combined claims of rhetoric and morality. Virtues and vices are starkly identified and vividly dramatized: Tacitus tells us that this is his goal. Moral philosophy, then, was one of the chief influences at work on him; and Virgilian epic, and tragic drama, were others. No wonder, therefore, that he saw history as something considerably elevated and exalted above the pedestrian trivialities of our mundane lives. As a result, he avoids language that seems to him lacking in appropriate dignity, and the subjects he chooses are those calculated to contribute to the dramatic grandeur of the whole pattern. The highest drama seemed to him to be centered upon the potent, sinister, glamorous imperial court. We also hear much of the Senate, for Tacitus is, in a sense, one of its traditional historians, a member of its order who writes from a senatorial standpoint. However, the prominence accorded to the Senate in his narrative only serves to illustrate its humiliating impotence and degeneracy under the heel of the imperial autocrats, whose power is thus thrown into even higher relief. While the empire's provinces and the lives of their many peoples are not neglected, they appear only when they can contribute to the general picture the historian wants to paint.

All the same, Tacitus remained in two minds about the despotic rule of the emperors. He admired the traditions and glories of the Republic. Yet he was also well aware that this Republic was a thing of the past—and could never be revived. Indeed, he even went farther, and stigmatized any sort of political opposition to the imperial régime, if it went beyond passive, resigned disapproval, as theatrical and pointless—thus implicitly justifying his own role as an imperial official under the tyrant Domitian. When Tacitus is dealing with post-Augustan emperors, he appears to admire the ostensibly more republican Augustus in contrast to these degraded characters. Nevertheless, his introductory survey of Augustus' own reign is a series of sneers directed against him, which have their value for us as a counterweight to the Augustan propaganda that flooded the world but which also contain grossly unfair suggestions and innuendoes.

While he expresses grateful awareness of his good fortune in being able to write during the relatively enlightened reigns of Nerva and Trajan, Tacitus, nevertheless, constantly insists upon the essentially evil nature of rule by one man; and perhaps this conviction is the central point of his philosophy. Since the autocrat, in the last resort, controls everything, Tacitus reserves his closest, coldest scrutiny for the motives and morals of emperors. Their oppressive domination—and the universal moral degeneracy that was both cause and effect—made him become embittered and pessimistic. On the question of divine guidance of the world or lack of it, Tacitus is inconsistent; clearly, however, he feels that there are some historical periods when everything seems to be at the mercy of a fate or deity (if such exists) that is blind—or even malignant. And human nature often seems as black to him as human destiny. On the other hand, he is far from skeptical about the potentialities of the human spirit. Even in times of civil war or oppressive government, he notes that men and women manage, on occasion, to act with extraordinary pertinacity, virtue, and courage—a vital emphasis that makes him one of the outstanding humanists of the ancient world.

Tacitus was too individual and demanding a writer to leave a school of followers, or indeed even to attract much interest at all, either in antiquity or in the medieval times that followed. In the later fourth century, it is true, Ammianus Marcellinus, another outstanding historian, was attentive to his memory and deliberately began his history where Tacitus left off. Nonetheless, for Books 1–6 of the *Annals* we depend upon the tenuous thread of a single Codex (the First Medicean), copied at Corvey in Saxony during the ninth century but not studied until after it had been taken to Rome (1508). The other half of what survives from the *Annals* (Books 11–16), together with the extant part of the *Histories,* has likewise come down to us in a single manuscript. This, the Second Medicean, was written at Monte Cassino (southwestern Italy) in the eleventh century and is perhaps identifiable with a text that was in the possession of Boccaccio three centuries later. It was printed in Venice, with the *Germania,* in about 1470. The *Agricola* followed in 1482, and a complete edition of Tacitus' surviving works was published at Rome in 1515.

Among the sixteenth century thinkers who felt his enormous impact were the Dutch scholar Erasmus and the Italian statesman and political philosopher Machiavelli. Tacitus was so versatile, and so complex, that he seemed to provide slogans both for and against every conceivable section of political opinion, all the way from autocracy to republicanism. In due course, he became the favorite historian of some of the Founding Fathers of the United States, including John Adams and Thomas Jefferson. By 1837, he had been translated into various languages by no less than four hundred different hands.

EDITIONS—Opera Minora (Agricola, Germania, Dialogus): R. M. Ogilvie and M. Winterbottom, 1975. Histories: Heubner, 1963, 1972; K. Wellesley, Book 3, 1972. Annals: H. Furneaux, 1896–1907, reprints; E. Koestermann, 1963– ; F. R. D. Goodyear, v 1 (Book 1, Chapters 1–54), 1972; N. P. Miller, Book 15, 1973; F. Romer, Books 15 and 16, 1976. *Translations*—M. Hutton, W. Peterson, C. H. Moore, R. M. Ogilvie, E. H. Warmington, M. Winterbottom (Loeb ed.), 1914, 1925, 1931, 1937, 1970; Agricola: H. Mattingly and S. A. Handford (Penguin ed.), 1970; Dialogus: D. A. Russell and M. Winterbottom, eds., Ancient Literary Criticism, 1972; Histories: K. Wellesley, 1972; Annals: D. R. Dudley, 1966; M. Grant (Penguin ed.), 1977; P. Wuilleumier (Budé ed.), 1974– .
ABOUT—K. Büchner, Tacitus: Die historischen Versuche, 1955; C. W. Mendell, Tacitus: The Man and His Work, 1958, reprint 1970; R. Syme, Tacitus, 1958, reprint 1970; B. Walker, The Annals of Tacitus: A Study in the Writing of History, revised ed., 1960, reprint 1968; F. Kuntz, Die Sprache des Tacitus und die Tradition der lateinischen Historikersprache, 1962; E. Paratore, Tacito, 2nd ed., 1962; C. Questa, Studi sulle fonti degli Annales di Tacito, 2nd ed., 1963; B. R. Voss, Der pointierte Stil des Tacitus, 1963; R. Häussler, Tacitus und das historische Bewusstsein, 1965; J. Tresch, Die Nerobücher in den Annalen des Tacitus, 1965; D. R. Dudley, The World of Tacitus, 1968; R. T. Scott, Religion and Philosophy in the Histories of Tacitus, 1968; T. A. Dorey, ed., Tacitus, 1969; V. Pöschl, Tacitus (Wege der Forschung, v 97), reprint 1969; F. R. D.

Goodyear, Tacitus (Greece & Rome: New Surveys in the Classics, no 4), 1970; M. Grant, The Ancient Historians, 1970; D. Flach, Tacitus in der Tradition der antiken Geschichtsschreibung, 1973; J. Lucas, Les obsessions de Tacite, 1974; H. W. Benario, An Introduction to Tacitus, 1975; U. Zuccarelli, Psicologia e semantica di Tacito, 2nd ed., 1975; I. Lana, Tacito: L'intellettuale e il potere, 1977; A. Momigliano, Essays in Ancient and Modern Historiography, 1977; K. C. Schellhase, Tacitus in Renaissance Political Thought, 1977.

TATIUS, ACHILLES. See Achilles Tatius

TERENCE (Publius Terentius Afer), Latin poet and dramatist, was born in about 195 or 185 and died in 159 B.C. He was born at Carthage in northern Africa (hence his surname *Afer* meaning African). He came to Rome as a slave in the household of a senator, Terentius Lucanus, by whom he was educated and then set free, at which time he assumed his liberator's family name. He was on friendly terms with highly placed Romans; his patrons were said to have included Scipio Aemilianus and Laelius, whose friendship was celebrated by Cicero in his *De Amicitia;* and it is clear from Terence's own prologues that he had noblemen among his friends. At the end of his life he visited Greece and never returned to Italy; according to one account, he died in a shipwreck.

Terence has left six plays, all of which were produced by Ambivius Turpio, who was also his leading actor. The music was written by a slave named Flaccus.

In the *Andria (Woman of Andros,* 166), Simo has chosen Chremes' daughter Philumena as the future wife of his son Pamphilus, whose own preference, on the other hand, is directed toward Glycerium, supposedly an orphan; Philumena is loved by Simo's friend Charinus. Chremes, learning of Pamphilus' attachment to Glycerium, decides to break off the young man's engagement to his daughter Philumena and does so when Pamphilus' slave Davus shows him the child Glycerium has borne to Pamphilus. However, Glycerium is proved to be
ter′ ens

Chremes' daughter and marries Pamphilus; Charinus and Philumena also get married.

In the *Heautontimorumenus (Self-Tormentor)*, Clinia, who loves the poor Corinthian girl Antiphila, is compelled to serve as a soldier abroad by his father Menedemus, who later regrets inflicting this exile upon him and imposes a hard and laborious life on himself by way of penance (it is he who is the self-tormentor of the title). Clinia returns to his hometown without his father's knowledge and stays at the house of his friend Clitipho (the son of Chremes), to which the wily slave Syrus brings a couple of girls: Antiphila, so that she can be reunited with Clinia, and Bacchis, a grasping prostitute whom Clitipho loves but of whom his father, Chremes, would not approve. In the course of a series of complicated intrigues, a sum of money is extracted from Chremes to pay for Bacchis, whom Clitipho marries; meanwhile Antiphila is discovered to be Clitipho's sister and becomes Clinia's wife.

In the *Eunuch* (161), the music girl Pamphila, whom the prostitute Thais wrongly believes to be her sister, is purchased and presented to her by the braggart soldier Thraso. A young Athenian, Phaedria, who loves Thais and has given her the eunuch Dorus as a present, leaves for the country when she requests him to give place to Thraso for two days. Phaedria's young brother Chaerea, falling in love with Pamphila, dresses up as a eunuch (on the suggestion of his family slave Parmeno) and seizes the opportunity to seduce his beloved. Pamphila is now discovered, however, not to be of humble birth after all, but to be the sister of a respectable Athenian named Chremes, who approves of her marriage to Chaerea. Thais agrees to have the young man's father Laches as her protector so that Phaedria can have free access to her; since Phaedria's funds are limited, however, the parasite Gnatho advises him to let Thraso have a share of her favors as well.

The *Phormio* (161) is named after a parasitic character who, in the absence of Antipho's father, arranges a lawsuit, in collaboration with the family slave Geta, that allows Antipho to marry the penniless orphan Phanium, whom he loves. But Antipho's father Demipho, on his return, is enraged to discover what has happened. Geta also manages to extort money from Chremes (Demipho's brother) to allow Chremes' son Phaedria to buy the flute girl Pamphila. Chremes is anxious to keep from his wife Nausistrata the fact that Phanium is his own clandestine daughter; but the secret comes out, because Phormio, dragged to court for his intrigues, gives him away. However, in the end Nausistrata pardons her husband.

The *Adelphi* (*Brothers*, 160), are the two sons of the strict Demea: Aeschinus has been given away for adoption to Micio, easygoing brother of Demea; Ctesipho remains with his father. As a favor to Ctesipho, who is in love with a girl harpist in Sannio's brothel, Aeschinus has abducted her. He has also seduced Pamphila, an Athenian girl in humble circumstances, and wishes to marry her. Demea grumbles but is won over; Aeschinus marries the girl Pamphila, whom he has wronged; Micio, somewhat reluctantly, agrees to marry her mother; and Ctesipho is allowed his music girl.

Although Terence came from northern Africa, the Latin he wrote was not colloquial like that of his forerunner Plautus but impeccably pure. Moreover, his aim was quite different from that of Plautus. Not only does he lack his vivid wit, but he has none of his vigor and rowdiness. As a dramatist, he is far closer to the contemplative sentimental "criticism of life" of the Athenian New Comedy. Indeed, like other Latin comedians, he derived his plots from the New Comedy playwrights, notably Menander (342–293 B.C.), for Terence was writing for a better educated audience than Plautus had been able to muster. With the backing of Scipio Aemilianus and his circle, who were knowledgeable admirers of Greek cultural achievement, he was able to appeal to a select public, which suited his less robust talent.

Select as they were, Terence's audiences, like those of earlier times, still did not require displays of morality in their theatre, and Terence is amoral—that is to say, he does not regard morality as relevant to his themes. Occasionally, however, he seems to reflect the humaneness of the Stoic ethics that were now beginning to be fashionable at Rome. Thus, when one of Terence's characters asserts in a famous line: "I am a man; I regard nothing human as beyond my scope," Seneca the Younger (d. A.D. 65), and others after him, chose to interpret it as an endorsement of the Stoic Brotherhood of Man (though this may not have been specifically in the dramatist's mind when he was writing those words).

Terence evidently encountered a good deal of criticism of his plays. This is clear from his Prologues, in which he justifies his practices as a playwright against various attacks. Answering criticisms of plagiarism, he admits that the Greek dramatists have said everything before—and he is certainly closer than Plautus to his Greek originals: he may even, perhaps, be regarded as standing somewhere between an independent creator and a translator. However, when accused of the "spoiling" *(contaminatio)* of these Greek originals by their combination, in a single play of his own, with extraneous matter derived from other comedies, he protests that Plautus had done just the same. He was also criticized for borrowing too extensively from earlier Latin adaptations of what the Greek comedians had written. Another reproach was that his aristocratic friends and supporters not only gave him general assistance in his literary activities but were actually the real authors of his plays, since his style exhibited a degree of cultivated refinement that he could not, it was felt, have achieved on his own account. But this slur is unlikely to be justified.

Terence's artistry and polish were something entirely new in Latin literature. They are displayed not only in his linguistic usage but in the fluency and grace of his dialogues and narrative passages. Moreover, although the plots of his comedies sound singularly fatuous and monotonous to us today, their construction was clever and sophisticated; and it is from him, rather than from Menander or from Plautus, that many subsequent generations came to understand the art of composing a play. In the first century, Cicero quoted him often. Caesar called him a "lover of pure language" but also "half-a-Menander" *(dimidiate Menander)* —by which he probably meant someone who did not rise to Menander's full stature, since Caesar, although ranking Terence among the greatest writers, nevertheless detected in him a certain deficiency. Horace, one of the greatest Roman poets, however, asserted that Terence "conquered by his art." From the end of the classical period onward, his plays, despite their lack of concern for ethical propriety, were studied everywhere as schoolbooks—for example, Hroswitha, poet, chronicler, and abbess of the Benedictine convent of Gandersheim, adapted them in the tenth century for the use of her convent. In the sixteenth century, Terence's works were extensively read and acted in England; his influence can be traced in early English comic drama, and again in the comedies of manners of the seventeenth century Restoration, notably those of the English dramatist William Congreve; and later it appears again in the work of Richard Steele (1672–1729) and Irish dramatist Richard Sheridan (1751–1816).

EDITIONS—Adelphi: R. H. Marin, 1976; Andria: G. P. Shipp, 2nd ed., 1960; Eunuch: Brown, 1977; Hecyra: T. F. Carney, 1963; R. Scarcia, 1966; Phormio: R. H. Martin, 1959. *Translations*—J. Sargeaunt (Loeb ed.), 1912; B. Radice (Penguin ed.), 1965, 1967; F. O. Copley, 1967; P. Borie, C. Carrier, and D. Parker, 1974.

ABOUT—G. Norwood, The Art of Terence, 1923, reprint 1965, *and* Plautus and Terence, 1931, reprint 1963; N. Terzaghi, Prolegomeni a Terenzio, 1931, reprint 1965; E. Reitzenstein, Terenz als Dichter, 1940; F. Arnaldi, Da Plauto a Terenzio, 1947; G. E. Duckworth, The Nature of Roman Comedy, 1952; W. Beare, The Roman Stage, 3rd ed. revised, 1961; O. Rieth, Die Kunst Menanders in den "Adelphen" des Terenz, ed. by K. Gaiser, 1964; H. J. Glücklich, Aussparung und Antithese: Studien zur terenzischen Komödie (Heidelberg, dissertation), 1966; D. Klose, Die Didaskalien und Prologe des Terenz (Freiburg, dissertation), 1966; B. Denzler, Der Monolog bei Terenz (Zurich, dissertation), 1968; P. Flury, Liebe und Liebessprache bei Menander, Plautus und Terenz, 1968; E. Lefèvre, Die Expositionstechnik in den Komödien des Terenz, 1969, *and* (as ed.) Die römische Komödie: Plautus und Terenz, 1973; C. Garton, Personal Aspects of the Roman Theatre, 1972; B. A. Taladoire, Térence: Un théatre de la jeunesse, 1972; L. Perelli, Il teatro rivoluzionario di Terenzio, 1973; K. Büchner, Das Theater des Terenz, 1974; W. G. Arnott, Menander, Plautus, Terence (Greece & Rome: New Surveys in the Classics, no 9), 1975; V. Pöschl, Das Problem der Adelphen des Terenz, 1975; D. Bo, Genitori e figli nelle commedie di Terenzio, 1977; F. H. Sandbach, The Comic Theatre of Greece and Rome, 1977.

TERENTIUS VARRO, MARCUS. See Varro, Marcus Terentius

TERPANDER, Greek lyric poet and musician, won a prize during the period 676–673 B.C. at the Games in honor of Apollo Carneius at Sparta. He had gone to Sparta from Antissa on the island of Lesbos, where he was born.

According to tradition, he was the inventor of the seven-stringed lyre *(kithara)*. This cannot be strictly true, since this instrument had already been known in the second millennium B.C., when it is depicted, for example, in a funeral scene on the sarcophagus of Hagia Triada in Crete; and a seven- or eight-stringed lyre also appears in Mycenaean art. However, the instrument no doubt vanished from use when the Mycenaean civilization disappeared, and it is likely enough that Terpander brought it back into use. It is represented on a vase painting from Smyrna which can be dated to the latter half of the seventh century B.C. The fifth century poet Pindar, in connection with Terpander's achievement, observed that the Lesbians got to know of the many-stringed lyre from the people of Lydia (western Asia Minor), when they encountered them at dinner parties.

At Sparta, as we learn from Pseudo-Plutarch in *On Music,* Terpander was believed to have founded the first of the two musical establishments or schools *(katastaseis)* ascribed to this period. What, if anything, he contributed to choral lyric we do not know. But there is some record of his composition of solo songs, for lyre accompaniment. The monograph *On Music,* which derives most of its information from the musical theorist of the fourth century B.C. Aristoxenus of Taras and from the grammarian Heraclides Ponticus, describes him as the composer-executant of hexameter "Preludes" to epic texts accompanied by the lyre; these preludes may have been somewhat similar to the Homeric Hymns. According to the same treatise, Terpander also set Homeric texts to music.

In addition, he developed the nome, an already existing type of vocal solo, with lyre accompaniment, dedicated to Apollo; tûr pan' dĕr

nomes were originally styles rather than definite melodies, but a form had emerged consisting of seven parts, the first four of which comprised choral chants and responses, reflecting and resolving the contemporary rivalry between vocal and instrumental music. So strong was the influence of Terpander's compositions on this traditional genre that nomes were henceforward regarded as his personal creation; and in due course competitions were established for their future composers. Terpander was also said to have invented the musical form of *skolia,* songs written for diners at banquets, who had to cap each other's pieces with another on a similar subject.

The fragments attributable to his authorship amount to no more than seven lines; and even among these it is doubtful whether any of them are genuine. It is not apparent that Terpander's writings were known later among the Hellenistic scholars at Alexandria.

EDITIONS (dubiously attributable fragments)—D. L. Page, Poetae Melici Graeci, 1962. *With translation:* J. M. Edmonds, Lyra Graeca (Loeb ed.), v 1, revised ed., 1928.
ABOUT—C. M. Bowra, Greek Lyric Poetry, 2nd ed., 1962; D. A. Campbell, Greek Lyric Poetry, 1967.

TERTULLIAN (Quintus Septimius Florens Tertullianus), Latin Christian writer, was born between A.D. 155 and 160 and may have died in about 240. He was born at Carthage in Africa (Tunisia) of pagan parents, his father being reputedly a centurion in the Roman army. Tertullian studied law and rhetoric and moved to Rome, where he probably worked as a lawyer. At first he was attracted to Stoicism; but his disgust with pagan immorality, combined with a strong admiration for the martyrs, converted him to Christianity (c. 193/5). Returning to Carthage, he used his brilliant gifts to become the leading defender of the faith against the state, and the Jews, and those Christian sects that he regarded as heretical. According to St. Jerome (c. 340–420), he became a priest, and despite modern doubts this remains likely. From then onward, however, his tûr tul' yàn writings show an ever-increasing extremism, which led him in about 207 to go over openly to the Montanists, a rigorous sect of Phrygian origin that combined a sensational apocalyptic message with emphasis on the glory of martyrdom, on liberation from the encumbrances of worldly life, and on ritual purification. Finally, he seems to have broken even with Montanism, to found his own sect of Tertullianists who were more fanatical still. His latest tracts became more and more violent, until after 220 they ceased to appear.

Thirty-one of Tertullian's treatises have survived (and more than a dozen others are known by name). A major group concentrates on the defense of the Christian faith against paganism. *To the Gentiles (Ad Nationes)* and the *Apology (Apologeticus)*, both written in about A.D. 197, are related to one another, approaching the same question from different angles. The former preserves material from the lost *Antiquities* of the scholarly Varro (who died 27 B.C.) but is for the most part a mere rehash of Greek defenses of Christianity. The treatise argues that pagans and their legislators condemn Christians (without any examination of their behavior) of all kinds of sins and crimes without the slightest justification and ignoring the fact that these very offenses are common among their own fellow pagans and are even ascribed to the gods whom they worship. The *Apologeticus,* the most renowned of Tertullian's works, is a highly individual and carefully finished production, reflecting not only its author's savage capacity for sarcasm but the influence of his legal training. Addressed to the Roman government of his province, the treatise contradicts pagan allegations that the Christians performed disgusting rites and insists that they are not only highly moral (because of their fear of God) but are excellent Roman citizens as well. On the issue of their recognition of the emperor's divinity, which they were accused of failing to honor, Tertullian retorts that they show their loyalty in a far more convincing fashion by the prayers they offer to God for the welfare of the emperor. Persecution, he declares in a famous passage, will only strengthen the church: "The blood of Christians is seed."

In the *Witness of the Soul (De Testimonio Animae),* composed shortly afterward, a different argument is put forward: that the fundamental doctrines of Christianity—including belief in the existence of God—appear in other faiths as well, and form a part of natural religion; so that the human soul is by its very nature Christian *(anima naturaliter Christiana).* This is the old Stoic doctrine of the commonwealth of humankind given a novel and ingenious twist. *To Scapula* delivers an admonition to the governor of Africa of that name who had imprisoned a soldier for refusing to wear a garland during a pagan festival. Tertullian (who had already defended the soldier's action in his earlier pamphlet entitled *On the Garland*) warns the governor of the divine penalties that would be visited upon him for this act of persecution. Nor does Tertullian neglect to attack Judaism as well: *Against the Jews (Adversus Judaeos),* drawing upon the *Dialogue With Trypho* of Justin Martyr (who died A.D. 168), declares that Jewish law is abolished by the New Covenant of Jesus.

Tertullian also devotes a great deal of attention to attacking heterodox Christians, whose deviations he regards as deplorable. *On the Prescription of the Heretics* relies on the technicality of the *praescriptio* (a legal term describing an objection that causes the dismissal of a case) as a way of dismissing the doctrines of all heretics; Tertullian asserts that heretics cannot and must not make use of the Gospels, because these are not theirs to use but belong to the Church, to which they have been handed down by the Apostles. In this treatise we find not only the basis for future western views of traditional authority but also a masterly onslaught on those who vainly hoped to combine pagan philosophy with Christian belief.

One of the earliest of these anti-heretical tractates, *Against Hermogenes,* directs its vituperation against a Carthaginian artist who believed that God had made the world out of matter already existing before the Creation. *The Antidote for Scorpion Stings (Scorpiace)* denounces the Gnostics, who believed that the world, being evil, cannot have been made by God; Tertullian compared them to menacing, destructive scorpions, beause they mistakenly considered that outward conformity to pagan practice might be allowed and failed to regard martyrdom as a positive duty (by this time he had retracted his earlier view that it was permissible to flee from persecution).

Against the Valentinians abuses the followers of the sect's founder, Valentinus, an Egyptian teacher of the second century A.D. *Against Marcion,* in five books, which draws upon Justin, Irenaeus, and others, is our chief (though biased) source of information about that even more significant second century personage Marcion of Sinope, who had enunciated the doctrine of two Gods—one, the Old Testament Creator and Judge (a comparatively inferior being), and the other, the God whom Jesus revealed—and who had claimed that Paul was the only true Apostle. Tertullian's most important polemic, this was subjected to repeated revisions as his thought continued to evolve. The targets of *On the Body of Christ (De Carne Christi)* were once again the Gnostics—together with Docetists, who believed that Jesus had only appeared to take on human flesh. The purpose of the work was to show that the soul is corporeal and material, that His body and sonship to the Virgin were real; Tertullian was even prepared to stress the Savior's human nature by declaring that He was ugly. In continuation, *On the Resurrection of the Flesh* denounces those who disbelieved in bodily resurrection. *Against Praxeas* adopts a particularly unpleasant tone because of Tertullian's personal dislike of this personage, who was an enemy of Montanism and a Monarchian or Patripassionist— that is to say, he held that God the Father shared in the sufferings of God the Son. This discussion contributed to the formulation of the Trinity; and in Tertullian's treatise the term *Trinitas* occurs in Latin literature for the first time.

On the Soul, which seeks to contradict heretical doctrines on this theme and is based on the views of a pagan physician named Soranus, is a clever piece of fireworks but very naive psychology.

Tertullian also produced a large series of pamphlets prescribing Christian behavior and morality in specific situations or circumstances. *On the Martyrs (Ad Martyras)* was addressed to Christians who were in prison awaiting trial and execution—perhaps including Saint Perpetua and Saint Felicitas, on whose martyrdoms a work was written that may possibly be of his authorship. *On Shows (De Spectaculis,* 197 or 203) contains an eloquent and violent condemnation of gladiatorial games and also an attack on all theatrical displays, which are declared to be cruel and immoral because founded on heathen rites. *On Idolatry (De Idololatria)* strikes out in all directions, denouncing the practice of astrology, the teaching of literature, the sculpting of statues, and the trade of selling perfumes.

A further group of treatises discusses doctrinal issues. Three of them, written between 200 and 206, *On Baptism, On Prayer,* and *On Penitence,* may be regarded as a trilogy. *On Baptism,* the only surviving monograph on any of the sacraments prior to the Nicene Creed, discusses a number of controversial points, including the problem whether baptism conferred by a heretic is valid, a question decided in the negative. *On Prayer (De Oratione),* which provides the earliest account of the Lord's Prayer in any language, deals, among other matters, with the correct posture to be adopted while praying and with the clothes that ought to be worn. *On Penitence* allows the baptized a single repentance; Tertullian has not yet, by this time, gone quite all the way to Montanism, which allowed no second chance at all but asserted that even one such single sin by a baptized person precluded salvation altogether. Another treatise of the same period, *On Patience,* maintains that this quality (in which the author admits that he finds himself deficient) is not, for a Christian, the same as the old pagan virtue of endurance but must be specifically related to the requirements of his own religion.

Tertullian also commented on sexual and matrimonial matters. *On the Adornment of Women* (between 197 and 201) reminds them that, since they are descended from sinful Eve, smart clothes—an invention of the fallen angels—are inappropriate for them; they must not allow themselves to be dominated by pagan fashions. *On the Veiling of Virgins* (c. 208) offers the view that marriageable young women (or married women

425

for that matter) will do well to wear veils when they appear in public. *To My Wife (Ad Uxorem),* in two books, suggests how as a widow she ought to behave after he is dead, expressing the opinion that a Christian widow, preferably, should not marry, but that, if she must, it is at least imperative that her choice should fall upon a fellow Christian. In a subsequent piece, however, the *Exhortation to Chastity (De Exhortatione Castitatis),* he rejects second marriage in categorical terms, as being contrary to the will of God; and then, in an essay entitled *On Monogamy* (213), he reiterates this view, denouncing such marriages with true Montanist narrowness and fervor as illicit and virtually adulterous.

Tertullian's views became increasingly rigorous; and his writings finally put forward doctrines that signalized an open breach with the church. *On Sexual Propriety (De Pudicitia),* for example, is more than an attack on adultery, for it is also a denunciation of an unnamed authority, perhaps Pope Callixtus himself (217–212), who had suggested that this sin, while grievous, was nevertheless not wholly unpardonable. *On Fasting: Against the Moderates (De Ieiunio Adversus Psychicos)* is explicitly a product of Montanism. In it one encounters the name *psychici* (natural men) applied to the more moderate Catholics, whose refusal to practice Montanist asceticism Tertullian fiercely rebukes. *On the Mantle (De Pallio)* (c. 210), although very different, may fit into the same picture. In this witty and sarcastic little work, the author explains, with many tricks of rhetoric and argument, why he has abandoned the Roman toga and adopted instead the traditional cloak of the Greeks, the *pallium,* that was worn by Greek philosophers and teachers and other professional men. Although various other interpretations have been suggested, Tertullian may have been celebrating his withdrawal from officialdom—here identified with the Catholic Church.

Everything he wrote recalls his legal education; his vigorous and incisive argumentation is that of a jurist—and a jurist of rather an unscrupulous kind, delighting in logical tricks and prepared to indulge in any verbal maneuvers that will make his opponents look foolish. For, more a lawyer than a creative philosopher or theologian, Tertullian makes no pretense of a judicial balance or impartial approach. Intolerant, ironic, exasperating, and formidably erudite, he pours forth torrents of highly individual and dramatic prose, accompanied by a wealth of lavish illustration and punctuated by frequent exclamatory outbursts, all often framed in a style that was pregnant, terse, and knotted to the point of obscurity.

Yet despite these excesses and exaggerations, Tertullian enjoys an exalted position: he was the first of all the great Latin churchmen—indeed, the first major Latin writer ever—to take up the cudgels on behalf of Christianity. Although he ended his days outside the Church, it was he who turned the thinking of the Christian West into the channels in which it continued to flow in later times. Thus Cyprian, bishop of Carthage (c. 200–58), for example, who followed him in discussing the Church from a legalistic point of view, was said to have called him "the master" and reportedly studied his writings every day of his life. Furthermore, Tertullian was also the father of the whole tradition of Puritan nonconformity and the pioneer of political protest based on the ideas of the Bible.

WORKS—For a list of Tertullian's lost works *see* M. Schanz, C. Hosius, and G. Krüger, Geschichte der römischen Literatur, v 3, 1905, pp 322–26. For treatises wrongly attributed to him *see* H. J. Rose, Handbook of Latin Literature, 1966, p 477 note 21.
EDITIONS—Corpus Christianorum (Series Latina), v 1, and v 2; Corpus Scriptorum Ecclesiasticorum Latinorum, v 19, v 47, and v 76; J. P. Migne, Patrologia Latina, v 1, and v 2. On the Soul: J. H. Waszink, 1947. Against the Gentiles: A. Schneider (Book I), 1968. *With translation:* A. Souter, Apology, 1917, *and* Against Praxeas, On Prayer, On Baptism, 1919, *and* On the Resurrection of the Body, 1922; T. R. Glover, Apology and On Shows (De Spectaculis), *in* T. R. Glover, W. C. A. Ker, and G. H. Rendall, Tertullian: Minucius Felix (Loeb ed.), 1931; E. Evans, many works, 1948–72; W. P. le Saint, Treatises on Marriage and Remarriage, 1951; J. H. Waszink, Against Hermogenes, 1956.
ABOUT—A. d'Alès, La théologie de Tertullien, 1905; J. Berton, Tertullien le schismatique, 1928; E. A. Isichei, Political Thinking and Social Experience: Some Christian Interpretations of the Roman Empire from Tertullian to Salvian, 1964; T. P. O'Malley, Tertullian and the Bible, 1967; R. Klein, Tertullian und das römische Reich, 1968; T. D. Barnes, Tertullian, 1971; R. D.

Sider, Ancient Rhetoric and the Art of Tertullian, 1971; J. E. L. van der Geest, Le Christ et l'Ancien Testament chez Tertullien, 1972; C. Aziza, Tertullien et le judaisme, 1977.

THALES. See Anaximander

THEMISTIUS, Greek philosopher and rhetorician, was born in about A.D. 317 and died in about 388. His birthplace was in Paphlagonia (northeastern Asia Minor), where his father, a pagan landowner with philosophical interests, ensured that he obtained a rhetorical education. From 337 he continued this training at Constantinople, where he himself inaugurated a school eight years later. His aim, which was to record the rival claims of rhetoric and philosophy, earned him criticism from both sides, to which he responded in a series of speeches defending his program. Though unwilling to accept a salary or fees, he was granted an official professorship, and the emperor Constantius II made him a member of the Senate at Constantinople (355). Moreover, in addition to serving, virtually, as public orator of the eastern court, Themistius traveled extensively with imperial personages and official delegations, notably a mission to the Roman Senate in 357—although, in contrast to the emperor, he still remained a pagan. As such, he applauded the reversion to paganism of the emperor Julian the Apostate (361–63), to whom he wrote an address, now lost, which evoked the emperor's well-known reply announcing his restoration of pagan practices. Nevertheless, Themistius remained in favor with the Christian emperors who followed, down to the time of Theodosius I (379–95), who appointed him prefect of the city (383/4) and entrusted him with the education of his elder son Arcadius, destined to become his successor in the eastern part of the empire.

As a philosopher, Themistius expressed an admiration for Plato and quoted him frequently, though his own thought remained remote from contemporary Neoplatonism, especially in its preoccupation with the
the mis′ ti us

supernatural. He was far more attracted to the pragmatic approach of Aristotle, of whose treatises he composed a series of paraphrases (ostensibly for his own convenience). Expanding, simplifying, and explaining the complicated language of the originals, these paraphrases embodied material from lost commentaries and established a pattern that scholars continued to find helpful throughout the Middle Ages. Themistius' versions of Aristotle's *Physics, Posterior Analytics,* and *On the Soul* have survived, and his renderings of *On the Heavens* and *Metaphysics* are extant in medieval Hebrew versions of an Arabic translation. The paraphrases were published in their compiler's lifetime but, according to him, without his consent.

Thirty-four of his speeches, too, have been preserved. Composed in a pure Attic style, they include a funeral encomium of his father and five orations addressed to various emperors. While inevitably full of complimentary remarks, the orations fall considerably short of groveling adulation and are mainly employed as a courteous means of familiarizing rulers with the philosophical ideal of monarchic responsibility. Thus, the first speech, addressed to Constantius II— one of a pair that constitute important documents for the political circumstances of the time—is subtitled *On Philanthropy.* Another oration, celebrating a consulship held by the emperor Jovian (363–64), who succeeded Julian on the throne and restored official Christianity, is an eloquent plea for religious tolerance, pointing out that, even if the bodies of human beings are mastered and slain by persecutors, their souls will still carry on.

Themistius was neither an original philosopher nor an influential politician. The value of his writings lies in their clear demonstration that the long tradition of Greek political philosophy was still alive in a Christian era.

EDITIONS—Paraphrases of Aristotle: M. Wallies, H. Schenkl, R. Heinze, S. Landauer, Commentaria in Aristotelem Graeca, v 5, 1899–1903. Speeches: H. Schenkl, G. Downey, and A. F. Norman, Orationes Quae Supersunt (Teubner ed.), v 1 and v 2, 1965, 1971. ABOUT—S. A. Stertz, Themistius: A Hellenic Philosopher Statesman in the Christian Roman Empire (Classical Journal, v 71), 1976.

THEOCRITUS

THEOCRITUS, Greek poet, was born between 310 and 300 B.C. and died between 260 and 250. His birthplace was probably Syracuse (Siracusa) in Sicily. Nothing is known about his life except what can be inferred from his own poems. From these it appears that he lived mostly away from his native island, first perhaps in southern Italy and later at Cos and Alexandria. Although he evidently built up a reputation as a poet and had influential friends, several initial attempts to find a patron proved unsuccessful, as he complained to King Hiero II of Syracuse, probably in 275/4. Not long afterward, however, he obtained recognition from King Ptolemy II Philadelphus of Egypt, for whom he composed a panegyric (before 270).

The thirty-one poems (other than epigrams) attributed to Theocritus and generically known as his *Idylls* (*eidullion* being the diminutive of *eidos,* a name given earlier to the Odes of Pindar) may be divided into those that are bucolic (pastoral) and those that are not. The former are half a dozen in number. The first Idyll ("Thyrsis") is a beautiful, dramatic dirge for the death of the shepherd Daphnis. Idyll No. 3 is a lyric monologue, on the theme of unhappy love, which is also the subject of No. 10. Idyll No. 4 is a dialogue, cleverly conveying a series of changes of emotional atmosphere, in which conflict between the two participants gives place to friendliness. In No. 5, on the other hand, mutual antipathy gradually increases, until Comatas triumphantly wins the poetry competition against his rival.

These pastoral poems are Theocritus' most characteristic work. The genre was said to have been created by the legendary Daphnis in Sicily, and partial precedents can be traced in the Sicilian poets Epicharmus and Sophron (as well as others in more easterly Greek regions); but it is in Theocritus that we first find mature poetry of this type. In a literary form of the Doric dialect, and a peculiar version of the epic hexameter, he introduces his rural themes, including such topics as shepherds' singing contests, mutual bantering, and lamentations for rustic lovers. These topics are enlarged upon in a spirit of artfully elegant simplicity; this is
thē ok' ri tus

428

the pastoral verse of an urban civilization, written for the townsman, with a subtle humor that combines an artificial bucolic naiveté with some of the traditional trappings of refined poetry, so that rural life is at one moment idealized and at the next presented with lusty realism. Theocritus has been described as the last of the Greeks to create and perfect a new kind of poetry, presenting a new pattern of life. Although the themes of some of these pastoral pieces are Sicilian and the settings of others ostensibly belong to southern Italy, there is no good reason to suppose that any of the series were written before he left for the west; most of the poems contain details suggesting connections with Cos and other parts of the east.

Theocritus exercised great influence on subsequent Greek exponents of the pastoral, such as Moschus of Syracuse (c. 150 B.C.) and Bion of Phlossa (c. 100 B.C.?); and it was he who provided the decisive inspiration for the Latin pastoral adapted by Virgil (70–19 B.C.), with marked originality, for his *Eclogues,* which in turn created the entire pastoral tradition of later Europe. Moreover, Idyll No. 1, the lament for Daphnis, left a special heritage of its own, including, in England, Milton's *Lycidas* (1638) on the death of his friend Edward King and Shelley's *Adonais* (1821) on the death of the poet Keats.

But many significant pieces by Theocritus cannot be described as pastoral or bucolic at all. Poem No. 2 (the *Pharmaceutria*), displaying a vivid contrast of moods, tells of the unhappy love of Simaetha and describes her incantations to recover the affections of her lover. In No. 7 ("Thalusia"), the author, under the name of Simichidas, sings of the loves of a certain Aratus of Cos; the poem seems to recall a mime, such as those of another third century poet, Herodas or Herondas. The same applies to No. 14 and No. 15, which have their scenes laid in towns. The latter of these pieces, the *Adoniazusae,* entertainingly depicts the visit of two contrastingly characterized women, Gorgo and Praxinoa, to the festival of Adonis at Alexandria, concluding with the hymn that they hear sung in honor of Aphrodite and Adonis. In No. 11 Theocritus performs a *tour de force* by presenting the physically repellent Polyphemus as a not unsympathetic lover of Galatea. Other mythical themes, treated with dramatic techniques, are the carrying off of Hylas by a nymph (No. 13), the first exploit of Heracles (No. 24), and the fight between Polydeuces and Amycus (No. 22); this last, like Nos. 13, 24, and 26, is a hymn or short epic *(epyllion)*. No. 16 and No. 17 are addressed to Hiero II of Syracuse and Ptolemy II of Egypt respectively. No. 18 is a wedding song *(epithalamium)* addressed to Helen. Nos. 28-31, the last of which is a fragment, are written in Aeolic dialect and meters.

Like so many other members of the Alexandrian school, Theocritus wrote short and highly finished poems, favored fresh and sometimes exotic themes, and preferred new structural forms or old forms utilized in novel ways. But except when special effects were required, he avoided the Alexandrian tendency to over-erudition, and he surpassed his contemporaries, not only by the creation of the virtually new bucolic genre but also in his fresh and sharp observation of human beings and nature alike, in his lyrical and lively narratives and descriptions and images, and above all in a dramatic vividness that amounted to genius.

WORKS dubiously attributed to Theocritus include Idylls No. 8 and No. 9 of the collection; No. 8 is partly in the elegiac meter.
EDITIONS—K. J. Dover, Theocritus: Select Poems, 1971; A. H. Griffiths, Theocritus: Selected Idylls, 1979. *With translation:* A. S. F. Gow, Theocritus, 2nd ed., 1952 (translation reprinted *in* The Greek Bucolic Poets, 1953). *Translations*—J. M. Edmonds, The Greek Bucolic Poets, revised ed., 1928; B. Mills, Idylls, 1963; A. Holden, Greek Pastoral Poetry (Penguin ed.), 1974; A. Rist, The Poems of Theocritus, 1979; P. E. Legrand, Bucoliques grecs (Budé ed.), 3rd ed., 1946–53.
ABOUT—E. Bignone, Teocrito, 1934; C. Gallavotti, Theocritus quique Ferentur Bucolici Graeci, 1946, *and* Lingua technica e poesia negli Idilli di Teocrito, 1952; M. Sanchez-Wildberger, Theocrit-Interpretationen (Zürich, dissertation), 1955; A. Köhnken, Apollonios Rhodios und Theokrit, 1965; A. Lesky, History of Greek Literature, 1966; G. Lawall, Theocritus' Coan Pastorals, 1967; T. G. Rosenmeyer, The Green Cabinet: Theocritus and the European Pastoral Lyric, 1969; G. Lawall *in* A. J. Boyle, ed., Ancient Pastoral, 1975; A. E.-A. Horstmann, Ironie und Humor bei Theokrit, 1976.

THEODORE OF STUDIUM, Saint (also known as **THEODORUS STUDITA** and **THEODORE THE STUDITE**), A.D. 759–826, Greek theologian of the Byzantine epoch, was born at Constantinople. His father, Photinus, was an official of the imperial treasury; and his mother, Theoctista, a society woman of extremely pious and austere character who gave her children an ascetic upbringing. Theodore also received a careful education, which was designed to secure his entry to the imperial civil service. At the age of twenty-two, however, at the prompting of his mother, he retired to an estate belonging to their family at Saccoudion on Mount Olympus in Bithynia (northwestern Asia Minor), where he joined a monastery previously founded by his uncle who was named Plato. By 794 Theodore had become abbot of this institution, by now greatly enlarged. However, when in the following year the monks, under his leadership, adopted a censorious attitude toward the allegedly adulterous second marriage of the emperor Constantine VI, they were sentenced to banishment. Theodore went into exile at Thessalonica (Salonika) but after Constantine's downfall in 797 was recalled by the empress Irene. However, the entire Saccoudion community was soon compelled by the government to leave once more and was transferred to a deserted foundation in the Psamathia quarter of Constantinople, the monastery of Studius (later known as the Studion). Under the leadership of Plato, and Theodore—who adopted many of his uncle's ideas—this monastery became a center of monastic reform, embodying meticulous organization, strict discipline, and a severe though not intolerable asceticism.

In 806, however, Theodore and his Studites objected strongly to an action of the emperor Nicephorus I (802–11), who had chosen a patriarch (of the same name as himself) directly from among the lay population. Condemned by a church council, Theodore went into exile for the second time (809–11). He returned, but when Leo V the Armenian (813–20) revived the policy of iconoclasm, which forbade the veneration of sacred images, Theodore became his leading opponent and was sentenced to a third pe-

thē′ ə dōr stū′ di um

429

riod of banishment (816–20). He was allowed back by the emperor Michael II the Amorian (820–29), but, since iconoclasm still remained the order of the day, he was never permitted to resume the leadership of his monastery. He died on the island of Büyükada (Prinkipo) in the Sea of Marmara.

A warm and humane character, with a regard for classical tradition, which many of his supporters rejected, he was recognized as a saint by the eastern and western churches alike. The principal importance of his career lay in his fight to preserve the independence of the church from interference by the emperors—and by the patriarchs who were often obliged to obey them. This was a cause for which Theodore, an untiring controversialist and archprotester, did not even hesitate to appeal over the heads of the Constantinople authorities to the Pope at Rome.

His collection of five hundred fifty letters, many of them "open," not only throw extensive light upon the theological disputes of the time but illuminate the intellectual climate and everyday life of Constantinople as a whole. The most popular of his other writings were his numerous sermons, comprising the Greater and Lesser *Catechisms (Catecheses)*, which demonstrate his ideals for a monastic community. Also extant are specialist works on monastic discipline and three polemics against the iconoclasts, as well as festival homilies and panegyrics of saints. In addition, Theodore composed impressive funeral orations for his mother Theoctista and his uncle Plato.

He also wrote long hymns of the characteristic form of his day, known as Canons. Compared to the efforts of previous hymnists, they display progress in refinement and elaboration; but a certain waning of spontaneity is now apparent. Theodore's further works included verse epigrams, mainly in the iambic meter, which concern themselves with every aspect of monastic life. Some of these pieces are addressed to the servants of the monastery, including its shoemaker and its cook; their aim is to point out the exalted function of such labors.

EDITIONS—J. P. Migne, Patrologia Graeca, v 99.

Hymns: J. Pitra, Analecta Sacra Spicilegio Solesmensi Parata, v 1, 1876.
ABOUT—A. Gardner, Theodore of Studium: His Life and Times, 1905; I. Hausherr, Saint Théodore Studite: L'homme et l'ascète, 1926; H. G. Beck, Kirche und theologische Literatur im byzantinischen Reich, 1959; D. Attwater, Saints of the East, 1963.

THEODORET (Theodoretus), Greek church historian, biographer and theologian, was probably born in about A.D. 393 and died in about 466. His native city was Syrian Antioch (Antakya in southeastern Turkey). After becoming a monk at an early age, in 423 he was appointed bishop of Cyrrhus (or Cyrrus; the modern Kurus), between Antioch and the River Euphrates, where, except for a brief period of banishment, he spent the rest of his life. When Cyril of Alexandria (376–444, noted for his orthodoxy) attacked Theodoret's friend Nestorius of Constantinople (patriarch of Constantinople, 428–31) for allegedly overstressing the independence and separation of the divine and human natures of Christ incarnate, Theodoret became involved in the dispute and henceforward figured as Cyril's leading critic. He maintained that the two natures in Christ, while united in one person, are not amalgamated in essence, but the Council of Ephesus (449) found this formula heretical, and deposed him from his bishopric. He was rehabilitated at the Council of Chalcedon (451)—though obliged to join in a pronouncement of anathema upon Nestorius and "upon all who. . . divide the one Son into two."

Theodoret's *Church History,* carrying the work of the church historian and scholar Eusebius of Caesarea from Constantine down to 428, reproduces many documents of great value. His *Religious History,* consisting of thirty biographies of ascetics, achieved widespread popularity. His most ambitious apologetic tract, the *Therapeutica (Graecarum Affectionum Curatio),* is a painstaking and impressive defense of the Christian faith. The *Mendicant (Eranistes, or Polymorphus)* comprises three dialogues directed against Cyril's views of the nature of Christ. Theodoret also refuted Cyril's

thē od' ō ret

twelve denunciations (anathematisms) of Nestorius. Long after his death, however, he still remained well enough known for his polemics in this cause to provoke the censure of the Second Council of Constantinople in 553.

Theodoret also wrote anti-pagan tracts *(Quaestiones et Responsiones ad Orthodoxos, De Providentia)* and brief commentaries on the Prophets, the Book of Psalms, the Song of Solomon, and the Pauline epistles. As a biblical scholar, he followed a tradition—combining literary and historical exegesis—that had been established at Antioch under the leadership of Diodorus of Tarsus and Theodore of Mopsuestia. Theodoret was not as forceful or consistent as Diodorus but wrote with considerable effectiveness all the same.

He also left a series of informative, well-composed, and elegantly formulated letters, in some of which he laments the plight of the western empire and notes the momentous significance, for all Christians, of the fall of northern Africa to the Vandals.

EDITIONS—J. P. Migne, Patrologia Graeca, v 80-84. *Translations*—B. Jackson, The Ecclesiastical History, Dialogues and Letters, 1892. Church History: L. Parmentier and F. Scheidweiler, 2nd ed., 1954. Therapeutica: T. Comber, A Treatise of Laws, 1776; P. Canivet, Thérapeutique des maladies helléniques, 1958. Eranistes: C. H. Ettlinger, 1975. Quaestiones et Responsiones ad Orthodoxos: A Papadopoulos-Kerameus, 1895. Letters: Y. Azéma, 1955–65.
ABOUT—M. M. Wagner, A Chapter in Byzantine Epistolography: The Letters of Theodoret of Cyrus (Dumbarton Oaks Papers, v 4), 1948; P. Canivet, Histoire d'une entreprise apologétique au Vᵉ siècle, 1957, *and* Le monachisme syrien selon Théodoret de Cyr, 1977; W. E. Kaegi, Byzantium and the Decline of Rome, 1968.

THEODORUS, PUBLIUS AELIUS. See Aristides, Aelius

THEODORUS STUDITA. See Theodore of Studium

THEODULF, Frankish churchman and statesman, and Latin poet, was born in

the′ ō dulf

about A.D. 750 and died in about 821. He appears to have been of Gothic origin; it is uncertain whether his birthplace was in southern France or northern Spain, but he spent his youth in the former country, at Narbonne. From there, he traveled northward to the court of Charlemagne, whose favor gained him the bishopric of Orléans, of whose historic schools (including Meung nearby) he was a pioneer and part founder. He was also abbot of Fleury and Saint-Aignan.

In 798 he was appointed *missus dominicus,* with the function of holding synods and carrying out judicial duties in southern France. Two years later he accompanied Charlemagne to Rome. Subsequently, however, he became involved not only in a disagreement with the monastery of St. Martin of Tours but also in a quarrel with the English scholar Alcuin over sanctuary rights (801); but Charlemagne intervened to support him. When Alcuin retired to Tours (and died in 804), Theodulf took his place as the emperor's counselor on theological matters, advising him on the Procession of the Holy Spirit (in preparation for the Council of Aachen) and receiving honors also from Pope Stephen IV. He sponsored a wide program of reform, patronized the arts and built and restored churches, and established a guesthouse for travelers and the poor. After Charlemagne's death, however, his son Louis I the Pious, believing Theodulf guilty of participation in a conspiracy (led by the king's nephew Bernard, king of Italy), detained him in a monastery at Angers; Theodulf died in prison (or shortly after an amnesty had enabled him to leave it).

His seventy-nine surviving poems include a piece comprising nearly a thousand lines about his tour of inspection as *missus dominicus.* It is entitled *Against the Judges* but includes not only criticisms of these personages—accompanied by vivid details of the judicial practices of the time—but many picturesque notes about the territories through which he traveled. Thus we are given an amusing enumeration of the various bribes he was offered—including Cordovan leather, Moorish gold, and a cup embossed with the labors of Hercules (he himself designed vases, including one which showed a beautiful woman suckling a child—an allegory of the bountiful earth).

To King Charlemagne (Ad Carolum Regem) presents a lively but somewhat idealized picture of that monarch surrounded by his children and grandchildren. Notable among his other poems are verses that tell how Theodulf received gifts of various flowers and fruits from his daughters Berta, Chrodtrudh, Gisla, and Rothaidh, while other daughters, Hiltrudh and Tetdrada, presented him with wheat and wine respectively. Although owing evident debts to the Latin Anthology, this is one of the comparatively few passages in these pieces that rises above the level of documentary interest to true poetry. But there is authentic lyricism in Theodulf's famous seventy-eight-line hymn named by its first lines "All glory, laud and honor to Thee, Redeemer, King" *(Gloria laus et honor tibi sit rex Christe redemptor)*, which passed into breviaries as a Palm Sunday processional. The story, which may or may not be apocryphal, was that Theodulf wrote the hymn in the Angers jail and that as Louis I passed the building he heard the poet singing it and released him. While still a prisoner, Theodulf had sent an elegiac poem to Bishop Modoin of Autun, to whom, in the name of his Muse, he appealed for help.

Theodulf had read not only the Christian poets, notably the fourth century Prudentius, but also Virgil; and he had studied Ovid, who inspired his address to Modoin and was allegorized in another of his poems, *Accessus ad Auctores.* Among the prose writers used by Theodulf were Aelius Donatus, the grammarian—and perhaps the Roman historian Pompeius Trogus. He set out an allegorical explanation of the Seven Arts and wrote "of the books I was accustomed to read and how the fables of the poets are to be philosophically interpreted in a mystic sense." Some of his learned colleagues he disliked, notably a Scot (or Irishman) known as Clement the Grammarian, but with others he exchanged erudite compliments, under their adopted names, such as Naso or Ovid (probably an Englishman) and Homer (St. Angilbert, Frankish Latin poet, privy councillor to Charlemagne).

At the palace academy, Theodulf himself went under the name of Pindar—which paid him too high a compliment, since his poems display, for the most part, commonsense and moral earnestness rather than poetic inspiration; perhaps the weight of his official responsibilities prevented them from rising to more notable heights. Yet he was a literary figure of considerable caliber, who mirrors in his poetry almost all the principal literary ideals of his time.

EDITIONS—J. P. Migne, Patrologia Latina, v 105. *Translations*—K. Langosch, Lyrische Anthologie des lateinischen Mittelalters, 1968.
ABOUT—C. Cuissard, Théodulphe évêque d'Orléans, 1892; H. Waddell, The Wandering Scholars, 1927; J. Ghellinck, Littérature latine au moyen âge, 1939.

THEOGNIS, Greek elegiac poet, was stated by the Suidas (Suda) Lexicon (of about the tenth century A.D.) to have flourished during the fifty-ninth Olympiad—that is to say, in the period 545–541 B.C. He came from Megara in mainland Greece. Plato's attribution of his origin to Megara in Sicily seems to be erroneous, although it is true that Theognis was said to have written a poem about Syracuse. At one time, he appears to have been exiled from his native city.

He was also believed to have been the author of twenty-eight hundred lines of verse—perhaps more. About fourteen hundred lines attached to his name have survived, divided into two books of unequal size. However, the authenticity of many of these passages is very dubious, since they are not only repetitive but include suspicious echoes of other poets and some of their topical references pose serious chronological difficulties. Evidently, therefore, the original work of Theognis has been considerably supplemented to form the collection as we have it. The presence of numerous variations on similar themes suggests that it was a group of *skolia* or drinking songs, by various authors, to be sung by banqueters who had to cap one song with another. Theognis himself was well aware of the likelihood of interpolation and plagiarism, since he writes
thē og' nis

of a "seal" set on his verses, which marks those that are authentic and cannot be stolen or replaced by a substitute. This allusion has been interpreted in different ways, but perhaps the most probable explanation is that a mention of his own name in a verse is the seal of genuineness to which he refers, though it is not clear why other authors could not fraudulently insert his name into poems or verses written by themselves.

Nevertheless, there remain many verses that are identifiable as Theognis' work, and a strong personality can be seen in them. In particular, he emerges as an extreme and indeed truculent conservative. At a time of social ferment, when the new rich were to be seen on all sides and at any moment the discontent of the masses might raise a tyrant to power, Theognis passionately supports the claims of aristocratic blood and breeding. In his view, all abilities come from inheritance: "the good" are the noblemen and "the bad" the lower classes—and the effect of wealth, in obliterating such class distinctions, is deplored. It is within this reactionary framework (praised by the nineteenth century German philosopher-poet Nietzsche) that the poet, worried about the fate of his beloved city—although it at one stage rejected him—spells out the characteristically Greek code according to which the greatest sin is *hubris,* arrogance or infatuation, a stranger to moderation: it destroyed many great cities, of which Megara, it seemed to Theognis, was likely to become the next.

These are hard times, we are told, for the great landowner of noble descent, brought up, as befits a gentleman, to take an interest in horses and dogs—and in boys too, for Theognis is a determined pederast. Many of his poems are addressed to the youth he loved, Cyrnus the son of Polypäus; and in one eloquent song, which is surely his own work, the poet tells Cyrnus that, despite his ingratitude, the youth has been given wings by these poems, which have saved his name from oblivion. Women are mentioned less often, though Theognis does complain that, while men take pains to secure suitable mates for their cattle, they themselves have now become accustomed to contracting marriages in which the old virtue of good

blood gets lost. Another poem is a dialogue between a loving woman and a man who cannot be bothered with her. In a more sympathetic mood, however, Theognis admits that there is no more satisfactory good fortune than to have a good wife.

He writes gracefully, displaying a taste for bold and vivid metaphors. He is very frank about his emotions and throws interesting light on the place of homosexuality in Greek life. Moreover, his poetry is also of wider social and political interest, because of the defensive action it so vigorously fights on behalf of an upper class whose clearly defined values were threatened on various fronts by the rise of more democratic ideas.

EDITIONS—T. Hudson-Williams, The Elegies of Theognis, 1910; B. A. van Groningen, Théognis: Le premier livre, 1966; M. L. West, Iambi et Elegi Graeci, v 1, 1971 (Theognidea). *With translation:* J. M. Edmonds, Greek Elegy and Iambus (Loeb ed.), v 1, 1931; D. Wender, Hesiod and Theognis (Penguin ed.), 1973; J. Carrière, Théognis: Poèmes élégiaques (Budé ed.), 1962.
ABOUT—E. Harrison, Studies in Theognis, 1902; F. Jacoby, Theognis, 1931; T. W. Allen, Theognis, 1934; J. Kroll, Theognisinterpretationen, 1936; C. M. Bowra, Early Greek Elegists, 1938; J. Carrière, Théognis et Mégare, 1948; K. J. Dover, Greek Homosexuality, 1978.

THEOPHANES THE CONFESSOR, Saint, Greek historian of the Byzantine epoch, was born in about A.D. 752 and died in about 818. His birthplace was Constantinople, where he came of a noble and wealthy house. After a brief marriage, he founded the monastery of the Greater Agros at Sigriane on the Sea of Marmara and became a monk there. A vehement leader and spokesman of the "iconodule" movement, which opposed the official policy of the destruction of holy images (iconoclasm), he was placed on trial by the emperor Leo V the Armenian (813–20) and then, after a spell of confinement in prison, was exiled to the island of Samothrace in the northern Aegean, where he died.

His *Chronographia,* written in 810–14 at the request of his friend George Syncellus (whose *Chronicle* it continues) covers the period from the accession of Diocletian (A.D.
thē of' á nēz

433

284) to the fall of Michael I Rhangabe in 813. The work gives tables of Byzantine emperors, Persian kings, Muslim caliphs, Roman popes, and patriarchs of Constantinople, Alexandria, Antioch, and Jerusalem. Moreover, Theophanes follows a strict chronological method narrating events year by year.

This scheme, however, leads him into a good many errors, since the authorities he relies upon had not invariably followed the annalistic scheme he employed, and he often finds the necessary adjustment beyond his powers.

Moreover, he is naive and uncritical, incapable of distinguishing between what is important and what is not, and ignorant of the processes of historical causation. Indeed, these processes scarcely interest him, since his own approach, which is exclusively theological, insists strongly upon the eastern orthodox viewpoint. His concern is to provide edification, which he supplies by pointing out that victories reward piety and disasters overwhelm heretics.

Yet within these anti-historical limitations Theophanes reports diligently enough, drawing upon many earlier writers of whom we should otherwise know nothing; and, for the final sections of his account, he depends usefully on eyewitness evidence and personal observation. He is thus our principal narrative source for Byzantium's ill-documented seventh and eighth centuries and is particularly valuable to religious historians because of the unusual amount of space he devotes to the iconoclastic movement.

As a narrator of events, he is a good deal more readable than most Byzantine historians, writing a straightforward Greek that is close to the spoken language of the time and relatively emancipated from classical references, in order to suit the taste and culture of his readership, which was for the most part monastic. His work was utilized, excerpted, and summarized by many subsequent Byzantine historians, and a Latin translation made by the papal librarian Anastasius in the second half of the ninth century served a similar purpose for chroniclers in the West.

A continuation of his work in four books by various writers, known as *Theophanes Continuatus* or *The Writers After Theophanes (Scriptores post Theophanem)*, was originally commissioned by the emperor Constantine VII Porphyrogenitus (912–59), who appended a fifth book dealing with the reign of Basil I (867–86)—a sixth book covering the period down to 961 was added later.

EDITIONS—C. de Boor, 1883–85 (including Anastasius' Latin translation); J. P. Migne, Patrologia Graeca, v 108–9. *German translations* (selections)—L. Breyer, Bilderstreit und Arabersturm in Byzanz: Das 8 Jahrhundert (717–813) aus der Weltchronik des Theophanes, 1957.
ABOUT—G. Ostrogorsky, History of the Byzantine State, 1956; C. Moravcsik, Byzantinoturcica, v 1, 2nd ed., 1958.

THEOPHRASTUS, Greek philosopher and scientist, was born in about 370 B.C. and died between 288 and 285. *Theophrastus* means marked by a god and was probably a pseudonym; his original name seems to have been Tyrtamus. His birthplace was at Eresus on the island of Lesbos, and he was the son of a fuller. He became a pupil of the philosopher Aristotle, probably at Assos in the Troad (northwestern Asia Minor), later accompanying him to Macedonia and from there going on with him to Athens (335). When Aristotle retired to Chalcis shortly before his death in 322, Theophrastus, in spite of competition from Eudemus of Rhodes, succeeded him as head of his school, the Lyceum or Peripatos; he remained its director until he died. He attracted as many as two thousand students at a time to his lectures, which were continually revised. Theophrastus gave practical attention to the technique of a lecturer, dressing and anointing himself with care and indulging in carefully thought out gestures. Although he lived at Athens as a metic (a resident alien), he acquired property through the intervention of his famous pupil Demetrius of Phaleron, whose extensive legislation he influenced (317–315). He also survived an action for impiety brought against him by an orator named Hagnonides. When Demetrius fell from power, the ō fras′ tus

THEOPHRASTUS

however, and a certain Sophocles moved a law forbidding the operation of philosophical schools without the permission of the Assembly (307/6), Theophrastus departed from Athens—but only temporarily, because the law was soon repealed. He was a friend of King Ptolemy I of Egypt (d. 283/2) and Cassander of Macedonia (d. 297). His successor as head of the Peripatetic school was Straton of Lampsacus.

Theophrastus' writings were based on his lectures. He was the only Peripatetic (with the exception of Eudemus) whose works covered almost as wide a range as those of Aristotle himself. Listed in four surviving catalogues, they covered rhetoric, ethics, politics, logic, religion, metaphysics, and numerous aspects of physics—the whole amounting to two hundred and forty separate writings, many of which ran to more than one book. Comparatively few of these compositions, however, have come down to us, and even when they have survived, their texts are often seriously defective.

The only two of his scientific studies that we can confidently regard as complete are both on botanical subjects. One of them, the *Inquiry Concerning Plants,* is in nine books. The first book attempts classification and represents the earliest surviving endeavor by any writer to solve this basic problem of arrangement. The next two books deal with propagation and wild trees respectively. The theme of Book 4 is botanical geography, a

field in which Theophrastus not only employed his own students as researchers but also to some extent utilized the extensive information made available by Alexander's campaigns. Book 5 treats of timber and its various uses, and Books 6-8 discuss plants smaller than trees, which he defines as shrubs, undershrubs, and herbs, and comments on methods of cultivation and on relations between wild and cultivated species. The last book reviews the products of plants other than timber, and offers observations on nonscientific aspects of the theme, including popular beliefs about the right ways and times to pick these plants and superstitions regarding their supposed magical properties.

Theophrastus' other extant botanical treatise is *Causes of Plants* or *How Plants Grow (De Causis Plantarum).* The work is divided into six books, the first five of which discuss propagation, with special attention to vines; the sixth describes their different juices and saps. This work and the *Inquiry Concerning Plants,* both planned on the general model of Aristotle's zoological monographs, are Theophrastus' acknowledged masterpieces. They illustrate his meticulous care in marshaling facts, his talent as an observer, and his characteristic caution as a theorist. While classifying the various types of plants, for example, he notes that definitions must only be taken in a general sense, since they sometimes overlap—and "nature does not go by any hard and fast law." The language Theophrastus employs for these topics is plain, lucid, and agreeable. He is the first botanical writer whose scientific interests are not dominated by medicine.

We also have extracts from a number of his shorter essays on scientific subjects. These include *On Paralysis, On Weariness, On Fainting, On Sweat, On Smells,* and *On Weather Signs.* Three others, *On Fire, On Wind,* and *On Stones,* may be extracts from his lost *Physics.* The last-named, a work on petrology, makes use of a framework derived from Plato and Aristotle, subdividing things found in the ground into two main groups: those (such as metals) in which water predominates, and those of which earth is the dominant element. His discussion embraces a huge range of data, including important material taken from industrial processes.

One of Theophrastus' two most important writings, now lost, was the *Doctrines of Natural Philosophy (Phusikon Doxai)* in eighteen books, which systematized the evidence presented by Aristotle into what became the standard history of the principal problems in ancient science and philosophy. It is not certain whether the fragment entitled *On Sense Perception,* which combines discussion with excellent criticism, ever belonged to that larger work. His other major work, likewise in eighteen books and likewise no longer extant, was his *Laws.* Founded on material set out by Aristotle in his *Politics* and *Constitutions,* this compilation presented a collection of laws and customs of Greek states.

In his *Ethics,* Theophrastus acknowledged the predominant importance of moral considerations. Yet, like Aristotle, he conceded that these considerations did not altogether prevent external good things, outside the moral sphere, from also possessing a certain significance on their own account. In consequence, the treatise attracted condemnation from the Stoics, who refused to accept that reservation: and it is to their hostile comments that we owe our knowledge of what he said, since once again the original is lost. So is his essay entitled *On Piety,* though a considerable proportion of its substance has been reconstructed from quotations and paraphrases by Porphyry (died c. A.D. 305).

Theophrastus' *Metaphysics,* on the other hand, has survived. This analysis, which briefly discusses the first cause of the universe and its relation to particular phenomena, illustrates the writer's attitude toward Aristotle. He is capable enough of criticizing the weaker points of the master's *Metaphysics* but rarely willing to offer original or constructive countersuggestions himself.

While *Metaphysics* is written in a manner as technical and thorny as Aristotle's, another of his writings offers a most attractive stylistic contrast and has enjoyed by far the most widespread popular favor of anything he wrote. This is the *Characters.* In this piece, generally (though not invariably) regarded as an independent work, rather than as part of some larger composition, he presents thirty sketches of character types—unidentified, generalized personalities, each distinguished by some more or less ludicrous fault or minor vice: the man who grumbles, or is avaricious, or is officious, or is timid, or is a flatterer, or invents news, or is late off the mark in finding things out. Each sketch is only a page long; within this brief compass Theophrastus neatly depicts these perennial moral and social failings with dry, satirical humor, razor-sharp observation and a lifelike practicality: the types are streamlined, but never unreal.

The *Characters* became so famous that they received the compliment of spurious additions, notably the preface and moralizing epilogues. A subsequent Peripatetic, Ariston of Ceos, who became head of the school in about 225 B.C., imitated Theophrastus by writing a *Characters* of his own, in the form of dietetics for the soul. Among many similar works in later times the most famous was *Les Caractères de Théophraste,* with topical allusions, by the French moralist Jean de la Bruyère in 1688.

Nevertheless, the scope and purpose of Theophrastus' *Characters* have been the subject of disagreement among scholars. In the past, they were usually interpreted as moral essays, prompted by Aristotle's classification of virtues in his *Ethics.* More recently, however, it has been pointed out that the personalities described in the work are similar to characters in the New Comedy of manners led by Menander, who was said to be a pupil of Theophrastus; and the resemblance certainly is there, though it is not necessary to assume a direct link between the two writers. Another theory has stressed the use of Theophrastus' material for rhetorical handbooks, and it is not impossible that he wrote with this purpose in mind. The field was by no means unfamiliar to him, since, as befitted an expert lecturer, he composed a considerable number of studies on rhetorical subjects, including an *Art of Rhetoric,* collections of rhetorical exercises, a monograph entitled *On Style* of which Cicero made repeated use, and *On the Ludicrous,* which probably influenced subsequent analyses of the nature of humor. All these works are now lost.

A researcher and teacher rather than an original philosopher, Theophrastus followed the lines already laid down by Aristotle. Yet he also began to shift the major emphasis further away from philosophy in the direction of scientific and empirical observation, in keeping with the spirit of his epoch in which purely philosophic studies were tending to degenerate into platitude. Next to Aristotle, Theophrastus remained not only the most prolific but the most famous of the Peripatetic school, and his writings continued to exercise a strong impact throughout the rest of antiquity.

EDITIONS—H. Diels, Doctrines of Natural Philosophy, 1879, reprint, 1929; A. Gercke, On Fire, 1896; R. E. Dengler, The Causes of Plants, Book 1, 1927; G. M. Stratton, On Sense Perception, 1927; W. D. Ross and F. H. Fobes, Metaphysics, 1929; P. Steinmetz, Characters, 1960; R. G. Ussher, Characters, 1960; W. Pötscher, On Piety, 1964; D. Eichholz, On Stones, 1965; L. Repici, La logica di Teofrasto, 1971; A. Graeser, Die logischen Fragmente des Theophrast, 1973. *With translation:* A. F. Hort, Enquiry into Plants (Loeb ed.) 1916; J. M. Edmonds, Characters *in* J. M. Edmonds and A. D. Knox, Theophrastus, Herodes, Cercidas . . . (Loeb ed.), 1946; W. Anderson, The Characters, Sketches, 1970; B. Einarson and G. K. K. Link, The Causes of Plants (Loeb ed.), v 1, 1976; V. Coutant and V. L. Eichenlaub, On Winds, 1977.
ABOUT—O. Regenbogen, Theophrastos *in* Pauly-Wissowa-Kroll, Real-Encyclopädie der klassischen Altertumswissenschaft, Supplement, v 7, 1940, columns 1354ff; J. M. Bochenski, La logique de Théophraste, 1947; E. Barbotin, La théorie aristotélicienne de l'intellect d'après Théophraste, 1954; C. Senn, Die Pflanzenkunde des Theophrastos von Eresos, 1956; G. Kennedy, The Art of Persuasion in Greece, 1963; G. Reale, Teofrasto e la sua aporetica metafisica, 1964; P. Steinmetz, Die Physik des Theophrastos von Eresos, 1964; A. A. Long, Hellenistic Philosophy, 1974; L. Repici, La logica di Teofrasto, 1977.

THEOPOMPUS, Greek historian, was born in about 378 or 376 B.C. and died some time after 323. His birthplace was on the island of Chios. As a young man, he and his father Damasistratus were compelled to go into exile, owing to the latter's friendly attitude to Sparta, to which Chios was hostile. During this part of his life Theopompus traveled extensively. At one time, he resided at Athens and was reputed, probably correctly, to have become a pupil of Isocrates

the ō pom' pus

(whom he was also said to have defeated in a rhetorical contest). He also stayed at the court of King Philip II of Macedonia (359–336). Because of Theopompus' opposition to the pro-Persian oligarchy on the island, Philip's son Alexander the Great arranged for him to return to Chios in 333, and for a time he acted as one of the leaders of local political life. But after Alexander's death in 323 he was expelled once again and took refuge with King Ptolemy I of Egypt, who did not, it appears, receive him very cordially.

Only fragments of Theopompus' historical writings survive. His *Hellenica,* in twelve books, narrated events of Greek history from the year 411, the point at which Thucydides had broken off, down to the naval history of the Athenian Conon at Cnidus in 394, which ended the period of Spartan hegemony over Greece, a period that provided the main theme of Theopompus' work.

A much more elaborate and important historical enterprise was his *Philippica* in fifty-eight books, beginning with the accession of King Philip II and ending with his death. In taking this theme and treating it comprehensively, the author claimed he had surpassed Herodotus himself (of whose history he was also said to have written a separate epitome). For although the *Philippica* were pervaded by the conception that the king had inaugurated a new epoch, the narrative of his deeds, as recounted by Theopompus, was only the framework for a general survey of contemporary history. Moreover, this survey was interlarded with digressions on various other countries (Persia, Greece, Sicily), so that when Philip V of Macedonia (221–179 B.C.) had a compilation made of the portions of the *Philippica* that concerned his own country, the result was a treatise comprising no more than sixteen books. Some of the digressions later acquired separate titles of their own, such as *Wonders (Thaumasia,* Books 8 and 9), *On the Sacking of Delphi,* and *On Demagogues.*

Theopompus was able to look at events in Greece from a relatively detached viewpoint, since Philip II, with whom he chiefly concerned himself, was an outsider as far as the city-states of that country were concerned. Examining the ruler's career, the historian gradually modified his initial aristocratic ideals in favor of the concept of a paternalistic monarchy—like Philip's—as the guarantor of a conservative society. Nevertheless, his work is by no means an unqualified encomium, since Philip II comes in for a good deal of severe criticism; Theopompus is very harsh and censorious in his historical verdicts (Plato is another of whom he does not approve). This willingness to censure Philip shocked the historian Polybius in the second century B.C., for, as a loyal Arcadian, he regarded the king with gratitude as the liberator of the Peloponnese from Sparta and therefore considered that Theopompus had shown very bad taste in attacking him and had failed, moreover, to maintain decent standards of controversy. At an earlier date, another historian, Duris (c. 340–c. 260 B.C.) had criticized Theopompus apparently because he had not adopted a dramatic enough manner of writing, though to us, to judge from the surviving fragments, his style is by no means lacking in vividness and even displays a measure of extravagance, betraying the influence of the rhetoric taught him by Isocrates, who remarked that Theopompus needed the bridle, whereas his other pupil Ephorus needed the spur.

In the broad sweep of his *Philippica,* achieved with the assistance of keen psychological insight into its central character, Theopompus had accomplished something distinctive. He must be regarded as an outstanding forerunner of Hellenistic historiography; and the disappearance of his writings is an extremely grave loss. In the Augustan age, the historian Pompeius Trogus borrowed his title, and a considerable amount of his material, for his own *Philippic Histories.*

WORKS (wrongly attributed to Theopompus)—It has been suggested that nine hundred lines of papyrus found at Oxyrhynchus in Egypt, *Hellenica Oxyrhynchia,* dealing authoritatively with events in the Greek world in 396–395 B.C., may have formed part of Theopompus' *Hellenica,* but the attribution has not been found generally acceptable. (Other historians, Cratippus of Athens [of fifth century B.C. or later date] and Daimachus of Plataea [third century] have also been suggested as authors.)
EDITIONS—F. Jacoby, Die Fragmente der griechischen Historiker, 2B, 115.

ABOUT—E. Meyer, Theopomps Hellenika, 1909; K. Fritz *in* Histoire et historiens dans l'antiquité (Entretiens Hardt, v 4), 1956; A. Momigliano, Teopompo, *in* Terzo contributo alla storia degli studi classici, 1966; W. R. Connor, Theopompus and Fifth Century Athens, 1968; H. D. Westlake, Essays on the Greek Historians and Greek History, 1969. On the Oxyrhynchus papyrus *see* I. A. F. Bruce, An Historical Commentary on the Hellenica Oxyrhynchia, 1967.

THESPIS, Greek tragic poet from the country region *(deme)* of Icaria in Attica (near Athens), can be dated from the information that he was the first to win the competition for tragedy at the city festival of Dionysus (his native district also cherished an ancient cult of Dionysus) in 535/3 B.C.

According to the rhetorician Themistius (fourth century A.D.), Aristotle, probably drawing upon Charon of Lampsacus (fifth century B.C.), reported that the earliest performances of tragic drama were restricted to a singing chorus but that Thespis introduced a prologue and speech *(rhesis)* for a speaker, impersonating a character, to perform with the chorus; in other words, he invented the first actor. The Greek word for actor, *hupokrites,* is generally translated as answerer, indicating that Thespis caused him to exchange words with the leader of the chorus, thus creating the first tragic dialogue. But it has alternatively been suggested that *hupokrites* rather signifies interpreter or explainer, in which case Thespis' spoken contribution may have taken the form of a messenger's speech. In either case, it is disputed how this separate spoken part came into existence: either it developed out of the choral sections or it was added to them as a supplementary entity, or (less probably) there was a division of the chorus into two groups singing responses in turn, one of which gradually dwindled to a single actor.

At least to begin with, Thespis was his own actor. According to the Suidas or Suda lexicon of the tenth century A.D., in his first plays he painted his face with white lead; then subsequently he introduced linen masks. This latter assertion cannot be literally true, since such masks, as vases show, were already in existence; their attribution to Thespis by Suidas merely means that
thes' pis

some kind of disguise earlier than the masks was still remembered in later times, when it seemed natural to attribute the invention to the reputed founder of this dramatic form. However, it also remains possible that Thespis did devise some novel type of mask.

Suidas also gives a few titles of his plays, including *Pentheus, The Contests of Pelias, The Youths,* and *The Priests*—themes not confined to the stories of Dionysus, with which tragic poetry was believed to have originated, but drawn from the whole mythological corpus; and a few surviving fragments are attributed to him. However, the authenticity of Thespis' titles and fragments alike is not above suspicion, since in the fourth century B.C. Aristoxenus of Taras censured the contemporary philosopher Heraclides Ponticus for having published tragedies of his own authorship under the false name of Thespis.

Horace, in his *Ars Poetica,* suggested that Thespis went around the villages of Attica to perform his plays, taking the members of his chorus along with him in a cart, their faces stained by wine dregs. This is part of a semi-legendary tradition stressing the picturesque rusticity of the origins of tragedy. By the same token, the original prize was said to have been a goat, *tragos* (an animal that could then be used for a sacrifice to Dionysus—and the banquet that followed). But it appears very probable that when Horace (or his source Neoptolemus of Parium, of the 3rd century B.C.) gives this account of the cart, he is confusing the origins of Greek tragedy with those of comedy.

EDITIONS—A. Nauck, Tragicorum Graecorum Fragmenta, new ed., 1964.
ABOUT—M. Bieber, The History of the Greek and Roman Theater, 2nd ed., 1961; H. Patzer, Die Anfänge der griechischen Tragödie, 1962; A. W. Pickard-Cambridge and T. B. L. Webster, Dithyramb, Tragedy and Comedy, 2nd ed., 1962; G. F. Else, The Origin and Early Form of Tragedy, 1965; A. Lesky, Greek Tragedy, 1965; T. B. L. Webster, Greek Theatre Production, 2nd ed., 1970; A. D. Trendall and T. B. L. Webster, Illustrations of Greek Drama, 1971.

THUCYDIDES, Greek historian, was probably born between 460 and 455 B.C. and thū sid' i dēz

is likely to have died in about 400. His father, although Athenian, had a Thracian name, Olorus, which suggests connections with that country; moreover, this was also the name of the grandfather of the leading Athenian statesman Cimon (d. 449), to whom Thucydides, therefore, was probably related. He obtained from his father (or his wife) a Thracian estate at Scapte Hyle, which was a base for the working of adjacent gold mines. When the Peloponnesian War broke out (431), Thucydides was at Athens, where he was a victim of the Great Plague (430–429), but he recovered. In 424 he was elected one of the ten generals *(strategoi)* for the year and, because of his Thracian links, was given command of the fleet in northern waters. On failing to prevent the capture of the important Macedonian city of Amphipolis by the Spartan Brasidas, he was called home, put on trial, and sent into exile for twenty years. During that period, he traveled extensively and made wide contacts. His banishment continued until Athens' final defeat in the war (404), after which he appears to have been allowed back. According to tradition, he died a violent death at the hands of a murderer. His tomb or cenotaph and a monument to his memory were still to be seen at Athens in the second century A.D.

Thucydides' *History of the Peloponnesian War* between Athens and Sparta (431–404 B.C.; his account ends at 411) consists of eight books. Book I contains an introduction, giving the author's motives for writing his history of the war, a brief summary of early Greek history, a description of the military incidents and diplomatic exchanges that led up to the outbreak of hostilities, and an account of the growth of Athenian power in the fifty years since the Persian invasions (490, 480–479). Books 2-4 describe the main events of the first part of the Peloponnesian War, known as the Archidamian War (431–421 B.C.), with the Plague and the Funeral Speech of Pericles (presenting an idealized picture of Athens) in Book 2, the revolt of Mitylene (Lesbos) in Book 3, and the capture of the Spartan garrison on Sphacteria (425 B.C.) and the loss of Amphipolis to Brasidas (424 B.C.) in Book 4. Book 5 contains the deaths of Brasidas and Cleon, the

Peace of Nicias (421), the Mantinean War, and the subjugation of Melos (416). Books 6 and 7 describe the disastrous Athenian expedition to Sicily (415–413), and Book 8, the revolt of the Athenian allies, followed by the oligarchic counterrevolution of 411. This book is unfinished, and the story of the rest of the Peloponnesian War, which terminated with the capitulation of Athens in 404, is not told.

Thucydides' work is based on a masterly idea, which has had a vast effect on subsequent historians: the idea of writing contemporary history. Like Herodotus, he chose a war as his subject—the Peloponnesian War, which he considered the greatest event of all time. The two preparatory studies he provides on Greece before and after the Persian invasions respectively, are intended to make this opinion clear. His conviction about the Peloponnesian War led him to criticize not only his contemporary, the chronicler Hellanicus, who had already dealt with the fifty years between the Persian and Peloponnesian wars in a manner Thucydides declared to be inaccurate, but also Herodotus, whose view that the Persian Wars were of supreme significance he was determined to counter. Thucydides' belief in the greater importance of the Peloponnesian War was justified up to a point, for this was the fatal convulsion heralding the downfall of the political structure of Greek civilization, based on a network of independent city-states.

Thucydides writes for those who require a "clear record of what had happened in the past and will, in due course, tend to be repeated with some degree of similarity"— that is to say, his history is designed to be instructive because a knowledge of the past will be a useful guide to the future. In his search below the surface for underlying causes, he resembles the Ionian natural scientists and the school of the contemporary physician Hippocrates (to which his remarkable analysis of the plague surely owes debts). He divides the causation of the Peloponnesian War into two parts, the causes of complaint (aitiai)—quarrels about the allegiance of subsidiary city-states, Corcyra and Potidaea—and the real or true reason (prophasis), which he identified as Sparta's fear of Athenian expansion.

In thus directing his readers' attention from immediate grievances to the fundamental realities of power, Thucydides made a major contribution to political thought. But his juxtaposition or antithesis of the two sorts of cause may also be partly due to the very long time it took him to write his history, since he started it, he tells us, at the outbreak of the war in 431 and was still at work, as internal evidence shows, after the final defeat of Athens in 404. Within this period, from the Peace of Nicias in 421, there was a break in hostilities for several years. However, at some stage Thucydides decided to argue that the entire twenty-seven-year period should be regarded as one unbroken unit—the single Peloponnesian War of which we speak today.

The dates when the various portions of his work were composed have been the subject of much argument. When completed, they were introduced to the public by recitation. Thinking of these, the historian concedes that the absence of a romantic element (such as was so prominent in Herodotus) may make his history less agreeable to the ear; but he emphasizes that it is intended as "a possession for ever." However, the work was apparently left incomplete, for the final book (Book 8) includes not only contradictions but verbatim citations, which it was his custom, in other books, to alter and adjust to his own style before insertion.

Book 8 is also totally lacking in the speeches that (following a tradition inherited from Herodotus) constituted a vital and integral element in the other books of Thucydides' history: he includes no less than forty, comprising a quarter of the whole work. He deliberately couples words with deeds as the twin materials of history, in which the principal actors base their decisions on verbal formulations. This point, that speech is the root of all political life, was illustrated by the contemporary Athenian scene, on which professional speakers—rhetoricians and sophists—had begun to be extremely active; their influence is clearly detectable in the techniques of Thucydides' speeches. He does not claim that these necessarily reproduce the exact words the various speakers employed—and indeed it is clear from their homogeneous, Thucydidean style that they do not. Instead, it is his purpose to make the speakers say what, in his opinion, was called for by each situation. Thus, the speechmakers are mouthpieces of the historian, their speeches being designed to penetrate to underlying causes and motives, reveal general truths, and bring out the viewpoints and characters of the major participants in events. Very often, these orations occur in balanced, antithetical pairs and present colliding theses, displaying emotional highlights in the manner of tragic drama: for instance, in the great debate on the doom of rebellious Melos, the arguments are put forward in a dramatic dialogue form, strongly reminiscent of the contemporary tragedies of Euripides.

The style of these climactic scenes, and of Thucydides' speeches in general, is archaic and harsh, the very opposite of the relaxed fluency of Herodotus. Crammed with meaning and overtone, sentence after sentence of this diction deliberately cultivates an astringent, abrupt unevenness. The diction of Thucydides' narrative passages, though less exaggerated than that of the speeches, is severe, grave, and terrifyingly intense.

Thucydides' method is cerebral, the product of an exceptionally powerful brain. And his *History,* throughout, is the glorification of intelligence; the word for understand or judgment *(gnome)* occurs more than three hundred times in the work. And just as he himself probes incessantly to comprehend events, so, too, this capacity to *understand* is the quality he admires most in the personages he is depicting. What he wants to do is to elucidate the *type* of persons who fix the characters of the city-states. In consequence, meticulous attention is devoted to the great Athenian statesman Pericles, whose famous "Funeral Speech" outlines what the historian regarded as the principal features of the Periclean ideal—in implied contrast to the inferior behavior that came to predominate later. Thucydides knew all too well the oppressive basis of Athenian imperialism, of which Pericles was the archrepresentative; yet he also admired the brilliant civilization that this imperialism had created. Moreover, he exonerated Pericles for Athenian failure in the war. Cleon, on the other hand, who succeeded him as the

most influential political leader, appears in the *History* as a clown unworthy of the dignity of history.

A more subtle character study is reserved for Nicias (d. 413 B.C.), the general who failed disastrously in the Sicilian expedition: it is implied that his piety and conventional virtue were insufficient qualifications. In the brilliant, unreliable general and politician Alcibiades, Thucydides detects both bad and good. On the whole, he sees the moderate oligarchic constitution and policy of the Five Thousand (411) as the best system he has known; and he praises its leader, the statesman and general Theramenes, for his cleverness.

Thucydides' psychological studies are directed not only to individuals but also, with particular effectiveness, to groups and masses. It is in analyzing the changing attitudes of states, councils, and armies that he is at his greatest. Thus, in battle scenes, we are given remarkable pictures of the soldiers' excitements, exaltations, and despairs, especially during the final stages of the disastrous Sicilian expedition. This catastrophe is described in the phrases and terms of high tragedy, with all its infatuations *(hubris),* ironies, and reversals. There is nothing supernatural about these developments, Thucydides tells us: they come from all too typical flaws in human nature. Certainly, he finds life a tragedy, but it is a secular one. Oracles influence what people think and do; but causes are entirely human. Men and women get ensnared, it is true, by Fate or Necessity—but that is the unavoidable result of a chain of events, something they have brought upon themselves. And while Chance, he concedes, plays a mighty part, he offers this reservation, with Pericles as his mouthpiece: "We commonly blame Chance for whatever belies our calculation." And, in wartime, Thucydides adds, our calculations go particularly badly astray, for war utterly perverts and overturns human psychology.

About the importance of the economic element Thucydides has no doubt; but he does not discuss this factor as much as we should like—first, because the statistics were just not available and, secondly, because in any case he saw the real, basic cause of the war as political rather than economic. The

History is unparalleled for its author's intense concentration on the matters that seemed to him essential—and his ruthless elimination of what he judged to be irrelevancies has left us no possibility of examining the evidence by which he reached his conclusions or forming alternative opinions for ourselves. Thucydides seeks to emphasize his objectivity by writing of himself in the third person; thus, he describes his own military failure in Macedonia, for example, with almost superhuman restraint. Yet, at the same time, he allows a certain amount of moral bias into his story—for example, in his savage detestation of Cleon, which seems by no means objective.

His historical method displayed impressive advances over that of his predecessors. For instance, he possessed clear and original ideas on chronology, inventing a method of dating the events of the war by winters and summers. As a personal observer, he had the advantage, first, of participating prominently in events and, then, of meeting many Peloponnesians and other non-Athenians during his long period of banishment. Although he rarely identifies his authorities and hardly ever indicates rival, contradictory, versions, his use of secondhand information is conscientious and critical.

No historian has ever equaled the penetration with which he analyzed this climactic period of Greek society, and no one has ever probed human motives with more intensive rigor. But Thucydides' tone was so sharp and his language so prickly that he had to wait a long time for recognition: it only came when the Greek historian Polybius, in the second century B.C., and the Roman authors Caesar and Sallust, in the first, approved his methods. Certain later Greek historians, notably Dexippus, Procopius, and Critobulus (third, sixth, and fifteenth centuries respectively), were strongly influenced by his work. The Italian statesman and political philosopher Machiavelli and the English philosopher Thomas Hobbes predictably respected his ruthless analyses of reasons of state; and in America Thomas Jefferson expressed his admiration in a letter to John Adams in 1812.

EDITIONS—A. W. Gomme, Historical Commentary on

Thucydides, v 1, 1945 and v 2-3, 1956; continued by A. Andrewes & K. J. Dover, v 4, 1970 (abridgment, 1965), v 5, 1979; K. J. Dover, Book 7, 1965, reprint 1978. *Translations*—C. F. Smith (Loeb ed.), 1919–30; B. Jowett (abridged and revised by P. A. Brunt), 1963; R. Warner (Penguin ed.; revised by M. I. Finley), 1972.

ABOUT—F. M. Cornford, Thucydides Mythistoricus, 1907, reprint 1965; C. N. Cochrane, Thucydides and the Science of History, 1929, reprint 1965; J. H. Finley, Thucydides, 1942, reprint 1947, *and* Three Essays on Thucydides, 1967; G. B. Grundy, Thucydides and the History of His Age, 1948; D. Grene, Man in His Pride: A Study in the Political Philosophy of Thucydides and Plato, 1950; C. Meyer, Die Urkunden im Geschichtswerk des Thukydides, 1955; D. de Romilly, Histoire et raison chez Thucydide, 1956, *and* Thucydides and Athenian Imperialism, 1963; F. E. Adcock, Thucydides and His History, 1963; C. Lichtenthaeler, Thucydide et Hippocrate, 1965; F. W. Walbank, Speeches in Greek Historians, 1965; P. J. Fliess, Thucydides and the Politics of Bipolarity, 1966; H. P. Stahl, Thukydides: Die Stellung des Menschen im geschichtlichen Prozess, 1966; L. E. Lord, Thucydides and the World War, 1967; H. Herter, ed., Thukydides, 1968; H. D. Westlake, Individuals in Thucydides, 1968; L. Canfora, Tucidide continuato, 1970; M. Grant, The Ancient Historians, 1970; O. Luschnat, Thukydides der Historiker, *in* Pauly-Wissowa-Kroll, Real-Encyclopädie der klassischen Altertumswissenschaft, (Supplementband, v 11), 1971; K. J. Dover, Thucydides (Greece & Rome: New Surveys in the Classics, no 7), 1973; H. F. Harding, The Speeches of Thucydides, 1973; V. J. Hunter, Thucydides the Artful Reporter, 1973; C. Schneider, Information und Absicht bei Thukydides, 1974; L. Edmunds, Chance and Intelligence in Thucydides, 1975; H. Drexler, Thukydides-Studien, 1976; W. den Boer, Progress in the Greece of Thucydides, 1977.

TIBERIANUS, Latin poet and philosopher, does not seem earlier than the third century A.D.: his work is quoted by the fourth century grammarian and commentator Servius. He should probably be identified with Gaius Annius Tiberianus, who was governor of Africa (325–27) and Spain (332, *vicarius* 335) and praetorian prefect in Gaul in 336–37, and who was described by St. Jerome as eloquent. Tiberianus appears to have been the author of philosophical dialogues, now lost, including one relating to Socrates. The four short extant poems attributed to him include a set of thirty-two correct hexameters that invoke an all-powerful deity *(omnipotens)* in a pantheistic manner. He also wrote a piece consisting of twenty trochaic tetrameters (i.e., based on the trochee, long-short foot); the subject is

tī bēr i ā′ nus

spring and the first line reads: "The river flowed among the meadows" *(Annis ibat inter arva)*.

Owing to its formal rhythm and other resemblances to this latter composition, the anonymous poem *The Vigil of Venus (Pervigilium Veneris),* consisting of ninety-three lines, has now been convincingly attributed to Tiberianus (its attribution to a second century poet and rhetorician Publius Annius Florus, perhaps identical with the historian Lucius Annaeus Florus, has less to be said for it). Although the order of the lines in the *Pervigilium* (divided into stanzas that may be of unequal length) is somewhat disputable, it was evidently punctuated by the refrain, "Tomorrow shall be love for the loveless, and for the lover tomorrow shall be love." Set in Sicily, the poem is a hymn to Venus, goddess of love and sexual fertility, on the occasion of her three-night spring festival on the island. In this festival the Graces and nymphs, Ceres, Bacchus, and Apollo—and Cupid without his arrows—all play their parts. Everywhere nature is arousing itself from the torpor of winter: the flowers are in blossom, birds are singing, and the chants of garlanded choirs ring through the woods. By the power of the foam-born Venus, all creatures mate and give increase; and Rome, in particular, is grateful to the benevolent goddess for her manifold blessings. But a sudden note of personal elegy and private sadness intrudes: "The nightingale sings, but we are mute: when shall my spring come?" This has sometimes been interpreted as a lament for the recession of paganism, throughout the Roman world.

The *Pervigilium,* greatly admired in the nineteenth century by the English essayist and critic Walter Pater, is notable for its haunting melodiousness and for a new kind of lyrical, romantic warmth that makes it a bridge between the two worlds of antiquity and the Middle Ages. Remarkable, too, is the experimental poetic form, making extensive use of devices such as assonance and the incantatory repetition of words and phrases—and even, occasionally, stress-accent and rhyme, in anticipation of the accentual Latin poetry of later epochs.

EDITIONS with translation—Minor poems: J. W. Duff and A. M. Duff, Minor Latin Poets (Loeb ed.), revised ed., 1935; Pervigilium Veneris: C. Clement, 3rd ed., 1937. *Translations*—Pervigilium Veneris: J. Auslander, 1931; F. L. Lucas, 1939, reprinted in Aphrodite, 1948; L. Gielgud, 1952; A. Tate in Poems: 1922–47, 1961; E. D. Blodgett and H. O. Weber (Arion, v 1), 1962; J. W. Mackail in F. W. Cornish, J. P. Postgate, J. W. Mackail, Catullus, Tibullus, Pervigilium Veneris, revised ed., 1962.

ABOUT—Tiberianus: A. H. M. Jones, J. R. Martindale, and J. Morris, Prosopography of the Later Roman Empire, v 1, 1971, p 911ff. About the Pervigilium Veneris: M. Schanz and C. Hosius, Geschichte der römischen Literatur, v 3, 3rd ed., 1922; M. Martini, La lunga veglia: Studio sul Pervigilium Veneris, 1977. Also, *see* Oxford Classical Dictionary, 2nd ed., 1970, p 806. (The attribution of the Pervigilium to Tiberianus was reasserted by A. Cameron at a meeting of the Greek and Roman Societies at Cambridge in August, 1978.)

TIBULLUS, ALBIUS, Latin elegiac poet, was born between 55 and 48 and died in 19 B.C. It is stated in a short *Life,* which perhaps goes back to Suetonius, that he belonged to a family of knightly (equestrian) rank. He himself tells us that he inherited an estate but lost it, perhaps, like Virgil and Propertius and Horace, through expropriation in the civil wars following Caesar's death, when the triumvirs Antony and Octavian (the later Augustus) confiscated land for their soldiers. But it has also been suggested that there is an element of conventional poetic fiction in Tibullus' protestations of poverty. In any case, Horace informs us that the poet possessed property at Pedum (Gallicano nel Lazio); either this estate was part of his inheritance or he was given it by the soldier-statesman Marcus Valerius Messalla Corvinus (64 B.C. –A.D. 8), who became his patron. After the victory of Octavian at Actium (31 B.C.), Tibullus accompanied Messalla to the east, though the poet fell ill on the way, at Corcyra, and had to return home. It is uncertain whether he subsequently served under Messalla's leadership in Gaul. However, he was the most prominent member of the literary circle of Messalla, who, although he played a prominent part in the early years of Augustus' sole rule, remained, unlike his fellow literary patron Maecenas, aloof from the Augustan court. Moreover, his circle apparently did the same. Indeed, Tibullus, de-

ti bul' lus

spite his hatred of the wars that Augustus had brought to an end, never pays the ruler a direct compliment or even mentions his name; and he derides worldly success, claiming to desire victory only as a lover. Thus, although there is no suggestion that he was persecuted by the emperor, it may be significant that the poet Ovid, in disgrace and exile, bracketed Tibullus with the lyric poet Catullus, who had abused Julius Caesar, and with the elegiac poet Cornelius Gallus—described by Ovid as Tibullus' elegiac predecessor—who had earned Augustus' fatal disfavor.

The *Corpus Tibullianum* contains three books, the first two of which comprise poems written by Tibullus himself. Their dates of publication are impossible to determine; the first book makes a reference to Messalla's Triumph in 27 B.C., and the second alludes to the installation of the statesman's son, Messallinus, as a priest, which he may not have become until shortly before Tibullus' death.

One of the main subjects of the first book is his love for a mistress whom he calls Delia (after whom the book was named in antiquity). If she is not just a literary invention but really existed—as seems likely enough—the name Delia is a pseudonym. The novelist Apuleius, in the second century A.D., said that she was really called Plania; this was the name of a freeborn Roman family. Delia appears, from the evidence of the poems, to be married, or at least to have a regular protector other than Tibullus himself—though he seems to have taken useful advantage of the man's absence in Cilicia.

The first piece, addressed to Messalla, declares the poet's love for the girl, amid characteristically elegiac contemplation of old age and death that lie ahead; and Tibullus reveals that he cares neither for riches nor warlike glory, praising the simple and carefree life of the countryside. Elegy No. 2 is a variation of the traditional serenade before his beloved's locked door and tells of a love philter a witch prepared for the poet to administer to her. No. 3 tells how lonely Tibullus was without Delia when he fell ill at Corcyra and hopefully pictures her glad greetings when he comes back. But, alas, she turned to a richer lover. However, in No. 5

the poet does not reproach her but is only angry with the woman, assailed as a procuress, who lured her away. In the sixth poem he suspects her again, but Delia swears both to him and to her husband as well, if that is what he was, that there is nobody else; and Tibullus prays that he and she will still be together when they are old.

Three poems in the first book, however, celebrate another of his loves: they are directed this time toward a beautiful youth, whom he calls by the probably fictitious name of Marathus. Elegy No. 4 is a discussion on the art of winning the love of boys, containing counsel attributed to the lecherous god of gardens, Priapus. In No. 8 Tibullus has come upon Marathus whispering with a girl named Pholoe, and he admonishes them. In No. 9 he discovers that Marathus has been carrying on secretly with a nasty but rich old man; the poet taxes the youth with perfidious, mercenary ingratitude and finally casts him off.

In the second book Tibullus reverts to heterosexuality, but now the object of his emotions is not Delia any longer. He calls his new love Nemesis. If she truly existed, as is once again a reasonable supposition, this was perhaps not a pseudonym but her real name; in which case its mythological, un-Roman character indicates that she did not belong to the free-born citizen class but may have been a professional prostitute. She is depicted as much tougher and greedier than her predecessor. In the third elegy of this book Tibullus curses a wealthy rival who has taken her away to the country; and in the abject fourth piece he can only pray that he will become hardened to misery, meanwhile admitting that he is so enslaved by the girl that he would perform any wild action or commit any crime in order to be able to go on seeing her. In the last poem of the cycle, No. 6, Tibullus confesses to his friend Macer, who is off to the wars, that his own hope has nothing to do with any warlike ambition: it is merely that Nemesis may still let him into her house.

This second book has very different themes as well. Elegy No. 1 is a charming picture of a lively country festival. No. 2 is a birthday poem to Cornutus, another member of Messalla's circle. No. 5, Tibullus' longest poem, celebrates the appointment of Messalla's son to a priestly office and tells how the Sibyl once prophesied to Aeneas of the future greatness of Rome.

Tibullus has a gentle, but distinct, charm. His attitude toward women shows a tenderness unusual in antiquity. He has no yearnings for an active life, and no ambition. His ideal is a tranquil retirement to the country, with his loved one by his side; he writes of the rural scene and its old religious rites very movingly—and no poet is more eloquent about the blessings of peace. His verse and language are smooth and melodious, and his passion, though restrained, is just vigorous enough to retain our interest. But, in respect of fire and vigor he falls far short of his contemporary Propertius—though Quintilian placed Tibullus first, partly no doubt because his style was much more polished.

WORKS in the Tibullan Corpus that are not by Tibullus himself—The third book of the Corpus contains poems by other members of Messalla's circle. These include six rather frigid elegies by a certain Lygdamus (which may be a pseudonym); a feeble and bombastic panegyric of Messalla by an unknown hand; five further anonymous poems—pleasant but rather ineffectual—about the love affair between Sulpicia, Messalla's ward and niece, and a young man who is given the name of Cerinthus; and seven wonderfully direct contributions by Sulpicia herself.
EDITIONS—K. F. Smith, 1913, reprint 1971; O. Tescari, 1968; M. C. J. Putnam, 1973; G. Lee, 1975; M. Wimmel, Tibull und Delia, 1976. *Translations*—J. P. Postgate *in* F. W. Cornish, J. P. Postgate, J. W. Mackail, Catullus, Tibullus, Pervigilium Veneris (Loeb ed.), 1962; C. Carrier, Poems, 1968; P. Dunlop, The Poems of Tibullus With the Tibullan Collection (Penguin ed.), 1972.
ABOUT—J. P. Elder *in* J. P. Sullivan, ed., Critical Essays, 1962; M. Schuster, Tibull-Studien, 1968; G. Williams, Tradition and Originality in Roman Poetry, 1968; W. Wimmel, Der frühe Tibull, 1968; G. Luck, The Latin Love Elegy, 2nd ed., 1969; D. F. Bright, Haec Mihi Fingebam: Tibullus in His World, 1979.

TIMAEUS, Greek historian, was born in about 356 and died in about 260 B.C. His birthplace was the eastern Sicilian city-town of Tauromenium (Taormina), of which his father Andromachus was the ruler, having gathered there the refugees from another Sicilian town, Naxos (358/7). Timaeus, however, was driven from his homeland by

tī mē′ us

the tyrant Agathocles of Syracuse (317–289) and moved to Athens, where he studied rhetoric under Isocrates' pupil Philiscus and where he spent the next half-century of his life. It is uncertain whether he ever returned to Sicily.

His *Histories,* in thirty-eight books, of which fragments are preserved in quotations and references, were centered on Sicilian events but also covered the story of the whole Greek west from its beginnings. Books 1-5 formed an introduction covering the early history of Italy and Sicily, including sections dealing with western geography as far as the extreme north; a large amount of mythical and legendary material was also introduced, and probably also an account of the earliest Greek colonizations. Books 6-33 narrated the history of Sicily from the foundations of the Greek colonies down to the accession of Agathocles, with digressions relating to events in Greece and elsewhere; and Books 34-38 gave a separate account of Agathocles. A supplementary portion of the work was added later, dealing with King Pyrrhus of Epirus and carrying on the story either until his death (272) or until the subsequent outbreak of the First Punic War between Rome and Carthage in 264.

The *Histories* probably drew upon a work entitled *On Sicily* by Lycus of Rhegium, the adoptive father of the poet Lycophron (third century B.C.). Timaeus was careful in his chronology, which he based largely on the four-year periods of the Olympiads. His *Victors at Olympia* was presumably a preliminary exercise in establishing this method of chronology. One of his achievements was to link together the histories of the western and eastern Mediterranean regions through the myths and Heracles, and the Argonauts, and Troy. It was also he who gave a decisive shape to the future of western Mediterranean historiography by stressing the contrast between Greeks and "barbarians."

We can discern from the surviving fragments of Timaeus' work that while he was a learned man—and very diligent in the collection of material (including inscriptions) —he showed little critical acumen, indulging in wild rationalizations of myths and etymologies of a puerile nature, producing an abundance of rhetorical commonplaces,

445

and inserting speeches that appear to be entirely fictitious. His pretensions to impartiality vanished whenever he dealt with persons he hated, such as Dionysius II and Agathocles of Syracuse; and he correspondingly exaggerated the merits of the Corinthian general Timoleon (d. 334), who subsequently liberated Syracuse. In the second century B.C., his fellow historian Polybius devoted a whole book of his own *Histories* to an elaborate criticism of Timaeus. While paying him the compliment of starting his work at the point where his predecessor had left off, and even conceding him a certain carefulness in chronology and research, Polybius believed that Timaeus was frequently ignorant and credulous and that he deliberately abandoned any claims to objectivity when he displayed, for example, a disrespectful and unfair attitude toward Aristotle and put forward niggling criticisms of his own historical forerunners, Theopompus and Ephorus. Polybius entertained an even more serious objection to the whole way in which Timaeus carried out his task, rooted to his study and his role of armchair historian for decade after decade, without obtaining any practical knowledge of warfare and the outside world.

Furthermore, Polybius, who belonged to the mainland of Greece, disapproved of the Sicilian Timaeus' location of the Greek west as the center of his narrative focus. Finally, he resented the reputation that Timaeus' work enjoyed as the standard history of western lands—his *Histories* became an important source, of which traces are detectable in the most widely scattered fields: for example, its stories about Troy exercised considerable influence on the legends concerning the origins of the Romans—a people whose significance Timaeus was quick to recognize—and it is evident that he was generally regarded as the first historian of Rome. In fact, he had to be taken seriously; and that was the main reason why his successor, for all his greater distinction, could not endure him.

EDITIONS—F. Jacoby, Die Fragmente der griechischen Historiker, 3 b, 566.
ABOUT—T. S. Brown, Timaeus of Tauromenium, 1958, *and* The Greek Historians, 1973; A. Momigliano, Ter-zo contributo alla storia degli studi classici, 1966, *and* Essays in Ancient and Modern Historiography, 1977; F. W. Walbank, Polybius, 1972.

TIMOCLES, Greek comic poet, worked in the latter part of the fourth century B.C. His native city was Athens. He was a writer of the Middle Comedy, the other leading representatives of which included Alexis, Anaxandrides, Antiphanes, and Eubulus. Timocles won the first prize at the Lenaea on a single occasion, sometime between 330 and 320 (the latest datable allusion in his plays falls between the years 317 and 307).

His comedies are lost, except for fragments, but twenty-seven of their titles are known. Two of these titles refer to stock characters: *Epichairekakos* (the man who rejoices in his neighbor's ills) and *Polypragmon* (the busybody). *Heroes, Centaurs,* and a couple of other works appear to have been parodies of mythical themes. *Orestautokleides* is an invented composite title; the play tells how Autoclides suffered the ordeal of Orestes but was haunted by old women instead of Furies. A long excerpt from an unidentified play by Timocles praises Tragedy as a consoler of our misfortunes; however bad these are, he declares, there is always a tragic person who has suffered more grievously. But almost half of the surviving fragments are personal allusions. In his attacks on contemporary politicians, including Demosthenes and Hyperides, Timocles is closer in spirit to the fifth century Old Comedy of Aristophanes than to the Middle Comedy.

EDITIONS—A. Meineke, Fragmenta Comicorum Graecorum, v 3, 1839–57; T. Kock, Comicorum Atticorum Fragmenta, v 2, 1880–88; J. M. Edmonds, The Fragments of Attic Comedy, v 2, 1957.

TIMOCREON, Greek lyric and elegiac poet, lived in the first half of the fifth century B.C. His birthplace was Ialysus on the island of Rhodes. When Rhodes fell to Persian invaders, he apparently collaborated with them and went to their capital Susa as guest

tī' mō klēz

ti mok' rē on

of their king. After 479 he mocked the Athenian statesman Themistocles' for the latter's political setbacks and because of a personal grudge: Themistocles had failed to rescue Timocreon and take him home after the Persian Wars had ended. These attacks on Themistocles incurred the disapproval of another poet, Simonides (c. 556–468 B.C.), who censured Timocreon for both his character and his literary style.

Timocreon's poems also included epigrams, written in a blend of literary and colloquial language. In addition, he composed drinking songs; and he gained notoriety as a glutton. However, he was a remarkable athlete, with victories to his credit in the all-round Five Events (Pentathlon).

EDITIONS—D. L. Page, Poetae Melici Graeci, 1962.
ABOUT—C. M. Bowra, Greek Lyric Poetry, 2nd ed., 1961.

TIMON, Greek popular philosopher and poet, was born in (perhaps) about 320 and died in 230 B.C. He came from Phlius in the northeastern Peloponnese. In his youth, he adopted the profession of a dancer but also studied at Megara under Stilpo (c. 380–300), the third head of its philosophical school, and at Elis under Pyrrho, the founder of Greek skepticism, of which Timon, too, became an adherent. Later, he was active as a lecturer (sophist) at Chalcedon (Kadiköy, northwestern Asia Minor) and subsequently spent the rest of his life at Athens. (He is not the same man as the misanthrope Timon of Athens—celebrated by Shakespeare—who apparently lived in the fifth century B.C.)

Only fragments survive of the abundant writings of Timon of Phlius. The most influential of them were his *Silloi* or "squint-eyed" pieces—that is to say, mockeries or lampoons. Following the example of the satirical *Silloi* of the poet-philosopher Xenophanes of Colophon (sixth-fifth centuries B.C.), whom he purports to engage in a dialogue, he attacked dogmatic philosophers, living and dead, in three books of hexameters. The first, after a prologue, parodied a heroic, Homeric battle between the expo-

ti' mən

nents of their rival creeds, followed, apparently, by a scene in which an old woman was shown fishing for a shoal of philosophers, including Plato. In the second book Timon descends to the underworld to meet these philosophers in person and abuse them. Book 3 continued the tale and wound it up with an epilogue. The *Silloi* cannot have been addressed to a popular audience, since they presuppose a wide knowledge of the history of philosophy. Other targets upon which they launched attacks included the scholarly writers of Hellenistic Alexandria, whom Timon described as "well-stuffed pedants quarreling endlessly in the hen coops of the Muses."

In addition to the *Silloi,* Timon is credited by Diogenes Laertius with a variety of poetical works, including epics, obscenities, satyr plays, and no less than thirty comedies and sixty tragedies. His plays seem to have been written to be read, not for performance on the stage. Another poem, which does not fit readily into these categories, was his *Indalmoi* in elegiac verse, dealing with the doctrines of Pyrrho, who, together with Xenophanes, was one of the few philosophers he did not deride. The title probably means illusions or fantasies, referring to the doctrines of rival schools. Timon also wrote a prose treatise entitled *Python,* on his career as an adherent of Pyrrho's school, and another entitled *The Funeral Banquet of Arcesilaus,* dealing appreciatively with the Academic philosopher of that name (c. 316–242 B.C.), whom he had previously mocked. Timon's other prose writings—which were said to total twenty thousand lines—included monographs entitled *On Sensations* and *Against the Physicists.*

EDITIONS—H. Diels, Poetarum Philosophicorum Fragmenta, 1901.
ABOUT—V. Brochard, Les sceptiques grecs, 1887, reprint 1959; M. M. Patrick, The Greek Sceptics, 1929.

TIMOTHEUS, Greek poet, was born in about 450 B.C. and died in about 360. His hometown was Miletus (southwestern Asia Minor). He became a friend of the playwright Euripides. When Timotheus was de-

ti moth' e us

447

pressed by early failures at Athens, it was said that Euripides encouraged him, and Euripides in his turn was believed to have been under Timotheus' influence. It was also believed, though on doubtful authority, that Timotheus, like Euripides, visited Macedonia.

Timotheus wrote dithyrambs (choral songs for accompaniment by the flute, originally in honor of Dionysus) and nomes (*nomoi,* solo songs for lyre accompaniment in honor of Apollo). The two forms of song were becoming increasingly similar, and Timotheus, who was consciously an innovator, played a leading part in developing the artistic character of both. This was a time when the musical component was being enhanced and intensified in nome and dithyramb alike, and it is recorded that Timotheus was the earliest poet to introduce a choral element into the previously solo nome, just as his contemporary Philoxenus was the first to insert solos into the hitherto choral dithyramb. Timotheus' meters and rhythms are varied, restless, and abrupt. His writings should be thought of as librettos rather than poems, and we are prevented from judging them adequately by the disappearance of the music, which, presumably, was as sensational as the text.

Although the greater part of his eighteen books of verse are lost, substantial portions of a nome by Timotheus entitled *The Persians* was discovered in 1902 at Abusir in Lower Egypt on a papyrus of the fourth century B.C. This is the oldest Greek book that has come down to us and our only clear source of evidence for this genre. Despite all innovations, however, the nome's conventional division into seven parts, made canonical by Terpander, poet and musician of Lesbos in the seventh century B.C., is retained.

The surviving two hundred fifty-three continuous lines of Timotheus' poem begin in the central section, the "navel" *(omphalos),* the most important part of the piece, which traditionally comprised its narrative element. The theme is the battle of Salamis (480 B.C.), seen not as a single historical event but as a series of separate pictures. They are presented in startlingly melodramatic fashion, foreshadowing the techniques of Hellenistic historians—for example, a drowning Persian delivers a passionate outburst against the sea which is engulfing him, and his stranded compatriots moan despairingly for their homeland. In these passages, Timotheus adopts a method for depicting foreign speech that recalls the practice of Euripides. In general, his language combines crude realism with a fantastic parody of the elevated style with a penchant for bold periphrases and surprising adjectives. At times, however, his work degenerates into turgid and wanton obscurity.

Among the other extant portions of the nome is its sixth traditional section, the *sphragis* (seal), in which the poet sang in his own person and about his own concerns. Here Timotheus, with dignified moderation, defends himself against criticisms that had been launched against him at Sparta; in particular, he seeks to explain and justify his novel employment of the eleven-stringed lyre.

The epilogue of *The Persians* offers good wishes for the victory of a city (no doubt Miletus) where the poem seems to have been written shortly after 400 B.C.

EDITIONS—D. L. Page, Poetae Melici Graeci, 1962.
ABOUT—U. von Wilamowitz-Moellendorf, Timotheos: Die Perser, 1903; A. Lesky, History of Greek Literature, 1966.

TRANQUILLUS, GAIUS SUETONIUS. See Suetonius

TROGUS, POMPEIUS,

TROGUS, POMPEIUS, Roman historian, worked in the latter part of the first century B.C. He came from Vasio (Vaison-la-Romaine), a town of the tribe of the Vocontii in southern Gaul. His grandfather received Roman citizenship from Pompey, and his father was one of Julius Caesar's secretaries.

Trogus wrote what appears to have been the first universal history ever composed in the Latin tongue. Comprising forty-four books, of which only fragments and a summary survive, it was named the *Philippic*

Histories (a title already used by both Theopompus and Anaximenes of Lampsacus) after the Macedonian empire established by Philip II (359–336 B.C.), which constituted its central theme. Books 1-6 dealt with earlier historical developments, including accounts of the Assyrians, Medes, Persians, Scythians, and Greeks. In Book 7 Trogus turned to Philip and began to describe his rise to power; Macedonia remains the subject of the next five books. The next twenty-eight continued the story of this and the other Hellenistic kingdoms down to the time of their suppression by Rome. Books 41 and 42 gave an account of Parthia, the Middle Eastern kingdom that remained independent, from its origins "following the death of Alexander the Great." The last two books narrated the history of Rome from the regal period and surveyed developments in Gaul and Spain down to the victories of Augustus over the northern Spanish Cantabrians. The initial portion of these books, which was devoted to the earliest Roman history, was curiously brief, as Trogus himself appreciated, since his aim, he said, was "not to exceed the limits of the task he had set himself, but also not to pass over in silence the origins of the city which is queen of the whole world." This brevity may have been due to his desire not to compete with the work of his eminent contemporary Livy, or to his belief that there was room for a companion history to Livy's that concentrated rather on the non-Italian peoples.

The synopsis from which our knowledge of the *Philippic Histories* is derived is an epitome that was compiled by a certain Justin (Marcus Junianus Justinus), a Roman historian, probably in the third century A.D., and was widely read in the Middle Ages. Justin's abridgment, though uneven, is useful, since in addition to preserving tables of contents, it retains the principal lines of the original. It is possible to deduce from it that Trogus favored an elaborate style of narrative, in the Hellenistic tradition, with a tendency toward melodrama and moralizing. He generally, though not invariably, employed indirect, third-person speech for the presentation of public discourses, criticizing historians, such as Livy and Sallust, who professed to reproduce them directly. His main source may well have been the *History of Kings* by Timagenes of Alexandria, a Greek work that is independent of the nationalist Roman tradition. (Timagenes was captured and taken to Rome [55 B.C.], where he subsequently became a friend of Octavian [Augustus], though later they became estranged from one another.)

Trogus' *Histories,* even in the summarized form in which they have come down to us, present facts not available elsewhere and add to our relatively scanty information about the Hellenistic world.

Trogus also wrote a zoological work *(De Animalibus)* in at least ten books; and, since Pliny the Elder reprimands him for stating that palms can be propagated from palm leaves, it appears that he compiled a botanic study as well.

EDITIONS—O. Seel, Pompei Trogi Prologi et Fragmenta, 1956, *and* Justin, Epitome, 1935.
ABOUT—L. E. Hallberg, De Trogo Pompeio, 1869; F. Seck, De Pompei Trogi Sermone, 1881; E. Schneider, De Trogi Historiarum Philippicarum Consilio et Arte, 1913; O. Seel, Die Praefatio des Pompeius Trogus (Erlanger Forschungen, A, 3), 1955; L. Santi Amantini, E. Salomone, Fonti e valore storico di Pompeo Trogo, 1972, 1973; M. G. B. Angeli and M. Giacchero, Atene e Sparta nella storiografia trogiana 415–400 B.C., 1974.

TYRTAEUS, Greek elegiac poet, wrote in the seventh century B.C. He evidently lived among the Spartans, whom his poetry rallied to put down the rebel Messenians in the Second Messenian War (c. 640–621 B.C.). There were, it is true, persistent ancient reports that he himself was not a Spartan but came from Athens or Miletus instead; however, these stories were probably invented at a later period, when other Greeks could no longer imagine that the Spartans could ever have produced poets of their own. It was also recorded that Tyrtaeus held the office of a Spartan general,. and surviving passages from his poems show him as handing out orders—this the Spartans would scarcely have accepted from a foreigner. Moreover, he usually speaks of them as "us"; the further fact that he says to them "*you* are of the race of unconquerable Heracles" suggests only that he may not have belonged to the
tûr tē' us

ruling (Spartiate) class, which alone claimed such descent. The conclusion that he was a native Spartan, receives additional support from his language, which, although for the most part traditionally epic, not only adapts its Homeric borrowings with a certain clumsiness but admits a number of Doric (Spartan) elements, which look like the slips of a poet who had learned to write the traditional Ionian dialect but occasionally relapsed into his own native Spartan form of speech.

Tyrtaeus' works were later collected into five books at Alexandria, under the general title of *Eunomia (Law and Order),* one of the characteristic catchwords of this postheroic epoch. The greater part of his fairly abundant surviving fragments, in elegiac verse, come from propagandist exhortations to be steadfast in battle and to endure unto death; the Spartans were said to have sung his songs on the march. But the *Iliad's* ideal of the individual knightly champion—a Hector or Achilles—has departed, and in its place we find a collective picture of citizens on foot, fighting as a team, shoulder to shoulder in phalanx—the beginnings of the hoplites, the upper middle-class infantry of Greece. Fragment No. 1 deals with some specific warlike occasion, citing orders for tactical dispositions and referring to a siege. Fragment No. 8 begins with a general eulogy of courage, apparently composed at a time of demoralization after a military setback; and the passage concludes with advice on conduct in battle.

The authenticity of other elegies has been doubted, mainly on the grounds that their character is not specifically Spartan; yet on the whole the authorship of Tyrtaeus still seems probable. From these poems come Fragments No. 6 and No. 7, which praise the virtue of dying for one's country and urge young men to valorous courage. Fragment No. 9, the longest and most elaborate of the elegiac pieces, enumerates various admirable personal assets—royal blood, fine appearance, athletic ability, eloquent speech —but none of these, the poet concludes, is a guarantee of manly virtue *(arete),* which can only be demonstrated by tenacious bravery in the face of the enemy.

Certain other fragments may have belonged to a poem called *Politeia (Constitu-*

tion) that was written by Tyrtaeus for the benefit of the Spartans and suggests that he was interested in the political reforms of his time. These passages include No. 1 on the beginnings of their community, No. 3 on the alleged Delphian origin of their constitution, and No. 4 and No. 5 on the semi-legendary First Messenian War of the eighth century B.C.

WORKS dubiously attributed to Tyrtaeus—Fragments No. 15 and No. 16 belong to war songs which are unmistakably Spartan but should not necessarily be regarded as the work of Tyrtaeus. For Fragments No. 6, No. 7, and No. 9, of which he is probably the author, *see* discussion in sketch above.
EDITIONS—M. L. West, Iambi et Elegi Graeci ante Alexandrum Cantati, v 2, 1972. *Translations*—J. M. Edmonds, Greek Elegy and Iambus, v 1, 1931.
ABOUT—C. M. Bowra, Early Greek Elegists, 1938; C. Prato, Tyrtaeus, 1968; B. Snell, Tyrtaios und die Sprache des Epos (Hypomnemata, v 22), 1969; G. Pfohl, Die griechische Elegie, 1972; J. Latacz, Kampfparänäse, Kampfdarstellunge und Kampfwirklichkeit in der Ilias bei Kallinos und Tyrtaios, 1977.

ULPIAN (Domitius Ulpianus), Roman jurist, was born after the middle of the second century A.D. and died in 223. He came of a family long established at Tyre in Phoenicia (now es-Sur in Lebanon). Under Septimius Severus (193–211), he served as assessor (together with another famous figure, Paulus) to their fellow jurist Papinian, when the latter was praetorian prefect (the emperor's principal adviser). The sources for the later part of Ulpian's career are unreliable, but it appears likely that he devoted himself during most of the reign of Caracalla (211–17) to literary activity; he seems to have been dismissed from some office by Elagabalus (218–22) but then in 221/2 became master of petitions *(magister libellorum)* to Elagabalus' heir-designate (with the title of Caesar), the twelve-year-old Severus Alexander. Less than three weeks after Alexander's accession to the throne in 222, however, Ulpian was holding the post of prefect of the grain supply *(praefectus annonae)* and very soon afterward became chief praetorian prefect. After carrying out certain reforms, he put to death his two subordinate prefects, Flavianus and Chrestus, but in 223 was himul' pi ăn self killed by mutinous praetorian guardsmen, who regarded his reformist measures as damaging to their privileges.

Ulpian was a prolific author, to whom nearly two hundred and eighty writings were ascribed, almost all attributable to the time of Caracalla. Two of these works were outstanding. One was an eighty-one-book study on the praetorian edicts *(Ad Edictum Libri 81)*, the declarations of policy and intent by the annually elected praetors, which Salvius Julianus (c. 130) had collected together in a revised edition. Appended to Ulpian's work is a two-book supplement on the edict of another group of magistrates, the curule aediles.

Ulpian's other major achievement was a comprehensive commentary entitled *On Sabinus (Ad Sabinum)*, so-called because it followed the system and disposition of the writings of Masurius Sabinus, the jurist of the first century A.D. after whom the Sabinian School of law took its name. *On Sabinus* may have been left incomplete by Ulpian; it was subsequently reedited by others with the addition of a number of monographs relating to various legislative enactments and particular branches of private law. *Ad Edictum* and *Ad Sabinum*, taken together, formed an ambitious and comprehensive restatement of edictal law—and, indeed, civil law in general.

Ulpian also wrote elementary handbooks for legal practitioners *(Disputationes, Responsa)* and a series of textbooks *(Institutiones, Definitiones* and *Regulae* or Legal Rules, in seven books), as well as special studies of particular magistracies.

It is to the *Digest* of the Byzantine emperor Justinian I (A.D. 527–65) that we owe our knowledge of Ulpian's work. Indeed, Justinian's compilers make much more use of him than of any other jurist: almost a third of the *Digest* is taken from his writings, more than twice as much as from his nearest competitor, Paulus. (It seems likely that he and Paulus were not on very good terms; for whereas both quote amply from other legal authorities, they never quote one another). Ulpian's gigantic output, reflecting the contemporary civil service trend toward codification, was planned to cover the entire range of the law, with the intention that reference to earlier authorities would become unnecessary. Although less original and acute than Paulus, he is trustworthy, businesslike, and unaffected, writing with superlative ease and clarity (even if also with a certain bureaucratic guardedness) and displaying a magisterial command of his voluminous, complex material.

WORKS (doubtfully or wrongly attributable to Ulpian) —The Opiniones, a further elementary handbook, and the Tituli ex Corpore Ulpiani (or Epitome Ulpiani), which is probably a fourth century summary of a treatise by someone other than Ulpian.
EDITIONS—Corpus Iuris Civilis. Digesta. (Quotations from Ulpian occupy more than one-third of the work.)
ABOUT—F. Schulz, Sabinus-Fragmente in Ulpians Sabinus-Commentar, 1906, *and* De Epitome Ulpiani, 1926, *and* Roman Legal Science, 1946; W. Kunkel, Herkunft und soziale Stellung der römischen Juristen, 1952, *and* Introduction to Roman Legal and Constitutional History, 1966.

VALERIUS ANTIAS, Latin historian, flourished in the first century B.C. For his date there is only one piece of external evidence: a later historical writer, Velleius Paterculus, describes him as a contemporary of the historian Sisenna and the annalist Claudius Quadrigarius—which would assign his period of work to c. 80–60 B.C. Modern arguments preferring a somewhat later chronology are less convincing. To judge from his name, Valerius came from Antium (Anzio, southeast of Rome), where he presumably belonged to a little-known local branch of the great Valerian clan.

Valerius Antias wrote an annalistic (year-by-year) history of Rome, from its beginnings down to about 60 B.C., comprising at least seventy-five books. As we learn from the surviving fragments, he had only reached the second legendary or mythical Roman king (Numa Pompilius) by the second book. The defeat of Gaius Hostilius Mancinus by the Spaniards in 137 B.C. and the activities of Tiberius Gracchus as quaestor in that country (136) were said to have been described in Book 22. If this last numeral is correct, Valerius must have treated the events of that, to him, comparatively

və lēr′ i us an′ ti əs

451

recent period much more fully than he had handled previous epochs.

Yet, even about early times, according to Livy (c. 59 B.C.–c. A.D. 12), he wrote at greater length than the available information warranted. Livy also criticized him for inexcusable exaggerations of numbers, notably of soldiers fighting or killed or captured —figures to which Valerius lent an air of plausibility by specifying them with ostensibly meticulous exactitude. This almost total indifference to veracity, which prompted Livy to employ a check source when confronted with some particularly implausible total, was part of Valerius' general tendency to write for melodramatic effect (for example, he loved, like Hellenistic historians of similar tendencies before him, to emphasize the role of Fortune and Nemesis in human affairs). Nevertheless Livy, despite his criticisms, cited Valerius no less than ten times in extant passages of his *History* and indeed —like another annalist, Tubero—used Valerius, throughout his work, as one of his principal authorities—and above all as a model for his own literary style, in which tragic and pathetic effects played such an extensive part. Another writer who made use of Valerius was the literary critic and historian Dionysius of Halicarnassus (first century B.C.). And in the first century A.D. Plutarch, too, may have been one of his readers.

On the credit side, it was useful that Valerius drew upon the history of Lucius Calpurnius Piso Frugi (consul in 133 B.C.), since Piso had possessed access to the official annals. And Valerius, fortunately, was by no means unwitting to accept and reproduce an account of events that he had derived from the national priestly and senatorial records, so that he preserved many invaluable details of Roman administrative practice. Yet he elaborated what he found without shame. Moreover, in addition to his general unreliability, he exhibited strong specific biases, which Livy does not sufficiently discount. In the first place, the Valerian clan at all epochs of Roman history was endowed by him with every possible virtue, and its role was preposterously and fraudulently overestimated. Secondly, where he found records of events and actions unaccompanied by

names, he fictitiously and fraudulently supplied them—enriching, for example, his accounts of ancient epochs by the names of nonexistent personages from clans that had not existed in those times but were prominent in the years when he himself was writing. Thirdly, Valerius lavishes a prodigious favoritism on the dictator Sulla, for whose measures (especially those intended to shore up the authority of the Senate) he invents many glorious antique precedents; indeed his whole character sketch of Servius Tullius, the monarch ascribed to the sixth century B.C., is updated to imply a favorable interpretation of the doings of Sulla half a millennium later. Valerius' enthusiasm for Sulla was partially motivated by the brutal sack of the historian's hometown Antium by Sulla's enemy Marius, the enemy of the Senate, in 87 B.C.

Valerius' style was regarded as unattractive by the lawyer-scholar Fronto in the second century A.D. Yet he had evidently possessed considerable rhetorical vigor; and he brought the writing of annalistic history to its highest degree of literary artistry before Livy.

EDITIONS—H. Peter, Historicorum Romanorum Reliquiae, v 1, 2nd ed., 1914.
ABOUT—A. Klotz, Livius und seine Vorgänger, 1940–41; R. M. Ogilvie, A Commentary on Livy Books 1-5, 1965; P. G. Walsh, Livy: His Historical Aims and Methods, 1967.

VALERIUS FLACCUS, GAIUS, Latin epic poet, worked in the period between about 70 and 92 A.D.: he refers to the Jewish War for which a triumph was held in 71 and to the eruption of Vesuvius in 79—and the rhetorician Quintilian, in the early nineties, alludes to his recent death. If we follow a Vatican manuscript in attributing to Valerius Flaccus the additional names of Balbus and Setinus, the latter name suggests that he came either from one of the two towns called Setia in Spain or from the colony of the same name (Sezze) on the borders of Latium and Campania—which is more probable, since he held office in Rome as a member of the **và lēr′ i us flak′ kus**

priestly Board of Fifteen. Nothing further is known about him.

His only surviving work is the *Argonautica,* an epic in 5,593 hexameter verses divided into eight books, dedicated to the emperor Vespasian (69–79). The poem describes the mythical voyage of the Argo, the ship in which Jason and other heroes sailed to Colchis, at the farthest extremity of the Black Sea, to seize the Golden Fleece and bring it back to Thessaly. Book 1 portrays the jealousy of the Thessalian king Pelias toward his nephew Jason, whom he plans to dispatch on the perilous quest for the Fleece. At Minerva's command Jason builds and launches the Argo, while the sun-god, father of King Aeëtes of Colchis, complains to Jupiter of the threat to his son's property. In Book 2 the Argonauts reach the island of Lemnos, loved by Vulcan and hated by Venus, where Hypsipyle falls in love with Jason; but the Argonauts press on through the strait to Cyzicus, ruled by a monarch of the same name. The third book is mainly concerned with the fight against King Cyzicus and the kidnapping by a water nymph of the youth Hylas, beloved by Hercules, who searches for him in vain. Book 4 tells how the Argonauts narrowly escape through the Clashing Rocks and emerge into the Black Sea. In Book 5, they traverse the sea and land on the shore of Colchis, where the queen's daughter Medea, awake early after a night of ominous dreams, has eyes only for Jason and guides him to the royal audience hall. Her father, Aeëtes, is angered by Jason's plan to seize the Fleece but concedes agreement on the condition that the Argonauts will help him against his hostile brother Perses. Book 6 is largely devoted to the fighting that follows, in which Perses is defeated, owing to Jason's deeds of valor.

Book 7 tells of the growth of Medea's passion for Jason and of her mental conflict resulting from her love for this stranger and her devotion to her father: she and Jason then avow their mutual love in a temple. Aeëtes breaks his promise and demands that Jason, in addition to the help he has already contributed, shall also yoke fire-breathing bulls and sow a crop of warriors from the dragon's teeth. Medea now leaves the city to join Jason and enables him by her magic counsel to overcome these ordeals. In the eighth book he duly seizes the Fleece and sets off homeward with Medea, whose surrender, however, to the pursuing Colchians he treacherously meditates if only they will let him keep the Fleece. With his falsely soothing words to her, the epic abruptly breaks off. If Valerius had continued it (perhaps he did not live to do so), it may be conjectured that he would have added four more books to complete the work, thus making the same total as in Virgil's *Aeneid.* There are internal reasons for supposing that the return journey of the Argonauts, which these books would have described, would have brought them back to the mouth of the Danube and then through eastern Europe to Italy.

This would have been quite different from the voyage described in the *Argonautica* of the Hellenistic poet Apollonius Rhodius (third century B.C.), with whom comparisons are inevitable. Valerius expands or contracts and otherwise seeks to improve Apollonius' narrative and is more attentive to dramatic plausibility and motivation, exhibiting particular skill in depicting the emotions that sway men and women *en masse*. His Jason, too, is more successfully portrayed as a leader of men than the wooden hero of Apollonius Valerius. Medea, on the other hand, though her growing love is sketched cleverly enough, is less subtly and vigorously presented than her prototype in Apollonius. The characterization owes something to the Dido of Virgil, to whom Valerius displays many debts, while the influence of the poets Ovid and Lucan and the statesman-philosopher Seneca, who wrote tragedies, is also apparent. All in all, however, he is as much innovator as borrower.

Valerius is able to tell a well-organized and dramatic story. His narrative is also relatively free of the worst rhetorical excesses of contemporary poetry; on the other hand, artificiality always prevails, his striving for point often ends in strained language, and his appreciation and criticism of life rarely rises over a banal and uninspiring level. Nevertheless, he strikes a more original note than his contemporary Statius; yet he never rises to Statius' poetic best. Both Statius and another epic poet of the day, Silius

453

Italicus, show traces of his influence; but otherwise the *Argonautica* suffered a prolonged oblivion, until the first three and a half books were "rediscovered" by the Italian humanist Poggio in 1417. In the seventeenth century a leading Dutch scholar, Heinsius, greatly admired the poem.

EDITIONS—P. Langen, 1897. *Translations*—J. H. Mozley (Loeb ed.), revised ed., 1936.
ABOUT—W. C. Summers, A Study of the Argonautica of Valerius Flaccus, 1894; F. Mehmel, Valerius Flaccus, 1934; J. Strang, Notes on Valerius Flaccus' Argonautica, 1972; S. Contino, Lingua e stile in Valerio Flacco, 1973; J. Adamietz, Zur Komposition der Argonautica des Valerius Flaccus, 1976.

VALERIUS MAXIMUS, Latin anecdotal historian, wrote during the reign of Tiberius (A.D. 14–37). He tells us that he was poor, but that he was befriended by Sextus Pompeius, a minor patron of literature who was consul in A.D. 14 and thirteen years later became governor of Asia, where he took Valerius as a member of his entourage.

His surviving work, *Memorable Deeds and Sayings (Factorum et Dictorum Memorabilium Libri)*, was published probably shortly after Sejanus' downfall in 31, which we infer from the fact that it contains abuse of the consul unthinkable while he was in power. It consists of a long series of anecdotes about Romans, for the most part well-known men (and some women), each story usually followed by a similar tale about a foreigner—in most cases Greek. Grouped loosely and amorphously according to theme, each story is prefaced in the manuscript by headings, which may have been supplied at a later epoch. Book 1 contains anecdotes that deal with matters of religion, prodigies, and miraculous or curious marvels; Book 2, *inter alia*, with points relating to matrimony, official and military matters, public games, and foreign customs. The third book is devoted to intellectual and moral qualities and discusses people who have risen from humble origins to greatness; and the fourth is concerned with moderation, temperance, married love, friendship, and generosity. The subjects of Book 5 are mercy, gratitude and the lack of it, filial and

và lēr' i us mak' si mus

454

brotherly and paternal love, and patriotic deeds and feelings. Book 6, after treating of justice, national honor, and other subjects, speaks of the faithfulness of wives—and of slaves—and the changeability of fortune. Book 7 celebrates wise or smart sayings, and actions and military tricks, and ends with a section on canceled or ratified wills. The widely varying topics of Book 8 include legal cases of different kinds, people who have been guilty of mistakes that they penalized in others, remarkable effects of the arts, and glory and renown. Book 9 covers a series of human faults or vices and goes on to note deaths of an uncommon nature.

Valerius Maximus emerges as a strong champion of the imperial regime—indeed, his praise of Tiberius is fulsome—and an equally convinced believer that he and his fellow Romans, though inferior to their ancestors, were nevertheless much superior to all foreigners. His principal historical authorities appear to have been Livy and Cicero, but there are also traces of many other Latin sources, including Caelius Antipater, Pompeius Trogus, Cato the Elder, Pomponius Rufus, and probably Varro; and a score of Greek writers are quoted as well. Although much of this evidence is interesting and useful, Valerius' use of his data is almost entirely uncritical and often inaccurate, and he is always prepared to falsify history in order to make a point. His style, too, is abominable—shallow, showy, sententious, bombastic, clumsy, and obscure—though he can produce, at rare intervals, a well-turned piece of narrative or dialogue and is even capable, on occasion, of an imaginative touch of fancy.

In spite of all its faults, the diversity and convenient organization of the work secured it a certain amount of attention in antiquity—notably from the encyclopedist Pliny the Elder and the biographer Plutarch—and then a remarkably high degree of popularity in the Middle Ages. A considerable number of medieval manuscripts of the work have come down to us; and at least two abridgments were in circulation. One of these, intended for schools, was compiled by Julius Paris, a writer who probably lived in the fourth century A.D.; and he attached to his summary a list of Roman first names, *De*

Praenominibus, attributed to a certain Gaius Titius Probus. The other epitome, by Januarius Nepotianus (possibly fifth century A.D.), breaks off early in the third book. The ninth century scholar Heiric of Auxerre and his pupil Rémi both produced selections from Valerius Maximus' work, in the first case in association with Suetonius and in the second, alone. A translation into German was made in 1369 (printed 1486), and a Spanish version in 1467 (printed 1495).

EDITIONS—P. Constant (with French translation), 1935; R. Faranda, 1971.
ABOUT—R. Helm in Pauly-Wissowa-Kroll, Real-Encyclopädie der klassischen Altertumswissenschaft, v 8, columns 90–116; C. Bosch, Die Quellen des Valerius Maximus, 1929; A. Klotz, Studien zu Valerius Maximus und den Exempla, 1942; C. J. Carter *in* T. A. Dorey, ed., Empire and Aftermath: Silver Latin, v 2, 1975; M. Fleck, Untersuchungen zu den Exempla des Valerius Maximus, 1976.

VARIUS RUFUS, LUCIUS, Latin epic, tragic, and elegiac poet, may have been born in the 70s B.C. and perhaps died in about 13. He was a member of the entourage of Octavian (the later Augustus) at the Conference of Tarentum with Antony in 37 B.C., at which the Second Triumvirate was renewed. The poets Virgil and Horace and the statesman and patron of literature Maecenas, who were all friends of Varius, were also with Octavian at the meeting.

When Virgil, on his deathbed in 19 B.C., concluded that the manuscript of the *Aeneid* would not be destroyed as he had wished, he inserted a clause in his will appointing Varius and Plotius Tucca, another member of Maecenas' circle, as his literary executors. He requested them not to publish anything left unpublished by himself. Augustus, however, gave directions for a compromise, according to which the *Aeneid* was published, but without extensive revision. Varius is on record as noting a point about Virgil's composition: that he worked very slowly, and only completed a few verses every day.

Only fragments of his poetry have survived. His epics included a piece entitled *On Death (De Morte),* written from the Epicurean viewpoint, with special reference to the

vâ' ri us rōō' fus

death of Julius Caesar; twelve hexameters have been preserved by the Latin grammarian Macrobius (who flourished after A.D. 400). Horace announced that Varius was also going to publish an epic in honor of Augustus' chief friend and adviser Agrippa, and, according to the grammarians Helenius Acro and Pomponius Porphyrio (second and third centuries A.D.), this poem duly materialized; moreover, Porphyrio refers to a *Panegyric of Augustus* by Varius. Horace declares that as an epic poet he "surpasses all in spirit"; it is true that he wrote this before the publication of the *Aeneid,* but elsewhere he twice couples him with Virgil. And Virgil himself, in one of his *Eclogues,* pronounced Varius to be his superior, to judge by their publications to that date.

Porphyrio refers to the tragedies of Varius, but only one, the *Thyestes,* is known. It was performed in 29 B.C. at the games celebrating the victory of Octavian and Agrippa over Antony and Cleopatra at the battle of Actium two years earlier. Octavian gave Varius a very large monetary gift (a million *sestertii*) as a reward for the production. Only one fragment from the play, or at most two, have survived, but the celebrated rhetorician Quintilian declared it worthy of comparison with anything from Greek drama; and the historian Tacitus bracketed the piece with Ovid's *Medea* (also lost) as deserving of the highest praise. The epigrammatist Martial, too, mentioned Varius as a tragic poet, and Junius Philargyrius, a commentator on Virgil in the fifth century A.D., pronounced him to be the greatest of all (Latin) practitioners of tragedy. Another scholar Pomponius Porphyrio, two centuries earlier, had referred to Varius as a writer of elegies also, but nothing is known of his activity in this field. However, his reputation as an epic and tragic poet was so conspicuous that the complete loss of his works in these genres is one of the strangest phenomena of ancient literary history.

EDITIONS—W. Morel, Fragmenta Poetarum Epicorum et Lyricorum, 1927; O. Ribbeck, Tragicorum Romanorum Fragmenta, 1962.
ABOUT—W. S. Teuffel, History of Latin Literature, v 1, 1873; E. Lefevre, Der Thyestes des Lucius Varius Rufus: Zehn Überlegungen zu seiner Rekonstruktion, 1976.

VARRO, MARCUS TERENTIUS (116–27 B.C.), one of the most learned of Roman scholars, was born of a wealthy senatorial, land-owning family, probably at the Sabine town of Reate (Rieti in central Italy), though the early Christian Church Father and philosopher Augustine said he was born at Rome. Augustine added that Rome was also the place where he was educated, and this part of his statement we know to be correct, for Varro, like Cicero, became a pupil of the pioneer Roman philological scholar Lucius Aelius Stilo Praeconinus (born c. 150 B.C.). Subsequently, he studied at Athens under teachers who included the Academic philosopher Antiochus of Ascalon (c. 138–68 B.C.). Thereafter, he entered upon a Roman public career, in which he rose to the high rank of praetor. He served on sea and on land as a subordinate commander *(legatus)* of Pompey in the war against Sertorius in Spain, where he was proquaestor (76), and in Pompey's campaign against the pirates (67), for which Varro received the high decoration of the rostral crown *(corona navalis)*. In 59 he served as a member of the Board of Twenty, established, with the connivance of Caesar as consul, to settle Pompey's veterans on Campanian land. However, he was not a supporter of the First Triumvirate of Pompey, Caesar, and Crassus and in the same year wrote a pamphlet entitled *The Three-Headed (Tricaranus),* denouncing it.

During the Civil War between Pompey and Caesar, he held a command on behalf of Pompey in Further Spain but, after Caesar had defeated his colleagues in the province of Nearer Spain, capitulated without fighting. Caesar pardoned him and in 47 made him director of his scheme for establishing magnificent public libraries. In 43, after Caesar's death, the Second Triumvirate—Antony, Octavian (the future Augustus), and Lepidus—proscribed him, but he was granted refuge in the house of Antony's friend Fufius Calenus. His collection of books was plundered, but Octavian showed no further desire to persecute him, and he spent the rest of his life studying and writing.

Varro was a scholar of enormous versatility. He was also (with the single exception of Origen, according to St. Jerome) the most prolific writer in the whole of antiquity. His total output has been estimated at about seventy-four separate works, covering a great range of different subjects and extending over approximately six hundred and twenty books. Only two of these works, however, survive to any substantial extent. One belongs to the philological field, on which his early Roman training had been centered. It is a study entitled *On the Latin Language (De Lingua Latina)* in twenty-five books, of which Nos. 2-4 were dedicated to Varro's second-in-command Publius Septimius (probably forming an earlier smaller work); the remaining books were dedicated to Cicero. Only Books 5-10 have come down to us, for the most part with considerable gaps (Books 5 and 6 alone are preserved in their entirety); but the overall plan can be reconstructed from various references by other writers. After an introductory first book, the treatise consisted of three main parts. Books 2-7 dealt with etymology; an assessment of its utility as a branch of learning was followed by an analysis of the origin and sources of words and a study of their application to things and ideas. The second main part, comprising books 8-13, dealt with the derivation of words from other words, including conjugations and declensions. Then Varro weighed the rival grammatical principles of analogy (regularity) and anomaly (irregularity), which had exercised the Hellenistic specialists (setting Aristophanes of Byzantium and Aristarchus against Chrysippus and Crates); and he went on to discuss place-names and terms relating to time. The third part of the work, covering the last twelve books, was devoted to syntax, particularly stylistic and rhetorical ornament. Within the general framework, the arrangement of the study was somewhat disorderly, and many of Varro's etymological derivations were no less superficial and erroneous than those of his contemporaries. Others, however, were correct, owing to Varro's wide knowledge of antique forms; and his treatise contained a mass of incidental information on a large variety of topics.

He also wrote a considerable number of

esser monographs in this same linguistic field; but except for occasional quotations they are lost, and their subject matter is not always discernible. *On the Similarity of Words (De Similitudine Verborum)* reverts to the conflict between analogy and anomaly. Another study, *On the Usefulness of Speech (De Utilitate Sermonis),* was apparently written to defend forms discordant with analogy, provided that they were guaranteed by usage. *On Latin Speech (De Sermone Latino)* attempted to assess what constitutes good Latin. *On the Origin of the Latin Tongue (De Origine Linguae Latinae)* apparently had something to say about foreign intrusions in the language.

Varro also extended his activities on a wide scale to literary history and criticism. These are the themes of his essays entitled *On Poems (De Poematis)* and *On the Characteristic Features of Writers (De Proprietate Scriptorum).* He also wrote a work entitled *On Recitations* (if that is the meaning of *De Lectionibus*)—dealing with the public readings that had become a characteristic feature of the times. What *De Descriptionibus* was about is not clear; but *On Libraries (De Bibliothecis)* was clearly related to the duties Varro had been allotted by Caesar. Fragments of *Plautine Questions,* or *On the Comedies of Plautus (Quaestiones Plautinae,* or *De Comoediis Plautinis)* show that both the biography and the vocabulary of the comic dramatist received treatment. Moreover, Varro wrote at least three treatises on matters relating generally to the stage: *On the Origins of Drama (De Scaenicis Originibus), On Dramatic Productions (De Actionibus Scaenicis),* and *On Dramatic Performances (De Actis Scaenicis)*—however, the validity of these English translations of the Latin headings cannot be regarded as certain, and it is possible that the two last-named pieces were not independent but formed sections of the first.

Varro also wrote a fifteen-book work entitled *On Portraits (De Imaginibus),* also known as the *Hebdomades (Sevens)* because that numeral played a leading part in its arrangement. The work was an illustrated biographical dictionary containing seven hundred designs portraying eminent Greeks and Romans, in equal numbers, each accompanied by a descriptive verse epigram and a text in prose. This appears to have been the first illustrated book in Latin, probably composed under the influence of contemporary Greek illustrated volumes on botany.

The *Hebdomades* spans the fields of literature and history, and it was as a historian and antiquarian that Varro achieved his greatest influence. His most important work in this sphere, the loss of which is indeed lamentable, was his *Human and Divine Antiquities (Antiquitates Rerum Humanarum et Divinarum).* This gigantic compilation, virtually a historical encyclopedia, filled forty-one books, which were divisible into two main parts. The first part, consisting of twenty-five books, dealt with human affairs, relating especially to the history of Rome and falling, after an introductory book, into a number of subdivisions: relating to human beings (Books 2-7), places (Books 8-13), times (Books 14-19), and actions (Books 20-25)—that is to say, Varro put the successive questions: Who? Where? When? and What? The second part of the work dealt with matters of cult and constituted a general discussion of Roman religion, which Varro, a Stoic, saw as the mirror of philosophical verities. Books 26-38 were subdivided once again into Who, Where, and When—three books being devoted to each—and then in the thirty-ninth to the forty-first book he considered religious rites, classified according to the gods concerned (whom Varro arbitrarily defined according to their supposed characteristics). (The *Book of Augurs [Augurum libri]* may or may not have been part of this larger work.)

In spite of the loss of the *Antiquities,* large portions of its contents have filtered through to us at second hand, largely because Christian writers took exception to Varro's views in the field of Roman religion—and their refutations have come down to us. Varro was also the author of numerous other historical writings, large and small. *The Manner of Life of the Roman People (De Vita Populi Romani),* dedicated to Atticus, was a history of Roman society and culture, prompted by the *Manner of Life in Greece* by Dicaearchus of Messana (c. 300 B.C.). Varro's treatise entitled *On the Roman Nation*

457

(De Gente Populi Romani) dealt with the prehistory and early chronology of Rome; while a kind of appendix entitled *On Trojan Families* discussed the Roman houses that claimed ancestry from this source. *The Annals* and *Roman Studies (Res Urbanae)* seem to have carried the story into later periods, and the *Book of Tribes* analyzed this aspect of the constitution. *Reasons for Customs (Aitia)* is a title taken from Callimachus (c. 305–240 B.C.) and subsequently revived by Plutarch.

Varro also composed an autobiography *(De Vita Sua)* and two pieces relating to Pompey, an essay that appears to have been a biographical study *(De Pompeio)* and *Advice to Pompey (Isagogicus ad Pompeium)*, written for his consulship of 70 B.C., in order to instruct him on proper procedures for dealing with the Senate.

A further important, and by no means unoriginal treatise that does not fall readily into any literary category, was his *Logistorica* in seventy-six books, a collection of pieces in dialogue form that deal with a vast range of subjects including history, religion, education, health, fortune, and Varro's own personal experiences during his career. Each essay bore its own title, such as *Pius on Peace, Curio on Worship, Cato on Education, Marius on Fortune, Orestes on Madness.*

Of this vast output, Varro's only work to survive complete is one of his last, a three-book study entitled *On Farming (De Re Rustica),* written in dialogue form during his eightieth year, and dedicated to his wife Fundania. The first book is devoted to agriculture, the second to cattle, and the third to smaller stock such as birds, bees, and fish. The style is unadorned, abrupt, and conversational. The treatise suffers from its author's tendency to multiply headings and subdivisions. However, his erudition bursts out impressively, often at unexpected points, and is accompanied by many a touch of dry wit. This monograph may have been used by Virgil as a sourcebook for the *Georgics.*

Geography, astronomy, law, and rhetoric also belong to the apparently endless list of subjects about which Varro wrote; and, in addition, he published collections of his own speeches and poems. Moreover, he produced one hundred fifty books of *Menippean Satires* (between 81 and 67 B.C.), humorous essays in mixed prose and verse (or in prose with verse adornments) after the fashion of Menippus of Gadara, the Cynic philosopher of the third century B.C. About six hundred fragments of Varro's *Menippean Satires* have survived and about ninety titles, and these reveal that the lively and varied settings were often Greek and that Varro, like Menippus, was seeking to express serious matters in comic form. Many of the titles bear the names of mythological personages (Endymion, Eumenides, Meleager, Prometheus, Tithonus), but others are more philosophically or proverbially explicit: "Tomorrow I Believe, Today Not," "Know Thyself," "You Don't Know What Late Evening Will Bring," "The Cynic as Preacher," "The Funeral of Menippus," "On Philosophical Sects." A further group shows an interest in eating and drinking: "The Pot Has Its Measure" (or "On Drunkenness"), "On Eatables," "The Water-Dog." Varro emerges as a rigorous conservative, making fun of absurd modernities; he also mocks at philosophical dogmas and preaches the simple, old-fashioned, unluxurious life. Extant fragments reveal a great diversity of style, a willingness, despite his conservatism, to entertain stylistic novelties, and considerable powers of poetic expression. Consequently the disappearance of the greater part of the *Mennipean Satires* must be seen as a major loss.

With the exception of these *jeux d'esprit*, however, it was to scholarship that Varro devoted his life; and he was the greatest scholar that Rome ever produced—the untiring and insatiably curious propagator of immense quantities of knowledge, in addition to numerous mistakes.

EDITIONS—F. della Corte, Saturae Menippeae, 1953; A. Traglia, Opere, 1974; B. Cardauns, Antiquitates Rerum Divinarum: Die Fragmente, 1976. *With translation:* R. G. Kent, De Lingua Latina (Loeb ed.), revised ed., 1951; W. D. Hooper and H. B. Ashe, Cato and Varro: On Agriculture (De Re Rustica), revised ed. 1935; J. P. Cèbe, Satires ménippées (Budé ed.), 1972-77. J. Heurgon, Varron: L'économie rurale (De Re Rustica) (Budé ed.), v 1, 1978.
ABOUT—J. Collart, Varron grammairien latin, 1954; Varron (Entretiens Hardt, v 9), 1963; R. Pfeiffer, History of Classical Scholarship, v 1, 1968; J. E. Skyds

gaard, Varro the Scholar (Studies in De Re Rustica, 1), 1968; F. della Corte, Varrone: Il terzo gran lume romano, 1970; B. Riposati, Marci Terentii Varronis De Vita Populi Romani, 1972; R. Gelsomino, Varrone e i sette colli di Roma, 1975; D. J. Taylor, Declinatio: A Study of the Linguistic Theory of Marcus Terentius Varro, 1975; B. Tilly, Varro the Farmer, 1976; L. Deschamps, Étude sur la langue de Varron dans les Satires ménippées, 1977.

VARRO ATACINUS, AULUS TERENTI-US, Latin poet, was born in 82 B.C.; it is not known when he died. He came from the valley of the River Atax (Aude) in Gallia Narbonensis (Provence).

Varro Atacinus wrote verse of various kinds, only fragments of which are preserved. His *Bellum Sequanicum (Sequanian War)* was a chronicle-epic (a genre familiar from the epic poets Naevius [third century B.C.] and Ennius [239–169 B.C.]) about Julius Caesar's campaign against the Gallic tribe of the Sequani in 58 B.C. He also wrote a didactic, geographical piece, the *Chorographia,* from which ten excerpts have come down to us; and he composed love poems (probably in elegiacs) addressed to a mistress whom he called Leucadia, as well as satires of which Horace expressed a negative opinion. In addition, perhaps at the age of about thirty-five (if this can be deduced from an assertion by Jerome—unlikely in itself—that Varro "knew no Greek" until he was that age), he was the author of a free translation or adaptation of the *Argonautica* of the Greek Alexandrian poet Apollonius Rhodius (c. 295–c. 215 B.C.); a dozen quotations have survived, including some excellent lines. Varro's choice of such a theme suggests that he might, at this stage of his life at least, be classed as a member of the Latin Alexandrian school, who modeled themselves on the Greek Alexandrians.

WORKS—An isolated reference to a poem called the Epimenides or Epimenis (or Ephemeris?) leaves it somewhat uncertain whether the piece should not instead be attributed to Varro of Reate.
EDITIONS (of fragments)—E. Baehrens, Fragmenta Poetarum Latinorum Epicorum et Lyricorum, ed. by W. Morel, 1927.

var' rō a tå kī' nus

VEGETIUS RENATUS, FLAVIUS, Latin military historian, can be dated approximately from his reference to the deification of the emperor Gratian, whose death (A.D. 383) had therefore taken place before he wrote; and from the fact that as early as 450 a certain Flavius Eutropius had published a critical revision so that Vegetius' original must have been finished by then. Indeed it was probably completed a good deal earlier. The single emperor to whom it is addressed is unnamed but has been plausibly identified as Theodosius I, whose presence in Italy in 388–91 may well have prompted the work. Theodosius was a devout adherent of Christianity, and Vegetius, too, was professedly a Christian. His work is the *Epitoma Rei Militaris* or *De Re Militari,* a manual on Roman military institutions, the only textbook on the subject to have come down to us complete. The first of its four books, on the training of recruits, was published separately and dedicated to the emperor, who gave it a favorable reception and encouraged Vegetius to continue. This he did, compiling three additional books on other branches of military activity: Book 2 discusses organization; Book 3, tactics and strategy; and Book 4, fortifications and naval warfare. Each book has a preface, and Books 1 and 2 also have epilogues of a courtierlike rhetorical character.

Vegetius was a civilian official—perhaps the functionary in charge of free distributions of imperial funds *(comes sacrarum largitionum).* Neither a soldier nor a historian, he writes as an amateur, providing a mass of information that is theoretical, and derivative, and antiquarian. He names a number of sources—Cato the Elder, Frontinus, and a certain Paternus—and quotes edicts of Augustus, Trajan, and Hadrian; but clearly he did not always consult these authorities at first hand, and besides, he used other, unnamed, sources as well, belonging to a variety of different periods. His work is a conglomeration of inconsistencies and anachronisms. He did not realize, for example, that the revival of the "ancient" organization of the legion—which he proposed—was quite incompatible with existing conditions of warfare. Moreover, his arrangement of all

ve gē' ti us re nä' tus

459

this unstratified material is slovenly and careless.

It is remarkable, therefore, that, after the ancient world had ended, his monograph became extremely popular and gained the respect of leading military thinkers. In the Middle Ages his instructions about siege-craft (which display a Maginot Line obsession with defense) received careful notice; and the ninth century scholar Sedulius Scotus included Vegetius among his recommended readings. We possess more than one hundred forty manuscripts of his work, the earliest being of the tenth century; and Jean de Meung translated him into French as early as 1300. During the Renaissance, his advice about training and tactics was studied with the greatest care, and the work continued to serve as a military bible for centuries. One of its chief weaknesses—a lack of attention to the potential of cavalry —which made the work obsolescent at the time of its composition, became, by a curious reversal, an up-to-date and relevant concept in contemporary warfare once crossbows and gunpowder had weakened the shock power of mounted knights. Translations became abundant—Caxton's English edition of 1489 was taken from a French paraphrase by Christine de Pisan (1363?–1431).

A work in four books on veterinary medicine, the *Mulomedicina* on the cure of diseases of mules, was also attributed to Vegetius, probably with justice, though it could also have been composed slightly before his time. Its author professes to have consulted every Latin author who ever wrote on this topic, but his actual authorities are Columella, the agricultural writer of the first century A.D.; a more recent veterinarian named Pelagonius; and a Latin rendering of a Greek veterinary handbook (also used by Pelagonius) known as the *Hippiatrika*. An anonymous Italian translation of the *Mulomedicina* was published in 1544.

EDITIONS (of the De Re Militari)—C. Lang, 2nd ed., 1885. *Translations—in* T. R. Phillips, Roots of Strategy, 1940.
ABOUT—D. Schenck, Die Quellen der Epitoma Rei Militaris (Kho, Beiheft 22), 1930; A. Anderson, Studia Vegetiana, 1938; V. A. Sirago, Galla Placidia, 1961; G. R. Watson, The Roman Soldier, 1969; G. Webster, The Roman Imperial Army, 1969; M. Grant, The Army of the Caesars, 1974.

VELLEIUS PATERCULUS (GAIUS ?),

Latin historian, was born in about 19 B.C. (in the reign of Augustus) and lived at least until A.D. 30. He was of Campanian descent, and he seems at one point to suggest that his family came from Capua. He is proud of the military and political record of his paternal and maternal ancestors alike, the Velleii and the Magii—in particular of the fact that some of them, as he points out, served under the forebears of Tiberius. After serving with the army in the Balkans and in the east, Velleius went to Germany with Tiberius as a cavalry officer in A.D. 4. Two years later, while quaestor-elect, he helped Tiberius to suppress the Dalmatian and Pannonian revolts (in what are now Yugoslavia and Hungary) and continued to serve under him, taking part in his Triumph in A.D. 15, the year in which Velleius and his brother both held the important office of praetor.

Velleius was also devoted to another distinguished soldier, Marcus Vinicius (the son-in-law of Germanicus, who in turn was the adopted son of Tiberius). When Vinicius became consul in A.D. 30, Velleius dedicated the *Historiae Romanae* to him. The work was a comparatively brief survey of the history of Rome in two books. Book 1, the initial portion of which comprising six hundred years of narrative are lost, began with the history of the east and of Greece and concluded with the destruction of Carthage and Corinth in 146 B.C. The second book, carrying events to A.D. 30, is much longer and more detailed, no doubt in preparation for another (and, as far as we know, unfulfilled) project, a more comprehensive history from the Civil War period onward.

His narrative is continually interrupted by digressions: on Roman colonization; on the provinces; three on literary themes—one each dealing with early Latin literature, the Ciceronian epoch, and the age of Augustus (in which he strangely brackets Virgil with the obscure poet Rabirius)—and one on the narrowness of the limits within which the most flourishing epochs of Greek and Ro-

ve lē′ yus pả tûr′ kə lus

man literary achievement had been confined. Velleius shows some knowledge of Greek literature but does not quote any sources in this field. Among Romans he cites only two authorities, Cato the Elder, whose speeches greatly influenced the development of Roman literature, and the orator Hortensius, Cicero's chief rival in the law courts; however, he evidently drew on the Republican (annalistic) historians as well, in addition to the treatises of Nepos, Atticus, and Pompeius Trogus, historians of the first century B.C.

Livy, whose comparative independence earned him the nickname of Pompeian from Augustus, was presumably not enthusiastic enough toward the imperial regime to be employed by Velleius, who was a passionate supporter of the system. In particular, he was a wholehearted and unreserved admirer of Tiberius. He also speaks warmly of Tiberius' chief adviser Sejanus (whose downfall in A.D. 31 the composition of his *History* must therefore precede). For such reasons he is a prime example of the gushing, eulogistic type of history—a form of writing denounced in the next century by Tacitus who, like all other ancient authorities, ignores Velleius completely (so that only a single, corrupt, manuscript of his work survives). When these biases are discounted, however, his keen interest in the biographical approach produces useful results concerning both eminent and lesser historical personages—for example, his favorable account of Tiberius provides a useful counterblast to the excessive hostility of Tacitus. Moreover, Velleius supplies our only continuous account of the lengthy stretches of Roman history for which the work of Livy is lost.

All the same, Velleius is too unprofessional as a historian to be more than intermittently useful. For one thing, he is very far from profound, a lack accentuated by the brevity he decided to impose upon himself (indeed he refers frequently to the hasty treatment his chosen scheme imposes). For another, his literary manner jars heavily, and his determination to achieve the flashy, pointed characteristics of the Silver Age of Latin (which was just coming into vogue at that time) fails abjectly. He learned contemporary rhetoric but learned it badly and perhaps late in life; his style (apart from a rare felicitous touch) is affected, artificial, clumsy, and sententious. He indulges in far too many exclamations and rhetorical questions; and he loves to use overlong periods that are little more than independent clauses strung together end to end, made more cumbersome still by the interspersion of abundant parentheses.

EDITIONS with translation—F. W. Shipley, Velleius Paterculus and the Res Gestae Divi Augusti, 1924; H. Watelet (French), 1932.
ABOUT—E. Bolaffi, De Velleiano Sermone, 1925; I. Lana, Velleio Patercolo o della propaganda, 1952; J. W. Duff, Literary History of Rome in the Silver Age, 2nd ed., 1960; A. J. Woodman *in* T. A. Dorey, ed., Empire and Aftermath: Silver Latin, v 2, 1975, *and* Velleius Paterculus: The Tiberian Narrative, 1977.

VENANTIUS FORTUNATUS (Venantius Honorius Clementianus Fortunatus), bishop and writer of Latin poems, hymns, and prose, was born in about A.D. 540 and died in about 600. His birthplace was Tarvisium (Treviso) in northern Italy, and he was educated at Ravenna, the schools of which were then famous. But in c. 565 he left the country—shortly before its invasion by the Lombards—and visited various cities including Metz and Paris, where he became the friend of leading ecclesiastics and functionaries. Then he went to Tours to the shrine of St. Martin, by whom he believed he had once been miraculously healed. Next he moved to Poitiers, where Radegunda, the widow of the Merovingian king Lothar I (511–61), had founded a monastery; she had made her daughter Agnes its abbess, and the two women, both subsequently canonized, became close friends of Venantius. He did not leave Poitiers until 587, when both mother and daughter were dead; and then, after a visit to the valley of the Moselle, he returned to Poitiers and became the local bishop, remaining in this post until his death. He is revered as a saint in parts of Italy and France.

Venantius' large literary output included a biography of St. Martin (in four books of hexameters), which he undertook at the urg-
ve nan′ ti us fôr tyū nä′ tus

461

ing of his friend Gregory of Tours, and eleven books (with an appendix) of *Miscellanea,* nearly all in verse, mainly elegiac. Many of these poems, especially in books 3, 5, 7, and 9, are versified letters; Book 4 is composed chiefly of epitaphs; and there are a number of fulsome panegyrics. The sixth book includes an epithalamium on the marriage of Sigebert and Brunhilda; a poem about the garden of the dowager queen Ultrogotho that shows a keen appreciation of nature; and a piece, suggested by Radegunda, dedicated to the memory of the princess Galswintha—she had been murdered, but Venantius glosses this over. In Book 8, a long and vigorous poem in praise of virginity is addressed to Agnes as the Bride of Christ. Other pieces in the *Miscellanea* are cast into the form of cruciform acrostics or center around puns; in still others again Venantius expends his energies on trivialities such as dinner services.

These poems in classical meters, though echoing earlier pagan and Christian authors as faithfully as they can, only manage to follow them haltingly, owing to Venantius' shakiness about metrical and grammatical forms, a characteristic he shared with his contemporaries. But, apart from this, Venantius' pieces lack, for the most part, any real poetic inspiration so that as a representative of classical poetry he emerges as an inferior, laborious, latecomer.

On the other hand, Venantius' two hymns in nonquantitative, postclassical, medieval meters (trochaic tetrameters, and partly rhyming couplets of iambic dimeters) provide a startling and noble contrast. Their initial lines, *Pange lingua gloriosi praelium certaminis* and *Vexilla regis prodeunt,* appear in English translations as "Sing my tongue the glorious battle" and "The royal banners forward go" (or "The standards of the King advance"). Written to celebrate the arrival of a fragment of the True Cross presented to Radegunda at Poitiers by the Byzantine emperor Justin II (A.D. 565–78), both these compositions are superb examples of hymnology, marking the triumph of religious passion over classical form; Venantius has crossed the threshold into medieval poetry. These verses were sung in later ages by generations of French and Spanish sol-

diers and were even parodied in a political attack on a favorite of the English king Edward II (1307–27). The authenticity of a number of other hymns attributed to Venantius is open to question. He also wrote numerous prose works, including biographies of Radegunda and other saints.

EDITIONS—J. P. Migne, Patrologia Latina, v 88; F. Leo and B. Krusch, Monumenta Germaniae Historica: Auctores Antiquissimi, v 4, 1881–85.
ABOUT—D. Tardi, Fortunat, 1927; F. J. B. Raby, History of Christian Latin Poetry, 2nd ed., 1953; K. Langosch, Profile des lateinischen Mittelalters, 1967.

VICTOR, SEXTUS AURELIUS, Latin historian, worked in the latter part of the fourth century A.D. He came from a poor family in northern Africa, but in 361, at Sirmium (Sremska Mitrovica in Yugoslavia) he met the recently appointed emperor Julian the Apostate, who instructed him to come to Naissus (Niš) to take up the governorship of Pannonia Secunda (northern Yugoslavia); like Julian, Victor was a pagan. After the Christian restoration, despite his religion, he was made prefect of the city of Rome by Theodosius I (389). He was described by his fellow historian Ammianus Marcellinus as a man of exemplary sobriety.

In 360 Victor wrote a brief imperial history, *The Caesars (De Caesaribus),* from Augustus to Constantius II (who died in the following year). *The Caesars* follows the biographical approach of the second century historian Suetonius, drawing upon him and other writers but adding moralizing reflections of Victor's own, following the pagan senatorial tradition of the earlier historians Sallust and Tacitus. Victor's style is for the most part tiresomely rhetorical. He also reveals an excessive, traditional interest in portents and prodigies. Yet he also adds scraps to our historical information. Moreover, he displays a number of independent attitudes and makes an attempt to be fair about the personages and questions he discusses, deliberately putting forward both favorable and unfavorable points of view. For example, although proud of his senatorial rank and regretful that Gallienus, in the third century A.D., had excluded the senators from military commands, he is also prepared to offer criticisms of the behavior of the Senate at that time.

Later writers have often, perhaps too often, followed his division of post-Augustan imperial history into four periods: the first century until Nerva (96–98), including subdivisions; the "good" epoch ending with Severus Alexander (222–35); the "soldier emperors" of the third century; and the new era introduced by Diocletian (284–305). In concluding his account of the Julio-Claudians, Victor observes, with unconscious humor, that an emperor ought to be both good and cultured, but if he cannot manage both, he ought at least to be cultured.

Not long afterward an unknown compiler inserted the *Caesars* into a larger survey of Roman antiquity known as the *Triple History (Historia Tripertita)*—thus ensuring the preservation of Victor's work. The other two elements of the *Triple History* were an *Origin of the Roman Race (Origo Gentis Romanae),* which narrated traditional legends from Saturn to Romulus, and a treatise entitled *On Famous Romans (De Viribus Illustribus Urbis Romae),* which provided sketchy biographies from the kings of Alba Longa down to Antony and Cleopatra. Subsequently, yet another work was added to the collection, *The Epitome on the Lives and Characters of the Emperors (De Vita et Moribus Imperatorum* or *Epitome de Caesaribus),* which goes down to the death of Theodosius I (A.D. 395). The first eleven chapters of this epitome follow Victor closely, and its author is sometimes described as the Second Victor—but the author is not the Victor who wrote the *Caesars.*

The relation between these various specimens of briefly, superficially summarized history has attracted a great deal of discussion. In 1884 the German scholar A. Enmann declared that Victor, and the *Epitome,* and certain other historical summaries, all went back to a single common source, which he named the imperial history *(Kaisergeschichte).* Whether this was correct, or partly correct, is still actively disputed today.

EDITIONS (of Victor)—F. Pichlmayr (Teubner ed.), 1911; Origo Gentis Romanae: G. Puccioni, 1958; Epitome de Caesaribus: J. Schlumberger, 1974. Transla-

tions—W. K. Sherwin, Victor: Deeds of Famous Men, 1973; P. Dufraigne, Aurelius Victor: Livre des Césars (Budé ed.), 1975.
ABOUT—A. Momigliano, Conflict Between Paganism and Christianity in the Fourth Century A.D., 1963; R. Syme, Ammianus and the Historia Augusta, 1968, *and* Emperors and Biography, 1971; W. den Boer, Some Minor Roman Historians, 1972.

VIRGIL (Publius Vergilius Maro), Latin poet, was born in 70 and died in 19 B.C. His birthplace was Andes near Mantua (Mantova) in northern Italy. He seems to have been partly of Etruscan stock. His father was a farmer or a potter; his mother's name was Magia Polla. They were well enough off to send their son to be educated at Cremona and Mediolanum (Milan); later, he studied philosophy, rhetoric, and literary subjects at Rome, where he became a friend of the historian Pollio. Virgil made one appearance as speaker at the bar but soon abandoned public life—possibly when the civil war broke out in 49 B.C.—and moved to Neapolis (Naples) to study philosophy under the Epicurean Siro, whose property he subsequently inherited. When land in Italy was confiscated for settlement by ex-soldiers in 41 B.C., Virgil's father was one of those whose holdings were expropriated (perhaps permanently, despite ancient reports to the contrary) and he went to live with his son near Neapolis. At the time of the publication of the *Eclogues* (37 B.C.), however, Virgil was living in Rome; he became a member of the literary circle of Maecenas, trusted counselor of Augustus and literary patron, to whom he dedicated the *Georgics.* He also recommended his friend Horace to Maecenas, whom the two poets accompanied on a journey to Brundusium (Brindisi) in 37.

Soon afterward Virgil withdrew again to Campania, where he spent most of the rest of his life, keeping away from Rome as much as possible: he had residences at Neapolis and Nola by favor of Augustus, to whom Maecenas had introduced him. After working for eleven years on the *Aeneid,* he left Italy in 19 B.C. to travel in Greece and Asia Minor, with the intention of staying away for three years while he polished the poem—

after which he proposed to devote himself to philosophy. At Athens, however, he met Augustus, who asked him to return home to him. But Virgil, whose health was never good, fell ill at Megara and was brought back as far as Brundusium, where he died. His body was buried outside Neapolis, where his tomb was greatly revered in later ages. He left instructions that the *Aeneid,* which was still incomplete, should be burned, but Augustus ordered Virgil's friends Varius Rufus and Plotius Tucca to publish it, with excisions where necessary.

According to Suetonius' *On Poets,* Virgil had a tall, large figure and looked like a countryman; he was subject to frequent stomach and throat troubles and headaches, and he often suffered from hemorrhages.

The earliest of Virgil's published works were the *Bucolics* or *Eclogues (eclogae*— meaning selections—was not Virgil's own title, which is unknown). They comprise a collection of ten short, unconnected, poems in hexameters, composed between about 42 and 37 B.C. The earliest of these pieces are apparently Nos. 2, 3, 5, and perhaps 7, imitating the Idylls of the Greek pastoral poet Theocritus (c. 300–260 B.C.), of whose tradition Virgil claims to be the Romanizer. In the second Eclogue, Corydon laments that his fellow shepherd Alexis does not reciprocate his love. The third and the seventh contain poetical competitions between shepherds. In the fifth, two shepherds celebrate the death and deification of Daphnis, who may perhaps be identifiable with Julius Caesar. Nos. 1 and 9, referring to confiscations of land, are generally believed to refer to the seizure of Virgil's own farm in the year 41; the dialogue between the shepherds reflects the misery of the former occupants. The sixth Eclogue, mainly consisting of a song of the god Silenus, who tells of the creation of the world, was perhaps composed at the house of Virgil's Epicurean teacher Siro. The famous "Messianic" fourth is addressed to Pollio, orator, literary patron, and author, during the latter's consulship of 40 B.C. and predicts the return, under Pollio's guidance, of a golden age, in which a newborn boy shall govern a pacified world. The identity of the infant has been the subject of age-long debate; he was perhaps the ex-

pected child of Antony and Octavia (the sister of Octavian, the future Augustus), whose marriage was intended to seal the Peace of Brundusium (40 B.C.) reconciling the two triumvirs (in fact, however, the baby turned out to be a girl). The eighth Eclogue, of the following year, containing the songs of two shepherds, was likewise addressed to Pollio. The tenth, probably written in 37, represents Virgil's friend and fellow poet Cornelius Gallus, dying for unrequited love of Lycoris (the Cytheris of Gallus' own poems) and lamented by the woodlands and rocks.

The *Eclogues* show the influence not only of Theocritus but of recent or contemporary writers as well, including Meleager (fl. c. 60 B.C.) among the Greeks, and Catullus, Gallus, and Lucretius among Latin poets of the same century. Yet Virgil's poems, unpretentious and unheroic, exercise a unique, enigmatic fascination displaying a satisfying and piquant balance between the apparent simplicity of their rustic subject and the consummate, conscious artistry with which it is treated. The post-Virgilian title *Eclogues,* meaning selections, implies a disunity and lack of connection between the ten poems, but they are united by an emotional, dreamlike, association of ideas; and each poem is an elaborate and well-rounded unity within itself. As the summary of their contents shows, the scenery of the *Eclogues* is composite and imaginative, nowhere in the real world; the references to the traditional bucolic Arcadia are blended with topographical allusions from Sicily and northern Italy, relating to the homelands of Theocritus and of Virgil himself; the evocative, sensuous "enchanted light" in which this poetically conceived countryside is bathed establish Virgil as one of the great poets of nature, the model of much subsequent European poetry.

The fourth Eclogue owed its overwhelming fame to the belief, in late antiquity and the Middle Ages, that Virgil was prophesying the birth of Christ. The other, pastoral, pieces were occasionally imitated in the ancient world but came into their own in the Renaissance. In England, they were echoed by Spenser's *Shepherd's Calendar* (1579), and the tenth Eclogue inspired the *Lycidas* (published in 1638) of Milton, who also wrote other poems reflecting the influence of the Virgilian collection. In 1690, at Rome, a society named Arcadia was founded in memory of Queen Christina of Sweden, who had passionately admired the pastoral tradition. And in France, too, the same Arcadian ideal, as transmitted by the *Eclogues,* took on an active literary life for hundreds of years. Works by Rousseau, Chénier, and Mallarmé testify to its persistence and pastoral opera and ballet have also enjoyed long popularity.

Much of the success of these poems is due to Virgil's brilliant development of the hexameter. With a thousand devices, he achieves previously unimaginable beauties and subtleties. And then, in his next work this metrical and linguistic achievement grew ever more complex and sensitive—and profound. This second masterpiece, written between 37 and 30 B.C. in Campania, bears the title of *Georgics* (*Georgica,* agricultural poems); it comprises a didactic poem of 2,188 lines, divided into four books, on the subject of farming. Book 1 deals with the cultivation of crops and with weather signs. The theme of Book 2 is the growing of trees, especially the vine and the olive. Book 3 is concerned with the rearing of cattle; and Book 4 discusses the keeping of bees.

The general idea of hexameter poetry on such agricultural subjects goes right back to the remote Greek past of Hesiod; and, indeed, it is the Roman Hesiod that Virgil claims to be. It was an essentially patriotic task to bring the Hesiodic spirit to the language and people of Rome, and the four books of the poem are paeans in praise of Rome and the Italian countryside. Italy has now become a concept carrying profound emotional associations. But Italian unity had only been recently achieved; within living memory the country had been shattered by the savage rebellion of the social (Marsian) war and the grim civil wars that followed. So a dominant, emphatic theme of the *Georgics* is peace. It would be given to the world, Virgil forecasts, by "our young prince," who is Octavian, the future Augustus; and the poem is dedicated to Octavian's and Virgil's friend Maecenas, whom the poet credits with the inspiration of the *Georgics.* Their moral is the need for hard work,

and their theme is the life of the men who labored on their native soil—certainly in the spirit of Hesiod. Virgil's debt is not only to the classical Greece of Hesiod's time but to the subsequent Alexandrian movement as well. Even his very title echoes that of a Greek poem of the Alexandrian epoch, the *Georgica* of Nicander (second century B.C.), and the contents of the *Georgics,* too, owe something to another Alexandrian, Aratus of Soli (born c. 315 B.C.). Like the Alexandrians, Virgil was a townsman playing at being a countryman and exhibits that same duality of nature and artistry that had characterized the *Eclogues,* but now enhanced by even more refinement of language and meter.

And yet, strangely enough, much of the material that Virgil's genius brought into brilliant life was derived from pedestrian prose textbooks on agriculture. These had been a feature of Hellenistic Egypt, and Cato the Elder and Varro had composed Latin examples. Indeed, the latter's *Res Rusticae* had been published only about a year before Virgil began the *Georgics,* and the latter's work owes a good deal to Varro's treatise and reflects the public interest that followed its publication. Yet the *Georgics* quite obviously were very far removed indeed from a technical monograph. For one thing, they include numerous passages that rise far above the agricultural theme: a famous eulogy of rustic life and a compliment to Lucretius, who was Virgil's forerunner as a Latin didactic poet (Book 2); an encomium of Octavian (Book 3); a description of the pirate from Corycus in Asia Minor, who retired and grew a garden near Tarentum (Book 4), and in the same book the tale of Aristaeus, the pursuer of Orpheus' wife Eurydice, who died and was brought back from the underworld by Orpheus—though on the return journey he looked back, which was forbidden, and so she vanished.

"Virgil did not seek to instruct farmers, but to delight his readers," as Seneca the Younger pointed out. Seneca deeply admired the *Georgics,* and they have fascinated all subsequent ages as well. In the sixteenth century, they were the French essayist Montaigne's favorite reading; and parts of the English poet Milton's *Paradise Lost,* written

465

in the seventeenth century, are deeply imbued with their spirit. The English poet John Dryden called the *Georgics* "the best poem of the best poet." There was an immense crop of eighteenth century imitations, and, more recently, Cecil Day Lewis (poet laureate for 1968–72) saw Virgil as "chiefly dear for his gift to understand earth's intricate, ordered heart."

The *Aeneid,* left unfinished at Virgil's death, describes how the Trojan Aeneas escaped from the Greek sack of Troy and after many wanderings reached Italy, where he won himself a home by fierce warfare and became the ancestor of the founders of Rome. The poem consists of twelve books.

Book I, after introducing the poem's main theme, describes the great storm that brought Aeneas and his followers to the coast of Carthage and the hospitality of Queen Dido. In a long flashback Aeneas recounts, in Book 2, the fall of Troy, and in Book 3 describes his subsequent wanderings from Troy to Sicily. Book 4 is devoted to the tragic love of Dido and Aeneas, which for a time seemed likely, in defiance of fate, to link the destinies of Rome and Carthage. But Aeneas, in obedience to instructions from Jupiter himself, sails away from the African shore, and Dido kills herself. Book 5, a description of the funeral games for Aeneas' father, Anchises, provides a break in the tension. But this builds up again in Book 6, in which Aeneas, with the Sybil of Cumae as his guide, goes down to the Underworld to receive from the spirit of Anchises a great revelation of the future of Rome.

In Book 7 the fleet of the Trojans reaches the Tiber, and the Italian peoples muster to drive them out. In Book 8 Aeneas sails up the river to the future site of Rome and spends his first night ashore in the humble abode of the local monarch, Evander (which Virgil places on the very spot where Augustus' own house stood). Vulcan forges for him a magic shield, engraved with designs revealing a second prophecy of the future grandeur of Rome. In the center was depicted the sea battle of Actium, in which Augustus defeated Antony and Cleopatra. The last four books are devoted to the wars of Aeneas and his Trojans against the Latins and their allies, led by Turnus. After many

vicissitudes, a truce results in Turnus' agreement to fight a personal duel with Aeneas, in order to end the war. After Jupiter has conciliated his wife Juno, who favored the Latins, with a decree that they and the Latins would become united, the two heroes fight; Book 12 ends with the death of Turnus at Aeneas' hands.

The first half of the *Aeneid* is a kind of counterpart of the Homeric *Odyssey,* and the second half an Italian version of the *Iliad.* Yet for all the echoes of Homer's classic epics, the difference between Homer and Virgil is infinitely great, for their two epochs were separated by gulfs of time and civilization, during which the Greek epics of the Alexandrian school had brought a new infusion of romantic personal feeling, scholarly elaborateness, and experiments in language and subject. Thus, in particular, the association of epic and romance by the Alexandrian Apollonius Rhodius (third century B.C.) inspired the story of Dido and Aeneas, which to many is the supreme achievement of the *Aeneid.* Another strand in the tradition inherited by Virgil was the early epic in the Latin language itself, the leading practitioners of which were Naevius (c. 270–201 B.C.) and Ennius (b. 239 B.C.). Naevius had prefaced his contemporary theme (the First Punic War) with a mythological account of the origins and past stories of Rome and Carthage. Ennius' *Annals,* revered for their rugged, if crude splendor, were consciously echoed by Virgil at many points.

These are only a few of the forerunners of whom Virgil, despite his own outstanding originality, offers abundant and complex echoes. The Carthaginian episode, for example, and the subsequent warfare in Italy, owe a good deal to Athenian tragedy. Fate overrides both Dido's love and Turnus' courage. The dilemmas embodied in these conflicts are harrowing. Indeed, many modern critics have seen Virgil's sympathy for losing sides to be so great that it obscures the main issue. Aeneas, it is felt, seems insipid compared to Dido and Turnus and is presented as merely the obedient servant of destiny whereas they, on the other hand, are both authentically human. Nevertheless, Aeneas is deliberately portrayed in this way so as to represent the Stoic ideal, greatly admired by the poet and many of his contemporaries, of the man who presses on regardless of the obstacles and buffets interposed by life. The *Aeneid* does show a gradual, dramatic evolution of its main character. Aeneas does not become the impregnable Stoic all at once, or even quickly. He has his weaknesses, and it takes him much time to overcome them. The turning point comes in Book 6, when Virgil, in conscious adaptation of Book 11 of the *Odyssey,* brings him to the Underworld. This experience grants him initiation into his new world and a prophetic vision of its glories, disclosed by his dead father Anchises. But first he has a desperately hard and fearful task to perform, since Turnus and the Italians take up arms against him. In the end, however, helped by providence, he prevails over all his enemies and troubles—and everything is set fair for the foundation of Rome by his eventual descendants—for this is a national epic.

With profound, heartfelt earnestness, the *Aeneid* glorifies Rome and Italy as the enlightened ruler of the world—just as the *Georgics* had glorified the land itself. And Virgil is also honoring Augustus: Aeneas is by no means his replica, but very clearly his forerunner, for Augustus, when he defeated Antony and Cleopatra at Actium, had ended the intolerable waste and tragedy of decades of civil war and disturbance. The epic is further bent to the purpose of national glorification by the figure of Dido, who not only personifies the coming Carthaginian confrontation with Rome in the Punic Wars but also suggests, as Virgil portrays her, the more recent challenge of Cleopatra—whose name in fact is uttered by Anchises as he foretells the future.

Victory, however, is no longer seen as a triumphant, Homeric affair; Virgil knows all too well the weariness, frustration, and harrowing pathos that fighting and winning wars involve, and he seems, at times, to find this contradiction almost unendurable: this may have been the reason why he wanted the poem destroyed at his death. He saw the true victory, it appears, not so much in military conquest as in the human spirit's conquest of itself. Thus, in addition to its being a national epic, the *Aeneid* is a philosophical poem; and its main intention is religious.

The stock epithet the poet applies to Aeneas, *pius,* is a term meaning loyalty—to family, to country, and to the gods. Virgil was attentive to the old stories of the native Italian cults. He also respected the traditional tales of the Olympian deities and made full use of them, as part of the traditional epic machinery, in order to heighten dramatic conflicts and tensions. But he was, at heart, a monotheist, who believed, like the Stoics, in the rule of the world by an omnipotent deity who was also Fate.

These philosophic concerns are conveyed by means of an unprecedented mastery of words and sounds. Here are subtleties infinitely removed from the ballad style of Homer. Harmonizing style and meter, Virgil made the utmost of the elaborate inflections and versatility of the Latin tongue. His groupings of several lines into a structural unit brought an almost symphonic grandeur into poetry. With the assistance of every possible device of resonance and rhythm and flexible word-order, phrases and sentences and periods are welded together and interlaced to achieve a many-faceted narrative that is without parallel in the whole of European literature.

The *Aeneid,* said Sir Maurice Bowra (British classical scholar, 1898–1971), contains "an unparalleled variety of appeal," which "has helped many generations to formulate their views on the chief problems of existence." At the very beginning, it is true, objections to Virgil's "affected" style (as Augustus' admiral Agrippa called it), and criticisms of his elaborate borrowings from other poets, sometimes tended to overlook his outstanding originality. However, by as early as the first century A.D. his fame had reached the level of veneration and reverence. A mass of superstitious legends described his activities as a magician and enlarged on his supposedly miraculous powers. At least as early as the time of Hadrian (A.D. 117–38), recourse was had to the *Sortes Vergilianae* (Virgilian Lots)—attempts to prophesy the future by opening a volume of his works at random and noting whatever the passage revealed. Virgil's *Aeneid* soon became, as indeed it has remained, one of the most widely used schoolbooks in the world; and it was the subject of a great many learned commentaries, among which those by the fourth century grammarians Donatus and Servius are the most famous.

The number and caliber of extant manuscripts of early date—between the third and fifth centuries A.D.—testify once again to the immeasurable esteem in which Virgil was held. Early Christian writers were caught between their admiration of his poems and their distrust of his paganism. But Dante (1265–1321) regarded him as a prophet of Christianity and made him his guide to the Gates of Paradise. The first edition of Virgil was printed in about 1464. In 1882, on the nineteenth centenary of his death, Tennyson paid a tribute to the "wielder of the stateliest measure ever moulded by the lips of man."

WORKS (doubtfully or wrongly ascribed to Virgil)—Fourteen short epigrams and other poems, known as the Catalepton (Greek *kata lepton,* on a small scale), have been attributed to his youthful years; among them is an address to Siro's house, where Virgil lived for a time, and other contemporary references, too, appear in the poems. It is possible, but no more than possible, that some of these pieces are by Virgil—for example, a clever parody of Catullus. However, other poems in the collection seem too clumsy to be attributable to his authorship.

The Catalepton was placed by editors in the Virgilian Appendix—an appendix to Virgil's major works—grouped together with a series of longer poems likewise regarded as juvenile publications of Virgil but now rejected from this category and mostly ascribed to dates in the late Augustan period or the first century A.D. They include the Ciris (a miniature epic about the story of Scylla who was turned into the sea bird of that name); Copa (Hostess—of a tavern—who dances to castanets); Culex (Gnat, who is killed by a shepherd it has befriended and, reappearing to him as a ghost, describes the underworld); Dirae (Curses, uttered by a farmer against the farm he has lost); Lydia (separation from whom the writer laments—transmitted in manuscripts with the Dirae); Elegiae in Maecenatem (two unimpressive elegies on Maecenas' death); Moretum (Salad—a vivid account of a peasant's early rising and breakfast on a winter morning); and Aetna (a didactic poem of 644 lines explaining the volcanic activity of the mountain, possibly written in the time of the emperor Nero). The Virgilian Appendix also includes three minor poems of an obscene nature (Priapea).
EDITIONS—Eclogues, Georgics, and Aeneid: J. Conington, revised by H. Nettleship and F. Haverfield, 1883–96; A. Sidgwick, 1894; T. E. Page, 1894–1900. Eclogues: R. Coleman, 1977. Georgics: W. Richter, 1959; H. H. Huxley, Books 1 and 4, 1963. Aeneid: J. W. Mackail, 1930; R. D. Williams, 1960–73; R. G. Austin, Book 1, Book 2, 1964, Book 4, 1955, Book 6,

1978; F. Fletcher, Book 6, 1941; C. J. Fordyce, Books 7-8, 1977; K. W. Gransden, Book 8, 1976; W. S. Maguinness, Book 12, 1953. Appendix Vergiliana—Culex: F. Leo, 1891; Ciris: D. Knecht, 1970; R. O. A. M. Lyne, 1978. Catalepton: R. E. H. Westendorp Boerma, 1949–63. *Translations* (of all works)—H. R. Fairclough (Loeb ed.), revised ed. 1934–35; C. Day Lewis, 1966 (reprints). Eclogues: G. Johnson, 1960; E. V. Rieu (Penguin ed.), revised ed., 1967; W. Berg, Early Virgil, 1974; A. J. Boyle, 1976. Georgics: L. A. S. Jermyn, The Singing Farmer, 1947; S. P. Bovie, 1956, reprint 1966; H. A. Hedges, 1959. Aeneid: R. Humphries, 1951; W. F. Jackson Knight (Penguin ed.), 1956; T. H. Delabère May, 1961; P. Dickinson, 1961; L. R. Lind, 1963; J. H. Martinband, 1964; M. Oakley, 1967; A. Mandelbaum, 1971–72; F. O. Copley, 2nd ed., 1975. Budé ed: E. de Saint-Denis, Bucoliques, 1942, *and* Géorgiques, 1956; J. Perret, Énéide, 1978.
ABOUT: E. Nitchie, Vergil and the English Poets, 1919; R. Heinze, Virgils epische Technik, 3rd ed., 1928; C. Bailey, Religion in Virgil, 1935, reprint 1969; H. J. Rose, The Eclogues of Virgil, 1942; C. M. Bowra, From Virgil to Milton, 1945, reprint 1962; J. H. Whitfield, Dante and Virgil, 1949, *and* Dante e Virgilio, 1965; J. Perret, Virgile: L'homme et l'oeuvre, 1952; P. Grimal, Pius Aeneas, 1960; V. Pöschl, The Art of Vergil: Image and Symbol in the Aeneid, 1962; P. Boyancé, La religion de Virgile, 1963; F. Klingner, Virgils Georgica, 1963; H. Oppermann, ed., Wege zu Vergil, 1963; B. Otis, Virgil: A Study in Civilized Poetry, 1963; H. W. Prescott, The Development of Virgil's Art, 1963; G. N. Knauer, Die Aeneis und Homer, 1964; M. C. J. Putnam, The Poetry of the Aeneid: Four Studies in Imaginative Unity and Design, 1965, *and* Virgil's Pastoral Art, 1970; P. F. Distler, Vergil and Vergiliana, 1966; W. F. Jackson-Knight, Roman Vergil, 2nd ed., 1966; R. D. Williams, Virgil, 1967; M. Crosby, Vergil: The Aeneid, 1968; K. Quinn, Virgil's Aeneid: A Critical Description, 1968; W. S. Anderson, The Art of the Aeneid, 1969; W. A. Camps, An Introduction to Virgil's Aeneid, 1969; D. R. Dudley, ed., Virgil, 1969; J. Sargeaunt, The Trees, Shrubs, and Plants of Virgil, 1969; L. P. Wilkinson, The Georgics of Virgil: A Critical Survey, 1969; A. G. McKay, Vergil's Italy, 1970–71; G. Highet, The Speeches in Virgil's Aeneid, 1972; E. W. Leach, Virgil's Eclogues: Landscape of Experience, 1974; A. J. Boyle, ed., Ancient Pastoral, 1975; C. Monteleone, L'Egloga quarta di Virgilio a Constantino, 1975; T. M. Andersson, Homer, Virgil and the Medieval Legacy, 1976; F. Cupaiuolo, Trama poetica nelle bucoliche di Virgilio, 1976; R. Häussler, Das historische Epos der Griechen und Römer bis Vergil, 1976; W. R. Johnson, Darkness Visible: A Study of Virgil's Aeneid, 1976; R. Kettemann, Bukolik und Georgik, 1977; W. Pötscher, Vergil und die göttlichen Mächte, 1977; A. Thornton, The Living Universe: Gods and Men in Virgil's Aeneid, 1977; R. Chevallier, ed., Présence de Vergile (Caesarodunum, v 13 bis), 1978.

VITRUVIUS (Marcus Vitruvius Pollio), Roman architect and engineer and Latin
vi trōō′ vi us

writer, dedicates his work to an emperor, who is probably Augustus. To fix its author's date more closely is difficult, but he appears to be writing between 27 and 13 B.C.; and he describes himself as already an old man. At one point, he had served as a military engineer, in charge of artillery. He also designed important buildings—including the basilica (hall for meetings) at Fanum Fortunae (Fano on the Adriatic coast)—and he played some part in the erection of aqueducts. He has been identified, though without universal acceptance, with Julius Caesar's chief engineer Mamurra.

Vitruvius' treatise, in ten books, bears the title *On Architecture (De Architectura),* but this designation is misleading since, in addition to dealing with matters of all kinds related to architecture, he discusses a number of subjects that cannot be brought under any such definition at all. Book 1 treats of the qualifications and training of an architect and the various subdivisions of the art and then turns to town planning and the appropriate locations for buildings. Book 2 is concerned with architectural history and surveys various types of building materials. Books 3 and 4 consider temples and the different kinds of columnar "Order." The fifth book concerns itself with other public and civic buildings such as theatres (including their acoustics) and baths and harbor constructions. The subject of Book 6 is domestic architecture, both inside and outside towns; Book 7 handles various aspects of interior decoration, notably mosaic pavements, ornamental plaster work, and the employment of coloring. Book 8 discusses water supply; and Book 9, geometry, mensuration, and astronomy, with special reference to dials and water clocks. Finally, Book 10 is devoted to mechanical engineering, offering descriptions of engines of war and other machines of various kinds.

Although Vitruvius manifestly writes from a sound theoretical knowledge as well as from extensive personal experience, he curiously refrains from mentioning the important edifices of Augustus' reign and offers more than one expression of contempt for contemporary architectural achievements. His desire was to preserve what he regarded as the pure, classical, traditions of design, and his outlook was essentially backward-looking and Hellenistic. Indeed, it seems clear that much of what he writes is based on the precepts or practice of a Greek architect, probably Hermogenes (c. 200 B.C.), who had designed the Ionic temples of Dionysus at Teos and Artemis Leucophryne at Magnesia on the Maeander (both in western Asia Minor).

While claiming to be a keen reader (even outside his special field), Vitruvius, as he frankly admits, is no stylist. Apart from his introductory remarks, in which he makes a misguided attempt at rhetorical elegance, his language displays a professional dreariness, and he has recourse to the jargon, sometimes partly Hellenized, of his trade. Nevertheless, much of the information he provides—for example, rules of proportion, building materials, and methods of construction—is of great value. Above all, he insists on high standards of professional behavior. Many observations in the *Natural History* of Pliny the Elder (A.D. 23–79)—for example, on constructional methods and on wall paintings—are derived from Vitruvius, though without acknowledgment. Later, the planning of Roman cities in northern Africa, such as Thamugadi (Timgad) and Thugga (Dougga) was evidently based on his precepts or influence. In the fourteenth century the Italian poet Petrarch possessed or had read his work, though it was something of a rarity at the time. However, after the Italian Renaissance had got into its stride, Vitruvius achieved great fame and influence, becoming the principal authority studied by the architects of the day, who read his verdicts in the edition of his work published in 1486 and regarded them as final. Consequently, he fixed the classical style for great areas of Europe. In Italy Bramante (1444–1514), Michelangelo (1475–1564), and Palladio (1508–1580) were among his careful students, reading him not for historical reasons—as a chapter in past architectural history—but in order to apply what he said directly to their own practice. Alberti, too, had read a manuscript of Vitruvius, which he used as the model for his own *Ten Books of Architecture* in Latin.

Vitruvius was translated into Italian at least four times between 1521 and 1590, and there were French and Spanish editions, too, before the middle of the same century. The term *Vitruvian man* (illustrated by drawings by the Florentine sculptor, painter, architect, engineer Leonardo da Vinci [1452–1519] and the English artist, poet, and mystic William Blake [1757–1827]) refers to his explanation of the theory of ideal human proportions by means of a square related to a circle.

EDITIONS—F. Krohn (Teubner ed.), 1912. *With translation:* F. Granger (Loeb ed.), 1931–34; A. Choisy (French), 1909; C. Fensterbuch (German), 1964. Budé ed.: J. Soubiran (Book 9), 1969; L. Callebat (Book 8), 1973. *Translations* (English)—M. H. Morgan, 1914, 1960.
ABOUT—G. Giovanni *in* C. Bailey, ed., The Legacy of Rome, 1924; W. Sackur, Vitruv und die Poliorketiker, 1925; F. Pellati, Vitruvio, 1938; A. Boëthius, Vitruvius and the Roman Architecture of His Age (*in* Dragma M. P. Nilsson Dedicatum), 1939, *and* (with J. B. Ward-Perkins) Etruscan and Roman Architecture, 1970; H. Koch, Vom Nachleben Vitruvs, 1951; H. Plommer, Vitruvius and Later Roman Building Materials, 1973.

VOPISCUS, FLAVIUS. See Spartianus, Aelius

WALAHFRID STRABO, Latin poet and theologian, was born in about A.D. 809 and died in 840. His education began at the monastery of Reichenau (Germany) under two distinguished teachers, Jatto and Wettin; after Wettin's death in 824 he was sent to study under the Frankish theologian and scholar Hrabanus Maurus at Fulda, where he became attached to his fellow pupil and theologian Gottschalk. Subsequently, however, he left to take up the tutorship of the future king and emperor Charles II the Bald, son of the emperor Louis I the Pious by his second wife Judith, whose favor Walahfrid gained. Later still he became abbot of Reichenau. At one point he was dismissed from this post, but he regained it and remained in office until his early death.

When he was only eighteen he composed a long hexameter poem entitled *The Visions of Wettin,* in which he describes with great vividness the dreams of hell, purgatory, and wôl′ à frid or vä′ lä frid strä′ bō

paradise that Wettin had experienced shortly before his death; the piece provides one of the earliest of those imaginary pictures of the afterlife that were to culminate in Dante's *Divine Comedy.* Walahfrid also commemorated the erudition and beauty of his patron Judith in many poems. In addition, he was the author of versified biographies of saints, including a popular life of the Irish Saint Gall (c. 600) written in about 833. The *Scintilla (The Spark)* is a dialogue between the poet and his Muse, drawing a contrast between a brutal tyrant and the devout emperor Louis I.

In his last years Walahfrid wrote his poem *De Cultu Hortorum (On Horticulture),* often known as the *Hortulus (Little Garden).* With a simpler charm than that of Virgil's *Georgics,* Walahfrid tells how he started to cultivate his garden plot at Reichenau; and he lists the twenty-two herbs and flowers the garden contained, concluding with the roses and lilies that the Church had chosen for its saints in heaven and martyrs on earth.

EDITIONS—L. Traube, Monumenta Germaniae Historica: Poetae Latini Aevi Carolini, v 2; R. Thuli, De Vita Beati Galli (Life of St. Gall), 1890; D. A. Traill, Walahfrid Strabo's Visio Wettini, 1974. *Translations* (of Hortulus)—R. S. Lambert, 1924; M. Joynt, 1927.
ABOUT—H. Waddell, The Wandering Scholars, 1927; F. A. Wright and T. A. Sinclair, 1931; W. Schroeder; Kritisches zu neuen Verfasserschaften Walahfrid Strabos, 1957.

WARNEFRID. See Paul the Deacon

XANTHUS, Greek historian, lived in the fifth century B.C. The son of a certain Candaules, he came from Sardes (Sart) in Lydia (western Asia Minor) and was not a Greek by extraction, but a Lydian. Dionysius of Halicarnassus brackets him with Hellanicus and Damastes as "extending down to the time of Thucydides (c. 460/55–400). Xanthus was a logographer *(logographos),* in the particular sense in which Thucydides employed the term, meaning one of these early historical writers who were the forerunners and contemporaries of Herodotus.
zan′ thus or ksän′ thus

Xanthus wrote a *History of the Lydians (Lydiaca),* extant fragments of which written in the Ionic dialect display an interest in anecdotes and folktales, frequently of non-Greek and oriental origin; Herodotus may have owed his own similar taste to Xanthus, of whose work, according to the later historian Ephorus (c. 405–330 B.C.) he made use. Characteristic of Xanthus' piquant stories was a tale of a Lydian king who ate his own wife, and then, waking up in the morning to discover her hand in his mouth, committed suicide. The work also contained scientific speculations about geological transformations of the countryside, once again after the manner of Herodotus, who had engaged in similar discussions. In the Augustan age, the historian Nicolaus of Damascus displayed a familiarity with details of Lydian legend and tradition that do not appear in Herodotus; these passages in Nicolaus' work contain traces of Ionic forms, and it seems probable that they are derived from Xanthus' *Lydian History* or from one of its later adaptations. It is not clear whether another treatise attributed to Xanthus, the *Magica,* on Persian religion, was part of his *History* or a separate monograph.

Diogenes Laertius, in the third century A.D., made a statement that can perhaps be regarded as an indication that Xanthus wrote the life of his older contemporary the philosopher-scientist Empedocles. "Aristotle," says Diogenes, "declares him [Empedocles] to have been a champion of freedom who did not favor rule of any kind, seeing that, as Xanthus reports in his account of him, he declined the kingship when it was offered to him, obviously because he preferred a frugal life." If that is correct, then Xanthus (for it may reasonably be assumed that he is the man to whom Diogenes is referring) takes his place with Stesimbrotus of Thasos and Ion of Chios (d. 422 B.C.) and Scylax of Caryanda (who was a Persian subject like himself) among the earliest representatives of the art of biography.

EDITIONS—F. Jacoby, Fragmente der griechischen Historiker, 3c, 765F 33, *and* 2A 90 (Nicolaus).
ABOUT—L. Pearson, Early Ionian Historians, 1939; H. Diller, Zwei Erzählungen der Lyder Xanthus *in* Navicula Chiloniensis: Studies in Honor of F. Jacoby, 1956; G. Bernagozzi, La storiografia greca dai logografi ad Erodoto, 1961; H. H. Scullard, Two Halicarnassians and a Lydian *in* Ancient Society and Institutions: Studies Presented to V. Ehrenberg, 1966; A. Momigliano, The Development of Greek Biography, 1971.

XENOPHANES, Greek theologian, scientist, and poet, was born in (perhaps) about 570 B.C. and died in about 475. He came from Colophon in Ionia (western Asia Minor), which he left at the age of twenty-five, probably after its capture by the Persians in 545. He then lived the life of an exile for at least sixty-seven years. On leaving his homeland, he resided first in Sicily—at Zancle (Messana, now Messina), Catana (now Catania), and perhaps also at the court of King Hiero I of Syracuse (478–467)—then at Elea (or Velia, the modern Castellamare di Bruca) in southwestern Italy, where Ionians (Phocaeans) had founded a Greek colony in about 540.

Diogenes Laertius, third century Greek biographer, states that Xenophanes recited his own poems. They included pieces entitled *The Founding of Colophon* and *The Colonization of Elea,* the latter being the earliest known epic relating to a more or less contemporary historical event. These works have not, however, survived; his existing writings belong either to elegiac compositions or to *Silloi* ("squints"), a satirical genre of hexameters and iambics, subsequently made famous by Timon of Phlius (c. 320–230 B.C.), who recognized Xenophanes to have been his literary ancestor.

As a theologian, Xenophanes ruthlessly pulls to shreds the concept of the gods as they are portrayed in the Homeric and Hesiodic epics. In the first place, as he points out, they are implausibly depicted in those poems as immoral and criminal. Secondly, there is no good reason for regarding the gods as anthropomorphic at all; they are only given human shape, he perceives, because it is humankind that is envisaging them; and in this connection he notes that different races credit their divinities with their own particular ethnic characteristics, the Ethiopians imagining their gods as black

ze nof' á nēz or kse nof' á nēz

and snub-nosed, and the Thracians as red-haired and blue-eyed. By the same token, he observes, oxen and lions, if they had hands and were able to make images of the gods, would likewise make them in their own image.

However, Xenophanes goes on to insist that there is a god—but only one—an eternal self-sufficient Consciousness that directs the universe (with which it is synonymous) by the power of thought and spirit—remaining in itself, without movement (and thus foreshadowing the Unmoved Mover of Aristotle). Whether Xenophanes saw this deity in a monotheistic or pantheistic sense, or even as only the supreme god among other gods (which is what one fragment suggests), it does appear that his conception, while owing considerable debts to Persian thought, represents an important step forward in the intellectual history of Greece.

Certain other fragments of Xenophanes treat of natural phenomena, in pursuance of the traditions of the Milesian pre-Socratic philosopher-scientists such as Thales, Anaximander, and Anaximenes. Despite the retention of some naive and rudimentary popular theories, he displays an unusually keen talent for scientific observation. Thus, from the discoveries of shells and fossils of sea creatures in rocks he infers a period in which the land was covered by the sea, a conclusion that led to his further belief that a process of alternate flooding and drying out had characterized the evolution of the earth.

However, Xenophanes also offers impressive warnings about the inevitable limitations of human knowledge. "No man knows, or will ever know, the truth about the gods and all that I speak about. For even if someone happened to tell the complete truth, yet oneself does not know it; but all things are matters of opinion. . . . Let what I say be interpreted as resembling the truth. . . . The gods have not revealed all things to men from the beginning; but by searching men find out better in time."

In his elegiac poems, Xenophanes, among other things, ridicules the doctrine of the transmigration of souls. He also comments on aspects of human society. For one thing, in anticipation of Euripides and Isocrates,

he courageously denounces the accepted standards of virtue *(arete),* which caused people to lavish so much applause on men of physical prowess such as wrestlers, boxers, and charioteers. In his view, the achievements of such persons were far less substantial and useful to the good government and material prosperity of the state than exploits of an intellectual character—such as his own. Elsewhere he deplores the introduction of Lydian luxury into Colophon. On a more private level, a pleasant description of a dinner party reveals him as displaying a blend of simple and fastidious tastes, favoring the reasonable enjoyment of social pleasures. He was regarded by Plato as one of the founders of the Eleatic school of philosophers.

EDITIONS—M. Untersteiner, Senofane: Testimonianze e frammenta, 1972. *With translation:* G. S. Kirk and J. E. Raven, The Presocratic Philosophers, 1960; A. Farina, Senofane di Colofone: Ione di Chio, 1961.
ABOUT—A. Lumpe, Die Philosophie des Xenophanes von Kolophon (Munich, dissertation), 1952; H. Thesleff, On Dating Xenophanes, 1957; H. Fränkel, Wege und Formen frühgriechischen Denkens, 1960; W. K. C. Guthrie, History of Greek Philosophy, v 1, 1962; E. Hussey, The Presocratics, 1972; M. C. Stokes, One and Many in Presocratic Philosophy, 1972.

XENOPHON, Greek historian and man of letters, was born in about 428 B.C. and died in about 354. He was the son of a well-born Athenian named Gryllus. Xenophon approached manhood during the last turbulent years of the Peloponnesian War (431–404), in which he himself took part as a cavalryman; and perhaps he was also present at the sea battle of Arginusae (406). He got to know Socrates and became his keen admirer, though probably not his pupil, since he possessed no aptitude for philosophy himself. Xenophon was a man of right-wing political tastes, with a simple belief in the virtues of strong leadership; he probably found life uncomfortable when the short-lived oligarchic revolution came to an end and democracy was restored in Athens (403). In any case, he moved away from the city.

In 401 his Boeotian friend Proxenus invited him to join the expedition (*anabasis,* zen' ə fun or ksen' ə fun march up country) of Cyrus the Younger who was in rebellion against his brother King Artaxerxes II of Persia. After Cyrus had been defeated and killed at Cunaxa (401), Xenophon was elected a general and played a major part in the evacuation of the Greek expeditionary force to Trapezus (Trabzon, northeastern Turkey). Then, after a brief period of service with the Thracian king Seuthes, he offered himself and his troops to Thibron—a general from Sparta, which was at war with Persia—and engaged as his ally, in operations that continued under Thibron's successor Dercylidas (399–397). In Xenophon's absence, however, at the time when Socrates had just been executed and his associates were discredited, the Athenians formally pronounced a sentence of exile upon him, involving the confiscation of his property. In 396–394 he fought against the Persian satrap Pharnabazus in the service of Agesilaus, king of Sparta (398–361), to whom he formed a strong attachment; and when Agesilaus was called home in 395 at the outset of the Corinthian War (in which Sparta was pitted against Thebes), Xenophon took part in the battle of Coronea (394), thus fighting against his own Athenian compatriots, who were in alliance with Thebes. Subsequently, he settled with his family at Sparta.

He was presented by the Spartans with an estate at Scillus in Elis (northwestern Peloponnese) where he spent the next two decades living the life of a literary country gentleman, dividing his time between hunting and writing. The Spartans appointed him as their envoy (proxenos) to look after such of their citizens as visited Olympia nearby. When, after its defeat by the Thebans at the battle of Leuctra (371), Sparta lost possession of Scillus, Xenophon and his family moved to a new residence on the isthmus of Corinth. However, relations between Athens and Sparta having now improved, the Athenians repealed his condemnation to exile (c. 365), and it seems likely that he returned to Athens and lived there. In 362 his sons Gryllus and Diodorus (by his wife Philesia) were members of an Athenian contingent fighting with the Spartans against the Thebans at Mantinea, and Gryllus was killed. Xenophon was probably on a visit to Corinth when he died.

The most important of his numerous literary works was his *Hellenica,* a history of Greece in seven books from 411 to 362 B.C. By starting the work at 411, he joined the group of writers who deliberately attempted the task of continuing the history of the great Athenian historian Thucydides (which terminated at that point). Like the others, however—notably Cratippus and Philistus in the fourth century—Xenophon is not in the same class as their forerunner and master. As his banal, sermonizing remedies for moral and social evils indicate, he is vastly inferior to Thucydides in intellectual depth; and his reliability has been discredited by the discovery, on a papyrus, of the so-called Oxyrhynchus Historian, who gives conflicting and evidently superior versions of some of the events Xenophon describes. Moreover, the latter's diction had moved away from the Attic way of speech, the medium of fifth century masterpieces, to a more relaxed and less distinctive language— anticipatory of the common tongue of later Greece—which, although it makes less demands on the reader, wholly lacks the tense brilliance of Thucydides.

Yet Xenophon does show a talent for the succinct and quick-moving description of exciting events: he is capable, at his best, of handling single episodes and scenes with an effectiveness that foreshadows the dramatic school of history, exemplified by Duris of Samos (c. 340–260 B.C.). The *Hellenica* is also of interest as the self-expression of an Athenian exile who, although sympathizing with his city's plight at the disastrous end of the Peloponnesian War, resembled many other upper-class Greeks in feeling a profound admiration for the Spartan foe. Xenophon expressed this sentiment in his *Spartan Constitution* (c. 388). Nevertheless, when the Spartans seized the citadel of Thebes (382), he was profoundly disillusioned and withdrew his support; but only for a time.

However, it is the *Anabasis* (March Up Country) that shows him at his best. Here is a fresh and vivid account of an adventurous enterprise in which he himself had played a leading part. Rarely has a good story been so well told by one of its major participants.

One of the passages that has remained in the memory of posterity describes the moment when the weary Greek column, after its long retreat through inhospitable lands, first catches sight of the welcome sea. For certain events during the march, Xenophon had to depend on others—notably the Persian court doctor Ctesias of Cnidus, for his version of the decisive battle of Cunaxa—but most of the narrative is based on his own experiences and observations, from which a great deal of picturesque description and ethnology emerge. He holds strong views on the desirability of discipline among the troops and yet, at the same time, shows great sympathy for the rank and file—indeed, in the opinion of his critics, a sympathy that was altogether excessive—so that their day-to-day existence receives a most unusual degree of attention in his work. A slightly jarring feature of the whole work, however, is Xenophon's continual self-righteousness about his own behavior. His account is a deliberate personal justification, intended as a riposte to the story told by another participant in the expedition, Sophaenetus of Stymphalus, which presented Xenophon in a much less favorable light.

The *Anabasis* exhibits Xenophon's deep interest in people's characters; his acutely observed sketches of Cyrus the Younger and the Greek leaders point the way to his later excursions into biographical writing, notably in his *Agesilaus*, a posthumous panegyric of the Spartan king of that name that is something of a landmark in the early history of biography. Another larger biographical work similarly concerned with a monarch and monarchy was the *Cyropaedia* or *Education of Cyrus* (the Elder, the founder of the Persian monarchy, d. 529 B.C.), which is now in eight books and is cast in the form of a historical novel. Designed (according to Gellius, the Latin writer of the second century A.D.) as a counterblast to Plato's *Republic,* this treatise presents an ideal ruler putting into practice Xenophon's Spartophile notions of authority, organization, moral reform, and family life. *The Hero,* in the form of a dialogue between King Hiero I of Syracuse and Simonides of Ceos who was his visitor in 476, is perhaps a postscript to the *Cyropaedia.* It discusses whether an

474

autocrat's position could be a happy one and how he could secure the loyalty of his subjects.

On *Horsemanship* (c. 380?), the oldest surviving complete work on this theme, is an authoritative production. A final chapter on the armor of horses and horsemen may have been added in c. 357, when Xenophon also wrote the *Hipparchicus,* dealing with a wide range of practical, topical questions relating to the state cavalry. *On Hunting (Cynegetica),* about hunting wild boar and deer, and especially hare, was either written early in Xenophon's career or was the work of another author. *On Ways and Means* (or *On Revenues,* c. 355/3) puts forward sensible views on the management of the state.

A further group of Xenophon's writings centers around the figure of Socrates, whom he was very proud to have known. The *Apology,* written in c. 384, some fifteen years after Socrates' condemnation and death, describes his conduct before, during, and after his trial. The compilation in four books known since Renaissance times as the *Memorabilia (Memoirs)* (c. 381, c. 355/4), comprises further recollections of Socrates. *Household Management (Oeconomicus)* (c. 362/1) purports to reproduce Socrates' discussions with Critobulus and Ischomachus, in the course of which he offers lessons on domestic affairs and proper behavior to Ischomachus' wife—who no doubt stands for Xenophon's own wife. The *Symposium* describes a fictitious party given by a rich Athenian named Callias in c. 422, at which Socrates is presented as one of the guests.

In the absence of other reliable information—we have only that of Plato, whose view of the man is often colored—Xenophon is of some importance as an interpreter of Socrates, though the information he provides is often as disconcerting and misleading in its own way as Plato's. Socrates appears in Xenophon's writings, especially in the *Memorabilia,* as a prosaic figure who displays a robust, paradoxical, common sense. Often, his alleged opinions—for example, on the Good and Beautiful—do not accord with those described by Plato; and Xenophon makes the point that Socrates was willing to die, not for the spiritual reasons given in Plato's *Apology,* but in order to escape the disabilities of old age. However, Xenophon should not necessarily be regarded as the more reliable of the two, since the discussions of wealth and household and state management, for example, which are attributed to Socrates in the last two books of the work, are too closely related to Xenophon's own tastes and interests to seem authentic—and the same applies to Socrates' alleged opinions and reflections in the *Oeconomicus.* Xenophon's refutation of the charges on which Socrates was tried and sentenced to death is based on a literary exercise by a certain Polycrates, and his account in the *Apology* of Socrates' last hours is derived from the dead man's friend Hermogenes, who attended him in his dying moments.

Xenophon was a country gentleman who enjoyed a good story, but he was also much more besides. Pious and superstitiously attentive to omens, he was nevertheless a competent man of affairs. The basic causes of events did not interest him greatly, but his assessment of current opinions and trends showed considerable acuteness. His versatility, too, was most impressive—and in one sphere, namely military affairs, although not a professional soldier by training, he made himself into something of an expert, especially in cavalry tactics. Thoroughly and un-self-consciously reactionary, he was a curious blend of extreme egotism and philanthropy, abounding in optimism about life and human nature. He wrote with unaffected charm and held up the clearest of mirrors to certain aspects of his times as he saw them.

Xenophon received little recognition in the early Hellenistic age but was greatly admired by eminent Romans including Scipio Africanus, Cato the Elder, Cicero, Julius Caesar, and Mark Antony. In the Roman imperial period interest in his work continued to rise, owing to the revival of an "Attic" approach, which favored his simple, intelligible prose, and because it was felt that Xenophon alone among earlier writers possessed all the qualifications of the historian who also led an active public life. In the first century A.D. the rhetorician Quintilian spoke warmly of his achievement; and in the following century the Greek satirist Lucian

even ranked him with Herodotus and Thucydides.

But he came truly into his own in the fifteenth century, from which thirty-eight codices of his works are known, as well as a whole series of Latin translations, while numerous vernacular versions followed from 1502 onward. Xenophon was one of the authors whom the great pioneer archeologist Johann Winckelmann (1717–68) studied in order to prepare himself for the visual arts, and Goethe went on from Homer not only to Plato but to Xenophon's *Memorabilia* as well. Moreover, when Greek was taught extensively in schools, the *Anabasis* figured very largely in elementary curricula.

WORKS (wrongly attributed to Xenophon)—The Constitution of Athens, preserved among his works, is not by his hand and is earlier in date: it was evidently written in c. 431 B.C., by an unidentifiable critic of the Athenian democracy who is described as the Old Oligarch. Seven fictitious letters of Xenophon were also in circulation in later antiquity.
EDITIONS—Hellenica: G. E. Underhill, 1906; T. Horn, Xenophon: The Fall of Athens (selections from Books I and II), 1978. Anabasis: W. Vollbrecht, 1907–12; J. Antrich and S. Usher, Xenophon: The Persian Expedition, 1978. Spartan Constitution: F. Ollier, 1934. On Horsemanship: F. Delebecque, 1950. Hiero: J. Luccioni, 1948. Cyropaedia, Oeconomicus: H. A. Holden, 1883–89. Ways and Means (Poroi): G. B. Giglioni, 1970 *and* P. Gauthier, 1976. Memorabilia, Symposium, Apologia, Oeconomicus: R. Laurenti, 1961. Constitution of Athens (Pseudo-Xenophon, Old Oligarch): L. Stecchini, 1950. *Translations* —Hellenica: R. Warner, History of My Times (Penguin ed.), 1966; Anabasis: W. H. D. Rouse, The March Up Country, 1948, reprint 1964, *and* R. Warner, The Persian Expedition, 1949; Spartan Constitution: J. M. Moore, Aristotle and Xenophon on Democracy and Oligarchy, 1975; On Horsemanship: E. Delebecque, Le commandant de la cavalerie (Budé ed.), 1978; Cynegeticus: E. Delebecque, La chasse (Budé ed.), 1978; Hiero: L. Strauss, On Tyranny, revised ed., 1968; Cyropaedia: R. Mongan, 1880–81 *and* P. Holland, 1936 (reprint from 1632), *and* E. Delebecque, Cyropédie (Budé ed.), 1978; Oeconomicus: B. J. Hayes, 1888; Memorabilia and Apologia: A. S. Benjamin, Recollections of Socrates, and Socrates' Defense Before the Jury, 1965; Memorabilia and Symposium: H. Tredennick, Memoirs of Socrates and the Symposium (Penguin ed.), 1970; Constitution of Athens: K. Hughes, M. Thorpe, M. Thorpe, The Old Oligarch: Pseudo-Xenophon's Constitution of Athens, 1968, *and* J. M. Moore, Aristotle and Xenophon on Democracy and Oligarchy, 1975, *and* C. Leduc, La Constitution d'Athènes attribuée à Xénophon, 1977.
ABOUT—L. V. Jacks, Xenophon: Soldier of Fortune, 1930; G. Colin, Xenophons Historien, 1933; K. M. T.

XENOPHON OF EPHESUS

Atkinson, The Respublica Lacedaemoniorum Ascribed to Xenophon: Its Manuscript Tradition and General Significance, 1948; J. Luccioni, Les idées politiques et sociales de Xénophon, 1948, reprint 1957; A. H. Chroust, Socrates, Man and Myth: The Two Socratic Apologies of Xenophon, 1957; F. Delebecque, Essai sur la vie de Xénophon, 1957; K. Widdra, Xenophon On Horsemanship, 1965; W. P. Henry, Greek Historical Writing: A Historiographical Essay Based on Xenophon's Hellenica, 1966; G. R. Nussbaum, The Ten Thousand, 1967; M. J. Fontana, L'Athenaion Politeia del quinto secolo a.c., 1968; S. Taragna Novo, Economia ed etica nell'Economico di Senofonte, 1968; J. K. Anderson, Military Theory and Practice in the Age of Xenophon, 1970, *and* Xenophon, 1974; M. Grant, The Ancient Historians, 1970; L. Strauss, Xenophon's Socratic Discourse: An Interpretation of the Oeconomicus, 1970, *and* Xenophon's Socrates, 1972; E. M. Soulis, Xenophon and Thucydides, 1972; L. Canfora, Erodoto Tucidide Senofonte: Letture critiche, 1975; C. H. Grayson, Did Xenophon Intend to Write History?, *in* B. M. Levick, ed., The Ancient Historian and His Materials, 1975; W. E. Higgins, Xenophon the Athenian, 1977.

XENOPHON OF EPHESUS (or **EPHESIUS),** Greek novelist, can be dated, within wide limits, by two pieces of internal evidence. In the first place, he mentions the Eirenarchy, an official post in Cilicia that did not exist before the time of the emperor Trajan (A.D. 98–117). Secondly, the Ephesian temple of Artemis plays an important part in his story, and no mention is made of its destruction, which took place in A.D. 263. On general grounds, too, he is likely to have lived and worked earlier, because he borrows very closely indeed from his fellow romancer Charito of Aphrodisias, whose papyri include at least one that belongs to the second century A.D.

Xenophon's novel is called the *Ephesian Tale (Ephesiaca)* or *The Adventures of Anthea and Habrocomes.* The novel tells how the youthful hero and heroine Habrocomes and Anthea meet on the occasion of the procession of Artemis, fall in love, and get married (although the bridegroom had earlier said that he wanted to "rise above" the world of Eros). They are warned, however, of perils in store for them by the oracle of Apollo of Colophon. In order to avoid these dangers, the relatives of the young couple send them on a journey. During the voyage,

zen′ ə fun or ksen′ ə fun   e′ fà sus

476

however, they become separated and are thereafter subjected to all the traditional tribulations of this genre. When all the hazards are overcome and the couple is finally reunited, Anthea declares to her husband, "I have escaped the threats of brigands, the plots of pirates, the outrages of brothelkeepers, and chains, and pits, and beams, and poisons, and burials—but you, Habrocomes, have you remained chaste?" The answer is, for both, yes, in spite of every trial. Even when Anthea was compelled to become the wife of another man, a poor shepherd, it turned out that despite his humble origins he was the possessor of a truly noble character and had therefore refrained from taking advantage of her purity.

Xenophon piles up sensations more thick and fast than any other Greek novelist; and they are crammed into so narrow a compass and narrated in such a staccato style that some have believed this work of five short books to be a mere abridgment of a lost original that consisted of ten. This proliferation of thrills imposes a severe strain on the reader's credulity, and Xenophon's poor, indeed almost nonexistent, characterization of his principal personages does not help. On the other hand, more careful attention is given to the lesser figures in the story than is usually the case in such romances; all of them are sympathetically presented as human beings—even the slave dealer and the brothelkeeper emerge as kindly enough people, whose hearts can be softened by a tale of misfortune.

There is less warfare in Xenophon's novel than in the work of Charito, but more religion. The young couple spend a lot of time praying to Aphrodite and Artemis, who, in turn, secure the eventual salvation of their loyal devotees. The world and its inhabitants are felt to be controlled by a providence which operates, admittedly, in a tardy and inscrutable fashion but is ultimately benevolent. Xenophon also cherishes a quasimystical belief that dedication to chastity and fidelity will mean a happy life in the hereafter—which was the predominant concern of his age.

Xenophon prefers to tell his story in plain terms without rhetorical frills. His language, however, is full of vulgarisms, and for the most part he writes deplorably badly. There are, however, some cheering exceptions, like the cleverly told though macabre short story, inserted into the main narrative, of Aegialeus the Spartan who, after the death of his beloved wife Thelxinoe, embalmed her body and talked and lay and ate with her every day.

EDITIONS—A. D. Papanikolaou (Teubner ed.), 1973. *With French translation:* G. Dalmeyda, Xénophon d'Éphèse, Les Éphésiaques ou le Roman d'Habrocomès et d'Anthia, 1926. *English translations*—M. Hadas, Three Greek Romances, 1964.
ABOUT—O. Schissel von Fleschenberg, Die Rahmenerzählung in den Ephesischen Geschichten des Xenophon Ephesius, 1909; B. Lavagnini, Le origini del romanzo greco, 1921, *and* Studi sul romanzo greco, 1950; B. E. Perry, The Ancient Romance, 1967.

YOSEPH BEN MATATYAHU. See Josephus Flavius

ZENO, Greek philosopher (Stoic), was born in 335/4 and died in about 262 B.C. He was a native of Citium in Cyprus and probably a Phoenician (Semitic) by extraction; he is sometimes known as Zeno the Phoenician. Moving to Athens in 313, he studied under Polemo, head of the Academy, and under Diodorus of Megara but was converted by Crates of Thebes to the Cynic philosophy, which he was said to have reflected in his early work. Later Zeno turned to Socratic doctrine through study of the writings of Antisthenes of Athens (who died c. 360 B.C.). Antisthenes had been one of Socrates' most devoted followers but was also regarded as the founder of the Cynic school. Subsequently, however, Zeno evolved his own system and taught it in a public hall known as the Stoa Poikile (Painted Porch), from which the Stoic school took its name. He soon attracted large audiences, although it was his intention to exclude the general public from his courses and teach no one except genuine philosophers. He became a friend of King Antigonus II Gonatas of Macedonia (284–239 B.C.), who invited him to his court at Pella, but Zeno declined and sent his

zē′ nō

ZENO

pupil Persaeus instead; while another of his students, Sphaerus, inspired the revolution of King Cleomenes III at Sparta (236–222 B.C.).

Zeno also declined an offer of citizenship from the Athenians; yet when he died they honored him with a public funeral, as a man who "had made his life an example to all, for hè acted upon his own teaching." He had also become the subject of many more or less legendary anecdotes, some dealing with his self-control and simple manner of life and others with the gusto with which he liked to put down presumptuous young men.

Zeno's literary works are all lost. The first of them, the *Republic* or *Political State (Politeia)* was concerned with the proper structure of society but eliminated from its scheme almost everything that earlier Greeks had regarded as typical of the city-state *(polis)* and the organized community. There were to be no lawcourts, gymnasia, temples, or money, for wise men, declared Zeno, are friends, and friends, according to a Greek proverb, share their possessions with one another: a commune of friends has no need of cash transactions or political struggles or legal institutions. Zeno was also believed to have advocated (as his successors certainly did) the communal possession of wives, pronouncing that "any man should have sexual relations with any woman," for, among the wise, children would not need the

477

particular protection of a matrimonial household.

Zeno's later writings included treatises entitled *On the Universe, On Substance,* and *On Vision,* but most of the titles are more indicative of his preoccupation with human behavior—for example, *On Human Nature, On Life That Is in Harmony With Nature, On Appropriate Action, On Passions, On Impulse, On Law, On Greek Education.* He also composed a collection of *Homeric Problems* in five books and wrote a study of Hesiod's *Theogony,* evidently accepting the theory that poets were teachers whose doctrines could be discovered by correct interpretation. Moreover, it was Zeno's practice, if he disapproved of a sentiment he found in an earlier author, to rewrite the passage until it suited him.

It is not always easy to distinguish between those doctrines that were laid down by Zeno and the beliefs that were introduced by his successors. But it is evident that he himself, in his written works and in his oral teaching, established the main features of the system we know as Stoicism. That system divided philosophy into three parts: Logic (including also the theory of knowledge, and rhetoric); Physics (which found a place for theology and psychology); and Ethics. By far the most important part of Stoic logic, indispensable for an understanding of the philosophy, is its theory of knowledge. It is on knowledge, Zeno believed, that virtue is based. Only the wise man, who not only knows the truth but knows that he knows it, can be really virtuous. It is the aim of the philosopher to live "in harmony," that is to say, according to a consistent design. (Zeno's successors, Cleanthes and Chrysippus, amended this to "in harmony with nature," and similar phrases.) Zeno meant that the plan by which life should be lived should be formed by correct reason; furthermore, the plan should be natural, in the sense that it accords both with the nature of humankind and with universal nature. Nature is indissolubly linked with reason, which is life's formative and guiding principle. Reason manifests itself as fate or necessity and is synonymous also with divine Providence, which animates and directs the organic entity comprising the world.

(The Universe, according to Stoic belief, experiences a never-ending series of cycles; at the end of each of them it is absorbed into a divine conflagration, after which it starts on a fresh course exactly reproducing the one that had gone before.)

God, or Providence, maintained Zeno, is a material object; indeed, Stoicism held that only material bodies, or objects, have a real existence and can act and become causes. The human soul is such a body; and every soul contains a share of the divine spark. This concept led to the important conclusion that all human beings are brothers and sisters—without distinction between Greek and barbarian or between free person and slave—and that people ought never to be at odds but should live within a framework of universal benevolence and justice. This Stoic cosmopolitanism emphasized the existence of the natural law, which comprises the universal decrees of the Divine Reason, which are the same for all men and women and should form the basis of all legal institutions. In this way Stoicism was a new expression of the concept of absolute moral law that had been nobly expressed in the *Antigone* of Sophocles and had constituted the foundation of the ethics of the philosophers Socrates and Plato.

In this spirit, Zeno and his Stoics formulated the moral imperative: to be virtuous—that is to say, to live in harmony with nature and reason—is the only good, and not to be virtuous is the only evil. Everything else, even life and death, is "indifferent" *(adiaphoron)* —though it was admitted (and elaborated by Zeno's successors) that some of these "indifferent" things are "preferable" to others, so that wise human beings will choose, for example, self-preservation and health rather than illness or pain, if they can do so without acting unvirtuously. Yet the presence or absence of these indifferent things does not affect their happiness: having acted in harmony with reason they are always in possession of the only real good—knowledge of the truth—and in consequence are not at the mercy of other persons but enjoy unperturbable tranquillity, proof against all the troubles and vicissitudes of the world. This means that Stoicism, despite its ethical demands and a solid theoretical foundation for public activity, was in the main a doctrine of detachment from the outer world and in this respect was very characteristic of the new Hellenistic philosophies in general, which aimed, above all, at achieving imperviousness to worldly circumstances.

Zeno's immediate successors, followed in later centuries by Panaetius, Posidonius, Seneca the Younger, Epictetus, and Marcus Aurelius, exercised an enormous influence on the thought of the ancient world.

EDITIONS—A. C. Pearson, The Fragments of Zeno and Cleanthes, 1891; J. ab (H. von) Arnim, Stoicorum Veterum Fragmenta, 1902–5.
ABOUT—S. Samburksy, Physics of the Stoics, 1959; B. Mates, Stoic Logic, 2nd ed., 1961; B. Watson, The Stoic Theory of Knowledge, 1966; L. Edelstein, The Meaning of Stoicism, 1967; J. M. Rist, Stoic Philosophy, 1969, reprint 1977; M. Pohlenz, Stoa und Stoiker, 4th ed., 1970, 1972; A. A. Long, ed., Problems in Stoicism, 1971, and Hellenistic Philosophy, 1974; A. Graeser, Zenon von Kition, 1974; A. Graeser, Zenon von Kition: Positionen und Probleme, 1975; F. H. Sandbach, The Stoics, 1975; H. A. K. Hunt, A Physical Interpretation of the Universe: The Doctrines of Zeno the Stoic, 1976; D. E. Hahm, The Origins of Stoic Cosmology, 1977.

ZENO OF ELEA, Greek philosopher, was born in (probably) about 500 B.C. The date of his death is unknown. His birthplace was Elea or Velia (the modern Castellamare di Bruca) in southwestern Italy. He was the son of Teleutagoras, and the pupil and friend of his fellow townsman and fellow philosopher Parmenides. Like Parmenides, Zeno was said to have been originally an adherent of the Pythagorean school; and like him again he was credited with political activity. There was a tradition (varying greatly in its details but persistent enough to merit some credence) that he took part in a plot against a tyrant and displayed courage under torture.

His best-known, and perhaps only, book was written when he was young, according to the *Parmenides* of Plato, who indicates that it was placed in circulation without Zeno's knowledge and puts into its author's mouth this presumably accurate explanation of its purpose: "The book is a sort of

zē′ nō   ē lē′ á

defense of Parmenides' arguments against those who try to make fun of them by seeking to demonstrate that, if a One [i.e. a single, unitary reality] is assumed, many ridiculous and contradictory consequences follow from this assumption. My book is a retort to those who instead believe in plurality [i.e., the existence of many distinguishable qualities and things capable of motion]; it pays them back in their own coin, and with something to spare, by attempting to prove that, if you investigate the matter carefully, even more absurd consequences follow from their supposition of plurality than from the theory of the One."

In this cause of defending Parmenides' theory of the One, Zeno was said to have offered a set of forty arguments, only a small number of which have been preserved. They come to the paradoxical conclusions or antimonies that, if it were true that many things existed, they would have to be both infinitely small and infinitely great, both limited and unlimited in number, both like and unlike, both one and many, both at rest and at motion.

It has been supposed by some that Zeno was arguing particularly against doctrines of his former associates the Pythagoreans, and this may be true. However, his chief aim was to develop and systematize Parmenides' condemnation of current beliefs in a pluralistic universe by demonstrating that it is impossible to define any such universe in convincing or acceptable terms. These tactics of deriving pairs of contradictory conclusions from the premises of his opponents caused Aristotle to call Zeno the inventor of dialectic. But the French poet Paul Valéry described him as "cruel."

EDITIONS—M. Untersteiner, Zenone: Testimonianze e frammenti, 1970. With translation: H. D. P. Lee, Zeno of Elea, 1936; G. S. Kirk and J. E. Raven, The Presocratic Philosophers, 1960.
ABOUT—H. Fränkel, Wege und Formen frühgriechischen Denkens, 1960; M. C. Stokes, One and Many in Presocratic Philosophy, 1972; G. E. L. Owen in R. A. Allen and D. J. Furley, Studies in Presocratic Philosophy, v 2, 1975.

ZENODOTUS, Greek scholarly writer, was born in about 325 B.C. It is not known when he died. He came from Ephesus (Selçuk) in Ionia (western Asia Minor) but lived under Ptolemy I Soter (304–283/2) and Ptolemy II Philadelphus (283/2–246) at Alexandria, where he was a pupil of Philetas of Cos and later became the first director of the Alexandrian Library (c. 284). There he directed the preliminary classification of its books, assigning the section containing the tragedies to Alexander of Pleuron and the collection of comedies to Lycophron of Chalcis but taking the epic and lyric poets for himself and compiling editions *(diorthoseis)* of some of their works.

His critical revisions of the *Iliad* and *Odyssey,* which he was the first to divide into twenty-four books each, constituted the first scientific attempt to reconstruct the original texts by the examination of more than one manuscript. After undertaking these comparisons, he affixed a mark invented by himself *(obelos)* to lines of dubious authenticity. He also transposed, telescoped or inserted further lines and offered new interpretations of his own. His edition exercised some influence on poets who were his younger contemporaries, Apollonius Rhodius (who succeeded him as Director of the Library) and Callimachus.

The evidence on which Zenodotus drew for his revisions was largely derived from not very ancient criticisms or notes *(scholia)* on the Homeric poems; and the highly subjective character of his criteria, which laid great stress on "propriety" (*to prepon*—i.e., the attribution to each character of words and actions suitable to him or her) resulted in incautious cuts that incurred severe censure from Aristarchus of Samothrace (c. 217–145 B.C.). Yet, as the pioneer of Homeric recension and, indeed, as the earliest of all textual critics, Zenodotus demands respect even when his critical zeal led him to what others regard as unacceptable conclusions. Moreover, some of the strange ideas ascribed to him may be based on misconceptions, since it is believed that he himself wrote no separate treatises on the texts but merely imparted his views orally to a group of students, who are very likely to have misrepresented them.

Zenodotus also prepared editions of Hesiod's *Theogony* and of the poems of Pindar and Anacreon; traces of the two last have survived. In addition, he produced *Foreign Terms,* a collection of non-Greek expressions occurring in literary texts, and a Homeric *Glossary,* which gave the meanings of difficult words and, although often dependent on guesswork, prepared the way for the further development of scholarly linguistic study. In producing these last two works, Zenodotus was the earliest person so far known to employ alphabetical order. He was also said to have written some epic verse himself.

EDITIONS (of fragments)—Oxyrhynchus Papyrus V, 841 (Pindar recension); G. M. Bolling, The Athetized Lines of the Iliad, 1944.
ABOUT—A. Römer, Über die Homerrecension des Zenodot, 1886; J. E. Sandys, History of Classical Scholarship, v 1, 3rd ed., 1921; M. van der Valk, Researches on the Text and Scholia of the Iliad, v 2, 1964; R. Pfeiffer, History of Classical Scholarship from the Beginnings to the End of the Hellenistic Age, 1968; K. Nickau, Untersuchungen zur textkritischen Methode des Zenodotos von Ephesus, 1977.

ZOILUS, Greek philosopher, orator, and historian, lived in the fourth century B.C. and was a citizen of Amphipolis in Macedonia. An adherent of the Cynic school founded by Diogenes of Sinope (c. 400–325 B.C.), he studied under the Athenian rhetorical teacher Polycrates and himself taught the historian and rhetorician Anaximenes of Lampsacus (c. 380–320 B.C.). He probably visited Alexandria at the time of the foundation of the Museum and Library. Claudius Aelianus (second-third centuries A.D.) called him a "rhetorical dog," a combination of rhetorician and Cynic (*kuon,* which means dog, was the nickname of Diogenes, and its plural *kunes* thus became the term for Cynics). Claudius also described him as "censorious."

In his writings, of which only fragments have survived, Zoilus particularly dedicated himself to the task of denouncing the Homeric poems, which were becoming the sub-

ze nod′ ō tus

zō′ i lus

ject of lively critical controversies now that interest in literary history had begun to intensify. His *Censure of Homer* appears to have been delivered in the form of a declamation. In addition, he wrote a treatise entitled *Against Homer* or *Against Homer's Poetry*—or it may even have been called *Homer's Scourge (Homeromastix)*, which in fact became Zoilus' own nickname. His onslaught on the Homeric poems, which was scathing and often unwarranted, was delivered on several fronts, belittling not only the poet's inventive gifts but his depiction of character and the credibility of his narratives. Aristotle's lost *Homeric Objections (Aporemata Homerika)* was an answer to Zoilus and to those who echoed his attitudes.

Other writers assailed by Zoilus' pamphlets included the orator and rhetorician Isocrates and the philosopher Plato; the work attacking the latter received favorable notice from the Greek scholar Dionysius of Halicarnassus. Zoilus also wrote a rhetorical treatise entitled *On Figures (of Speech),* in which he was, apparently, the first writer to use the word *schema.* According to the first century Roman rhetorician Quintilian, the term meant "a form of expression to which a new aspect is given by art"—that is, a rational change in meaning or language away from the ordinary or simple form. Quintilian believed that Zoilus had restricted his definition of *schema* too narrowly, because he had limited its employment to cases when the speaker pretends to say something other than what he actually says.

Zoilus also wrote an ambitious historical work, an account of Greece from its mythological beginnings to the death of Philip II of Macedonia in 323 B.C. In addition, he was the author of a monograph entitled *On Amphipolis* (his hometown) and a *Panegyric on the People of Tenedos* (island off the Troad, northwestern Asia Minor).

EDITIONS—F. Jacoby, Fragmente der griechischen Historiker, 2a, 71.
ABOUT—U. Friedländer, De Zoilo Aliisque Homeri Obtrectatoribus, 1895.

ZOSIMUS, Greek historian of the early Byzantine epoch, must have completed his work after A.D. 498, since he mentions an event of that year. He must also have written it before the *Chronicle* of Eustathius of Epiphaneia was compiled during the first decades of the sixth century A.D.—because Eustathius quoted him. Zosimus held the superior rank of *Comes* in the Byzantine hierarchy and occupied an important post on the legal side of the financial administration *(exadvocatus fisci).* It is uncertain whether he should be identified with either of two sophists of the same name, who came respectively from Ascalon and Gaza in Palestine.

Zosimus wrote a *New History (Historia Nova)* of the Roman Empire, in six books, from the time of the Trojan wars onward. Beginning with a brief survey of ancient history, including a review of the victories over Macedonia and Carthage during the Roman Republic, Book 1 summarizes the history of the first three centuries of the principate (the passage relating to Diocletian, A.D. 284–305, has not survived). The rest of the work goes into greater detail about the fourth century A.D. and some of the fifth, particularly concentrating on the period from 395 to 410, for which this work is our most important source. The principal event of the latter year, the sack of Rome by Alaric the Visigoth, is now missing, but it is unlikely that Zosimus carried his account much further than that climactic landmark.

He was a pagan; indeed, he appears to have been the last of the pagan historians (on the assumption that the slightly later Procopius adhered officially to Christianity). He consistently attributes the decay of the empire not to objective physical factors but to its rejection of the pagan faith. In pursuing this line, he made extensive use of two pagan Greek predecessors, the sophist Eunapius of Sardes (d. 420), whose anti-Christian attitudes he intensifies, and the historian Olympiodorus of Thebes (d. 425). For an excursus on the Secular Games (celebrated at intervals to renew divine support for the Roman state), he also drew upon Phlegon of Tralles (second century A.D.). Claiming the role of the historian of Rome's

zō´ si mus

481

decline, he regarded himself as a latter-day counterpart of Polybius, who, in the second century B.C., had analyzed its rise.

However, being a man of conservative, oligarchic political views, Zosimus ignores Polybius' view that the Roman Republic owed its successes to a "mixed [balanced] constitution"; he himself prefers, instead, to treat it quite simply as an aristocracy. As a consequence of this view, he believes that Augustus, who put an end to the Republic, caused certain "evils" to appear. Nevertheless, Zosimus regards a period as late as the third century A.D.—in particular the reign of Septimius Severus (193–211)—as a victorious, happy, and prosperous time in Roman history; and, although his account of Diocletian is missing, it is clear that he regarded that reign, too, with favor.

On the other hand, Constantine the Great, who made the empire officially Christian, receives stern condemnation from Zosimus for actions that supposedly caused the withdrawal of divine favor and brought about Rome's decline. Constantine is blamed for pursuing harmful political, military, and financial policies, but the principal complaint is that he neglected pagan religious practices, notably the celebration of the Secular Games, which Zosimus considered indispensable for the survival of Roman power. He further declares that Constantine had not embraced Christianity until he stood in dire need of expiation, when pagan priests had refused to absolve him for the execution of his wife Fausta and eldest son Crispus: Constantine's subsequent pious acts were regarded, from this pagan standpoint, as attempts to atone.

Naturally enough, Zosimus takes a favorable view of Julian the Apostate (361–63) and goes so far as to maintain that the death of this pagan emperor caused greater political harm to the Roman state than any other event since the imperial regime had begun. However, he is able to interpret the reigns of the Christian rulers Valentinian I (364–75) and Valens (364–78) as an epoch when paganism still retained a hopeful purpose and meaning, although, at the same time, he notes that there were many signs, omens, and visions predicting ruinous disaster. Under the devout Theodosius I (378–95), al-

though Zosimus concedes him occasional resourcefulness, he sees the process of deterioration rapidly accelerating. Next, he finds that Athens, a stronghold of paganism, was preserved by divine action against capture by Alaric; whereas Rome, where the rites of the pagans had been neglected and acts of sacrilege committed against their temples and holy emblems, was allowed by the gods to fall to the Visigoths.

However, although Zosimus regards the Christians as guilty of pernicious immorality and fanatical intolerance, he does not explicitly blame them for the catastrophes that had befallen the Roman empire, causing its western half (as he is the earliest historian to note) to vanish altogether. Instead he takes the broader view that, because the Romans had generally neglected the gods, the divinities in turn had withdrawn their support from the state. In his historical analysis, Zosimus was faced with an awkward problem of logic: why, if Rome had fallen for these reasons, had the devoutly Christian, eastern, Byzantine empire survived and prospered? To solve this question, on which he admits perplexity, he somewhat tortuously envisages the possibility that Constantinople, despite its adherence to Christianity, had managed to come under the special protection of the pagan gods, which Rome had enjoyed in earlier times.

It is remarkable, all the same, that a pagan felt able to write bitter attacks on the Christian regime at this late date; the existence of his work and the enthusiastic propaganda it contains reveal that all the efforts of Christian apologists and legislators had not yet silenced the adamant convictions of eastern pagans. Zosimus' thesis provoked one such apologist, Evagrius Scholasticus (c. A.D. 536–600), to attempt a vigorous refutation of his arguments in his *History of the Church (Historia Ecclesiastica)*, covering the period from 431 to 594.

In 1576 the German scholar Johann Löwenklau (Launclavius), who had discovered a text of Zosimus while on a mission to Turkey, wrote an important *Apology in Defense of Zosimus*, which in many ways anticipates the eighteenth century English historian Edward Gibbon.

EDITIONS—L. Mendelssohn, 1887. *With translation:* J. J. Buchanan and H. T. Davis, Zosimus: Historia Nova, The Decline of Rome, 1967; F. Paschoud, Zosime: Histoire nouvelle (Budé ed.), 1971, 1979; F. Conca, Zosimo: Storia nuova, 1977.

ABOUT—S. Mazzarino, The End of the Ancient World, 1966, W. E. Kaegi, Byzantium and the Decline of Rome, 1968; R. J. Ridley, Zosimus the Historian, 1970: F. Paschoud *in* O. Reverdin, ed., Polybe (Entretiens Hardt, v 20, 1974, *and* Cinq études sur Zosime, 1976; L. C. Ruggini, Zosimo; Ossia il rovesciamento delle storie ecclesiastiche (Augustinianum, v 16), 1976.

APPENDIX A
WORKS OF DOUBTFUL ATTRIBUTION

ALEXANDER ROMANCE. See Callisthenes

ANTHOLOGY (GREEK, PALATINE, PLANUDEAN). See Agathias; Asclepiades; Cephalas; Meleager; Philip

CONSTITUTION OF ATHENS ("OLD OLIGARCH"). See Xenophon

EINSIEDELN ECLOGUES. See Calpurnius Siculus

EPIC CYCLE. See Arctinus; Hesiod; Homer

EPITOME DE CAESARIBUS. See Victor

HELLENICA OXYRHYNCHIA. See Theopompus

HISTORIA AUGUSTA. See Spartianus, Aelius

HOMERIC HYMNS. See Homer

LAUS PISONIS. See Calpurnius Siculus

"OLD OLIGARCH." See Xenophon

OXYRHYNCHUS HISTORIAN. See Theopompus

PERVIGILIUM VENERIS. See Tiberianus

PRAISE OF PISO. See Calpurnius Siculus

SCRIPTORES HISTORIAE AUGUSTAE. See Spartianus, Aelius

VIGIL OF VENUS. See Tiberianus

APPENDIX B
CHRONOLOGICAL LIST OF AUTHORS
ARRANGED BY CENTURY

Authors whose lives spanned parts of two centuries are listed under both.

8th Century B.C.

Hesiod

Homer

7th Century B.C.

Alcaeus
Alcman
Archilochus
Arctinus of Miletus

Arion
Mimnermus
Semonides
Solon

Terpander
Tyrtaeus

6th Century B.C.

Aesop
Alcaeus
Anacreon
Anaximander
Anaximenes
Arctinus of Miletus
Epicharmus
Hecateus

Heraclitus
Hipponax
Ibycus
Mimnermus
Phrynicus (tragic poet)
Sappho
Scylax
Semonides

Simonides
Solon
Stesichorus
Theognis
Thespis
Xenophanes

5th Century B.C.

Aeschylus
Agathon
Anaxagoras
Andocides
Antiphon
Antisthenes
Aristophanes
Bacchylides
Corinna(?)
Cratinus
Ctesias
Democritus
Empedocles
Epicharmus
Eupolis
Euripides

Gorgias
Hecataeus
Hellanicus
Heraclitus
Herodotus
Hippias
Hippocrates
Isocrates
Lysias
Melissus
Panyassis
Parmenides
Philistus (or Philiscus)
Phrynichus (comic poet)
Phrynichus (tragic poet)
Pindar

Plato
Plato (Comicus)
Pratinas
Prodicus
Protagoras
Simonides
Sophocles
Sophron
Thucydides
Timocreon
Timotheus
Xanthus
Xenophanes
Xenophon
Zeno of Elea

4th Century B.C.

Aeneas Tacticus
Aeschines
Alexis
Andocides
Antisthenes
Archytas
Aristophanes
Aristotle
Aristoxenus
Asclepiades
Bion the Borysthenite
Callisthenes
Cleanthes
Cleitarchus
Demetrius of Phaleron
Democritus
Demosthenes

Dicaearchus
Diphilus
Duris
Ephorus
Epicurus
Erinna
Euclid
Eudoxus
Euhemerus
Gorgias
Heraclides Ponticus
Hieronymus
Hyperides
Isocrates
Lycurgus
Lysias
Menander

Philemon
Philistus (or Philiscus)
Philochorus
Plato
Plato (Comicus)
Pytheas
Rhinthon
Theophrastus
Theopompus
Timaeus
Timocles
Timotheus
Xenophon
Zeno
Zenodotus
Zoilus

3rd Century B.C.

Aeneas Tacticus
Alexis
Apollonius Rhodius
Aratus of Soli
Archimedes
Aristophanes of Byzanti
Asclepiades
Bion the Borysthenite
Callimachus
Cato (the Censor)
Cercidas
Chrysippus
Cleanthes
Cleitarchus
Corinna(?)
Demetrius of Phaleron
Dicaearchus
Diphilus

Duris
Ennius
Epicurus
Erasistratus
Eratosthenes
Erinna
Euclid
Euhemerus
Euphorion
Fabius Pictor
Herodas
Herophilus
Hieronymus
Isaeus
Leonidas
Livius Andronicus
Lycophron
Menander

Menippus
Naevius
Philemon
Philetas
Philochorus
Phylarchus
Plautus
Rhianus
Rhinthon
Satyrus
Sotades
Strato (Physicus)
Theocritus
Theophrastus
Timaeus
Timon
Zeno
Zenodotus

2nd Century B.C.

Accius
Afranius
Apollodorus of Athens
Aristarchus of Samothrace
Aristides of Miletus
Aristophanes of Byzantium
Caecilius Statius
Cato (the Censor)
Crates of Mallus

Dionysius Thrax
Ennius
Eratosthenes
Hermagoras
Hipparchus
Lucilius
Meleager
Moschus

Nicander
Pacuvius
Panaetius
Plautus
Polybius
Posidonius
Satyrus
Terence

1st Century B.C.

Accius
Augustus
Caesar, Gaius Julius
Catullus
Cicero
Cinna
Cremutius Cordus
Didymus
Diodorus Siculus
Dionysius of Halicarnassus
Dionysius Thrax
Gallus
Horace
Hyginus
Labeo

Livy
Lucretius
Macer
Manilius
Meleager
Nepos
Nicolaus of Damascus
Ovid
Parthenius
Philo
Philodemus
Pollio
Posidonius
Propertius

Publilius Syrus
Sallust
Seneca the Elder
Sisenna
Strabo
Sulpicia
Tibullus
Trogus
Valerius Antias
Varius Rufus
Varro
Varro Atacinus
Virgil
Vitruvius

1st Century A.D.

Aufidius Bassus
Augustus
Calpurnius Siculus
Celsus
Claudius
Clement of Rome, Saint
Cluvius Rufus
Columella
Cremutius Cordus
Curtius Rufus
Dio Chrysostom
Dioscorides
Fabius Rusticus
Frontinus
Germanicus
Hero

Hyginus
Ignatius, Saint
Josephus
Juvenal
Labeo
Livy
Longinus
Lucan
Manilius
Martial
Mela
Ovid
Persius
Petronius
Phaedrus
Philip

Philo
Pliny the Elder
Pliny the Younger
Plutarch
Pollio
Quintilian
Seneca the Elder
Seneca the Younger
Silius Italicus
Statius
Strabo
Suetonius
Tacitus
Valerius Flaccus
Valerius Maximus
Velleius Paterculus

2nd Century A.D.

Achilles Tatius
Aelian
Appian
Apuleius
Aristides, Aelius
Arrian
Artemidorus
Athenaeus
Aurelius, Marcus
Babrius
Chariton
Clement of Alexandria
Dio Cassius
Dio Chrysostom
Favorinus

Florus
Frontinus
Fronto
Gaius
Galen
Gellius
Hadrian
Hermogenes
Herodian
Ignatius, Saint
Irenaeus, Saint
Julianus
Justin Martyr
Juvenal
Lucian

Martial
Papinian
Pausanias
Philostratus
Pliny the Younger
Plutarch
Pollux
Ptolemy
Sextus Empiricus
Silius Italicus
Suetonius
Tacitus
Tertullian
Ulpian
Xenophon of Ephesus

3rd Century A.D.

Aelian
Alexander of Aphrodisias
Arnobius
Clement of Alexandria
Cyprian, Saint
Dexippus
Dio Cassius
Diogenes Laertius

Eusebius
Heliodorus
Herodian
Iamblichus
Lactantius
Longus
Minucius Felix
Nemesianus

Origen
Papinian
Paulus
Philostratus
Plotinus
Porphyry
Tertullian
Ulpian

4th Century A.D.

Ambrose, Saint
Ammianus Marcellinus
Athanasius, Saint
Augustine, Saint
Ausonius
Basil, Saint
Claudian
Donatus
Eusebius
Eutropius
Firmicus Maternus
Gregory of Nazianzus,
    Saint

Gregory of Nyssa, Saint
Hilary, Saint
Iamblichus
Jerome, Saint
John Chrysostom, Saint
Julian the Apostate
Lactantius
Libanius
Nonius Marcellus
Olympiodorus
Oribasius
Paulinus of Nola, Saint
Porphyry

Prudentius
Sallustius
Servius
Spartianus
Sulpicius Severus
Symmachus
Synesius
Themistius
Tiberianus
Vegetius Renatus
Victor

5th Century A.D.

Augustine, Saint
Caelius
Jerome, Saint
John Chrysostom, Saint
Macrobius
Martianus Capella
Musaeus Grammaticus
Nonnus

Olympiodorus
Orosius
Paulinus of Nola, Saint
Paulinus of Pella
Priscian
Proclus
Prudentius
Rutilius Namatianus

Salvian
Sidonius Apollinaris, Saint
Sulpicius Severus
Symmachus
Synesius
Theodoret
Zosimus

6th Century A.D.

Agathias
Benedict, Saint
Boethius
Cassiodorus
Cosmas Indicopleustes
Gregory of Tours, Saint
Gregory the Great, Saint
Isidore of Seville. Saint

John Climax, Saint
John Moschus
Jordanes
Leontius of Byzantium
Malalas
Menander Protector
Musaeus Grammaticus
Paul the Silentiary

Philoponus
Priscian
Procopius
Romanus the Melode
Simplicius
Venantius Fortunatus
Zosimus

7th Century A.D.

George the Pisidian
Gregory the Great, Saint
Isidore of Seville, Saint

John Climax, Saint
John Damascene, Saint
John Moschus

Leontius
Maximus Confessor, Saint

8th Century A.D.

Einhard
John Damascene, Saint
Paul the Deacon

Theodore of Studium,
   Saint
Theodulf

Theophanes the Confessor,
   Saint

9th Century A.D.

Cephalas
Einhard
Erigena, John Scotus
George the Monk
Gottschalk
Hrabanus Maurus

Leo VI, the Wise
Lupus of Ferrières
Notker Balbulus
Photius
Sedulius Scotus

Theodore of Studium,
   Saint
Theodulf
Theophanes the Confessor,
   Saint
Walahfrid Strabo

10th Century A.D.

Cephalas
Constantine VII (Byz-
   antine emperor)
Gerbert

Hroswitha
Leo VI, the Wise
Liutprand
Notker Balbulus

Rather
Symeon the New Theologian

11th Century A.D.

Gerbert

Symeon the New Theologian